American Foreign Relations

VOLUME 2

A History • Since 1895

SEVENTH EDITION

Thomas G. Paterson

J. Garry Clifford

Shane J. Maddock

Deborah Kisatsky

Kenneth J. Hagan

D0025538

WADSWORTH
CENGAGE Learning™

Australia • Brazil • Japan • Korea • Mexico • Singapore • Spain • United Kingdom • United States

American Foreign Relations, Volume 2: A History • Since 1895, Seventh Edition
Thomas G. Paterson, J. Garry Clifford, Shane J. Maddock, Deborah Kisatsky, Kenneth J. Hagan

Editor in Chief: PJ Boardman
Senior Publisher: Suzanne Jeans
Sponsoring Acquisitions Editor: Ann West
Development Manager: Jeffrey Greene
Assistant Editor: Megan Curry
Editorial Assistant: Megan Chrisman
Senior Media Editor: Lisa Ciccolo
Senior Marketing Manager:
    Katherine Bates
Marketing Coordinator: Lorreen Pelletier
Marketing Communications Manager:
    Christine Dobberpuhl
Senior Managing Editor: Kathy Brown
Senior Content Project Manager: Aileen
    Mason
Senior Art Director: Cate Rickard Barr
Print Buyer: Linda Hsu
Senior Rights Acquisition Account
    Manager: Katie Huha
Text Researcher: Terri Hampton
Production Service: S4Carlisle Publishing
    Services
Senior Photo Editor: Jennifer Meyer Dare
Photo Researcher: Pembroke Herbert
Cover Designer: Faith Brosnan
Cover Image: The Granger Collection
Compositor: S4Carlisle Publishing Services

For product information and technology assistance, contact us at **Cengage Learning Customer & Sales Support, 1-800-354-9706**

For permission to use material from this text or product, submit all requests online at **www.cengage.com/permissions.** Further permissions questions can be emailed to **permissionrequest@cengage.com.**

Library of Congress Control Number: 2009922145
ISBN-13: 978-0-547-22569-2
ISBN-10: 0-547-22569-5

Wadsworth
20 Channel Center Street
Boston, MA 02210
USA

Cengage Learning products are represented in Canada by Nelson Education, Ltd.

For your course and learning solutions, visit **www.cengage.com.**
Purchase any of our products at your local college store or at our preferred online store **www.ichapters.com.**

Printed in Canada
1 2 3 4 5 6 7 13 12 11 10 09

for

Suzanne Monchamp Paterson

Thomas Paterson, Jr.

Carol Davidge

Vera Low Hagan

Emily Rose Maddock

Benjamin Quinn Maddock

About the Authors

Thomas G. Paterson, professor emeritus of history at the University of Connecticut, graduated from the University of New Hampshire (B.A., 1963) and the University of California, Berkeley (Ph.D., 1968). He has written *Soviet-American Confrontation* (1973), *Meeting the Communist Threat* (1988), *On Every Front* (1992), *Contesting Castro* (1994), *America Ascendant* (with J. Garry Clifford, 1995), and *A People and a Nation* (with Mary Beth Norton et al., 2001). Tom has also edited *Cold War Critics* (1971), *Kennedy's Quest for Victory* (1989), *Imperial Surge* (with Stephen G. Rabe, 1992), *The Origins of the Cold War* (with Robert McMahon, 1999), *Explaining the History of American Foreign Relations* (with Michael J. Hogan, 2004), and *Major Problems in American Foreign Relations* (with Dennis Merrill, 2010). With Bruce Jentleson, he served as senior editor for the *Encyclopedia of American Foreign Relations* (1997). A microfilm edition of *The United States and Castro's Cuba, 1950s–1970s: The Paterson Collection* appeared in 1999. He has served on the editorial boards of the *Journal of American History* and *Diplomatic History.* Recipient of a Guggenheim fellowship, he has directed National Endowment for the Humanities Summer Seminars for College Teachers. In 2000 the New England History Teachers Association recognized his excellence in teaching and mentoring with the Kidger Award. Besides visits to many American campuses, Tom has lectured in Canada, China, Colombia, Cuba, New Zealand, Puerto Rico, Russia, and Venezuela. He is a past president of the Society for Historians of American Foreign Relations, which in 2008 honored him with the Laura and Norman Graebner Award for "lifetime achievement" in scholarship, service, and teaching. A native of Oregon, Tom is now informally associated with Southern Oregon University.

J. Garry Clifford teaches at the University of Connecticut, where he is a professor of political science and director of its graduate program. Born in Massachusetts, he earned his B.A. from Williams College (1964) and his Ph.D. in history from Indiana University (1969). He has also taught at the University of Tennessee and Dartmouth College and has participated in two National Endowment for the Humanities seminars for high school teachers at the Franklin D. Roosevelt Library. For his book *The Citizen Soldiers* (1972), he won the Frederick Jackson Turner Award of the Organization of American Historians. With Norman Cousins, he has edited *Memoirs of a Man: Grenville Clark* (1975), and with Samuel R. Spencer, Jr., he has written *The First Peacetime Draft* (1986). He also co-authored *America Ascendant* (with Thomas G. Paterson) in 1995. With Theodore A. Wilson, he edited and contributed to *Presidents, Diplomats, and Other Mortals: Essays in Honor of Robert H. Ferrell* (2007). Garry's chapters have appeared in Gordon Martel, ed., *American Foreign Relations Reconsidered* (1994), Michael J. Hogan and Thomas G. Paterson, eds., *Explaining the History of American Foreign Relations* (1991 and 2004), Arnold A. Offner and Theodore A. Wilson, eds., *Victory in Europe, 1945* (2000), and in the *Journal of American History, Review of Politics, Mid-America, American Neptune,* and *Diplomatic History.* Garry has served on the editorial board of *Diplomatic History* as well as on the editorial board of the Modern War Series of the University Press of Kansas. He is currently writing a book on FDR and American intervention in World War II.

Shane J. Maddock is professor of history at Stonehill College in Easton, Massachusetts, where he also serves on the faculty of the Martin Institute for Law and Society. Born in North Dakota, he earned his B.A. from Michigan State University (1989) and his Ph.D. from the University of Connecticut (1997). He also taught at the U.S. Coast Guard Academy. Shane edited *The Nuclear Age* (2001) and contributed a chapter to G. Kurt Piehler and Rosemary Mariner, eds., *The Atomic Bomb and American Society* (2008). He has also published in the *Journal of American History, International History Review, Pacific Historical Review, New England Journal of History, Presidential Studies Quarterly, Mid-America, Journal of Military History, American Jewish History, Canadian Journal of Latin American and Caribbean Studies, History in Dispute,* and *The Encyclopedia of U.S. Foreign Relations.* He received fellowships from the Institute for the Study of World Politics, the U.S. Arms Control and Disarmament Agency, and the Hoover, Truman, Eisenhower, Kennedy, and Johnson presidential libraries. His book, *Nuclear Apartheid: The American Quest for Atomic Supremacy* will be published by University of North Carolina Press.

Deborah Kisatsky is associate professor of history at Assumption College in Worcester, Massachusetts. Born in Pennsylvania, she earned her B.A. (1990) and her Ph.D. (2001) from the University of Connecticut. Deborah published *The United States and the European Right, 1945–1955* with Ohio State University Press in 2005. She has published as well in *The American Historical Review, Intelligence and National Security, The Historian, Presidential Studies Quarterly, The Journal of Interdisciplinary History,* and the *Encyclopedia of U.S. Foreign Relations.* Deborah has received fellowships from the Alexander von Humboldt Foundation, the Center for European Integration Studies (University of Bonn), the Society for Historians of American Foreign Relations, the Franklin D. Roosevelt Library, and the Harry S. Truman Institute. She is currently writing a book about the life, thought, and transnational legacy of the nineteenth-century communitarian and social radical Adin Ballou.

Kenneth J. Hagan is a professor of strategy and policy at the U.S. Naval War College, Monterey Program, and professor of history and museum director emeritus at the U.S. Naval Academy, Annapolis. He previously taught at Claremont McKenna College, Kansas State University, and as an adjunct at the U.S. Army Command and General Staff College. A native of California, he received his A.B. and M.A. from the University of California, Berkeley (1958, 1964) and his Ph.D. from the Claremont Graduate University (1970). Ken is the author of *This People's Navy: The Making of American Sea Power* (1991), a comprehensive history of American naval strategy and policy since the Revolution, and *American Gunboat Diplomacy and the Old Navy, 1877–1889* (1973), and co-author with Ian J. Bickerton of *Unintended Consequences: The United States at War* (2007), a critical reassessment of ten American wars from the Revolution to Iraq. His scholarship also includes two edited collections of original essays: *In Peace and War: Interpretations of American Naval History, 30th Anniversary Edition* (2008) and, with William Roberts, *Against All Enemies: Interpretations of American Military History from Colonial Times to the Present* (1986). He has lectured on the history of U.S. naval strategy at the Canadian Forces College, the Defence Academy of the United Kingdom, and the U.S. National War College. Ken has given papers on naval and diplomatic history at professional meetings in Sweden, Greece, Turkey, France, Spain, and the United Kingdom. In 2006 and 2007 he spoke on naval history at conferences hosted by the Royal Australian Navy in Sydney and Canberra. In 2007 and 2008 he discussed the unintended consequences of war at Oxford University and at Strathclyde University in Glasgow, Scotland. For thirty years he has advised the Naval ROTC college program on its naval history course. He currently is writing a biography of Admiral William S. Sims, who served as President Theodore Roosevelt's naval aide and as the commander of U.S. naval forces in Europe in World War I. A retired captain in the naval reserve, Ken served on active duty with the Pacific Fleet from 1958 to 1963.

Contents

Preface   xv

1 *Imperialist Leap, 1895–1900*   1

DIPLOMATIC CROSSROAD: **The *Maine*, McKinley,
and War, 1898**   2

The Venezuela Crisis of 1895   5

Men of Empire   8

Cleveland and McKinley Confront *Cuba Libre*, 1895–1898   10

WHAT IF ... **Spain had granted independence in
Cuba in 1898?**   15

The Spanish-American-Cuban-Filipino War   16

Men Versus "Aunties": The Debate over Empire in the
    United States   18

Imperial Collisions in Asia: The Philippine Insurrection and the
    Open Door in China   21

The Elbows of a World Power, 1895–1900   28

FURTHER READING FOR THE PERIOD 1895–1900   29

NOTES TO CHAPTER 1   30

2 *Managing, Policing, and Extending
the Empire, 1900–1914*   33

DIPLOMATIC CROSSROAD: **Severing Panama from
Colombia for the Canal, 1903**   34

Architects of Empire   39

Cuba's Limited Independence Under the Platt Amendment   43

The Constable of the Caribbean: The Roosevelt Corollary, Venezuela,
    and the Dominican Republic   45

Ordering Haiti and Nicaragua   47

Resisting Revolution in Mexico   49

Japan, China, and Dollar Diplomacy in Asia   53

Anglo-American Rapprochement and Empire Building   57

vii

WHAT IF ... manliness and civilization had not become linked in the minds of American leaders in the period 1900–1917?   63

FURTHER READING FOR THE PERIOD 1900–1914   64
NOTES TO CHAPTER 2   66

3   *War, Peace, and Revolution in the Time of Wilson, 1914–1920*   **70**

DIPLOMATIC CROSSROAD: The Sinking of the *Lusitania*, 1915   71

The Travails of Neutrality   75

Submarines, Neutral Rights, and Mediation Efforts   79

Wilson's Choices Bring America into World War   81

The Debate over Preparedness   84

The Doughboys Make the Difference in Europe   87

The Fourteen Points and a Contentious Peace Conference   90

Principle, Personality, Health, and Partisanship:
    The League Fight   94

WHAT IF ... the president had accepted Senate reservations and the United States had joined the League of Nations in 1919–1920?   99

Red Scare at Home and Abroad: Bolshevism and Intervention
    in Russia   100

The Whispering Gallery of Global Disorder   103

FURTHER READING FOR THE PERIOD 1914–1920   106
NOTES TO CHAPTER 3   108

4   *Descending into Europe's Maelstrom, 1920–1939*   **111**

DIPLOMATIC CROSSROAD: Roosevelt Extends America's Frontier to the Rhine, 1939   112

"Prize Fighters with a Very Long Reach": The Independent
    Internationalists   115

Economic and Cultural Expansion in a Rickety World   120

Seekers of a World Without War   125

Cold as Steel: Soviet-American Encounters   127

Hitler's Germany, Appeasement, and the Outbreak of War   130

American Isolationism and Myopic Neutrality   133

WHAT IF ... President Franklin D. Roosevelt had vetoed the Neutrality Acts in the 1930s? 135

Roosevelt Shifts and Congress Balks on the Eve of War 136

FURTHER READING FOR THE PERIOD 1920–1939 139
NOTES TO CHAPTER 4 141

5 *Asia, Latin America, and the Vagaries of Power, 1920–1939* 144

DIPLOMATIC CROSSROAD: **The Manchurian Crisis, 1931–1932** 145

A Question of Power 147

Facing Japan: The Washington Naval Disarmament Conference and China 149

Japan's Footsteps Toward Pacific Hegemony 152

WHAT IF ... Americans had not sympathized with China over Japan after 1931? 156

Being "Neighborly" in Latin America 157

Creating "Frankenstein" Dictators in the Dominican Republic, Nicaragua, and Haiti 162

Subverting Nationalism in Cuba and Puerto Rico 167

Accommodating Mexico 169

Pan Americanism and Hemispheric Defense on the Eve of War 171

FURTHER READING FOR THE PERIOD 1920–1939 173
NOTES TO CHAPTER 5 174

6 *Survival and Spheres: The Allies and the Second World War, 1939–1945* 177

DIPLOMATIC CROSSROAD: **The Atlantic Charter Conference, 1941** 178

Juggling Between War and Peace, 1939–1941 181

The Road to Pearl Harbor: Japanese-American Relations, 1939–1941 186

The Big Three: Strategies and Fissures, 1941–1943 190

WHAT IF ... the Allies had opened a second front in France before 1944? 192

China Tangles 196

Bystanders to the Holocaust 200

Planning the Postwar Peace, 1943–1945 203

Compromises at Yalta   207

To Each Its Own: Allied Divergence and Spheres of Influence   210

The Potsdam Conference and the Legacy of World War II   214

FURTHER READING FOR THE PERIOD 1939–1945   217
NOTES TO CHAPTER 6   220

7   *All-Embracing Struggle: The Cold War Begins, 1945–1950*   225

DIPLOMATIC CROSSROAD: **Atomic Bombs at Hiroshima and Nagasaki, 1945**   226

Truman, Stalin, and the U.S.–Soviet Clash   231

Challenging the Soviets in Eastern Europe   235

"Getting Tough": Early Cold War Crises   238

WHAT IF ... **the United States and the Soviet Union had reached an agreement in 1946 to prevent the spread of atomic weapons?**   242

"A Bolt of Lightning": The Truman Doctrine, Israel, and Containment   243

Europe Divided: The Marshall Plan, Germany, and NATO   246

Allies and Adversaries in Asia   251

The People's Republic of China and U.S. Nonrecognition   254

A Cold War Culture Emerges   256

FURTHER READING FOR THE PERIOD 1945–1950   259
NOTES TO CHAPTER 7   263

8   *Cold War Prism: The Korean War and Eisenhower-Dulles Foreign Relations, 1950–1961*   267

DIPLOMATIC CROSSROAD: **The Decision to Intervene in the Korean War, 1950**   268

The Korean War and the "Trojan Horse" of American National Security   269

"The Great Equation": Eisenhower's Foreign Policy   275

Dulles, the New Look, and McCarthyism   279

The Glacier Grinds On: Eisenhower, Khrushchev, and the Cold War   281

Missiles, Berlin, and the U-2 Mess   287

To the Brink with China, To the Market with Japan   292

Nationalism, Neutralism, and the Third World   295

"Batten Down the Hatches": Reform and Resistance in the Middle
   East and Latin America   300

**WHAT IF ... the United States had used diplomacy
rather than covert action to confront Third World
nationalism during the 1950s?**   306

American Cultural Expansion and the Cold War   307

FURTHER READING FOR THE PERIOD 1950–1961   311
NOTES TO CHAPTER 8   314

9   *Passing the Torch: The Vietnam Years,
1961–1969*   **319**

**DIPLOMATIC CROSSROAD: The Tet Offensive
in Vietnam, 1968**   320

Vietnamese Wars Before 1961   324

Bear Any Burden? John F. Kennedy and His Foreign
   Policy Team   328

Arms Buildup, Berlin Crisis, and Nation Building   331

The Most Dangerous Area in the World: The Cuban Revolution
   and Latin America   336

Spinning Out of Control: The Cuban Missile Crisis   338

Laos, Vietnam, and the Kennedy Legacy   343

**WHAT IF ... John F. Kennedy had lived to make key decisions
on the Vietnam War?   348**

Nose to Nose: Lyndon B. Johnson and the World   349

"The Biggest Damned Mess": Johnson's War   350

Hawks, Doves, Comrades, and Adversaries   356

FURTHER READING FOR THE PERIOD 1961–1969   359
NOTES TO CHAPTER 9   363

10   *Détente and Disequilibrium, 1969–1981*   **367**

**DIPLOMATIC CROSSROAD: Richard M. Nixon's Trip
to China, 1972**   368

Nixon, Kissinger, and Their Critics   371

Détente, SALT, and the Nuclear Arms Race   373

Regional Tails Wagging the Superpower Dogs:
   The Middle East   378

Thinking Globally: Relations with Latin America and Africa   382

Number One Challenged: Economic Competition, Environmental
Distress, and the North-South Debate   385

No Mere Footnote: Vietnamization, Cambodia, and a Wider War   390

The Peace Agreement, Withdrawal, and Defeat   392

The Many Lessons and Questions of Vietnam   394

Mixed Signals: Carter's Contradictory Course   398

Engaging the Third World: Latin America and Africa   401

Middle East Highs and Lows: Camp David and the Iranian
Hostage Crisis   406

**WHAT IF ... the Iranian Hostage Rescue Mission
Had Succeeded?**   410

Détente's Downfall: Soviet-American Rivalry, Afghanistan,
and the Carter Record   411

FURTHER READING FOR THE PERIOD 1969–1981   415
NOTES TO CHAPTER 10   416

**11   *A New World Order? Reagan, Bush,
and Clinton, 1981–2001*   421**

**DIPLOMATIC CROSSROAD: The Berlin Wall
Comes Down, 1989**   422

Gorbachev and the Earthquakes of 1989–1991   423

Ronald Reagan's Mission to Revive American Hegemony   425

Soviet-American Crises and the Antinuclear Movement   429

Civil Wars and Interventionism: Central America
and the Caribbean   434

Hornets' Nests in the Middle East, Africa, and Asia   438

Indispensable Nation: Bush, Clinton, and the Post–Cold
War World   443

Russian Disintegration, German Reunification, NATO Expansion,
Balkan Hell   447

Hope and Tragedy in Africa   451

**WHAT IF ... the United States had killed Osama bin Laden
in August 1998?**   454

Invasions and Implosions in Latin America   455

Mideast Imbroglios   459

Feuding and Trading with China, Vietnam, and Japan   463

Between Two Worlds: Reagan, Bush, Clinton, and the
Legacies of the Cold War   465

FURTHER READING FOR THE PERIOD 1981–2001   471
NOTES TO CHAPTER 11   474

12 *Millennial America: Foreign Relations Since 2001* **479**

DIPLOMATIC CROSSROAD: **9/11 and After** 480

Rise of the Vulcans: Bush and His War Cabinet 483

Present at a New Creation: The War on Terror, Afghanistan, and the Bush Doctrine 487

"Slam Dunk": Justifying the Iraq War 490

Mission Accomplished? The Invasion and Occupation of Iraq 493

Containing Evil and Spreading Freedom: The Bush Policy Toward the Middle East and Asia 501

Getting a Sense of Their Souls: Europe, Latin America, and Africa in the Twenty-First Century 508

Transnational Challenges and Opportunities 515

WHAT IF ... **Al Gore had become president in 2001?** **518**

FURTHER READING FOR THE PERIOD SINCE 2001 524
NOTES TO CHAPTER 12 526

Appendix: Makers of American Foreign Relations **531**

General Bibliography **535**

General Reference Works 535

Overviews of Relations with Countries, Regions, and Other Places of the World, Including Atlases and Gazetteers (A), Annual Surveys and Chronologies (AS), Bibliographies (B), Biographical Aids (BA), Chronologies (C), Encyclopedias and Dictionaries (E), and Statistics (S) 536

Overviews of Subjects, Including Atlases (A), Annual Surveys (AS), Bibliographies (B), Biographical Aids (BA), Chronologies (C), Encyclopedias (E), and Statistics (S) 546

Index **559**

Maps and Graphs

The Great Powers in Asia, 1900   27

Panama Canal Zone   37

U.S. Interventions in the Caribbean and Central America   48

The *Lusitania* and *U-20*   74

The Outbreak of World War I Summer 1914   78

Europe Reshaped by War and Peace   95

The Weight of the United States in the World Economy   122

The Contracting Spiral of World Trade   123

Japanese Expansion to 1941   155

The German Onslaught, 1939-1942   183

The Allies Push Japan Back, 1942-1945   212

Changes in Europe After World War II   237

Changes in Asia After World War II   253

The Korean War, 1950-1953   271

Africa in 1945   296

Africa in 2000   297

Southeast Asia and the Vietnam War   355

The Middle East   379

The United States and Latin America Since 1945   402

Transformations: Russia, the Former Soviet Republics,
    Eastern Europe, and Germany   424

World Arms Exports, 1992–1994   467

Preface

Much has happened to challenge and to redirect American foreign relations since the sixth edition of this text appeared in 2005. A seemingly endless war in Iraq and Afghanistan; continued confrontations with putative nuclear threats from so-called "rogue" states and terrorist networks; fluctuating relations with former Cold War adversaries China and Russia; a possible new relationship with Cuba after Fidel Castro; complaints from allies about Washington's unilateral behavior as a "hyperpower"; ongoing debates about "globalization" and its myriad effects; increased alarm over fast-spreading deadly diseases, global warming, and environmental decline; controversial new definitions of national security and "homeland defense" that include preemptive war as well as "rendition" and torture of prisoners; anguished questioning as to why our enemies "hate" us; a financial meltdown and economic recession of international proportions; and the election and inauguration of a new president promising to rectify the mistakes of his predecessor—all have riveted attention on America's global travails and how they came to be. These urgent contemporary developments, along with new scholarship and encouraging comments from instructors and students, have again prompted us to revise *American Foreign Relations.* As before, in this seventh edition we engage current perspectives on the United State's engagement with the world. We seek to explain foreign relations in the broadest manner as the many ways that peoples, organizations, states, and systems interact—economic, cultural, strategic, environmental, political, and more.

We continue to emphasize the theme of expansionism, exploring its myriad manifestations. We also show that on almost every issue in the history of American foreign relations, alternative voices unfailingly sounded among and against official policymakers. Americans have always debated their place in the world, their wars, their overseas commitments, and the status of their principles and power, and they have always debated the people of other nations about the spread of U.S. influence. We try to capture with vivid description and quotation the drama of these many debates.

A historical overview such as this one necessarily draws on the copious work of scholars in the United States and abroad. Their expertise informs this book and lends it the authority that instructors and students have come to expect. Our "Further Reading" and "Endnotes" sections provide one way to thank them for their books, articles, and conference papers. We have also appreciated their recommendations for text revisions and their suggestions for teaching the courses for which this book is intended. We thank them, too, for challenging us to consider the many different approaches and theories that have commanded attention in this field, including world systems, corporatism, dependency, culture, ideology, psychology and personality, medical biography, lessons from the past, bureaucratic politics, public opinion, executive-legislative competition, race, gender, national security and power, and the natural environment. This book also presents the findings of our own ongoing archival research and writing as we continually discover the past.

The subjects of diplomacy, war, economic intercourse, and politics remain central to our presentation of the foreign-relations story. We have made this edition more comprehensive by further extending our discussion of the cultural dimensions of foreign relations: how race-based and gendered thinking conditions the decision-making environment; how media and film reflect cultural myths and capture public perceptions of international events; how American mass culture (such as rock and roll and sports) proliferates world-wide with its innumerable effects; the relationship between travel, tourism, and expansionism; and the ways in which "public diplomacy"—the presentation of a positive image of the United States through media propaganda—reflects official U.S. efforts to employ culture in service to American foreign policy.

We have also increased our coverage of the self-conscious expansion of American "empire" from its westward displacement of Native Americans in the eighteenth and nineteenth centuries to its overseas incarnations in the twentieth and twenty-first centuries. We add new details about "makers" of American foreign relations from presidents such as John Adams, Theodore Roosevelt, and George W. Bush to diplomats such as Nicholas Trist, Sumner Welles, and Condoleeza Rice. We take note, for example, of recent scholarship that shows how the "iconography" of empire after the Spanish-American-Cuban-Filipino War of 1898 often depicted opponents of empire in gendered terms—as carping old "aunties" (a pun on "anti-imperialists") dressed in skirts and bonnets—in sharp contrast to a virile Uncle Sam who willingly took up the burdens of empire.

Amid such recent catastrophes as Hurricane Katrina, tsunamis in the Indian Ocean, earthquakes in China, and typhoons in Myanmar, we pay greater attention to issues that spring from human interaction with the natural environment and the international conferences convened to deal with damage to the environment. American relations with Middle East countries before and after World War II receive more coverage, as do linkages between the civil rights movement and American relations with the Third World in the 1940s through the 1960s. Recent scholarship prompted by such anniversaries as the Louisiana Purchase and Lewis and Clark Expeditions, the Spanish-American-Cuban-Filipino War, the cruise of the Great White Fleet, Korean War, the Cuban Missile Crisis, and the Vietnam War, among others, have brought fresh insights to these important events.

Equally important, with the Cold War International History Project providing scholars with a treasure trove of declassified documents from foreign archives (Russian, East German, Cuban, and Chinese among them), we have enriched our treatment of Joseph Stalin's goals and tactics during and after World War II, the origins of the Korean War, Nixon's opening to China in 1972, Cuban policy toward Africa, the Soviet invasion of Afghanistan, the failure of détente in the 1970s, and the end of the Cold War in 1989–1991. Similarly, recently declassified U.S. government documents made available via "electronic briefing books" from the National Security Archive have added nuance to our coverage, for example, of the attempted Hungarian Revolution (1956), U.S. reactions to secret contacts between North and South Vietnam in 1963, the India-Pakistan War of 1971, and the Indonesian invasion of East Timor in 1976, as well as new evidence regarding Washington's Cold War initiatives toward the Soviet Union, the People's Republic of China, and Castro's Cuba. The declassification, duplication, and public release of presidential audio tapes from the Kennedy, Johnson, and Nixon years help to recapture those leaders' colorful language and reveal how the assumptions, styles, and emotions of presidents have influenced decision-making. We have reorganized the final three chapters of Volume II, reflective of an emerging consensus that the terrorist attacks of September 11, 2001, commenced a new era in U.S. foreign relations history. Chapter 10 now covers the period 1969–1981, while Chapter 11 runs from 1981 to 2001. Our final chapter concentrates on events from 2001 to the present and includes expanded treatment of the Iraq War and U.S. policies toward Iran, North Korea, and Afghanistan.

In preparing this edition, we once again immersed ourselves in the memoirs, diaries, letters, speeches, recorded tapes, and oral histories of U.S. and international leaders. We often let them speak for themselves in the frankest terms, guarded and unguarded. We have sought to capture their anger and their humor, their cooperation and their competitiveness, their truths and their lies, their moments of doubt and times of confidence, their triumphs and setbacks. *American Foreign Relations,* in short, strives to capture the erratic pulse of international relations through peoples' struggles to plan, decide, and administer. We study not only the leaders who made influential decisions, but also the world's peoples who welcomed, resisted, or endured the decisions that profoundly influenced their lives. In this regard, we have drawn on the growing scholarship that studies non-state actors, including peace groups, African Americans, and international bodies such as the World Health Organization.

Each chapter opens with a significant and dramatic event—a "Diplomatic Crossroad"—that helps illustrate the chief characteristics and issues of the era. The introductory and concluding sections of each chapter set the themes. Illustrations—several of them new to this edition—from collections around the world, are closely tied to the narrative in image and caption description. Also in this seventh edition, to generate student debate, we have added a new feature called "What If" to every chapter. We intend these speculative counterfactual essays to spark the reader's imagination as to what might have happened had leaders made different decisions or if conditions or events had turned out differently. What consequences might have followed had the British recognized the Confederacy during the Civil War? What if the United States had joined the League of Nations in 1919–1920? What if John F. Kennedy had lived to make the key decisions on Vietnam after 1963? What if Bill Clinton had succeeded in capturing or killing Osama Bin Laden? We make no claim to definitive scholarly answers in these mini-essays. We hope, however, to excite appreciation for the counterfactual reasoning implicit in all historical writing and to stimulate discussion of many contingencies that together comprise the history of American foreign relations.

The maps, graphs, and "Makers of American Foreign Relations" tables in each chapter provide essential information. The updated chapter bibliographies guide further reading and serve as a starting point for term or research papers. The "General Bibliography" at the end of the book is also a place to begin research or seek more information. The "General Bibliography" consists of three parts: first, general reference works, such as biographical dictionaries, atlases, statistics, encyclopedias, and bibliographies; second, overviews of U.S. relations with countries and regions, from Afghanistan to Zimbabwe; and, third, overviews of subjects, such as Air Force and air power, CIA and covert action, Congress, cultural relations, ethnic conflict, human rights, isolationism, Manifest Destiny, Monroe Doctrine, oil, refugees, slave trade and slavery, terrorism, and United Nations.

In the late 1970s, the People's Republic of China adopted a new system for rendering Chinese phonetic characters into the Roman alphabet. Called the Pinyin method, it replaced the Wade-Giles technique, which had long been used in English. Use of the Pinyin method is now common, and we use it in *American Foreign Relations.* Many changes are minor—Shantung has become Shandong and Mao Tse-tung has become Mao Zedong, for example. But when we have a possibly confusing Pinyin spelling, we have placed the Wade-Giles spelling in parentheses—for example, Beijing (Peking) or Jiang Jieshi (Chiang Kai-shek).

Instructors and students interested in the study of foreign-relations history are invited to join the Society for Historians of American Foreign Relations (SHAFR). This organization publishes a superb journal, *Diplomatic History,* and a newsletter; offers book, article, and lecture prizes and dissertation research grants; and holds an annual conference where scholars present their views and research results. For information, contact the SHAFR Business Office, Department of History, Ohio State University, 106 Dulles Hall, 230 West 17th Avenue, Columbus, OH 43210, or email to shafr@osu.edu.

Another informative web site is H-Diplo: Diplomatic History, found at www.h-net.org/~diplo/. Besides presenting provocative online discussions on foreign-relations history, including "Round Table" reviews of important recent books, this site also provides research and bibliographic aids and an extensive list of links to other useful resources, including journals, newspapers, archives and presidential libraries, research organizations such as the National Security Archive, and government agencies such as the Central Intelligence Agency and Department of State. Readers should also note our citations to relatively new scholarly journals in foreign relations history—*Cold War History, Journal of Cold War Studies, Diplomacy & Statecraft, International History Review, Intelligence and National Security, Journal of the Gilded Age and Progressive Era, Journal of Military History,* among others. Such journals often publish fresh perspectives from younger scholars before they appear in book form.

Many colleagues, friends, students, and editors contributed to this edition of *American Foreign Relations* by providing research leads, correction of errors, reviews of the text, library searches, documents and essays, and editorial assistance. We give our heartiest thanks to Ian Bickerton, Mark Boyer, David Brown, Frank Costigliola, Carol Davidge, Robert H. Ferrell, Irwin Gellman, Robert E. Hannigan, Christine Luberto, Marc O'Reilly, Heather Perry and other members of the interlibrary loan staff of Stonehill College's MacPháiden Library, Jeremy Pressman, Larry Spongberg and Janice Wilbur of Assumption College's d'Alzon

Library, Jennifer Sterling-Folker, Mark Stoler, and Hal Wert. We also thank the following reviewers, who gave many helpful comments and suggestions for this new edition: David Fogelsong, Rutgers University; Max Friedman, American University; Barbara Keys, California State University – Sacramento; and Lorraine Lees, Old Dominion University. Wadworth/Cengage Learning's talented team merits the highest of praise: Jeff Greene, Leslie Kauffman, and Aileen Mason. Ken Hagan generously shared naval illustrations from his latest edition of *In Peace and War* (2008).

We are also eager to thank the many people who helped us in previous editions: Philip J. Avillo, Jr., Richard Baker, Ann Balcolm, Michael A. Barnhart, Robert Beisner, Michael Butler, R. Christian Berg, Kenneth J. Blume, Linda Blundell, Richard Bradford, Kinley J. Brauer, John Burns, Richard Dean Burns, Robert Buzzanco, Charles Conrad Campbell, Chen Jian, John Coogan, Alejandro Corbacho, Frank Costigliola, Carol Davidge, Mark Del Vecchio, Ralph Di Carpio, Justus Doenecke, Michael Donaghue, Xavier Franco, Frances Gay, Paul Goodwin, James Gormly, Eric Hafter, Hope M. Harrison, Alan Henrikson, Gregg Herken, George Herring, Ted Hitchcock, Joan Hoff, Kristin Hoganson, Reginald Horsman, Michael Hunt, Edythe Izard, Holly Izard, Richard Izard, Leith Johnson, Mary Kanable, Burton Kaufman, Melville T. Kennedy, Jr., Thomas Lairson, Lester Langley, Jane Lee, Thomas M. Leonard, Li Yan, Terrence J. Lindell, Florencia Luengo, Paul Manning, Martha McCoy, David McFadden, Charles McGraw, Elizabeth McKillen, Matt McMahon, Robert McMahon, James T. McMaster, Elizabeth Mahan, Herman Mast, Dennis Merrill, Jean-Donald Miller, William Mood, Jay Mullen, Carl Murdock, Brian Murphy, R. Kent Newmyer, Arnold Offner, John Offner, Marc O'Reilly, Chester Pach, Jerry Padula, Carol Petillo, David Pletcher, Salvadore Prisco, Stephen G. Rabe, Carol S. Repass, Wayne Repeta, Barney J. Rickman III, Michael Roskin, John Rourke, Evan Sarantakes, Kenneth E. Shewmaker, Kent M. Schofield, David Sheinin, Anna Lou Smethurst, Elbert B. Smith, Kevin Smith, Thomas G. Smith, Kenneth R. Stevens, Mark A. Stoler, William W. Stueck, Jr., Duane Tananbaum, Chris Thornton, George Turner, Jonathan G. Utley, Thomas Walker, Wang Li, Kathryn Weathersby, Ralph E. Weber, Edmund S. Wehrle, Immanuel Wexler, Lawrence Wittner, Sol Woolman, Jean Woy, Sherry Zane, and Thomas Zoumaras.

We welcome comments and suggestions from students and instructors.

T. G. P.
J. G. C.
S. J. M.
D. K.
K. J. H.

CHAPTER 1

Imperialist Leap, 1895–1900

The Battleship Maine Explodes.   *This imaginative contemporary artwork depicts the U.S. battleship blowing up in the early morning of February 15, 1898, in the harbor of Havana, Cuba. The warship had arrived three weeks earlier to protect American citizens caught up in the Cuban rebellion against Spanish rule. The deaths of 266 U.S. sailors in the explosions helped feed popular passions for war with Spain. (Naval Historical Foundation)*

DIPLOMATIC CROSSROAD

◆ *The Maine, McKinley, and War, 1898*

THE BURLY U.S. battleship *Maine* steamed into Havana harbor on January 25, 1898. "A beautiful sight," reported the American consul-general Fitzhugh Lee, who had requested the visit ostensibly to protect the lives of Americans living in war-torn Cuba.[1] President William McKinley had sent the vessel to Havana hoping to calm tensions with Spain, then in its third year of battling Cuban rebels fighting for national independence. The *Maine* was to stay three weeks and then depart for New Orleans in time for Mardi Gras. But at 9:40 P.M. on February 15, a "dull sullen" roar followed by massive explosions ripped through the 6,700-ton ship, killing 266 Americans.[2] McKinley, who had been taking sedatives to sleep, awoke an hour before dawn to take a phone call from Secretary of the Navy John D. Long reporting the event. "The *Maine* blown up! The *Maine* blown up!" the stunned president kept muttering to himself.[3] Even though "the country was not ready" for it, the war with Spain would begin three months later.[4]

McKinley ordered an official investigation of the *Maine* disaster and tried to gain time. With no evidence but with considerable emotion, many Americans assumed that the *Maine* had been "sunk by an act of dirty treachery on the part of the Spaniards."[5] In early March, U.S. Minister Stewart L. Woodford protested strongly to the Spanish about the *Maine*. "End it at once—*end it at once—end it at once,*" he exhorted Madrid regarding the war in Cuba.[6] On March 6 the president met with Joe Cannon, chair of the House Appropriations Committee, and asked for $50 million for war preparedness. "It seemed as though a hundred Fourths of July had been let loose in the House," a clerk noted, as Congress enthusiastically obliged three days later.[7]

In mid-March Senator Redfield Proctor of Vermont, a friend of McKinley reportedly opposed to war, graphically told his colleagues about his recent visit to Cuba. He recounted ugly stories about Spain's notorious reconcentration policy (the forced settlement of Cubans into fortified camps): "Torn from their homes, with foul earth, foul air, foul water, and foul food or none, what wonder that one-half died and one-quarter of the living are so diseased that they cannot be saved?"[8] Shortly after this moving speech, which convinced many members of Congress and business leaders that Spain could not restore order to Cuba, the American court of inquiry on the *Maine* concluded that an external mine of unknown origin had destroyed the vessel. A Spanish commission at about the same time attributed the disaster to an internal explosion. More than a century later, after several more investigations, experts still disagree whether the *Maine* blew up because of "a coal bunker fire" or from an "undership mine."[9] In 1898 vocal Americans pinned "the crime" squarely on Spain. "Remember the *Maine,* to hell with Spain" became a popular slogan.

A decorated veteran of the Civil War, President McKinley once asserted: "I have been through one war; I have seen the dead piled up, and I do not want to see another."[10] He quietly explored the possibility of purchasing Cuba for $300 million— or some other means "by which Spain can part with Cuba without loss of respect and with certainty of American control."[11] But a jingo frenzy had seized Congress. Interventionist critics increasingly questioned the president's manhood, claiming, as did Teddy Roosevelt, that he "had no more backbone than a chocolate eclair."[12] One member of Congress called the president's policies on Cuba "lame, halting, and impotent," while another said of McKinley: "He wobbles, he waits, he hesitates. He changes his mind."[13] Following one stormy Senate session, Vice President Garrett Hobart warned McKinley: "They will act without you if you do not act at once." "Say no more," McKinley responded.[14]

On March 27, Washington cabled the president's demands to Madrid: an armistice, Cuban–Spanish negotiations to secure a peace, McKinley's arbitration of the conflict if there was no peace by October, termination of the reconcentration policy, and relief aid to the Cubans. Implicit was the demand that Spain grant Cuba its independence under U.S. supervision. As a last-ditch effort to avoid American military intervention, the scheme had little chance of success. Spain's national pride and interest precluded surrender. The Cubans had already said they would accept "nothing short of absolute independence."[15] Madrid's answer nonetheless held some promise: Spain had already terminated reconcentration, would launch reforms, and would accept an armistice if the rebels did so first. Yet by refusing McKinley's mediation and Cuban independence, the Spanish reply did not satisfy the president or Congress. McKinley began to compose a war message in early April. On April 9, Spain made a new concession, declaring a unilateral suspension of hostilities "for such a length of time" as the Spanish commander "may think prudent."[16] Too qualified, the declaration still sidestepped Cuban independence and U.S. mediation. Any chance of European support for Spain faded when the British told Washington that they would "be guided [on Cuban issues] by the wishes of the president."[17]

On April 11, McKinley asked Congress for authority to use armed force to end the Cuban war. Since neither Cubans nor Spaniards could stem the flow of blood, Americans would do so to serve the "cause of humanity" and prevent "very serious injury to the commerce, trade, and business of our people, and the wanton destruction of property." Citing the *Maine,* he described the conflict as "a constant menace to our peace." He conspicuously made no mention of Cuban independence, defining the U.S. purpose as "forcible intervention … as a neutral to stop the war." At the very end of the message, McKinley asked Congress to give "your just and careful attention" to news of Spain's recently offered armistice.[18]

As Congress debated, McKinley beat back a Senate attempt to recognize the rebels. He strongly believed that Cuba needed American tutelage to prepare for self-government. And he wanted a Cuba subservient to the United States. Indeed, as the historian Louis A. Pérez, Jr., has argued, McKinley's decision for war seemed directed "as much against Cuban independence as it was against Spanish sovereignty."[19] Congress did endorse the Teller Amendment, which disclaimed any U.S. intent to annex the island. Even Teddy Roosevelt supported the amendment lest "it seem that we are merely engaged in a land-grabbing war."[20] On April 19 Congress proclaimed Cuba's independence (without recognizing the Cuban junta), demanded Spain's evacuation from the island, and directed the president to use force to secure these goals. Spain broke diplomatic relations on April 21. The next day U.S. warships began to blockade Cuba; Spain declared war on April 24. Congress issued its own declaration the next day.

William McKinley (1843–1901). In one of his last speeches before his death in 1901, McKinley peered into the next century: "How near one to the other is every part of the world. Modern inventions have brought into close relations widely separated peoples … distances have been effaced. … The world's products are being exchanged as never before … isolation is no longer possible or desirable." (Library of Congress)

Because of the Teller Amendment, the choice for war seemed selfless and humane, and for many Americans it undoubtedly was. But the decision had more complex motives. McKinley cited humanitarian concern, property, commerce, and the removal of a regional disturbance. Senator Henry Cabot Lodge invoked politics, telling the White House that "if the war in Cuba drags on through the summer … we [Republicans] shall go down to the greatest defeat ever known."[21] Important business leaders, initially hesitant, shifted in March and April to demand an end to Cuban disorder. Farmers and entrepreneurs ogling Asian and Latin American markets thought a U.S. victory over Spain might open new trade doors by eliminating a colonial power. Republican Senator George F. Hoar of Massachusetts, later an anti–imperialist, could not "look idly on while hundreds of thousands of innocent human beings … die of hunger close to our doors. If there is ever to be a war it should be to prevent such things."[22] Another senator claimed that "any sort of war is better than a rotting peace that eats out the core and heart of the manhood of this country."[23] Christian missionaries dreamed of new opportunities to convert the "uncivilized." Imperialists hoped that war would add new territories to the United States and encourage the growth of a larger navy. "Warriors" differed from "imperialists" in that some people opposed empire and sincerely thought war would halt the protracted conflict in Cuba, whereas imperialists seized on war as an opportunity to expand the American empire.

Emotional nationalism also made an impact. The *Maine* and de Lôme (see page 216) incidents ignited what one educator called the "formidable inflammability of our multitudinous population."[24] Imperialist senator Albert Beveridge waxed ebullient: "At last, God's hour has struck. The American people go forth in a warfare holier than liberty—holy as humanity."[25] Excited statements by people such as Roosevelt, who regarded war as a sport, aroused martial fevers. War would surely redeem national honor and repudiate those "old women of both sexes, shrieking cockatoos" who made virile men "wonder whether" they lived "in a free country or not."[26] Newspapers of the "yellow press" variety, such as William Randolph Hearst's *New York Journal* and Joseph Pulitzer's *New York World,* sensationalized stories of Spanish lust and atrocities. Others proudly compared the Cuban and American revolutions. The American public, already steeped in a brash nationalism and prepared by earlier diplomatic triumphs, reacted favorably to the hyperbole.

Both Washington and Madrid had tried diplomacy without success. McKinley wanted "peace" and independence for Cuba under U.S. tutelage. The first Spain could not deliver because the Cuban rebels sensed victory and complete independence, while Spanish forces remained weak. The second Spain could not grant immediately because ultranationalists might overthrow the constitutional Bourbon monarchy. Spain promised to fight the war more humanely and grant autonomy, but McKinley and Congress wanted more. They believed they had the right and duty to judge the affairs of Spain and Cuba. "To save Cuba, we must hold it," noted one reporter.[27]

Well-meaning or not, American meddling prevented Cubans and Spaniards from settling their own affairs. Sending the *Maine* and asking Congress for $50 million probably encouraged the Cuban rebels to resist any compromise. McKinley could have given Spain more breathing space. Spain, after all, did grant partial autonomy, which ultimately might have led to Cuban independence. Some critics said the president should have recognized the Cuban insurgents and covertly aided them. American matériel, not men, might have liberated Cuba from Spanish rule. By April 1898, one U.S. official concluded that Spain had become "absolutely hopeless, … exhausted financially and physically, while the Cubans are stronger."[28] McKinley wanted to avoid war and chose it reluctantly only after trying other options. That he adamantly refused to recognize the insurgency or the republic indicates also that he did not endorse outright Cuban independence. He probably had two goals in 1898: to remove Spain from Cuba and to control Cuba in some manner yet ill-defined. When the Spanish balked at a sale and both belligerents rejected compromise, McKinley chose war—the only means to oust Spain *and* to control Cuba. A new and enlarged American empire shimmered on the horizon.

The Venezuela Crisis of 1895

Three years earlier, during the administration of an avowedly anti-imperialist president, a seemingly insignificant cartographic controversy in South America had served as a catalyst for empire. In July 1895, Secretary of State Richard Olney personally delivered a 12,000-word draft document to President Grover Cleveland on the Venezuelan boundary dispute. The president, thinking it "the best thing of its kind I ever read," suggested some "softened verbiage here and there" and directed that Olney send the document to London, which he did on July 20.[29]

What became known as Olney's "twenty-inch gun" pointed directly at Great Britain, which had long haggled with Venezuela over the boundary separating that country from British Guiana. The British drew a line in the 1840s, but nobody liked it. In the 1880s, the discovery of gold in the disputed region raised the stakes. At issue, too, was control of the mouth of the Orinoco River, gateway to the potential trade of northern South America. Since the 1870s, Venezuela had appealed to the United States over Britain's alleged violation of the Monroe Doctrine. Washington repeatedly asked the British to submit the issue to arbitration but met constant rebuff. London's latest refusal in December 1894 led to Olney's "twenty-inch gun" rejoinder.

The Venezuelans had hired William L. Scruggs, a former U.S. minister to Caracas, to propagandize their case before the American public. His widely circulated pamphlet *British Aggression in Venezuela, or the Monroe Doctrine on Trial* (1895) stirred considerable sympathy for the South American nation. Stereotypes soon replaced reasoned analysis: The land-grabbing British were robbing a poor hemispheric friend of the United States. A unanimous congressional resolution of February 1894 called for arbitration, underscoring U.S. concern. Cleveland's Democratic party had lost badly in the 1894 elections, and Republicans were attacking his administration as cowardly for not annexing Hawai'i. Bold action might deflect criticism and recoup Democratic losses. One Democrat advised Cleveland: "Turn this Venezuelan question up or down, North, South, East or West, and it is a 'winner.'"[30]

The global imperial competition of the 1890s also pushed the president toward action. The British, already holding large stakes in Latin America, seemed intent on enlarging their share. Like the French intervention in Mexico a generation earlier, London's claim against Venezuela became a symbol of European intrusion

"The Real British Lion."   This is a popular American depiction of the British global presence during the crisis over Venezuela. A few years later, President Cleveland himself recalled British behavior as "mean and hoggish." (*New York Evening World,* 1895)

into the hemisphere. The economic depression of the 1890s also caused concern. Many Americans, including Cleveland, thought that overproduction had caused the slump and that expanding foreign trade could cure it. The National Association of Manufacturers, organized in 1895 to encourage exports, chose Caracas as the site of its first overseas display of American products. Might the British close this potential new market?

Nor did Cleveland like bullies. He had already rejected Hawaiian annexation in part because he thought Americans had bullied the Hawaiians. Now the British were arrogantly slapping the Venezuelans. Defense of the Monroe Doctrine became his and Olney's maxim. In unvarnished language, the "twenty-inch gun" of July 20, 1895, warned that European partition of Africa should not repeat itself in Latin America. The "safety," "honor," and "welfare" of the United States were at stake, and the Monroe Doctrine stipulated that "any permanent political union between a European and an American state [was] unnatural and inexpedient." The Cleveland–Olney message stressed that "the states of America, South as well as North, by geographical proximity, by natural sympathy, by similarity of government constitutions, are friends and allies, commercially and politically, of the United States. To allow the subjugation of any one of them by a European power … signifies the loss of all the advantages incident to their natural relations with us." The forceful overriding theme of the note boldly addressed an international audience. "To-day the United States is practically sovereign on this continent, and its fiat is law upon the subjects to which it confines its interposition." And more: The United States's "infinite resources combined with its isolated position render it master of the situation and practically invulnerable as against any or all other powers."[31] Finally, the message

"If There Must Be War."   Lord Salisbury and President Grover Cleveland slug it out during the Venezuelan crisis of 1895. Britain's ambassador, Sir Julian Pauncefote, simplistically blamed the war scare on sensationalist U.S. newspapers whose "stream of mendacity and audacity and ignorance and malice and general blackguardism … is swallowed by millions and does infinite mischief." (*Life,* 1896)

demanded arbitration, threatened U.S. intervention, and requested a British answer before Cleveland's annual message to Congress in December.

British Prime Minister Lord Salisbury received the missive with some surprise and sent it to the Foreign Office for study. Distracted by crises in South Africa, Salisbury saw no urgency. In the late nineteenth century, American Anglophobic bombast was not unusual, especially before elections. Thus, by ignoring the problem in the hope that the "conflagration will fizzle away," Salisbury did not reply until after Cleveland's annual message, which was actually quite tame on Venezuela.[32] The British note, which smacked of the "peremptory schoolmaster trying—with faded patience—to correct the ignorance of dullards in Washington," denied the applicability of the Monroe Doctrine and dismissed any U.S. interest in the controversy.[33]

On reading the note, Cleveland became "mad clean through."[34] His special message to Congress on December 17 rang the alarm bell: England must arbitrate; the United States would create an investigating commission to set the true boundary line; unless London acquiesced, the United States would intervene by "every means in its power."[35] Congress quickly voted funds for the commission. Republicans and Democrats rallied behind the president, and New York City police commissioner Theodore Roosevelt boomed: "Let the fight come if it must; I don't care whether our sea coast cities are bombarded or not; we would take Canada."[36] With Irish Americans volunteering to fight their ancient foe, the British ambassador reported: "Nothing is heard but the voice of the Jingo bellowing defiance to England."[37]

War fevers cooled rapidly in early 1896. Many bankers and business leaders grew alarmed when the stock market plummeted, in part because British investors were pulling out. The *New York World* put out a special Christmas issue with portraits of the Prince of Wales and Lord Salisbury under the headline "PEACE AND GOOD WILL," suggesting the irrationality of war with Britain, a country so close in race, language, and culture.[38] Even the U.S. ambassador in London feared the president had been "too *precipitate*" in joining "the camp of aggressiveness."[39] But Cleveland never wanted war. He wanted peace on his terms.

What followed seemed anticlimactic. The British cabinet in early January 1896 decided to seek an "honourable settlement" with the United States.[40] Facing a new dispute with Germany over South Africa, England needed friends, not enemies. Formal talks continued until November 1896, when the United States and Britain agreed to set up a five-person arbitration board to define the boundary. Finally, in October 1899, the tribunal reached a decision that rejected the extreme claims of either party and generally followed the original line from the 1840s. The mouth of the Orinoco went to Venezuela, which came out of the dispute rather well, considering that neither the United States nor Britain cared much about Venezuela's national interest. In fact, both parties excluded Venezuela's duly accredited minister in Washington from the talks. Lobbyist William Scruggs complained that the United States sought to "*bull-doze*" Venezuela."[41] He had it right, but Washington's "sledgehammer subtlety" targeted others besides that South American nation.[42] The overweening theme of the "twenty-inch gun" merits repeating: "To-day the United States is practically sovereign on this continent, and its fiat is law upon the subjects to which it confines its interposition."[43]

Men of Empire

The Venezuelan crisis and the war with Spain punctuated an era of imperialist competition when, as one senator grandiosely put it: "The great nations are rapidly absorbing … all the waste areas of the earth. It is a moment which makes for civilization and the advancement of the race."[44] Cleveland and McKinley helped move the United States toward world-power status. As examples of forceful, even aggressive, diplomacy, both events accelerated important trends. Besides ignoring the rights and sensibilities of small countries, both episodes revealed a United States more certain about the components of its "policy" and more willing to confront rivals. Both events stimulated what critics at the time called "jingoism." The Monroe Doctrine gained new status as a warning to curb European meddling in the Western Hemisphere. Just as Cleveland went to the brink of war over Venezuela without consulting Congress, so too did McKinley, despite a jingoist Congress and inflamed public opinion, reinforce presidential control over foreign policy.

In both crises Latin Americans learned again that the United States sought supremacy in the Western Hemisphere and would intervene when it saw fit. The Venezuela crisis and the outbreak of revolution in Cuba in 1895 intensified North American interest in the Caribbean, a significant dimension of which was economic. Coinciding with a severe economic depression at home, the potential loss of markets

Makers of American Foreign Relations, 1895–1900

Presidents	Secretaries of State
Grover Cleveland, 1893–1897	Walter Q. Gresham, 1893–1895
	Richard Olney, 1895–1897
William McKinley, 1897–1901	John Sherman, 1897–1898
	William R. Day, 1898
	John Hay, 1898–1905

in Venezuela and Cuba brought more attention to the theory of overproduction as a cause of depression, which increased exports could allegedly cure. Commercial expansion, always a trend in American history, received another boost.

The discord with Britain over Venezuela ironically helped foster Anglo-American rapprochement. Cooperation and mutual interest increasingly characterized relations between Washington and London. British diplomats cultivated U.S. friendship as a possible counterweight to growing German power, and Britain's support over Cuba and its subsequent deference to the United States regarding the Caribbean facilitated the emerging entente.

The chief mechanism by which the United States sought to manage events in that area was through naval power. The Venezuelan crisis, joined by crises in Asia and the belief that naval construction would employ those idled by the depression, stimulated additional naval expansion. The Navy Act of 1896, for example, provided for three new battleships and ten new torpedo boats, several of which contributed to naval victories over Spain two years later.

By the end of the decade the United States had gained new U.S. colonies in the Pacific, Asia, and the Caribbean, a protectorate over Cuba, and Europe's recognition of U.S. hegemony in the Caribbean. By 1900, too, the United States had pledged itself to preserve the "Open Door" in China; it had built a naval armada that had just annihilated the Spanish navy and ranked second in the world only to Great Britain's "mammoth imperial fleet"; and it had developed an export trade amounting to $1.5 billion.[45] Steel and iron production exemplified its industrial might, which almost equaled that of Britain and Germany combined. U.S. acquisition of new colonies after the Spanish-American-Cuban-Filipino War suggests that *only then,* about 1898, did the United States become an imperialist world power. But what actually happened, one scholar writes, was a "culmination" not an "aberration."[46] Having taken halting steps toward empire before the depression of the 1890s, the United States now took a giant imperialist leap.

Assistant Secretary of the Navy Theodore Roosevelt described the anti-imperialists in 1897 as "men of a by-gone age" and "provincials."[47] Indeed, anti-imperialism waned in the late nineteenth century. Increasing numbers of educated, economically comfortable Americans made the case for formal empire (colonies or protectorates) or informal empire (commercial domination). Naval officers, diplomats, politicians,

Grover Cleveland (1837–1908). This portrait of the two-term president, overweight from frequenting saloons as a young man, exhibits the gruff American attitude toward Britain during the Venezuelan crisis. The historian Dexter Perkins has written that Cleveland was "so honest, so brave, so independent ..., but also so rigid and inflexible in his thinking, so unimaginative, so dogmatic." (Library of Congress)

farmers, skilled artisans, business leaders, and clergy made up what political scientists call the "foreign-policy public," who influenced mass opinion through their management of the printing press and the public lectern. This "elite," aided by the hawkish clamoring of the "yellow press," helped the McKinley administration maneuver America towards war and empire.

Analysis of the phrase "public opinion" helps explain the *hows* as distinct from the *whys* of decision making. One often hears that "public opinion" or "the man in the street" influenced a leader to follow a certain course of action. But "public opinion" did not comprise a unified, identifiable group speaking with one voice. Political leaders and other articulate, knowledgeable people often shaped the "public opinion" they wanted to hear by their very handling of events and their control over information. In trying to determine who the "people" are and what "public opinion" is, social scientists have demonstrated that in the 1890s the people who counted, who expressed their opinion publicly in order to influence policy, numbered no more than 1.5 million to 3 million, or between 10 and 20 percent of the voting public. This percentage—upper- and middle-income groups, highly educated, active politically—constituted the "foreign-policy public." Secretary of State Walter Q. Gresham observed in 1893: "After all, public opinion is made and controlled by the thoughtful men of the country."[48] The public opinion the president heard in the 1890s did not come from the "people," but rather from a small, articulate segment of the American population alert to foreign-policy issues. Although these educated elites included anti-imperialists, the foreign-policy public leaned heavily toward the side of imperialism.

The president ultimately dominates policymaking and may even disregard advice from the foreign-policy public itself. President Cleveland, for example, successfully resisted pressure to annex Hawai'i and withdrew the treaty from the Senate, and he never let Congress or influential public opinion set the terms of his policy toward the Venezuelan crisis. But while the initiative in foreign affairs finally rests in executive hands—with Cleveland and McKinley appearing "unabashed in their resistance" to public pressure (unlike their seemingly more pliant predecessors of the 1860s and 1870s)—no president formulates policy in a vacuum.[49] Explanations of the 1898 war are inadequate that specifically designate the yellow press or public vengeance towards Spain as *the* reason the United States fought. So, too, are explanations that stress executive leadership absent other factors. Emotional nationalism, sensationalist journalism, and a visible, active foreign policy elite did not force McKinley into war. But they did help create an environment that helped condition McKinley's perceived range of options and that enabled him, once he chose war, to disperse responsibility—and blame—for the outcomes.

Cleveland and McKinley Confront *Cuba Libre,* 1895–1898

The year 1895 brought momentous events. The Venezuelan crisis, Japan's defeat of China in the Sino-Japanese War, and the outbreak of revolution in Cuba—all carried profound meaning for U.S. foreign relations. The sugar-rich island of Cuba, since the close of its unsuccessful war for independence (1868–1878), suffered political repression and poverty. After that war Cuban nationalists prepared for a new assault on their Spanish overlords. From 1880 to 1895, the Cuban national hero José Martí plotted from exile in the United States. In 1892 he organized the Cuban Revolutionary party, using U.S. territory to recruit men and money. Martí's opportunity came when Cuba's economy fell victim in 1894 to a new U.S. tariff, which raised duties on imported sugar and hence reduced Cuban sugar shipments to the United States. On February 24, 1895, with cries of *"Cuba Libre,"* the rebels reopened their drive for independence.

Cuban revolutionaries kept a cautious eye on the United States, well known for its relentless interest in the island, and they feared an ultimate U.S. attempt to control their nation's destiny. José Martí's fifteen-year stay in the United States had turned him into a critic of what he called "the monster"—an "aggressive" and "avaricious" nation "full of hate" and "widespread spiritual coarseness." If the North Americans intervened, they might not leave. "To change masters is not to be free," he warned.[50] On May 19 Martí died in battle.

Cuban and Spanish military strategies wreaked destruction and death. Led by General Máximo Gómez, a veteran of the 1868–1878 war, the *insurrectos* burned cane fields, blew up mills, and disrupted railroads, with the goal of rendering Cuba an economic liability to Spain. "The chains of Cuba have been forged by her own richness," Gómez proclaimed, "and it is precisely this which I propose to do away with soon."[51] Spain, in turn, vowed to "use up the last peseta in her treasury and sacrifice the last of her sons" to retain Cuba.[52] Although outnumbered (about 30,000 Cuban troops fought 200,000 Spanish) and lacking adequate supplies, the insurgents, with the sympathy of the populace, wore the Spanish down through guerrilla tactics. By late 1896, rebels controlled about two-thirds of the island, with the Spanish concentrated in coastal and urban regions. That year, to break the rebel stronghold in the rural areas, Governor-General Valeriano y Nicolau Weyler instituted the brutal reconcentration program. He divided the island into districts and then herded a half-million Cubans into fortified camps, where frightful sanitation conditions, poor food, and disease contributed to the death of perhaps 200,000 people. Weyler's soldiers regarded any Cubans outside the camps as rebels and hence targets for death; they also killed livestock, destroyed crops, and polluted water sources. This effort to starve the insurgents and deprive them of physical and moral support, combined with the rebels' destructive behavior, made a shambles of Cuba's society and economy. "Blood on the roadsides, blood in the fields, blood on the doorsteps, blood, blood, blood," wrote a *New York World* reporter in 1896.[53]

The Cleveland administration could have recognized Cuban belligerency. But such an act, Olney noted, would relieve Spain of any responsibility for paying claims filed by Americans for properties destroyed in Cuba. Cleveland and Olney found recognition of Cuban independence even less appetizing, for they believed the Cubans ("the most inhumane and barbarous cutthroats in the world") incapable of self-government and feared anarchy and even racial war.[54] That course might also arouse a Spanish declaration of war or force U.S. belligerency because, legalistically, a Spanish attempt to conquer an "independent" Cuba would constitute a violation of the Monroe Doctrine. Olney toyed with buying the island at one point.

The Cleveland administration settled on a dual policy of hostility to the revolution and pressure on Spain to grant some autonomy. Diplomacy and lecturing to a foreign government seemed to work in the Venezuelan crisis; perhaps it would work with Cuba.

Prodded by a Republican Congress and by Spanish obstinacy in refusing reforms and adhering to force, Olney sent a note to Spain in April 1896. He urged a political solution that would leave "Spain her rights of sovereignty" while securing to the Cubans "all such rights and powers of local self-government as they [could] ask."[55] Spain should initiate reforms short of independence. Olney showed particular concern for the interests of Americans, not Cubans. With American property estimated at $50 million, the decline in sugar production wrought disaster to Cuban-American trade relations. In 1892 Cuba had shipped to the United States goods worth $79 million; by 1898 that figure had slumped to $15 million.

When Spain rejected Olney's advice, the Cleveland administration seemed flummoxed. It did not desire war, but it meant to protect U.S. interests. Congress kept asking for firm action. And in Havana, hotheaded Consul-General Fitzhugh Lee clamored for U.S. annexation. Cleveland did not fire Lee, nephew of General Robert E. Lee, because the incumbent president needed political friends at a time when Democrats were dumping him in favor of William Jennings Bryan. Consul-General Lee also warned that "there may be a revolution within a revolution," noting that Cuban insurgents vowed to redistribute property, which U.S. officials (and Creole elites) would not tolerate.[56] It further nettled Cleveland and Olney that Spain had approached the courts of Europe for diplomatic support, with the argument that the Monroe Doctrine threatened all European powers.

British ambassador to Spain H. Drummond Wolff accurately claimed that for Cuba the United States wanted "peace with commerce."[57] In December 1896, Cleveland reported that neither the Spanish nor the Cuban rebels had established their authority over the island. Americans felt a humanitarian concern, he said, and their trade and investments ("pecuniary interest") faced destruction. Further, to maintain its neutrality, the United States had to police the coastline to intercept unlawful expeditions. Spain must grant autonomy or "home rule," but not independence, to "fertile and rich" Cuba in order to end the bloodshed and devastation. Otherwise, the United States, having thus far acted with "restraint," might abandon its "expectant attitude."[58]

But Cleveland had more bark than bite. Through Olney he successfully buried a Senate resolution urging recognition of Cuban independence and contented himself with some limited Spanish reforms of February 1897. Thereafter he let the Cuban issue fester, bequeathing it to the incoming McKinley administration.

William McKinley had defeated William Jennings Bryan in the election of 1896. The teetotaling Ohioan seemed a stable, dignified figure in a time of crisis. He projected deep religious conviction, personal warmth, sincerity, commitment to economic development and the revival of business, party loyalty, and support for expansion abroad. Yet McKinley often gave the appearance of being a pliant follower, a mindless flunky of the political bosses. Cartoonists depicted him in women's dress and called him a "goody-goody" man.[59] Such an image was created in large part by bellicose imperialists who believed that McKinley was not moving fast

Uncle Sam—"All That You Need Is Backbone."   This cartoon depicts a tall, erect Uncle Sam shoving a rifle down President McKinley's coat to provide him with a backbone. As the historian Kristin Hoganson points out in *Fighting for American Manhood* (1998), expansionist critics of McKinley often accused the president of being weak, flabby, and vacillating because he did not immediately leap into war with Spain. (*Chicago Chronicle,* in *Cartoons of the War of 1898 with Spain,* Chicago, 1898)

enough. Certainly a party regular and friend of large corporations, the president was no lackey. A manager of diplomacy who wanted expansion and empire without war and a settlement of the Cuban question without U.S. military intervention, McKinley acted as "his own man."[60]

McKinley shared America's image of itself as an expanding, virile nation of superior institutions and as a major power in Latin America. He agreed that the United States must have a large navy, overseas commerce, and foreign bases. He believed strongly that America must export its surplus goods. As a tariff specialist, he favored high tariffs on manufactured goods, low tariffs on raw materials, and reciprocity agreements. The Republican party platform of 1896 overflowed with expansionist rhetoric. It urged American control of Hawai'i, a Nicaraguan canal run by the United States, an enlarged navy, purchase of the Virgin Islands, and Cuban independence. Between election and inauguration, however, McKinley quietly joined Cleveland and Olney in sidetracking a Senate resolution for recognition of Cuba. He wanted a free hand, and he did not believe that Cubans could govern themselves. His inaugural address vacuously urged peace, never mentioning the Cuban crisis.

Beginning in March 1897, congressional resolutions on Cuba sprang up repeatedly, but the new president managed to kill them. McKinley did satisfy imperialists by sending a Hawaiian annexation treaty to the Senate. In June Madrid received an American reprimand for Weyler's uncivilized warfare and for his disruption of the Cuban economy. Spain, however, showed no signs of tempering its military response to the insurrection. American citizens languished in Spanish jails; American property continued to be razed. In July McKinley instructed Minister Woodford to demand that the Spanish stop the fighting. Increasingly convinced that the Cuban *insurrectos* would not compromise, the president implored Spain to grant autonomy. A new Spanish government soon moderated policy by offering Cuba a substantial degree of self-government. Even more significantly, it removed the hated Weyler and promised to end reconcentration. Such reforms actually encouraged intransigence, as Cuban leaders saw them as "a sign of Spain's weakening power and an indication that the end is not far off."[61]

McKinley's December 6, 1897, annual message to Congress discussed the Cuban insurrection at great length. Voicing the "gravest apprehension," McKinley rejected annexation of the island as "criminal aggression." He argued against recognition of belligerency, because the rebels hardly constituted a government worthy of recognition. And he ruled out intervention as premature at a time when the Spanish were traveling the "honorable paths" of reform. He asked for patience to see if Spanish changes would work, but he hinted that the United States would keep open all policy options, including intervention "with force."[62]

By mid-January 1898, it became evident that Spanish reforms had not moderated the crisis; in fact, insurgents, conservatives, and the Spanish army all denounced them. After antireform Spaniards rioted in Havana, McKinley sent the *Maine* to the Cuban city to protect American lives and property. On February 9, the State Department received a copy of a private letter written in late 1897 by the Spanish minister to the United States, Enrique Dupuy de Lôme, and sent to a senior Spanish politician touring Cuba. Intercepted in Cuba by a rebel sympathizer who forwarded it to the Cuban junta in New York City, the letter not only reached the State Department, but William Randolph Hearst's flamboyant *New York Journal* published it that day with the banner headline: "Worst Insult to the United States in its History." De Lôme labeled McKinley "weak," a "bidder for the admiration of the crowd," and a "would-be politician."[63] McKinley particularly resented another statement that suggested that Spain did not take its reform proposals seriously and would persist in fighting to defeat the rebels. Spain, it appeared, could not be trusted. De Lôme's hasty recall hardly salved the hurt. Less than a week later the *Maine* blew up, setting in motion events and decisions that led to war and overseas empire for the United States.

What if ... *Spain had granted independence to Cuba in 1898?*

Had Madrid offered full independence instead of autonomy to Cuban insurgents in 1898, subsequent history might have been different. Even if full Cuban independence had come after the *Maine* explosion, the ostensible reason for U.S. military intervention would have been removed. Although President William McKinley might have preferred a U.S. protectorate rather than complete independence for Cuba, it would have been difficult, if not impossible, to justify a military occupation without war with Spain. The Cuban revolutionaries could have built their own democratic, multiracial republic and pursued social and economic reforms without having to accommodate the class and racial biases of a North American overlord. Cubans would not have perceived their apparent victory over the Spanish snatched from them by Washington, and Cuban nationalism might not have developed the strong strain of anti-Americanism that leaders such as Fidel Castro later exploited.

Of course, given the devastation of Cuba's infrastructure after three years of war, the influx of entrepreneurs and investments from the United States might have been inevitable while perhaps resulting in less overt dominance over the island's economy. Even without a Platt Amendment mandating U.S. intervention under certain circumstances, marines and "money doctors" might still have temporarily occupied Cuba, as they actually did in 1906, 1912, and 1917, whenever revolutionary disorder seemed to threaten American lives and investments. One other outcome would certainly have been different, for without the perpetual lease agreement included in the Platt Amendment of 1903, the U.S. government could not have set up an internment camp a century later at the Guantánamo Bay naval base where Afghani and other prisoners of war were tortured in the name of a U.S. "war on terror."

Cuban independence without U.S. intervention in 1898 might also have affected American policies elsewhere. Theodore Roosevelt's celebrated order to Commodore George Dewey's Far Eastern Squadron to attack the Spanish fleet in Manila Bay would not have been carried out. Nor would Puerto Rico have become a war prize. Unburdened by the conflict in Cuba, Spanish forces might have defeated Filipino insurgents, but Emilio Aguinaldo's guerrillas would likely have emerged victorious. A Philippines Republic proclaimed in 1899 might not have survived surrounded by imperial predators. The Germans, Americans, British, French, and perhaps the Japanese might have partitioned Spain's Pacific possessions among themselves, just as the Germans and Americans divided Samoa that same year. The United States might still have annexed Guam and parts of the Philippines. Such imperial arrangements might have prompted Washington to seek its own leasehold in China, similar to Hong Kong or Port Arthur, instead of promulgating the Open Door Notes to preserve America's share of the China trade. In such a context, the rationale for annexing Hawai'i to reinforce Dewey would have been less compelling, but U.S. commercial and strategic interests in the Pacific would have kept those islands within a growing informal empire.

An unfought war over Cuba would also have meant less prominence for such would-be war heroes as Teddy Roosevelt. Someone other than the Rough Rider in the White House would surely have negotiated with England, Colombia, Panama, and Nicaragua with less flamboyance and pugnacity on behalf of an isthmian canal. Nonetheless, the same arguments about commercial and strategic needs and benefits to civilization from such a canal would likely have prevailed. An American-built canal would still symbolize U.S. hemispheric preeminence. Similarly, a Roosevelt Corollary by another name (and possibly with less imperial language) would still have articulated the economic, strategic, and legal arguments to justify U.S. intervention under the Monroe Doctrine. In short, the year 1898 would likely have remained a springboard for American imperial expansion even without an American-Spanish war over Cuba.

The Spanish-American-Cuban-Filipino War

Americans enlisted in what they trumpeted as a glorious expedition to demonstrate U.S. right and might. They were cocky. Theodore Roosevelt, who resigned as assistant secretary of the navy to lead the flashy but overrated Rough Riders, said that it was not much of a war but it was the best Americans had. It was a short war, April to August 12, but 5,462 Americans died in it—only 379 of them in combat. Most expired from malaria and yellow fever. Camera operators for Thomas Edison and Biograph shot "moving pictures" of the war, and crowds flocked to see flickering images of battleships at sea, the wreck of the *Maine,* and triumphant victory parades.[64] Led by officers seasoned in the Civil War and in campaigns against Native Americans, the new imperial fighters embarked from Florida in mid-June. Seventeen thousand men, clutching their Krag-Jörgensen rifles, landed on Cuban soil unopposed because Cuban insurgents had driven Spanish troops into the cities. Cubans cooperated warily with their new American allies.

Commodore George Dewey (1837–1917) at the Battle of Manila Bay, May 1, 1898. From the bridge of his 5,386-ton flagship, U.S.S. *Olympia,* Dewey directs the battle that destroyed Spanish naval power in the Pacific. This dramatic action turned the modest sailor from Vermont into a national hero and soon led to the American acquisition of the Philippines. This print is from the original painting that is on display at the Vermont State House in Montpelier. The *Olympia* is now a floating museum in Philadelphia. (Naval Historical Foundation)

"Cuba Reconciling the North and South." Captain Fritz W. Guerin's 1898 photograph depicted nationalism in the Spanish-American-Cuban-Filipino War. Golden-haired Cuba, liberated from her chains by her North American heroes, oversees the reconciliation of the Union and Confederacy in a splashy display of patriotism. Nevertheless, as the historian David W. Blight has written in *Race and Reunion* (2001), "national unity in foreign policy … gave the promoters of Jim Crow in the South a freer hand than ever in fashioning a segregated social system." (Library of Congress)

Yet the big news had already arrived from the Philippine Islands, Spain's major colony in Asia. Only days after the American declaration of war, Commodore George Dewey sailed his Asiatic Squadron from Hong Kong into Manila Bay, where he smashed the Spanish fleet with the loss of one U.S. sailor. Slipping by the Spanish guns at Corregidor, Dewey entered the bay at night. Early in the morning of May 1, with the laconic order, "You may fire when ready, Gridley," his flagship *Olympia* began to demolish the ten incompetently handled Spanish ships. "PHILIPPINES OURS, WHAT WILL WE DO WITH THEM?" ran the headline of the *New York Journal*.[65] Some people, ignorant of U.S. interests in the Pacific, wondered how a war to liberate Cuba saw its first action in Asia. Naval officials had pinpointed the Philippines in contingency plans as early as 1896. Often credited alone with ordering Dewey on February 25, 1898, to attack Manila if war broke out, Assistant Secretary of the Navy Theodore Roosevelt actually set in motion preexisting war plans already known and approved by the president. After the war, when the Navy Department balked at revealing its advance preparations, Roosevelt was "naturally delighted at shouldering the responsibility."[66]

By late June, U.S. troops in Cuba had advanced toward Santiago, where dispirited Spanish soldiers manned antique guns. Joined by experienced Cuban rebels, the North Americans on July 1 battled for San Juan Hill. American forces, spearheaded by the Rough Riders and the black soldiers of the Ninth Cavalry, finally captured the strategic promontory overlooking Santiago after suffering heavy casualties. Two days later the Spanish squadron, penned in Santiago harbor for weeks by U.S. warships, made a desperate daylight break for open sea. Some U.S. vessels nearly collided as they hurried to sink the helpless Spanish craft, which went down with 323 dead. Its fleet destroyed, Spain surrendered—but only to the Americans. Cubans were forbidden from entering towns and cities to celebrate. Historians still debate whether Cubans could have won their independence without U.S. intervention. Louis A. Pérez, Jr., has argued that McKinley intervened because he was "alarmed at the prospect of a Cuban victory," whereas a recent multi-archival account by John Lawrence Tone suggests that "the Cuban insurgency was in a nearly terminal condition by 1897 and had no chance of victory without outside help" and therefore only "the rather small American expeditionary army … could have destroyed the Spanish army at Santiago."[67] With victory, however, came U.S. occupation and U.S. hegemony.

"Porto Rico is not forgotten and we mean to have it," wrote Senator Lodge in May 1898.[68] Thus did U.S. troops also invade another Spanish colony, Puerto Rico, which expansionists coveted as the "Malta of the Caribbean"—an ideal base for a proper navy and a strategic outpost to protect a Central American canal. In nineteen days General Nelson A. Miles, in what was described as "a picnic" and a "*fete des fleurs,*" captured the sugar- and coffee-exporting island.[69] At least at first, the Puerto Rican elite welcomed their new North American masters as an improvement over their Spanish rulers.

Manila capitulated in mid-August, after the Spanish put up token resistance in a deal that salvaged Spanish pride by surrendering to Americans and not to the "niggers," thereby keeping Filipino nationalist Emilio Aguinaldo from the walled city.[70] Washington soon ordered Aguinaldo and other Filipino rebels, who had fought against the Spanish for independence since 1896 and had surrounded Manila for weeks, to remain outside the capital and to recognize the authority of the United States.

In July, ostensibly to ensure uninterrupted reinforcement of Dewey, the United States officially absorbed Hawai'i, where troop transports took on coal en route to Manila. From 1893 to 1897, while Cleveland refused annexation, politics in Hawai'i had changed little. Despite a 556-page antiannexation petition from native Hawaiians, the white revolutionaries clung to power. Once elected, McKinley proclaimed: "We need Hawai'i … a good deal more than we did California. It is manifest destiny."[71] After negotiating a new treaty with the white-led Hawaiian government, he side-stepped the constitutional requirement of a two-thirds vote in the Senate in favor of a joint resolution. On July 7, 1898, Congress passed the resolution for annexation by a majority vote (290 to 91 in the House and 42 to 21 in the Senate), thereby formally attaching the strategically and commercially important islands to the United States. Annexation was "not a change" but "a consummation," said McKinley.[72]

Men Versus "Aunties": The Debate over Empire in the United States

Spain sued for peace, and on August 12 the belligerents proclaimed an armistice. To negotiate with the Spanish in Paris, McKinley appointed a "peace commission" loaded with imperialists and headed by Secretary of State William R. Day, friend and

"The Fools Are Not All Dead Yet" *Los Angeles Times*, May 14, 1899

"The Fools Are Not All Dead Yet." This cartoon from the *Los Angeles Sunday Times* lampoons anti-imperialists by drawing them as fussy old women, often called "aunties" (a pun on "anti"). Here they are worshipping a statue of Emilio Aguinaldo, whom some anti-imperialists hailed as the George Washington of Philippine Independence. (*Los Angeles Sunday Times,* May 14, 1899)

follower of the president's wishes. As negotiations continued into autumn, and after McKinley tested public opinion by touring the Midwest (his ear "so close to the ground that it was full of grasshoppers"), he demanded all of the Philippines ("the whole Archipelago or none"), plus the island of Guam in the Marianas, and Puerto Rico, as well independence for Cuba.[73] Articulate Filipinos pleaded for their country's freedom but met a stern U.S. rebuff. Spanish diplomats accepted this American land grab after the United States offered $20 million as compensation. In early December, U.S. delegates signed the treaty and walked out of the elegant French conference room clutching the Philippines, Puerto Rico, and Guam.

Opponents protested vigorously. They had organized the Anti-Imperialist League in Boston in November 1898, but they never acted in unison. They counted among their number such unlikely bedfellows as the steel magnate Andrew Carnegie, the labor leader Samuel Gompers, the agrarian spokesman William Jennings Bryan, the Massachusetts Senator George Hoar, Harvard president Charles W. Eliot, and the humorist Mark Twain—people who had often disagreed among themselves on domestic issues. Some anti-imperialists took inconsistent positions. Hoar, the most outspoken senator opposed to the treaty, had voted for war and annexation of

Carl Schurz (1829–1906).
Born in Germany, Schurz
emigrated to the United States
after the failed revolutions of 1948.
Journalist, diplomat, reformer,
Union General during the Civil
War, the first German-American
U.S. senator, and Secretary
of the Interior under President
Rutherford B. Hayes, he became
an outspoken leader of the
American Anti-Imperialist League
during the debates over Philippine
annexation in 1899–1900. "Our
country right or wrong," Schurz
once said. "When right, to be kept
right. When wrong, to be put right."
(Library of Congress)

Hawai'i. An expansionist, Carnegie apparently would accept colonies if they could be taken without force. He even offered to write a personal check for $20 million to buy the independence of the Philippines. And the anti-imperialists could not overcome the *fait accompli,* possession and occupation of territory, handed them by McKinley. After all, argued the president, could America really relinquish this valuable real estate so nobly taken in battle?

Imperialists ridiculed anti-imperialists as "unmanly aunties," often caricaturing their opponents as "carping old ladies" or pygmies in skirts and bonnets.[74] Many opponents did want trade, but not at the cost of subjugating other peoples or of formally absorbing non-white races into the United States. The anti-imperialist David Starr Jordan, president of Stanford University, spoke of "peaceful conquest" by trade rather than by annexation.[75] Some anti-imperialists insisted that serious domestic problems demanded attention and resources first. Labor leader Samuel Gompers feared that annexation would bring "hordes" of "semi-savage races" with "coolie" labor standards "swarming into the United States."[76] Representative Champ Clark of Missouri could not stomach the prospect of "almond eyed, brown skinned United States Senators" from the Philippines: "No matter whether they are fit to govern themselves or not, they are not fit to govern us."[77] Mark Twain referred to the $20 million payment for the Philippines as the U.S. "entrance fee into the Society of the Sceptered Thieves."[78]

Prominent women also participated in the debate, hoping to build a distinct foreign-policy constituency out of existing networks of women's clubs and organizations. The New Hampshire pacifist Lucia True Ames Mead pronounced it immoral for "any nation … which buys or takes by conquest another people, and dominates them without promise of granting them independence."[79] The social reformer Jane Addams saw children playing war games in the streets of Chicago. The kids were *not freeing Cubans,* she protested, but rather *slaying Spaniards* in their not-so-innocent play. Although unsuccessful in preventing U.S. colonization of former Spanish territories in Asia and the Caribbean, peace activists raised public consciousness about the moral quandaries of imperialism. Due to their efforts, tens of thousands of women and men were inspired to become activists, and a discourse of peace and reform became articulated that persisted into the next century.

The imperialists, led by Roosevelt, Lodge, and McKinley, and backed strongly by business leaders, engaged their opponents in vigorous debate in early 1899. These empire builders stressed geostrategic considerations, although they communicated common ideas of racial superiority and national destiny to civilize the savage world. "For a thousand years," boasted Senator Albert Beveridge, "God had prepared Americans to be the "master organizers of the world," possessors of what he called "the blood of government," which could be transfused into "their Malay [Filipino] veins."[80] The Philippines provided stepping-stones to the rich China market and strategic ports for the expanding navy that protected American commerce and demonstrated U.S. prestige. International competition also dictated that the United States keep the fruits of victory, argued the imperialists; otherwise, a menacing Germany or expansionist Japan might pick up what America discarded. Few believed that the United States should relinquish territory acquired through blood. To the charge that no one had asked the Filipinos if they desired annexation to the United States, Roosevelt delighted in telling Democratic anti-imperialists that President Thomas Jefferson took Louisiana without a vote by its inhabitants. McKinley put it simply: "Duty determines destiny."[81]

Pro-imperialist Senator Lodge described the treaty fight in the Senate as the "closest, most bitter, and most exciting struggle."[82] Shortly before the vote, word reached Washington that Filipino insurrectionists and American soldiers had begun to fight. The news apparently stimulated support for the Treaty of Paris. Democrats tended to be anti-imperialists and Republicans imperialists, yet enough of the former endorsed the treaty on February 6, 1899, to pass it, just barely, by the necessary two-thirds vote, 57 to 27. William Jennings Bryan, believing that rejection of the treaty would prolong the war and that the Philippines could be freed after terminating the hostilities with Spain, urged an aye vote on his anti-imperialist friends. The Republicans probably had enough votes in reserve to pass the treaty even if Bryan had opposed it.

Imperial Collisions in Asia: The Philippine Insurrection and the Open Door in China

Controlling, protecting, and expanding the enlarged U.S. empire became a major chore. The Filipinos resisted most forcefully. By the end of the war, Aguinaldo and rebel forces controlled most of the islands, having routed the Spanish and driven them into Manila. Aguinaldo had arrived from exile in a U.S. warship and believed that American leaders, including Dewey, had promised his country independence

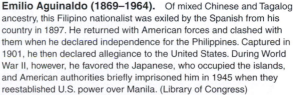

Emilio Aguinaldo (1869–1964). Of mixed Chinese and Tagalog ancestry, this Filipino nationalist was exiled by the Spanish from his country in 1897. He returned with American forces and clashed with them when he declared independence for the Philippines. Captured in 1901, he then declared allegiance to the United States. During World War II, however, he favored the Japanese, who occupied the islands, and American authorities briefly imprisoned him in 1945 when they reestablished U.S. power over Manila. (Library of Congress)

if he joined U.S. forces in defeating the Spanish. Ordered out of Manila by U.S. authorities after the Spanish-American armistice, he and his cohorts had to endure racial insults, including "nigger" and "gu gu" (the linguistic ancestor of "gook").[83] American soldiers considered the Filipinos inferior, the equivalent of Indians and blacks at home. Although one Methodist missionary boasted that the Americans had found Manila "a pesthole, and made it a health resort," critics claimed that imperialism exported the worst in American life.[84] The Treaty of Paris angered the Filipinos, as did McKinley's decree asserting the supreme authority of the United States in the Philippines. In open defiance of Washington, Aguinaldo and other prominent Filipinos organized a government at Malolos, wrote a constitution, and proclaimed the Philippine Republic in late January 1899.

McKinley deemed his new subjects unfit for self-government and proposed "benevolent assimilation" instead.[85] In February 1899 the Filipinos began fighting better armed American troops. After bloody struggles in which "the boys go for the enemy as if they were chasing jack-rabbits," U.S. forces captured Aguinaldo in March 1901.[86] Before the insurrection collapsed in 1902, some 4,165 Americans and more than 200,000 Filipinos died. One hundred twenty-five thousand American troops quelled the insurrection, which cost the United States at least $160 million. In Batangas province south of Manila, General J. Franklin Bell drove insurrectionists into the hills and killed their livestock. Thus malaria-transmitting mosquitoes "were forced to get their meals from people" instead of cattle. The result: an "epidemiological catastrophe" wherein the Batangas population declined by 90,000 (one-quarter of the people) over a six-year period.[87] Andrew Carnegie caustically deplored the pacification of the Filipinos: "About 8,000 of them have been completely civilized and sent to heaven. I hope you like it."[88] The Harvard philosopher William James similarly mocked "Civilization" as "the big, hollow, resounding, corrupting, sophisticating, confusing torrent of brutal momentum and irrationality that brings forth fruits like this!"[89]

What one U.S. general called the "most legitimate and humane war ever conducted" was hardly that.[90] After Filipinos massacred an American regiment on Samar and stuffed molasses into disemboweled corpses to attract ants, General Jacob Smith told his officers: "I want no prisoners. I wish you to kill and burn, the more you kill and burn the better you will please me."[91] With "the judicious application of the torch," U.S. soldiers burned *barrios* to the ground, placing villagers in reconcentration camps like those that had defaced Cuba.[92] To get information, Americans administered the "water cure," by which "men are pumped so full of water as to nearly drown him [sic], and then are brought back to life by thumping them over the stomach with the butts of muskets."[93] Senator Lodge defended such practices as legitimate responses to the alleged "torture and castration of [U.S.] prisoners" by Filipinos.[94] Racist notions of white superiority proliferated. "Civilize 'em with a Krag" went a popular army song, as one officer urged the same "remedial measures that proved successful with the Apaches."[95] The civil governor of the Philippines from 1901 to 1904, William Howard Taft used loftier language to make the same point. It was the American mission, he said, to "teach those people individual liberty, which shall lift them up to a point of civilization ..., and which shall make them rise to call the name of the United States blessed."[96] Taft simultaneously administered a sedition act to suppress

William Howard Taft (1857–1930) Astride a Water Buffalo. The first U.S. civil governor of the Philippines, Taft weighed more than 300 pounds. He once proudly reported to Washington that he had ridden twenty-five miles to a high mountain spot. Secretary of War Elihu Root cabled back: "HOW IS HORSE?" Regarding Filipino self-rule, Taft wrote in 1907: "The principles of the Declaration of Independence do not require the immediate surrender of a country to a people like this. If they did, then it would be utterly impossible to defend the rules which exclude women, … minors, … [and] ignorant and irresponsible male adults from the ballot." (U.S. Army Military History Institute)

criticism of the United States. American colonial authorities censored newspapers and jailed dissenters in the name of bringing freedom to the Philippines.

For years, the Moros would not submit to American rule. One military expert predicted that "the Moro question will eventually be settled in the same manner as the Indian question, that is by gradual extermination."[97] In a June 1913 battle on the island of Jolo, U.S. forces killed 500 Moros. The army's premier "guerrilla warrior," General John J. Pershing, called that bloody encounter "the fiercest [fighting] I have ever seen."[98] Until 1914, moreover, the followers of Artemio Ricarte harassed the U.S. military with their hit-and-run tactics. Imprisoned from 1904 to 1910 and then deported to Japan, Ricarte himself refused allegiance to the United States, set up a government-in-exile, and "was continually imagined to be plotting an invasion with Japanese financial and military aid."[99]

The carrot joined with the stick to repress the Philippine insurrections. Local self-government, social reforms, and American schools, where American educators (called "Thomasites") taught Filipinos of all social classes English and arithmetic, helped win over elites ("*ilustrados*") and key minorities.[100] A general amnesty proclaimed by President Theodore Roosevelt on July 4, 1902, also encouraged accommodation. By restricting suffrage at the outset to Filipinos with wealth, education,

"The Metamorphosis of a Bontoc Igorot."   Dean Worcester, an American zoology professor who served as the U.S. assistant secretary of the interior for the Philippines from 1900 to 1913, included these two photographs of "Pit-a-pit," a Bontoc Igorot, in his 1914 book to illustrate his conclusion that U.S. policies and programs had a civilizing effect on Filipinos. The two pictures were taken nine years apart. Worcester classified the islands' population of 8 million into eighty-four tribes, including the Bontoc Igorot. As the historian Paul A. Kramer has noted, by "tribalizing" the Filipinos, Americans "rhetorically eradicate[d] the Philippine Republic as a legitimate state whose rights the United States might have to recognize under international law." (Dean Worcester, *The Philippines Past and Present* [New York: Macmillan Company, 1914], vol. 2, frontispiece)

and previous government service, U.S. administrators successfully wooed Filipino elites, including former revolutionaries. American roads, bridges, port improvements, and sanitation projects soon followed. Rebellion was gradually confined to the "boondocks," a Tagalog term for remote areas.[101] At the St. Louis World's Fair in 1904, a thousand Filipinos were put on display as "living exhibits," and photographs and dioramas depicted their "rapid social, educational and sanitary development" under "the kindly tutelage of the United States."[102] By 1911, Cebu City could boast an electric railway, telephone service, English-language newspapers, Fords and Buicks, movie houses, and a baseball park, but "I would prefer a government run like hell by Filipinos to one run like heaven by Americans," commented future president Manuel Quezon.[103] By the 1920s, a journalist described America's colonial project as an attempt to turn the Philippines into "a sort of glorified Iowa."[104] The Jones Act of 1916 promised eventual Philippine independence. It did not arrive until 1946.

The proximity of the Philippines to China whetted commercial appetites. In early 1898 business leaders organized the American Asiatic Association to stimulate public and governmental protection and enlargement of U.S. interests in China. Treasury official Frank Vanderlip typically lauded the Philippines as the "pickets of the Pacific, standing guard at the entrances to trade with the millions of China."[105]

American Cigarettes in China. An American soldier in China peddles cigarettes. After the invention of the cigarette machine in 1881, the tobacco tycoon James B. Duke asked to see an atlas. Leafing through the pages, he noticed China's large population of 430 million. "That," he said, "is where we are going to sell cigarettes." Nine years later came the first exports; by 1916 Duke and other American entrepreneurs were selling 12 billion cigarettes per year in China. (Edward J. Parrish Papers, Duke University Library)

Although China attracted only 2 percent of U.S. foreign commerce, American traders had long dreamed of an unbounded China market, and missionaries romanticized a Christian kingdom. These ambitions remained dreams more than reality. Yet dreams spurred action, and during the 1890s the United States, despite limited power, sought to defend its Asian interests, real and imagined.

During that decade the European powers and Japan divided China, rendered helpless in 1895 after the Sino-Japanese War, into spheres of influence (zones) that established discriminatory trading privileges. The McKinley administration in early 1898 watched anxiously as Germany grabbed Jiaozhou (Kiaochow) and Russia gained a lease at Port Arthur on the Liaodong Peninsula. "Partition would destroy our markets," the U.S. minister to China cabled apprehensively.[106] France, already ensconced in Indochina, leased Guangzhou Bay in southern China in April of that year. Japan already had footholds in Formosa (Taiwan) and Korea. The British in March 1898 suggested a joint Anglo-American declaration on behalf of equal commercial opportunity in China. In the midst of the Cuban crisis, Washington ignored the request. Britain, which already had Hong Kong, then forced China to give up part of the Shandong Peninsula.

American interests in China seemed threatened. The American Asiatic Association and missionary groups appealed to Washington for help. Drawing on

John M. Hay (1838–1905).
The author of the Open Door notes graduated from Brown University and served as one of President Abraham Lincoln's secretaries. He became a newspaper editor and diplomat and, in 1897, ambassador to Great Britain. The following year McKinley named him secretary of state, a post he held until his death. Hay's support of the Open Door policy underscored the confidence Americans had in their ability to compete in the globalizing economy. Hay presciently told Congress in 1902 that "the financial center of the world, which required thousands of years to journey from the Euphrates to the Thames and Seine, seems [to be] passing to the Hudson between daybreak and dark." (Library of Congress)

recommendations from William W. Rockhill, an adviser on Asian policy, who in turn consulted his British friend and officer of the Chinese customs service, Alfred Hippisley, Secretary of State John Hay tried words. He sent an "Open Door" note on September 6, 1899, to Japan, Germany, Russia, Britain, France, and Italy, asking them to respect equal trade opportunity for all nations in their spheres. It was, of course, a traditional American principle, born of the nation's comparative military and economic weakness during much of its history. Lacking world economic or military status before the 1890s, the United States could pry back international trade barriers neither through force nor sheer economic might—particularly in Asia, where America's reach remained short. Hay nonetheless read into the non-committal replies what he wanted and proclaimed definitive acceptance of the Open Door proposal.

Although frail, the Open Door policy carried meaning. Americans discerned a delicate balance of power in East Asia. Excluding American commerce altogether from China might cause Washington to tip that balance by joining one of the powers against the others. A world war might even erupt from competition in Asia. Americans hoped the Open Door policy would serve their goals in an area where they had little military power. The United States wanted the commercial advantages without having to employ military force, as it did in Latin America. This policy of playing others off to U.S. advantage did not always work, but it fixed itself in the American mind as a guiding approach to Chinese affairs.

The Open Door note of 1899 notwithstanding, the Manchu dynasty (1644–1912) was nearing death, unable to cope with the foreign intruders. Resentful nationalistic Chinese, led by a secret society called *Yihequan* ("Boxers"), undertook in 1900 to throw out the imperialist aggressors. The Boxers murdered hundreds of Christian missionaries and their Chinese converts and laid siege to the foreign legations in Beijing (Peking). The foreigner "often treats the Chinese as though they were dogs," wrote the wife of the U.S. minister in Peking. "No wonder that they growl and sometimes bite."[107] To head off a complete gouging of China by vengeful Europeans and Japanese, McKinley, without consulting Congress, sent 2,500 American troops to Beijing from the Philippines to join 15,500 soldiers from other nations to lift the siege. Hay then issued another Open Door note on July 3, 1900. He defined U.S. policy as the protection of American life and property, the safeguarding of "equal and impartial trade," and the preservation of China's "territorial and administrative entity."[108] In short, keep the trade door open for the United States by keeping China intact.

Certainly these actions did not save China, which had to pay foreign governments more than $300 million for the Boxers' damages. The United States itself even asked for a territorial concession in late 1900 at Sansha Bay, Fujian Province, but then shelved the request. Thereafter Washington buttressed its support for the Open Door by increasing the Asiatic Squadron to forty-eight warships, some of which routinely patrolled the Yangtze River, and earmarking army forces in the Philippines for future emergency deployment in China. Even Buffalo Bill Cody extended America's frontier to China by reenacting the suppression of the Boxer Rebellion in his Wild West Show to depict the "triumph of Christian civilization over paganism."[109]

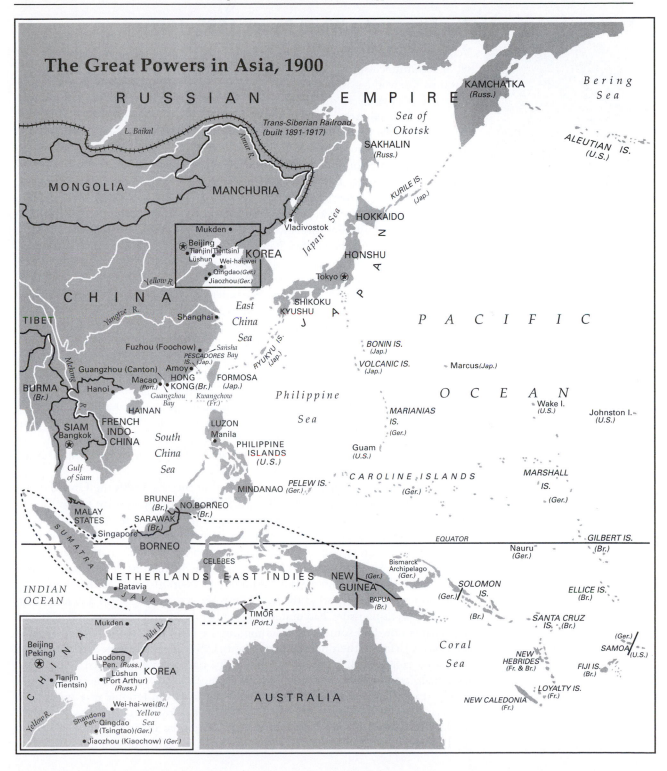

The Great Powers in Asia, 1900

RUSSIAN EMPIRE

Bering Sea

KAMCHATKA *(Russ.)*

L. Baikal

Trans-Siberian Railroad
(built 1891–1917)

Amur R.

Sea of Okotsk

SAKHALIN *(Russ.)*

ALEUTIAN IS. *(U.S.)*

MONGOLIA   MANCHURIA

KURILE IS. *(Jap.)*

HOKKAIDO

Mukden

Vladivostok

Beijing
Tianjin (Tientsin)   KOREA
Lüshun   Wei-hai-wei
Qingdao *(Ger.)*
Jiaozhou *(Ger.)*

HONSHU

Tokyo

Japan Sea

CHINA

TIBET

Yellow R.

Yangtze R.

Shanghai

East China Sea

SHIKOKU
KYUSHU

J A P A N

P A C I F I C

BONIN IS. *(Jap.)*

VOLCANIC IS. *(Jap.)*

Marcus *(Jap.)*

Fuzhou (Foochow)
Sansha Bay
PESCADORES IS. *(Jap.)*

RYUKYU IS. *(Jap.)*

Guangzhou (Canton)   Amoy
Macao *(Port.)*   HONG KONG *(Br.)*   FORMOSA *(Jap.)*

BURMA *(Br.)*

Hanoi

Mekong R.

Guangzhou Bay   Kwangchow *(Fr.)*

HAINAN

FRENCH INDO-CHINA

SIAM
Bangkok

South China Sea

Philippine Sea

MARIANAS IS. *(Ger.)*

Wake I. *(U.S.)*

Johnston I. *(U.S.)*

O C E A N

Gulf of Siam

LUZON
Manila

PHILIPPINE ISLANDS *(U.S.)*

Guam *(U.S.)*

C A R O L I N E   I S L A N D S *(Ger.)*

MARSHALL IS. *(Ger.)*

MALAY STATES

SUMATRA

Singapore

MINDANAO

PELEW IS. *(Ger.)*

BRUNEI *(Br.)*
NO. BORNEO *(Br.)*
SARAWAK *(Br.)*

BORNEO

EQUATOR

Nauru *(Ger.)*

GILBERT IS. *(Br.)*

INDIAN OCEAN

CELEBES

NETHERLANDS   EAST   INDIES

Batavia
JAVA

NEW GUINEA *(Ger.)*

Bismarck Archipelago *(Ger.)*

SOLOMON IS. *(Ger.)*

ELLICE IS. *(Br.)*

PAPUA *(Br.)*

TIMOR *(Port.)*

SANTA CRUZ IS. *(Br.)*

AUSTRALIA

Coral Sea

NEW HEBRIDES *(Fr. & Br.)*

LOYALTY IS. *(Fr.)*

NEW CALEDONIA *(Fr.)*

SAMOA *(Ger.)* *(U.S.)*

FIJI IS. *(Br.)*

Inset

Mukden

CHINA

Yalu R.

Beijing (Peking)

Liaodong Pen. *(Russ.)*   KOREA

Tianjin (Tientsin)

Lüshun (Port Arthur) *(Russ.)*

Yellow R.

Wei-hai-wei *(Br.)*

Shandong Pen.   *Yellow Sea*

Qingdao (Tsingtao) *(Ger.)*

Jiaozhou (Kiaochow) *(Ger.)*

Pears Soap advertisement.
This telling mixture of commercial and diplomatic advertising salutes Anglo-American rapprochement. (*Life,* 1898)

The Elbows of a World Power, 1895–1900

Venezuela, Cuba, Hawai'i, the Philippines, Open Door notes—an unprecedented set of commitments brought new responsibilities for the United States. Symbolic of this thrust to world-power status was the ascendancy of the imperialists' imperialist, Theodore Roosevelt, to the presidency in 1901. Peering into the twentieth century, Roosevelt warned Americans to avoid "slothful ease and ignoble peace." Never "shrink from the hard contests"; "let us therefore boldly face the life of strife."[110] Indeed, many diplomats looked back on the 1890s as a time of testing when the United States met the international challenge and rightfully asserted its place as a major world power. Europeans watched anxiously. Some, especially Germans, warned of a new "American peril."[111] Russia, however, supported U.S. annexation of Hawai'i because it kept the islands from becoming Japanese. Acquisition of Hawai'i and the Philippines also meant, in TR's words, that "we would have the Japs on our back."[112] With the United States becoming key factor in the global "balance of power," other states wondered: With whom would the United States ally itself?

The odds seemed to favor Great Britain, although the Anglo-American courtship would be prolonged and marriage something for the future. Ever since the eye-opening Venezuelan crisis, the British had applauded Washington for "entering the lists and sharing the task which might have proved too heavy for us alone."[113] Seeking support against an expansionist Germany, John Bull thought Uncle Sam a fit partner and counterweight. During the War of 1898 the British conspicuously tilted toward the American side and encouraged the subsequent U.S. absorption of Spanish colonies. U.S. leaders, in turn, compared the British suppression of the Boers in South Africa (1899–1902) with their own war against the Filipinos, saying that both peoples were equally "incapable of statehood."[114] Articulate Americans welcomed Britain's implicit acceptance of their imperialism. "Germany, and not England, is the power with whom we are apt to have trouble over the Monroe Doctrine," wrote Roosevelt in 1898.[115]

Britain still ranked first in naval power, but in the late 1890s the United States was growing, standing sixth by 1900. In 1898 alone, spurred by the war with Spain, the United States added 128 vessels to its navy, at a cost of $18 million. As one contemporary scholar put it: "Barriers of national seclusion are everywhere tumbling like the great wall of China. Every nation elbows other nations to-day."[116] The steel baron Andrew Carnegie boasted that "the old nations of the earth creep at a snail's pace," but the United States "thunders past with the rush of the express."[117] Many commentators reported that the United States, although still divided North and South on many issues, had united as never before. Southern racists and northern imperialists now had something in common: the need to keep inferior peoples in their place. Befitting their new imperial status, U.S. leaders often used gendered and age-based language that presumed superiority over peoples deemed "emotional, irrational, irresponsible, unbusinesslike, unstable, childlike."[118] If Americans played "the part of China, and [were] content to rot by inches in ignoble ease within our borders," warned Roosevelt, they will "go down before other nations which have not lost the manly and adventurous qualities."[119] Imperial annexation, bragged Senator Beveridge in 1900, "means opportunity for all the glorious young manhood of the republic, the most virile, ambitious, impatient, militant manhood the world has ever seen."[120]

The events of the 1895–1900 period further altered the process of decision making. Both Cleveland and McKinley conducted their own foreign policies to an extent not seen since the presidency of Abraham Lincoln, and they often thwarted or manipulated Congress. "Expansion and disorder abroad equaled centralization at home," one historian has written.[121] Woodrow Wilson, as president of Princeton University, later noted that 1898 had "changed the balance of powers. Foreign questions became leading questions again … Our President must always, henceforth, be one of the great powers of the world."[122] Wilson also welcomed the "primeval" Philippines as a new "frontier on which to turn loose the colts of the race."[123] From "a provincial huddle of petty sovereignties held together by a rope of sand," one editor boasted, "we rise to the dignity and prowess of an imperial republic incomparably greater than Rome."[124]

Indeed, the allure of empire seemed to offer the "most merciful of the world's great race of administrators" an exceptionalist mission—that of "teaching the world how to govern dependent peoples through uplift, assimilation, and eventual self-government."[125] Thus did the optimistic leaders of the "new world power" after 1900 see themselves as reforming an international system that they believed to be "working in their favor."[126] After 1900 the task of managing the expansive empire and the global responsibilities that came with it consumed U.S. foreign policy. The United States, having completed its project of contiguous imperialism, commenced the business of informal and formal global empire that would preoccupy it for much of its remaining history.

FURTHER READING FOR THE PERIOD 1895–1900

For the 1890's push for empire and the coming and waging of the Spanish-American-Cuban-Filipino War, see Ronald J. Barr, *The Progressive Army* (1998); Edward J. Berbusse, *The United States and Puerto Rico, 1898–1900* (1966); H. W. Brands, *The Reckless Decade* (1985); Cesar J. Ayala and Rafael Bernabe, *Puerto Rico in the American Century* (2007); Ada Ferrer, *Insurgent Cuba* (1999); Lillian Guerra, *The Myths of José Martí* (2005); Richard F. Hamilton, *President McKinley, War, and Empire* (2006); Robert E. Hannigan, *The New World Power* (2002); Kenneth E. Hendrickson, Jr., *The Spanish-American War* (2003); Sylvia Hilton and S. J. Ickringell, eds., *European Perceptions of the Spanish-American War* (1999); Kristin L. Hoganson, *Fighting for American Manhood* (1998); Robert Kagan, *Dangerous Nation* (2006); John M. Kirk, *José Martí* (1983); Gerald F. Linderman, *The Mirror of War* (1974); Paul T. McCartney, *Power and Progress* (2006); Ivan Musicant, *Empire by Default* (1998); John L. Offner, *An Unwanted War* (1992); Louis A. Pérez, Jr., *The War of 1898* (1998), *Cuba and the United States* (2003), and *Cuba Between Empires, 1878–1902* (1983); Hyman G. Rickover, *How the Battleship* Maine *Was Destroyed* (1976); Emily Rosenberg, *Spreading the American Dream* (1982); Peggy Samuels and Harold Samuels, *Remembering the* Maine (1995); Thomas Schoonover, *Uncle Sam's War and the Origins of Globalization* (2003); David J. Silbey, *A War of Frontier and Empire* (2007); Noenoe K. Silva, *Aloha Betrayed* (2004); Angel Smith and Emma Davila-Cox, eds., *The Crisis of 1898* (1999); James Lawrence Tone, *War and Genocide in Cuba, 1895–1898* (2006); David F. Trask, *The War with Spain in 1898* (1981); David Traxel, *1898* (1998); and Warren Zimmermann, *First Great Triumph* (2002).

For U.S. leaders, see John Braeman, *Albert J. Beveridge* (1971); H. W. Brands, *T.R.* (1997); Charles W. Calhoun, *Gilded Age Cato* (1988) (Gresham); Kathleen Dalton, *Theodore Roosevelt* (2002); Gerald Eggert, *Richard Olney* (1973); Lewis L. Gould, *The Presidency of William McKinley* (1981); Nathan Miller, *Theodore Roosevelt* (1992); H. Wayne Morgan, *William McKinley and His America* (1963); Ronald Spector, *Admiral of the*

New Empire (1974) (Dewey); Richard E. Welch, Jr., *The Presidencies of Grover Cleveland* (1988); and William C. Widenor, *Henry Cabot Lodge and the Search for an American Foreign Policy* (1980).

Anti-imperialism is treated in Kendrick A. Clements, *William Jennings Bryan* (1983); Amy Kaplan, *The Anarchy of Empire in the Making of U.S. Culture* (2002); Frank Ninkovich, *The United States and Imperialism* (2001); Thomas J. Osborne, *"Empire Can Wait": American Opposition to Hawaiian Annexation, 1893–1898* (1981); Hans L. Trefousse, *Carl Schurz* (1982); and Joseph F. Wall, *Andrew Carnegie* (1970).

The Open Door policy and Asia are discussed in Thomas A. Breslin, *China, American Catholicism, and the Missionary* (1980); Sherman Cochran, *Big Business in China* (1980) (cigarette industry); Paul A. Cohen, *History in Three Keys* (1997) (Boxers); Michael Hunt, *Frontier Defense and the Open Door* (1973) and *The Making of a Special Relationship* (1983); Thomas McCormick, *China Market* (1967); Valentin H. Rabe, *The Home Base of American China Missions, 1880–1920* (1978); and Marilyn Blatt Young, *The Rhetoric of Empire* (1968).

The Philippine rebellion and the American debate receive scrutiny in Teodoro Agoncillo, *Malolos* (1960); A. J. Bacevich, *Diplomat in Khaki* (1989) (General Frank McCoy); Vincent Cirillo, *Bullets and Bacillus* (2004); Kenton J. Clymer, *Protestant Missionaries in the Philippines, 1898–1916* (1986); John M. Gates, *Schoolbooks and Krags* (1973); Servando D. Halili Jr., *Iconography of the New Empire* (2006); Paul A. Kramer, *The Blood of Government* (2007); Brian M. Linn, *Guardians of Empire* (1997), *The U.S. Army and Counterinsurgency in the Philippine War, 1899–1902* (1989), and *The Philippine War* (2000); Glenn A. May, *Battle for Batangas* (1991) and *Social Engineering in the Philippines* (1980); Stuart C. Miller, *"Benevolent Assimilation"* (1982); Resil B. Mojares, *The War Against the Americans* (1999); Alfredo Rocas, *Adios, Patria Adorada* (2006); Angel Velasco Shaw and Luis Francia, eds., *Vestiges of War* (1999); Peter Stanley, *A Nation in the Making* (1974) and ed., *Reappraising an Empire* (1984); and Richard E. Welch, *Response to Imperialism* (1979).

For the Venezuelan crisis and Anglo-American relations, see Stuart Anderson, *Race and Rapprochement* (1981); Charles S. Campbell, *From Revolution to Rapprochement* (1974); Judith Ewell, *Venezuela and the United States* (1996); Richard B. Mulanax, *The Boer War in American Politics and Diplomacy* (1994); R. G. Neale, *Great Britain and United States Expansion, 1800–1900* (1966); Thomas J. Noer, *Briton, Boer, and Yankee* (1978); Bradford Perkins, *The Great Rapprochement* (1968); Serge Ricard and Hélène Christol, eds., *Anglo-Saxonism in U.S. Foreign Policy* (1991); and Joseph Smith, *Illusions of Conflict* (1979).

See also the General Bibliography, the following notes, and Robert L. Beisner, ed., *Guide to American Foreign Relations Since 1600* (2003).

NOTES TO CHAPTER 1

1. Quoted in H. Wayne Morgan, *William McKinley and His America* (Syracuse: Syracuse University Press, 1963), p. 359.
2. Lt. Blandin quoted in David Traxel, *1898* (New York: Knopf, 1998), p. 102.
3. Quoted in Walter Millis, *The Martial Spirit* (Boston: Houghton Mifflin, 1931), p. 102.
4. McKinley quoted in Morgan, *McKinley,* p. 361.
5. Quoted in John L. Offner, *An Unwanted War* (Chapel Hill: University of North Carolina Press, 1992), p. 123.
6. Quoted in Louis A. Pérez, Jr., *The War of 1898* (Chapel Hill: University of North Carolina Press, 1998), p. 15.
7. Quoted in Offner, *Unwanted War,* p. 129.
8. *Congressional Record, XXXI* (March 17, 1898), 2916–2919.
9. Thomas B. Allen, ed., "What Really Sank the Maine?" *Naval History, XII* (March/April 1998), 38.
10. McKinley quoted in Warren Zimmermann, *First Great Triumph* (New York: Farrar, Straus and Giroux, 2002), p. 252.

11. Quoted in Louis A. Pérez, Jr., *Cuba Between Empires, 1878–1902* (Pittsburgh: University of Pittsburgh Press, 1983), p. 172.
12. Quoted in Edmund Morris, *The Rise of Theodore Roosevelt* (New York: Coward, McCann, & Geoghegan, 1979), p. 610.
13. Sen. George Turner and Rep. William Sulzer quoted in Kristin L. Hoganson, *Fighting for American Manhood* (New Haven: Yale University Press, 1998), p. 91.
14. Quoted in Pérez, *Cuba Between Empires,* p. 174.
15. Tomás Estrada Palma quoted in Pérez, *War of 1898,* p. 9.
16. *Foreign Relations, 1898,* p. 746.
17. Quoted in Walter LaFeber, *The American Search for Opportunity, 1865–1913* (New York: Cambridge University Press, 1993), p. 143.
18. *Congressional Record, XXXI* (April 11, 1898), 3699–3702.
19. Pérez, *Cuba Between Empires,* p. 178.
20. Roosevelt quoted in H. W. Brands, *The Reckless Decade* (New York: St. Martin's, 1995), p. 336.
21. Quoted *ibid.,* p. 174.

22. Quoted in H. Wayne Morgan, *America's Road to Empire* (New York: Wiley, 1965), p. 63.

23. Senator Hernando de Soto Money quoted in Hoganson, *Fighting for Manhood*, p. 73.

24. Charles W. Eliot quoted in Frank Ninkovich, *The United States and Imperialism* (Malden, Mass.: Blackwell, 2001), p. 14.

25. Quoted in John Braeman, *Albert J. Beveridge* (Chicago: University of Chicago Press, 1971), p. 23.

26. Max O'Rell quoted in Hoganson, *Fighting for Manhood,* p. 35.

27. Quoted in Joseph A. Fry, "Late Nineteenth Century U.S. Foreign Relations," in Charles W. Calhoun, ed., *The Gilded Age* (New York: Rowman & Littlefield, 2007), p. 323.

28. William Day quoted in Pérez, *War of 1898*, p. 12.

29. Quoted in Gerald G. Eggert, *Richard Olney* (College Park: Penn State University Press, 1974), p. 208.

30. Quoted in Ernest R. May, *Imperial Democracy* (New York: Harper and Row, [1961], 1973), p. 33.

31. *Foreign Relations, 1895,* Part I (Washington, D.C.: Government Printing Office, 1896), pp. 545–562.

32. Quoted in Paul Gibb, "Unmasterly Inactivity?" *Diplomacy & State-craft,* XVI (January 2005), 29.

33. Richard E. Welch, Jr., *The Presidencies of Grover Cleveland* (Lawrence: University Press of Kansas, 1988), p. 184.

34. Quoted in Robert L. Beisner, *From the Old Diplomacy to the New, 1865–1900* (Arlington Heights, Ill.: Harlan Davidson, 1986; 2nd ed.), p. 111.

35. Quoted in Gibb, "Unmasterly Inactivity?", 35.

36. Quoted in H. W. Brands, *T.R.* (New York: BasicBooks, 1997), p. 289.

37. Quoted in Stuart Anderson, *Race and Rapprochement* (Rutherford, N.J.: Fairleigh Dickinson University Press, 1981), p. 97.

38. Quoted in Joyce Milton, *The Yellow Kids* (New York: Harper and Row, 1989), p. 27.

39. Quoted in Allan Nevins, *Grover Cleveland* (New York: Dodd, Mead, 1932), p. 644.

40. Quoted in Joseph Smith, *Illusions of Conflict* (Pittsburgh: University of Pittsburgh Press, 1979), p. 207.

41. Quoted in George Young, "Intervention Under the Monroe Doctrine," *Political Science Quarterly,* LVII (June 1942), 277.

42. Lars Schoultz, *Beneath the United States* (Cambridge: Harvard University Press, 1998), p. 115.

43. Quoted in Mark T. Gilderhus, "The Monroe Doctrine," *Presidential Studies Quarterly,* XXXVI (March 2006), 10.

44. Henry Cabot Lodge quoted in Fredrick B. Pike, *The United States and Latin America* (Austin: University of Texas Press, 1992), pp. 158–159.

45. Lisle A. Rose, *Power at Sea: The Age of Navalism, 1890–1918* (Columbia: University of Missouri Press, 2007), p. 14.

46. Joseph A. Fry, "From Open Door to World Systems," *Pacific Historical Review,* LX (May 1996), 282.

47. Quoted in Richard E. Welch, Jr., *George Frisbie Hoar and the Half-Breed Republicans* (Cambridge: Harvard University Press, 1971), p. 209.

48. Walter Q. Gresham to Carl Schurz, October 6, 1893, Walter Q. Gresham Papers, Library of Congress, Washington, D.C.

49. Pérez, *War of 1898*, p. 74.

50. Quoted in Louis A. Pérez, Jr., *Cuba and the United States,* 2nd ed. (Athens: University of Georgia Press, 1997), p. 80; quoted in Pérez, *War of 1898*, p. 20; John M. Kirk, *José Martí* (Gainesville: University of Florida Press, 1983), pp. 52, 56, 58, 90, 118; and George C. Herring, *From Colony to Superpower* (New York: Oxford University Press, 2008), p. 310.

51. Quoted in Philip S. Foner, *The Spanish-Cuban-American War and the Birth of American Imperialism* (New York: Monthly Review Press, 1972; 2 vols.), *I,* 21.

52. P. M. Sagasta quoted in Angel Smith, "The People and the Nation," in Angel Smith and Emma Davila-Cox, eds., *The Crisis of 1898* (New York: St. Martin's, 1999), p. 165.

53. Quoted in McCartney, *Power and Progress,* p. 92.

54. Olney quoted in Schoultz, *Beneath the United States,* p. 128.

55. Quoted in Offner, *Unwanted War,* p. 26.

56. Quoted in LaFeber, *American Search,* p. 132.

57. Quoted in Eggert, *Olney,* p. 265.

58. James D. Richardson, ed., *A Compilation of the Messages and Papers of the Presidents, 1789–1897* (Washington, D.C.: Government Printing Office, 1896–1899; 10 vols.), *IX,* 716–722.

59. *Atlanta Constitution* quoted in Hoganson, *Fighting for Manhood,* p. 90.

60. Eric Rauchway, "William McKinley and Us," *Journal of the Gilded Age and Progressive Era,* IV (July 2005), 15.

61. General Calixto García quoted in Pérez, *War of 1898*, p. 9.

62. *Congressional Record, XXXI* (December 6, 1897), 3–5.

63. *Foreign Relations, 1898* (Washington D.C.: Government Printing Office, 1901), pp. 1007–1008.

64. Amy Kaplan, *The Anarchy of Empire in the Making of U.S. Culture* (Cambridge: Harvard University Press, 2002), p. 147.

65. Quoted in John Byrne Cooke, *Reporting the War* (New York: Palgrave Macmillan, 2007), p. 70.

66. Quoted in John A. S. Grenville and George B. Young, *Politics, Strategy, and American Diplomacy* (New Haven: Yale University Press, 1966), p. 278.

67. Louis A.Pérez, Jr., *Cuba and the United States,* 3d ed. (Athens: University of Georgia Press, 2003), p. 94; and John Lawrence Tone, *War and Genocide in Cuba, 1895–1898* (Chapel Hill: University of North Carolina Press, 2006), pp. xii, 280.

68. Quoted in César J. Ayala and Rafael Bernabe, *Puerto Rico in the American Century* (Chapel Hill: University of North Carolina Press, 2007), p. 15.

69. Richard Harding Davis quoted in Stephen Kinzer, *Overthrow* (New York: Times Books, 2006), p. 46.

70. Quoted in Kenneth J. Hagan and Ian J. Bickerton, *Unintended Consequences* (London: Reaktion Press, 2007), p. 93.

71. Quoted in Walter A. McDougall, *Promised Land, Crusader State* (Boston: Houghton Mifflin, 1997), pp. 111–112.

72. Quoted in Ninkovich, *United States and Imperialism,* p. 29.

73. Quoted in McCartney, *Power and Progress,* p. 217; quoted in Hagan and Bickerton, *Unintended Consequences,* p. 95.

74. Quoted in Amy S. Greenberg, *Manifest Manhood and the Antebellum American Empire* (New York: Cambridge University Press, 2005), p. 280; quoted in Servando D. Halili, Jr., *Iconography of the New Empire* (Manila: University of the Philippines Press, 2006), p. 127.

75. Quoted in Robert L. Beisner, "1898 and 1968," *Political Science Quarterly, LXXV* (June 1970), 200.

76. Quoted in Kramer, *Blood of Government,* p. 119.

77. Clark quoted in David Mayers, *Dissenting Voices in America's Rise to Power* (New York: Cambridge University Press, 2007), pp. 200–201.

78. Quoted in Jose D. Fermin, *1904 World's Fair* (Manila: University of the Philippines Press, 2004), p. 23.

79. Quoted in John M. Craig, "Lucia True Ames Mead," in Edward P. Crapol, ed., *Women and American Foreign Policy* (Westport, Conn.: Greenwood, 1992; 2nd ed.), p. 72.

80. Quoted in Paul A. Kramer, *The Blood of Government* (Chapel Hill: University of North Carolina Press, 2007), p. 2.

81. Quoted in Anders Stephanson, *Manifest Destiny* (New York: Hill & Wang, 1995), p. 87.

82. Quoted in Morgan, *McKinley*, p. 322.

83. Quoted in Paul A. Kramer, "Race-Making and Colonial Violence in the U.S. Empire: The Philippine-American War as Race War," *Diplomatic History, XXX* (April 2006), 181.

84. Quoted in Kenton J. Clymer, *Protestant Missionaries in the Philippines, 1898–1916* (Urbana: University of Illinois Press, 1986), p. 159.

85. Quoted in Kramer, *Blood of Government*, pp. 127–128.

86. Gen. Frederick Funston quoted in Brian Daizen Victoria, "When God[s] and Buddha Go to War," in Mark Selden and Alvin Y. So, eds., *War & State Terrorism* (New York: Rowman & Littlefield, 2004), p. 97.

87. Glenn A. May, *Battle for Batangas* (New Haven: Yale University Press, 1991), pp. 267, 291.

88. Quoted in Ronald J. Barr, *The Progressive Army* (New York: St. Martin's, 1998), p. 56.

89. *Boston Evening Transcript*, March 1, 1899.

90. Arthur MacArthur quoted in Patrice Higonnet, *Attendant Cruelties* (New York: Other Press, 2007), p. 186.

91. Quoted in James Chace, "Tomorrow the World," *New York Review of Books*, November 21, 2002, p. 36.

92. General S. B. M. Young quoted in Brian McAllister Linn, *The Philippine War, 1899–1902* (Lawrence: University Press of Kansas, 2000), p. 220.

93. Quoted in Cooke, *Reporting the War*, p. 83.

94. Lodge quoted in Kathleen Dalton, *Theodore Roosevelt* (New York: Knopf, 2002), p. 228.

95. S. B. M. Young quoted in Linn, *Philippine War*, p. 211; quoted in John M. Gates, *Schoolboys and Krags* (Westport, Conn.: Greenwood, 1979), p. vii.

96. Henry F. Graff, ed., *American Imperialism and the Philippine Insurrection* (Boston: Little, Brown, 1969), p. 36.

97. Benjamin Foulois quoted in Brian Linn, *Guardians of Empire* (Chapel Hill: University of North Carolina Press, 1997), p. 36.

98. Quoted in Donald Smythe, *Guerrilla Warrior* (New York: Charles Scribner's Sons, 1973), p. 198.

99. Kramer, *Blood of Government*, p. 297.

100. Fermin, *1904 World's Fair*, p. 172.

101. Kramer, "Race-Making," 197.

102. Robert W. Rydell, *World of Fairs* (Chicago: University of Chicago Press, 1993), pp. 75–76.

103. Quoted in Mayers, *Dissenting Voices*, p. 196.

104. Nicholas Roosevelt quoted in Michael Adas, "Improving on the Civilization Mission?" in Lloyd C. Gardner and Marilyn B. Young, eds., *The New American Empire* (New York: The New Press, 2005), p. 173.

105. Quoted in Thomas J. McCormick, *China Market* (Chicago: Quadrangle, 1967), p. 119.

106. Charles Denby quoted in Thomas Schoonover, *Uncle Sam's War of 1898 and the Origins of Globalism* (Lexington: University Press of Kentucky, 2003), p. 69.

107. Sarah Pike Conger quoted in Carol C. Chin, "American Women Missionaries in China at the Turn of the Twentieth Century," *Diplomatic History, XXVII* (June 2003), 350.

108. *Foreign Relations, 1901* (Washington, D.C.: Government Printing Office, 1902), Appendix, p. 12.

109. J. G. Blair, "First Steps Toward Globalization," in Reinhold Wagnleitner and Elaine Tyler May, eds., *"Here, There and Everywhere": The Foreign Politics of American Popular Culture* (Hanover, N.H.: University Press of New England, 2000), p. 25.

110. Quoted in Beale, *Theodore Roosevelt*, p. 84.

111. Quoted in Fareed Zakaria, *From Wealth to Power* (Princeton: Princeton University Press, 1998), p. 133.

112. Quoted in Serge Ricard, "The Roosevelt Corollary," *Presidential Studies Quarterly, XXXVI* (March 2006), 21–22.

113. Quoted in Anderson, *Race and Rapprochement*, p. 127.

114. A. T. Mahan quoted in Paul A. Kramer, "Empires, Exceptions, and Anglo-Saxons," *Journal of American History, LXXXVIII* (March 2002), 1335.

115. Quoted in Edward P. Crapol, "From Anglophobia to Fragile Rapprochement," in Hans-Jürgen Schröder, ed., *Confrontation and Cooperation* (Providence, R.I.: Berg, 1993), p. 21.

116. American Historical Association, *Annual Report, 1898* (Washington, D.C.: Government Printing Office, 1899), p. 288.

117. Quoted in Smith, *Illusions of Conflict*, p. 40.

118. Emily S. Rosenberg, "Walking the Borders," in Michael J. Hogan and Thomas G. Paterson, eds., *Explaining the History of American Foreign Relations* (New York: Cambridge University Press, 1991), p. 33.

119. Quoted in Gail Bederman, *Manliness & Civilization* (Chicago: University of Chicago Press, 1995), p. 193.

120. Quoted in Cecilia Elizabeth O'Leary, *To Die For* (Princeton: Princeton University Press, 1999), p. 142.

121. LaFeber, *American Search*, p. 117.

122. Quoted in Arthur Link's essay in *Wilson's Diplomacy* (Cambridge: Schenkman, 1973), p. 6.

123. Quoted in Robert Hannigan, *The New World Power* (University Park: Pennsylvania State University Press, 2002), p. 282.

124. Henry Watterson quoted in Alan Brinkley, "The Concept of an American Century," in R. Laurence Moore and Maurizio Vaudagna, eds., *The American Century in Europe* (Ithaca: Cornell University Press, 2003), p. 8.

125. A. J. Beveridge quoted in Kramer, "Empires," p. 1351.

126. Hannigan, *New World Power*, p. xii.

CHAPTER 2

Managing, Policing, and Extending the Empire, 1900–1914

"The Thirteenth Labor of Hercules." With this official poster by Perham Nahl, the Panama-Pacific Exposition in San Francisco in 1915 celebrated the opening of the Panama Canal. The artist commemorates the ten-year construction project using symbols that reflect the era's themes of empire-building and male hegemony: A powerful, muscular Hercules (the United States) forcibly parts the land (a yielding Panama) to make space for the canal. (Library of Congress)

DIPLOMATIC CROSSROAD

❖ *Severing Panama from Colombia for the Canal, 1903*

"REVOLUTION IMMINENT" WARNED the cable from the American consul at Colón, a normally quiet Colombian seaport on the Atlantic side of Panama. Acting Secretary of State Francis B. Loomis fired off an inquiry to the U.S. consul at Panama City, on the Pacific slope: "Uprising on Isthmus reported. Keep Department promptly and fully informed." The response came back in four hours: "No uprising yet. Reported will be in the night. Situation is critical." Loomis's anxiety soon increased when he learned that troops of the Colombian government had landed in Colón.

In Washington, D.C., it was now 8:20 P.M., November 3, 1903. As far as Loomis knew, a revolution had not yet broken out on the isthmus. Nonetheless, he hurriedly drafted instructions for the consuls at Panama and Colón. "Act promptly" to convey to the commanding officer of the U.S.S. *Nashville* this order: "In the interests of peace make every effort to prevent [Colombian] Government troops at Colón from proceeding to Panama [City]." Loomis agonized for another hour. Finally, a new cable arrived: "Uprising occurred to-night … no bloodshed. … Government will be organized to-night." Loomis had done his part to ensure success in the scheme to acquire a canal controlled by the United States.

November 3 was far more hectic for the conspirators in Panama. A tiny band of Panamanians and Americans living on the isthmus had actively plotted revolution since August, when the Colombian congress rejected the treaty that would have permitted the United States to construct an isthmian canal. By late October, they had become convinced that the North American colossus, frustrated in its overtures to Colombia, would lend them moral and physical support. Confident that U.S. naval vessels would be at hand, they selected November 4 as the date of their coup d'état. To their dismay, however, the Colombian steamer *Cartagena* disembarked about 400 troops at Colón early on November 3. Because the "important message" directing him to prevent the "landing of any armed force … at Colón" had not reached him, Commander John Hubbard of the *Nashville* did not interfere with the landing.

Forced to improvise, the conspirators deviously separated the Colombian commanding general from his troops, lured him aboard a train, and sped him across the isthmus to Panama City, where they arrested their guest, formed a provisional government, and paraded before a cheering crowd at the Cathedral Plaza. But the revolution would remain perilously unfinished so long as armed Colombian soldiers occupied Colón. Too weak to expel the soldiers by force, the insurgents gave the colonel in charge $8,000 in gold, whereupon he ordered his troops aboard a departing steamer. The U.S. consul at Panama City cabled: "Quiet prevails." At noon the next day, Secretary of State John Hay recognized the sovereign Republic of Panama.

The new Panamanian government appointed as its minister plenipotentiary a Frenchman, Philippe Bunau-Varilla, an engineer of an earlier failed Panama canal project. With Gallic flourish, Bunau-Varilla congratulated Secretary Hay for rescuing Panama "from the barbarism of unnecessary and wasteful civil wars to consecrate it to the destiny assigned to it by Providence, the service of humanity, and the progress of civilization."[1] On November 18, 1903, less than two weeks after U.S. recognition of Panama, Hay and Bunau-Varilla signed a new treaty by which the United States would build, fortify, and operate a canal linking the Atlantic and Pacific oceans. Washington also guaranteed the "independence of the Republic in Panama," thereby ensuring against any threat from Colombia.[2]

Hay had at last achieved a goal set by his chief, President Theodore Roosevelt, several years earlier. If an unfortified, neutral canal had existed in Central America during the recent war with Spain, Roosevelt had argued, the United States would have spent the war in "wild panic," fearful that the Spanish fleet would slip through the waterway and rush to the Philippines to attack Commodore Dewey. "Better to have no canal at all, than not give us the power to control it in time of war," Roosevelt decided.[3]

"No other arm may go around this waist." This artistic rendering by W. A. Rogers of a lascivious Uncle Sam abducting a female Panama appeared on the cover of *Harper's Weekly* on December 29, 1900. The gendered imagery actually anticipated President Theodore Roosevelt's forceful intervention in 1903 to gain U.S. control of a canal to be built across the Isthmus of Panama. When TR subsequently tried to justify his actions in support of Panamanian independence, Secretary of War Elihu Root observed: "You have shown that you have been accused of seduction and you have conclusively proved that you were guilty of rape." (Library of Congress)

The Clayton–Bulwer Treaty of 1850, stipulating joint Anglo-American control of any isthmian canal, seemed to block the way. In December 1898, flushed with victory over Spain, President William McKinley had directed Secretary Hay to seek a modification of that agreement with the British ambassador, Sir Julian Pauncefote. The Hay-Pauncefote Treaty of February 1900 permitted the United States to build a canal but forbade its fortification, much to the dismay of Roosevelt who spearheaded an attack that defeated the treaty in the Senate. On November 18, 1901, with Roosevelt now president, Hay and Pauncefote signed a satisfactory new pact.

Then began the complex process of determining the route. In November 1901, after a two-year investigation, the Walker Isthmian Canal Commission reported in favor of Nicaragua. The decisive criterion—cost—seemed exorbitant for Panama because of the obduracy of the New Panama Canal Company, a French-chartered firm that held the Colombian concession for canal rights. The company estimated its assets on the isthmus at $109 million—machinery, property, and excavated soil left by the defunct de Lesseps organization in 1888. Purchase of the company's rights and holdings would make construction of a Panama canal prohibitively expensive if technologically easier. For these reasons, plus travelers' depiction of Panama as "a hideous dung heap of physical and moral degradation," the House passed the Hepburn Bill in January 1902 authorizing a canal through Nicaragua.[4]

The New Panama Canal Company's American lawyer, William Nelson Cromwell, schemed to sell the assets of his French client for the highest possible price. Lobbying hard, Bunau-Varilla even exposed the unsuitability of Nicaraguan terrain by deluging Congress with Nicaraguan postage stamps that depicted a belching volcano. On January 18, 1902, the Walker Commission reversed itself and decided for the technologically preferable Panama passage, citing the company's willingness to sell out for the reduced sum of $40 million. Guided by Roosevelt and Cromwell, Congress five months later chose the Panama route. The State Department soon opened negotiations with Colombia. The annual rent became a stumbling block, which Hay removed only by delivering an ultimatum to the Colombian chargé d'affaires, Tomás Herrán, in January 1903. On January 22 he and Hay signed a treaty granting Colombia an initial payment of $10 million and $250,000 annually. The United States would control the six-mile-wide Canal Zone for one hundred years, renewable at the "sole and absolute option" of the North American republic.[5]

The U.S. Senate approved the Hay-Herrán Treaty on March 17, 1903, but the Colombian government attempted to extract a $10 million payment from the New Panama Canal Company for permitting the transfer of its assets to the U.S. government. Cromwell promptly cried foul, whereupon Hay bluntly announced that any payment to Colombia was "not permissible."[6] The Colombians next tried to raise the initial American cash payment from $10 million to $15 million. Roosevelt exploded against "those contemptible little creatures in Bogotá."[7] The president believed that "you could no more make an agreement with the Colombian rulers than you could nail currant jelly to the wall."[8] TR's intransigence and Hay's extraordinary intercession on behalf of a privately owned foreign corporation increased the Colombians' resentment against U.S. infringement on their sovereignty over Panama. The Colombian congress unanimously rejected the treaty on August 12, 1903.

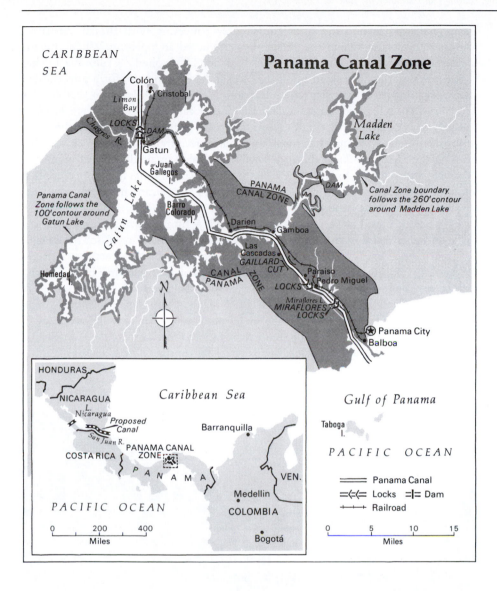

Roosevelt was already pondering undiplomatic alternatives. In June the frenetic Cromwell had met with Roosevelt and then planted a story in the *New York World* reporting that, if Colombia rejected the treaty, Panama would secede and grant to the United States "the equivalent of absolute sovereignty over the Canal Zone," and that "President Roosevelt is said to strongly favor this plan."[9] By now the president was privately castigating Colombia for its "squalid savagery," combined with "the worst forms of despotism and of anarchy, of violence and of fatuous weakness, of dismal ignorance, cruelty, treachery, greed, and utter vanity."[10]

Roosevelt now considered two options: seizure of Panama by force, or instant recognition and support for any revolutionary regime in Panama. The president inclined sharply toward the latter course after a meeting with Bunau-Varilla on October 10, during which the Frenchman predicted an uprising. When Bunau-Varilla asked what the United States would do, TR replied: "Colombia by her action has forfeited any claim upon the U.S. and I have no use for a government that would do what that government has done."[11] One week later, on October 16, Secretary Hay informed Bunau-Varilla that American naval vessels were heading toward the isthmus. Calculating the steaming time, Bunau-Varilla cabled the revolutionaries on the isthmus that warships would arrive by November 2. Early that evening the U.S.S. *Nashville* dropped anchor at Colón as predicted. Although the *Nashville* landed troops to keep order *after* the Panamanian junta had gained control, a Colombian diplomat rightfully complained: "The Americans are against us. What can we do against the American Navy?"[12]

Roosevelt urged swift ratification of the Hay–Bunau-Varilla Treaty, claiming that Colombia had forced the United States to take "decisive steps" for the benefit of "civilized mankind."[13] When critics complained about his "Bowery-boy" behavior toward Colombia, Roosevelt denounced the "small body of shrill eunuchs who consistently oppose" his "righteous" policies.[14] On February 23, 1904, the Senate approved the treaty by a vote of 66 to 14. The treaty granted the United States "power and authority" within the zone "in perpetuity" as "if it were the sovereign of the territory."[15] Later, in 1911, TR reportedly boasted that "I took the Canal Zone and let Congress debate; and while the debate goes on the Canal does also."[16]

Panama Canal. The U.S.S. *Ohio* passes through the Culebra Cut (now called the Gaillard Cut) of the Panama Canal about a year after the canal opened to traffic—both warships and commercial vessels. "For the next seven decades," the scholar Lars Schoultz has noted, "the Panama Canal Zone stands as the most obvious legacy of the age of imperialism in United States policy toward Latin America." (Library of Congress)

In what has been called "the greatest liberty Man has taken with nature," construction of the fifty-mile-long canal began in 1904, and the locks were formally opened on August 15, 1914.[17] During the first year of operation alone, 1,058 merchant vessels slid through the locks, while the Atlantic and Pacific fleets of the U.S. Navy freely exchanged ships. San Francisco in 1915 hosted the extravagant Panama-Pacific International Exposition with the theme "The Land Divided—The World United."[18] In 1922 the United States paid "conscience money" or "canalimony" of $25 million to Colombia but did not formally apologize for having taken the Canal Zone. Most Americans have applauded Roosevelt's bold venture against Colombia. TR ranked it alongside the Louisiana Purchase and the acquisition of Texas. The canal, Woodrow Wilson later asserted, shifted "the center of gravity of the world."[19]

Architects of Empire

The taking of Panama symbolized the new activism characteristic of American foreign policy after the Spanish-American-Cuban-Filipino War, and construction of the canal intensified U.S. influence over Latin America. It also accelerated Washington's participation in the global contest for empire among the great powers. "The United States will be attacked as soon as you are about to complete the canal," Germany's Kaiser Wilhelm II predicted in 1907, identifying Japan as the most likely culprit.[20] Britain, which had the power to challenge U.S. preeminence in the hemisphere, acquiesced in the hope of gaining a Yankee ally to deter a growing political and naval threat from Germany. In turn, the vigorous German Empire, having expanded its markets and investments in Central and South America to more than 2 billion marks by 1900, seemed "desirous of obtaining a foothold in the Western Hemisphere," noted the General Board of the U.S. Navy.[21] Revolutionary upheavals in Russia, China, and Mexico further shifted the international balance of power. In an era of tumultuous transformation, as European alliances consolidated and lurched toward a world war, President Roosevelt and his successors thought it imperative to defend, develop, and enlarge the new U.S. empire.

In the late nineteenth century, Roosevelt had associated closely with the most vocal pressure group agitating for an American canal, the uniformed "professors of war" at the Naval War College.[22] He corresponded regularly with Admiral Alfred

Makers of American Foreign Relations, 1900–1914

Presidents	Secretaries of State
Theodore Roosevelt, 1901–1909	John Hay, 1898–1905
	Elihu Root, 1905–1909
	Robert Bacon, 1909
William Howard Taft, 1909–1913	Philander C. Knox, 1909–1913
Woodrow Wilson, 1913–1921	William Jennings Bryan, 1913–1915

Thayer Mahan, who tirelessly touted the strategic advantages of a canal. During the war of 1898, the warship *Oregon* dashed at full speed from San Francisco around South America to Cuba in time to help destroy the Spanish fleet off Santiago. The race of more than 14,000 miles fired American imaginations, but it also consumed sixty-eight days and underscored the need for an interoceanic canal across Central America.

Roosevelt's sense of isthmian strategic necessity reflected a broad worldview he shared with many "progressives" in the early twentieth century. A patrician reformer, he "feared that unrest caused by social and economic inequities would impair the nation's strength and efficiency."[23] With similar danger lurking in disorder abroad, he sought influence to create a U.S.-friendly order on a global scale through "proper policing."[24] Roosevelt talked about doing the "rough work of the world" and the need to "speak softly and carry a big stick."[25] Imbibing Darwinist doctrines of "natural selection," he proclaimed "our duty toward the people living in barbarism [is] to see that they are freed from their chains, and we can free them only by destroying barbarism itself."[26] Anglo-Saxon superiority was best expressed in war. "All the great masterful races have been fighting races," TR lectured.[27] Not all Progressive-era reformers joined Roosevelt in advocating a vigorous activism abroad. Wisconsin's Senator Robert M. La Follette, for example, opposed imperialism and contended that the same corporate monopolists they battled at home were dragging the United States into perpetual intervention overseas. Activists in women's organizations bemoaned the "present intoxication with the hashish of conquest" as they urged "women's values" on a male government so as to rein in the "champing steeds" of American militarism and expansion.[28]

Roosevelt vigorously debated his critics. Exuberant and calculating, he centralized foreign-policy decision making, frequently bypassed Congress, and believed "the people" so ignorant about foreign affairs that they should not direct an informed president like himself. At the same time, he kept favorite journalists and other "intelligent observers sufficiently enlightened to prevent their going wrong."[29] Seeking world stability, Roosevelt advocated "minimizing the chances of war among civilized people" and "multiplying the methods and chances of honorably avoiding war in the event of controversy."[30] Indeed, he won the Nobel Peace Prize in 1906 for his mediation of the Russo-Japanese War at the Portsmouth Conference (see pages 253). The robust Roosevelt relished debate with those he considered his intellectual equals, and he invited favored foreign diplomats to be members of his boisterous Tennis Cabinet. "The biggest matters," this progenitor of the imperial presidency later wrote, "I managed without consultation with anyone; for when a matter is of capital importance, it is well to have it handled by one man only."[31]

Roosevelt and other shapers of American foreign policy before World War I were members of an American quasi-aristocracy who moved comfortably in the affluent, cosmopolitan, upper-class society of the Atlantic seaboard. Roosevelt, a graduate of Harvard College and prolific author, had served as assistant secretary of the navy and governor of New York. His successor, Ohioan William Howard Taft, a graduate of Yale, had served as a federal circuit court judge, governor general of the Philippines (1901–1904), and secretary of war (1904–1908). Woodrow Wilson earned a Ph.D. from Johns Hopkins, wrote books on government and history, and

Jules Jusserand (1855–1932). This distinguished scholar and diplomat served capably as France's ambassador to the United States from 1903 to 1924. An old friend of Theodore Roosevelt, he often joined the president in his celebrated "scrambles" through Washington's Rock Creek Park. TR's motto on such excursions was "over, under, or through, but never around," which meant jumping, wading, or swimming across any watery obstacle. On one occasion, as Roosevelt's entourage stripped to plunge into a pond, the president noticed that the ambassador had removed all clothes except his lavender gloves. "It would be embarrassing if we should meet ladies," Jusserand explained. His diplomatic memoir *What Me Befell* (1933) remains a classic. (Library of Congress)

was president of Princeton and governor of New Jersey before entering the White House. Each president believed that "we owe to our less fortunate [international] neighbors" the same "neighborly feeling and aid that a successful man in a community owes to his less fortunate fellow citizens."[32]

Their secretaries of state, with one exception, belonged to the same elite. John Hay, secretary from 1898 to 1905, was educated at Brown University. A poet, novelist, biographer, and editor of the *New York Tribune,* the wealthy Hay had served as Lincoln's personal secretary during the Civil War and much later as McKinley's ambassador to Great Britain, becoming a chief architect of the Anglo-American rapprochement. His successor, Elihu Root (1905–1909), graduated from Hamilton College, took a law degree at New York University, and became one of America's most successful corporation lawyers. As secretary of war from 1899 to 1904, Root created mechanisms, such as the Platt Amendment for Cuba, for managing the

American empire. Like TR, he believed that the "main object of diplomacy is to keep the country out of trouble" and maintain order abroad.[33] Philander C. Knox (1909–1913) followed Root. A corporation lawyer, Knox served as attorney general and U.S. senator before entering the State Department. He liked to play golf at Chevy Chase, spend summers with his trotters at his Valley Forge Farms estate, vacation in Florida in the winter, and delegate departmental work to subordinates. He advocated "dollar diplomacy" as a means of creating order in revolution-prone areas—that is, using private financiers and business leaders to promote foreign policy, and using diplomacy to promote American commerce and investment abroad. As his *second* secretary of state, President Wilson named New Yorker Robert Lansing (1915–1920), a graduate of Amherst College, son-in-law of a former secretary of state, and practitioner of international law. Reserved and conservative, Lansing also abhorred disorder in the U.S. sphere of Latin America.

William Jennings Bryan, Wilson's *first* appointment (1913–1915), lacked such conservative elite status. The "boy orator" of Nebraska could mesmerize crowds by decrying the "cross of gold" on which eastern capitalists were crucifying western and southern farmers, but he could not win a presidential election (he ran in 1896, 1900, and 1908). The "Great Commoner" languished for years as the most prominent has-been of the Democratic party until Wilson named him secretary of state as a reward for support at the convention of 1912. The president let Bryan appoint "deserving Democrats" to diplomatic posts and indulge his fascination with "cooling off" treaties, but Wilson bypassed him in most important diplomatic decisions, even to the point of composing overseas cables on his own White House typewriter.

The conservative managers of American foreign policy believed that a major component of national power was a prosperous, expanding economy invigorated by a healthy foreign trade. The principle of the "Open Door"—to keep open trade and investment opportunities—became a governing tenet voiced globally, if often tarnished in application. In 1900 the United States exported goods valued at $1.5 billion. By 1914 that figure stood at $2.5 billion. Exports to Latin America increased markedly, from $132 million at the turn of the century to $309 million in 1914. Investments there in sugar, transportation, and banking shot up. By 1913 the United Fruit Company, the banana empire, had some 130,000 acres in cultivation in Central America, a fleet of freighters, and substantial political influence as well. By 1914 U.S. entrepreneurs dominated nickel mining in Canada and sugar production in Cuba, and total American investments abroad stood at $3.5 billion.

But those statistics meant more than fat pocketbooks for the corporate elite. Americans believed that economic expansion also carried abroad positive values of industriousness, honesty, morality, and private initiative. Thus Yale University-in-China and the Young Men's Christian Association (YMCA) joined Standard Oil Company and Singer Sewing in China as advance agents of civilization. Taft said about the Chinese: "The more civilized they become the more active their industries, the wealthier they become, and the better market they will become for us."[34] President Wilson, adding missionary paternalism to the quest for order, said simply that he would "teach the South American Republics to elect good men."[35] Not all foreigners viewed Americans as benevolent. One Venezuelan writer characterized "Yanquis" as "rough and obtuse Calibans, swollen by brutal appetites, the enemies of idealism, furiously enamored of the dollar," whiskey-soaked sots, "overwhelming, fierce, [and] clownish."[36] The Russian novelist Fyodor Dostoevsky depicted the United States as "a geographic outlaw, a place where his fictional protagonists fled never to return."[37] Whatever Americans' intentions, their compulsion to shape the lives of other peoples while denying any selfish desire to dominate showed a persistent and often glaring disjunction between the practices and professed ideals of U.S. foreign policy.

Cuba's Limited Independence Under the Platt Amendment

In December 1898, President McKinley promised a "free and independent" status for Cuba once the U.S. occupation had established "complete tranquility" and a "stable government."[38] To accelerate Cuban democracy and stability, he appointed General Leonard Wood as the military governor of the island. A Harvard graduate with a degree in medicine, Wood favored outright annexation of Cuba, but he loyally carried out the administration's policy of patrician tutelage. During his tenure as military governor (1899–1902), he worked to eradicate yellow fever, Americanize education, construct highways, and formulate an electoral law. He even added "before" and "after" photographs of public toilets in his reports. The general defined his objectives narrowly: "When money can

"If General Wood Is Unpopular with Cuba, We Can Guess the Reason."   General Leonard Wood (1860–1927) joined the army as a surgeon in 1886 and earned the Congressional Medal of Honor for helping to capture the Apache leader Geronimo. Wood commanded the Rough Riders at San Juan Hill before his appointment as the military governor of Cuba. As this cartoon suggests, he saw his role in Cuba as the "paternalistic" supervision of what he sanctimoniously described as a Cuban "race that has been steadily going down for a hundred years." Later he served as governor general of the Philippines. (*Minneapolis Tribune* in *Literary Digest,* 1901)

be borrowed at a reasonable rate of interest and when capital is willing to invest in the Island, a condition of stability will have been reached."[39] Only the North Americans had the resources to reconstruct war-ravaged Cuba. Those Cuban elites who spoke English and knew American ways could serve as local managers, traders, agents, and advisers. The occupation stressed English in public schools because "the Cuban people will never understand the people of the United States until they appreciate our institutions."[40]

Secretary of War Elihu Root sought a Cuban-American political relationship that would weather the storms of independence. Working closely with Senator Orville Platt, Root fashioned the Platt Amendment to the Army Appropriation Bill of 1901. By the amendment's terms, Cuba could not make a treaty with any nation that might impair its independence. Should Cuban independence ever be threatened, or should Cuba fail to protect "life, property, and individual liberty," the United States had the right to intervene. For these purposes, Cuba would cede to the United States "lands necessary for coaling or naval stations."[41]

Cubans protested. On Good Friday 1901, the front page of Havana's *La Discusión* carried a cartoon of "The Cuban Calvary" depicting the Cuban people as Christ and Senator Platt as a Roman soldier. Root piously denied any "intermeddling or interference with the affairs of a Cuban government," but Wood privately conceded that "little or no independence [was] left Cuba under the Platt Amendment."[42] A reluctant Cuban convention adopted the measure as an amendment to the new constitution on June 12, 1901, and the two governments signed a treaty embodying the Platt Amendment on May 22, 1903. That same year the U.S. Navy constructed a naval base at Guantánamo Bay; "Gitmo," as the marines christened it, was leased to the United States in perpetuity for a small annual fee. With North American investments pouring into capital-starved Cuba, extending control over sugar, tobacco, mining, transportation, utilities, and cattle ranching, the Reciprocity Treaty of 1902 permitted Cuban products to enter the United States at specially reduced tariff rates, thereby further interlocking the two economies.

The first president of the Republic of Cuba, Tomás Estrada Palma, acted "more plattish than Platt himself" until discontented Cuban nationalists rebelled.[43] In September 1906, the U.S. consul general in Havana reported Estrada Palma's inability to "protect life and property."[44] "I am so angry with that infernal little Cuban republic," exploded Roosevelt, "that I would like to wipe its people off the face of the earth." All he wanted was for the Cubans to "behave themselves."[45]

Into this turmoil stepped the portly Secretary of War William Howard Taft, sent by TR to mediate between the warring factions. Estrada Palma resigned, permitting Taft to establish a new government with himself as governor. Likening Cuban efforts at self-rule to "making bricks without straw," Taft concluded that Cubans woefully lacked a "mercantile spirit," a "desire to make money, to found great enterprises."[46] He returned home in mid-October, leaving behind a government headed by an American civilian, administered by U.S. Army officers, and backed by 5,000 American soldiers. For twenty-eight months Governor Charles E. Magoon attempted to reinstate Leonard Wood's electoral and humanitarian reforms, while Roosevelt worried that "those ridiculous dagoes would flare up over some totally unexpected trouble and start to cutting one another's throats."[47]

Under his successor, Taft, and under Taft's successor, Woodrow Wilson, U.S. policy toward Cuba reflexively supported existing governments, by force if necessary. Order took precedence over democracy; no serious effort was made to expand participatory politics or to empower historically disenfranchised poor, black, and mixed-race populations. The United States instead used "dollar diplomacy" to foster stability in Cuban politics and security for investments and commerce, particularly in sugar. The $50 million invested by Americans in 1896 jumped to $220 million in 1913. By 1920 American-owned mills produced about half of Cuba's sugar. Annual Cuban exports to the United States in 1900 equaled $31 million, by 1914 $131 million, and by 1920 $722 million, thus confirming José Martí's dictum that "*el pueblo que compra, manda*" ("the country which buys, commands").[48] U.S. entrepreneurs helped establish missionary schools (such as the Candler school in Havana, named after the founder of Coca-Cola) that, in effect, trained Cubans for employment in North American companies. When revolution threatened these interests, as in May 1912 and February 1917, marines went ashore. After Havana followed Washington's lead and declared war against Germany in April 1917, some 2,500 U.S. troops occupied the island, ostensibly to protect the sugar plantations that helped feed the Allied armies.

The Constable of the Caribbean: The Roosevelt Corollary, Venezuela, and the Dominican Republic

In his first annual message, on December 3, 1901, President Roosevelt called the Monroe Doctrine "a guarantee of the commercial independence of the Americas." The United States, however, as protector of that independence, would "not guarantee any state against punishment if it misconducts itself, provided that punishment does not take the form of the acquisition of territory by any non-American power."[49] If a Western Hemispheric country misbehaved toward a European nation, Roosevelt promised to "let the European country spank it."[50]

The president was thinking principally of Germany and Venezuela. The flamboyant Venezuelan dictator Cipriano Castro had perpetually deferred payment on $12.5 million in bonds held by European investors, once showing olfactory contempt during negotiations by "breaking wind" against indignant German diplomats.[51] In December 1902, after clearing the way with Washington, Germany and Britain delivered an ultimatum demanding immediate settlement of their claims, seized several Venezuelan vessels, bombarded two forts, and blockaded all ports. To all of this Roosevelt initially acquiesced, despite the doctrine of Argentina's Foreign Minister Luis M. Drago that "physical force cannot be used to compel the collection of public debt under any circumstances."[52]

In mid-January 1903, the German navy bombarded two more forts. This time Roosevelt delivered a quiet warning to desist. He also sent Admiral George Dewey on naval maneuvers in the Caribbean, which were intended, Dewey later boasted, as "an object lesson to the Kaiser."[53] TR worried that the "fuss-cat" kaiser might spark war through his "incessant hysterical vacillations."[54] Impressed by the U.S. reaction, the kaiser replaced his ill-informed ambassador with Hermann Speck von Sternburg, an old friend of Roosevelt. The president urged on him a quick settlement. Thereupon, Britain and Germany in February lifted the blockade and submitted the dispute to the Permanent Court of Arbitration at The Hague. Speck von Sternburg averred that the kaiser "would no more think of violating that [Monroe] doctrine than he would of colonizing the moon."[55] When the Hague arbiters found in favor of Germany and England in early 1904, a State Department official complained that this decision put "a premium on violence" and made likely similar European interventions in the future.[56]

TR also fretted about the Dominican Republic, revolution-torn since 1899 and seemingly vulnerable to German interests. "I have about the same desire to annex it," Roosevelt confessed privately, "as a gorged boa constrictor might have to swallow a porcupine wrong-end to."[57] An American firm claimed damages of several million dollars, and European creditors demanded action by their governments. The president prayed that the Dominicans "would behave so that I would not have to act in any way." By spring 1904 he thought he might have to do "what a policeman has to do."[58] If he said "'Hands off' to the powers of Europe, then sooner or later we must keep order ourselves," he told Root.[59]

On December 6, 1904, Roosevelt described to Congress his conception of the United States as hemispheric policeman. "Chronic wrongdoing, or an impotence which results in a general loosening of the ties of civilized society," he proclaimed, "may in America, as elsewhere, ultimately require intervention by some civilized nation, and in the Western Hemisphere the adherence of the United States to the Monroe Doctrine may force the United States, however reluctantly, in flagrant cases of such wrongdoing or impotence, to the exercise of an international police power."[60] James Monroe "certainly would no longer recognize" his own doctrine because TR had transformed the ban on European meddling into a brash assertion of U.S. military and political hegemony over the Americas.[61]

The Rough Rider soon donned his constable's badge. He appointed a U.S. collector of Dominican customs. "The Constitution," Roosevelt later explained, "did not explicitly give me the power to bring about the necessary agreement with Santo Domingo. But the Constitution did not forbid me."[62] Yet "policing" and "civilizing" the Dominican Republic by presidential order provoked national-ist resentment, as Dominicans soon quieted "their children with the threat 'There comes an American. Keep quiet or he will kill you.'"[63] Taft's secretary of state, Philander C. Knox, applauded the customs receivership in the Dominican Republic for curing "century-old evils" and halting corruption.[64] The assassination of the Dominican president in November 1911 suggested that Knox spoke prematurely. And in 1912 revolutionaries operating from contiguous Haiti marauded throughout the Dominican Republic, forcing the closure of several customs houses. To restore order, Taft in September 1912 sent a commission backed by 750 marines. The com-missioners redefined the Haitian-Dominican border, forced the corrupt Dominican president to resign, and avoided direct interference in a new election.

His denunciation of "dollar diplomacy" notwithstanding, Woodrow Wilson's search for stability in Latin America retraced familiar steps. When, in September 1913, revolution again threatened the Dominican government, Secretary of State

Bryan promised "every legitimate means to assist in the restoration of order and the prevention of further insurrections."[65] When Wilson ordered naval intervention after further Dominican disorders in May 1916, he said: "If a man will not listen to you quietly in a seat, sit on his neck and make him listen."[66] As the 400 marines of Admiral William Caperton's landing force entered the city of Santo Domingo at dawn on May 15, they found empty streets, bolted doors, shuttered windows, and Dominican flags festooned with black crepe. A new treaty was imposed giving the United States full control over Dominican finances. In November, as U.S. participation in the European war became increasingly probable, Wilson proclaimed the formal military occupation of the Dominican Republic, ostensibly to suppress revolutionaries suspected of a pro-German bias. The U.S. Navy formally governed the country until 1922. The main legacy of the occupation, in the historian Bruce Calder's understated judgment, was "a strong anti-U.S. feeling" among the Dominican people.[67]

Ordering Haiti and Nicaragua

The Dominican Republic shares the island of Hispaniola with Haiti, where revolution became an increasingly popular mode of changing governments in the early twentieth century. American investments in Haiti were limited to ownership of a small railroad and a one-third share in the Haitian National Bank. Nationals of France and Germany controlled the bank, and disorder thus could give either European nation a pretext for intervention. After the outbreak of World War I, the Wilson administration worried about "the ever present danger of German control" of Haiti and its deepwater harbor of Môle Saint Nicolas.[68] The Navy Department, content with bases in Cuba and Puerto Rico, nonetheless remembered the German gunboat *Panther*'s sinking a Haitian gunboat in 1902. The State Department sought to buy the Môle "to take it out of the market."[69] Wilson also pressed for an American customs receivership on the Dominican model.

The Haitians resisted successfully until July 1915, when the regime of Guillaume Sam fell in an orgy of grisly political murders. Wilson ordered the navy to "amicably take charge" of the "dusky little republic."[70] After 2,000 troops imposed martial law and seized the customshouses, the African American activist-historian W. E. B. Du Bois admonished: "SHAME ON AMERICA!" because "murder in Port-au-Prince is no worse than ... lynching in Georgia."[71] Subsequent fighting between occupiers and native guerrillas, which critics perceived as "a racial war of extermination," killed more than 2,250 Haitians compared to 16 marine casualties.[72] Until the marines finally departed in 1934, U.S. officials observed "the intense feeling ... practically everywhere against the American occupation."[73]

The United States also intervened, virtually at will, in Nicaragua. In 1907 Roosevelt and Mexico's president jointly proposed a peace conference to end the incessant warfare among Central American states. As Secretary of State Root explained, their conduct mattered because the Panama Canal put them "in the front yard of the United States."[74] When President José Santos Zelaya solicited funds to build a second interoceanic canal, especially from Germany (whose capital investments were three times greater than U.S. properties in Nicaragua), Washington turned against a leader whom some Nicaraguans had compared to Roosevelt

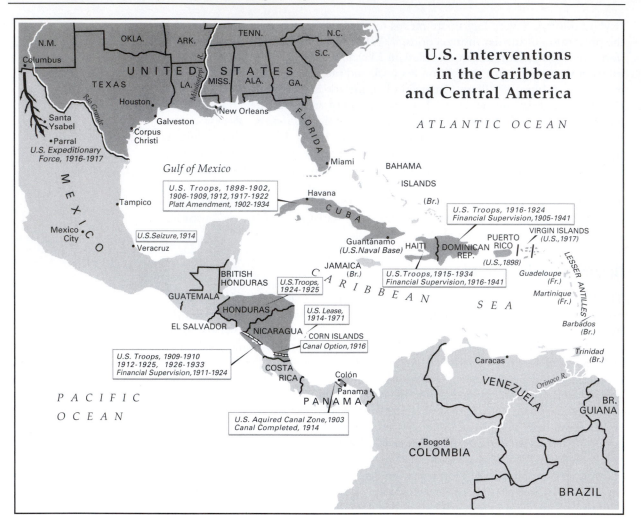

U.S. Interventions
in the Caribbean
and Central America

himself. For Zelaya's crime of seeking a "better economic position for Nicaragua outside the U.S. economic subsystem," Secretary of State Knox called his regime "a blot upon the history of Nicaragua" and President Taft said he would no longer deal with "such a medieval despot."[75]

After Zelaya executed two Americans for aiding rebels, Washington broke diplomatic relations in November 1909, sent a battleship for "moral effect," forced Zelaya into exile, and threatened to "knock heads together until they should maintain peace."[76] Secretary Knox then negotiated a treaty with the victorious conservatives led by Adolfo Díaz, providing for U.S. control of the customs service and an American loan. Instead of gratitude, "the natural sentiment of an overwhelming majority of Nicaraguans is antagonistic to the United States," the U.S. envoy reported.[77] Rebuffed by the U.S. Senate, Knox and a group of bankers simply went ahead without a treaty. In September 1912, the administration sent 354 marines into battle on behalf of the Díaz regime, which the State Department deemed representative of "the ablest people of the country."[78] After routing the newest revolutionary army, the leathernecks returned home, leaving one hundred behind as a legation guard in Managua. The marines could prevent a coup d'état, but "*keeping* a surrogate in power in Central America was often as problematical as *putting* him in power."[79]

The Wilson administration did much the same. In the spring of 1913 Secretary Bryan dusted off a shelved draft treaty granting the United States a canal option in Nicaragua in exchange for $3 million. The secretary also added a clause similar to the Platt Amendment before sending the Bryan-Chamorro Treaty to the Senate. When the upper house balked, Bryan deleted the U.S. right of intervention. Ratification in February 1916 did help Nicaragua's finances. The treaty also effectively excluded European powers from naval bases in the Gulf of Fonseca, and to make that point stick, Wilson ordered U.S. warships to cruise offshore during the 1916 Nicaraguan presidential campaign. Although nominally independent, Nicaragua remained a U.S. protectorate until 1933.

Resisting Revolution in Mexico

Revolution in Mexico posed major problems for Washington. In 1911 Francisco I. Madero toppled Porfirio Díaz, the aged dictator who had maintained order, personal power, and a healthy environment for North American investments since the late 1870s. U.S. citizens owned more than 40 percent of Mexico's property, and Mexico had become the world's third largest oil producer, thanks to the Standard Oil Company, Texas Oil Company (Texaco), and other firms. The revolution thus inevitably took on an anti–Yankee tinge. Despite the threat to American lives and property, Taft determined to "sit tight on the lid and it will take a good deal to pry me off."[80] One of Taft's diplomats, however, soon reversed the president's policy of nonintervention. In February 1913, Ambassador Henry Lane Wilson encouraged one of Madero's trusted generals, Victoriano Huerta, to overthrow the revolutionary nationalist. Indeed, Huerta had Madero shot and then set about to consolidate his own power. The German ambassador called these events "the usual American policy of replacing hostile regimes with pliable ones through revolutions without taking official responsibility for it."[81] But one of the state governors, Venustiano Carranza, organized the "Constitutionalist" revolt on February 26, igniting a period of vicious internal conflict. When American residents became caught in the crossfire, the departing Taft administration refused recognition until Huerta punished the "murderers of American citizens" and ended "discriminations against American interests."[82]

Appalled by Madero's murder, President Woodrow Wilson vowed not to recognize a "government of butchers."[83] He privately described his purpose as that of a benevolent neighbor who would help Mexico "adjust her unruly household."[84] Seemingly unconcerned about private American properties in Mexico worth some $1.5 billion, Wilson refused to act as "the servant of those who wish to enhance the value of their Mexican investments."[85] When Ambassador Wilson continued to urge recognition of Huerta to protect those U.S. interests, the president recalled him in July 1913 for "treason, perfidy, and assassination in an assault on constitutional government."[86] The president thereafter treated with Mexico through special emissaries, only one of whom spoke fluent Spanish.

William Jennings Bryan (1860–1925), Woodrow Wilson (1856–1924), and Franklin D. Roosevelt (1882–1945), 1913. President Wilson, in white trousers and dark jacket, speaks while Secretary of State Bryan, to the president's right, and Assistant Secretary of the Navy Roosevelt, at the far right of the picture, look on. Wilson spoke proudly of his "missionary diplomacy," for he believed that "every nation needs to be drawn into the tutelage of America." To achieve this goal, Wilson sent more U.S. warships into more Caribbean harbors than did any other president. (Franklin D. Roosevelt Library)

In August one such representative, John Lind, arrived in Mexico City. A former governor of Minnesota without diplomatic experience, Lind delivered Wilson's proposal for an armistice between Huerta's federalist troops and all revolutionary groups, "an early and free election," and Huerta's promise not to run for president. In exchange, the United States pledged recognition and aid to "the administration chosen and set up … in the way and on the conditions suggested." With sublime arrogance, Woodrow Wilson wondered: "Can Mexico give the civilized world a satisfactory reason for rejecting our good offices?"[87] "Where in the hell does he get the right to say who shall or shall not be President of Mexico," wrote one Mexican after Wilson's "counsels" were rebuffed.[88] After this snub, Woodrow Wilson announced a restrained policy of "watchful waiting."[89]

Undeterred, Huerta in October held a special election, which returned an entirely submissive congress ready to extend his presidency indefinitely. Wilson then turned to Carranza in northern Mexico, but the latter contemptuously refused Wilsonian mediation and rejected any solution short of his own triumph. Wilson informed the other powers in November of his renewed policy "to isolate General Huerta entirely … and so to force him out."[90]

Most European powers, especially Germany, had recognized Huerta in defiance of Wilson. "Good. Finally unity against the Yankee," the kaiser had noted in July 1913.[91] The British, however, their capital investments in Mexico ranking second only to those of the United States and their navy relying on Mexican oil, did not want to antagonize Wilson, with tensions mounting in Europe. The British

Foreign Office therefore notified Huerta that it would not support him against the United States, and urged him to resign—all the while viewing Wilson's policies as "most impractical and unreasonable."[92]

With British compliance assured, Wilson lifted the U.S. arms embargo in February 1914 and permitted large quantities of arms to flow to both factions, although mostly to Carranza. As the latter's resupplied forces pushed south, the president sent U.S. naval vessels to the oil-producing town of Tampico on the Gulf of Mexico. On April 9, at Tampico, Huerta's troops arrested several American sailors loading gasoline onto a whaleboat docked provocatively near a Mexican military installation. The Mexican colonel in charge quickly freed the sailors and apologized orally. The hotheaded U.S. squadron commander, Rear Admiral Henry T. Mayo, demanded a formal twenty-one-gun salute because Mexico had insulted the flag. When Huerta refused, the president on April 20 requested congressional approval to use armed force to obtain "the fullest recognition of the rights and dignity of the United States."[93] Without waiting for congressional authorization, Wilson then ordered U.S. warships to the port of Veracruz to stop a German arms shipment intended for Huerta.

On April 21, 1914, 800 American sailors and marines landed. Huerta's troops withdrew but cadets from the naval academy, joined by prisoners liberated from jails and other irregulars, put up a bloody resistance. Nineteen Americans and several hundred Mexicans died. An anguished Wilson bemoaned that "it was I who ordered those young men to their deaths."[94] Despite his intent to undermine Huerta, the capture of Veracruz temporarily rallied Mexicans behind the dictator. Rejecting advice from his military advisers, who wanted to march to Mexico City, Wilson accepted mediation when proposed by Argentina, Brazil, and Chile (the ABC powers) on April 25. These mediation talks, held on the Canadian side of Niagara Falls that summer, accomplished little, but in mid-July Huerta fled to Europe, and on August 20 a triumphant Carranza paraded before enthusiastic throngs in Mexico City.

The Constitutionalist triumph did not last. One of Carranza's northern generals, Francisco (Pancho) Villa, soon broke from the ranks, marched south, and in December occupied Mexico City. Wilson saw Villa as "the only instrument of civilization in Mexico" whose "firm authority allows him to create order and to educate the turbulent masses of peons so prone to pillage."[95] Because Villa had not criticized the U.S. assault on Veracruz, the president facilitated arms exports to him and refused to recognize Carranza. To prevent a military clash with any Mexican faction, all American troops withdrew from Veracruz on November 23, 1914. Once again, Wilson watched and waited.

U.S. relations with Mexico remained tense during early 1915. Carranza's forces gradually drove Villa north, but in the process Mexico City became a no-man's-land, with bread riots and starvation threatening its inhabitants, including 2,500 Americans and 23,000 other foreign residents. Further complications arose along the Mexico-U.S. borderland, especially in southern Texas, where the massive influx of refugees and revolutionaries exacerbated local tensions between Anglos and *Tejanos*. The Plan of San Diego, an anarchist manifesto broadcast in early 1915, demanded return of all lands "robbed in a most perfidious manner," execution of every North American "over sixteen years of age," restoration of Indian lands, and sovereign territory for blacks.[96] The ensuing raids and counterraids turned south Texas into a war zone as vigilantes and Texas rangers killed at least 150 Mexicans. A new verb—"rangered"—described summary treatment of suspects by Texas authorities.[97] Preoccupied by the *Lusitania* crisis with Germany after May 1915 (see page 271), Wilson reluctantly concluded that "Carranza will somehow have to be digested."[98] With American oil fields under Carranza's protection, Wilson extended de facto recognition to the Constitutionalist regime in June 1915, permitted arms exports (while banning them to opponents), and beefed up the U.S. military presence along the border.

Francisco (Pancho) Villa (1878–1923).   The intelligent, dedicated revolutionary nationalist bedeviled both Mexico and the United States. His daring raid on an American border town was calculated to outrage President Wilson, whom he mocked as "an evangelizing professor of philosophy who is destroying the independence of a friendly people." This photograph was taken in 1908. (Library of Congress)

Egged on by German agents who envisaged a Mexican–American war as "a noose … to tie the United States to the American continent," Villa denounced *Carranzistas* as "vassals" of the United States.[99] In the predawn hours of March 9, 1916, Villa led a band of *Villistas* across the border into Columbus, New Mexico, initiating a battle that left seventeen Americans and more than a hundred Mexicans dead. Within hours of the attack, Wilson unleashed the Punitive Expedition of 7,000 soldiers, commanded by General John J. Pershing, which soon penetrated 350 miles into Mexico in a vain search for Villa. Nonetheless, a clash with *Carranzista* troops occurred at Carrizal in June 1916. Wilson resisted demands to withdraw Pershing's forces until February 1917. Later that month, the secret Zimmermann telegram, proposing an anti-American alliance between Germany and Mexico, came into the hands of the State Department, courtesy of British intelligence. This German threat prompted the United States to extend de jure recognition of the Carranza government on August 31, 1917, in order to ensure Mexican neutrality during the fight against Germany. After four futile years, Wilson had finally given up trying to tutor the Mexicans.

Japan, China, and Dollar Diplomacy in Asia

Managing Asian affairs proved even more difficult after 1900. Secretary of State John Hay's Open Door notes did not prevent the further humiliation of China. During the Boxer Rebellion Russia stationed 175,000 troops in Manchuria and demanded exclusive rights from China, including a commercial monopoly. Roosevelt and Hay disingenuously acquiesced because the Open Door had "always recognized the exceptional position of Russia" in Manchuria and had merely sought the commercial freedom "guaranteed to us by … the whole civilized world."[100] Thinking it folly "to play the role of an Asian power without military power," Roosevelt retreated because the American people would not fight for nebulous principles of Chinese integrity in Manchuria.[101] His successors in the White House did not always follow his example.

Japan viewed the question quite differently. Russia blocked Japanese economic expansion into Manchuria, posed a potential naval menace, and endangered the Japanese position in Korea. Tokyo covered its flanks with an Anglo–Japanese Alliance in 1902 and prepared for war. On February 8, 1904, the Japanese navy destroyed Russia's Asian fleet and naval base in a surprise attack at Port Arthur. At first Roosevelt cheered privately, "for Japan is playing our game," but he worried about "the creation of either a yellow peril or a Slav peril."[102] By spring 1905, Japanese soldiers had taken Mukden, where Russia lost 97,000 men. Revolutionary stirrings had hit St. Petersburg, and Admiral Heihachiro Togo had sunk the Russian Baltic fleet at Tsushima Strait (between Japan and Korea). On May 31, Japanese envoy Kogoro Takahira requested Roosevelt "to invite the two belligerents to come together" for direct peace negotiations.[103]

Hoping to balance the belligerents "so that each may have a moderative action on the other" and thus protect U.S. access to the Pacific and Asia, Roosevelt assembled Japanese and Russian diplomats at Portsmouth, New Hampshire, in August 1905.[104] Japan demanded Russia's leasehold on the Liaodong Peninsula and the railroad running from Harbin to Port Arthur, evacuation of Russian

"Spread-eagleism" in China. The missionary teacher Grace Roberts teaches a Bible class in 1903 in Manchuria. Americanism and religious work, flag and mission, became partners. The missionary force was thus feminized—the majority of missionaries were women. (By permission of the Houghton Library, Harvard University, ACB 78.1)

troops from Manchuria, and recognition of Japan's control of Korea. The Russians quickly conceded these points but rejected demands for an indemnity and cession of the island of Sakhalin. Roosevelt broke the deadlock by proposing a division of Sakhalin and agreement "in principle" on an indemnity. Tsar Nicholas II agreed to partition but "not a kopeck of compensation."[105] Japan yielded and in late August signed a peace treaty. Roosevelt had earned the Nobel Peace Prize.

The president's search for equipoise in East Asia did not end at Portsmouth. As early as March 1904, the president had conceded to Japan a relationship with Korea "just like we have with Cuba."[106] Secretary of War Taft reaffirmed the concession with Prime Minister Taro Katsura on July 27, 1905. In the Taft-Katsura "agreed memorandum of conversation," Japan denied any designs on the Philippines, and Taft thereby put an American "seal on the death warrant of an independent Korea."[107] A year later the Japanese reopened southern Manchuria to foreign and American trade but discouraged foreign capital investments. Japan formally annexed Korea in 1910.

A domestic dispute in California soon soured Japanese–American amity. On October 11, 1906, the San Francisco School Board created a special "Oriental Public

School" for all Japanese, Chinese, and Korean children. Japan immediately protested, and TR denounced the "infernal fools in California" whose exclusion of
Japanese from all other public schools was "as foolish as if conceived by the mind
of a Hottentot."[108] Given existing federal-state jurisdictions, however, he could do
little more than rail against the recalcitrant school board, apply political pressure to
the governor and California legislature to prevent statewide discriminatory measures, and propose federal legislation to naturalize Japanese residing permanently in
the United States. Defending segregation, the *San Francisco Examiner* editorialized:
"Californians do not want their growing daughters to be intimate in daily school
contact with Japanese young men. Is this remarkable?"[109] Always the political realist, Roosevelt accepted what he personally disliked and sought accommodation
with Japan. In February 1907, he reached a "Gentlemen's Agreement" with Tokyo,
sharply restricting Japanese immigration on a voluntary basis.

Because "the Japanese jingoes are ... about as bad as ours," the president
shrewdly pressed for more battleships and fortification of Hawai'i and the vulnerable Philippines, now America's "heel of Achilles," so that the United States
would "be ready for anything that comes."[110] He also dramatized the importance
of a strong navy to Congress and to Japan by ordering the battle fleet to the
Pacific and around the world. An armada of sixteen battleships steamed out of
Hampton Roads, Virginia, in December 1907, not to return until February 1909.
Germany's kaiser predicted that U.S. warships in the Pacific "will upset all British
and Japanese calculations."[111] Just after the "Great White Fleet" visited Tokyo in
October 1908, Japan's ambassador received instructions to reach an agreement
with the United States recognizing the Pacific Ocean as an open avenue of trade,
pledging the integrity of Japanese and American insular possessions in the Pacific,
and promising equal opportunity in China. The ensuing Root-Takahira declaration of November 30, 1908, seemed to restore Japanese-American harmony.

The promising new epoch was spoiled by conflicting Japanese-American goals
toward China. Despite the Open Door notes, American commerce with China
stalled during the Roosevelt era, in part because of resurgent nationalism. When
Congress barred Chinese immigration in 1904, the Chinese staged a short-lived boycott of American goods. A protest song against "American Flour-Made Mooncakes"
became popular in Chinese cities.[112] In addition, prostitution flourished in China's
treaty ports. This illegitimate China trade ("deeply corrupt, overtly predatory, transnational, transracial, conducted without regard to a 'national interest'") undercut
the gains of legitimate American commerce in China.[113] Because Roosevelt viewed
the Chinese as passive and effete, "sunk in Oriental stagnation and corruption," he
placed strategic interests first and refused to antagonize Japan over China.[114]

Roosevelt's successor thought otherwise. Instead of a decrepit China in decay,
President Taft envisioned expanded trade with a "young China, rousing from a
centuries-old slumber and rubbing the sand of its past from its eyes."[115] During a
1905 trip to East Asia, Taft had met the intensely anti-Japanese American consul general in Mukden, Willard Straight. Two years later, after calling the Root-Takahira
agreement "a terrible diplomatic blunder" because it accepted Japan's exploitation
of Manchuria, Straight proposed the creation of a Manchurian bank, to be financed
by the American railroad magnate E. H. Harriman.[116] Under Taft, Straight and the

Elihu Root (1845–1937).
Root served as secretary of
state (1905–1909). He helped
devise methods for managing
the American empire. (Library of
Congress)

State Department quickly inspired several New York banks to form a combination, headed by J. P. Morgan, to serve as the official agency of American railroad investment in China. As acting chief of the department's new Far Eastern Division, Straight demanded admission of the American bankers into a European banking consortium undertaking construction of the Huguang Railway linking Beijing and Guangzhou (Canton). Straight then resigned from the State Department to become the Morgan group's roving representative.

In November 1909, Washington had proposed to Britain the neutralization of Manchurian railroads through extending a large international loan to China for the purchase of the lines. Britain, however, joined both Japan and Russia to reject the proposal. Instead of an open door in Manchuria, Secretary of State Knox had "nailed that door closed with himself on the outside."[117] In the fall of 1910, an agreement expanded the Huguang Railway consortium to include American bankers, but the Chinese Revolution broke out in May 1911 against the Manchu dynasty and foreign interests and delaying railroad construction until 1913. "Dollar diplomacy," Straight ruefully admitted, "made no friends" in the Huguang matter.[118]

Hoping to reap tangible benefits by dissociating the United States from the other powers, President Wilson and Secretary Bryan repudiated American participation in the international consortium on March 18, 1913—to do otherwise would have cost the United States "the proud position … secured when Secretary Hay stood for the Open Door in China after the Boxer Uprising." Wilson extended formal diplomatic recognition to the Chinese Republic in May.[119] He had thereby renewed America's commitment to the political integrity of China, a goal pragmatically abandoned by Roosevelt, unsuccessfully resuscitated by Taft, and consistently opposed by Japan.

Wilson's Asian policy started out tentatively, but events at home and abroad eventually caused it to resemble Taft's more than Roosevelt's. In April 1913, Democratic and Progressive politicians placed before the California legislature a bill denying residents "ineligible to citizenship" the right to own land. The measure struck directly at the 50,000 Japanese living in California. Racist passions erupted, with one farmer recoiling from the prospect of racial intermarriage: "What is that baby? It isn't a Japanese. It isn't white."[120] Basically sharing the Californians' anti-Japanese prejudices and sensitive to states' rights, Wilson nonetheless sent Bryan to Sacramento to beg for a milder statute. But the California legislature passed the offensive bill on May 3, 1913. When Japan protested the "unfair and intentionally racially discriminatory" measure, Wilson and Bryan lamely argued that one state's legislation did not constitute a "national discriminatory policy."[121]

Wilson's antipathy toward Japan reappeared in fall 1914 when Japan declared war on Germany, seized the German Pacific islands north of the equator, and swept across China's Shandong Peninsula to capture the German leasehold of Jiaozhou. "When there is a fire in a jeweller's shop," a Japanese diplomat arrogantly theorized, "the neighbours cannot be expected to refrain from helping themselves."[122] Tokyo immediately followed with the Twenty-One Demands of January 18, 1915, asserting extensive political and economic rights in Shandong, southern Manchuria, and Mongolia. Preoccupied with Mexico and the *Lusitania* crisis, the Wilson administration refused to recognize Japan's gains, which amounted to a repudiation of the Open Door policy.

Wilson's nonrecognition policy ran counter to secret treaties in which the European Allies promised to support Japan's conquests at the peace conference after World War I. Washington soon compromised. In an agreement with Viscount Kikujiro Ishii, signed November 2, 1917, Secretary Lansing admitted that "territorial propinquity creates special relationships between countries, and consequently … Japan has special interests in China," while Ishii reiterated his nation's dedication to the Open Door and integrity of China.[123] The Wilson administration also revived the international banking consortium as the only way to check further unilateral Japanese economic penetration of China proper. The wheel had turned full circle for Wilson. Like Taft before him, Wilson failed to protect China's fragile sovereignty because he could neither conciliate nor deter Japan.

Anglo-American Rapprochement and Empire Building

American policies toward Asia and Latin America often fell short of their proclaimed goals because of the pseudoscientific thinking about race characteristic of the early twentieth century. Americans viewed Asians as "inscrutable and somnolent," depicted Latin Americans as black children or alluring maidens, imagined Africa as the "dark continent" of "savage beasts and beastly savages," and referred to Filipinos as "our little brown brothers." These biased stereotypes inevitably aroused resentment from Bogotá to Beijing, from Managua to Manila.[124] Yet such Darwinist racial attitudes also facilitated much closer relations between the United States and Great Britain. Because victory "in the international competition among the races … might not go to the refined and peaceful peoples but rather to the amoral, the cunning, the fecund, and the power hungry," England and the United States sought to "cultivate a sense of solidarity and a capacity for cooperation."[125] "Buffalo Bill" Cody certainly thought the "hatchet" had been "buried" when Queen Victoria attended his Wild West Show and "bowed" before the American flag.[126] So too did the British, as shown by their willingness to accept exclusive U.S. control of a canal in Panama. Also prompted by Britain's search for allies against Germany (evidenced in the Anglo-Japanese Alliance of 1902 and the Entente Cordiale with France in 1904), London's pursuit of "the most cordial and constant cooperation" with the United States led to a celebrated "great rapprochement."[127]

The tenuous new Anglo-American affinity nearly dissolved in 1903 over the Alaska boundary controversy, which stemmed from Canadian claims to large areas of the Alaskan panhandle. As the power responsible for the Dominion's foreign relations (Canada did not establish a foreign office until 1909), Britain found itself backing Ottawa's dubious contention that much of the panhandle's coastline actually belonged to Canada. Expostulating that Canada had less claim "than the United States did to Cornwall or Kent," President Roosevelt refused arbitration and sent 800 soldiers to Alaska to awe his opponents, both foreign and domestic.[128] London finally agreed in January 1903 to an American proposal for a mixed boundary commission composed of six jurists, three from each side. Taking no chances, Roosevelt appointed Senator Henry Cabot Lodge and Secretary Root, hardly disinterested judges, to the commission. He informally warned London he would demarcate the line himself if the

John Bull in Need of Friends.   Battered by criticism over its war against the Boers in South Africa and challenged by a rising Germany, Great Britain found a new friend in the United States. Not all Britons embraced Anglo-American affinity. "Only 1/4 of the population of the United States are what you might call natives," wrote a British admiral in 1901. "The rest are Germans, Irish, Italians, and the scum of the earth! all of them hating the English like poison." (*Des Moines Leader* in *Literary Digest,* 1901)

commissioners failed to agree. One British commissioner sided with the Americans, and on October 20, 1903, by a vote of 4 to 2, the commission panel officially decided for the United States. The British "made the inevitable choice to please a power ten times the size of Canada and with more than ten times the wealth."[129]

Canadian-American relations did improve with the Migratory Bird Treaty of 1916. Conservationists and scientists, alarmed by a decline in North American birds caused by reckless sport and commercial hunting, pressed for this agreement under the principle of "common property resources." The death of the last passenger pigeon, in the Cincinnati Zoo in 1914, symbolized the crisis. Because the treaty restricted hunting, especially during the mating season, it sparked some opposition in the United States. Representative John Tillman, a Democrat from Arkansas who defended duck hunting in gendered terms, cried that the accord "should be bedecked with skirts" because it "would feminize our boys."[130] The bird population increased, and similar wildlife protection, evident in the Inland Fisheries Treaty (1908) and the North Pacific Fur Seal Convention (1911), became landmarks in international environmental history.

Entente also characterized the Anglo-American settlement of the North Atlantic fisheries dispute. Since 1782, American fishermen had insisted on retaining their pre-Revolutionary privileges off Canada's Newfoundland. Indeed, "a gilded wooden cod" still hung from the ceiling of the Massachusetts State House.[131] The modus vivendi of 1888, under which they had fished for several years, collapsed in 1905 when Newfoundland placed restrictions on American fishing vessels. Senator Lodge cried for warships to protect his constituents' livelihood. Instead, Roosevelt proposed, and London accepted, arbitration at The Hague Tribunal. In 1910 the arbiters ruled that Britain could oversee fishing off Newfoundland if it established reasonable regulations, that a fisheries commission would hear cases, and that Americans could fish in large bays if they remained three miles from shore. This compromise defused the oldest dispute in American foreign relations and symbolized London's political withdrawal from the Western Hemisphere.

The naval retreat had occurred earlier, when the Admiralty abolished the North Atlantic station based at Jamaica. After 1902 the Royal Navy patrolled the Caribbean only with an annual visit by a token squadron of cruisers. Admiral Sir John Fisher wanted to concentrate his heavy ships in the English Channel and North Sea as monitors of the growing German navy. He regarded the United States as "a kindred state with whom we shall never have a parricidal war."[132]

Even the aggressive hemispheric diplomacy of Taft and Wilson did not undermine the Anglo-American rapprochement. Britain criticized both dollar diplomacy in Latin America and Wilson's quixotic efforts to dislodge Huerta. But Foreign Secretary Sir Edward Grey tersely laid to rest all talk of a challenge: "His Majesty's Government cannot with any prospect of success embark upon an active counterpolicy to that of the United States, or constitute themselves the champions of Mexico or any of these republics against the United States."[133] In reciprocation, Wilson protected British oil interests in Mexico and made it a "point of honor" to eliminate the one potentially dangerous British grievance inherited from his predecessor.[134] Late in the Taft administration, Congress had exempted American intercoastal shippers from payment of Panama Canal tolls. British opinion condemned this shifting of canal maintenance costs to other users. Because it unfairly discriminated against foreign shipping, Wilson persuaded Congress to revoke the law in June 1914.

In the end, rapprochement meant mutual respect for each other's empires. In addition to having the "Great White Fleet" visit "white man's country" in New Zealand and Australia, Roosevelt encouraged London to frustrate native aspirations for independence in India, while the British accepted the American suppression of the Filipinos and U.S. hegemony in Latin America.[135] American leaders usually spoke favorably of independence for colonial peoples—but independence only after long-term tutelage to make them "civilized" enough to govern. In 1910 in Egypt, a country that the ex-president considered "years, even generations" away from self-government, he lectured Muslim nationalists about Christian respect for womanhood.[136] In chronically unstable Liberia, where the United States in 1912 instituted a financial receivership in the African nation resembling that in the Dominican Republic, the British encouraged Washington to use a strong hand in what London called America's "protectorate."[137]

While building an empire, U.S. policymakers largely adhered to the tradition of aloofness from continental European political and military affairs. Even Roosevelt overtly tampered only once with Europe's balance of power. In 1904 France acquiesced in British control of Egypt in exchange for primacy in Morocco. A year later, Germany decided to test the solidity of the new Anglo-French entente by challenging France's claims in Morocco. The kaiser belligerently demanded a German political role in Morocco, which France at once refused. After a brief European war scare, in which Britain stood by its ally, Germany asked Roosevelt to induce France and England to convene a conference to settle Morocco's future. Worried about Kaiser Wilhelm's "violent and often wholly irrational zigzags," Roosevelt accepted the personal invitation only after assuring Paris that his "sympathies … at bottom [were] with France."[138] During the conference, held in early 1906 at Algeciras, Spain, Roosevelt devised a pro-French compromise and persuaded the kaiser to accept it. This political intervention isolated Germany and reinforced the Anglo-French entente, but it generated criticism at home. Roosevelt's successors made sure they did not violate the American policy of nonentanglement with Europe during the more ominous second Moroccan and Balkan crises preceding the First World War.

Nonentanglement also doomed the sweeping arbitration treaties that Secretary Hay negotiated with several world powers. When the Senate attached crippling amendments, Roosevelt withdrew the treaties because they did "not in the smallest degree facilitate settlements by arbitration."[139] After 1905 Secretary Root persuaded Roosevelt to accept watered-down bilateral arbitration treaties, and Secretary Bryan later negotiated a series of supplementary "cooling-off" treaties by which nations pledged to refrain from war during international investigations of serious disputes. None of these arrangements, however, effectively bound signatories, and like the Permanent Court of Arbitration at The Hague, they represented a backwater in international diplomacy. Ambassador Whitelaw Reid compared U.S. participation in the Hague Peace Conference of 1907 to a farmer taking his hog to market: "That hog didn't weigh as much as I expected he would, and I always knew he wouldn't."[140]

The mainstream of American foreign policy between 1900 and 1914 flowed through the Panama Canal, a momentous political, military, and technological achievement. The United States became the unchallenged policeman of the Caribbean region, empowering Washington, in Taft's words, "to prevent revolutions" so that "we'll have no more."[141] Although German authorities thought that the canal would shift American priorities to Asia and "today's Atlantic fleet will become the Pacific fleet," the United States still lacked the power to challenge Japan or Britain.[142] As Roosevelt understood, the Open

Naval Arms Race. The international naval competition in the early twentieth century was foreboding. Disarmament talks at The Hague Conferences in 1899 and 1907 and arbitration treaties did not curb the arms buildup. Roosevelt's decision to send the "Great White Fleet" around the world in 1907–1908 may have encouraged both Japan and Germany to speed up their naval programs. (*Detroit News* in *Literary Digest,* 1904)

Door "completely disappears as soon as a powerful nation determines to disregard it."[143] One military officer told Congress in 1910: "We have grown from a little frontier army to one spread all over the world—in America, Puerto Rico, Hawai'i, Alaska, the Philippines, and sometimes in Cuba—and we have not got the officers and men to do it."[144]

American insensitivity to the nationalism and distinct cultural identities of other peoples became another imperial legacy. Filipino resistance to American domination, Cuban anger at the Platt Amendment, Colombian outrage over Panama, and Mexican rejection of Wilsonian intervention bore witness to the depth of nationalistic sentiments and to resentment at U.S. efforts to control. Like the European powers who were carving up Asia, Africa, and the Middle East, the United States developed its empire by subjugating peoples and compromising their sovereignty in Latin America and the Pacific. As a Panamanian diplomat later explained: "When you hit a rock with an egg, the egg breaks. Or when you hit an egg with a rock, the egg breaks. The United States is the rock. Panama is the egg. In either case, the egg breaks."[145] With the exception of the Virgin Islands, purchased from Denmark for $25 million in 1917 to forestall any wartime German seizure, the empire grew little from outright territorial gains. It was, instead, an informal empire administered by troops, financial advisers, and reformers who frequently ran roughshod over the culture, politics, and economies of the peoples they dominated. The U.S. governor of Guam captured the prevailing outlook when he depicted the indigenous Chamorros as children, "easily controlled and readily influenced by example, good or bad."[146]

Puerto Rico thus seemed the "good" territorial possession, and political cartoons portrayed the populace as a "polite schoolchild, sometimes female, in contrast to ruffian boys" in Cuba and the Philippines.[147] Under the Foraker Act (1900), Puerto Rico and its naval base on Culebra became a "new constitutional animal"—an "unincorporated territory" subject to the will of the U.S. Congress and governed by the War Department (until 1934).[148] In a series of decisions called the Insular Cases (1901–1904), the Supreme Court upheld the Foraker Act, providing Washington with a means to govern people it did not wish to organize as a state. In March 1917, Congress granted Puerto Ricans U.S. citizenship just in time for them to be drafted into the U.S. armed forces in the war against Germany. "Increasingly tied to the United States and insistently defined as not part of it," Puerto Rico still remains a colony, or "commonwealth," and Puerto Ricans remain divided in their views about statehood, independence, and commonwealth status.[149]

The adventurous nature of American foreign relations under an imperial ideology and the male ethos in the years 1900–1914 attracted many capable, well-educated young men to diplomatic service. "It was TR's call to youth which lured me to Washington," the diplomat William Phillips later recalled.[150] Career ambassador Joseph C. Grew first gained presidential favor by shooting a tiger in China. Several of these young foreign-service career officers, virtually all graduates of Ivy League colleges, including Phillips, Grew, Willard Straight, former Rough Rider Henry P. Fletcher, and soldier-diplomat Frank R. McCoy, lived in an exclusive bachelors' townhouse at 1718 H Street during their Washington service. Known among themselves as "the Family," these youthful professionals blended camaraderie with careers and "became the elite or legendary 'inner circle' of the State Department" for the next forty years.[151] The New York attorney Henry L. Stimson, himself a protégé of Elihu Root, served as secretary of war under Taft (1911–1913) and continued this tradition of recruiting some of the brightest public servants to a succession of high-level posts through the end of World War II.

The American empire burgeoned culturally, as well as militarily and economically, during these years. Just as Buffalo Bill Cody's Wild West Show had "hyped" American cultural myths abroad since the 1890s, Wilbur Wright's airplane tour of Europe in 1908 set records, thrilled crowds, and impressed military strategists.[152] The cruise of the "Great White Fleet" provided as much pageantry as statecraft—"a feast, a frolic, or a fight," as Admiral Robley D. Evans put it.[153] Colonial subjects became popular on college campuses, as anthropologists and ethnographers offered courses on "Savage Childhood" and "Peoples of the Philippines."[154] When academic exchanges with European universities expanded after 1900, Harvard University commemorated its new Germanic Museum by bestowing an honorary doctorate on Prince Henry of Prussia, the kaiser's brother—"a simple, natural person who got used in a day to our troublesome democratic ways."[155]

Hundreds of thousands of U.S. tourists ("the world's wanderers") traveled abroad clutching their Baedeker guidebooks, spending American dollars, and sometimes acquiring foreign titles through marriage, as in the case of Jennie Jerome and Lord Randolph Churchill, whose son Winston valued Anglo–American partnership.[156] A French humorist commented that for American women "the freedom to flirt is as sacred and inalienable … as the immortal principles of 1789 are in our country."[157] Civic leaders took pride in hosting the Olympic Games in St. Louis in 1904, hailed an American victory in the 1908 Round-the-World Automobile race, became weekend frontiersmen after organizing the Boy Scouts of America in 1910, and cheered the gold medals won by Native American Jim Thorpe at the Stockholm Olympics in 1912. Just as they seemed to take up the great game of empire from Great Britain, so too did Americans become proficient in that most diplomatic of athletic competitions, the royal and ancient Scottish sport of golf. For some Americans, true Anglo-American entente did not occur until young Francis Ouimet bested British champions Harry Vardon and Ted Ray in the U.S. Open at Brookline, Massachusetts, in 1913.

Yet beneath the glitter lurked danger. Winston Churchill later wrote of living in two different worlds: "the actual, visual world with its peaceful activities" and "a hypothetical world 'beneath the threshold'"—"a world at one moment utterly fantastic, at the next seeming to leap into reality—a world of monstrous shadows moving in convulsive combination through vistas of fathomless catastrophe."[158] Once the world started spinning around the catastrophic assassination in Sarajevo, Bosnia, it became difficult for the growing American empire to escape the maelstrom of world war.

What if ...   *manliness and civilization had not become linked in the minds of American leaders in the period 1900–1917?*

Without the heavy emphasis on virility and civilization as a rationale for U.S. empire after 1898, certain features of that imperial experience might have been different. Had imperialists such as Theodore Roosevelt, William Howard Taft, and Gen. Leonard Wood not regarded Filipinos and Cubans as racial inferiors, as weak women and children who needed American tutelage, Americans might have opted to negotiate with them—a process that implies equal partnership—instead of using coercion, including the "water cure" and forcing the Platt Amendment upon Cuba. By treating peoples of Asia and Latin America as equals rather than subordinates, U.S. leaders might have appeared less self-righteous and aroused less anti-Americanism in the long term. The United States, in short, might have secured its interests in the area without violating its own best principles of fair play and self-determination. It is also improbable that a president of less blatant *machismo* than Theodore Roosevelt would have crudely impugned the masculinity of anti-imperialists by calling them mollycoddles and "nice old women of both sexes." Such gender-based language mattered because it undermined legitimate criticism, exalted the presidency over Congress in the checks-and-balance U.S. system, and stifled debate—the very stuff of the democratic process. A less conspicuously virile Roosevelt might not have imagined his own manhood challenged by Colombian "dagoes" and might have renegotiated a canal treaty with Bogotá instead of "taking" Panama.

For masculinity not to have mattered, though, would have required the undoing of gendered and race-based attitudes and practices that had been refined and affirmed through centuries of slavery, Indian removal, and institutionalized female inequality. In both rhetoric and practice, gendered language helped shape and give meaning to an official American worldview that envisaged conflict and competition as consistent with democracy and capitalism, and that assumed a natural hierarchy of power and order in the world where white males of European descent asserted supremacy over all others.

Nonetheless, we should be careful not to attribute too much weight to the masculinity factor alone. True, Roosevelt's nemesis Woodrow Wilson—whose commitment to the strenuous life consisted largely of throwing out baseballs on opening day and ineffectual attempts at golf—rejected Roosevelt's straightforward strategic rationale of policing the Caribbean to forestall European intervention, favoring instead the less bellicose alternative of missionary diplomacy (wherein Wilson would presumably teach Latin Americans to elect better men). Yet Wilson also sent more U.S. marines into more foreign ports than TR ever did. Even as he demonstrated modest anti-imperialist credentials by supporting the Jones Acts of 1916 and 1917 (which promised eventual Philippines independence and granted citizenship to Puerto Ricans), Wilson subscribed to notions of masculine honor that sanctioned the use of military force. When Mexican authorities refused to salute the U.S. flag at Tampico in April 1914, Wilson sent marines ashore at Veracruz, resulting in more resistance and more deaths than the shocked president expected. Although Wilson spoke about a nation being too proud to fight in rejecting war with Germany after the *Lusitania* sinking in 1915, he demanded "pledges" from Berlin that Germans would adhere to "civilized" rules of warfare. When Germany violated these pledges in 1917, the president whom Roosevelt called a college sissy led the country into a crusade to make civilization safe for democracy. Core values of manliness and civilization thus proved flexible in application. While their presence was ubiquitous, their manifestation varied in accordance with leadership and historical context.

FURTHER READING FOR THE PERIOD 1900–1914

See studies listed in the last two chapters and Michael C. C. Adams, *The Great Adventure* (1990); A. J. Bacevich, *Diplomat in Khaki* (1989) (General Frank McCoy); William H. Becker, *The Dynamics of Business-Government Relations* (1982); Gail Bederman, *Manliness & Civilization* (1995); Frances A. Boyle, *Foundations of World Order* (1999); Lester H. Brune, *The Origins of American Security Policy* (1981); Richard D. Challener, *Admirals, Generals, and American Foreign Policy, 1898–1914* (1973); Kendrick A. Clements, *William Jennings Bryan* (1982); Kurkpatrick Dorsey, *The Dawn of Conservation Diplomacy* (1999); Lloyd C. Gardner, *Safe for Democracy* (1984); Frank H. Goday, *Face of Empire* (2004); Robert E. Hannigan, *The New World Power* (2002); Robert C. Hilderbrand, *Power and the People* (1981); Kevin Murphy, *Political Manhood* (2008); David Traxel, *Crusader Nation* (2006); Cyrus Veeser, *A World Safe for Capitalism* (2002); Richard H. Werking, *The Master Architects* (1977) (foreign service); William C. Widenor, *Henry Cabot Lodge and the Search for an American Foreign Policy* (1980); and Mira Wilkins, *The Emergence of Multinational Enterprise* (1970).

Theodore Roosevelt is the subject of Howard K. Beale, *Theodore Roosevelt and the Rise of America to World Power* (1956); H. W. Brands, *T.R.* (1997); Richard H. Collin, *Theodore Roosevelt* (1985); John M. Cooper, Jr., *The Warrior and the Priest* (1983); Kathleen Dalton, *Theodore Roosevelt* (2002); Thomas G. Dyer, *Theodore Roosevelt and the Idea of Race* (1980); Raymond A. Esthus, *Theodore Roosevelt and the International Rivalries* (1970); Lewis L. Gould, *The Presidency of Theodore Roosevelt* (1991); Jonathan Hawley, *Theodore Roosevelt* (2008); Henry J. Hendrix, *Theodore Roosevelt's Naval Diplomacy* (2009); James R. Holmes, *Theodore Roosevelt and World Order* (2006); Frederick W. Marks, *Velvet on Iron* (1979); Edmund Morris, *Theodore Rex* (2001); Natalie A. Naylor et al., eds., *Theodore Roosevelt* (1992); and William N. Tilchin, *Theodore Roosevelt and the British Empire* (1997).

For the Taft administration, see David H. Burton, *William Howard Taft* (2004); Paolo E. Coletta, *The Presidency of William Howard Taft* (1973); Ralph E. Minger, *William Howard Taft and American Foreign Policy* (1975); and Walter V. Scholes and Marie V. Scholes, *The Foreign Policies of the Taft Administration* (1970).

For Wilson policies, see the next chapter and Frederick S. Calhoun, *Power and Principle* (1986) and *Uses of Force and Wilsonian Foreign Policy* (1993); Kendrick A. Clements, *The Presidency of Woodrow Wilson* (1990); and Edward S. Kaplan, *U.S. Imperialism in Latin America* (1997) (on Bryan's policies).

U.S. relations with Latin America are examined in Laura Briggs, *Reproducing Empire* (2002) (Puerto Rico); José A. Cabranes, *Citizenship and the American Empire* (1979) (Puerto Rico); Bruce J. Calder, *The Impact of Intervention* (1984) (Dominican Republic); Raymond A. Carr, *Puerto Rico* (1984); Arturo M. Carrión, *Puerto Rico* (1983); Mark T. Gilderhus, *Pan American Visions* (1986) (Wilson); David Healy, *Drive to Hegemony* (1989) and *Gunboat Diplomacy in the Wilson Era* (1976) (Haiti); Warren G. Kneer, *Great Britain and the Caribbean, 1901–1913* (1975); Walter LaFeber, *Inevitable Revolutions* (1993) (Central America); Lester D. Langley, *Struggle for the American Mediterranean* (1976), *The United States and the Caribbean, 1900–1970* (1980), and *The Banana Wars* (2002); Lester D. Langley and Thomas Schoonover, *The Banana Men* (1995); Nancy Mitchell, *The Danger of Dreams* (1999); Dana Munro, *Intervention and Dollar Diplomacy* (1964); Thomas F. O'Brien, *The Revolutionary Mission* (1996); Fredrick B. Pike, *The United States and Latin America* (1992); Brenda G. Plummer, *Haiti and the United States* (1992) and *Haiti and the Great Powers, 1902–1915* (1988); Mary Renda, *Taking Haiti* (2001); Emily Rosenberg, *Financial Missionaries to the World* (1999) (dollar diplomacy); Hans Schmidt, *The United States Occupation of Haiti, 1915–1934* (1971); Thomas D. Schoonover, *The United States in Central America, 1860–1911* (1991); David Sheinin, *Searching for Authority* (1998) (Argentina) and *Beyond the Ideal* (2000) (Pan Americanism); Lars Schoultz, *Beneath the United States* (1998); and Richard P. Tucker, *Insatiable Appetite* (2000).

For the Panama Canal, see Richard H. Collin, *Theodore Roosevelt's Caribbean* (1990); Michael L. Conniff, *Panama and the United States* (1992); and *Panama and the United States* (2001); James Howe, *The People Who Would Not Kneel* (1998); Richard L. Lael, *Arrogant Diplomacy* (1987); Walter LaFeber, *The Panama Canal* (1989); John Lindsay-Poland, *Emperors in the Jungle* (2003); John Major, *Prize Possession* (1993); David McCullough, *The Path Between the Seas* (1977); Matthew Parker, *Panama Fever* (2008); and Stephen J. Randall, *Colombia and the United States* (1992).

U.S. hegemony in Cuba is discussed in David Healy, *The United States in Cuba, 1898–1902* (1963); José M. Hernández, *Cuba and the United States* (1993); James H. Hitchman, *Leonard Wood and Cuban Independence, 1898–1902* (1971); Allan R. Millett, *The Politics of Intervention* (1968); and Louis A. Pérez, Jr., *Cuba and the United States* (2003), *On Becoming Cuban* (1999), and *Cuba Under the Platt Amendment, 1902–1934* (1986).

Relations with Mexico are treated in Jonathan C. Brown, *Oil and Revolution in Mexico* (1993); Jules Davids, *American Political and Economic Penetration of Mexico, 1877–1920* (1976); Jorge Domínguez and Rafael Fernandez de Castro, *United States and Mexico* (2001); Joseph M. Gilbert, *Revolution from Without* (1982); Mark T. Gilderhus, *Diplomacy and Revolution* (1977); John M. Hart, *Revolutionary Mexico* (1988) and *Empire and Revolution* (2002); Friedrich Katz, *The Life and Times of Pancho Villa* (1998) and *The Secret War in Mexico* (1981); Alan Knight, *U.S.–Mexican Relations, 1910–1940* (1987); Daniel Nugent, ed., *Rural Revolt in Mexico and U.S. Intervention* (1988); Ramón E. Ruíz, *The Great Rebellion* (1980); Karl M. Schmitt, *Mexico and the United States, 1821–1973* (1974); Joseph A. Stout, Jr., *Border Conflict* (1999); Paul J. Vanderwood and Frank N. Samponaro, *Border Fury* (1988); and Josefina Vázquez and Lorenzo Meyer, *The United States and Mexico* (1985).

For America's interactions with Asia and China, see William R. Braisted, *The United States Navy in the Pacific, 1897–1909* (1958) and *1909–1922* (1971); Jongsuk Chay, *Diplomacy of Asymmetry* (1990) (Korea);

Warren I. Cohen, *America's Response to China* (2000); Daniel M. Crane and Thomas A. Breslin, *An Ordinary Relationship* (1986); Jose D. Fermin, *1904 World's Fair* (2004); Jonathan Goldstein et al., eds., *America Views China* (1991); Michael H. Hunt, *The Making of a Special Relationship* (1983); Akira Iriye, *Across the Pacific* (1967); Delber L. McKee, *Chinese Exclusion Versus the Open Door Policy, 1900–1906* (1976); Dennis L. Noble, *The Eagle and the Dragon* (1990); Noel H. Pugach, *Paul S. Reinsch* (1979); Eileen Scully, *Bargaining with the State from Afar* (2001) (Extraterritoriality); and Guanhua Wang, *In Search of Justice* (2002).

Japanese-American relations are studied in Burton F. Beers, *Vain Endeavor: Robert Lansing's Attempt to End the American-Japanese Rivalry* (1962); Raymond A. Esthus, *Double Eagle and Rising Sun* (1988) (Portsmouth) and *Theodore Roosevelt and Japan* (1966); Akira Iriye, *Pacific Estrangement* (1972); Walter LaFeber, *The Clash* (1997); Charles E. Neu, *An Uncertain Friendship* (1967) and *The Troubled Encounter* (1975); and E. P. Trani, *The Treaty of Portsmouth* (1969).

American missionaries, especially in Asia, are covered in Kenton J. Clymer, *Protestant Missionaries in the Philippines, 1898–1916* (1986); Gael Graham, *Gender, Culture, and Christianity* (1995); Patricia R. Hill, *The World Their Household* (1985) (women); Jane Hunter, *The Gospel of Gentility* (1984) (women in China); Xi Lian, *The Conversion of Missionaries* (1997); and James Reed, *The Missionary Mind and American East Asia Policy, 1911–1915* (1983).

U.S. relations with Europe and Great Britain, and rivalry with Germany, are discussed in Stuart Anderson, *Race and Rapprochement* (1981); A. E. Campbell, *Great Britain and the United States, 1895–1903* (1960); Charles S. Campbell, *Anglo-American Understanding, 1898–1903* (1957); David Dimbleby and David Reynolds, *An Ocean Apart* (1989); Holger H. Herwig, *Politics of Frustration* (1976); Manfred Jonas, *The United States and Germany* (1984); B. J. C. McKercher and Lawrence Aronson, eds., *The North Atlantic Triangle in a Changing World* (1996); Bradford Perkins, *The Great Rapprochement* (1968); Hans–Jürgen Schröder, ed., *Confrontation and Cooperation* (1993) (Germany); and Frederick F. Travis, *George Kennan and the Russian-American Relationship, 1865–1924* (1990).

The peace movement and the role of The Hague are discussed in Peter Brock, *Pacifism in the United States* (1968); Charles Chatfield, *The American Peace Movement* (1992); Calvin Davis, *The United States and the First Hague Conference* (1962) and *The United States and the Second Hague Peace Conference* (1975); Charles DeBenedetti, *The Peace Reform in American History* (1980); Sondra R. Herman, *Eleven Against War* (1969); Charles F. Howlett and Glen Zeitzer, *The American Peace Movement* (1985); C. Roland Marchand, *The American Peace Movement and Social Reform, 1898–1918* (1973); and David S. Patterson, *Toward a Warless World* (1976).

See also the General Bibliography, the following notes, and Robert L. Beisner, ed., *Guide to American Foreign Relations Since 1600* (2003).

NOTES TO CHAPTER 2

1. All quotations from U.S. Congress, *Diplomatic History of the Panama Canal*, Senate Doc. 474 (1914), pp. 345–363.
2. Quoted in John Major, *Prize Possession* (New York: Cambridge University Press, 1993), p. 45.
3. Elting E. Morison, ed., *The Letters of Theodore Roosevelt* (Cambridge: Harvard University Press, 1951–1954; 8 vols.), II, 1185–1187.
4. James A. Froude quoted in John Lindsay-Poland, *Emperors in the Jungle* (Durham: Duke University Press, 2003), p. 5.
5. *Diplomatic History of the Canal*, p. 261.
6. Quoted in Dwight C. Miner, *The Fight for the Panama Route* (New York: Columbia University Press, 1940), p. 275.
7. Quoted in Henry F. Pringle, *Theodore Roosevelt* (New York: Harcourt, Brace, 1931), p. 311.
8. Quoted in Howard K. Beale, *Theodore Roosevelt and the Rise of America to World Power* (Baltimore: Johns Hopkins Press, 1956), p. 33.
9. *New York World*, June 14, 1903.
10. Quoted in Lars Schoultz, *Beneath the United States* (Cambridge: Harvard University Press, 1998), p. 164.
11. Quoted in Thomas Schoonover, "Max Farrand's Memorandum on the U.S. Role in the Panamanian Revolution of 1903," *Diplomatic History*, XII (Fall 1988), 505.
12. Quoted in Stephen J. Randall, *Colombia and the United States* (Athens: University of Georgia Press, 1992), p. 88.
13. Quoted in Serge Ricard, "The Roosevelt Corollary," *Presidential Studies Quarterly*, XXXVI (March 2006), 20.

14. C. F. Adams to Moorfield Story, December 9, 1903, Moorfield Story Papers, Massachusetts Historical Society, Boston; Roosevelt quoted in H. W. Brands, *T.R.* (New York: BasicBooks, 1997), p. 487.

15. Quoted in Walter LaFeber, *The Panama Canal* (New York: Oxford University Press, 1989; updated ed.), pp. 225–226.

16. *New York Times*, March 25, 1911.

17. Lord Bryce quoted in Michael Adas, *Dominance by Design* (Cambridge: Harvard University Press, 2006), p. 186.

18. Quoted *ibid*, p. 198.

19. Quoted in Robert E. Hannigan, *The New World Power* (Philadelphia: University of Pennsylvania Press, 2002), p. 46.

20. Quoted in Wayne A. Wiegand, *Patrician in the Progressive Era* (New York: Garland, 1988), p. 120.

21. Quoted in Stephen R. Rock, *Why Peace Breaks Out* (Chapel Hill: University of North Carolina Press, 1989), p. 132.

22. Ronald H. Spector, *Professors of War* (Newport, R.I.: Naval War College Press, 1977).

23. John Milton Cooper, Jr., "Progressivism and American Foreign Policy," *Mid-America, LI* (October 1969), 261.

24. Quoted in John Morton Blum, *The Republican Roosevelt* (New York: Atheneum [1954], 1973), p. 127.

25. Quoted in Beale, *Theodore Roosevelt*, p. 77; G. Wallace Chessman, *Theodore Roosevelt and the Politics of Power* (Boston: Little, Brown, 1969), p. 70.

26. Quoted in Frank Ninkovich, *Modernity and Power* (Chicago: University of Chicago Press, 1994), p. 6.

27. Quoted in Beale, *Theodore Roosevelt*, p. 140.

28. Quoted in Judith Papachristou, "American Women and Foreign Policy, 1896–1905," *Diplomatic History, XIV* (Fall 1990), 499, 501, 509.

29. Quoted in Frederick F. Travis, *George Kennan and the Russian-American Relationship, 1865–1924* (Athens: Ohio University Press, 1990), p. 266.

30. Quoted in Ninkovich, *Modernity*, p. 13.

31. Quoted in John Milton Cooper, Jr., *The Warrior and the Priest* (Cambridge: Harvard University Press, 1983), p. 75.

32. Taft quoted in Hannigan, *New World Power*, p. 282.

33. Quoted in Richard W. Leopold, *Elihu Root and the Conservative Tradition* (Boston: Little, Brown, 1954), p. 50.

34. Quoted in Ralph E. Minger, *William Howard Taft and United States Foreign Policy* (Urbana: University of Illinois Press, 1975), p. 179.

35. Quoted in Ray S. Baker, *Woodrow Wilson* (Garden City, N.Y.: Doubleday, Doran, 1927–1939; 8 vols.), *IV*, 289.

36. Jesus Samprun quoted in David M. Pletcher, *The Diplomacy of Trade and Investment* (Columbia: University of Missouri Press, 1998), p. 393.

37. Jessica C. E. Gienow-Hecht, "Always Blame the Americans," *American Historical Review, CXI* (October 2006), 1074.

38. William Shafter quoted in Louis A. Pérez, Jr., *The War of 1898* (Chapel Hill: University of North Carolina Press, 1898), p. 29; *Foreign Relations, 1898* (Washington, D.C.: Government Printing Office, 1901), pp. lvi–lvii.

39. Quoted in David F. Healy, *The United States in Cuba, 1898–1902* (Madison: University of Wisconsin Press, 1963), p. 133.

40. U.S. Commissioner Robert P. Porter quoted in Louis A. Pérez, Jr., *Cuba and the United States* (Athens: University of Georgia Press, 1997, 2nd ed.), p. 127.

41. *Congressional Record, XXXIV* (February 26, 1901), 3036.

42. Quoted in H. Hagedorn, *Leonard Wood* (New York: Harper, 1931; 2 vols.), *I*, 362; Healy, *United States in Cuba*, p. 178.

43. Quoted in R. H. Fitzgibbon, *Cuba and the United States, 1900–1935* (New York: Russell & Russell, 1964), p. 112.

44. Quoted in Allan R. Millett, *The Politics of Intervention* (Columbus: Ohio State University Press, 1968), p. 72.

45. Quoted in David H. Burton, *Theodore Roosevelt* (Philadelphia: University of Pennsylvania Press, 1968), p. 106.

46. James D. Richardson, ed., *A Compilation of the Messages and Papers of the Presidents, 1789–1897* (Washington, D. C.: Government Printing Office, 1896–1899; 10 vols.), *X*, 7436–7437; quoted in David H. Burton, *William Howard Taft* (Philadelphia: St. Joseph's University Press, 2004), p. 44.

47. Quoted in Schoultz, *Beneath*, p. 201.

48. Quoted in Alistair Hennessy, "The Origins of the Cuban Revolt," in Angel Smith and Emma Davila-Cox, eds., *The Crisis of 1898* (New York: St. Martin's, 1999), p. 85.

49. Fred L. Israel, ed., *The State of the Union Messages* (New York: Chelsea House, 1967; 3 vols.), *II*, 2038.

50. Morison, *Letters of Roosevelt, III*, 116.

51. William Haggard quoted in Nancy Mitchell, *The Danger of Dreams* (Chapel Hill: University of North Carolina Press, 1999), p. 69.

52. Francis Anthony Boyle, *Foundations of World Order* (Durham: Duke University Press, 1999), p. 81.

53. Quoted in John G. Clifford, "Admiral Dewey and the Germans, 1903," *Mid–America, XLIX* (July 1967), 218.

54. Quoted in Kathleen Dalton, *Theodore Roosevelt* (New York: Knopf, 2002), p. 238.

55. Quoted in Manfred Jonas, *The United States and Germany* (Ithaca: Cornell University Press, 1985), p. 73.

56. Quoted *ibid.*, p. 420.

57. Quoted in Brands, *T.R.*, p. 524.

58. Quoted in Dexter Perkins, *The Monroe Doctrine, 1867–1907* (Baltimore: Johns Hopkins Press, 1937), p. 420.

59. Quoted in Warren G. Kneer, *Great Britain and the Caribbean, 1901–1913* (East Lansing: Michigan State University Press, 1975), p. 103.

60. Quoted in Ricard, "Roosevelt Corrollary," p. 23.

61. Jules Jusserand, quoted in Cyrus Veeser, "Inventing Dollar Diplomacy," *Diplomatic History, XXVII* (June 2003), 320.

62. Theodore Roosevelt, *An Autobiography* (New York: Charles Scribner's Sons, 1926), p. 511.

63. Quoted in Richard D. Challener, *Admirals, Generals, and American Foreign Policy, 1898–1914* (Princeton: Princeton University Press, 1973), p. 142.

64. *Foreign Relations, 1912* (Washington, D.C.: Government Printing Office, 1919), p. 1091.

65. *Foreign Relations, 1913* (Washington, D.C.: Government Printing Office, 1920), p. 426.

66. Quoted in Frederick S. Calhoun, *Uses of Force and Wilsonian Foreign Policy* (Kent, Ohio: Kent State University Press, 1993), p. 53.

67. Bruce Calder, *The Impact of Intervention* (Austin: University of Texas Press, 1984), p. 250.

68. Quoted in Dana G. Munro, *Intervention and Dollar Diplomacy in the Caribbean* (Princeton: Princeton University Press, 1964), p. 336.

69. Quoted in Brenda G. Plummer, *Haiti and the Great Powers, 1902–1915* (Baton Rouge: Louisiana State University Press, 1988), p. 188.

70. Quoted in Hannigan, *New World Power*, p. 49.

71. Quoted in Alan McPherson, "Americanism against American Empire," in Michael Kazin and Joseph A. McCartin, eds., *Americanism* (Chapel Hill: University of North Carolina Press, 2006), p. 181.

72. Alexander DeConde, *Ethnicity, Race, and American Foreign Policy* (Boston: Northeastern University Press, 1993), pp. 79–80.

73. Victor Hoiser quoted in Mary Renda, *Taking Haiti* (Chapel Hill: University of North Carolina Press, 2001), p. 34.

74. Quoted in Munro, *Intervention*, p. 155.

75. Thomas D. Schoonover, *The United States in Central America, 1860–1911* (Durham: Duke University Press, 1991), p. 130; Knox quoted in Michel Gobat, *Confronting the American Dream* (Durham: Duke University Press, 2005), p. 70; Taft quoted in Stephen Kinzer, *Overthrow* (New York: Times Books, 2006), p. 66.

76. Zelaya quoted in Lester D. Langley and Thomas D. Schoonover, *The Banana Men* (Lexington: University Press of Kentucky, 1995), p. 89; quoted in Emily S. Rosenberg, *Financial Missionaries to the World* (Cambridge: Harvard University Press, 1999), p. 67; Taft quoted in Burton, *William Howard Taft*, p. 66.

77. Elliott Northcott quoted in Walter LaFeber, *The American Search for Opportunity, 1865–1913* (New York: Cambridge University Press, 1993), p. 219.

78. Quoted in John E. Findling, *Close Neighbors, Distant Friends* (Westport, Conn.: Greenwood, 1987), p. 61.

79. Langley and Schoonover, *Banana Men*, p. 114.

80. Quoted in Paolo E. Coletta, *The Presidency of William Howard Taft* (Lawrence: University Press of Kansas, 1973), p. 176.

81. Quoted in Friedrich Katz, *The Secret War in Mexico* (Chicago: University of Chicago Press, 1981), p. 113.

82. *Foreign Relations, 1912*, p. 846.

83. Quoted in David Traxel, *Crusader Nation* (New York: Knopf, 2006), p. 86.

84. Quoted in Michael H. Hunt, *The American Ascendancy* (Chapel Hill: University of North Carolina Press, 2007), p. 57.

85. Quoted in Arthur S. Link, *Wilson: Confusions and Crises, 1915–1916* (Princeton: Princeton University Press, 1964), p. 317.

86. William Bayard Hale quoted in Schoultz, *Beneath*, p. 240.

87. Quoted in Arthur S. Link, *Wilson: The New Freedom* (Princeton: Princeton University Press, 1956) p. 358.

88. Quoted in Elizabeth McKillen, "Wilsonian Internationalism Reconsidered," *Diplomatic History, XXV* (Fall 2001), 567.

89. Quoted in Kenneth J. Grieb, *The United States and Huerta* (Lincoln: University of Nebraska Press, 1969), p. 137.

90. Quoted in Link, *Wilson: New Freedom*, pp. 386–387.

91. Quoted in Katz, *Secret War*, p. 216.

92. Quoted in Grieb, *United States and Huerta*, p. 135.

93. Quoted in Mark T. Gilderhus, *Diplomacy and Revolution* (Tucson: University of Arizona Press, 1977), p. 11.

94. Quoted in Cary T. Grayson, *Woodrow Wilson* (New York: Holt, Rinehart and Winston, 1960), p. 30.

95. Wilson quoted in Hannigan, *New World Power*, p. 177.

96. Quoted in Douglas Monroy, "Fence Cutters, *Sedicioso*, and First Class Citizens," in Paul Buhle and Dan Georgakis, eds., *The Immigrant Left in the United States* (Albany: State University of New York Press, 1996), pp. 21–22.

97. Quoted in James A. Sandos, *Rebellion in the Borderlands* (Norman: University of Oklahoma Press, 1992), p. 92.

98. Quoted in Arthur S. Link, *Wilson: The Struggle for Neutrality, 1914–1915* (Princeton: Princeton University Press, 1960), p. 491.

99. Katz, *Secret War*, p. 560; Villa quoted in Friedrich Katz, "Pancho Villa and the Attack on Columbus, New Mexico," *American Historical Review, LXXXIII* (February 1978), 111, 114.

100. Morison, *Letters of Roosevelt, III*, 497–498.

101. Akira Iriye, *The Cold War in Asia* (Englewood Cliffs, N.J.: Prentice Hall, 1974), p. 35.

102. Morison, *Letters of Roosevelt, IV*, 724, 761.

103. Quoted in Raymond A. Esthus, *Double Eagle and Rising Sun* (Durham: Duke University Press, 1988), p. 39.

104. Quoted in Brands, *T.R.*, p. 534.

105. Quoted in Norman Saul, *Concord and Conflict* (Lawrence: University Press of Kansas, 1996), p. 504.

106. Quoted in Raymond A. Esthus, *Theodore Roosevelt and Japan* (Seattle: University of Washington Press, 1966), p. 101.

107. John Edward Wilz, "Did the United States Betray Korea in 1905?" *Pacific Historical Review, LIV* (August 1985), 252.

108. Quoted in Akira Iriye, *Across the Pacific* (New York: Harcourt, Brace & World, 1967), p. 107.

109. Quoted in Ian Mugridge, *The View from Xanadu* (Montreal: McGill–Queen's University Press, 1995), p. 51.

110. Quoted in Walter A. McDougall, *Let the Sea Make a Noise* (New York: BasicBooks, 1993), p. 479; Morison, *Letters of Roosevelt, V*, 729–730, 761–762.

111. Quoted in Ute Mehnert, "German *Weltpolitik* and the American Two Front Dilemma," *Journal of American History, LXXXII* (March 1996), 1458.

112. Quoted in Guanhua Wang, *In Search of Justice* (Cambridge: Harvard University Press, 2001), p. 90.

113. Quoted in Eileen P. Scully, "Taking the Low Road" *Journal of American History, LXXXII* (June 1995), 63–64.

114. Anders Stephanson, *Manifest Destiny* (New York: Hill & Wang, 1995), p. 97.

115. Ninkovich, *Modernity*, p. 25.

116. Quoted in Herbert Croly, *Willard Straight* (New York: Macmillan, 1925), p. 276.

117. A. Whitney Griswold, *The Far Eastern Policy of the United States* (New Haven: Yale University Press, 1938), p. 157.

118. Quoted in Croly, *Straight*, pp. 392–393.

119. Quoted in Daniel M. Crane and Thomas A. Breslin, *An Ordinary Relationship* (Miami: Florida International University Press, 1986), p. 122.

120. Quoted in Roger Daniels, *The Politics of Prejudice* (New York: Atheneum, [1962], 1968), p. 59.

121. Quoted in Link, *Wilson: New Freedom*, pp. 300–301.

122. Quoted in George C. Herring, *From Colony to Superpower* (New York: Oxford University Press, 2008), p. 384.

123. *Foreign Relations, 1922* (Washington, D.C.: Government Printing Office, 1938; 2 vols.), II, 591.

124. Quoted in Michael H. Hunt, *Ideology and U.S. Foreign Policy* (New Haven: Yale University Press, 1987), pp. 69, 71, 79, 81.

125. *Ibid.*, p. 79.

126. Cody quoted in Robert W. Rydell and Rob Kroes, *Buffalo Bill in Bologna* (Chicago: University of Chicago Press, 2005), p. 108.

127. Herbert Asquith quoted in Rock, *Why Peace*, p. 51; Bradford Perkins, *The Great Rapprochement* (New York: Atheneum, 1968).

128. Roosevelt quoted in Frederick W. Marks, *Velvet on Iron* (Lincoln: University of Nebraska Press, 1979), p. 168.

129. Robert Bothwell, *Canada and the United States* (New York: Twayne, 1992), p. 8.

130. Quoted in Kurk Dorsey, "Scientists, Citizens, and Statesmen," *Diplomatic History, XIX* (Summer 1995), 426.

131. Mark Kurlansky, *Cod* (New York: Walker, 1997), p. 79.

132. Quoted in Arthur Marder, *From the Dreadnought to Scapa Flow* (London: Oxford University Press, 1961–1970; 5 vols.), I, 125.

133. Quoted *ibid.*, p. 201.

134. Quoted in Link, *Wilson: New Freedom,* p. 308.

135. Quoted in Lisle A. Rose, *Power at Sea: The Age of Navalism, 1890–1918* (Columbia: University of Missouri Press, 2007), p. 145.

136. Quoted in Michael B. Oren, *Power, Faith, and Fantasy* (New York: Norton, 2007), p. 318.

137. Quoted in Emily S. Rosenberg, "The Invisible Protectorate," *Diplomatic History, IX* (Summer 1985), 194, 198.

138. Quoted in Tilchin, *Theodore Roosevelt,* p. 67; quoted in Hannigan, *New World Power,* p. 204.

139. Morison, *Letters of Roosevelt, IV,* 1119.

140. Quoted in Calvin Davis, *The United States and the Second Hague Peace Conference* (Durham: Duke University Press, 1975), p. 296.

141. Quoted in Minger, *William Howard Taft,* p. 106.

142. Quoted in Mehnert, "German *Weltpolitik,*" p. 1461.

143. Quoted in Jerry Israel, *Progressivism and the Open Door* (Pittsburgh: University of Pittsburgh Press, 1971), p. 96.

144. General William Carter quoted in Brian Linn, *Guardians of Empire* (Chapel Hill: University of North Carolina Press, 1997), p. 62.

145. Quoted in Michael L. Conniff, *Panama and the United States* (Athens: University of Georgia Press, 1992), p. 3.

146. G. L. Dyer quoted in Julian Go, "Modes of Rule in America's Overseas Empire," in Sanford Levinson and Bartholomew H. Sparrow, eds., *Louisiana Purchase and American Expansion, 1803–1898* (New York: Rowman & Littlefield, 2005), p. 278.

147. Laura Briggs, *Reproducing Empire* (Berkeley: University of California Press, 2002), p. 2.

148. Raymond Carr, *Puerto Rico* (New York: Vintage, 1984), p. 36.

149. Cesar J. Ayala and Rafael Bernabe, *Puerto Rico in the American Century* (Chapel Hill: University of North Carolina Press, 2007), p. 28.

150. William Phillips, *Ventures in Diplomacy* (Boston: Beacon Press, 1952), p. 6.

151. Quoted in A. J. Bacevich, *Diplomat in Khaki* (Lawrence: University Press of Kansas, 1989), p. 48.

152. Emily S. Rosenberg, *Spreading the American Dream* (New York: Hill & Wang, 1982), p. 35.

153. Quoted in Robert A. Hart, *The Great White Fleet* (Boston: Little, Brown, 1965), p. 45.

154. Quoted in Franklin Ng, "Knowledge for Empire," in Robert David Johnson, ed., *On Cultural Ground* (Chicago: Imprint Publications, 1994), p. 135.

155. Charles W. Eliot quoted in Frank Trommler, "Inventing the Enemy," in Hans-Jürgen Schröder, *Confrontation and Cooperation* (Providence, R.I.: Berg, 1993), p. 101.

156. Quoted in Christopher Endy, "Travel and World Power," *Diplomatic History, XXII* (Fall 1998), 574.

157. Crosnier de Varigny quoted in Philippe Roger, *The American Enemy* (Chicago: University of Chicago Press, 2005), p. 186.

158. Winston S. Churchill, *The World Crisis* (New York: Charles Scribner's Sons, 1927; 6 vols.), I, 18.

CHAPTER 3

War, Peace, and Revolution in the Time of Wilson, 1914–1920

Mass Grave of Lusitania Victims. *In Cork, Ireland, a large burial ground holds more than a hundred victims of the Lusitania disaster of 1915, which rudely brought World War I to American consciousness. It did not, however, lead to an immediate declaration of war. (U.S. War Department, National Archives)*

DIPLOMATIC CROSSROAD

◈ *The Sinking of the* **Lusitania***, 1915*

"PERFECTLY SAFE; SAFER than the trolley cars in New York City," claimed a British Cunard Line official the morning of May 1, 1915.[1] More than twice as long as an American football field, the majestic *Lusitania,* with its watertight compartments and swiftness, seemed invulnerable. The British Admiralty had stipulated that the 30,396-ton vessel could be armed if necessary, but "Lucy's" priority was pleasure, not war. Resplendent with tapestries and carpets, the luxurious floating palace dazzled. One American found the ship "more beautiful than Solomon's Temple—and big enough to hold all his wives."[2]

A crew of 702 attended the 1,257 travelers who departed from New York's Pier 54 on May Day. Deep in the *Lusitania's* storage area rested a cargo of foodstuffs and contraband (4.2 million rounds of ammunition for Remington rifles, 1,250 cases of empty shrapnel shells, and eighteen cases of nonexplosive fuses). The Cunarder thus carried, said a U.S. State Department official, both "babies and bullets."[3]

In the morning newspapers of May 1 a rather unusual announcement, placed by the German Embassy, appeared beside the Cunard Line advertisement. The German "Notice" warned passengers that the waters around the British Isles constituted a war zone wherein British vessels were subject to destruction. Only a handful of passengers transferred to the *New York,* ready to sail under the American flag that same day. The *New York* was slow and for the American "smart set" socially unacceptable. The State Department did not warn the 197 American passengers away from the *Lusitania.* Most Americans accepted the Cunard Line statement: "She is too fast for any submarine. No German war vessel can get her or near her."[4]

Captained by William T. Turner, the *Lusitania* steamed into the Atlantic at half past noon on May 1. Manned by an ill-trained crew (the best men now on war duty), "Lucy" enjoyed a smooth crossing in calm water. Despite lifesaving drills, complacency about the submarine danger lulled captain, crew, and passengers alike. Passengers joked about torpedoes, played cards, consumed liquor, and listened to concerts on deck. On May 6, as the *Lusitania* neared Ireland, Turner received a warning from the Naval Centre at Queenstown: "Submarines active off south coast of Ireland."[5] The captain posted lookouts but took no other precautions, despite follow-up warnings. He had standing orders from the Admiralty to take a zigzag path, to steer a mid-channel course, and to steam at full speed to keep lurking German submarines from zeroing in on their prey. But Turner steered straight ahead.

Unusually good visibility, recorded Lieutenant Walter Schwieger in his log on May 7. The young German commander was piloting his *U-20* submarine along the southern Irish coast. That morning it had submerged because British ships capable of ramming the fragile, slender craft were passing nearby. He surfaced at 1:45 P.M. and soon spotted a four-funneled ship in the distance. Schwieger quickly submerged and set a course toward the *Lusitania.* At 700 meters the *U-20* released a torpedo. The deadly missile plunged through the water tailed by bubbles. A watchman on the starboard

The *Lusitania* and *U-20*.
The majestic passenger liner was sunk by the German submarine *U-20* off the coast of Ireland on May 7, 1915. "Suppose they should sink the *Lusitania* with American passengers on board," King George V had mused to Colonel Edward M. House on that fateful morning. (The Lusitania Courtesy of the Peabody Essex Museum, Salem, MA)

bow of the *Lusitania* cried out one minute before the torpedo struck, but Captain Turner did not hear the megaphone. Had he heeded the warning, the ship *might* have veered sharply and avoided danger. Turner felt the explosion as it ripped into the *Lusitania*. Panic swept the passengers as they stumbled about the listing decks or groped in the darkness below. Steam whistled from punctured boilers. Less than half the lifeboats were lowered; some capsized or cast off only partially loaded. Within eighteen minutes the "Queen of the Atlantic" sank, killing 1,198—128 of them Americans. A survivor recalled that the *Lusitania* went down with "a terrible moan."[6]

Captain William T. Turner (1856–1933). His command of the *Lusitania* led to disaster. (U.S. War Department)

Lieutenant Walter Schwieger (1885–1917). His *U–20* sank the *Lusitania*. (Bundesarchiv)

President Woodrow Wilson had just ended a cabinet meeting when he learned of the disaster. His special assistant, Colonel M. Edward House, then in London, predicted: "We shall be at war with Germany within a month."[7] Fearing war, Secretary of State William Jennings Bryan advised the president that "ships carrying contraband should be prohibited from carrying passengers.... [I]t would be like putting women and children in front of an army."[8] Ex-president Theodore Roosevelt bellowed that "this represents ... piracy on a vaster scale of murder than old-time pirates ever practiced."[9] American after American voiced horror, but few wanted war. Wilson secluded himself to ponder a response to the ghastly event. Just months before, he had said he would hold Berlin strictly accountable for any American ships or lives lost due to submarine warfare. Thereafter, Wilson found himself trying to fulfill America's "double wish"—"to maintain a firm front ... [toward] Germany and yet do nothing that might by any possibility involve us in war."[10]

Wilson spoke in Philadelphia on May 10. His words, much misunderstood, suggested he had no backbone: "There is such a thing as a man being too proud to fight. There is such a thing as a nation being so right that it does not need to convince others by force that it is right."[11] He quickly regretted his impromptu remarks. Preoccupied by his intense courtship of his future second wife, Wilson did "not know just what I said in Philadelphia ... because my heart was in such a whirl."[12] The next morning he told the cabinet that he would send a note to Berlin insisting that Americans had a right to travel on the high seas and demanding a German disavowal of the inhumane acts of its submarine commanders. Secretary Bryan, long troubled about an apparent American double standard in protesting more against German than British violations of American neutral rights, pleaded for a simultaneous protest to London. But only one note went out on May 13—to

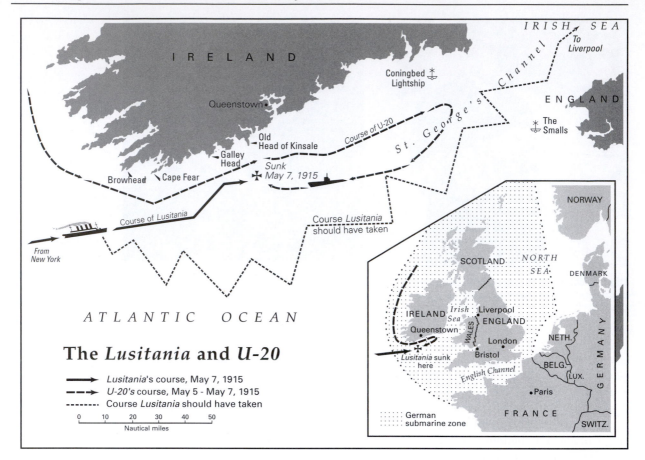

The *Lusitania* and U-20

→ *Lusitania*'s course, May 7, 1915
– – – U-20's course, May 5 - May 7, 1915
· · · · · Course *Lusitania* should have taken

0   10   20   30   40   50
Nautical miles

Berlin: "The Imperial Government will not expect the United States to omit any word or any act necessary to the performance of its sacred duty of maintaining the rights of the United States and its citizens and of safeguarding their free exercise and enjoyment."[13] In short, end submarine warfare, or else.

The German government took no pleasure in the destruction of the *Lusitania*. Chancellor Theobold von Bethmann-Hollweg had more than once chastised the navy for inviting war with the United States through submarine attacks on neutral or Allied merchant vessels. On May 28 he sent an evasive reply to Wilson's note. The *Lusitania* case could not be settled until they clarified certain questions. The German note claimed that the ship was armed, carried munitions, and had orders to ram submarines. Germany asked Washington to investigate. That same day, in a secret meeting with German Ambassador Johann von Bernstorff, Wilson proposed that if Germany would settle the *Lusitania* crisis favorably, he would press the British to suspend their blockade and then call a conference of neutrals to mediate an end to the war on the following basis: "1. The status quo in Europe; 2. Freedom of the seas. … 3. Adjustments concerning colonial possessions."[14]

Wilson convened his cabinet on June 1. One member recommended a strong note demanding observance of American rights, while another suggested a note to England to protest British interference with American commerce. Debate grew heated. A majority rejected simultaneous notes. When the U.S. ambassador in Berlin reported that the Germans wanted to keep the issue "'jollied' along until the American papers get excited by baseball or a new scandal and forget," Wilson sent a second "*Lusitania* note" that vigorously demanded an end to warfare by submarines.[15] He rejected Bryan's plea for a warning to passengers and a protest note to England. The secretary of state then quietly resigned in protest on June 8, and Wilson went to the golf links to free himself from the blinding headaches of the past several days. "He is absolutely *sincere,*" the president said of Bryan. "That is what makes him dangerous."[16]

More correspondence on the *Lusitania* followed. The United States insisted that Germany must admit it had committed an illegal act; but Germany, unwilling to abandon one of its few effective weapons against British mastery of the ocean, refused and asked for arbitration. "Utterly impertinent," sniffed Kaiser Wilhelm II, who preferred victory to Wilson's mediation.[17] Eventually Germany sought compromise. On February 4 it expressed regret over the American deaths and offered an indemnity (ultimately paid in the early 1920s). Wilson accepted the German concession.

The horrible deaths from the *Lusitania* remained etched in American memories. For Germany, the torpedoing of the magnificent Cunarder marked a "naval victory worse than a defeat," as Britons and Americans alike depicted the "Huns" as depraved.[18] The sinking also hardened Wilson's opinion against Germany. After Germany spurned his secret mediation offer, Wilson no longer made diplomatic life easier for the Germans by simultaneously protesting British infractions. The British were violating property rights, he held, but the Germans violated rights of life and liberty. Wilson stubbornly refused to warn Americans away from belligerent ships. In short, if a U-boat attacked a British ship with Americans aboard, Germany would have to take the consequences. Wilson did not spell out those consequences, but the logical implication was war—just what Bryan feared. His successor, pro-Allied Robert Lansing, expected "that we would ultimately become an ally of Great Britain."[19] The sinking of the *Lusitania* exposed, for all to see, the complexities, contradictions, and uncertainties inherent in American neutrality during the European phase of the First World War, 1914–1917. Such complications had been apparent prior to the War of 1812, and they would reemerge between 1939 and 1941.

The Travails of Neutrality

Woodrow Wilson acted virtually as his own secretary of state during the First World War. "Wilson makes confidant of no one. No one gets his whole mind," an aide wrote.[20] British Prime Minister Lloyd George put it less kindly: Wilson "believed in mankind but … distrusted all men."[21] The president encapsulated an approach to American foreign policy—what historians call "Wilsonianism"—that anticipated major themes of twentieth-century U.S. diplomacy. Above all else, Wilson promoted an *open* world unencumbered by imperialism, war, or revolution. Barriers to trade and democracy had to come down, and secret diplomacy and alliances—like those that had triggered world war—had to give way to public negotiations. The right of self-determination (national self-rule) would force the collapse of empires. Constitutional procedures would replace revolution. A free-market, humanized capitalism would ensure economic, as well as political democracy. Disarmament would restrict weapons. The Open Door of equal trade and investment would harness the economic competition that led to war. Wilson, like so many Americans, saw the United States as exceptional—its mission was "to redeem the world and make it fit for free men like ourselves to live in."[22] His "semi-divine power to select the right" incongruously blended with realism.[23] The president calculated the nation's economic and strategic needs and devised a foreign policy to protect them. Yet many Americans feared that his world-reforming efforts might invite war, dissipate American resources, and undermine reform at home. Wilson led a divided nation.

Few Americans, Wilson included, desired war. Most watched in shock as the European nations savagely slashed at one another in 1914. The conviction that civilization had advanced too far for such bloodletting was ruthlessly challenged. Before 1914 the new machine guns, howitzers, submarines, and dreadnoughts seemed too awesome for leaders to launch them. The outbreak of World War I smashed illusions and tested innocence. Progressive-era Americans nonetheless exuded optimism, and the crusading Wilson sought to retrieve a happier past by assuming the role of civilized instructor: America would help Europe come to its senses by teaching it the rules of humane conduct. The war's carnage justified the mission. In 1915 alone France suffered 1.3 million casualties, including 330,000 deaths. Germany suffered 848,000 casualties, 170,000 of them deaths. Britain followed with 313,000 casualties, and 73,000 deaths. By war's end 12 million soldiers had died—"half the seed of Europe," in poet Wilfred Owen's mournful phrase.[24]

Americans had reason, then, to believe that Europe needed help in cleaning its own house. The outbreak of the war seemed so senseless. By June 1914, the great powers had constructed two blocs, the Triple Alliance (Germany, Austria-Hungary, and Italy) and the Triple Entente (France, Russia, and Great Britain). Some called this division of Europe a balance of power, but an assassin's bullet unbalanced it. Between Austria and Serbia lay Bosnia, a tiny province in the Austro-Hungarian Empire. Slavic nationalists sought to build a greater Serbia—an independent Slavic state—by annexing Bosnia, which the Austro-Hungarian Empire had absorbed in 1909. A Slavic terrorist group, the Black Hand, decided to force the issue. On June 28 the

Makers of American Foreign Relations, 1914–1920

President	Secretaries of State
Woodrow Wilson, 1913–1921	William Jennings Bryan, 1913–1915
	Robert Lansing, 1915–1920
	Bainbridge Colby, 1920–1921

heir to the Hapsburg Crown of Austria-Hungary, Archduke Franz Ferdinand, visited Sarajevo, the capital of Bosnia. As his car moved through the streets of the city, a Black Hand assassin gunned him down.

Austria-Hungary sent impossibly harsh demands to Serbia. The Serbs rejected them. Austria-Hungary had already received encouragement from Germany, and Serbia had a pledge of support from Russia, which in turn received backing from France. A chain reaction followed. On July 28 Austria-Hungary declared war on Serbia; on August 1 Germany declared "preventive" war on Russia and two days later on France; on August 4 Germany invaded Belgium, and Great Britain declared war on Germany. In a few weeks Japan joined the Allies (Triple Entente) and Turkey the Central Powers (Triple Alliance), and Italy entered on the Allied side the next year. Wilson's friend Colonel House, visiting Europe that May, had reported "jingoism run stark mad ... there is some day to be an awful cataclysm."[25]

Wilson issued a Proclamation of Neutrality on August 4, followed days later by an appeal to Americans to be neutral in thought, speech, and action. Laced with patriotic utterances, the decree sought to cool the passions of immigrant groups who identified with the belligerents. America must demonstrate to a troubled world that it was "fit beyond others to exhibit the fine poise of undisturbed judgment, the dignity of self-control, the efficiency of dispassionate action."[26] It was a lofty call for restraint, an expression of America as the beacon of common sense in a world gone mad, a plea for unity at home—but altogether difficult to achieve.

Few Americans proved capable of neutral thoughts. Loyalties to fatherlands and motherlands did not abate. German Americans identified with the Central Powers. Many Irish Americans, nourishing their traditional Anglophobia at a time when Ireland chafed under British rule and readied itself for rebellion, wished catastrophe on Britain. But Anglo-American traditions and cultural ties, as well as slogans such as "Remember Lafayette," pulled most Americans toward a pro-Allied position. Since the 1890s, Anglophobia had weakened in the face of the calming Anglo-American rapprochement. Woodrow Wilson himself harbored pro-British sentiment, telling the British ambassador that a German victory "would be the crowning calamity."[27] Wilson's advisers, House and Lansing, were ardently pro-British. The U.S. ambassador to England, Walter Hines Page, even wanted Americans "to hang our Irish agitators and shoot our hyphenates and bring up our children with reverence for English history."[28]

German war actions, exaggerated by British propaganda, also undermined neutrality. To Americans, the Germans, led by arrogant Kaiser Wilhelm II (who later boasted to the U.S. ambassador that "there was no longer any international law"), became symbols of the dreaded militarism and conscription of the Old World.[29] Germany seemed an upstart nation, an aggressive latecomer to the scramble for imperialist prizes, and a noisy intruder in the Caribbean where the British had already acknowledged U.S. hegemony. Eager to grasp world power and encouraging Austria-Hungary to war, Berlin certainly had little claim on virtue. The European powers had guaranteed Belgium its neutrality by treaty, but Bethmann-Hollweg dismissed it as a "scrap of paper."[30] On August 4, 1914, hoping to outflank the French, the Germans attacked Belgium and, angered that the Belgians resisted, ruthlessly razed villages, unleashed firing squads against townspeople, and deported young workers

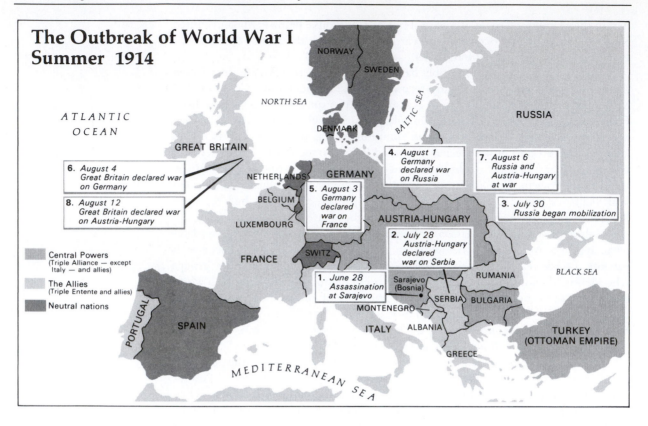

The Outbreak of World War I Summer 1914

6. *August 4*
Great Britain declared war on Germany

8. *August 12*
Great Britain declared war on Austria-Hungary

4. *August 1*
Germany declared war on Russia

7. *August 6*
Russia and Austria-Hungary at war

5. *August 3*
Germany declared war on France

3. *July 30*
Russia began mobilization

2. *July 28*
Austria-Hungary declared war on Serbia

1. *June 28*
Assassination at Sarajevo

Central Powers
(Triple Alliance — except Italy — and allies)

The Allies
(Triple Entente and allies)

Neutral nations

to Germany. One magazine called Belgium "a martyr to civilization, sister to all who love liberty, or law; assailed, polluted, trampled in the mire, heel-marked in her breast, tattered, homeless."[31] American hearts and hands went out in the form of a major relief mission headed by a young, wealthy, and courageous mining engineer, Herbert Hoover.

American economic links with the Allies also undermined neutrality. England had always been America's best customer, and wartime conditions simply intensified the relationship. The Allies needed both war matériel and consumer goods. Americans, inspired by huge profits and a chance to pull out of a recession, obliged. In 1914 U.S. exports to England and France equaled $754 million; in 1915 the figure shot up to $1.28 billion; and in 1916 the amount more than doubled to $2.75 billion. Comparable statistics for Germany reveal why Berlin believed the United States was taking sides. In 1914 U.S. exports to Germany totaled $345 million; in 1915 they plummeted to $29 million; and in 1916 they fell to $2 million. In 1914–1917 New York's banking house of J. P. Morgan Company served as an agent for England and France and arranged for the shipment of more than $3 billion worth of goods. By April 1917, British purchasing missions were spending $83 million a week for American copper, steel, wheat, oil, and munitions.

Britain and France sold many of their American securities and liquidated investments to pay for these goods. This netted them several billion dollars. In appeals to prominent American bankers and State Department officials, they also sought loans. In 1914 Bryan discouraged private American loans to the belligerents, observing that "money is the worst of all contrabands because it commands everything else."[32] After Bryan's resignation, Robert Lansing argued that loans to the Allies would prevent "restriction of output, industrial depression, idle capital, idle labor, numerous failures, financial demoralization, and general unrest and suffering among the laboring classes."[33] Because U.S. industries "will burst their jackets if they cannot find a free outlet to the markets of the world," Wilson approved $2.3 billion in loans to the Allies during 1914–1917—a sharp contrast to loans of only $27 million to Germany.[34] Once it joined the war as a belligerent, the American economic powerhouse became even more the dispenser of munitions, food, and money to the Allies.

Berlin, of course, protested such "unneutral" economic ties. Yet curbing trade with Britain, which ruled the seas, would have constituted unneutral behavior in favor of the Germans, for under international law a belligerent could buy, at its own risk, contraband and noncontraband goods from a neutral. Neutral or not, the United States had become the arsenal of the Allied war effort.

Submarines, Neutral Rights, and Mediation Efforts

To strangle Germany, the British invoked legal doctrines of retaliation and contraband without ever technically declaring a blockade. They mined the North Sea, expanded the contraband list to include foodstuffs and cotton, forced American ships into port for inspection, seized "contraband" from neutral vessels, halted American trade with Germany's neutral neighbors Denmark and Holland, armed British merchant ships, used decoy ships to lure U-boats into traps, flew neutral (often American) flags on their merchant vessels, and rammed whenever possible any U-boats that complied with international law by surfacing to warn a British merchant vessel of an imminent attack. The Wilson administration issued protests, some mild, some tough, against these illegalities. The Foreign Office usually paid appropriate verbal deference to international law and went right on with its restrictive behavior. Britain sometimes compensated U.S. businesses for damages and purchased large quantities of goods at inflated prices. Americans thus came to tolerate the indignities of British economic warfare. By these measures, Britain managed brilliantly to sever American economic lines to the Central Powers without rupturing Anglo-American relations.

Germans protested vehemently against American acquiescence in the British "hunger" blockade. To continue the war, Germany had to have imports and had to curb the flourishing Anglo-American trade that fueled the Allied war machine. The German surface fleet, bottled up in ports, seemed inadequate for the task, so German leaders hesitantly turned to a relatively new experimental weapon of limited maneuverability: the submarine. At the start they possessed just 21 U-boats, and at peak strength in October 1917 they had but 127. Only a third of this fleet operated at sea at any one time. On February 4, 1915, Berlin announced that it was retaliating against British strangulation by declaring a war zone around Britain. All *enemy* ships

William Jennings Bryan (1860–1925). The great agrarian reformer went to Congress in 1890 as a Democrat from Nebraska. After several unsuccessful runs for the presidency, Bryan endorsed Wilson in the 1912 election and became secretary of state the following year. He favored the arbitration of international disputes, and he perpetuated U.S. interventionist policy in Latin America. Believing that Wilson was tilting toward the British after the *Lusitania* disaster of 1915, Bryan resigned in protest. A colleague called him "too good a Christian to run a naughty world." (Library of Congress)

in the area would be destroyed. Germany warned neutral ships to *stay out* of the zone because of possible mistaken identity. Passengers from neutral countries were urged, moreover, to *stay off* enemy passenger vessels. Six days later Wilson held Germany to strict accountability for the loss of American life and property.

The British continued to arm their merchant vessels, which thereby became warships and theoretically ineligible to take on arms or munitions in neutral ports. But Washington invoked a fine distinction between offensive and defensive armaments and permitted such "defensively" armed British craft to carry war supplies from American ports. Crying foul, the Germans also argued that old international law, which Wilson invoked, did not fit the submarine. Rules adopted during the era of sailing ships held that an attacking cruiser about to sink or capture enemy merchant vessels had to give adequate warning so as to ensure the safety of passengers and crew. Yet if a submarine surfaced in its sluggish fashion, the merchant ship's crew might sink it with a deck gun. This was the problem bewildering Schwieger of *U-20* when he spotted the *Lusitania*. Had he surfaced to warn the ship, the *Lusitania* probably would have attempted to ram *U-20* or flee and would have sent distress signals to British warships in the vicinity. Even if the *Lusitania* had submitted to the warning, it might have taken an hour for passengers to get into lifeboats before Schwieger could torpedo the *Lusitania,* by which time British warships might have closed in. In short, from the German point of view, to comply with an international law that failed to anticipate the submarine was not possible. Wilson retorted that differences over international law could be "adjusted after the war," whereas Germany's "sheer acts of piracy on the high seas … might easily lead to actual hostilities."[35]

Secretary Bryan tried diplomacy in early 1915, asking Germany to give up use of unannounced submarine attacks in exchange for a British promise to disarm its merchant carriers and permit food to flow to Germany. The Germans seemed interested, but London refused. In March 1915, Wilson did send Colonel House to Europe to sound out possibilities for mediation, but to no avail. Nonetheless, Wilson failed to adjust or shelve traditional international law, which had no provision for the submarine. He accepted British modifications but not German ones, for both economic and humanitarian reasons.

Between February and May 1915, marauding submarines sank ninety ships in the war zone. One American citizen, on the British passenger ship *Falaba,* died in the sinking of that vessel on March 28. Then came the *Lusitania* in May with 128 American deaths. Through Wilson's many protest notes, a U.S. posture took shape: uneasy tolerance of British violations of property rights and rejection of German violations of what later generations would call human rights. Despite secret German orders to submarine commanders to avoid a repetition of the *Lusitania* incident, on August 19 the *Arabic,* another British liner, was torpedoed with the loss of two American lives. A worried Ambassador Bernstorff publicly pledged that U-boats would now spare passenger ships.

In early 1916, calling the United States ideally suited to be the "mediating nation of the world," Wilson tried to bring the warring parties to the conference table.[36] Colonel House talked with British officials in London but departed with no promises for peace. He journeyed next to Berlin, where German leaders gave no assurances. Both sides would fight on. "Hell will break loose in Europe this spring and summer as never before," House informed Wilson.[37] House then traveled to Paris, where he rashly informed his skeptical French hosts: "If the Allies obtain a small success this spring or summer, the U.S. will intervene to promote a peaceful settlement, but if the Allies have a setback, the United States will intervene militarily and will take part in the war against Germany."[38] House did not report his prediction to the president.

House returned to London to press Sir Edward Grey, the British foreign secretary, to heed Wilson's call for a peace conference. The American envoy recorded their agreements in the House-Grey Memorandum of February 22, 1916, a document loaded with "ifs." The first paragraph read: "Colonel House told me that President Wilson was ready, on hearing from France and England that the moment was opportune, to propose that a Conference should be summoned to put an end to the war. Should the Allies accept the proposal, and should Germany refuse it, the United States would probably enter the war against Germany." The record of conversation also reported that House had said that the peace conference would secure terms "not unfavourable to the Allies" and should the conference failed to achieve peace, "the United States would leave the Conference as a belligerent on the side of the Allies, if Germany was unreasonable."[39] Wilson pronounced the memorandum a diplomatic triumph, but he clouded its uncertain meaning all the more by inserting a "probably" before the word "leave" in the sentence quoted above. He took the document much more seriously than did the British or French, who shelved it, snubbed American mediation, and vowed victory over Germany.

As House moved among European capitals, Lansing informed the Allied governments that the United States sought a modus vivendi to defuse naval crises: The Allies would disarm merchant vessels, and the Germans would follow international law by warning enemy merchant ships. This suggestion revealed that Wilson understood the German argument that armed merchant vessels actually operated as offensive craft—that is, warships. The British and Colonel House protested when they received this news from Washington. The Germans seemed to endorse the proposal by declaring on February 10 that submarines would henceforth attack only *armed* merchant ships without warning. Suddenly Wilson reversed policy. He abruptly abandoned the modus vivendi in order to restore his standing with the British and sustain House's mediation efforts in London. Lansing announced, furthermore, that the United States would not ban its citizens from traveling on "defensively" armed merchant ships.

Edward M. House (1858–1938). This Texas "colonel" served as Wilson's trusted emissary abroad. In the House-Grey Memorandum of 1916 he showed signs of the deviousness that led to his break with the president after the Versailles conference of 1919. President Wilson once identified House as "my second personality. He is my independent self. If I were in his place I would do just as he suggested." An opponent called House "an intimate man … even when he was cutting your throat." (National Portrait Gallery, Smithsonian Institution/Art Resource, N.Y.)

Wilson's Choices Bring America into World War

Why let one American passenger and a trigger-happy U-boat captain start a war? Why not keep Americans off belligerent ships and require them instead to sail on American vessels? From August 1914 to mid-March 1917 only three Americans (on the oil tanker *Gulflight,* May 1, 1915) had lost their lives on an American-flagged ship torpedoed by a U-boat. In contrast, about 190 Americans, including the *Lusitania*'s 128, died on belligerent-owned ships. After the *Falaba* was sunk, Bryan had acknowledged the right of neutrals to travel on belligerent vessels, but he wanted Wilson to forgo that right. Americans on belligerent ships seemed no different than

Woodrow Wilson (1856–1924). Scholar, professor, president of Princeton University, and Democratic governor of New Jersey, Woodrow Wilson was usually cocksure once he made a decision. "I would rather fail in a cause that will ultimately triumph than triumph in a cause that will ultimately fail," he once said. (*Cartoons,* 1912)

"those who by remaining in a belligerent country assume risk of injury."[40] Wilson had, after all, urged Americans to leave war-torn Mexico. Ambassador James W. Gerard in Berlin also wondered: "Why should we enter a great war because some American wants to cross on a ship where he can have a private bathroom?"[41]

In January 1916, Congressman Jeff McLemore of Texas, a Democrat, introduced a resolution to prohibit Americans from traveling on armed belligerent vessels. In February Senator Thomas P. Gore of Oklahoma, another Democrat, submitted a similar resolution in his chamber. Wilson bristled at this challenge from Congress. He unleashed cabinet members with patronage muscle on timid legislators, suggesting that Gore-McLemore was a pro-German ploy. To halt American passage on belligerent ships, Wilson declared, would be to accept national humiliation and destruction of the "whole fine fabric of international law."[42] In short, he stuck with rigid, archaic concepts, refusing to adjust to the new factor of the submarine or to appreciate the impact on Germany of the obvious British violations of the same law. In early March, the Gore-McLemore resolution lost 68 to 14 in the Senate and 276 to 142 in the House. The resolution had asked America to give up very little. Wilson's message to Berlin rang loud and clear: Do not use your submarines.

In March 1916, another passenger ship, another U-boat, another torpedo, more American injuries: The French ship *Sussex,* moving across the English Channel, took a hit but did not sink. Aboard was a young American scholar, Samuel Flagg Bemis, later a renowned historian of foreign relations but then fresh from archival research on Jay's Treaty. Bemis glimpsed the swirling wake of a torpedo. "The entire bow was blown off and with it the people who were in the dining room," he recalled.[43] Four Americans sustained injuries, but Bemis escaped serious harm by jumping overboard while holding on to his research notes.

The *Sussex* attack violated the "*Arabic* pledge," even though the U-boat commander mistook the ship for a minelayer. Wilson delivered an ultimatum warning the Germans on April 18 that he would sever relations if they did not halt their submarine warfare against passenger and merchant vessels. With the unsuccessful German offensive at Verdun costing more than half a million lives, Berlin did not want war with the United States. With the "*Sussex* Pledge" in early May, Germany promised that submarines would not attack passenger or merchant ships without prior warning. The Germans also nagged Washington to stop British infractions of international law.

The British clamped down even harder on trade with the Central Powers. In July London issued a "blacklist" of more than eighty American companies that had traded with the Central Powers. Even Wilson now fumed that he was "about at the end of my patience with Great Britain and the Allies."[44] He contemplated a ban on loans and exports to them, but he did little. Many Americans also condemned the brutal British smashing of the Irish Easter Rebellion in April 1916.

Shortly after his reelection in 1916, under the slogan "He Kept Us Out of War," the president boldly asked the belligerents to state their war aims. Neither side, still seeking military victory, welcomed Wilson's mediation. Germany coveted Poland, Lithuania, Belgium, and the Belgian Congo; Britain sought German colonies; France wanted Alsace-Lorraine. On January 22, 1917, however, Wilson instead called for a "peace without victory" because only through a peace founded on the "equality of nations" could a lasting world order be achieved. He regarded victory as "an intoxicant that fires the national brain and leaves a craving for more."[45] The French novelist Anatole France responded cynically: "Peace without victory is bread without yeast …, love without quarrels, a camel without humps, night without moon, roof without smoke, town without brothel."[46]

In early 1917, crises mounted quickly. On January 31, Berlin announced that German submarines would attack without warning and sink all vessels, enemy and neutral, found near British waters. This declaration of unrestricted submarine warfare expressed Germany's calculated risk that it could defeat England and France before the United States could mobilize and send soldiers overseas. The supremely arrogant German naval minister remarked: "From a military standpoint, America's entrance is as nothing."[47] German naval officers persuaded the kaiser that the U-boats, now numbering about one hundred, could knock Britain out of the war in six months. Army officers, bogged down in trench warfare, hoped to end their costly immobility through a bold stroke.

On February 3, Washington severed diplomatic relations with Berlin. According to Lansing, Wilson became "more and more impressed with the idea that 'white civilization' and its domination over the world rested largely on our ability to keep this country intact, as we would have to build up the nations ravaged by the war."[48] Yet Wilson had also committed himself to stand firmly against unrestricted submarine warfare. Allied ships carrying war supplies soon suffered increasing losses, and the few American vessels carrying contraband languished in port or shifted to trade outside the European war zones. The U.S. economy seemed imperiled.

Next came an apparent challenge to U.S. security. Washington had already endured espionage and sabotage by German agents, most notably the explosions at the Black Tom munitions factories across from the Statue of Liberty in July 1916. In late February the British passed to Ambassador Walter Hines Page an intercepted telegram dated January 16 and sent to Mexico by German foreign minister Arthur Zimmermann. The message proposed that Mexico and Germany "make war together, make peace together," and then Berlin would help Mexico "to reconquer the lost territories in Texas, New Mexico, and Arizona."[49] Although the skeptical Mexican government never took up the German offer, Wilson now saw Germany as a "madman that should be curbed."[50]

Wilson now asked Congress for authority to arm American merchant vessels. On March 1, to create a favorable public opinion for the request, he released the Zimmermann telegram to the press. But antiwar senators Robert La Follette and George Norris led a filibuster—a "little group of willful men," Wilson snarled—that killed the armed ship legislation.[51] Stubbornly ignoring the Senate, Wilson ordered the arming anyway. To no avail: during March 16–18 alone, U-boats sunk the American ships *City of Memphis, Illinois,* and *Vigilancia.* Buttressed by the unanimous support of his cabinet, the president decided for war.

After several intense days writing his own speech with help from Colonel House, Wilson addressed a special joint session of Congress on the evening of April 2. He asked for a declaration of war against Germany—a war that Berlin had "thrust" on the United States. The "unmanly business" of using submarines, he asserted, constituted "warfare against mankind." Freedom of the seas, commerce, American lives, human

Jeannette Rankin (1880–1973). A native of Montana, Rankin, in 1916, became the first woman to be elected to the House of Representatives. A lifelong pacifist, she voted against war in 1917, only to lose her seat the following year. In the interwar period she lobbied for peace and was again elected to Congress in 1940. This time she cast the only vote against war in 1941. She later marched against the Vietnam War. Rankin took pride in being "the first woman who was ever asked what she thought about war [and] said 'NO.'" (Library of Congress)

rights—the "outlaw" U-boats challenged all. Economic self-interest, morality, and national honor compelled Americans to fight. He characterized the German government as a monster tearing at the "very roots of human life." The "Prussian autocracy" stirred up trouble through spies and the Zimmermann telegram. He also hailed the Russian Revolution of March, which created a democratic government and made Russia "a fit partner for a league of honor" in a crusade against autocracy. Then came the potent and unforgettable words: "The world must be made safe for democracy."[52]

Although the oration simplified issues and promised too much from American intervention, the moment evoked patriotic fervor. "It is [Kaiser] Bill against Woodrow, Germany against America, Hell against Heaven," proclaimed the evangelist Billy Sunday, as he demonized the "wolfish Huns, whose fangs drip with blood."[53] By votes of 82 to 6 in the Senate on April 4 and 373 to 50 in the House on April 6, Congress endorsed Wilson's call for a war for peace.

Submarine warfare precipitated the American decision to enter the war. Had no submarine menaced American lives, property, and the U.S. definition of international law, no American soldiers would have gone to France. Critics have argued, however, that from the German perspective, the submarine became necessary because of the long list of unfriendly American acts: acquiescence in the British blockade, which was part of a general pro-British bias; huge munitions shipments to the Allies; large loans; an interpretation of neutral rights that insisted that American passengers could sail anywhere on any ship, even into a war zone. Take away those acts, which the Germans considered unneutral, and they might not have unleashed the U-boats. To dissenters it seemed wrong that American ideals and interests could depend so perilously on armed ships carrying contraband, heading for Britain, and steaming through a war zone. Yet Wilson and his advisers had so defined the problem.

Permeating Wilson's policies was the traditional American belief that others must conform to U.S. prescriptions and that America's ideals served as a beacon for the world. "We created this Nation," the president once proclaimed, "not to serve ourselves, but to serve mankind."[54] When the Germans defied America's rules, ideals, and property, and threatened its security through a proposed alliance with Mexico, they had to be punished. Here was an opportunity to protect both humane principles and commercial interests. When Wilson spoke passionately of the right of a neutral to freedom of the seas, he demonstrated the perceived interconnections among American moral, economic, and strategic interests. Wilson sought the role of peacemaker and promised to remake the world in the American image—a world order in which barriers to political democracy and the Open Door came down, in which revolution and aggression no longer threatened. The war coincided with the Progressive Era of energetic social and political reformism in the nation's history—a "plastic juncture," in the philosopher John Dewey's words, that rendered Americans particularly receptive to the idea of fighting to reshape the world according to democratic principles.[55]

The Debate over Preparedness

Berlin's assumption that massive numbers of U.S. soldiers could not reach France fast enough to reverse an expected German victory proved a gross misjudgment. American military muscle and economic power decisively tipped the balance against

Germany. Given the information available in early 1917, however, the German calculation did not seem so unrealistic. In April the United States had no capacity to send a major expedition to the western front. At that date the Regular Army counted only 130,000 officers and men, backed by 180,000 national guardsmen. Although some officers had been seasoned by interventions in Cuba, the Philippines, and Mexico, many soldiers lacked adequate training. Arsenals had meager supplies of such modern weapons as the machine gun. The "Air Service," then part of the army, did not have an airplane of modern design with a machine gun, and some warships had never fired a gun.

An American "preparedness movement" had been underway for months, encouraged by prominent Americans such as General Leonard Wood, who argued that America's military weakness invited attack. After 1914, Wood, Theodore Roosevelt, the National Security League, the Army League, and the Navy League lobbied for bigger military appropriations with the argument that "preparedness" offered insurance against war. When the hit pacifist song "I Didn't Raise My Boy to Be a Soldier" became "an icon of popular antiwar sentiment" in 1915, preparedness proponents countered with "I Didn't Raise My Boy to Be a Coward."[56] One propaganda film, *The Battle Cry of Peace* (1916), depicted spike-helmeted soldiers rampaging through New York City. That same year a U.S. admiral claimed that a single hostile dreadnought could "knock down all the buildings in New York …, smash all the cars, break down all the bridges, and sink all the shipping."[57]

Convinced that "a great standing army" was "antidemocratic," Wilson belatedly sought moderate preparedness.[58] He asked for a half-billion-dollar naval expansion program in late 1915, including ten battleships. The new force would surpass Britain as "incomparably the greatest navy in the world."[59] He also urged that land forces be enlarged and reorganized.

Senator La Follette, Representative Claude Kitchin, and prominent reformers such as William Jennings Bryan, Lillian Wald, and Oswald Garrison Villard spurred a movement against these measures. These peace advocates, especially the Women's Peace Party (representing "the mother half of humanity"), prophetically argued that war would interrupt reform at home, benefit big business, and curtail civil liberties.[60] Several peace leaders also joined the auto manufacturer Henry Ford in December 1915 as he sailed to Europe on his peace ship, *Oscar II,* to establish a Neutral Conference for Continuous Mediation—a quixotic attempt to end the war and get "the boys out of the trenches by Christmas."[61] The American Union Against Militarism agitated against preparedness with its papier-mâché dinosaur, "Jingo," whose collar read "ALL ARMOR PLATE—NO BRAINS."[62] Because his support of mediation, disarmament, and a postwar association of nations appealed to antiwar liberals and socialists ("progressive internationalists"), Wilson hoped that moderate preparedness would not alienate them. Chicago's famed social reformer Jane Addams remembered "moments of uneasiness," but she and others endorsed Wilson in the 1916 presidential campaign, for it seemed "at last that peace was assured and the future safe in the hands of an executive who had received an unequivocal mandate from the people 'to keep us out of war.'"[63]

In January 1916, Wilson set out on a two-month speaking tour, often criticizing members of his own party for their opposition to a military buildup. U-boat sinkings aided the president's message. In May 1916, Congress passed the National Defense Act, increasing the Regular Army to some 200,000 men and 11,000 officers, and the National Guard to 440,000 men and 17,000 officers. The act also authorized summer training camps, modeled after one held in Plattsburg, New York, in 1915 for the social and economic elite. Despite Jane Addams's query, "Why spend $45,000,000 for warships, when they will only be reduced to scrap heap after this war?" the naval appropriations bill passed in August 1916.[64]   Theodore Roosevelt thought the measures inadequate, but the anarchist Emma Goldman saw no difference between Roosevelt, "the born bully who uses a club," and Wilson, "the history professor who uses the smooth polished mask."[65] TR denounced pacifists as "active agents of the devil."[66]

Once in the war, after learning what the Allies "want and need is men, whether trained or not," Wilson relied on the Selective Service Act of May 1917.[67] National military service, proponents believed, would not only prepare the nation for battle but also instill respect for order, democracy, and sacrifice. Under the selective service system, 24,340,000 men eventually registered for the draft. Some 3,764,000 men received draft notices, and 2,820,000 were inducted. Over all, 4,744,000 soldiers, sailors, and marines served. "The Jews, the Wops, and the Dutch and the Irish cops,/ They're all in the Army now!" went a popular tune.[68] The typical serviceman was a white, single, poorly educated draftee between twenty-one and twenty-three years of age. Officer training camps turned out "ninety-day wonders," thousands of

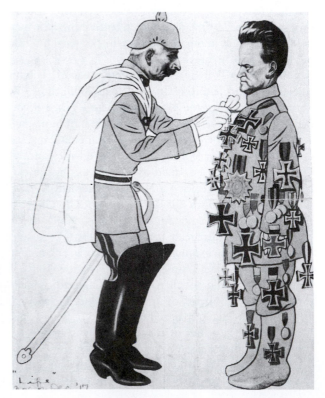

Senator Robert M. La Follette (1855–1925). This *Life* magazine cartoon depicted the antiwar, progressive reformer as a traitor. La Follette wanted a referendum on the war, certain that the American people would vote no. Some Americans thought that he should be expelled from the Senate. Others claimed that he took orders from the German kaiser, here shown pinning medals on the Wisconsin senator. La Follette withstood the intolerance of dissent and continued to speak against organized power and for the powerless, who, he said, were the people destined to do the fighting and dying abroad. (State Historical Society of Wisconsin)

commissioned officers drawn largely from people of elite background. Although excluded from military combat, women became navy clerks, telephone operators in the Army Signal Corps, and nurses and physical therapists to the wounded and battle-shock cases (the term then used for post-traumatic stress syndrome).

With the Allies begging for soldiers, General John J. "Black Jack" Pershing, now head of the American Expeditionary Forces to Europe, soon sent a "show the flag" contingent to France to boost Allied morale. Neither Wilson nor Pershing, however, would accept the European recommendation that U.S. troops be inserted in Allied units. American units would cooperate in joint maneuvers with other forces, but the U.S. Army would remain separate and independent. National pride dictated this decision, but so did the realization that Allied commanders had for years wasted the lives of hundreds of thousands in trench warfare. For more than two years officers had been ordering their men to charge out of the trenches, cross a "no man's land" of barbed wire and shell holes, and attack defenders off enemy trenches. Too often the assaulters were mowed down by machine gun fire, blown apart by artillery, or asphyxiated by chlorine gas, first used by Germany in 1915. Nor did Wilson endorse exploitative Allied war aims. Thus did the United States call itself an "associated" rather than an "allied" power in the war.

The Doughboys Make the Difference in Europe

On July 4, 1917, General Pershing reviewed the first battalion to arrive in France, as nearly a million Parisians tossed flowers, hugged the "doughboys" (apparently so-called because their buttons resembled dumplings made of dough), and cheered wildly. *"Lafayette, nous sommes ici!"* ("we are here!") shouted Pershing's aide.[69]

To the dismay of American leaders, taverns and brothels quickly surrounded military camps in the United States, even as alcohol and prostitution, remained taboo during the Progressive era. "Fit to Fight" became the government's slogan, as it moved to close "red-light districts," designated "sin-free zones" around camps, and banned the sale of liquor to men in uniform. Super patriots condemned those "treacherous Germans: Pabst, Schlitz, Blatz, and Miller."[70] The YMCA and the Jewish Welfare Board sent song leaders to camps. Movies, athletic programs, and well-stocked stores sought to keep soldiers on the base by making them feel "at home."

Success against venereal disease in the United States contrasted with a major flu epidemic, which first struck camps in spring 1918. The extremely contagious flu virus cut across race, gender, and class lines. At Camp Sherman, Ohio, one of the bases hit hardest, 1,101 people died between September 27 and October 13. Whereas about 51,000 soldiers died in battle during the war, some 62,000 soldiers died from diseases. Doughboys infected with the virus carried the flu with them to the European war, where it ignored national boundaries and turned into a global pandemic that killed more than 21 million people by spring 1919.

The approximately 400,000 African-American troops suffered racism and discrimination during this war "to make the world safe for democracy." Military camps were segregated and "white only" signs posted. In 1917 in Houston, Texas, whites provoked blacks into a riot that left seventeen whites and two blacks dead. In the army, three out of every four black soldiers served in labor units, where they wielded a shovel, not a gun, or where they cooked or unloaded supplies. African Americans endured second-class citizenship and the glaring contradiction between America's war-time rhetoric and reality. A statistic revealed the problem: 382 black Americans were lynched in the period 1914–1920. Segregation nonetheless did score one diplomatic success when the polyrhythms of the 169th Infantry's Harlem Hellcats marching band "touched off France's passion for jazz."[71]

The first official American combat death in Europe came only ten days after Congress declared war—that of Edmund Charles Clinton Genet, the great-great-grandson of French Revolutionary diplomat Citizen Genet and member of the famed American volunteer air squadron, the Lafayette Escadrille. Despite Allied impatience, General Pershing hesitated to commit his green soldiers to full-scale battle. As it was, great numbers of troops shipped over in British vessels and had to borrow French weapons. Disease continued to stalk U.S. forces. American reformers hoped soldiers had enough social armor not to be tempted by "sin" overseas, but the venereal-disease rate spiraled up. French premier Georges Clemenceau offered licensed—health-inspected—prostitutes. When Secretary of War Newton Baker

Red Cross Postcard. Women served in many roles in the war. They became workers in weapons factories. They sold Liberty Bonds and publicized government mobilization programs as members of the Women's Committee of the Council of National Defense. In France, women nurses and canteen workers became envoys of the U.S. home front, representing the mothers, wives, and sisters left behind. As the historian Susan Zeiger has written, the government's sponsorship of these wartime roles for women cleverly blunted the feminist-pacifist claim that women were "inherently more peaceful than men and would oppose war out of love for their children." (Library of Congress)

received the Gallic proposal, he exclaimed: "For God's sake … don't show this to the President or he'll stop the war."[72] Prevention programs and the threat of court-martial eventually reduced the "VD" problem.

By early 1918, the Allies had become mired in a murderous strategy of throwing ground forces directly at enemy ground forces. German troops were mauling Italian forces, and the French army was still suffering from mutinies of the year before. In March, after Germany swallowed large chunks of European Russia through the Brest-Litovsk Treaty, Wilson warned of a German "empire of force" out to "dominate the world itself" and urged Americans to "arm and prepare themselves to contest the mastery of the world."[73] In April he called for the national exertion of "Force, Force to the utmost, Force without stint or limit."[74] U.S. forces soon trooped into battle.

In March the German armies, swollen by forty divisions from the Russian front, launched a great offensive. Allied forces retreated, and by late May the kaiser's soldiers encamped near the Marne River, less than fifty miles from Paris. Saint-Mihiel, Belleau Wood, Cantigny, Château-Thierry—French sites where U.S. soldiers shed their blood—soon became household words for Americans. In June at Château-Thierry the doughboys dramatically stopped a German advance. From May through September 1918 more than 1 million American troops went to France—2 million by the November armistice. In mid-July the Allies launched a counteroffensive; nine American divisions fought fiercely near Château-Thierry, helping to lift the German threat from Paris. In the Meuse-Argonne offensive (begun in late September), more than 1 million doughboys joined French and British units in a six-week struggle that

First Division Troops Encounter German Gas Warfare, 1918. Near Soissons, France, U.S. soldiers attacked German lines through air contaminated with poisonous gas. The soldier in the foreground, wounded by fire, tore off his gas mask. Before U.S. intervention, President Wilson had deplored "this vast, gruesome contest of systematized destruction" and denied any "glory commensurate with the sacrifice of millions of men." The last surviving U.S. combat veteran of World War I, Corporal Harold V. Ramsay, died in 2008 at age 108. (Library of Congress)

cost 26,277 American deaths and 95,786 wounded—the "deadliest battle in all of American history."[75] "The American infantry in the Argonne won the war," German Marshal Paul von Hindenburg later commented, perhaps with overstatement.[76] Not only was the German army in retreat, but the U-boats had been defeated at sea and the Atlantic had become an uninterrupted highway for the reinforcement of men and war supplies from the United States. The logistical avalanche would soon bury Germany, so Berlin sought peace.

On October 4, the German chancellor asked Wilson for an armistice. German troops had mutinied; revolution and riots plagued German cities; Bulgaria had left the war in September. Then Turkey dropped out in late October, and Austria-Hungary surrendered on November 3. Germany had no choice but to seek terms. The kaiser fled to Holland. On November 11, in a railroad car in the Compiègne Forest, German representatives capitulated.

The Fourteen Points and a Contentious Peace Conference

During the combat, President Wilson had begun to explain his plans for the peace. He trumpeted his vision most dramatically in his "Fourteen Points" speech before Congress on January 8, 1918. The first five points promised an "open" world after the war, a world distinguished by "open covenants, openly arrived at," freedom of navigation on the seas, equal trade opportunity and the removal of tariffs, reduction of armaments, and an end to colonialism. Points six through thirteen called for self-determination for national minorities in Europe. Point fourteen stood paramount: a "general association of nations" to ensure "political independence and territorial integrity to great and small states alike."[77] His Fourteen Points signaled a generous, nonpunitive postwar settlement. They served, too, as effective American propaganda against revenge-fueled Allied aims and Russian Bolshevik appeals for European revolution.

Despite secret treaties that promised German colonies and other territorial gains, Allied leaders feared that Wilson would deny them the spoils of war. Nor did they appreciate his promises to slay the "dragons of reaction" in Europe.[78] In view of the comparative wartime losses, Europeans believed that Wilson "had bought his seat at the peace table at a discount."[79] When, in September and October 1918, Wilson exchanged notes with Germany and Austria-Hungary about an armistice, the Allied powers expressed strong reservations about the Fourteen Points. Wilson hinted at a separate peace with the Central Powers and even threatened to publicize the exploitative Allied war aims. Facing possible reduced American shipments to Europe, London, Paris, and Rome reluctantly accepted, in the armistice of November, peace negotiations on the basis of the Fourteen Points.

Wilson relished his opportunity. The United States could now claim a major role in deciding future international relations. The pictures of dying men dangling from barbed-wire fences and the battle-shock victims who staggered home persuaded many Americans of the need to prevent another conflagration. Wilson's call for a just peace commanded the backing of countless foreigners as well. Italians hoisted banners reading *Dio di Pace* ("God of Peace") and *Redentore dell' Humanità* ("Redeemer of Humanity") to welcome Wilson to Europe.

Yet the president weakened his position even before the peace conference. Congressional leaders wanted him to stay home to handle domestic problems. Lansing feared that Wilson would have only one vote in the day-to-day conference bickering, whereas from Washington he could symbolically marshal the votes of humankind. Wilson retorted that "England and France have not the same views with regard to peace that we have," so he had to attend personally to defend the Fourteen Points.[80]

Domestic politics soon set Wilson back. In October 1918, Wilson "hurled a brick into a beehive" by asking Americans to return a Democratic Congress loyal to him.[81] Partisan Republicans proceeded to capture the November election and majorities in both houses of Congress; they would sit in ultimate judgment of Wilson's peacemaking. The president also made the political mistake of appointing neither an important Republican nor a senator to the American Peace Commission. Wilson, House, and Lansing sat on it; so did Henry White, a seasoned diplomat and nominal Republican. Some concessions to his political opposition, and to senatorial prerogatives in foreign affairs, might have smoothed the path later for his peace treaty.

On December 4, with great fanfare, Wilson departed from New York aboard the *George Washington*. He settled into a quiet voyage, surrounded by advisers and nearly 2,000 reports produced by "The Inquiry," a group of scholars who had studied issues likely to arise at the peace conference. Confident that "we can force" the Allies "to our way of thinking" because they will be "financially in our hands," the president had made few concrete plans.[82] After reaching France on December 15, Wilson basked in the admiration of enthusiastic Parisian crowds. Later, thousands in Italy and England cheered him with near religious fervor. Wilson assumed that this generous outpouring meant that *his* peace aims were universally popular and that Americans "would be the only disinterested people" at Versailles.[83] Such "man-in-the-street" opinion did not impress David Lloyd George, prime minister of Britain, French Premier Georges Clemenceau, or Italian Prime Minister Vittorio Orlando, Wilson's antagonists at the peace conference.

With Germany and Bolshevik Russia (see page 300) excluded from the Versailles conference, thirty-two nations sent delegations, which essentially followed the lead of the "Big Four." Most sessions worked in secrecy, hardly befitting Wilson's first "point." Clemenceau resented Wilson's "sermonettes" and preferred to work with the more compliant Colonel House. "The old tiger [Clemenceau] wants the grizzly bear [Wilson] back in the Rocky Mountains before he starts tearing up the German Hog," commented Lloyd George, who sought to build a strong France and to ensure German purchases of British exports.[84] A fervent Italian nationalist, Orlando concerned himself primarily with enlarging Italian territory. These leaders sought a vengeful peace. Lloyd George complained of a chameleonlike Wilson—"the noble visionary, the implacable and unscrupulous partisan, the exalted idealist and the man of rather petty personal rancour."[85] Wilson, in turn, thought the Europeans "too weatherwise to see the weather."[86]

Much wrangling occurred over the disposition of colonies and the creation of new countries. "Tell me what's right and I'll fight for it," said Wilson as he appealed

David Lloyd George (1863–1945). "America," said the British prime minister, referring to the League of Nations, "had been offered the leadership of the world, but the Senate had tossed the sceptre into the sea." (Library of Congress)

for self-determination.[87] After hard negotiating, the conferees mandated former German and Turkish colonies to the countries that had conquered them, to be loosely supervised under League of Nations auspices. Under the mandate system—a compromise between outright annexation and complete independence—France (with Syria and Lebanon) and Britain (with Iraq, Trans-Jordan, and Palestine) received parts of the Middle East. Wilson voiced support for Britain's Balfour Declaration that promised "a national home for the Jewish people" in Palestine, and he briefly considered an American mandate for Armenia (where the Turks had committed genocidal atrocities during the war) but rejected it because he could "think of nothing that the people of the United States would be less inclined to accept than military responsibility in Asia."[88] Japan acquired China's Shandong Province and some of Germany's Pacific islands. After Wilson's reluctant acceptance of the Shandong arrangement, the president deemed it "the best that could be accomplished out of a 'dirty past'" and expected the League of Nations to "decide the matter later."[89] Outraged Chinese students in Beijing protested by launching the May Fourth Movement, claiming that "we could no longer depend upon the principle of any so-called great leader like Woodrow Wilson."[90]

With his rhetoric combining the "text of modern liberalism with the subtext of racism," Wilson conspicuously ignored a petition calling for self-determination in French Indochina and signed by, among others, Nguyen Al Quoc—later famous under the name Ho Chi Minh.[91] France gained the demilitarization of the German

Wilson in Dover, England, 1919. Wilson received flowers from English schoolchildren. The biographer Louis Auchincloss has written that "the ringing shouts in the streets and squares of the Old World must have made him [Wilson] feel like a messiah endowed with the vision to understand that the multitude was on the side of the merciful angels of a fair and lasting peace and that only a minority of stubborn old men wanted to crush the enemy to dust. He never learned that the only leader who can take advantage of the momentary enthusiasm of the common man is a dictator who can use its force to blast his way to power; a democrat must abide by the decision of those whom the common man has elected to represent him." (U.S. Signal Corps, National Archives)

Rhineland and a stake in the coal-rich Saar Basin. Italy annexed South Tyrol and Trieste from the collapsed Austro-Hungarian Empire. Some 1,132,000 square miles changed hands. Newly independent countries also emerged from the defunct Austro-Hungarian Empire: Austria, Czechoslovakia, Hungary, Romania, and Yugoslavia. The Allies further exploited nationalism to recognize a ring of hostile states already established around Bolshevik Russia: Finland, Poland, Estonia, Latvia, and Lithuania, all formerly part of the Russian empire (see map on page 295). The mandate system smacked of imperialism, in violation of the Fourteen Points, but the new states in Europe fulfilled Wilson's self-determination pledge. To assuage French fears of a revived Germany, Britain and the United States signed a security pact with France guaranteeing its borders, but Wilson never submitted it for Senate approval.

Reparations proved a knotty issue. The United States wanted a limited indemnity for Germany to avoid a harsh peace that might arouse long-term German resentment or debilitate the German economy and politics. "Excessive demands," Wilson predicted, "would most certainly sow the seeds of war."[92] To cripple Germany, France pushed for a large bill of reparations. The conferees composed a "war guilt clause," which held Germany responsible for all of the war's damages. Rationalizing that the League would ameliorate any excesses, Wilson gave in on both reparations and war guilt. It was a major mistake. The Reparations Commission in 1921 presented a hobbled Germany with a huge reparations bill of $33 billion, thereby helping to destabilize international economic relations for more than a decade.

The Allies played to Wilson's priorities: "Give him the League of Nations and he will give us all the rest."[93] Drafted largely by Wilson, the League's covenant provided for an influential council of five big powers (permanent) and representatives from smaller nations (by election) and an assembly of all nations for discussion. Wilson saw the heart of the covenant as Article 10, a provision designed to curb aggression and war: "The Members of the League undertake to respect and preserve as against external aggression the territorial integrity and existing political independence of all Members of the League." In case of aggression or threat, "the Council shall advise upon the means by which this obligation shall be fulfilled."[94] Wilson persuaded the conferees to merge the League covenant and the peace terms in a package, with the charter constituting the first 26 articles of a 440-article Treaty of Paris. Wilson deemed the League covenant the noblest part of all—"It is practical, and yet it is intended to purify, to rectify, to elevate."[95]

The Germans, without having previously participated in the deliberations, signed sullenly on June 28 in the elegant Hall of Mirrors at Versailles. By stripping Germany of 13 percent of its territory, 10 percent of its population, and all of its colonies, and by demanding reparations, the treaty humiliated the Germans without crushing them. In one historian's words, the treaty contained "a witches' brew" with "too little Wilsonianism to appease, too little of Clemenceau to deter; enough of Wilson to provoke contempt, enough of Clemenceau to inspire hatred."[96] When Wilson died on February 3, 1924, the Weimar Republic in Berlin refrained from issuing an official condolence, and the German Embassy in Washington broke custom by not lowering its flag to half-mast.

Principle, Personality, Health, and Partisanship: The League Fight

Wilson spent almost six months in Europe negotiating the postwar peace. From February 24 to March 14, 1919, however, he returned to the United States for executive business. On arrival, he asserted that any U.S. failure to back the League "would break the heart of the world."[97] In Washington, Republicans peppered Wilson with questions about the degree to which the covenant limited American sovereignty. When Wilson spoke vaguely, Senator Frank Brandegee of Connecticut said he felt as if he had been "wandering with Alice in Wonderland and had tea with the Mad Hatter."[98] In early March, Republican Senator Henry Cabot Lodge of Massachusetts engineered a "Round Robin," a statement by thirty-nine senators (enough to deny the treaty a two-thirds vote) that questioned the League covenant and requested that the peace treaty and the covenant be acted on separately. Many of Lodge's signers feared that the League would limit U.S. freedom to act independently in international affairs.

A defiant Wilson sailed again for France, determined that "little Americans," full of "watchful jealousies [and] of rabid antagonisms," would not destroy his beloved League.[99] Still, he was politician enough to seek changes in Paris. He amended the covenant so that League members could refuse mandates, League jurisdiction over purely domestic issues was precluded, and the Monroe Doctrine was safeguarded against League interference. But he would not alter Article 10. When he returned to the United States in July, Wilson submitted the long Treaty of Versailles to the Senate on July 10, with an address that resembled an evangelical sermon: "The stage is set, the destiny disclosed. It has come about by no plan of our conceiving, but by the hand of God, who led us into this way."[100] Asked if he would accept senatorial "reservations" to the treaty, Wilson snapped: "Anyone who opposes me in that, I'll crush."[101] "If it won't work," he said of the League, "it must be made to work."[102]

Wilson, against strong odds in Paris, gained a good percentage of his goals as outlined in the Fourteen Points. Self-determination for nationalities was advanced as never before in Europe, and the League ranked as a notable achievement. But Wilson did compromise, especially with Clemenceau. Both Italy and Japan had threatened to walk out unless they realized some territorial goals. Still, Wilson had so built up a case for an unselfish peace that when the conquerors' hard bargaining and harsh terms dominated the conference, observers could only conclude that the president had failed badly to live up to his millennial rhetoric. Critics said that Wilson should have left Paris in protest, refusing to sign, or that he might have threatened the Allies with U.S. economic pressure. Believing desperately that the League, with Article 10, would rectify all, Wilson warned Congress that without it, "the United States and every other country will have to arm to the teeth."[103]

He would not compromise at home, however. And he seldom provided systematic, technical analysis to treaty clauses. He simply expected the Senate dutifully to ratify his masterwork. Yet his earlier bypassing of that body and his own partisan speeches and self-righteousness ensured debate, if not defeat. Progressive internationalists protested that "the capitalists wanted the League as a superstate to protect their exploitative concessions in underdeveloped countries."[104] Henry Cabot Lodge

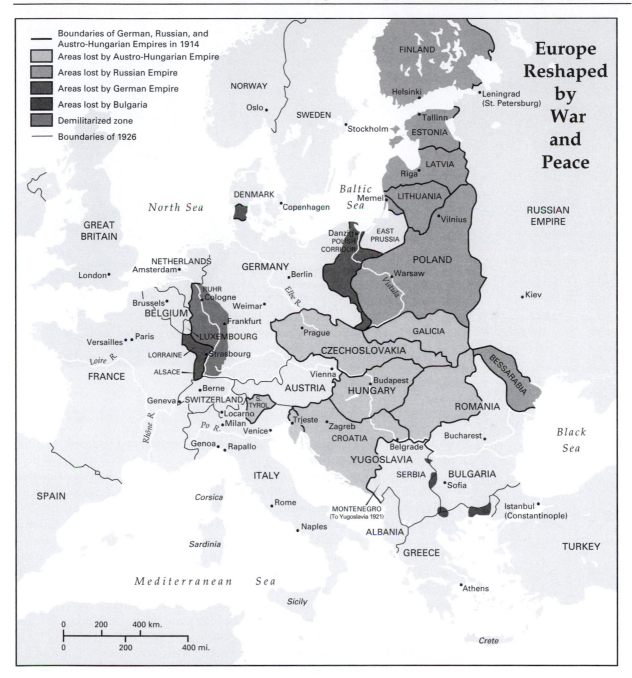

Europe
Reshaped
by
War
and
Peace

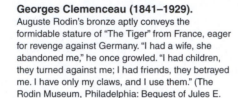

Georges Clemenceau (1841–1929).
Auguste Rodin's bronze aptly conveys the
formidable stature of "The Tiger" from France, eager
for revenge against Germany. "I had a wife, she
abandoned me," he once growled. "I had children,
they turned against me; I had friends, they betrayed
me. I have only my claws, and I use them." (The
Rodin Museum, Philadelphia: Bequest of Jules E.
Mastbaum, 1929)

asked a key question: "Are you willing to put your soldiers and your sailors at the disposition of other nations?"[105] Senator James Reed of Missouri feared racial peril from a League initially comprising fifteen white nations and seventeen nations of "black, brown, yellow, and red races," which, he claimed, ranked low in "civilization" and high in "barbarism."[106]

Article 10 seemed to rattle everybody. The article did not require member states to use force, but it implied they should. Senator William Borah complained that "I may be willing to help my neighbor …, but I do not want him … [to] decide for me when and how I shall act or to what extent I shall make sacrifice."[107] Because of its apparent commitment to territorial integrity, Senator Hiram Johnson of California claimed that Article 10 would "freeze the world into immutability and put it in a straightjacket," keeping "subject peoples … subject until the crack of doom."[108] The article seemed too open-ended to most opponents.

Henry Cabot Lodge towered as Wilson's chief legislative obstacle. Chair of the Senate Foreign Relations Committee, nationalist-imperialist, author, Republican partisan, like Wilson a scholar in politics, Lodge packed his committee with anti-League senators, dragged out hearings for weeks, kept most Republicans together on treaty votes, and nurtured a personal animosity toward Wilson matched only by Wilson's detestation for Lodge. He attacked obliquely by proposing "reservations" to the League covenant. Although in retrospect these reservations, intended to guard

American sovereignty, do not appear to have been death blows to the League, at the time they stirred impassioned debate. They addressed the central question of American national interest—the degree to which the United States would limit its freedom of action, the degree to which the United States should engage in collective security. In fact, many of the fourteen reservations stated the obvious—that Congress would retain its constitutional role in foreign policy. Another denied the League jurisdiction over American domestic legislation. The reservation on Article 10 disclaimed any obligation to preserve the territorial integrity or political independence of another country unless authorized by Congress. For Wilson this meant "nullification of the treaty."[109] He was wrong.

The Senate divided into four groups. Wilson counted on about forty loyal Democrats called the Non-Reservationists. Another group, the Mild-Reservationists, led by Frank B. Kellogg, numbered about thirteen Republicans. The third faction, managed by Lodge, stood together as the Strong-Reservationists—some twenty Republicans and a few Democrats. The fourth group, consisting of sixteen Irreconcilables, ardently opposed the treaty with or without reservations. Most of them were Republicans, including Borah, La Follette, George Norris of Nebraska, and Hiram Johnson of California. "If the Savior of mankind would revisit the earth and declared for a League," vowed Borah, "I would be opposed to it."[110]

Wilson met individually with some twenty-three senators over two weeks, but he suffered a minor stroke on July 19, 1919. He thereafter rigidly refused to accept any reservations. He argued that a treaty ratified with reservations would have to go back to another conference for acceptance and every nation would then rush in with its pet reservations. The British punctured this hollow claim by announcing that they would accept American reservations. In September 1919, Wilson set off on a 10,000-mile train trip across the United States. Growing more exhausted with each day, suffering severe headaches and nighttime coughing spells, Wilson pounded the podium in forty speeches. He blasted his traducers as "absolute, contemptible quitters."[111] He confused his audiences when he stated that Article 10 meant that the United States had a moral, not a legal, obligation to use armed force, and that Congress was "absolutely free to put its own interpretation on it."[112] Failure to join the League, he prophesied "with absolute certainty" meant that "within another generation there will be another world war."[113] On September 26, after an impassioned speech in Pueblo, Colorado, he awoke to nausea and uncontrollable facial twitching. When his doctor ordered him to cancel the rest of his trip, Wilson wept.

After Wilson returned to Washington, a massive stroke paralyzed his left side. He lay flat in bed for six weeks and saw virtually no one except his wife and Dr. Cary Grayson. For months Edith Bolling Galt Wilson ran her husband's political affairs, screening messages and banishing House and Lansing, among others, from presidential favor. The president should have resigned, as Dr. Grayson advised him to do in early 1919. As it was, his concentration diminished and his stubbornness accentuated by the stroke, Wilson adamantly refused to change his all-or-nothing position.

In November 1919, the Senate balloted on the complete treaty *with* reservations and rejected it, 39 to 55 (Irreconcilables and Non-Reservationists in the

Henry Cabot Lodge (1850–1924). Wilson's partisan rival observed of the League Covenant that "it might get by at Princeton," Wilson's alma mater, "but certainly not at Harvard," where Lodge had earned a Ph.D. Lodge's opposition to Wilson's League, was motivated in part by his belief that the United States should control the Americas and act cautiously in European political and military affairs. He was a long-time expansionist who had declared in 1895: "From the Rio Grande to the Arctic Ocean there would be but one flag and one country." (Library of Congress)

Woodrow Wilson After His Stroke. Recent scholarly assessments of medical evidence reveal that Wilson had a long history of cerebrovascular disease. Wilson remained in the White House after his massive stroke in October 1919, while his wife and doctor tried to keep secret the severity of his physical incapacity. Dr. Edwin A. Weinstein, who has studied the effects of Wilson's health and personality on his decision making, has noted that the president after his stroke could not maintain his train of thought and was prone to bursts of temper. An increasingly paranoid president broke with such close advisers as Colonel House and Secretary Lansing for alleged slights and betrayals. (Library of Congress)

negative). Then it voted on the treaty *without* reservations and also rejected it, 38 to 53 (Irreconcilables and Reservationists in the negative). The president had instructed loyal Democrats not to accept any "reserved" treaty. In March 1920, another tally saw some Democrats vote in favor of reservations. Not enough, the treaty failed, 49 to 35, several votes short of the two-thirds majority required for approval. When his wife urged him to accept reservations, Wilson admonished: "Little girl, don't you desert me. That I cannot stand."[114] Still a fighter, the president claimed that the election of 1920 would be a "solemn referendum" on the treaty. Other questions actually blurred the League issue in that campaign, and Republican Warren G. Harding, who as a senator had supported reservations, promptly condemned the League after his election as president. In July 1921, Congress officially terminated the war, and in August, by treaty with Germany, the United States claimed as valid for itself the terms of the treaty of Versailles— exclusive of the League articles.

The memorable League fight had ended. The tragic dénouement occurred because of political partisanship, personal animosities, senatorial resentments, the president's failing health, popular adherence to traditional unilateralism, and disinterest and confusion in the public mind. Progressive internationalists, many of them harassed by wartime restrictions on civil liberties and disappointed by Wilson's compromises with the imperial powers, no longer backed a president they thought reactionary. Then, of course, there was Wilson himself—stubborn, pontificating, combative, and increasingly ill. He might have conceded that the peace had imperfections. He might have provided more careful analysis of a long, complicated document. He might, further, have admitted that his opponents held a respectable intellectual position. Instead, he often chose shrill rhetoric and rigid self-righteousness. Most importantly, he saw the difference between himself and his critics as fundamental: whether it was in America's national interest to participate in collective security or seek safety unilaterally. As one critic put it, Wilson sought "collective security without forming an alliance." He wanted the "omelet" without "cracking the eggs."[115]

Although the League came into being without the United States as a member, none of the great powers wished to bestow significant authority on the new organization. Japan's foreign minister called it "nothing but a great hypocritical monster under the cloak of justice and humanity."[116] Even if Washington had joined, the United States most likely would have acted outside the League's auspices, especially regarding its own empire in Latin America. No international association at that time could have outlawed war, dismantled empires, or scuttled navies. Wilson overshot reality in thinking that he could reform world politics through a new international body. The League represented a commendable restraint against war, but hardly a panacea for world peace.

What if ... *the president had accepted Senate reservations and the United States had joined the League of Nations in 1919–1920?*

Had Woodrow Wilson resigned following his stroke in October 1919, as his personal physician Dr. Cary Grayson urged him to do, the Senate and Vice President Thomas Marshall almost certainly would have reached some agreement on admission to the League, probably with reservations to Article 10 of the Covenant. Similar to the veto in the United Nations since 1945, the United States could have decided if and when it would follow League recommendations. Contemporary observers would not have misinterpreted the divisive presidential election of 1920 as a solemn referendum for or against League membership, even though Republicans most likely would have won because of public disenchantment with Wilsonian rhetoric, the Red Scare, wartime inflation, postwar recession, and failed promises. The Senate might also have ratified the Anglo-American treaty of guarantee of France, which Wilson had refused to submit until the Senate approved the League. As Senator Henry Cabot Lodge actually preferred, a de facto alliance among the United States, France, and Britain might have continued into the 1920s. As with the Locarno Treaty of 1925, such a treaty would have guaranteed Germany's western boundaries with France and Belgium but not its eastern boundaries with Poland and Czechoslovakia. Washington could probably have joined the World Court with minimum controversy, albeit with little practical effect.

Would U.S. membership in the League have altered the history of the interwar period? Washington's hegemony within the Western Hemisphere would surely not have changed. Participation by U.S. experts in the League's Reparations Commission in 1920–1921 might have resulted in a total bill of much less than $33 billion and an easier schedule of payments for Weimar Germany. If so, Germany's default by inflation, the Franco-Belgian occupation of the Ruhr in 1923, and readjustment of reparations payments and private U.S. bank loans to Germany under the Dawes Plan of 1924 need not have occurred. Nonetheless, without Washington's willingness to lower its tariff walls, to grant generous reconstruction aid to Europe, or to write off wartime debts to the allies, the jerry-rigged recycling of loans, reparations, and debts would still have left the international economy vulnerable to the stock market crash and depression after 1929. Notwithstanding U.S. participation in multiple League-sponsored forums culminating in the London Economic Conference of 1933, cooperative efforts offered no effective solutions to the Great Depression. Similarly, it is difficult to imagine that direct U.S. participation would have bolstered the League's tepid response to the Manchurian Crisis of 1931 or to the Italian invasion of Ethiopia in 1935. In fact, some American diplomats viewed League membership as an excuse for such countries as Britain and France not to act more forcefully. In any event, the peace lobby, continued public disillusionment with World War I, and New Deal domestic priorities would still have constrained President Franklin D. Roosevelt from multilateral initiatives to deter German and Japanese expansion until later in the decade.

When "independent internationalism" failed to prevent a second world war (see next chapter), Americans readily grasped a second chance to rectify the apparent mistakes of 1919–1920 by embracing a new version of the League. Spurred on by a resurgence of Wilsonianism, including the lavish Hollywood film *Wilson* (1944), the Roosevelt administration sought bipartisan support from Republicans and successfully persuaded Americans to join a modified collective security organization known as the United Nations. American participation and leadership, it was hoped, would ensure a peaceful international order. The checkered history of the United Nations since 1945, however, suggests that earlier membership would have made little difference. Despite Wilson's messianic vision, the League was never more than the sum of its collective parts.

Red Scare at Home and Abroad: Bolshevism and Intervention in Russia

"Paris cannot be understood without Moscow [Russia]," wrote Wilson's press secretary Ray Stannard Baker.[117] As he traveled to France aboard the *George Washington,* President Wilson depicted Bolshevism as "the poison of disorder, the poison of revolt, the poison of chaos."[118] Revolutionary and anticapitalist, the Bolsheviks, or Communists, threw fright into the leaders of Europe and America. At home and abroad the peacemakers battled the radical left. In the United States the Wilson administration trampled on civil liberties during an exaggerated "Red Scare," which sent innocent people to jail or deported them. Wilson himself seemed to think that "the only way to kill Bolshevism is … to open all the doors to commerce."[119] Only belatedly, after authorizing secret aid and espionage against the "Reds," did the president openly "cast in his lot" with the other powers in a futile attempt to destroy the new revolutionary regime.[120]

Most Americans applauded the Russian Revolution of March 1917, which toppled Tsar Nicholas II. Wilson himself viewed it as a thrust against autocracy, war, and imperialism. But when the moderate Provisional government under Alexander Kerensky fell to the radical Bolsheviks in October, Americans responded first with irritation and then anger. Their disapproval became acute in March 1918 after the Bolsheviks signed the Brest-Litovsk Treaty with Germany and ceded Ukraine and Finland, among other territories—a total of 1,267,000 square miles, 62 million people, and one-third of Russia's best agricultural land. A necessary peace for a devastated Russia from the Bolshevik perspective, the treaty seemed a stab in the back for the Allies, a decisive victory for Berlin. Because German authorities had allowed Vladimir I. Lenin to travel to Russia via Germany in 1917, some irate American officials even considered Bolsheviks pro-German. Others recoiled after Ambassador David Francis's testimony that Bolsheviks had "nationalized women."[121]

Lenin actually treated the United States as a special, favored case, and he consistently sought accommodation with Washington. Soviet representatives held a series of cordial conversations from December 1917 to May 1918 with Red Cross official Raymond Robins, a de facto U.S. representative, and reached agreements on food relief, purchase of strategic materials, and exemption of American corporations from

ТОВ. Ленин ОЧИЩАЕТ землю от нечисти.

"Comrade Lenin Sweeps the Globe Clean." Vladimir Ilyich Lenin (1870–1924) is shown in this Bolshevik art as a revolutionary ridding the world of monarchs and capitalists. But Lenin also craved Western trade and investment to spur his nation's economic reconstruction. As he said in 1919: "We are decidedly for an economic understanding with America—with all countries, but especially with America." (By Mikhail Cheremnykh and Victor Deni in Mikhail Guerman, comp., *Art of the October Revolution,* Leningrad: Aurora Art Publishers, 1979)

Bolshevik nationalization decrees. Prior to Brest-Litovsk, Robins urged prompt recognition of the Bolshevik government to keep Russia in the war, but President Wilson paid more heed to Francis's prediction that the Bolshevik regime would soon collapse.

Although American officials in Russia engaged in propaganda and espionage and cooperated with Allied and "White" agents in anti-Bolshevik activities after November 1917, Wilson knew only broad outlines of this "secret war" when he sent U.S. troops to Archangel in northern Russia in August 1918. Ordered to avoid military action in the Russian civil war, they inevitably cooperated with British and French forces in attempts to roll back Bolshevik influence. Wilson said publicly that he authorized the expedition only to prevent German seizure of military supplies and a railroad, but he quickly approved $50 million in secret payments to White armies fighting the Bolsheviks. Wilson's motives were thus "simultaneously anti-German and anti-Bolshevik."[122] Some 5,000 American troops suffered through a bitter winter of fifty-below-zero temperatures. Their morale sagged; mutiny threatened. In December 1918, Senator Hiram Johnson introduced a resolution to withdraw them from Russia. It failed by one vote. U.S. soldiers did not leave Russia until June 1919. Two hundred twenty-two American soldiers died in what critics dubbed "Mr. Wilson's little war with Russia."[123]

A. Mitchell Palmer (1872–1936). When U.S. troops were intervening in Bolshevik Russia, Wilson's attorney general, A. Mitchell Palmer, was chasing suspected radicals at home. An architect of the "Red Scare," Palmer believed that the "blaze of revolution" was "eating its way into the homes of the American workmen, its sharp tongues of revolutionary heat … licking the altars of the churches, leaping into the belfry of the school bell, crawling into the sacred corners of American homes, burning up the foundations of society." After jailing and deporting thousands with little or no due process, Palmer claimed that the government could not "stand idly by and wait for the actual throwing of bombs or the actual use of arms in military operations before it can defend itself." (Library of Congress)

Wilson claimed to be "sweating blood over the question of what is right and feasible … in Russia. It goes to pieces like quicksilver under my touch."[124] Pressure from the deeply anticommunist French and British and expansionist Japanese and his own anti-Bolshevism inclined him to send another expedition, this time to Siberia, where many envisioned the growth of a non-Bolshevik Russian bastion. In July 1918, he approved the expedition, later officially explaining to the American people that he was sending the troops (eventually numbering 10,000) to rescue a group of 70,000 Czechs stranded in Russia. Organized earlier as part of the tsarist Russian army to fight for a Czech homeland in Austria-Hungary, the Czech legion was battling Bolsheviks along the Trans-Siberian Railroad in an effort to reach Vladivostok and possible transportation to the western front. Wilson's avowed purpose of evacuating the Czech legion derived also from his "friendly feelings" for Professor Thomas Masaryk and Czechoslovakia's independence, which Wilson soon recognized in October.[125]

Despite his disingenuous official explanation, Wilson believed that "a limited, indirect intervention to help the Russian people overcome domination by Bolsheviks and Germans would not contradict, but rather [would] facilitate self-determination."[126] Yet intervention in Siberia became openly anti-Bolshevik because the Czechs were fighting Lenin's forces. Once Wilson found it impossible to evacuate the Czechs in time for them to fight in Europe, he reluctantly bowed to Allied pressure and gave support to the anti-Bolshevik White Russian leader Admiral A.V. Kolchak in the hope that he could form a pro-Western constitutional government. Despite money and supplies from the Allies, Kolchak faltered and his armies were routed before they could reach Moscow in June 1919. U.S. troops finally withdrew from Siberia in 1920, with one departing soldier noting that Vladivostok looked better in photographs because "the 'smell' ain't in the pictures or it m't be 'good night' when you opened the letter that contained them."[127]

At the Paris peace conference, the victors tried to isolate what they considered revolutionary contagion. The organization of the Third International in Moscow in early 1919 alarmed postwar leaders, as did communist Bela Kun's successful revolution in Hungary in March 1919, which lasted only until August. Accordingly, the conferees granted territory to Russia's neighbors (Poland, Romania, and Czechoslovakia) and recognized the nations of Finland, Estonia, Latvia, and Lithuania as a ring of states unfriendly to Russia. During the conference, besides the military interventions, the Allies imposed a strict economic blockade on Russia, sent aid to the White forces, and extended relief assistance to Austria and Hungary to stem political unrest.

Even though Wilson perceived the Soviets as the "negation of everything that is American," he never settled on a definitive, workable policy to co-opt or smash Bolshevism.[128] By not leading decisively, the president allowed subordinates and circumstances to determine U.S. policy toward Russia. His growing estrangement at Versailles from Colonel House, a conduit for pro-Soviet liberals, meant that the interventionist Allies and the rabidly anti-Bolshevik Secretary Lansing exerted greater influence.

Wilson's one serious effort to end the civil war in Russia through diplomacy came in January 1919 when he invited the warring groups to meet on Prinkipo

Island off the Turkish coast. The Bolsheviks cautiously accepted the invitation, but the anti-Bolsheviks rejected any meeting. Next, in February, House helped arrange a trip by William C. Bullitt, a member of the U.S. delegation at Versailles, and Lincoln Steffens, the radical muckraking journalist, to Russia. Wilson envisioned only a fact-finding mission. The ambitious Bullitt nonetheless negotiated a proposal whereby the Allies would withdraw their troops, suspend military aid to White forces, and lift the economic blockade; in return the Soviets promised a cease-fire in which their opponents would hold the territories they occupied. Bullitt and Steffens returned to Paris convinced that their agreement would satisfy all parties. Lloyd George opposed it; Wilson ignored it. Bullitt resigned in protest.

The Allied counterrevolution proved costly. "It intensified the civil war and sent thousands of Russians to their deaths," the British official Bruce Lockhart later wrote. "Its direct effect was to provide the Bolsheviks with a cheap victory, ... and to galvanize them into a strong and ruthless organism."[129] Kremlin leaders also nurtured long memories. "Never have any of our soldiers been on American soil," Premier Nikita S. Khrushchev lectured Americans as late as 1959, "but your soldiers were on Russian soil."[130] Participation by such young men as Allen and John Foster Dulles in Wilson's "secret war" against the Bolsheviks provided "the formative experiences that inclined [them] to rely on propaganda and covert action" when they later directed U.S. policies during the Cold War.[131] Such tactics ultimately backfired, as Wilson recognized before his death. "Bolshevism is a mistake," Wilson said. "If left alone it will destroy itself. It cannot survive because it is wrong."[132]

The Whispering Gallery of Global Disorder

More than 116,000 American soldiers died in World War I, which cost the U.S. government more than $30 billion. A third of the figure was paid through taxes; the other two-thirds represented borrowed money, which postwar generations would have to pay back. If one counts the long-term expense of veterans' benefits, the cost to the United States probably equaled three times the immediate direct costs. What President Dwight D. Eisenhower would later call the "military-industrial complex" had its origins in a high degree of government-business cooperation during the war; economic decision making for the nation became centralized as never before; and the increased application of efficient methods in manufacturing contributed to U.S. economic power. The era of World War I witnessed other domestic events that impinged on foreign affairs: racial conflict, evidenced by twenty-five race riots in 1919; suppression of civil liberties under the Espionage and Sedition Acts, by which people who dissented from the war were silenced; the stunting of radical commentary (Socialist leader Eugene Debs and the pacifist Alice Paul, among others, went to jail for opposing the war) and hence the imposition of coercive consensus; and the withering of the reform impulse.

In foreign affairs, the White House assumed more authority in initiating policy and controlling its execution. The State Department read diplomatic messages that Wilson had typed on his own machine. Wilson bypassed Congress on a number of occasions, failing to consult that body about the Fourteen Points, the goals at Paris,

The Cambridge American Cemetery and Memorial. The American Doughboy-poet John McCrae famously wrote: "In Flanders Field the poppies blow / Between the crosses row on row." England's Cambridge University donated thirty acres that contain the graves of 3,812 American war dead. Even though these concentric circles of white gravestones evoke an atmosphere of serenity and repose, the wartime ambulance driver Ernest Hemingway later wrote: "I had seen nothing sacred, and the things that were glorious had no glory and the sacrifices were like the stockyards at Chicago." (Courtesy American Battle Monuments Commission)

and the intervention in Russia. He acted "like a divine-right monarch in the conduct of foreign relations."[133] The Senate finally rebelled by rejecting the League of Nations, but that negative decision did not reverse the trend of growing presidential power over foreign policy.

World War I took the lives of some 14,663,400 people—8 million soldiers and 6.6 million civilians, not including victims of the influenza pandemic. Russia led with 3.7 million dead; Germany followed with 2.6 million; then came France with 1.4 million, Austria-Hungary with 950,000, and Britain with 939,000. One out of every two French males who would have been between the ages of twenty and thirty-two in 1914 died during the war. It had been a total war, involving whole societies, not merely their armies. Never before had a war left the belligerents so exhausted, so battered. New destructive weapons made their debut—tanks, airplanes, poison gas, and submarines—"a preview of the Pandora's box of evils that the linkage of science with industry in the service of war was to mean."[134] The war reinforced American desires to avoid foreign entanglement. Captain of Artillery Harry S. Truman of Missouri claimed that most soldiers "don't give a whoop (to put it mildly) whether Russia has a Red Government or no government and if the King of the Lollipops wants to slaughter his subjects or his Prime Minister it's all the same to us."[135] Disillusioned clergy regretted their participation in the "shrieking and hysterical patriotism."[136] The war had ended "the artificial glow of past American idealism," wrote the novelist Ellen Glasgow.[137]

World War I stacked the cards for the future by bequeathing "time bombs" of political instability.[138] "Empires cannot be shattered and new states raised upon their ruins without disturbance," noted Colonel House.[139] The Europe-oriented international order of the turn of the century fragmented and left, in Thomas Masaryk's words, "a laboratory atop a vast cemetery" that included several new states in central and eastern Europe.[140] In what the historian Erez Manela has called the "Wilsonian Moment," anticolonial nationalists in Egypt, India, Korea, Indochina, and elsewhere capitalized on Wilson's rhetoric of self-determination to set goals of "full-fledged" autonomous nationhood based in part on Wilson's ideal of self-determination.[141] "Wilson's proposals, once set forth, could not be recalled," said Sun Zhongshan (Sun Yat-Sen) in 1924 as his China battled imperialist domination.[142] In Latin America, prewar economic ties with Europe withered, inviting the United States to expand its interests there, even though nationalists resented the greater North American presence. The rise of Bolshevism in Russia and the hostility it aroused around the world made an already fluid international system even more so. Because of fear of a revived Germany, European leaders tried to strip it of power, creating bitter resentments among the German people. Facing reconstruction problems at home, the victors tagged Germany with a huge reparations bill that would disorient the world economy. Nobody seemed happy with the postwar settlement; many would attempt to recapture lost opportunities or to redefine the terms. Yet to blame World War II on Wilson's failures, as the historian Margaret MacMillan has noted, "is to ignore the actions of everyone—political leaders, diplomats, soldiers, ordinary voters—for twenty years between 1919 and 1939."[143]

World War I made the United States the world's leading economic power. Wilson confidently predicted: "The financial leadership will be ours. The industrial primacy will be ours. The commercial advantage will be ours."[144] During the war years, to meet the need for raw materials, American companies expanded operations in developing nations. Goodyear went into the Dutch East Indies for rubber, Swift and Armour reached into South America, tin interests tapped Bolivia, copper companies penetrated Chile, and oil firms sank new wells in Latin America and gained new concessions in the Middle East. Washington encouraged this economic expansion by building up the merchant marine, which by 1919 had grown 60 percent larger than its prewar size. By 1920 the United States produced about 40 percent of the world's coal and 50 percent of its pig iron.

Because the U.S. government and American citizens loaned heavily to the Allies during the war, the nation shifted from a debtor to a creditor, with New York replacing London as the world's financial center. Whereas before the war Americans owed foreigners some $3 billion, after the conflict foreigners owed Americans and the U.S. government about $13 billion ($10 billion of which represented other governments' debts). Americans had devised plans to seize the apparent economic opportunities given them by the war—the Edge Act to permit the establishment of foreign branch banks, and the Webb–Pomerene Act to allow trade associations to continue to combine for export trading without fear of antitrust action, for example—but a key question remained: How could Europeans liquidate their enormous indebtedness to the United States? The answer lay somewhere in a complicated tangle of loans, reparations, tariffs, and world trade.

Economic disorder and political instability thus became the twin legacies of global war. "The world is all now one single whispering gallery," Wilson asserted in September 1919. "All the impulses ... reach to the ends of the earth; ... with the tongue of the wireless and the tongue of the telegraph, all the suggestions of disorder are spread." More than most Americans, Woodrow Wilson understood that global interdependence exposed America to "disorder and discontent and dissolution throughout the world."[145] And, he admitted with supreme regret, "democracy has not yet made the world safe against irrational revolution."[146]

FURTHER READING FOR THE PERIOD 1914–1920

Many of the works listed in the last chapter also explore the themes, events, and personalities in the era of World War I. See also Anthony Boyle, *Foundations of World Order* (1999); John W. Chambers, *The Tyranny of Change* (1992); Alan Dawley, *Changing the World* (2003); Robert E. Hannigan, *The New World Power* (2002); Ellis W. Hawley, *The Great War and the Search for a Modern Order* (1992); Clayton D. James and Anne Sharp Wells, *America and the Great War* (1998); Bernadotte E. Schmitt and Harold C. Vedeler, *The World in the Crucible, 1914–1919* (1984); Tony Smith, *America's Mission* (1994); David Stevenson, *Cataclysm* (2004); and Spencer C. Tucker, *The Great War* (1998).

For Woodrow Wilson and his foreign-policy views, consult Lloyd E. Ambrosius, *Wilsonianism* (2002); Louis Auchincloss, *Woodrow Wilson* (2000); H. W. Brands, *Woodrow Wilson* (2003); Kendrick A. Clements, *The Presidency of Woodrow Wilson* (1990) and *Woodrow Wilson* (1987); John Milton Cooper, Jr., *The Warrior and the Priest* (1983); Ross Kennedy, *The Will to Believe* (2008); Thomas J. Knock, *To End All Wars* (1992); Phyllis Lee Levin, *Edith and Woodrow* (2001); Arthur S. Link, *Wilson* (1960–1965) and *Woodrow Wilson* (1979); Barksdale Maynard, *Woodrow Wilson* (2008); Frank Ninkovich, *The Wilsonian Century* (1999); Jan Willem Schulte Nordholt, *Woodrow Wilson* (1991); and John A. Thompson, *Woodrow Wilson* (2001).

Wilson's health problems and their relationship to decision making are examined in Robert H. Ferrell, *Ill-Advised* (1992), and Edwin A. Weinstein, *Woodrow Wilson: A Medical and Psychological Biography* (1981). See also the essays by Dr. Bert E. Park in volumes of Arthur S. Link et al., eds., *The Papers of Woodrow Wilson,* and Park's *Ailing, Aging, and Addicted* (1993) and *The Impact of Illness on World Leaders* (1986).

Central actors in the period's drama are presented in LeRoy Ashby, *William Jennings Bryan* (1987); Kendrick A. Clements, *William Jennings Bryan* (1982); Paolo Coletta, *William Jennings Bryan* (1956–1969); John Milton Cooper, Jr., *Walter Hines Page* (1977); Ross Gregory, *Walter Hines Page* (1970); Geoffrey Hodgson, *Woodrow Wilson's Right Hand* (2006) (Edward House); Jim Lacey, *Pershing* (2008); Gerald Leinwand, *William Jennings Bryan* (2007); George H. Nash, *The Life of Herbert Hoover* (1996); Ronald Steel, *Walter Lippmann and the American Century* (1981); David P. Thelen, *Robert M. La Follette and the Insurgent Spirit* (1976); and William C. Widenor, *Henry Cabot Lodge and the Search for an American Foreign Policy* (1980).

For European questions and the neutrality issue on the U.S. road to World War I, see Thomas A. Bailey and Paul B. Ryan, *The Lusitania Disaster* (1975); Henry Blumenthal, *Illusion and Reality in Franco-American Diplomacy, 1914–1945* (1986); John W. Coogan, *The End of Neutrality* (1981); David M. Esposito, *The Legacy of Woodrow Wilson* (1996); Robert H. Ferrell, *Woodrow Wilson and World War I* (1985); Richard M. Gamble, *The War for Righteousness* (2003); Ross Gregory, *The Origins of American Intervention in the First World War* (1971); Ernest R. May, *The World War and American Isolation, 1914–1917* (1959); Diana Preston, *Lusitania* (2002); David Ramsey, *Lusitania* (2002); Hew Strachan, *The First World War* (2003); and Robert W. Tucker, *Woodrow Wilson and the Great War* (2007).

The German-American relationship is spotlighted in Reinhard R. Doerries, *Imperial Challenge* (1989); Manfred Jonas, *The United States and Germany* (1984); Hans-Jürgen Schröder, ed., *Confrontation and Cooperation* (1993); and Barbara Tuchman, *The Zimmermann Telegram* (1958).

The Anglo-American relationship is featured in Kathleen Burk, *Britain, America, and the Sinews of War, 1914–1918* (1985); G. R. Conyne, *Woodrow Wilson: British Perspectives, 1912–21* (1992); and Joyce G. Williams, *Colonel House and Sir Edward Grey* (1984).

For the peace movement, see works cited in the previous chapter and Charles DeBenedetti, ed., *Peace Heroes in Twentieth-Century America* (1986); Allen F. Davis, *American Heroine* (1974) (Addams); Frances H. Early, *A World Without War* (1997); Barbara S. Kraft, *The Peace Ship* (1978); Kathleen Kennedy, *Subversive Mothers and Scurrilous Citizens* (1999); Erika A. Kuhlman, *Petticoats and White Feathers* (1997); Ernest A. McKay, *Against Wilson and War* (1996); David S. Patterson, *The Search for a Negotiated Peace* (2008); and Allison L. Sneider, *Suffragettes in an Imperial Age* (2008).

America's preparedness and warmaking experiences are discussed in Robert B. Bruce, *A Fraternity of Arms: America & France in the Great War* (2003); John W. Chambers, *To Raise an Army* (1987); J. Garry Clifford, *The Citizen Soldiers* (1972); Wesley K. Clark, *Pershing* (2008); Edward M. Coffman, *The War to End All Wars* (1968); Byron Farrell, *Over There* (1999); Robert H. Ferrell, *America's Deadliest Battle* (2007); Kenneth J. Hagan, *This People's Navy* (2008); Jennifer D. Keene, *The Doughboys, the Great War, and the Remaking of America* (2002); Thomas C. Leonard, *Above the Battle* (1978); Bullitt Lowry, *Armistice, 1918* (1997); William N. Still, *The Crisis at Sea* (2007); David F. Trask, *The AEF and Coalition Warmaking* (1993), *Captains & Cabinets: Anglo-American Naval Relations, 1917–1918* (1980), and *The United States in the Supreme War Council* (1961); Jonathan Reed Winkler, *Nexus* (2008) (strategic communications); David R. Woodward, *Trial by Friendship: Anglo-American Relations, 1917–1918* (1993); Susan Zeiger, *In Uncle Sam's Service* (1999) (women); and Robert H. Zieger, *America's Great War* (2001).

For the wartime home front, civil-liberties issues, and propaganda, see Allan M. Brandt, *No Magic Bullet* (1985) (venereal disease); Alfred W. Crosby, *America's Forgotten Pandemic* (1989); Leslie Midkiff DeBauche, *Reel Patriotism* (1997); Mark Ellis, *Race, War, and Surveillance* (2002); David M. Kennedy, *Over Here* (1980); Elizabeth McKillen, *Chicago Labor and the Quest for a Democratic Diplomacy* (1995); Joseph A. McCartin, *Labor's Great War* (1998); Paul L. Murphy, *World War I and the Origin of Civil Liberties* (1979); Richard Polenberg, *Fighting Faiths* (1987); Ronald Schaffer, *America in the Great War* (1991); John A. Thompson, *Reformers and War* (1986); and Stephen Vaughn, *Hold Fast the Inner Lines* (1980) (Committee on Public Information).

The Versailles peacemaking and League debate are discussed in Lloyd E. Ambrosius, *Wilsonian Statecraft* (1991) and *Woodrow Wilson and the American Diplomatic Tradition* (1987); Manfred F. Boeneke et al., eds., *The Treaty of Versailles* (1998); John M. Cooper, Jr., *Breaking the Heart of the World* (2002); Inga Floto, *Colonel House in Paris* (1973); Lawrence E. Gelfand, *The Inquiry* (1963); Derek Heater, *National Self-Determination* (1994); Warren F. Kuehl, *Seeking World Order* (1969); Warren F. Kuehl and Lynne K. Dunne, *Keeping the Covenant* (1997); Antony Lentin, *Lloyd George, Woodrow Wilson, and the Guilt of Germany* (1985); Margaret MacMillan, *Paris 1919* (2002); Erez Manela, *The Wilsonian Moment* (2007); Herbert F. Margulies, *The Mild Reservationists* (1989); Daniela Rossini, *Woodrow Wilson and the American Myth in Italy* (2007); Klaus Schwabe, *Woodrow Wilson, Revolutionary Germany, and Peacemaking* (1985); Alan Sharp, *The Versailles Settlement* (1991); Ralph A. Stone, *The Irreconcilables* (1970); Marc Trachenberg, *Reparations in World Politics* (1986); and Arthur Walworth, *America's Moment, 1918* (1977) and *Wilson and His Peacemakers* (1986).

The U.S. response to Bolshevism, intervention in Russia, and the Red Scare are investigated in Kenneth D. Acherman, *Young J. Edgar* (2007); Leo Bacino, *Reconstructing Russia* (1999); Donald E. Davis and Eugene P. Trani, *The First Cold War* (2000); Victor M. Fic, *The Collapse of American Policy in Russia and Siberia, 1918* (1995); David S. Foglesong, *America's Secret War Against Bolshevism* (1995); Lloyd Gardner, *Safe for Democracy* (1984); George F. Kennan, *Russia Leaves the War* (1956) and *The Decision to Intervene* (1958); Linda Killen, *The Russian Bureau* (1983); N. Gordon Levin, Jr., *Woodrow Wilson and World Politics* (1968); Arthur S. Link, ed., *Woodrow Wilson and a Revolutionary World, 1913–1921* (1982); Arno Mayer, *Politics and Diplomacy of Peacemaking* (1967); David W. McFadden, *Alternative Paths* (1993); William Pencak, *For God and Country* (1989) (American Legion); Benjamin D. Rhodes, *The Anglo-American Winter War with Russia, 1918–1919* (1988); Neil V. Salzman, *Reform and Revolution* (1991) (Robins); Norman Saul, *War and Revolution* (2001); Ilya Somin, *Stillborn Crusade* (1996); John Thompson, *Russia, Bolshevism, and the Versailles Peace* (1966); and Betty Miller Unterberger, *America's Siberian Expedition* (1956) and *The United States, Revolutionary Russia, and the Rise of Czechoslovakia* (1989).

U.S. economic expansion abroad during the war is studied in Burton I. Kaufman, *Efficiency and Expansion* (1974); Emily S. Rosenberg, *World War I and the Growth of United States Predominance in Latin America* (1987); and Jeffrey J. Safford, *Wilsonian Maritime Diplomacy, 1913–1921* (1978).

Also see the General Bibliography, the following notes, and Robert L. Beisner, ed., *Guide to American Foreign Relations Since 1600* (2003).

NOTES TO CHAPTER 3

1. Quoted in Thomas Bailey and Paul Ryan, *The* Lusitania *Disaster* (New York: Free Press, 1975), p. 81.
2. Quoted in Edward Ellis, *Echoes of Distant Thunder* (New York: Coward, McCann & Geoghegan, 1975), p. 195.
3. Quoted in Bailey and Ryan, Lusitania *Disaster*, p. 94.
4. Quoted *ibid.*, p. 82.
5. Quoted *ibid.*, p. 133.
6. Quoted in C. L. Droste and W. H. Tantum, eds., *The* Lusitania *Case* (Riverside, Conn.: 7 C's Press, 1972), p. 172.
7. Quoted in Burton J. Hendrick, *Life and Letters of Walter Hines Page* (Garden City, N.Y.: Doubleday, Page, 1922–1925; 3 vols.), *II*, 2.
8. William Jennings Bryan and Mary B. Bryan, *Memoirs* (Chicago: Winston, 1925), pp. 398–399.
9. Quoted in William Harbaugh, *The Life and Times of Theodore Roosevelt* (New York: Oxford University Press, 1975), p. 448.
10. John Milton Cooper, Jr., *The Warrior and the Priest* (Cambridge: Harvard University Press, 1983), p. 288.
11. R. S. Baker and W. E. Dodd, eds., *Public Papers of Woodrow Wilson* (New York: Harper & Brothers, 1926; 2 vols.), *I*, 321.
12. Quoted in August Hecksher, *Woodrow Wilson* (New York: Charles Scribner's Sons, 1991), p. 365.
13. *Foreign Relations, 1915, Supplement* (Washington, D.C.: Government Printing Office, 1928), p. 396.
14. Quoted in Richard R. Doerries, *Imperial Challenge* (Chapel Hill: University of North Carolina Press, 1989), p. 105.
15. Robert W. Tucker, *Woodrow Wilson and the Great War* (Charlottesville: University of Virginia Press, 2007), p. 110.
16. Quoted in LeRoy Ashby, *William Jennings Bryan* (Boston: Twayne, 1987), p. 161.
17. Quoted in Doerries, *Imperial Challenge*, p. 111.
18. Bailey and Ryan, Lusitania *Disaster*, p. 340.
19. Robert Lansing, *War Memoirs* (Indianapolis: Bobbs-Merrill, 1935), p. 128.
20. Ray S. Baker quoted in Arthur S. Link et al., eds., *The Papers of Woodrow Wilson* (Princeton: Princeton University Press, 1989), *LXI*, 383.
21. Quoted in Rohan Butler, "The Peace Settlement of Versailles, 1918–1933," in C. L. Mowat, ed., *The New Cambridge Modern History*, vol. *XII* (Cambridge, Eng.: Cambridge University Press, 1968), p. 214.
22. Quoted in Zara Steiner, *The Lights That Failed: European International History, 1919-1933* (New York: Oxford University Press, 2005), p. 35.
23. Lansing quoted in Margaret MacMillan, *Paris 1919* (New York: Random House, 2002), p. 10.
24. Quoted in C. D. Lewis, ed., *The Collected Poems of Wilfred Owen* (New York: New Directions, 1965), p. 42.
25. Quoted in Robert E. Hannigan, *The New World Power* (Philadelphia: University of Pennsylvania Press, 2002), p. 228.
26. Baker and Dodd, *Public Papers, I*, 157–159.
27. Wilson quoted in Michael H. Hunt, *The American Ascendancy* (Chapel Hill: University of North Carolina Press, 2007), p. 59.
28. Quoted in Alexander DeConde, *Ethnicity, Race, and American Foreign Policy* (Boston: Northeastern University Press, 1992), p. 86.
29. Quoted in Alan Kramer, *Dynamic of Destruction* (New York: Oxford University Press, 2007), p. 46.
30. Quoted in Barbara Tuchman, *The Guns of August* (New York: Dell [1962], 1963), p. 153.
31. *Life* quoted in Mark Sullivan, *Our Times* (New York: Charles Scribner's Sons, 1926–1937; 6 vols.), *V*, 59.
32. Quoted in Ray Stannard Baker, *Woodrow Wilson* (New York: Doubleday, Doran, 1927–1939; 8 vols.), *V*, 175.
33. Quoted in Elisabeth Glaser, "J. P. Morgan & Company and Aid for the Allies, 1914–1916," in Elisabeth Glaser and Hermann Wellenreuther, eds., *Bridging the Atlantic* (New York: Cambridge University Press, 2002), p. 230.
34. Quoted in Ross A. Kennedy, "Woodrow Wilson, World War I, and an American Conception of National Security," *Diplomatic History, XXV* (Winter 2001), 23.
35. Frederick Dixon quoting Wilson in G. R. Conyne, *Woodrow Wilson* (New York: St. Martin's, 1992), p. 51.
36. Quoted in Frederick S. Calhoun, *Uses of Force and Wilsonian Foreign Policy* (Kent, Ohio: Kent State University Press, 1993), p. 100.
37. Quoted in Arthur S. Link, *Woodrow Wilson and the Progressive Era, 1910–1917* (New York: Harper and Row, 1954), p. 203.
38. French report quoted in Joyce G. Williams, *Colonel House and Sir Edward Grey* (Lanham, Md.: University Press of America, 1984), p. 83.
39. Quoted in Arthur S. Link, *Wilson: Confusions and Crises, 1915–1916* (Princeton: Princeton University Press, 1964), pp. 134–135.
40. Bryan and Bryan, *Memoirs*, p. 397.
41. *Foreign Relations, 1915, Supplement*, p. 461.
42. Link, *Papers of Wilson, XXXVI* (1981), 213–214.
43. Samuel Flagg Bemis, "A Worcester County Student in Wartime London and Paris (via Harvard): 1915–1916," *New England Galaxy, XI* (Spring 1970), 20.
44. Quoted in Patrick Devlin, *Too Proud to Fight* (New York: Oxford University Press, 1975), p. 517.
45. Quoted in Frank Ninkovich, *Modernity and Power* (Chicago: University of Chicago Press, 1994), p. 50.
46. Quoted in Arthur S. Link, *Wilson: Campaigns for Progressivism and Peace, 1916–1917* (Princeton: Princeton University Press, 1965), p. 274.
47. Quoted *ibid.*, p. 289.
48. Lansing, *War Memoirs*, p. 212.
49. Quoted in Fred Anderson and Andrew Cayton, *The Dominion of War* (New York: Viking, 2005), p. 347.
50. Quoted in Manfred F. Boeneke, "Woodrow Wilson's Image of Germany," in Manfred F. Boeneke, Gerald D. Feldman, and Elisabeth Glaser, eds., *The Treaty of Versailles* (New York: Cambridge University Press, 1998), p. 610.
51. Quoted in Thomas W. Ryley, *A Little Group of Willful Men* (Port Washington, N.Y.: Kennikat Press, 1975), p. 2.
52. Link, *Papers of Wilson, XLI* (1983), 519–527.
53. Quoted in Alan Dawley, *Changing the World* (Princeton: Princeton University Press, 2003), pp. 145–146.
54. Quoted in Robert E. Osgood, *Ideals and Self-Interest in American Foreign Relations* (Chicago: University of Chicago Press, 1953), p. 177.
55. Quoted in Michael S. Sherry, *In the Shadow of War* (New Haven: Yale University Press, 1995), p. 8.
56. Susan Zeiger, "She Didn't Raise Her Boy to Be a Slacker," *Feminist Studies, XXII* (Spring 1996), 11–12.

57. Bradley Fiske quoted in Kenneth J. Hagan, ed., *In Peace and War* (3d. ed., Westport, Conn.: Praeger, 2008), p. 146.

58. Quoted in Kennedy, "Conception of National Security," p. 4.

59. Quoted in Kenneth J. Hagan, *The People's Navy* (New York: Free Press, 1991), p. 252.

60. Quoted in Dawley, *Changing the World*, p. 94.

61. Quoted in Barbara S. Kraft, *The Peace Ship* (New York: Macmillan, 1978), p. 1.

62. Quoted in Thomas J. Knock, *To End All Wars* (New York: Oxford University Press, 1992), p. 63.

63. Jane Addams, *Peace and Bread in Time of War* (New York: King's Crown Press, 1945), p. 58.

64. Erika Kuhlman, *Petticoats and White Feathers* (Westport, Conn.: Greenwood, 1997), p. 56.

65. Quoted in J. Garry Clifford, *The Citizen Soldiers* (Lexington: University Press of Kentucky, 1972), p. 123.

66. Quoted in Clifford Putney, *Muscular Christianity* (Cambridge: Harvard University Press, 2001), p. 172.

67. General Tasker Bliss quoted in Calhoun, *Uses of Force*, p. 114.

68. Quoted in David Traxel, *Crusader Nation* (New York: Knopf, 2006), p. 296.

69. Colonel Charles Stanton quoted in Robert B. Bruce, *A Fraternity of Arms* (Lawrence: University Press of Kansas, 2003), p. 94.

70. James A. Marone, *Hellfire Nation* (New Haven: Yale University Press, 2003), p. 313.

71. Richard T. Arndt, *The First Resort of Kings* (Washington: Potomac Books, 2006), p. 25.

72. Quoted in Allen F. Davis, "Welfare, Reform, and World War I," *American Quarterly, XIX* (Fall 1967), 531.

73. Quoted in Ninkovich, *Modernity and Power*, p. 52.

74. Link, *Papers of Wilson, XLVII* (1984), 270.

75. Robert H. Ferrell, *America's Deadliest Battle* (Lawrence: University Press of Kansas, 2007), p. xi.

76. Quoted in Donald Smythe, *Pershing* (Bloomington: Indiana University Press, 1986), p. 237.

77. Link, *Papers of Wilson, XLV* (1984), 529.

78. Quoted in Selig Adler, *The Isolationist Impulse* (New York: Collier Books, [1957], 1961), pp. 60–61.

79. H. G. Nicholas essay in *Wilson's Diplomacy* (Cambridge: Schenkman, 1973), p. 81.

80. Quoted in James D. Startt, "American Propaganda in Britain During World War I," *Prologue, XXVIII* (Spring 1996), 20.

81. Knock, *To End All Wars*, p. 180.

82. Quoted in Inbal Rose, *Conservatism and Foreign Policy During the Lloyd George Coalition 1918–1922* (London: Frank Cass, 1999), p. 121.

83. Quoted in William C. Widenor, "The Structure of the American Interpretation: The Pro-Treaty Version," in Boeneke, *Treaty of Versailles*, p. 550.

84. Quoted in David W. McFadden, *Alternative Paths* (New York: Oxford University Press, 1993), p. 209.

85. Quoted in Herbert Hoover, *The Ordeal of Woodrow Wilson* (New York: McGraw-Hill, 1958), p. 254.

86. Quoted in Walter A. McDougall, *Promised Land, Crusader State* (Boston: Houghton Mifflin, 1997), p. 139.

87. Quoted in Neil Smith, *American Empire* (Berkeley: University of California Press, 2003), p. 169.

88. Quoted in Michael B. Oren, *Power, Faith, and Fantasy* (New York: Norton, 2007), pp. 365, 382.

89. Quoted in John Milton Cooper, Jr., *Breaking the Heart of the World* (New York: Cambridge University Press, 2001), p. 85; quoted in Noriko Kawamura, *Turbulence in the Pacific* (Westport, Conn.: Praeger, 2000), p. 148.

90. Quoted in Erez Manela, "Imagining Woodrow Wilson in Asia: Dreams of East-West Harmony and the Revolt against Empire in 1919," *American Historical Review, CXI* (December 2006), 1349.

91. Quoted in Mark Philip Bradley, *Imagining Vietnam and America* (Chapel Hill: University of North Carolina Press, 2000), p. 10.

92. Quoted in Lawrence E. Gelfand, "Where Ideals Confront Self-Interest," *Diplomatic History, XVIII* (Winter 1994), 133.

93. Billy Hughes quoted in David Reynolds, *Britannia Overruled* (New York: Longman, 2000), p. 110.

94. U.S. Congress, Senate, *Treaties,* Senate Doc. 348 (Washington, D.C.: Government Printing Office, 1923), pp. 3336–3345.

95. Link, *Papers of Wilson, LV* (1985), 177.

96. Antony Lentin, *Lloyd George, Woodrow Wilson, and the Guilt of Germany* (Baton Rouge: Louisiana State University Press, 1984), p. 132.

97. Wilson quoted in Cooper, *Breaking the Heart*, p. 62.

98. Quoted in D. F. Fleming, *The United States and the League of Nations, 1918–1920* (New York: Russell & Russell, 1968), p. 134.

99. Quoted in Beth McKillen, "The Corporatist Model, World War I, and the Debate over the League of Nations," *Diplomatic History, XV* (Spring 1991), 174.

100. Link, *Papers of Wilson, LXI* (1989), 436.

101. Quoted in Louis Auchincloss, *Woodrow Wilson* (New York: Viking, 2000), p. 112.

102. Quoted in Michael Lind, *The American Way of Strategy* (New York: Oxford University Press, 2006), p. 97.

103. Quoted in Kennedy, "Conception of National Security," p. 30.

104. Robert David Johnson, *The Peace Progressives and American Foreign Relations* (Cambridge: Harvard University Press, 1995), p. 102.

105. Quoted in William C. Widenor, "The United States and the Versailles Peace Settlement," in John M. Carroll and George C. Herring, Jr., eds., *Modern American Diplomacy* (Wilmington, Del.: Scholarly Resources, 1986), p. 49.

106. Quoted in Lloyd E. Ambrosius, *Woodrow Wilson and the American Diplomatic Tradition* (New York: Cambridge University Press, 1987), p. 139.

107. Quoted in Osgood, *Ideals and Self-Interest*, p. 286.

108. Johnson, *Peace Progressives*, p. 96.

109. Wilson quoted in Frank Ninkovich, *The Wilsonian Century* (Chicago: University of Chicago Press, 1999), p. 74.

110. Quoted in David Mayers, *Dissenting Voices in America's Rise to Power* (New York: Cambridge University Press, 2007), p. 247.

111. Link, *Papers of Wilson, LXIII* (1990), 35.

112. Quoted in Lloyd E. Ambrosius, "Woodrow Wilson, Alliances, and the League of Nations," *Journal of the Gilded Age and Progressive Era, V* (April 2006), 9.

113. Quoted in Stephen C. Schlesinger, *Act of Creation* (Boulder, Col: Westview Press, 2003), p. 25.

114. Quoted in Auchincloss, *Wilson*, p. 118.

115. Walter Lippmann quoted in Walter LaFeber, "Age of American Unilateralism," in R. Laurence Moore and Maurizio Vaudagna, eds., *The American Century in Europe* (Ithaca: Cornell University Press, 2003), p. 34.

116. Goto Shimpei quoted in Sadao Asada, "Between the Old Diplomacy and the New, 1918-1922," *Diplomatic History, XXX* (April 2006), 213.

117. Quoted in John M. Thompson, *Russia, Bolshevism, and the Versailles Peace* (Princeton: Princeton University Press, 1966), pp. 3–4.

118. Quoted in David S. Foglesong, *America's Secret War Against Bolshevism* (Chapel Hill: University of North Carolina Press, 1995), p. 25.
119. Quoted in McFadden, *Alternative Paths,* p. 247.
120. Winston Churchill quoting Wilson in Lloyd C. Gardner, *Safe for Democracy* (New York: Oxford University Press, 1984), p. 239.
121. Quoted in Foglesong, *Secret War,* p. 43.
122. *Ibid.,* p. 77.
123. Quoted in Alexander DeConde, *Presidential Machismo* (Boston: Northeastern University Press, 2000), p. 106.
124. Quoted in Leo J. Bacino, *Reconstructing Russia* (Kent, Ohio: Kent State University Press, 1999), p. 76.
125. Betty Miller Unterberger, "Woodrow Wilson and the Russian Revolution," in Arthur S. Link, ed., *Woodrow Wilson and a Revolutionary World, 1913–1921* (Chapel Hill: University of North Carolina Press, 1982), p. 70.
126. Foglesong, *Secret War,* p. 190.
127. Verne Bright quoted in Norman Saul, *War and Revolution* (Lawrence: University Press of Kansas, 2001), p. 329.
128. Quoted in David S. Foglesong, *The American Mission and the "Evil Empire"* (New York: Cambridge University Press, 2007), p. 51.
129. Quoted in McFadden, *Alternative Paths,* p. 154.
130. Quoted in Benjamin D. Rhodes, *The Anglo-American War with Russia, 1918–1919* (Westport, Conn.: Greenwood, 1988), p. 123.
131. Foglesong, *Secret War,* p. 296.
132. Quoted *ibid.,* p. 291.

133. Arthur S. Link, *The Higher Realism of Woodrow Wilson* (Nashville: Vanderbilt University Press, 1971), p. 83.
134. Quoted in Gordon A. Craig, "The Revolution in War and Diplomacy," in Jack J. Roth, ed., *World War I* (New York: Knopf, 1967), p. 12.
135. Quoted in Robert H. Ferrell, *Woodrow Wilson and World War I* (New York: Harper and Row, 1985), p. 180.
136. Ozora Davis quoted in Putney, *Muscular Christianity,* p. 192.
137. Quoted in Lloyd E. Ambrosius, *Wilsonianism* (New York: Palgrave, 2002), p. 6.
138. David Stevenson, *Cataclysm* (New York: 2004), p. 477.
139. Quoted in Patrick O. Cohrs, *The Unfinished Peace after World War I* (New York: Cambridge University Press, 2006), p. 24.
140. Quoted in Tony Smith, *America's Mission* (Princeton: Princeton University Press, 1994), p. 102.
141. Erez Manela, *The Wilsonian Moment: Self-Determination and the Origins of Anticolonial Nationalism* (New York: Oxford University Press, 2007), p. 224.
142. Quoted in Hans Schmidt, "Democracy in China," *Diplomatic History,* XXII (Winter 1998), 28.
143. MacMillan, *Paris 1919,* p. 493.
144. Link, *Papers of Wilson,* LXII (1990), 47.
145. Quoted in Foglesong, *Secret War,* p. 1.
146. Quoted in Donald E. Davis and Eugene P. Trani, *The First Cold War* (Columbia: University of Missouri Press, 2002), p. 201.

CHAPTER 4

Descending into Europe's Maelstrom, 1920–1939

A-20 Boston Attack Bomber.   Nearly fifty feet long, the mid-wing, twin-engine medium bomber was the most produced attack bomber built during World War II, with more than 7,000 constructed in the United States. President Franklin D. Roosevelt hoped to expedite rearmament in 1938 by secretly selling hundreds of these planes to the French. Some 162 of the aircraft en route to France in 1940 were diverted to the British Royal Air Force. More than half of the Boston Bombers went into the service of other countries, especially the Soviet Union. The plane earned a reputation for returning its crews home safely. (U.S. Air Force Museum Photo Archives)

DIPLOMATIC CROSSROAD

❖   *Roosevelt Extends America's Frontier to the Rhine, 1939*

DAUBED WITH RED, white, and blue U.S. Army Air Corps paint, the new A-20 ("Boston") twin-engine light bomber performed high-speed acrobatics over Los Angeles's municipal airport on January 23, 1939. The sleek craft climbed to 3,000 feet at more than 300 miles per hour. Test pilot John Cable then apparently cut one motor attempting a climb on half power. Suddenly the plane went into a spin and hurtled toward the ground. Cable bailed out at 400 feet but died on impact.

Onlookers extricated a civilian-clad survivor from the crashed bomber before it burst into flames. Reporters soon learned that the man with the broken leg belonged to a secret French purchasing mission sent to buy American-made warplanes for the French air force. The French were getting ready for World War II, which began in September.

Controversy engulfed Washington. General Henry "Hap" Arnold of the U.S. Army Air Corps happened to be testifying before the Senate Military Affairs Committee. One senator asked how a French officer could be aboard the "secret" bomber that had just crashed. Arnold disingenuously replied that the Frenchman had gone "out there under the direction of the Treasury Department with a view of looking into possible purchase of airplanes by the French Mission."[1] Formal authorization, he added, had come from the War Department, and all secret equipment was removed from the plane before the French saw it.

Senator Gerald P. Nye of North Dakota then summoned Treasury Secretary Henry Morgenthau, Jr., and Secretary of War Harry Woodring for further grilling. Morgenthau acidly pointed out that the army had not yet placed orders for the plane, which remained the sole property of the Douglas Aircraft Company and could hardly be termed "secret" if flown from a municipal airport where anyone could see it. Woodring admitted that the air corps had originally opposed the French mission but that "everyone [was] … in accord before the French went to the West Coast."[2] President Franklin D. Roosevelt muddied matters further by denying to the press that "this Government [had] taken any steps to assist or facilitate France in buying planes in this country." But French plane purchases "would be an excellent idea" to help "in building up" U.S. foreign trade, he mused.[3]

A devotee of poker, the president "wasn't ready publicly to show his hand."[4] In seeking to deter a major war through nonmilitary methods, he had talked publicly in recent years about quarantines against aggressors, held secret naval talks with the British, and toyed with calling a conference in Washington of major world leaders. His invitation to the king and queen of England to visit America in June 1939 seemed a clever "way of dramatizing Anglo-American amity for the benefit of the dictators and the American public."[5] Roosevelt had mentioned "methods short of war" to Congress in early January but gave no details of what would amount to a shift in foreign policy in the months prior to World War II.[6]

Ever since the disastrous Munich Conference of September 1938, when England and France had agreed to German territorial demands against Czechoslovakia, FDR had seized on air power as a possible deterrent against another European war. "Had we ... 5,000 planes and the immediate capacity to produce 10,000 per year," he had speculated, "[Adolf] Hitler would not have dared to take the stand he did."[7] When the French financier-diplomat Jean Monnet visited in October 1938, the president confided that France needed "20–30,000 more" planes per year "to achieve decisive superiority over Germany and Italy; and they'll have to be found here, in the United States."[8] He urged England and France to place orders, thereby stimulating the lagging U.S. aviation industry and jump-starting military rearmament. When War Department officials balked at showing top-secret prototypes to foreign buyers, Roosevelt argued that "the only check to a world war, which would be understood by Germany, would be the creation of a great [French] air force and a powerful force in this country."[9] Only after a direct presidential order did General Arnold permit the French to inspect the Douglas bomber.

FDR also wanted to revise U.S. neutrality laws to permit the sale of arms and munitions to belligerents on a cash-and-carry basis. France and Britain could buy weapons legally in peacetime, but the current law forbade such sales in wartime. The president had secretly promised British prime minister Neville Chamberlain "the industrial resources of the American nation ... in the event of war with the dictatorships."[10] The crash of the airplane with the French officer aboard put Roosevelt's plans in jeopardy and threatened to expose rifts in his administration. The designation of his close friend Morgenthau to oversee all foreign purchases had aroused criticism. The bespectacled Treasury secretary served as an "intellectual rough-neck" who "bulled things through" with little regard for bureaucratic sensitivity. In this instance, the chief obstruction proved to be Secretary of War Woodring, a "fourth-rate" former governor of Kansas, "who not only couldn't see that our frontier was the Rhine, but couldn't see across the Hudson River."[11]

On January 31, 1939, a day after Hitler had told the German Reichstag that "international finance Jewry" was plotting a second "world war" that would result in the "annihilation of the Jewish race in Europe," Roosevelt invited the Senate Military Affairs Committee to the White House.[12] FDR asked for confidentiality so as not "to frighten the American people." During the meeting, he asserted that the growing menace from Germany, Italy, and Japan necessitated fundamental changes in U.S. policies. He denied that "we can draw a line of defense around this country and live completely and solely to ourselves." Americans might hope that "somebody would assassinate Hitler or that Germany will blow up from within." Or they could "try to prevent the domination of the world—prevent it by peaceful means."

Strengthening America's "first line of defense" offered the best approach. In the East, that defense consisted of "a series of islands, with a hope that through the Army and Navy and the airplanes we can keep the Japanese" from dominating the Pacific. In the Atlantic, the line of defense rested on "the continued independence" of countries from Finland to Turkey. If England and France fell, however, the others would "drop into the [German] basket." Colonial Africa would "automatically" capitulate. The president claimed that the Germans could dominate South and Central America through subversion and economic penetration. He warned: "The Germans have 1,500 bombing planes that can go from Germany to Colombia inside of forty-eight hours. We have, I think, about eighty that can go down there."

Franklin D. Roosevelt (1882–1945). Although stricken by polio in the 1920s, Roosevelt remained energetic and optimistic. A talented politician who won four presidential elections, he moved haltingly to shore up Britain and France as they faced an aggressive Germany. Here FDR relaxes with stamp collecting, his favorite hobby. During World War II the president once showed British Prime Minister Winston Churchill a favorite stamp "from one of your colonies." Churchill asked: "Which one?" Roosevelt replied: "One of your last. … You won't have them much longer, you know." (Franklin D. Roosevelt Library)

Roosevelt emphatically defended the sale of aircraft, saying that "it is to our interest … to help the British and French maintain their independence." The American aviation industry also needed foreign orders to expedite mass production and "turn out nine or ten thousand planes per year" without delaying the buildup of U.S. air forces. He vowed to send Britain and France "all they can pay for on the barrelhead. … Now, that is the foreign policy of the United States."

One member of the Senate committee clapped, but the "rest sat stony-faced."[13] When asked if he meant that the United States had the "duty" to "maintain the independence of these nations … by whatever efforts may be necessary," Roosevelt shot back: "No. No! Listen: I probably saw more of the war [World War I] in Europe than any other living person." Describing his three-month tour of the battle zones as assistant secretary of the navy in 1918, "I spent days on the Belgian front, on the British front, on the French front, and on the American front. … Therefore, you may be quite sure that about the last thing this country should do is ever to send an army to Europe again."[14] Senator Nye, listening intently, went back to his office and immediately wrote a nine-page memorandum. "Get the uniforms ready for the boys," he noted. "I saw troops moving even though the Pres[ident] had declared he had no intent to go to war."[15]

The next day word leaked to the press that FDR had proclaimed that "the frontiers of the United States are on the Rhine."[16] The president angrily called the leak "a deliberate lie" that "some boob got off." Accusing isolationists of trying to "make political capital" out of words he never spoke, he specifically singled out Senator Nye as "an unscrupulous person."[17]

Did FDR lie? According to a stenographic transcript of his meeting with the senators, he never said exactly that America's frontier extended to the Rhine, but his assertions about the independence of France and England was "so closely akin to it" that "it is difficult to distinguish the difference," as one senator noted.[18] Several times, Morgenthau later recalled, the president did say privately: "Our frontier is on the Rhine."[19] A deft "juggler" who always kept options open, FDR wanted above all else to deter a European war while at the same time preparing for possible U.S. participation.[20] He sought "methods short of war" because "sending a large army abroad was ... politically out of the question."[21] Roosevelt persisted in selling aircraft to the French and British, even threatening to exile General Arnold to Guam if he did not "play ball."[22] Although the 555 combat planes eventually delivered to France did not deter war, French orders quadrupled American airplane production and laid the foundation "for the gigantic later expansion of the U.S. aircraft industry."[23]

The bomber episode also caused FDR to abandon any sustained personal effort to educate Congress and guide public opinion about revising American neutrality laws before the outbreak of war in Europe. Only after the German invasion of Poland in September 1939 did the administration succeed in repealing the arms embargo, and even then the president remained conspicuously in the background. The French airplane fiasco reinforced his timidity. "Recall the colorful and untrue reports of over a year ago about our frontier being on the Rhine; ... about the death of a French officer caused by the crash of an airplane in California," he told a prominent publisher in June 1940. "The government ... cannot change its 'editorial' policy overnight. ... Governments, such as ours, cannot swing so far or so quickly."[24] Of course, the French officer had not died, but Roosevelt sometimes exaggerated for effect.

Some six years and two months after FDR made his alleged remarks about America's frontier on the Rhine, U.S. soldiers seized the bridge at Remagen and crossed the Rhine into Germany. Another European war, which American diplomacy and arms sales to France had failed to prevent, definitively extended the defense perimeter of the United States.

"Prize Fighters with a Very Long Reach": The Independent Internationalists

The French airplane incident of 1939 illustrated salient themes of interwar foreign relations. It demonstrated that even on the eve of World War II in Europe, the United States still sought methods short of war to deter potential aggressors in areas vital to the national interest. Because foreign airplane orders also meant "prosperity in this country and we can't elect a Democratic Party unless we get prosperity," as Roosevelt put it, the episode revealed the impact of the Great Depression on foreign trade, domestic politics, and international security.[25] It also showed how an activist president can use subterfuge and surrogates to circumvent bureaucratic rivalries and congressional opposition. The episode underlined the lessons learned from American intervention in World War I and the determination of U.S. leaders to avoid the mistakes attributed to Woodrow Wilson. In view of FDR's claim that America's national security had become tied to the independence of France and England, it also demonstrated that important U.S. leaders recognized global interdependence and rejected an ostrichlike isolationist course during the interwar years.

The United States had emerged from World War I as a recognized world power. Under the Versailles treaty, U.S. military forces even occupied the left bank of the Rhine near Koblenz until early 1923. Postwar U.S. diplomats, closer to a global perspective than ever before, knew that even if they wanted to, Americans could not be bystanders in world affairs. True, between World Wars I and II Americans hoped to avoid foreign entanglements and concentrate on domestic matters. But, within the limits of U.S. power, American leaders pursued an active foreign policy befitting their nation's high international status. They worked to create a community of peaceful nations characterized by legal processes, economic openness, and political stability. Washington emphasized nonmilitary means—treaties, conferences, disarmament, economic and financial agreements, banking reform—in its pursuit of world order based on Open Door principles. A British diplomat likened the United States to a "prize fighter with a very long reach. He stands with his left arm stretched out, and the opponent may dance round and round in the ring and never come to close quarters."[26] America between the wars wanted to isolate itself from war, to scale down foreign military interventions, and to preserve the freedom to make independent decisions in international affairs. "Independent internationalism," rather than "isolationism," best characterizes American practice—active on an international scale, but independent in direction.[27]

Where the United States lacked viable power, such as in Asia, it moved haltingly. Where it possessed abundant power, as in Latin America, it moved vigorously. As for Europe, "economic imperatives, humanitarian instincts, and ideological impulses compelled American officials to take an active interest."[28] Until 1933 the Republican administrations worked to contain but rehabilitate Germany, relieve French strategic anxieties, tame Soviet radicalism, advance disarmament, resolve controversies over war debts and reparations, stabilize European currencies, foster American exports, showcase American culture, and systematize the flow of private American capital abroad. In pursuing peace and prosperity, the U.S. government encouraged private experts in business, finance, labor, and agriculture to cooperate with public officials in a system of "corporatism." By the mid-1930s, with international stability shattered by the Great Depression and Europe torn by conflict, Americans tried to protect themselves from war through neutrality laws. Not until 1939 did policymakers again risk war to achieve a U.S.-friendly international order.

In the 1920s especially, weak presidential leadership, congressional-executive competition, and increased professionalism in the Foreign Service characterized U.S. policymaking. Presidents Warren G. Harding and Calvin Coolidge gave minimal attention to foreign affairs, leaving that field to their secretaries of state. Harding's world was his hometown of Marion, Ohio. Wilson's League of Nations fiasco persuaded Harding to eschew a conspicuous role in foreign policy. On one occasion, when a European correspondent talked with Harding, the president cut him short: "I don't know anything about this European stuff."[29]

Reflecting foreign policy's low priority, Calvin Coolidge managed in his autobiography to avoid mentioning it altogether. The taciturn president once shocked Britain's ambassador by saying he would "never visit Europe" because America had "everything he needed to know."[30] Coolidge's relaxed approach to problems, exemplified by long afternoon naps in the White House and by his fawning worship of American business, created a deceptively passive image. The simple man

Charles Evans Hughes (1862–1948) and Warren G. Harding (1865–1923). The secretary of state (left) and president were quite different in background and intellect, but as conservatives both sought a stable, nonrevolutionary world order. (Ohio Historical Society)

from Vermont, preaching self-reliance, had little patience with Europeans—who, he believed, always looked to the United States to bail them out. "We couldn't help people very much until they showed a disposition to help themselves," he noted in 1926.[31]

A rarity among presidents because of his extensive experience abroad, Herbert Hoover believed that disarmament would promote peace, and the money saved by not purchasing armaments could be used to pay war debts and restore prosperity. His distinguished career included international business (mining), food relief (Belgium and Russia), and diplomacy (reparations adviser at Versailles). As secretary of commerce under Harding and Coolidge, he energetically expanded America's economic presence abroad. True to his Quaker background, he sought nonmilitary, noncoercive solutions to international crises and emphasized cooperative economic relations. Known as the "Great Engineer," Hoover had a telephone installed at his desk in the White House, further enhancing his reputation for administrative efficiency. A plodding speaker with a shy personality, Hoover entered the presidency as the Great Depression struck, wrecking his political career.

Secretaries of state during the 1920s often compensated for presidential shortcomings. Magisterial Charles Evans Hughes was a distinguished jurist (Supreme Court), an experienced politician (unsuccessful Republican candidate for president in 1916), and a confirmed nationalist and expansionist. Under Harding and Coolidge the patient, pragmatic Hughes enjoyed considerable freedom in diplomacy, receiving little presidential instruction. International law and the sanctity of treaties served as his primary guides to world order. Frank B. Kellogg succeeded Hughes. Ingloriously called "Nervous Nellie" because of a trembling hand, the former senator and ambassador to Britain moved cautiously, often consulting a major critic of interventionism,

Makers of American Foreign Relations, 1920–1939

Presidents	Secretaries of State
Woodrow Wilson, 1913–1921	Bainbridge Colby, 1920–1921
Warren G. Harding, 1921–1923	Charles Evans Hughes, 1921–1925
Calvin Coolidge, 1923–1929	Frank B. Kellogg, 1925–1929
Herbert C. Hoover, 1929–1933	Henry L. Stimson, 1929–1933
Franklin D. Roosevelt, 1933–1945	Cordell Hull, 1933–1944

William E. Borah, chair of the Senate Foreign Relations Committee. Because of jurisdictional disputes with Hoover's Commerce Department, one of Kellogg's subordinates complained: "Diplomatic functions today are mainly economic; this places the Department of Commerce in control of the substance of diplomacy, and leaves the State Department with social relationships."[32]

In 1929 President Hoover named as secretary of state mustachioed Henry L. Stimson, one of America's most distinguished public servants. The reserved, punctual, sexist, mannered Stimson lived on his Long Island estate like an English squire. His résumé included Phillips Andover Academy, Yale University, Harvard Law School, and tutelage under the eminent Elihu Root. Before becoming secretary, Stimson headed the War Department under Taft. In 1927 he went as a diplomatic troubleshooter to Nicaragua, and during 1927–1929 he served as governor-general of the Philippines. He had been Colonel Stimson in World War I—and let few forget it. Hoover came to dislike Stimson's combative personality and his eagerness to "march toward the guns."[33]

Franklin D. Roosevelt came to office with some foreign-affairs experience, having served in the Navy Department under Woodrow Wilson. He admired both the big-sticking of his cousin Theodore and the liberal internationalism of Wilson. As a vice-presidential candidate in 1920, Roosevelt had defended the League and the Versailles treaty, but in the 1932 campaign he abandoned the League ("an emasculated constituency") to garner the endorsement of the influential newspaper magnate William Randolph Hearst.[34] "I am not a Wilsonian idealist, I have problems to solve," he once said.[35] Though fully conscious of the war clouds billowing in Europe and Asia, FDR gave priority to his domestic New Deal recovery program.

With his "happy-go-lucky, snap-of-the-moment style," FDR relished personal diplomacy, often taking command of negotiations and more than once failing to tell the Department of State what he was doing.[36] He centralized decision making in the White House; but dangers lurked in his methods because too often he possessed only a superficial understanding of other nations' cultures and histories. Sometimes he misled diplomats with his easy smile; sometimes his agreements lacked precision, depending for their authority on the honor of gentlemen's words; sometimes the formal diplomatic document did not properly capture the "spirit" of a meeting; sometimes U.S. diplomacy moved forward with the dizziness of a confused

Herbert Hoover (1874–1964). The thirty-first president graduated from Stanford University. Cautious and stubborn, Hoover advocated healthy trade relations, military retrenchment, and foreign loans to stimulate industrial growth and prosperity as routes to peace. Conversation with the increasingly morose president, frustrated by his inability to alleviate the Great Depression during his final two years, was "like sitting in a bath of ink," noted Secretary of State Henry L. Stimson. (Library of Congress)

bureaucracy. A consummate politician, Roosevelt compromised frequently and resorted to deception if it served his goals. One historian has called Roosevelt "an intellectual jumping-jack ... hopping helter-skelter in several directions at once"; another scholar has likened him to a college professor who prefers teaching without a syllabus.[37]

Roosevelt chose Tennessean Cordell Hull as his secretary of state. A powerful senator devoted to free trade, the chronically ill sexagenarian (he secretly suffered from diabetes, tuberculosis, and claustrophobia) reluctantly accepted. FDR picked Hull because the appointment would please old Democratic party members, southern conservatives, and unreconstructed Wilsonians. Roosevelt often undercut him, although Hull and the State Department remained dominant in formulating Asian and Latin American policy. Indeed, Roosevelt sent Hull to the World Economic Conference in London in June 1933 without consulting him on the makeup of the delegation, and then embarrassed him by rejecting a currency stabilization plan and effectively ending the conference. Once dubbed "Miss Cordelia Dull" for his "congenital procrastination," the secretary had contemplated resigning earlier that spring when the president delayed sending to Congress Hull's pet project, the reciprocal trade bill.[38] Hull's deliberate methods wearied the president, who preferred quickness and repartee. The secretary resented the president's practice of dispatching personal envoys overseas, of conspicuously excluding Hull from summit conferences, and of relying on friends such as Sumner Welles (after 1937, under secretary of state), Morgenthau, and Ambassador William C. Bullitt, instead of Hull himself. "They all come at me with knives and hatchets," Hull once complained.[39] But he stayed on until 1944, the longest tenure of any secretary of state, forever disliking the pomp of official dinners, always charming his listeners with his hill-country drawl and lisp, and impressing all with his personal dignity, hard work, and deep commitment to eradicating the perceived root of war, international economic constraints.

The Foreign Service over which Hull presided improved during the interwar period. It certainly needed reform. Frequenting the dark corridors and Victorian furnishings of the old State, War, and Navy Building on Pennsylvania Avenue were U.S. diplomats noted for their elite backgrounds (urban, wealthy, eastern, and Ivy League–educated). Invoking a trope that falsely conflated homosexuality with intellect and patrician status, critics derided Foreign Service officers as "cookie pushers" and "striped pants," as purveyors of "pink peppermint and protocol." Despite their limited influence on policy, these professional diplomats believed that "they belonged to a pretty good club" with "a healthy *esprit de corps*."[40] Under the spoils system, faithful politicians still received top diplomatic posts and seldom spoke the language of the country to which they were assigned.

The heavy workload imposed on Foreign Service personnel during World War I had exposed serious shortcomings. The immigration laws of 1921 and 1924, establishing quotas, demanded a more efficient consular staff; the revolution in China required observers who could intelligently interpret that convulsion; and economic expansion depended on sound reporting about market conditions abroad. The Rogers Act of 1924 merged the previously unequal consular and diplomatic corps into the Foreign Service of the United States and provided for examinations, increased salaries, promotion by merit, and overseas living allowances. At about the same time, the State

Secretary of State Cordell Hull (1871–1955) and Under Secretary Sumner Welles (1892–1961). President Franklin D. Roosevelt tried to manage the State Department through unorthodox administrative methods. Even though the courtly Hull (on left) acted as the titular head of the department for nearly twelve years, the president preferred to work through Under Secretary Welles (right), an old friend and fellow Groton and Harvard graduate. Resentful of Welles's power and influence, the secretary finally had his revenge on learning that his subordinate was a homosexual. "For God's sake, get rid of this degenerate," Hull demanded. When the scandal threatened to become public, FDR reluctantly accepted Welles's resignation in August 1943. As a result, Roosevelt relied even less on the State Department for the rest of his presidency. (FDR Library)

Department began training specialists in Soviet affairs, with initiates George F. Kennan and Charles E. Bohlen (both later ambassadors to the Soviet Union) who mastered the language and culture of Russia. Despite persistent cliques, political favoritism, snobbery, sexism, anti-Semitism, and lower salaries and staff cutbacks during the depression, the Foreign Service slowly became more efficient and professional.

Economic and Cultural Expansion in a Rickety World

The Foreign Service facilitated conspicuous American economic expansion abroad after World War I. Measured by statistics, the United States had become the most powerful nation in the world, accounting for 70 percent of the world's petroleum and 40 percent of its coal production. Most impressively, the United States produced 46 percent of total world industrial goods (1925–1929 figures). It also ranked first as an exporter, shipping more than 15 percent of total world exports in 1929, and it replaced Great Britain as the largest foreign investor and financier of world trade. Throughout the decade the United States enjoyed a favorable balance of trade, exporting more than it imported. In the period 1914–1929, the value of exports more than doubled, to $5.4 billion, and American private investments abroad grew from $3.5 billion in 1914 to $17.2 billion by 1930.

As the historian Mira Wilkins has noted, U.S. companies in the 1920s "were (1) going to *more countries,* (2) building *more plants* in a particular foreign country,

(3) manufacturing or mining *more end products* in a particular foreign land, (4) investing in a single alien nation in a *greater degree* of integration, and (5) diversifying on a *worldwide* basis."[41] U.S. Rubber bought its first Malayan plantation; Anaconda moved into Chilean copper mining; General Electric joined international cartels and invested heavily in Germany; Americans controlled 83 percent of the automobile industry in Canada; General Motors purchased Opel, by 1929 the best-selling automobile in Germany; Henry Ford helped build an automobile plant in Soviet Russia; and American firms handled about one-third of oil sales in France. In 1928 the seven largest U.S. oil companies joined leading European firms to form a new cartel, the Iraq Petroleum Company (IPC), and under the subsequent "red line agreement," U.S. firms received 23.75 percent of all petroleum extracted from the Middle East. The arrangement allowed Americans to exploit the black riches without assuming political responsibilities in such turbulent countries as Iraq, which Winston Churchill famously called "an ungrateful volcano."[42]

American material culture—including household appliances, foods, sports, language, music, film, and appreciation for machines—also spread worldwide. "Today we go to America as the Japanese once came to Germany," an industrialist from Weimar Germany wrote after visiting Detroit to observe American mass-production techniques.[43] U.S. government support for the expanding communications industry helped International Telephone and Telegraph (ITT), Radio Corporation of America (RCA), Associated Press (AP), and United Press (UP) become international giants by 1930. American movies so dominated the global market that the "sun … never sets on the British Empire and the American motion picture." Indeed, movies became "silent salesmen of American goods" and so effectively advertised U.S. products and lifestyles abroad that some overseas nationals feared "the tempting image of a mass consumption society."[44] As "the most pervasive and persuasive of American contributions to European culture," Hollywood movies "epitomized American culture in its mass orientation, tempo, monumentalism, sensationalism and profit urge."[45] Thus did street urchins in London adopt American slang: "O.K., kid" and "What are you doing tonight, babe?"[46] In 1929 alone, some 251,000 American tourists visited Europe, where they spent $323 million. F. W. Woolworth had opened 350 stores in England, with nothing priced above a sixpence. For German women "Americanization" produced, among other things, an advertisement from Siemens describing "How the Buschmüllers Got a Vacuum."[47] With the rise of what one historian has called "a great imperium with the outlook of a great emporium," American products from jazz to gym shoes claimed an eager international clientele.[48] Even in the realm of athletics, despite U.S. indifference to the global appeal of soccer, American dominance at the Olympic Games and leadership in boxing, swimming, track, and winter sports helped transform "international sport from an elite cultural pursuit to a mass cultural phenomenon based on commercialism and the new consumer culture."[49]

Through philanthropic programs in preventive medicine and public health the Rockefeller Foundation also introduced America to the world. Under Rockefeller auspices, for example, "Kentucky closets" (outdoor toilets) became ubiquitous in Croatian villages.[50] The foundation also battled yellow fever in Latin America and supported colleges to train doctors in Lebanon and China—all under the philosophy that adoption of culture, economic expansion, and social and political stability went hand in hand.

This expansion did encounter obstacles. Mexican nationalism, confiscation of property in Soviet Russia, European resentments, a wrecked German economy, wartime destruction in Europe, growing tariff walls, and the dislocation of international finance caused by World War I debts and reparations—all hindered enterprising Americans. U.S. government decisions offered welcome but limited help. The Webb-Pomerene Act (1918) permitted American companies to combine for purposes of foreign trade without prosecution under the antitrust laws; the Edge Act of 1919 legalized branch banks abroad; and the Merchant Marine Act of 1920 authorized the federal government to sell vessels to private companies and to make loans for the construction of new ships. New tax laws also permitted foreign tax credits for American investors abroad. The Department of Commerce provided businesses with research data and advice. To help financiers avoid unproductive foreign lending and risky foreign bonds, official Washington tried to oversee loans and bond sales, but the practice never became consistent or thorough. For example, the government discouraged the sale in the United States of the bonds of a Czech brewery because it would violate the "spirit" of prohibition laws, but tolerated an unproductive loan for a sports palace in Germany.

Believing trade essential to domestic prosperity, Washington continued to proclaim the Open Door but applied it selectively. U.S. officials usually invoked the maxim where the United States faced vigorous competition, as in Asia and the Middle East. In Latin America and the Philippines, however, where American capital and trade predominated, something approximating a "closed door" developed. Europeans complained bitterly that the United States followed a double standard.

The Weight of the United States in the World Economy

Relative Value of Industrial Production, 1925–1929

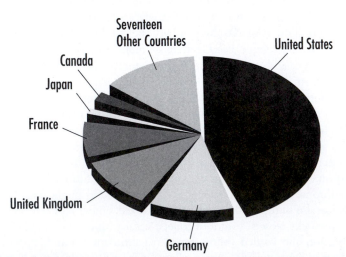

Source: U.S. Department of Commerce, *The United States in the World Economy* (Washington, D.C.: Government Printing Office, 1943), p. 28.

They also resented American tariff policy, which made it difficult to sell to the United States—as they had to do in order to obtain the dollars necessary to buy American goods. The tariff acts of 1922 (Fordney-McCumber) and 1930 (Hawley-Smoot) raised duties to protect domestic producers and invited retaliation against American products. Economists predicted "a tariff war" that would disturb world peace.[51] Some twenty-five nations by 1932 had retaliated against American imports. Secretary of Commerce Hoover held that high tariffs and overseas economic expansion could proceed hand in hand, and until the Great Depression struck in 1929, the two practices did seem harmoniously to coexist.

The depression played havoc with the world economy. Only two countries might have led the world out of depression, but the "British couldn't and the Americans wouldn't."[52] Economic nationalism guided most countries as they tried to protect themselves from the cataclysm with higher tariffs and import quotas. World trade from 1929 to mid-1933 declined 40 percent in value and 25 percent in volume. In 1933 the United States exported goods worth $2.1 billion, down from the 1929 figure of $5.4 billion. American capital stayed at home, and foreign

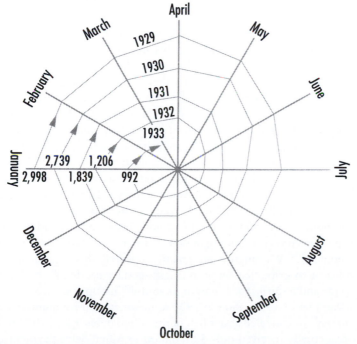

The Contracting Spiral of World Trade

January 1929 to March 1933
Total Imports of 75 Countries in Millions of Dollars

Source: Charles P. Kindleberger, *The World in Depression*, 1929–1939 (Berkeley and Los Angeles: University of California Press,1973), p. 172. Copyright © 1973 by the Regents of the University of California; reprinted by permission of the University of California Press.

holders of American loans defaulted. American private investments abroad slumped to $13.5 billion, down from the $17.2 billion figure of 1930. President Hoover flatly—and wrongly—called it a "patently European crisis."[53] His successor, Franklin D. Roosevelt, confronting 13 million unemployed Americans in 1933, also succumbed to economic nationalism as he created his New Deal recovery program. He abruptly sabotaged the London Economic Conference, indicating that the United States would henceforth "pursue domestic recovery by means of a policy of unilateralism."[54] But Hull gradually persuaded him that lowered tariffs would spur U.S. foreign trade and spark an economic upturn at home. Hull further preached that healthy world trade would contribute to stable politics and peace at a time when Japan, Germany, and Italy were turning to political extremism and threatening aggression, and when Bolshevism seemed poised to exploit European unrest.

In 1934 Hull piloted through Congress the Reciprocal Trade Agreements Act, which empowered the president to reduce tariffs by as much as 50 percent after negotiating agreements with other nations under the doctrine of the most-favored nation. This principle, which had guided American trade since the Model Treaty of 1776, meant that the United States was entitled to the lowest tariffs imposed by a country (in short, the best favor that country granted any other nation) with which the United States had a reciprocal agreement. The reciprocal trade program did slow down the deterioration of world trade, but, as President Roosevelt confessed, "those trade treaties are just too goddamned slow. The world is moving too fast."[55] Hull also created in 1934 the Export-Import Bank, a governmental agency designed to provide loans to expand foreign trade. Yet in 1937, FDR skeptically concluded that "an economic approach to peace is a weak reed."[56]

The reciprocal trade program and the bank came too late to help solve the interwar debts-reparations tangle. Whereas before the war U.S. citizens owed some $3 billion to Europeans, after the war European citizens owed private Americans $3 billion and their governments owed another $10 billion, largely because of wartime loans. America had gone dramatically from a debtor to a creditor nation. But how would Europeans earn dollars to pay such a huge sum? American investments, sale of goods to the United States, U.S. tourist spending, and income from German reparations payments ranked as the most promising sources. But the Germans proved unwilling to meet the indemnity of $33 billion, so in the early 1920s the British began quoting Scripture: "Forgive us our debts," arguing that Americans should write them off as a contribution to the Allied victory.[57] Europeans, then, looked on the war loans as essentially political in character, rather than as business transactions. Anyway, they pointed out, they had suffered huge losses of lives and property, while "thanks to the war, America more than doubled her power and laid the foundation for a new empire."[58] Washington indignantly rejected this argument, prompting one British leader to gripe that "even in its gifts and its goodness" the United States "has an attitude and a spirit that makes one's soul shrink up and shrivel."[59] Congress created the War Debt Commission in 1922 to negotiate full payment, but that body ultimately forgave or canceled about half of the Allied debts. From 1918 to 1931, the United States actually received only $2.6 billion in Allied debts payments.

By stabilizing European finances, restoring trade, and encouraging the flow of private capital to Germany, U.S. diplomats sought to "harness Germany's resources to the cause of European recovery without restoring its prewar hegemony or reinvigorating the economic nationalism and autarky" that could lead to war.[60] The debts-reparations imbroglio eventually undercut this strategy. Wild inflation, a crippled economy, inadequate exports, and anti-Versailles hostility prompted the Germans to default on reparations payments in 1922–1923. France and Belgium aggravated Germany's plight by seizing the rich Ruhr Valley. In 1924 the State Department encouraged the businessman Charles G. Dawes to negotiate the Dawes Plan, whereby American investors such as the J. P. Morgan Company loaned millions to Germany, and Berlin accepted a reparations payment schedule. But the European economy simply could not bear the heavy debts and the reparations. Nor could American capital keep Europe afloat. Under the Young Plan of 1929, another salvaging effort reduced German reparations to $9 billion. That year, too, Hoover informed the British that he would cancel their debt if they transferred Bermuda, British Honduras (Belize), and Trinidad to the United States. London refused. In 1931 he declared a one-year moratorium on debts payments. Thereafter only Finland met its debt obligations.

Debtors defaulted, Germany stopped paying reparations, and the world settled into the devastating depression of the 1930s. "While the United States was hardly the only culpable party," the historian Zara Steiner has written, "the failure of the world's leading creditor to offer any radical solution to the reparations-war-debt imbroglio contributed to its ongoing destructive effects." In both economic and security terms, the United States refused to be "an offshore balancer" to Europe.[61]

Seekers of a World Without War

Despite the international economic turmoil, peace sentiment ran high in the United States between the wars. In 1923, when the publisher Edward Bok sponsored a contest for the best peace plan, he received more than 22,000 entries. Some peace advocates, including the Carnegie Endowment for International Peace, placed their hopes in such global institutions as the World Court and the League of Nations. Educational exchanges, such as Smith College's Junior Year in France, worked to prove that "isolationism is no longer possible even for 'mind your own business' Americans."[62] Pacifists in the Fellowship of Reconciliation, the War Resisters League, and the Women's Peace Union, in contrast, renounced individual participation in war. Religious groups pointed to the un-Christian character of war. Salmon Levinson, a Chicago lawyer who organized the American Committee for the Outlawry of War, argued that "war is an institution in the same sense as the church, the school or the home. It will never cease to be an institution until it becomes illegal."[63] Women gravitated to their own organizations, such as the Committee on the Cause and Cure of War and the Women's International League for Peace and Freedom (WILPF), among others, because they lacked influence in male-dominated groups and because of the popular assumption that women—as life givers and nurturing mothers—had a unique aversion to violence and war. Disarmament and anticolonialism became the goals of many peace-oriented people. Radical pacifists and antiwar advocates agitated for fundamental social and economic change in order to alleviate social injustice, the perceived wellsprings of imperialism and war.

"Come on in. I'll treat you right. I used to know your daddy." C. D. Batchelor's cartoon won a Pulitzer Prize in 1937. As the historian Michael Sherry has noted, the depiction of war as "a diseased whore luring men to their death" revealed the "strikingly—sometimes maliciously—gendered ways in which war was often portrayed in modern American culture." (Library of Congress)

The National Council for the Prevention of War, founded in 1921, acted as an organizational umbrella for the divergent peace groups.

Most peace activists believed that the United States could regenerate habitually war-prone Europe. In the 1920s, such reformist ideas did not seem farfetched: arms seemed controllable (technology had not yet produced global bombers or atomic weapons); domestic economies still did not rely heavily for their prosperity on defense production; the revulsion against World War I remained intense; and few warmongers had yet seized governments. Yet when Dorothy Detzer of WILPF threatened the loss of a million female votes in 1932 if President Hoover did not name Mount Holyoke College president Mary Woolley as a delegate to the Geneva Disarmament Conference, Secretary Stimson grumbled that Woolley "knows nothing about the subject."[64] Notwithstanding Woolley's active participation, and a WILPF-sponsored Transcontinental Peace Caravan that forwarded several hundred thousand signatures to Geneva, the disarmament talks ran afoul of the Manchurian crisis (see Chapter 5) and accomplished little.

One of the peace movement's few achievements was the Kellogg-Briand Pact of 1928. France, prodded by James T. Shotwell, a trustee of the Carnegie Endowment for International Peace, asked the United States to sign a bilateral treaty renouncing war between the two nations. The security-conscious French, ever worried about a revived Germany, seemed to want a "defensive treaty" that would permit them to "leave it open … to take what action she [France] liked in Europe" while ensuring U.S. "neutrality."[65] Washington coolly received the request. But a publicity campaign for a multilateral treaty launched by Shotwell, Salmon Levinson, and Senator William Borah, as well as pressure from women's delegations ("a set of God-damned fools" in Kellogg's view), finally prodded the secretary to action.[66] In February 1928, he sent a draft treaty to France and other powers. Foreign Minister Aristide Briand fumed; Kellogg and the peace advocates had transformed his Franco-American security treaty into a universal declaration against war. That August in Paris, the signatories, eventually numbering sixty-two, agreed to renounce war "as an instrument of national policy."[67]

The Kellogg-Briand Pact required no real sacrifices and established no precise responsibilities. On January 15, 1929, the Senate approved it 85 to 1. With one bemused supporter dismissing the treaty as "the last stage of nervous and degenerate effeminacy," the Senate that same day approved funds for fifteen new warships.[68] Peace advocates did not naively believe that Kellogg-Briand guaranteed a peaceful world. Dorothy Detzer of the WILPF regarded it as a first step in a long process and championed the pact as a way of alerting the American people to think once again of the costs of war. Thus it held educational value. And the pact gave the Allies the legal grounds after World War II to punish Axis leaders for plotting aggressive war.

The League of Nations, itself designed to check wars, opened in Geneva in 1920 without the United States as a member. Washington at first ignored League communications. But by 1925, U.S. diplomats were discreetly participating in League functions. By 1930 unofficial American "observers" had attended more than forty League conferences on such questions as health, prostitution, codification of international law, and opium traffic. In October 1931, U.S. envoy Prentiss B. Gilbert formally participated in League Council meetings on the Manchurian crisis, but Washington would only push the League to cite the Kellogg–Briand Pact and condemn Japan for aggression (see Chapter 5). The United States nearly did join the League-sponsored Permanent Court of International Justice (World Court), which sought to arbitrate international disputes when requested to do so. In 1926 the Senate approved U.S. membership but so qualified it that the court could not accept the American proposal. In 1935, aided by FDR's claim that "the sovereignty of the United States [would] in no way be diminished or jeopardized," a treaty of membership fell just short of the two-thirds majority needed to pass.[69] That eminent jurists such as Charles Evans Hughes sat as judges in the World Court offered internationalists some solace.

American participation in disarmament conferences in 1922 (Washington), 1927 (Geneva), 1930 (London), 1932–1933 (Geneva), and 1935–1936 (London) also demonstrated America's international but independent diplomatic course. At those conferences, the United States sought arms limitations, especially on navies, in part because it hoped to shackle others at a time when a parsimonious Congress restrained U.S. military growth. Except for some naval restrictions negotiated at the Washington and London conferences, little was accomplished. Without building to treaty limits, the United States sought to check the quantitative growth of other navies; France would not endorse disarmament until it received security guarantees; the British had a huge empire to protect and police by sea; Italy and Germany plotted military buildups; Japan eyed naval expansion in the Pacific. German rearmament under Adolf Hitler after 1933 and Japanese renunciation of Washington treaty provisions in 1934 signaled the failure of the peace seekers as the world lurched toward global war.

Cold as Steel: Soviet-American Encounters

The Soviet Union signed the Kellogg–Briand Pact and joined the League of Nations in 1934. Yet most European nations and the United States treated the Communist regime as a revolutionary disease to be isolated. It was like "having a wicked and disgraceful neighbor," Hoover wrote. "We did not attack him, but we did not give him a certificate of character by inviting him into our homes."[70] Only when Europe tottered on the brink of war in 1939 did Germany on the one hand and France and Britain on the other attempt to forge ties with Soviet Russia.

Washington in the 1920s adhered to the nonrecognition policy set by Woodrow Wilson. The Bolsheviks had confiscated American-owned property valued at $336 million, and Russia owed another $192 million to the U.S. government and still another $107 million to American nationals (Tsarist and Provisional government debts). Until Moscow paid, recognition would be denied. Many Americans, moreover, saw the Bolsheviks as godless, uncivilized, anticapitalist, violent revolutionaries who chained their workers like slaves to an authoritarian system. Secretary Stimson, wary of the American Communist party, promised in 1930 to deny recognition until Russia "ceased to agitate for the overthrow of American institutions by revolution."[71] Some Americans, such as Senator Borah and leaders of the International Ladies Garment Workers Union, urged tolerance and recognition while they criticized the Soviet system.

If most Americans shunned the Bolsheviks, others edged closer. In 1921 Russia suffered a devastating famine. Fearful that hunger "breeds anarchy" that "will yet spread to the United States," Secretary of Commerce Hoover organized shipments of food and medicine to needy areas.[72] The humanitarian Hoover also believed that this aid would help implant American influence in Russia and serve as a counterrevolutionary force. From 1921 to 1924 under Hoover's aegis, the American Relief Administration collected $50 million from the federal government and private citizens for assistance to 10 million Russians. African-American jazz musicians also visited the USSR in 1923–1926, as audiences in Moscow and Leningrad were "bedazzled" by the likes of Sam Wooding and the Chocolate Kiddies.[73]

American businesses seemed willing to "sell the misguided [Soviet] fanatics all they are willing to pay for."[74] International Harvester, General Electric, and Du Pont signed trade and technical assistance contracts with the Soviet government, often through its purchasing agency in New York, the Amtorg Trading Corporation. By 1924 Soviet purchases of American products had jumped seven times over the 1923 figure. The entrepreneur W. Averell Harriman obtained monopolistic rights to rich manganese deposits in Soviet Georgia valued at $1 billion, from which Harriman eventually earned a "reasonable profit."[75] In 1928 Americans accounted for 24 percent of all foreign investment in the Soviet Union. With Joseph Stalin urging Soviet cadres to combine "Russian revolutionary scale" with the "American business approach," industrialization and collectivization could not have advanced without American machinery, technology, and engineers (1,000 by 1931).[76] Henry Ford's contract with the Soviet Union seemed remarkable. In the 1920s, the auto magnate agreed to supply technical information needed for the large Nizhni-Novgorod automobile factory, which would buy Ford parts and produce a car like the Model A and a truck like the Model AA. Ford eventually lost $578,000 on this multimillion-dollar venture, which was terminated in 1934. Expecting a "market for Ford products which … may someday surpass in volume all the rest of Europe and Asia combined," the auto entrepreneur did sell the Soviets on mass-production techniques (*Fordizatsia*).[77] By 1927, 85 percent of the Soviets' tractors were "Fordsons." Once Moscow acquired Western skills and technology, the Soviet leader Leon Trotsky fantasized, "Americanized Bolshevism will defeat and crush imperialist Americanism."[78]

U.S.–Soviet economic ties began to fray in the early 1930s. With the Great Depression causing widespread unemployment, government and business officials resented Soviet announcements in the United States that jobs were available in Russia. The Soviets also began selling goods ("dumping") in the world market below American prices. The United States banned imports of Soviet paper pulp, claiming that convict labor produced it. In retaliation the Soviets reduced drastically their buying of American products. In another abortive venture, the famed Russian director Sergei Eisenstein came to Hollywood in 1930 to film Theodore Dreiser's novel *An American Tragedy,* only to have Paramount terminate his contract and U.S. authorities deport him to Mexico. Eisenstein thereafter always expressed contempt for capitalist "Californica."[79] By 1932 American exports to Russia had declined 90 percent from the 1931 trade volume. Business executives eager for markets began to argue that official diplomatic recognition might restart stalled commercial relations. The Reconstruction Finance Corporation, a U.S. government agency, helped nudge along normalization by extending Russia a $4 million credit for the purchase of American cotton.

"So You're the Big Bad Bear!" Roosevelt and Soviet commissar for foreign affairs Maxim Litvinov met in Washington in 1933. The atmosphere was friendly and U.S. recognition of the Soviet Union followed. (*Washington Evening Star,* Library of Congress)

The Roosevelt administration, seeking to improve trade while deterring further Japanese encroachment on China, formally recognized the Soviet Union in November 1933. Despite foot-dragging from an "unfriendly" State Department, Roosevelt himself conducted the negotiations.[80] "Tell Stalin that the antireligious attitude is wrong," said FDR as he insisted on the rights of Americans to worship freely inside the USSR. "God will punish you Russians if you go on persecuting the church."[81] But the exchange of embassies neither smoothed relations nor halted Japan. American trade with Russia improved little, despite the signing of a trade treaty in 1935 and the establishment of the Export-Import Bank. The loan or credit discussed at the time of recognition never materialized because of disagreement over compensation for World War I debts. When American communists spoke critically of the United States at Moscow's Seventh International Communist (Comintern) Congress in 1935, Secretary Hull charged a violation of Russia's no-propaganda pledge. The Kremlin foolishly expected governments to "fall like ripe fruit from their capitalist treetops," noted another U.S. diplomat.[82]

Other issues disrupted Soviet-American relations. Named the first ambassador to Moscow, William Bullitt left America in 1933 as a friend of Russia. Two years later he resigned, convinced that the Soviet government "is a conspiracy to commit murder and nothing else."[83] He had changed his mind because of difficult living conditions in Moscow, spies among his servants, indignities inflicted by rude Soviet bureaucrats, his own volatile prejudices (he called one Soviet commissar "a wretched little kike"), and the ubiquitous Soviet tyranny.[84] Bullitt soon "deviled the Russians. I did all I could to make things unpleasant."[85] He mocked the Comintern's call for a popular front against Germany as similar to the tiger's "historic ride with the young lady of Niger. The Communists feel sure they will come back from the ride with the Socialists and Democrats inside."[86]

Stalin's purges of Communist and Red Army leaders on trumped-up charges of treason also moved Bullitt and others to a hard line. "The last mass trials were a great success. There are going to be fewer but better Russians," quipped an unsmiling Greta Garbo in the movie *Ninotchka* (1939).[87] Bullitt's successor as ambassador, the wealthy Joseph E. Davies, thought Soviet Premier Joseph Stalin "cold as steel" and the Soviet government "oriental in its cruelty and in its complete disregard for individual human life."[88] George F. Kennan, a member of the embassy staff, at first extolled "the romance of economic development" among the Russian people before he acquired a "liberal education in the horrors of Stalinism."[89] Kennan, who had much enjoyed the "fraternity-like atmosphere" and "homosocial bonding" of 1933–1934, attended the purge trials in person. So intense was the outrage of Kennan, Bullitt, and others at official Soviet cruelties, a scholar writes, that they employed a highly impassioned "eroticized discourse" that reflected their sense of having been spurned as suitors in their wooing of the Russian people.[90]

The Nazi-Soviet Pact of August 1939 also outraged Americans. Stalin believed that the Western European powers and the United States had let Hitler expand without restraint in order to encourage the German leader's design to conquer Russia. Stalin had so depleted the officer ranks of his army through the purges that he was in no position to stave off an expected German attack. In the United States, the nonaggression pact, which secretly divided Poland, reinforced charges that Stalin had become Hitler's friend. When World War II erupted in September 1939, many Americans blamed the Soviet Union.

Hitler's Germany, Appeasement, and the Outbreak of War

By exploiting the depression-afflicted economy and vehement popular resentment against the Versailles treaty in Germany, the Nazi leader Adolf Hitler came to power in January 1933. Racist toward Jews and emphatically anticommunist, Hitler alarmed diplomats with his "fanatic chauvinism coupled with his hatred of democratic government and the parliamentary system."[91] In October 1933, Hitler withdrew Germany from the faltering League of Nations and denounced disarmament talks. He told an associate that the European powers would "never act! They'll just protest. And they will always be too late."[92] Indeed, France and Britain settled on a timid policy of "appeasement," hoping to satisfy what they thought were Hitler's limited goals and to avert another European war. By 1935 Britain, France, Italy, and the League of Nations had censured Germany for building a huge army and air force. Yet at the same time, Britain agreed that Germany could rebuild its navy to 35 percent of the size of the British navy, another costly concession to German militarism.

Adolf Hitler (1889–1945). When Hitler took power in 1933, some Americans likened his face and mustache to the actor Charlie Chaplin. One political scientist described Hitler's oratory as a "combination of Ku Klux Klan, Negro revival meeting, and Billy Sunday harangue." In this propagandistic German painting, the anticommunist, anti-Semitic Nazi leader is surrounded by swastikas and saluting followers. Hitler judged Americans to be "very good at refrigerators and razor blades," but said they could never build airplanes. He learned otherwise. (U.S. Army)

Hardly adjusted to the rise of Nazi Germany, the world watched as Italy invaded the African state of Ethiopia in October 1935. The fascist dictator Benito Mussolini had governed Italy since 1922, and he had long dreamed of creating an Italian empire. Already holding Somaliland and Eritrea as African colonies, Mussolini pressed Ethiopian leader Haile Selassie until military skirmishes broke out. Then Mussolini invaded and annexed Ethiopia. The League imposed an embargo on the shipment of war-related goods (except oil) to Italy. But the French, with their own empire in Africa, and the British, fearful that Italy might disrupt their imperial life-line in the Mediterranean, seemed willing to sacrifice Ethiopia, a mere "corridor for camels."[93] They also feared that further hostilities would "play into Germany's hands" and "might mean a general war in Europe."[94]

Apparently encouraged by Anglo-French docility over Ethiopia, Hitler in March 1936 ordered his goose-stepping troops into the Rhineland, the area bordering Belgium and France that the Versailles treaty had declared permanently demilitarized. After World War I, the French had erected the Maginot Line, a series of large guns and defensive bunkers along the German-French border. By seizing the Rhineland, Germany could outflank the line. The French, fearful of igniting another war, did not resist the German advance. Meanwhile, in June, the League of Nations lifted economic sanctions against Italy. Victories by German athletes at the Berlin Olympiad in the summer of 1936 proved "as conducive to [Hitler's] self-esteem as a 98 percent plebiscite," even as the African American sprinter Jesse Owens became "the darling of the Berlin crowds."[95] That same fall, after Hitler signed the Rome–Berlin Axis agreement with Italy and the Anti-Comintern Pact with Japan, U.S. military attachés sent ominous reports on German military maneuvers, including *Panzer* brigades, warning of "a revolution in military methods."[96]

Spain became contested ground, too. "Nationalist" soldiers under General Francisco Franco started the Spanish civil war in July 1936 by attacking the "Loyalist" Republican government. Eager for a Franco government hostile to France, Hitler

Joachim von Ribbentrop (1893–1946) and Joseph Stalin (1879–1953). The German foreign minister (left) and Soviet premier smile their approval of the Nazi-Soviet nonaggression pact signed in August 1939. The news angered but did not surprise American officials, who monitored the secret negotiations through reports from a cooperative German diplomat in Moscow. (World War II Collection of Seized Enemy Records, National Archives)

and Mussolini poured military equipment and troops into the Nationalist effort. The tepid Anglo-French response produced an International Non-Intervention Committee of twenty-seven nations, remarkably including Germany and Italy. Hitler and Mussolini continued covert aid, and France and Britain lived with the fiction that they had isolated the Spanish civil war. The Soviet Union and Mexico sent help to the Republicans, and some 3,000 American volunteers fought alongside them in the Abraham Lincoln Brigade. Franco and his brand of fascism nonetheless prevailed in early 1939.

When Neville Chamberlain became British prime minister in 1937, he enshrined the appeasement policy. He believed that Germany had good reason to want to reject the humiliating Versailles treaty and to claim status as a major power. Tolerant of Hitler's demand for mastery over people of German descent living in Austria, Czechoslovakia, and Poland, Chamberlain also judged that Germany could be "weaned from aggression by his blend of conciliation and firmness, carrot and stick."[97] An appeased Germany could also serve as a useful restraint on the Soviet Union.

In March 1938, German troops crossed into Austria and annexed it to the German Reich. Months of terrorism against Jews and opponents of Nazism in Austria followed. Hitler next demanded the Sudeten region of Czechoslovakia, where 3 million ethnic Germans lived. Hitler assured Chamberlain that this marked Germany's last territorial demand. Britain and France (which had a defense treaty with Prague) granted the Nazi this additional prize. At the Munich Conference of September 29–30, 1938, Italy, Germany, France, and Britain agreed never to make war against one another and to sever the Sudetenland from Czechoslovakia. The Czechs were not consulted. Unwilling to wage "a war today in order to prevent a war hereafter," Chamberlain flew back to England to proclaim "peace for our time."[98] Opponents gibed: "if at first you can't concede, fly, fly, fly again."[99] Hitler soon accelerated his persecution of German Jews, and in March 1939 Germany swallowed the rest of Czechoslovakia. The following month Italy annexed Albania.

Poland came next. Refusing Hitler's demands for the city of Danzig, the Poles soon faced German pressure. Jolted by the Nazi seizure of all of Czechoslovakia, London and Paris announced in March 1939 that they would stand behind an independent Poland. A grim Chamberlain judged it "impossible to deal with Hitler after he had thrown all his own assurances to the wind."[100] The Soviet Union then emerged as a central actor in the European tumult. Germany, Britain, and France opened negotiations with Moscow in attempts to gain Soviet allegiance. Stalin chose Germany. "Britain and France wanted us to be their hired hand … and without pay," he remarked.[101] On August 23, Nazi Germany and Soviet Russia signed the Molotov-Ribbentrop nonaggression pact. Poland, the immediate victim, found itself divided between the two powers. A U.S. senator wrote privately: "If Germany can organize Russia and they make England give up her fleet, look out—we'll have a Nazi, or nasty, world."[102] On September 1, German soldiers invaded Poland. Two days later Britain and France declared war against Germany. On September 17, Soviet troops struck Poland, taking half the nation.

Throughout these years of descent into World War II, Hitler both admired and underrated the United States. Impressed by anti-Semite Henry Ford and his production techniques, he sent German car designers to Detroit before launching the *Volkswagen*. He nonetheless underrated U.S. influence in world affairs. Although his advisers told him that American isolationism might not last, he deemed the United States "incapable of conducting war"—a "Jewish rubbish heap," incapacitated by economic and racial crises, crime, and inept political leadership.[103] Hitler's Nazis also viewed emancipated American women as "egoistic, manipulative, overly sexual, and unerotic," in stark contrast to "the Nazi ideal of a devoted Gretchen bearing future soldiers for the Third Reich's wars of conquest."[104] Despite the popularity of "swing" music and American films (especially those of Shirley Temple and "Micky Maus"), the Nazis outlawed "Nigger-Jew jazz" and soon banned importation of Hollywood movies.[105] Although the *Fuehrer*'s long-range goals probably included aggressive war against the United States, his initial perceptions of America as a "half-Judaized, half negrified" country with a large navy and minuscule army caused him to discount growing U.S. support for England and France.[106]

American Isolationism and Myopic Neutrality

"This nation will remain a neutral nation," President Roosevelt announced on September 3, 1939, "but I cannot ask that every American remain neutral in thought as well."[107] Second thoughts about neutrality came only late in the decade. During the early 1930s, the United States attempted to shield itself from conflict in Europe by remaining rigidly neutral. Although most Americans strongly disapproved of Hitler and his "brutal, beer swilling people," they tried to isolate themselves from a continent they thought prone to self-destruction.[108] If Britain and France could not handle German aggression on their own continent, America would not do the job for them.

Americans also drew lessons from World War I. Disillusioned writers and historians argued that Germany had not solely precipitated war in 1914, that business leaders

Senator Hiram W. Johnson (1866–1945). The California progressive reformer, anti-imperialist, and firm isolationist served in the U.S. Senate for twenty-eight years. He opposed U.S. membership in the League of Nations and the World Court and called for strict U.S. neutrality toward Europe. The United States, Johnson insisted, "cannot strut as a knight-errant to reform the world." In 1941, however, he voted for U.S. entrance into World War II after the Japanese attack on Pearl Harbor. (Library of Congress)

and propagandists had influenced a pro-British Wilson from 1914 to 1917, and that the costs and results of war did not justify American participation. In their best-selling book *Merchants of Death* (1934) Helmuth Englebrecht and Frank Hanighen argued that profiteering arms manufacturers had exploited the American economic and political system to compromise U.S. neutrality. Encouraged by President Roosevelt, Senator Gerald P. Nye held hearings during 1934–1936 to determine if munitions makers and bankers had lobbied Wilson into war. The committee never proved the allegation, but it did uncover substantial evidence that these entrepreneurs had exerted influence on behalf of the Allies. By identifying an "unhealthy alliance" among business, the military, and the government, the Nye Committee anticipated "with remarkable accuracy … the growth of the structure later called the military-industrial complex."[109] Popular sentiment held that World War I had been a tragic blunder and that Americans "must think of the next war as they would of suicide."[110]

A diverse coalition of isolationists and peace advocates shared the traditional belief in political and military nonentanglement—"a north star, constant and steady, which will hold us true to our course."[111] The antiwar movement grew strong on college campuses and among women. Princeton University students organized the Veterans of Future Wars in 1936 and demanded $1,000 each as a bonus *before* going into battle, because few, they predicted, would live through the next war. The journalist William Allen White wrote with bitter irony that "war is the devil's joke on humanity. So let's celebrate Armistice Day by laughing our heads off."[112] In 1938 Representative Louis Ludlow introduced a constitutional amendment calling for a national referendum on decisions for war. Roosevelt claimed that the amendment "would cripple any President in his conduct of our foreign relations," and even the isolationist Senator Arthur Vandenberg protested that it "would be as sensible to require a town meeting before permitting the fire department to put out the blaze."[113] A motion to discharge Ludlow's resolution from the Rules Committee failed by only a vote of 209 to 188.

Many progressive isolationists believed that American entry into a European war would undercut the New Deal's attempts to recover from the depression. They also remembered how the Wilson administration had savaged critics in World War I. Convinced that business expansionists helped create the conditions that spawned war, progressive isolationists sought to curb business adventures abroad that entangled the United States. By 1937, for example, twenty of the top one hundred American corporations had negotiated important agreements with Nazi Germany, some with the core of the German military machine, the I. G. Farben Company. Du Pont, Union Carbide, and Standard Oil signed contracts, with Standard Oil helping Germany develop synthetic rubber and aviation fuel. "American businessmen publicly opposed war as much as anyone else," one scholar has concluded, "but it would seem that the one price they would not pay for peace was private profit."[114]

Although sharply critical of fascism abroad, Dorothy Detzer, the dynamic executive secretary of the WILPF, also feared a "peculiar type of American Fascism" in which "women would be thrown back into the kitchen, as … in Germany."[115] Detzer and other peace progressives worked behind the scenes on behalf of the Nye Committee and neutrality legislation. Roosevelt wanted a neutrality law that banned sales of arms to aggressors. Congress instead passed the Neutrality Act of

1935, requiring an American arms embargo against all belligerents after the president had officially proclaimed the existence of war. "Leave as little to the discretion of the President as possible," urged Detzer.[116] Subsequent legislation banned loans to countries at war (Act of 1936) and required belligerents wishing to trade with the United States to carry away U.S. goods in their own ships ("cash and carry"), after payment on delivery (Act of 1937). The latter also forbade U.S. citizens to travel on belligerent vessels. An amendment of 1937 made the United States neutral in the Spanish civil war, even though FDR privately winked at unsuccessful "covert" schemes to supply Loyalist forces with warplanes.[117]

The Neutrality Acts erred in providing for no discrimination among the belligerents, no punishment of the aggressor. They denied the United States any forceful word in the cascading events in Europe. They amounted to an abdication of international responsibility. Yet, at the same time, much of what the isolationists said about the fruits of war rang true. Their criticisms of imperialism and business expansion were honest and telling. They scorned the British Empire and U.S. intervention in Latin America. They compared Italy's subjugation of Ethiopia to Britain's supremacy in India. Many of them warned about extending the power of the president in foreign affairs beyond congressional reach. Denounced by Neville Chamberlain as "those pig-headed and self-righteous nobodies," isolationists nonetheless comprised "a large, responsible, and respectable segment of the American people."[118] In condemning all imperialism—American, British, or German—the isolationists often refused to make the choice of the lesser of two or three evils. As a result, however praiseworthy their thought, their formulas for the 1930s proved as myopic as Britain's appeasement policy.

What if ...   *President Franklin D. Roosevelt had vetoed the Neutrality Acts in the 1930s?*

Suppose the president had not made New Deal recovery from the Great Depression a higher priority than foreign policy during his first term and well into his second. FDR might have heeded the State Department's advice and vetoed the first Neutrality Act in August 1935 because it called for a mandatory arms embargo that did not differentiate between aggressors and victims. Yet he signed this bill and subsequent legislation in 1936 and 1937 in large part because midwestern progressives in the Senate and House threatened to block key New Deal reforms, including Social Security, unless he accepted strict neutrality. Openly repudiating Woodrow Wilson's neutral rights policy prior to U.S. entry into World War I, Roosevelt signed legislation that required an embargo on arms and munitions, banned private loans to belligerents, forbade travel by U.S. citizens on belligerent vessels, and limited trade with belligerents to noncontraband materials on a "cash and carry" basis. Historians generally agree that such neutrality laws, had they existed in 1914–1917, might well have kept the United States out of World War I—but not out of World War II. The president himself changed his mind in late 1938 and worked to revise and repeal the neutrality laws he had so recently championed.

It is unlikely, however, that different U.S. neutrality rules would have deterred Axis aggression in the 1930s. As it was, the Neutrality Act of 1935 halted U.S. arms sales to fascist Italy but had no effect on its conquest of Ethiopia. Adolf Hitler's commitment to military expansion was absolute, and thus any shift in policy by "mongrel" America elicited only his contempt. In Asia, the president pointedly did not apply the neutrality laws to the undeclared Sino-Japanese War after 1937, thus permitting American loans and arms to go to embattled China, but also resulting in even greater sales of petroleum and scrap metals to Japan until 1940.

Nonetheless, it is possible that if FDR had spoken out more forcefully against Germany's occupation of the Rhineland in 1936, the takeover of Austria in 1938, and even the Munich Agreement to dismember Czechoslovakia, promises of further U.S. support might have emboldened the French, British, and possibly even the Soviet Union to stand firm against Hitler's demands. Instead of sacrificing his popularity with his abortive plan to "pack" the Supreme Court in 1937, the president might have issued a clarion call for rearmament and for hemispheric defense, much as he later asked for thousands of war planes in 1939 and a two-ocean navy in 1940. Such a policy of massive military spending could have stimulated the economy, ended the depression, and encouraged potential allies. Expanded arms sales to the British and French might have prompted their military support of Czechoslovakia in September–October 1938, in which case dissident officers within Germany's high command might have conspired to assassinate Hitler and overthrow the Nazi regime.

Such an earlier turnaround would have required a different political strategy at home. Instead of wooing midwestern isolationists such as Senators Gerald P. Nye, Robert M. La Follette, Jr., and George W. Norris, all of whom supported the New Deal but insisted on strict neutrality, FDR would have needed to cultivate Republican internationalists and Southern Democrats (several of whom he unsuccessfully tried to purge from the party in 1938 because of their opposition to the New Deal). The president belatedly adopted that very strategy in 1940 when he invited prominent Republicans Henry L. Stimson and Frank Knox into his Cabinet. By then, France had fallen, the swastika flew over most of Europe, Roosevelt was running for an unprecedented third term, isolationists were calling him a warmonger, and it was nearly too late for the United States to assert its influence in a world at war.

Roosevelt Shifts and Congress Balks on the Eve of War

President Roosevelt, sensitive to American sentiment against U.S. entanglement in Europe and sharing much of the pacifist loathing of war, responded haltingly to the "hair-trigger times" of the 1930s.[119] His foreign policy at first fed appeasement. When Italy attacked Ethiopia, Roosevelt stated that the United States sought above all to avoid war. America would set a peaceful example for other nations to follow. He and Hull invoked the Neutrality Act, warned Americans not to travel on belligerent ships, and suggested a moral embargo against trade with the warring parties. Perversely, American businesses ignored the moral embargo and increased commerce with Italy, especially in oil. At the same time, European aggression in Africa sparked a "great manifestation" of African American protest.[120] In addition to anti-Italian boycotts and petitions by black churches to the pope, the black poet Langston Hughes composed a "Ballad of Ethiopia" in support of pan-African solidarity.[121] In August 1936, the president gave a stirring speech at Chautauqua, New York, recalling World War I: "I have seen war. ... I have seen blood running from the wounded. I have seen men coughing out their gassed lungs. ... I hate war."[122]

In January 1937, Roosevelt asked Congress for an arms embargo against Spain. Congress obliged, but the decision sparked considerable debate. It produced "malevolent neutrality" that worked against the "Loyalist" Republican government and in favor of Franco.[123] In this case, many isolationists protested neutrality— the sacrifice of Spanish democracy. They agonized: How can one be committed to both peace and liberty? Roosevelt and Hull chose strict neutrality, in essence backing feeble British-French efforts to contain the civil war and aligning themselves with the pro-Franco views of the Catholic hierarchy at home. Yet Roosevelt privately pondered ways to curb the aggressors.

In July, when Japan plunged into undeclared war against China, Roosevelt favored China by not invoking the Neutrality Act, thereby permitting the Chinese government to buy and import American war goods (see Chapter 5). Then in October he delivered his famous "quarantine" speech, calling for the isolation of international lawbreakers. FDR also approached the British ambassador about a joint cruiser blockade against Japan and sent a naval officer to London for secret staff talks. Under Secretary of State Sumner Welles also proposed a world conference on disarmament and international law in Washington, at which Roosevelt might quietly stiffen British diplomacy. Chamberlain, however, blocked the meeting in early 1938 because it interfered with his efforts to negotiate with the aggressors. Convinced that America was "a nation of cads," Chamberlain gave FDR a "douche of cold water" and continued to pursue appeasement.[124] The spectacular first-round knockout of Germany's Max Schmeling in June 1938 by the African American boxing champion Joe Louis nonetheless temporarily thwarted Nazi plans to celebrate "the innate superiority of the Nordic" race.[125]

During the Czech crisis that autumn, President Roosevelt appealed for negotiations to head off war, telling Hitler that the United States had "no political involvements in Europe and will assume no obligations in the conduct of the present negotiations."[126] "Good man," FDR cabled Chamberlain when he heard that the prime minister would go to Munich.[127] Yet the dismemberment of Czechoslovakia, combined with the Japanese terror in China, prompted the president to confess privately that Munich had failed and that Hitler was "a pure unadulterated devil" who must be stopped.[128] Worried about the insidious effects of "too much Eton and Oxford," FDR thought the British needed "a good stiff grog, inducing not only the desire to save civilization but the continued belief that they can do it."[129]

Benito Mussolini (1883–1945). *Il Duce* excited a revival of Italian imperial grandeur by attacking Ethiopia in 1935. In the mistaken belief that Mussolini would help to stabilize Europe, President Roosevelt had earlier referred to *Il Duce* as "that admirable Italian gentleman." British Foreign Secretary Anthony Eden more accurately called him "the complete gangster [whose] pledged word means nothing." (National Archives)

"Uncomfortable Grandstand."   The British cartoonist David Low obviously did not think that a neutral United States could remain safe after the outbreak of war in Europe. President Roosevelt turns a quizzical face to Secretary of State Hull as the bombs burst in air. (*London Evening Standard/ Solo*)

In October 1938, Roosevelt asked Congress for $300 million for national defense. He encouraged the State Department and Senator Key Pittman, the hard-drinking, gun-packing, incompetent chair of the Foreign Relations Committee, to lobby for the repeal of the arms embargo law. In November, in protest against Hitler's vicious persecution of the Jews, he recalled Ambassador Hugh Wilson from Berlin and never let him return. That same month, FDR initiated a program to build more than 10,000 warplanes per year, in order "to have something to back up my words."[130] He also secretly arranged for the French government to place orders for planes.

In January 1939, Roosevelt again urged revision of the Neutrality Act so that it would not in effect "give aid to an aggressor and deny it to the victim."[131] The crash of the A-20 bomber in Los Angeles and FDR's garbled statement about America's frontier on the Rhine stalled this initiative. The president thus delayed until March the introduction of a bill specifically repealing the arms embargo, and throughout the spring he allowed the erratic Pittman to direct legislative strategy. Reluctant to fight against sizable political odds, FDR failed to lead at a critical time. In April he asked Hitler and Mussolini to refrain from attacking countries named on a list, but his request met open derision when Hitler repeated the countries one by one to a raucous Reichstag. The Senate Foreign Relations Committee, by a 12 to 11 vote, refused in July to report out a bill repealing the arms embargo. "I've fired my last shot," the president groaned.[132] Not until November 1939—after Germany's conquest of Poland—did Congress finally revise the Neutrality Act so that England and France, as belligerents, could purchase American arms on a cash-and-carry basis.

Even in the fall of 1939, however, most Americans joined their president in wanting to avoid participation in World War II. "We cannot expect ... the United States to evolve quicker than we did," the British ambassador reported.[133] By sending Sumner Welles to Berlin, London, Paris, and Rome in the winter of 1940, FDR evidently thought there might be "one chance in a thousand" of mediating a compromise peace.[134] Hitler's *blitzkrieg* in the west that spring killed any such possibility. The Democratic party platform of 1940, on which Roosevelt ran for an unprecedented third term, reflected the American desire to avoid war but also to prepare for it: "We will not participate in foreign wars, and we will not send our army, naval or air forces to fight in foreign lands outside of the Americas except in case of attack."[135] As in World War I, because of their international interests, because U.S. power became intertwined in the war, and because they gradually abandoned neutrality to aid the Allies, Americans once again found themselves risking major war. The interwar quest for world order and peace had failed; the Neutrality Acts had failed; independent internationalism had failed.

FURTHER READING FOR THE PERIOD 1920–1939

Overviews include Warren I. Cohen, *Empire Without Tears* (1987); Patrick O. Cohrs, *The Unfinished Peace after World War I* (2006); Robert A. Divine, *The Reluctant Belligerent* (1979); Justus D. Doenecke and John E. Wilz, *From Isolation to War* (2003); Robert H. Ferrell, *American Diplomacy in the Great Depression* (1957) and *Peace in Their Time* (1952); Conan Fischer, *After the Versailles Treaty* (2007); Margaret Louria, *Triumph and Downfall* (2001); Arnold Offner, *The Origins of the Second World War* (1975); Brenda Gayle Plummer, *Rising Wind* (1996) (African Americans); Benjamin D. Rhodes, *United States Foreign Policy in the Interwar Period, 1918–1941* (2001); Robert Schulzinger, *The Making of the Diplomatic Mind* (1975); and Zara Steiner, *The Lights That Failed* (2005).

The presidents and their presidencies are treated in John Dean, *Warren G. Harding* (2004); Martin Fausold, *The Presidency of Herbert C. Hoover* (1985); Robert H. Ferrell, *The Presidency of Calvin Coolidge* (1998); Alonzo L. Hamby, *For the Survival of Democracy* (2004) (Roosevelt); Ellis W. Hawley, ed., *Herbert Hoover* (1981); William E. Leuchtenburg, *Herbert Hoover* (2009); and Joan Hoff Wilson, *Herbert Hoover* (1975).

For Franklin D. Roosevelt, see H. W. Brands, *Traitor to His Class* (2008); Wayne S. Cole, *Roosevelt and the Isolationists* (1983); Robert Dallek, *Franklin D. Roosevelt and American Foreign Policy, 1933–1945* (1979); Kenneth R. Davis, *FDR* (1972–1993); Robert A. Divine, *Roosevelt and World War II* (1969); Frank Freidel, *Franklin D. Roosevelt* (1990); Frederick W. Marks III, *Wind over Sand* (1988); George McJimsey, *The Presidency of Franklin Delano Roosevelt* (2000); Arthur M. Schlesinger, Jr., *The Age of Roosevelt* (1957–1960); and Cornelius A. van Minnen and John F. Sears, eds., *FDR and His Contemporaries* (1992).

For the secretaries of state, see Michael Butler, *Cautious Visionary* (1998) (Hull); Robert H. Ferrell, *Frank B. Kellogg* (1963) and *Henry L. Stimson* (1963); Elting E. Morison, *Turmoil and Tradition* (1960) (Stimson); Julius Pratt, *Cordell Hull* (1964); and David F. Schmitz, *Henry L. Stimson* (2001).

Other diplomats and politicians are studied in Leroy Ashby, *The Spearless Leader* (1972) (Borah); Fred A. Bailey, *William Edward Dodd* (1997); Will Brownell and Richard N. Billings, *So Close to Greatness* (1988) (Bullitt); Wayne S. Cole, *Senator Gerald P. Nye and American Foreign Relations* (1962); Ralph de Bedts, *Ambassador Joseph Kennedy* (1985); Irwin Gellman, *Secret Affairs* (1995) (Hull and Welles); Betty Glad, *Key Pittman* (1986); Frank W. Graff, *Strategy of Involvement* (1988) (Welles); Waldo Heinrichs, *American Ambassador* (1966) (Grew); Kenneth P. Jones, *Diplomats in Europe, 1919–1941* (1981); Richard C. Lower, *A Bloc of One* (1993) (Hiram

Johnson); Elizabeth K. MacLean, *Joseph E. Davies* (1992); Peter Schlinger and Holman Hamilton, *Spokesman for Democracy* (2000) (Claude Bowers); Jesse H. Stiller, *George S. Messersmith* (1987); Michael Weatherson and Hal W. Bochin, *Hiram Johnson* (1995); and Benjamin Welles, *Sumner Welles* (1997).

Economic foreign relations receive attention in Frederick Adams, *Economic Diplomacy* (1976); Derek H. Aldcroft, *From Versailles to Wall Street, 1919–1929* (1977); Patricia Clavin, *The Failure of Economic Diplomacy* (1996); Lloyd C. Gardner, *Economic Aspects of New Deal Diplomacy* (1964); Michael J. Hogan, *Informal Entente* (1977); Burton I. Kaufman, *Efficiency and Expansion* (1974); Charles P. Kindleberger, *The World in Depression, 1929–1939* (1986); Stephen J. Randall, *United States Foreign Oil Policy, 1919–1948* (1986); William Stivers, *Supremacy and Oil* (1982); Mira Wilkins, *The Maturing of Multinational Enterprise* (1974); Joan Hoff Wilson, *American Business and Foreign Policy, 1920–1933* (1971); and Gilbert Ziebura, *World Economy and World Politics, 1924–1931* (1990).

The German reparations issue is explored in Bruce Kent, *The Spoils of War* (1989); Stephen Schuker, *American "Reparations" to Germany* (1988); and Marc Trachtenberg, *Reparation in World Politics* (1980).

Cultural issues and industries are highlighted in Seth D. Amus, *French Anti-Americanism* (1930–1948) (2007); Frank Costigliola, *Awkward Dominion* (1984) (Europe); David H. Culbert, *News for Everyman* (1976); Victoria de Grazia, *Irresistible Empire* (2005); George Q. Flynn, *Roosevelt and Romanism* (1976); Barbara J. Keys, *Globalizing Sport* (2006); Lucy Moore, *Anything Goes* (2008); Emily S. Rosenberg, *Spreading the American Dream* (1982); Thomas J. Saunders, *Hollywood in Berlin* (1994); Lawrence Spinelli, *Dry Diplomacy* (2008) (Prohibition); Richard W. Steele, *Propaganda in an Open Society* (1985); and Robert C. Williams, *Russian Art and American Money* (1980).

Defense preparedness and arms-control questions are discussed in James L. Abrahamson, *America Arms for a New Century* (1981); Thomas Buckley, *The United States and the Washington Conference* (1970); Thomas Richard Davies, *The Possibilities of Transnational Activism* (2007); Roger Dingman, *Power in the Pacific* (1976); Richard W. Fanning, *Peace and Disarmament* (1995); Emily O. Goldman, *Sunken Treaties* (1994) (naval arms control); Robert Kaufman, *Arms Control During the Pre-Nuclear Age* (1990); Paul A. C. Koistinen, *Planning War, Pursuing Peace* (1998); Ernest R. May, *Knowing One's Enemy* (1984) (intelligence assessment); Stephen Pelz, *Race to Pearl Harbor* (1974) (Second London Naval Conference); and Michael S. Sherry, *The Rise of American Air Power* (1987).

For peace advocates and the League of Nations, see Harriet H. Alonso, *The Women's Peace Union and the Outlawry of War* (1989); Jason Berger, *A New Deal for the World* (1981) (Eleanor Roosevelt); Charles Chatfield, *For Peace and Justice* (1971); Blanche Wiesen Cook, *Eleanor Roosevelt* (1992, 1999); Charles DeBenedetti, *Origins of the Modern American Peace Movement, 1915–1929* (1978) and *The Peace Reform in American History* (1980); Michael Dunne, *The United States and the World Court* (1988); Carrie Foster, *The Women and the Warriors* (1995); Catherine Foster, *Women for All Seasons* (1989); Robert D. Johnson, *The Peace Progressives and American Foreign Relations* (1995); Harold Josephson, *James T. Shotwell and the Rise of Internationalism in America* (1976); Warren F. Kuehl and Lynne K. Dunn, *Keeping the Covenant* (1997) (League); Cecilia Lynch, *Beyond Appeasement* (1999); Gary B. Ostrower, *Collective Insecurity* (1979) (League); Lois Scharf, *Eleanor Roosevelt* (1987); Linda K. Schott, *Reconstructing Women's Thoughts* (1997) (WILPF); Joan Hoff Wilson and Marjorie Lightman, eds., *Without Precedent* (1984) (Eleanor Roosevelt); and Lawrence S. Wittner, *Rebels Against War* (1984).

For American isolationism, see overviews cited in the first paragraph and Warren I. Cohen, *The American Revisionists* (1967); Thomas Guinsburg, *The Pursuit of Isolationism* (1981); Manfred Jonas, *Isolationism in America* (1966); Thomas C. Kennedy, *Charles A. Beard and American Foreign Policy* (1975); and John Wiltz, *In Search of Peace* (1963) (Nye Committee).

Relations with Europe and Germany and the coming of World War II are studied in many of the works cited above and in James J. and Patience P. Barnes, *Hitler's* Mein Kampf *in Britain and America* (1980); Alfred M. Beck, *Hitler's Ambivalent Attaché* (2005); Edward W. Bennett, *German Rearmament and the West, 1932–1933* (1979); Peter H. Buckingham, *International Normalcy* (1983); Bernard Burke, *Ambassador Frederick Sackett and the Collapse of the Weimar Republic* (1995); James V. Compton, *The Swastika and the Eagle* (1967); Jean-Baptiste Duroselle, *France and the United States* (1978); Barbara R. Farnham, *Roosevelt and the Munich Crisis* (1997); John Haight, Jr., *American Aid to France, 1938–1940* (1970); Linda Killen, *Testing the Peripheries* (1994) (Yugoslavia); Melvyn Leffler, *The Elusive Quest* (1979) (France); Charles S. Maier, *Recasting Bourgeois Europe* (1975); Brian McKercher, ed., *Anglo-American Relations in the 1920s* (1991); and *Transition of Power* (1999); William C. McNeil, *American Money and the Weimer Republic* (1986); Wolfgang Mommsen and Lothar Kettenacker, eds., *The Fascist Challenge and the Policy of Appeasement* (1983); John E. Moser, *Twisting the Lion's Tail* (1999); Mary Nolan,

Visions of Modernity (1994) (American business in Germany); Arnold Offner, *American Appeasement* (1969); R. A. C. Parker, *Chamberlain and Appeasement* (1993); Neal Pease, *Poland, the United States, and the Stabilization of Europe, 1919–1933* (1986); David Reynolds, *The Creation of the Anglo-American Alliance, 1937–41* (1982); David Reynolds and David Dimbleby, *An Ocean Apart* (1989); William R. Rock, *Chamberlain and Roosevelt* (1988); J. Simon Rofe, *Franklin D. Roosevelt's Foreign Policy and the Welles Mission* (2006); David F. Schmitz, *The United States and Fascist Italy* (1988); David F. Schmitz and Richard D. Challener, eds., *Appeasement in Europe* (1990); D. C. Watt, *How War Came* (1989); Gerhard Weinberg, *The Foreign Policy of Hitler's Germany* (1970, 1980); and Marvin Zahniser, *Then Came Disaster* (2002).

Soviet-American relations and recognition are discussed in Edward Bennett *Franklin D. Roosevelt and the Search for Security* (1985); Peter G. Boyle, *American-Soviet Relations* (1995); Michael Cassella-Blackburn, *The Donkey, the Carrot and the Club* (2004) (William C. Bullitt); Dennis Dunn, *Caught Between Roosevelt and Stalin* (1998); Keith D. Eagles, *Ambassador Joseph E. Davies and American-Soviet Relations, 1937–1941* (1985); David C. Engerman, *Modernization from the Other Shore* (2003); Beatrice Farnsworth, *William C. Bullitt and the Soviet Union* (1967); Peter Filene, *Americans and the Soviet Experiment* (1967); John Lewis Gaddis, *Russia, the Soviet Union, and the United States* (1990); Jonathan Haslam, *The Soviet Union and the Struggle for Collective Security in Europe* (1984); (1960); Melvyn Leffler, *The Specter of Communism* (1994); James K. Libbey, *Alexander Gumberg and Soviet-American Relations* (1977); Thomas R. Maddux, *Years of Estrangement* (1980); David Mayers, *The Ambassadors and America's Soviet Policy* (1995); Bertrand Patenaude, *The Big Show in Bololand* (2002) (Relief for Russia); Hugh Ragsdale, *The Soviets, the Munich Crisis, and the Coming of World War II* (2004); Norman Saul, *Friends or Foes* (2006); Katherine Siegel, *Loans and Legitimacy* (1996); Christine A. White, *British and American Commercial Relations with Soviet Russia* (1993); and Joan Hoff Wilson, *Ideology and Economics* (1974).

For the Spanish civil war, see Michael Alpert, *A New International History of the Spanish Civil War* (1998); Peter N. Carroll, *The Odyssey of the Abraham Lincoln Brigade* (1994); Mark Falcoff and Fredrick B. Pike, *The Spanish Civil War, 1936–1939* (1982); Allen Guttman, *The Wound in the Heart* (1962); Douglas Little, *Malevolent Neutrality* (1985); and R. Dan Richardson, *Comintern Army* (1982).

See also "Further Reading" in Chapters 5 and 6, the General Bibliography, Robert L. Beisner, ed., *Guide to American Foreign Relations Since 1600* (2003), and the following notes.

NOTES TO CHAPTER 4

1. Quoted in Kenneth S. Davis, *FDR: Into the Storm* (New York: Random House, 1993), p. 401.
2. Quoted *ibid.*, p. 402.
3. Quoted *ibid.*, p. 401.
4. Henry Morgenthau, Jr., quoted in conference transcript, March 21, 1946, Box 391, Henry Morgenthau, Jr., Papers, Franklin D. Roosevelt Library, Hyde Park, N.Y.
5. David Reynolds, *The Creation of the Anglo-American Alliance, 1937–1941* (Chapel Hill: University of North Carolina Press, 1982), p. 43.
6. Quoted in Wayne S. Cole, *Roosevelt and the Isolationists* (Lincoln: University of Nebraska Press, 1983), p. 297.
7. Quoted in Michael S. Sherry, *The Rise of American Air Power* (New Haven: Yale University Press, 1987), pp. 79–80.
8. Quoted in Jean Monnet, *Memoirs* (London: Collins, 1978), p. 119.
9. Quoted in Sherry, *Air Power*, p. 80.
10. Quoted in Cole, *Roosevelt and Isolationists*, p. 301.
11. Quoted in conference transcript, "The French Airplane Mission," April 25, 1946, Box 391, Morgenthau Papers.
12. Quoted in David Reynolds, "The Origins of Two 'World Wars,'" *Journal of Contemporary History, XXXVIII* (January 2003), 38.
13. Bennett C. Clark journal, January 31, 1939, Bennett C. Clark papers, Western Manuscripts Collection, University of Missouri Library, Columbia, Missouri.
14. Transcript of "Conference with Senate Military Affairs Committee, Executive Offices of the White House, January 31, 1939, 12:45 P.M.," Personal Files, PPF 1-P, Franklin D. Roosevelt Papers, Roosevelt Library.
15. Quoted in J. Garry Clifford, "A Note on the Break Between Senator Nye and President Roosevelt in 1939," *North Dakota History, XLIX* (Summer 1982), 17.
16. *New York Times*, February 1, 1939.
17. Quoted in Clifford, "A Note," 14.
18. Bennett Clark journal, February 2, 1939.
19. Transcript, "French Airplane Mission."
20. Warren F. Kimball, *The Juggler* (Princeton: Princeton University Press, 1991), p. 7.
21. Quoted in Sherry, *Air Power*, p. 79.
22. Henry Arnold quoted in John M. Haight, Jr., *American Aid to France, 1938–1940* (New York: Atheneum, 1970), p. 204.
23. Francois Duchêne, *Jean Monnet* (New York: Norton, 1994), p. 69.
24. Franklin D. Roosevelt to Helen Rogers Reid, June 6, 1940, Reid Papers, Library of Congress, Washington, D.C.
25. Quoted in John M. Blum, *From the Morgenthau Diaries* (Boston: Houghton Mifflin, 1959–1967; 3 vols.), *I*, 118.
26. Ambassador Ronald Lindsey quoted in Greg Kennedy, *Anglo-American Strategic Relations and the Far East, 1933–1939* (Portland, Ore.: Frank Cass, 2000), p. 229.

27. Joan Hoff Wilson, *American Business and Foreign Policy, 1920–1933* (Boston: Beacon Press, 1973), p. x.

28. Melvyn P. Leffler, *The Elusive Quest* (Chapel Hill: University of North Carolina Press, 1979), p. 362.

29. Quoted in L. Ethan Ellis, *Republican Foreign Policy, 1921–1933* (New Brunswick, N.J.: Rutgers University Press, 1968), p. 40.

30. Quoted in B. J. C. McKercher, "'A Certain Irritation'," *Diplomatic History, XXXI* (November 2007), 835.

31. Howard H. Quint and Robert H. Ferrell, eds., *The Talkative President* (Amherst: University of Massachusetts Press, 1964), p. 298.

32. Quoted in Frank Ninkovich, *Modernity and Power* (Chicago: University of Chicago Press, 1994), p. 80.

33. Stimson quoted in David F. Schmitz, *Henry L. Stimson* (Wilmington, Del.: Scholarly Resources, 2001), p. 79.

34. Warren F. Kuehl and Lynne K. Dunne, *Keeping the Covenant* (Kent, Ohio: Kent State University Press, 1997), p. 196.

35. Quoted in Warren F. Kimball, "The Second World War," in Dale Carter and Robin Clifton, eds., *War and Cold War in American Foreign Policy, 1942–62* (New York: Palgrave, 2002), p. 40.

36. Stimson quoted in Justus D. Doenecke and John E. Wilz, *From Isolation to War, 1931–1941* (Wheeling, Ill.: Harlan Davidson, 2003; 3d ed.), p. 49.

37. Willard Range, *Franklin D. Roosevelt's World Order* (Athens: University of Georgia Press, 1959), p. xii.

38. Benjamin Welles, *Sumner Welles* (New York: St. Martin's, 1997), p. 199.

39. Quoted in Jordan A. Schwarz, *Liberal* (New York: The Free Press, 1987), p. 191.

40. Wilbur Carr quoted in Martin Weil, *A Pretty Good Club* (New York: Norton, 1978), p. 47.

41. Mira Wilkins, *The Maturing of Multinational Enterprise* (Cambridge: Harvard University Press, 1974), p. 138.

42. Quoted in Ronald Hyam, *Britain's Declining Empire* (New York: Cambridge University Press, 2006), p. 34.

43. Quoted in Mary Nolan, *Visions of Modernity* (New York: Oxford University Press, 1994), p. 24.

44. Rob Kroes, "French Views of American Modernity," in Michael Kazin and Joseph A. McCartin, eds., *Americanism* (Chapel Hill: University of North Carolina Press, 2006), p. 227; Edward G. Lowry, "Trade Follows the Film," *Saturday Evening Post, CXCVIII* (November 7, 1925), 12; quoted in Michael H. Hunt, *The American Ascendancy* (Chapel Hill: University of North Carolina Press, 2007), p. 87.

45. Thomas Saunders, *Hollywood in Berlin* (Berkeley: University of California Press, 1994), p. 11.

46. Quoted in David Reynolds and David Dimbleby, *An Ocean Apart* (New York: Vintage, 1989), p. 116.

47. Quoted in Nolan, *Visions*, p. 216.

48. Victoria de Grazia, *Irresistible Empire* (Cambridge: Harvard University Press, 2005), p. 3.

49. Barbara J. Keys, *Globalizing Sports* (Cambridge: Harvard University Press, 2006), p. 65

50. Quoted in Paul Weindling, "Public Health and Political Stabilization," *Minerva, XXXI* (Autumn 1993), 261.

51. *New York Times,* May 5, 1930.

52. Charles Kindleberger, *The World in Depression, 1929–1939* (Berkeley: University of California Press, 1973), p. 222.

53. Quoted in Patricia Clavin, *The Failure of Economic Diplomacy* (New York: St. Martin's, 1996), p. 16.

54. Quoted in Robert A. Hathaway, "1933–1945: Economic Diplomacy in a Time of Crisis," in William H. Becker and Samuel F. Wells, Jr., eds., *Economics and World Power* (New York: Columbia University Press, 1984), p. 285.

55. Quoted in Blum, *Morgenthau Diaries, I,* 151.

56. Quoted in Richard A. Harrison, "The United States and Great Britain," in David F. Schmitz and Richard D. Challener, eds., *Appeasement in Europe* (Westport, Conn.: Greenwood, 1990), p. 116.

57. Ambassador Ronald Lindsay quoted in Doenecke and Wilz, *From Isolation,* p. 54.

58. Andrei Tardieu quoted in Philippe Roger, *The American Enemy* (Chicago: University of Chicago Press, 2005), p. 307.

59. Ramsay MacDonald quoted in B. J. C. McKercher, *Transition of Power* (New York: Cambridge University Press, 1999), p. 32.

60. Michael J. Hogan, "Revival and Reform," *Diplomatic History, VIII* (Fall 1984), 289.

61. Zara Steiner, *The Lights That Failed* (New York: Oxford University Press, 2005), pp. 621–622.

62. Marcus Marks quoted in Whitney Walton, "Internationalism and the Junior Year Abroad," *Diplomatic History, XXIX* (April 2005), 262.

63. Quoted in Harold Josephson, *James T. Shotwell and the Rise of Internationalism in America* (Rutherford, N.J.: Fairleigh Dickinson University Press, 1975), p. 140.

64. Quoted in Rhodri Jefferys-Jones, *Changing Differences* (New Brunswick, N.J.: Rutgers University Press, 1995), p. 53.

65. Frank B. Kellogg quoted in Patrick O. Cohrs, *The Unfinished Peace after World War I* (New York: Cambridge University Press, 2006), p. 448.

66. Kellogg quoted in Doenecke and Wilz, *From Isolation,* p. 14.

67. *The General Pact for the Renunciation of War* (Washington, D.C.: Government Printing Office, 1928).

68. James Cabell Bruce quoted in Robert David Johnson, *The Peace Progressives and American Foreign Relations* (Cambridge: Harvard University Press, 1995), p. 178.

69. Quoted in Michael Dunne, *The United States and the World Court* (New York: St. Martin's, 1988), p. 264.

70. Quoted in Melvyn P. Leffler, *The Specter of Communism* (New York: Hill & Wang, 1994), p. 19.

71. Quoted in David J. Danelski and Joseph S. Tulchin, eds., *The Autobiographical Notes of Charles Evans Hughes* (Cambridge: Harvard University Press, 1973), p. 262.

72. Quoted in Nick Cullather, "The Foreign Policy of the Calorie," *American Historical Review, CXI* (April 2007), 350.

73. Norman E. Saul, *Friends or Foes* (Lawrence: University Press of Kansas, 2006), pp. 169–170.

74. Loy Henderson quoted in Peter G. Boyle, *American-Soviet Relations* (London: Routledge, 1995), p. 23.

75. Katherine A. S. Siegel, *Loans and Legitimacy* (Lexington: University Press of Kentucky, 1996), p. 126.

76. Quoted in Vladislav M. Zubok, *A Failed Empire* (Chapel Hill: University of North Carolina Press, 2007), p. 12.

77. Quoted in Christine A. White, *British and American Commercial Relations with Soviet Russia, 1918–1924* (Chapel Hill: University of North Carolina Press, 1992), p. 223.

78. Quoted in Reynolds and Dimbleby, *Ocean Apart,* p. 118.

79. Quoted in David Bordwell, *The Cinema of Eisenstein* (Cambridge: Harvard University Press, 1993), p. 19.

80. FDR quoted in Mary Glance, *FDR and the Soviet Union* (Lawrence: University Press of Kansas, 2005), p. 19.

81. Quoted in David S. Foglesong, *The American Mission and the "Evil Empire"* (New York: Cambridge University Press, 2007), p. 77.

82. John Wiley quoted in Thomas R. Maddux, *Years of Estrangement* (Tallahassee: University Presses of Florida, 1980), p. 21.

83. Quoted in Irwin Gellman, *Secret Affairs* (Baltimore: Johns Hopkins University Press, 1995), p. 141.

84. Quoted in David Mayers, *The Ambassadors and America's Soviet Policy* (New York: Oxford University Press, 1995), p. 113.

85. Quoted in Beatrice Farnsworth, *William C. Bullitt and the Soviet Union* (Bloomington: Indiana University Press, 1967), p. 153.

86. Quoted in Mayers, *Ambassadors*, p. 115.

87. Quoted in Melvin Small, "Buffoons and Brave Hearts," *California Historical Quarterly, LII* (Winter 1973), 327.

88. Davies quoted in Elizabeth Kimball MacLean, *Joseph E. Davies* (Westport, Conn.: Praeger, 1992), p. 50; and quoted in Glance, *FDR and the Soviet Union*, p. 27.

89. Kennan quoted in David C. Engerman, *Modernization from the Other Shore* (Cambridge: Harvard University Press, 2003), p. 5; George F. Kennan, *Memoirs, 1925–1950* (Boston: Little, Brown, 1967), p. 67.

90. Frank Costigliola, "'Unceasing Pressure for Penetration,'" *Journal of American History, LXXXIII* (March 1997), 1316, 1321, 1329.

91. Ambassador Frederick Sackett quoted in Margot Louria, *Triumph and Downfall* (Westport, Conn: Greenwood Press, 2001), p. 220.

92. Quoted in Arnold A. Offner, *American Appeasement* (New York: Norton, 1976 [c. 1969]), p. 50.

93. Quoted in Raymond J. Sontag, *A Broken World, 1919–1939* (New York: Harper and Row, 1971), p. 290.

94. Ambassador Robert Bingham quoted in David F. Schmitz, *The United States and Fascist Italy, 1922–1940* (Chapel Hill: University of North Carolina Press, 1988), pp. 161–162.

95. Ambassador William Dodd quoted in George Eisen, "The Voices of Sanity: American Diplomatic Reports from the 1936 Berlin Olympiad," *Journal of Sports History, XI* (Winter 1984), 75; and Barbara J. Keys, "Spreading Peace, Democracy, and Coca-Cola," *Diplomatic History, XXVIII* (April 2004), 92.

96. Col. Truman Smith quoted in Thomas G. Mahnken, *Uncovering Ways of War* (Ithaca: Cornell University Press, 2002), p. 104.

97. Reynolds, *Creation*, p. 9.

98. Quoted in David Reynolds, *Britannia Overruled* (New York: Longman, 2000), p. 127.

99. Quoted *ibid.*, p. 129.

100. Quoted in Roy Douglas, "Chamberlain and Appeasement," in Wolfgang J. Mommsen and Lothar Kettenacker, eds., *The Fascist Challenge and the Policy of Appeasement* (London: Allen & Unwin, 1983), p. 87.

101. Quoted in Leffler, *Specter*, p. 26.

102. Harry S. Truman quoted in Robert H. Ferrell, ed., *Dear Bess* (New York: Norton, 1983), p. 419.

103. Quoted in James V. Compton, *The Swastika and the Eagle* (Boston: Houghton Mifflin, 1967), pp. 17, 25.

104. V. R. Bergahn, "Germany's America," *American Heritage, XLVI* (May/June 1995), 68; Uta G. Poiger, *Jazz, Rock, and Rebels* (Berkeley: University of California, Press, 2000), p. 15.

105. Quoted *ibid.*, p. 26; and movie poster quoted in Sabine Hake, *Popular Cinema of the Third Reich* (Austin: University of Texas Press, 2001), p. 133.

106. Quoted in Michael Lind, *The American Way of Strategy* (New York: Oxford University Press, 2006), p. 103.

107. Samuel I. Rosenman, ed., *Public Papers ... of Franklin D. Roosevelt, 1939* (New York: Macmillan, 1938–1950; 13 vols.), VIII, 463.

108. Thomas Wolfe quoted in Michaela Honicke Moore, "American Interpretations of National Socialism, 1939–1945," in Allen E. Steinweiss and Daniel E. Rogers, eds., *The Impact of Nazism* (Lincoln: University of Nebraska Press, 2003), p. 10.

109. Paul A. C. Koistinen, *Planning War, Pursuing Peace* (Lawrence: University Press of Kansas, 1998), p. 301.

110. Eleanor Roosevelt quoted in Blanche Wiesen Cook, "Eleanor Roosevelt and Human Rights," in Edward P. Crapol, ed., *Women and American Foreign Policy* (Wilmington, Del.: Scholarly Resources, 1992; 2nd ed.), p. 97.

111. Ernest Lundeen quoted in Thomas N. Guinsburg, "The Triumph of Isolationism," in Gordon Martel, ed., *American Foreign Relations Reconsidered, 1890–1993* (London: Routledge, 1994), p. 99.

112. Quoted in David G. Haglund, "Roosevelt as 'Friend of France'— But Which One?'" *Diplomatic History, XXXI* (November 2007), 893.

113. Quoted in Robert A. Divine, *The Reluctant Belligerent* (New York: Wiley, 1979; 2nd ed.), p. 52; and in Justus D. Doenecke and John E. Wilz, *From Isolation to War* (Arlington Heights, Ill.: Harlan Davidson, 1991; 2nd ed.), p. 15.

114. Offner, *American Appeasement*, p. 103.

115. Quoted in Carrie Foster, *The Women and the Warriors* (Syracuse: Syracuse University Press, 1995), p. 190.

116. Quoted in Linda K. Schott, *Reconstructing Women's Thoughts* (Syracuse: Syracuse University Press, 1997), p. 115.

117. Dominic Tierney, "Franklin D. Roosevelt and Covert Aid to the Loyalists in the Spanish Civil War, 1936-39," *Journal of Contemporary History, XXXIX* (September 2004), 99.

118. Chamberlain quoted in Thomas E. Mahl, *Desperate Deception* (New York: Brassey's, 1998), p. 5; Manfred Jonas, *Isolationism in America, 1935–1941* (Ithaca: Cornell University Press, 1966), p. viii.

119. FDR quoted in Alonzo L. Hamby, *For the Survival of Democracy* (New York: Free Press, 2004), p. 393.

120. Brenda Gayle Plummer, *Rising Wind* (Chapel Hill: University of North Carolina Press, 1996), p. 37.

121. Quoted in Alexander DeConde, *Ethnicity, Race, and American Foreign Policy* (Boston, Northeastern University Press, 1992), p. 107.

122. Rosenman, *Public Papers, 1936, V*, 289.

123. Douglas Little, *Malevolent Neutrality* (Ithaca: Cornell University Press, 1985), p. 265.

124. Chamberlain quoted in Hugh Ragsdale, *The Soviets, the Munich Crisis, and the Coming of World War II* (New York: Cambridge University Press, 2004), p. 40; and Sumner Welles quoted in J. Simon Rofe, *Franklin Roosevelt's Foreign Policy and the Welles Mission* (New York: Palgrave, 2007), p. 25.

125. Quoted in Keys, *Globalizing Sport*, p. 118.

126. *Foreign Relations, 1938, I* (Washington, D.C.: Government Printing Office, 1955), 685.

127. *Ibid.*, p. 688.

128. Roosevelt quoted in Hunt, *American Ascendancy*, p. 118.

129. Quoted in Reynolds, *Creation*, p. 43.

130. Quoted in Blum, *Morgenthau Diaries, II*, 49.

131. Rosenman, *Public Papers, 1939, VIII*, 4.

132. Quoted in Robert Dallek, *Franklin D. Roosevelt and American Foreign Policy, 1932–1945* (New York: Oxford University Press, 1979), p. 192.

133. Lord Lothian to Lord Halifax, September 27, 1939, vol. 24, Halifax Papers, Public Record Office, Kew, Eng.

134. FDR quoted in Rofe, *Welles Mission*, p. 12.

135. Kirk H. Porter and Donald B. Johnson, eds., *National Party Platforms, 1840–1972* (Urbana: University of Illinois Press, 1973), p. 382.

CHAPTER 5

Asia, Latin America, and the Vagaries of Power, 1920–1939

William E. Borah (1865–1940) and Henry L. Stimson (1867–1950). *The Idaho senator (left) chaired the Foreign Relations Committee (1925–1933). An isolationist, he opposed U.S. membership in the League of Nations and promoted neutrality; an anti-imperialist, he condemned U.S. interventions in Latin America; a peace advocate, he saluted the Kellogg-Briand Pact. A noted orator, Borah said much on most issues. "Borah this and Borah that, Borah here and there, Borah does and Borah doesn't, until you wish that Borah wasn't," wrote a journalist. In a February 1932 public letter to Borah, Secretary of State Stimson defended the Open Door policy during the Manchurian crisis. (Library of Congress)*

DIPLOMATIC CROSSROAD

❖ *The Manchurian Crisis, 1931–1932*

IT APPARENTLY STARTED with thirty-one inches of steel. At 10:20 P.M., just outside the Manchurian capital of Mukden on September 18, 1931, an explosion apparently blasted a short section from the South Manchurian Railway. Japanese soldiers apparently killed some Chinese attempting to escape from the area. Apparently? Yes, because Japanese army officers had a most difficult time explaining the events of that dark night. The Mukden Express somehow crossed over that very section of track *after* the alleged explosion. In fact, independent-minded young Japanese officers of the Guandong army, stationed in Manchuria ostensibly to protect the railroad, fabricated the "Mukden Incident" of September 18. They had plotted for months to seize Manchuria from China. Feverish in their quest for Japanese grandeur and Asian power, they or their followers had already, in 1930, assassinated the Japanese premier. So when the news from Mukden reached Tokyo, one civilian official remarked, "They've done it at last."[1]

For the Japanese—civilian or military—Manchuria ranked as a vital interest where the unprecedented "harmony of the five races" (Japanese, Chinese, Manchu, Mongolian, and Korean) might be perfected.[2] As large as France and Germany, with a population of 30 million (28 million Chinese), Manchuria served as a defensive buffer against the Soviet Union. The territory teemed with coal, iron, timber, and soybeans so desperately needed by the import-hungry Japanese islands. Manchuria accounted for more than half of Japan's foreign investments. The Japanese-run South Manchurian Railway interlaced these large economic holdings. Ever since their 1905 victory in the Russo-Japanese War, the Japanese had been driving in their imperial stakes. By treaty they had acquired the right to station troops along the railroad. Indeed, as early as 1910 Theodore Roosevelt had predicted: "As regards Manchuria, if the Japanese … follow a course of conduct to which we are adverse, we cannot stop it unless we are prepared to go to war."[3] Concurrently, Washington recognized Japan's primacy in Manchuria through the Root-Takahira and Lansing-Ishii agreements (see Chapter 2).

Chinese nationalists throughout the 1920s had resisted Japanese intrusions. Nationalist leader Jiang Jieshi (Chiang Kai-shek) encouraged his countrymen to move to Manchuria and sought to build a railroad to compete with the South Manchurian. The Chinese boycotted Japanese products, a particularly alarming practice during the Great Depression, when Japan's foreign trade slumped. Chinese and Japanese blood was spilled in isolated incidents. As Japanese schoolbooks would soon explain, because of aggression by the Pigs (Chinese), the land of the Sheep (Manchuria) had to "call in the Dogs" (Japanese) to protect the Sheep and Goats (Mongolians) from both Pigs and Bears (Soviet Union).[4]

The Mukden news of September 18, 1931, reached an irritable Secretary of State Henry L. Stimson, worn low by Washington's hot, humid temperatures. The weather accentuated what President Herbert Hoover called Stimson's "combat psychology."[5] The forthright secretary shared prevalent American attitudes that

"The Open Door."   The Japanese thrust into Manchuria in 1931 called into question the peace and disarmament agreements of the previous decade. A. U.S. diplomat described Japan in 1934 as "the combination of national centralization with feudal loyalty, of mysticism with technical efficiency, of medievalism with tanks and airplanes. … They dwell in a no-man's zone of time, their springs of action in the Middle Ages, their instruments of action out of the twentieth century." (*The Outlook,* 1931)

characterized Asians and the "Oriental mind" as "inferior."[6] He also embraced the Open Door policy and the sanctity of law. Japanese aggression in Manchuria violated treaties signed at the Washington Conference (1922), which endorsed the Open Door, and the Kellogg–Briand Pact (1928), which outlawed war.

Stimson hoped at first that the "Mukden Incident" would remain a localized mutiny of the Japanese army. No American wanted to become ensnarled in this hazardous terrain so "full of hidden explosives, dense underbrush, [and] quicksand."[7] The United States possessed little power in Asia. The British, interested in preserving their own Asian empire and hobbled by economic crisis at home, preferred to appease Japan. The French foundered in their frequent domestic political confusion. The Soviet Union, still not recognized by the United States, could hardly be called on for help. And the feeble League of Nations seemed unable to discipline "the big fellows."[8]

Stimson decided on a meek policy of letting "the Japanese know we are watching them."[9] On September 24, 1931, he urged the Chinese and Japanese to cease hostilities. A few days later the League began to discuss the Manchurian crisis, and a U.S. representative sat at the League table, if only as an "observer." Despite Stimson's fear that the international organization would "dump" the "Manchurian baby" in Washington's lap, the League passed mild peace resolutions and set up the Lytton Commission to investigate.[10] After Japanese forces occupied all of Manchuria by early December, Stimson thought Japan "in the hands of virtually mad dogs," with its army "running amok."[11]

The secretary had few options. He could not intervene militarily. Economic sanctions seemed a possibility. Stimson knew that the island empire depended on imports of American oil, that it was the third largest buyer of American exports, and that the United States took about 40 percent of Japan's exports. Maybe economic pressure would force Tokyo to disengage from Manchuria. Hoover, however, refused to stick "pins in tigers."[12] On January 7, 1932, Stimson issued what became known as the Stimson Doctrine. He threw tradition and law against Japan: The United States would not recognize any arrangements in China that might impair American treaty rights, violate the Open Door policy, or subvert the Kellogg-Briand Pact. Defiantly, on January 28, the Japanese marched into Shanghai, far to the south of Manchuria. A belligerent Stimson persuaded Hoover to reinforce the American military garrison in that city. Reminded of the German attack on Belgium in 1914, the secretary set his jaw against this new aggression.

Armed only with "spears of straw and swords of ice," Stimson tried to bluff.[13] On February 23, 1932, he sent a public letter to Senator William Borah, chair of the Senate Foreign Relations Committee—a letter the secretary hoped would "encourage China, enlighten the American public, exhort the League, stir up the British, and warn Japan."[14] Citing the Open Door policy, Stimson chastised Japan for violating the administrative and territorial integrity of China and the Kellogg-Briand agreement. He threatened to fortify Guam and build up the U.S. Navy in the Pacific if Japan did not halt its aggression. Although Japan soon signed an armistice in Shanghai and the League endorsed nonrecognition, this protest made little impact. In February, Japan actually reconstituted Manchuria as the puppet state of Manchukuo. That October the Lytton Commission censured the Japanese for misconduct in Manchuria. Evoking the image of a "crucified Japan," Tokyo ostentatiously resigned from the League in early 1933.[15] "In Japan," Stimson wrote, "the cause of Mr. Hyde [Japanese militants] against Mr. Jekyll has in large measure been victorious, and my efforts on behalf of the latter without much seeming result."[16] "No one here gives a two-penny d—n about" Manchuria, admitted a British diplomat.[17]

A Question of Power

Stimson's diplomatic efforts raise questions about the choices facing U.S. leaders during 1920–1939. Was it wise for Stimson to rail against Japanese machinations in Manchuria? Did it perhaps help the Japanese military gain support from civilian nationalists who also considered Manchuria vital? Did nonrecognition reveal just how weak the United States was in Asia? Did it not also expose China's abandonment by other nations? Yet, should and could Stimson have ignored treaty violations? Or should he have let the Asians settle their own differences? Did the Manchurian crisis threaten U.S. national interests?

Stimson soon admitted that nonrecognition had not worked. Moral exhortation may only have soothed the American conscience and stirred up the aggressor, to nobody's benefit. As the diplomat Hugh Wilson reflected: "Condemnation creates a community of the damned who are forced outside the pale, who have nothing to lose by the violation of all laws of order and international good faith." Those nations that "feel strongly enough to condemn … should feel strongly enough to use force,"

Makers of American Foreign Relations, 1920–1939

Presidents	Secretaries of State
Woodrow Wilson, 1913–1921	Bainbridge Colby, 1920–1921
Warren G. Harding, 1921–1923	Charles Evans Hughes, 1921–1925
Calvin Coolidge, 1923–1929	Frank B. Kellogg, 1925–1929
Herbert C. Hoover, 1929–1933	Henry L. Stimson, 1929–1933
Franklin D. Roosevelt, 1933–1945	Cordell Hull, 1933–1944

he judged.[18] Still, despite minimal U.S. interests in Manchuria, the principle of the Open Door, both as diplomatic tool and as symbol, stood at risk. If Tokyo could violate the Open Door in Manchuria, it could do so elsewhere, Stimson argued.

America's limited response to the Manchurian crisis demonstrated that the United States could not manage affairs in Asia. U.S. gunboats still chugged on Chinese rivers, American troops were garrisoned on Chinese soil, American business interests formed the Shanghai Power Company in 1928 and thus "Americanized" that city, and the Philippines remained a colony, but in Asia the Japanese exercised hegemony. The United States could lecture but not enforce.

By contrast, the United States held considerable power—economic, cultural, naval, military, political—in Latin America. Central America and the Caribbean were to the United States what China, especially Manchuria, was to Japan—resource-rich neighboring territories deemed vital to the national interest, where a proprietary relationship came to be assumed by the dominant power. Hence the United States in Latin America, like Japan in mainland Asia, practiced a version of the "closed door," seeking preponderant economic and political power to the exclusion of other states. In Asia, by contrast, where American power was comparatively weak, U.S. leaders appealed for the "Open Door" as a means of leveraging expanded influence.

The United States favored a world characterized by legal, orderly processes, economic openness, and political stability, all achieved through nonmilitary means. The Hoover-Stimson response to the Manchurian episode typified these goals and methods. Americans hoped to muzzle the dogs of war in order to stimulate domestic prosperity, expand foreign trade, and ensure national security. Yet the Manchurian crisis also revealed the ineffectiveness of the treaties of the 1920s and the reluctance of the European powers to check aggression in the 1930s, when appeasement became the policy of the day (see Chapter 4). What frightened Stimson and Hoover was "not so much China's fate as the specter of the great powers seizing new empires to rescue themselves from economic depression."[19] Japan's violation of the Nine Power Treaty eroded "the Washington Conference system," threatening global instability.[20] Given the timidity of the Europeans and the League, Americans recognized the limits of their own power and nurtured their independent internationalism, still hoping to create a peaceful international order. As in Europe, so in Asia would U.S. global aspirations fall short.

Facing Japan: The Washington Naval Disarmament Conference and China

The American pursuit of independent internationalism began conspicuously at the Washington naval conference of November 12, 1921, through February 6, 1922. After World War I a naval arms race loomed among the United States, Britain, and Japan. All parties recoiled from the spiraling financial costs. Japan was pumping as much as one-third of its national budget into naval construction. The United States, possessing the second largest navy in the world, occasionally menaced third-ranked Japan by stationing most of its heaviest battleships in the Pacific Fleet and by developing the base at Pearl Harbor. First-ranked Britain already had Singapore but lacked funds to engage in a sustained naval arms race. The U.S. Congress wanted to spend less on armaments, too. Thus all three powers welcomed arms control to check one another. Hoping to achieve a comprehensive agreement, the Harding administration thus invited Britain, France, Italy, Japan, China, Belgium, the Netherlands, and Portugal to Washington to discuss naval arms limitations and competition in Asia.

The conclave opened with dramatic words from bewhiskered Secretary of State Charles Evans Hughes, who announced that the United States would scrap thirty heavy ships. Then he turned to the British and eliminated twenty-three of their warships. The secretary next scuttled twenty-five large Japanese vessels. One commentator wrote that "Hughes sank in thirty-five minutes more ships than all the admirals of the world have sunk in a cycle of centuries."[21] Despite grumblings of doom from navy officers, the diplomats hammered out a naval limitations pact—the Five Power Treaty. It set a ten-year moratorium on the construction of capital ships—defined as battleships and battle cruisers—and limited the tonnage for aircraft carriers. The treaty also established a tonnage ratio for capital ships of 5 : 5 : 3 : 1.75 : 1.75 (United States : Britain : Japan : France : Italy; 1 equaling approximately 100,000 tons displacement). The top three naval powers agreed to dismantle sixty-six capital ships, many of them battleships. They also pledged not to build new fortifications in their Pacific possessions, such as the Philippines and Hong Kong, thus reassuring the Japanese, who had sarcastically accepted naval inferiority by translating 5 : 5 : 3 as Rolls Royce : Rolls Royce : Ford.

Another treaty—the Four Power—abolished the Anglo-Japanese Alliance of 1902 and simply obligated signatories to respect each other's Pacific territories. Washington secretly promised Tokyo: "no change whatsoever in Japan's present position in Manchuria."[22] All delegations also signed the Nine Power Treaty, an endorsement of the Open Door for the preservation of China's administrative integrity and equal trade opportunity. In other agreements, Japan consented to evacuate troops from the Shandong Peninsula as well as from Russian Siberia and the northern half of Sakhalin Island. Hughes's diplomatic success owed much to the State Department's "Black Chamber" code-breakers, who deciphered some 1,600 secret Japanese cables during the conference, proving that "stud poker is not a very difficult game after you've seen your opponent's hole card."[23]

The treaties signed in Washington essentially recognized the status quo in Asia. Japan had regional superiority, and the other powers could not challenge it without undertaking massive naval construction and expensive fortifications. Geography worked in Japan's favor in Asia, as it did for the United States in Latin America. The United States gave up only the *potential* of naval superiority—ships that Congress had no intention of funding ("phantom vessels sailing on seas of fancy," as one diplomat remarked).[24] The United States secured temporary verbal protection of the vulnerable Philippines and abolition of the Anglo-Japanese Alliance.

Shortcomings surfaced. The Five Power Treaty did not limit submarines, destroyers, or cruisers, thus sparking in those categories an arms race that agreements at the London conference of 1930 only partly curbed. Nor did the naval treaty provide means for verification. The Soviet Union, with major stakes in Asia, was not invited to attend the Washington conference, since the major powers were still attempting to isolate the Bolsheviks. None of the pacts contained enforcement provisions. In the mid-1930s, the Washington treaties succumbed to what one historian has called the "Icarus Factor"—the "waxwork of political webs" that sustained disarmament at the beginning and later "melted" before the "Rising Sun" of Japanese expansion.[25]

China, torn by civil war between Sun Zhonghan's (Sun Yat-sen's) Guomindang and regional warlords, lost the most. Chinese pleas for tariff autonomy, withdrawal of foreign troops, and an end to extraterritoriality fell on stony ground. Washington helped by negotiating the Japanese out of Shandong, but the imperial powers rejected full sovereignty for China and continued to do so even as the Guomindang (Nationalists) triumphed over its rivals by 1927. The Washington conference took a worthy step toward disarmament, but the absence of enforcement provisions and the refusal to recognize full Chinese territorial integrity left China vulnerable to military encroachment.

U.S. relations with the anti-imperialist, nationalist Chinese government proved nettlesome. In 1898 Americans had perceived the Philippines as stepping-stones to China; three decades later, in a historical flip-flop, a strong, friendly China appeared necessary to protect the U.S.-controlled islands from an expanding Japan. China thus took on new strategic importance for Americans in the late 1920s and 1930s. Also, many Americans remained mesmerized by the mirage of the China market and the inviolability of the Open Door principle. Sentimental considerations partly accounted for the attachment to China. Pearl Buck's best-selling *The Good Earth* (1931), made into a powerful movie six years later, captured for Americans the romance of hard-working, persevering Chinese peasants. One diplomat recalled this "righteous infatuation" with China, stemming from years of religious missionary activity and a self-congratulatory belief that the United States had become China's special friend by virtue of the Open Door, about which "Washington preached to everyone, including the Chinese."[26]

Washington sermonized fervently to the Japanese, Soviets, and Chinese Nationalists, all of whom strove to check Western imperialists in Asia. For the United States, peaceful change, the Open Door, protection of American property and citizens, and the treaty rights of trade and judicial extraterritoriality seemed threatened by local resistance, and Washington coupled its rhetoric of peace with shows of force. Sun Zhongshan, leader of the Chinese Revolution from its outbreak in 1911 until his death in 1925, bristled when U.S. gunboats visited Guangzhou in 1923 to thwart a potential Chinese takeover of foreign-dominated customshouses. Instead of "an American Lafayette" who would "fight on our side in this good cause," Sun lamented, "there comes not a Lafayette but an American Admiral with more ships of war than any other nation in our waters."[27]

Americans, caught between hostility to nationalists who wanted them out and a perceived need to advance U.S. economic opportunities in China, did little to assist the Guomindang at first. When Washington insisted on retaining its treaty privileges, the Chinese turned to another possible source of support, the Soviet Union. Seeking to restrain Japan, counter capitalist-imperialists, and implant communism, Moscow sent Soviet emissary Michael Borodin (alias of Mikhail Markovich Gruzenberg) to help the Nationalists centralize the structure of the Guomindang party. Americans understood neither the depth of Chinese nationalism nor Sun's use of Soviet agents for Chinese purposes; some Americans attributed China's intense anti-foreign sentiment to Bolshevik agitation.

In 1925, Sun died and the Nationalist outpouring in the May 30th Movement of that year led to attacks on foreign nationals and missionaries. Lieutenant Colonel George C. Marshall summed up his experience with the Fifteenth Infantry in China over the next two years: "We are either just out of near trouble with the Chinese or trouble is just hovering near us."[28] The outbreak of civil war within the Guomindang ranks soon prompted Washington to reconsider treaty privileges. In 1926–1927 the ambitious Nationalist leader Jiang Jieshi (Chiang Kai-shek) turned fiercely on his communist allies, booting Borodin back to Moscow and killing Chinese communists by the thousands. The communist leader Mao Zedong (Mao Tse-tung) fled south to Kiangsi Province, where he set up a rebel government and denounced Americans as imperialists "one hundred times worse than England or Japan."[29] Jiang told U.S. officials that only American assistance could buttress China in "holding off" Japan and Soviet Russia and averting "a great war in the Pacific."[30] Washington signed a trade treaty in 1928 that restored tariff autonomy to China and granted most-favored-nation treatment. By 1930 more than 500 American companies were operating in China, with investments amounting to $155 million, still only 1 percent of total American foreign investments. From 1923 to 1931 the United States sent only 3 percent of its exports to China. American trade with Japan totaled twice as much.

Although at least one U.S. sailor left China having "seen enough of this yeller race to suit me a while," Washington policymakers waxed hopeful because American-trained Chinese "cosmopolitans" such as H. H. Kung (Kŏng Xiángx), Hū Shi, and T. V. Soong (Sóng Zivén) were gaining influence in the Guomindang.[31] The Rockefeller Foundation was training an English-speaking elite through institutions such as the Peking Union Medical College, where American "modernizers" introduced "scientific medicine" and purported to "make over a medieval society in terms of modern knowledge."[32] Jiang had joined the crusade against communism. In 1930, furthermore, he converted to Christianity and married Meiling Soong, daughter of the American-educated, prominent Chinese businessman Charles Soong. "Part dreamy lotus flower, part sullen tiger lily, and part American rose," the Wellesley College honors graduate, with her "fluency in English and attractive femininity," soon established ties with prominent Americans, later called the China Lobby.[33] With flattering photographs of China's first couple appearing in *Life* magazine, the beautiful,

Two First Ladies. In this photograph taken in 1943, Eleanor Roosevelt (1884–1962) and Madame Jiang Jieshi (1897–2003) exemplified the friendly relations between the United States and China. Mrs. Roosevelt described her counterpart as "this very beautiful, very charming, very gentle woman." Madame Jiang's feminine charms and "her American popularity," writes the historian Karen J. Leong," were "valuable tools in promoting" the Sino-American alliance. (Library of Congress)

intelligent, and "Westernized" Madame Jiang became the perfect "damsel in distress" as she—and the new God-fearing China—appealed to American notions of "mission, chivalry, and machismo."[34]

Japan's Footsteps Toward Pacific Hegemony

Fearing the future, Japanese leaders became zealous expansionists. With 65 million people living in an area smaller than Texas in 1931, Japan had become dependent on outside sources for vital raw materials. The Japanese also complained that Western nations had for years intruded into their sphere of influence and controlled products central to their economy, such as oil. Japan sought self-sufficiency because "a tree must have its roots," citing U.S. "roots" in Latin America as an example.[35] Japan was only doing what the Western powers had done, Tokyo rationalized. The imperialists had taught Japan the game of poker but then, after winning most of the chips, pronounced the game immoral and took up contract bridge. As a Japanese diplomat noted during the Manchurian crisis: "Did not the United States send 6,000 troops into Nicaragua to protect only 600 Americans … for the same reason as the Japanese are acting?"[36] In August 1936, Tokyo secretly adopted the "Fundamental Principles of National Strategy," which called for both southern expansion by peaceful "footsteps" toward the British, Dutch, and French empires of Southeast Asia (favored by the navy) and a northern advance into China and Mongolia (favored by the army).[37] Three years later, Japan announced its imperial ambitions by proclaiming the "Greater East Asia Co-Prosperity Sphere" wherein Japan would gain raw materials and markets from the rest of East Asia.

Despite the spectacular success of Babe Ruth's 1934 baseball tour in which the famed Yankee slugger became a "household name" in Japan, the United States soon ranked first on Tokyo's list of potential enemies.[38] A Japanese navy study of 1936 stated that "in case the enemy's [America's] main fleet is berthed at Pearl Harbor the idea should be to open hostilities by surprise attacks from the air."[39] Ambassador Joseph Grew predicted that Japanese extremists "might well" commit "national hara-kiri."[40] Japan became the enemy on the war-game board at the U.S. Naval War College. Naval competition intensified in 1935–1936 when the London conference broke up without agreement and Japan announced its abrogation of earlier treaties. The Immigration Act of 1924, blatantly discriminatory in excluding Japanese citizens from entering the United States, also rankled Tokyo "right down to the bone."[41] A Japanese nationalist predicted an "inevitable clash of civilizations" in which Japan and the United States "are destined to fight each other as Greece had to fight against Persia, and Rome against Carthage."[42] Trade disputes intensified. Inexpensive Japanese goods, especially textiles, entered the American market, undercutting some domestic producers. "Buy America" campaigns and public boycotts of Japanese goods followed. Japan began to close the trade and investment door in China.

President Franklin D. Roosevelt continued Stimson's nonrecognition policy, reflecting American weakness in Asia. But at least until 1937, the long lull in fighting between China and Japan did not seem to require U.S. action. Roosevelt did move to bring the navy up to the strength permitted by the Washington and London conference treaties. Under New Deal programs in 1933, the president allocated funds for thirty-two new vessels, including two aircraft carriers, and by 1937 naval appropriations had doubled. Isolationists called it "relief for the munitions makers."[43] Two years earlier the United States staged large-scale naval maneuvers near Midway Island in the Pacific to impress the Japanese. Instead of deterring Tokyo, these naval activities reinforced Japan's secret decision in May 1937 to outbuild the Americans and construct warships "above and beyond the quantitative and qualitative limits of the naval treaties"—including the huge 64,000-ton battleships *Yamato* and *Musashi*.[44] FDR's diplomatic recognition of the Soviet Union in 1933 aimed in part to cow Japan by arousing suspicion that Moscow and Washington had linked arms in Asia. Four years later, Captain Claire Chennault, retired from the U.S. Army Air Corps, joined the Chinese air force as chief adviser. By 1940 American volunteer pilots manned his "Flying Tigers" unit.

On July 7, 1937, Japanese and Chinese troops clashed at the Marco Polo Bridge near Beijing. This skirmish grew quickly into the "China Incident" (not a "war" because the Kellogg-Briand Pact outlawed wars). Fighting spread throughout China. Shanghai fell to Japan in November after a costly battle and the indiscriminate bombing of civilians. The "rape" of Nanjing followed in December, when the order to "Kill All Captives" resulted in beheadings, bayoneting, burnings, sexual violence, and live burials.[45] Journalists reported "wholescale atrocities," as Japanese soldiers raped 80,000 women and massacred some 300,000 residents of China's then capital city.[46] A U.S. military observer recoiled at bloated corpses—"like grotesque

Shanghai, China, 1937.
This photograph of a baby amid the ruins of North Station after Japanese bombing galvanized American opinion against Tokyo. Because of such scenes, the U.S. ambassador to China, Nelson T. Johnson, complained about the "terrible ordeal just to have to sit helplessly by and watch men, women, and children killed in cold blood by these cowards of the sky who float in safety high in the air dropping their death where they will." (National Archives)

inflated rubber figures which children sometimes play with … at seaside resorts. The stench was almost unbearable."[47]

Civil war between Jiang's Guomindang forces and Mao Zedong's communists further sapped China. The communists had declared war on Japan in 1932, charging Jiang with appeasing Tokyo. Until 1937 Jiang fought the communists more than he fought the Japanese. From 1935 to 1937, the communists took the dramatic "Long March" from their southern haven to Yan'an (Yenan) in the north—an expedition of 6,000 miles. In late 1936, dissident Chinese army forces in Manchuria kidnapped Jiang, hoping to end the civil war by creating a coalition government. Joseph Stalin and the Chinese communists soon secured his release and persuaded him to institute a tenuous united front against Japan in early 1937. Thereafter Moscow increased arms sales and technical assistance to Jiang and Soviet troops delivered a "firm rebuff" to the Japanese in border clashes along the Manchurian and Mongolian frontiers in 1938 and 1939.[48]

Having refused to invoke American neutrality after the Marco Polo Bridge incident, thereby permitting valuable trade to continue with China, Roosevelt addressed a Chicago audience on October 5, 1937. He dramatically called for a "quarantine" against aggressors to check the "epidemic of world lawlessness."[49] After the speech, FDR privately toyed with economic warfare—a naval blockade or embargo—but drew back following isolationist protests over his speech. In November Roosevelt sent representatives to an eighteen-nation conference in Brussels to defuse the Sino-Japanese crisis, but it disbanded without taking a stand—only the Soviet Union pushed for reprisals against Japan. In December the American gunboat *Panay,* escorting on the Yangtze River three Standard Oil Company tankers flying American flags, took destructive fire from Japanese pilots. Two U.S. sailors died. With Secretary Hull blasting the perpetrators

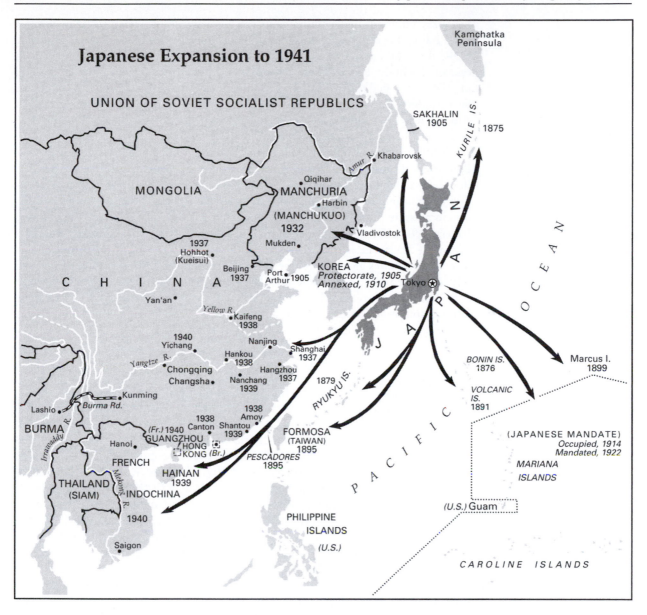

Japanese Expansion to 1941

as "wild, runaway, half-insane men," Tokyo quickly apologized and paid an indemnity.[50]

Japan plunged deeper into China in 1938 in what was called the "Three-All" campaign—"Kill All, Burn All, Loot All."[51] Amid reports that "the Japanese fly has at last got himself well entangled in the Chinese flypaper," the Roosevelt administration cautiously initiated new measures.[52] By purchasing Chinese silver, the United States gave China dollars with which to buy American military equipment.

Secretary Hull imposed a "moral embargo" on the sale of aircraft to Japan, while a naval bill authorized two new aircraft carriers and the doubling of naval airplanes. FDR also sent a secret naval emissary to London to discuss contingency plans in case of war in the Pacific. These actions did not deter the Japanese, who by the end of 1938 controlled virtually all major Chinese seaports, had established exploitative development companies, and had begun to install a puppet Chinese regime. An American trade commissioner in Shanghai accurately noted that the "Open Door" was being "banged, barred, and bolted."[53]

With war clouds billowing in Europe in the summer of 1939 (see Chapter 4), Roosevelt abrogated the Japanese-American commercial treaty of 1911. Because the United States was supplying Japan with 44 percent of its imports, mostly automobiles, machinery, copper, oil, iron, and steel, FDR hoped that the threat of economic pressure might temper Japan's onslaught in China. The abrogation, effective January 1940, did not immediately curtail bilateral trade, but Ambassador Grew's talks with the Japanese foreign minister in the fall of 1939 elicited a Japanese pledge to cease brutalities against foreigners. In November 1939, another American naval bill authorized two more battleships. By then World War II had begun in Europe, and Japanese-American relations had stalemated. Unwilling to fight over China, Washington had to decide what to do if Japan expanded beyond China. Those fateful decisions would come in 1941.

What if ... *Americans had not sympathized with China over Japan after 1931?*

Had the Japanese not seized Manchuria in 1931–1932, the positive images that Americans had projected onto Japan over the previous three decades might have continued: the plucky Japan that defeated Russia in the Russo-Japanese War; the grateful Japanese whose gift of 3,000 cherry trees in 1912 would beautify Washington's Tidal Basin for the next century; the "associate" power that shared in the victory over Imperial Germany in World War I; the co-interventionist against Bolshevik Russia after 1918; the cooperative and commercial Japan that abided by the Washington Conference rules in the 1920s; the helpless victim of earthquakes that elicited donations from millions of U.S. school children; the one Asian country that embraced American baseball and exuberantly applauded a visiting Babe Ruth in 1934.

China's comparatively negative image might have endured as well—the inscrutable and sinister "other" of Hollywood films; the fractured land of battling warlords, of Generalissimo Jiang Jieshi and his "red" advisers; the barbaric nation that mistreated foreign missionaries and issued bellicose anti-Western demands; the teeming embodiment of the "Yellow Peril." Jiang's marriage to Meiling Soong, his conversion to Christianity, and Japan's lightning conquest of Manchuria quickly changed attitudes. The brutal Japanese invasion of China in 1937 accelerated the perceptual turnaround, punctuated by the "rape" of Nanjing and such searing photographs as that of the helpless Chinese child in the ravaged Shanghai railroad station (see p. 154). The "sneak attack" on Pearl Harbor in December 1941 solidified the inverted imagery of China as victim and Japan as monster.

Yet popular sympathies need not have determined American diplomacy in the 1930s. The pro-China fervor rested as much on illusion and exaggeration as on reality. Conditioned by Henry Luce's influential publications *Time* and *Life,* Americans imagined China as a gallant victim of bloodthirsty aggression, a magical land inhabited by hard-working peasants as portrayed in the award-winning film *The Good Earth* (1937). Photographs of the beautiful Madame Jiang standing loyally beside her husband masked the ineptitude, divisions, and corruption of Guomindang China. Despite these perceptions, had President Herbert Hoover won a second term in 1932, Japanophiles in the State Department might have persuaded Hoover to mediate between Japan and China, thus delaying or avoiding the vicious undeclared war that broke out in 1937. Mutual opposition to the Soviet Union might have provided the glue for a Republican administration's rapprochement with Tokyo. Even under President Franklin D. Roosevelt, the State Department largely ignored pro-China opinion and worked doggedly until 1941 to keep the Sino-Japanese conflict from expanding beyond China. Beating Hitler first and avoiding a two-ocean war seemed more important than rescuing a mythical China. If Washington had not cut off oil to Japan, perhaps the Japanese warlords might not have embarked on their ultimately suicidal Pacific War. In the end, cultural images mattered less than Japan's decision to roll the dice for larger empire and enter the war on the side of Nazi Germany.

Notwithstanding official U.S. wartime propaganda that accentuated the images of China as democratic friend and Japan as subhuman foe, these popular perceptions proved ephemeral within a decade as a newly communist China morphed into an American enemy and Japan became a Cold War ally. The example of movie actor Richard Loo underscored the irony of this evolution. Born in Hawai'i of Chinese-Korean descent, Loo had portrayed the archetypal Japanese whom American audiences loved to hate in such wartime films as *Purple Heart* (1944) and *First Yank in Tokyo* (1945). His accented and idiomatic English, delivered in a sneering, mocking manner, personified the malevolent wartime enemy. Yet by the time of the Korean War in 1950, Loo had ceased playing Japanese roles and switched to impersonating sinister Chinese and North Koreans. Prior to his death in 1983, he had become a television pitchman for Toyota commercials. Such fluctuating popular sentiments toward China and Japan during the mid-twentieth century alternately reflected, facilitated, and strained American relations with each country.

Being "Neighborly" in Latin America

In contrast with Asia, U.S. power in the Western Hemisphere remained unmatched. Indeed, shortly after World War I, U.S. armed forces used the Caribbean for maneuvers—to rehearse for a possible Pacific war with Japan. And when Germany and Japan marched aggressively in the 1930s, the United States brought most of

Latin America into a virtual alliance to resist foreign intrusions into the hemisphere. The imperial net in Latin America had been stitched together before and during World War I, especially in Central America and the Caribbean, through military occupations, naval demonstrations, the Panama Canal, management of national finances, threat of intervention, nonrecognition, and economic ties. A U.S. diplomat in Guatemala, revealing endemic U.S. attitudes of racial condescension, reported in 1921 that "the bacillus of revolution is in the blood of these people, and will never be eradicated until some strong hand is placed over them and the serum of hard work is injected into them by force."[54] The Roosevelt Corollary to the Monroe Doctrine provided the overriding justification for U.S. hegemony (see Chapter 2). Swaggering American marines in the streets of Havana, Managua, or Port-au-Prince represented the most conspicuous evidence of North American imperial management.

The use of marines as instruments of policy, however, became unpopular and counterproductive, and nationalist sentiment, especially in Mexico and Argentina, placed limits on U.S. power. Anti-imperialists such as Senators George Norris and William Borah demanded self-determination for Latin Americans. Congress resented both the costs of military incursion and the president's usurpation of congressional prerogatives when he unilaterally dispatched troops to the Caribbean. Business leaders came to believe that military expeditions, because they aroused anti–U.S. sentiment and violence, endangered rather than protected their properties. Referring to Japan's seizure of Manchuria, and alert to a double standard, Secretary Stimson commented in 1932: "If we landed a single soldier among those

Charles A. Lindbergh (1902–1974) Returns from Latin America, 1928. Lindbergh made aviation history on May 20, 1927, when he flew nonstop from New York to Paris in the *Spirit of St. Louis.* To promote U.S. goodwill toward Latin America, the aviator began a tour in December 1927 that first took him to Mexico. There he met Anne Morrow, the daughter of Ambassador Dwight Morrow; later Lindbergh married her. After visiting Guatemala, Panama, Venezuela, and other countries, Lindbergh returned from Cuba in February 1928. In the late 1930s, Lindbergh became an outspoken isolationist opponent of U.S. intervention in World War II, and in his last years he earned yet another reputation as a conservationist. (Lindbergh Picture Collection, Yale University Library)

South Americans now … it would put me absolutely in the wrong in China, where Japan has done all this monstrous work under the guise of protecting her nationals with a landing force."[55]

Between the world wars, therefore, Washington forswore overt armed inter-ference and employed economic penetration, political subversion, nonrecognition, support for dictators who kept order, clandestine military aid to rebels, arbitration treaties, Pan Americanism, financial supervision, Export-Import Bank loans, and the training of indigenous national guards. At times U.S. officials pressed for negoti-ated settlements, as, in 1929, when Secretary Kellogg helped settle the Tacna-Arica dispute between Chile and Peru. These tactics translated into a catchy phrase popu-larized by Franklin D. Roosevelt—the Good Neighbor policy. In early 1933, FDR hailed "the policy of the good neighbor—the neighbor who resolutely respects himself and, because he does so, respects the rights of others—the neighbor who respects his obligations and respects the sanctity of his agreements in and with a world of neighbors."[56] Although Latin Americans welcomed the new spirit, the goal of U.S. hegemony in the hemisphere had not changed, only the means for maintain-ing it, namely, by economic and political rather than military pressure.

Economic decisions by U.S. leaders, private and governmental, held immense importance for Latin American nations. In the Dominican Republic, Cuba, and Haiti, for example, officials had to obtain U.S. consent before borrowing foreign capital. With its ambassador in Washington working to influence U.S. decisions on copper purchases and Chilean bonds, both vital to his nation's livelihood, Chile in the 1930s had never "felt so totally controlled by the unpredictable attitudes of a foreign power."[57] In Cuba, where North American interests accounted for about two-thirds of sugar production, U.S. investments helped lock the country into a risky one-crop economy subject to fluctuating world sugar prices. In Honduras, U.S. companies provided cannon and machine guns to one political group that conducted a successful coup in 1924. In 1929 U.S. firms produced more than half of Venezuela's oil. Their bribery of Venezuelan government officials, including the president, was not uncommon. In Guatemala, the arrogance of American shipping and rail executives caused a State Department official in 1938 to question "the pro-priety of an American corporation, possessing a monopoly of essential transporta-tion facilities in a foreign country, and operating in virtually complete independence of … either the American or Guatemalan governments."[58]

In a process sometimes called "colonialism by contract," professional economists such as Edward Kemmerer of Princeton University served as financial advisers (or "money doctors") to Colombia, Chile, Ecuador, and Peru during the 1920s, usually recommending gold-exchange currency reforms managed by a central bank, new taxes, revised tariffs, and private American loans for public-works projects tied to U.S. firms.[59] Popular at first, such programs aroused nationalist backlashes in the 1930s when declining exports, excessive indebtedness, and contracting capital mar-kets caused massive defaults throughout Latin America, where Wall Street's "diaboli-cal machine" was viewed as "emasculating" ("*desvirilizado*") local elites and turning them into "*los estrangulados*" ("strangled ones").[60]

The Argentine writer Manuel Ugarte bluntly identified a "new Rome" in the mid-1920s. The United States, he explained, annexed wealth rather than territory,

Marine Recruiting Poster.   Marines landed in many parts of Latin America, especially the Caribbean. But battle and occupation conditions were hardly as pleasant as depicted in James Montgomery Flagg's drawing. And, asked critics, once you are on the jaguar's back, how do you get off? (Library of Congress)

thus enjoying the "essentials of domination" without the "dead-weight of areas to administrate and multitudes to govern." U.S. economic penetration always "invoked peace, progress, civilization and culture; but its motives, procedure, and results have frequently been a complete negation of these premises."[61] Nonetheless, Hollywood movies and other manifestations of U.S. popular culture held a unique appeal, as Argentine newspapers, for example, featured such comic strips as "El Chiquito ['Li'l'] Abner" and "El Raton Mickey ['Mouse']."[62] Similarly, President Roosevelt's smiling personification of the Good Neighbor seemed to make the Yankee presence more palatable—"a gringo in the Latin mold, a man they could understand and empathize with as a projection of their own political style," the scholar Fredrick B. Pike has written. "The man was so *simpatico*: and that papered over a multitude of sins."[63]

Although Latin American intellectuals often regarded North American "intruders as crass émigrés from a materialist culture," a U.S. consul in Brazil appreciated one of the ways the United States cultivated ruling elites.[64] He praised Rotary International, whose "meetings are attended by members of the Federal Cabinet, mayors of cities, and other officials who … welcome our support and cooperation."[65] Still, too many North Americans resembled the boorish member of Congress who insulted a Latin American diplomat's wife: "Señora, I regret that I know only two words of your beautiful language: mañana, which means tomorrow, and pyjama, which means tonight."[66] When a young Nelson Rockefeller visited Venezuela in the early 1930s to look after his oil investments, he noticed that U.S. citizens there seldom learned Spanish. "Why should I?" asked one American. "Who would I talk to in Spanish?"[67] Rockefeller thereupon hired twelve Berlitz instructors to begin

Nelson A. Rockefeller (1908–1979) and Anastasio Somoza García (1896–1956). The grandson of Standard Oil millionaire John D. Rockefeller, Sr., Nelson (second from right) functioned as director of the family oil business in Venezuela during the 1930s. An advocate of improved U.S. cultural, scientific, and educational relations within the hemisphere, Rockefeller served as coordinator of the Office of Inter-American Affairs for the State Department during World War II. Elected governor of New York in 1958, Rockefeller became vice president in 1974 under President Gerald Ford following President Richard Nixon's resignation during the Watergate scandal. Rockefeller is dining here with Nicaraguan strongman Somoza, who ruled from 1937 to 1956, aligned himself with the United States, and created a corrupt family dynasty in his country. (National Archives)

Spanish classes for company employees. Unless U.S. corporations used "its ownership of assets to reflect the best interests of the [Latin American] people," Rockefeller warned in 1937, "they will take away our ownership."[68]

Less successful was auto manufacturer Henry Ford's attempt in the late 1920s to establish Fordlandia, a huge rubber plantation in the Amazon rain forest of Brazil. On terrain three times the size of Rhode Island, Ford tried to replicate the same mass production techniques he had perfected in Detroit, soon building an American-style town with sidewalks, fire hydrants, modern hospital, and bungalows for 4,000 agricultural workers. Yet Ford's managers ignored Brazilian botanists who urged that rubber trees be scattered at safe distances to prevent South American leaf blight. Instead, the overseers planted trees in tightly regimented rows. As a result, by 1934 the disease had spread from tree to tree, devastating the plantation and another similar enterprise downriver. After investing $20 million and planting more than 3 million rubber trees over seventeen years, Ford's company sold its property to the Brazilian government for $250,000, and "hardly any Fordlandia latex ever found its way into a Ford tire."[69]

U.S. investments in and trade with Latin America reached a "boom" stage after World War I. The direct investments of U.S. citizens (excluding bonds and securities) jumped from $1.26 billion in 1914 to $3.52 billion in 1929, mostly in electric power, railroads, bananas, sugar, oil, and minerals. By 1936, because of the devastating impact of the global depression, the amount dropped to $2.77 billion. These figures represented about one-third of total U.S. investments abroad. One of the nation's largest corporations, Standard Oil of New Jersey, operated in eight countries, and United Fruit Company held a large stake in the "banana republics" of Central America. International Telephone and Telegraph controlled communications in Cuba, where, between 1919 and 1933, overall U.S. investments increased 536 percent. Worried about diminishing domestic oil reserves after World War I, Washington urged U.S. firms to preempt foreign competitors in South America. "A conference of the leading oil producers was called," recorded Commerce Secretary Hoover, "and such action taken that most of the available oil lands in South America were acquired by Americans."[70] In the period 1925–1929 in Latin America, the average annual income outflow from U.S. investments totaled $100 million more than the U.S. capital inflow.

With trade following investments, U.S. exports to Latin America tripled in value from 1914 to 1929, reaching the billion-dollar figure, approximately 20 percent of total U.S. exports. Although this impressive trade slumped during the Great Depression, for many Latin American countries commercial relationships with the United States remained critical. Nicaragua, for example, shipped 96 percent of its exports to the United States by 1941. In 1920 the United States supplied Cuba with 73 percent of its imports; that trade shrank to 59 percent in 1929 because of the depressed Cuban sugar economy. Cuba's exports to the United States also dropped off, although they still comprised 68 percent of all the island's exports. American investments in and trade with Venezuela moved the British out and helped that country to become the world's leading exporter of oil. Trade with Chile in nitrates and copper jumped after U.S. investments there doubled from $200 million in 1920 to $400 million in 1928. To stem declining world trade during the 1930s, Secretary Hull sought wider markets in Latin America when he launched the Export-Import Bank (directing loans to inter-American commerce) and the Reciprocal Trade Agreements Program. His efforts helped increase exports to Latin America from $244 million in 1933 to $642 million in 1938.

Creating "Frankenstein" Dictators in the Dominican Republic, Nicaragua, and Haiti

Until World War I, corrupt politics in the Dominican Republic and mismanagement of national revenues produced economic stagnation, political factionalism, foreign indebtedness, and U.S. intervention (see Chapter 2). In May 1916, to quell local disorder, American marines went ashore. Although U.S. forces occupied the major cities and established martial law, the peasants and caudillos in the mountainous east waged bloody guerrilla war from 1917 to 1922. The marines retaliated in kind against rebels who "are almost all touched with the tarbrush," as Military Governor Harry Knapp crudely put it.[71] Marine atrocities against Dominican people of color usually went unpunished. Sumner Welles, the American commissioner to the Dominican Republic (1922–1924), later criticized the U.S. officers who ran the occupation—"the great majority of whom could not even speak the language of the country."[72]

The military intervention in the Dominican Republic became a hot political issue at home and abroad. Warren G. Harding accused Wilson of the "rape of Haiti" in the 1920 campaign but continued the Dominican and Haitian occupations as president.[73] When Washington ended the occupation in 1924, after forcing on the Dominican government a stabilization loan to liquidate past debt, and when the new national guard consumed a quarter of the Dominican budget, Hughes ingeniously claimed that the departure proved that the United States was "anti-imperialistic."[74] Franklin D. Roosevelt agreed in a 1928 article in *Foreign Affairs:* "We accomplished an excellent piece of constructive work, and the world ought to thank us."[75] With Americans running the country's fiscal affairs until 1941, FDR ignored "the lasting hostility towards the American people which the occupation created in the hearts of … the Dominican people."[76]

The U.S. occupation also begot Rafael Leonidas Trujillo. In early 1919, he received a commission as a second lieutenant in the U.S.-created national guard. The onetime thief, forger, and pimp earned high marks from U.S. military officers and became chief of staff of the army in 1928. Through the rigged election of 1930, Trujillo won the presidency. The State Department initially looked on Trujillo as "a kind of Frankenstein, brought to life by the marines" and likely to spawn new insurrections, but Washington gradually warmed to him when his strong-arm tactics obviated the need for U.S. military intervention.[77] Thanks to beneficent U.S. control of the customs, Trujillo could divert funds to his army for the suppression of domestic dissent. Political corruption, military muscle, torture, murder, nepotism, commercial monopolies, and raids on the national treasury enabled Trujillo to quiet opponents and amass a fortune of $800 million.

From 1930 until his assassination in 1961, sometimes as president, sometimes through puppets, Trujillo became "the dictatingest dictator who ever dictated," as *Time* called him.[78] U.S. military arms filled Dominican arsenals. U.S. business leaders, who dominated sugar production, endorsed him. Most of the country's imports came from the United States. The National City Bank became the official depository for Dominican revenues. By World War II, the Dominican Republic stood as a success story for the new Good Neighbor policy. But good neighbors with whom? Roosevelt reportedly gave an answer in reference to Trujillo: "He may be an S.O.B., but he is our S.O.B."[79]

Nicaragua, like the Dominican Republic, felt the weight of U.S. military occupation and Good Neighbor pressures. From 1912 to 1925 the United States ruled Nicaragua and kept in power the pliant Conservative party. Nicaragua by 1925 appeared to be solvent, secure, and stable. The marines departed, but in late 1926 they returned because, in President Coolidge's words, Nicaragua "went to hell in a hack."[80] In an overstated report titled "Bolshevik Aims and Policies in Mexico and Latin America," Secretary Kellogg alleged that communists were fomenting trouble in Nicaragua. The U.S. embassy in Mexico had greatly exaggerated the activities of American leftists in Mexico, and Washington found the anti-Bolshevik rationale irresistible. In fact, it was Nicaraguan Liberals, not communists, who had used Mexico as a sanctuary to challenge the Conservatives. "We are not making war on Nicaragua," Coolidge opined, "any more than a policeman on the street is making war on passersby."[81] Nicaraguans in the Coco River basin saw it differently: "The Machos are coming," they said of the marines. "They will burn our houses."[82]

The Nicaraguan intervention generated rancorous debate in the United States. The allegation of a communist plot persuaded few. Congress again resented presidential initiatives that ignored the legislature's power to declare war. Senator Burton K. Wheeler suggested that if U.S. soldiers intended to "stamp out banditry,

Rafael Trujillo (1891–1961). The strongman of the Dominican Republic graduated from an American military training school and went on to rule his nation from 1930 to 1961, when he was assassinated. The historian Eric Paul Roorda explains that a "group of pro-Trujillo businessmen, legislators, and paid advocates constituted a kind of 'Dominican Lobby' in the United States with Joseph E. Davies at the center." In 1933 Davies became Trujillo's counsel—negotiating, lobbying, and propagandizing for the regime in the United States. Four years later, President Roosevelt appointed his friend Davies as the U.S. ambassador to the Soviet Union. (*The Reporter,* 1961. Copyright 1961 by The Reporter Magazine Co.)

César Augusto Sandino (1895–1934). President Hoover called him a "cold-blooded bandit," but Nicaraguans have hailed Sandino as a hero. Determined that Nicaragua control its natural resources and help the poor, Sandino blasted the Monroe Doctrine as meaning "America for the Yankees." Accused of administering "machete justice" to members of the Guardia Nacional, Sandino countered that "liberty is not conquered with flowers." The revolutionaries who overthrew the Somoza dictatorship in 1979 called themselves "Sandinistas." (Library of Congress)

let's send them to Chicago to stamp it out there. … I wouldn't sacrifice … one American boy for all the damn Nicaraguans."[83] Bloodshed and destruction in Nicaragua raised further outcries after Secretary of the Navy Curtis D. Wilbur matter-of-factly reported in 1928: "Several houses were destroyed in the village of Quilali in order to prepare a landing field for airplanes so that 19 wounded Marines could be evacuated to a hospital."[84] From 1927 to 1933 the Liberal insurgent Cèsar Augusto Sandino, who railed against the "dastardly invaders," earned an international reputation as he waged guerrilla war against U.S. troops, numbering 5,000 in early 1929.[85] Two Hollywood films in 1929, *Flight* and *Cock-eyed World,* turned Nicaragua into "Indian country" by casting burly Victor McLaglen as a virile U.S. marine who battled sinister and swarthy rebels, and proclaimed that "we can't have any peace until we capture this bandit Lobo (Sandino)."[86]

With critics urging Washington to trade the "big bully" for the "big brother" in Nicaragua, special emissary Henry L. Stimson brought Liberals and Conservatives together in the "Peace of Tipitapa" (1927) and provided for U.S. supervision of the election of 1928.[87] Most importantly, he and General Frank R. McCoy created an American-trained national guard to perpetuate the authoritarian order that the marines had helped to impose. Shortly after U.S. troops withdrew in 1933, Sandino signed a truce with the Nicaraguan government. But General Anastasio Somoza, who had studied at a business school in Philadelphia and knew colloquial English, gained command of the U.S.-trained Guardia Nacional. Somoza then captured and executed Sandino, notwithstanding his "word of honor" that no harm would come to him.[88] In 1936 Somoza seized power and established a self-enriching family dictatorship that lasted until 1979. A U.S. collector-general remained to handle customs collections until 1944, and the United States retained a naval base. The Roosevelt administration in 1939 constructed an interoceanic highway (the Rama Road) to spur economic development.

Few benefits accrued to the United States from its years of interference in Nicaragua. Trade never reached important levels, although the United States dominated the Central American nation's economy. From 1914 to 1930 U.S. investments grew from $4.5 million to $13 million. Although the stormy occupation of Nicaragua may have indirectly fostered the Good Neighbor policy, for Nicaraguans that policy meant continued foreign financial management and replacement of the U.S. Marine Corps by a home-grown dictator who used extreme violence to "preserve order" and who was "insistently '*Americanista*'" in following Uncle Sam.[89]

Haiti, too, drew Washington's hegemonic gaze. A marine officer depicted the Haitians as "real nigger and no mistake."[90] When U.S. soldiers went abroad, of course, they carried American prejudices as well as canteens. For nineteen years, from 1915 to 1934, marines governed the tiny French-speaking nation of Haiti in the Caribbean. The Wilson administration ordered U.S. marines ashore on July 28, 1915, because it feared German intrigue during World War I and sought to protect American financial interests in the Caribbean. The venture only deepened Haiti's distress.

The occupiers built highways, technical schools, lighthouses, hospitals, and railroads. Americans improved public health and sanitation, but never eradicated Haiti's profound human squalor. By the mid-1960s, Haiti had the lowest life expectancy (thirty-five years) and the lowest literacy rate (10 percent) in Latin

Comic Strips in Nicaragua. In this 1927 photograph of the cultural side of intervention, marines read newspaper comic strips to Nicaraguan children. Said Clifford Hamm, collector-general of customs in Nicaragua: "Three cheers for the American marine who is teaching baseball and sportsmanship! It is the best step towards order, peace, and stability." (Marine Corps, National Archives)

America. Many of the roads had been built in 1916–1918 by forced labor—the *corvée* system under which Admiral William Caperton ordered workers into labor gangs. The NAACP official James Weldon Johnson, who investigated conditions in Haiti, protested: "They were maltreated, beaten and terrorized … [like] the convicts in the Negro chain gangs that are used to build roads in many of our southern states."[91] Haitians repeatedly rebelled against the *corvée;* in 1919 alone the marines killed 2,000 to quell the insurrection.

American racism also penetrated Haiti. U.S. personnel introduced to Haitians the words "nigger," "gook," and "coon" and enforced segregation between blacks and whites. When an aide objected to inviting Haitian diplomats to tea, Secretary Hull responded in both race and class terms: "When they [blacks] speak French, that's different."[92] Americans bestowed higher status on mulattos (the mixed-race "elites") than on the *authentiques* (blacks) but neither wooed nor fraternized with the Haitian bourgeoisie. They avoided doing so because of intense hostility to mixed bloods based on the belief "that such persons, as links between the races, endangered the established order in what should be a rigidly color-defined world."[93] Anthropological research in the 1930s by Franz Boaz and others that showed complex linkages among African, European, and indigenous cultures could not displace the prevailing Hollywood film stereotype of Haiti as "America's Africa"—the land of voodoo and zombies.[94]

Transportation improvements expanded commercial contacts between cities and rural farmers. Pan American Airways began flights between Miami and Port-au-Prince. Irrigation systems and a telephone network contributed to economic growth. Sugar and cotton exports increased, although the heavy dependence on

"The Rights of Small Nations: Haiti."   This cartoon provides a harshly critical view of the marine occupation of Haiti, 1915–1934. Mary Renda, in *Taking Haiti* (2001), writes that paternalistic language became "the cultural flagship of the United States in Haiti." By referring to Haitians as wards, U.S. officials asserted their "authority, superiority, and control expressed in the metaphor of a father's relationship with his children. It was a form of dominance … masked as benevolent by its reference to paternal care and guidance." (*Good Morning,* 1921)

one crop, coffee, left Haiti susceptible to fluctuations in world prices. The United States became Haiti's largest trading partner. With the Banque Nacional owned by the National City Bank of New York, American capital investments grew from $11.5 million in 1914 to $28.5 million in 1930. Under U.S. financial supervision, Haiti actually paid its foreign debts (largely French) ahead of schedule.

U.S. military authorities trained a national guard, the Garde d'Haiti. U.S. officers so dominated this *gendarmerie* that no Haitian had reached captain's rank by 1930. The first commandant, Major Smedley D. Butler of the marines, had experience in putting down "natives" in China, Honduras, Nicaragua, Panama, and Mexico. The brash Butler worked "hard with my little black Army" and began to "like the little fellows" who did well "as long as white men lead them."[95] The national guard served as judges, tax collectors, and paymasters for teachers, enforced martial law, and wielded deciding political force.

The United States failed to establish or demonstrate respect for honest government in Haiti. Washington officials drafted the 1918 constitution and then suspended the legislature for thirteen years. When President Philippe Sudre Dartiguenave's term ended in 1922, Americans jilted him in favor of Louis Borno, an acquiescent lawyer who collaborated with the American high commissioner, General John H. Russell of Georgia, to rule Haiti from 1922 to 1930. Borno "has never taken a step without first consulting me," Russell boasted.[96] The marines had made Haiti "safe for almost everybody but the Haitians," taunted *The Nation* in 1926.[97]

Haitians resented their colonial status. The peaking of discontent in 1929 came after a slump in coffee exports and exposure of Borno's political machinations. Protests and strikes spread across the country. President Hoover appointed an investigating commission chaired by W. Cameron Forbes, former governor-general of the Philippines. His report of 1930 noted "the failure of the Occupation to understand the social problems of Haiti."[98] The commission promoted "Haitianization" to ease Haitians into positions of responsibility. Hoover started the military withdrawal; Roosevelt completed it in 1934. Thereafter strong-arm presidents ruled with the help of Export-Import Bank loans and ties with Washington. During World War II, the United States used Haitian bases, and until 1947 U.S. officials supervised Haitian national finances. A revolution in 1946 placed the government in the hands of the Garde, and the revolution of 1956–1957 produced the callous dictatorship of Dr. François ("Papa Doc") Duvalier. He ruled with the ruthless help of his secret police force, the Touton Macoutes, until his death in 1971, when his son "Baby Doc" assumed power. Driven out in 1986, he left behind abject poverty and rampant civil strife. In 1994 U.S. armed forces once again invaded Haiti to stabilize politics.

Subverting Nationalism in Cuba and Puerto Rico

Cubans chafed under the Platt Amendment and U.S. military interventions. Through the 1920s and into the 1930s, the United States helped conduct elections, enlarged the national army, managed the national budget, and maintained economic control over the island. North American investment, particularly in sugar, soared to $1.5 billion in 1929. Approximately half a million fun-seeking Americans a year visited the capital city of Havana, where, according to the American song-writer Irving Berlin, "dark-eyed Stellas/Light their fellers' panatelas."[99]

Gerardo Machado ruled from 1924 to 1933, suppressing free speech, jailing and murdering dissidents, and wielding the army as a political weapon. Obtaining loans from U.S. bankers, he prohibited strikes and looked after North American business interests "as if they were my own."[100] Cuban resentment against Machado intensified in the late 1920s when sugar prices began to drop. Dependent on sugar and exports to the United States, Cuba sank further into economic crisis when the United States instituted the restrictive Smoot-Hawley Tariff of 1931. Unemployment rates shot up. Machado's army beat back protesters. Because armed intervention would violate the newly stated Good Neighbor policy, Roosevelt and his advisers chose to ease out the unpopular Machado.

Sumner Welles, a Groton School friend of Roosevelt, went as ambassador to Havana in 1933. While U.S. warships patrolled Cuban waters and a general strike rocked the country, Welles persuaded Machado to flee. But Welles lost control; his handpicked government lasted less than a month. Military dissidents, commanded by Sergeant Fulgencio Batista, staged the "Sergeants' Revolution" of September 1933 and installed Professor Ramón Grau San Martín as president.

An exile under Machado and critic of the Platt Amendment, Grau stood as "the hope and the symbol of the forces of nationalism, patriotism, and reform."[101] Yet Welles refused recognition because "we owe it to the Cuban people not to assist in saddling upon them for an indefinite period a government which every responsible element in the country violently opposed."[102] When Grau suspended payment on Chase National Bank loans and seized some North American–owned sugar mills, Welles decried the "confiscatory" decrees of this "social revolution" and conspired with Batista, who toppled Grau in January 1934.[103] A Batista-backed president took over, and the United States quickly granted recognition.

Disdained by the upper classes as "an adventurer, an upstart, and a despicable mulatto," Batista ruled Cuba, sometimes as president, sometimes from the shadows, from 1934 to 1959.[104] At the start of the Batista era, the United States abrogated the unpopular Platt Amendment (1934), lowered the sugar tariff, granted a

Fulgencio Batista (1901–1973). Born of impoverished parents in the United Fruit Company town of Banes, Batista joined the Cuban army at age twenty. A smiling, ruthless dictator, he became a staunch U.S. ally, cooperated with the Mafia, bought real estate in Daytona Beach, Florida, and turned Havana into a playground of casinos and brothels for American tourists. Fidel Castro's 26th of July Movement overthrew the corrupt regime in 1959. Batista died in exile in Portugal. (National Archives)

favorable quota to Cuban sugar imports (1934), and issued Export–Import Bank loans ($8 million in 1934). In 1940 Cuba granted American armed forces the use of ports and airfields (besides Guantánamo) in exchange for military aid. Even popular Hollywood movies influenced Cuban politics, as *gangsterismo* passed into the vernacular to describe the shoot-outs and political gun battles in the Batista era.

Elsewhere in the Caribbean, Puerto Rico stagnated under American paternalism. Throughout the interwar years, mediocre and often crude U.S. governors who could not speak Spanish castigated Puerto Ricans as "unsteady, unprincipled children" unable to govern themselves.[105] Although the Jones Act of 1917 had granted Puerto Ricans U.S. citizenship, Washington stiff-armed requests for the colony's independence or statehood. Puerto Ricans did not gain the right to elect their own governor until 1947. Absentee American landowners and sugar barons ran the island's economy. Despite improved roads and new schools, Governor Theodore Roosevelt, Jr. (1929–1932) observed "farm after farm where lean underfed women and sickly men repeated again and again the same story—little food and no opportunity to get more."[106] Eighty percent of peasants remained landless and many crowded into urban slums.

Encouraged by New Deal reformers to act "as a cultural bridge between the Americas," faculty and alumni of the University of Puerto Rico actually became increasingly critical of U.S. hegemony.[107] The Harvard-educated lawyer Pedro Albizu Campos headed the Nationalist party, which advocated the violent overthrow of U.S. rule. On Palm Sunday, 1937, police fired on unarmed Nationalist

Ponce, Puerto Rico, 1938. The U.S. Farm Security Administration photographer Edwin Rosskam captured class divisions in Puerto Rico, where U.S. neglect helped perpetuate the island's poverty. At the top of the hill sits the villa of the owner of a sugar plantation and refinery. The shacks of workers cling to the hillside. (Library of Congress)

marchers, killing nineteen in the "Ponce Massacre." Albizu went to federal prison until 1947. Other Puerto Ricans rallied behind the socialist Luis Muñoz Marín, whose Popular Democratic party ultimately advocated "commonwealth" status, which was attained in 1952. New Deal relief and public works projects brought in $1 million a month, along with funds to attract mainland tourists to Puerto Rico—to don a "coat of tan" and to mingle with "beautiful señoritas" on San Juan's beaches.[108] By 1940 the perceived German threat to the hemisphere brought increased defense construction and turned Puerto Rico into "a beehive for war-related activity."[109] Yet when Governor Rexford Tugwell arrived in 1941, he found the island "still sunk in hopeless poverty."[110]

Accommodating Mexico

The ongoing Mexican Revolution, which began in 1910, presented the United States with a test of the nonmilitary emphasis of the Good Neighbor policy. Before the 1920s it had appeared that Mexico would be treated like other U.S. neighbors—invaded, occupied, and owned by Americans, who by 1910 controlled 43 percent of Mexican property and produced more than half of Mexico's oil. Hollywood films perpetuated stereotypes by portraying the Mexican as a bandit or villainous "greaser."[111] Scholars and artists promoted cultural interaction to counter such negative images. Professor Herbert E. Bolton of the University of California, Berkeley, emphasized a shared borderlands history, drawing large numbers of students to his course on "Greater America." Throughout the United States in the 1930s, the Mexican artists José Clemente Orozco and Diego Rivera, the latter accompanied by his wife, the talented Mexican painter Frida Kahlo, created colorful murals of revolutionary struggle. A decade earlier Mexico City had become a "Yankee Bohemia" where expatriate writers and artists sympathetically interpreted Mexican politics and culture.[112] These contacts did not diminish the nationalism of either nation, but they probably did encourage an environment of tolerance and understanding based on mutual experience that undercut war hawks bent on military confrontation.

The Mexican Constitution of 1917 alarmed capitalist Americans, because Article 27 held that all "land and waters" and all subsoil raw materials belonged to the Mexican nation, thereby jeopardizing $300 million in American investments in oil and mines. Mexico also began to tax American oil producers heavily. Washington continued to claim economic rights for its nationals in Mexico and refused to recognize the government of Alváro Obregón. In 1923, however, Mexico and the United States signed the Bucareli Agreements. In exchange for U.S. recognition, Mexico agreed that Americans who held subsoil rights before the 1917 Constitution could continue those concessions and that Americans whose agricultural lands were expropriated would receive Mexican bonds in compensation. Americans owned at that time about 60 percent of Mexico's oil industry. But a new law passed by the Mexican congress in 1925 stated that oil lands secured before 1917 could be held for a maximum of only fifty years. In part because American oil companies had begun to exploit the oil fields of Venezuela, Washington rejected intervention and resorted to nonmilitary methods instead.

In early 1927, President Coolidge selected Dwight W. Morrow, an old college chum and Wall Street banker, as the new ambassador to Mexico City. In the belief that "we can best defend the right of our own country when we understand the rights of other countries," Morrow engaged in "ham-and-eggs diplomacy" by having breakfast with the Mexican president instead of sending formal notes.[113] Learning a little Spanish, having "Lone Eagle" Charles Lindbergh fly nonstop from Washington, D.C., and even bringing the humorist Will Rogers (that "most *simpatico* citizen") to the Mexican capital, Morrow ingratiated himself.[114] The ambassador then negotiated an agreement that confirmed pre-1917 ownership of petroleum lands and tacitly conceded that Mexico legally controlled its own raw materials. This arrangement lasted until 1938, when President Lázaro Cárdenas defiantly expropriated the property of all foreign oil companies. "No more humble pie, no more kowtowing to arrogant foreign officials," crowed one Mexican journalist.[115]

Roosevelt's ambassador, Josephus Daniels, did his best to defuse the crisis. He balked at Hull's "get tough" policies, softening an intemperate State Department blast when he delivered it to the Mexican foreign minister and opposing any reduction of U.S. purchases of Mexican silver. For their part the American oil companies refused to sell petroleum equipment to Mexico, and they persuaded shipping firms not to carry Mexican oil. Standard Oil of New Jersey financed false propaganda in the United States with the message that Cárdenas plotted to turn Mexico into a communist domain. In 1938 Daniels cabled Hull that "some of the oil men are predicting revolution" so that they can "return to conditions here as existed under Díaz or Huerta."[116]

Viewing Cárdenas as "one of the few Latin leaders who was actually preaching and trying to practice democracy," FDR ruled out intervention and sought compensation.[117] Increased purchases of Mexican oil by Germany, Italy, and Japan underscored the urgent need for a diplomatic settlement. Indeed, once war broke out in Europe in September 1939, FBI director J. Edgar Hoover reported false

Lázaro Cárdenas (1895–1970) and Josephus Daniels (1862–1949). A former newspaper publisher and secretary of the navy during the Wilson administration, Daniels (second from left) donned Mexican national costumes, adopted a warm, folksy style, and became a popular ambassador to Mexico (1933–1941) under his friend President Franklin D. Roosevelt. As president of Mexico (1934–1940), Cárdenas (center with mustache) attempted to regain control of his nation's oil resources from multinational corporations. In contrast to the frightened pro-business attitudes of professional diplomats in Mexico, and to FBI director J. Edgar Hoover's warning that Cárdenas was "anti-foreign due to his Indian antecedents," Daniels assured FDR that Cárdenas was simply another "New Dealer" trying to improve his country's living conditions. According to the historian Friedrich E. Schuler, Daniels, through his defense of Cárdenas's expropriation of U.S. oil companies in 1938, "represented the proverbial good neighbor in Mexico more than any other U.S. ambassador to Latin America during all of Roosevelt's administrations." (Library of Congress)

rumors about 250 Nazi pilots in Mexico, eight German submarines operating out of Veracruz, and Hitler's promise of British Honduras if Mexico agreed to supply Germany with petroleum. Protracted Mexican-American talks finally produced an agreement in 1941 that recognized Mexico's ownership of its own raw materials, plus Mexico's promise to pay for expropriated properties. The Export-Import Bank extended a $30 million loan. Compromise with Mexican nationalism became a strategic necessity as the United States readied itself for World War II, and Daniels's sympathetic diplomacy facilitated the accommodation.

Pan Americanism and Hemispheric Defense on the Eve of War

Notwithstanding occasional conferences and high hopes for improved trade and hemispheric solidarity, the Pan American movement had accomplished little since its inception in the 1880s. One Argentine diplomat sneered that "there is no Pan Americanism in South America; it exists only in Washington."[118] The declarations of neutrality during World War I by seven Latin American governments suggested the hollowness of Pan American solidarity.

In 1923 the Fifth International Conference of American States met in Santiago, Chile. The United States controlled the agenda, and the delegates endorsed the Gondra Treaty to Avoid or Prevent Conflicts Between the American States. The Havana conference of 1928 proved quite different, because it convened shortly after U.S. troops had landed in Nicaragua. Anticipating trouble, the popular former secretary of state Charles Evans Hughes headed the U.S. delegation, and even President Coolidge traveled to Cuba to address the conference with soothing banalities. At the conference, the delegate from El Salvador boldly moved that "no state has the right to intervene in the internal affairs of another."[119] Mexico and Argentina backed this challenge to the United States. Hughes defended the right of "interposition of a temporary character," and he manipulated the conference to table the resolution.[120]

The seventh Pan American conference, in Montevideo, Uruguay (1933), met under the positive aura of the newly announced Good Neighbor policy. The nonintervention resolution was once again introduced. Secretary Hull cast an affirmative vote but retained a U.S. right to intervene "by the law of nations as generally recognized and accepted."[121] Further confusion about the meaning of the nonintervention pledge became evident at the 1936 Buenos Aires conference, where the United States seemingly endorsed an unequivocal statement. The U.S. definition, however, intended to outlaw military intervention, whereas many Latin American countries argued that Washington could not interfere through economic or political pressure when countries nationalized American-owned property.

Pan Americanism took a decided turn toward hemispheric security in the late 1930s, when Germany, Italy, and Japan attempted to improve their economic and political standing in Latin America. As Germany's trade with Latin America climbed, Hull saw the most "acute" threat "in its indirect form of propaganda, penetration, organizing political parties, buying some adherents, and blackmailing others."[122] With Adolf Hitler dreaming of "a new Germany" in Brazil and instigating subversive activities there and in Uruguay, Argentina, and Mexico, Washington tried to form "a north-south axis" at the Lima Pan American conference of 1938.[123] The anti-German sentiment of most delegates, aroused by the recent Munich crisis, helped Hull to fashion the Declaration of Lima, a pledge to resist foreign intervention in the Americas. A secret U.S. Army Air Corps study in early 1939 warned that "airdromes in the north-west part of Brazil … would place Nazi-Fascist bombers less than 1,000 miles from the Panama Canal, well within their operating radius of action with [a] heavy load of bombs."[124] That autumn the Declaration of Panama established a security belt around the Western Hemisphere to rebuff possible German intrusions. At the same time, the United States persuaded Latin American nations to reduce or cease trade with the Axis powers and to ship strategic raw materials to the United States. To advance hemispheric unity even more, Roosevelt in 1940 appointed Nelson Rockefeller coordinator of inter-American affairs. His office encouraged Hollywood to produce films, such as *The Three Caballeros* (1944) and *Simon Bolivar* (1941), which "strengthened popular support for U.S. foreign policy."[125]

The post–World War I search for international order had broken down by 1939. In both Asia and Latin America, fervent nationalists challenged the United States. In both areas the viability of American diplomacy was proportional to the power the United States possessed and exercised. In Asia, after the Manchurian crisis of 1931–1932, the United States sought, without success, to build a counterforce to Japan. Even the Philippines became a virtual hostage that the U.S. military said it could not defend. By spring 1939, the possibility of simultaneous war with Germany, Italy, and Japan prompted the U.S. Joint Army-Navy Board to modify war plan ORANGE (which emphasized a naval offensive in the Pacific) in favor of RAINBOW plans for hemispheric defense based on the primacy of the Atlantic and Caribbean approaches.

The Great Depression prostrated international relations. World trade and investment collapsed; tariffs went up. The island-bound and trade-conscious Japanese accelerated efforts to build a "co-prosperity" sphere in Asia and the western Pacific. In Latin America, where many countries depended on the exportation of one commodity, revolutions and coups erupted, feeding on incipient nationalism. Social unrest and political instability rocked the area from which the United States was withdrawing its marines. While U.S. culture was spreading, political upheavals in the Dominican Republic, Argentina, Brazil, and Chile in 1930, Peru in 1931, Cuba in 1933—all threatened U.S. hegemonic pretensions. Devastated by the depression, Latin Americans gained a new awareness of the extent to which foreigners made their national choices and the degree to which foreign companies drained profits from them. By World War II, Latin Americans held a more favorable image of the United States, which seemed to have abandoned military intervention under the Good Neighbor policy and in the face of the growing global threat of Axis expansion. But they harbored fresh suspicions that invigorated inter-American economic relations meant intensified U.S. meddling. Yankeephobia simmered even as Latin Americans joined the United States in the fight against the Axis.

FURTHER READING FOR THE PERIOD 1920–1939

For general studies and biographies for this period, see works cited in Chapter 4.

For Asia, see Tokomo Akami, *Internationalizing the Pacific* (2000); Irvine H. Anderson, *The Standard-Vacuum Oil Company and United States East Asia Policy* (1974); Richard D. Burns and Edward M. Bennett, eds., *Diplomats in Crisis* (1974); Roger Dingman, *Power in the Pacific* (1976); Akira Iriye, *Across the Pacific* (1967), *After Imperialism* (1969), and *The Origins of the Second World War in Asia and the Pacific* (1987); Greg Kennedy, *Anglo-American Strategic Relations and the Far East, 1933–1939* (2002); Brian M. Linn, *Guardians of Empire* (1997); Jonathan Marshall, *To Have and Have Not* (1995); and William R. Nestor, *Power Across the Pacific* (1996).

For relations with Japan, consult Sadao Asada, *Culture Shock and Japanese-American Relations* (2007); Cemil Aydin, *The Politics on Anti-Westernism in Asia* (2007); Michael Barnhart, *Japan Prepares for Total War* (1987); Piers Brandon, *The Dark Valley* (2000); Dorothy Borg and Shumpei Okamoto, eds., *Pearl Harbor as History* (1973); Jon Thares Davidann, *Cultural Diplomacy in U.S.-Japanese Relations, 1919–1941* (2007); Roger Dingman, *Deciphering the Rising Sun* (2009); Justus D. Doenecke, *When the Wicked Rise* (1984) (Manchurian crisis); Peter Duus et al., eds., *The Japanese Wartime Empire, 1931–1945* (1996); Marc S. Gallichio, ed., The *Unpredictability of the Past* (2008); Carol Gluck and Stephen Graubard, eds., *Showa* (1992); Izumi Hirobe, *Japanese Pride, American Prejudice* (2001) (exclusion clause); Walter LaFeber, *The Clash* (1997); James W. Morley, ed., *Deterrent Diplomacy* (1977); Ian Nish, *Japanese Foreign Policy in the Interwar Period* (2002); Mark R. Peattie, *Sunburst* (2003); Nicholas Tarling, *A Sudden Rampage* (2001); Christopher Thorne, *The Limits of Foreign Policy* (1972); Haruo Tohmatsu and H. P. Wilmott, *A Gathering Darkness* (2004); Jonathan G. Utley, *Going to War with Japan, 1937–1941* (2006); and Dandra Wilson, *The Manchurian Crisis and Japanese Society, 1931–1933* (2002).

China and the United States are explored in David P. Barrett and Larry N. Shyu, eds., *Chinese Collaboration with Japan, 1932–1945* (2001); William Braisted, *Diplomats in Blue* (2009); Mary B. Bullock, *An American Transplant* (1980) (Rockefeller Foundation); Warren I. Cohen, *America's Response to China* (1990) and *The Chinese Connection* (1978); Bernard Cole, *Gunboats and Marines* (1983); John W. Garver, *Chinese-Soviet Relations, 1937–1945* (1988); David H. Grover, *American Merchant Ships on the Yangtze* (1992); Shizhang Hu, *Stanley K. Hornbeck and the Open Door Policy* (1995); T. Christopher Jespersen, *American Images of China* (1996); Karen J. Leong, *The China Mystique* (2005); Fei Fei Li et al., *Nanking 1937* (2002); Xi Lian, *The Conversion of Missionaries* (1997); Kathleen Lodwink, *Educating the Women of Hainan* (1995); Patricia Neils, *China Images in the Life and Times of Henry Luce* (1990); David Pong, ed., *Resisting Japan* (2008); Youli Sun, *China and the Origins of the Pacific War* (1993); and Stephen J. Valone, "*A Policy Calculated to Benefit China*" (1991).

Inter-American relations and the Good Neighbor policy are treated in Cole Blasier, *The Hovering Giant* (1976); John A. Britton, *Carleton Beals* (1987); Marcos Cueto, ed., *Missionaries of Science* (1994) (Rockefeller Foundation); Alexander DeConde, *Herbert Hoover's Latin American Policy* (1951); Lauren Derby, *The Dictator's Seduction* (2009) (Trujillo); Irwin F. Gellman, *Good Neighbor Diplomacy* (1979); Mark T. Gilderhus, *The Second Century* (2000); Greg Grandin, *Empire's Workshop* (2006); David G. Haglund, *Latin America and the Transformation of U.S. Strategic Thought, 1936–1940* (1984); Gilbert M. Joseph et al., *Close Encounters of Empire* (1998); Thomas L. Karnes, *Tropical Enterprise* (1978); Michael L. Krenn, *U.S. Policy Toward Economic Nationalism in Latin America* (1990); Lester D. Langley, *America and the Americas* (1989); Abraham F. Lowenthal, ed., *Exporting Democracy* (1991); John Major, *Prize Possession* (1993) (Panama Canal); Carlos Marichal, *A Century of Debt Crises in Latin America* (1989); Thomas O'Brien, *The Revolutionary Mission* (1996); Fredrick B. Pike, *FDR's Good Neighbor Policy* (1995); Emily S. Rosenberg, *Financial Missionaries to the World* (1999); Lars Schoultz, *Beneath the United States* (1998); David F. Schmitz, *Thank God They're on Our Side* (1999) (dictatorships); James Schwoch, *The American Radio Industry and Its Latin American Activities* (1990); Sarah E. Sharbach, *Stereotypes of Latin America* (1993); Peter H. Smith, *Talons of the Eagle* (1996); and Joseph Tulchin, *The Aftermath of War* (1971).

For the Caribbean and Central America, see G. Pope Atkins and Larman C. Wilson, *The Dominican Republic and the United States* (1998); Jorge Rodriguez Beruff, *Strategy As Politics* (2007) (Puerto Rico); Bruce Calder, *The Impact of Intervention* (1984) (Dominican Republic); Raymond Carr, *Puerto Rico* (1984); Arturo Morales Carrión, *Puerto Rico* (1983); Andrew Crawley, *Somoza and Roosevelt* (2007); Laura Derby, *The Dictator's*

Seduction (2008) (Trujillo); Paul J. Dosal, *Doing Business with the Dictators* (1993) (United Fruit, Guatemala); Ronald Fernandez, *The Disenchanted Island* (1992) (Puerto Rico); Walter LaFeber, *Inevitable Revolutions* (1993); Lester D. Langley, *The United States and the Caribbean* (1980); A. W. Maldonado, *Teodoro Moscoso and Puerto Rico's Operation Bootstrap* (1997); Dana Munro, *The United States and the Caribbean Republics, 1921–1933* (1974); Brenda G. Plummer, *Haiti and the United States* (1992); Mary Renda, *Taking Haiti* (2001); Eric Paul Roorda, *The Dictator Next Door* (1998) (Trujillo); Robert I. Rotberg, *Haiti* (1971); Richard V. Salisbury, *Anti-Imperialism and International Competition in Central America* (1989); and Hans Schmidt, *The United States Occupation of Haiti* (1971) and *Maverick Marine* (1987) (Butler).

For Nicaragua and the U.S. intervention, see Paul C. Clark, Jr., *The United States and Somoza* (1992); Thomas J. Dodd, *Managing Democracy in Central America* (1992); Michel Gobat, *Confronting the American Dream* (2005); William Kamman, *A Search for Stability* (1968); Richard Millett, *Guardians of the Dynasty* (1977); Marco Aurelia Narro-Genie, *Augusto "Cesar" Sandino* (2002); and Knut Walter, *The Regime of Anastasio Somoza* (1993).

For South America, see Elizabeth A. Cobbs, *The Rich Neighbor Policy* (1992); Paul W. Drake, *The Money Doctor in the Andes* (1988); Stanley Hilton, *Brazil and the Great Powers* (1975); Michael Grow, *The Good Neighbor Policy and Authoritarianism in Paraguay* (1981); Michael Montéon, *Chile in the Nitrate Era* (1982); Stephen G. Rabe, *The Road to OPEC* (1982) (Venezuela); Stephen J. Randall, *The Diplomacy of Modernization* (1977) (Colombia); and David M. K. Sheinin, *Argentina and the United States* (2006).

Studies of U.S.-Mexican relations include Leslie Bethell, ed., *Mexico Since Independence* (1991); John A. Britton, *Revolution and Ideology* (1995); Helen Delpar, *The Enormous Vogue of Things Mexican* (1992) (culture); Linda B. Hall, *Oil, Banks, and Politics* (1995); Catherine E. Jayne, *Oil, War, and Anglo-American Relations* (2001); Dan LaBotz, *Edward L. Doheny* (1991) (oil); Lorenzo Meyer, *Mexico and the United States in the Oil Controversy* (1977); Stephen R. Niblo, *War, Diplomacy, and Development* (1995); W. Dirk Raat, *Mexico and the United States* (1996); Matthew A. Redinger, *American Catholics and the Mexican Revolution, 1924–1936* (2005); Friedrich E. Schuler, *Mexico Between Hitler and Roosevelt* (1998); Robert F. Smith, *The United States and Revolutionary Nationalism in Mexico* (1972); and Daniela Spencer, *The Impossible Triangle* (1999).

For Cuba, see Jules R. Benjamin, *The United States and Cuba* (1978); Irwin F. Gellman, *Roosevelt and Batista* (1973); Louis A. Pérez, Jr., *Cuba and the United States* (1997), *Cuba Under the Platt Amendment*, (1968), *Becoming Cuban* (1999), and *Cuba in the Imperial Imagination* (2008); and Ramón Ruíz, *Cuba* (1968).

See also the General Bibliography, Robert L. Beisner, ed., *Guide to American Foreign Relations Since 1600* (2003), and the following notes.

NOTES TO CHAPTER 5

1. Quoted in Elting E. Morison, *Turmoil and Tradition* (New York: Atheneum, 1964), p. 312.
2. Quoted in John W. Dower, "Occupation," in Lloyd C. Gardner and Marilyn B. Young, eds., *The New American Empire* (New York: The New Press, 2005), p. 194.
3. Sadao Asada, "Between the Old Diplomacy and the New, 1918–1922," *Diplomatic History, XXX* (April 2006), 221.
4. Quoted in Maruo Tohmatsu and H. P. Willmott, *A Gathering Darkness* (Wilmington, Del: Scholarly Resources, 2004), p. 16.
5. Quoted in Richard N. Current, "Henry L. Stimson," in Norman A. Graebner, ed., *An Uncertain Tradition* (New York: McGraw-Hill, 1961), pp. 169, 171.
6. Quoted in Frank Freidel, *Franklin D. Roosevelt: Launching the New Deal* (Boston: Little, Brown, 1973), p. 120.
7. Stanley K. Hornbeck quoted in Richard Dean Burns, "Stanley K. Hornbeck," in Richard Dean Burns and Edward M. Bennett, eds., *Diplomats in Crisis* (Santa Barbara: ABC-CLIO Press, 1974), p. 103.

8. Will Rogers quoted in Justus D. Doenecke, *When the Wicked Rise* (Lewisburg, Pa.: Bucknell University Press, 1984), p. 37.
9. Quoted in Christopher Thorne, *The Limits of Foreign Policy* (New York: Capricorn, 1973), p. 158.
10. Quoted in Morison, *Turmoil and Tradition*, p. 310.
11. Quoted in Zara Steiner, *The Lights That Failed* (New York: Oxford University Press, 2005), p. 728.
12. Quoted in Justus D. Doenecke and John E. Wilz, *From Isolation to War, 1931–1941* (Wheeling, Ill.: Harlan Davidson, 2003; 3d ed.), p. 37.
13. Stimson quoted in David F. Schmitz, *Henry L. Stimson* (Wilmington, Del.: Scholarly Resources, 2001), p. 111.
14. Quoted in Norman A. Graebner, "Hoover, Roosevelt, and the Japanese," in Dorothy Borg and Shumpei Okamoto, eds., *Pearl Harbor as History* (New York: Columbia University Press, 1973), p. 30.
15. Quoted in Steiner, *Lights*, p. 741.

16. Quoted in Walter LaFeber, *The Clash* (New York: Norton, 1997), p. 173.

17. Miles Lampson quoted in Steiner, *Lights*, p. 745.

18. Hugh R. Wilson, *Diplomat Between the Wars* (New York: Longmans, Green, 1941), p. 280.

19. Michael Schaller, *The U.S. Crusade in China, 1938–1945* (New York: Columbia University Press, 1979), p. 5.

20. Akira Iriye, *The Origins of the Second World War in Asia and the Pacific* (London: Longman, 1987), p. 16.

21. Quoted in Thomas H. Buckley, *The United States and the Washington Conference, 1921–1922* (Knoxville: University of Tennessee Press, 1970), p. 73.

22. Elihu Root quoted in Asada, "Between the Old Diplomacy and the New," 226.

23. Cryptographer Herbert Yardley quoted in LaFeber, *Clash*, p. 140.

24. Robert Vansittart quoted in Richard W. Fanning, *Peace and Disarmament* (Lexington: University Press of Kentucky, 1995), p. 153.

25. Thomas H. Buckley, "The Icarus Factor," *Diplomacy & Statecraft*, *IV* (November 1993), 125.

26. John Paton Davies, *Dragon by the Tail* (New York: Norton, 1972), p. 95.

27. Quoted in Akira Iriye, *Across the Pacific* (New York: Harcourt Brace & World, 1967), p. 148.

28. Quoted in Dennis L. Noble, *The Eagle and the Dragon* (Westport, Conn.: Greenwood, 1990), p. 192.

29. Quoted in Warren I. Cohen and Nancy Bernkopf Tucker, "America in Asian Eyes," *American Historical Review, CXI* (October 2006), 1097.

30. Quoted in Bernard D. Cole, *Gunboats and Marines* (Newark: University of Delaware Press, 1983), p. 145.

31. Ernie Place quoted in Noble, *Eagle*, p. 150; James L. Huskey, "The Cosmopolitan Connection," *Diplomatic History, XI* (Summer 1987), 228.

32. Mary B. Bullock, *An American Transplant* (Berkeley: University of California Press, 1980), pp. 44, 47; Raymond Fosdick quoted in Frank Ninkovich, *The Wilsonian Century* (Chicago: University of Chicago Press, 1999), p. 40.

33. Karen J. Leong, *The China Mystique* (Berkeley: University of California Press, 2006), p. 134; Clare Boothe Luce quoted in T. Christopher Jesperson, *American Images of China, 1931–1949* (Stanford: Stanford University Press, 1996), p. 54.

34. Jesperson, *American Images*, p. 91; and quoted in James E. Taylor, "The Production of the Chiang Kai-shek Personality Cult, 1929–1975," *The China Quarterly, CLXXXV*, (March 2006), 100.

35. Quoted in Justus D. Doenecke and John E. Wilz, *From Isolation to War, 1931–1941* (Arlington Heights, Ill.: Davidson, 1991; 2nd ed.), p. 23.

36. Consul Uchiyama Kiyoshi quoted in Sandra Wilson, *The Manchurian Crisis and Japanese Society, 1931–1933* (New York: Routledge, 2002), p. 94.

37. Quoted in Nicholas Tarling, *A Sudden Rampage* (Honolulu: University of Hawai'i Press, 2001), p. 43.

38. Barbara J. Keys, *Globalizing Sport* (Cambridge: Harvard University Press, 2006), p. 75.

39. Quoted in Sadao Asada, "The Japanese Navy and the United States," in Borg and Okamoto, *Pearl Harbor*, p. 238.

40. Quoted in Piers Brandon, *The Dark Valley* (New York: Knopf, 2000), p. 45.

41. Eugene Dooman quoted in Izumi Hirobe, *Japanese Pride, American Prejudice* (Stanford: Stanford University Press, 2001), p. 35.

42. Okama Shumai quoted in Cemil Aydin, *The Politics of Anti-Westernism in Asia* (New York: Columbia University Press, 2007), p. 153.

43. Senator Gerald P. Nye quoted in Lisle A. Rose, *Power at Sea: The Breaking Storm, 1919–1945* (Columbia: University of Missouri Press, 2007), p. 63.

44. Robert G. Kaufman, *Arms Control During the Pre-Nuclear Era* (New York: Columbia University Press, 1990), p. 181.

45. Quoted in Peter Li, ed., *Japanese War Crimes* (New Brunswick, NJ: Transaction Publishers, 2003), p. 232.

46. Archibald Steele and F. Tilman Durdin quoted in Daqing Yang, "The Nanjing Massacre in Postwar China and Japan," in T. Fujitani, Geoffrey M. White, and Lisa Yoneyama, eds., *Perilous Memories: The Asia Pacific War(s)* (Durham: Duke University Press, 2001), p. 51.

47. Roger B. Jeans, ed., *Good-Bye to Old Peking* (Athens: Ohio University Press, 1998), p. 11.

48. John W. Garver, *Chinese-Soviet Relations 1937–1945* (New York: Oxford University Press, 1988), p. 15; Soviet commander quoted in Albert L. Weeks, *Stalin's Other War* (Lanham, Md.: Rowman & Littlefield, 2002), p. 55.

49. Samuel I. Rosenman, ed., *Public Papers and Addresses of Franklin D. Roosevelt* (New York: Macmillan, 1938–1943; 13 vols.), *VI*, 406–411.

50. Quoted in Benjamin D. Rhodes, *United States Foreign Policy in the Interwar Period, 1918–1941* (Westport, Conn.: Praeger, 2001), p. 150.

51. Quoted in Tohmatsu and Wilmott, *Gathering Darkness*, p. 58.

52. Major David Barrett quoted in Youli Sun, *China and the Origins of the Pacific War* (New York: St. Martin's, 1993), p. 134.

53. Quoted in Frederick C. Adams, *Economic Diplomacy* (Columbia: University of Missouri Press, 1976), p. 233.

54. Quoted in Stephen M. Streeter, "Waging the Counterrevolution: The United States and Guatemala, 1954–1961" (Ph.D. diss., University of Connecticut, 1994), p. 4.

55. Quoted in Arthur P. Whitaker, "From Dollar Diplomacy to the Good Neighbor Policy," *Inter-American Economic Affairs, IV* (Spring 1951), 18.

56. Rosenman, *Public Papers, II*, 14.

57. Fredrick B. Pike, *Chile and the United States* (South Bend, Ind.: University of Notre Dame Press, 1963), p. 236.

58. Sumner Welles quoted in Paul J. Dosal, *Doing Business with Dictators* (Wilmington, Del.: Scholarly Resources, 1993), p. 8.

59. Emily S. Rosenberg and Norman L. Rosenberg, "From Colonialism to Professionalism," *Journal of American History, LXXIV* (June 1987), 79; Paul W. Drake, *The Money Doctor in the Andes* (Durham: Duke University Press, 1989).

60. Hernan Robleto and Salvador Mendiata quoted in Michel Gobat, *Confronting the American Dream* (Durham: Duke University Press, 2005), pp. 133–134.

61. C. Neale Ronning, ed., *Intervention in Latin America* (New York: Knopf, 1970), pp. 42–49.

62. David M. K. Sheinin, *Argentina and the United States* (Athens: University of Georgia Press, 2006), pp. 60–61.

63. Fredrick B. Pike, *FDR's Good Neighbor Policy* (Austin: University of Texas Press, 1995), p. 137.

64. Lester D. Langley, *America and the Americas* (Athens: University of Georgia Press, 1989), p. 125.

65. Quoted in Emily S. Rosenberg, *Spreading the American Dream* (New York: Hill & Wang, 1982), p. 112.

66. Quoted in Benjamin Welles, *Sumner Welles* (New York: St. Martin's, 1997), p. 93.

67. Quoted in Elizabeth A. Cobbs, *The Rich Neighbor Policy* (New Haven: Yale University Press, 1992), p. 28.

68. Quoted in Greg Grandin, "Your Americanism and Mine," *American Historical Review, CXI* (October 2006), 1052.

69. Greg Grandin, *Empire's Workshop* (New York: Henry Holt Company, 2006), p. 13.

70. Herbert Hoover, *Memoirs* (New York: Macmillan, 1952), p. 69.

71. Quoted in Bruce J. Calder, *The Impact of Intervention* (Austin: University of Texas Press, 1984), p. 124.

72. Sumner Welles, *Naboth's Vineyard* (New York: Payson and Clark, 1928; 2 vols.), II, 797–798.

73. Quoted in Magdaline W. Shannon, *Jean Price-Mars, the Haitian Elite, and the American Occupation, 1915–1935* (New York: St. Martin's, 1996), p. 166.

74. Quoted in Joseph R. Juárez, "United States Withdrawal from Santo Domingo," *Hispanic American Historical Review, XLII* (May 1962), 180.

75. Franklin D. Roosevelt, "Our Foreign Policy," *Foreign Affairs, VI* (July 1928), 583.

76. Sumner Welles quoted in Calder, *Impact of Intervention*, p. 252.

77. Eric Paul Roorda, "The Cult of the Airplane," in Gilbert M. Joseph, Catherine C. LeGrand, and Ricardo D. Salvatore, eds., *Close Encounters of Empire* (Durham: Duke University Press, 1998), p. 286.

78. Quoted in Eric Paul Roorda, *The Dictator Next Door* (Durham: Duke University Press, 1998), p. 106.

79. Quoted in Robert F. Smith, *The United States and Cuba* (New York: Bookman, 1960), p. 184.

80. Quoted in Benjamin T. Harrison, *Dollar Diplomat* (Pullman: Washington State University Press, 1988), p. 91.

81. Quoted in Albert K. Weinberg, *Manifest Destiny* (Chicago: Quadrangle, 1963 [c. 1935]), p. 441.

82. Quoted in Carleton Beals, "This Is War, Gentlemen!" *The Nation, CXXVI* (April 11, 1928), 406.

83. Quoted in Ivan Musicant, *The Banana Wars* (New York: Macmillan, 1990), p. 328.

84. U.S. Navy, *Operation of Naval Service in Nicaragua* (Senate Doc. 86, 70 Cong., 1 Sess., 1928), pp. 5–6.

85. Quoted in Michael J. Schroeder, "The Sandino Rebellion Revisited," in Gilbert, *Close Encounters*, p. 210.

86. Emily S. Rosenberg, *Financial Missionaries to the World* (Cambridge: Harvard University Press, 1999), p. 209; quoted in Gobat, *American Dream*, p. 252.

87. Senator Clarence C. Dill quoted in Robert David Johnson, *The Peace Progressives and American Foreign Relations* (Cambridge: Harvard University Press, 1995), p. 125.

88. Quoted in Walter LaFeber, *Inevitable Revolutions* (New York: Norton, 1993; 2nd ed.), p. 70.

89. Ambassador Capus Waynick quoted in David F. Schmitz, *Thank God They're on Our Side* (Chapel Hill: University of North Carolina Press, 1999), p. 156.

90. Colonel Littleton Waller quoted in Robert I. Rotberg, *Haiti* (Boston: Houghton Mifflin, 1971), pp. 137–138.

91. James Weldon Johnson, "The Truth About Haiti," *The Crisis, XX* (September 1920), 223.

92. Quoted in Brenda G. Plummer, *Rising Wind* (Chapel Hill: University of North Carolina Press, 1996), p. 100.

93. Brenda G. Plummer, *Haiti and the United States* (Athens: University of Georgia Press, 1992), p. 129.

94. William F. Jordan quoted in Mary Renda, *Taking Haiti* (Chapel Hill: University of North Carolina Press, 2001), p. 124.

95. Quoted *ibid.*, p. 201.

96. Quoted in Donald B. Cooper, "The Withdrawal of the United States from Haiti, 1928–1934," *Journal of Inter-American Studies, V* (January 1963), 83.

97. Quoted in Johnson, *Peace Progressives*, p. 224.

98. Quoted in Dana G. Munro, *The United States and the Caribbean Republics, 1921–1933* (Princeton: Princeton University Press, 1974), pp. 314–315.

99. Quoted in Louis A. Pérez, Jr., *On Becoming Cuban* (Chapel Hill: University of North Carolina Press, 1999), p. 190.

100. Quoted in Thomas F. O'Brien, *The Revolutionary Mission* (New York: Cambridge University Press, 1996), p. 228.

101. Quoted in Luis E. Aguilar, *Cuba 1933* (New York: Norton, 1974), p. 167.

102. Sumner Welles quoted in Irwin F. Gellman, *Secret Affairs* (Baltimore: Johns Hopkins University Press, 1995), p. 80.

103. Quoted in Louis A. Peréz, Jr., *Cuba Under the Platt Amendment, 1902–1934* (Pittsburgh: University of Pittsburgh Press, 1986), pp. 323–324.

104. Quoted in Frank Argote-Freyre, *Fulgencio Batista* (New Brunswick, NJ: Rutgers University Press, 2004), p. 124.

105. Arturo Morales Carrión, *Puerto Rico* (New York: W. W. Norton, 1983), p. 206.

106. Quoted in Raymond Carr, *Puerto Rico* (New York: Vintage, 1984), p. 54.

107. Ernest Gruening quoted in Robert David Johnson, "Anti-Imperialism and the Good Neighbor Policy," *Journal of Latin American Studies, XXIX* (February 1997), 109.

108. Tourist brochures quoted in Dennis Merrill, "Negotiating Cold War Paradise," *Diplomatic History, XXV* (Spring 2001), 1.

109. Jorge Rodriguez Beruff, *Strategy as Politics* (San Juan: La Editorial Universidad de Puerto Rico, 2007), p. ix.

110. Quoted in Carr, *Puerto Rico*, p. 61.

111. Quoted in Helen Delpar, *The Enormous Vogue of Things Mexican* (Tuscaloosa: University of Alabama Press, 1992), p. 5.

112. John A. Britton, *Revolution and Ideology* (Lexington: University Press of Kentucky, 1995), p. 52.

113. Morrow quoted in Daniela Spenser, *The Impossible Triangle: Mexico, Soviet Russia, and the United States in the 1920s* (Durham: Duke University Press, 1999), pp. 139–140.

114. Lars Schoultz, *Beneath the United States* (Cambridge: Harvard University Press, 1998), p. 282.

115. Verna Carlton Millan quoted in Britton, *Revolution*, p. 130.

116. Quoted in Stephen R. Niblo, *War, Diplomacy, and Development* (Wilmington, Del.: Scholarly Resources, 1995), p. 45.

117. Quoted in Pike, *FDR's Good Neighbor*, p. 192.

118. Quoted in J. Lloyd Mecham, *A Survey of United States–Latin American Relations* (Boston: Houghton Mifflin, 1965), p. 100.

119. Quoted in Samuel Guy Inman, *Inter-American Conferences* (Washington, D.C.: University Press, 1965), p. 117.

120. Quoted in Richard V. Salisbury, *Anti-Imperialism and International Competition in Central America, 1920–1929* (Wilmington, Del.: Scholarly Resources, 1989), p. 121.

121. Quoted in Bryce Wood, *The Making of the Good Neighbor Policy* (New York: Columbia University Press, 1961), p. 119.

122. Cordell Hull, *Memoirs* (New York: Macmillan, 1948; 2 vols.), I, 602.

123. Quoted in Jordan A. Schwarz, *Liberal* (New York: Free Press, 1987), p. 123.

124. Quoted in John Major, *Prize Possession* (New York: Cambridge University Press, 1993), p. 295.

125. Peter H. Smith, *Talons of the Eagle* (New York: Oxford University Press, 1996), p. 85.

CHAPTER 6

Survival and Spheres: The Allies and the Second World War, 1939–1945

Church Service on the Prince of Wales. *On August 10, 1941, President Franklin D. Roosevelt and Prime Minister Winston S. Churchill, with their staffs, attended a stirring service aboard the British warship during the Atlantic Charter Conference. (Franklin D. Roosevelt Library)*

◆ *The Atlantic Charter Conference, 1941*

IN HIS LONGEST walk since contracting polio twenty years earlier, President Franklin D. Roosevelt slowly limped along the length of the battleship H.M.S. *Prince of Wales.* More than 1,500 men, including British Prime Minister Winston S. Churchill, stood at rigid attention as the president took tortured steps, "determined to walk along that deck even if it killed him."[1] Roosevelt finally reached his seat near the bow, next to Churchill. British and American chiefs of staff stood behind them. Roosevelt and Churchill were attending church services in Placentia Bay near the harbor of Argentia, Newfoundland, on August 10, 1941.

The Sunday services aboard the *Prince of Wales* marked the "keynote" of the four-day summit meeting between the two leaders (August 9–13, 1941), some four months before Pearl Harbor catapulted the United States into World War II as a formal belligerent.[2] The sermon, from Joshua 1:1–9, seemed directed at the president: "As I was with Moses, so I will be with thee: I will not fail thee, nor forsake thee." Further suggesting the need for U.S. aid in the war against Hitler was the hortatory hymn, "Onward Christian Soldiers," which called for "marching as to war." For Roosevelt, who had already supplied destroyers, Lend–Lease, and other aid short of war, the moment evoked a rush of emotion. "If nothing else had happened," he later told his son, "that would have cemented us. 'Onward Christian Soldiers.' We *are,* and we *will,* go on, with God's help."[3] Churchill found symbolic unity that morning— "the Union Jack and the Stars and Stripes draped side by side; … British and American sailors … joining fervently in the prayers and hymns familiar to both."[4] Nobody aboard the *Prince of Wales* could know that Japanese bombs would destroy the majestic battleship off the coast of Malaya on December 10, 1941.

The four-day meeting in Placentia Bay was the first of many between Roosevelt and Churchill during World War II. Notwithstanding the fears that the meeting might spark a clash of "prima donnas," the personalities blended well.[5] Churchill's willingness to pay deference to a man he regarded "almost with religious awe" and his own pride in being half-American on his mother's side made him an ardent advocate of Anglo-American solidarity.[6] Roosevelt reciprocated Churchill's friendship. Under their leadership the two countries became "mixed up together … for mutual and general advantage" to a degree unmatched in modern times.[7] "No lover ever studied the whims of his mistress as I did those of President Roosevelt," Churchill later boasted.[8]

Aside from the personal intimacy and cultural symbolism, Argentia produced few decisive results. The British asked for men, ships, planes, and tanks. Churchill urged the U.S. Navy to extend its convoying of British vessels farther into the German submarine-infested North Atlantic. The British military chiefs, citing the frightful casualties of World War I, argued that bombing, blockades, and propaganda might so weaken the Germans that they would surrender without a full-scale invasion. The Americans favored a more direct strategy, insisting on large ground armies. Army Chief of Staff General George C. Marshall declared that a U.S. military buildup had to take priority over British requests for weapons and equipment; otherwise, "we might have lost everything we owned, including our pants."[9] FDR did promise to convoy British merchant ships as far as Iceland, but he delayed any public declaration until September, when a German submarine fired torpedoes at the destroyer U.S.S. *Greer* near Iceland. Neglecting to mention that the *Greer* had stalked the U-boat for three hours prior to the attack, Roosevelt announced on September 11 that henceforth American naval vessels would shoot at German submarines—"the rattlesnakes of the Atlantic."[10] Undeclared naval action was as far as Roosevelt would go in the months before Pearl Harbor. Hitler himself reacted to the Argentia meeting by ordering the deportation of German and Austrian Jews to the East, a "massive step" in his genocidal Final Solution.[11]

At Argentia, discussions about Japan exposed British and American differences. Foreign Office diplomats argued that Japan, which had recently occupied the southern half of French Indochina, should receive an explicit U.S. warning against further encroachments, and that the United States should commit to war if the Japanese attacked British or Dutch territory in Southeast Asia. Roosevelt did promise a "mighty swat" at Japan, but instead of announcing that continued Japanese aggression would cause the United States to take measures that "might result in war," the watered-down statement merely read that Washington would take steps necessary "toward insuring the safety and security of the United States."[12] Roosevelt preferred to delay a confrontation in the Pacific until he strengthened his army and navy and cultivated a more favorable public opinion. He also intended to beat Hitler first.

The most famous product of the summit came in the eight-point statement of war aims—the Atlantic Charter. Reminiscent of Woodrow Wilson's Fourteen Points, the charter reaffirmed the principles of collective security, national self-determination, freedom of the seas, and liberal trading practices (see Chapter 3). The signatories also disclaimed any territorial aggrandizement and pledged economic collaboration. Behind the vision of a postwar world, however, lay Anglo-American differences. The Americans, particularly Under Secretary of State Sumner Welles, pressed for a statement explicitly endorsing freer trade. The British wanted to protect their discriminatory system of imperial preferences. The compromise called for "access, on equal terms, to the trade and to the raw materials of the world," leaving the British an escape clause that promised "due respect for their existing obligations." Churchill failed to gain Roosevelt's backing for a new League. FDR endorsed only "the establishment of a wider and permanent system of general security."[13] As "both realist and idealist, both fixer and preacher, both a prince and a soldier," the president wanted to be as cautious as he was eloquent about postwar goals.[14]

The Atlantic Charter became a propaganda tool against the Axis. Soon Voice of America radio broadcasts hailed the charter's call to "fight on all the world's battlefields for these essential liberties: liberty of expression, of religion, and the right to live protected from need and from fear."[15] In September 1941, representatives of the nations battling Hitler formally adhered to the "common principles" set forth in the Atlantic Charter.[16] The Soviet Union gave qualified approval. Twenty-six nations, on January 1, 1942, signed the Declaration of the United Nations, which pledged cooperation in achieving the aims of the Atlantic Charter. Churchill and Roosevelt,

**Winston S. Churchill
(1874–1965) at Placentia
Bay, August 1941.** Churchill
claimed later that after he and
Roosevelt signed the Atlantic
Charter, "America could not
honourably stay out" of the war.
American support for Churchill and
Britain, FDR said privately, rested
on "a mathematical proposition. If
Hitler organizes Europe and Africa
with their 400 million people, plus
Japan, we would stand no chance
with our 175 million (Canada and
Mexico included). Not only would
we have to reduce our standard of
living, but in the end we would be
beaten because of the manpower
superiority of the other side.
Therefore we *cannot* let Britain be
defeated." (Franklin D. Roosevelt
Library)

however, provided no procedures for enforcement or implementation. Indeed, the prime minister insisted that the charter applied only to "nations of Europe now under the Nazi yoke," not to "the regions and peoples which owe allegiance to the British Crown."[17] Roosevelt came to view the principles as a "beautiful idea" rather than as set rules, and he seemed willing to postpone their application to accommodate pressing military and diplomatic priorities.[18] "I dream dreams but am, at the same time, an intensely practical person," he once admitted.[19]

By meeting publicly with Churchill on a British battleship, Roosevelt demonstrated America's commitment to the defense of Britain by all means short of war. Whatever his hopes that the theatrics of Argentia would galvanize American opinion for a firmer stance, Roosevelt maintained a "policy of influence without belligerence."[20] Not "a single American officer has shown the slightest keenness to be in the war on our side," one British participant noted.[21] Yet the Atlantic Charter, the Churchill-Roosevelt friendship, the Anglo-American strategic conversations, even the divergent views on international organization and postwar economic policy—all struck chords that would echo through the next four years of war. That the Soviet Union, invaded by Germany some six weeks earlier, sent no representatives to Argentia did not inhibit discussion of Soviet cooperation against the Axis. Presidential aide Harry Hopkins had visited Moscow two weeks before the Argentia conference, and his assurances that the USSR would withstand the Nazi onslaught buoyed the two leaders. In a joint communication to Joseph Stalin from Argentia, Churchill and Roosevelt hailed "the splendid defense that you are making against the Nazi attack" and promised the "very maximum" of supplies.[22] This Anglo-American commitment to the Soviet Union also carried large implications for the future.

Juggling Between War and Peace, 1939–1941

The conversations at Placentia Bay exemplified Roosevelt's distinctly personal approach to diplomacy during World War II. A deft juggler who "could keep all his balls in the air without losing his own," FDR delighted in face-to-face confrontations, always confident in his ability to charm even those who accused him of "messianic" delusions.[23] It mattered little that Secretary of State Cordell Hull learned of the conference when he read about it in the newspapers. With selfless subordinates such as Sumner Welles and Harry Hopkins to do his bidding, Roosevelt relished shining the spotlight on himself. British foreign secretary Anthony Eden once compared FDR to "a conjurer, skillfully juggling with balls of dynamite, whose nature he failed to understand."[24]

The juggling act had begun two years earlier, when Germany started World War II by attacking Poland. FDR had avowed on September 3, 1939, just two days after the German invasion, that "this nation will remain a neutral nation." Still, "I cannot ask that every American remain neutral in thought as well."[25] Thus, in words pointedly different from Wilson's in 1914, did Roosevelt project the next twenty-six months of U.S. policy toward the war in Europe. Roosevelt proceeded from neutrality to nonbelligerency to undeclared war in the Atlantic and finally, after Pearl Harbor, to full-scale war against the Axis. Hoping to avoid war while giving as much aid as possible to Hitler's opponents, FDR did not always speak candidly about the inherent contradiction between these two goals.

On September 21, 1939, Roosevelt asked Congress to repeal the arms embargo in the Neutrality Act as the best way to stay out of the war. He stressed this deceptive argument, knowing that his real purpose was to permit England and France, with their superior sea power, to purchase arms and munitions on a cash-and-carry basis. He persuaded William Allen White, the Republican sage from Kansas, to form a Non-Partisan Committee for Peace Through Revision of the Neutrality Act. Although isolationists such as Republican Senator Charles Tobey of New Hampshire opposed "our changing the rules after the war has broken out," FDR's tactics worked.[26] By a vote of 63 to 30 in the Senate and 243 to 181 in the House, the revised Neutrality Act became law on November 4, thus permitting Britain and France to buy arms.

The Pan American Conference at Panama City (September 23–October 3, 1939) also signaled the pro-Allied emphasis of U.S. policy. The conferees proclaimed neutrality, established a committee for economic coordination, and created a neutral zone 300 miles wide along the entire coast of the Western Hemisphere (except Canada), in which belligerent naval operations were prohibited. Roosevelt had mockingly told his cabinet in April 1939 that the Atlantic fleet would patrol such areas and "if we fire and sink an Italian or German [submarine] … we will say

Makers of American Foreign Relations, 1939–1945

Presidents	Secretaries of State
Franklin D. Roosevelt, 1933–1945	Cordell Hull, 1933–1944
	Edward R. Stettinius, Jr., 1944–1945
Harry S. Truman, 1945–1953	James F. Byrnes, 1945–1947

it the way the Japs do, 'so sorry.' 'Never happen again.' Tomorrow we sink two."[27] These "neutrality patrols" actually became the first step toward Anglo-American naval cooperation. By late summer 1940, conversations between staff officers began in London, soon followed by exchanges of personnel and cryptographic intelligence, actual coordination against German naval operations, and, in the autumn of 1941, convoying merchant ships across the Atlantic. Ostensibly justified in terms of contingency planning and aid short of war, such naval measures nonetheless led the chief of naval operations, Admiral Harold R. Stark, to conclude in early 1941: "We cannot avoid having it [war] thrust upon us or our deliberately going in."[28]

Germany's *blitzkrieg* humbled Poland in two weeks, and then from November 1939 to March 1940 the Soviet Union defeated Finland in the "Winter war." Roosevelt sent his sympathies but little else to Finland. Hitler's conquest of France in June 1940 stung FDR into bold measures. In a speech on June 10, Roosevelt condemned Italy for wielding the dagger that "struck … the back of its neighbor," and he pledged to England "the material resources of this nation."[29] A week later, he respectively named the prominent Republicans Henry L. Stimson and Frank Knox, both vocal advocates of aid to Britain, as secretary of war and secretary of the navy. Then, after intricate negotiations, the president announced on September 3, 1940, that he was transferring to England some fifty old destroyers in exchange for leases to eight British bases stretching from Newfoundland to British Guiana. Two weeks later, he signed into law the Selective Service Act of 1940, the first peacetime military draft in American history.

That Roosevelt could accomplish so much at a time when isolationist sentiment still prevailed and he was seeking a controversial third presidential term testifies to his political astuteness. As for both selective service and the destroyers-for-bases agreement, FDR learned that his Republican presidential opponent, Wendell L. Willkie, would not make them campaign issues. In both cases, Roosevelt also encouraged private citizens groups to lobby for his objectives. The Committee to Defend America by Aiding the Allies, headed by William Allen White, soon rallied behind the president to counter the isolationist America First Committee set up in September 1940. FDR avoided congressional scrutiny of the destroyers deal by presenting it as an executive agreement rather than as a treaty, and he deflected political opposition to conscription by having men of integrity, such as Secretary Stimson and General Marshall, attest to the military's need for a draft. Further, Roosevelt continued to promise that he would keep America out of war. Although Germany could regard the destroyers deal as an act of war, FDR called it instead "the most important action in the reinforcement of our national defense … since the Louisiana Purchase."[30] At the end of the fall campaign, Roosevelt promised American mothers: "Your boys are not going to be sent into any foreign wars." Willkie exploded: "That hypocritical son of a bitch! This is going to beat me!"[31] It did.

After the election Churchill cabled: "The moment approaches when we shall no longer be able to pay cash for shipping and other supplies."[32] Roosevelt held one of his breezy, jaunty press conferences, saying that he favored lending or leasing

The German Onslaught 1939–1942

Lend-Lease to the USSR. A U.S. lend-lease official checks American food destined for the Soviet Union's hard-pressed people. Recipients of $11.3 billion in lend-lease goods, the Soviets eventually lost nearly 27 million lives in the war. (U.S. Information Agency, National Archives)

supplies to Britain. He likened the practice to lending a garden hose to a neighbor whose house was burning. Once the fire is out, "he gives it back to me and thanks me very much."[33] In a radio fireside chat on December 29, FDR admitted that sending armaments to Britain risked war, but the "sole purpose is to keep war away from our country and our people." Then, in a ringing phrase, Roosevelt called on the United States to "become the great arsenal of democracy."[34]

Over the next two months, Americans debated the Lend-Lease bill "in every newspaper, on every wave length—over every cracker barrel in all the land."[35] Although the vote of 60 to 31 in the Senate and 317 to 71 in the House seemed substantial, the White House did not win easily. Senator Burton K. Wheeler, an isolationist Democrat from Montana, warned that aid short of war was a dangerous delusion—"You can't put your shirt tail into a clothes wringer and pull it out suddenly when the wringer keeps turning."[36] Right-wing women's groups accused interventionists of "'bundling,' 'balling,' and curtseying for Britain."[37] Senator Hiram Johnson grumbled: "Like the dog gone back to his vomit, the country has become English again."[38]

To overcome such opposition, some deception became necessary. The administration's floor manager, Representative John W. McCormack, worried that his Irish constituents in South Boston would protest any "McCormack Bill" designed to aid the British Empire, induced the House parliamentarian to tag the Lend-Lease bill H.R. 1776. When one irate constituent still berated him, the future Speaker of the House thought quickly: "Madam, do you realize that the Vatican is surrounded on all sides by totalitarianism? Madam, this is not a bill to save the English, this is a bill to save Catholicism."[39]

The Lend-Lease Act became law on March 11, 1941. Under its terms the president could "sell, transfer title to, exchange, lease, lend, or otherwise dispose of" defense articles to "any country whose defense the President deems vital to the defense of the United States."[40] Although the initial appropriation totaled $7 billion, by war's end the United States had expended more than $50 billion on Lend-Lease. England eventually received $31.6 billion of that amount.

With German U-boats sinking 500,000 tons of shipping a month, it seemed logical that the United States would use its navy to ensure that Lend-Lease supplies reached England safely. FDR hesitated, partly because of public opinion, but also because the Atlantic fleet lacked operational readiness. Instead, he extended naval "patrols" halfway across the Atlantic, announcing in April that U.S. vessels would monitor German warships. "We have got a tadpole that someday may be a frog," noted Secretary Hull.[41] U.S. troops also occupied Greenland the same month. FDR declared a national emergency in late May but took no new action. He told the cabinet that "he expected a clash sooner or later but said the Germans would have to fire the first shots."[42]

When Hitler occupied the Balkans and invaded the Soviet Union in June 1941, the president announced the next month that 4,000 American marines would occupy Iceland for hemispheric defense. Roosevelt also began military Lend-Lease aid to the USSR in November, notwithstanding opinions from military advisers that the Soviet Union would resist for a "maximum [of] *three months*."[43] FDR gambled that prolonged Soviet resistance would eventually result in "the liberation of Europe from Nazi domination."[44] When bureaucratic tangles inhibited the flow of goods to the USSR, Roosevelt insisted that supplies be sent "even if the Army and Navy authorities in America did not like it."[45] Then the president held his dramatic meeting with Churchill at Placentia Bay, and in early September, after German torpedoes just missed the *Greer,* he publicly ordered naval convoys as far as Iceland and issued a "shoot-on-sight" command to the navy.

By autumn 1941, Roosevelt probably anticipated an "incident" to induce U.S. entry into the war against Hitler. After the Placentia Bay conference, the president told Churchill that "he would wage war, but not declare it, and that he would become more and more provocative. If the Germans did not like it, they could attack American forces."[46] When a U-boat torpedoed the destroyer *Kearny* off Iceland on October 17, killing eleven men, the president seized the moment: "History has recorded who fired the first shot. ... Hitler's torpedo was directed at every American."[47] Roosevelt also spoke of a Nazi plan to "abolish all existing religions— Catholic, Protestant, Mohammedan, Hindu, Buddhist, and Jewish alike."[48] The president hoped to persuade Congress to repeal the sections of the 1939 Neutrality Act that prohibited the arming of merchant ships and banned all vessels from war zones. After a U-boat sank the destroyer *Reuben James* on October 31, killing more than one hundred men, the isolationist America First Committee charged that the White House was "asking Congress to issue an engraved drowning license to American seamen."[49] Following bitter debate, repeal passed in November by narrow margins, 50 to 37 in the Senate and 212 to 194 in the House. For the first time since the outbreak of war in 1939, U.S. merchant vessels could legally carry munitions to England.

Roosevelt charted an oblique course toward war because he believed he had no other choice. "Haranguing the country doesn't help," he said. "It will take a 'shock' like 1932" to change isolationist attitudes.[50] In October 1941, he bluntly told the British ambassador that "if he asked for a declaration of war, he wouldn't get it, and opinion would swing against him."[51] FDR thus chose indirection over candor and relied on events and his own manipulative ability to inch ahead. By the autumn of 1941, 80 percent of the American people still opposed entering the war, while a higher percentage wanted an Axis defeat. So long as FDR touted aid to the Allies as the best way to avoid war, Americans could apparently fulfill both goals. The narrow vote over repeal of the Neutrality Act in November reinforced the president's reluctance to ask for outright intervention. "The day of the white rabbits has passed," one senator wrote, "and the great magician who could pull them out of any silk hat … cannot find the rabbit."[52]

The Road to Pearl Harbor: Japanese-American Relations, 1939–1941

Events in Asia, not Europe, plunged the United States into World War II. Ambassador Joseph C. Grew expressed surprise at increased anti-Japanese sentiment during a trip home in the summer of 1939 when President Roosevelt talked truculently of intercepting the Japanese fleet if it moved against the Dutch East Indies. With the announcement in July that the 1911 commercial treaty with Japan would be terminated in six months, Grew feared that economic sanctions and war might follow. "Sparks will fly before long," he predicted.[53]

Grew misjudged the Europe-first emphasis of Roosevelt's foreign policy. After 1937, when Japan marched deeper into China, Washington angrily reacted with protests but lacked the power to challenge Japanese predominance in East Asia and the Western Pacific. Even Roosevelt's much-heralded refusal to apply the Neutrality Act to the undeclared war in China, thus making it legal to sell arms to Jiang Jieshi's government, could not obscure the preponderance of U.S. trade with Japan. As late as 1940, $78 million in American exports went to China, whereas $227 million were shipped to Japan. Ending the 1911 commercial treaty permitted economic sanctions against Japan, but oil, the most vital ingredient in Japan's war machine, flowed until July 1941. In keeping with Roosevelt's policy of all-out aid to England short of war, the navy revised its strategic thinking in November 1940. "Plan Dog" called for a defensive posture in the Pacific, depicted Germany as the country's primary enemy, and made preservation of England its principal goal. Roosevelt still hoped to avoid a confrontation with Japan, because "I simply have not got enough Navy to go around."[54] During 1941 he mentioned Hitler and the Nazis on more than 150 public occasions, but made only "four references" to Japan so as not to divert public attention from Europe.[55]

Japanese movement into Southeast Asia placed Washington and Tokyo on a collision course. With the Asian colonies of France and the Netherlands lying unprotected, Japanese expansionists demanded a thrust southward, thus completing the strangulation of China and creating what Hull called "a self-sufficient trading bloc" that made "a mockery of … the Open Door."[56] Japan pressed England and France to close down supply routes to the Guomindang through Burma and Indochina.

Tokyo also demanded economic concessions from the petroleum-rich Dutch East Indies. Then, only four days after Vichy France allowed Japanese troops to occupy northern Indochina, Japan signed the Tripartite Pact with Germany and Italy on September 27. The signatories pledged to aid one another "if attacked" by a nation not currently "involved in the European War or the Sino-Japanese Conflict."[57] Because the pact explicitly exempted the Soviet Union, Washington had no doubt about being its target. Indeed, Hitler told the Japanese that "enemy number 1 was America."[58]

A new, more militant Japanese government, with Prince Fumimaro Konoe as prime minister and General Hideki Tojo as war minister, took the fateful steps. Foreign Minister Yosuke Matsuoka articulated the advantages of boldness—"one cannot obtain a tiger's cub unless he braves the tiger's den."[59] Matsuoka intended the Tripartite Pact to deter the United States from intervening in the Atlantic or the Pacific, and to facilitate a rapprochement between Japan and the Soviet Union, which remained aligned with Germany in the Nazi-Soviet Pact. Tokyo might then induce Jiang Jieshi to join the Co-Prosperity Sphere, after which Japanese troops would gradually withdraw from China and civilian authorities could reassert control over the army.

Washington flashed warnings. In July 1940, Roosevelt withheld aviation fuel and top-grade scrap iron from Japan. In September, after the Tripartite Pact, he extended the embargo to all scrap metals. Even Grew urged firmness, labeling Japan "one of the predatory powers," lacking "all moral and ethical sense."[60] Administration "hawks" pressed the president to end oil exports as well. Backed by Hull and the Joint Chiefs, however, Roosevelt kept the oil flowing to Japan. Recognizing the interdependence of Asian and European events, FDR expedited aid to China to keep Japan's army "busy and more or less tied up" so it could not "move southward in full force."[61] The president hoped to aid England while avoiding a showdown in the Pacific, which an oil embargo would likely precipitate.

In February 1941, Admiral Kichisaburo Nomura became ambassador to Washington. A personal friend of President Roosevelt, Nomura accepted the appointment only when assured by Konoe and Matsuoka that peace with the United States took precedence over Japan's commitment to the Axis. Despite protracted negotiations between Hull and Nomura that spring and summer, Japan's determination to hold China and to advance beyond China doomed any diplomatic solutions. In early July 1941, Roosevelt thought the Japanese were about to decide "which way they are going to jump—attack Russia, attack the South Seas … or whether they will sit on the fence and be more friendly with us."[62] FDR knew how grave the situation was because he received intelligence reports indicating that in the event of war between the United States and Japan, "Germany would declare war on U.S.A."[63] When Japan seized southern Indochina in late July, he signed an order freezing all Japanese funds to deter further expansion. Hard-line bureaucrats interpreted the order to mean stopping all trade with Japan—including oil. Thereafter, Washington and Tokyo steered "a collision course that even statesmen of great flexibility would find it difficult to avoid."[64]

Unless the sale of American oil resumed, Japan was determined to seize Dutch and British petroleum fields. "If we are going to fight," the navy chief of staff told Emperor Hirohito, "then the sooner … the better because our supplies are dwindling anyway."[65] But the United States would not turn on the oil spigot until Tokyo agreed to respect China's sovereignty and territorial integrity. Key American officials also knew from cracking the Japanese diplomatic code (Operation MAGIC) that Japan's forces were massing to strike southward after mid-November, although most officials did not think Japan would attack any U.S. territory, certainly not as far east as the Hawaiian Islands. As late as November 27, when MAGIC intercepts revealed the imminence of a Japanese strike somewhere, State Department Asian expert Stanley K. Hornbeck challenged his colleagues: "Tell me of one case in history when a nation went to war out of desperation."[66] Amid this atmosphere, the urging of army and navy leaders to string out negotiations until the Philippines could be reinforced went unheeded. An eleventh-hour U.S. modus vivendi coupled a trickle of oil to Japan with negotiations between Chóngqing and Tokyo, while maintaining American aid to China; Japan would have to abrogate the Tripartite Pact and accept basic principles of international conduct. Exhausted from months of negotiations, Hull advised the president to shelve the proposal. "It is now in the hands of … the Army and Navy," he said.[67]

After months of discussion, the Japanese Imperial Conference of September decided to fight the United States if Washington did not lift its embargo by October 15—a date later extended to November 25 and then to November 29. Tokyo's final decision to attack the United States did not stem from irrationality or suicidal tendencies. Japan required 12,000 tons of oil each day, and moderates and militants alike read U.S. pressure as provocative and life-strangling. In a choice between fighting the United States or pulling out of China, no Japanese leader recommended the latter. They knew America's power and industrial potential well enough, but as Emperor Hirohito put it: "An arrow is about leave a bow. Once an arrow is fired, it will become a long-drawn out war."[68] The Japanese did not expect a U.S. surrender, but they hoped Americans would see them as "a crazed and reckless

The PURPLE Machine. In September 1940, U.S. cryptanalysts of the Signal Intelligence Service cracked Japan's most secret diplomatic code. The American code-breakers, under Operation MAGIC, not only deciphered thousands of intercepted messages sent by Japanese officials around the world, but also duplicated the machine, called PURPLE, that generated the codes. Although these dispatches revealed through 1941 that Japan expected all-out war with the United States, they did not reveal military plans or the planned attack on Pearl Harbor. By facilitating the formation of better strategies, the intelligence gathered from MAGIC and British ULTRA intercepts of German signals may have shortened the war by two or three years. (National Archives)

people against whom it would not pay to fight."[69] "We would become a third-class nation … if we just sat tight," asserted Tojo.[70]

On November 25, 1941, a huge task force that included six carriers bearing some 350 airplanes headed across 3,000 miles of the Pacific Ocean. The target: Pearl Harbor, Hawai'i. After receiving the message "Climb Mt. Niitake" on December 2, every ship maintained radio silence to avoid detection and ensure complete surprise. In the early morning of Sunday, December 7, the carriers launched their planes. After a flight of 220 miles, the aircraft swept down on the unsuspecting American naval base. Within a few hours eight U.S. battleships had been sunk or damaged and 2,403 Americans had died. The stunning news shot around the world. In London, Churchill thought: "So we had won after all!"[71] In Chongqing, Jiang Jieshi "sang an old opera air, and played the Ave Maria all that day," also rejoicing in his new ally.[72] "Those little yellow bastards," exclaimed Navy Secretary Frank Knox when he learned of the attack.[73]

Critics have charged that Roosevelt and his top advisers deliberately sacrificed the Pacific fleet to get into the war with Hitler via the "back door."[74] Most scholars reject the conspiracy theory and explain Pearl Harbor as the consequence of mistakes, missed clues, overconfidence, and plain bad luck. Better intelligence in Washington might have alerted Hawai'i, but American errors weighed less than the enormous care and skill with which the Japanese planned the attack. MAGIC intercepts on November 30, for example, read that "war may suddenly break out between the Anglo-Saxon nations and Japan …; this war may come quicker than anyone dreams."[75] Yet the intercepts never revealed military plans, and Washington

Pearl Harbor. A Japanese aerial reconnaissance view of the torpedo plane attack on "Battleship Row" taken at about 8:00 a.m., Sunday, December 7, 1941, at Pearl Harbor, Hawai'i. The three Pacific U.S. aircraft carriers were not in port and escaped the attack. Of the eight battleships hit at Pearl Harbor, six were repaired and eventually participated in the war. The historian John Fousek writes that "Pearl Harbor would enter U.S. public discourse as one of the code words for the almost universally accepted 'lessons' of World War II—never appease aggressors and always remain militarily prepared." (Naval Historical Foundation)

thought Japan would strike Southeast Asia, where troop ships were spotted heading for Malaya. No one thought Tokyo could undertake two major operations at once. As for hints of major Japanese interest in Pearl Harbor, including Grew's warning in February 1941 of a possible sudden attack, one scholar has written: "After the event a signal is always crystal clear. … But before the event it is obscure and pregnant with conflicting meanings. … In short, we failed to anticipate Pearl Harbor not for want of the relevant materials, but because of a plethora of irrelevant ones."[76] Many "ifs" cloud the question. If the radar operator had convinced his superiors on Oahu that the blips really were planes, if General Marshall had sent his last-minute warning by navy cable instead of Western Union telegraph, if MAGIC could have read Japan's naval communications as well as its diplomatic cables, if …

For Japan, Pearl Harbor proved a tactical victory but a strategic disaster. It was also a "relief to the Boss," as one Cabinet member noted, because FDR had promised to aid the British if the Japanese attacked Singapore.[77] He could now cite Japan's infamous attack on American territory in asking for a declaration of war. Congress responded on December 8 with a unanimous vote in the Senate for war against Japan and only one dissent in the House. For Senator Arthur H. Vandenberg, the Japanese attack on Hawai'i "ended isolationism for any realist."[78] Spewing venom against FDR and "the circle of Jews surrounding him," Hitler declared war on the United States on December 11.[79] Congress's immediate declaration of war on Germany confronted the now united Americans with a daunting two-theater conflict.

The Big Three: Strategies and Fissures, 1941–1943

The events of 1939–1941 darkly foreshadowed the themes of wartime diplomacy. Giving material aid to Hitler's opponents became the main U.S. contribution to victory in Europe. Washington's commitment to a "Europe First" strategy derived from Anglo-American staff discussions prior to Pearl Harbor, as did the different American and British conceptions of that strategy. Americans favored a "massive thrust at the enemy's heart," and the British preferred "successive stabs around the periphery … like jackals worrying a lion before springing at his throat."[80] During the war Americans also revived Wilsonianism but combined it with a pragmatic determination to avoid Wilson's mistakes. This time the United States would join an international organization to maintain peace, even if it meant adding blatant balance-of-power features to the institution under Roosevelt's concept of the "Four Policemen" (United States, USSR, Britain, and China), each of which would maintain peace in a sphere of influence. This time there would be no debts-reparations tangle because Lend-Lease would eliminate the dollar sign. This time the enemy must surrender unconditionally. This time tariff walls must fall and trade doors must open. This time there would be postwar cooperation with the Soviets. FDR encouraged Hollywood to produce such pro-Soviet films as *Mission to Moscow* (1943), which he sent to Stalin with the message that Washington was "on the level—no axes to grind."[81] *Life* magazine described Russians as "one hell of a people" who "look like Americans, dress like Americans, and think like Americans."[82] They reportedly had "a terrific interest in anything American."[83]

Global war brought new power and confidence to U.S. diplomacy. The Atlantic Charter reflected a commitment to shaping the postwar world in an American image. As Henry Luce's best-selling *American Century* phrased it in 1941, the United States must "exert upon the world the full impact of our influence, for such purposes as we see fit and by such means as we see fit."[84] By rearming, acquiring new bases, raising an army of more than 2 million, welding hemispheric unity, and revving up its industries, the United States built the sinews of global power even before Pearl Harbor. By 1944 Churchill would tell Roosevelt: "You have the greatest navy in the world … the greatest air force … the greatest trade. You have all the gold." But Churchill hoped that the Americans would avoid "vainglorious ambitions, and that justice and fair-play will be the lights that guide them."[85] FDR irritated his European allies by his anticolonial pronouncements, claiming, for example, that "after 100 years of French rule in Indochina, the inhabitants were worse off than they were before."[86] Churchill retorted: "I have not become the King's First Minister in order to preside over the liquidation of the British Empire."[87]

American-British-Soviet diplomacy in the "Grand Alliance" centered on boundaries in Eastern Europe and the timing of an Anglo-American "second front" in Western Europe. Shortly after Pearl Harbor, Stalin said he had no objections to the "algebra" of the Atlantic Charter, but he preferred "practical arithmetic"—that is, an agreement guaranteeing Soviet boundaries with Eastern Europe as they stood prior to Hitler's attack in 1941.[88] The British seemed inclined to grant what Stalin wanted, but Roosevelt vetoed any secret or public treaty on boundaries "until the war had been won."[89] Content with "a free hand," Stalin noted that "our frontiers" would be "decided by force."[90]

FDR viewed the establishment of a second front as a matter of great urgency. The Soviets, fighting some 200 German divisions and dying by the hundreds of thousands, pleaded for a cross-channel attack as quickly as possible. Assuring Soviet foreign minister V. M. Molotov in May 1942 that Roosevelt wanted to help, Harry Hopkins urged the diplomat to paint a deliberately "gloomy picture of the Soviet position to make the American generals understand the gravity of the situation."[91] Roosevelt promised Molotov a second front that year, but the Anglo-American invasion of France did not take place until June 6, 1944. In the interim, as FDR acknowledged, "the Russian armies are killing more Axis personnel and destroying more Axis material than all other twenty-five United Nations put together."[92] The delay produced serious fissures in the Grand Alliance.

American military leaders urged a cross-channel attack by the spring of 1943 at the latest, but the British, with Roosevelt's reluctant compliance, decided otherwise. A new plan, Operation TORCH, called for the invasion of French North Africa in November 1942, a decision that became, in Churchill's words, "a springboard and not a sofa" for operations against Sicily and Italy in the summer of 1943 and effectively postponed a cross-channel attack (later dubbed Operation OVERLORD) until 1944.[93] When General Dwight D. Eisenhower learned that the second front had been postponed, he pronounced it the "blackest day in history."[94] At numerous military conferences in 1942–1943, the Americans always suspected that Britain's fixation on the Mediterranean demonstrated a desire to shore up imperial lifelines and not, as the British claimed, a coherent strategy to bleed Germany on the

"Jap … You're Next!" James Montgomery Flagg, already famous for his "I Want You" poster of World War I, offered this version of Uncle Sam in 1942. After Pearl Harbor, posters such as Flagg's helped focus public resentment on Japan, rather than on Hitler. "I can see why we are fighting the Japanese," observed one Gallup Poll respondent, "but I can't see why we are fighting the Germans." Yet Roosevelt did not want to adopt a "Pacific First" strategy and kept his "Europe First" strategy alive by supporting British proposals to invade North Africa in November 1942. (National Archives)

periphery before launching a full-scale invasion of France. Churchill said he no longer needed to woo the United States; "now that she is in the harem, we talk to her quite differently."[95] What Eisenhower called Britain's "scatteration" strategy predominated in the two years after Pearl Harbor because England had fully mobilized, whereas America had not. Any combined operation had to depend largely on British troops, shipping, and casualties; any landing in Western Europe had to be staged from the British Isles.[96] U.S. matériel and forces, moreover, were being diverted to the Pacific theater at the insistence of General Douglas MacArthur and Admiral Ernest King. Once American production and manpower surged by 1943, combined strategy gradually shifted toward Operation OVERLORD. A symbolic clash between the two competing strategies occurred in early 1944. Churchill insisted on an invasion of Rhodes, off the Turkish coast. "Not one American soldier is going to die on [that] God Damned beach," barked General Marshall.[97] None did.

Roosevelt and Churchill knew how intensely Stalin wanted a second front in France, not in North Africa or Italy. The Red Army had stopped the Germans short of Moscow in 1941, but in the summer of 1942 German *panzers* drove into the Caucasus oil fields and laid siege to Stalingrad. Churchill told Stalin in August 1942, just as U.S. marines were landing on Guadalcanal in the southwest Pacific, that a cross-channel attack was planned for spring 1943. After another year's procrastination, Stalin claimed that "Churchill is intent on the defeat of the USSR in order to then come to terms with … Hitler … at our expense," while the Soviet ambassador in Washington concluded that "the military calculations of both powers are based on the striving for the maximum exhaustion and wearing down" of the USSR "in order to diminish its role in deciding postwar problems."[98]

What if ...   *the Allies had opened a second front in France before 1944?*

Had the Americans persuaded British leaders to forego the North African landings in November 1942, the alternative strategy called for the buildup in England of Anglo-American forces to prepare for a full-scale cross-Channel attack in spring 1943. A successful invasion of Nazi-occupied France in 1943, combined with a Soviet counteroffensive after their victory at Stalingrad, might have ended the war a year earlier with Allied and Soviet forces meeting somewhere in central Europe. An earlier second front might have allayed Stalin's suspicions that his Anglo-American allies wanted the Red Army and the *Wehrmacht* to bleed each other to death on the Russian steppes. Victory in Europe by 1944 would have saved millions of lives, including countless victims of the Nazi death camps, and reduced the devastation that so destabilized Europe at war's end.

The North African victory instead prompted President Franklin D. Roosevelt unexpectedly to announce at Casablanca in January 1943 the Unconditional Surrender Doctrine—a proclamation that many observers believed encouraged the Germans to fight fanatically to the end. This new policy undercut U.S. intelligence agents in Switzerland who might have pursued closer contacts with anti-Hitler conspirators. Had plotters successfully assassinated the *Fuehrer*, a negotiated peace might have followed with a German government headed perhaps by the popular war hero General Erwin Rommel, though such a scenario would surely have alienated Moscow.

Without the North African landings, the buildup in the British Isles would have meant fewer reinforcements in the Pacific where Japanese conquests by summer 1942 had reached as far as New Guinea and the Solomon Islands, threatening Australia. Constrained by "Europe First" priorities, FDR might not have authorized the August 1942 invasion of Guadalcanal or the subsequent Australian-American thrust northward up the Solomon Islands toward the Philippines. Even had the U.S. Navy deployed its growing carrier task forces in a limited island-hopping campaign in the central Pacific, Allied battle lines would still have remained thousands of miles from the Japanese home islands if the European war ended in 1944. Two more years of war against a seemingly merciless Asian foe would have meant excessive casualties, nuclear warfare, Soviet intervention, or all three—unless Tokyo prudently sought peace terms after Nazi Germany, its crucial Axis ally in Europe, had surrendered.

It is also possible, even likely, that an Allied assault on Fortress Europe in 1943 would have failed. Without the Allied bombing campaign of 1942–1944 that so wore down the *Luftwaffe*, and without the massive German losses on the Eastern front, General Dwight D. Eisenhower's troops might have landed in 1943 only to be pushed back by German counterattacks. The disastrous 6,000 man commando raid on Dieppe in August 1942, in which half of the attacking forces were killed, wounded, or captured, provided an ominous precedent. Given the previous evacuation of British armies from Dunkirk in 1940 and from Greece in 1941, a worse debacle in 1943 might have caused the Churchill government to fall and thus postponed another invasion attempt for at least two years, by which time Hitler's heretofore "secret" weapons (jet aircraft, guided and ballistic missiles, snorkel submarines, and transatlantic bombers) might have repulsed any Allied assault. Such defeats might have led to a separate peace between the Soviet Union and Germany. Other worst case scenarios might have followed.

What is clear is that the Normandy landings in June 1944 proved decisive in bringing the European war to its final stage by having Allied forces storm Europe from the West and draw German forces away from Southern and Eastern fronts. The delayed opening of a second front, by necessitating that the Soviet Union fight in Central and Eastern Europe alone, also enabled the expansive and protracted occupation by the Red Army of defeated Axis zones that cleared the way for Europe's postwar division.

Tensions increased that summer of 1943, when the Soviet Union announced the "interruption" of diplomatic relations with the Polish exile government in London after the Poles asked the International Red Cross to investigate charges that the Russians had murdered more than 10,000 Polish prisoners in the Katyn Forest in 1941.[99] Stalin claimed the victims had escaped "to Manchuria," but Russian archives later revealed that he had ordered the murders.[100] The Soviets also protested when the Allies suspended convoys carrying vital Lend-Lease supplies to Murmansk because of shipping needs in the Mediterranean and Pacific. In August 1943, Stalin complained to Roosevelt that he was only "informed" about separate peace talks with Italy.[101] The Italians formally surrendered in early September, then declared war against Germany, only to have German forces occupy most of the peninsula before Anglo-American troops could land in force.

Stalin had to be "courted, wooed, constantly chatted up," so Churchill urged the Poles not to protest because "nothing you can do will bring them [the dead POWs] back."[102] FDR expedited Lend-Lease supplies to Russia without the usual quid pro quo arrangements, even though Soviet officials resented having "to beg for crumbs from the lord's table."[103] At the Casablanca Conference in January 1943, the president announced that "the elimination of German, Japanese, and Italian war power means the unconditional surrender by Germany, Italy, and Japan."[104] Coming shortly after the Anglo-Americans made an agreement with the Vichy French collaborator Admiral Jean-François Darlan to gain French cooperation in North Africa, Roosevelt's "unconditional surrender" announcement signaled to a suspicious Stalin that Britain and the United States would not make a separate German peace with one of Hitler's subordinates. The doctrine brought a modicum of Allied unity by concentrating on a total military victory over Hitler, deferring troublesome peace terms until afterward. "Roosevelt is more friendly to us than any other prominent American," the Soviet ambassador reported in 1943.[105] Nonetheless, one U.S. official compared dealing with the Russians to playing "golf—the more you try, the more you press, and the worse you score."[106]

The foreign ministers' meeting in Moscow (October 19–30) did establish an Advisory Council for Italy to coordinate Allied policy and a European Advisory Commission to make recommendations for a final peace settlement. The Soviets told Hull that the 200,000 American battle casualties did not amount to much—"we lose that many each day before lunch. You haven't got your teeth in the war yet."[107] Hull replied: "I knew a bully in Tennessee. He used to get a few things his way by being a bully and bluffing other fellows. But he ended up by not having a friend in the world."[108] Suffering from tuberculosis, the seventy-two-year-old Hull got what he wanted: a Declaration of Four Nations on General Security (China included), the first definite commitment to a postwar replacement for the defunct League of Nations.

The Moscow Conference seemed a mere prologue for "the turning point" at Teheran, Iran, November 28–December 1, 1943.[109] Meeting the Soviet leader for the first time, FDR thought Stalin "very confident, very sure of himself."[110] Stalin emphatically told Churchill and Roosevelt that he favored a firm commitment to OVERLORD as opposed to any Anglo-American operations in the Balkans. When Churchill backed an Adriatic landing, Stalin asked whether "the British really believed in Operation OVERLORD or simply speak of it to reassure the Russians?"[111] Churchill lamely replied that "it was the duty of the British Government to hurl every scrap of strength across the channel."[112] At a dinner party two nights later Stalin playfully advocated the summary execution of 50,000 German officers, whereupon the prime minister protested that the British would "never tolerate mass execution."[113] When Roosevelt joked that only 49,500 should be shot, Churchill walked out in a huff. The prime minister complained that the "great Russian bear" and the "great American buffalo" were squeezing the "poor little English donkey."[114]

Major Wartime Conferences, 1941–1945

Conference	Date	Participants	Results
Argentia, Newfoundland	August 9–12, 1941	Roosevelt, Churchill	Atlantic Charter
Washington, D.C.	December 22, 1941– January 14, 1942	Roosevelt, Churchill	Combined Chiefs of Staff; priority in war effort against Germany; United Nations Declaration
Washington, D.C.	June 19–25, 1942	Roosevelt, Churchill	North African campaign strategy
Moscow, USSR	August 12–15, 1942	Churchill, Stalin, Harriman	Postponement of second front
Casablanca, Morocco	January 14–24, 1943	Roosevelt, Churchill	Unconditional surrender announcement; campaign against Sicily and Italy
Washington, D.C.	May 12–25, 1943	Roosevelt, Churchill	Scheduling of cross-channel landing for May 1, 1944
Quebec, Canada	August 14–24, 1943	Roosevelt, Churchill	Confirmation of cross-channel landing (OVERLORD)
Moscow, USSR	October 19–30, 1943	Hull, Eden, Molotov	Postwar international organization to be formed; Soviet promise to enter the war against Japan after Germany's defeat; establishment of European Advisory Commission
UNRRA, Washington, D.C.	November 9, 1943	44 nations	Creation of UNRRA
Cairo, Egypt	November 22–26, 1943	Roosevelt, Churchill, Jiang	Postwar Asia: China to recover lost lands; Korea to be independent; Japan to be stripped of Pacific islands
Teheran, Iran	November 27– December 1, 1943	Roosevelt, Churchill, Stalin	Agreement on cross-channel landing and international organization; Soviet reaffirmation of intent to enter the war against Japan
Bretton Woods, New Hampshire	July 1–22, 1944	44 nations	Creation of World Bank and International Monetary Fund
Dumbarton Oaks, Washington, D.C.	August 21– October 7, 1944	U.S., Britain, USSR, China	United Nations Organization
Quebec, Canada	September 11–16, 1944	Roosevelt, Churchill	"Morgenthau Plan" for Germany
Moscow, USSR	October 9–18, 1944	Churchill, Stalin	Spheres of influence in Balkans (percentage scheme)
Yalta, USSR	February 4–11, 1945	Roosevelt, Churchill, Stalin	Polish governmental structure, elections, and boundaries; United Nations; German reparations; USSR pledge to declare war against Japan and to recognize Jiang's government; some Japanese territories to USSR
San Francisco, California	April 25–June 26, 1945	50 nations	United Nations Organization Charter
Potsdam (Berlin), Germany	July 17– August 2, 1945	Truman, Churchill/Attlee, Stalin	German reconstruction and reparations; Potsdam Declaration to Japan; Council of Foreign Ministers established

At Teheran, FDR called for a new international organization dominated by the "Four Policemen," who would deal immediately with threats to peace. The president said that the United States would only supply air and naval support in the event of a crisis in postwar Europe; troops would have to come from Britain and the USSR. The conferees also discussed the postwar status of Eastern Europe and Germany. Churchill had proposed moving Poland's boundaries a considerable distance to the west, incorporating German lands. Polish territory in the east would pass to the Soviets to secure their western frontier. Roosevelt acquiesced in these plans for Poland but said he could not "publicly take part in any such arrangement at the present time." The election of 1944 loomed, and "as a practical man," he would not risk the votes of millions of Polish-Americans. When he mentioned self-determination for the Baltic states, Stalin insisted that they belonged to the Soviet Union. To Roosevelt's remark that the American people "neither knew nor understood," Stalin shot back that "some propaganda work should be done."[115] But FDR never did explain publicly the differences between the Atlantic Charter and Soviet demands for security in Eastern Europe. On Germany, the conferees debated ways to divide the nation, but they left specific plans for "retribution" against Germany to the future.[116]

Although inconclusive on many points, the Teheran discussions pleased the Americans, particularly because Stalin had confirmed that once Hitler was defeated, the USSR would fight against Japan. Stalin's preference for OVERLORD instead of a Balkans operation also resolved the Anglo-American debate over strategy. A peace dictated by the big powers, an international organization, and a weakened postwar Germany signified important Allied cohesion. Stalin also paid tribute to Lend-Lease, "without which … our victory [over the Nazi invaders] would have been impossible."[117] After Teheran the president remarked: "We are going to get along very well with him [Stalin] and the Russian people—very well indeed."[118] The Big Three had temporarily closed some fissures.

China Tangles

Visiting Washington in December 1941, Winston Churchill was astonished that his hosts "rated the Chinese armies as a factor to be mentioned in the same breath as the armies of Russia."[119] America's infatuation with China, the legacy of the Open Door, the false image of China as "one of the great democracies of the world"—all reinforced an American determination that China should be a high wartime priority.[120] Also viewing China as a bridge to Asian peoples freeing themselves from colonialism, FDR wanted to keep that country "as a friend because in 40 or 50 years time China might easily become a powerful military nation."[121] China's military importance soon diminished, however, as Japanese victories in early 1942 sent the British and Americans reeling. The fall of Burma in May closed the last remaining land route to Chongqing. The Americans wanted to keep China in the war, yet Roosevelt could not send troops needed elsewhere. He sent General Stilwell instead.

Joseph W. Stilwell arrived in Chongqing with the impressive title of Commanding General of the United States Forces in India, Burma, and China. As a junior officer he had served two tours of duty in China, had become fluent in Chinese, and had developed great admiration for the Chinese people. But he thought Jiang an untrustworthy scoundrel. In his diary, the always blunt Stilwell called the British "pig fuckers" and Roosevelt "old Rubberlegs."[122] In Chongqing "Vinegar Joe" sought to train and equip Chinese divisions. With these modernized forces, plus British help from India, Stilwell planned to reopen Burma, increase supplies to China, and thus make the mainland the staging point for the final invasion of Japan.

Stilwell's plans for military reform cut at the heart of the Guomindang system. The general sputtered in his diary: "Why doesn't the little dummy [Jiang] realize that his only hope is the 30-division plan, and the creation of a separate, efficient, well-equipped, and well-trained force?"[123] Most of Jiang's armies were actually controlled by twelve commanders, several of them virtually autonomous warlords. Before making a decision, the generalissimo always had to ask: "What orders will my generals accept from me?"[124] Jiang actually preferred a U.S. Navy program that trained the Guomindang's secret police in counterguerilla tactics. Some 500,000 of Jiang's best troops were blockading the communists in Yan'an as he waited out the war and mustered his strength for a final showdown with Mao Zedong. Jiang refused to fight in Burma without more Allied support, and the British balked at a Burma campaign. Shortly after the Anglo-American landings in North Africa, Stilwell described his strategic dilemma: "Peanut [Jiang] and I are on a raft, with one sandwich between us, and the rescue ship is heading away from the scene."[125]

President Roosevelt sought conciliation. To Chongqing he sent personal emissaries to buoy Chinese morale. Jiang received a half-billion-dollar loan in 1942, and in 1943 the State Department negotiated a treaty abolishing the U.S. right of extraterritoriality in China. Next Roosevelt hosted Madame Jiang at the White House. Hollywood also feted China's First Lady, whose "hands, a woman's hands,

The Cairo Conference. Jiang Jieshi (1887–1975) and Madame Jiang (1897–2003) with Roosevelt and Churchill in November 1943. Although President Roosevelt publicly heaped praise on the Chinese leader, FDR privately told General Stilwell at the Cairo meeting: "If you can't get along with Chiang [Jiang], and can't replace him, get rid of him once and for all. You know what I mean, put someone in you can manage." (Franklin D. Roosevelt Library)

have helped to shape a nation's destiny," and whose "heart, a woman's heart, whispers a simple woman's hope and all the world must pause and heed."[126] At the Cairo Conference in November 1943, Churchill and Roosevelt met with Jiang and formally pledged the return, after the war, of Taiwan, Manchuria, and other areas "stolen by Japan."[127] In December Congress repealed the exclusion laws, which had prohibited Chinese immigration. FDR spoke confidently of postwar China as one of his "Four Policemen" that would keep the peace.

FDR also endorsed a plan of General Claire Lee Chennault, the famed "Flying Tiger" who claimed that with "a very modest American air force equipped with modern airplanes" he could destroy Japanese air power in "six months."[128] When Chennault's bombers began to draw blood in the spring of 1944, Japanese armies launched a massive counterattack and nearly overran all U.S. air bases. Jiang then refused to fight. This time Roosevelt made the extraordinary proposal that Jiang give Stilwell unrestricted command of all forces, Chinese and foreign, in China. Roosevelt sent an ultimatum that Stilwell delivered in person. "I handed this bundle of paprika to the Peanut and then sank back with a sigh," Stilwell wrote in September. "The harpoon hit the little bugger right in the solar plexus, and went right through him."[129] Rather than antagonize the unyielding Jiang further after such humiliation, FDR replaced Stilwell.

In November 1944, General Patrick J. Hurley became ambassador to China and concentrated on forming a coalition between Jiang's nationalists and the communists. Even though the Soviets, like the Americans, sent military supplies to Jiang's forces and not to Mao Zedong's communists, the communist-led troops had waged successful guerrilla war against the Japanese. The Yan'an communists had an effective intelligence network that extended behind Japanese lines. Members of the U.S. "Observer Mission" to Yan'an found it easier to talk with Mao and Zhou Enlai "than with the Nationalists. You knew the Nationalists were lying most of the time. The communists never lied."[130] The communist revolutionary leadership, according to Foreign Service Officer John S. Service, "has improved the political, economic and social status of the peasant [and] ... the Communists are certain to play a large, if not dominant, part in China's future."[131] Because most Americans in China shared the belief that the communists might defeat Jiang in a postwar struggle for power, Hurley's initial efforts at coalition building received widespread support.

On Hurley's first visit to communist Yan'an, in November 1944, the "genbassador" alighted from his plane "with enough ribbons on his chest to represent every war ... in which the United States had ever engaged except possibly Shays's Rebellion."[132] Then the Oklahoma Republican completely discombobulated the worldly wise Zhou Enlai by letting out Choctaw war whoops. Later, after the communists rejected Jiang's offer of a virtually worthless seat on the National Military Council in return for merging the Yan'an army under Guomindong control, Hurley first accepted and then rejected Mao's counterproposal for full coalition and communist sharing in Lend-Lease supplies. Mao concluded that U.S. policy had changed from "uniting with the CCP [Communists] and pressuring Jiang" to "supporting Jiang, dragging the CCP along [in order to] beat the Japanese."[133]

Hurley began to diverge markedly from the Foreign Service Officers. The ambassador decided on his own that his objective was not to mediate but rather to

Mao Zedong (1893–1976) and Patrick J. Hurley (1883–1963). The Chinese communist leader (second from left) seems less than moved by Ambassador Hurley's dramatic gesture of welcome at Chongqing in 1945. Mao thought Hurley a "clown" who favored Jiang. Hurley once bellowed that Mao was a "motherfucker." The U.S. embassy staff considered the ambassador a "Colonel Blimp" and accused him of "crass stupidity," of being a "stuffed shirt playing at being a great man." The Office of Strategic Services (OSS) in China gave Hurley the code name "Albatross." In November 1945, Hurley suddenly resigned and flung charges of treason at Foreign Service Officers who had disagreed with him. (National Archives)

"sustain" Jiang Jieshi and "to prevent the collapse of the Nationalist government."[134] During an earlier visit to Moscow in August 1944, Molotov had told Hurley that the Chinese communists "had no relation whatever to Communism" and the Soviets would support Jiang Jieshi.[135] Other U.S. officials in China feared that if denied aid, Mao would obtain assistance from Moscow and cause a postwar squabble between the United States and the USSR over China. Contrary to Hurley, these "China hands" believed that the rift between the communists and Guomindang ran deep, and that they could obtain Chinese unity only by dealing with Yan'an separately as a way of pressing Jiang. Preliminary talks had already begun in Yan'an, and in January 1945, the head of the American Military Observers Mission cabled that "Mao and Zhou will be immediately available … should President Roosevelt express desire to receive them at White House as leaders of a primary Chinese party."[136] By "clearly offering himself," Mao hoped that if American forces landed in China, Roosevelt would abandon the "militarily impotent Nationalists" and choose "military cooperation" with the communists.[137]

The predictable explosion occurred when Hurley returned to Washington in February 1945 after the Yalta Conference. In Hurley's absence, the embassy officers at Chongqing cabled the president urging him to inform Jiang "in definite terms that we are required by military necessity to cooperate with and supply the communists against Japan."[138] These young "China hands" did not know that Stalin had reaffirmed future Soviet entry into the Japanese war at Yalta and, accordingly, that the military rationale for a Guomindang-communist coalition now became less urgent. When Hurley read the telegram, he charged that his subordinates had betrayed him. The dying president gave him what he wanted—unqualified backing for Jiang's regime. The embassy diplomats soon found themselves transferred out of China as a timid State Department bowed to the demands of the rambunctious ambassador. Mao's communists grew more suspicious of the United States.

Roosevelt's wartime policy toward China exposed the disparity between his military strategy and postwar political goals. When it became obvious in 1944 that China would not play a major role in the Japanese war and hardly deserved rank as one of the "Four Policemen," he faced a choice. He could accelerate American military activities in China, giving the United States more leverage, and press Jiang to undertake the reforms necessary to maintain him in power. Or he could scale down his political expectations for China and limit military operations there. In fact, Roosevelt "tried to do both and ran the risk of succeeding in neither," and he kept disingenuously portraying China as a great power even as he gave higher and higher priorities to "other military theaters."[139] When the feud between Hurley and the "China hands" ignited, moreover, Roosevelt drifted with existing policy rather than take a hard look at Chinese politics.

Bystanders to the Holocaust

Another problem finessed for the future was that of European refugees, hundreds of thousands of them Jews from Nazi-occupied territories. Many sought asylum in the United States. Although most Americans denounced Hitler's crusade to preserve the purity of the "Aryan race" through the persecution and extermination of European Jews, translating moral revulsion into effective policy proved difficult. U.S. immigration laws, traditional anti-Semitism, the Depression, bureaucratic procedures, wartime fear of spies, and domestic politics shaped the tentative American response.

In April 1933, Hitler boasted to an American visitor that he would do what "the rest of the world would like to do. It doesn't know how to get rid of the Jews. I will show them."[140] Thereafter the Nazis systematically eliminated Jews from the professions and denied them ownership of businesses. In 1935 the Nuremberg Laws stripped Jews of their civil and political rights. Hate mongers plastered signs on buildings: "Whoever buys from a Jew is a traitor."[141] In November 1938, a distraught Jewish youth living in Paris entered the German embassy and killed a German official. Nazi thugs beat up Jews on the streets, sacked and burned synagogues, and destroyed Jewish shops. After this *Kristallnacht* (or "night of the broken glass") the German government fined its Jewish subjects $400 million and sent 50,000 Jews to concentration camps at Dachau and Buchenwald, detention centers where tortures and executions became common. Roosevelt called the U.S. ambassador home in protest, exclaiming, "I myself could scarcely believe that such things could occur in a twentieth century civilization."[142]

Such brutal events occurred again in Austria, Czechoslovakia, Poland, Hungary, and elsewhere as the Third Reich overran Europe. Urgent requests for transit of refugees to the United States flooded U.S. embassies and consulates. American immigration law, however, prescribed a quota for each country. The National Origins Act of 1924 openly discriminated against immigrants from eastern and southern Europe. The annual quota for Great Britain and Ireland was 83,575, for Germany and Austria 27,370, for Poland 6,000, for Italy 5,500, and for Romania 300. American consular officers also rigidly denied entry to people "likely to become a public charge," which meant that persons could gain a place on the quota list only if they proved that they could support themselves once in the United States. Yet under Nazi law Jews could not take their property or savings from Germany. These restrictions, combined with the evaporation of American jobs during the depression, created a revealing statistic for the period 1933–1938: 174,067 people entered the United States and 221,239 departed, or a net *loss* of 47,172. To have opened America's doors to refugees, in short, would not have inundated a nation of 130 million.

The American Federation of Labor lobbied against any revision in the quotas or visa requirements. Foreigners should not compete with U.S. citizens for scarce jobs—a telling argument during the depression. Longstanding anti-Semitism fed such nativist thought. Father Charles E. Coughlin, a fiery Catholic priest from Michigan, equated Judaism and communism in his radio broadcasts, which reached 3.5 million listeners a week. Opinion polls revealed that more than 80 percent of Americans opposed revision of the quotas to admit European refugees. Congress stood firmly behind the quota system. Already blistered by charges that his domestic reform program was a "Jew Deal," a label attached because he appointed such Jews as Henry Morgenthau, Jr., and Felix Frankfurter to prominent positions, the president played it safe.

Roosevelt mostly left the refugee problem to the Department of State, which "clung to a policy that was timid, rigidly legal, and without innovation."[143] In 1934 the department lobbied successfully against a Senate resolution condemning Germany's treatment of the Jews, fearful that the resolution would spark German comment about the segregation of black Americans. Despite his own wife's Jewish heritage, Secretary Hull opposed boycotts organized by American Jews against German products because such behavior interrupted normal trade. FDR "quietly manipulate[d] at the margins" with executive orders that combined German and Austrian quotas in 1938–1939 and temporarily relaxed enforcement of the "likely to become a public charge" clause, but many Jews still could not obtain documents.[144] The result: the German-Austrian quota went unfilled in 1933–1938 and 1940–1945.

In 1938 Roosevelt did call for an international conference on refugees, which met in Evian, France, to establish an Intergovernmental Committee on Refugees (IGC). Plans for refugee havens in Latin America and central Africa faltered. Hitler sneered that "the entire democratic world dissolves in tears of pity, but then, in spite of its obvious duty to help, closes its heart to the poor, tortured people."[145] In early 1939, Senator Robert Wagner of New York introduced a bill to allow 20,000 German refugee children to enter above the quota. With revision of the Neutrality Act then pending, the president scratched "File No action FDR," and the bill died in committee.[146]

In mid-1939 the ship *St. Louis* steamed toward Cuba from Hamburg carrying 930 Jewish refugees. Havana officials, however, would not permit them to land without proper visas. The ship then headed for Miami, tailed by U.S. Coast Guard cutters. American immigration officials would not let the passengers disembark, so the *St. Louis* had to return to Europe. Its passengers ultimately scattered to Britain, the Netherlands, Belgium, and France after refugee societies pressed their governments. One-third of these passengers later died in the Holocaust.

The plight of Jewish refugees deepened after the outbreak of war. State Department visa regulations actually tightened. Refugee questions came under the jurisdiction of Breckinridge Long, a State Department official and political supporter

Buchenwald Concentration Camp, Germany. This large Nazi concentration camp held Jews and others who served as slave labor for local factories during World War II. Although Buchenwald did not have death-dealing gas chambers, many prisoners died there from disease, malnutrition, beatings, medical experiments, and executions. When Generals Omar Bradley and Dwight Eisenhower viewed the "naked, emaciated bodies ... flung into shallow graves," the scene "both stunned and numbed us." Eisenhower, himself of German descent, wrote to his wife: "The German is a beast. ... God, I hate the Germans." (Library of Congress)

of FDR, who feared a potential fifth column of refugees in the United States. He and other officials blocked private efforts to admit them and later erected a "wall of silence" about Hitler's genocidal policies.[147] U.S. consuls increasingly rejected visa applications, and ships returned to America half empty. When asked to approach Portugal about opening its African colony of Angola to Jewish refugees, British ambassador Lord Halifax snapped: "Let the Americans do it."[148] Resettlement proposals for British Guiana, French Madagascar, and the Philippines also fell through; Britain restricted the movement of Jews to Palestine. Some 75,000 to 90,000 Jewish refugees did find havens in Latin American countries.

Reliable reports reached Washington in August 1942 that Germany had begun to exterminate the entire Jewish population in Europe. What followed revealed a large "gap between information and knowledge, even after the information had been received," as one historian puts it.[149] When Jan Karski, a Pole who had witnessed mass executions at Belzec and Treblinka, briefed FDR and Hull, they could not grasp the enormity of the Holocaust. Even Justice Felix Frankfurter, a Zionist, confessed that "he didn't believe what he was being told."[150] Yet the evidence mounted. The Jewish ghetto in Warsaw, with only 70,000 of its 380,000 residents still alive, desperately rebelled in the spring of 1943. Using Zyklon B gas and large crematoria, German officials murdered a million victims in the most notorious extermination camp at Auschwitz, Poland. Scholars have debated the feasibility of bombing Auschwitz and surrounding rail lines. The U.S. Army Air Forces probably could have destroyed these installations by August 1944, but FDR reportedly vetoed the proposal because it "wouldn't have done any good" and "we would have been accused of destroying Auschwitz [by] bombing these innocent people."[151] The War Department also rejected any "diversion" that would delay victory, seen as the best hope for the Jews.[152] Indeed, Allied victories in Egypt and North Africa in 1942 prevented Hitler from carrying out his promised destruction ("*Vernichtung*") of all the Jews in Palestine and other parts of the Middle East.[153] In early 1943, British and U.S. representatives met in Bermuda and concluded that they had done all they could to rescue refugees. As Hull informed FDR: "The unknown cost of moving an undetermined number of persons from an undisclosed place to an unknown destination … is … out of the question."[154] By 1944 perhaps only the assassination of Hitler might have saved hundreds of thousands of Jews—if not more—but the Allies never tried, and attempts by German dissidents failed. By war's end at least 6 million Jews in Nazi-occupied Europe had been murdered.

Secretary of the Treasury Henry Morgenthau, Jr., did what he could. At his request, Treasury general counsel Randolph Paul submitted the *Report to the Secretary on the Acquiescence of This Government in the Murder of the Jews,* a frank critique of the State Department. "It takes months and months to grant the visa and then it usually applies to a corpse," Paul wrote. The rescue of Jews should not "remain in the hands of men indifferent, callous and perhaps hostile," warned Morgenthau, who persuaded FDR to create the War Refugee Board, outside the auspices of the State Department.[155] Using private and public funds, board operatives established refugee camps in Italy, Morocco, Hungary, Sweden, Palestine, and Switzerland. The board thus saved some 200,000 Jews and 20,000 non-Jews by war's end. "What we did was little enough. … Late and little," its director concluded.[156] Jewish refugees themselves took command of their survival after the war by leading the "exodus" to Palestine and creating the new nation of Israel in 1948.[157] Nearly a half century later the film director Steven Spielberg in *Schindler's List* (1993) depicted what a few heroic individuals might have done to save thousands more.

Henry Morgenthau, Jr. (1891–1967). A long-time friend of Franklin D. Roosevelt, Morgenthau served as FDR's secretary of the treasury (1933–1945) but often participated in the making of foreign policy. A deft bureaucratic infighter, Morgenthau pressed during World War II for an active U.S. stance against the genocide in Europe and for harsh peace terms against the Nazis after the war. Although successful in creating the War Refugee Board, he failed to impose the Morgenthau Plan on defeated Germany. (Franklin D. Roosevelt Library)

Planning the Postwar Peace, 1943–1945

The great European military battles of 1944, wherein the Anglo-American D-Day invasion of France in June coincided with a massive Soviet offensive that reached the Vistula River by August, gave postwar planning higher priority. Taking advantage of a "second chance" to overcome isolationism, economic depression, and war, U.S. officials helped launch several international organizations to secure peace and prosperity. Indeed, when FDR saw the Hollywood film *Wilson* (1944), with vivid scenes of his predecessor losing his health and the League, he exclaimed, "By God, that's not going to happen to me."[158] He thus made the Atlantic Charter a more flexible guide than the Fourteen Points. During 1943–1945 the United Nations Relief and Rehabilitation Administration (UNRRA), World Bank, International Monetary Fund, and United Nations Organization took form. Unlike World War I, this time the establishment of postwar institutions would not await the grand deliberations of one conference.

On November 9, 1943, at the White House, forty-four nations signed the UNRRA agreement for the "relief of victims of war … through the provision of food, fuel, clothing, shelter and other basic necessities, medical and other essential services."[159] Some leaders, fearing that hungry, displaced people might, in desperation, turn to political extremes like communism, hoped that food and medicine would help stem postwar political chaos. Operating in Europe until mid-1947, UNRRA had a budget of $4 billion, $2.7 billion of which the United States donated. UNRRA dispensed 9 million tons of food; built hundreds of hospitals; prevented epidemics of diphtheria, typhoid, cholera, and venereal disease; revived transportation systems; and cared for at least a million displaced persons. China, Italy, Greece, and Austria absorbed about half of UNRRA's assistance. The other half went to Poland, other Eastern European nations, and the Soviet Union. American critics protested that an international organization was spending taxpayers' dollars to shore up communist governments. In fact, UNRRA tried to avoid politics, refusing to apply political tests to the needy. But Americans expected food aid to bring political returns. When it did not, Washington killed UNRRA by cutting off funds.

Two other organizations proved more permanent. From July 1 to 22, 1944, the delegates of forty-four nations negotiated at Bretton Woods in New Hampshire. Working from an Anglo-American proposal, the conferees created the International Bank for Reconstruction and Development (World Bank) and the International Monetary Fund (IMF). The World Bank could extend loans to "assist in the reconstruction and development" of members, to "promote private investment," and to "promote the long-range balanced growth of international trade."[160] The IMF was intended to facilitate world trade by stabilizing the international system of payments through currency loans. After much debate, Congress passed the Bretton Woods Agreement Act by wide margins in July 1945.

From the start, U.S. economic power dominated the two organizations. Located in Washington, D.C., the World Bank has always had an American as president. The United States also possessed one-third of the votes in the bank by committing $3.175 billion of the total of $9.100 billion initial subscriptions. The United States also held one-third of the votes in the fund. As payer of the "piper," the United States would "call the tune."[161] Britain begrudged U.S. control but joined. The USSR did not join the bank or fund because the Soviets practiced state-controlled trade and finance, feared having to divulge economic data, and could not accept the emphasis on "private" enterprise or U.S. domination. Moscow's absence augured poorly for postwar Allied cooperation.

From August to October 1944, representatives of the United States, Britain, the Soviet Union, and China met in the Dumbarton Oaks mansion in Washington, D.C., to shape the United Nations Organization (UN). Public opinion polls indicated that Americans strongly endorsed a new collective-security organization, and Congress had passed favorable enabling resolutions. The conferees hammered out the UN's charter, providing for a powerful Security Council dominated by the great powers and a weak General Assembly. The Security Council, empowered to use force to settle crises, had five permanent members (United States, USSR, China, France, and Britain). When Washington pushed China as a permanent

United Nations Symbol.
A sign of peace for the new international organization.
(United Nations)

member, Churchill proposed France, calling China a "faggot vote on the side of the United States."[162]

Two other issues also proved contentious: voting procedures in the Security Council and membership in the General Assembly. The Soviet Union advocated an absolute veto for permanent members of the Council, whereas the United States argued that parties to a conflict should not veto discussion or action. Not until the Yalta Conference in early 1945 did the Allies agree that the veto would apply only to substantive questions such as economic or military sanctions, not to procedural questions. As for membership in the Assembly, Moscow brazenly requested seats for all sixteen Soviet republics. That outlandish request derived from Soviet fears of being badly outnumbered in the Assembly by the British Commonwealth "bloc" and the U.S.–Latin America "bloc." At Yalta the Soviets accepted a compromise of three votes in the Assembly (see page 210).

Seeking bipartisan support, Secretary Hull successfully appealed to GOP presidential candidate Thomas E. Dewey to keep the issue of international organization out of the political campaign. The resulting nonpartisanship and the inclusion of senators in the Dumbarton Oaks delegation helped the Roosevelt administration build its case for the UN. On January 10, 1945, the influential Senator Arthur H. Vandenberg of Michigan, an arch prewar Republican isolationist, delivered a stunning speech urging U.S. participation in collective security as a curb on aggression. He further advised the major Allies to sign a security treaty to keep the Axis nations permanently demilitarized; he hoped thereby to allay Soviet fears of a revived Germany and hence render Soviet expansion unnecessary. Vandenberg could accept membership in the United Nations because "this is anything but a wild-eyed internationalist dream of a world State."[163]

Vandenberg served as a delegate to the San Francisco Conference of April 25–June 26, 1945, convened to launch the United Nations. The new secretary of state, Edward R. Stettinius, Jr., managed the conference. The 282 delegates did not make decisions without prior approval of the representatives of the big powers, who met each evening in Stettinius's penthouse at the Fairmont Hotel. The United States refused to admit Poland, because its government had not reorganized as required by Yalta. But then Stettinius shocked all by requesting participation for Argentina, which had only declared war against Germany in March. The United States, believing that the Latin American republics would not vote for three Soviet seats in the Assembly unless Argentina were included, would not relent. By the lopsided vote of 32 to 4, with 10 abstentions, Argentina won its seat. Notwithstanding Soviet protests, Stettinius boasted privately that "we gave [them] a good public licking."[164]

Journalists detected an American "steamroller" at San Francisco.[165] So did the Soviet Union, which objected in blunt language. And so did smaller states, which protested their exclusion from key decisions and their impotence in the new United Nations Organization. Fifteen nations abstained in the vote on the veto formula. The UN Charter, as finally adopted, included the Economic and Social Council and the Trusteeship Council. The latter looked to the eventual independence of colonial areas but left the British and French empires intact and permitted the United States to absorb former Japanese-dominated islands in the Pacific (Marianas, Carolines, and Marshalls). The Charter included Article 51, which permitted regional alliances such

"Uncle Sam Pulls the Lever at the UN." Many foreign commentators believed that the United States dominated the new United Nations Organization. (*Ta Kung Pao* of Shanghai–Hong Kong in *United Nations World,* 1951)

as the one United States and Latin America had outlined in the Act of Chapultepec in March. The United States would "have our cake and eat it too"—freedom of action in the Western Hemisphere and an international organization to curb aggression in Europe.[166] Amid memories of 1919, the Senate approved the UN Charter on July 28, 1945, by a vote of 89 to 2.

While these plans for the victors unfolded, the debate over how to "uproot Nazism" in a defeated Germany centered on a "constructive" policy (rehabilitation, economic unity, and integration into the European economy) or a "corrective" policy (strict reduction of industry, large reparations, and a decentralized economy).[167] At the center of the controversy stood Treasury Secretary Morgenthau, who proposed a "corrective" plan designed to despoil Germany of industries having potential military value. In early September 1944 he had advised Roosevelt that the coal- and iron-rich Ruhr area should be stripped of industry. At the Quebec Conference in September 1944, the president gained Churchill's reluctant signature to a memorandum "eliminating the war-making industries in the Ruhr and in the Saar" and "converting Germany into a country primarily agricultural and pastoral in its character."[168] Churchill apparently had approved the Morgenthau scheme in exchange for the promise of a postwar American loan.

Leaked to the press, the Morgenthau Plan caused "a hell of a hubbub" because Secretaries Hull and Stimson both opposed a harsh economic peace.[169] Believing that "poverty in one part of the world induces poverty in other parts," Hull and Stimson contended Germany had to revive to spur postwar prosperity in Western Europe.[170] Morgenthau nonetheless persuaded Roosevelt to approve an interim Joint Chiefs of Staff directive (JCS/1067), which ordered denazification and demilitarization, the dismantling of iron, steel, and chemical industries, a controlled economy, and limited rehabilitation. The new president, Harry S. Truman, however, thought "Morgenthau didn't know sh—from apple butter" and began a gradual retreat from the Morgenthau Plan and from JCS/1067, especially after he eased Morgenthau out of office in July 1945.[171] By the end of the war, then, U.S. plans for postwar Germany remained unsettled.

Compromises at Yalta

Near the end of the European war Churchill, Roosevelt, and Stalin met once again from February 4 to 11, 1945, at the Livadia Palace near Yalta in the Soviet Crimea—"the Riviera of Hades," in Churchill's words.[172] The Big Three entered the conference with different goals. Britain sought a zone in Germany for France, a curb on Soviet expansion into Poland, and protection of the British Empire. The Soviet Union wanted reparations to rebuild its devastated economy, possessions in Asia, influence over Poland, and a Germany so weakened that it could never again march eastward. The United States wanted a U.S.-managed United Nations, a Soviet declaration of war against Japan, a reduction of communist political power in Poland, and elevation of China to big-power status. Despite mutual suspicions, Yalta did produce agreements.

The Big Three, after considerable compromise, made important decisions for the war against the Axis and for the postwar configuration of international affairs, the Yalta "system." After the conclave, Yalta aroused heated controversy akin to the Munich Conference. To some critics, Yalta symbolized a "sellout" to the Soviets, an example of Roosevelt's coddling of the communist dictator. Worn low by the illness that would take his life two months later, critics have claimed, Roosevelt gave in to a guileful Stalin and failed to use superior U.S. economic power to force concessions.

The Yalta Conference. In this meeting with Churchill, a haggard Roosevelt betrayed symptoms of the cardiovascular disease that would kill him in April 1945. Robert H. Ferrell's *The Dying President* (1998), utilizing the records and diaries of FDR's heart doctor, concludes that the president was "arguably as incapacitated as President Wilson had been, a shell of his former self, unable to keep abreast of the great decisions he had left to the end of the war, too ill or too arrogant to inform his successor about them." (Franklin D. Roosevelt Library)

The president's detractors also pointed an accusing finger at Alger Hiss, a U.S. official at Yalta who later went to jail on a perjury charge for testifying that he had not served Moscow as a spy.

The "consensus" at Yalta reflected the military and diplomatic realities of the moment. Just prior to Yalta, Anglo-American troops had bogged down in the Battle of the Bulge in Belgium. Asked to take pressure off the western front by stepping up the Soviet winter offensive in the east, Stalin obliged on January 12. "I am most grateful to you for your thrilling message," a relieved Churchill replied.[173] Indeed, Russian soldiers were sweeping westward along a wide front through Poland, Czechoslovakia, and Hungary, with Romania already freed from German clutches. The Red Army, not Roosevelt, gave the Soviet Union influence in Eastern Europe.

Asian military realities also shaped diplomatic decisions. Japan was fiercely battling American forces in Luzon and the Marianas, and still had 1 million soldiers in China, 2 million in the home islands, and another 1 million in Manchuria and Korea. The atomic bomb was still an unproven secret known only to Roosevelt's and Churchill's closest advisers. With some 54 percent of American battle deaths in the Pacific occurring in the last year of the war, both sides fought with increasing savagery. Japanese authorities depicted Americans as "albino apes" and "carnivorous beasts," and U.S. film audiences cheered when Popeye the Sailor punched out the "Jap-pansy" navy in *You're a Sap, Mr. Jap* (1942).[174] U.S. Admiral William E. ("Bull") Halsey called the Japanese "little yellow monkeys" and said that "the only good Jap is a Jap who's been dead for six months."[175] Japan's suicidal *Kamikaze* resistance on Okinawa still lay in the future. In short, Roosevelt and Churchill still needed Soviet help to defeat Japan.

The Yalta meetings proceeded amicably, although Stalin once became ruffled when he took Roosevelt's name for him—"Uncle Joe"—as ridicule rather than as a term of endearment, and Molotov wore his customary stone face. At the final dinner, Churchill informed Stalin that with general elections scheduled soon, "I shall have to speak very harshly about the Communists. ... You know we have two parties in England." "One party is much better," Stalin deadpanned.[176]

For Churchill, Poland counted as "the most urgent reason for the Yalta Conference."[177] The British and Americans recognized the conservative exiled government in London, led by Stanislas Mikolajczyk. Moscow recognized the communist-led provisional government in Lublin. Repeatedly reminding everyone that Germany had attacked the Soviet Union through the Polish corridor twice in the century, Stalin insisted not only on Allied support for the Lublin government but also "a mighty, free and independent Poland" that included part of Germany (with the Oder-Neisse line in the west) but gave Russia Polish territory in the east (the Curzon line).[178] Churchill and Roosevelt opposed a communist Poland but had little bargaining power because Soviet troops occupied much of the country. Roosevelt said he had several million Polish voters back home who demanded a more representative Polish government. Stalin remained adamant.

Compromises emerged. The Curzon line was temporarily set as the eastern boundary. The Yalta agreement stipulated also that the provisional government should be "reorganized on a broader democratic basis with the inclusion of democratic leaders from Poland itself and from Poles abroad," with "free and unfettered

"The Two Thousand Yard Stare."   Combat artist Tom Lea captures the zombie-like demeanor of a young marine who has endured too much. Lea painted this portrait during the battle for Peleliu in the Palau Islands (September–November 1944), in which 2,000 Americans were killed and more than 8,500 were wounded. Some 11,000 Japanese also died. The journalist Ernie Pyle also described the same "look of dullness, eyes that look without seeing, eyes that see without conveying any image to the mind. It's a look that is the display room for what lies behind it—exhaustion, lack of sleep, tension for too long, weariness that is too great, fear beyond fear, misery to the point of numbness, a look of surpassing indifference to anything anybody can do." (U.S. Army, Center of Military History)

elections" held as soon as possible.[179] Until such an election the communist Lublin group would comprise the nucleus of the Polish government. When later asked about the Polish agreement, FDR said "it was the best I could do."[180] Churchill swallowed the bitter pill, in part because Stalin assured him that the Soviet Union would not intrude in British-dominated Greece, then rocked by civil war. Compromises on other issues also made the Polish settlement tolerable.

Britain reluctantly accepted Germany's dismemberment so long as France received a zone of occupation. Noting that Roosevelt had said that American troops would not long remain in Europe, Churchill cited France as a bulwark against Germany. Stalin grudgingly accepted a French zone. On reparations from Germany, which the Soviets vigorously demanded, Britain and America agreed that they should be "in kind" and approved the creation of a Reparations Commission, but they refused to set a figure until they determined Germany's ability to pay.

The conferees reached compromises on Asia and the Pacific. By February 1945, the Japanese were retreating northward as General MacArthur's amphibious forces pressed them from the southwest Pacific and Admiral Chester Nimitz's carrier-backed amphibians pushed them northward from the Marianas in the central Pacific. The home islands came under sustained attack by U.S. heavy bombers, but the Americans still feared very high casualties in the planned invasion of Japan. Soviet intervention and a Red Army thrust across Manchuria would draw off defenders and materially reduce American casualties during the landings in Kyushu and Honshu. A grateful FDR won Stalin's promise to declare war against Japan two or three months after Hitler's defeat, enough time to transfer his troops to Asia. Stalin also agreed to sign a pact of friendship and alliance with Jiang Jieshi's regime, not with Mao Zedong's rival communists. In return, the Soviet Union regained what Russia had lost in 1905: the southern part of Sakhalin, Dairen (Dalian) as a free port, Port Arthur as a naval base, and joint operation of Manchurian railroads. The Soviet Union also obtained the Kurile Islands. On these issues the Big Three never consulted China, a clear loser at Yalta.

The Allies reached agreement on the United Nations Organization. Dumbarton Oaks had added France and China as "permanent" members of the Security Council, each possessing the veto. Although Churchill thought China would vote with the United States, FDR and Stalin expected France to support British positions. Thus outnumbered in the council, Stalin asked at Yalta for membership of all sixteen Soviet republics in the General Assembly. He also insisted on an absolute veto in the council on all issues, procedural and substantive. Roosevelt agreed to three Soviet seats in the General Assembly, and Stalin shelved the veto for procedural questions. The conference also reaffirmed national self-determination in the "Declaration of Liberated Europe," which Stalin signed because "we will implement it in our own way later. The essence is in the correlation of forces."[181]

Yalta marked the "dawn of the new day," said Harry Hopkins. "We were absolutely certain that we had won the first great victory of the peace."[182] "Poor Neville Chamberlain believed he could trust Hitler," Churchill commented after Yalta. "He was wrong. But I don't think I'm wrong about Stalin."[183] Roosevelt, Churchill, and Stalin had deftly played the great-power game of building spheres of influence. Each went home with some major objectives satisfied. Although they had postponed some tough questions and written some vague language, they had squarely faced military and political realities.

Later, when the Yalta agreements collapsed, critics ignored U.S. gains from the conference—broadening of the Polish government, a UN voting formula, delay of the reparations question, the significant Soviet pledge to enter the Pacific war—and charged that FDR had conceded too much in "saying 'nice kitty' to Stalin."[184] The United States might have used reconstruction aid as a diplomatic weapon, but such tactics would have spoiled the spirit of compromise at Yalta, which served American interests. Churchill recognized the necessity of conciliation: "What would have happened if we had quarreled with Russia while the Germans still had three or four hundred divisions on the fighting front?"[185] The spheres-of-influence agreement, the Yalta leaders believed, would serve as a transition to peace.

To Each Its Own: Allied Divergence and Spheres of Influence

Throughout World War II, the Allies attempted to protect and, if possible, extend their spheres of influence. Churchill's defense of the British Empire, from the initial conference at Argentia through Yalta, reflected this characteristic of wartime diplomacy. "If the Americans want to take Japanese islands," he remarked, "let them do so with our blessing. … But 'Hands Off the British Empire' is our maxim."[186] Some

Americans suspected that Churchill's constant postponement of the second front and his strategies for North Africa and Italy aimed at preserving British interests. His advice to U.S. military leaders, near war's end, that they drive quickly to Berlin, and if possible even farther into Eastern Europe, to beat the Soviets there, also aroused suspicion.

The Churchill-Stalin percentage agreement of October 1944 was emblematic. In early 1944, Churchill concluded that "we are approaching a showdown with the Russians" in the Balkans, and he called for a frank settlement. Roosevelt agreed to a trial division of authority. Instability plagued Romania, where Soviet troops dominated; Yugoslavia, where independent communist Josip Tito and his Partisans were emerging; Bulgaria, where an indigenous communist movement grew with Soviet influence; and Greece, a British-dominated area plagued by civil war. At an October conference with Stalin in Moscow, Churchill scribbled some percentages on a piece of paper. In Romania, Russia would get 90 percent of the power and Britain 10 percent; in Greece, Britain would enjoy 90 percent and Russia 10 percent; in Yugoslavia and Hungary, a 50–50 split; and in Bulgaria, 75 percent would go to Russia and 25 percent to "others." Churchill "pushed this across to Stalin," who "took his blue pencil and made a large tick upon it."[187] Upon learning of the agreement, Roosevelt did not protest.

Soviet support for the Lublin government, demands for Polish and Romanian territory, efforts to exclude the United States and Britain from the joint control commissions in Eastern Europe, and seizure of German-operated property underscored the growing power of the Soviet Union among its neighbors. Soviet handling of the Warsaw uprising of July 1944, alarmed Western observers. With Soviet armies some twelve miles from Warsaw, the Polish underground gambled and attacked German forces, hoping that Soviet troops would dash to their aid. But the Red Army stopped. Over the next two months the Germans leveled half the city and killed 166,000 Poles, most of whom owed allegiance to the exiled government in London. Stalin dropped supplies to the besieged city in September but refused at first to let Allied planes land at Soviet airfields after carrying supplies to Warsaw.[188] He called the uprising a "foolish adventure" by "power-seeking criminals."[189] Stalin's callous contempt for the Warsaw Poles prompted Ambassador W. Averell Harriman to view the Soviets as a "world bully" who "misinterpreted our generous attitude toward them."[190] The liberation of Poland by Soviet forces in 1944 ultimately fixed a communist regime in Warsaw—one that Roosevelt's compromises at Yalta essentially recognized.

The United States itself was expanding and building spheres of influence during the war. Having drawn most of the Latin American states into a defensive community at the Lima Conference (1938) and in the Declaration of Panama (1939), the United States moved to drive German investments and influence from the Western Hemisphere. The Export-Import Bank loaned $130 million to twelve Latin American nations in 1939–1941 to help them expel German businesses, cut trade with the Axis, stabilize their economies, and bring them into alignment with U.S. foreign policy. During the war, the United States increased its stake in Bolivian tin, helped build Brazilian warships, expanded holdings in Venezuelan oil, acquired bases in Panama and Guatemala, and nourished the Dominican dictatorship of Rafael

The Allies Push Japan Back, 1942–1945

Japanese-held areas

Limit of Japanese conquest

Norman Adams

Pacific Fleet Carriers. After Japan's attack on Pearl Harbor ended the U.S. Navy's addiction to the irresistible masculine sensuality of battleships, the air superiority provided by aircraft carriers proved to be a major reason for U.S. victories in the Pacific and for a substantial American role in postwar Asia. The light aircraft carrier *Langley* and the heavy carrier *Ticonderoga* led this Pacific fleet task group. From 1940 to June 1945, the U.S. Navy grew from 1,099 to 50,759 vessels, including 8 new battleships, 92 new aircraft carriers, and 43,255 new landing craft. (Navy Department, National Archives)

Trujillo. Despite warnings that "lethal toys" might be used "for a very different purpose than they were intended," the U.S. military dispensed arms and training to Latin American forces.[191] During the war Latin America shipped 50 percent of its exports, largely much needed raw materials, to the United States. At the Rio de Janeiro Conference (January 15–28, 1942), all but Chile and Argentina voted to break diplomatic relations with the Axis nations. Yet despite the pro-Nazi sympathies of dictator Juan Perón, ample food exports and massive pro-Allied demonstrations in Buenos Aires qualified even Argentina as "a closet Ally."[192] In March 1945, in the Act of Chapultepec, the United States and Latin America took another step toward a regional defense alliance.

U.S. leaders also sought to direct events in postwar Italy and Asia. They essentially excluded the Soviets from the Italian surrender agreement in 1943 and denied them a role in the control commission, thereby setting a precedent for later Soviet predominance in Romania and Hungary. U.S. officials also insisted on holding the conquered Japanese islands in the Pacific and in unilaterally governing postwar Japan. With U.S. forces spearheading the counteroffensive in the southwest Pacific, Australian Prime Minister John Curtin acknowledged allegiance "to America, free of any pangs to our traditional links with the United Kingdom."[193] Thus did Washington envisage closer postwar ties with India, Australia, New Zealand, and Jiang's China.

In the Middle East the United States also expanded. In 1939 the Arabian-American Oil Company (Aramco) began to tap its 440,000-square-mile concession in Saudi Arabia's rich oil fields. By 1944 U.S. corporations controlled 42 percent of the proved oil reserves of the Middle East, a nineteen-fold increase since 1936. In 1944 American companies, with Washington's encouragement, applied for an oil

Harry Hopkins (1890–1946).
A progressive reformer, the Iowa-born Hopkins became one of Franklin D. Roosevelt's most trusted New Deal administrators and advisers. During World War II, Roosevelt sent Hopkins on special missions and utilized his counsel at international conferences, including Yalta. When he traveled to Moscow for Truman in May 1945, Hopkins was suffering from the cancer that would cause his death within months. (Courtesy of FDR Library)

concession in Iran, then occupied by British and Soviet troops and used as a corridor for Lend-Lease shipments to the Soviet Union. This request touched off a three-cornered competition for influence in the heretofore British-dominated country. When Roosevelt promised in 1944 not to deprive the British of their traditional stakes in the Middle East, Churchill tartly thanked him "for your assurances about no sheeps' eyes at our oil fields in Iran and Iraq. Let me reciprocate by giving you fullest assurance that we have no thought of trying to horn in upon your interests or property in Saudi Arabia."[194] FDR actually met the Saudi king on the way home after Yalta and learned more about Arab matters "by talking with Ibn Saud for five minutes than I could have learned in … two or three dozen letters."[195] The establishment of a U.S. air base at Dhahran in 1945 began a tacit alliance that rendered oil and "the defense of Arabia vital to the defense of the United States."[196]

With Germany's surrender on May 8, 1945, the Third Reich collapsed in the rubble of bombed-out Berlin. President Harry S. Truman quickly ended Lend-Lease aid to the Soviet Union (he soon partially restarted it), thereby angering Moscow. With this issue and the Polish question troubling Soviet-American relations, the president sent Harry Hopkins to see Stalin in May, to "use diplomatic language or a baseball bat."[197] An irate Stalin warned the Americans had made "a fundamental mistake" in halting Lend-Lease "as pressure on the Russians in order to soften them up."[198] Hopkins expressed growing U.S. dismay about Stalin's obstruction of the Yalta agreement on elections in Poland—a symbol of Soviet-American trust. Stalin would not permit the anti-Soviet London Poles to govern postwar Poland, because Poland had twice "served as a corridor for German attacks. … It is therefore in Russia's vital interest that Poland should be both strong and friendly."[199] Stalin did agree that a few ministries should go to non-Lublin Poles. He also reiterated his Yalta promises to enter the war against Japan and respect Jiang's government. Truman then noted in his diary: "I'm not afraid of Russia. … They've always been our friends and I can't see any reason why they shouldn't always be."[200]

The Potsdam Conference and the Legacy of World War II

The Big Three gathered near Berlin for the Potsdam Conference (July 16–August 2, 1945). Truman's first impression of his Soviet counterpart was favorable: "I can deal with Stalin. He is honest—but smart as hell."[201] That impression soon changed, as Truman wrote that "you never saw such pigheaded people as are the Russians."[202] Churchill took a liking to the new president, whom he described as a "man of exceptional character and ability with … simple and direct methods of speech, and a great deal of self-confidence and resolution."[203] Reports of the successful explosion of an atomic device in New Mexico had "tremendously pepped up" the president at Potsdam.[204]

By the time of Potsdam, American intentions toward postwar Germany had moved a good distance from the Morgenthau Plan and JCS/1067. Reconstruction now became the watchword. U.S. officials saw Germany as a vital link in the economic recovery of Western Europe. When Germany came up for discussion, Truman thus resisted dismemberment and large reparations. The final Potsdam accord stated that Germany would be managed by military governors in four zones, treated as "a single economic unit," and permitted a standard of living higher than its low level of 1945.[205] Transportation, coal, agriculture, housing, and utilities industries were to be rehabilitated. As for reparations, desired by the Soviet Union for both revenge and the recovery of its hobbled economy, Stalin had to settle for an agreement that each occupying power would take reparations from its own zone and that the USSR would get some industrial equipment from the Western zones. In return, the Soviet Union would send food to the other three zones. The diplomat George F. Kennan described the reparations deal as "catch as catch can."[206]

When Churchill complained that no elections had been held in Poland, Stalin mentioned the British domination of Greece. They did agree, however, to set the Oder-Neisse line as Poland's temporary western boundary, thereby granting Poland large chunks of German territory. The Soviet Union agreed to accept Italy as a member of the United Nations. The big powers also established the Council of Foreign Ministers to continue discussion on issues not resolved at Potsdam: peace treaties for the former German satellites; withdrawal of Allied troops from Iran; postwar control of the Dardanelles; internationalization of inland waterways; and disposition of Italian colonies. After learning that the Americans had successfully tested a new atomic weapon. Britain and the United States issued the "Potsdam Declaration," demanding Japan's unconditional surrender and threatening it with destruction.

The seemingly minor issue of waterways became for Truman a test of Soviet intentions. At Potsdam he pushed for an international authority to govern the 800-mile-long Danube River, which wound its way through several countries, including the Soviet Union, to the Black Sea. Essentially combining two traditional American principles—free navigation and the Open Door—the proposal antagonized Moscow, which countered with a commission limited to those states through which the river flowed. The president simplistically concluded that Stalin's attitude on waterways showed "what he was after. ... The Russians were planning world conquest."[207] For his part, Stalin interpreted London and Washington as wanting to "force us" to accept "their plans on questions affecting Europe and the world. Well, that's not going to happen."[208]

Potsdam left the world much as it had found it—divided and devastated. World War II ended on August 14, 1945, with Japan's surrender after the Soviets invaded Manchuria and two atomic bombs decimated Hiroshima and Nagasaki. But peace remained elusive because of the war's vast social, economic, and political dislocations in Europe and Asia. World War II claimed the lives of at least 55 million people—26.6 million in the USSR alone. Poland and Germany lost 6 million each; Yugoslavia suffered at least 1.6 million dead; Britain lost 400,000. The toll mounted in Asia, too: 15 million Chinese, 4 million Indonesians, 3 million Japanese, 1 million Vietnamese, 120,000 Filipinos, and thousands more elsewhere. A total of 405,395 Americans died fighting in the war—approximately one American death for every fifteen Germans and fifty-three Russians. Indeed, "20,000 Russians died *per day*" during four years of war.[209]

Bombed-out French Town, 1944. Europe lay in ruins at the end of the war, and American help became essential to the reconstruction effort. (U.S. Office of War Information, National Archives)

Millions of displaced persons became separated from their homelands. Transportation systems, communications networks, and factories shut down. Cities entered the postwar era as rubble heaps, including the German city of Dresden, which Allied planes had incinerated in February 1945 in a merciless attack of questionable necessity. The "most destructive single bombing raid in history" on Tokyo on March 9, 1945, killed at least 83,793 civilians and left more than 1 million homeless.[210] When General Dwight D. Eisenhower flew into the Soviet Union after V-E Day, he "did not see a house standing between the western borders of the country and the area around Moscow."[211] An unprecedented global reconstruction task lay ahead.

With the imperial powers in disarray, their Asian colonies, encouraged by Japan during the waning days of the war, became rebellious. Without the necessary resources and manpower to curb the nationalist revolutions, the European empires began to crumble. The Dutch battled their Indonesian subjects; France fought the Vietnamese in Indochina; Britain reluctantly began its exit from Burma (Myanmar), India, and Ceylon (Sri Lanka).

The rise of the Soviet Union as a major international player counts as another legacy of World War II. Thanks to Hitler, said Truman at Potsdam, "we shall have a Slav Europe for a long time to come."[212] The Soviets resented any intimation that they should not have an influential voice in postwar questions. Reeling from heavy wartime losses, they asked for much—"like a greedy kid, never satisfied," noted one U.S. official.[213] "Whoever occupies a territory imposes on it his own social system," said Stalin. "It cannot be otherwise."[214]

The USSR rose, Britain declined, China floundered, and the United States galloped. "Unbombed, unoccupied, and relatively unbloodied," America had its economy moving in high gear at war's end.[215] The U.S. gross national product jumped from $90.5 billion in 1939 to $211.9 billion in 1945. Observers spoke of an American production miracle. By the end of the war the United States had become "the global workshop and banker, umpire and policeman, preacher and teacher."[216]

Alone in a position to provide the capital and goods for recovery abroad, Washington exuded confidence in the future. Vice President Henry Wallace predicted a century for the "common man" in which science and technology could enable "all the people of the world [to] get enough to eat."[217] Americans looked forward to creating the stable world order that had eluded them between the two world wars. State Department official Dean Acheson observed that "peace is possible only if countries work together and prosper together. That is why the economic aspects are no less important than the political aspects of the peace."[218] Through the war years the United States had constructed institutions—UNRRA, World Bank, International Monetary Fund, United Nations—to ensure that peace.

The war also wrought changes in the policy-making process in the United States. Government agencies handling national security matters ballooned in size. The defense establishment became more active in making diplomatic choices. "Obstruction, understaffing, and rival ambitions" distracted a State Department too often bypassed by FDR.[219] The war spawned a large espionage establishment, beginning with the Office of Strategic Services (OSS) in 1942 and culminating in the Central Intelligence Agency (CIA) five years later. The president centralized decision making in the White House, while Congress neglected its foreign-affairs prerogatives in the constitutional system and applauded bipartisanship. Another consequence of the war was an enlarged "military-industrial complex," a partnership between business executives eager for lucrative defense contracts and military brass eager for increased budgets. The recruitment of universities bequeathed a long-term legacy. Science professors had developed the atomic bomb at the Universities of Chicago and California, Berkeley. Princeton received grants for ballistics research. Postwar federal subsidies flowed to colleges for arms development, research on Soviet studies, and intelligence gathering.

"The world was fluid and about to be remade" in 1945, the journalist Theodore White remembered.[220] Just before FDR's death on April 12, 1945, one of the president's speechwriters observed: "It is practically impossible to be unpatriotic these days—in fact it is difficult not to be an eagle-screaming, flag-waving chauvinist."[221] America now could forge ahead as the world's strongest power.

FURTHER READING FOR THE PERIOD 1939–1945

Biographical studies include Rudy Abrahamson, *Spanning the Century* (1992) (Harriman); Conrad Black, *Franklin Delano Roosevelt* (2003); H. W. Brands, *Traitor to His Class* (2008); Dik Alan Daso, *Hap Arnold and the Evolution of American Air Power* (2000); Kenneth R. Davis, *FDR* (1972–1993); Martin Gilbert, *Winston S. Churchill* (1983); Waldo H. Heinrichs, *American Ambassador* (1966) (Grew); John Huston, *American Air Power Comes of Age* (2002) (Hap Arnold); Warren F. Kimball, *The Juggler* (1991) (FDR); Joseph P. Lash, *Roosevelt and*

Churchill, 1939–1941 (1976); William Lasser, *Benjamin V. Cohen* (2002); John Lukacs, *Churchill* (2002); George McJimsey, *Harry Hopkins* (1987); Jon Meacham, *Franklin and Winston* (2003); Forrest C. Pogue, *George C. Marshall* (1963–1987); Edward J. Renehan, *The Kennedys at War* (2002); Neil Smith, *America's Empire* (2003) (Isaiah Bowman); Mark A. Stoler, *George Marshall* (1989); and works cited in Chapters 4 and 5.

FDR's health is the subject of Robert H. Ferrell, *The Dying President* (1998) and *Ill-Advised* (1992); and Bert E. Park, *The Impact of Illness on World Leaders* (1986).

For the United States and Europe, 1939–1941, and debates at home, see Alfred M. Beck, *Hitler's Ambivalent Attaché* (2005); J. Garry Clifford and Samuel R. Spencer, Jr., *The First Peacetime Draft* (1986); Wayne S. Cole, *Roosevelt and the Isolationists* (1983); Justus Doenecke, *The Battle Against Intervention* (1997) and *Storm on the Horizon* (2001); Max Paul Freidman, *Nazis and Good Neighbors* (2003); Richard F. Hill, *Hitler Attacks Pearl Harbor* (2002); Ian Kershaw, *Fateful Choices* (2007); Warren F. Kimball, *The Most Unsordid Act* (1969) (Lend-Lease); James R. Leutze, *Bargaining for Supremacy* (1977); Mark A. Lowenthal, *Leadership and Indecision* (1988); John Lukacs, *Five Days in London: May 1940* (2001), *June 1941* (2006), and *Blood, Toil, Tears, and Sweat* (2008); Thomas Mahl, *Desperate Deception* (1998); Thomas Mahnken, *Uncovering Ways of War* (2002); Norman Moss, *Nineteen Weeks* (2003); Arnold A. Offner, *The Origins of the Second World War* (1975); Thomas Parrish, *FDR's Men in Churchill's London, 1941* (2008); David L. Porter, *The Seventy-Sixth Congress and World War II, 1939–1940* (1979); Anthony Read and David Fisher, *The Deadly Embrace* (1989) (Nazi-Soviet Pact); David Reynolds, *The Creation of the Anglo-American Alliance, 1937–1941* (1982) and *From Munich to Pearl Harbor* (2001); J. Simon Rofe, *Franklin Roosevelt's Foreign Policy and the Welles Mission* (2007); James C. Schneider, *Should America Go to War?* (1989); Ivo Tasovac, *American Policy and Yugoslavia, 1939–1941* (1999); D. C. Watt, *How War Came* (1989); and Theodore A. Wilson, *The First Summit* (1991).

For the advent of war with Japan, see Michael A. Barnhart, *Japan Prepares for Total War* (1987); Antony Best, *Britain, Japan, and Pearl Harbor* (1995); Fred Borch and Daniel Martinez, *Kimmel, Short, and Pearl Harbor* (2005); Robert J. C. Butow, *Tojo and the Coming of the War* (1961) and *The John Doe Associates* (1974); Hilary Conroy and Harry Wray, eds., *Pearl Harbor Reexamined* (1990); Henry G. Gole, *The Road to Rainbow* (2003); Michael D. Gordin, *Five Days in August* (2007); Akira Iriye, *The Origins of the Second World War in Asia and the Pacific* (1987); Walter LaFeber, *The Clash* (1997); Martin V. Melosi, *The Shadow of Pearl Harbor* (1977); Edward S. Miller, *Bankrupting the Enemy* (2007); James Morley, ed., *The Fateful Choice* (1980), ed., *The Final Confrontation* (1994), and, ed., *Japan's Road to the Pacific War* (1994); Gordon W. Prange, *At Dawn We Slept* (1981) and *Pearl Harbor* (1986); Emily Rosenberg, *A Date Which Will Live* (2003); Paul W. Schroeder, *The Axis Alliance and Japanese-American Relations, 1941* (1958); Youli Sun, *China and the Origins of the Pacific War* (1993); Nicholas Tarling, *A Sudden Rampage* (2001); Haruo Tohmatsu and H. P. Wilmott, *A Gathering Darkness* (2004); Jonathan Utley, *Going to War with Japan* (2005); and Roberta Wohlstetter, *Pearl Harbor* (1962).

Allied relations and postwar planning are explored in David Alvarez, *Secret Messages* (2000) (code-breaking); Rick Atkinson, *An Army at Dawn* (2002); Alan H. Bath, *Tracking the Axis Enemy* (1998); Edward M. Bennett, *Franklin D. Roosevelt and the Search for Victory* (1990); Michael Bercuson and Holger Herwig, *One Christmas in Washington* (2006); Michael Beschloss, *The Conquerors* (2002); Elizabeth Borgwardt, *A New Deal for the World* (2007); Douglas Brinkley and David Facey-Crowther, eds., *The Atlantic Charter* (1994); Susan A. Brewer, *To Win the Peace* (1997); Raymond Callahan, *Churchill and His Generals* (2006); Mark J. Conversino, *Fighting with the Soviets* (1997); Robert Dallek, *Franklin D. Roosevelt and American Foreign Policy* (1979); Norman Davies, *No Simple Victory* (2007); Richard L. DiNardo, *Germany and the Axis Powers* (2005); Robert A. Divine, *Second Chance* (1967) and *Roosevelt and World War II* (1969); Alan P. Dobson, *U.S. Wartime Aid to Britain* (1986); Robin Edmonds, *The Big Three* (1991); Lloyd C. Gardner, *Spheres of Influence* (1993); Mary Glantz, *FDR and the Soviet Union* (2005); Patrick Hearden, *Architects of Globalism* (2002); George C. Herring, Jr., *Aid to Russia, 1941–1946* (1973); Gary R. Hess, *The United States at War, 1941–1945* (1986); Gregory Hooks, *Forging the Military-Industrial Complex* (1990); Barry M. Katz, *Foreign Intelligence* (1989); Warren F. Kimball, ed., *America Unbound* (1992); Eric Larrabee, *Commander in Chief* (1987); Ralph Levering, *American Opinion and the Russian Alliance* (1976); Vojtech Mastny, *Russia's Road to the Cold War* (1979); Christopher Mauch, *The Shadow War Against Hitler* (2003); Steven M. Miner, *Between Churchill and Stalin* (1988) and *Stalin's Holy War* (2003); Wilson Miscamble, *From Roosevelt to Truman* (2007); Williamson Murray and Allen Millett, *A War to Be Won* (2000); Arnold A. Offner and Theodore A. Wilson, eds., *Victory in Europe*

1945 (2000); William O'Neill, *A Democracy at War* (1993); Christopher D. O'Sullivan, *Sumner Welles, Postwar Planning, and the Quest for a New World Order, 1937–1945* (2007); Robert Persico, *Roosevelt's Secret War* (2001); R. C. Raack, *Stalin's Drive to the West, 1938–1945* (1995); David Reynolds et al., eds., *Allies at War* (1994) and *Rich Relations* (1995); Andrew Roberts, *Masters and Commanders* (2008); Geoffrey Roberts, *Stalin's Wars* (2006); Kenneth D. Rose, *Myth and the Greatest Generation* (2008); Norman Saul, *Friends or Foes?* (2006); Ronald Schaffer, *Wings of Judgment* (1985) (U.S. bombing); Michael S. Sherry, *Preparing for the Next War* (1977); Ronald Smelser, *The Myth of the Eastern Front* (2008); Bradley F. Smith, *Sharing Secrets with Stalin* (1996); Mark A. Stoler, *The Politics of the Second Front* (1977), *Allies and Adversaries* (2000), and *Allies in War* (2005); Gerhard L. Weinberg, *A World at Arms* (1994) and *Visions of Victory* (2006); Steve Weiss, *Allies in Conflict* (1996); and Randall B. Woods, *A Changing of the Guard* (1990) (U.S.-Britain).

For the Churchill–Roosevelt relationship and assessments of Churchill, see John Charmley, *Churchill's Grand Alliance* (1995); Martin Gilbert, *Winston S. Churchill* (1983–1986); Roy Jenkins, *Churchill* (2001); Warren F. Kimball, *Forged in War* (1997); and Keith Sainsbury, *Churchill and Roosevelt at War* (1994).

Big Three summit meetings are treated in Russell O. Buhite, *Decisions at Yalta* (1986); Diane Shaver Clemens, *Yalta* (1970); Keith Eubank, *Summit at Teheran* (1985); Fraser J. Harbutt, *Yalta, 1945* (2008); Keith Sainsbury, *The Turning Point* (1985) (Cairo and Teheran); and John L. Snell, ed., *The Meaning of Yalta* (1956).

For the creation of new international organizations, see Thomas Campbell, *Masquerade Peace* (1973) (UN); Robert C. Hilderbrand, *Dumbarton Oaks* (1990); Townsend Hoopes and Douglas Brinkley, *FDR and the Creation of the U.N.* (1997); Greg Schild, *Bretton Woods and Dumbarton Oaks* (1995); and Stephen C. Schlesinger, *Act of Creation* (2003).

Propaganda and the mobilizing of public opinion in the era of World War II are studied in Steven Casey, *Cautious Crusade* (2001); Nicholas Cull, *Selling War* (1995) (British propaganda in the United States); Clayton Koppes and Gregory Black, *Hollywood Goes to War* (1987); Clayton Laurie, *The Propaganda Warriors* (1996); George H. Roeder, Jr., *The Censored War* (1993); Holly C. Shulman, *The Voice of America* (1991); Richard Steele, *Propaganda in an Open Society* (1985); and Michael S. Sweeney, *Secrets of Victory* (2000).

For the Pacific theater, China, and decolonization, see Wesley M. Bagby, *The Eagle-Dragon Alliance* (1992); Günter Bischof and Robert Dupont, eds., *The Pacific War Revisited* (1997); Herbert P. Bix, *Emperor Hirohito and the Making of Modern Japan* (2001); Russell D. Buhite, *Patrick J. Hurley and American Foreign Policy* (1973); Carolle Carter, *Mission to Yenan* (1997); Francis B. Cogan, *Captured* (1999); Roger Dingman, *Deciphering the Rising Sun* (2009); John W. Dower, *War Without Mercy* (1986); Charles Fenn, *At the Dragon's Gate* (2004); T. Fujitani et al., *Perilous Memories: The Asia-Pacific War(s)* (2001); Marc S. Gallichio, ed., *The Unpredictability of the Past* (2007) and *The Scramble for Asia* (2008); Max Hastings, *Retribution* (2008); Gerald Horne, *Race War* (2004); Akira Iriye, *Power and Culture* (1981); John D. Kuehn, *Agents of Innovation* (2008); Karen J. Leong, *The China Mystique* (2005); Laura Tyson Li, *Madame Chiang Kai-Shek* (2006); Peter Li, ed., *Japanese War Crimes* (2003); Xiaoyuan Liu, *A Partnership for Disorder* (1996) (China); William R. Louis, *Imperialism at Bay* (1978) (decolonization); Sean Malloy, *Henry L. Stimson and the Decision to Use the Atomic Bomb against Japan* (2008); Greg Robinson, *By Order of the President* (2001); Mark Roehrs and William Renzl, *World War II in the Pacific* (2003); Michael Schaller, *The U.S. Crusade in China, 1938–1945* (1978); Peter Schrijvers, *The GI War Against Japan* (2002); Sterling Seagrave and Peggy Seagrave, *The Yamato Dynasty* (2001); Michael M. Sheng, *Battling Western Imperialism* (1997); Leon V. Sigal, *Fighting to the Finish* (1988); Ronald H. Spector, *Eagle Against the Sun* (1984); Christopher Thorne, *Allies of a Kind* (1977) and *The Issue of War* (1985); Barbara Tuchman, *Stilwell and the American Experience in China, 1911–1945* (1971); Frederick Wakeman, Jr., *Spymaster* (2003); Odd Arne Westad, *Cold War and Revolution* (1993) (China); Maochun Yu, *The Dragon's War* (2006); and Thomas Zeiler, *Unconditional Defeat* (2004).

For wartime relations with Latin America, see works cited in Chapter 5; Michael J. Francis, *The Limits of Hegemony* (1977) (Argentina and Chile); Michael Grow, *The Good Neighbor Policy and Authoritarianism in Paraguay* (1981); Thomas M. Leonard and Robert F. Bratzel, eds., *Latin America During World War II* (2007); Frank D. McCann, Jr., *The Brazilian-American Alliance, 1937–1945* (1973); Stephen R. Niblo, *War, Diplomacy, and Development* (1995) (Mexico); María Emilia Paz, *Strategy, Security, and Spies* (1997) (Mexico); David Rock, ed., *Latin America in the 1940s* (1994); Charlie Witham, *Bitter Rehearsal* (2002) (British West Indies); and Randall B. Woods, *The Roosevelt Foreign Policy Establishment and the "Good Neighbor"* (1980) (Argentina).

For U.S. interest in the Middle East and oil, consult Irvine H. Anderson, *Aramco, the United States, and Saudi Arabia* (1981); Philip J. Baram, *The Department of State in the Middle East, 1919–1945* (1978); Rachel Bronson, *Thicker Than Oil* (206); Aaron D. Miller, *Search for Security* (1980) (Saudi Arabia); and Michael B. Stoff, *Oil, War, and American Security* (1980).

The Holocaust and refugee problem are recounted in Robert H. Abzug, *Inside the Vicious Heart* (1985); Yehuda Bauer, *Jews for Sale?* (1994) and *Rethinking the Holocaust* (2001); Richard Breitman and Alan M. Kraut, *American Refugee Policy and European Jewry* (1987); Richard Breitman, *Official Secrets* (1998); Christopher Browning, *The Path to Genocide* (1992); Leonard Dinnerstein, *America and the Survivors of the Holocaust* (1982); Henry L. Feingold, *Bearing Witness* (1995) and *Politics of Rescue* (1970); Saul Friedlander, *Nazi Germany and the Jews* (1997) and *Years of Extermination* (2007); Martin Gilbert, *Auschwitz and the Allies* (1981); Ian Kershaw, *Hitler, the Germans, and the Final Solution* (2008); Walter Laqueur, *The Terrible Secret* (1980); Deborah E. Lipstadt, *Beyond Belief* (1993); Louise London, *Whitehall and the Jews, 1933–1948* (2002); Arthur D. Morse, *While Six Million Died* (1968); William E. Nawyn, *American Protestantism's Response to Germany's Jews and Refugees* (1982); Verne Newton, ed., *FDR and the Holocaust* (1995); Monty N. Penkower, *The Jews Were Expendable* (1983); Brian M. Rigg, *Hitler's Jewish Soldiers* (2002); Robert N. Rosen, *Saving the Jews* (2006); David Wyman, *The Abandonment of the Jews* (1984), *Paper Walls* (1968), and ed., *The World Reacts to the Holocaust* (1996); and David S. Wyman and Rafael Medoff, *A Race Against Death* (2002).

See also the General Bibliography, the following notes, and Robert L. Beisner, ed., *Guide to American Foreign Relations Since 1600* (2003).

NOTES TO CHAPTER 6

1. Quoted in Theodore A. Wilson, *The First Summit* (Lawrence: University Press of Kansas, 1991), p. 98.
2. FDR quoted in Warren F. Kimball, *Forged in War* (New York: Morrow, 1997), p. 98.
3. Elliott Roosevelt, *As He Saw It* (New York: Duell, Sloan, and Pearce, 1946), p. 33.
4. Winston S. Churchill, *The Grand Alliance* (Boston: Houghton Mifflin, 1950), p. 431.
5. Quoted in Robert E. Sherwood, *Roosevelt and Hopkins* (New York: Harper & Brothers, 1948), p. 236.
6. Harold Nicolson, *Diaries and Letters* (New York: Atheneum, 1966–1968; 3 vols.), II, 385.
7. David Reynolds, *Rich Relations* (New York: Random House, 1995), p. 438
8. Quoted in "Briefly Noted," *New Yorker*, LXXIX (December 22 and 29, 2003), 157
9. Diary entry, August 14, 1941, in John W. Huston, ed., *American Air Power Comes of Age* (Maxwell Air Force Base: Air University Press, 2002, 2 vols.), I, 234.
10. FDR quoted in Lisle A. Rose, *Power at Sea: The Breaking Storm, 1919–1945* (Columbia: University of Missouri Press, 2007), p. 250.
11. David Reynolds, "The Origins of the Two 'World Wars,'" *Journal of Contemporary History*, XXXVIII (January 2003), 40.
12. Quoted in Raymond Esthus, "President Roosevelt's Commitment to Britain to Intervene in a Pacific War," *Mississippi Valley Historical Review*, L (June 1963), 31.
13. *Foreign Relations, 1941* (Washington, D.C.: Government Printing Office, 1958), I, 368–369.
14. James M. Burns, *Roosevelt* (New York: Harcourt Brace Jovanovich, 1970), p. 550.
15. Quoted in Holly C. Shulman, *The Voice of America* (Madison: University of Wisconsin Press, 1990), p. 72.
16. *Foreign Relations, 1941, I,* 378.
17. Quoted in William H. McNeill, *America, Britain, & Russia* (London: Oxford University Press, 1953), p. 41.
18. Quoted in Lloyd C. Gardner, *Spheres of Influence* (Chicago: Ivan R. Dee, 1993), p. 241.
19. Quoted in Burns, *Soldier,* p. 609.
20. Mark A. Lowenthal, *Leadership and Indecision* (New York: Garland, 1988), p. 633.
21. Ian Jacob quoted in Martin Gilbert, *Winston S. Churchill* (Boston: Houghton Mifflin, 1983), p. 1161.
22. Quoted in Wilson, *First Summit,* p. 182.
23. Henry Wallace quoted in J. Garry Clifford, "Juggling Balls of Dynamite," *Diplomatic History*, XVII (Fall 1993), 636; Charles De Gaulle quoted in Deborah Kisatsky, "The United States, the French Right, and American Power in Europe, 1946–1958," *The Historian, LX* (Spring 2003), 627.
24. Anthony Eden, *The Reckoning* (Boston: Houghton Mifflin, 1965), p. 433.
25. Samuel I. Rosenman, ed., *Public Papers … of Franklin D. Roosevelt, 1939* (New York: Macmillan, 1938–1950; 13 vols.), VIII, 463.
26. Charles Tobey to James Richardson, September 28, 1939, Tobey Papers, Dartmouth College Library, Hanover, N.H.
27. Quoted in John M. Blum, *From the Morgenthau Diaries: Years of Urgency* (Boston: Houghton Mifflin, 1965), p. 91.
28. Quoted in B. Mitchell Simpson, *Admiral Harold R. Stark* (Columbia: University of South Carolina Press, 1989), p. 99.
29. Rosenman, *Public Papers, 1940, IX,* 263.
30. FDR and Willkie quoted in David Reynolds, *From Munich to Pearl Harbor* (Chicago: Ivan R. Dee, 2001), p. 101.

31. FDR quoted in Robert A. Divine, *Foreign Policy and U.S. Presidential Elections, 1940–1948* (New York: New Viewpoints, 1974), pp. 82–83.

32. Warren F. Kimball, ed., *Churchill & Roosevelt* (Princeton: Princeton University Press, 1984; 3 vols.), I, 108.

33. Rosenman, *Public Papers, 1940,* IX, 607.

34. *Ibid.,* pp. 640–643.

35. Quoted in George C. Herring, Jr., *Aid to Russia, 1941–1946* (New York: Columbia University Press, 1973), p. 4.

36. Quoted in Nicholas Cull, *Selling War* (New York: Oxford University Press, 1995), p. 75.

37. Elizabeth Dilling quoted in June Melby Benowitz, *Days of Discontent* (Dekalb: Northern Illinois University Press, 2002), p. 43.

38. Quoted John E. Moser, *Twisting the Lion's Tail* (New York University Press, 1999), p. 143.

39. Quoted in Warren F. Kimball, *The Most Unsordid Act* (Baltimore: Johns Hopkins University Press, 1969), p. 153.

40. *Congressional Record, LXXVII* (March 8, 1941), 2097.

41. Breckinridge Long Diary, May 12, 1941, Long Papers, Library of Congress, Washington, D.C.

42. Claude Wickard Diary, May 2, 1941, Wickard Papers, Franklin D. Roosevelt Library, Hyde Park, N.Y.

43. Col. Ivan Yeaton quoted in Mary Glantz, *FDR and the Soviet Union* (Lawrence: University Press of Kansas, 2005), p. 65.

44. Quoted in Calvin L. Christman, "Franklin D. Roosevelt and the Craft of Strategic Assessment," in Williamson Murray and Allen R. Millett, eds., *Calculations* (New York: Free Press, 1992), p. 256.

45. Harry Hopkins quoted in Mark A. Stoler, *Allies and Adversaries* (Chapel Hill: University of North Carolina Press, 2000), p. 53.

46. August 19, 1941, CAB 65/19, War Cabinet Records 84, Public Record Office, London.

47. Quoted in Ian Kershaw, *Fateful Choices* (New York: Penguin, 2007), p. 325.

48. Quoted in Philip Chen, "Religious Liberty in U.S. Foreign Policy," in David B. Woolner and Richard G. Kurial, eds., *FDR, the Vatican, and the Roman Catholic Church in America, 1933–1945* (New York: Palgrave, 2003), p. 134.

49. Quoted in Wayne S. Cole, *America First* (Madison: University of Wisconsin Press, 1953), p. 163.

50. FDR quoted in Joseph Lash Diary, February 5, 1940, Joseph Lash Papers, Roosevelt Library.

51. Quoted in Steven Casey, *Cautious Crusade* (New York: Oxford University Press, 2001), p. 44.

52. Josiah Bailey to I. M. Meekins, September 6, 1941, Bailey Papers, Duke University Library, Durham, N.C.

53. Quoted in Edward M. Bennett, "Joseph C. Grew," in Richard Dean Burns and Edward M. Bennett, eds., *Diplomats in Crisis* (Santa Barbara: ABC-CLIO, 1974), p. 78.

54. Quoted in Kershaw, *Fateful Choices,* p. 300.

55. Casey, *Cautious Crusade,* p. 39.

56. Quoted in Richard L. DiNardo, *Germany and the Axis Powers* (Lawrence: University Press of Kansas, 2005), p. 93.

57. Quoted in Christopher Layne, *The Peace of Illusions* (Ithaca: Cornell University Press, 2006), p. 162.

58. Quoted in John Lukacs, *June 1941* (New Haven: Yale University Press, 2006), p. 37.

59. Quoted in Charles E. Neu, *The Troubled Encounter* (New York: Wiley, 1975), p. 168.

60. *Foreign Relations, 1940* (Washington, D.C.: Government Printing Office, 1955), IV, 602.

61. Quoted in Christopher Thorne, *The Issue of War* (New York: Oxford University Press, 1985), p. 22; Jonathan Marshall, *To Have and Have Not* (Berkeley: University of California Press, 1995), p. 251.

62. Quoted in Herbert Feis, *The Road to Pearl Harbor* (New York: Atheneum, 1967), p. 206.

63. *Magic* report quoted in Timothy Wilford, "British and Commonwealth Intelligence Before Pearl Harbor," *Intelligence and National Security, XVII* (Winter 2002), 137.

64. Jonathan Utley, *Going to War with Japan, 1937–1941* (Knoxville: University of Tennessee Press, 1984), p. 156.

65. Osami Nagano quoted in Herbert P. Bix, *Emperor Hirohito and the Making of Modern Japan* (New York: HarperCollins, 2000), p. 202.

66. Quoted in James C. Thomson, Jr., "The Role of the Department of State," in Dorothy Borg and Shumpei Okamoto, eds., *Pearl Harbor as History* (New York: Columbia University Press, 1973), p. 101.

67. Quoted in Kimball, *Forged in War,* p. 118.

68. Quoted in Noriko Kawamura, "Emperor Hirohito and Japan's Decision to Go to War with the United States," *Diplomatic History, XXXI* (January 2007), 78.

69. Admiral Yamamoto quoted in Warren I. Cohen and Nancy Bernkopf Tucker, "America in Asian Eyes," *American Historical Review, CXI* (October 2006), 1098.

70. Quoted in Nicholas Tarling, *A Sudden Rampage* (Honolulu: University of Hawai'i Press, 2001), p. 77.

71. Quoted in Thorne, *Issue of War,* p. 10.

72. Youli Sun, *China and the Origins of the Pacific War* (New York: St. Martin's, 1993), p. 155.

73. Quoted in David J. Bercusen and Holger H. Herwig, *One Christmas in Washington* (New York: Overlook Press, 2005), p. 88.

74. Charles Tansill, *Back Door to War* (Chicago: Regnery, 1952).

75. Quoted in Carl Boyd, *Hitler's Japanese Confidant* (Lawrence: University Press of Kansas, 1993), p. 36.

76. Roberta Wohlstetter, *Pearl Harbor* (Stanford: Stanford University Press, 1962), p. 387.

77. Frank Walker quoted in Frances Perkins memorandum of Pearl Harbor Cabinet Meeting, December 8, 1941, Frances Perkins Papers, Butler Library, Columbia University, New York City, New York.

78. Arthur H. Vandenberg, Jr., ed., *The Private Papers of Senator Vandenberg* (Boston: Houghton Mifflin, 1952), p. 1.

79. Quoted in Saul Friedlander, *The Years of Extermination* (New York: HarperCollins, 2007), p. 279.

80. Samuel E. Morison, *Strategy and Compromise* (Boston: Little, Brown, 1958), p. 25.

81. Quoted in Todd Bennett, "Culture, Power, and *Mission to Moscow,*" *Journal of American History, LXXXVIII* (September 2001), 504.

82. Quoted in George H. Roeder, Jr., *The Censored War* (New Haven, Yale University Press, 1993), p. 129.

83. Kathleen Harriman quoted in David S. Foglesong, *The American Mission and the "Evil Empire"* (New York: Cambridge University Press, 2007), p. 100.

84. Quoted in Geoffrey Perrett, *Days of Sadness, Years of Triumph* (Baltimore: Penguin, 1973), p. 197.

85. Quoted in Warren F. Kimball, "Churchill and Roosevelt," *Prologue, VI* (Fall 1971), 181.

86. Quoted in Mark Bradley, "Culture, Diplomacy, and the Origins of the Cold War in Vietnam," in Christian G. Appy, ed., *Cold War Constructions* (Amherst: University of Massachusetts Press, 2000), p. 21.

87. Quoted in Warren F. Kimball, *The Juggler* (Princeton: Princeton University Press, 1991), p. 136.

88. Eden, *Reckoning*, pp. 336–337.

89. Quoted in Stephen M. Miner, *Between Churchill and Stalin* (Chapel Hill: University of North Carolina Press, 1988), p. 217.

90. Quoted in David Reynolds, "The Wartime Alliance and Post-War Transitions, 1941–1947," *The Historical Journal, XLV* (Winter 2002), 217.

91. Quoted in Oleg Rzheshevsky, ed., *War and Diplomacy* (Amsterdam, Neth.: Harwood, 1996), p. 120.

92. Quoted in Herbert Feis, *Churchill, Roosevelt, Stalin* (Princeton: Princeton University Press, 1957), p. 42.

93. Quoted in Mark A. Stoler, *Allies at War* (London: Hodder Arnold, 2005), p. 86.

94. Quoted in Mark Perry, *Partners in Command* (New York: Penguin, 2007), p. 117.

95. Quoted in Kimball, *Forged in War*, p. 130.

96. Quoted in Dale R. Herspring, *The Pentagon and the Presidency* (Lawrence: University Press of Kansas, 2005), p. 33.

97. Quoted in Stoler, *Allies at War*, p. 139.

98. Stalin quoted in Geoffrey Roberts, *Stalin's Wars* (New Haven: Yale University Press, 2006), p. 141; and Maxim Litvinov quoted in Geoffrey Roberts, "Litvinov's Lost Peace, 1941–1946," *Journal of Cold War Studies, IV* (Spring 2002), 32.

99. Quoted in Wlodzimierz Borodziej, *The Warsaw Uprising of 1944* (Madison: The University of Wisconsin Press, 2006), p. 32.

100. Quoted in Steven Merritt Miner, *Stalin's Holy War* (Chapel Hill: University of North Carolina Press, 2003), p. 107.

101. Quoted in Robert Beitzell, *The Uneasy Alliance* (New York: Knopf, 1972), p. 159.

102. D. C. Watt, *Succeeding John Bull* (Cambridge: Cambridge University Press, 1984), p. 1; Winston S. Churchill, *The Hinge of Fate* (Boston: Houghton Mifflin, 1950), p. 759.

103. V. A. Golikov quoted in Vladislav M. Zubok, *A Failed Empire* (Chapel Hill: University of North Carolina Press, 2007), p. 13.

104. Quoted in Raymond G. O'Connor, *Diplomacy for Victory* (New York: Norton, 1971), p. 52.

105. Maxim Litvinov quoted in John Lewis Gaddis, *We Now Know* (New York: Oxford University Press, 1997), p. 15.

106. General John Dean quoted in Stoler, *Allies and Adversaries*, p. 187.

107. Memorandum of Conversation with Cordell Hull, November 30, 1943, "Black Notebooks," Box 1, Arthur Krock Papers, Princeton University Library, Princeton, N.J.

108. Cordell Hull, *Memoirs* (New York: Macmillan, 1948; 2 vols.), *II,* 1297.

109. Keith Sainsbury, *The Turning Point* (New York: Oxford University Press, 1985), p. 307.

110. Quoted in Keith Eubank, *Summit at Teheran* (New York: Morrow, 1985), p. 248.

111. Quoted in Geoffrey Roberts, "Stalin at the Tehran, Yalta, and Potsdam Conferences," *Journal of Cold War Studies, IX* (Fall 2007), 15.

112. Quoted in Mark A. Stoler, *The Politics of the Second Front* (Westport, Conn.: Greenwood Press, 1977), p. 149.

113. Churchill, *Hinge of Fate*, p. 374.

114. Quoted in David Reynolds, "The Erosion of British Influence," in Charles Brower, ed., *World War II in Europe: The Final Year* (New York: St. Martin's, 1998), p. 40.

115. Quoted in Norman Davies, *No Simple Victory* (New York: Viking, 2007), p. 185; *Foreign Relations, Cairo and Teheran* (Washington, D.C.: Government Printing Office, 1961), pp. 594–595.

116. Churchill quoted in Sainsbury, *Turning Point*, p. 300.

117. Quoted in Michael Adas, *Dominance by Design* (Cambridge: Harvard University Press, 2006), p. 224.

118. Rosenman, *Public Papers, 1943, XII,* 558.

119. Churchill, *Hinge of Fate*, p. 133.

120. FDR quoted in George McJimsey, *The Presidency of Franklin D. Roosevelt* (Lawrence: University Press of Kansas, 2000), p. 225; Nevile Butler quoted in LaFeber, *The Clash*, p. 231.

121. FDR quoted in Gerhard L. Weinberg, *Visions of Victory* (New York: Cambridge University Press, 2005), p. 186.

122. Quoted in Jonathan Spence, *To Change China* (Boston: Little, Brown, 1969), p. 236; Christopher Thorne, "Indochina and Anglo-American Relations, 1942–1945," *Pacific Historical Review, XLIV* (February 1976), 76.

123. Theodore H. White, ed., *The Stilwell Papers* (New York: William Sloane Associates, 1948), p. 157.

124. Quoted in Robert P. Newman, *Owen Lattimore and the "Loss" of China* (Berkeley: University of California Press, 1992), p. 70.

125. Quoted in Herbert Feis, *The China Tangle* (Princeton: Princeton University Press, 1953), p. 51.

126. Walter Huston quoted in Laura Tyson Li, *Madame Chiang Kai-shek* (New York: Grove Press, 2006), p. 224.

127. Quoted in Maochun Yu, *OSS in China* (New Haven: Yale University Press, 1996), p. 66.

128. Quoted in Martha Byrd, *Chennault* (Tuscaloosa: University of Alabama Press, 1987), p. 174.

129. White, *Stilwell Papers*, p. 333.

130. John Melby quoted in Nancy Bernkopf Tucker, ed., *China Confidential* (New York: Columbia University Press, 2001), p. 27.

131. *Foreign Relations, 1944* (Washington, D.C.: Government Printing Office, 1967), *VI,* 631–632.

132. David D. Barrett, *Dixie Mission* (Berkeley: University of California, 1970), p. 56.

133. Quoted in Michael M. Sheng, *Battling Western Imperialism* (Princeton: Princeton University Press, 1997), p. 94.

134. Quoted in Feis, *China Tangle*, p. 213.

135. Quoted in Russell D. Buhite, *Patrick J. Hurley and American Foreign Policy* (Ithaca: Cornell University Press, 1973), p. 152.

136. Quoted in Carolle J. Carter, *Mission to Yenan* (Lexington: University Press of Kentucky, 1997), p. 147.

137. Pyotr Vladimirov quoted in Wesley M. Bagby, *The Eagle-Dragon Alliance* (Newark: University of Delaware Press, 1992), p. 122; Michael H. Hunt, *The Genesis of Chinese Communist Foreign Policy* (New York: Columbia University Press, 1996), p. 156.

138. Quoted in Feis, *China Tangle*, p. 269.

139. Burns, *Soldier*, p. 545.

140. James G. MacDonald, entry of April 8, 1933, in Richard Breitman et al., eds., *Advocate for the Doomed* (Bloomington: Indiana University Press, 2007), p. 48.

141. Quoted in Moshe Gottlieb, "The Berlin Riots and Their Repercussions in America," *American Jewish Historical Quarterly, LIX* (March 1970), 306.

142. Quoted in Cyrus Adler and Aaron M. Margalith, *With Firmness in the Right* (New York: American Jewish Committee, 1946), p. 381.

143. Arnold A. Offner, *American Appeasement* (New York: Norton, 1976 [c. 1969]), p. 92.

144. Richard Breitman quoted in Verne Newton, ed., *FDR and the Holocaust* (New York: St. Martin's, 1996), p. 14.

145. Quoted in Friedman, *No Haven*, p. 83.

146. Quoted in David Wyman, *Paper Walls* (Amherst: University of Massachusetts Press, 1968), p. 97.

147. Quoted in Henry L. Feingold, *Bearing Witness* (Syracuse University Press, 1995), p. 173.

148. Quoted in A. J. Sherman, *Island Refuge* (Berkeley: University of California Press, 1973), p. 207.

149. Yehuda Bauer, *Rethinking the Holocaust* (New Haven: Yale University Press, 2001), p. 221.

150. Quoted in Henry L. Feingold, "Courage First and Intelligence Second," in Michael Marrus, ed., *The Nazi Holocaust: Bystanders to the Holocaust* (Westport, Conn.: Meckler, 1989; 9 vols.) II, 781.

151. John J. McCloy quoting FDR in Robert N. Rosen, *Saving the Jews* (New York: Thunder Mouth Press, 2006), p. 405.

152. McCloy quoted in Friedlander, *Years of Extermination*, p. 627.

153. Hitler quoted in Gerhard L. Weinberg, "'Gray Zones' in Raul Hilberg's Work," in Jonathan Petropolous and John K. Roth, eds., *Gray Zones* (New York: Bergahn Books, 2005), p. 72.

154. Quoted in Arthur D. Morse, *While Six Million Died* (New York: Random House, 1968), p. 63.

155. Quoted *ibid.*, pp. 93, 95; Morgenthau quoted in David S. Wyman and Rafael Medoff, *A Race Against Death* (New York: The New Press, 2002), p. 48.

156. Quoted in David Wyman, "The United States," in Wyman, ed., *The World Reacts to the Holocaust* (Baltimore: Johns Hopkins University Press, 1996), p. 707.

157. Feingold, *Bearing*, p. 8.

158. Quoted in Frank Costigliola, "Broken Circle," *Diplomatic History*, XXXII (November 2008), 740.

159. Quoted in George Woodbridge et al., *The History of the United Nations Relief and Rehabilitation Administration* (New York: Columbia University Press, 1950), I, 4.

160. *Treaties and Other International Acts* (Washington, D.C.: Government Printing Office, 1946), series 1501–1502.

161. *Manchester Guardian* quoted in Richard N. Gardner, *Sterling-Dollar Diplomacy* (New York: McGraw-Hill, 1969; rev. ed.), p. 267.

162. Quoted in Diane Shaver Clemens, *Yalta* (New York: Oxford University Press, 1970), p. 48.

163. Quoted in Gabriel Kolko, *The Politics of War* (New York: Random House, 1968), pp. 270–271.

164. Quoted in Stephen C. Schlesinger, *Act of Creation* (Boulder, Col.: Westview Press, 2003), p. 140.

165. Walter Lippmann quoted in Robert A. Divine, *Second Chance* (New York: Atheneum, 1967), p. 291.

166. John J. McCloy quoted in Kolko, *Politics of War*, p. 470.

167. Arnold Wolfers, *United States Policy Toward Germany* (New Haven: Yale Institute of International Studies, 1947), p. 3; Cordell Hull quoted in Deborah Kisatsky, *The United States and the European Right, 1945–1955* (Columbus: Ohio State University Press, 2005), p. 13.

168. *Foreign Relations, Conference at Quebec, 1944* (Washington, D.C.: Government Printing Office, 1972), p. 467.

169. John J. McCloy quoted in Michael Beschloss, *The Conquerors* (New York: Simon & Schuster, 2002), p. 144.

170. Henry L. Stimson to the president, September 15, 1944, Box 100, James Forrestal Papers, Princeton University Library.

171. Notebooks, Interview with Harry S. Truman, November 12, 1949, Box 85, Jonathan Daniels Papers, University of North Carolina Library, Chapel Hill.

172. Quoted in Davies, *No Simple Victory*, p. 192.

173. *Correspondence Between the Chairman*, I, 295.

174. Quoted in Alexander, *Ethnicity, Race, and American Foreign Policy* (Boston: Northeastern University Press, 1992), p. 123; *You're a Sap, Mr. Jap* (New York: King Features, 1942).

175. Quoted in Kenneth D. Rose, *Myth and the Greatest Generation* (New York: Routlege, 2008), p. 24.

176. Quoted in Martin Gilbert, *Winston S. Churchill: Road to Victory, 1941–1945* (Boston: Houghton Mifflin, 1986), p. 1208.

177. Churchill, *Triumph and Tragedy*, p. 366.

178. Stalin quoted in Anthony Beevor, *The Fall of Berlin 1945* (New York: Viking, 2002), p. 81.

179. *Foreign Relations, Yalta* (Washington, D.C.: Government Printing Office, 1955), p. 973.

180. Quoted in William L. O'Neill, *A Democracy at War* (New York: Free Press, 1993), p. 196.

181. Quoted in Zubok, *Failed Empire*, p. 22.

182. Quoted in Sherwood, *Roosevelt and Hopkins*, p. 870.

183. Quoted in Reynolds, "Erosion," p. 51.

184. Isaiah Bowman quoted in Neil Smith, *American Empire* (Berkeley: University of California Press, 2003), p. 379.

185. Churchill, *Triumph and Tragedy*, p. 402.

186. Quoted in Kolko, *Politics of War*, p. 465.

187. Churchill, *Triumph and Tragedy*, pp. 227–228.

188. Stalin quoted in Vojtech Mastny, *The Cold War and Soviet Insecurity* (New York: Oxford University Press, 1996), p. 20.

189. Stalin quoted in Borodziej, *Warsaw Uprising*, p. 92; also quoted in Mark J. Conversino, *Fighting with the Soviets* (Lawrence: University Press of Kansas, 1997), pp. 136–137.

190. Quoted in Rudy Abrahamson, *Spanning the Century* (New York: Morrow, 1992), p. 383.

191. John M. Cabot quoted in Thomas M. Leonard, "The New Pan Americanism in U.S.-Central American Relations, 1933–1954," in David Sheinin, ed., *Beyond the Ideal* (Westport, Conn.: Praeger, 2000), p. 103.

192. David Sheinin, "Argentina: The Closet Ally," in Thomas E. Leonard and Robert F. Bratzel, eds., *Latin America during World War II* (Lanham, Md.: Rowman & Littlefield, 2007), p. 184.

193. Quoted in Kimball, *Forged in War*, p. 134.

194. *Foreign Relations, 1944* (Washington, D.C.: Government Printing Office, 1965), III, 103.

195. Quoted in Ross Gregory, "The United States and Saudi Arabia," in J. Garry Clifford and Theodore A. Wilson, eds., *Presidents, Diplomats, and Other Mortals* (Columbia: University of Missouri Press, 2007), p. 131.

196. James F. Byrnes quoted in Rachel Bronson, *Thicker Than Oil* (New York: Oxford University Press, 2006), p. 24.

197. Harry S. Truman, *Memoirs* (Garden City, N.Y.: Doubleday, 1955–1956; 2 vols.), I, 258.

198. *Foreign Relations, Berlin* (Washington, D.C.: Government Printing Office, 1960; 2 vols.), I, 33.

199. *Ibid.*, I, 39.

200. Quoted in James L. Gormly, *From Potsdam to the Cold War* (Wilmington, Del.: Scholarly Resources, 1990), p. 21.

201. Quoted in Robert H. Ferrell, ed., *Off the Record* (New York: Harper and Row, 1980), p. 53.

202. Truman, *Memoirs*, I, 402.

203. "Note of the Prime Minister's Conversation with President Truman at Luncheon, July 18, 1945," Prem. 3, Prime Minister's Office Records, Public Record Office.

204. Quoted in Robert L. Messer, "World War II and the Coming of the Cold War," in John M. Carroll and George C. Herring, eds., *Modern American Diplomacy* (Wilmington, Del.: Scholarly Resources, 1986), p. 121.

205. *The Tehran, Yalta & Potsdam Conferences: Documents* (Moscow: Progress Publishers, 1969), p. 323.

206. George F. Kennan, *Memoirs, 1925–1950* (Boston: Little, Brown, 1967), p. 260.

207. Truman, *Memoirs*, I, 412.

208. Stalin quoted in Andrei Gromyko, *Memoirs* (New York: Doubleday, 1989), p. 110.

209. Kenneth J. Hagan and Ian R. Bickerton, *Unintended Consequences* (London: Reaktion Press, 2007), p. 127.

210. Thomas W. Zeiler, *Unconditional Defeat* (Wilmington, Del.: Scholarly Resources, 2004), p. 151.

211. Quoted in Donald W. White, *The American Century* (New Haven: Yale University Press, 1996), p. 43.

212. Quoted in Marc Trachtenberg, "New Light on the Cold War?" *Diplomacy & Statecraft, XII* (December 2001), 12.

213. James F. Byrnes quoted in Huston, ed., *American Air Power, II*, 378.

214. Quoted in Peter G. Boyle, *American-Soviet Relations* (New York: Routledge, 1993), p. 45.

215. David Reynolds, "World War II and Modern Meanings," *Diplomatic History, XXV* (Summer 2001), 470.

216. Thomas J. McCormick, *America's Half-Century* (Baltimore: Johns Hopkins University Press, 1989), p. 33.

217. Wallace quoted in Nick Cullather, "The Foreign Policy of the Calorie," *American Historical Review, CXII* (April 2007), 362.

218. *Department of State Bulletin, XXII* (April 22, 1945), 738.

219. Isaiah Bowman quoted in Smith, *American Empire*, p. 385.

220. Theodore H. White, *In Search of History* (New York: Warner, 1979), p. 224.

221. Robert E. Sherwood to Harry Hopkins, April 4, 1945, Box 4, Series III, Harry Hopkins papers, Lauinger Library, Georgetown University, Washington, D.C.

CHAPTER 7

All-Embracing Struggle: The Cold War Begins, 1945–1950

Atomic Blast. *The second atomic bomb fell on Nagasaki August 9, 1945, killing almost 74,000. The theoretical physicist J. Robert Oppenheimer, a leading architect of the bomb, later reflected that "we knew the world would not be the same. … I remembered the line from the Hindu scripture, the Bhagavad-Gita … 'Now I am become death, the destroyer of worlds.'" (U.S. Air Force)*

◈ *Atomic Bombs at Hiroshima and Nagasaki, 1945*

THE CREW OF the B-29 group on the Pacific island of Tinian scrawled graffiti on the "Little Boy." A major, thinking about his son and a quick end to the war, scratched "No white cross for Stevie" on the orange and black bomb.[1] At last, the United States's secret atomic development program (Manhattan Project) neared fruition. On the evening of August 5, 1945, Colonel Paul Tibbets informed his crew that their rare cargo was "atomic." He did not explain the scientific process by which two pieces of uranium (U-235), placed at opposite ends of a cylinder, smashed together to create tremendous energy. Yet they knew what the equivalent of 20,000 tons of TNT meant.

At 2:45 A.M. on August 6, 1945, the *Enola Gay,* a heavily laden B-29 named after Tibbets's mother, lifted ponderously off the Tinian runway. The six-hour flight was uneventful except for the nerve-wracking final assembly of the bomb's inner components. The *Enola Gay* spotted the Japanese coast at 7:30 A.M. A weather plane assigned to Hiroshima, the primary target, reported that "everything was peachy keen."[2] Tibbets headed for that city.

"This is history," Tibbets intoned over the intercom, "so watch your language."[3] At 31,600 feet and 328 miles per hour the *Enola Gay* began its run on Hiroshima. Bombardier Thomas Ferebee prepared to cross the hairs in his bombsight. At 8:15 A.M. he shouted "bombs away." "Little Boy" fell for fifty seconds and then exploded about 2,000 feet above ground, a near perfect hit at hypocenter. A brilliant flash temporarily blinded the fliers. The aircraft trembled. "It looked like a pot of black, boiling tar," thought navigator Theodore Van Kirk, as he watched the huge mushroom cloud of smoke, dust, and debris rise 40,000 feet.[4]

Hiroshima ranked as Japan's eighth largest city, with 250,000 people. Manhattan Project director Brigadier General Leslie Groves had put it first on the target list because, though largely a residential and commercial city, Hiroshima housed regional military headquarters. On the cloudless, warm morning of August 6, few of Hiroshima's inhabitants heard the *Enola Gay* overhead. Suddenly a streak of light raced through the sky. A blast of lacerating heat traveling near the speed of light rocked the city. The temperature soared to suffocating levels. Trees were stripped of their leaves. Buildings blew apart like firecrackers. Permanent shadows etched themselves into concrete. The sky grew dark, lighted only by the choking fires that erupted everywhere. Victims experienced gaping wounds, vomiting and diarrhea, intense thirst, and skin peeling off in ribbons. "This was like the hell I had always heard about," a survivor recalled.[5] The nightmare registered in statistics: about 130,000 dead, as many wounded, and 81 percent of the city's buildings destroyed. Some twenty-three U.S. prisoners of war also perished there. Nine days later in Fukuoka, Japan, seventeen captured American airmen were beheaded by Japanese soldiers, allegedly in retaliation for the "indiscriminate bombing" of civilians.[6]

Enola Gay. On August 6, 1945, just before takeoff, Colonel Paul Tibbets waved from the cockpit of his aircraft *Enola Gay.* Upon returning to their base on Tinian Island, Tibbets and his crew were greeted with medals and a large beer bash. Tibbets received the Distinguished Service Cross for commanding the Hiroshima mission. (U.S. Air Force)

"Little Boy." The nuclear weapon detonated over Hiroshima measured 120 inches long and 28 inches in diameter and weighed about 10,000 pounds. (Los Alamos Scientific Laboratory, courtesy of the Harry S. Truman Library)

When President Harry S. Truman heard about the successful detonation over Hiroshima, he exclaimed: "This is the greatest thing in history."[7] On August 9, a second atomic bomb smashed the industrial and commercial center of Nagasaki, killing 73,884. The next day, shaken after "killing all those kids," Truman decided not to unleash a third nuclear attack.[8] Japan surrendered four days later. "We cried with relief and joy," a young American lieutenant recalled. "We were going to grow up to adulthood after all."[9]

Truman later defended the use of the bomb as necessary to end the war quickly and save "half a million" or more American lives.[10] But some advisers and scientists at the time believed that the bomb was unnecessary because Japan tottered on the verge of defeat. Fearing that by using such weapons, the United States "would sacrifice public support throughout the world" and precipitate a postwar arms race, they suggested several alternatives: (1) follow up Japanese peace feelers; (2) blockade and bomb Japan conventionally; (3) have the USSR declare war on Japan; (4) warn Tokyo about the bomb and threaten its use; (5) demonstrate the bomb on an unpopulated island or area with international observers, including Japanese; (6) conduct a military landing on the southernmost Japanese island of Kyushu.[11] The physicist Robert Wilson, who had helped direct the Manhattan Project, recalled feeling "betrayed" that "the bomb was exploded over Japan without [international] discussion or some peaceful demonstration of its power" to Japan's leaders. "I remember being just ill … sick … to the point that I thought I would be—you know, vomit."[12]

No military or naval adviser, however, told Truman before Hiroshima that "the use of the A-bomb was unnecessary, or that the weapon should not be used, or both."[13] Quite the contrary, officials in charge of the $2 billion Manhattan Project, which had commenced in 1942 after European scientists had warned President Franklin D. Roosevelt that Germany might develop nuclear weapons, always assumed that the United States would use the bomb once it was ready. Doing so was consistent with the "routinization of slaughter" by both Axis and Allied powers throughout the war, as evidenced in the Holocaust, in Nazi air raids on London, in Japanese incendiary raids on Chinese cities, and in the U.S. and British firebombing of Dresden.[14] The conventional bombing of Tokyo and other Japanese cities in 1945 killed as many as 600,000 Japanese and wounded more than 1 million. The battle for Okinawa, which ended in June 1945, saw 12,000 American deaths and 60,000 wounded; 70,000 Japanese soldiers died along with 150,000 Okinawan noncombatants. Such horrific events "lowered the moral threshold by obliterating

Mother and Child at Nagasaki. A mother and her son received a boiled rice ball from an emergency relief party, one mile southeast of Ground Zero, on August 10, 1945. Manhattan Project Director Leslie Groves and Lieutenant Colonel Charles Rea initially dismissed as "propaganda" news reports of widespread radiation sickness among atomic bombing victims. "They just got a good thermal burn, that's what it is," Rea told Groves. "A lot of these people … they don't notice it much." In fact, the vast majority—71 percent in Hiroshima and 69 percent in Nagasaki—suffered acute radiation sickness immediately after the explosions. (National Archives)

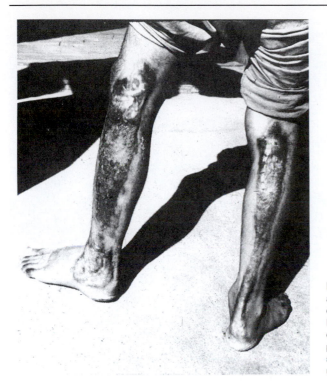

Radiation Burns on a Hiroshima Victim's Legs. The anthropologist Hugh Gusterson notes that images like this "helped display the military power of those who control nuclear weapons." Photographic close-ups of mangled flesh obscure the race, age, and sex of the victim, making it "hard for us to identify with the power in another person's suffering body." But "these bodies are also booby-trapped," for such pictures "can excite feelings of sympathy and terror that work to undermine the nuclear state." (National Archives)

the distinction between combatants and noncombatants."[15] Truman, who inherited these practices and plans from his predecessor, never really *decided* to drop the atomic bomb. Rather, as Groves put it, the president practiced "noninterference—basically a decision not to upset the existing plans."[16] Truman's acquiescent approach helped ensure that the pace towards usage quickened following the successful atomic test at Alamogordo, New Mexico, on July 16, even though Germany had surrendered and Japan faced imminent defeat.

A second factor—emotion—reinforced the military momentum towards a nuclear assault. Vengeful Americans never forgave Japan's attack on Pearl Harbor, which, as one historian writes, seemed to confirm popular beliefs that "the Japanese were a uniquely treacherous people" who "used sneaky methods to gain an unfair advantage."[17] The Bataan death march and other Japanese atrocities against Allied troops "came to signify a unique form of Japanese perversity: a manic intention to humiliate the West by brutal treatment and slaughter," while *Kamikaze* suicide raids in 1945 persuaded many that Japanese "fanatics" would never surrender.[18] The Japanese, too, demonized their enemies, depicting the Americans and British as hairy, horned devils, "lawless savages," who must be annihilated, in the words of a Japanese editorial, to "make the world safe for civilization."[19] Within this context, the Pacific War was not only a political and a military conflict; it was also a "race war," which

Hiroshima. The ruins of Japan's eight largest city bespoke the birth of the atomic age. The total of immediate and longer-term deaths caused by the Hiroshima and Nagasaki bombings may be as high as 300,000. Official Japanese registries in the 1980s recognized 368,259 *hibakusha* (survivors). (U.S. Air Force)

"exposed raw prejudices" and "was fueled by racial pride, arrogance, and rage on many sides."[20] Truman reflected the American convention of equating the Japanese with apes: "When you have to deal with a beast you have to treat him as a beast," he privately commented on August 11, 1945.[21]

The third factor that helped unleash the atomic bomb was the prospect of a diplomatic "bonus"—a strengthened U.S. bargaining position with the Soviets after the war.[22] Two advantages seemed possible. Truman hoped, first, that the bomb would preempt Allied plans for the Soviets to invade Japan and thereby limit Moscow's postwar influence in Asia. "Japs will fold up before Russia comes in," Truman wrote on learning of the successful test at Alamogordo. "I am sure they will when Manhattan appears over their homeland."[23] Japan's surrender of August 14 did obviate a full-fledged Soviet occupation of Japanese-controlled Asia. But the Soviets had already declared war against Japan on August 8 and invaded Manchuria on August 9. "Soviet entry into the war shocked the Japanese even more than the atomic bombs," one historian argues, because it ended hopes of achieving a Moscow-mediated settlement short of unconditional surrender.[24] The Red Army's offensive, combined with the bombs, compelled Japan's leaders to "face the reality of defeat."[25] U.S. officials also anticipated a second opportunity in the bomb: An intimidated USSR might offer concessions on Eastern Europe—the region liberated and now controlled by Soviet troops—if the bomb's destructiveness were revealed on a Japanese city. Throughout the war, Churchill and Roosevelt had tried to keep

Japanese Surrender Document (September 2, 1945). Japanese dignitaries signed the act of unconditional surrender in the presence of 50 Allied generals aboard the U.S.S. *Missouri* in Tokyo Bay. Under terms of the surrender, Japan acknowledged the sovereignty of the U.S. Supreme Commander for Japan, General Douglas MacArthur, though Hirohito was permitted to remain as nominal head of state. Japan's prime minister, Prince Higashikuni Naruhiko, appealed to Japan's people to "suffer even the insufferable" in complying with the surrender proclamation. (National Archives)

the bomb a secret from the Soviet Union, in part for use as diplomatic leverage in the postwar period. Churchill noted that at the Potsdam Conference of July–August 1945, when Truman first heard the news from Alamogordo, "he was a changed man" who "told the Russians just where they got on and off."[26] Truman cryptically informed Stalin at Potsdam that the United States had "a new weapon of unusual destructive force."[27] But while the Soviets had already penetrated the Manhattan Project through espionage, Stalin did not grasp the importance of atomic weapons until Hiroshima and Nagasaki had "shaken the whole world."[28] He then authorized an accelerated program to catch up, an initiative that culminated in the Soviets' own explosion of an atomic device in August 1949.

Military momentum, emotion, and diplomatic advantage together impelled the United States towards a nuclear attack on Japan. The rapidity and totality of Japan's surrender caught U.S. officials by surprise but enabled Truman later to claim that the bomb had saved American lives by averting a land invasion of Japan. Regardless of whether Japan's depleted forces could have held out until November 1, when that invasion was scheduled to begin, many U.S. soldiers believed that the bomb cut short the war and saved them from certain death. Still, the atomic bomb's costs were not inconsequential. Some of the alternatives, perhaps in combination, might have terminated the war without substantial American casualties and without the massive suffering of Japanese civilians. The atomic bombings and the failure to discuss atomic issues with the Soviets during the war bequeathed a nuclear age of division and fear.

Truman, Stalin, and the U.S.-Soviet Clash

"World War II changed everything," writes the historian Tony Judt.[29] Some 35 million people in Europe alone died during the war, and many more homeless refugees trekked through a "blasted landscape of broken cities and barren fields."[30]

War Secretary Henry L. Stimson, Army Chief of Staff George C. Marshall, and President Harry S. Truman Show the Surrender Documents to the Press (September 7, 1945). Truman publicly insisted throughout his life that he never had qualms about his atomic bomb decisions. A former U.S. diplomat in 1962 alleged that Truman confessed to "recurring nightmares about the dropping of the bombs and that he considered that it was the greatest mistake of his life." (Harry S. Truman Library)

The international system was shattered, and competing models for the future produced wrenching political turmoil. The war so weakened the French, British, and Dutch that they began to retreat from empire. Britain granted independence to India in 1947 and Burma in 1948, and the Dutch left Indonesia a year later. France clung precariously to Indochina in the face of nationalist rebellion. The contrast with a prosperous and expanding America, untouched by enemy bombers or soldiers, appeared stark.

As Washington moved to fill power vacuums left by the defeated Axis and retreating colonial powers, it encountered an obstreperous competitor in Joseph Stalin's Soviet Union. The Soviets's pushy behavior and blunt language rankled Americans. A bipolar international structure emerged from the Soviet-American rivalry—the Cold War. The Soviet Union lacked an effective navy or air force and had no atomic bomb, but it possessed strong regional power by virtue of its military exploits. At the end of the war, Red Army troops occupied several East European countries and part of Germany. Motivated by traditional Russian nationalism and communist ideology, craving security against a revived Germany, and facing a major task of reconstruction, the Kremlin determined to make the most of its limited power. Still, compared with the United States, as the diplomat George F. Kennan reported from Moscow, the Soviet Union stood as the "weaker force."[31]

In fact, an asymmetry—not a balance—of power existed. Because of domestic public pressure, Washington may have demobilized its troops faster than Truman

Makers of American Foreign Relations, 1945–1950

President	Secretaries of State
Harry S. Truman, 1945–1953	Edward R. Stettinius, Jr., 1944–1945
	James F. Byrnes, 1945–1947
	George C. Marshall, 1947–1949
	Dean G. Acheson, 1949–1953

wished (he later called it "disintegration"), but the Soviet Union also demobilized millions of soldiers.[32] With troops in Asia and Europe, the world's largest navy and air force, a monopoly of the atomic bomb, and a high-gear economy, the United States claimed first rank in world affairs. In contrast, a Moscow study estimated that total Soviet war damages surpassed "the national wealth of England or Germany" and constituted "one-third of the overall national wealth of the United States."[33] The estimated 27 million Soviet war dead amounted to roughly 90 times the number of Americans who died. So devastated, "Russia couldn't turn a wheel in the next ten years without our aid," bragged Truman.[34]

American ideology held that world peace and order depended on the existence of prosperity and political democracy. Poverty and economic depression bred totalitarianism, revolution, communism, the disruption of world trade, and war. Growth became the handmaiden of stability, political freedom, unrestricted trade, and peaceful international relations. Americans had long believed that they were prosperous because they were democratic and democratic because they were prosperous.

Economic needs influenced postwar expansionism. Many Americans, remembering the Great Depression, predicted economic catastrophe unless foreign trade continued and expanded. By 1947 U.S. exports accounted for one-third of total world exports at $14 billion a year. Pivotal industries such as automobiles, steel, and farm machinery relied heavily on foreign trade. Farmers exported about half of their wheat, and imports of manganese, tungsten, and chromite became essential to America's industrial system. Foreign trade, however, was threatened by the sickness of America's best customer, Europe, which lacked the resources to purchase American products, and by nationalists in former colonial areas, who controlled raw materials for both Europe and America.

American leaders determined that *this time,* unlike after World War I, the United States would seize the opportunity to mold a world order in its own image. As the diplomat Dean Acheson saw it, "only the United States had the power to grab hold of history and make it conform."[35] The lessons of the 1920s and 1930s taught the leaders of the 1940s to make the most of a second chance to promote American-style peace and prosperity worldwide.

President Truman felt the flush of American power, shared the peace-and-prosperity outlook, and knew well the economic needs of the country. A Democratic party regular from the Pendergast machine in Kansas City, Missouri,

"What Next?" Jack Lambert's 1946 cartoon of Harry S. Truman captured the feeling of many Americans that the president, new at his job, was overwhelmed by postwar problems. FDR had kept Truman in the dark on foreign affairs. Recalling their first contentious meeting in April 1945, Molotov thought Truman "half-witted" and "far behind Roosevelt in intellect." Stalin called the president a "gentleman shopkeeper." (Courtesy of Chicago Sun-Times. Reprinted with permission)

Truman had long experienced rough-and-tumble politics. "The buck stops here" read a sign on his desk. He prided himself on blunt language and quick decisions. With intense eyes peering through thick lenses, Truman relished the verbal brawl. His peppery style spawned jokes that sometimes fit the truth. Somebody rewrote a proverb: "To err is Truman." Although intelligent and energetic, Truman was a provincial nationalist of narrow vision who believed he could win the Cold War through the projection of U.S. power. He expected the world to go America's way, and when it did not, he sometimes lost his temper.

In April 1945, Soviet foreign minister V. M. Molotov visited the White House for the first meeting between the new president and a high-ranking Soviet official. Truman gave Molotov a vigorous tongue-lashing, charging that Moscow had not honored the Yalta accords on Poland. After the encounter, the president gloated: "I gave it to him straight 'one-two to the jaw.' I let him have it straight."[36] He did not fear the Soviets, Truman told Ambassador W. Averell Harriman, because they "needed us more than we needed them." The new president did not expect to win 100 percent of the American case, but "we should be able to get 85 percent."[37]

The Soviets, too, projected power in a world newly transformed by war. If the Soviets and Americans "can collaborate in war," Stalin asked American dignitaries as late as 1947, "why can't they collaborate in peacetime?"[38] But he also warned against Soviet "servility before the West."[39] The Red Army occupied half of Europe, and Stalin, recalling the hostile encirclement of Russia by neighboring states during two world wars, intended to maintain a sphere of influence in the countries that bordered Eurasian Russia. He saw this objective as consistent with both the percentages agreement (1944) and the Yalta accords (1945; see Chapter 6). At the same time, he and his subordinates viewed with mounting suspicion the United States's sprawling global presence. "There is no corner of the world in which the USA cannot be seen," Molotov complained to Byrnes in May 1945 while ticking off a list of new U.S. bases in Iceland, Greece, Turkey, Italy, and elsewhere. "This is evidence of a real expansionism and expresses the striving of certain American circles towards an imperialist policy."[40]

The confrontation between the United States and the Soviet Union derived from the different postwar needs, ideology, style, and power of the two rivals. Each displayed what one historian calls "ethnocentric arrogance," a belief in the superiority of its own ideals and institutions.[41] Each saw the other, in mirror image, as the world's bully. Americans compared Hitler and Stalin, coining the phrase "Red Fascism." Stalin made a parallel analogy, warning that "the use of A-bombs ... depends on Trumans and Hitlers being in power."[42] Moscow and Washington became trapped in a "security dilemma": Every step taken by one side to ensure its interests appeared to the other to be provocative.

The advent of the air and nuclear ages made all nations vulnerable to surprise attack. "We are for all time de-isolated," wrote one observer.[43] Soviet and American quests for spheres of influence kindled a global contest for advantage—what Truman called an "all-embracing struggle"—with an expensive arms race, military alliances, trade restrictions, and repeated interventions and client-state wars.[44] The Cold War era lasted more than forty years, claimed millions of victims, and sent the protagonists into perilous debt. Globalist foreign policies sacrificed domestic social and economic health to the perceived exigencies of worldwide political and military conflict, at great cost to infrastructures, and to human life itself.

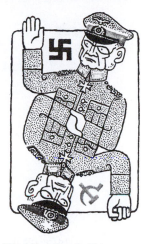

"Red Fascism." This popular notion among Americans suggested that German Nazism and Soviet communism were really one and the same and that the 1940s would suffer totalitarian aggression like that of the 1930s. Such thinking aroused fears of another "Munich" or "appeasement" and hindered negotiations. (*The Reporter,* 1950. Copyright 1950 by Fortnightly Publishing Co., Inc.)

Challenging the Soviets in Eastern Europe

The Soviet presence in Eastern Europe before 1947–1948 was neither uniform nor consistent. Soviet documents from 1945–1946 suggest that Stalin acted as a "ruthless opportunist rather than a revolutionary ideologue."[45] Poland, with the Lublin communists in control, fell firmly within the Soviet grasp. Stalin said repeatedly that Poland had been a corridor for attack and that a secure Poland meant life or death for the Soviets. The Red Army also imposed communist rule in Romania, while in Bulgaria indigenous communists easily won elections.

Yet Stalin also urged local communists not to "precipitate conflict, alienate the Americans, or challenge the British" so long as "time was on his side."[46] Hungary and other nations hence developed differently. The conservative Hungarian Smallholders' party of Ferenc Nagy won national elections in November 1945 by routing the communists, who gained only 17 percent of the vote. Toward Finland, Stalin practiced "generosity by calculation," telling Finnish leaders "when we treat our neighboring countries well, they respond in kind."[47] So long as Helsinki remained neutral vis-à-vis the Soviet-American confrontation, the Finns retained their independence

Joseph Stalin (1879–1953).
General secretary of the Soviet
Communist party since 1922, he
ran an authoritarian state and
conducted a foreign policy of
suspiciousness. Because Stalin
often played "good cop" to Foreign
Minister V. M. Molotov's "bad cop,"
President Truman once called
the Soviet dictator a "prisoner
of the Politburo." Ambassador
Averell Harriman wrote that if
"it were possible to see [Stalin]
more frequently ... many of our
difficulties would be overcome."
(*The Reporter*, 1952. Copyright
1952 by Fortnightly Publishing
Co., Inc.)

and in 1948 even ousted the lone communist from their cabinet. In Czechoslovakia, democratic socialist officials sought to steer a middle course in the developing Cold War. A coalition government under noncommunist president Eduard Beneš and Foreign Minister Jan Masaryk assumed office after free elections in May 1946. With Czech communists holding a minority position in the Prague government, the Soviet Union refrained from meddling directly in Czech affairs until a communist coup in February 1948 sharply intensified the Cold War. Yugoslavia, although a communist state, established its independence from Moscow under the leadership of Josip Broz Tito. When Belgrade and Moscow rancorously split in 1948, U.S. officials noted with satisfaction that the "germ of Titoism is growing."[48]

Although Soviet control in Eastern Europe was far from absolute, U.S. leaders believed that Moscow sought total domination there. Such prospects conflicted with U.S. hopes for political and economic democracy in the form of free elections and Open Door (or multilateral) trade relations. Free elections proved difficult in the region, however, because, as Stalin bluntly put it, "a freely elected government in any of these countries would be anti-Soviet," and "that we cannot allow."[49] The noncommunist Nagy delayed elections in 1946 precisely because he knew that the communists would lose badly, alarming Moscow and perhaps triggering Soviet intervention.

Molotov charged the United States with a double standard in preaching Western-style democracy for Eastern Europe. "How governments are being organized in Belgium, France, Germany, etc., we do not know," he grumbled. "We have not been asked. ... We have not interfered."[50] As for widening the door for trade, Molotov held that a multilateral system invited American economic domination of a region where the United States historically lacked strong commercial ties. The Soviets signed with many East European states preferential bilateral treaties that discriminated against the Western powers.

Throughout 1945–1946, the United States sought to counter Soviet power in Eastern Europe. Washington abandoned its initial strategy of not recognizing pro-Soviet governments when Stalin agreed to allocate a few ministries to noncommunists. But American officials quietly planned "the judicious use of covert operations applied at the appropriate time."[51] And they publicly engaged in atomic shadow-boxing with their Soviet counterparts. At the London Conference in October 1945, Byrnes jokingly warned Molotov that "if you don't cut out all this stalling and let us get down to work, I am going to pull an atomic bomb out of my hip pocket and let you have it."[52] Washington never practiced a blatant atomic diplomacy of direct threat, and the U.S. nuclear monopoly did not budge the Soviets from Eastern Europe. But as Henry L. Stimson advised Truman in September 1945, negotiating with "this weapon rather ostentatiously on our hip" increased Soviet distrust.[53] Stimson, unlike Byrnes, rejected the bomb as a diplomatic weapon, and he urged Truman to share atomic data and spur postwar cooperation. Vice President Henry Wallace agreed, but Secretary of the Navy James V. Forrestal opposed any effort to "buy [Soviet] understanding and sympathy. We tried that once with Hitler."[54] Truman sided with Forrestal.

The United States also used foreign aid as a diplomatic weapon in Eastern Europe. Byrnes stated the policy in 1946: "We must help our friends in every way

Changes in Europe
After World War II

Territorial Changes After World War II

Notes: -The United States, British, and French Zones
of Germany merged in 1949 as the Federal
Republic of Germany.

-The Russian Zone of Germany became the
German Democratic Republic in 1949.

-The four zones of Austria merged in 1955 to
become the Federal Republic of Austria.

NORWAY

SWEDEN

FINLAND
To Russia

*Leased to Russia
until 1955*

*L.
Ladoga*

Gulf of Finland

• Leningrad

NORTH
SEA

DENMARK

ESTONIA
to Russia

L. Pskov

To Russia
LATVIA

BALTIC SEA

LITHUANIA
To Russia
Niemen R.

To Russia

SOVIET RUSSIA

U.S. ZONE

NETH.

BRITISH
ZONE

Berlin •

G E R M A N Y

W.

BEL.

E.

RUSSIAN
ZONE

LUX.

FRENCH
ZONE

Rhine R.

FRANCE

UNITED
STATES
ZONE

SWITZ.

Danzig •
*To
Oder R.*
Poland

Nisse R.

EAST
PRUSSIA
To Poland

Vistula R.

P O L A N D

To Russia

NORTHERN
BUKOVINA

C Z E C H O S L O V A K I A

RUSSIAN
U.S.
Vienna •
FRENCH
A U S T R I A
BRITISH

BRATISLAVA
BRIDGEHEAD
To Czech.

H U N G A R Y

SUBCARPATHIAN
RUTHENIA

Dniester R.

BESSARABIA
To Russia

Pruth R.

VENEZIA-GIULIA
To Yugoslavia

To France

Trieste •

Po R.

Dravu R.

R O M A N I A

Don R.

I T A L Y

CORSICA

Rome •

ADRIATIC SEA

Y U G O S L A V I A

Danube R.

BLACK
SEA

DOBRUJA
*To
Bulgaria*

SARDINIA

ALBANIA

BULGARIA

G R E E C E

TURKEY

*AEGEAN
SEA*

SICILY

MALTA (Br.)

DODECANESE IS.
*(To Greece
from Italy)*

CRETE

M E D I T E R R A N E A N   S E A

237

"I Can't Give You All Up for One Angel of Peace."   The burly Soviet savors the attention of the Eastern Europeans in this critical Turkish cartoon. The brutish caricature suggests a certain truth. According to the historian Norman Naimark, "women in the Eastern zone" of Germany "shared an experience for the most part unknown in the West, the unbiquitous threat and reality of rape, over a prolonged period of time." The raping by Soviet troops of an estimated 2 million German women prompted the U.S. military governor Lucius Clay to write: "We began to look like angels, not because we were angels, but we looked [like] that in comparison to what was going on in Eastern Europe." (*ULUS*, Ankara, in *United Nations World*, 1947)

and refrain from assisting those who … are opposing the principles for which we stand."[55] In short, no loans or aid for Eastern Europe. This policy backfired, for it left those countries dependent on Soviet aid and drove them deeper into the Soviet orbit. In Czechoslovakia, for example, the United States abruptly severed an Export-Import Bank loan. Noncommunist foreign trade minister Hubert Ripka objected bitterly when U.S. officials offered 500,000 tons of wheat to "throw the Communists out of the Czechoslovak Government." Instead, "these idiots in Washington have driven us straight into the Stalinist camp."[56] Truman's pressure tactics helped intensify the Cold War because Moscow leaders read them as threats to their own security and thus tightened their grip.

"Getting Tough": Early Cold War Crises

At the London Conference of Foreign Ministers (September–October 1945), Byrnes demanded representative governments in Bulgaria and Romania before he would sign any peace treaties with the former German satellites. Molotov countered with questions about British-dominated Greece and American-dominated Japan. At the Moscow Conference in December 1945, however, Stalin permitted a token broadening of the Romanian and Bulgarian regimes in exchange for U.S. recognition. He also accepted Byrnes's proposals for a general peace conference to be held in Paris and a United Nations Atomic Energy Commission to prepare plans for international control.

Domestic critics blasted the Moscow agreement as "an appeasement document," a "typical American giveaway."[57] In early 1945, an impatient Truman ordered Byrnes to "stiffen up" and "stop babying" the Soviets.[58] News that a Canadian spy ring had sent atomic secrets to Moscow broke in February, about the time that Stalin gave a speech persuading some Americans that the Soviets had become intractable. From Moscow, on February 22, chargé d'affaires George F. Kennan wrote an alarmist cable that described an adversary "committed fanatically to the belief that with [the] US there can be no permanent modus vivendi."[59] Widely read in Washington, this "long telegram," the historian Frank Costigliola writes, depicted a rapacious, aggressive, hypermasculine Soviet Union, guided by an implacable communist ideology and a "neurotic view of world affairs." To reassure the "tired and frightened" Europeans, Kennan urged the United States to "tighten" up, assert greater "cohesion, firmness and vigor," and exhibit manly "courage, detachment, [and] objectivity" in dealing with Moscow.[60]

On March 5, ex-Prime Minister Winston Churchill spoke in Fulton, Missouri. President Truman heard the eloquent orator ominously intone: "From Stettin in the Baltic to Trieste in the Adriatic, an iron curtain has descended across the Continent."[61] Most Americans liked Churchill's stern anti-Soviet message, but they warmed much less to his call for an Anglo-American alliance outside the fledgling United Nations Organization. Stalin told *Pravda* magazine that Churchill was a "firebrand of war" who resembled "Hitler and his friends" with his "racial theory … that only nations speaking the English language" should "decide the destinies of the entire world."[62]

A crisis over Iran disturbed Soviet-American relations at the same time. The standoff began quietly in 1944 when British and American oil companies applied for Iranian concessions. In a classic example of spheres-of-influence rivalry, the

Winston S. Churchill (1874–1965) in Fulton.   Churchill (far left) received applause from President Harry S. Truman (far right) during the former British prime minister's visit to Westminster College in Fulton, Missouri. There Churchill delivered his provocative oration against the "iron curtain." (Truman Library and Westminster College)

Soviet Union soon applied as well. By 1944 U.S. corporations controlled 42 percent of proven oil reserves of the Middle East, a nineteenfold increase since 1936. A 1942 treaty with Iran allowed the British and Soviets to occupy the country and required them to leave six months after the end of the war. U.S. personnel also went to Iran, primarily to facilitate Lend-Lease shipments to the Soviet Union. After the Soviets in mid-1945 backed an indigenous rebellion in northern Iran (Azerbaijan) against the central government, Iran took the question to the new United Nations Organization in early 1946. Teheran and Moscow could not reach an accord by March 2, when all foreign troops, by treaty, had to depart. With U.S. and British troops already gone, Truman vowed to use "an iron fist and strong language" to expel the remaining Soviet forces from the region.[63] In April, however, Soviet forces agreed to withdraw; in exchange, Iran offered to establish a joint Iranian-Soviet oil company, subject to approval by its parliament. Stalin abandoned his Azerbaijani clients. In late 1946, Iranian troops, advised by U.S. Army officers, crushed the insurrection in northern Iran. Not until October 1947 did Iran's legislature consider the joint oil company, rejecting it by a vote of 102 to 2.

The Soviets exploded in anger. Moscow wanted what the British and Americans already had—oil and influence—and they feared foreign penetration of a neighboring state. Yet they had departed Iran while Britain and the United States had driven in stakes. Years later, Truman embellished the Iranian story by claiming that he had sent the Soviets an ultimatum to get out of Iran or face U.S. troops, but no record of such a message exists. This myth nonetheless suggests the simple lesson Americans drew: "Get tough" and the Soviets will give way. Secretary Wallace told a Madison Square Garden audience in September 1946 that "'getting tough' never brought anything real and lasting. … The tougher we get, the tougher the Russians will get."[64] Truman thereupon fired Wallace, lumping the "cat bastard" with "parlor pinks and soprano-voiced men" as a "national danger" and "a sabotage front for Uncle Joe Stalin."[65]

Other fractious issues in 1946 illustrated Truman's "get tough" policy at work. During the war, Moscow asked Washington for a major postwar reconstruction loan. Seeing U.S. aid as one of America's cards in the Cold War game, Truman decided to withhold assistance in hopes of leveraging gains in Eastern Europe. But as Ambassador Harriman admitted, U.S. rejection of the Soviet loan request in early 1946 actually "may have contributed to their avaricious policies" in Eastern Europe.[66] Later that year, Washington granted Britain a $3.75 billion loan in return for British promises to open trade in their Sterling Bloc.

The Baruch Plan of July 1946 also divided Washington and Moscow. The plan emerged from months of intra-administration talks, but its final touches belonged to Bernard Baruch, the uncompromising American negotiator. He outlined a proposal for the control of atomic weapons: (1) creation of an international authority; (2) international control of fissionable raw materials by this authority; (3) inspections to prevent violations; (4) no Security Council vetoes of control or inspections; (5) global distribution of atomic plants for peaceful purposes; (6) cessation of the manufacture of atomic bombs; (7) destruction of existing bombs; and (8) execution of these procedures in stages, with abandonment of the U.S. atomic bomb monopoly coming last.

W. Averell Harriman (1891–1986). Graduate of Yale, heir to the Harriman railroad empire, investment banker of Brown Brothers, and diplomat, Harriman was one of America's great public servants in the twentieth century. He served as ambassador to Russia (1943–1946), ambassador to Great Britain (1946), secretary of commerce (1946–1948), and U.S. representative in Europe for the Marshall Plan. Later he advised Presidents John F. Kennedy and Lyndon B. Johnson. As early as May 1945, Dean Acheson described Harriman as "ferocious about the Rouskis." (*The Reporter,* 1950. Copyright 1950 by Fortnightly Publishing Co., Inc.)

Not until after the Soviets had given up all fissionable materials and submitted to inspections would the United States relinquish its "winning weapon."[67] "We are telling the Russians that if they are 'good boys' we may eventually turn over our knowledge of atomic energy to them," Wallace wrote to the president.[68] About the same time, the Soviet ambassador in Washington, Nikolai Novikov, warned his superiors that the United States was "striving for world supremacy."[69] Moscow rejected the Baruch Plan, and the stalemate persisted until 1949, when the Soviets successfully exploded their first atomic device.

The key issue of Germany deepened the schism. The Allied occupation consisted of British, French, American, and Soviet zones, wherein each occupying power did what it liked. The United States sought to treat Germany as one economic unit to speed reconstruction. The British generally wanted a strong Germany oriented towards social democracy. The Soviets tried with mixed success to grab reparations, thereby weakening the entire German economy. The French, fearing both German revival and Soviet control of any unified German government, adopted a "hard-line policy," refusing to permit any centralized German agencies and pushing for permanent dismemberment.[70] All four occupiers dismantled war-related industries at first. But with the Morgenthau Plan shelved, Anglo-American plans evolved to reconstruct steel- and coal-rich Germany as the vital center of a revived European economy. Project Paperclip, meanwhile, recruited ex-Nazi scientists to assist in the "development of new types of weapons."[71] And thousands of GIs "fraternized" or "went frattin" with German women in the U.S. zone.[72] The 94,000 total offspring that resulted prompted a German joke that "if America ever got into another war in Europe, it would not be necessary to send any troops—just the uniforms."[73]

In May 1946, U.S. military governor Lucius Clay halted all reparations shipments from the American zone to pressure the Soviets to accept German economic unity. In December 1946, the British and Americans combined their zones into "Bizonia." "We really do not intend to accept German unification in any terms that the Russians might agree to," one U.S. diplomat wrote privately.[74] The Federal Republic of Germany (West Germany), a consolidation of Bizonia and the French zone, was formed in May 1949. The Soviets, after looting their zone, created their own client, the German Democratic Republic (East Germany), in October 1949.

Perhaps we can kick them out, Stalin told a German communist as he initiated the Berlin blockade (June 1948–May 1949) to impede unification of the western zones. Fearful of a Germany linked to the West, the Soviets sealed off land, rail, and water access to Berlin (inside the Soviet zone). Truman answered with an airlift. U.S. planes soon swept into the western part of the city with food, fuel, and other provisions. He also ordered B-29 bombers to England, concealing the fact that they went without any of the fifty atomic bombs then in the U.S. arsenal. The Soviet ambassador reported a "war psychosis" rampant in Washington.[75] Yet Stalin never interfered with the airlift and even permitted a half-million tons of supplies to reach Berlin from the Soviet zone. Moscow eventually lifted the blockade, but only after suffering worldwide reproach and the creation of the West Germany it had so wanted to prevent. Americans drew another Cold War lesson: To win, never flinch in the face of communist aggression.

Berlin Airlift. In May 1949, at the close of the crisis over the Berlin blockade, American military personnel celebrate victory for "Operation Vittles." Unlike 1944 and 1945, when Berliners rushed to air raid shelters at the sound of approaching Allied aircraft, German children during the airlift ran to catch candy dropped from U.S. transport planes, which they affectionately dubbed *Rosinenbomber* (raisin bombers). The historian Petra Goedde has written that the Germany encountered by American GIs after the war was "weak, submissive, and disproportionately female," and the ensuing interactions with German women and children helped the United States "create a new monolithic image of Germany: feminine victim of war and the Soviet menace." (U.S. Air Force)

What if ... *the United States and the Soviet Union had reached an agreement in 1946 to prevent the spread of atomic weapons?*

The Baruch Plan provided that the American nuclear arsenal would only be disbanded once other powers agreed not to pursue their own atomic programs. And it required international monitoring to ensure compliance while denying UN Security Council members the right to veto inspections. Fearing threats to Soviet sovereignty and security, Moscow rejected Baruch's proposals and countered with a Soviet plan that required the United States to end its program as a precondition to Soviet concessions. The Soviets exploded their first nuclear device in 1949. Not until the Strategic Arms Limitation Treaty (1972) did the two powers formally agree to limit atomic weapons production (see Chapter 10). By then, both states had tens of thousands of warheads to deliver via missiles, and Britain (1952), France (1960), and China (1964) all had nuclear arsenals of their own. By the year 2008, Israel (1968), India (1974), Pakistan (1998), and North Korea (2006) had atomic weapons, and other states, including Iran, Iraq, Libya, and South Africa had conducted nuclear weapons research as well.

In missing a chance to prevent a nuclear arms race, U.S. and Soviet leaders bequeathed a terrible burden to the world. Consider: the U.S. arsenal was still quite small in 1946—probably no more than nine partially dismantled plutonium bombs, as compared with an historic high of 32,200 U.S. warheads in 1966. The American image of nuclear strength, cultivated by U.S. leaders, nonetheless convinced Moscow that, as the Soviet physicist German Goncharov put it, "we must not lag behind. ... An absolutely insane task was set for us. ... We must have everything Americans have. ... And it resulted in the mindless arms race." By 1996 the United States had spent more than $5.4 trillion building and maintaining its nuclear weapons complex; the Soviets had expended a similar amount. Laid end to end, bricks of $1 bills equaling this sum could encircle the earth at the equator almost 105 times, making a wall more than 8.7 feet high. Some historians have credited atomic weapons for ushering in a Soviet-American "long peace" by deterring a superpower war and a possible nuclear Armageddon. But the economic costs, combined with the environmental and human effects of nuclear testing and accidents such as Chernobyl (see Chapter 11) and with the security risks that accompanied nuclear gambles as during the Cuban Missile Crisis (see Chapter 9), raise questions about whether atomic weapons made the world more safe after 1945—or less so.

"A Bolt of Lightning": The Truman Doctrine, Israel, and Containment

On March 12, 1947, President Harry S. Truman spoke dramatically to a joint session of Congress. Unless the United States offered help to Greece and Turkey, "we may endanger the peace of the world—and we shall surely endanger the welfare of this Nation." His most famous words became known as the Truman Doctrine: "It must be the policy of the United States to support free peoples who are resisting attempted subjugation by armed minorities or by outside pressures." Truman implied that the Greek and Turkish governments were democratic and that "totalitarian regimes" would sprout wherever the United States withheld its support. As an "investment in world freedom and world peace," the president requested $400 million, which Congress granted in May by votes of 62 to 23 in the Senate and 287 to 107 in the House, following vigorous debate.[76] Truman's under secretary of state, Dean Acheson, helped craft the message, using universalistic language that he hoped was "clearer than truth."[77] The speech cut "like a bolt of lightning ... through the confused international atmosphere," *Life* magazine declared.[78]

A British request for help in Greece and a lingering squabble over the Dardanelles served as immediate catalysts for the Truman Doctrine. When the Germans withdrew from Greece in 1944, much of the countryside had come under the control of communist and other leftist Greek nationalist resistance fighters. Intent on preserving their influence in the eastern Mediterranean, the British soon reinstated the Greek government-in-exile. Violence erupted in December 1944. British troops, transported to Greece on U.S. ships, engaged the leftists in vicious warfare. The rebels, hoping to gain political power through elections, signed a peace treaty in February 1945.

From then until March 1946, when civil war flared again, the British-sponsored Athens regime persecuted its political foes. The United States sent warships to Greek ports and aid through the Export-Import Bank. In September, Navy Secretary Forrestal announced a permanent U.S. fleet in the Mediterranean. Although the Greek government was reportedly "reactionary, ... weak, stupid, and venal," Washington preferred a friendly regime to a leftist or communist one.[79] Greece limped along, staggered by war-wrought devastation and civil turmoil. On February 21, 1947, the economically hobbled British informed Washington that they were pulling out. Truman's special message to Congress answered London's appeal with uncommon alacrity.

Critics charged that Truman backed a ruthless Greek regime. Others preferred economic over military aid, recommended UN action, and feared that the Soviets would interpret the Truman Doctrine as threatening a world crusade. Critics also doubted that Soviet aggression threatened Greece and Turkey. Greek leftists, though communist-led, had minimal ties with the Soviet Union. Churchill always credited Stalin for keeping the bargain he made at their 1944 Moscow conference to stay out of the Greek imbroglio. In fact, Stalin disliked the nationalist Greek communists because the independent-minded Yugoslav leader Tito gave them aid. Yet Truman simplistically claimed that all communists took their orders from Moscow.

The Dardanelles question also had greater complexity than Truman acknowledged. The Soviets complained that Turkey had permitted German warships to pass through the Dardanelles straits into the Black Sea during World War II. Stalin insisted at Yalta that he could not "accept a situation in which Turkey had a hand on Russia's throat."[80] When Turkey refused joint control with the Soviets, Moscow threatened action. The presence of Soviet troops near the Turkish border in August 1946 prompted the U.S. State-War-Navy Coordinating Committee to assert that "the only thing which will deter the Russians will be the conviction that the United States is prepared ... to meet aggression with the force of arms."[81] The ostentatious dispatch of a U.S. carrier task force to Istanbul may have caused the Soviets to moderate their demands. Ignoring legitimate Soviet concerns about the Dardanelles, Truman reflexively concluded that Stalin sought to subjugate Turkey. Aid to Turkey under the Truman Doctrine pulled that Soviet neighbor into the U.S. orbit.

American aid and advisers flowed to Greece after 1947, with U.S. officials taking charge of the Greek government. More than 350 American officers accompanied the Greek army in its counterinsurgency campaign. Truman claimed another Cold War victory. Yet the Greek rebels lost in October 1949 not only because of U.S. intervention but because the Soviet Union refused to help them and because Tito sealed off the Yugoslav border to deny them a sanctuary.

U.S. interest in the Mediterranean region also entangled the United States in the Palestine question (see map, p. 379). Zionists around the world had long sought a Jewish homeland, and at the end of World War II they pressed London and Washington to open British-mandated Palestine to Holocaust survivors. When the British blocked immigration and turned back ships such as the *Exodus* loaded with Jewish refugees, some Zionists resorted to arms. Valuing Mideast oil and Arab anticommunism, Washington at first sought to satisfy Arabs who opposed increased Jewish immigration and a new Jewish state. Yet many Americans, including President

Truman, welcomed the humanitarian opportunity to assist displaced persons once terrorized by Nazism. Truman also noted in a not-so-subtle remark about Jewish voters in the United States: "I do not have hundreds of thousands of Arabs among my constituents."[82] The president groped for a policy while fending off angry charges from Zionists that he did too little to back an independent Jewish state. "Jesus Christ couldn't please them when he was here on this earth, so how would anyone expect that I would have any luck?" Truman griped.[83] The beleaguered British meanwhile referred the Palestine question to a special UN commission that recommended partition into Jewish and Arab states, with 56 percent of the mandate area assigned to the Zionists. In fall 1947, Truman endorsed partition. Fighting between Arabs and Jews escalated, and millions of private dollars from Jewish Americans flowed to co-religionists in Palestine to buy weapons.

Truman tilted further toward the Zionists after Chaim Weizmann visited in March 1948. This Zionist leader (soon to be the first president of Israel) initially thought Truman "will never jeopardize his oil concessions for the sake of the Jews, although he may need them when the time of election arrives."[84] For reasons of politics and Cold War strategy, however, Truman formally extended diplomatic recognition to Israel on May 14, 1948. Presidential aides Clark Clifford, David Niles, and Max Lowenthal had persuaded Truman that Israel would "line up on the side of the United States a far abler force" than the Arabs, thereby bolstering the American position vis-à-vis the Soviet Union in the Middle East.[85] Although Secretary of State George Marshall bluntly warned the president that he "would vote against

Founders of the New Israel, 1948. Formerly the High Commissioner for Refugees under the League of Nations, America's first ambassador to Israel James G. MacDonald (1886–1964; on left) enjoys tea after presenting his credentials to Israel's President Chaim Weizmann (1874–1952) and Prime Minister David Ben-Gurion (1886–1973; on right). The historian Michelle Mart has observed that "Jews in the postwar period first symbolized a complete lack of masculinity for their role as victims and then masculine resurgence in their survival and construction of a new state," an image that commanded respect from Americans. (National Archives)

George F. Kennan (1904–2005). Graduate of Princeton, Pulitzer Prize–winning historian, career diplomat, and recognized expert on Soviet affairs, Kennan was Mr. "X" in 1947 when he first articulated the containment doctrine. This brilliant man served Ambassador Harriman in Moscow and then headed the State Department's Policy Planning Staff (1947–1949). Later he became ambassador to Russia (1952) and Yugoslavia (1961–1963). In the 1970s and 1980s he emerged as a leading critic of the nuclear arms race. The biographer Bruce Kuklick calls Kennan "the first intellectual middleman of postwar national security studies, someone with an interest in ideas and a knack for conveying them to a less scholarly audience in Washington and elsewhere." (Library of Congress)

you" in the election if Truman recognized Israel, subsequent Israeli military victories over the armies of five Arab states prompted the State Department to reassess Israel's importance as a potential ally in the containment of the Soviet Union. By war's end in early 1949, some 780,000 of 1,300,000 Palestinians had become refugees in Lebanon and Jordan, while Israel came to occupy 77 percent of Palestine.

Containment became the byword of the time, and George F. Kennan, director of the State Department's Policy Planning Staff, wrote the definitive statement. The July 1947 issue of the major journal *Foreign Affairs* carried "The Sources of Soviet Conduct," written by a mysterious Mr. "X," soon revealed as Kennan. The United States must adopt a "policy of firm containment," he wrote, "designed to confront the Russians with unalterable counterforce, at every point where they show signs of encroaching upon the interests of a peaceful and stable world." Such pressure might force the "mellowing" of Soviet policy. Kennan sketched a picture of an aggressive, uncompromising Soviet Union driven by ideology, moving "inexorably along a prescribed path, like a persistent toy automobile wound up and headed in a given direction, stopping only when it meets some unanswerable force."[86] Although Kennan opposed military means to implement containment, his muscular language suggested otherwise. Most U.S. leaders shared the view put forth by one analyst: "Containment allowed no role for diplomacy until the climactic final scene in which the men in the white hats accepted the conversion of the men in the black hats."[87]

One of Kennan's most vocal critics, the journalist Walter Lippmann, called containment a "strategic monstrosity" because it did not distinguish vital from peripheral areas. Lippmann prophetically observed that the "policy can be implemented only by recruiting, subsidizing and supporting a heterogeneous array of satellites, clients, dependents and puppets." He proposed the removal of all foreign troops from Europe to ease tension. Denying that Soviet forces stood poised to attack Western Europe, Lippmann sadly concluded that Truman and Mr. "X" had abandoned their essential responsibility—diplomacy. "For a diplomat to think that rival and unfriendly powers cannot be brought to a settlement is to forget what diplomacy is about."[88]

Europe Divided: The Marshall Plan, Germany, and NATO

In 1947–1948 U.S. goals for Western Europe crystallized under the banner of containment. Economic reconstruction, hunger relief, the merging of Germany's western zones with a Western European economic system, reinvigorated trade with the United States, the ouster of communists from government in Italy and France, the settlement of colonial disputes, the blockage of neutralist tendencies, and the building of military alliances all became linked with the prevention of leftist gains across the continent. By 1947 the United States had already spent $9 billion in the region. Despite assistance through the United Nations Relief and Rehabilitation Administration (UNRRA), World Bank, and International Monetary Fund, plus the loan to Britain and expenditures for the military occupation of Germany, Europe's continued economic prostration left it vulnerable to communist exploitation.

A multibillion-dollar deficit also meant that Europeans could not buy American products unless they received dollars from the United States.

On June 5, 1947, at Harvard University, Secretary of State George C. Marshall called for a comprehensive, coordinated program to revive Europe. A halting orator, Marshall delivered his historic message in only 1,500 words. Europe, he said, needed help to overcome "economic, social and political deterioration of a very grave character." He urged the European nations to initiate a collective plan to spur productivity and ensure the survival of "free institutions" on the Continent.[89] Conservative U.S. critics lambasted the proposal as a "preposterous scheme for a worldwide redistribution of wealth," while Henry Wallace warned that the "Martial Plan" could only deepen Europe's ideological divide.[90] But British Foreign Secretary Ernest Bevin and French Foreign Minister Georges Bidault conferred and soon accepted Marshall's proposal, shaping it according to American specifications. They reluctantly invited Soviet Foreign Minister V. M. Molotov to join them for a meeting in Paris in June.

Smelling a capitalist trap, Molotov suggested loosely structured arrangements designed to protect national sovereignties. Bevin and Bidault, knowing that Washington insisted on an integrated effort, rejected national shopping lists. Molotov then abruptly left Paris. Moscow ultimately rejected the Marshall Plan because the plan sought to revive West Germany and envisioned Eastern Europe shipping raw materials to industrial Western Europe (thereby becoming "a tool against the USSR," in Stalin's words), while a large influx of dollars into the Soviet sphere of influence potentially undercut Soviet power and interests.[91] Truman, in fact, had never wanted Soviet participation in the European Recovery Program (ERP), as the Marshall Plan became known. "At best," the historian Michael J. Hogan has written, "American officials saw Marshall's plan as a way to break Soviet influence in Eastern Europe; at worst, they were counting on Soviet opposition to galvanize support for the plan in Congress."[92] Congress in any case would probably have opposed an initiative that included the Soviet Union and its clients. The effect was nonetheless to widen the Cold War chasm. Stalin declared that the world had now been split irrevocably into "two camps." He demanded "total conformity" from his allies and instituted a feeble Molotov Plan for Eastern Europe.[93] Congress passed the Economic Cooperation Act in March 1948, against the backdrop of the coup in Czechoslovakia, divisive Italian elections, and the growing crisis over Germany. After a bellicose speech to a joint session of Congress, Truman garnered the Marshall Plan a vote of 69 to 17 in the Senate and 329 to 74 in the House. Congress approved $4 billion for the program's first year. Before ending in December 1951, the Economic Cooperation Administration had sent $12.4 billion into the needful European economy.

The Marshall Plan sparked impressive Western European industrial production and investment and started the region toward self-sustaining economic growth. The ERP, noted the administrator Paul Hoffman, "got Europe on its feet and off our backs."[94] It also stimulated the American economy by requiring recipients to spend some of the U.S. aid on American goods; in this way, the profitable flow of U.S. exports to traditional European markets continued. The program accelerated the anticommunist shift of the European trade union movement, and it won votes for political parties that backed the generous U.S. project.

V. M. Molotov (1890–1986). Popularly known as "stone ass," the Soviet foreign minister (1939–1949; 1952–1956), a tough-minded negotiator, cleared most decisions with Stalin. When he became angry, a bump appeared on his forehead, alerting adversaries of trouble. In his memoirs Molotov stressed *realpolitik:* "What we did … we did superbly, we strengthened the Soviet state. That was my chief task. My task as minister of foreign affairs was to see to it that we weren't cheated." (*The Reporter,* 1956. Copyright 1956 by The Reporter Magazine Co.)

Critics have noted shortcomings as well. The price of a "revved-up capitalist economy," writes the historian Victoria de Grazia, were decreased wages, higher commodity prices, a weakened labor movement, and an increasingly homogeneous consumer landscape that reflected American products and styles.[95] Europe remained, at least for the short term, dependent on American aid, less able to make its own choices. And while the plan's authors trumpeted its democratic promise, some American money funded European colonial wars. The program bypassed the United Nations and the Economic Commission for Europe, where it might have operated with less divisiveness. The ERP encouraged restrictions on East-West trade and helped revive West Germany, heightening Moscow's fears of its nemesis. In 1951 the Economic Cooperation Administration merged into the Mutual Security Administration, with 80 percent of American aid to Western Europe becoming military in nature. To U.S. contemporaries involved in crafting the plan, it culminated a "brief season of daring and wisdom" that had commenced with the Truman Doctrine—a period wherein "the United States forsook isolationism and assumed leadership of the West in the Cold War."[96] "Scholarly scrutiny has stripped some Herculean features from this view," writes the historian Robert L. Beisner, but "the rapidity of the administration's response remains striking."[97]

Essen, Germany. In the rubble of this German city rested a new citizen, who because of American reconstruction aid could expect to have a full stomach. According to the historian Thomas A. Schwartz, "the United States pursued a 'dual containment' policy in Europe, designed to keep both the Soviet Union and Germany from dominating the Continent. … The two policies, which were inextricably linked, were always in a delicate balance; the United States could not contain the Soviet Union in Europe without German strength, and it could not maintain its hold over the German Federal Republic without the Soviet threat." (Harry S. Truman Library)

Unaware that "the Soviet army in Germany was configured for defensive," not offensive, operations, and believing the Soviets capable of overrunning Western Europe in six months, the Pentagon sought intensified U.S. rearmament.[98] In July 1947, Congress passed the National Security Act, which streamlined the military establishment. The act created the Department of Defense and the National Security Council (NSC) to advise the president, as well as the Central Intelligence Agency (CIA) to gather and collate information. The CIA's vague, open-ended mandate prompted some members of Congress to fear an "American Gestapo" run amok, even as that agency secretly recruited ex-Nazis and other agents for subversive activities across Europe.[99] In Europe in March 1948, Britain, France, and the three Benelux nations, with U.S. encouragement, signed the Brussels Treaty for collective defense. In June the Senate passed (64 to 4) Vandenberg's resolution applauding that effort and suggesting American participation.

U.S. leaders fought the Cold War not only through "power politics, but also with words and images."[100] The United States implemented the Fulbright Program in 1948. The brainchild two years earlier of Senator J. William Fulbright, Democrat of Arkansas and a former Rhodes scholar, this example of "public diplomacy" sought to breach cultural barriers and inculcate a favorable image of the United States worldwide. The Fulbright Program sponsored educational exchanges. Faculty and students went abroad to teach and study, and their counterparts from other countries came to the United States. By 1953 elites in twenty-eight nations participated in the program in Europe, Asia, and the Middle East. In some countries, former Fulbrighters achieved political prominence and helped keep their governments friendly to Washington. To combat anti-American propaganda in what Truman described as a "great campaign of truth," some American and European intellectuals organized the Congress of Cultural Freedom in 1950.[101] The CIA secretly subsidized this effort to promote America in Europe.

The United States also endorsed in 1948 the World Health Organization (WHO), a specialized United Nations agency that fulfilled a "two-pronged strategy of education and disease-fighting." Targeting borderless epidemic diseases such as malaria, tuberculosis, and syphilis, with a "sense of international fellowship," WHO physicians blanketed the earth to promote prevention and administer vaccines.[102] Washington has traditionally supplied the largest share of the WHO's budget.

Truman summarized American foreign policy in his inaugural address of January 20, 1949, listing four central points. First, he endorsed the United Nations. Second, he applauded the European Recovery Program. Third, he revealed that the United States was planning a North Atlantic defense pact. And fourth, he announced a "bold new program" of technical assistance for "underdeveloped areas."[103] Under the ensuing Point Four Program, launched in 1950, countries such as Afghanistan and Iran received millions in loans for hydroelectric dams and other modernization projects to create "an environment in which societies which directly or indirectly menace ours will not evolve."[104]

On April 4, 1949, the United States, Canada, and ten European countries signed the North Atlantic Treaty in Washington. Article 5 provided "that an armed attack against one or more … shall be considered an attack against them all."[105] A skeptical Senator Robert Taft, Republican from Ohio, saw NATO as a threat to

Dollars and Atomic Diplomacy. In this Soviet view of U.S. foreign policy, Truman wields the atomic bomb and the money bag. Note Winston S. Churchill on the right. (*Krokodil,* USSR)

Dean Acheson (1893–1971).
A graduate of Yale and Harvard and a wealthy lawyer, Acheson became secretary of state in 1949. Polished and arrogant, he served as secretary of state until 1953. The historian Robert L. Beisner writes that Acheson's "fingerprints—whole hand and footprints are all over the president's diplomacy and national security policies." Acheson told Truman that in the Cold War there are no "rules, no umpire, no prizes for good boys, no dunce caps for bad boys. … Good intentions are not worth a damn, moral principles are traps, weakness and indecision are fatal." (National Portrait Gallery, Smithsonian Institution, Washington D.C./Art Resource, NY)

the Soviet Union that would eventually spur an arms race, and he feared that the president could now commit American troops almost at will without constitutional restraint. Other dissenters questioned the precise nature of the Soviet threat: Was it military, political, or ideological? After all, no Soviet military attack seemed imminent. Was the United States overextending itself?

The Truman administration welcomed NATO as much for political as for military purposes. A popular saying quipped that NATO kept the Soviets out, the Americans in, and the Germans down. In other words, the alliance prevented a revival of "appeasement psychology" by permitting the United States to rearm West Germany while reassuring Europeans that Germany would be controlled by a multinational organization.[106] U.S. officials also believed that Western Europe needed a "general stiffening of morale" through the creation of NATO, not only to deter the Soviets, but to stimulate capital investment and encourage an energetic reconstruction effort in the newly launched Marshall Plan.[107] Depicting new allies as insecure members of the same family, Kennan recommended that "we must exhibit more confidence in them than we may actually feel—string them along a little."[108] On July 21, 1949, the Senate approved the NATO Treaty by an 82 to 13 margin. Two days later, Truman sent a Mutual Defense Assistance Bill to Congress requesting more than a billion dollars for European military aid. Containment had taken a distinctly military turn, and the stakes grew bigger.

After the Soviets exploded an atomic device in August 1949, Truman ordered development of a thermonuclear or hydrogen "superbomb," saying that "since we can't obtain international control we must be strongest in atomic weapons."[109] By mid-1950 the U.S. arsenal already held some 300 atomic bombs and more than 260 aircraft that could drop them on Soviet targets. The Soviets responded to NATO with the Warsaw Pact in 1955, the same year that they detonated their first hydrogen bomb, three years after the U.S. H-bomb. The major National Security Council Paper Number 68 (NSC-68), an April 1950 report requested by Truman, predicted prolonged global tension, Soviet military expansion, and relentless communist aggression. Washington had to persuade the public to support larger defense budgets and higher taxes. Paul Nitze, who replaced Kennan as head of the Policy Planning Staff, wrote most of NSC-68, and he glossed over complexities. The document treated communism as a monolith. It spoke of the "free world," overlooking the many undemocratic nations allied with the United States. It postulated that communism orchestrated the world's troubles, ignoring the indigenous origins of anticolonial rebellions. It made sweeping assumptions about Soviet motives and capabilities, exaggerating the communist "threat." But how to convince Americans to support the report's prescriptions? "We were sweating over it, and then—with regard to NSC-68—thank God Korea came along," recalled an Acheson aide (see Chapter 8).[110] Shortly thereafter Truman ordered NSC-68's implementation.

Stalin initially viewed NATO with disdain. Though the United States "screams war," he told Chinese Premier Mao Zedong in December 1949, it "is actually afraid of war."[111] Yet even as the two superpowers consolidated their respective spheres, Moscow appealed in spring 1950 for a dialogue to reduce tensions. Secretary Dean Acheson ridiculed the Soviet "Trojan dove," vowing to build U.S. "situations of strength" throughout the world.[112] As Lippmann had predicted, diplomacy became a victim of the Cold War.

Allies and Adversaries in Asia

Asia experienced a major reconfiguration after World War II. In Indochina, Burma, and Indonesia the old imperial system crumbled. The colonial powers looked to the United States to help them salvage what they could. Japan suffered defeat and occupation. Korea, formerly dominated by Japan, was divided along the thirty-eighth parallel by the Soviet Union and the United States. Civil war loomed in China.

If the Soviets ran some of the Eastern European countries, the Supreme Commander for the Allied Powers, General Douglas MacArthur, ran Japan. Unlike Germany, Japan had no zones. A Far Eastern Advisory Commission included Soviet members, but MacArthur treated Moscow's representative like "a mere piece of furniture."[113] The United States also assumed control over Micronesia (the Marianas, Marshalls, and Carolines), Okinawa, Iwo Jima, and more than a hundred other Pacific outposts. The Pacific Ocean was becoming an "Anglo-Saxon lake."[114] As if to demonstrate the point, on July 7, 1946, the United States tested an atomic bomb on the Marshall Island of Bikini.

General Douglas MacArthur (1880–1964) and Emperor Hirohito (1901–1989). This famous photograph of the first meeting of the Japanese emperor and the American supreme commander on September 27, 1945, has been called the "wedding photo" because, as the scholar Yoshikuni Igarashi points out, it suggests the "sexualized power relations" between a conquering United States and a submissive Japan. The meeting provided "the necessary ingredients for a melodrama—humiliation and the heroic acceptance of humiliation" by Hirohito. (Courtesy of the General Douglas MacArthur Foundation)

The first two years of occupation brought *demokurashii* to Japan: a new constitution, war crimes trials, women's rights, the dismantling of feudalism, the liberalization of education, even American censorship of Japanese films so as to depict Emperor Hirohito not as a god but as a constitutional monarch. Japan seemed to bury its militarism, and a more pacifist culture emerged. As the Cold War escalated, U.S. officials reversed course because they needed a "stable Japan, integrated into the Pacific, friendly to the U.S."[115] During 1947–1950, labor unions were restricted, production controls in war-related industries relaxed, the antitrust program suspended, communists barred from government and university positions, and former Japanese leaders reinstated. A pro-American outlook was inculcated, as millions learned conversational English from the radio program "Come, Come English," "Tokyo Boogie-Woogie" became the hit song of 1948, and such U.S.-based philanthropic organizations as the Ford Foundation and the Carnegie Corporation promoted cross-cultural exchanges to "bridge the postwar divide."[116] Mutual suspicions endured, however, as shown in the racial discrimination experienced in both cultures by the some 200,000 Japanese-American children born during the occupation. In the end, the historian John W. Dower has noted, "the ideals of peace and democracy took root in Japan—not as a borrowed ideology or imposed vision, but as a lived experience and a seized opportunity."[117]

The restoration of Japan had international ramifications. Chinese communists feared a Western scheme to rebuild Japan for aggression against China. Japanese recovery, U.S. officials argued in early 1950, required the development of Asian markets for Japanese products and containment strategies to undercut communists throughout the region. Moscow suspiciously eyed U.S. expansion in Asia and protested separate peace negotiations with Japan. In September 1951, the United States and fifty other nations signed a peace treaty that restored Japanese sovereignty, gave the United States a base on Okinawa, and permitted the retention of foreign troops in Japan. Stalin refused to sign. A bilateral security pact also permitted U.S. troops and planes on Japanese soil. From Pearl Harbor, a merciless war, and the atomic blasts to a peaceful occupation and Japanese-American cooperation—how to explain the dramatic shift? Continued demonic images and punishment no longer served the interests of either party. Americans sought a Cold War ally, and the Japanese sought a helping hand. Symbolic of Japan's new status as "ally and subordinate partner," the *Saturday Review* editor Norman Cousins, beginning in 1953, raised money from readers in a well-publicized effort to fund reconstructive surgery in the United States for twenty-five Japanese females disfigured by the atomic blasts. The "Hiroshima Maidens" showed that the Japanese were "no longer vermin" but "innocent virgins, victims, and patients" with whom "Americans could identify and feel sympathy, and their femininity distanced them from the masculinity of the Japanese military."[118]

Americans also wanted a peaceful China within the U.S. sphere of influence. For decades Americans had preached the Open Door, dreamed of vast Chinese markets and Christian converts, and considered China a special friend. A recovering Japan needed Asian markets, necessitating friendly ties with China. The Chinese communists had other ideas, challenging the American-backed regime of Jiang Jieshi. During 1945–1949, the United States became a counterrevolutionary force in a revolutionary country.

American postwar goals sought a united noncommunist country under Jiang as a U.S. ally. At the end of the war, American forces transported Jiang's soldiers to Manchuria in a race to beat Mao Zedong's communists there. As he had promised at Yalta, Stalin signed a treaty of friendship with Jiang's regime in August 1945, hoping to deter a Japan expected to "restore her might in 20, 30 years."[119] Stalin pressed Mao to cooperate with Jiang. Calling Mao a "cave-dweller-like Marxist," the Soviet premier preferred a cooperative China that would pose no threat along the 4,150 miles of the Sino-Soviet border.[120] U.S. Foreign Service Officers reported from China that relations between Moscow and Mao remained fractious and that the communists would probably defeat Jiang without much help from Soviet troops in Manchuria.

Swashbuckling Ambassador Patrick J. Hurley managed to bring Mao and Jiang together for talks in fall 1945, but Jiang refused to make concessions, confident of American backing. In November, Hurley, with his typical blast-furnace approach, resigned and charged that pro-communist U.S. diplomats were plotting in favor of "Mouse Dung" and "Joe N. Lie" (as he called Mao and Mao's communist liaison to Jiang's government, Zhou Enlai).[121] Hurley's attack on the professional diplomats provided scapegoats for the American frustration over China. The "China experts" had not preferred Mao; they had simply reported that Jiang was corrupt, reactionary, and unlikely to gain the allegiance of the Chinese people, and that the communists would probably triumph. Criticized for having "warm hearts, but soft heads," the China hands eventually were forced from the State Department under pressure from red-baiting Senator Joseph McCarthy.[122]

After the Hurley debacle, in December 1945, Truman sent the "Marshall Mission" to China. Headed by the highly respected General George C. Marshall, it sought to unite the factions under a noncommunist government. The communists, seeing coalition government as a nonviolent route to power, accepted Marshall's cease-fire in January 1946. A grateful Mao praised Marshall's "fairness," reflecting

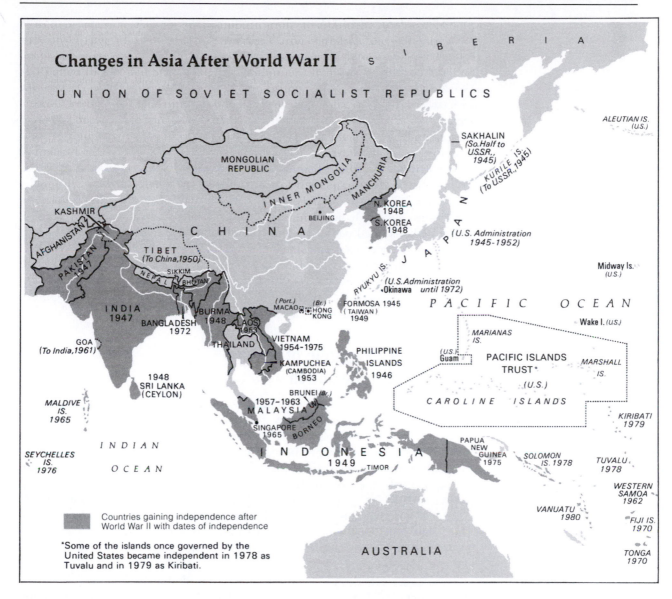

Changes in Asia After World War II

Countries gaining independence after World War II with dates of independence

*Some of the islands once governed by the United States became independent in 1978 as Tuvalu and in 1979 as Kiribati.

that "there are so many things I could learn from America" and assuring the general that although "in theory we support socialism, … at present we do not intend to put it into practice."[123] By May 1946, after Soviet forces had pulled out, 90 percent of Manchuria rested in communist hands. Jiang's decision to "give up a political solution" and storm Manchuria to challenge Mao doomed the cease-fire.[124] Marshall and the 1,000 U.S. military and naval personnel in China could not restrain the overconfident generalissimo, especially once Congress approved $51.7 million in "pipeline" equipment to nationalist forces in June 1946. "We were taken in," an embittered Mao said of U.S. mediation efforts. "We won't be cheated again."[125] A chagrined Marshall returned to Washington in January 1947 to become secretary of state.

Still hopeful of preventing a communist victory, Truman dispatched the "Wedemeyer Mission" to China in July 1947. General Albert C. Wedemeyer criticized the disarray of the Nationalists but concluded that China, like Greece, needed an aid program to curb the communist menace. That autumn Marshall released undelivered Lend-Lease goods to Jiang and sent more arms, advisers, and ammunition. To answer critics who wondered why Greece, but not China, should be saved from communism, the White House asked Congress in early 1948 for $570 million in China aid. China obtained $400 million in April.

Despite $3 billion in aid to Jiang since V-J Day, Washington failed to stop the communists' ascent. Jiang's American defenders called him a "great and genuine patriot" who wanted peace, but the Guomindong leader permitted inflation to run rampant, neglected tax and land reforms, launched risky military expeditions, tolerated corruption, and shunned negotiations.[126] Dispirited soldiers defected, and U.S. military equipment fell into communist hands. In this roundabout way, Mao's troops ironically got more aid from America than from the Soviet Union. "We picked a bad horse," President Truman lamented.[127]

The People's Republic of China and U.S. Nonrecognition

In June 1949, Mao Zedong stated that he was leaning to the side of socialism (the Soviet Union) against that "one great imperialist power" (the United States).[128] For many Americans, Mao's strident address simply confirmed Moscow's creation of another puppet state. Despite limited Soviet military aid ("not even a fart," Mao groused), Americans maintained that, as Acheson put it in the *China White Paper* of August 1949, "the Communist regime serves not [Chinese] interests but those of Soviet Russia."[129] The *White Paper* documents revealed that the United States could have done little because Jiang himself would do so little. In January 1949, Jiang sent China's gold supplies to the island of Formosa (Taiwan); in December, his Nationalist government followed. Mao's People's Republic formally assumed power in October.

Critics screeched that "China had been sold down the Yangtze" River by the Democrats.[130] Senator Styles Bridges (Republican of New Hampshire) and Representative Walter Judd (Republican of Minnesota) headed an informal and influential "China Lobby," which for years had advocated a major U.S. intervention in the Chinese civil war. They asked: If Truman sought to contain communism without geographical limit, as stated in the Truman Doctrine, why no intervention in China? Truman officials answered that China was too large, a land war in Asia unthinkable, Jiang unmanageable, and the monetary costs prohibitive. Jiang's mishandling of U.S. funds confirmed Truman's private view of the Guomindang as "grafters and crooks," and a Gallup poll of late 1948 showed "more people opposed to than supporting military aid to the Nationalists."[131] Still, as charges mounted that the president's administration was soft on communism in Asia, Truman rejected calls for a "realistic" U.S.-China policy of recognition, choosing instead to withhold formal diplomatic ties.[132]

Behind the nonrecognition policy lay growing Sino-American animosities. Anti-American Chinese sentiments mounted throughout the postwar half-decade, especially among students who protested the postwar U.S. military presence in Manchuria, denounced sexual misconduct by American troops, resented the "dumping" of American goods on Chinese markets, and branded as "imperialist" U.S. aid to the Guomindong.[133] In June 1949, when communist leaders asked to meet American Ambassador J. Leighton Stuart, Truman vetoed contact. He resented bombastic communist speeches that reminded Americans of their imperialist past, including military participation in the Boxer Rebellion and naval gunboat patrols on Chinese rivers in the 1920s and 1930s. Confiscating American property, the Chinese communists kept the U.S. consul general at Mukden under house arrest for two years before expelling him as a spy in October 1949.

From December 1949 through February 1950, in Moscow, Mao negotiated a treaty of friendship and alliance with the Soviet Union. Fearing a revived Japan and an expanded U.S. presence in Asia, Mao needed an ally. Stalin treated Mao like an inferior "younger brother" until the latter blurted in exasperation: "I only have had three tasks here: the first was to eat, the second was to sleep, and the third

"Sanmao Was 'Clobbered' by a Drunken American Sailor" (1947). *The Adventures of Sanmao, The Orphan*, a comic strip created by the famous Chinese cartoonist Zhang Leping, "typified the negative Chinese images of America military personnel" as "reckless, drunken, lascivious, and haughty," writes the historian Hong Zhang. In this strip, the hungry and miserable orphan boy Sanmao is clobbered over the head by a hairy, big-nosed American sailor with a whiskey bottle. (From Zhang Leping, Adventures of Sammao, The Orphan [1947; reprint, Hong Kong: Joint Publishing Co., 1981], p. 153.)

was to shit."[134] Mao eventually obtained an alliance obligating both parties to come to each other's assistance if attacked by a third party. U.S. observers played down the meager foreign aid that Moscow promised and dismissed Sino-Soviet differences over Mongolia and Manchuria. Despite Acheson's changed view that the "basic objectives of Moscow are very hostile to the basic objectives of China," Truman denounced the treaty as the Soviet conquest of China.[135] Assistant Secretary of State Dean Rusk mocked the new government in early 1951: "The Peiping regime may be a colonial Russian government—a Slavic Manchukuo on a larger scale. It is not the Government of China. It does not pass the first test. It is not Chinese."[136] The "Chi Commies," as official U.S. cables tagged China's leadership, did not merit U.S. diplomatic recognition.

A Cold War Culture Emerges

"We were heirs to a smiling and victorious confidence," noted a U.S. writer who recalled the end of World War II.[137] In a world ravaged by war, business and government officials cooperated to expand U.S. foreign trade. By 1947 the United States accounted for one-third of the world's exports. Americans exploited Middle Eastern oil and tapped the raw materials of the Third World, importing manganese ore from Brazil and India, for example. Open Door pronouncements helped spur this trade and facilitate the investment of $12 billion abroad by 1950. Liberated countries usually welcomed, or "invited," a limited American presence, and U.S. agents eagerly flooded Europe and Asia not only with dollars and soldiers, but also with jazz and baseball, "blue jeans and T-shirts, Coca-Cola and chewing gum, U.S. comics and movie stars."[138] "The American occupation [in Austria] cannot be complete without Mickey Mouse and Donald Duck," an official cabled Washington in 1945.[139]

The American belief that "Stalin was out to dominate the world" seemed to justify U.S. expansionism.[140] Austere, intransigent, and ruthless, Stalin executed strong-arm rule in Eastern Europe while Moscow churned out crude communist propaganda that dramatized the East-West rift. With threats more common than compromises, the rude Soviet diplomatic style caused Western diplomats to respond in a similar "crabbed and rancorous" manner.[141] The containment doctrine became commanding dogma in the United States. "Like medieval theologians," Senator Fulbright noted, "we had a philosophy that explained everything to us in advance, and everything that did not fit could be readily identified as a fraud or a lie or an illusion."[142]

Yet Americans exaggerated the Soviet threat, claiming for it a strength it did not possess, blaming it for trouble it did not start, and identifying a communist monolith that did not exist. The tough-talking Soviets eventually turned Eastern Europe into client states and tested Western resolve in Berlin, but right after World War II the Soviets acted cautiously, lacking a long-range air force, air defenses, the atomic bomb, and a surface fleet. "The most important thing," Stalin told an Albanian communist in January 1948, "is not to provoke our former allies."[143] Moscow actually snubbed independent communists such as Tito and Mao and could not control communists in Western Europe. And even in the

Third World (the former colonial and "semicolonial" countries of Africa, Asia, and Latin America), where communists sometimes led movements for independence, revolutions sprang not from the Kremlin but from indigenous sources—colonial, ethnic, religious, political, cultural, and economic.[144] Whereas Washington explained its mission as containment, Moscow charged "strangulation" and deemed the "Open Door policy as dangerous to a nation as foreign military invasion."[145]

Americans nonetheless came to believe that Moscow ignited, fueled, and exploited unrest around the world. Erecting a global wall against communism, the United States supported imperialist allies such as France, which attempted to restore its colonial power in Vietnam against a popular nationalist movement. Believing that the Soviet Union masterminded revolutions, Washington sniffed international conspiracy and refused to recognize the People's Republic of China, hardly a Soviet puppet. Dependent on imports of uranium from South Africa to sustain a Cold War nuclear strategy and economy, the Truman administration backed white, anticommunist regimes that suppressed black nationalism, acting "as a reluctant uncle—or godparent—at the baptism of apartheid."[146]

Even in Latin America, indirect U.S. intervention to oust communists from the Costa Rican government in 1948 "mirrored the hardening" of Washington's Cold War policies elsewhere.[147] In 1945–1946 Washington had given tacit support for democratic interventions by exile groups against Caribbean dictatorships, but by the end of the decade it "placed a premium on stability out of concern that Communists might exploit situations of unrest."[148] Panama thus received Point Four assistance in 1950 to combat "Communist-influenced subversive elements," and U.S. military aid flowed to the Péron regime in Argentina after 1947 because of Cold War fears.[149] As the United States "extended the hemispheric purview of the Monroe Doctrine to every corner of the globe," anti-Americanism—defined as "an antagonism to the United States that is systemic, seeing it as completely and inevitably evil"—intensified, both among disempowered overseas groups who came to identify the United States with political repression, and among indigenous elites who found "an ideal tool for delegitimizing critics: branding them as American agents."[150] Because Kremlin leaders also believed that "the world was going our way" and covertly sought to undermine U.S. allies in Latin America, Asia, and Africa, Moscow must also share responsibility for the Cold War's devastating human and political costs.[151]

The American Cold War mentality rested on a binary outlook that "defined America's national identity by reference to the un-American 'other,'" namely the Soviet Union.[152] Federally funded behavioral studies depicted the Soviet Union as a "predatory expansionist power" and the United States as a "defensive status quo power."[153] Hollywood released films about World War II in which "the real unseen enemy was Communism," and postwar movies such as *Sands of Iwo Jima* (1949) and *Twelve O'Clock High* (1949) stressed the "psychological conditioning necessary for a new kind of war."[154] Television became both a "popular medium of shared experience" for families and communities but also a venue for challenging the emergent Cold War consensus, as such media personalities as Rod Serling produced shows that depicted atomic testing as "something volatile and potentially catastrophic."[155] Civil defense planners worked to curb atomic anxiety by drawing cartoon "icons of the friendly atom or congenial mushroom cloud" to "train youngsters and parents alike

"Uncle Sam's World Wide Umbrella."   The United States undertook new global responsibilities after World War II. The depiction of smaller countries as children and Uncle Sam as the adult protector suggests a favorite American metaphor of family in which difficult allies were seen as naive children in need of tutelage and nurturing from the altruistic United States. *(The Reporter,* 1950. Copyright 1950 by Fortnightly Publishing Co., Inc.)

to trust the nuclear authorities without question." Whether targeting children or adults, such depictions "seemed to turn nuclear hazards into child's play."[156]

The Cold War reshaped political priorities at home. The perennial need for "national security" came to justify huge military budgets that starved the infrastructure and fostered a presidential secrecy that undermined the constitutional checks-and-balances system. Even strident anticommunists wondered whether America was becoming like "the very power we are trying to combat; intolerant, secretive, suspicious, cruel, and terrified of internal dissension because we have lost our own belief in ourselves and in the power of our ideals."[157] Race became an issue of global importance, as the "ferment of freedom" in the decolonizing world exposed America's own "Achilles heel" of institutionalized inequality evident in segregation.[158] With the United Nations calling racial discrimination a "burning question" of "immense importance," the President's Committee on Civil Rights warned that "the treatment which our Negroes receive" plays "into the hands of the Communist propagandists."[159] In a brilliant stroke, Truman appointed Eleanor Roosevelt to the United Nations, where she exhibited "the will, the clout, and the skill" to push through the UN Declaration on Human Rights, adopted in 1948.[160] Yet too often Truman's administration used scare tactics to get its way. Most foreign policy debates centered on how much to spend, not whether to spend. Presidential authority expanded accordingly. Bipartisanship also allowed Truman to depict any critic as "a son-of-a-bitch and not a true patriot." If people "will swallow that," Acheson observed, "then you're off to the races."[161]

People swallowed it. Debate became shallow. Tolerance of dissenting views and the fearless inquiry so essential to democracy deteriorated during the early Cold War. Unprincipled agitators exploited public anxiety, charging that communist conspiracies wormed through official Washington. Consistent with Cold War rhetoric that put a "premium on hard masculine toughness and rendered anything less than that soft, timid, feminine, and as such a real or potential threat to the security of the nation," the demagogic Republican Senator Joseph McCarthy leveled hundreds of false accusations that equated political dissidence, "sexual perversion," and social nonconformity with communism.[162] During the 1948 campaign, the president himself practiced the "red-baiting" so common to Cold War politics when he deliberately linked Progressive party candidate Henry A. Wallace, a dissenter from the "get-tough" policy, to the communists. Three years before Senator McCarthy charged government officials with treason, the Truman administration itself instituted a federal employee loyalty program to identify and ferret out suspected subversives. By not clearly distinguishing dissent from subversion, Truman opened the door for McCarthyism.

As the Cold War grew more perilous, so too did the ominous presence of the atomic bomb. Advertisers depicted a "world of tomorrow" that blithely linked rocket technology with such modern household conveniences as washing machines.[163] But military estimates exposed the dangers of a growing arms race, with analysts projecting that Soviet stockpiles of "10, 50, 100" atomic bombs could devastate American cities and kill tens of millions by 1953.[164] Government officials, magazine editors, strategic analysts, scientists, and fiction writers alike, again and again, issued apocalyptic forecasts, sketching pictures of a radioactive global wasteland if nuclear weapons were not controlled. In late 1949, after the Soviet atomic success, the *Bulletin of the Atomic Scientists* moved the hands of its "doomsday clock" to three minutes before midnight. A few months after the United States exploded the first hydrogen bomb in 1953, the hands moved one minute closer.

FURTHER READING FOR THE PERIOD 1945–1950

Some works cited in Chapter 6 cover particular leaders and the transition from war to peace.

For general studies of the Cold War era relevant to this chapter and others that follow, see A. C. Bacevich, *The Long War* (2007); Alfred E. Eckes and Thomas W. Zeiler, *Globalization and the American Century* (2003); David S. Fogelsong, *The American Mission and the "Evil Empire"* (2007); Michael H. Hunt, *The World Transformed* (2004); Walter LaFeber, *America, Russia, and the Cold War* (2006); John Lewis Gaddis, *The Cold War* (2005); Klaus Larres and Ann Lane, eds., *The Cold War* (2001); David Leebaert, *The Fifty-Year Wound* (2002); Melvyn P. Leffler, *For the Soul of Mankind* (2007); Ralph B. Levering, *The Cold War* (2005); Martin Medhurst and H. W. Brands, eds., *Critical Reflections on the Cold War* (2001); Robert J. McMahon, *The Cold War* (2003); Thomas J. McCormick, *America's Half Century* (1994); David S. Painter, *The Cold War* (1999); Thomas G. Paterson, *Meeting the Communist Threat* (1988) and *On Every Front* (1992); Ronald E. Powaski, *The Cold War* (1997); David Reynolds, *One World Divisible* (2000); Michael S. Sherry, *In the Shadow of War* (1995); Marc Trachtenberg, ed., *Between Empire and Alliance* (2003); Odd Arne Westad, *The Global Cold War* (2006); and Vladislav M. Zubok, *A Failed Empire* (2007).

U.S. leaders and influential Americans of the early Cold War period are studied in Rudy Abrahamson, *Spanning the Century* (1992) (Harriman); Kai Bird and Martin J. Sherwin, *American Prometheus* (Oppenheimer); Robert L. Beisner, *Dean Acheson* (2006); Russell D. Buhite, *Douglas MacArthur* (2008); David Callahan, *Dangerous Capabilities* (1990) (Nitze); James Chace, *Acheson* (1998); John C. Culver and John Hyde, *American Dreamer* (2000) (Henry Wallace); Irwin F. Gellman, *The Contender* (1999) (Nixon); Mary Ann Glendon, *A World Made New* (2001) (Eleanor Roosevelt); Peter Goodchild, *Edward Teller* (2004); James G. Hershberg, *James B. Conant and the Birth of the Nuclear Age* (1993); Robert E. Herzstein, *Henry R. Luce, Time, and the American Crusade in Asia* (2005); Townsend Hoopes and Douglas Brinkley, *Driven Patriot* (1992) (Forrestal); Walter Isaacson and Evan Thomas, *The Wise Men* (1986) (various); Bruce Kuklick, *Blind Oracles* (various); Nelson D. Lankford, *The Last American Aristocrat* (1996) (David Bruce); Jeffery C. Livingston, *Swallowed by Globalism* (2001) (John Vorys); Kyle Longley, *Senator Albert Gore, Sr.* (2004); John Lukacs, *George Kennan* (2007); David McCullough, *Truman* (1992); John T. McNary, *Acheson and Empire* (2001); Robert J. McMahon, *Dean Acheson and the Creation of an American World Order* (2008); Arnold Offner, *Another Such Victory* (2002) (Truman); James C. Olson, *Stuart Symington* (2003); Forrest C. Pogue, *George C. Marshall* (1963–1987); Darlene Rivas, *Missionary Capitalist* (2002) (Nelson Rockefeller); David Robertson, *Sly and Able* (1994) (Byrnes); T. Michael Ruddy, *The Cautious Diplomat* (1986) (Bohlen); Elizabeth Edwards Spalding, *The First Cold Warrior* (2006) (Truman); Mark A. Stoler, *George C. Marshall* (1989); and Charles Thorpe, *Oppenheimer* (2006).

Many books include and critique the Soviet leader's foreign policy, most recently: Robert Conquest, *Stalin* (1991); Yoram Gorlizki and Oleg V. Khlevniuk, *Cold Peace* (2004); Walter Laqueur, *Stalin* (1990); Edward Radzinsky, *Stalin* (1996); Geoffrey Roberts, *Stalin's Wars* (2006); and Robert Service, *Stalin* (2005).

For the origins of the Cold War, see John Lewis Gaddis, *The United States and the Origins of the Cold War* (1972); James L. Gormly, *The Collapse of the Grand Alliance* (1987); Michael J. Hogan, *A Cross of Iron* (1998); Michael H. Hunt, *The World Transformed* (2004); John Ikenberry, *After Victory* (2001); Caroline Kennedy-Pipe, *The Origins of the Cold War* (2007); Melvyn P. Leffler, *A Preponderance of Power* (1992) and *The Specter of Communism* (1994); Ralph B. Levering et al., *Debating the Origins of the Cold War* (2002); Vojtech Mastny, *The Cold War and Soviet Insecurity* (1996); Wilson D. Miscamble, *From Roosevelt to Truman* (2007); Thomas G. Paterson, ed., *Cold War Critics* (1971); David Reynolds, ed., *The Origins of the Cold War in Europe* (1994); Patrick Wright, *Iron Curtain* (2007); Vladislav Zubok, *A Failed Empire* (2007); and Vladislav Zubok and Constantine Pleshakov, *Inside the Kremlin's Cold War* (1996).

For the early years of the United Nations Organization, see Carol Anderson, *Eyes off the Prize* (2003) (African Americans); Robert C. Hilderbrand, *Dumbarton Oaks* (1990); Townsend Hoopes and Douglas Brinkley, *FDR and the Creation of the U.N.* (1997); and Stephen Schlesinger, *Act of Creation* (2003).

The atomic bomb, nuclear questions, and their cultural impact are discussed in Gar Alperovitz, *The Decision to Use the Atomic Bomb* (1995); Kai Bird and Lawrence Lifschultz, eds., *Hiroshima Shadows* (1998); Paul Boyer, *By the Bomb's Early Light* (1986) and *Fallout* (1998); Craig Campbell, *The Atomic Bomb and the Origins of the Cold War* (2008); Gerald J. De Groot, *The Bomb* (2005); Michael D. Gordin, *Five Days in August* (2007) and *Red Cloud at Dawn* (2009); Hugh Gusterson, *People of the Bomb* (2004); Tsuyoshi Hasegawa, *Racing the Enemy* (2005) and ed., *The End of the Pacific War* (2007); Margot A. Henriksen, *Dr. Strangelove's America* (1997); Michael J. Hogan, ed., *Hiroshima in History and Memory* (1996); David Holloway, *Stalin and the Bomb* (1994); David F. Krugler, *This is Only a Test* (2006); Robert Jay Lifton and Greg Mitchell, *Hiroshima in America* (1995); Robert J. Maddox, *Hiroshima in History* (2007) and *Weapons for Victory* (2004); Sean Malloy, *Atomic Tragedy* (2008); Rosemary B. Mariner and G. Kurt Piehler, eds., *The Atomic Bomb and American Society* (2009); Robert S. Norris, *Racing for the Bomb* (2002) (Leslie Groves); Richard Rhodes, *Dark Sun* (1987); Joe O'Donnell, *Japan 1945* (2005); Andrew J. Rotter, *Hiroshima* (2008); Martin Sherwin, *A World Destroyed* (1975); Ronald Takaki, *Hiroshima* (1995); Nina Tannenwald, *The Nuclear Taboo* (2005); J. Samuel Walker, *Prompt and Utter Destruction* (1997); Allan M. Winkler, *Life Under a Cloud* (1993); and Lawrence S. Wittner, *The Struggle Against the Bomb* (1993) (disarmament movement).

Studies that focus on Eastern Europe and Finland include Debra J. Allen, *The Oder-Neisse Line* (2003); László Borhi, *Hungary in the Cold War* (2004); James Jay Carafano, *Waltzing into the Cold War* (2002) (Austria); Jussi M. Hanhimäki, *Containing Coexistence* (1997) (Finland); Richard Lukacs, *Bitter Legacy* (1982) (Poland); Sabrina P. Ramet, *The Three Yugoslavias* (2006); and Eric Roman, *Hungary and the Victor Powers* (1996).

Anglo-American relations are discussed in Terry H. Anderson, *The United States, Great Britain, and the Cold War* (1981); Andrew Defty, *Britain, America, and Anti-Communist Propaganda, 1945–1953* (2004); Jeffrey A. Engel, *Cold War at 30,000 Feet* (2007); Fraser J. Harbutt, *The Iron Curtain* (1986); Michael F. Hopkins, *Oliver Franks and the Truman Administration* (2003); Arieh Kochavi, *Post-Holocaust Politics* (2002) (Britain and U.S.); Klaus Larres, *Churchill's Cold War* (2002); W. Roger Louis and Hedley Bull, eds., *The Special Relationship* (1986); Ritchie Overdale, *The English Speaking Alliance* (1985); and Randall B. Woods, *A Changing of the Guard* (1990).

The United States in the world economy and economic expansion are treated in William H. Becker, *The Market, the State, and the Export-Import Bank* (2003); Jacqueline Best, *The Limits of Transparency* (2005) (international finance); Kevin M. Casey, *Saving International Capitalism* (2001) (Truman years); Alan P. Dobson, *U.S. Economic Statecraft* (2002); Marc Flandreau, *International Financial History in the Twentieth Century* (2003); Diane Kunz, *Butter and Guns* (1997); David S. Painter, *Oil and the American Century* (1986); and Thomas Zeiler, *Free Trade, Free World* (1999).

Cultural relations are specifically explored in Christian G. Appy, *Cold War Constructions* (2000); Richard T. Arndt, *The First Resort of Kings* (2005); Laura A. Belmonte, *Selling the American Way* (2008); Lori Lyn Bogle, *The Pentagon's Battle for the American Mind* (2004); David Caute, *The Dancer Defects* (2005); Stanley Corkin, *Cowboys as Cold Warriors* (2004); Nicholas J. Cull, *The Cold War and the United States Information Agency* (2008); Thomas Doherty, *Cold War Cool Medium* (2005) (television); Chistopher Endy, *Cold War Holidays* (2004); Benjamin O. Fordham, *Building the Cold War Consensus* (1998); John Fousek, *To Lead the Free World* (2000); Jessica C. E. Gienow-Hecht, *Transmission Impossible* (1999); T. Jeremy Gunn, *Spiritual Weapons* (2009); Cynthia Lee Henthorn, *From Submarines to Suburbs* (2006); Willian Inboden, *Religion and American Foreign Policy, 1945-1960* (2008); Peter J. Kuznick and James Gilbert, eds., *Rethinking Cold War Culture* (2001); Raina Mitter and Patrick Major, eds., *Across the Blocs* (2004); Ruth Oldenziel and Karin Zachmann, *Cold War Kitchen* (2009); Richard Pells, *Not Like Us* (1997); Shawn J. Parry-Giles, *The Rhetorical Presidency* (2002) (propaganda); Uta G. Poiger, *Jazz, Rock, and Rebels* (2000); Andrew Ross and Kristin Ross, *Anti-Americanism* (2004); Barry Rubin, *Hating America* (2004); Frances Stoner Saunders, *The Cultural Cold War* (1999); William W. Savage, Jr., *Commies, Cowboys, and Jungle Queens* (1998); James Swoch, *Global TV* (2009); and Reinhold Wagnleitner, *Coca-Colonization and the Cold War* (1994) (Austria).

For Western European issues, including economic reconstruction, Austria, and the Marshall Plan, see Günter Bischof and Anton Pelinka, *The Americanization/Westernization of Austria* (2003); John Bledsoe Bonds, *Bipartisan Strategy* (2002); James Jay Carafano, *Waltzing into the Cold War* (2002); Francis M. Carroll, *The American Presence in Ulster* (2005); Michael Creswell, *A Question of Balance* (2006) (France); Victoria de Grazia, *Irresistible Empire* (2005); David W. Ellwood, *Rebuilding Europe* (1992); Dominik Geppert, *The Postwar Challenge* (2003); John L. Harper, *America and the Reconstruction of Italy* (1986) and *American Visions of Europe* (1994); William I. Hitchcock, *France Restored* (2001) and *The Struggle for Europe* (2003); Michael J. Hogan, *The Marshall Plan* (1987); Tony Judt, *Postwar* (2005); John Killick, *The United States and European Integration, 1945–1960* (1998); Deborah Kisatsky, *The United States and the European Right, 1945–1955* (2005); Brian A. McKenzie, *Remaking France* (2005); James E. Miller, *The United States and Italy* (1986); Alan S. Milward, *The Reconstruction of Western Europe, 1945–51* (1984); Thomas G. Paterson, *Soviet-American Confrontation* (1973); Sallie Pisani, *The CIA and the Marshall Plan* (1991); Alexander Stephan, *The Americanization of Europe* (2006); Marc Trachtenberg, *A Constructed Peace* (1999); Irwin M. Wall, *The United States and the Making of Postwar France* (1991); and Imanuel Wexler, *The Marshall Plan Revisited* (1983).

For Germany, see Andrei Cherny, *The Candy Bombers* (2008) (Berlin airlift); Jeffrey M. Diefendorf et al., eds., *American Policy and the Reconstruction of West Germany* (1993); Carolyn Eisenberg, *Drawing the Line* (1996); Heide Fehrenbach, *Race after Hitler* (2005); Petra Goedde, *GIs and Germans* (2003); Norman J. W. Goda, *Nazi Criminals and the Cold War* (2007); William Glenn Gray, *Germany's Cold War* (2003); Maria Hohn, *GIs and Frauleins* (2002); Patrick Thaddeus Jackson, *Civilizing the Enemy* (2006); James McAllister, *No Exit* (2002); David Monod, *Settling Scores* (2005) (music); Norman Naimark, *The Russians in Germany* (1995); Thomas Parrish, *Berlin in the Balance, 1945–1949* (1998); Timothy L. Schroer, *Recasting Race after World War II* (2007); Thomas A. Schwartz, *America's Germany* (1991); and John Willoughby, *Remaking the Conquering Heroes* (2001).

For the Truman Doctrine and containment, consult Denise M. Bostdorff, *Proclaiming the Truman Doctrine* (2008); John Lewis Gaddis, *Strategies of Containment* (2005); John O. Iatrides, ed., *Greece at the Crossroads* (1995); Judith S. Jeffery, *Ambiguous Commitments and Uncertain Policies* (1999); Jon V. Kofas, *Intervention and Underdevelopment* (1989) (Greece); and Bruce R. Kuniholm, *The Origins of the Cold War in the Near East* (1980).

NATO and military questions are studied in Christopher Layne, *The Peace of Illusions* (2006); Lawrence S. Kaplan, *The Long Entanglement: NATO's First Fifty Years* (1999) and *NATO 1948* (2007); Raymond P. Ojserkis *Beginnings of the Cold War Arms Race* (2003); S. V. Papacosma et al., *NATO After Fifty Years* (2001); Steven L. Rearden, *History of the Office of the Secretary of Defense* (1984); Gustav Schmidt, *A History of NATO* (2001); Edward J. Sheehy, *The U.S. Navy, the Mediterranean, and the Cold War* (1992); E. Timothy Smith, *The United States, Italy, and NATO* (1991); and Joseph Smith, ed., *The Origins of NATO* (1990).

U.S. relations with Asia, including decolonization, are discussed Nick Cullather, *Illusions of Influence* (1994) (Philippines); Hal M. Friedman, *Creating an American Lake* (2000); Richard J. Jensen, *Trans-Pacific Relations* (2003); Christina Klein, *Cold War Orientalism* (2003); Robert J. McMahon, *Colonialism and Cold War* (1981) (Indonesia), *The Cold War on the Periphery* (1994) (India and Pakistan) and *The Limits of Empire* (1999) (Southeast Asia); Allan R. Millett, *Their War for Korea* (2005); Andrew Roadnight, *United States Policy Toward Indonesia in the Truman and Eisenhower Years* (2002); Andrew J. Rotter, *Comrades at Odds* (2000) (India); Mark Selden, *War and State Terrorism* (2004); William Stueck, *The Road to Confrontation* (1981); and Nicholas Tarling, *Britain, Southeast Asia and the Onset of the Cold War, 1945–1950* (1998). For works on Vietnam and Indochina, see Chapter 9.

For Japan and the American occupation, see Ian Baruna, *Investigating Japan* (2003); John W. Dower, *Embracing Defeat* (1999); Robert D. Eldridge, *The Origins of the Bilateral Okinawa Problem* (2001); Mire Koikuri, *Pedagogy of Democracy* (2008); Yukiko Koshiro, *Trans-Pacific Racisms and the U.S. Occupation of Japan* (1999); Walter LaFeber, *The Clash* (1997); Tim Maga, *Judgment at Tokyo* (1999); Michael S. Molasky, *The American Occupation of Japan and Okinawa* (1999); Nicholas E. Sarantakes, *Keystone* (2000) (Okinawa); Michael Schaller, *The American Occupation of Japan* (1985); Masako Shibata, *Japan and Germany under the U.S. Occupation* (2005) (education); Naoko Shibusawa, *America's Geisha Ally* (2006); John Swenson-Wright, *Unequal Allies* (2005); and Tadashi Yamamoto, *Philanthropy and Reconciliation* (2006).

For China and the recognition question, see Carolle J. Carter, *Mission to Yenan* (1997); Gordon Chang, *Friends and Enemies* (1990); Thomas J. Christensen, *Useful Adversaries* (1996); Sergei Goncharov, John Lewis, and Xue Litai, *Uncertain Partners* (1993); Michael H. Hunt, *The Genesis of Chinese Communist Foreign Policy* (1996); T. Christoper Jesperson, *American Images of China* (1996); Chen Jian, *Mao's China and the Cold War* (2001); Ronald C. Keith, *The Diplomacy of Zhou Enlai* (1989); Robert P. Newman, *Owen Lattimore and the "Loss" of China* (1992); Simei Qing, *From Allies to Enemies* (2007); Priscilla Roberts, *Behind the Bamboo Curtain* (2006); Michael M. Sheng, *Battling Western Imperialism* (1998); William Stueck, *The Wedemeyer Mission* (1984); Nancy B. Tucker, *Patterns in the Dust* (1983) and *Taiwan, Hong Kong, and the United States* (1994); Odd Arne Westad, *Cold War and Revolution* (1993) and *Decisive Encounters: The Chinese Civil War* (2003); Hong Zhang, *America Perceived* (2002); and Shu Guang Zhang, *Deterrence and Strategic Culture* (1992).

For the Middle East, Iran, and the new state of Israel, see Irvine H. Anderson, *Biblical Interpretation and Middle East Policy* (2005); Uri Bialer, *Cross on the Star of David* (2005) (Israel); Michael J. Cohen, *Truman and Israel* (1990); Lawrence Davidson, *America's Palestine* (2001); Michael J. Devine et al., *Israel and the Legacy of Harry S. Truman* (2008); Louise L. Fawcett, *Iran and the Cold War* (1992) (1946 crisis); James F. Goode, *The United States and Iran, 1946–51* (1989); Peter L. Hahn, *The United States, Great Britain, and Egypt* (1991), *Caught in the Middle East* (2004), and *Crisis and Crossfire* (2005); Burton I. Kaufman, *The Arab Middle East and the United States* (1996); Douglas Little, *American Orientalism* (2002); Mark H. Lytle, *The Origins of Iranian-American Alliance, 1941–1953* (1987); Rafael Medoff, *Militant Zionism in America* (2002); Michael B. Oren, *Power, Faith, and Fantasy* (2007); William A. Rugh, *American Encounters with Arabs* (2006); and David Schoenbaum, *The United States and the State of Israel* (1993).

Relations with other Third World nations, including Latin America, are explored in Charles D. Ameringer, *The Caribbean Legion* (1996); Scott L. Bills, *The Libyan Arena* (1995); Thomas Borstelmann, *Apartheid's Reluctant Uncle* (1993) (South Africa); Laura Briggs, *Reproducing Empire* (2002) (Puerto Rico); Mary Ann Heiss and Peter L. Hahn, eds., *Empire and Revolution* (2001); Zachary Karabell, *Architects of Intervention* (1999); Michael L. Krenn, *The Chains of Interdependence* (1996) (Central America); Kyle Longley, *The Sparrow and the Hawk* (1997) (Costa Rica); Jason Parker, *Brother's Keeper* (2008) (British Caribbean); Stephen Schwartzberg, *Democracy and U.S. Policy Toward Latin America in the Truman Years* (2003); Gaddis Smith, *The Last Years of the Monroe Doctrine* (1994); and Odd Arne Westad, *The Global Cold War* (2005).

For Canada-U.S. relations, see Greg Donaghy, ed., *Canada and the Early Cold War, 1943–1957* (1998); Joseph Jockel, *No Boundaries Upstairs* (1989); and John H. Thompson and Stephen J. Randall, *Canada and the United States* (1998).

For espionage and the origins of the Central Intelligence Agency, see Richard Aldrich, *The Hidden Hand* (2001); Christopher Andrew, *The World Was Going Our Way* (2005) (KGB); Jeffrey G. Barlow, *From Hot War to Cold* (2009) (U.S. Navy); David M Barrett, *The CIA and Congress* (2005); Richard Breitman, *U.S. Intelligence and the Nazis* (2005); Sarah-Jane Corke, *U.S. Covert Operations and Cold War Strategy* (2008); R. Bruce Craig, *Treasonable Doubt* (2004) (Harry Dexter White); Peter Grose, *Operation Rollback* (2000); S. J. Hamrick, *Deceiving the Deceivers* (2004) (spies); John Earl Haynes and Harvey Klehr, *Venona* (1999) and *Early Cold War Spies* (2006); Peter A. Huchthausen, *Hide and Seek* (2009) (naval espionage); Susan Jacoby, *Alger Hiss and the Battle for History* (2009); Rhodri Jeffreys-Jones, *Cloak and Dollar* (2002); Ernest R. May, Philip Zelikow, et al., *Dealing with Dictators* (2006); Alfred W. McCoy, *A Question of Torture* (2006); Gregory Mitrovich, *Undermining the Kremlin* (2000); Katherine S. Olmsted, *Red Spy Queen* (2002) (Elizabeth Bentley); Jeffrey Richelson, *Spying on the Bomb* (2006); David F. Rudgers, *Creating the Secret State* (2000); Katherine A. Sibley, *Red Spies in America* (2004); Athan Theoharis, *Chasing Spies* (2002); Evan Thomas, *The Very Best Men* (1995); Thomas F. Troy, *Wild Bill and Intrepid* (1996); Hugh Wilford, *The CIA, the British Left, and the Cold War* (2003) and *The Mighty Wurlitzer* (2008); and G. Edward White, *Alger Hiss's Looking-Glass Wars* (2004).

For domestic politics, anticommunism, interest groups, and public opinion in the early Cold War period, see Jonathan Bell, *The Liberal State on Trial* (2004); David Ciepley, *Liberalism in the Shadow of Totalitarianism* (2006); Robert W. Cherny et al., *American Labor and the Cold War* (2004); Kyle Courdileone, *Manhood and American Political Culture* (2005); Bruce E. Field, *Harvest of Dissent: The National Farmers Union and the Early Cold War* (1998); Richard M. Fried, *Nightmare in Red* (1990) and

The Russians Are Coming! The Russians Are Coming! (1998); Aaron L. Friedberg, *In the Shadow of the Garrison State* (2003); John E. Haynes, *Red Scare or Red Menace?* (1996); Robert David Johnson, *Congress and the Cold War* (2006); Harvey Klehr and Ronald Radosh, *The Amerasia Spy Case* (1996); David F. Krugler, *The Voice of America and the Domestic Propaganda Battles, 1945–1953* (2000); Helen Laville, *Cold War Women* (2002) (international organizations); Azza Salama Layton, *International Politics and Civil Rights in the United States, 1941–1960* (1999); Scott Lucas, *Freedom's War* (1999); David Allan Mayers, *Dissenting Voices in America's Rise to Power* (2007); Brenda G. Plummer, *Rising Wind* (1996) (African Americans) and *Windows on Freedom* (2003); Ron Robin, *The Making of a Cold War Enemy* (2001); Timothy E. Smith, *Opposition Beyond the Water's Edge* (1999); Penny von Eschen, *Race Against Empire* (1997) (African Americans); and Wendy Wall, *Inventing the American Way* (2007).

See also the General Bibliography, Robert L. Beisner, ed., *Guide to American Foreign Relations Since 1600* (2003), and the following notes.

NOTES TO CHAPTER 7

1. Quoted in Hanson W. Baldwin, "Hiroshima Decision," in *Hiroshima Plus 20* (New York: Delacorte, 1965), p. 41.
2. Harold M. Agnew quoted in *Time*, CXXVI (July 29, 1985), 46.
3. Quoted in John Toland, *The Rising Sun* (New York: Random House, 1970), p. 780.
4. Quoted in *New York Times*, August 6, 1995.
5. Quoted in Peter Goodchild, *Edward Teller* (Cambridge: Harvard University Press, 2004), p. 108.
6. Quoted in Timothy L. Francis, "The Japanese Execution of American Aircrew at Fukuoka, Japan, During 1945," *Pacific Historical Review, LXVI* (November 1997), 481.
7. Quoted in Michael D. Gordin, *Five Days in August* (Princeton: Princeton University Press, 2007), p. 82.
8. Quoted in John M. Blum, ed., *The Price of Vision* (Boston: Houghton Mifflin, 1973), p. 474.
9. Paul Fussell, "Hiroshima," in Michael B. Stoff, ed., *The Manhattan Project* (New York: McGraw-Hill, 1991), p. 276.
10. Harry S. Truman, *Memoirs* (Garden City, NY: Doubleday, 1955–56; 2 vols.), I, 417.
11. Document 16, "Memorandum from Arthur B. Compton to the Secretary of War," June 12, 1945, in National Security Archive, ed., Electronic Briefing Book No. 162, "The Atomic Bomb and the End of World War II," (2005/2007).
12. Quoted in Kai Bird and Martin J. Sherwin, *American Prometheus* (New York: Knopf, 2005), p. 317.
13. Barton J. Bernstein, "Understanding the Atomic Bomb," *Diplomatic History*, XIX (Spring 1995), 267.
14. Mark Selden, "The United States and Japan in Twentieth-Century American Wars," in Mark Selden and Alvin Y. So, eds., *War and State Terrorism* (New York: Rowman & Littlefield, 2004), p. 30.
15. Robert Messer, "'Accidental Judgments, Casual Slaughters'" in *A World at Total War*, eds. Roger Chickering et al., (New York: Cambridge University Press, 2005), p. 298.
16. Quoted in Michael S. Sherry, *The Rise of American Air Power* (New Haven: Yale University Press, 1989), p. 341.
17. Naoko Shibusawa, *America's Geisha Ally* (Cambridge: Harvard University Press, 2006), p. 2.
18. *Ibid.*, p. 93.
19. Quoted in John Dower, *War Without Mercy* (New York: Random House, 1986), p. 73.
20. *Ibid.*, p. 4.
21. Quoted in Barton J. Bernstein, "Roosevelt, Truman, and the Atomic Bomb, 1941–1945," *Political Science Quarterly, XC* (Spring 1975), 61.
22. Barton J. Bernstein, "Japanese Buildup on Southern Kyushu," *Pacific Historical Review, LXVIII* (December 1999), 903.
23. Quoted in Lloyd C. Gardner, "Unconditional Surrender," in Dale Carter and Robin Clifton, eds., *War and Cold War in American Foreign Policy, 1942–62* (New York: Palgrave, 2002), p. 71.
24. Tsuyoshi Hasegawa, *Racing the Enemy* (Cambridge: Harvard University Press, 2005), p. 3.
25. Sadao Asada, "The Shock of the Atomic Bomb and Japan's Decision to Surrender—A Reconsideration," in Robert James Maddox, ed., *Hiroshima in History* (Columbia: University of Missouri Press, 2007), p. 46.
26. Quoted in Martin J. Sherwin, *A World Destroyed* (New York: Knopf, 1975), p. 224.
27. Truman, *Memoirs*, I, 416.
28. Stalin quoted in David Holloway, *Stalin and the Bomb* (Stanford: Stanford University Press, 1994), p. 132.
29. Tony Judt, *Postwar* (New York: Penguin, 2005), p. 40.
30. *Ibid.*, p. 13.
31. *Foreign Relations, 1946* (Washington, D.C.: Government Printing Office, 1969), VI, 707,
32. Quoted in Raymond P. Ojserkis, *Beginnings of the Cold War Arms Race* (Westport: Praeger, 2003), p. 8.
33. Quoted in Vladislav Zubok and Constantine Pleshakov, *Inside the Kremlin's Cold War* (Cambridge: Harvard University Press, 1996), p. 31.
34. Quoted in Arnold A. Offner, *Another Such Victory* (Stanford: Stanford University Press, 2002), p. 129.
35. Quoted in Gaddis Smith, *Dean Acheson* (New York: Cooper Square, 1972), p. 46.
36. Quoted in John Lewis Gaddis, *The United States and the Origins of the Cold War* (New York: Columbia University Press, 1972), p. 205.

37. Quoted in John Lewis Gaddis, "Harry S. Truman and the Origins of Containment," in Frank Merli and Theodore Wilson, eds., *Makers of American Diplomacy* (New York: Charles Scribner's Sons, 1974), p. 500.

38. Quoted in Geoffrey Roberts, *Stalin's Wars* (New Haven: Yale University Press, 2006), p. 24.

39. Quoted in Yoram Gorlizki and Oleg Khlevniuk, *Cold Peace* (New York: Oxford University Press, 2004), p. 35.

40. Quoted in Roberts, *Stalin's Wars*, p. 305.

41. T. H. Von Laue quoted in Ralph B. Levering, *The Cold War*, 2nd ed. (Wheeling, IL: Harlan Davidson, 2005), p, 23.

42. Quoted in John Lewis Gaddis, *The Cold War* (New York: Penguin, 2005), p. 57.

43. Lester Markel, "Opinion—A Neglected Instrument," in Lester Markel et al., *Public Opinion and Foreign Policy* (New York: Harper, 1949), p. 4.

44. Quoted in Elizabeth Edwards Spalding, *The First Cold Warrior* (Lexington: University Press of Kentucky, 2006), p. 1.

45. Vladimir O. Pechatnov, "Foreign Policy Correspondence Between Stalin and Molotov and Other Politburo Members, September 1945–December 1946," Working Paper no. 26, Cold War International History Project (Washington, D.C., September 1999), p. 25.

46. Quoted in Melvyn P. Leffler, "The Beginning and the End" (unpublished paper, 2002), p. 9.

47. Stalin quoted in Ralph B. Levering et al., *Debating the Origins of the Cold War* (New York: Rowman & Littlefield, 2002), p. 121.

48. George F. Kennan quoted in Gregory Mitrovich, *Undermining the Kremlin* (Ithaca: Cornell University Press, 2000), p. 39.

49. Quoted in Edward Pessen, *Losing Our Souls* (Chicago: Ivan R. Dee, 1993), p. 62.

50. Quoted in Marc Trachtenberg, *A Constructed Peace* (Princeton: Princeton University Press, 1999), p. 36.

51. Kennan quoted in Mitrovich, *Undermining*, p. 39.

52. Quoted in Gregg Herken, *The Winning Weapon* (New York: Knopf, 1980), p. 48.

53. Henry L. Stimson and McGeorge Bundy, *On Active Service in Peace and War* (New York: Harper & Brothers, 1948), p. 644.

54. Walter Millis, ed., *The Forrestal Diaries* (New York: Viking, 1951), p. 96.

55. *Foreign Relations, 1946, VII* (Washington, D.C.: Government Printing Office, 1969), 223.

56. Quoted in Alexander Werth, *Russia* (New York: Taplinger, 1971), pp. 328, 329.

57. William D. Leahy and Arthur Vandenberg quoted in Edward S. Mihalkanin, "James F. Byrnes," in Edward S. Mihalkanin, ed., *American Statesmen* (Westport: Greenwood Press, 2004), p. 93.

58. Quoted in James L. Gormly, *The Collapse of the Grand Alliance, 1945–1948* (Baton Rouge: Louisiana State University Press, 1987), p. 147.

59. Quoted in Thomas G. Paterson, *Meeting the Communist Threat* (New York: Oxford University Press, 1988), pp. 114, 115.

60. Frank Costigliola, "'Unceasing Pressure for Penetration,'" *Journal of American History, LXXXIV* (March 1997), 1333.

61. Quoted in Fraser J. Harbutt, *The Iron Curtain* (New York: Oxford University Press, 1986), p. 186.

62. "Churchill's Iron Curtain Speech and Stalin's Reply, March 1946," in Jussi Hanhimäki and Odd Arne Westad, eds., *The Cold War*, (New York: Oxford University Press, 2003), pp. 48, 49.

63. Quoted Michael B. Oren, *Power, Faith, and Fantasy* (New York: W.W. Norton, 2007), p. 480.

64. *Vital Speeches, XII* (October 1, 1946), 738–741.

65. Quoted in Arnold A. Offner, "Another Such Victory," *Diplomatic History, XXIII* (Spring 1999), 138.

66. W. Averell Harriman, "Certain Factors Underlying Our Relations with the Soviet Union," November 14, 1945, Harriman Papers, Library of Congress, Washington, D.C.

67. Baruch quoted in Shane J. Maddock, "The Nth Country Conundrum" (Ph.D. diss., University of Connecticut, 1997), p. 123.

68. Henry A. Wallace, "The Path to Peace with Russia," *The New Republic, CXV* (September 30, 1946), 401–406.

69. "The Novikov Telegram, Washington, September 27, 1946," *Diplomatic History, XV* (Fall 1991), 527.

70. Michael Creswell, *A Question of Balance* (Cambridge: Harvard University Press, 2006), p. 8.

71. Quoted in John Gimbel, "Project Paperclip," *Diplomatic History, XIV* (Summer 1990), 351.

72. Quoted in John Willoughby, *Remaking the Conquering Heroes* (New York: Palgrave, 2001), p. 33.

73. Heide Fehrenbach, *Race After Hitler* (Princeton: Princeton University Press, 2005), p. 1; Petra Goedde, *GIs and Germans* (New Haven: Yale University Press, 2003), p. 94.

74. Walter Bedell Smith quoted in Carolyn Eisenberg, *Drawing the Line* (New York: Cambridge University Press, 1996), p. 488.

75. Alexander Paniushkin quoted in Vojtech Mastny, *The Cold War and Soviet Insecurity* (New York: Oxford University Press, 1996), p. 59.

76. "The Truman Doctrine, March 1947," in Westad and Hanhimäki, *Cold War*, pp. 117–118.

77. Quoted in James Chace, "Dean Acheson," in Mihalkanin, ed., *American Statesmen*, 10.

78. Quoted in Dennis Merrill, "The Truman Doctrine," *Presidential Studies Quarterly, XXXVI* (March 2006), 34.

79. Paul A. Porter quoted in Howard Jones, *"A New Kind of War"* (New York: Oxford University Press, 1989), p. 30.

80. *Foreign Relations, Yalta*, 903.

81. Quoted in Eduard Mark, "The War Scare of 1946," *Diplomatic History, XXI* (Summer 1997), 383.

82. Quoted in Oren, *Power, Faith, and Fantasy*, p. 484.

83. Quoted *ibid.*, p. 488.

84. Quoted in Michael J. Cohen, *Truman and Israel* (Berkeley: University of California Press, 1990), p. 122.

85. Quoted *ibid.*, p. 193.

86. "X," "The Sources of Soviet Conduct," *Foreign Affairs, XXV* (July 1947), 13, 21, 60.

87. Henry Kissinger quoted in Frederik Logevall, "A Critique of Containment," *Diplomatic History, XXVIII* (September 2004), 473.

88. Walter Lippmann, *The Cold War* (New York: Harper & Brothers, 1947), pp. 18, 21, 60.

89. *Department of State Bulletin, XVI* (July 15, 1947), 1159–1160.

90. Senator George Malone quoted in Robert David Johnson, *Congress and the Cold War* (New York: Cambridge University Press, 2006), p. 23; Wallace quoted in David Mayers, *Dissenting Voices in America's Rise to Power* (New York: Cambridge University Press, 2007), p. 296.

91. Stalin quoted in Mikhail Narinskii, "The Soviet Union and the Marshall Plan," in Antonio Varsori and Elena Calandri, eds., *The Failure of Peace in Europe, 1943–48* (New York: Palgrave, 2002), p. 285.

92. Michael J. Hogan, *The Marshall Plan* (New York: Cambridge University Press, 1987), p. 52.

93. Quoted in Vladislav Zubok, "Stalin's Plans and Russian Archives," *Diplomatic History, XXI* (Spring 1997), 299.

94. Quoted in John Ikenberry, *After Victory* (Princeton: Princeton University Press, 2001), p. 201.

95. Victoria de Grazia, *Irresistible Empire* (Cambridge: Harvard University Press, 2005), p. 338.

96. Robert L. Beisner, *Dean Acheson* (New York: Oxford University Press, 2006), p. 55.

97. *Ibid.*

98. Matthew Evangelista, "The 'Soviet Threat,'" *Diplomatic History*, *XXII* (Summer 1998), 444.

99. Senator Edward Robertson quoted in David M. Barrett, *The CIA and Congress* (Lawrence: University Press of Kansas, 2005), p. 9.

100. Dominik Geppert, "'Proclaim Liberty Throughout all the Land," in Geppert, ed., *The Postwar Challenge* (New York: Oxford University Press, 2003), p. 339.

101. Quoted in Frances Stoner Saunders, *The Cultural Cold War* (New York: New Press, 1999), p. 85.

102. Amy L. S. Staples, "Constructing International Identity" (Ph.D. diss., Ohio State University, 1998), pp. 361, 373.

103. *Public Papers, Truman, 1949* (Washington, D.C.: Government Printing Office, 1964), p. 114.

104. Quoted in Nick Cullather, "Damming Afghanistan," *Journal of American History, LXXXXIX* (September 2002), 527.

105. *Department of State Bulletin, XX* (March 20, 1949), 340.

106. Quoted in Thomas G. Paterson, *On Every Front* (New York: Norton, 1992; rev. ed.), p. 87.

107. John D. Hickerson (Director, State Department Office of European Affairs) in *Foreign Relations, 1948* (Washington, D.C.: Government Printing Office, 1974), *III*, 183.

108. Quoted in Frank Costigliola, "The Nuclear Family," *Diplomatic History, XXI* (Spring 1997), 165, 166.

109. Quoted in Samuel R. Williamson and Steven L. Reardon, *Origins of U.S. Nuclear Strategy, 1945–1953* (New York: St. Martin's, 1993), p. 109.

110. Edward W. Barrett (Assistant Secretary of State for Public Affairs) in "Princeton Seminar," October 10–11, 1953, Box 65, Dean Acheson Papers, Truman Library.

111. Conversation between Stalin and Mao, December 16, 1949, in *Cold War International History Project Bulletin*, nos. 6–7 (Winter 1995/1996), p. 5.

112. Dean Acheson, *Present at the Creation* (New York: Norton, 1969), p. 379; *Department of State Bulletin, XXII* (March 20, 1950), 1037.

113. Stalin quoted in D. Clayton James, *The Years of MacArthur* (Boston: Houghton Mifflin, 1985), pp. 26–27.

114. MacArthur quoted in John W. Dower, "Occupied Japan and the American Lake, 1945–1950," in Edward Friedman and Mark Selden, eds., *America's Asia* (New York: Vintage, 1971), p. 170.

115. John Paton Davies quoted in Michael Schaller, "Securing the Great Crescent," *Journal of American History, LXXIX* (September 1982), 395.

116. Yamamoto Tadeshi, "The Role of Philanthropy in Postwar U.S.-Japan Relations," in Tamamoto Tadashi et al., eds., *Philanthropy and Reconciliation* (New York: Japan Center for International Exchange, 2006), p. 21.

117. Dower, *Embracing Defeat*, p. 23.

118. Christina Klein, *Cold War Orientalism* (Berkeley: University of California Press, 2003), p. 150.

119. Quoted in Sergei Goncharov, John Lewis, and Xue Litai, *Uncertain Partners* (Stanford: Stanford University Press, 1993), p. 10.

120. Quoted in Ilya V. Gaiduk, *Confronting Vietnam* (Stanford: Stanford University Press, 2003), p. 4.

121. Quoted in John Maxwell Hamilton, *Edgar Snow* (Bloomington: Indiana University Press, 1988), p. 171; Robert A. Hart, *The Eccentric Tradition* (New York: Charles Scribner's Sons, 1976), p. 156.

122. Clare Boothe Luce quoted in T. Christopher Jesperson, *American Images of China* (Stanford: Stanford University Press, 1996), p. 181.

123. Quoted in Simei Qing, *From Allies to Enemies* (Cambridge: Harvard University Press, 2007), p. 78.

124. Jiang quoted *ibid.*, p. 83.

125. Quoted in He Di, "The Evolution of the Chinese Communist Party's Policy Toward the United States," in Harry Harding and Yuan Ming, eds., *Sino-American Relations, 1945–1955* (Wilmington, Del; Scholarly Resources, 1989), p. 40.

126. Henry R. Luce quoted in Robert E. Herzstein, *Henry R. Luce, Time, and the American Crusade in Asia* (New York: Cambridge University Press, 2005), p. 53.

127. Quoted in Thomas G. Paterson, "If Europe, Why Not China?" *Prologue, XIII* (Spring 1981), 37.

128. Quoted in William Stueck, *The Road to Confrontation* (Chapel Hill: University of North Carolina Press, 1981), p. 124.

129. Mao quoted in Li Zhisui, *The Private Life of Chairman Mao* (New York: Random House, 1994), p. 117; *United States Relations with China* (Washington, D.C.: Department of State, 1949), p. xvii.

130. Geraldine Fitch quoted in Jesperson, *American Images*, p. 179.

131. Quoted in Gordon H. Chang, *Friends and Enemies* (Stanford: Stanford University Press, 1990), p. 13; Ernest R. May, "China, 1945–1958: Making Hard Choices," in May and Philip D. Zelikow, eds., *Dealing with Dictators* (Cambridge: MIT Press, 2006), p. 47.

132. Anti-nuclear activist Maud Russell quoted in Karen Garner, *Precious Fire* (Amherst: University of Massachusetts Press, 2003), p. 202.

133. Quoted in Hong Zhang, *America Perceived* (Westport: Greenwood, 2002), pp. 66, 120.

134. Mao quoted in Chen Jian, *Mao's China and the Cold War* (Chapel Hill: University of North Carolina Press, 2001), p. 53; Memorandum of Mao Conversation, July 22, 1958, in *Cold War International History Project Bulletin*, nos. 6–7 (Winter 1995/1996), p. 156.

135. Quoted in John Lewis Gaddis, *We Now Know* (New York: Oxford University Press, 1997), p. 62.

136. *Department of State Bulletin, XXIV* (May 28, 1951), 847.

137. L.E. Sissman, "Missing the Forties," *Atlantic Monthly, CCXXXIX* (October 1973), 35.

138. Geir Lundestad, "'Empire by Invitation' in the American Century," *Diplomatic History, XXIII* (Spring 1999), 189–217; Reinhold Wagnleitner, "The Irony of American Culture Abroad," in Lary May, ed., *Recasting America* (Chicago: University of Chicago Press, 1989), p. 295.

139. Quoted in Yukiko Koshiro, *Trans-Pacific Racisms and the U.S. Occupation of Japan* (New York: Columbia University Press, 1999), p. 159.

140. J. William Fulbright quoted in Daniel Yergin, "Fulbright's Last Frustration," *New York Times Magazine*, November 24, 1974, p. 87.

141. British Ambassador Clark Kerr quoted in Frank Costigliola, "'Mixed Up' and 'Contact'," *International History Review, XX* (December 1998), 803.

142. Quoted in Saunders, *Cultural Cold War*, p. 212.

143. Quoted in Mastny, *Soviet Insecurity*, p. 38.

144. Odd Arne Westad, *The Global Cold War* (New York: Cambridge University Press, 2005), p. 3.

145. Quoted in Levering, *Debating the Origins*, p. 130; Stalin quoted in W. Averell Harriman and Elie Abel, *Special Envoy to Churchill and Stalin* (New York: Random House, 1975), p. 528.

146. Thomas Borstelmann, *Apartheid's Reluctant Uncle* (New York: Oxford University Press, 1993), p. 197.

147. Kyle Longley, *The Sparrow and the Hawk* (Wilmington, Del; Scholarly Resources, 1997), p. 159.

148. Charles D. Ameringer, *The Caribbean Legion* (University Park; Pennsylvania State University Press, 1996), p. 197.

149. Ambassador Monnet Davis quoted in John Major, *Prized Possession* (New York: Cambridge University Press, 1993), p. 273.

150. Andrew Ross and Kristin Ross, "Introduction," in Andrew Ross and Kirstin Ross, eds., *Anti-Americanism* (New York: New York University Press, 2004), p. 3; Barry Rubin and Judith Colp Rubin, *Hating America* (New York: Oxford University Press, 2004), pp. ix, 117.

151. Christopher Andrew and Vasili Mitrokhin, *The World Was Going Our Way* (New York: BasicBooks, 2005), p. 24.

152. Michael J. Hogan, *A Cross of Iron* (New York: Cambridge University Press, 1998), p. 17.

153. Ron Robin, *The Making of a Cold War Enemy* (Princeton: Princeton University Press, 2001), p. 71.

154. Garry Wills, *John Wayne's America* (New York: Simon & Schuster, 1997), p. 154.

155. Andrew J. Falk, "Reading Between the Lines," *Diplomatic History, XXVIII* (April 2004), 200, 213.

156. Cynthia Lee Henthorn, *From Submarines to Suburbs* (Athens: Ohio University Press, 2006), pp. 250, 251.

157. Kennan quoted in Falk, "Reading," p. 209.

158. Walter White quoted in Jonathan Rosenberg, *How Far the Promised Land* (Princeton: Princeton University Press, 2006), p. 163; Azza Salama Layton, *International Politics and Civil Rights in the United States, 1941–1960* (New York: Cambridge University Press, 2000), p. 141.

159. Quoted in Paul Gordon Lauren, "The International Perspective," in Brenda Gayle Plummer, *Window on Freedom* (Chapel Hill: University of North Carolina Press, 2003), pp. 29, 31.

160. Carol Anderson, *Eyes off the Prize* (New York: Cambridge University Press, 2003), p. 133.

161. Dean Acheson Oral History Interview, Truman Library.

162. K.A. Courdileone, *Manhood and American Political Culture in the Cold War* (New York: Routledge, 2005), p. viii; David K. Johnson, *The Lavender Scare* (Chicago: University of Chicago Press, 2004), p. 5.

163. Henthorn, *Submarines to Suburbs*, p. 221.

164. Kennan quoted in Mitrovich, *Undermining*, p. 50.

CHAPTER 8

Cold War Prism: The Korean War and Eisenhower-Dulles Foreign Relations, 1950–1961

United Nations Leaflet in Korean War. *This leaflet, dropped by UN forces over North Korea, aimed to incite hostility in the Korean War among Chinese "volunteer" forces against their nation's leaders. The flyer shows a "Soviet advisor" manipulating the "Chinese Puppet" marionettes Liu Shaoqi, Mao Zedong, and Zhou Enlai. Such "psychological warfare," according to the scholar Ron Robin, was a "futuristic strategy for defeating the enemy" with images and words "rather than bullets." This propaganda piece reflected the widespread U.S. assumption that Joseph Stalin and his cohorts pulled the strings in China, North Korea, and other communist regimes. During the first eighteen months of the Korean War, U.S. aircraft dropped a billion leaflets on North Korean and Chinese forces. (Courtesy General Douglas MacArthur Foundation)*

DIPLOMATIC CROSSROAD

❖ *The Decision to Intervene in the Korean War, 1950*

AMERICAN AMBASSADOR TO South Korea John J. Muccio picked up the phone at 8:00 A.M. "Brace yourself for a shock," he heard his chief deputy say. "The Communists are hitting all along the front!"[1] At 4:00 A.M. that rainy Sunday morning of June 25, 1950, some 75,000 troops of the Democratic People's Republic of Korea (North Korea) "struck like a cobra" with armor and heavy artillery across the thirty-eighth parallel into South Korea.[2] As Soviet-made tanks rumbled forward along a 150-mile front, South Korean forces collapsed in a rout.

Around 10:00 P.M. the bad news reached Secretary of State Dean Acheson, resting at his Maryland farm. Acheson quickly requested an emergency session of the United Nations Security Council. The United States dominated that body, and the principle of collective security in the face of aggression seemed at issue. At 11:20 P.M. Acheson rang up President Harry S. Truman, at home in Independence, Missouri, and asked him to come to Washington the next day. State Department personnel worked through the night drafting a Security Council resolution that charged North Korea with "breach of the peace" for violating the boundary between north and south that the United States and the Soviet Union had drawn after World War II, and for trying to reunify the nation by force.[3] The Pentagon and State Department debated courses of action. Orders went out to evacuate Americans from Seoul. World War III had started, thought some American officials.

President Truman possessed "an appetite, too much of one, really, for unhesitating decision."[4] He stood low in opinion polls, in part because Senator Joseph McCarthy of Wisconsin charged Truman with "softness toward communism."[5] Former State Department official and accused Soviet spy Alger Hiss had been convicted of perjury in January, and China had gone communist a few months before. Bold action now would disarm the president's critics. Truman pondered history and drew facile lessons from the past: "Communism was acting in Korea just as Hitler, Mussolini, and the Japanese had acted ten, fifteen, and twenty years earlier."[6] No appeasement this time! Meanwhile, the Security Council passed the U.S. resolution condemning North Korea. Except for Yugoslavia's abstention, all members present voted "yes." The Soviet delegation, which could have vetoed the measure, remained surprisingly absent, boycotting the UN over its refusal to seat China's new communist government.

A stern, short-tempered Truman deplaned in Washington and headed for a meeting with top officials. "By God, I'm going to let them have it!" he told aides.[7] Nobody present doubted that the Soviet Union had engineered the attack, using its North Korean allies to probe for a soft spot in the American containment shield. The relationship between the Soviet Union and North Korea, one official remarked, was like "Walt Disney and Donald Duck."[8] "If we let Korea down," Truman predicted, "the Soviet [*sic*] will keep right on going and swallow up one piece of Asia after another. ... [Then] the Near East would collapse and no telling what would happen in Europe."[9]

The president and his advisers believed that the United States's reputation stood at risk. To falter would forfeit world leadership. Truman ordered General Douglas MacArthur in Japan to send military equipment to South Korea and to use U.S. war planes to attack the North Korean spearhead. He sent the Seventh Fleet into the waters between the Chinese mainland and Formosa (Taiwan) to forestall conflict between the two Chinas. Despite strong bipartisan support for Truman's decisions, some conservative Republicans indulged in McCarthyite recriminations. "The Korean debacle," Senator William E. Jenner of Indiana blustered, "reminds us that the same sell-out-to-Stalin statesmen … are still in the saddle, riding herd on the American people."[10] By Monday evening, North Korean forces neared Seoul. Truman learned about a downed North Korean plane, which he hoped "was not the last."[11]

Truman ordered U.S. aircraft and warships into full-scale action below the thirty-eighth parallel. He declared Formosa off limits to the mainland Chinese, and he dispatched military aid to Indochina and the Philippines. The president informed key legislators about his decisions, but he did not request a congressional declaration of war to stop a few "bandits in Korea."[12] Democratic Senator Tom Connally of Texas, chair of the Foreign Relations Committee, agreed: "If a burglar breaks into your house, you can shoot him without going down to the police station and getting permission."[13] Though Republican Senator Robert A. Taft complained that the president had done "the right thing the wrong way," most Americans applauded Truman's quick response.[14] The United Nations passed another U.S.-sponsored resolution urging members to aid South Korea, in essence endorsing actions the United States had already taken. Seoul fell nonetheless.

The continued North Korean push into the South sparked talk on June 28 and 29 of sending U.S. troops. Presidential supporters cited historical precedent: Jefferson had ordered action against the Barbary pirates and McKinley had sent troops into China during the Boxer Rebellion without prior congressional sanction. On the twenty-ninth, Truman ordered U.S. pilots to attack above the thirty-eighth parallel. On Friday, June 30, after visiting the war front, MacArthur asked Truman to send U.S. soldiers to Korea. The president gave the order amid reports of a North Korean surge southward into the Pusan perimeter. "We will hurl back the North Koreans, and if the Russkies intervene we will hurl them back, too!" declared one general.[15] The nation mobilized for an undeclared but initially popular war against communism. Truman tagged it a "police action."[16]

The Korean War and the "Trojan Horse" of American National Security

At first the war went badly for the United States, South Korea, and the small number of allied troops, all nominally under UN auspices. America's combat units took heavy losses, buying time to equip and transport a substantial offensive force. Discussions began on whether U.S. troops should cross the thirty-eighth parallel and attempt to liberate the North from communism. In August the president approved this drastic change in U.S. war aims.

Meanwhile, MacArthur persuaded the reluctant Joint Chiefs of Staff to approve a difficult amphibious assault at Inchon, hundreds of miles behind North Korean lines. On September 15, U.S. marines landed, pushed the North Koreans back, and quickly cut to Seoul. North Korean troops retreated north. "We want you to feel unhampered tactically and strategically to proceed north of the 38th Parallel," Secretary of Defense George C. Marshall cabled MacArthur.[17]

The Chinese warily watched events. When Truman sent the Seventh Fleet to neutralize Formosa on June 27, Beijing railed that the United States had exposed its "true imperialist face."[18] Shortly after the Inchon landing, Mao Zedong vowed not to wait "year after year unsure of when the enemy will attack us."[19] "We must repair the house before it rains," he said, informing his generals that "we may have no other options but to send our troops across the Yalu."[20] Mao and China's premier, Zhou Enlai, then insisted the United States keep away from that river boundary, a warning MacArthur dismissed as a bluff. The U.S. general's assessment might initially have been correct. When Stalin cabled Mao on October 1, urging the Chinese to "move at least five or six divisions toward the 38th parallel at once," the Chinese Communist Party chairman cabled back that immediate intervention would provoke "open conflict" with the United States. "The wounds inflicted on the people by the [Chinese Civil] war have not healed, we need peace."[21] Stalin then promised Soviet air support: "If war is inevitable, then let it be waged now, and not in a few years, when Japanese militarism will be restored as an ally of the USA."[22] After intense debate in Beijing, Mao reversed course because the "Americans would run more rampant" unless stopped.[23]

On October 8, United Nations forces under U.S. command trooped across the thirty-eighth parallel and drove deep into North Korea. Some 250,000 Chinese troops quietly crossed the Yalu on October 19, even after Stalin reneged on his promise of air support. On October 26, Chinese forces attacked. After fierce fighting, they retreated—"purposely showing ourselves to be weak," as their commander put it, "increasing the arrogance of the enemy, letting him run amuck, and luring them deep into our area."[24] U.S. officials abandoned caution. On November 8, for the first time, B-29 bombers struck bridges across the Yalu—bridges that linked North Korea and China. Then, on November 24, MacArthur launched a major offensive that would "have the boys home by Christmas."[25] Two days later, what one U.S. general called "a glut of Chinamen" swept down on MacArthur's unsuspecting armies.[26] Within weeks Chinese troops engulfed the North, propelling UN forces southward. "We are not retreating," one harried commander told a reporter. "We are merely attacking in another direction."[27] "It's mean and nasty," a U.S. soldier wrote his mother. "Muddy ground and rain do not make for good bedfellows … Still sleep with our boots on. … The rattle of rifle fire means someone nearby is having a rough go."[28]

MacArthur unsuccessfully requested Washington's approval of air strikes against China, now branded an "aggressor" by the United Nations. Truman hinted publicly that nuclear retaliation was under "active consideration."[29] "You can use the atomic bomb," Mao reportedly boasted. "I will respond with my hand grenade. I will catch the weak point on your part and defeat you."[30] British Prime Minister Clement Attlee urged negotiations. To Truman's assertion that the Chinese communists were "complete satellites" of Moscow, British Ambassador Oliver Franks argued

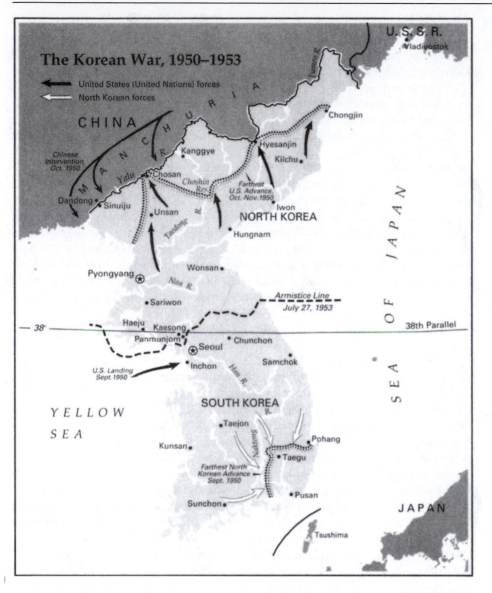

The Korean War, 1950–1953

→ United States (United Nations) forces
← North Korean forces

U.S.S.R.
Vladivostok

C H I N A

M A N C H U R I A

Chinese
Intervention
Oct. 1950

Tumen R.

Chongjin

Kanggye   Hyesanjin
Kilchu

Yalu   Chosan   Choshin
Res.
Dandong   Sinuiju   Unsan   Farthest
U.S. Advance.
Oct.-Nov. 1950

Taedong R.   Iwon

NORTH KOREA

Hungnam

Pyongyang   Wonsan
Nan R.

Sariwon   Armistice Line
July 27, 1953

Haeju   Kaesong
38°   Panmunjom   38th Parallel

Chunchon

Seoul   Samchok

U.S. Landing
Sept. 1950   Inchon

Han R.

SEA   OF   JAPAN

YELLOW
SEA

SOUTH KOREA
R.

Taejon

Naktong R.   Pohang

Kunsan   Taegu

Farthest North
Korean Advance
Sept. 1950

Sunchon   Pusan

JAPAN

Tsushima

that war with China would tighten a Sino-Soviet alliance based "on a coincidence of Chinese and Russian views, not Chinese subservience to Russian views."[31] In fact, Truman and his advisers rejected a wider war because they deemed the nuclear arsenal too small and feared Soviet retaliation in Europe.

By March 1951, MacArthur had shoved communist forces back across the thirty-eighth parallel. With fighting stabilized at roughly the prewar boundary, Truman contemplated negotiations, but "Mr. Prima Donna, Brass Hat, Five Star MacArthur" was hell-bent on reversing earlier defeats and slashing communist China.[32] MacArthur began publicly suggesting that his commander in chief

Douglas MacArthur (1880–1964). The West Point graduate commanded U.S. troops in Asia during World War II, directed the postwar occupation of Japan, and headed forces in Korea until relieved of duty by the president in April 1951. MacArthur later claimed he could have ended the Korean War in ten days: "I would have dropped between 30 and 50 atomic bombs" on China. (Library of Congress)

preferred appeasement. "There is no substitute for victory," he wrote Representative Joseph Martin in a letter made public in April.[33] On April 11 Truman, backed strongly by the Joint Chiefs, fired the seventy-one-year-old MacArthur for insubordination. "The son of a bitch should be impeached," MacArthur shot back.[34]

The general who had so badly miscalculated Chinese reactions returned home to ticker-tape parades. In a televised address he told Congress on April 19 that the war must be expanded. He closed famously: "Old soldiers never die; they just fade away."[35] Congressional hearings soon revealed that many Americans shared MacArthur's frustrations over Truman's "limited war," fought without atomic weapons, in Korea. Debate focused on different strategies for rolling back communism. "There was MacArthur's, which resembled a locomotive with no brakes. And there was Acheson's, a controlled rollback limited to Korea."[36]

Truman and Acheson pointed to the risk of world war. The Joint Chiefs of Staff Chairman, General Omar Bradley, warned that escalation might bring the Soviets in and cost the United States allies. A showdown with Soviet communism in Korea, he said, would be "the wrong war, at the wrong place, at the wrong time, and with the wrong enemy."[37] As one scholar observes, Bradley implied that the *right war* should be against the Soviet Union, "the *right place* to fight it was not at the periphery, but at the heart of Soviet power," and the *right time* was only after a U.S. military buildup.[38]

Peace talks began at Panmunjom in July 1951 but made little headway, and the fighting continued. Americans "want to subjugate the world," scoffed Stalin, "yet they cannot subdue little Korea."[39] Republican presidential candidate Dwight D. Eisenhower pledged in 1952, if elected, to go to Korea and seek an end to the conflict. Ike won, in part due to American frustration with limited war. He went to Korea, but found no easy solution. The most serious obstacle centered on prisoners of war (POWs). A few hundred American captives in the North, having undergone communist "brainwashing," remained above the thirty-eighth parallel. Thousands of Chinese and North Korean soldiers, encouraged by a "re-education" program in the South, likewise refused repatriation.

By 1953 the military buildup under NSC-68 had erased doubts about U.S. capabilities that had earlier precluded escalation. Announcing that the United States considered "the atomic bomb as simply another weapon in our arsenal," Eisenhower tried to intimidate the Chinese.[40] Jiang Jieshi's forces attacked the mainland, with Washington's approval. The death of Stalin in March probably helped bring the peace talks to a conclusion. A more flexible Moscow urged Beijing to settle the prisoner question. When South Korean President Syngman Rhee tried to sabotage the talks by releasing thousands of North Korean POWs, the Chinese launched a final offensive against South Korean positions.

On July 27, 1953, the adversaries signed an armistice. They agreed to turn over the POW issue to a committee of neutral nations (ultimately the POWs stayed where they chose, including twenty-one Americans in North Korea). The conferees drew a new boundary line close to the thirty-eighth parallel, which gained South Korea 1,500 square miles of territory. The agreement also provided for a demilitarized zone between the two Koreas.

The Korean War ranks as one of the costliest in twentieth-century history. More than 4 million died: 2 million North Korean civilians and 500,000 North Korean soldiers; 1 million South Korean civilians and some 47,000 South Korean soldiers; and official Chinese statistics list 148,000 dead. The United States, with 54,246 dead and 105,000 wounded, spent some $20 billion. The United States supplied 80 percent of the naval power and 90 percent of the air support, as well as 90 percent of foreign combat troops in this "United Nations" effort.

The Korean War has left many questions, some of which the partial opening of Chinese and Russian archives are helping to answer. Did Moscow start the Korean War? Truman officials claimed that the Soviet Union induced its North Korean client to attack. Moscow sensed an opportunity, some scholars have reasoned, because Acheson had, in a speech of January 12, 1950, implied that South Korea lay outside the American defense perimeter. Acheson's remarks could have "produced a certain influence" on the North Korean leader Kim Il Sung, who visited Moscow in April and promised a surprise attack that would win the war in three days.[41] A cautious Stalin told Kim to check with Mao, who anticipated American intervention but endorsed Kim's plans. Stalin then backed Kim's scheme, gambling that North Korea could score a quick victory and widen Soviet leverage in the East while strengthening Stalin's stature at home.

This "gamble thesis" raises difficult questions. Moscow did provide secret air cover, supplies, and training to North Korean and Chinese forces, but only after China's intervention on October 19. If Stalin engineered the initial attack, why did the Soviets not veto the Security Council's June condemnation of North Korea, which paved the way for a UN-sponsored intervention? Why did Stalin delay aiding communist forces, and why was all such assistance kept covert? Why would Moscow launch a European movement for peaceful coexistence and then torpedo that effort by provoking war in Asia? "We are thus left to reconcile the ubiquitous American assumption that Stalin started the war," one scholar notes, "with the unambiguous evidence that he distanced Soviet interests, prestige, and armed might from the conflict, allowing the United States ultimately to pulverize North Korea."[42]

Soviet relations with China influenced Stalin's decisions on Korea. If he refused to support Korean unification, Stalin invited charges that he hindered revolution in Asia and boosted Mao's China as a Soviet rival. Stalin may further have calculated that, even if the United States did not defend South Korea, Washington would never permit the additional loss of Taiwan. American efforts to protect Jiang Jieshi's government on Formosa would prevent rapprochement between Washington and Beijing and ensure China's continued reliance on Soviet economic and military aid. Perhaps, by endorsing North Korean actions while limiting Soviet visibility in the fighting, Stalin "covered all his bets," advancing the desired goal of a reunified, communist-controlled Korea while minimizing chances for "World War III"—a nuclear war with the United States.[43] Whatever Stalin's precise motives, he knew that war in Korea risked Soviet economic and strategic interests in northeast Asia. As for Mao, who expected imminent U.S. aggression against China, he leaned toward intervention *after* Truman sent the Seventh Fleet into the Taiwan Strait.

The initiative, and probably the timing, for the war came from Pyongyang, not from Moscow or Beijing. This interpretation seems plausible because since 1945 a two-part civil war had wracked Korea: the conflict in the South and the conflict between South and North. In the South, "people's committees" resisted the rightist state backed by the United States. Peasant uprisings, leftist-initiated labor strife, and guerrilla warfare claimed tens of thousands of lives. The North encouraged the rebellions in the South, and skirmishes between northern and southern soldiers intensified in 1949 along the dividing parallel. Both Kim's North Korean communist government and Rhee's Republic of Korea in the South craved national unification. Both tapped foreign sources for material aid. Rhee, who had lived in the United States for almost four decades, used his American political connections well. In February 1950, Congress authorized $60 million in economic aid for South Korea; in March it voted almost $11 million in military assistance; and on June 5 it added another $100 million in military aid. Although U.S. occupation troops had departed in mid-1949, a U.S. Military Advisory Group remained to train Rhee's forces. In May elections, Rhee lost his majority in the South Korean National Assembly. With a 150,000-soldier army well supplied with Soviet arms, including 150 T-34 tanks, Kim's authoritarian regime probably decided to strike before Rhee could utilize U.S. aid and stabilize his precarious political position. In any case, scholars interpret the major war that exploded in June 1950 as an extension of the ongoing civil war waged by North and South Korea, not simply as a conflagration ignited by the two Cold War superpowers.

Despite uncertainty over the war's origins, we *can* measure its consequences. Korea's staggering death tolls highlighted the war's human costs, as did lingering refugee questions in the wake of Korea's protracted division. That American soldiers fired upon noncombatants at No Gun Ri and elsewhere during summer 1950 showed that the conflict "was anything but a limited war for Koreans."[44] Human rights abuses persisted in both the South and the North long after hostilities had ended, as both the United States and the Soviet Union cultivated authoritarian regimes that perpetuated Cold War bipolarity more than they advanced the cause of democracy.

Global transformations quickly followed the war. The Korean conflict poisoned Sino-American relations. The Taiwan question became "locked in place" as the United States continuously intervened in China's civil war by aiding Jiang and adamantly refusing to recognize Mao's government, which now had shed American blood.[45] The war enabled the Chinese communists to consolidate their revolution at home and gain international prestige by battling the Americans to a draw. The conflict also bolstered Japan and its alliance with the United States. Some $3 billion in U.S. procurement orders during the war revived Japanese industry. South Korea also became a key American ally, receiving, in 1953–1972, $5.5 billion in foreign aid. Viewing all nationalist movements as potential Soviet auxiliaries, and determined to back Western allies in the enlarged Cold War, Washington increased aid to the French in their battle against Vietnamese nationalists (see Chapter 9).

The war also brought momentous change to the United States. "Like the Trojan horse sent into Troy," writes one historian, "President Harry S. Truman's June 1950 decision to intervene" in Korea "laid the nation bare to a bombardment of economic, political, military, and social changes."[46] The war "put an end to Truman's 'Fair Deal' [domestic reform program] and to a Democrat[ic] political hegemony that extended back two decades."[47] Public exasperation with the Korean stalemate led to the repudiation of the Democrats and the election of the Republican Eisenhower in

Makers of American Foreign Relations, 1950–1961

Presidents	Secretaries of State
Harry S. Truman, 1945–1953	Dean G. Acheson, 1949–1953
Dwight D. Eisenhower, 1953–1961	John Foster Dulles, 1953–1959
	Christian A. Herter, 1959–1961

1952. The war wounded bipartisanship and fueled McCarthyism. It helped set off a major debate during the early 1950s over whether Europe or Asia ranked higher in the struggle against communism and whether the United States had overcommitted itself globally. Truman's handling of the Korean War also confirmed presidential supremacy in foreign policy. He neither consulted Congress nor asked for a declaration of war. Acheson did not wish to answer "ponderous questions" in drawn-out hearings that might have "muddled up" presidential policy.[48] The war "gave teeth to the mobilization planning process" already begun under Truman.[49] The Defense Department budget for fiscal year 1953 reached $52.6 billion, up from $17.7 billion in 1950. U.S. military expansion included a much enlarged army; development of tactical nuclear weapons; four more army divisions for Europe, making a total of six there; the 1952 maiden flight of a new jet bomber, the B-52; the explosion of a thermonuclear device in November 1952; and expansion of the Strategic Air Command (SAC) to 1,600 aircraft (nearly all atomic capable). The United States also acquired bases in Saudi Arabia and Morocco, began successful talks with authoritarian Spain for an air base, and initiated plans for the rearmament of West Germany. In 1951 the United States, Australia, and New Zealand formed the ANZUS Pact. The United States created a military alliance with Pakistan in 1954. The Korean War bequeathed the militarization of the Cold War.

"The Great Equation": Eisenhower's Foreign Policy

The stalemated Korean War energized the 1952 Republican presidential race. Eisenhower conducted a smiling, moderate campaign. But his party's right wing vehemently attacked the Truman administration as "soft" on communism. Vice-presidential candidate Richard M. Nixon ridiculed the Democratic presidential candidate, Illinois Governor Adlai E. Stevenson, as "Adlai the Appeaser."[50] John Foster Dulles, who had authored the Republican platform condemning Truman's leadership, proposed the "liberation" of "captive peoples" in Eastern Europe as an alternative to "futile and immoral" containment, which, like a "treadmill," kept Americans "in the same place until we dropped."[51] He never explained precisely how liberation would be achieved, but Eisenhower's promise to go to Korea helped the Republican candidate win 55 percent of the popular vote. The journalist David Brinkley recalled that Eisenhower frequently mangled syntax and grammar when he spoke, so that his "ad-libbed sentences bounced around like dodgem cars at a carnival."[52]

Richard M. Nixon (1913–1994). Before being elected vice president in 1952, Nixon graduated from Whittier College, earned a law degree from Duke University, and represented California in the U.S. House of Representatives (1947–1950) and Senate (1950–1953). An anticommunist alarmist who often used excessive language to score debating points, Nixon was, said Adlai Stevenson, "the kind of politician who would cut down a redwood tree, and then mount the stump and make a speech for conservation." (*The Reporter,* 1960. Copyright 1960 by The Reporter Magazine Co.)

But this soon-to-be "first true television president" deftly orchestrated a media campaign to advance an image of sincerity, modesty, integrity, and decisiveness.[53] A waggish jingle mocked the strategy: "Eisenhower hits the spot/One full General, that's a lot/Feeling sluggish, feeling sick?/Take a dose of Ike and Dick/Philip Morris, Lucky Strike/Alka Seltzer, I like Ike."[54] Because the Cold War seemed more than ever a military matter, this amiable soldier and war hero outshone the comparatively bland Stevenson, who later wondered, "Who did I think I was, running against George Washington?"[55]

The first Republican president since Hoover proved a skillful politician, whose rhetorical bumbling masked a "hidden-hand" management of the policy process.[56] Raised in Abilene, Kansas, Eisenhower graduated from West Point and led an obscure military life until appointed the supreme allied commander in Europe during World War II. After the war he served as army chief of staff, president of Columbia University, and NATO commander. As president, Eisenhower was guided by what he called "The Great Equation," namely that "spiritual force, multiplied by economic force, multiplied by military force, is roughly equal to security. If one of these factors falls to zero … the resulting product does likewise."[57] Eisenhower admired business leaders and appointed many to high policy offices. Believing that only through "free enterprise" could "democracy be preserved" and communism deterred, the president extended the reciprocal trade agreements program, expanded the lending authority of the Export-Import Bank, and relaxed controls on trade with Eastern European nations.[58] Total American exports expanded from $15 billion in 1952 to $30 billion in 1960. During the 1950s, the United States spent more than $3 billion a year on foreign military assistance under the Mutual Security program. The "Food for Peace" program, inaugurated in 1954, accounted for $12.2 billion in farm exports over ten years. Beginning in 1959 the Inter-American Development Bank spurred hemispheric economic projects.

Eisenhower waged "psychological warfare" in a "battle for men's minds" against the Soviets and their allies.[59] Voice of America (VOA), Radio Free Europe (RFE), Radio Liberty, and the United States Information Agency (USIA) employed news stories, music, film, trade fairs, print journalism, and other media to juxtapose American material abundance and freedom against the lives of "'Soviet drones,' locked in a despotic system plagued by … forced labor camps and oppressive working conditions."[60] The Smithsonian Institution aided the U.S. government in promoting cross-cultural ties, reasoning that, as one supporter put it, "the arts provide fall-out shelters for the human spirit more urgently needed and at infinitely less cost than those needed for the human body."[61] Dizzy Gillsepie, Louis Armstrong, Duke Ellington, and other American jazz musicians conducted high-profile, U.S.-sponsored international tours in a "self-conscious campaign against worldwide criticism of U.S. racism" and to "build cordial relations with new African and Asian states." The "glaring contradiction in this strategy," writes the historian Penny Von Eschen, "was that the U.S. promoted black artists as goodwill ambassadors—symbols of the triumph of American democracy—when America was still a Jim Crow nation."[62]

While VOA, the USIA, and other cultural programs openly acknowledged U.S. sponsorship, psychological warfare experts also advanced a "camouflaged" approach

Dwight D. Eisenhower (1890–1969). Well experienced in world affairs before entering the White House, Eisenhower became preoccupied as president with preventing "falling dominoes"—halting the spread of communism—in Asia and elsewhere. He stockpiled thousands of nuclear and conventional weapons, even as he eloquently criticized the burgeoning U.S.-Soviet nuclear arms race. Eisenhower suffered a coronary thrombosis in September 1955 but went on to win reelection in 1956 against Democratic candidate Adlai Stevenson. (Dwight D. Eisenhower Library)

that used the news media and private enterprises as "surrogate communications" for the United States on grounds that, in Eisenhower's words, "the hand of government must be carefully concealed, and in some cases wholly eliminated, to be persuasive."[63] In parallel fashion, Eisenhower elevated the CIA as a major instrument of foreign policy. Under CIA Director Allen W. Dulles, brother of the secretary of state, the agency engaged in intelligence analysis—assessing other countries' policies, motives, and capabilities—as well as covert action, which aimed to influence political, economic, or military conditions abroad without publicly acknowledging the U.S. role. Working on the assumption that the Cold War had "no rules" and that "longstanding American concepts of 'fair play' must be reconsidered," the CIA mobilized to "subvert, sabotage, and destroy our enemies."[64] The agency hired mercenaries, co-opted labor unions, planted news stories, and bribed foreign leaders such as King Hussein of Jordan. Operatives successfully staged coups in Iran (1953) and Guatemala (1954) while failing to overthrow governments in Syria (1957) and Indonesia (1958) or to counter a growing "Filipino First" nationalist movement. The CIA also provided the president with the "quiet option" of "termination with extreme prejudice" or "health

John Foster Dulles (1888–1959). Watching Dulles "grapple with a problem," an aide recalled, "was like watching a bird dog sniffing for its prey. He got a little excited as he worked over a solution, breathed a little faster, and obviously enjoyed the thinking process." (*The Reporter,* 1956. Copyright 1956 by The Reporter Magazine Co.)

alteration"—that is, assassination.[65] Among those included on the CIA's assassination hit list were the Congo's Patrice Lumumba and Cuba's Fidel Castro.

At home, the CIA put American journalists and professors on its payroll, published books, recruited business executives as "fronts," financed the National Student Association, funded research projects at universities, and used philanthropic foundations to pass money to organizations for anticommunist activities. In the name of Cold War research and without the knowledge of victims, the agency used Americans as guinea pigs. Under a program called MKULTRA, researchers subjected unwitting Americans to the mind-altering drug LSD. Other projects secretly exposed unsuspecting soldiers, prisoners, children, and sick people to radiation. Eisenhower remarked that he "knew so many things that I am almost afraid to speak to my wife."[66] He worked to keep his participation secret "on the theory of why put burdens on people that they don't need to know about."[67] While sometimes portrayed as a "rogue elephant" acting on its own, the CIA's "mahout, the driver who sits on top and steers," as two scholars put it, "is always the president."[68]

Unlike Truman and Acheson, Eisenhower at least seemed willing to negotiate with the Soviets. Stalin's death in March 1953 removed one of the original Cold War instigators, and in April the president's earnest "Chances for Peace" speech revealed Ike's discomfort with militarism. "Every gun that is made, every warship launched, every rocket fired signifies, in the final sense, a theft from those who hunger and are not fed."[69] But Soviet analysts deemed Eisenhower's remarks "irritating and provocative," unworthy of serious attention, while a tougher speech by Secretary Dulles two days later confirmed Moscow's suspicion that the administration contained "resolute enemies" of peace.[70] Fearing that "there aren't enough bulldozers to scrape the bodies off the street" following a nuclear war, especially once the Soviets exploded a thermonuclear device in August 1953, Eisenhower urged arms control measures.[71] "The only way to win World War III is to prevent it," he said.[72] The president's "Atoms for Peace" speech in December 1953 led to U.S. agreements with thirty-nine nations to develop nuclear energy for peaceful purposes. In 1954 the president rejected advice to use nuclear weapons or send troops to Indochina to forestall a Vietnamese victory over France, and in 1958 he unilaterally halted atomic tests. In his "Farewell Address" of early 1961, Eisenhower warned against a "military-industrial complex" and a government-university scientific complex that threatened the "democratic process" and "possible domination of the nation's scholars by federal employment, project allocations, and the power of money."[73]

But Ike's peace initiatives fizzled, and his antimilitarist sentiments seldom translated into effective policies. Interagency divisions impeded progress towards arms control, with the Defense Department and Joint Chiefs of Staff "generally opposed" to U.S.-Soviet bans on nuclear testing and Eisenhower usually siding with the military—hardly surprising, given the nation's growing reliance on atomic defense.[74] America's stockpile of nuclear weapons during Eisenhower's presidency rose from 1,200 to 22,229, and by 1959 a million Americans served overseas in forty-two countries. By 1960 the Defense Department controlled 35 million acres of land at home and abroad. Defense budgets averaged more than $40 billion a year, even as Eisenhower, who feared "busting ourselves" by overspending, angered generals by authorizing cuts in army personnel.[75]

Dulles, the New Look, and McCarthyism

Although Secretary of State John Foster Dulles (1953–1959) seemed a less flexible and more articulate Cold Warrior than Eisenhower, the two "held strikingly parallel views," and "the documents confirm that it was the president who made the decisions."[76] Forceful, ambitious, sharp, and self-righteous, Dulles blended moral "idealism" with hard-nosed political "pragmatism."[77] One official mused that Dulles thought he had a "pipeline on high" and that he received "his instructions from a superior source."[78] Tutelage from his Presbyterian minister father, education at Princeton and George Washington Law School, service as a negotiator on reparations at the Paris Peace Conference at Versailles, membership in the prestigious Wall Street firm of Sullivan and Cromwell, and worldwide activity on behalf of the Federal Council of Churches gave Dulles a varied pre-World-War-II international background. "Foster has been studying to be Secretary of State since he was five years old," Eisenhower once joked.[79] What Dulles possessed in experience he lacked in personal skills. A dull, flat speaker with a lecturing tone, Dulles favored face-to-face diplomacy, yet showed, according to Eisenhower, a "curious lack of understanding as to how his words and manner may affect another personality."[80] After the war Dulles promoted bipartisanship, but in 1952 he assailed the very policies of the Truman administration that he

Titan II Missile. Ten stories high and packing in one nuclear warhead the explosive power of 9 million tons of TNT (equivalent to 700 Hiroshima bombs), this intercontinental ballistic missile (ICBM) was successfully tested in 1959. The Titan II became part of the Strategic Air Command in 1963. Jay W. Kelley, lieutenant general of the U.S. Air Force (ret.), recalled "the tremendous, healthy rivalry that existed between the six Minuteman [missile] wings and the three Titan II wings. Inevitably, the argument would start with size and work its way to who had the biggest warhead." (U.S. Air Force)

Joseph McCarthy (1909–1957). Graduate of Marquette University, judge, and marine, the Republican senator from Wisconsin (1947–1957) was known as the "Pepsi-Cola Kid" for protecting the interests of that company. The scholar Ellen Schrecker, noting that anticommunist excesses were widespread, argues that the demagogic McCarthy was the "creature" not the "creator" of the 1950s Red Scare. But as the journalist Cabell Phillips wrote, McCarthy used "lies, slander, and innuendo to smash his opponents and to build his own image of invincibility." The Senate formally condemned McCarthy in December 1954. (*The Reporter,* 1951. Copyright 1951 by Fortnightly Publishing Co., Inc.)

had helped to shape. He later admitted that his desire to elect Eisenhower had fueled this political gambit.

Dulles helped Eisenhower craft a revised military strategy, which they dubbed "The New Look." Prompted by Defense Department predictions that Moscow by 1955 could cause as many as 12 million U.S. casualties in a surprise attack, the New Look coupled conventional military forces adequate to "deter" or "counter aggression" with a cost-saving "massive atomic capability" that permitted the United States to "respond vigorously" to threats "at places and with means of its own choosing."[81] What Dulles called "massive retaliation," the president described as "blow the hell out of them in a hurry if they start anything."[82] With nuclear missiles delivering more "bang for the buck" than did conventional weapons, the strategy appeared fiscally sound.[83] As Eisenhower reasoned, "if we let defense spending run wild, you get inflation … then controls … then a garrison state … and *then* we've lost the very values we were trying to defend."[84] Ike's secretary of state also urged "brinkmanship" as a political counterpart to nuclear deterrence. "Victory goes to him who can keep his nerve to the last fifteen minutes," wrote Dulles.[85] "Three brinks and he's brunk," jibed critics.[86]

Eisenhower and Dulles viewed the Third World, like everything else, "through the prism of the Cold War."[87] In 1954, the president theorized: "You have a row of dominoes set up, you knock over the first one, and … the last one … will go over very quickly."[88] If one more country in Asia fell to communism, others supposedly would topple in succession. The 1957 "Eisenhower Doctrine" stipulated that the United States would intervene in the Middle East if any government threatened by a communist takeover requested aid. Sold as dynamic departures from Truman policies, such slogans offered only tactical changes in a continuing containment strategy.

At home, as abroad, the administration perpetuated Truman-era policies, particularly in rooting out presumed "subversives" from the U.S. government. Playing on public anxieties that falsely conflated communism with social nonconformity, political dissent, and moral weakness, the expression "security risk" became a pretext for firing any federal worker who challenged prevailing norms.[89] Most notably targeted were homosexuals, who had come to Washington amidst the influx of single young professionals serving in the burgeoning federal bureaucracy of the New Deal and World War II, and who had retained a visible presence in Washington, D.C. during the postwar years. Under the crusading leadership of Senators Styles Bridges (R–NH) and Kenneth Wherry (R–Neb.), a "Lavender Scare" fused with the "Red Scare" gripping Washington during the early 1950s.[90] Accusations and innuendo wrongly linking so-called "sexual perversion" with communism destroyed the careers, reputations, and in some cases, the lives of as many as 5,000 federal employees, while chilling debate at a crucial historical juncture. Among those targeted was the 1952 Democratic presidential candidate Adlai Stevenson, an alleged "egghead" with a "fruity" voice, nicknamed "Adelaide" by the Republican opposition during the 1952 campaign.[91] In the end, not a single federal employee accused during the 1950s was ever convicted of treasonous actions against the U.S. government.

McCarthyism claimed other victims as well. One tragic case centered on Foreign Service Officer John Carter Vincent, an independent-minded "China hand" who during World War II reported that Jiang Jieshi would probably lose in a civil war with the communists. McCarthyites took this professional analysis to mean that Vincent plotted to defeat Jiang. A State Department Loyalty Board cleared Vincent, but the Civil Service Loyalty Review Board, by a vote of 3 to 2, doubted his loyalty to the United States. Dulles forced Vincent out. Another China specialist, John Paton Davies, also lost his job even though nine security reviews had cleared him. McCarthyism left deep wounds. "The wrong done," the journalist Theodore H. White has written, "was to poke out the eyes and ears of the State Department on Asian affairs, to blind American foreign policy."[92]

The Glacier Grinds On: Eisenhower, Khrushchev, and the Cold War

Like a huge glacier, the Cold War ground across the international landscape—occasionally receding amidst brief thaws in U.S.-Soviet relations, only to harden and advance in the chill of mutual fear and distrust. Signs of a possible warming trend appeared following Stalin's death. Although the Red Army crushed an East Berlin riot in June 1953, Moscow helped end the deadlock over Korea, opened diplomatic relations with Yugoslavia and Greece, abandoned territorial claims against Turkey, toned down its anti-American rhetoric, launched a "peace offensive," and freed victims from forced labor camps. Soviet leaders scrambled for position in the

Margaret Chase Smith (1897–1995). The only female member of the U.S. Senate during the 1950s, Smith, a Republican of Maine who served four terms (1949–1973), led six other Republican moderates in advancing a "Declaration of Conscience" against McCarthyism, delivered on June 1, 1950: "Those of us who shout the loudest about Americanism in making character assassinations are all too frequently those who, by our own words and acts, ignore some of the basic principles of Americanism—The right to criticize; ... The right to protest; The right of independent thought. The exercise of these rights should not cost one single American citizen his reputation. ... Otherwise none of us could call our souls our own. Otherwise thought control would have set in." Five of Smith's six supporters bolted when McCarthy assailed Smith; only Senator Wayne Morse (R-OR) remained loyal. Smith suffered thereafter in her committee assignments and was "further marginalized for her apostasy," writes the historian Lewis L. Gould. (Margaret Chase Smith Library Archives)

"I Hear There's Something Wrong with Your Morale."   Secretary Dulles launched a damaging purge of Foreign Service Officers. President Eisenhower, refusing to get into "a pissing contest with that skunk" McCarthy, whom he privately viewed as "a pimple on [the] path of progress," did nothing to halt the political onslaught against the State Department. ("I HEAR THERE'S SOMETHING WRONG WITH YOUR MORALE"—A 1954 Herblock Cartoon, copyright by The Herb Block Foundation)

post–Stalin succession crisis. Nikita S. Khrushchev, for years the Communist party boss of the Ukraine, climbed to the top of the Kremlin hierarchy. By September 1953, Khrushchev had become first secretary of the Central Committee of the party; five years later he became premier. "A short, stocky man with an almost perfectly spherical bald head," Khrushchev impressed Americans as competitive and coarse.[93] Eisenhower found him "tough, and coldly deliberate even when he was pretending to be consumed by anger."[94]

On European problems after Stalin, neither side budged much. "Our asses aren't freezing in the wind," bragged Khrushchev.[95] "We are not dancing to any Russian tune," said Dulles.[96] Neither Moscow nor Washington had the power to force significant changes in continental alignments, and neither wanted a hot war to alter the status quo. Both nations continued their military buildups. Though Soviet ground forces outnumbered the Americans' by a 2 to 1 margin, the United States possessed many more strategic bombers and nuclear weapons. In an attempt to bolster Western defenses through greater integration, Dulles promoted a European Defense Community (EDC) that included West German troops in integrated units. He warned that French resistance would prompt an "agonizing reappraisal" of U.S. security commitments.[97] A London cartoon mocked Dulles's threat, depicting a jewelry store sign: "Appraisals $2; Agonizing Reappraisals $5."[98] Paris called Dulles's bluff and rejected EDC, but in May 1955 the secretary gained West German membership in NATO. That same year witnessed the U.S. defense treaty with nationalist China, formation of the Southeast Asia Treaty Organization (SEATO) (see p. 326) and the Baghdad Pact (see p. 299). The Soviets forged their own military alliance, the Warsaw Pact of Eastern European states. In May 1955, the Soviet Union and the United States seemed close to a treaty to prohibit the use and manufacture of nuclear weapons, reduce conventional forces, and create an inspection system to monitor compliance—all terms that the United States had insisted on for years. Within months, however, Washington backed away from the disarmament proposal, convinced that the Soviets would cheat.

At the same time, one "test case for détente" produced a rare display of Cold War cooperation.[99] The two powers agreed in May 1955 to end their ten-year occupation of Austria and create an independent, neutral state. Both the Soviets and the Americans found elements of victory: Each side effectively denied Austria to the other's sphere; Moscow demonstrated a commitment to peaceful coexistence; and Washington welcomed a possible model for Eastern European nations eager to roll back Soviet power. Also throughout 1954–1955 came calls for a summit meeting of the great powers. Winston Churchill made an eloquent plea, and Democrats in Congress urged negotiations. Dulles countered: A summit conference would empower the Soviets and encourage neutralism, for other countries would fear less and align less. But while Eisenhower agreed that Moscow should not be permitted to "hit the free world in the face," he thought the present moment "propitious" to negotiate.[100]

The Soviet Union, the United States, Britain, and France met in Geneva, Switzerland, July 18–23, 1955. In the end, a participant recalled, "not much was achieved at the meeting except that it had occurred."[101] Everybody tried to score points for prestige. East and West wanted Germany united, but each on its own terms. Both sides favored arms control, parting over methods. Eisenhower's dramatic "Open Skies" proposal called for the Soviet Union and the United States to exchange maps and submit their military installations to aerial inspection. Eisenhower later remarked: "We knew the Soviets wouldn't accept" but "thought it was a good move."[102] "A bald espionage plot," sniffed Khrushchev.[103] The Soviets kept Americans guessing on whether Moscow had caught up in airborne striking power. That secrecy ended in 1956 when the United States began covert surveillance flights by high-altitude U-2 planes over the Soviet Union.

Eisenhower nonetheless applauded a "new spirit of conciliation and cooperation" and assured Americans that he had not penned any secret agreements.[104] Soviets and Americans at Geneva drank "coexistence cocktails"—vodka and Coke.[105] After the largely ceremonial conference, Moscow recognized West Germany and Khrushchev endorsed "détente." Still, he added, "if anybody thinks" that "we shall forget about

Nikita S. Khrushchev (1894–1971). "I made speeches to bolster the morale of my people," Premier Khrushchev recalled. "I wanted to give our enemy pause. … I exaggerated a little. I said that we had the capability of shooting a fly out of space with our missiles." He fell from power in 1964 and until his death aired his views through his memoirs. (*The Reporter*, 1956. Copyright 1956 by The Reporter Magazine Co.)

Marx, Engels, and Lenin, he is mistaken. This will happen when shrimps learn to whistle."[106]

The Geneva summit did initiate cultural exchanges, most notably Vice President Nixon's 1959 trip to the Soviet Union where, at a display of U.S. products in a Moscow exhibition, he engaged Khrushchev in the "kitchen debate" on capitalism, communism, and the "commodity gap."[107] At the Moscow Youth Festival of 1957, some 30,000 young people danced to U.S. musicians, picking up slang ("see ya later, alligator"), and calling themselves *bitniki* (beatniks).[108] Washington's containment strategists, one wry commentator wrote, never imagined "rollback as rock 'n' roll back."[109]

Soviet leaders themselves seemed eager for progress. In February 1956, the once loyal supporter of Stalin's bloody purges during the 1930s delivered a secret speech to the Twentieth Party Congress. Khrushchev denounced Stalin as "monstrous" for his "grave abuse of power." He initiated "de-Stalinization," embraced peaceful coexistence, and seemed to endorse different brands of communism.[110] The abolition of the Cominform in April implied a new Soviet tolerance for diversity. But international and regional events exposed the limits of Khrushchev's vision for change. The CIA published Khrushchev's speech, emboldening nationalists and victims of Stalinism to challenge autocratic leaders in Eastern Europe. In Poland, a labor dispute in mid-1956 evolved into national resistance to Soviet dominance. After using force to put down riots, Moscow compromised with Polish nationalism by reluctantly accepting Wladyslaw Gomulka as the Polish Communist party chairman, heretofore denied influence because Stalin thought

Preparation for the "Kitchen Debate."   Khrushchev and Vice President Richard M. Nixon sip Pepsi-Cola at the American National Exhibition in Moscow in July 1959, just before their "kitchen debate" in which the Soviet leader admitted American superiority in consumer goods but boasted "when we catch you up, in passing you by, we will wave to you." (Pepsi-Cola is a registered trademark of Pepsico, Inc. Used with permission)

him too "Titoist." The United States, which had been giving aid to Tito himself for years, soon offered Poland economic assistance.

Revolt erupted next in Hungary, where "hatred of the political police, declining standard of living, the desperate housing situation, [and] the dull regimented and poor quality of everyday existence" fed "the yearning for political and cultural pluralism."[111] A new government, backed by Budapest street demonstrators and countrywide local revolutionary councils, dramatically announced Hungary's pullout from the Warsaw Pact and declared neutrality in the Cold War. Reasoning that the unfolding Suez crisis (see p. 301) offered the Red Army a "favorable moment" to act, and fearing that a successful Hungarian revolt would "give a great boost to Americans, English, and French," an initially reluctant Khrushchev endorsed intervention because Soviet apparatchiks "would not understand a failure to respond with force."[112] In early November some 20,000 under-armed Hungarian students

Propaganda Balloons for Eastern Europe. Although the United States did not send troops or military supplies to Hungary during the 1956 uprising, in the 1950s the Free Europe Committee floated message-filled balloons across the Iron Curtain from West Germany to stir up unrest. The CIA-front organization launched its first polyethylene balloons in 1951; its leaflets read: "Freedom will rise again." (Franklin D. Roosevelt Library)

"I'll Be Glad to Restore Peace to the Middle East, Too." The ugly Soviet suppression of the Hungarian rebellion of 1956 prompted this telling cartoon by Herblock. (I'LL BE GLAD TO RESTORE PEACE TO THE MIDDLE EAST TOO"—A 1956 Herblock Cartoon, copyright by The Herb Block Foundation)

and workers and 3,000 Soviet troops died as Soviet tanks crushed the rebellion in the streets of Budapest.

The Polish and Hungarian rebellions seemed to embody Dulles's dream of "liberation." In 1953, Congress had passed the first annual Captive Peoples' Resolution to spur self-determination in Eastern Europe. The Eisenhower administration had been encouraging discontent through Voice of America and CIA-financed Radio Free Europe. "Sure we never said rise up and revolt," one CIA agent recalled.[113] But during Christmas 1955, Eisenhower had declared that "any East European" displaying "visible opposition" to "Soviet oppression … can count on our help."[114] And the covert CIA program RED SOX/RED CAP trained East European émigrés for paramilitary action—despite the fact that the agency stationed only one operative in Hungary, where he mainly performed such cover duties as purchasing stamps and interviewing visitors. Hungary thus exposed liberation as a sham slogan "fashioned to appeal to domestic ethnic audiences."[115] One critic quipped: "The initials 'NATO' could summarize" the administration's approach: "No Action, Talk Only."[116] To counter complaints of a "do-nothing attitude," the administration permitted more than 20,000 Hungarian refugees to enter the United States and introduced a UN resolution denouncing Soviet force.[117] Still, condemnations "rained down" upon Eisenhower for publicly promoting but not supporting anticommunist revolution in Eastern Europe.[118]

Missiles, Berlin, and the U-2 Mess

In 1956–1957, the United States seemed on the defensive and the Soviets on the offensive. Washington hastened to patch up its crumbling European alliance, rocked by U.S. disapproval of British-French military actions in the Middle East. Washington reinvigorated NATO by deploying intermediate-range ballistic missiles in Britain and tactical nuclear weapons in Western Europe. The French foundered amidst a colonial war in Algeria and shifted French NATO contingents to Africa. Many Western Europeans distrusted the U.S. push for German rearmament, worried about resurgent McCarthyism, and resented U.S. strictures on trade with communist countries. An American economic recession in 1957 further sapped Western vitality. John Foster Dulles's cancer surgery in November 1956 meant that President Eisenhower had to steer the United States through Eastern European and Mideast crises without his trusted adviser, who died in May 1959.

On October 4, 1957, the Soviets launched the world's first artificial space satellite, *Sputnik*. Twenty-two inches around and weighing 184 pounds, this apparent display of Soviet ingenuity dealt a "severe blow" to American "pride."[119] Eisenhower himself was taken aback by "the wave of near hysteria" that consumed the United States in the wake of *Sputnik*'s inaugural orbit.[120] Michigan's Democratic Governor G. Mennen Williams versified American anxiety: "Oh Little Sputnik, flying high / With made-in Moscow beep / You tell the world it's a commie sky / And Uncle Sam's asleep."[121] Two months earlier the Soviets had launched the first intercontinental ballistic missile (ICBM). Critics lambasted Eisenhower for allowing American power to slip. Khrushchev bragged about turning out rockets "like sausages," even though the USSR had test-fired only six ICBMs and deployed just four unwieldy ICBMs by 1960.[122] Eisenhower knew that *Sputnik* had not endangered U.S. security because high-flying U-2 spy planes had been photographing Soviet military capabilities since 1956. A presidentially commissioned study, the Gaither Report of November 1957, nonetheless urged an expensive military buildup to improve U.S. deterrent power. Eisenhower rejected the report's alarmist tone as "far-fetched," but he followed by building more missiles, dispersing Strategic Air Command bombers, improving radar technology, beefing up antimissile defense, and reorganizing the Defense Department.[123] In January 1958, rocket scientists successfully launched an American satellite named Explorer I. In July, Congress created the National Aeronautics and Space Administration (NASA), which soon became, alongside the Pentagon, the chief federal funding source for high-tech government-sponsored research in universities such as Stanford and Massachusetts Institute of Technology. The National Defense Education Act (NDEA), enacted in September 1958, financed new educational programs in the sciences, mathematics, and foreign languages. U.S. government-sponsored civil defense preparedness schemes urged Americans to build fallout shelters, stockpile food, and practice classroom "duck and cover drills" to prepare for a possible nuclear Armageddon, thus heightening popular anxiety about the dangers of atomic war.

The continued militarization of the Cold War alarmed George F. Kennan, a leading architect of containment. In 1957 Kennan, building on a proposal of Polish Foreign Minister Adam Rapacki earlier that year, delivered the "Reith Lectures"

"So Russia Launched a Satellite, But Has It Made Cars with Fins Yet?" Ross Lewis's cartoon suggested that Americans had become too fascinated by 1950s consumer products while the Soviets were advancing missile technology. It did not take long for the United States to establish superiority in the nuclear arms race through new intercontinental ballistic missiles. (Courtesy Ross Lewis and the "Milwaukee Journal" October 1957)

in London, calling for the removal of all foreign troops from Eastern Europe and Germany, restrictions on nuclear weapons in that area, and the creation of a unified, nonaligned Germany. Although Dulles and Eisenhower had already rejected Rapacki's plan for a "denuclearized zone" in Central and Eastern Europe as "highly dangerous," Kennan urged the administration to "put our military fixations aside," to exercise diplomacy rather than to strengthen NATO.[124]

Kennan's suggestions sparked furious debate. Should Kennan's plan become reality, former Secretary of State Dean Acheson scolded, the Soviet Union might reintroduce troops into Eastern Europe, threaten Western Europe, and sign an anti-American military pact with the new united Germany. A rearmed West Germany must remain in the U.S. camp. The United States, Kennan answered, would never know Moscow's intentions unless it negotiated. The journalist Walter Lippmann, who had criticized Kennan's containment in 1947, stood by him in 1957. Lippmann compared Acheson and other hard-liners to "old soldiers trying to relive the battles in which they won their fame and glory. … Their preoccupation with their own past history is preventing them from dealing with the new phase of the Cold War."[125]

A new crisis over divided Berlin substantiated Kennan's admonition to defuse European issues. West Berlin, 110 miles inside communist East Germany, had become a "malignant tumor," in Khrushchev's words.[126] Some 3 million East German defectors, many of them skilled workers, had used West Berlin as an escape route since 1949. For Americans and their allies, the city operated as an espionage and

"Braggers." In this Japanese cartoon, Khrushchev and Eisenhower brag about their missiles. Despite his menacing public boasts, Khrushchev, like Eisenhower, dreaded the consequences of nuclear war. "We could never possibly use these weapons," he told an Egyptian journalist, "but all the same we must be prepared." (Nasu, courtesy of the State Historical Society of Missouri)

propaganda center. West Berlin's prosperity, induced by billions of dollars in U.S. aid, glittered next to drab East Berlin. Washington piqued Soviet tempers by crowing about West Berlin's economic success and applauding the East German exodus. The continued rearmament of West Germany, including U.S. planes capable of dropping nuclear bombs, further alarmed Moscow, which had endorsed the Rapacki Plan. The United States also insisted that the two Germanies unite under free elections and refused to recognize the East German government.

In November 1958, the Soviet Union boldly issued an ultimatum. Within six months, warned Khrushchev, unless East–West talks on Germany had begun, Moscow would sign a peace treaty with East Germany, end occupation agreements still in effect from World War II, and turn East Berlin over to the East German regime. He recommended that Berlin become a "free city" without foreign troops. Washington knew that to deal with East Germany would confirm the Soviet claim of two Germanies and throw into question U.S. occupation rights in West Berlin and West Germany. Eisenhower feared that "if we let the [West] Germans down they might shift their own position and even go neutralistic."[127] Urged to test Soviet intentions by sending U.S. military units through the corridors to West Berlin, the president stalled. "In this gamble," he vowed, "we are not going to be betting white chips, building up the pot gradually and fearfully. Khrushchev should know that when we decide to act, our whole stack will be in the pot."[128] Khrushchev wanted to talk, not fight. "Do not hurry," he told East German leaders. "The conditions are not ripe as yet for a new scheme of things."[129] He agreed to a foreign ministers conference for May 1959, which proved inconclusive, a trip in September 1959 to the United States to speak directly with Eisenhower, and ultimately a Paris summit meeting in May 1960.

Warmly welcomed by Eisenhower, whom Khrushchev grudgingly deemed "not without decency," the Soviet leader began his U.S. visit of September 1959 with a dramatic speech at the United Nations, where he proposed "general and complete disarmament in three years."[130] More in the forefront of diplomacy following Dulles's death in May, Eisenhower hoped that firsthand exposure to America's vastness and variety would make a "favorable chip in the granite."[131] The portly premier inspected an IBM plant, marveled at the fecundity of Midwest grain fields, gaped at the bare legs exposed on the Hollywood film set of *Can Can* (a sign to him of Western decadence), and sulked that for security reasons he was denied a visit to Disneyland. "Somebody here ought to hire" him, a movie producer laughed. "He's the biggest ham actor in the world."[132] The Soviet leader plugged "peaceful coexistence" and said that no one should take his "we will bury capitalism" statement in a literal or military sense.[133] After ten days on the road, the Soviet premier went to Camp David, a quiet, secluded presidential retreat near the Catoctin Mountains in Maryland. For two days the two leaders traded war stories and discussed Berlin. Eisenhower would not agree to a new summit meeting until Khrushchev abandoned his Berlin ultimatum. The premier agreed to do so, evoking the "Spirit of Camp David"—a willingness on both sides to talk their way to détente. Eisenhower "sincerely wanted to liquidate the 'cold war' and improve relations," Khrushchev later told the Politburo, adding that the moderates who advised Eisenhower had gained the upper hand over the "madmen."[134]

In 1959–1960 Eisenhower himself took goodwill trips abroad in a deliberate effort to ease tensions. Just before Khrushchev's visit to the United States, the president flew to London, Paris, and Bonn for talks with European leaders. In December he traveled 22,000 miles to eleven nations in Europe, Asia, and North Africa. In February 1960, he toured Latin America for two weeks, encountering a mixed reception. He then departed for the Paris summit meeting in May.

Two weeks before that international gathering, on May 1, 1960, an American airplane carrying high-powered cameras and other reconnaissance instruments was shot down over Sverdlovsk in the Ural Mountains of northern Russia, 1,200 miles inside the Soviet Union. On a CIA mission, the U-2 intelligence plane flew from a base in Pakistan to one in Norway. Although such flights had gone on for four years and the Soviets knew about them, this was the first time that Soviet firepower had reached the high-altitude craft. Pilot Francis Gary Powers's U-2 evidently had engine trouble and dropped several thousand feet before being shot down. He parachuted and was captured immediately, unable or unwilling to kill himself by taking his CIA-issued poison, then interrogated, but not tortured, by the KGB for several days. When Khrushchev publicly declared that a U.S. plane on a mission of "aggressive provocation aimed at wrecking the summit conference" had violated Soviet air space and been shot down, the State Department fabricated a claim that a civilian weather plane had simply flown off course.[135] On May 6, Khrushchev displayed photographs of the uninjured pilot, his spy equipment, and the crashed U-2. The president defended the flights as necessary to prevent "another Pearl Harbor"—a "surprise attack" on "the United States and the Free World."[136] But for many the affair "reinforced the prevailing view that Eisenhower was not minding the store."[137]

Francis Gary Powers with a Model U-2 Plane. Shot down in his U-2 over Sverdlovsk on May 1, 1960, Powers was convicted by the Soviet Union of espionage and sentenced to three years imprisonment and seven years of hard labor. On February 10, 1962, he and American student Frederic Pryor were exchanged for the U.S.-captured Soviet KGB Colonel Vilyam Fischer (alias Rudolf Abel). The CIA, the U.S. Air Force, and the Senate Armed Services Committee then grilled Powers about his failure to destroy his plane's spy equipment before capture. The Senate Committee in March 1962 deemed Powers "a fine young man" who had performed well "under dangerous circumstances." In August 1977, Powers died in a helicopter crash while reporting for KNBC television (Los Angeles) on local brush fires. He was posthumously awarded the Distinguished Flying Cross, the Prisoner of War Medal, and the National Defense Service Medal. When asked throughout his life by his son, Gary F. Powers, how high he had been flying when shot down over Soviet airspace, the father would reply, "not high enough." (AP Images)

The Berlin "can of worms" and nuclear-testing controls stood high on the Paris summit meeting's agenda.[138] Apparently preferring to wait until a new president took office, perhaps seizing an opportunity to show domestic hard-liners and Chinese critics of peaceful coexistence that he could be tough, and certainly angry about U.S. violations of Soviet air space, Khrushchev denounced American aggression, demanded an apology for the U-2 flights, and stalked out. He had hoped, he told Soviet officials, to show Eisenhower his "dacha" and "to take him for a motorboat ride on the Moscow River." But the overflights convinced him "that our pride and dignity would be damaged if we went ahead with the conference as if nothing had happened."[139] Thinking that a real opportunity to wind down the Cold War had been lost, Eisenhower bemoaned "the stupid U-2 mess" and looked forward to retirement on his Gettysburg farm.[140] Both Eisenhower and Khrushchev had spoken optimistically of peace. But in the end, neither "could liberate himself from his fears or transcend his ideological makeup. The world seemed too frightening; it also seemed too full of opportunity."[141]

To the Brink with China, To the Market with Japan

The People's Republic of China (PRC) did not mourn this deterioration in Soviet-American relations. Beijing frequently criticized Khrushchev for "yielding to evil" in dealing with the United States.[142] John Foster Dulles hoped to profit from the growing Sino-Soviet rift, which widened over Moscow's refusal to help China develop nuclear capability and Mao's growing conviction that Khrushchev was a "revisionist" who favored peaceful Western ties over communist expansionism.[143] The Eisenhower-Dulles strategy of "exploiting potential jealousies, rivalries, and disaffection" heightened Sino-American tensions, stalling détente.[144]

In early 1953, to press the PRC to accept an armistice in the Korean War, President Eisenhower announced that the Seventh Fleet would no longer block Jiang Jieshi's attempts to attack the mainland. The decision alarmed Beijing, especially after Nationalist bombing raids began to hit the coast. Throughout the 1950s, Jiang pledged a return to China and received more than $250 million annually in U.S. economic and military aid. The Seventh Fleet remained in the Taiwan Strait. In December 1954, Taiwan and the United States signed a mutual defense treaty. The following month, Congress, by a vote of 83 to 3 in the Senate and 410 to 3 in the House, authorized the president in the Formosa Resolution to "stand up to Communist aggression" by employing American troops as needed to defend Taiwan and the adjoining islands.[145] By granting the president so open-ended a mandate to commit U.S. forces overseas, both parties contributed to the "eroding" of the "legislative role in international affairs." Subsequent events in the Middle East (1957), Cuba (1962), and Vietnam (1964) prompted similar presidential efforts to broaden executive war-making power, and "these legislatures would find it much harder, given the Formosa Resolution precedent, to resist."[146]

In 1954 the United States created the Southeast Asia Treaty Organization (SEATO), which formally allied France, Britain, Australia, New Zealand, Thailand, Pakistan, and the Philippines against "Red China" and its support of revolution in Indochina. Mao later grumbled about "all the bases, like nails pounded in around us."[147] Washington also forbade American journalists to accept Beijing's 1956 invitation to visit the mainland and prohibited the shipment of a panda to the United States from China. At the 1954 Geneva Conference on Indochina (see Chapter 9), Foreign Minister Zhou Enlai approached Secretary Dulles intending to shake hands, but Dulles turned away, lest photographers record this contaminating gesture. Washington further imposed a total trade embargo in order to increase China's "ostracism" from the world.[148]

China and the United States lurched toward the brink in 1954–1955. Jinmen (Quemoy) and Mazu (Matsu) lay just a few miles off southeastern China in the Taiwan Strait, two of some thirty small offshore islands that the Nationalists had managed to hold when they fled to Taiwan in 1949. Jiang had fortified the two islands with thousands of troops and used the outposts to raid the mainland. As the United States negotiated the defense treaty with Jiang in summer 1954, Beijing unfurled a "Liberate Taiwan" global propaganda campaign and prepared to invade another offshore island group called the Dachens. Chinese shore batteries began to bombard Jinmen early in September. Deeming the offshore islands militarily valuable to Taiwan (some 100 miles away), Washington nonetheless cautioned Jiang against escalating coastal warfare. "Quemoy is not our ship," Eisenhower said at first. People would ask: "What do we care what happens to those yellow people out there?"[149] But Senator William F. Knowland of California insisted: "The defense ... cannot wait until the team with the ball crosses the line of scrimmage before resisting."[150]

Despite British warnings that Jiang might ignite war "through impulsiveness," the United States signed the defense treaty with Taiwan, and Congress gave the president a blank check in the Formosa Resolution.[151] Mao also practiced brink-manship. Boasting that "the U.S. cannot annihilate the Chinese nation with a small stack of atom bombs," Mao in mid-January 1955 sent his army to overrun the Dachens.[152] Heeding U.S. advice, Jiang pulled his troops out. Then Washington took up Mao's challenge. Eisenhower brandished nuclear weapons, stating publicly that he would use them "just exactly as you would use a bullet or anything else."[153] The Joint Chiefs of Staff readied plans to drop several Hiroshima-size bombs on coastal cities with expected casualties in the millions.

Lacking guaranteed support from the Soviet Union and reacting to alarms voiced by Asian nations attending the Bandung Conference (see p. 300), China of-fered in April to discuss tensions with the United States. The crisis quickly quieted. At Geneva, and after 1958 in Warsaw, Chinese and American officials talked at the ambassadorial level about Taiwan, trade, and other topics. But relations ruptured once again.

After the deployment of U.S. tactical nuclear weapons on Taiwan, and after Jiang had augmented his forces to more than 100,000 on the offshore islands, Mao answered in August 1958 by shelling Jinmen and Mazu anew. Khrushchev leveled a "barrage of criticism" against Beijing, whose actions jeopardized Moscow's "peace offensive" with the West, while Soviet Foreign Minister Andrei Gromyko urged Mao to seek a peaceful settlement.[154] Eisenhower nonetheless perceived a "long-range plan, 'with Soviet backing,' to retake Taiwan."[155] Possibly heeding European

Mao Zedong (1893–1976). Chief of the Communist party in "Red China," father of the successful Communist Revolution, and radical philosopher-poet, Mao said of the Taiwan Strait crisis: "I did not expect that the whole world would be so deeply shocked." (National Archives)

allies' voices of caution, the president resisted military advice to strike China with "low yield" nuclear weapons and cause "millions of noncombatant casualties."[156] Eisenhower instead ordered airlifts and Seventh Fleet escorts for Nationalist supply ships while Beijing vowed "resolute blows" against Jiang's "clique."[157] Mao told Gromyko that "it's getting so hot, and we want Eisenhower to take a shower."[158] "Those damned little offshore islands," the president griped. "I wish they'd sink."[159]

Eisenhower, Mao, and Jiang stepped back from the brink. After Dulles and Jiang agreed in October that Jiang would not use force against the mainland, the Nationalist leader withdrew some troops from Jinmen and Mazu, and Eisenhower suspended escorts of Nationalist vessels. Beijing relaxed bombardment of the islands. But the People's Republic accelerated efforts to acquire nuclear weapons "even if the Chinese people have to pawn their trousers for this purpose."[160]

As it went to the brink with Beijing, the United States worked to "keep the Japanese on our side."[161] American television replaced images of the "treacherous, myopic, bucktoothed Jap of World War II" with "A Guy Named Mickey," a handsome, pro-American Japanese college student in the United States who appeared in December 1956 on ABC TV's *Navy Log*.[162] Two September 8, 1951, agreements formalized peaceful ties. The first, a peace treaty signed by the United States and forty-seven other nations, ended the American occupation of Japan as of April 28, 1952. The second, the Mutual Security Treaty signed by Washington and Tokyo, provided for U.S. defense of Japan and the stationing of American arms and forces on Japanese soil. Japan agreed to create a 110,000-strong military (Self-Defense Forces), which could not be used outside the nation. Many Japanese resented the U.S. bases and the U.S. pressure to rearm, and throughout the 1950s mass street demonstrations strained relations. Meanwhile, American leaders who insisted that Japan pay for more of its own defense sharply criticized the Tokyo government for obstructing rearmament.

The plight of the *Fukuryu Maru* (*Lucky Dragon*), a Japanese fishing boat, heightened tensions. On March 1, 1954, the United States tested its new hydrogen bomb in the Bikini Atoll (Marshall Islands), some distance from the fishing area. A huge fireball spread outside the 50,000 square mile restricted zone around the island and showered radioactive fallout on the crew, causing severe nausea, fever, and blisters, and eventually killing one crew member. Ike's careless remark at a press conference that "something must have happened that we never experienced before, and must have surprised and astonished scientists," did little to quell the ensuing international outcry against nuclear testing.[163] Disparaging Japan's "fancied martyrdom," Washington waited months to compensate the victims.[164] The movie *Godzilla*, which debuted in Japan in 1954, offered a "realistic recalling" of the *Lucky Dragon* affair, as a prehistoric monster, revived by atomic tests, rampaged through Tokyo.[165]

After negotiators signed a renewed Japanese-American defense pact in January 1960, hundreds of thousands marched and rioted against the retention of U.S. bases. The Japanese government pushed the new treaty through the Diet (parliament), but the prime minister was forced to resign, and President Eisenhower cancelled his goodwill trip to Japan.

Even though huge U.S. military purchases in Japan during the Korean War— for Toyota trucks, for example—spurred economic recovery, Secretary Dulles

Neighborhood Street and Coca-Cola in Tokyo, Japan. Although Japan developed a booming export economy in the 1950s, it also imported famous U.S. products. Wherever U.S. troops were stationed during the Cold War, Coca-Cola followed, as the Georgia-based company greatly expanded its global marketing. Despite complaints about "Coca-colonization," the beverage quickly became a popular soft drink abroad. "One could swallow it," one scholar notes, "without giving up one's cultural loyalties or sense of national identity." (Library of Congress)

complained in 1954 that Japan expected "merely to be taken care of by [the] U.S."[166] Eager to lower the costs of subsidizing Japanese reconstruction and to blunt possible communist exploitation of economic instability, American officials encouraged Japan to develop a prosperous export-oriented economy. By the mid-1950s, Japan experienced double-digit economic growth by using substantial U.S. aid to buy and adapt American technology (Motorola helped start the electronics industry), improving labor-management coordination to enhance efficiency and quality, and investing in research and development rather than in weapons. Americans "helped the Japanese reinvent themselves as 'people of plenty'—to use the historian David Potter's celebrated term."[167] With Japan's populace striving for the "three sacred treasures" (television, washing machine, and refrigerator), and with 2,500 Japanese intellectuals visiting the United States through academic exchange programs in the 1950s, Japan became not only America's military ally but also eventually its economic competitor.[168]

Nationalism, Neutralism, and the Third World

Between 1946 and 1960, thirty-seven new nations emerged from colonial status in Asia, Africa, and the Middle East. Eighteen countries gained independence in 1960 alone. In 1958, twenty-eight prolonged guerrilla insurgencies raged. Revolutions and the collapse of empires claimed a central place in global affairs. These great changes occurred in the "Third World"—a term for nations that belonged neither to the capitalist "West" nor to the communist "East." At first called "backward" and

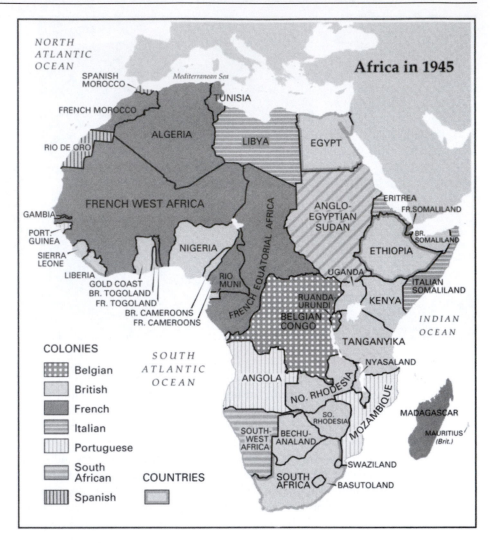

then "developing" countries, Third World nations generally consisted of nonwhite, agricultural peoples in the Southern Hemisphere. Such countries provided industrial nations with bountiful raw materials, military bases, intelligence facilities, and markets for manufactured goods. In 1959 more than one-third of American direct private investments abroad was in the Third World.

Volatile nationalist movements flourished in these emerging nations, often led by anticolonial revolutionaries who sought economic improvement without foreign ownership. Eisenhower warned Churchill that "should we try to dam [nationalism] up completely it would, like a mighty river, burst through the barriers and could create havoc."[169] Yet many U.S. leaders "doubted the capacity of darker-skinned peoples to practice self-government."[170] Nixon in 1960 remarked that "some

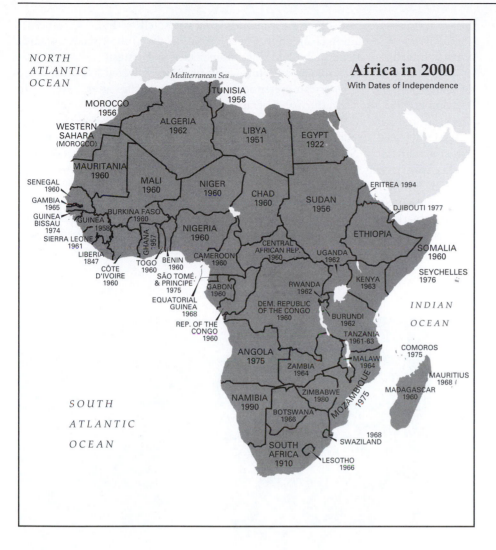

Africa in 2000
With Dates of Independence

NORTH ATLANTIC OCEAN

Mediterranean Sea

MOROCCO 1956

WESTERN SAHARA (MOROCCO)

TUNISIA 1956

ALGERIA 1962

LIBYA 1951

EGYPT 1922

MAURITANIA 1960

SENEGAL 1960

GAMBIA 1965

GUINEA BISSAU 1974

GUINEA 1958

SIERRA LEONE 1961

LIBERIA 1847

CÔTE D'IVOIRE 1960

MALI 1960

BURKINA FASO 1960

GHANA 1957

TOGO 1960

BENIN 1960

NIGER 1960

NIGERIA 1960

CAMEROON 1960

SÃO TOMÉ & PRINCIPE 1975

EQUATORIAL GUINEA 1968

GABON 1960

REP. OF THE CONGO 1960

CHAD 1960

CENTRAL AFRICAN REP. 1960

DEM. REPUBLIC OF THE CONGO 1960

SUDAN 1956

ERITREA 1994

DJIBOUTI 1977

ETHIOPIA

UGANDA 1962

RWANDA 1962

BURUNDI 1962

SOMALIA 1960

SEYCHELLES 1976

KENYA 1963

TANZANIA 1961-63

ANGOLA 1975

ZAMBIA 1964

NAMIBIA 1990

BOTSWANA 1966

ZIMBABWE 1980

MOZAMBIQUE 1975

MALAWI 1964

COMOROS 1975

MAURITIUS 1968

MADAGASCAR 1960

SOUTH AFRICA 1910

LESOTHO 1966

1968 SWAZILAND

INDIAN OCEAN

SOUTH ATLANTIC OCEAN

African peoples had only been out of the trees for fifty years."[171] Anticolonial revolutions frequently produced regimes that declared themselves nonaligned or neutral in the Cold War, a stance that Washington condemned as helpful to communism. Convinced that Moscow caused much upheaval in the Third World and that "premature independence" would facilitate "Soviet colonialism," the administration endorsed a "middle path" of "acceding to continued colonial rule by anticommunist allies while verbally backing eventual self-determination" in Africa.[172] The practice of blaming communists for nationalist explosions, one scholar has written, "is like blaming the inherent danger in a huge mass of exposed combustible materials on the possible presence of arsonists."[173] U.S. officials nonetheless privately acknowledged favoring "propertied classes who place a premium on order and trade."[174] Hence, in late 1960, when forty-three African and Asian states, led by India, sponsored a United Nations resolution championing decolonization, the United States abstained from voting, lest it offend such Cold War colonial allies as Portugal.

American racism, symbolized by Jim Crow practices, hovered like "the sword of Damocles … over American pretensions to world leadership after 1945."[175] In December 1952, the U.S. attorney general asked the Supreme Court to strike down segregation in public schools, arguing that "it is in the context of the present world struggle between freedom and tyranny that the problem of racial discrimination must be viewed."[176] So it was. In 1955 the dark-skinned Indian ambassador G. L. Mehta was "racially abused" at an airport restaurant in Texas.[177] Two years later, a Howard Johnson's in Dover, Delaware in 1957 denied food to newly independent Ghana's finance minister K. A. Gbedemah, a notable irony, given Martin Luther King's recent remark to Vice President Richard Nixon that in Alabama, "we are seeking the same kind of freedom Ghana is celebrating."[178] That same year, the president sent federal troops to escort black children to school in Little Rock, Arkansas, amidst ugly

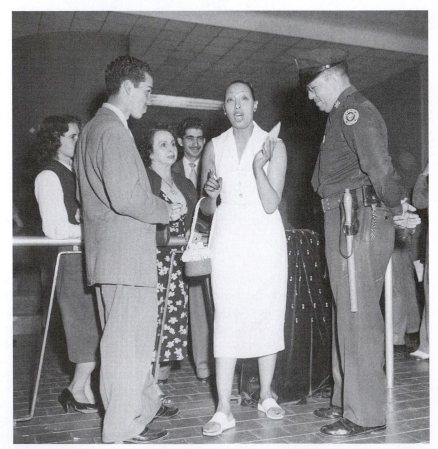

Josephine Baker in Cuba. The "saga" of jazz vocalist Josephine Baker, writes the historian Mary Dudziak, "underscores the importance to Cold War international politics of maintaining control over the narrative of race and American democracy." Outspoken at home and abroad on American racial inequality, Baker found herself surveilled and harassed by the FBI, the State Department, and the USIA, which together used disinformation falsely to discredit her as a communist in order to silence her allegedly "anti-American" views. She is shown protesting near a Havana, Cuba, radio station in February 1953 after the U.S. embassy successfully pressured her hosts to cancel Baker's scheduled performances on the island. (Corbis)

white protests. Dulles bemoaned American racial strife as "worse for us than Hungary was for the Russians."[179] International observers concluded that "the United States has no moral claim to be leader of Western democracies," for "one can't be world champion of the colonial peoples while championing inequality in one's backyard."[180] At the Brussels World's Fair of 1958, the "lily-white" State Department extolled "positive progress" on race with a controversial life-size photo of multiracial children playing ring-around-the-rosy.[181] Despite favorable European reactions, Eisenhower withdrew the display when segregationists in Congress protested the "unimaginable stupidity" of America's government "[apologizing] for racial segregation in the United States."[182] The image of the "Ugly American" exacerbated international resentment. In 1958 William J. Lederer and Eugene Burdick wrote a novel with that title to satirize "fat," "ostentatious," "loud," and "stupid" American tourists abroad and U.S. diplomats who lived lavishly in a "Golden Ghetto."[183] The authors appealed for Foreign Service Officers who spoke the language of the host country. Unless U.S. officials moved more among their host populations, they argued, Washington would lose the struggle against communism.

Gender stereotypes joined racism and other cultural biases in shaping U.S. policies toward the Third World. In South Asia, for example, American officials thought that the "vigorous" and "virile" Pakistan, which had joined the Baghdad Pact and SEATO, showed "more masculinity" than the "mystics, dreamers, [and] hypocrites" of nonaligned India, who displayed an "almost feminine hypersensitiveness" regarding national prestige.[184] Israel, having shed the stereotype of passive victim of the Holocaust for that of the "tough Jew" or "virile, throbbing civilization" surrounded by "hostile enemies," assumed the role of America's "democratic bulwark" in the Middle East.[185] U.S. leaders conversely portrayed oil-rich Arab states as cowardly "marauders," "devious" and undisciplined soldiers, or "problem [children]" in need of "an intelligent parent."[186]

Eisenhower and Prime Minister Jawaharlal Nehru (1889–1964). The Indian prime minister and the American president are shown during Nehru's U.S. visit in 1956. The British-educated Brahmin enjoyed cordial personal relations with Eisenhower, but the two remained far apart on such issues as Washington's military alliance with India's rival Pakistan (1954) and Nehru's leadership of the nonaligned movement in the Third World. According to the historian Andrew Rotter, U.S. leaders viewed Nehru's wearing of the traditional kurta, his preference for fruit juice instead of alcohol, and above all his refusal to ally with the West in the Cold War as confirming American stereotypes of Indians as lacking male "potency." (Dwight D. Eisenhower Library, White House Album)

The Soviets paid attention to the Third World, too. Both Marxism and the USSR's professed anticolonialism enjoyed wide appeal. In the mid-1950s Khrushchev toured India, Burma (Myanmar), and Afghanistan. Moscow granted some quarter billion dollars to Indonesia between 1954 and 1959 and funded an Indian steel plant and the Aswan Dam in Egypt. The Soviets also praised the Bandung Conference of April 1955, which convened twenty-nine nonaligned states (about one-quarter of the world's population) at the "first international conference of colored peoples in the history of mankind."[187] "While Washington and London fumble feebly, obsessed by visions of colored hordes clouding a lily-white horizon like locusts," the *Times of India* reported, "Moscow, Moses-like, beckons the dispossessed hosts onwards to the Promised Land."[188] U.S. information agents took note and hastened publicly to discredit the conference as "a Communist propaganda maneuver."[189]

Yet the Soviets also struggled to control Third World nationalists who refused to be the "pawn" or "plaything" of either side.[190] As one Khrushchev aide recalled, "the idea of having a whole set of Titos running the Third World was not very palatable from the Kremlin's perspective."[191] When, during his 1955 trip to India, Khrushchev vehemently denounced the West, neutralist-minded Indians under the leadership of Prime Minister Jawaharlal Nehru resented this blatant effort to bring the Cold War into their country. Arab nationalism, not communism, dominated the Middle East under the leadership of such dynamic individuals as Egypt's president Gamal Abdel Nasser. And in Latin America, between 1945 and 1955, sixteen nations outlawed the Communist party. The Soviets, like the Americans, viewed independent nationalism with suspicion. Nor could the Kremlin explain away the contradiction between its own promise of self-determination and its hypocritical performance in suppressing independence in Eastern Europe.

American officials remained fearful nonetheless that communists would exploit nationalistic sentiment and poverty in the Third World. Foreign aid became a primary U.S. tool. Whereas during the 1949–1952 period some three-quarters of total U.S. economic assistance went to Europe, in the years 1953–1957 three-quarters flowed to developing countries. By 1961 more than 90 percent of U.S. aid targeted the Third World. To Washington's distress, many recipients refused to choose sides in the Cold War. To Dulles, neutralism seemed but an "immoral and shortsighted" stage on the road to communism.[192]

"Batten Down the Hatches": Reform and Resistance in the Middle East and Latin America

Crises in the Middle East strained U.S.–Third World relations and elevated covert action and propaganda as major instruments of foreign policy. In 1952 Colonel Nasser led young Egyptian army officers against King Farouk, who fled to Europe with his harem and his wealth. Nasser initiated land reform and pledged to end British control of the Suez Canal. London reluctantly agreed in 1954 to a phased withdrawal. To prevent a defense "vacuum" in the Middle East, Washington in 1955 promoted the Baghdad Pact, a military alliance of Britain, Turkey, Iran, Iraq, and Pakistan.[193] An expansive public diplomacy campaign simultaneously used pamphlets, posters, media outlets, books, music, film, educational exchanges, and religious appeals in order to guide "revolutionary and nationalistic pressures throughout the area into orderly channels not antagonistic to the West."[194] Iran was won over in 1953 when the CIA and British intelligence jointly overthrew the nationalist regime of Mohammed Mossedegh. This alleged "elderly lunatic" unsettlingly fainted and wept, pajama-clad, during meetings with Westerners, and had pushed to nationalize foreign oil interests.[195] U.S. companies produced about 50 percent of the Middle East's petroleum. Eighty-nine percent of Europe's crude oil imports came from that region.

Israel drew closer to the United States through foreign aid totaling $374 million from 1952 to 1961. Yet bitter Arab-Israeli conflict thwarted U.S. hopes for order in the Middle East. After the Israelis raided the Gaza Strip in 1955 and exposed Egypt's military weakness, Cairo signed an arms agreement with Czechoslovakia, ending the Western arms sales monopoly in the Middle East. Meanwhile, Palestinian refugees languished in squalid camps, growing more militant each year. The State Department's Henry Byroade lectured Israelis to "drop the attitude of conqueror" toward their neighbors. But he also implored Arabs to accept the "accomplished fact" of Israel's existence.[196] "Snared in the middle of a nasty fight," the United States sought to avoid alienating either side, and in the process of trying, strained relations with both.[197]

Fluctuating U.S. views of Nasser reflected American efforts to balance competing objectives in the Middle East. While disliking Nasser's Pan-Arabism and neutralism, Dulles initially tried to entice him toward the West with foreign aid. In December 1955, the secretary offered to fund Nasser's dream of the Aswan Dam as a potential source of electricity and irrigation on the Nile. The next year the World Bank crafted a $1.3 billion project utilizing British, American, and World Bank monies. Egypt concurrently joined an anti-Israeli military alliance with Saudi Arabia, Syria, and Yemen. Jewish Americans protested in Washington, while southern members of Congress balked at a project that permitted Egypt to produce competitive cotton. Eisenhower and Dulles worried that a Czech-Egyptian arms deal signified alignment with the Soviets. Nasser viewed the weapons as "a defensive rather than an offensive means vis-a-vis Israel," and he countered that nationalism offered the best defense against communism.[198] But on July 19, 1956, a distrustful Dulles told the Egyptian ambassador that the United States had changed its mind about funding the Aswan Dam. The State Department publicly insulted the Egyptians by declaring their credit no good—despite the World Bank's decision that the dam represented a sound investment. "May you choke to death on your fury," Nasser fumed.[199] He quickly seized the Suez Canal, intent on using its $25 million annual profit to help build the dam. Washington's hard-knuckled economic diplomacy had failed.

Without consulting Washington, Britain and France huddled with Israel to plan a military operation. The British sought to preserve their joint ownership with France over the canal and to maintain access to strategic bases in the Indian Ocean. "If we do not move now," Israeli President David Ben-Gurion decided, "we will have to fight Nasser in the future, without France."[200] French officials offered Israel an additional incentive: a nuclear reactor, enabling eventual progress towards an Israeli atomic arsenal. In late October and early November 1956, forces from all three states invaded Egypt and nearly captured the canal. "Nothing

Gamal Abdel Nasser (1918–1970). The bold Egyptian leader once told John Foster Dulles that the Russians "have never occupied our territory ... but the British have been here for seventy years." Nasser went on: "How can I go to my people and tell them I am disregarding a killer with a pistol sixty miles from me at the Suez Canal to worry about somebody who is holding a knife a thousand miles away?" (*The Reporter*, 1956. Copyright 1956 by The Reporter Magazine Co.)

justifies double-crossing us," raged Eisenhower.[201] With Dulles in the hospital for cancer treatment, the president publicly upbraided Britain and France for military action that invited Soviet interference in the Middle East and diverted attention from the simultaneous Soviet invasion of Hungary (see p. 286). Tensions mounted in the West as Moscow issued an implied ultimatum on behalf of its Egyptian ally: "We are full of determination to crush the aggressor and reestablish peace in the East by using force," read telegrams wired from Moscow to Washington, Paris and London on November 5.[202] The Soviets, preoccupied with Eastern Europe and lacking capability to hit England or France with long-range missiles, actually did little during the Suez crisis except rail against the invaders, though Khrushchev, architect of the bluffing strategy, viewed the British-French withdrawal in late December as a personal vindication. Only after Washington threatened sanctions (economic aid had already been suspended) did Israel disengage from the Sinai in March 1957. A UN peacekeeping force then took positions and returned the canal, now clogged with sunken ships, to Egypt.

Suez reordered power relations in Europe and the Middle East. The crisis accelerated Britain's postwar decline. Britain's chancellor of the exchequer Harold Macmillan gloomily told the U.S. ambassador that at Suez, "we are probably witnessing the end of Western civilization. … In another 50 years yellow and black men would take over. … On the whole we had all had a very good time of it for about 500 years."[203] In efforts to force a British retreat, U.S. officials had introduced a UN resolution demanding withdrawal, and Washington had refused Britain oil shipments to compensate for the closing of the Suez Canal and the destruction of oil pipelines. The United States also had denied aid to Britain when its currency (the pound) faltered and Bank of England reserves dwindled because of a dollar drain. The British after Suez "had to face the fact that the days of the United Kingdom acting as a great power were over."[204]

The affair complicated U.S.-Arab relations as well. Although retaining its oil interests, Washington after Suez failed to dissuade many Arabs from seeing Uncle Sam as anything more than another Western usurper. After all, the United States still stood at odds with the region's most popular figure, Nasser. After withdrawing the High Dam offer and letting Moscow build the imposing structure, Eisenhower urged a U.S. role as Middle East policeman because "the Bear is still the central enemy."[205] Anti-imperialist and anti-Israeli Arabs bristled at the U.S. presumption that they needed a protective sheriff. But Eisenhower coveted Israel as an anticommunist ally, and in August 1958 Washington made its first arms sale to the Jewish state.

The administration simultaneously cultivated Saudi Arabia's King Saud bin Abdel Aziz as "the best counter to Nasser."[206] As king of the country which nurtured Islam, the State Department noted, Saud "commands the respect of more than 200 million Muslims" worldwide and could offer an "alternative to Nasser's pan-Arabism."[207] Some U.S. leaders even described Saud as "the Islamic pope," despite his prolific drinking, spending, political unpopularity, poor health, promiscuity (he fathered some 107 children), and personal eccentricities (including driving through the desert throwing money from his car to watch the locals scramble after it).[208]

Nasser, by contrast, was "clean as a whistle," a former U.S. ambassador recalled, "very fond of his children, used to plan his vacations so he could take them to the beach."[209] The administration's enthusiasm dimmed following King Saud's visit in 1958 to Washington, D.C., which convinced Eisenhower that Saud lacked the charisma and power to challenge Nasser. But the administration continued viewing Saudi Arabia as a valued anticommunist partner in protecting bases, petroleum access, and transportation and communication lines in the Middle East.

Claiming that "it is 'curtains' for Israel" if the United States did not thwart Soviet-backed Arab radicals by endorsing alternatives everywhere in the region, the president and a recuperating Dulles revitalized containment in the Eisenhower Doctrine.[210] On January 30, 1957, both houses approved Eisenhower's request (72 to 19 in the Senate and 350 to 60 in the House) to help Middle East nations resist "overt armed aggression from any nation controlled by International Communism."[211] Although Iran and Lebanon endorsed the doctrine, Syria, Egypt, and Jordan soundly rejected it, while Iraq and Saudi Arabia seemed lukewarm. Macmillan called the policy a "gallant effort to shut the stable door after the horse had bolted."[212]

Tests of the new doctrine soon arose. In April 1957, when pro-Nasser Jordanians threatened to overthrow King Hussein, Eisenhower ordered the Sixth Fleet to patrol off the coast of Lebanon and suggested that he would send U.S. marines, too. Although the king had appealed for implementation of the Eisenhower Doctrine, this first application actually targeted Nasserite Arabs, not communists. In any case, the revolt failed. The second test came in Syria, where pro-Nasser military officers gained power and negotiated aid from the Soviet Union. Syrian officials exposed a CIA plot to oust them, and Dulles declared Syria a virtual Soviet satellite. In fact, the anticommunist Syrians looked mostly to Cairo, not Moscow. In February 1958, Syria and Egypt merged as the United Arab Republic; Nasser quickly banished the Communist party from Syria.

Iraq and Lebanon claimed attention next. In July 1958, Washington swallowed "a bitter pill" when Nasserites overthrew Iraq's government.[213] Fearing that Arab radicalism could spread, the United States acted unilaterally to save the Christian-led, pro-American government in multireligious Lebanon, where a civil war pitted Christians against pro-Nasser Muslims. On July 15, 14,000 U.S. marines waded ashore, "confronting ice-cream vendors, gawkers, and bikini-clad sunbathers, not hostile gunmen."[214] "You are doing a Suez on me," Macmillan told Eisenhower upon learning that the Sixth Fleet was already headed to Lebanon.[215] Lebanese politicians soon resolved the dispute, and U.S. forces departed in fall 1958. This instance of the Eisenhower Doctrine at work offered "little more than ideological window dressing for American action" on behalf of status quo forces, because, as Dulles privately acknowledged, the country was never "under the control of international communism."[216] The incident thus set "dangerous precedents" by "misrepresenting the Third World nationalism as Soviet inspired, and by waging what amounted to a limited but undeclared presidential war."[217]

Nationalism also challenged U.S. power in Latin America, a region viewed by U.S. leaders as a "tinderbox" of communist revolution due to massive poverty, malnutrition, and mounting population pressures.[218] Through the Rio Pact (a defensive military alliance formed in 1947), the Organization of American States (launched in 1948 but formally established in 1951 to help settle inter-American disputes), investments of $8.2 billion by 1959, economic assistance totaling $835 million for the period 1952–1961, and support for military dictators such as Fulgencio Batista in Cuba, the United States perpetuated hegemony over its neighbors. But Latin American destitution remained stark; illiteracy rates stood high; health care proved inadequate; productivity showed minuscule growth; and profits from raw materials such as sugar and oil flowed through American companies to the United States. To reverse the resulting "drift in the area toward radical and nationalistic regimes," Dulles said, the United States would intervene, the Good Neighbor policy notwithstanding.[219]

For Washington, Guatemala became a litmus test for combating supposed communism in Latin America. Jacobo Arbenz Guzmán won election as president by a wide margin, and after his inauguration in spring 1951, he set land reform as his central goal. Only 2 percent of the population owned 70 percent of the land. Under the agrarian reform law of mid-1952, Arbenz expropriated about one-quarter of the nation's arable land and distributed it to some 500,000 peasants. Food production increased. But Arbenz soon clashed with the United Fruit Company (UFCO), the U.S.-owned banana exporter and Guatemala's largest landholder. UFCO had to give up more than 400,000 acres of uncultivated land. When Arbenz offered compensation in government bonds, using the value of the land the company itself, for tax purposes, set at $1.2 million, UFCO claimed the expropriated properties represented $19 million. The State Department backed UFCO: "If the Guatemalans want to handle a Guatemalan company roughly that is none of our business, but if they handle an American company roughly it is our business."[220] UFCO propagandists spread the false word: Communism had secured a beachhead in Central America.

The Soviet Union, faced with superior U.S. regional power, and skeptical of anti-Yankee leftists such as Arbenz who seemed more reformist than communist, showed little interest in Latin America in the 1950s. Still, indigenous communists backed Arbenz against entrenched interests, and he appointed some of them to administer land reform projects. Given their Cold War mentality, U.S. diplomats thought the worst. As Ambassador John Peurifoy remarked, Arbenz "talked like a Communist, he thought like a Communist, he acted like a Communist, and if he is not one …, he will do until one comes along."[221] "They would have overthrown us even if we had grown no bananas," Arbenz's friend José Manuel Fortuny recalled.[222]

Fearful that Arbenz's program of aid to workers and peasants could threaten U.S. hegemony throughout the region, Eisenhower approved the CIA plan PBSUCCESS to overthrow the Guatemalan leader. CIA-recruited Guatemalan exiles trained in Nicaragua and Honduras for an invasion. Colonel Carlos Castillo Armas, a graduate of the army staff school at Fort Leavenworth, Kansas, won favor as the president-to-be. In early 1954 Washington prodded the Organization of American States to declare, by a 17 to 1 vote, that the domination of any American state by the international communist movement would constitute a threat to the hemisphere. When

Washington also cut off technical assistance to Guatemala, Arbenz accepted a large arms shipment from Czechoslovakia. "If Paul Revere were living today," a member of Congress declared, "he would view the landing of Red arms in Guatemala as a signal to ride."[223]

On June 18, after the CIA had bribed Guatemalans, planted fictitious news stories about Arbenz's submission to the Soviets, and dropped supplies at United Fruit facilities, Castillo Armas's small force attacked from Honduras. U.S.-supplied rebel planes bombed Guatemala City. Abandoned by his military and fearful that Washington would order U.S. marines to Guatemala if Castillo Armas's invasion failed, an anguished Arbenz fled to Mexico, where he died in 1971. Castillo Armas soon returned UFCO lands, jailed his detractors, and set Guatemala on a course of government-sponsored terror that by 1990 had left 200,000 Guatemalans dead. In 1957 he fell to assassination, but the new regime remained a staunch U.S. ally. When one cabinet member following the coup urged that "we ... stop talking so much about democracy" and simply "support dictatorships of the right if their policies are pro-American," Eisenhower interjected: "You mean they're OK if they're *our* s.o.b.s?"[224]

Vice President Richard Nixon felt Latin American resentment firsthand in April–May 1958 when he traveled south on a goodwill tour. In Montevideo, Uruguay, anti-Yankee pickets mingled with the cheering crowds when Nixon motored through the city. In Venezuela all hell broke loose. Earlier in 1958 a military junta had overthrown the dictatorship of U.S. ally Marcos Pérez Jiménez ("P.J."), to whom the Eisenhower administration then gave asylum. Into a volatile environment of Venezuelen bitterness stepped Nixon, emboldened by earlier tangles with protesting students at Peru's San Marcos University. "Communists, hoodlums, and thrill seekers" blocked Nixon's motorcade en route to a wreath-laying ceremony at Simón Bolívar's tomb.[225] Demonstrators spit, threw stones, shattered windows, smashed fenders, rocked the automobile, and threatened the vice president's life. Nixon's car somehow sped away. But USIA Director George Allen worried that the United States continued to "act like adolescents. We boast about our richness, our bignesss, and our strength. ... Nations, like people, who boast can expect others to cheer when they fail."[226]

After Nixon's trip, Washington began to send more economic and military aid to the hemisphere while remaining mostly inflexible toward grassroots nationalism. To combat communist propaganda and dissuade Latin American critics, Nixon recommended that Washington distance itself from unpopular rulers: "a formal handshake for dictators; an *embrazo* [embrace] for leaders in freedom."[227] In 1959 the United States subscribed $500 million to the new Inter-American Development Bank. U.S. infantry and Panamanian Zone police in 1959 beat back efforts by students and other nationalists to gain control of the Canal Zone. Eisenhower eventually permitted the Panamanian flag to fly over the zone for the first time since the early twentieth century. In Cuba, however, the United States prepared to resist Fidel Castro, who overthrew Batista in 1959 and launched a revolution to expel U.S. economic and military interests from the island. "Batten down the hatches," Assistant Secretary Thomas Mann told Latin American specialists in the State Department. "There's going to be some real stormy weather."[228]

What if ... *the United States had used diplomacy rather than covert action to confront Third World nationalism during the 1950s?*

The administration of Dwight D. Eisenhower was the first to use covert action systematically to influence politics in the Third World. Beginning with the overthrow of Iran's Mohammed Mossedegh in 1953 and Guatemala's Jacobo Arbenz Guzmán in 1954, the CIA increasingly sought, in Latin America, Africa, and Asia, to dislodge governments that appeared unwilling to do the United States's bidding, all the while publicly denying that Washington interfered in the affairs of other states. Despite the commonly invoked justification—communist containment—many targeted leaders, including Mossedegh, Arbenz, and the Congo's Patrice Lumumba (who was overthrown in 1960 and later assassinated with CIA complicity), were not communists. They were, rather, nationalists, who sought to align with neither side in the Cold War, but who sometimes worked with leftist forces at home and abroad in order to widen their political base or to gain coveted economic or military resources. Nationalists did pose a challenge to U.S. power, insofar as their desire to control their countries' political destinies and economies exposed the reality that U.S. interests in the world were not always identical with those of recently decolonized peoples. But the subversion of nationalistic governments, including democratically elected ones, seldom served the people that covert action purported to benefit—or even the interests of the United States over the long term.

The Iranian and Guatemalan coups were, at the time, viewed by U.S. officials as successful, which emboldened the CIA to pursue regime change in Cuba (1959–1961), South Vietnam (1963), Chile (1973), Nicaragua (1981–1987), and elsewhere during the Cold War. But the the Guatemalan coup prefaced three decades of U.S.-backed revolving door military dictatorships that prompted a bitter civil war, unspeakable human rights abuses, and protracted regional chaos—exactly the conditions widely believed by American officials to provide the seedbed for communist victory. The Iranian coup legitimized as that country's leader Shah Reza Pahlevi, a monarch who used SAVAK—the U.S.-trained and funded secret police—to intimidate, harass, interrogate, torture, and imprison political dissidents. Thwarted democratic aspirations and resentment of the U.S. role exploded in 1978 into an anti-American, theocratic revolution more damaging to U.S. prestige and power in the Middle East than Mossedegh and his supporters had ever been (see Chapter 10).

What is notable is that neither Arbenz nor Mossedegh sought communism for their country, only independence, an ideal cherished by Americans themselves. Nor did U.S. covert action remain covert. Contemporaries at the time and historians since amassed substantial evidence of the American role in clandestine enterprises, and widespread knowledge of U.S. action spawned popular hostility towards an American government that came to be seen by many as hypocritical at best, and, at worst, as an agent of political disorder and civilian suffering.

What if U.S. officials had engaged Mossedegh and Arbenz in diplomacy and dialogue? What would have happened if, instead of staging the ousters of these leaders, the United States participated in a diplomatic give-and-take that brought gradual, rather than immediate results? What if such efforts indeed compromised U.S. efforts to profit limitlessly from unrestricted access to oil, fruit, or other resources, but generated diplomatic goodwill and cemented a functional political alliance? Why was formal diplomacy the norm for the United States in Europe, but less so in the decolonizing world? What role did racial assumptions play in conditioning different U.S. responses?

We may debate the answers to these questions, but the sorrowful outcomes of U.S.-backed coups in the Third World are evident today, including "blow-back"—in intelligence jargon, unintended, negative consequences for the United States and its people, which have followed from an institutionalized practice of discarding America's highest proclaimed ideals in favor of short-term political, economic, and strategic gain.

American Cultural Expansion and the Cold War

By decade's end, one of the most conspicuous signs of U.S. influence abroad came in the proliferation of American mass culture and the globalization of American ways. As economies recovered in Western Europe and Japan, people spent proportionally more of their incomes on luxuries such as electrical appliances, hi-fi phonographs, televisions, leisurewear, even glossy, befinned American cars. Although some international elites sneered at "fast-food emporiums" and "sugar-saturated soft drinks," youth made clear choices—"worn-out jeans vs. neat trousers, 'Elvis-quiff' and ponytail vs. orderly … hairstyles, uninhibited rock 'n' roll vs. civilized ballroom dancing, comic strips vs. Goethe."[229] At trade fairs, the USIA touted "People's Capitalism," or middle-class consumerism. At the Moscow exhibition of 1959, site of the Nixon-Khrushchev debate, the Miracle Kitchen of Today served up "17,500 dishes ranging from ready-to-bake biscuits and oven-ready vegetable pies to instant coffee and Jello."[230] The continued appeal of American films demonstrated what one Austrian scholar has called the "Marilyn Monroe Doctrine."[231] "Is the World 'Going American'?" *U.S. News & World Report* asked, as it described Hula-Hoops in France, canned beer in British pubs, and traffic jams in Rome, Bonn, and Sydney.[232] Americanization became a component of national security policy, equating consumerism with freedom. "By the mid 1950s, West European youths, who flocked to American universities" and consumed American exports ranging "from Dr. Spock to Dr. Seuss, … from coca cola to ketchup, from the raucous sounds of Elvis Presley to the moral exhortations of Dr. Martin Luther King" were "building a world that had begun to transcend local and national borders."[233]

Yet cultural expansion spawned both adoption *and* rejection, as demonstrated by Europeans who bemoaned the "tyranny of the herd" that debased U.S. politics, and who scorned the "intellectual fodder offered to the American masses, from scandal magazines to digests of books."[234] Humorist Art Buchwald satirized the contradictory aspects of Britain's cultural critique: "If Americans would stop spending money, talking loudly in public places, telling the British who won the war, adopt a pro-colonial policy, back future British expeditions to Suez, … stop taking oil out of the Middle East, stop chewing gum, ... move their air bases out of Britain, settle the desegregation problem in the South, ... put the American woman in her proper place, not export Rock n' Roll, and speak correct English, the tension between the two countries might ease and the British and Americans would like each other again."[235]

The Eisenhower administration promoted Americanization as one of several means to contest and undermine the appeal of Arab nationalism, Latin American revolution, Third World neutralism, communism, the Soviet Union, and China. Despite the catchy phrases of the Eisenhower-Dulles years, however, no dramatic new departures occurred in foreign policy. "Liberation" and "rollback" had always been the ultimate goal of "containment." The "Eisenhower Doctrine" extended the "Truman Doctrine." Dulles's strictures against neutralism sounded very much like Truman's declaration that all nations must choose between two ways of life. The "domino theory" in Asia differed little from Truman's alarmist predictions that if Greece fell, the Middle East would fall and Europe would collapse. Eisenhower and Dulles reinforced the Truman–Acheson hostility to "Red China." Both administrations intervened, with different methods, in the Middle East. Both bolstered the nation's nuclear arsenal. Both nourished overseas economic interests as essential to U.S. and world stability. Both sought to draw West Germany into Western Europe. America's Cold War institutions, its high defense budgets, its large foreign-affairs bureaucracy, its assumptions from the past, its export of culture—all ground on.

Martha Graham in *Lamentation*.
The famous modern dance choreographer Martha Graham, shown here in her solo piece *Lamentation* (1939), was among dozens of performing artists enlisted by the Eisenhower administration to help fight the Cold War. The President's Emergency Fund for International Affairs exported dance as a form of "cultural diplomacy," which, according to the scholar Naima Prevots, used "the arts—rather than bullets, occupying armies, or A-bombs—to win friends and influence policy" abroad. (© Barbara Morgan, Barbara Morgan Archive/ Library of Congress LC-USZ62-92948)

But the world had changed. In 1945 the United States sat atop the international system. Few restraints obstructed its power. As the Soviet Union and the United States built their economies and military forces toward a stalemate, particularly in Europe, the bonds of stability loosened elsewhere. Throughout the 1950s new nations claimed independence, threw off colonialism, and charted an independent course in the Cold War. Troubles for the two major powers also erupted in their own spheres of influence, as client states and allies contested great-power hegemony in Latin America while political turmoil and anti-Yankeeism grew apace. The 1959 victory of nationalists in the Cuban Revolution symbolized the new challenge (see Chapter 9). Japanese rioters forced Eisenhower to cancel his trip to Japan, and Europeans such as Charles de Gaulle of France resisted U.S. influence. The Soviets faced growing discontent in Eastern Europe and the Sino-Soviet split. Nuclear proliferation scared both sides. "Soon even little countries will have a stockpile of these bombs," Eisenhower worried in 1954, "and then we *will* be in a mess."[236] Britain (1952), France (1960), and China (1964) independently developed atomic bombs. Amidst these potentially dangerous developments, American pacifist movements, such as the War Resisters League, pressed for nonviolent solutions to international problems. Though largely ignored by Eisenhower officials, such groups eventually helped animate antiwar and nuclear freeze movements of the 1960s, 1970s, and 1980s.

The world was becoming multipolar. Neither the Soviet Union nor the United States, tied to rigid policies and military programs, adjusted well to the more fluid international system. Although each professed sympathy with Third World needs and aspirations, both sought to curb national self-determination in decolonizing areas. U.S. antipathy toward revolutionary nationalism, socialism, and neutralism created an anti-American backlash among non-Western peoples. So did CIA activities in Iran and Guatemala, the training of counterrevolutionaries in South Vietnam (see Chapter 9), the sending of troops into Lebanon, and alliances such as SEATO and the Baghdad Pact. Both the United States and the Soviet Union, in their drive to win friends through foreign aid and subversion, saw Third World nations manipulate Cold War rivalries to gain economic assistance and military hardware from both sides.

Unimaginative in dealing with the Third World, the Eisenhower administration also lacked innovation in its relations with the Soviet Union and China. The arms race evolved into a space race and missile race. Washington seemed only minimally interested in reducing tension in Central Europe and Germany, quickly rejecting the Rapacki Plan and its disengagement proposals. The Soviet Union seemed serious about cooling the arms race, but Moscow, too, so distrusted the other side that negotiations produced little. Nonrecognition of China simply isolated the United States from one of the world's important nations. Standing firmly with Jiang on Formosa revealed obstinacy, not wisdom, when many other Western nations recognized Beijing and traded with the People's Republic.

McCarthyism inhibited movement toward détente, but it had waned by 1954. The president also deflected another challenge, a proposed amendment to the Constitution. The Bricker Amendment, first offered in 1951 by Republican senator John Bricker of Ohio, sought primarily to limit the effects in the United

States of UN-sponsored agreements on human rights. But it included restrictions on executive agreements to ensure that presidents did not skirt the treaty-making power of the Senate. Hoping to force the president to consult more with Congress on foreign-policy issues and to forestall another Yalta, the amendment's backers insisted that executive agreements be voted on like treaties. Vowing to "fight up and down the country" against this "stupid, blind violation of [the] Constitution by stupid, blind isolationists," Eisenhower, with help from liberal Democrats and moderate Republicans, beat back the amendment in a close Senate vote in February 1954.[237] Eisenhower thereafter consulted regularly with legislators on major foreign policies, with the conspicuous exception of covert operations. Congress usually granted his requests.

Eisenhower also found himself both emboldened and restrained by the "atomic culture" that flourished during the 1950s in the realms of advertising, comic books, board games, film, television, popular music, and daily life. As the U.S. nuclear arsenal grew and the Cold War intensified, Americans both romanticized the power of nuclear energy and expressed growing anxiety about its harmful effects.[238] The Western film genre that reached its apogee with such films as *High Noon* (1952), *Shane* (1953), and *The Searchers* (1956), for instance, "accommodated the persistence of militarism" by celebrating the myth of the Western gunslinger. At the same time, the contemplative tone of such movies exposed "the cracks that began to disrupt the Cold War consensus" as, amidst the Korea stalemate, the "realities of containment policies were beginning to erode a sense of the nation marching inexorably to greatness."[239]

In the election of 1960, the Democratic Party capitalized upon American ambivalence about Eisenhower's Cold War strategy. The Democratic Party and its presidential candidate, Senator John F. Kennedy, embraced the anticommunist absolutes of the era as heartily as John Foster Dulles ever had. But Eisenhower's political critics charged that he and his secretary of state had caused the United States to fall behind in the missile race and that they had squandered American power. They differed from Eisenhower over methods to continue the old fight and to reverse the declining position of the United States in the Third World, but not over the perceived need for a globalist U.S. foreign policy.

Historical assessments of the Eisenhower administration used to stress its rigid conservatism, passive style, limited achievements, and hesitancy to adjust to new circumstances. Many scholars now emphasize Eisenhower's "prudence and sober judgment"—his moderate approach to most problems, his command of policymaking, his political savvy, and his commitment to arms control.[240] Yet Eisenhower's loyalty program damaged the Foreign Service. His expansion of the CIA and covert operations proved dangerous and shortsighted. Whatever his doubts about the insanity of the nuclear arms race, he accelerated it and left a legacy of nuclear fear. Eisenhower distrusted Jiang's Nationalists and preferred a "two Chinas" policy, but a hard-line posture toward the People's Republic of China risked nuclear war more than once. Eisenhower revisionism has stimulated healthy reconsideration of the period. But while Ike did not stumble over the brink, he remained a zealous anticommunist of little flexibility and little innovation whose diplomatic record is at best mixed.

FURTHER READING FOR THE PERIOD 1950–1961

Some works cited in Chapter 7 also cover this period.

The Korean War is explored in Gregg Brazinsky, *Nation Building in South Korea* (2007); Steven Casey, *Selling the Korean War* (2008); Jian Chen, *China's Road to the Korean War* (1994); Grace M. Cho, *Haunting the Korean Diaspora* (2008); Chae-ho Chong, *Between Ally and Partner* (2007); Bruce Cumings, *The Origins of the Korean War* (1981 and 2004), *Korea's Place in the Sun* (1997), and ed., *Child of Conflict* (1983); Rosemary Foot, *The Wrong War* (1985) and *A Substitute for Victory* (1990); Sergei N. Goncharov, John W. Lewis, and Xue Litai, *Uncertain Partners* (1994); John Halliday and Bruce Cumings, *Korea* (1988); A.N. Lan'kov, *From Stalin to Kim Il Sung* (2002); Allan R. Millett, *Their War for Korea* (2002) and *The War for Korea* (2005); Bonnie B. C. Oh, ed., *Korea Under the American Military Government* (2002); Michael D. Pearlman, *Truman and MacArthur* (2008); Gordon L. Rottman, *The Korean War Order of Battle* (2002); Michael Schaller, *Douglas MacArthur* (1989); William Stueck, *Rethinking the Korean War* (2002) and *The Korean War in World History* (2004); Richard C. Thornton, *Odd Man Out* (2000); John Toland, *In Mortal Combat* (1991); Richard Whelan, *Drawing the Line* (1990); and Shu Guang Zhang, *Mao's Military Romanticism* (1996).

For the 1950s and President Dwight D. Eisenhower, see Valerie L. Adams, *Eisenhower's Fine Group of Fellows* (2006); Stephen E. Ambrose, *Eisenhower* (1983–1984); Michael R. Beschloss, *MAYDAY* (1986) (U-2); Günter Bischof and Stephen E. Ambrose, eds., *Eisenhower* (1995); Elizabeth Borgwardt, *A New Deal for the World* (2005) (human rights); Peter G. Boyle, *Eisenhower* (2005); H. W. Brands, Jr., *Cold Warriors* (1988); Ira Chernus, *General Eisenhower* (2002) and *Apocalypse Management* (2008); J. Garry Clifford and Theodore A. Wilson, eds., *Presidents, Diplomats, and Other Mortals* (2007); Blanche W. Cook, *The Declassified Eisenhower* (1981); Richard V. Damms, *The Eisenhower Presidency* (2002); Carlo D'Este, *Eisenhower* (2002); Mary L. Dudziak, *Cold War Civil Rights* (2002); Fred I. Greenstein, *The Hidden-Hand Presidency* (1982); Michael H. Hunt, *The American Ascendancy* (2007); Burton I. Kaufman, *Trade and Aid* (1982); Michael L. Krenn, *Black Diplomacy* (1998); Christopher Layne, *The Peace of Illusions* (2006); Michael Lind, *The American Way of Strategy* (2008); Elaine Tyler May, *Homeward Bound* (2008); Chester J. Pach, Jr. and Elmo Richardson, *The Presidency of Dwight D. Eisenhower* (1991); Brenda G. Plummer, *Rising Wind* (1996) (African Americans); Caroline Pruden, *Conditional Partners* (1998) (United Nations); Jonathan Rosenberg, *How Far the Promised Land?* (2006) (civil rights); Amy L. S. Staples, *The Birth of Development* (2006); and Tom Wicker, *Dwight D. Eisenhower* (2002).

Biographical studies of U.S. and world leaders include Lee Feigon, *Mao* (2002); A. A. Fursenko and Timothy J. Naftali, *Khrushchev's Cold War* (2006); Yoram Gorlizki and O. V. Khlevniuk, *Cold Peace* (2004) (Stalin); Richard H. Immerman, ed., *John Foster Dulles and the Diplomacy of the Cold War* (1990) and *John Foster Dulles* (1999); Frederick W. Marks, *Power and Peace* (1993) (J. F. Dulles); Geoffrey Roberts, *Stalin's Wars* (2006); William Taubman, *Khrushchev* (2003); and Clarence E. Wunderlin, *Robert A. Taft* (2005).

For the Soviet Union and Europe, consult Volker R. Berghahn, *America and the Intellectual Cold Wars in Europe* (2001); James J. Carafano, *Waltzing into the Cold War* (2002) (Austria); Günter Bischof and Saki Dockrill, eds., *Cold War Respite* (1999); Günter Bischof and Anton Pelinka, eds., *The Americanization/Westernization of Austria* (2003); Frank Costigliola, *France and the United States* (1992); Michael Creswell, *A Question of Balance* (2006) (France); Victoria de Grazia, *Irresistible Empire* (2005); Carole Fink and Frank Hadler, eds., *1956*; David S. Foglesong, *The American Mission and the 'Evil Empire'* (2007); Charles Gati, *Failed Illusions* (2006) (Hungary 1956); Christopher Endy, *Cold War Holidays* (2004) (tourism in France); Jeffrey Glen Giauque, *Grand Designs and Visions of Unity* (2002) (European Union); Johanna C. Granville, *The First Domino* (2004) (Hungary 1956); William Glenn Gray, *Germany's Cold War* (2003); Wolfram F. Hanrieder, *Germany, America, Europe* (1989); Hope M. Harrison, *Driving the Soviets Up the Wall* (2003) (East Germany); Maria Höhn, *GIs and Fräuleins* (2002); Patrick T. Jackson, *Civilizing the Enemy* (2006) (Germany); Tony Judt, *Postwar* (2005); Klaus Larres, *Churchill's Cold War* (2002); Klaus Larres and Kenneth Osgood, eds., *The Cold War After Stalin's Death* (2006); Melvyn P. Leffler, *For the Soul of Mankind* (2007); Andrei S. Markovits, *Uncouth Nation* (2007) (anti-Americanism); Philippe Roger, *The American Enemy* (2005) (French anti-Americanism); Victor Rosenberg, *Soviet-American Relations, 1953–1960* (2005); Victor Sebestyen, *Twelve Days* (2006) (Hungary 1956); Alexander Stephan, *The Americanization of Europe* (2006); Irwin M. Wall, *France, the United States, and the Algerian War* (2001) and *The*

United States and the Making of Postwar France, 1945–1954 (1991); Daniel C. Williamson, *Separate Agendas* (2006) (Britain); and Vladislav M. Zubok, *A Failed Empire* (2007) (USSR).

Defense issues, including nuclear arms and antinuclear views, are treated in Matthew Brzezinski, *Red Moon Rising* (2008); Ira Chernus, *Apocalypse Management* (2008); Ian Clark, *Nuclear Diplomacy and the Special Relationship* (1994) (U.S.-Britain); Tracy C. Davis, *Stages of Emergency* (2007) (civil defense); Gerard J. De Groot, *The Bomb* (2005); Robert A. Divine, *Blowing on the Wind* (1978) and *The Sputnik Challenge* (1993); Jeffrey A. Engel, *Cold War at 30,000 Feet* (2007); Dee Garrison, *Bracing for Armageddon* (2006) (civil defense); Sharon Ghamari-Tabrizi, *The Worlds of Herman Kahn* (2005); Peter Goodchild, *Edward Teller* (2005); Michael S. Goodman, *Spying on the Nuclear Bear* (2007); Benjamin P. Greene, *Eisenhower, Science Advice, and the Nuclear Test Ban Debate, 1945–1963* (2007); Mary Ann Heiss and S. Victor Papacosma, *NATO and the Warsaw Pact* (2008); Richard G. Hewlett and Jack M. Holl, *Atoms for Peace* (1989); Michael I. Karpin, *The Bomb in the Basement* (2006) (Israel); Scott Kirsch, *Proving Grounds* (2005); Dean W. Kohlhoff, *Amchitka and the Bomb* (2002); David F. Krugler, *This is Only a Test* (2006); Gunnar Skogmar, *The United States and the Nuclear Dimensions of European Integration* (2004); David Tal, *The American Nuclear Disarmament Dilemma, 1945–1963* (2008); Marc Trachtenberg, *History and Strategy* (1991); Andreas Wenger, *Eisenhower, Kennedy, and Nuclear Weapons* (1997) and *Transforming NATO in the Cold War* (2007); Zuoyue Wang, *In Sputnik's Shadow* (2008); and Lawrence S. Wittner, *The Struggle Against the Bomb* (1998).

For propaganda, culture and cultural expansion, see works cited in Chapter 7 and Michael Adas, *Dominance by Design* (2006) (technology); Richard T. Arndt, *The First Resort of Kings* (2005) (cultural diplomacy); Laura Belmonte, *Selling the American Way* (2008); Allan M. Brandt, *The Cigarette Century* (2007); Stanley Corkin, *Cowboys as Cold Warriors* (2004) (westerns); Thomas Doherty, *Cold War, Cool Medium* (2005) (television); Alfred E. Eckes and Thomas W. Zeiler, *Globalization and the American Century* (2003); Cynthia Lee Henthorn, *From Submarines to Suburbs* (2006); Walter L. Hixson, *Parting the Curtain* (1997); William Inboden, *Religion and American Foreign Policy, 1945–1960* (2008); Matthew Frye Jacobson, *What Have They Built You to Do?* (2006) ("Manchurian Candidate"); Michael Krenn, *Fall-Out Shelters for the Human Spirit* (2005); Rob Kroes, *If You've Seen One, You've Seen the Mall* (1996); Laura McEnaney, *Civil Defense Begins at Home* (2000); Shawn J. Parry-Giles, *The Rhetorical Presidency* (2002) (propaganda); Yale Richmond, *Cultural Exchange and the Cold War* (2003); Ron Robin, *The Making of the Cold War Enemy* (2001) (military–industrial complex); Kenneth D. Rose, *One Nation Underground* (2001) (fallout shelters); Andrew Ross and Kristin Ross, *Anti-Americanism* (2004); Barry M. Rubin, *Hating America* (2004); Giles Scott-Smith and Hans Krabbendam, eds., *The Cultural Cold War in Western Europe, 1945–1960* (2003); Chris Tudda, *The Truth is Our Weapon* (2006) (propaganda); Penny Von Eschen, *Satchmo Blows Up the World* (2004); and Scott C. Zeman and Michael A. Amundson, *Atomic Culture* (2004).

Asian questions are studied in Robert Accinelli, *Crisis and Commitment* (1996) (Taiwan); Russell D. Buhite, *Douglas MacArthur* (2008); Roger Buckley, *U.S.-Japan Alliance Diplomacy, 1945–1990* (1992); Gordon H. Chang, *Friends and Enemies* (1990); Thomas J. Christensen, *Useful Adversaries* (1996); Warren I. Cohen, *America's Response to China* (1990); Nick Cullather, *Illusions of Influence* (1994) (Philippines); Robert E. Herzstein, *Henry R. Luce, Time, and the American Crusade in Asia* (2005); Richard J. Jensen, *Trans-Pacific Relations* (2003); Audrey R. Kahin and George McT. Kahin, *Subversion as Foreign Policy* (1995) (Indonesia); Christina Klein, *Cold War Orientalism* (2003); Simei Qing, *From Allies to Enemies* (2007) (China); Naoko Shibusawa, *America's Geisha Ally* (2006) (Japan); Nancy B. Tucker, *Taiwan, Hong Kong, and the United States* (1994), *Dangerous Strait* (2005), and *Strait Talk* (2009) (both Taiwan); Odd Arne Wested, ed., *Brothers in Arms* (1999); Mari Yoshihara, *Embracing the East* (2003) (gender and Orientalism); Qiang Zhai, *The Dragon, the Lion, & the Eagle* (1994); Hong Zhang, *America Perceived* (2002) (Chinese images of U.S.); and Shu Guang Zhang, *Deterrence and Strategic Culture* (1992) and *Economic Cold War* (2001) (both China). Studies of Indochina/Vietnam appear in Chapter 9.

For U.S. relations with the Middle East, including the Suez crisis, see Jon B. Alterman, *Egypt and American Foreign Assistance, 1952–1956* (2002); Irvine H. Anderson, *Biblical Interpretation and Middle East Policy* (2005); Nigel J. Ashton, *Eisenhower, Macmillan, and the Problem of Nasser* (1996); Roby C. Barrett, *The Greater Middle East and the Cold War* (2007); Uri Bialer, *Cross on the Star of David* (2005); Rachel Bronson, *Thicker Than Oil* (2006) (Saudi Arabia); Nathan A. Citino, *From Arab Nationalism to OPEC* (2002); Lawrence Davidson, *America's*

Palestine (2001); Steven Freiberger, *Dawn Over Suez* (1992); Zvi Ganin, *An Uneasy Relationship* (2004) (Israel); Mark Gasiorowski, ed., *Mohammed Mossadeq and the 1953 Coup in Iran* (2004), Irene Gendzier, *Notes from the Minefield* (1997) (Lebanon); Peter L. Hahn, *Caught in the Middle* (2004), *Crisis and Crossfire* (2005), and *The United States, Great Britain, and Egypt, 1945–1956* (2008); Rashid Khalidi, *Sowing Crisis* (2009); Stephen Kinzer, *All the Shah's Men* (2003) (Iran coup); Diane B. Kunz, *The Economic Diplomacy of the Suez Crisis* (1991); Zach Levey, *Israel and the Western Power, 1952–1960* (1997); Douglas Little, *American Orientalism* (2002); William Roger Louis and Roger Owen, eds., *Suez 1956* (1989); Steve Marsh, *Anglo-American Relations and Cold War Oil* (2003) (Iran); Melani McAlister, *Epic Encounters* (2005); Michael B. Oren, *The Origins of the Second Arab-Israeli War* (1993) and *Power, Faith, and Fantasy* (2007) (Middle East); William A. Rugh, *American Encounters with Arabs* (2006); Bonnie Saunders, *The United States and Arab Nationalism* (1996) (Syria); Patrick Tyler, *A World of Trouble* (2009) (Middle East); Selwyn Troen, ed., *The Sinai-Suez Crisis, 1956* (1990); and Salim Yaqub, *Containing Arab Nationalism* (2004).

Latin American–U.S. relations are treated in Laura Briggs, *Reproducing Empire* (2002) (Puerto Rico); Marcelo Bucheli, *Bananas and Business* (2005) (United Fruit); Elizabeth A. Cobbs, *The Rich Neighbor Policy* (1992); Bradley Lynn Coleman, *Colombia and the United States* (2008); Nick Cullather, *Secret History* (1999) (CIA in Guatemala); Michael D. Gambone, *Eisenhower, Somoza, and the Cold War in Nicaragua* (1997); Piero Gleijeses, *Shattered Hope* (1991) (Guatemala); Greg Grandin, *Empire's Workshop* (2006) and *The Last Colonial Massacre* (2004); Michael Grow, *U.S. Presidents and Latin American Interventions* (2008); Michael R. Hall, *Sugar and Power in the Dominican Republic* (2000); Gerald Horne, *Cold War in a Hot Zone* (2007) (British West Indies); Richard Immerman, *The CIA in Guatemala* (1982); G.M. Joseph and Daniela Spencer, eds., *In From the Cold* (2008); John V. Kofas, *The Sword of Damocles* (2002) (Colombia, Chile); Walter LaFeber, *The Panama Canal* (1989) and *Inevitable Revolutions* (1993) (Central America); A.W. Maldonado, *Teodoro Moscoso and Puerto Rico's Operation Bootstrap* (1997); Alan L. McPherson, *Intimate Ties, Bitter Struggles* (2006); Jason C. Parker, *Brother's Keeper* (2008) (British Caribbean); Thomas G. Paterson, *Contesting Castro* (1994); Henry Raymont, *Troubled Neighbors* (2005); Stephen G. Rabe, *Eisenhower and Latin America* (1988) and *U.S. Intervention in British Guiana* (2005); Darlene Rivas, *Missionary Capitalist* (2002) (Venezuela); Stephen C. Schlesinger and Stephen Kinzer, *Bitter Fruit* (2005) (Guatemala); David F. Schmitz, *Thank God They're on Our Side* (1999) (right-wing dictatorships); Lars Schoultz, *Beneath the United States* (1998); David Sheinin, *Argentina and the United States* (2006); and Peter H. Smith, *Talons of the Eagle* (2007).

For South Asia, Africa, and surveys of the Third World policies, see Christopher M. Andrew and Vasili Mitrokhin, *The World Was Going Our Way* (2005) (KGB); H. W. Brands, *The Specter of Neutralism* (1989); Richard P. Dauer, *A North-South Mind in an East-West World* (2005) (Chester Bowles); Kevin Kelly Gaines, *American Africans in Ghana* (2006); Brian T. Edwards, *Morocco Bound* (2005); Gabriel Kolko, *Confronting the Third World* (1988); Robert J. McMahon, *The Cold War on the Periphery* (1994) (India and Pakistan); Francis N. Nesbitt, *Race for Sanctions* (2004) (African Americans and apartheid); Andrew J. Rotter, *Comrades at Odds* (2000) (India); Elizabeth Schmidt, *Cold War and Decolonization in Guinea, 1946–1958* (2007); Kathryn C. Statler, *The Eisenhower Administration, the Third World, and the Globalization of the Cold War* (2006); Odd Arne Westad, *The Global Cold War* (2005); George White, *Holding the Line* (2005) (Africa); and Stanley Wolpert, *Nehru* (1997). See also works cited in Chapters 7, 9–12.

For intelligence and covert action, see Chapter 7 bibliography and Stephen E. Ambrose, *Ike's Spies* (1981); Sigmund Diamond, *Compromised Campus* (1992); Peter Grose, *Gentleman Spy* (1994) (Allen Dulles); Rhodri Jeffreys-Jones, *Cloak and Dollar* (2002); Loch K. Johnson, *America's Secret Power* (1989); Loch K. Johnson and James J. Wirtz, *Intelligence and National Security* (2007); Stephen Kinzer, *Overthrow* (2006); Ludwell L. Montagne, *General Walter Bedell Smith as Director of Central Intelligence* (1992); Timothy Naftali, *Blind Spot* (2005) (counterterrorism); Kenneth Osgood, *Total Cold War* (2006); John Ranelagh, *The Agency* (1986); Frances Stonor Saunders, *The Cultural Cold War* (2000); Michael J. Sullivan, III, *American Adventurism Abroad* (2007); Evan Thomas, *The Very Best Men* (1995); Hugh Wilford, *The CIA, the British Left, and the Cold War* (2003); and Robin W. Winks, *Cloak & Gown* (1987).

For McCarthyism and domestic politics, consult works cited in Chapter 7 and Kyle A. Cuordileone, *Manhood and American Political Culture in the Cold War* (2005); Lewis L. Gould, *The Most Exclusive Club* (2005)

(U.S. Senate); Robert Griffith, *The Politics of Fear* (1987); M. J. Heale, *McCarthy's Americans* (1998); David K. Johnson, *The Lavender Scare* (2003); Robert D. Johnson, *Congress and the Cold War* (2006); Stanley I. Kutler, *The American Inquisition* (1982); David A. Mayers, *Dissenting Voices in America's Rise to Power* (2007); Thomas C. Reeves, *The Life and Times of Joe McCarthy* (1982); Ellen W. Schrecker, *No Ivory Tower* (1986) and *Many Are the Crimes* (1998); Athan Theoharis and John S. Cox, *The Boss* (1988) (J. Edgar Hoover); and Stephen J. Whitfield, *The Culture of the Cold War* (1991).

See also the General Bibliography, Robert L. Beisner, ed., *Guide to American Foreign Relations Since 1600* (2003); and the following notes.

NOTES TO CHAPTER 8

1. Quoted in Glenn D. Paige, *The Korean Decision* (New York: Free Press, 1968), p. 32.

2. Glenn D. Paige, ed., *1950: Truman's Decision* (New York: Chelsea House, 1970), p. 49.

3. *Ibid.*, p. 63.

4. Robert J. Donovan, *Tumultuous Years* (New York: Norton, 1982), p. 202.

5. Quoted in Athan Theoharis, *Chasing Spies* (Chicago: Ivan R. Dee, 2002), p. 202.

6. Harry S. Truman, *Memoirs* (Garden City, N.Y.: Doubleday, 1955–1956; 2 vols.), II, 333.

7. Quoted in David Halberstam, *The Coldest Winter* (New York: Hyperion, 2007), p. 93.

8. Quoted in *New York Times*, June 26, 1950.

9. Quoted in Melvyn P. Leffler, *A Preponderance of Power* (Stanford: Stanford University Press, 1992), p. 366.

10. *Congressional Record, XCVI* (June 26, 1950), 9188.

11. *Foreign Relations, 1950, VII* (Washington, D.C.: Government Printing Office, 1976), 179.

12. Quoted in Halberstam, *Coldest Winter*, p. 99.

13. Quoted in Stanley Sandler, *The Korean War* (Lexington: University Press of Kentucky, 1999), p. 54.

14. Quoted in Gary R. Hess, *Presidential Decisions for War* (Baltimore: Johns Hopkins University Press, 2001), p. 26.

15. John H. Church quoted in William Stueck, *The Korean War* (Princeton: Princeton University Press, 1995), p. 47.

16. Quoted in Bruce Cumings, *Korea's Place in the Sun* (New York: Norton, 1997), p. 265.

17. Quoted in D. Clayton James, *Refighting the Last War* (New York: Free Press, 1993), p. 265.

18. Mao Zedong quoted in Hao Yufan and Zhai Zhihai, "China's Decision to Enter the Korean War," *China Quarterly, CXXI* (May 1990), 101.

19. Quoted in Rosemary Foot, "Leadership, Perception, and Interest," *Diplomatic History, XX* (Summer, 1996), 479.

20. Quoted in Simei Qing, *From Allies To Enemies* (Cambridge: Harvard University Press, 2007), p. 154.

21. Stalin quoted in Shen Zhihua, "The Discrepancy on Chinese Entry into the Korean War," *Cold War International History Project Bulletin*, nos. 8–9 (Winter 1996/1997), p. 238; Mao quoted in Vladislav M. Zubok, "Stalin and the Nuclear Age," in John Lewis Gaddis et al., eds., *Cold War Statesmen Confront the Bomb* (New York: Oxford University Press, 1999), p. 57.

22. Quoted in Zubok, "Stalin," p. 57.

23. Quoted in Thomas G. Paterson, "The Korean War," in Bruce W. Jentleson and Thomas G. Paterson, eds., *Encyclopedia of U.S. Foreign Relations* (New York: Oxford University Press, 1997), III, 31.

24. Quoted in Melvyn P. Leffler, *The Specter of Communism* (New York: Hill & Wang, 1994), p. 107

25. Quoted in Hess, *Presidential Decisions*, p. 59.

26. Edward Almond quoted in Bruce Cumings, *The Origins of the Korean War* (Princeton: Princeton University Press, 1981, 1990; 2 vols), II, p. 742.

27. O. P. Smith quoted in Stueck, *Korean War*, p. 128.

28. Capt. Norman Allen, "The Chinese Counter-Attack, November 1950," in Jussi Hanhimäki and Odd Arne Westad, eds., *The Cold War* (New York: Oxford University Press, 2003), p. 192.

29. Quoted in Callum A. MacDonald, *Korea* (New York: Free Press, 1987), p. 71.

30. Quoted in Philip West, "Confronting the West," *Journal of American-East Asian Relations, II* (Spring 1993), 6–7.

31. Truman quoted in Arnold A. Offner, "Another Such Victory," *Diplomatic History, XXIII* (Spring 1999), 151; Oliver Franks quoted in Thomas J. Christensen, *Useful Adversaries* (Princeton: Princeton University Press, 1996), p. 184.

32. Truman quoted in David Mayers, *Dissenting Voices in America's Rise to Power* (New York: Cambridge University Press, 2007), p. 300.

33. Quoted in Michael Schaller, *Douglas MacArthur* (New York: Oxford University Press, 1989), p. 335.

34. Quoted in Lewis L. Gould, *The Most Exclusive Club* (New York: Basic Books, 2005), p. 203.

35. *Congressional Record, XCVII* (April 19, 1951), 4125.

36. Cumings, *Origins*, II, 713.

37. Quoted in Michael D. Pearlman, *Warmaking and American Democracy* (Lawrence: University Press of Kansas, 1999), p. 293.

38. Marc Trachtenberg, "A 'Wasting Asset,'" *International Security, XIII* (Winter 1988/1989), 27.

39. Quoted in Kathryn Weathersby, "Stalin, Mao, and the End of the Korean War," in Odd Arne Westad, ed., *Brothers in Arms* (Stanford: Stanford University Press, 1998), 105.

40. Quoted in Thomas Risse-Kappen, *Cooperation Among Democracies* (Princeton: Princeton University Press, 1995), p. 62.

41. General Chung Sang-chin of North Korea quoted in Kathryn Weathersby, "Soviet Aims in Korea and the Origins of the Korean War, 1945–1950," Working Paper no. 8, *Cold War International History Project* (Washington, D.C., November 1993), p. 26.

42. Cumings, *Origins*, II, 643.

43. Lloyd Gardner, "Korean Borderlands," in William Stueck, ed., *The Korean War in World History* (Lexington: University of Kentucky Press, 2004), p. 140.

44. Sahr Conway-Lanz, "Beyond No Gun Ri," *Diplomatic History, XXIX* (January 2005), 51.

45. Stueck, *Korean War*, p. 6.

46. Paul G. Pierpaoli, *Truman and Korea* (Columbia: University of Missouri Press, 1999), p. 1.

47. Sandler, *Korean War*, p. 4.

48. "Princeton Seminar," February 13–14, 1954, Box 66, Dean Acheson Papers, Harry S. Truman Library, Independence, Missouri.

49. Aaron L. Friedberg, *In the Shadow of the Garrison State* (Princeton: Princeton University Press, 2000), p. 216.

50. Quoted in Ronald R. Krebs, *Dueling Visions* (College Station: Texas A&M University Press, 2002), p. 20.

51. Quoted *ibid.*, p. 17.

52. David Brinkley, *David Brinkley* (New York: Ballantine, 1995), p. 125.

53. Thomas Doherty, *Cold War, Cool Medium* (New York: Columbia University Press, 2003), p. 97.

54. Quoted *ibid.*, pp. 99–100.

55. Quoted in Krebs, *Dueling Visions*, p. 16.

56. Fred I. Greenstein, *The Hidden-Hand Presidency* (New York: Basic-Books, 1982).

57. Quoted in Valerie Adams, *Eisenhower's Fine Group of Fellows* (New York: Lexington Books, 2006), p. 2.

58. Eisenhower quoted in David L. Snead, *The Gaither Committee, Eisenhower, and the Cold War* (Columbus: Ohio State University Press, 1999), p. 15.

59. Kenneth A. Osgood, "Form Before Substance," *Diplomatic History, XXIV* (Summer 2000), 412; Frances Stonor Saunders, *The Cultural Cold War* (New York: New Press, 1999), p. 2.

60. Laura Belmonte, "Selling Capitalism," in David C. Engerman et al., eds., *Staging Growth* (Amherst: University of Massachusetts Press, 2003), p. 114.

61. Lloyd Goodrich quoted in Michael Krenn, *Fall-Out Shelters for the Human Spirit* (Chapel Hill: University of North Carolina Press, 2005), p. 1.

62. Penny Von Eschen, *Satchmo Blows Up the World* (Cambridge: Harvard University Press, 2004), p. 4.

63. Kenneth Osgood, *Total Cold War* (Lawrence, Kansas: University of Kansas Press, 2006), pp. 5, 77.

64. Hoover Commission quoted in Loch K. Johnson, *America's Secret Power* (New York: Oxford University Press, 1989), p. 10.

65. Quoted *ibid.*, pp. 17, 27.

66. Quoted in Stephen E. Ambrose, *Eisenhower, the President* (New York: Simon & Schuster, 1984), p. 226.

67. Quoted in Alexander DeConde, *Presidential Machismo* (Boston: Northeastern University Press, 2000), p. 160.

68. Audrey R. Kahin and George McT. Kahin, *Subversion as Foreign Policy* (New York: New Press, 1995), p. 8.

69. *Public Papers, Eisenhower, 1953* (Washington, D.C.: Government Printing Office, 1960), pp. 182–183.

70. Quoted in Vojtech Mastny, "NATO in the Beholder's Eye," Working Paper no. 35, *Cold War International History Project* (Washington, D.C., March 2002), p. 6; Vladislav Zubok, "Soviet Intelligence and the Cold War," *Diplomatic History, XIX* (Summer 1995), 461.

71. Eisenhower quoted in Gregg Herken, "Commentary: In the Service of the State," *Diplomatic History, XXIV* (Winter 2000), 112.

72. Quoted in Peter G. Boyle, *Eisenhower* (New York: Pearson, 2005), p. 78.

73. *Public Papers, Eisenhower, 1960–61* (Washington, D.C.: Government Printing Office, 1961), pp. 1035–1040.

74. Martha Smith Norris, "The Eisenhower Administration and the Nuclear Test Ban Talks, 1958–1960," *Diplomatic History, XXVII* (September 2003), 504.

75. "Discussion at the 309th Meeting of the National Security Council, Friday, January 11, 1957," Box 7, NSC Summaries, NSC Series, Ann Whitman File, Dwight D. Eisenhower Papers, Dwight D. Eisenhower Library, Abilene, Kansas.

76. Richard H. Immerman, "Conclusion," in Immerman, ed., *John Foster Dulles and the Diplomacy of the Cold War* (Princeton: Princeton University Press, 1990), p. 266.

77. Richard H. Immerman, *John Foster Dulles* (Wilmingon, Del.: Scholarly Resources, 1999), pp. 2–3.

78. Ambassador George V. Allen quoted in Andrew J. Rotter, "Christians, Muslims, and Hindus," *Diplomatic History, XXIV* (Fall 2000), 599.

79. Quoted in Amy Portwood, "John Foster Dulles," in Edward S. Mihalkanin, ed., *American Statesmen* (Westport, CT: Greenwood Press, 2004), p. 168.

80. Eisenhower quoted in Robert R. Bowie and Richard H. Immerman, *Waging Peace* (New York: Oxford University Press, 1998), p. 84.

81. Quoted in Saki Dockrill, *Eisenhower's New-Look National Security Policy, 1953–61* (New York: St. Martin's, 1996), p. 4, and in William B. Pickett, *Dwight D. Eisenhower and American Power* (Arlington Heights, Ill.: Harlan Davidson, 1995), p. 104.

82. Quoted in Ronald E. Powaski, *The Cold War* (New York: Oxford University Press, 1998), p. 102.

83. Quoted in Michael Lind, *The American Way of Strategy* (New York: Oxford University Press, 2006), p. 120.

84. Eisenhower quoted in Shane J. Maddock, "The Fourth Country Problem," *Presidential Studies Quarterly, XXVIII* (Summer 1998), 554.

85. Quoted in Gordon H. Chang, *Friends and Enemies* (Stanford: Stanford University Press, 1989), p. 70.

86. Quoted in Nigel John Ashton, *Eisenhower, Macmillan, and the Problem of Nasser* (New York: St. Martin's, 1996), p. 5.

87. Michael R. Adamson, "The Most Important Single Aspect of Our Foreign Policy," in Kathryn C. Statler and Andrew L. Johns, eds., *The Eisenhower Administration, the Third World, and the Globalization of the Cold War* (Lanham, Md.: Rowman & Littlefield, 2006), p. 57.

88. *Public Papers, Eisenhower, 1954* (Washington, D.C.: Government Printing Office, 1960), p. 383.

89. David K. Johnson, *The Lavender Scare* (Chicago: University of Chicago Press, 2004), pp. 7–10.

90. *Ibid.*, p. 2.

91. Quoted *ibid.*, p. 121.

92. Theodore H. White, *In Search of History* (New York: Warner, 1978), p. 395.

93. Aleksandr Fursenko and Timothy Naftali, *Khrushchev's Cold War* (New York: Norton, 2006), p. 16.

94. Quoted in Steven I. Levine, "Soviet Asian Policy in the 1950s," in Warren I. Cohen and Akira Iriye, eds., *The Great Powers in East Asia, 1953–1960* (New York, 1990), p. 298.

95. Quoted in Vladislav Zubok and Constantine Pleshakov, *Inside the Kremlin's Cold War* (Cambridge: Harvard University Press, 1996), p. 180.

96. Quoted in Vojtech Mastny, "The Elusive Détente," in Klaus Larres and Kenneth Osgood, eds., *The Cold War after Stalin's Death* (New York: Rowman & Littlefield, 2006), p. 5.

97. Quoted in Alessandro Brogi, *A Question of Self-Esteem* (Westport, Conn.: Praeger, 2002), p. 151.

98. Quoted in Ashton, *Eisenhower*, p. 5.

99. Eisenhower quoted in Günter Bischof, "The Making of the Austrian Treaty and the Road to Geneva," in Bischof and Saki Dockrill, eds., *Cold War Respite* (Baton Rouge: Louisiana State University Press, 2000), p. 154.

100. Quoted in Richard H. Immerman, "Trust in the Lord but Keep Your Powder Dry," *ibid.*, p. 41.

101. Raymond L. Garthoff, *A Journey Through the Cold War* (Washington, D.C.: Brookings Institution Press, 2000), p. 24.

102. Quoted in Herbert S. Parmet, *Eisenhower and the American Crusades* (New York: Macmillan, 1972), p. 406.

103. Quoted in Michael R. Beschloss, *MAYDAY* (New York: Harper and Row, 1986), p. 103.

104. *Public Papers, Eisenhower, 1955*, p. 730.

105. Quoted in James T. Patterson, *Grand Expectations* (New York: Oxford University Press, 1996), p. 302.

106. Quoted in Denis Healey, "'When Shrimps Learn to Whistle,'" *International Affairs, XXXII* (January 1956), 2.

107. Elaine Tyler May, *Homeward Bound* (New York: BasicBooks, 1988), p. 164.

108. Walter L. Hixson, *Parting the Curtain* (New York: St. Martin's, 1997), p. 159.

109. Reinhold Wagnleitner, *Cocacolonization and the Cold War* (Chapel Hill: University of North Carolina Press, 1994), p. 4.

110. Quoted in William Taubman, *Khrushchev* (New York: Norton, 2003), p. 397.

111. László Borhi, *Hungary in the Cold War, 1945–1956* (New York: Central European University Press, 2004), p. 239.

112. Quoted *ibid.*, p. 208; in Mark Kramer, "New Evidence on Soviet Decision-Making and the 1956 Polish and Hungarian Crises," *Cold War International History Project Bulletin*, nos. 8–9 (Winter 1996/1997), p. 370; and in Malcolm Byrne, "The 1956 Hungarian Revolution," *National Security Archive Electronic Briefing Book* (November 4, 2002).

113. Thomas Polgar quoted in Evan Thomas, *The Very Best Men* (New York: Simon & Schuster, 1995), p. 147.

114. Quoted in Arch Puddington, *Broadcasting Freedom* (Lexington: University Press of Kentucky, 2000), p. 113.

115. Krebs, *Dueling Visions*, p. xi.

116. Charles Gati, *Failed Illusions* (Stanford: Stanford University Press, 2006), p. 2.

117. Radio Free Europe survey quoted in Lászió Borhi, "Rollback, Liberation, Containment, or Inaction?" *Journal of Cold War Studies*, *I* (Fall 1999), 67.

118. Gregory Mitrovich, *Undermining the Kremlin* (Ithaca: Cornell University Press, 2000), p. 189.

119. Campbell Craig, *Destroying the Village* (New York: Columbia University Press, 1998), p. 70.

120. Quoted in Christopher Andrew and Vasili Mitrokhin, *"The World Was Going Our Way"* (New York: BasicBooks, 2005), p. 6

121. Quoted *ibid.*

122. Quoted in Gregg Herken, *Counsels of War* (New York: Oxford University Press, 1987), p. 130.

123. Quoted in Bruce Kuklick, *Blind Oracles* (Princeton: Princeton University Press, 2006), p. 66.

124. Noble Frankland, ed., *Documents on International Affairs, 1957* (London: Oxford University Press, 1960), p. 157; Dulles quoted in Piotr Wandycz, "Adam Rapacki," in Gordon A. Craig and Francis L. Loewenheim, eds., *The Diplomats, 1939–1979* (Princeton: Princeton University Press, 1994), p. 300; Kennan quoted in George F. Kennan, *Russia, the Atom, and the West* (New York: Harper & Brothers, 1958), p. 92.

125. Quoted in Thomas G. Paterson, ed., *Containment and the Cold War* (Reading, Mass.: Addison-Wesley, 1973), p. 116.

126. Quoted in Taubman, *Khrushchev*, p. 397.

127. Quoted in William Burr, "New Sources on the Berlin Crisis, 1958–1962," *Cold War International History Bulletin*, no. 2 (Fall 1992), p. 22.

128. Quoted in Townsend Hoopes, *The Devil and John Foster Dulles* (Boston: Little, Brown, 1973), p. 470.

129. Quoted in Hope M. Harrison, "Ulbricht and the Concrete 'Rose'," Working Paper no. 5, *Cold War International History Project* (Washington, D.C., May 1993), p. 21.

130. Khrushchev quoted in David Wolff, "'One Finger's Worth of Historical Events,'" Working Paper no. 30, *Cold War International History Project* (Washington, D.C., May 1993), p. 21.

131. Dwight D. Eisenhower, *The White House Years: Waging Peace, 1956–1961* (Garden City, N.Y.: Doubleday, 1965), p. 432.

132. Quoted in Victor Rosenberg, *Soviet-American Relations, 1953–1960* (Jefferson, N.C.: McFarland and Company, 2005), p. 218.

133. Nikita Khrushchev, *Khrushchev in America* (New York: Crosscurrente, 1960), p. 120.

134. Quoted in Deborah Welch Larson, *Anatomy of Distrust* (Ithaca: Cornell University Press, 1997), p. 96.

135. Quoted in Fursenko and Naftali, *Khrushchev's Cold War*, p. 272.

136. Quoted in Philip Taubman, *Secret Empire* (New York: Simon & Schuster, 2003), p. 312.

137. *Ibid.*, p. 310.

138. Eisenhower quoted in Marc Trachtenberg, *A Constructed Peace* (Princeton: Princeton University Press, 1999), p. 260.

139. Quoted in William B. Pickett, "Eisenhower, Khrushchev, and the U-2 Affair," in J. Garry Clifford and Theodore A. Wilson, eds., *Presidents, Diplomats, and Other Mortals* (Columbia: University of Missouri Press, 2007), p. 151.

140. Quoted in Ambrose, *Eisenhower, President*, p. 580.

141. Melvyn P. Leffler, *For the Soul of Mankind* (New York: Hill and Wang, 2007), p. 150.

142. Quoted in Edward Crankshaw, *The New Cold War* (Baltimore: Penguin, 1965 [c. 1963]), p. 81.

143. Dong Wang, "The Quarrelling Brothers," Working Paper no. 49, *Cold War International History Project* (Washington, D.C., December 2006), pp. 29, 33.

144. Dulles quoted in Shu Guang Zhang, *Economic Cold War* (Washington, D.C.: Woodrow Wilson Press, 2001), p. 115.

145. Senator William F. Knowland quoted in Gayle B. Montgomery and James W. Johnson, *One Step from the White House* (Berkeley: University of California Press, 1998), p. 98.

146. Robert David Johnson, *Congress and the Cold War* (New York: Cambridge University Press, 2006), p. 67.

147. Quoted in David Wolff, "'One Finger's Worth,'" p. 55.

148. Dulles quoted in Zhang, *Economic Cold War*, p. 123.

149. Quoted in Waldo Heinrichs, "Eisenhower and the Sino-American Confrontation," in Cohen and Iriye, *Great Power*, p. 99.

150. Quoted in Montgomery and Johnson, *One Step*, p. 184.

151. Quoted in Qiang Zhai, *The Dragon, the Lion, & the Eagle* (Kent, Ohio: Kent State University Press, 1994), p. 161.

152. Quoted in Shu Guang Zhang, "Between 'Paper' and 'Real Tigers,'" in Gaddis, *Cold War Statesmen*, p. 200.

153. Quoted in Shu Guang Zhang, *Deterrence and Strategic Culture* (Ithaca: Cornell University Press, 1992), p. 214.

154. Odd Arne Westad, "The Sino-Soviet Alliance and the United States," in Westad, ed., *Brothers in Arms* (Washington, D.C.: Woodrow Wilson Center Press, 1998), p. 176.

155. Quoted in Dockrill, *Eisenhower's New-Look*, p. 242.

156. Quoted in Melvyn Gurtov, "The Taiwan Strait Crisis Revisited," *Modern China, II* (January 1976), 79.

157. From Andrew J. Goodpaster's notes, quoted in Dockrill, *Eisenhower's New-Look*, p. 242.

158. Quoted in Zhang, *Deterrence*, p. 255.

159. Quoted in Victor S. Kaufman, *Confronting Communism* (Columbia: University of Missouri Press, 2001), p. 92.

160. Chen Yi quoted in Zhang, "'Between 'Paper' and 'Real Tigers,'" pp. 210–211.

161. Ambassador John M. Allison quoted in Aaron Forsberg, *America and the Japanese Miracle* (Chapel Hill: University of North Carolina Press, 2000), p. 30.

162. Naoko Shibusawa, *America's Geisha Ally* (Cambridge: Harvard University Press, 2006), p. 176.

163. Quoted in Benjamin P. Greene, *Eisenhower, Science Advice, and the Nuclear Test-Ban Debate, 1945–1963* (Stanford: Stanford University Press, 2007), p. 53.

164. Allison quoted in Lawrence S. Wittner, *Resisting the Bomb* (Stanford: Stanford University Press, 1997), p. 146.

165. Margot Henrikson, *Dr. Strangelove's America* (Berkeley: University of California Press, 1997), p. 58.

166. Quoted in Stuart Auerbach, "How the U.S. Built Japan, Inc.," *Washington Post National Weekly Edition*, July 26–August 1, 1993.

167. Sayuri Shimizu, *Creating People of Plenty* (Kent: Kent State University Press, 2001), p. 9.

168. Quoted in *Washington Post Weekly Edition*, August 21–26, 1995.

169. Quoted in Deborah Kisatsky, *The United States and the European Right, 1945–1955* (Columbus: Ohio State University Press, 2005), p. 116.

170. Dennis Merrill, "The Ironies of History," in David Ryan and Victor Pungong, eds., *The United States and Decolonization* (New York: St. Martin's, 2000), p. 102.

171. Quoted in John Kent, "The United States and the Decolonization of Black Africa, 1945–1953," *ibid*, p. 178.

172. Henry Byroade quoted in James H. Meriwether, *Proudly We Can Be Africans* (Chapel Hill: University of North Carolina Press, 2002), pp. 132, 166.

173. Robert L. Heilbroner, "Making a Rational Foreign Policy Now," *Harper's*, CCXXXVII (September 1968), 65.

174. SWNCC, "Political and Military Problems in the Far East," November 29, 1945, James F. Byrnes Papers, Clemson University Library, Clemson, South Carolina.

175. Cary Fraser, "Crossing the Color Line in Little Rock," *Diplomatic History*, XXIV (Spring 2000), 235.

176. Quoted in Thomas Borstelmann, *The Cold War and the Color Line* (Cambridge: Harvard University Press, 2001), p. 93.

177. Andrew J. Rotter, *Comrades at Odds* (Ithaca: Cornell University Press, 2000), p. 166.

178. King quoted in Jonathan Rosenberg, *How Far the Promised Land* (Princeton: Princeton University Press, 2006), p. 207.

179. Quoted in Azza Salama Layton, *International Politics and Civil Rights Policies in the United States, 1941–1960* (New York: Cambridge University Press, 2000), p. 131.

180. Nigerian newspaper quoted in Fraser, "Crossing," p. 250.

181. Michael Krenn, *Black Diplomacy* (New York: Sharpe, 1999), p. 44; Cambridge Study Group quoted on p. 106.

182. Representative L. Mendel Rivers and Senator Herman Talmadge quoted *ibid.*, p. 107.

183. Authors quoted in Hixson, *Parting*, p. 126; William J. Lederer and Eugene Burdick, *The Ugly American* (New York: Fawcett, 1958), 234.

184. Harold Isaacs quoted in Rotter, *Comrades*, p. 217; Elbert Matthews and Eustace Seligman quoted in Rotter, "Gender Relations, Foreign Relations," *Journal of American History*, LXXXI (September 1994), 525, 538.

185. Quoted in Michelle Mart, "Tough Guys and American Cold War Policy," *Diplomatic History*, XX (Summer 1996), 366, 371, 376.

186. Scott Lucas, "The Limits of Ideology," in Ryan and Pungong, *United States*, p. 141.

187. Paul Robeson quoted in Layton, *International Politics*, p. 71.

188. Quoted *ibid.*, p. 70.

189. Quoted in Jason Parker, "Cold War II," *Diplomatic History*, XXX (November 2006), 875.

190. Gamal Abdel Nasser and Jawaharlal Nehru quoted in Robert J. McMahon, *The Cold War on the Periphery* (New York: Columbia University Press, 1994), p. 38.

191. Oleg Troianovskii, former Soviet UN ambassador, quoted in Odd Arne Westad, *The Global Cold War* (New York: Cambridge University Press, 2005), p. 103.

192. *Department of State Bulletin, XXXIV* (June 18, 1956), 1000.

193. Quoted in Thomas G. Paterson, *Meeting the Communist Threat* (New York: Oxford University Press, 1988), p. 161.

194. State Department quoted in Joyce Battle, ed., "Documentation on Early Cold War U.S. Propaganda Activities in the Middle East," *National Security Archive Electronic Briefing Book*, no. 78 (December 13, 2002).

195. John Foster Dulles quoted in Immerman, *John Foster Dulles*, p. 67; Foreign Office quoted in Mary Ann Heiss, *Empire and Nationhood* (New York: Columbia University Press, 1997), p. 74.

196. Byroade quoted in William R. Polk, *The Arab World Today* (Cambridge: Harvard University Press, 1991), p. 388.

197. Peter Hahn, *Caught in the Middle East* (Chapel Hill: University of North Carolina Press, 2006), p. 2.

198. Guy Laron, "Cutting the Gordian Knot," Working Paper no. 55, *Cold War International History Project* (Washington, D.C.: February 2007), p. 38.

199. Quoted in Gail E. Meyer, *Egypt and the United States* (Rutherford, N.J.: Farleigh Dickinson University Press, 1980), p. 146.

200. Quoted in Michael Karpin, *The Bomb in the Basement* (New York: Simon and Schuster, 2006), p. 86.

201. Eisenhower quoted in Peter L. Hahn, *The United States, Great Britain, and Egypt, 1945–1956* (Chapel Hill: University of North Carolina Press, 1991), p. 230.

202. Quoted in Fursenko and Naftali, *Khrushchev's Cold War*, p. 134.

203. Quoted in Rachel Bronson, *Thicker than Oil* (New York: Oxford University Press, 2006), p. 72.

204. Daniel C. Williamson, *Separate Agendas, 1953–1955* (New York: Lexington Books, 2006), p. 1.

205. Quoted in David Schoenbaum, *The United States and the State of Israel* (New York: Oxford University Press, 1993), p. 117.

206. Dulles quoted *ibid.*, p. 74.

207. Quoted *ibid.*

208. Quoted in Michael B. Oren, *Power, Faith, and Fantasy* (New York: Norton, 2007), p. 514.

209. Raymond A. Hare quoted in Salim Yaqub, *Containing Arab Nationalism* (Chapel Hill: University of North Carolina Press, 2004), p. 15.

210. John Foster Dulles quoted in Douglas Little, "The Making of a Special Relationship," *International Journal of Middle East Studies*, XXV (1993), 564.

211. Quoted in Ray Takeyh, *The Origins of the Eisenhower Doctrine* (New York: St. Martin's, 2000), p. 139.

212. Quoted in Ashton, *Eisenhower*, p. 109.

213. Khrushchev quoted in Wolff, "'One Finger's Worth,'" p. 57.

214. Salim Yaqub, "Imperious Doctrines," *Diplomatic History*, XXVI (Fall 2002), 578.

215. Quoted in E. Bruce Geelhoed and Anthony O. Edmonds, *Eisenhower, Macmillan, and Allied Unity, 1957–1961* (New York: Palgrave, 2003), 53.

216. Quoted in Ashton, *Eisenhower*, p. 110.

217. Douglas Little, "His Finest Hour?" *Diplomatic History*, XX (Winter 1996), 28.

218. David M. K. Sheinin, *Argentina and the United States* (Athens: University of Georgia Press, 2006), p. 90.

219. Quoted in Thomas G. Paterson, *Contesting Castro* (New York: Oxford University Press, 1994), p. 10.

220. Quoted in Nick Cullather, *Secret History: The CIA's Classified Account of Its Operations in Guatemala, 1952–1954* (Stanford: Stanford University Press, 1999), p. 35.

221. Quoted in Richard H. Immerman, *The CIA in Guatemala* (Austin: University of Texas Press, 1982), p. 181.

222. Quoted in Piero Gleijeses, *Shattered Hope* (Princeton: Princeton University Press, 1991), p. 365.

223. Quoted in Cullather, *Secret History*, p. 79.

224. Quoted in Stephen M. Streeter, *Managing the Counterrevolution* (Athens: Ohio University Press, 2000), p. 33.

225. White House statement quoted in Michael D. Gambone, *Eisenhower, Somoza, and the Cold War in Nicaragua, 1953–1961* (Westport, Conn.: Praeger, 1997), p. 141.

226. Quoted in Alan McPherson, *Yankee, No!* (Cambridge: Harvard University Press, 2003), p. 35.

227. Quoted in Stephen G. Rabe, *Eisenhower and Latin America* (Chapel Hill: University of North Carolina Press, 1988), p. 104.

228. Quoted in Robert A. Stevenson Oral History, Foreign Affairs Oral History Program, Lauinger Library, Georgetown University, Washington, D.C., p. 29.

229. Richard Pells, "American Culture Abroad," in Rob Kroes et al., *Cultural Transmissions and Receptions* (Amsterdam, Neth.: Vu University Press, 1993), p. 78; Kaspar Maase, "American Mass Culture in the Federal Republic of Germany," *ibid.*, p. 167.

230. Robert J. Haddow, *Pavilions of Plenty* (Washington, D.C.: Smithsonian Institution Press, 1997), pp. 212–213.

231. Wagnleitner, *Cocacolonization*, p. 4.

232. *U.S. News and World Report* quoted in Donald W. White, *The American Century* (New Haven: Yale University Press, 1996), p. 241.

233. Carole Fink, "Cold War Culture and Politics in Europe in 1956," in Fink et al., eds., *1956* (Leipzig, Leipziger Universitätsverlag, 2006), 42–43.

234. Bertrand Russell quoted in Michael H. Hunt, *The American Ascendancy* (Chapel Hill: University of North Carolina Press, 2007), p. 181; Franz Joseph and Raymond Aron quoted in Jessica C. E. Gienow-Hecht, "Shame on U.S.?" *Diplomatic History*, XXIV (Summer 2000), 468.

235. Quoted in Jessica C. E. Gienow-Hecht, "Always Blame the Americans," *American Historical Review*, CXI (October 2006), 1081–1082.

236. Quoted in Shane J. Maddock, "The Nth Country Conundrum" (Ph.D. diss., University of Connecticut, 1997), p. 189.

237. Quoted in DeConde, *Presidential Machismo*, p. 158.

238. Scott C. Zeman and Michael A. Amundson, "Introduction," in Zeman and Amundson, eds., *Atomic Culture* (Boulder: University Press of Colorado, 2004), pp. 1–2.

239. Stanley Corkin, *Cowboys as Cold Warriors* (Philadelphia: Temple University Press, 2004), pp. 128 and 162–163.

240. Bowie and Immerman, *Waging Peace*, p. 6.

CHAPTER 9

Passing the Torch: The Vietnam Years, 1961–1969

Lyndon Baines Johnson (1908–1973). *In July 1968, an exhausted president listens to tapes his son-in-law Chuck Robb had sent home from Vietnam. Johnson once told his vice president, Hubert Humphrey, "I'm not temperamentally equipped to be Commander in Chief. ... I'm too sentimental to give the orders." (Lyndon B. Johnson Presidential Library)*

DIPLOMATIC CROSSROAD

❖ *The Tet Offensive in Vietnam, 1968*

"THEY'RE COMING IN! VC in the compound," the young MP shouted into his radio.[1] Seconds later Vietcong (VC) commandos killed him. Moments before, about 3:00 A.M. that January 30, 1968, the U.S. Embassy in Saigon, South Vietnam, was quiet, the only noise coming from the air conditioners and the fireworks exploding in celebration of Tet, the Lunar New Year. Completed in 1967 at a cost of $2.6 million, the six-story embassy building was protected by shatterproof windows, a concrete sun shield covering the entire structure, and a thick, eight-foot-high outer wall. The fortified building had become "the symbol of America's power" in Vietnam.[2]

At 2:45 A.M., a taxi cab and truck moved into the darkness from a repair shop near the embassy. About fifteen Vietcong leaped out after a huge explosion blew a three-foot hole in the wall. The VC scrambled through, firing automatic rifles at two embassy MPs (military police), who radioed for help before they died. The invaders then unleashed their antitank guns and rockets, transported into Saigon weeks before under shipments of tomatoes and firewood. The thick embassy doors took a direct hit, sending the U.S. seal crashing to the ground. Inside, a crew of Central Intelligence Agency and Foreign Service officials felt as if they were "in a telephone booth in the *Titanic.*"[3] A few blocks away, aides roused Ambassador Ellsworth Bunker and whisked him away to a secret hiding place.

The news of the attack quickly reached the United States. Few U.S. leaders could believe that the enemy had breached "Bunker's bunker." On January 17, in his State of the Union message, President Lyndon B. Johnson himself had called most of South Vietnam secure, and the embassy seemed the most secure of all.

In Saigon's dim morning light, American soldiers counterattacked. Paratroopers landed by helicopter on the roof. By 9:15 A.M., with the compound pacified, General William C. Westmoreland counted nineteen dead Vietnamese (four were friendly embassy employees), five dead Americans, and two Vietcong prisoners. He then declared an American victory. One reporter described the compound as a "butcher shop in Eden."[4]

The bold sally against the embassy comprised but one part of the massive, well-coordinated Tet offensive. The forays struck thirty-six of the forty-four provincial capitals, some one hundred other villages, the gigantic Tan Son Nhut air base, and numerous sites in Saigon (see map, page 355). The communist forces attacked after half of the South Vietnamese Army (ARVN) had gone on leave for the Tet holiday. The VC, or National Liberation Front (NLF), and North Vietnamese hoped to seize the cities, foment a general sympathetic uprising, force ARVN and U.S. troops to move to the cities—leaving a vacuum in the countryside—and disrupt the governmental bureaucracy. In the end, Washington would presumably negotiate American withdrawal.

Yet the ARVN and U.S. armies struck back: "Forced to fight in the cities, they bombed, shelled, and strafed the most populous districts as if they saw no distinction

"What the Hell's Ho Chi Minh Doing Answering Our Saigon Embassy Phone ...?" Paul Conrad's cartoon of President Lyndon B. Johnson expressed well the startled American response to the attack on the U.S. Embassy in South Vietnam in January 1968. Johnson had earlier reported that most of South Vietnam had been secured against the Vietcong and North Vietnamese. But General Earl Wheeler explained that "in a city like Saigon people can infiltrate easily. ... This is about as tough to stop as it is to protect against individual muggings in Washington, D.C." (Paul Conrad © 1968 Tribune Media Services, Inc. All Rights Reserved. Reprinted with permission.)

between them and the jungle."[5] Americans at home watched on television, and many recoiled from the carnage. To fight enemy troops in Hue, South Vietnam's old imperial capital, U.S. and ARVN forces used everything from nausea gas to rockets. After three weeks of vicious warfare, the communists fled, 100,000 people had become refugees, thousands lay dead, and American bombings had reduced a once-beautiful city to rubble. The NLF executed hundreds, perhaps thousands, of civilians, most of them connected with the South Vietnamese government or Americans. The NLF commander at Hue later wrote: "There is never an easy 'political' victory ... without first having to shed blood and scatter bones on the battlefield."[6]

In the northwest corner of South Vietnam, U.S. soldiers bravely resisted a siege of their base at Khe Sanh, which, according to Westmoreland, "served to lure North Vietnamese to their deaths."[7] North Vietnamese General Vo Nguyen Giap claimed in contrast that Khe Sanh was important "only to the extent" that America put its "prestige" at stake.[8] Hundreds of Americans died during the first months of 1968, as enemy rockets zeroed in on the strategic but vulnerable position. American B-52s countered by dropping tons of bombs on the surrounding area. By April, remembered a colonel, "the jungle had become literally a desert."[9] Khe Sanh held, just barely.

The provincial capital of Ben Tre symbolized the costs of the Tet offensive. To ferret out the VC, American and ARVN forces leveled Ben Tre, killing a thousand civilians. In unforgettable words, a U.S. officer declared that "it became necessary to destroy the town to save it."[10] That statement joined a visual image to sear American memory. The NBC Huntley-Brinkley news program of February 2 showed a film clip of the national police chief of South Vietnam pointing a pistol at the head of a suspected VC. General Nguyen Ngoc Loan pulled the trigger and blasted the young man. The fifty-two seconds of footage, said an NBC producer, broadcast the "rawest, roughest film anyone had ever seen."[11] Secretary of State Dean Rusk, after viewing NBC's coverage, asked journalists, "Whose side are you on?"[12]

The Johnson administration, having claimed before Tet that South Vietnam had gained the upper hand in the war, suffered an ever-growing "credibility gap." January proved a bad month for Lyndon B. Johnson. On the twenty-third the North Koreans captured the American spy ship *Pueblo* and its entire crew off the Korean coast (Johnson secured their release in December 1968 after eleven months of captivity and torture). The international balance of payments for the United States, Johnson learned, was running at an annual deficit of $7 billion. And Senator Eugene McCarthy, a "dove" on Vietnam, challenged Johnson's renomination to the presidency.

Critics probed the administration's assertion that Tet counted as a triumph. Senator Robert F. Kennedy, soon to become a candidate for the Democratic presidential nomination, said: "It is as if James Madison [had claimed] victory in 1812 because the British only burned Washington instead of annexing it to the British Empire."[13] When the popular television newscaster Walter Cronkite of CBS judged the war a stalemate, LBJ moaned: "If I've lost Cronkite, I've lost middle America."[14] The North Vietnamese had hoped for "a mass uprising in Saigon," quipped one analyst. "What they got, of course, was a mass uprising in the United States."[15]

Some 45,000 NLF, 2,000 ARVN, and 1,000 American soldiers died. Vietnamese civilians suffered a heavy toll, too. More than 14,000 died and 24,000 were wounded. One-eighth of the South Vietnamese people became homeless refugees in their own land. "Giap was callous," Westmoreland later charged. "Had any American general taken such losses he wouldn't have lasted three weeks."[16] Giap had actually opposed an ambitious offensive when NLF military leaders first proposed it in April 1967. Ho Chi Minh, the most eminent figure in the North Vietnamese government, sympathized with the Southern cadres' impatience with protracted war and overruled his chief general. But seeing the NLF devastated as a fighting force in the wake of Tet staggered Ho, who "silently regretted not having listened to Giap." Ho's health declined and "[u]nable even to sleep, he died the next year."[17]

Despite a brave front, the U.S. president also reeled from the impact of the Tet offensive. Johnson authorized 10,500 more troops for Vietnam, gave hawkish speeches against quitting under fire, and flamboyantly toured U.S. military bases. "Give me the lesser of evils," said LBJ as he asked the new secretary of defense, Clark Clifford, to undertake a major review of Vietnam policy.[18] In late February, General Westmoreland had recommended that an additional 206,000 American troops join the more than 500,000 already there. The generals planned a major new ARVN-U.S. offensive. Within the Pentagon, formerly timid dissenters pleaded for deescalation, while Secretary Rusk suggested curtailing the bombing of North Vietnam to induce peace talks. In the New Hampshire Democratic primary on March 12,

"Wise Men."   From 1965 to 1968, President Lyndon Johnson periodically received advice on Vietnam from experienced members of the foreign policy establishment (most were Truman-era diplomats and generals)—a group christened the "Wise Men." Dean Acheson (with mustache) and Secretary of State Dean Rusk (on the far right) are pictured here in a meeting with Johnson and aides. This group's consistent support for escalation led Assistant Secretary of Defense John McNaughton to remark that "a feeling is widely and strongly held" around the country that "the Establishment is out of its mind." After the Tet Offensive, when the Wise Men reversed course and urged LBJ to withdraw, the president grudgingly accepted their advice. (Lyndon Baines Johnson Presidential Library)

McCarthy made a strong showing by winning 42 percent of the vote to Johnson's 49 percent. Speaking for the "Wise Men," former secretary of state Dean Acheson put it bluntly: "We can no longer do the job we ought to do in the time we have left and we must begin to take steps to disengage."[19] Regarding the Wise Men's reversal, hawkish Walt Rostow, LBJ's national security advisor, remarked contemptuously: "The American Establishment is dead."[20]

Clifford nonetheless concurred with the Wise Men. "Nothing had prepared me for the weakness of the military's case," he recalled.[21] His Ad Hoc Task Force on Vietnam recommended in early March sending 20,000 additional American troops. But Clifford's group found "no reason to believe" that 206,000 more troops—"or double or triple that quantity"—could achieve victory. The strategy of attrition had created "a sinkhole," said the report.[22] Johnson's advisers also expressed alarm that the Vietnam War had initiated a gold and dollar crisis that threatened the economic well-being of the United States. Nervous foreigners—especially Europeans—rushed to exchange their dollars for gold. On March 14 alone, international investors redeemed $372 million for gold in the "largest gold rush in history."[23] Rusk asked "what this troop increase would mean in terms of increased taxes, the balance of payments picture, inflation, gold, and the general economic picture."[24] One economist sensed "dangerous overtones of the 1929/31 disaster."[25] Clifford's friends in the business community found America "in a hopeless bog."[26] The sheer accumulation of negative views from advisers, opinion polls, the news media, and Congress turned Johnson toward deescalation. In a dream he saw himself as Woodrow Wilson paralyzed from the neck down.

On March 31, LBJ spoke on television. "We are prepared to move immediately toward peace through negotiations," he announced. Although another 13,500 soldiers would go to South Vietnam, U.S. airplanes would halt their bombing of a major portion of North Vietnam. "Even this limited bombing of the North could come to an early end—if our restraint is matched in Hanoi [the North Vietnamese capital]."[27] To the amazement of viewers, Johnson also declared that he would not seek reelection. French President Charles de Gaulle labeled the speech "courageous" and the American public responded positively too, transforming LBJ's 57 percent disapproval rating into a 57 percent approval rating overnight.[28] On April 3, the North Vietnamese agreed to go to the conference table. Discussions began on May 14. The fighting and talking—and dying—would go on for several years more. Many GIs no longer thought the war worth fighting, as they said in their familiar slogan: "It don't mean nothin'."[29]

Vietnamese Wars Before 1961

Why Vietnam? Why did this Southeast Asian land of peasant farmers become the site of America's longest war? The origins are found in the centuries-long story of Vietnamese resistance to foreigners—Chinese, French, Japanese, and American. In 1867 France colonized Vietnam and soon began to exploit the country's raw materials, as well as those of Laos and Cambodia, which became protectorates in 1883 and part of French Indochina in the 1890s. Rice, rubber, tin, and tungsten from the area flowed to European markets. France constructed a repressive imperial government and monopolized land holdings, while some 80 percent of the Vietnamese people subsisted as poor, rural peasants. From 1867 onward, the embittered Vietnamese battled their French overlords.

Vietnam's most famous nationalist leader was Ho Chi Minh, born in 1890 to a low-level government employee. Described by a U.S. intelligence officer as a "wisp of a man … intelligent, well-versed in the problems of his country, rational, and dedicated," Ho traveled to Europe and at the time of World War I lobbied for independence.[30] At the Paris peace conference, Ho's appeal to Wilson's principle of self-determination did not move the conferees. Because the Communist party seemed the only political force vigorously denouncing colonialism, Ho and other nationalists joined it. Throughout the twenties and thirties he lived and agitated in China and Russia. In 1930–1931 the French brutally suppressed a Vietnamese peasant rebellion, killing 10,000 and deporting another 50,000.

During 1940–1941 the Japanese took over Vietnam but left collaborating French officials in charge. Vietnamese nationalists, including Ho's communists, went underground, used China as a base, and in 1941 organized the Vietminh, a coalition of nationalist groups led by the Communist party. In the final days of World War II, Vietminh guerrillas tangled with Japanese troops, liberated some northern provinces, and cooperated with the U.S. Office of Strategic Services (OSS). The agency later judged Ho "a convinced Democrat."[31] Ho sent formal messages to Washington, asked for recognition of Vietnamese independence, and often spoke in understandable English about America—its history, its political ideals, its support for "free, popular governments all over the world."[32] In late August 1945, Ho's Vietminh organized the Democratic Republic of Vietnam (DRV) in Hanoi. On September 2, he proclaimed Vietnam's independence, borrowing phrases from America's document of July 4, 1776. Still, Ho remained privately suspicious of Americans as "only interested in replacing the French. … They are capitalists to the core."[33]

During World War II, President Franklin D. Roosevelt often remarked that France should relinquish Indochina. He toyed with the idea of a trusteeship. The Department of State valued the Southeast Asian countries as "potentially important markets for American exports, and some American officials worried that denying France its empire would alienate a potential European ally.[34] Prime Minister Winston Churchill, moreover, informed Roosevelt in no uncertain terms that Britain opposed the breakup of empires. Just before he died, Roosevelt decided he "did not want to get mixed up in any Indochina decision."[35] The French, with British military help and American acquiescence, soon returned to Vietnam. Ignored by the United States, receiving no support from Moscow, and now facing French forces, the Vietminh accepted a compromise with France in March 1946: Democratic Republic of Vietnam status as a "free state" in the French Union and French military occupation of northern Vietnam. By December the agreement broke down and the First Indochina War began. One French bombardment of Haiphong killed several thousand civilians. The Vietminh responded with guerrilla terror. For the next eight years Vietnam endured bloody combat, with the French holding the cities and the Vietminh the countryside. One French military commander compared fighting the Vietminh "to ridding a dog of its fleas. We can pick them, drown them, and poison them, but they will be back in a few days."[36]

To win Paris's favor for its postwar policies in Europe, Washington tolerated the return of French colonialism to Vietnam. As the Cold War intensified in 1946–1947, Ho's Moscow "training" became a topic of American discussion. The Department of State designated him an agent of international communism, although some diplomats pointed out that Vietnamese leaders were primarily nationalists. Ho himself had earlier described himself to an OSS officer as a "progressive-socialist-nationalist"—that is, the leader of both a colonial rebellion against France and a social revolution for Vietnam.[37]

In 1948 the French "coaxed" Emperor Bao Dai, who had served as a Japanese puppet in World War II, "out of his paradise of wine, women and thongs in Hong Kong" and installed him as their Vietnamese leader.[38] Paris actively lobbied for U.S. backing of this client regime, arguing that if the Vietnamese "believe we are supported by the United States," then "they will be more disposed to reach an agreement with France [and abandon the Vietminh]."[39] In February 1950, in a move inspired by fear of Communist Chinese expansion, Washington committed its "original sin" in Vietnam and recognized the Bao Dai government.[40] In May, moreover, the Truman administration extended aid to the French for their war in Vietnam.

The Korean War accentuated Washington's interest in the Vietnamese rebellion. In 1950 Truman sent $150 million and a contingent of military advisers to

Ho Chi Minh (1890–1969). His full name meant "enlightened one" and was merely the most famous of more than fifty shifting aliases he used throughout his life. Described by the journalist David Halberstam as "part Gandhi, part Lenin, all Vietnamese," Ho often cited the United States as an example of a successful anticolonial revolution. His biographer William Duiker, however, argues that Ho might not have been completely sincere in his overtures to Washington, contending that he "was quite willing to make tactical alliances with potential adversaries in the full understanding that such arrangements might only be temporary in character." After 1955 Ho delegated more and more authority to younger party members and took an increasingly ceremonial role in the affairs of North Vietnam. (Private Collection/ Picture Research Consultants & Archives)

Vietnam. For 1945–1954 the United States gave $2 billion of the $5 billion that Paris spent to battle Ho's forces. In 1954 U.S. aid covered 78 percent of the cost of the war, and some 300 Americans went to Vietnam as part of the Military Assistance Advisory Group—all to no avail.

In spring 1954, at Dienbienphu, a fortress where the besieged French had chosen to stand or fall, Vietminh forces moved toward a major, symbolic victory. To save the fortress, the French sought U.S. intervention. President Eisenhower received conflicting advice. The chair of the Joint Chiefs of Staff, Admiral Arthur Radford, urged massive night attacks on Vietminh positions by 300 U.S. carrier aircraft, possibly including tactical nuclear weapons. Army Chief of Staff Matthew Ridgeway, however, judged intervention a "hare-brained tactical scheme," while a Defense Department analyst warned that "one cannot go over Niagara Falls in a barrel only slightly."[41]

Eisenhower cited the "falling domino" analogy to explain U.S. interests in Southeast Asia and then sounded out Congress, France, and Britain about internationalizing the war through "United Action." Members of Congress warned against an air strike that might lead next to ground troops and another Korea. London also balked. Without U.S. intervention, French forces at Dienbienphu surrendered on May 7.

A few days earlier, on April 26, 1954, representatives from France, the Soviet Union, Britain, China, the United States, Bao Dai's Vietnam, the DRV, Laos, and Cambodia met in Geneva to discuss Asian issues. The Eisenhower administration, fearing a French retreat, reluctantly agreed to discuss Vietnam at the conference. In fact, a new French government committed to ending the war came to power on June 12. President Eisenhower expected to "gag" on any Geneva agreement but vowed to "salvage something."[42] China's Zhou Enlai pressed Ho's Vietminh (now controlling two-thirds of Vietnam) to make peace so as to "consolidate and develop our forces in order to make further progress later on."[43] On July 20 the DRV and France signed the Geneva agreements. The terms: temporary partition of Vietnam at the seventeenth parallel; French withdrawal to below that latitude; neither North nor South Vietnam to sign military alliances or permit foreign bases on Vietnamese soil; national elections to be held in 1956; unification of the country after elections; and elections also in neighboring strife-torn Laos and Cambodia. Refusing to endorse the accords, the United States did state that it would "refrain from the threat or the use of force."[44] John Foster Dulles disavowed the "'Yalta business' of guaranteeing Soviet conquests" and sought ways to prevent Ho's forces from uniting Vietnam.[45] In September 1954, Eisenhower established the Southeast Asia Treaty Organization to protect Cambodia, Laos, and South Vietnam from communist subversion and aggression. SEATO violated the spirit of the Geneva Accords by specifying the defense of the southern half of Vietnam—now treated as a separate state. Although Great Britain, France, Pakistan, the Philippines, Thailand, Australia, and New Zealand joined the United States in the pact, only the last three later sent troops to fight in Vietnam. (SEATO disbanded in 1977.)

In the South, the United States pressed Bao Dai to install Ngo Dinh Diem, a Vietnamese nationalist and Catholic, as his prime minister. Diem proved a controversial choice. U.S. diplomats labeled him "a Messiah without a message," and an American journalist thought him a "screwball" whose "eyes don't even focus."[46] A four-year residence in the United States gained him prominent friends such as Cardinal Francis Spellman, Supreme Court Justice William O. Douglas, and Senators Mike Mansfield and John F. Kennedy. An enlarged contingent of American advisers, in violation of Geneva, began to train a South Vietnamese army, and millions of dollars in U.S. military and economic aid flowed to Diem. In mid-1955 the North proposed preliminary talks toward the national election scheduled by Geneva for 1956. Diem refused, and the Eisenhower administration, certain that Ho would win an election, endorsed cancellation of the electoral provisions of the Geneva Accords. In October 1955, Diem used "lofty promises of equal rights and self-rule" in combination with blatant fraud to garner 98.2 percent of the vote in a referendum that deposed Bao Dai and installed himself as president.[47] Later the gap between his democratic promises and his repressive rule would help spark insurrection.

Ngo Dinh Diem (1901–1963). The South Vietnamese nationalist Diem, from a mandarin and Catholic family, spent time in exile in the United States before returning to his country as premier (1954–1963). Eisenhower and John Foster Dulles supported Diem when most people in the U.S. and West European foreign policy establishments dismissed him as "not overly intelligent" and "a fanatic." One American diplomat complained that Diem's "only present emotion, other than a lively appreciation of himself, is a blind hatred of the French." Although Diem claimed that many of the people imprisoned by his regime were communists, a large number had actually supported the French prior to 1954. (National Archives)

The two Vietnams went their separate ways, with Ho's North receiving aid from both the Soviet Union and China, cautiously avoiding excessive reliance on either. Ho launched land reform, ending a landlord system that had largely excluded peasants. Diem's Republic of Vietnam became so dependent on U.S. aid of about $300 million a year (80 percent of it for the military) that one CIA officer commented that "he would have fallen in a day without it."[48] Working under CIA contract, Michigan State University police experts trained a "Civil Guard" to capture suspected Vietminh. Air Force Colonel Edward Lansdale, on loan to the CIA, inaugurated a propaganda campaign. Slogans such as "Christ has gone to the South" along with disinformation about impending communist bloodbaths served to scare Catholics in the North into moving to the South.[49] Some 900,000 people, most of them Catholics, made the trek. Lansdale also directed sabotage operations in the North and helped Diem defeat local rivals, including the heavily armed Cao Dai and Hoa Hao religious sects, through bribes and threats. In 1956 Diem jailed 20,000 to 30,000 suspected communists in "reeducation" camps. Torture became routine. In 1957 and 1958 southern rebels retaliated by killing village teachers, police officers, and government officials.

Capitalizing on general anti-Diem dissent, the Vietminh organized the National Liberation Front (NLF) in December 1960. Hanoi encouraged this communist-dominated group. In the rural areas they controlled, NLF cadres won favor from peasants by distributing land and reducing rents. In contrast, Diem's land reform efforts proved meager and he openly favored Catholic refugees from the North and close family members, both economically and politically. Ambassador Elbridge Dubrow actually criticized Diem and his brother Nhu for establishing a political party, the Can Lao, "an authoritarian organization largely modeled on Communist lines."[50] The party also served as a means to line the Ngo family's pockets. But U.S. military advisers continued to defend Diem despite numerous signs of opposition to his rule from all sectors of Vietnamese society. The Vietnamese organized crime network Binh Xuyen had nearly toppled him in the Battle of Saigon in 1955. He survived an assassination attempt in 1957, and three years later he was held captive for several hours by his best troops in an abortive coup. Still the Eisenhower administration lavished $1.65 billion in aid on South Vietnam from 1955 to 1961 "making it the fifth largest recipient of aid" during that period. Saigon also hosted the largest U.S mission in the entire world.[51]

U.S. officials charged that Hanoi had initiated this violence in the South, but most scholars conclude that the NLF sprang from the peculiar, repressive environment of Diem's regime. Vietnam's history had thus evolved from a colonial rebellion to expel the French into several interacting wars and revolutions: post-Geneva social revolution in the North; civil war within Diem's South; civil war between North and South; and, finally, an anti-imperialist war to force the Americans out. Imbued with the Cold War mentality that shoehorned events into an East-West frame, however, Americans failed to understand the singularly *Vietnamese* character of these conflicts. Senator John F. Kennedy in 1956 called Diem's Vietnam the "cornerstone of the free world in Southeast Asia, the keystone of the arch, the finger in the dike."[52] In 1961, Kennedy became president.

Bear Any Burden? John F. Kennedy and His Foreign Policy Team

John F. Kennedy (1917–1963). Before becoming president, JFK represented Massachusetts in the House (1947–1953) and the Senate (1953–1961). His ghostwritten book *Profiles in Courage* (1957) won a Pulitzer Prize. One of the president's unheralded achievements was the Trade Expansion Act of 1962 and the subsequent "Kennedy Round" of trade negotiations, which reduced tariffs. (*The Reporter*, 1962. Copyright 1962 by the Reporter Magazine Co.)

Vietnam figured little in the 1960 presidential contest between Richard M. Nixon and John F. Kennedy, two Cold Warriors who differed more in style than on policy. Kennedy, who won by a narrow margin, aroused support through the slogan "I think it's time America started moving again," a promise to restore "the nation's vitality, and by extension American men's virility, through strenuous—in this case *vigorous*—endeavor."[53] Both Nixon and Kennedy belonged to the "containment generation" that imbibed the popular lessons of World War II and the Cold War. Both had won seats in Congress in 1946 and endorsed the Truman Doctrine. In 1960 Kennedy charged that the Eisenhower-Nixon administration had neglected the Third World, losing it to communism. With the U-2 affair, the collapse of the Paris summit meeting, an adverse balance of payments, and crises in Cuba, the Congo, and Indochina as the immediate backdrop, Kennedy claimed that the United States was losing the Cold War. Warning that the country had "gone soft—physically, mentally, spiritually soft," he ridiculed Nixon for saying in the kitchen debate with Khrushchev that, although behind in space, "we were ahead in color television." Asserted Kennedy: "I would rather take my television black and white and have the largest rockets in the world."[54]

Kennedy did not mind being called Truman with a Harvard accent. Born in 1917 to wealthy, Catholic, politically active parents, John Fitzgerald Kennedy graduated from Harvard College and skippered a PT-boat in World War II. While his father served as ambassador to Great Britain, his senior thesis appeared as a book titled *Why England Slept* (1940), with the theme that England should have resisted Nazi aggression with force. For Kennedy's generation, the Munich agreement became the "Munich syndrome." As he once said: "The 1930s taught us a clear lesson: aggressive conduct, if allowed to go unchecked and unchallenged, ultimately leads to war."[55]

Kennedy and Kwame Nkrumah (1909–1972). Shown here greeting the president of Ghana in 1961, Kennedy won praise from African leaders because of his previous support of Algerian independence and for speeches advocating "a world safe for diversity." A student in the United States (1935–1945) before becoming his country's first president in 1957, Nkrumah welcomed American Peace Corps volunteers to train Ghana's educators and U.S. aid to build hydroelectric dams. On a visit to China in 1966 as a self-appointed mediator of the Vietnam War, Nkrumah was deposed by his own army. In exile, he praised the Black Power movement in the United States as "part of the world rebellion of the oppressed against the oppressor." (John F. Kennedy Library)

The new president exuded charisma. "All at once you had something exciting," recalled a student campaigner for Kennedy.[56] Call it psychology, charm, image, or mystique, Kennedy had it. Photogenic and quick-witted, he became a television star. Handsome, articulate, dynamic, competitive, athletic, cultured, bright, self-confident, analytical, zealous—these were the traits universally ascribed to the president. People often listened not to what he said but to how he said it, and he usually said it with verve. Dean Rusk remembered him as an "incandescent man. He was on fire, and he set people around him on fire."[57] For the historian and presidential assistant Arthur M. Schlesinger, Jr., JFK had "enormous confidence in his own luck."[58]

Style and personality influence diplomacy. Many of his friends commented that a desire for power drove John F. Kennedy because power ensured victory. His father, Joseph P. Kennedy, "pressed his children hard to compete, never to be satisfied with anything but first place."[59] Although Kennedy secretly suffered from near-fatal Addison's disease and received a "staggering" number of injections and medications, JFK nonetheless projected the image of a healthy, vigorous man.[60] His appearances with Hollywood actresses such as Marilyn Monroe and his frequent extramarital sexual liaisons reflected his macho self-image. John F. Kennedy also saw foreign affairs as an arena for proving his toughness. "Who gives a shit about the minimum wage?" he once asked.[61] Kennedy soon gave Americans box scores on the missile race, the arms race, and the space race. He introduced new slogans: "The Grand Design" for Europe; the "New Africa" policy; "Flexible Response" for the military; and the "Alliance for Progress" for Latin America. Kennedy's alarmist inaugural address pledged that "the torch has been passed to a new generation." Then came

Makers of American Foreign Relations, 1961–1969

Presidents	Secretary of State
John F. Kennedy, 1961–1963	Dean Rusk, 1961–1969
Lyndon B. Johnson, 1963–1969	

those moving, but in hindsight dangerously expansive, words: "We shall pay any price, bear any burden, meet any hardship, support any friend, oppose any foe to assure the survival and the success of liberty."[62]

The Kennedy team considered themselves "can-do" types who with careful calculation could manage crises and revive an ailing nation and world. Theodore H. White tagged them "the Action Intellectuals."[63] They had an inordinate faith in data. When a White House assistant attempted to persuade Secretary of Defense Robert McNamara, the "whiz kid" from Ford Motor Company, that the Vietnam venture would fail, McNamara shot back: "Give me something I can put in the computer. Don't give me your poetry."[64] Danger lurked in a heavy reliance on quantified information. "Ah, *les statistiques,*" said a Vietnamese general to a U.S. official. "If you want them to go up, they will go up. If you want them to go down, they will go down."[65] Despite McNamara's high standing with both JFK and LBJ, some experienced Washington hands were unimpressed. J. William Fulbright, chair of the Senate Foreign Relations Committee, recalled that McNamara "didn't know a thing" about international relations. "[H]e'd had a great success making cars" and then suddenly "he's running the whole military."[66]

Kennedy's secretary of state, Dean Rusk, worked uncomfortably with the crusading "action intellectuals" but remained a loyal member of the team. Rusk had served as a military intelligence officer in Asia during World War II, as an assistant secretary of state under Truman, and as president of the Rockefeller Foundation in the 1950s. A native of Georgia and son of a Presbyterian minister, Rusk agonized over Vietnam, opposing Americanization of the war but refusing to advise withdrawal until a noncommunist government stood secure. So, he ended up backing military escalation.

Next to Attorney General Robert F. Kennedy, the president's brother who served as troubleshooter and confidant, McGeorge Bundy became Kennedy's chief foreign-relations counselor. The forty-one-year-old former Harvard dean had helped Henry L. Stimson write his memoirs and had worked for the Marshall Plan. As national security affairs adviser, Bundy centralized decision making in the White House. Colleagues stood in awe of Bundy's "mathematical mind," while others thought him "cold as ice and snippy about everything."[67] "Mac's intellectual cocksureness might be putting-off," one diplomat commented, but "they are all cocksure here."[68] A self-professed member of the well-born elite, Bundy arrogantly asserted that "the United States is the engine of mankind, and the rest of the world is the caboose."[69]

Arms Buildup, Berlin Crisis, and Nation Building

The Kennedy administration emphasized military expansion. Kennedy lambasted Eisenhower for tolerating a "missile gap" favorable to the Soviets. Eisenhower knew the politically motivated and unsubstantiated charge was nonsense. U-2 intelligence flights revealed a modest Soviet missile program. Beginning in July 1961, the first U.S. spy satellites also confirmed that "Khrushchev was playing an extremely weak hand" with only eight missile launching pads spread over two ICBM sites.[70] Despite Washington's immense superiority, Kennedy and McNamara, worried by Soviet boasting and Third World insurgencies, began a mighty expansion of the military arsenal.

The administration called its defense strategy "flexible response," with a method for every kind of war. The Special Forces, or Green Berets, would conduct counterinsurgency against wars of national liberation; conventional forces would handle limited wars; more and better missiles would deter war or serve as primary weapons in nuclear war; at home, fallout shelters would protect Americans under a civil defense plan. In 1961 Kennedy increased the defense budget by 15 percent. By 1963 the United States had 275 major bases in 31 nations, 65 countries hosted U.S. forces, and the U.S. military trained soldiers in 72 countries. Also, 1.25 million military-related American personnel were stationed overseas. In 1961 the United States had 63 ICBMs; by 1963, 424. During 1961–1963, NATO's nuclear firing power increased 60 percent. Kennedy also created the U.S. Arms Control and Disarmament Agency, but his military buildup took priority.

The more missiles Americans acquired, the more vulnerable Americans seemed to become as the Soviets tried to catch up by also building more. With Khrushchev about to test a fifty-megaton bomb "to hang over the heads of the capitalists," Kennedy sought to reassure Americans about nuclear supremacy as well as to warn Moscow not to miscalculate.[71] On October 21, 1961, Secretary McNamara's deputy, Roswell Gilpatric, announced that the United States had such a powerful nuclear retaliatory force that it could withstand a Soviet nuclear strike and still have enough missiles remaining to annihilate the Soviet Union. Moscow reacted by speeding up its ICBM program.

Kennedy met with Khrushchev at Vienna in June 1961 to discuss a test ban treaty, Berlin, and Laos. Some aides warned that Khrushchev's moods ranged from "cherubic to choleric," but Ambassador at Large W. Averell Harriman advised JFK to "have some fun, get to know him a little. … His style will be to attack and then see if he can get away with it. Laugh about it, don't get into a fight."[72] But Kennedy went to Vienna attempting to prove his toughness and show the Soviets that they "must not crowd him too much."[73] Khrushchev arrived in Austria determined to resolve a festering problem in Berlin. With 30,000 refugees each month escaping from East Germany to West Berlin, Khrushchev speculated that "soon there will be nobody left in the GDR [East Germany] except for [Communist boss Walter] Ulbricht and his mistress."[74] He told Kennedy that Berlin must become a "free city," thereby ending Western occupation. Otherwise, Moscow would sign a separate treaty with East Germany, terminating the Soviet commitment to postwar occupation rights in Berlin. "Berlin is the testicles of the West," Khrushchev

The Berlin Wall. This photograph, taken a decade after the concrete wall went up, shows a trench filled with oil and barbed-wire fencing, all designed to deter East Germans from scaling the Wall. From 1961 to 1989, East German guards killed eighty people trying to escape across the Wall. Mayor Willy Brandt, later West Germany's chancellor, grew disillusioned with the United States because it "merely frowned" when the Wall went up. "What was called my *Ostpolitik* was formed against this background. … Traditional formulas of Western policies had been shown to be ineffective and unrealistic." (National Archives)

privately quipped. "Every time I want to make the West scream, I squeeze on Berlin."[75] Although the Kremlin leader may have left Vienna thinking that he had outdueled the young president, records of their meetings reveal that a tenacious Kennedy gave as good as he got. Still, because news accounts depicted Kennedy as "shaken and angry," the public perception developed that the Soviet leader had pushed Kennedy around.[76]

After Vienna the administration decided to force the Berlin question. On July 25, calling Berlin "the great testing place of Western courage and will," the president asked Congress for a $3.2 billion addition to the regular defense budget and authority to call up military reservists.[77] He also requested $207 million to begin a civil defense program. In a meeting with East German comrades, Khrushchev snorted that if Kennedy "starts a war then he would probably become the last president of the United States of America."[78]

On August 13, the East Germans, backed by Moscow, suddenly put up a temporary barbed wire barricade, and later an ugly concrete barrier, between the two Berlins. Worried that his East German ally Walter Ulbricht might try to capture West Berlin, Khrushchev welcomed the wall as a solution to the crisis. The Wall did shut off the exodus of refugees. Kennedy remarked that "it seems particularly stupid to risk killing millions of Americans … because Germans want Germany to be reunified."[79] So he begrudgingly accepted the Wall. Unbeknownst to the president, his special representative in Berlin, General Lucius Clay, had armed U.S. tanks with bulldozer attachments to knock down the Wall. Soviet intelligence soon learned of these preparations. Ten American M-48 tanks suddenly found themselves facing ten Russian tanks on opposite sides of Checkpoint Charlie on October 27, nearly precipitating "a nuclear-age equivalent of the Wild West Showdown at the OK Corral."[80] With the NSC staff simulating war games in which European fatalities reached tens of millions and some officials urging a U.S. first strike while it still held an overwhelming nuclear advantage, Kennedy used a secret channel to negotiate with Khrushchev. After sixteen tense hours, both Soviet and U.S. tanks withdrew and the crisis passed. Khrushchev later told a U.S. official that "it's been a long time since you could spank us like a little boy. Now we can swat your ass."[81] Kennedy visited West Berlin in 1963 to assuage bruised West German feelings.

Kennedy also attended to the Third World, the region he thought most vulnerable to revolution and communism and at the same time most susceptible to U.S. influence. "Nation building" became his watchword. Recognizing the force of nationalism in the Third World, the "action intellectuals" sought to use or channel it. They hoped that through modernization, or what the Kennedy team called middle-class revolution, Third World nations would grow from economic and political infancy to maturity, and that evolutionary economic development would ensure noncommunist political stability. As one official put it: "We weren't just against the Reds; we were for democracy and we believed ourselves to have a missionary duty to export it."[82] Kennedy targeted populous India because it followed a noncommunist model of economic development, bordered the People's Republic of China, and led the nonaligned movement. Although dollar assistance to India

G. Mennen "Soapy" Williams (1911–1988). Governor of Michigan and a noted champion of civil rights, Williams became assistant secretary of state for African affairs under Kennedy and Johnson. Pictured here being invested as an honorary chief of the Kpelle tribe in Liberia, Williams angered Europeans and white residents of South Africa, Rhodesia, and Angola when he said that the United States "only want for the Africans ... what the Africans want for themselves." The South African foreign minister called for his firing and Portuguese officials called his comments "irresponsible lunacy." Republican Senator Barry Goldwater sarcastically praised JFK for sending Williams to Africa, claiming "if we'd been elected, that's exactly where we'd have sent him!" (Bentley Historical Library, University of Michigan)

angered Pakistan, a U.S. ally, Washington nonetheless tilted toward New Delhi, especially during the Sino-Indian border war of fall 1962. In the early 1960s, India became the world's largest recipient of U.S. economic aid because Kennedy feared that if "we lose" the neutrals, "the balance of power could swing against us."[83]

Khrushchev's pledge of January 1961 to support wars of national liberation seemed to raise the stakes in the Third World. To meet this test, U.S. counterinsurgency took several forms: the training of native police forces and bureaucrats, flood control, transportation and communications improvements, and community action projects. U.S. Special Forces units—Green Berets—received special attention. Kennedy personally elevated their status in the military and supervised their choice of equipment.

World hunger also became a battlefront for Third World sympathies. Kennedy created the Food for Peace program and appointed George McGovern, a former South Dakota congressional representative, its first director. McGovern disliked his designated task of agricultural "surplus disposal" because "we were in the business of feeding hungry children, not disposing of garbage."[84] By mid-1962 his program fed 35 million children daily. By mid-1964 in "arguably the greatest humanitarian achievement of the Kennedy-Johnson era," McGovern had used the program to aid 1 million children in Peru, 2 million in Korea, 3.5 million in Egypt, 4.5 million in Brazil, 9 million in India, and over 10 million in Southeast Asia.[85] Kennedy also advocated using U.S. science to aid the Third World in feeding itself. In a speech to the World Food Congress in June 1963, he called for an agricultural revolution "which may well rival, in its social consequences, the industrial revolution" and ultimately lead to the liberation of "the talents and creative abilities of half of mankind."[86]

Kennedy's other nation building initiative, the Peace Corps, arrived with greater fanfare. Established by executive order in 1961, this volunteer group of mostly young Americans numbered 6,646 by mid-1963 and 15,000 by mid-1966. Seeking "to live out the ideals of their culture," as one volunteer put it, they went into developing nations as teachers, agricultural advisers, and technicians.[87] Peace Corps officials heeded Vice President Lyndon Johnson's admonition to reject any volunteers who matched the "three C's—the Communists, the consumptives, and the cocksuckers."[88] But they won plaudits for their efforts to improve Third World living conditions. Peace Corps monuments—irrigation systems, water pumps, larger crops—arose throughout Latin America and Africa, even as the corps's humanitarian efforts fell far short of eradicating the Third World's profound squalor.

The Alliance for Progress focused on Latin America in hopes of heading off Cuban-style revolution and communist subversion. Launched in August 1961, the alliance envisioned spending $20 billion in funds from the United States and international organizations. In return, Latin Americans promised land and tax reform, housing, and health improvements. Despite its initial promise, the alliance soon sputtered. American businesses did not invest as expected; the State Department dragged its feet; Latin American nationalists disliked U.S. control; elites resisted reforms and pocketed U.S. dollars; middle-class Latin Americans, whom Washington counted on, proved selfish. In the end, adult literacy and infant mortality rates improved, but Latin American economies registered unimpressive growth rates, class divisions widened, unemployment climbed, and agricultural production per person declined.

The difficulties of nation building appeared dramatically in the Congo, which obtained hurried independence from Belgium in mid–1960. Civil war quickly erupted. Backed by U.S. and European cobalt and copper interests, Moise Tshombe tried to detach Katanga Province from the new central government headed by Patrice Lumumba, a fervent anti–colonialist deemed too leftist by Washington. The United States, fearing Soviet influence in "another Cuba," helped a UN mission quell the Katanga insurrection and ultimately defeat Tshombe in 1963.[89] Lumumba's assassination in 1961 aroused suspicions of U.S. complicity. In February, protestors filled the visitors' gallery at the UN building in New York, interrupting the U.S.

The New Frontier in the Third World. Tom Qualia, a Peace Corps volunteer in Bolivia, illustrates the belief, described by the historian Fritz Fischer, that the United States was "sending American youth into the new frontier of the third world." Not just a rhetorical device, "the volunteers were trained to expect conditions … similar to those of the mythic American West." The Peace Corps proved to be one of Kennedy's most popular programs and came to exemplify his reputed idealism. But he had little affection for the program, especially after the first director, his brother-in-law Sargent Shriver, persuaded Congress to make it independent of the State Department. After JFK lost that bureaucratic battle, Shriver complained that the president refused to give him any help, not even so much as a "light for a cigarette." (National Archives)

Ambassador Adlai Stevenson with cries of "Murderers of Lumumba, you Ku Klux Klan motherfuckers!"[90] Stevenson blamed the scene on Soviet machinations. In 1964 a major leftist revolt in the Congo supported by the Soviet Union, China, and Ghana broke out. With UN forces gone, the CIA soon bolstered former enemy Tshombe as the new leader of the central government, and with direct U.S. aid, including military advisers, he recruited white mercenaries. The rebels responded by terrorizing white foreigners. In November 1964, a small force of Belgian paratroopers dropped from U.S. aircraft into the Congo to rescue Belgian and U.S. citizens. The historian Thomas Borstelmann has noted that "Africans, African Americans, and antiracists around the world condemned Tshombe as a stooge of Belgian mining interests and were outraged by Lumumba's assassination, which they likened to an international lynching."[91] Nation building thus met resistance on both nationalist and racial grounds.

The Most Dangerous Area in the World: The Cuban Revolution and Latin America

In Latin America, events surrounding the Cuban Revolution claimed center stage. Because Cuba might export revolution to its neighbors, Kennedy considered Latin America "the most dangerous area in the world," and Khrushchev crowed that "Latin American reminds one of an active volcano."[92] On July 26, 1953, a young Cuban nationalist, Fidel Castro, attempted to overthrow the American-backed regime of Fulgencio Batista. Imprisoned and later released, Castro fled to Mexico. In late 1956, under the banner of the 26th of July Movement, he returned to Cuba. Almost captured, he escaped into the mountains, where for two years he augmented his guerrilla forces, gained popular support, and fought Batista's U.S.-supplied army. In January 1959, despite CIA plots to deny him power, the bearded rebel marched into Havana and initiated social and economic programs designed to reduce extensive U.S. interests that had developed since 1898 and had come to dominate Cuba's sugar, mining, and utilities industries.

Determined to dilute the North American cultural influence that they believed had undermined Cuba's national identity, the Castroites crippled the Mafia-run gambling casinos and ousted from government the *batistianos* who had profited from close contact with U.S. investors. Castro avowed that "we no longer live in times when one had to worry when the American Ambassador visited the [Cuban] Prime Minister."[93] Indeed, "what happened in Guatemala will not happen here."[94]

Fearing that a successful Cuban revolution would cause the United States to "get kicked around in the hemisphere," but finding no evidence that Castro was a communist, Washington soon applied a series of tests: Cuba must respect North American–owned property, continue alignment with the United States on international questions, and adhere to a democratic politics that permitted pro-U.S. "moderates" to sustain ties with Washington.[95] Cuba failed the U.S. tests. Land reform struck at U.S. interests, the execution of Batista supporters reduced U.S. influence, and the moderates faltered in their competition with Castroite radicals. After telling Vice President Richard Nixon that "the people of Cuba don't want free elections, they produce bad governments," Castro cancelled scheduled balloting and evicted the U.S. military missions that had supported Batista.[96] In vehement anti-Yankee orations, Castro also called for revolutions throughout Latin America. Washington warned against his "Nasser-like ambition."[97] In late 1959, the CIA began to work with Castro's rivals to "replace" the revolutionary regime.[98] In January 1960, Eisenhower labeled Castro a "mad man … who is going wild and harming the whole American structure."[99]

In March 1960, Eisenhower ordered the CIA to train Cuban exiles for an invasion of their homeland—this shortly after Cuba signed a trade treaty with the Soviet Union. In mid-1960, as the revolutionary government nationalized foreign properties, the United States suspended imports of Cuban sugar and then forbade U.S. exports to the island. These measures pushed Cuba toward a new economic lifeline—the Soviet Union. As Khrushchev later told Kennedy, Castro was no communist but "you are well on your way to making him a good one."[100] In the belief that Castro had moved from neutralism to communism, Washington broke diplomatic relations with Cuba in January 1961.

"The Castro regime is a thorn in the flesh," Senator J. William Fulbright argued, but "not a dagger in the heart."[101] Still, ignoring the U.S. contribution to Castro's anti-Americanism, President Kennedy defined Cuba as a test of will and gave the green light for a "covert" assault, dubbed "Operation Castration" by White House aide Arthur Schlesinger.[102] The CIA assured him that it could deliver another Guatemala. The agency predicted that the Cuban people would rise up against Castro and a CIA-hired assassin's bullet would kill him. The CIA pinpointed Bahía de Cochinos (Bay of Pigs) as the invasion site and organized a Cuban Revolutionary Council to take office. Kennedy, without consulting Congress, approved the invasion plan. He also prohibited U.S. military participation. The CIA did not protest this restriction because "we felt that when the chips were down," Allen Dulles later wrote, "any action required for success would have been authorized [by the president] rather than permit the enterprise to fail."[103] Kennedy worried that the trained exiles would embarrass him politically if he scotched the expedition. Secretary Rusk dissented that "U.S. policy should not be driven" to drastic action by "a single battalion of men."[104]

In mid-April 1961, 1,453 CIA-trained commandos departed from Nicaragua for Cuba (see map, page 402). They met early resistance from Castro's militia, no sympathetic insurrection occurred, and within two days the invasion had become a fiasco. One hundred fourteen commandos died, and more than 1,100 were captured. Some 150 Cuban defenders were killed. Four American pilots also died in the operation. Kennedy fumed: "I was assured by every son of a bitch I checked with … that the plan would succeed."[105] One intelligence veteran lamented that the Bay of Pigs had brought "the end of the golden age of covert action."[106] Khrushchev could not believe that the United States did not pursue the invasion to its ultimate end, telling his son, "Can he [Kennedy] really be that indecisive?"[107] After the disaster, despite having vetoed a desperate CIA request for U.S. air attacks during the last hours of the failing invasion, the president blamed the CIA and Joint Chiefs of Staff for faulty intelligence and sloppy execution. Cuban exiles cried betrayal, saying it was "like John Wayne backing down from a gunfight with an evil dwarf."[108] But

Cheddi Jagan (1918–1997). Premier of British Guiana from 1961 to 1964, as it awaited its independence, Jaggan at times referred to himself as a communist and raised U.S. fears of a "second Cuba." According to the historian Stephen G. Rabe, Robert Kennedy conceded that British Guiana was "a small country," but Cuba was also small, and "it's caused us a lot of trouble." The United States fomented racial, labor, and political unrest to prevent Jaggan from taking power in an independent Guyana. Washington, instead, backed the openly undemocratic and despotic Forbes Burnham, whose dictatorial regime lasted from 1966 to 1985. After Guyana held its first free elections in 1992, Jaggan emerged as president and held that office until his death in 1997. (John F. Kennedy Library)

even if the president had ordered more air strikes, then what? The brigade's meager forces would have had to face Castro's army of 25,000 and the nation's 200,000-strong militia.

Little sobered by the Bay of Pigs setback, the president issued secret orders making Cuba the "top priority … no time, money, effort, or manpower is to be spared."[109] Under Operations Mongoose and Northwoods, the Pentagon and CIA planned anti-Castro assassination plots and invasions while cooperating with anti-Castro exiles to stage hit-and-run sabotage raids against oil facilities and other island targets. Washington also tightened the economic embargo. This multitrack campaign did not knock Castro from his perch. What next? "If I had been in Moscow or Havana at that time," Secretary of Defense McNamara later remarked, "I would have believed the Americans were preparing for an invasion."[110] And rightly so, given that the Joint Chiefs of Staff in the spring of 1962 vigorously advocated "early military intervention in Cuba" even if the United States had to foment an incident to justify war.[111]

Spinning Out of Control: The Cuban Missile Crisis

Critical to understanding the missile crisis of fall 1962 is the relationship and timing between U.S. activities and Soviet-Cuban decisions to place on the island nuclear weapons that could strike areas of the United States where 92 million people lived. In May 1962, Soviets and Cubans first discussed the idea of such weapons; in July, during a trip by Raúl Castro to Moscow, representatives initialed a draft agreement; in late August–early September, during a trip by the Cuban leader Che Guevara to Moscow, an accord became final. These steps were taken while the United States was pressing Cuba on all fronts.

Not only did Castro learn about the assassination plots and witness the sabotage attacks, but his spies heard about possible U.S. military action against Cuba. The director of Operation Mongoose, Brigadier General Edward Lansdale, planned to ignite a revolt against Castro in October 1962 and recommended the use of U.S. forces to ensure success. American military maneuvers heightened Cuban fears. One well-publicized U.S. exercise, staged during April, included 40,000 troops and an amphibious landing on a small island near Puerto Rico. "Were we right or wrong to fear direct invasion?" Castro later asked.[112]

After the Bay of Pigs invasion, Moscow had begun military shipments that included small arms, howitzers, armored personnel carriers, patrol boats, MiG jet fighters, and tanks. Under the Moscow-Havana agreement, the Soviets sent to Cuba surface-to-air missiles (SAMs), 36 medium-range (SS-4) missiles, 42 light IL-28 jet bombers, Luna tactical nuclear weapons, nuclear warheads, and more than 42,000 Soviet military personnel. Only 24 intermediate range (SS-5) missiles, also part of the agreement, did not reach Cuba by mid-October. "I think we will win this operation," Khrushchev mused after looking over the military power that Moscow would now be able to project from Cuba.[113] Kennedy rejected immediate action against the military buildup because the Soviets "may try to blockade Berlin and we would then try to blockade Cuba."[114]

NOW IT'S OFFICIAL!

The Sun-Telegram, San Bernardino, Ca.

"Now It's Official." Jeff Yohn's anti-Castro, anti-Soviet cartoon appeared in the *San Bernadino Sun-Telegram* (California) newspaper in 1961. In July 1960, when the Soviet Union agreed to purchase Cuban sugar after the Eisenhower administration ended sugar imports from the island, Soviet premier Nikita Khrushchev declared the Monroe Doctrine dead and pledged military aid to Cuba "if it became necessary." During the April 1961 Bay of Pigs crisis, Khrushchev told President Kennedy that the Soviets would give "to the Cuban government all the necessary assistance to repel aggression." In 1962 such aid included nuclear-tipped SS-4 missiles, setting off yet another crisis. (Library of Congress)

Had there been no Bay of Pigs invasion, no destructive covert activities, no assassination plots, no military maneuvers and plans, and no economic and diplomatic steps to harass, isolate, and destroy the Castro government, there might have been no Cuban missile crisis. The origins of the October 1962 crisis derived largely from the concerted U.S. campaign to quash the Cuban Revolution and from the Soviet-Cuban effort to deter the United States through missile deployment. Many of Khrushchev's colleagues have commented on the importance of Castro to the Soviet premier, with one recalling that "Castro made Khrushchev feel like a young Bolshevik again."[115] Scholars have attributed other motives to the Soviets, such as their wanting to force negotiations on Berlin, to compel a trade for U.S. missiles stationed in Turkey, or to undermine Chinese criticism that Moscow had become too tolerant of the West. Perhaps because Pentagon officials had publicly announced decisive American nuclear superiority, Moscow also may have hoped to catch up in the nuclear arms race. But to stress only the global, Cold War dimension slights the local or regional sources of the conflict and misses the central point: Khrushchev would never have had the opportunity to install dangerous nuclear weapons in the Caribbean if the United States had not been attempting to overthrow the Cuban government. The United States helped precipitate what Dean Rusk called "an utterly crashing crisis."[116]

On October 14, a U-2 reconnaissance plane photographed medium-range (1,100-mile) missile sites under construction in Cuba. After gathering more data, American officials informed the president on October 16 that the Soviet Union had indeed placed missiles in Cuba. Kennedy quickly created an Executive Committee of the National Security Council (Ex Comm), consisting of his "action intellectuals" and experienced diplomats from the Truman years. Joining McNamara, brother Robert, and McGeorge Bundy were Dean Acheson, Paul Nitze, and Robert Lovett, among others. Scholars have speculated that Ex Comm might have been a means to keep potential right-wing dissenters from a diplomatic solution "inside the tent" and implicate them in any plan to resolve the crisis. If Kennedy saw it playing such a role, it would help explain "why men like Richard Goodwin, Chester Bowles, and Arthur Schlesinger were excluded from the group" and why "softer solutions" were only discussed outside Ex Comm meetings.[117]

Kennedy's immediate preference became clear: "We're certainly going … to take out these … missiles."[118] After JFK left the meeting, Robert McNamara exclaimed, "This is a domestic *political* problem. … We said we'd *act*. Well, how will we *act?*"[119] Ex Comm considered four options: "talk them out," "squeeze them out," "shoot them out," and "buy them out."[120] Ex Comm advisers initially gave only slight attention to negotiations and concentrated on military action. Acheson, among others, favored an air strike. Under Secretary of State George Ball countered that even a successful air strike would mean "carrying the mark of Cain on your brow for the rest of your life."[121] Air Force officials reported that some missiles might survive and still threaten the United States. The Joint Chiefs of Staff recommended a full-scale

Soviet Missile Site at San Cristóbal, Cuba. This revealing U-2 photograph was taken in October 1962, when Soviet technicians were busily trying to assemble the various components of medium-range missiles. (U.S. Air Force)

Adlai Stevenson (1900–1965). Governor of Illinois and twice a Democratic presidential candidate, Stevenson became ambassador to the United Nations under Kennedy. During the missile crisis, Stevenson urged removal of Soviet missiles from Cuba and U.S. missiles from Turkey—advice that prompted President Kennedy to tell journalists that "Adlai wanted a Munich." Because Kennedy, in the final settlement, secretly promised the Soviets that the Jupiter missiles would be withdrawn from Turkey, the historian Mark White ranks Stevenson as "the unsung hero of the missile crisis." (Library of Congress)

military invasion. Although alluring, such a scheme could mean a prolonged war with Cuba, heavy U.S. casualties, and a Soviet retaliatory attack on Berlin. Ex Comm ruled out a private overture to Castro. Ambassador to the United Nations Adlai Stevenson's proposal that the United States publicly offer to trade the missiles in Turkey for those in Cuba met open derision. Ex Comm members, tired and irritable, finally settled on a naval blockade or quarantine of future arms shipments to Cuba. The quarantine, pushed ardently by McNamara as "a communications exercise, not a military operation," left open options for further escalation.[122]

Kennedy went on national television on October 22, announcing a blockade and insisting that Khrushchev "halt and eliminate this clandestine, reckless and provocative threat to world peace."[123] More than 180 warships patrolled the Caribbean, and marines reinforced the U.S. naval base at Guantánamo, on Cuba. A B-52 bomber force loaded with nuclear bombs took to the skies. On October 24, Soviet vessels approached the blockade, but the ships stopped. Assembly of the missiles already in Cuba continued. Secretary General of the United Nations U Thant urged talks; Khrushchev called for a summit meeting. Kennedy demanded removal of the

Robert Strange McNamara (b. 1916). The mathematically minded secretary of defense graduated from the University of California, Berkeley. A former Ford Motor Company executive, who according to the journalist David Halberstam "epitomized booming American technological success," McNamara applied efficiency methods to his department and served as war minister for Vietnam. In 1968 he became president of the World Bank. In the 1980s he criticized the nuclear arms race that he had accelerated in the 1960s. McNamara finally published a memoir, *In Retrospect* (1995), wherein he confessed that America's war in Vietnam had been "wrong, terribly wrong." (*The Reporter*, 1967. Copyright 1967 by The Reporter Magazine Co.)

missiles first. On October 26, in a confusing episode, ABC News correspondent John Scali heard a Soviet agent suggest one possible solution whereby Moscow would disengage its missiles if Washington publicly pledged not to invade Cuba. Scali reported the conversation to U.S. officials as a genuine Soviet proposal from "very high sources," but the KGB agent had not been authorized to make the offer.[124] Yet a long letter from Khrushchev soon arrived proposing much the same settlement.

The next day, October 27, the crisis intensified. A Soviet surface-to-air missile shot down a U-2 plane over Cuba. The Americans prepared to retaliate, not knowing that Soviet commanders had tactical nuclear weapons ready to use against an invasion. Later in the day, a U.S. spy aircraft strayed into Soviet air space, nearly sparking a dogfight with Soviet MiGs. More ominous, the commander of a Soviet submarine harassed by American warships prepared his nuclear torpedo, telling his crew "we will die but we will sink them all."[125] Another officer fortunately calmed him down and persuaded the commander to await further instructions from Moscow. By this time U.S. officials were analyzing another Khrushchev letter. The premier raised the stakes: He would withdraw the missiles from Cuba if the United States removed its missiles from Turkey. "We can't very well invade Cuba," JFK mused, "when we could have gotten them [Soviet ballistic missiles] out by making a deal on … Turkey."[126] Sidestepping this proposal, the president endorsed Khrushchev's first offer: removal of the missiles in Cuba in exchange for a public U.S. pledge not to invade Cuba. Robert Kennedy assured the Soviets in private that the Jupiter missiles would be withdrawn from Turkey, but he warned that if Moscow divulged this secret deal, Washington would disavow it. A "very upset" Bobby said that "time is of the essence," that "many unreasonable heads" are "itching for a fight," in which "millions of Americans and Russians will die."[127] The president was pursuing multiple initiatives to resolve the crisis. If Khrushchev had balked, Rusk had secretly arranged for the United Nations to propose removing missiles from both Turkey and Cuba; "Kennedy would not let the Jupiters in Turkey become an obstacle," Rusk later insisted.[128] Khrushchev agreed to withdraw the missiles because Soviet forces could not prevent an invasion. A livid Castro led crowds in chanting "*Nikita, mariquita, lo que se da no se quita!*" ("Nikita, you little homosexual, what is given should not be taken back!").[129] The Chinese charged the Soviets with both "adventurism" and "capitulationism."[130] Having secured Cuba from invasion, Khrushchev said he was no "czarist officer who has to kill himself if I fart at a masked ball. It is better to back down than go to war."[131]

"We were in luck," John Kenneth Galbraith later commented, "but success in a lottery is no argument for lotteries."[132] Kennedy's team proved "pretty good at improvising," sniffed Dean Acheson, "but God help us … if they are given time to think!"[133] As McGeorge Bundy remembered, the crisis came "so near to spinning out of control."[134] Declassified recordings of the Ex Comm meetings confirm that Washington never had a firm handle on the crisis. As the scholar James Nathan has noted: "The voices are halting. The sentences are incomplete. Thoughts ramble. Memories slip and options ooze into the ether."[135] NATO allies, moreover, pointedly complained that they "can live with Soviet MRBMS, why can't [Americans]?"[136] Why not reduce tensions by publicly trading missiles in Turkey that U.S. officials privately considered "a pile of junk" and "worse than useless"?[137] Even the aftermath proved messy. Washington demanded that the IL-28 bombers that the Soviets had given to Cuba must be removed along with the missiles. Not until November 13 did Khrushchev agree to pull the IL-28s out. The three protagonists, moreover, never signed a formal agreement, leaving enough ambiguity to cause later crises in Cuban-Soviet-American relations (see Chapter 10). A quarter-century later, McNamara offered a somber reassessment: "You *can't* manage" crises because of all the "misinformation, miscalculation, misjudgment, and human fallibility."[138]

The Cuban missile crisis both slowed and accelerated the Cold War. Having found communication difficult during the event, the antagonists installed a "hot line" or Teletype link between the White House and the Kremlin. Both sides seemed frightened enough by nuclear danger to move toward a more accommodating relationship, producing the Limited Test Ban Treaty of July 1963, which prohibited atmospheric and underwater nuclear testing. In a speech at American University in June ("the best … by any president since Roosevelt," according to Khrushchev), Kennedy revealed uneasiness with large weapons spending, appealed for arms control, and asked Americans to reexamine Cold War attitudes.[139] Subsequent Kennedy speeches, however, sounded hawkish once again.

The missile crisis carried long-term detrimental effects. The Soviet Union, revealed as a nuclear inferior, pledged to catch up in the arms race. That part of the Cold War contest was ratcheted up with new and more dangerous weapons systems. As for Cuba, despite a Castro initiative for rapprochement, U.S. officials vowed to intensify "our present nasty course."[140] The CIA quickly launched new dirty tricks and revitalized its assassination option by making contact with a cooperative Cuban official, Rolando Cubela Secades. Bearing the code name AM/LASH, he plotted with the CIA to kill Fidel Castro. On the very day that President Kennedy fell to assassination, AM/LASH rendezvoused with CIA agents in Paris, where he received a ballpoint pen rigged with a poisonous hypodermic needle. Like all other assassination plots against Castro, this one failed. The new Johnson administration put exploratory Cuban-American contacts at the United Nations on ice. Thereafter, U.S.-Cuba relations remained frozen.

In the afterglow of the missile crisis, Kennedy's civilian advisers ignored the close calls of October and rationalized their improvisations as masterful "crisis management." Proud of keeping their generals "on a short leash," they believed they could confidently avoid nuclear holocaust, confine actual combat to Third World insurgencies, and win the Cold War through a calculated "display of superior American nerve and resolve."[141] Or so they thought, until Vietnam changed many of their minds.

General Curtis LeMay (1906–1990). After supervising the air attacks against Japan in World War II and leading the Strategic Air Command during the 1950s, LeMay became the U.S. Air Force Chief of Staff from 1961 to 1965. During the Cuban Missile Crisis, he advocated a massive military strike against Cuba and Soviet forces. He pontificated: "The Russian bear has always been eager to stick his paw in Latin American waters. Now we've got him in a trap, let's take his leg off right up to his testicles. On second thought, let's take his testicles off too." When JFK and Khrushchev resolved the crisis, LeMay blasted their agreement as "worse than Munich." Sometimes called General "Dismay," he ran unsuccessfully as a vice-presidential candidate along with third party presidential candidate Governor George Wallace in 1968. (U.S. Air Force Museum Photo Archives)

Laos, Vietnam, and the Kennedy Legacy

As continued unrest destabilized Laos and Vietnam, those countries climbed higher on President Kennedy's agenda. Rostow saw an opportunity to use "our unexploited counterguerrilla assets"—helicopters and Special Forces units. "We are not saving them for the Junior Prom," he told Kennedy.[142] Laos, wracked by civil war, became a testing ground. Granted independence at Geneva in 1954, Laos chose nonalignment in the Cold War when the nationalist leader Souvanna Phouma organized a coalition government of neutralists and the procommunist Pathet Lao in 1957. The Eisenhower administration opposed the government and built up the right-wing Laotian army. In 1958 CIA-backed rightists displaced Souvanna Phouma and shaped a pro-U.S. government. Washington dispatched military advisers to the new regime. Souvanna Phouma did return to power after a coup in 1960, but the United States again undermined him by equipping rightist forces. Souvanna soon took assistance from Moscow and North Vietnam. But in December he fled his country. For Eisenhower, Laos constituted the "cork in the bottle."[143]

The incoming Kennedy administration shared this perception of the Laotian problem. As conspicuous Soviet aid flowed to the Pathet Lao, Kennedy ordered the Seventh Fleet into the South China Sea and moved marines with helicopters into Thailand. Then the Bay of Pigs disaster struck. With one arm tied down in Cuba, Kennedy swung the other in Laos. The president instructed the several hundred U.S. military advisers in Laos, heretofore restricted to covert operations, to discard their civilian clothes and dress in more ostentatious military uniforms as a symbol of U.S. resolve. The Soviets wanted no fight in Laos. In April 1961, they endorsed Kennedy's appeal for a cease-fire. But the Pathet Lao battled on alone. The Joint Chiefs of Staff told Kennedy that they could win in Laos so long as they sent "120,000 to 140,000 men, with authority to use nuclear weapons if necessary."[144] Kennedy, however, listened to those who argued that "it would be a mistake to fight in Laos" because the Chinese threat would be too great.[145]

After more than a year of continued bloodshed in Laos and hard bargaining in Geneva, W. Averell Harriman helped produce "a good, bad deal" among the major powers.[146] Laos, under a government led by Souvanna Phouma, would become neutral. Still, peace did not come. Both the United States and North Vietnam quickly violated the accords. Hanoi continued to supply the Pathet Lao and failed to remove all its troops from Laos. Washington secretly shipped arms to Souvanna's government, and the CIA also armed and trained Hmong mountain clans, an ethnic minority that suffered "one of the highest mortality rates in modern war."[147] Without informing the American people, the United States began secret bombing raids against Pathet Lao forces in 1964. By then the problem of Laos derived from the country's proximity to Vietnam.

After the Bay of Pigs, the Berlin Wall, and the neutralization of Laos, Vietnam seemed to assume greater urgency. Rejecting French President Charles de Gaulle's warning that in Vietnam "we failed and you will fail," Kennedy advisers judged the corrupt Ngo Dinh Diem a liability, but as Vice President Lyndon B. Johnson put it, "Sh—, man, he's the only boy we got out there."[148] Even as JFK questioned the domino theory, his private doubts about Cold War verities hid behind bellicose words and policies. Fearing that if he abandoned Saigon, he would be "damned everywhere as a Communist appeaser," he steadily expanded the U.S. presence in South Vietnam.[149] In January 1961, Kennedy authorized $28.4 million to enlarge the South Vietnamese army and another $12.7 million to improve the civil guard. In May he ordered 400 Special Forces soldiers and another 100 military "advisers" to South Vietnam. Meanwhile, the NLF captured more territory and accelerated the violence through assassinations of village chiefs. In October a U.S. intelligence study indicated that 80 to 90 percent of the 17,000 Vietcong in South Vietnam came

Strategic Hamlet, South Vietnam. Introduced by the Diem regime in 1962 and funded by the United States, the strategic hamlet program sought to separate the NLF from its supporters among the people. The 6,000 hamlets, according to the historian David Trask, "isolated some Vietnamese from outside influences in ways reminiscent of reservations. ... There was an effort to 'kill the Vietnamese' culturally that recalled earlier attitudes toward Native Americans." A Native American veteran agreed: "We were involved in the same kind of colonization process that was carried out by whites in this country." Many of the hamlets were poorly built, "more suited to fencing the cattle in" than keeping "the Viet Cong out," according to a British military officer. (National Archives)

from the South, not from North Vietnam, and that most of their supplies originated in the South.

The president in October 1961 dispatched two hawks, General Maxwell Taylor and Walt Rostow, to South Vietnam to study the war firsthand. Diem asked for more American military aid. The duo recommended sending 8,000 U.S. combat troops. Rusk questioned such a "major additional commitment of American prestige to a losing horse."[150] Conscious that his decision violated the Geneva Accords and uncertain whether a larger U.S. military commitment could stabilize the Saigon government, Kennedy in November authorized a much smaller increase in U.S. advisers. By the end of 1961, they numbered 3,205. During the next year the figure jumped to 9,000, and at the time of Kennedy's death in November 1963 these forces had reached 16,700. American troops, helicopter units, minesweepers, and air reconnaissance aircraft went into action. In 1962, 109 Americans died and in 1963, 489. A nation building effort, the strategic hamlet program, intended to resettle 15 million people in fortified villages, but it proved disruptive and unpopular with villagers and permitted the NLF to appear as Robin Hoods. In February 1963, Rusk nonetheless announced that the "momentum of the Communist drive has been stopped."[151]

As aid to Saigon increased, Diem and his brother Nhu worried that it "could become a sort of opium paralyzing the country."[152] Anti-Americanism grew apace. The Diem government passed a "Social Purification Law" against alleged vice that Diem's sister-in-law Madame Nhu blamed on Americans, such as dancing and sexual relationships between American men and Vietnamese women. Diem himself complained about "all these soldiers I never asked to come here."[153] By early 1963, Nhu told multiple foreign officials that the United States had sent too many troops and half of them should go home. Americans exhibited similar negative

A Suicide in Protest, Saigon. Thich Quang Duc, a Buddhist monk aged seventy-three, set his gasoline-drenched yellow robes afire in June 1963 to protest Diem's restrictions on Buddhists. (AP Images)

attitudes toward Diem's nepotistic practices; indeed "our relations with the Ngo family … [were] like dealing with a whole platoon of de Gaulles," recalled one embassy official.[154] Diem's growing unpopularity at home and his refusal to ease the repressive nature of his regime prompted Senator Wayne Morse (D-Oregon) to cite "cumulating evidence" that Diem had not instituted "a democratic government."[155] By 1963 one diplomat claimed that Diem had gone "off his rocker."[156] In May 1963, tension between Saigon and Washington reached a peak, when South Vietnamese troops opened fire on unarmed Buddhist protestors in the city of Hue, massacring nine. The incident erupted after a Catholic provincial chief had enforced an old decree prohibiting the flying of Buddhist flags. The Buddhist demonstrations also expressed longstanding nationalist sentiment, an appeal for peace talks with the NLF, and resentment against U.S. interference in Vietnamese politics. In early June, Thich Quang Duc, a Buddhist monk, sat in a Saigon street, poured fuel over his body, and immolated himself. Appalled, Kennedy reportedly warned a confidant that the Vietnamese "hate us … [and] they'll kick our asses out of there."[157] During summer and fall the protest spread; so did Diem's suppression. Kennedy publicly chastised Diem and reduced aid.

Diem proved more and more resistant to U.S. advice. Nhu had already intimated a willingness to negotiate with both the NLF and North Vietnam, claiming that "the communists" were "brothers, lost sheep."[158] Evidence soon mounted that Nhu and Diem were not bluffing. Convinced that Washington desired their

Robert F. Kennedy (1925–1968) and Ngo Dinh Nhu (1910–1963). Pictured here together in Saigon, Kennedy and Nhu both emerged as the most influential advisors to their presidential siblings. In October 1963, Vice President Lyndon B. Johnson observed that Saigon and Washington were quite similar. Both capitals had chief executives in trouble because of "very strong" brothers. As early as 1960, British officials lamented that if Diem remained president, Nhu could continue "messing everything up." As the United States's relationship with Diem soured and policymakers pondered replacements, they listed as one of their top requirements that the new leader "should be an only child." (National Archives)

ouster after the Buddhist crisis, they sent out multiple peace feelers to the NLF and Hanoi. A settlement that neutralized both halves of Vietnam and reunified the country under a federated government that left Ho and Diem the dominant political figures in their zones seemed possible. Hanoi made only one nonnegotiable demand: "The Americans have to leave."[159] French President Charles de Gaulle's public call for a similar solution in late August increased Washington's paranoia. When Diem explored contacts with Hanoi and the NLF through India in late September, Kennedy officials feared that Diem and Nhu would choose a negotiated settlement rather than "abject surrender to U.S. demands."[160] Others believed that Nhu merely sought to bluff Washington into backing down.

Senior South Vietnamese generals, now aware that Diem no longer had American favor, asked how the Kennedy administration would respond to a coup d'état. The new ambassador, Henry Cabot Lodge, wanted to dump Diem, but officials in Washington hesitated—if the coup failed then "Diem throws us out."[161] As more evidence mounted of "secret contacts between Diem-Nhu and Ho Chi Minh," Washington gave the Vietnamese generals the green light.[162] On November 1, as Diem "desperately radioed for assistance," he found no one listening except the "unsympathetic and the hostile."[163] The generals later took Diem and Nhu prisoner and murdered them. In Washington, McGeorge Bundy remarked on how "the Saigonese people threw garlands of roses on the tanks and seemed genuinely pleased with the revolt."[164] A few weeks later, on November 22, Kennedy himself was assassinated in Dallas.

Kennedy and Charles de Gaulle (1890–1970).
De Gaulle, who served as France's chief executive from 1958 to 1969, first raised the subject of Vietnam with Kennedy when they met in Paris in 1961. He warned that Southeast Asia would quickly become a "bottomless military and political quagmire." Kennedy found de Gaulle's warning troubling enough to raise it during subsequent deliberations over Vietnam. Later confrontations with France over nuclear nonproliferation and British entry into the European Common Market, however, chilled relations and led U.S. policymakers to conclude that de Gaulle's proposal in August 1963 to neutralize Vietnam merely sought to embarrass Washington and curry favor with newly emerging nations in the Third World. (John F. Kennedy Library)

 What if ...   *John F. Kennedy had lived to make key decisions on the Vietnam War?*

Since JFK's sudden death, many have pondered what might have been if he had lived to finish his term and served another. Vietnam figures prominently in those speculations. Some see little change if JFK instead of LBJ had made the crucial decisions. They see two cold warriors, obsessed with appearing tough, who would have heard the same voices giving them the same options. Shortly before he died Kennedy had affirmed his determination not "to see a war lost" in Vietnam. If Kennedy really wished to leave Vietnam, Diem and Nhu had offered him a golden opportunity and he rejected it in a most decisive manner.

Others, however, point to JFK's many expressions of ambivalence about escalation and other decisions he made while alive that seem to indicate a willingness to negotiate and compromise. The president who rejected military intervention in Laos and who explored multiple options to end the Cuban Missile Crisis peacefully likely would have sought a solution in South Vietnam that avoided committing a half million American troops to the struggle. He might well have embraced the many opportunities that LBJ spurned to sign an agreement neutralizing South Vietnam.

If this speculation is correct and JFK had rejected escalation, what would have been the consequences? A shorter, less intense war certainly would have spared many, many lives on all sides of the conflict. The massive destruction that Vietnam experienced also would have been avoided. Other effects are less clear. Might the budding détente symbolized by the Limited Test Ban Treaty have continued without the impediment of the Vietnam War? Would Vietnam be viewed as a potential catastrophe narrowly avoided? Or would the "action intellectuals" have seen it as further proof of their ability to fashion finely calibrated solutions to foreign policy crises? So emboldened, might they have gambled in other instances where their luck did not hold out? Without massive antiwar protests and a "Vietnam Syndrome" to catalyze doubts about American expansionism and militarism, would future presidents have been more willing to intervene with large numbers of American troops in future civil wars or use massive military force to depose regimes seen as hostile to U.S. interests, such as in El Salvador, Nicaragua, and the Balkan wars of the 1990s? (See Chapter 11.)

The tragic consequences of the Vietnam War will continue to spawn speculations about lost opportunities for peace. Whether different decisions on Vietnam would have prevented the breakdown of the bipartisan foreign policy consensus or merely delayed it hinges on the prism through which one views the conflict. If Vietnam is seen as an aberration in U.S. foreign relations, then Washington officials could have avoided its wrenching escalation. If Vietnam represents the culmination of multiple trends in U.S. foreign relations, then a peaceful solution in the 1960s would have merely deferred the painful lessons of that conflict.

Nose to Nose: Lyndon B. Johnson and the World

Johnson kept on many of Kennedy's advisers. McNamara stayed until early 1968; Rusk until the end; replacing Bundy in 1966 was the zealous Walt Rostow. Alliance partners immediately sensed the change in presidential style. A British diplomat commented, "President Johnson is not at home in international affairs."[165] Less generous, Charles de Gaulle dismissed Johnson as "a cowboy radical" who "doesn't even take the trouble to pretend he's thinking."[166] Dean Acheson once called Johnson "a real centaur—part man, part horse's ass."[167] Soviet Ambassador Anatoly Dobrynin, however, noted that "in Johnson's time we had no serious conflicts in Soviet American relations" such as the Berlin and Cuban missile crises.[168]

An experienced political operator, Johnson came from the poor hill territory of Texas between Fort Worth and San Antonio. LBJ, projected "a sense of perpetual motion" and was known for thrusting "his face close to the face of the person he was talking to, practically touching the other's nose."[169] Receiving the "Johnson Treatment," as it came to be known, was "like being licked by a Great Dane," a subordinate recalled.[170] A "credibility gap" dogged the administration, not so much because Johnson told barefaced lies, but because he consciously downplayed his commitment to "that bitch of a war" in Vietnam lest it divert attention from the "woman I really loved—the Great Society" domestic reform program.[171]

Johnson left relations with the Soviet Union and China much as he had found them—calmer after the Cuban missile crisis but still strained and based on intense military competition. In 1967 LBJ attempted to slow the arms race when he met with Soviet Premier Alexsei Kosygin in Glassbro, New Jersey. But the movement toward negotiations stalled in June 1968 when the Soviets invaded Czechoslovakia the day before a Johnson-Kosygin summit was to be announced. It "was like throwing a dead fish" in the president's face, said Rusk.[172] LBJ, however, hoped the invasion proved merely "an accident on the road to détente."[173] The United States, the Soviet Union, and more than fifty other nations still signed a nuclear nonproliferation treaty in 1968 (ratified in 1969), a pledge not to spread nuclear weapons to other nations. But France and China, both members of the nuclear club, refused to sign.

In Latin America, smoldering nationalism, frequent military coups, and Castro's defiant survival defined Johnson's policies. Johnson put Assistant Secretary of State Thomas C. Mann in charge of the Alliance for Progress, and it soon withered away from neglect. Mann's declaration that the United States would support anticommunist military regimes received its first test in 1964, when the United States embraced a military coup in Brazil. That same year, Panamanians rioted against U.S. control of the Canal Zone. Neither LBJ nor Mann wanted to back down from what they considered a communist challenge ("Kids started it and the communists got into it," LBJ contended).[174] "I know my Latinos," claimed Mann. "They understand only two things—a buck in the pocket and a kick in the ass."[175] Nonetheless, the administration brokered a peaceful settlement.

Johnson fueled another crisis in Latin America when rebels launched a civil war in the Dominican Republic in 1965. Bragging that "he had just taken an action that will prove that Democratic presidents can deal with Communists as strongly as any Republican," he sent 24,000 soldiers to the Caribbean island.[176] He wanted to prevent the return of Juan Bosch as president. Bosch had initially won an election in 1962, but a coup ousted him in 1963. LBJ believed that a small number of communists controlled the rebels. "Our choice is … Castro or intervention," he claimed, although McNamara doubted that "fifty-eight people" can control a rebellion.[177] In the end, a military regime quashed the democratic rebellion with U.S. support.

Proud of his actions, Johnson announced that the United States would henceforth prevent any communist government from taking office in the hemisphere. This frank statement of hegemony attempted to maintain the U.S. sphere in Latin America. In 1968, the Soviets issued a similar statement after their invasion of Czechoslovakia, justifying their dominance of Warsaw Pact countries.

"The Biggest Damned Mess": Johnson's War

During Johnson's five years in office, Vietnam consumed his energies, his ambitions, his reputation. After Diem's death, "the NLF was ready and eager" to form a neutralist coalition government, according to a former North Vietnamese diplomat. He chided Americans: "There was an opportunity and you missed it."[178] Despite calls for such a solution from American allies, the United Nations, and some U.S. officials, Johnson would have none of it. In December 1963, he insisted on "victory" to prevent "a communist takeover."[179] For Johnson and his advisers, Vietnam occupied only one front in the Cold War; to falter in Southeast Asia, they believed, would send a false signal that the United States would retreat elsewhere, too.

By early 1964, however, the war was going badly. Washington grew alarmed when the new military government seemed even more determined than had Diem and Nhu to bring an end to the fighting. The Army of the Republic of Vietnam (ARVN) proved ineffective in the field, and desertions ran high. The strategic hamlet program collapsed. In late January 1964, with tacit U.S. support, General Nguyen Khanh seized power in a coup, but little changed. Secretary McNamara reported that the NLF controlled 40 percent of the South Vietnamese countryside by March 1964. "We're getting into another Korea," LBJ grumbled. "I don't think it's worth fighting for and I don't think we can get out. It's just the biggest damned mess."[180] The president worried a great deal about a resurgent American right wing, arguing that the loss of China and the stalemate in Korea may have sparked McCarthyism, but they "were chicken shit compared to what might happen if we lost Vietnam."[181] He also feared that if he withdrew U.S forces, Robert Kennedy would soon be "telling everyone … that I was a coward. An unmanly man. A man without a spine."[182] Deterioration in Vietnam gave Johnson's political foes an issue in the 1964 presidential race. Conservative Republican candidate Barry Goldwater urged military action against Ho Chi Minh's North. The president publicly chided Goldwater as a dangerous warmonger.

In private, however, the Johnson administration was already implementing plans to increase the U.S. presence in South Vietnam and U.S. pressure against North Vietnam. In early 1964, Washington dispatched more military advisers (reaching 23,000 by the end of the year). Air strikes hit Laos, through which supplies flowed south from Ho's North. In February a covert operation, tagged OPLAN 34-A, began to air-drop commandos into the North to conduct sabotage. To stiffen the Khanh government, aides urged the president in June to ask Congress for a resolution "conveying our firmness of purpose in Southeast Asia."[183]

On August 2, 1964, North Vietnamese torpedo patrol boats opened fire on the American destroyer *Maddox* some ten miles offshore. U.S. forces drove off the attackers, sinking one boat and damaging others, with no American casualties. The *Maddox* was on an espionage mission, called a "DeSoto patrol," collecting intelligence on radar and coastal defenses. As the president admitted privately, "we were playing around up there" in support of an OPLAN 34-A operation against two islands.[184] After the incident, almost as if to bait North Vietnam, the *Maddox* and *C. Turner Joy* steered to within four miles of the islands. After dark on August 4, the captain of the *Maddox* interpreted his sonar data to mean that North Vietnamese gunboats had attacked the two ships. The *Maddox* and *C. Turner Joy* fired away wildly and American warplanes flew in to help. No evidence has ever confirmed a North Vietnamese attack. The ship's radar may have picked up a "Tonkin Spook," a radar anomaly that some have theorized is produced by weather patterns and seabirds.[185] James B. Stockdale, who flew a Crusader jet from the the U.S.S. *Ticonderoga* that night, saw "nothing but black sea and American firepower."[186] LBJ scoffed, "For all I know our navy might be shooting at whales out there," but ultimately he accepted Walt Rostow's assessment that "our golden opportunity is at hand."[187] Beijing, wanting to avoid a wider war, informed Hanoi that the second incident was "not an intentional act by the Americans" but "based on wrong information."[188]

A NLF Fighter in His Tunnel.   One writer described "a formless war against a formless enemy who evaporated into the morning jungle mists only to materialize in some unexpected place." When a Vietnamese communist was told that his side had never beaten U.S. troops in a major battle, he replied: "That is correct. It is also irrelevant." Guerrillas win as long as they do not lose. Well-hidden tunnels helped the NLF defy superior U.S. military power. The most famous tunnels, in the Cu Chi region near Saigon, served as a staging area for the Tet offensive. (National Archives)

Despite the CIA's report that the North Vietnamese certainly acted defensively, Johnson moved quickly to punish North Vietnam and to seek passage of a congressional resolution. On August 4, the president announced air strikes against the North. Saying nothing about U.S. naval provocations, he charged the enemy with deliberate aggression in international waters. Johnson consciously misled the American people and the Congress. The "Tonkin Gulf Resolution" passed on August 7 by huge margins, 416 to 0 in the House and 88 to 2 in the Senate. Many voted "aye" only after receiving assurances from J. William Fulbright, chair of the Senate Foreign Relations Committee, that the resolution simply sought to insulate LBJ from Republican attacks during the forthcoming presidential campaign. Only Senators Ernest Gruening of Alaska and Wayne Morse of Oregon dissented. The resolution authorized the president to "take all necessary measures to repel armed attack against the forces of the United States and to prevent further aggression."[189] The resolution, said Johnson, was "like grandma's nightshirt—it covered everything."[190] (In 1970, regretting this open-ended concession, the Senate repealed it.)

After LBJ safely won reelection in November 1964, the Pentagon expected him to escalate quickly in Vietnam. But the president hesitated after his new ambassador Maxwell Taylor told him that a rapid escalation might actually further destabilize the Saigon government. As conditions worsened in South Vietnam in January 1965, and fears mounted that Khanh might open negotiations with Hanoi and the NLF,

LBJ approved a major escalation, "stable government or no stable government," and awaited an incident to use as a pretext.[191] On February 7, 1965, LBJ got what he needed when the NLF attacked the American airfield at Pleiku and killed eight Americans. By March the United States had initiated a sustained bombing program— Operation Rolling Thunder—against the North. When the Joint Chiefs of Staff in April urged calling up the reserves to "show the American people we were serious," the president said: "You leave the American people to me. I know more about … [them] than anybody in this room."[192] With 80,000 U.S. troops in the South by July, the military asked for 100,000 more. On July 21, 1965, the president convened his high-level advisers. Only Under Secretary of State George W. Ball argued that the United States could not win a protracted war in an Asian jungle. Sending more troops would be "like giving cobalt treatment to a terminal cancer case," he warned.[193] Johnson heard a powerful opposing opinion from former President Dwight Eisenhower who told him "You have to go all out! … We are not going to be run out of a free country that we helped to establish."[194] Fearful of the political consequences of withdrawal, LBJ opted for going "full blast down a wrong-way street."[195]

Friction between Johnson and his military advisers accompanied the decision to escalate. "Bomb, bomb, bomb. That's all you know," LBJ bellowed at one point.[196] Unwilling to let "some military idiots talk him into World War III," the president once told the Joint Chiefs to "get the hell out of my office."[197] Cowed by tirades in which the president "used the f-word more freely than a marine in boot camp," the military professionals ("five silent men") never confronted Johnson with "the total forces they believed would ultimately be required in Vietnam."[198] LBJ also feared an all-out war's effect on public opinion because strategic air power could blow the

Caught in Battle. A Vietnamese peasant mother and her children emerge after a battle between ARVN forces and NLF guerrillas near the village of Phung Hiep on July 23, 1965. Such a photograph is an exception to the caricatured images of the Vietnamese at war—"the shadowy foe darting through the underbrush or lying crumpled on the ground, the prostitute or crowd of children outside an American base camp, the venal official hobbling the Saigon government's war effort, the child in frightful flight from napalm," as the historian Michael H. Hunt has observed. (National Archives)

enemy "out of the water tonight. [But] I don't think our citizens would want us to do it."[199] The result: A McNamara-dominated strategy of graduated pressure, in which ground forces went to Vietnam in increments. By the end of the year nearly 200,000 American troops were fighting in Vietnam; a year later the number reached 385,000. The defense secretary rationalized: "It won't be that the South Vietnamese can win. But it will be clear to Hanoi that Hanoi can't win."[200] Incremental escalation also aimed at minimizing the chance of Chinese intervention. LBJ knew "that if escalation brought about a major Chinese attack, it would also involve use of nuclear arms."[201]

In 1966 American bombers hit oil depots in the North, and by midyear 70 percent of the North's storage capacity had been destroyed. With North Vietnamese and NLF forces increasing from 116,000 to 282,000 during the 1965–1967 period, the heavy bombing apparently had little impact on the enemy's ability to resist. During 1965–1968 the United States tried, in General Curtis Lemay's infamous phrase, "to bomb them back into the stone age" by dropping 400 tons of ordnance per day.[202] But the United States lost 918 aircraft valued at $6 billion. By war's end more than 7 million tons of U.S. bombs had battered Vietnam, the equivalent of 400 Hiroshima atomic blasts. Averell Harriman warned that aerial bombardment was "applying the stick without the carrot," but the bombing continued without serious efforts at negotiations.[203] The number of ground troops also continued to grow, peaking at 543,400 in early 1969, despite reports that "pacification has, if anything, gone backward."[204] According to Democratic Senator Frank Church of Idaho, Johnson came to view Vietnam as "some kind of Asian Alamo."[205] LBJ clearly saw the war as a challenge to his masculinity as well as a threat to his domestic and international standing. On one infamous occasion, when journalists asked why the United States needed to persist in Vietnam, the president "unzipped his fly, drew out his substantial organ and declared, 'This is why!'"[206]

In this period of escalation, 1965–1968, the bloodshed and dislocation staggered the Vietnamese people. Despite more Buddhist protests, the fighting only intensified. Under General William Westmoreland's ("Waste-more-men") questionable strategy of "attrition," U.S. and South Vietnamese forces bombed and destroyed villages that harbored suspected Vietcong, the "Charlie."[207] Hundreds of thousands of civilians died, many from fiery napalm attacks in areas called "free fire zones." One South Vietnamese villager lamented, "We gave up our sons and then had villages destroyed by allies. … It was a nightmare that never seemed to end."[208] To deny the enemy food and to expose hideouts, American defoliation teams sprayed 12 million gallons of chemicals such as Agent Orange on crops and forests, denuding the landscape and exposing GIs and the South Vietnamese population to the dioxin-tainted herbicide. (After the war, some 39,000 veterans with cancer and nerve diseases filed claims with the U.S. government and the Vietnamese government reported severe birth defects and multiple miscarriages in affected areas.) Beginning in 1967, the CIA supervised the Phoenix program, in which South Vietnamese operatives infiltrated rural areas and "neutralized," or assassinated, thousands of suspected Vietcong. "Infiltration of a couple of guys into our ranks created tremendous difficulties," a NLF leader later admitted.[209]

To many Americans, the My Lai massacre of March 16, 1968, where a U.S. Army platoon commanded by Lieutenant William Calley shot to death scores of helpless

Southeast Asia and the Vietnam War

■ Major U.S. bases during the Vietnam War

0   100   200   300
miles

**The Tet Offensive
January–February 1968**

☆ Major battles

women and children, or "gooks," represented a depravity unbecoming a civilized nation. Because of official cover-ups, the My Lai story only surfaced twenty months later. In late 1967, the military also successfully covered up a wave of murders by the 101st Airborne's elite Tiger Force. Its gruesome rampage included scalping corpses and removing ears. The unit escaped punishment and its acts did not become public until 2003. Despite documented incidents of the deliberate shooting, raping, and torturing of civilians and prisoners, however, most U.S. soldiers were not committing atrocities. They were trying instead to save their young lives—the average age of the Vietnam GI was only nineteen—from snipers, booby traps, ambushes, mortar attacks, and firefights. Etched in their memories, too, was the inhospitable environment, "as if the sun and land were in league with the Vietcong," recalled the marine officer Philip Caputo in *A Rumor of War* (1977), "wearing us down, driving us mad, killing us."[210]

Hawks, Doves, Comrades, and Adversaries

"Can the tortoise of progress in Vietnam stay ahead of the hare of dissent at home?" one official asked.[211] It could not. Students and faculties at universities began to hold "teach-ins" in 1965, first at the University of Michigan in March. Hundreds refused military draft calls and went to jail or fled to Canada. Others obtained deferments. Sit-ins greeted representatives of major corporations such as Dow Chemical, a maker of napalm, when they attempted to recruit on campus. In early 1967, 300,000 demonstrators marched in New York City; in November, 100,000 surrounded the Pentagon. Fed disinformation from the FBI and CIA, LBJ told sympathetic senators that communists stirred up protests among "the faculties and the student bodies."[212]

Prominent intellectuals, such as the linguist Noam Chomsky, the political scientist Hans Morgenthau, Jr., and the disaffected advisor-historian Arthur M. Schlesinger, Jr., called for withdrawal from Vietnam. Business executives, lawyers, and members of the clergy, too, joined antiwar groups. The singers Pete Seeger and Joan Baez, along with the pediatrician Benjamin Spock added their voices to the protest. In April 1967, the civil rights crusader Martin Luther King, Jr., spoke at the Riverside Church in New York City, stating "I could never again raise my voice against the violence of the oppressed in the ghettos without having first spoken clearly to the greatest purveyor of violence in the world today—my own government."[213] A White House aide dismissed these dissenting views, telling the president that "King—in desperate search of a constituency—has thrown in with the commies."[214] Radical pacifists, liberal reformers, conservative constitutionalists, strategic realists, religious moralists, hippies, trade unionists, and many others melded into a national, largely unstructured antiwar movement. Often stereotyped as the haven for long-haired, bearded college-age youth, the movement actually encompassed a wide spectrum of people. The strongest opposition to the war came from four groups: older, black, female, and lower-class Americans. Younger, white, male, and middle-class citizens tended to support escalation of the war and follow the president's lead—at least until 1968. In February of that year, after Tet, a majority of polled Americans for the first time said that the United States had made a "mistake" in sending troops to Vietnam.

The critics offered multifaceted arguments: the war cost too much and weakened needed reform at home; America's youth was dying—30,000 by 1968; inflation

"Black Power" and the War. At the March on the Pentagon in 1967, a protester carries a sign symbolizing the coincidence of the civil rights and antiwar movements. Beginning in 1965, the slogan Black Power marked a more radical turn in the fight to end racial discrimination. New groups such as the Black Panther Party protested racism and the war, stating that "we will not fight and kill other people of color in the world, who, like black people, are being victimized by the white racist government in America." (Frank Wolfe, LBJ Library Collection)

Vietnam War "Doves." Left to right, Senators J. William Fulbright, Mike Mansfield, Frank Church, and Wayne Morse—all members of the Foreign Relations Committee and critics of U.S. intervention in Vietnam. Church holds a portrait of Senator William E. Borah, who chaired the committee from 1925 to 1933. An unrepentant maverick, Morse claimed that Vietnam "makes my blood boil. That purges me; it keeps me fit." Of Fulbright, Morse said: "Bill's a bleeder. He keeps agonizing over it." (Frank Church Collection, Boise State University Library)

and a worsening balance of payments undermined the economy; the ghastly bloodshed and U.S. conduct of the war were immoral; the war damaged relations with allies and foes alike; Washington and Saigon could not win the war; the president was undermining the constitutional system of checks and balances; U.S. behavior in Vietnam debased the American principles of fair play and right to self-determination; and dissension was ripping domestic America apart. Above all else, the United States had succumbed to a debilitating globalism of anticommunism, overcommitment, and overextension. In short, some critics complained about how the war was being conducted, whereas others, more searching, criticized globalism and the containment doctrine itself.

The growing public disaffection encouraged dissent in Congress. Lingering doubts about the Tonkin Gulf Resolution prompted Senator Fulbright to hold publicly televised hearings before his committee. LBJ became incensed at Fulbright's "vapid sophomoric bitching" and ridiculed him as "a crybaby" because "I can't ... kiss him every morning."[215] The president also used threats to quash questions from Congress, shouting at Senator Robert Kennedy, "I'll destroy you and every one of your dove friends."[216] But dissenting senators kept asking the administration to explain exactly what in Vietnam the United States was trying to contain. The Soviet Union? China? North Vietnam? The Vietcong? Rusk settled on China as the main culprit, especially after the Chinese leader Lin Biao declared in 1965 that China would encourage Third World wars of national liberation. China did urge a protracted struggle in Vietnam. But Hanoi and Beijing proved to be "both comrades and adversaries" in a contentious relationship.[217] Through 1966, China sent supplies along with 320,000 noncombat troops into the North. Mao also assured Hanoi that more would be forthcoming if the U.S. forces crossed into North Vietnam: "The Chinese also have legs, and legs are used for walking?"[218] Hanoi's distrust of Beijing nonetheless limited their relationship throughout the war. Tired of Mao's and Zhou's patronizing attitude, one Vietnamese diplomat snapped, "we are the ones who are fighting against the U.S. and defeating them."[219] By 1966, North Vietnam tilted toward Moscow in the Sino-Soviet split and dubbed China "La Grand Impuissance" (Great Non-Power).[220] In response, Beijing gradually withdrew its troops from the North from 1968 to 1970. No matter which power Hanoi favored, it acted as a puppet of neither. As one North Vietnamese diplomat noted, "We needed Soviet and Chinese support as a deterrent against further U.S. aggression, but we never wanted to depend on Moscow or Beijing."[221]

The administration's warning about Beijing carried little weight with Congress, especially after George F. Kennan, in his testimony at the Fulbright hearings, insisted that containment would not work in Asia and recommended gradual withdrawal. By early 1968, Senators Eugene McCarthy and Robert F. Kennedy mounted antiwar candidacies to displace LBJ as the Democratic nominee. Despite Johnson's insistent claims of victory over this "raggedy-ass little fourth-rate country," doubters grew more numerous within administration ranks.[222] McNamara's increasing disenchantment and 1967 resignation angered the president, who blamed the defense secretary's departure on Robert Kennedy's telling McNamara he was "a murderer."[223] Yet Johnson resisted anything that would appear to be defeat in Vietnam.

Throughout the 1965–1968 escalation period, international groups suggested avenues for peace. "Everybody thinks Hanoi is ready; the Pope, the Poles, the Russians, but when you really get down to it," Johnson lamented, Hanoi would not "budge."[224] For the president, the North Vietnamese would be serious about

Johnson and Nguyen Van Thieu (1923–2001). Thieu, who served as Vietnam's president from 1967 to 1975, met with Johnson in Hawai'i in July 1968. President Johnson's attempts to use his formidable physique to cajole and persuade became known as the Johnson treatment. Hubert Humphrey joked that LBJ at his most effective was like "a cowboy making love." In 1968 LBJ worked to get Thieu to accept U.S. efforts to negotiate a ceasefire. The South Vietnamese leader, much like his predecessor Diem, proved able to resist U.S. entreaties. He remained in power until just a few days before Saigon fell to North Vietnamese forces in 1975. He later moved to Newton, Massachusetts, where he died in 2001. (Lyndon B. Johnson Presidential Library photo by Yoichi R. Okamoto)

negotiating only when it "gave clear signals that they were willing to meet American terms."[225] Moscow, for its part, pushed negotiations to eliminate the war as an obstacle to warmer ties with Washington and out of fear that China would not "show restraint if the war continued to escalate."[226] Although the United States and North Vietnam continued to make gestures toward negotiations, mistrust and fears about the domestic consequences of compromise hindered success. Johnson believed that "we know, from Munich on, that when you give, the dictators feed on raw meat."[227] The NLF leadership felt similarly "haunted" by the Geneva Conference, where they believed Ho Chi Minh had treated the South "as a sacrificial animal."[228] In 1966 General Giap warned a Polish diplomat that if North Vietnam opened talks with the United States, it could face NLF "accusations of 'selling' their interests in return for ending the bombing in the North."[229] Despite internal divisions among the Vietnamese, Washington appears to bear the greatest responsibility for squandering opportunities to end the war in 1966 and 1967. Two promising initiatives, MARIGOLD and SUNFLOWER, collapsed because Washington, especially National Security Adviser Walt Rostow, insisted on "capitulation by a Communist force that is far from beaten."[230] The bombing of the North and Hanoi's aid to the NLF proved to be key sticking points. MARIGOLD died when LBJ failed to call off a previously scheduled round of bombings, and SUNFLOWER withered when the United States insisted that Hanoi would have to prove it had stopped sending personnel and supplies down the jungle paths known as the Ho Chi Minh Trail (see map, page 355) before Washington would halt its aerial bombardment.

And then the Tet offensive of early 1968 wrought its havoc; military escalation and Johnson's political career derailed; the bombing scaled down; and the peace talks finally began in Paris. In November, Richard M. Nixon defeated Vice President Hubert Humphrey for the presidency. In 1961 John F. Kennedy had asked Americans to "pay any price" and "bear any burden." By 1969 many refused. The new Nixon administration faced the task of maintaining U.S. interests abroad while at the same time mollifying the mounting discontent with globalism and the Vietnam War.

FURTHER READING FOR THE PERIOD 1961–1969

Several works cited in Chapters 7 and 8 on the Cold War and the Third World also survey this period, and not all are repeated here.

For John F. Kennedy and his foreign relations, see Irving Bernstein, *Promises Kept* (1991); Michael Beschloss, *The Crisis Years* (1991); Douglas Brinkley and Richard T. Griffiths, eds., *John F. Kennedy and Europe* (1999); Robert Dallek, *An Unfinished Life* (2003); Lawrence E. Freedman, *Kennedy's Wars* (2000); James N. Giglio, *The Presidency of John F. Kennedy* (2006); James N. Giglio and Stephen G. Rabe, *Debating the Kennedy Presidency* (2003); Barbara Leaming, *Jack Kennedy* (2006); Timothy P. Maga, *John F. Kennedy and New Frontier Diplomacy* (1994); Michael O'Brien, *John F. Kennedy* (2005); Thomas G. Paterson, ed., *Kennedy's Quest for Victory* (1989); Richard Reeves, *President Kennedy* (1993); Thomas C. Reeves, *A Question of Character* (1991); W. J. Rorabaugh, *Kennedy and the Promise of the Sixties* (2002); and Mark J. White, ed., *Kennedy* (1998). For Kennedy and specific countries and crises, see below.

For Lyndon B. Johnson and his administration (see Vietnam below), see Irving Bernstein, *Guns or Butter* (1996); H. W. Brands, *The Wages of Globalism* (1995) and ed., *The Foreign Policies of Lyndon Johnson* (1999); Warren I. Cohen and Nancy B. Tucker, eds., *Lyndon Johnson Confronts the World* (1995); Robert Dallek, *Flawed Giant* (1998) and *Lyndon B. Johnson* (2005); Robert A. Divine, ed., *The Johnson Years* (1987–1994);

John Dumbrell, *President Lyndon Johnson and Soviet Communism* (2004); Paul Y. Hammond, *LBJ and the Presidential Management of Foreign Relations* (1993); Diane Kunz, ed., *The Diplomacy of the Crucial Decade* (1994); Mitchell B. Lerner, ed., *Looking Back at LBJ* (2005); and Randall B. Woods, *LBJ* (2006).

For other prominent Americans, see Leroy Ashby and Rod Gramer, *Fighting the Odds* (1994) (Frank Church); William C. Berman, *William Fulbright and the Vietnam War* (1988); James A. Bill, *George Ball* (1997); Kai Bird, *The Color of Truth* (1998) (Bundy); Douglas Brinkley, *Dean Acheson* (1992); Jeff Broadwater, *Adlai Stevenson* (1994); Richard P. Dauer, *A North-South Mind in an East-West World* (2005) (Chester Bowles); David L. DiLeo, *George Ball, Vietnam, and the Rethinking of Containment* (1991); Mason Drukman, *Wayne Morse* (1997); Gilbert C. Fite, *Richard B. Russell, Jr.* (1991); Dorothy Fosdick, ed., *Staying the Course* (1987) (Henry Jackson); Robert A. Goldberg, *Barry Goldwater* (1995); Walter Isaacson and Evan Thomas, *The Wise Men* (1986); Robert David Johnson, *Ernest Gruening and the American Dissenting Tradition* (1998); John B. Martin, *Adlai Stevenson and the World* (1977); David Milne, *American Rasputin* (2008) (Walt W. Rostow); Jonathan Nashel, *Edward Lansdale's Cold War* (2005); Thomas J. Noer, *Soapy* (2005) (G. Mennen Williams); John Prados, *Lost Crusader* (2003) (William Colby); Barry Riccio, *Walter Lippmann* (1989); Howard B. Schaffer, *Chester Bowles* (1993) and *Elsworth Bunker* (2003); Thomas J. Schoenbaum, *Waging Peace and War* (1988) (Rusk); Deborah Shapley, *Promise and Power* (1993) (McNamara); Carol Solberg, *Hubert Humphrey* (1984); Ronald Steel, *Walter Lippmann and the American Century* (1980); Evan Thomas, *Robert Kennedy* (2000); Randall B. Woods, *Fulbright* (1995); and Thomas W. Zeiler, *Dean Rusk* (1999).

Economic issues and trade policy are scrutinized in David P. Calleo, *The Imperious Economy* (1982); Frances J. Gavin, *Gold, Dollars, and Power* (2003); and Thomas Zeiler, *American Trade and Power in the 1960s* (1992).

Europe, the Berlin crisis, and the nuclear arms race are the subjects of Jonathan Colman, *A "Special Relationship"?* (2004) (Great Britain); Frank Costigliola, *France and the United States* (1992); Arne Hofman, *The Emergence of Détente in Europe* (2007); Erin Mahan, *Kennedy, De Gaulle, and Western Europe* (2002); Frank A. Mayer, *Adenauer and Kennedy* (1996); Kendrick Oliver, *Kennedy, Macmillan, and the Nuclear Test Ban Treaty* (1998); Christopher A. Preble, *John F. Kennedy and the Missile Gap* (2005); Andrew Priest, *Kennedy, Johnson, and NATO* (2006); Thomas Risse-Kappen, *Cooperation Among Democracies* (1995); Thomas A. Schwartz, *Lyndon Johnson and Europe* (2003); David Brandon Shields, *Kennedy and Macmillan* (2006); W. R. Smyser, *Kennedy and the Berlin Wall* (2009); Jeremi Suri, *Power and Protest* (2003); Frederick Taylor, *The Berlin Wall* (2007); Andreas Wenger, *Living with Peril: Eisenhower, Kennedy, and Nuclear Weapons* (1997); Andreas Wenger and Christian Nunlist, *Transforming NATO in the Cold War* (2007); and Peter Wyden, *The Wall* (1989).

Aspects of relations with the Third World in the 1960s include Kristin L. Ahlberg, *Transplanting the Great Society* (2008) (Food for Peace); Warren Bass, *Support Any Friend* (2003) (Israel); Abraham Ben-Zvi, *Decade of Transition* (1998) (Israel); Herbert Druks, *John F. Kennedy and Israel* (2005); Isabella Ginor and Gideon Remez, *Foxbats over Dimona* (2007) (Middle East); Gabriel Kolko, *Confronting the Third World* (1988); Michael F. Latham, *Modernization as Ideology* (2000); Timothy P. Maga, *John F. Kennedy and the New Pacific Community* (1990); Robert J. McMahon, *Cold War on the Periphery* (1994) (India and Pakistan) and *The Limits of Empire* (1999); Michael B. Oren, *Six Days of War* (2002) (Middle East); David L. Schalk, *War and the Ivory Tower* (1991) (Algeria); and Penny M. Von Eschen, *Race Against Empire: Black Americans and Anticolonialism* (1998).

For the Cuban Revolution, Fidel Castro, Bay of Pigs, and missile crisis, see Jules Benjamin, *The United States and the Origins of the Cuban Revolution* (1990); James G. Blight, *The Shattered Crystal Ball* (1990); James G. Blight and Philip Brenner, *Sad and Luminous Days* (2002); James G. Blight and Peter Kornbluh, eds., *Politics of Illusion* (1998) (Bay of Pigs); James G. Blight and David A. Welch, *On the Brink* (1989); James G. Blight et al., *Cuba on the Brink* (1993); Michael Dobbs, *One Minute to Midnight* (2008); Jorge Domínguez, *To Make a World Safe for Revolution* (1989); Alexander Fursenko and Timothy Naftali, *"One Hell of a Gamble"* (1997); Max Frankel, *High Noon in the Cold War* (2004); Samuel Farber, *Origins of the Cuban Revolution Reconsidered* (2006); Alexander L. George, ed., *Avoiding War* (1991); Alice L. George, *Awaiting Armageddon* (2003); Howard Jones, *Bay of Pigs* (2008); Donna R. Kaplowitz, *Anatomy of a Failed Embargo* (1998); Richard Lebow and Janice G. Stein, *We All Lost the Cold War* (1994); Ernest R. May and Philip D. Zelikow, eds., *The Kennedy Tapes* (1997); William S. McConnell, *Living through the Cuban Missile Crisis* (2005); Philip Nash, *The Other Missiles of October* (1997) (Jupiters); James A. Nathan, *Anatomy of the Cuban Missile Crisis* (2001); James A. Nathan, ed., *The Cuban Missile Crisis Revisited* (1992); Peter Pavia, *The Cuba Project* (2006); Louis A. Pérez, Jr., *Cuba and the United States* (2003); Norman Polmar and John Gresham, *Defcon-2* (2006); Daryl G. Press, *Calculating Credibility* (2007);

Scott D. Sagan, *The Limits of Safety* (1993); Len Scott, *Cuban Missile Crisis and the Threat of Nuclear War* (2008); Sheldon M. Stern, *Averting "The Final Failure"* (2003) and *The Week the World Stood Still* (2005); Tad Szulc, *Fidel* (1986); Lucien S. Vandenbroucke, *Perilous Options* (1993) (Bay of Pigs); Robert Weisbrot, *Maximum Danger* (2002); David Welch and Don Munton, *A Concise History of the Cuban Missile Crisis* (2006); and Mark J. White, *The Cuban Missile Crisis* (1996) and *Missiles in Cuba* (1997).

U.S.–Latin America relations, including the Alliance for Progress, are explored in Eric Thomas Chester, *Rag-Tags, Scum, Riff-Raff, and Commies* (2001) (Dominican Republic); Walter LaFeber, *Inevitable Revolutions* (1993); Ruth Leacock, *Requiem for Revolution* (1990) (Brazil); Abraham F. Lowenthal, *Exporting Democracy* (1991); Alan McPherson, *Intimate Ties, Bitter Struggles* (2006); Stephen G. Rabe, *The Most Dangerous Area in the World* (1999) (JFK) and *U.S. Intervention in British Guiana* (2005); Henry Raymont, *Troubled Neighbors* (2005); Lars Schoultz, *Beneath the United States* (1998); David Sheinin, *Argentina and the United States* (2006); Jeffrey Taffet, *Foreign Aid as Foreign Policy* (2007) (Alliance for Progress); and W. Michael Weis, *Cold Warriors & Coups D'État* (1993) (Brazil).

Studies of U.S. relations with Africa include David N. Gibbs, *The Political Economy of Third World Intervention* (1991) (Congo); Francis Njubi Nesbitt, *Race for Sanctions* (2004); Thomas J. Noer, *Cold War and Black Liberation* (1985); and Joseph E. Thompson, *American Policy and African Famine* (1990) (Nigeria).

For the Peace Corps, see Julius A. Amin, *The Peace Corps in Cameroon* (1992); Fritz Fischer, *Making Them Like Us* (1998); and Elizabeth Cobbs Hoffman, *All You Need Is Love* (1998).

For Vietnam, especially the experience of the 1960s, see David L. Anderson, ed., *Shadow on the White House* (1993); David Anderson and John Ernst, eds., *The War That Never Ends* (2007); David M. Barrett, *Uncertain Warriors* (1993); Thomas A. Bass, *The Spy Who Loved Us* (2009); Larry Berman, *Lyndon Johnson's War* (1989); Anne Blair, *Lodge in Vietnam* (1995); James G. Blight, Janet M. Lang, and David A. Welch, *Vietnam If Kennedy Had Lived* (2009); Mark Philip Bradley and Marilyn Young, eds., *Making Sense of the Vietnam War* (2008); Robert K. Brigham, *Guerrilla Diplomacy* (1999) and *ARVN* (2006); Peter Busch, *All the Way with JFK?* (2003); Robert Buzzanco, *Vietnam and the Transformation of American Life* (1999); Robert Buzzanco and Marilyn Young, eds., *Companion to the Vietnam War* (2002); James M. Carter, *Inventing Vietnam* (2008); Philip E. Catton, *Diem's Final Failure* (2002); Andreas Daum and Lloyd C. Gardner, eds., *America, the Vietnam War, and the World* (2003); Gerard De Groot, *A Noble Cause?* (2000); John Ernst, *Forging a Fateful Alliance* (1998) (Michigan State University contracts and Vietnam); Joseph A. Fry, *Debating Vietnam* (2006); Ilya V. Gaiduk, *The Soviet Union and the Vietnam War* (1996) and *Confronting Vietnam* (2003); Lloyd C. Gardner, *Pay Any Price* (1995); Lloyd Gardner and Ted Gittinger, eds., *International Perspectives on the Vietnam* (1999) and *The Search for Peace in Vietnam* (2005); William C. Gibbons, *The U.S. Government and the Vietnam War* (1986–1994); Marc Jason Gilbert, ed., *Why the North Won the Vietnam War* (2002); Gordon M. Goldstein, *Lessons in Disaster* (2008); George C. Herring, *LBJ and Vietnam* (1994) and *America's Longest War* (2001); Paul Hendrickson, *The Living and the Dead* (1996); Gary R. Hess, *Vietnam and the United States* (1998); David Hunt, *Vietnam's Southern Revolution* (2009); Michael H. Hunt, *Lyndon Johnson's War* (1996); Seth Jacobs, *America's Miracle Man in Vietnam* (2004) and *Cold War Mandarin* (2006); Howard Jones, *Death of a Generation* (2003); George McT. Kahin, *Intervention* (1986); David Kaiser, *American Tragedy* (2000); Yuen Foong Khong, *Analogies of War* (1992); A. J. Langguth, *Our Vietnam* (2000); Walter LaFeber, *Deadly Bet* (2005); Mark Atwood Lawrence, *The Vietnam War* (2008); Fredrik Logevall, *Choosing War* (1999); Robert Mann, *A Grand Delusion* (2001); H. R. McMaster, *Dereliction of Duty* (1997); Robert S. McNamara et al., *Argument Without End* (1999); Edwin F. Moïse, *Tonkin Gulf and the Escalation of the Vietnam War* (1996); Joseph G. Morgan, *The Vietnam Lobby* (1997); Mark Moyar, *Triumph Forsaken* (2006); Charles E. Neu, *America's Lost War* (2005); John M. Newman, *JFK and Vietnam* (1992); John Prados, *Vietnam* (2009); Gareth Porter, *The Perils of Dominance* (2005); Andrew Preston, *The War Council* (2006); Priscilla Roberts, ed., *Behind the Bamboo Curtain* (2006); David Schmitz, *Tet Offensive* (2005); Robert D. Schulzinger, *A Time for War* (1997); Lawrence Serewicz, *America at the Brink of Empire* (2006); Ronald H. Spector, *After Tet* (1993); Gary Stone, *Elites for Peace* (2007); Sandra Taylor, *Vietnamese Women at War* (1999); Robert Topmiller, *Lotus Unleashed* (2006); Frank E. Vandiver, *Shadows of Vietnam* (1997); Edmund F. Wehrle, *Between a River and a Mountain* (2005) (AFL–CIO and Vietnam); Jayne S. Werner and Luu Doan Huynh, eds., *The Vietnam War* (1992); Andrew Wiest, ed., *Rolling Thunder in a Gentle Land* (2006); James Willbanks, *Tet Offensive* (2007);

Randall B. Woods, ed., *Vietnam and the American Political Tradition* (2003); Marilyn Young, *The Vietnam Wars* (1991); and Qiang Zhai, *China and the Vietnam Wars* (2000).

Laos and Cambodia are discussed in many of the studies above and in Timothy N. Castle, *At War in the Shadow of Vietnam* (1993) (Laos); David P. Chandler, *The Tragedy of Cambodian History* (1991); Michael Haas, *Cambodia, Pol Pot, and the United States* (1991); Jane Hamilton-Merritt, *Tragic Mountain* (1993) (Laos); Marie A. Martin, *Cambodia* (1994); William Shawcross, *Sideshow* (1979) (Cambodia); and Charles Stevenson, *The End of Nowhere* (1972) (Laos).

The colonial history of Vietnam, its wars against foreigners, and the development of its politics are examined in many of the books above and in Dixee Bartholomew-Feis, *The OSS and Ho Chi Minh* (2006); Christopher Bayly and Tim Harper, *Forgotten Wars* (2007); Mark Bradley, *Imagining Vietnam and America* (2000); Pierre Brocheux, *Ho Chi Minh* (2007); Arthur J. Dommen, *The Indochinese Experience of the French and the Americans* (2001); William J. Duiker, *The Communist Road to Power in Vietnam* (1981), *Sacred War* (1995), and *Ho Chi Minh* (2000); Bernard Fall, *The Two Viet-Nams* (1967); David Marr, *Vietnamese Anti-Colonialism, 1885–1925* (1971) and *Vietnamese Tradition on Trial, 1920–1945* (1981); and Douglas Pike, *History of Vietnamese Communism* (1978) and *Viet Cong* (1972).

Specific studies of the Truman and Eisenhower administrations and Vietnam are David L. Anderson, *Trapped by Success* (1991) (Eisenhower); Melanie Billings-Yun, *Decision Against War* (1988) (Dienbienphu); Lloyd C. Gardner, *Approaching Vietnam* (1988); Lloyd C. Gardner and Ted Gittinger, eds., *Vietnam: The Early Decisions* (1998); Lawrence S. Kaplan et al., eds., *Dien Bien Phu and the Crisis of Franco-American Relations* (1990); Mark Atwood Lawrence, *Assuming the Burden* (2005); Mark Atwood Lawrence and Fredrik Logevall, eds., *First Vietnam War* (2007); David G. Marr, *Vietnam 1945* (1995); Andrew J. Rotter, *The Path to Vietnam* (1987); Martin Shipway, *The Road to War* (1996) (French policy); Kathryn Statler, *Replacing France* (2007); and Stein Tönnesson, *The Vietnamese Revolution of 1945* (1991).

For the My Lai massacre, see David L. Anderson, *Facing My Lai* (1998); Seymour M. Hersh, *Cover-Up* (1972); James S. Olson and Randy Roberts, *My Lai* (1998); and Kevin Sim and Michael Bilton, *Four Hours in My Lai* (1992).

For province- and village-level studies that probe American interactions with a peasant society, see William Andrews, *The Village War* (1973); Eric M. Bergerud, *The Dynamics of Defeat* (1991); Jeffrey Race, *War Comes to Long An* (1972); and James W. Trullinger, Jr., *Village at War* (1980).

Military decisions and operations and the soldier's experience in Vietnam are studied in Christian G. Appy, *Working Class War* (1993) and *Patriots* (2003); Sheryl Buchanan, *Vietnam Zippos* (2007); Robert Buzzanco, *Masters of War* (1996); Eric Dean, *Shook Over Hell* (1997) (posttraumatic stress disorder); Ronald B. Frankum, Jr., *Like Rolling Thunder* (2005); Douglas Kinnard, *The Certain Trumpet* (1991) (Taylor); Otto J. Lehrack, *No Shining Armor* (1992) (marines); Donald J. Mrozek, *Air Power & the Ground War in Vietnam* (1989); John A. Nagl, *Learning to Eat Soup with a Knife* (2005); Deborah Nelson, *The War Behind Me* (2008); Rick Newman and Don Shepperd, *Bury Us Upside Down* (2006); Douglas Pike, *PAVN: People's Army of Vietnam* (1986); John Prados and Ray Stubbe, *Valley of Decision* (1991) (Khe Sanh); Jeffrey Record, *The Wrong War* (1998); Michael Sallah and Mitch Weiss, *Tiger Force* (2006); Ronald H. Spector, *United States in Vietnam* (1983); and Harry G. Summers, *On Strategy* (1981).

American public opinion, media, and the antiwar movement are discussed in many of the works above and specifically in Milton J. Bates, *The Wars We Took to Vietnam* (1996); Charles DeBenedetti and Charles Chatfield, *An American Ordeal* (1990) (antiwar movement); Terry Dietz, *Republicans and Vietnam* (1986); Patrick Hagopian, *The Vietnam War in American Memory* (2009); Kenneth J. Heineman, *Campus Wars* (1993); Robert E. Herzstein, *Henry R. Luce, Time, and the American Crusade in Asia* (2005); Susan Jeffords, *The Remasculinization of America* (1989); Rhodri Jeffreys-Jones, *Peace Now!* (1999); Katherine Kinney, *Friendly Fire* (2000); Scott Laderman, *Tours of Vietnam* (2009); Melvin Small, *Johnson, Nixon, and the Doves* (1988); *Antiwarriors* (2002) and *At the Water's Edge* (2005); Melvin Small and William D. Hoover, eds., *Give Peace a Chance* (1992); William Prochnau, *Once upon a Distant War* (1995) (journalists); Amy Swerdlow, *Women Strike for Peace* (1993); Robert R. Tomes, *Apocalypse Then: American Intellectuals and the Vietnam War, 1954–1975* (1998); Fred Turner, *Echoes of Combat* (1996); Jeremy Varon, *Bringing the War Home* (2004); Tom Wells, *The War Within* (1994); Philip West et al., *America's Wars in Asia* (1998); Lawrence S. Wittner, *Rebels Against War* (1984); and Clarence R. Wyatt, *Paper Soldiers* (1993).

See also the General Bibliography; Robert L. Beisner, ed., *Guide to American Foreign Relations Since 1600* (2003); and the following notes.

NOTES TO CHAPTER 9

1. Quoted in J. L. Dees, "The Viet Cong Attack That Failed," *Department of State News Letter,* no. 85 (May 1968), 22.

2. Tran-van Dinh, "Six Hours that Changed the Vietnam Situation," *Christian Century, LXXXV* (March 6, 1968), 289.

3. Don Oberdorfer, *Tet!* (Garden City, N.Y.: Doubleday, 1971), p. 25.

4. Quoted *ibid.,* p. 33.

5. Frances FitzGerald, *Fire in the Lake* (New York: Vintage, 1972), p. 524.

6. Tran Van Tra, "Tet," in Jayne Werner and Luu Doan Huynh, eds., *The Vietnam War* (Armonk, N.Y.: Sharpe, 1992), p. 58.

7. William C. Westmoreland, *A Soldier Reports* (Garden City, N.Y.: Doubleday, 1976), p. 348.

8. Giap quoted in Frank Vandiver, *Shadows of Vietnam* (College Station: Texas A&M University Press, 1997), p. 276.

9. Quoted in Townsend Hoopes, *The Limits of Intervention* (New York: McKay, 1969), p. 213.

10. Quoted in George Kahin and John Lewis, *The United States in Vietnam* (New York: Dell, 1969), p. 373.

11. Quoted in George A. Bailey and Lawrence W. Lichty, "Rough Justice on a Saigon Street," *Journalism Quarterly, XLIX* (Summer 1972), 222.

12. Quoted in James H. Willbanks, *The Tet Offensive* (New York: Columbia University Press, 2007), p. 37.

13. Quoted in *Newsweek, LXXI* (February 19, 1968), 24.

14. Quoted in Philip B. Davidson, *Vietnam at War* (Novato, Cal.: Presidio Press, 1988), p. 486.

15. Sir Robert Thompson quoted in Gary Stone, *Elites for Peace* (Knoxville: University of Tennessee Press, 2007), p. 163.

16. Quoted in David Lamb, *Vietnam, Now* (New York: Public Affairs, 2002), p. 148.

17. Gerard J. De Groot, *A Noble Cause?* (New York: Longman, 2000), p. 182.

18. Quoted in George C. Herring, *LBJ and Vietnam* (Austin: University of Texas Press, 1994), p. 158.

19. Quoted in David M. Barrett, ed., *Lyndon B. Johnson's Vietnam Papers* (Austin: University of Texas Press, 1998), p. 713.

20. Quoted in Andrew Preston, *The War Council* (Cambridge: Harvard University Press, 2006), p. 12.

21. Clark Clifford, *Counsel to the President* (New York: Random House, 1991), p. 494.

22. Quoted in Robert Buzzanco, *Masters of War* (New York: Cambridge University Press, 1996), p. 333; quoted in Herring, *LBJ and Vietnam,* p. 160.

23. Quoted in George C. Herring, "Fighting without Allies," in Marc Jason Gilbert, ed., *Why the North Won the Vietnam War* (New York: Palgrave, 2002), p. 87.

24. Quoted in Walter LaFeber, *The Deadly Bet* (Lanham, Md.: Rowman & Littlefield, 2005), p. 56.

25. Quoted in Francis J. Gavin, *Gold, Dollars, and Power* (Chapel Hill: University of North Carolina Press, 2004), p. 5.

26. David M. Barrett, *Uncertain Warriors* (Lawrence: University Press of Kansas, 1993), p. 111.

27. *Public Papers, Johnson, 1968* (Washington, D.C.: Government Printing Office, 1970), p. 470.

28. De Gaulle quoted in Stephen Graubard, *Command of Office* (New York: Basic Books, 2004), p. 377; polling data from Randall B. Woods, *LBJ* (New York: The Free Press, 2006), p. 837.

29. Quoted in Christian G. Appy, *Working-Class War* (Chapel Hill: University of North Carolina Press, 1993), p. 208.

30. Archimedes Patti quoted in Stein Tönnesson, *The Vietnamese Revolution of 1945* (Newbury Park, Cal.: Sage, 1991), p. 311.

31. Quoted in Mark Philip Bradley, *Imagining Vietnam and America* (Chapel Hill: University of North Carolina Press, 2000), p. 139.

32. Quoted in David Marr, *Vietnam, 1945* (Berkeley: University of California Press, 1995), p. 289.

33. Quoted in Lloyd C. Gardner, *Approaching Vietnam* (New York: Norton, 1988), p. 65.

34. Quoted in Christopher Thorne, "Indochina and Anglo-American Relations, 1942–1945," *Pacific Historical Review, XLIV* (February 1976), 93.

35. Quoted in Richard H. Immerman, "Why and Why Not Vietnam," *New England Journal of History, LII* (April 1998), 25.

36. Quoted in Jeffrey Record, *The Wrong War* (Annapolis, Md.: Naval Institute Press, 1998), p. 60.

37. Quoted in Archimedes L. A. Patti, *Why Vietnam?* (Berkeley: University of California Press, 1980), p. 203.

38. Chester Cooper, *In the Shadows of History*, (Amherst, N.Y.: Prometheus Books, 2005), p. 120.

39. Quoted in Mark Atwood Lawrence, "Transnational Coalition-Building and the Making of the Cold War in Indochina, 1947–1949," *Diplomatic History, XXVI* (Summer 2002), 469.

40. Vietnames historian Luu Doan Huynh quoted in Mark Atwood Lawrence, *Assuming the Burden*, (Berkeley: University of California Press, 2005), p. 281.

41. Quoted in Robert Buzzanco, *Vietnam and the Transformation of American Life* (Malden, Mass.: Blackwell, 1999), p. 53; quoted in George C. Herring, *America's Longest War*, (New York: Knopf, 1996; 3rd ed.) p. 34.

42. Quoted Herring, *America's Longest War,* p. 41.

43. Zhou Enlai quoted in Qiang Zhai, *China and the Vietnam Wars, 1950–1975* (Chapel Hill: University of North Carolina Press, 2000), p. 61.

44. Quoted in Marilyn Young, *The Vietnam Wars* (New York: Harper-Collins, 1991), p. 42.

45. Quoted in Mark Moyar, *Triumph Forsaken* (New York: Cambridge University Press, 2006), p. 31.

46. Chargé Robert McClintock in David Anderson, *Trapped by Success* (Columbia: University of Missouri Press, 1991), pp. 60–61; journalist quoted in Seth Jacobs, *America's Miracle Man in Vietnam* (Durham, N.C.: Duke University Press, 2004), p. 32.

47. Jessica M. Chapman, "Staging Democracy," *Diplomatic History, XXX* (September 2006), 676.

48. Quoted in Seth Jacobs, *Cold War Mandarin* (Lanham, Md.: Rowman & Littlefield, 2006), p. 7.

49. Quoted in Robert D. Schulzinger, *A Time for War* (New York: Oxford University Press, 1997), p. 81.

50. Quoted in David Kaiser, *American Tragedy* (Cambridge: Harvard University Press, 2000), p. 61.

51. Michael E. Latham, "Redirecting the Revolution?" *Third World Quarterly, XXVII* (2006), 29.

52. Quoted in George W. Ball, *The Past Has Another Pattern* (New York: Norton, 1982), p. 364.

53. Quoted in Theodore C. Sorensen, *Kennedy* (New York: Harper and Row, 1965), p. 199; K.A. Cuordileone, *Manhood and American Political Culture in the Cold War* (New York: Routledge, 2005), p. 170.

54. Quoted in Robert D. Dean, *Imperial Brotherhood* (Amherst: University of Massachusetts Press, 2001), p. 181.

55. *Public Papers, Kennedy, 1962* (Washington, D.C.: Government Printing Office, 1963), p. 807.

56. Don Ferguson in Peter Joseph, *Good Times* (New York: Morrow, 1974), p. 4.

57. Quoted in Thomas G. Paterson, "Introduction," in Thomas G. Paterson, ed., *Kennedy's Quest for Victory* (New York: Oxford University Press, 1989), p. 14.

58. Arthur M. Schlesinger, Jr., *A Thousand Days* (Boston: Houghton Mifflin, 1965), p. 259.

59. James Barber, *The Presidential Character* (Englewood Cliffs, N.J.: Prentice-Hall, 1992; 4th ed.), p. 345.

60. James N. Giglio, *The Presidency of John F. Kennedy* (Lawrence: University Press of Kansas, 2006; 2nd ed.), p. 282.

61. Quoted in Michael Beschloss, *The Crisis Years* (New York: Harper-Collins, 1991), p. 48.

62. *Public Papers, Kennedy, 1961* (Washington, D.C.: Government Printing Office, 1962), pp. 1–3.

63. Theodore H. White, "The Action Intellectuals," *Life, LXII* (June 1967), 43.

64. Quoted in David Halberstam, "The Programming of Robert McNamara," *Harper's, CCXLII* (February 1971), 62.

65. Quoted in Roger Hilsman, *To Move a Nation* (Garden City, N.Y.: Doubleday, 1967), p. 523.

66. Quoted in Paul Hendrickson, *The Living and the Dead* (New York: Vintage, 1996), p. 167.

67. Harvard Professor and Chester Cooper quoted in Kai Bird, *The Color of Truth* (New York: Simon and Schuster, 1998), pp. 190–191.

68. Quoted in Preston, *War Council*, p. 51.

69. Quoted in Michael H. Hunt, *Lyndon Johnson's War* (New York: Hill & Wang, 1996), p. 48.

70. Aleksander Fursenko and Timothy Naftali, *Khrushchev's Cold War* (New York: Norton, 2006), p. 370.

71. Khrushchev quoted in Viktor Adamsky and Yuri Smirnov, "Moscow's Biggest Bomb," *Cold War International History Project Bulletin*, no. 4 (Fall 1994), p. 120.

72. Briefing Book, June 1961, Box 126, President's Office File, John F. Kennedy Papers, John F. Kennedy Library, Boston, Mass.; Harriman quoted in Graubard, *Command of Office*, p. 337.

73. Schlesinger, *Thousand Days*, p. 348.

74. Vladislav M. Zubok, "Khrushchev and the Berlin Crisis," Working Paper no. 6 *Cold War International History Project*, (May 1993), p. 20.

75. Quoted in Dean Rusk, *As I Saw It* (New York: Penguin, 1991), p. 227.

76. James Reston quoted in James N. Giglio, *The Presidency of John F. Kennedy* (Lawrence: University Press of Kansas, 1991), p. 78.

77. *Public Papers, Kennedy, 1961*, p. 534.

78. "Khrushchev's Secret Speech on the Berlin Crisis," *Cold War International History Project Bulletin*, no. 2 (Fall 1993), p. 59.

79. Quoted in James Nathan, *Anatomy of the Cuban Missile Crisis* (Westport, Conn.: Greenwood, 2001), p. 59.

80. Raymond L. Garthoff, "Berlin 1961," *Foreign Policy*, no. 84 (Fall 1991), 142.

81. Quoted in William Taubman, *Khrushchev* (New York: Norton, 2003), p. 539.

82. Wallice Irwin, Jr. quoted in Ralph B. Levering, *The Cold War* (Wheeling, Ill..: Harlan Davidson, 2005, 2nd ed.), p. 66

83. Quoted in Robert J. McMahon, *The Cold War on the Periphery* (New York: Columbia University Press, 1994), p. 273.

84. Quoted in Kristin L. Ahlberg, "'Machiavelli with a Heart,'" *Diplomatic History, XXXI* (September 2007), 670.

85. Thomas J. Knock, "'Come Home America'" in Randall B. Woods, ed., *Vietnam and the American Political Tradition* (New York: Cambridge University Press, 2003), p. 98.

86. Quoted in Nick Cullather, "Miracles of Modernization," *Diplomatic History, XXVIII* (April 2004), 240.

87. Lawrence Fuchs quoted in Elizabeth A. Cobbs, "The Foreign Policy of the Peace Corps," *Diplomatic History, XX* (Winter 1996), 104.

88. Johnson quoted in Elizabeth Cobbs Hoffman, *All You Need Is Love* (Cambridge: Harvard University Press, 1998), p. 70.

89. Quoted in Thomas Noer, "New Frontiers and Old Priorities in Africa," in Paterson, *Kennedy's Quest*, p. 262.

90. Quoted in Francis Njubi Nesbitt, *Race for Sanctions* (Bloomington: University of Indiana Press, 2004), p. 42.

91. Thomas Borstelmann, "John Kennedy and Racial Revolutions in the American South and Southern Africa," *Diplomatic History, XXIV* (Summer 2000), 453.

92. Kennedy quoted in Stephen G. Rabe, *The Most Dangerous Area in the World* (Chapel Hill: University of North Carolina Press, 1999), p. 19; Khrushchev quoted in Alan McPherson, *Intimate Ties, Bitter Struggles* (Washington, D.C.: Potomac Books, 2006), p. 46.

93. Quoted in Jules Benjamin, *The United States and the Origins of the Cuban Revolution* (Princeton: Princeton University Press, 1990), p. 182.

94. Quoted in Thomas G. Paterson, *Contesting Castro* (New York: Oxford University Press, 1994), p. 242.

95. Roy R. Rubottom, Jr., in *Foreign Relations of the United States, 1958–1960: Cuba* (Washington, D.C.: U.S. Government Printing Office, 1991), *VI*, p. 656.

96. Quoted in David M. Barrett, *The CIA & Congress* (Lawrence: University Press of Kansas, 2005), p. 427.

97. Quoted in Paterson, *Contesting*, p. 257.

98. Quoted in Piero Gleijeses, "Ships in the Night," *Journal of Latin American Studies, XXVII* (February 1995), 3.

99. Quoted in Stephen G. Rabe, *Eisenhower and Latin America* (Chapel Hill: University of North Carolina Press, 1988), p. 128.

100. Quoted in Anatoli I. Gribkov and William Y. Smith, *Operation Anadyr* (Chicago: Edition Q, 1994), p. 12.

101. Quoted in Schlesinger, *Thousand Days*, p. 251.

102. Quoted in Robert D. Dean, "Masculinity as Ideology," *Diplomatic History, XXII* (Winter 1998), 48.

103. Quoted in Lucien S. Vandenbroucke, "The 'Confessions' of Allen Dulles," *Diplomatic History, VIII* (Fall 1984), 369.

104. Quoted in Mark J. White, ed., *The Kennedys and Cuba* (Chicago: Ivan R. Dee, 1999), p. 19.

105. Quoted in Alexander DeConde, *Presidential Machismo* (Boston: Northeastern University Press, 2000), p. 174.

106. William J. Daugherty, *Executive Secrets* (Lexington: University of Kentucky Press, 2004), p. 154.

107. Quoted in Graubard, *Command of Office*, p. 646.

108. Quoted in James G. Blight and Peter Kornbluh, eds., *Politics of Illusion* (Boulder, Colo.: Lynne Rienner, 1998), p. 150.

109. Richard Helms memorandum, January 30, 1962, *ibid.*, p. 247.

110. Quoted in *New York Times*, February 5, 1989.

111. Lyman Lemnitzer quoted in White, *Kennedys and Cuba*, p. 119.

112. Quoted in Frank Mankiewicz and Kirby Jones, *With Fidel* (New York: Ballantine, 1975), p. 130.

113. Quoted in Fursenko and Naftali, *Khrushchev's Cold War*, p. 440.

114. Quoted in Timothy Naftali, ed., *John F. Kennedy: The Great Crises* (New York: Norton, 2001), *II*, 22.

115. Sergo Mikoyan quoted in Don Munton and David A. Welch, *A Concise History of the Cuban Missile Crisis* (New York: Oxford University Press, 2006), p. 24.

116. Quoted in Ernest R. May and Philip D. Zelikow, eds., *The Kennedy Tapes* (Cambridge: Harvard University Press, 1997), p. 258.

117. The historian Mark White quoted in Eric Alterman, *When Presidents Lie* (New York: Viking, 2004), pp. 111–112.

118. Transcript, "Off-the-Record Meeting on Cuba," 11:50 A.M.–12:57 P.M., October 16, 1962, Presidential Recordings, Kennedy Library.

119. Sheldon M. Stern, *The Week the World Stood Still* (Stanford: Stanford University Press, 2005), p. 52.

120. Maxwell Taylor quoted in J. Anthony Lukacs, "Class Reunion," *New York Times Magazine,* August 30, 1987, p. 58; Abram Chayes quoted in James A. Nathan, "The Heyday of the New Strategy," in Nathan, ed., *The Cuban Missile Crisis Revisited* (New York: St. Martin's, 1992), p. 24.

121. Quoted in May and Zelikow, *Kennedy Tapes,* p. 149.

122. Quoted in H. R. McMaster, *Dereliction of Duty* (New York: HarperCollins, 1997), p. 30.

123. *Public Papers, Kennedy, 1962,* p. 808.

124. Quoted in James T. Graham, "Kennedy, Cuba, and the Press," *Journalism History, XXIV* (Summer 1998), 64.

125. Quoted in William Burr and Thomas S. Blanton, eds., "The Submarines of October," *National Security Archive Electronic Briefing Book No. 75* (October 31, 2002).

126. Transcript, "Cuban Missile Crisis meetings," October 27, 1962, Presidential Recordings, Kennedy Library.

127. Anatoly Dobrynin cable to Soviet Foreign Ministry, October 27, 1962, *Cold War International History Project Bulletin,* no. 5 (Spring 1995), p. 79.

128. Quoted in Barton J. Bernstein, "Reconsidering the Missile Crisis," in Nathan, *Cuban Missile Crisis,* p. 100.

129. Quoted in James G. Blight and Philip Brenner, *Sad and Luminous Days* (Lanham, Md.: Rowman & Littlefield, 2002), p. 25.

130. Quoted in Odd Arne Westad, "The Sino-Soviet Alliance and the United States," in Westad, ed., *Brothers in Arms* (Stanford: Stanford University Press, 1998), p. 179.

131. Quoted in Richard Ned Lebow and Janice Gross Stein, *We All Lost the Cold War* (Princeton: Princeton University Press, 1994), p. 110.

132. John Kenneth Galbraith, "The Plain Lessons of a Bad Decade," *Foreign Policy,* no. 1 (Winter 1970–1971), 32.

133. Quoted in Graubard, *Chain of Command,* p. 647.

134. Quoted in McGeorge Bundy, *Danger and Survival* (New York: Random House, 1988), p. 426.

135. Nathan, *Anatomy,* p. 96.

136. McGeorge Bundy quoted in Thomas Risse-Kappen, *Cooperation Among Democracies* (Princeton: Princeton University Press, 1995), p. 148.

137. McNamara and Bundy quoted in Philip Nash, *The Other Missiles of October* (Chapel Hill: University of North Carolina Press, 1997), p. 3.

138. Quoted in James Blight and David Welch, *On the Brink* (New York: Hill & Wang, 1989), p. 100; Marc Trachtenberg, "Commentary," *Diplomatic History, XIV* (Spring 1990), 242.

139. Quoted in Raymond L. Garthoff, *A Journey Through the Cold War* (Washington, D.C.: Brookings Institution Press, 2001), p. 165.

140. McGeorge Bundy quoted in Stephen G. Rabe, "The Caribbean Triangle," *Diplomatic History, XX* (Winter 1996), 77.

141. Michael S. Sherry, *In the Shadow of War* (New Haven: Yale University Press, 1995), p. 243.

142. Walt W. Rostow, Memorandum, March 29, 1961, Box 193, National Security File, Kennedy Papers.

143. Quoted in Edmund F. Wehrle, "'A Good, Bad Deal,'" *Pacific Historical Review, LXVII* (April 1998), 353.

144. Quoted in Timothy N. Castle, *At War in the Shadow of Vietnam* (New York: Columbia University Press, 1993), p. 41.

145. Douglas MacArthur quoted in Noam Kochavi, "Kennedy, China, and the Laos Crisis, 1961–1963," *Diplomatic History, XXVI* (Winter 2002), 109.

146. Quoted in Wehrle, "Good, Bad Deal," 349.

147. Alfred W. McCoy, "America's Secret Wars in Laos, 1955–1975," in Marilyn B. Young and Robert Buzzanco, eds., *A Companion to the Vietnam War* (Malden, MA.: Blackwell, 2002), p. 284.

148. Quoted in Frank Costigliola, *France and the United States* (Boston: Twayne, 1992), p. 140; quoted in David Halberstam, *The Best and the Brightest* (Greenwich, Conn.: Fawcett, 1973), p. 77.

149. Quoted in James M. Burns, *Running Alone* (New York; Basic Books, 2006), p. 53.

150. Quoted in Howard Jones, *Death of a Generation* (New York: Oxford University Press, 2003), p. 113.

151. U.S. Senate, Foreign Relations Committee, *Foreign Assistance Act of 1968,* Part 1: *Vietnam* (Washington, D.C.: Government Printing Office, 1968), p. 218.

152. Quoted in Robert K. Brigham, *ARVN* (Lawrence: University Press of Kansas, 2006), p. 6.

153. Quoted in Stephen Kinzer, *Overthrow* (New York: Times Books, 2006), pp. 155–156.

154. John Mecklin quoted in Jacobs, *Cold War Mandarin,* p. 87.

155. Quoted in Robert David Johnson, *Congress and the Cold War* (New York: Cambridge University Press, 2006), p. 105.

156. Paul Kattenburg quoted in Christian G. Appy, *Patriots,* (New York: Penguin, 2003), p. 81.

157. Charles Bartlett quoting Kennedy in Seymour Hersh, *The Dark Side of Camelot* (Boston: Little, Brown, 1997), p. 418.

158. Quoted in Kinzer, *Overthrow,* p. 156.

159. North Vietnamese Prime Minister Pham Van Dong quoted in Jacobs, *Cold War Mandarin,* p. 165.

160. Chester Cooper quoted in Fredrik Logevall, *Choosing War* (Berkeley: University of California Press, 1999), p. 49.

161. Robert Kennedy quoted in Logevall, *Choosing War,* quoted, *ibid,* p. 63.

162. Polish diplomat Mieczyslaw Maneli quoted *ibid.,* p. 7.

163. Philip E. Catton, *Diem's Final Failure* (Lawrence: University Press of Kansas, 2002), p. 202.

164. Quoted in Preston, *War Council,* p. 128.

165. Matthew Jones, *Conflict and Confrontation in South East Asia, 1961–1965* (New York: Cambridge University Press, 2002), p. 262.

166. Quoted in Thomas A. Schwartz, *Lyndon Johnson and Europe* (Cambridge: Harvard University Press, 2003), pp. 28–29.

167. Quoted in Douglas Little, "Crackpot Realists and Other Heroes," *Diplomatic History, XIII* (Winter 1989), 103.

168. *Ibid,* p. 226.

169. The journalist Marianne Means quoted in John Dumbrell, *President Johnson and Soviet Communism* (New York: Manchester University Press, 2004), p. 5; Anatoly Dobrynin, *In Confidence* (New York: Random House, 1995), p. 120.

170. Ben Bradlee, *A Good Life* (New York: Simon & Schuster, 1995), p. 263.

171. Quoted in Hunt, *Johnson's War,* p. 72.

172. Quoted in Mitchell Lerner, "'Trying to Find the Guy Who Invited Them,'" *Diplomatic History, XXXII* (January 2008), 78.

173. Quoted in Vojtech Mastny, "Was 1968 a Strategic Watershed in the Cold War?," *Diplomatic History, XXIX* (January 2005), 149.

174. Quoted in Mark Atwood Lawrence, "Exception to the Rule?" in Mitchell B. Lerner, ed., *Looking Back at LBJ* (Lawrence: University Press of Kansas, 2005), p. 25.

175. Quoted in Michael H. Hunt, *The American Ascendancy* (Chapel Hill: University of North Carolina Press, 2007), p. 213.

176. Quoted in Eric Thomas Chester, *Rag-Tags, Scum, Riff-Raff, and Commies* (New York: Monthly Review Press, 2001), p. 80.

177. Quoted in Michael Beschloss, ed., *Reaching for Glory* (New York: Simon & Schuster, 2001), pp. 301, 317.

178. Luu Van Loi quoted in Robert S. McNamara, James G. Blight, and Robert K. Brigham, *Argument Without End* (New York: Public Affairs, 1999), p. 202.

179. Quoted in Kahin and Lewis, *U.S. and Vietnam*, p. 152.

180. Quoted in Michael Beschloss, *Taking Charge* (New York: Simon & Schuster, 1997), p. 370.

181. Quoted in Logevall, *Choosing*, pp. 76–77.

182. Quoted in Cuordileone, *Manhood*, p. 233.

183. McGeorge Bundy in Summary Record of Meeting, June 10, 1964, in Barrett, *LBJ's Vietnam Papers*, p. 54.

184. Quoted in Beschloss, *Taking Charge*, p. 493.

185. Edwin E. Moïse, *Tonkin Gulf and the Escalation of the Vietnam War* (Chapel Hill: University of North Carolina Press, 1996), p. 107.

186. Quoted in George Kahin, *Intervention* (New York: Knopf, 1986), p. 223.

187. LBJ quoted in Mark Hamilton Lytle, *America's Uncivil Wars* (New York: Oxford University Press, 2006), p. 165; Rostow quoted in Appy, *Patriots*, p. 116.

188. Quoted in Zhai, *China and the Vietnam Wars*, p. 132.

189. *Congressional Record*, CX (August 7, 1964), 18471.

190. Quoted in Stanley Karnow, *Vietnam* (New York: Viking, 1991; rev. ed.), p. 374.

191. Quoted in Logevall, *Choosing War*, p. 318.

192. Quoted in Lewis Sorley, *Honorable Warrior: General Harold K. Johnson* (Lawrence: University Press of Kansas, 1998), p. 202.

193. Quoted in Jack Valenti, *A Very Human President* (New York: Norton, 1975), p. 334.

194. Quoted in Edward Cuddy, "Vietnam: Mr. Johnson's War—Or Mr. Eisenhower's?" *Review of Politics*, LXV (Fall 2003), 368.

195. Chester Bowles quoted in Richard P. Dauer, *A North-South Mind in an East-West World* (Westport, Conn.: Praeger, 2005), p. 85.

196. Quoted in Herring, *LBJ and Vietnam*, p. 31.

197. Quoted in Robert Dallek, *Flawed Giant* (New York: Oxford University Press, 1998), p. 342.

198. Charles Cooper quoted in Appy, *Patriots*, p. 122; McMaster, *Dereliction*, pp. 328, 330.

199. Quoted in Michael Adas, *Dominance by Design* (Cambridge: Harvard University Press, 2006), p. 291.

200. Quoted in Beschloss, *Reaching*, p. 282.

201. Dean Rusk quoted in Daniel Ellsberg, *Secrets* (New York: Viking, 2002), p. 64.

202. Quoted in James P. Harrison, "History's Heaviest Bombing," in Werner and Huynh, *Vietnam War*, p. 135.

203. Quoted in David Milne, "'Our Equivalent of Guerrilla Warfare,'" *Journal of Military History*, XLL (January 2007), 189.

204. McNamara quoted in Eric M. Bergerud, *The Dynamics of Defeat* (Boulder, Colo.: Westview Press, 1991), p. 163.

205. Quoted in David F. Schmitz, "Congress Must Draw the Line," in Woods, ed, *Vietnam and the American Political Tradition*, p. 131.

206. Quoted in Alterman, *When Presidents Lie*, p. 181.

207. Quoted in Buzzanco, *Masters*, p. 350.

208. Quoted in Brigham, *ARVN*, p. 21.

209. Quoted in Karnow, *Vietnam*, p. 617.

210. Phillip Caputo, *A Rumor of War* (New York: Ballantine, 1977), p. 100.

211. Nicholas Katzenbach quoted in Melvin Small, *Antiwarriors* (Wilmington, Del.: Scholarly Resources, 2002), p. 67.

212. Quoted in Beschloss, *Reaching*, p. 295.

213. Quoted in Taylor Branch, *At Canaan's Edge* (New York: Simon and Schuster, 2006), p. 592.

214. John Roche quoted in Melvin Small, "Who Gave Peace a Chance," in Lloyd C. Gardner and Ted Gittinger, eds., *The Search for Peace in Vietnam* (College Station: Texas A & M University Press, 2004), p. 84.

215. Quoted in Joseph A. Fry, *Debating Vietnam* (Lanham, Md.: Rowman & Littlefield, 2006), p. 77; quoted in Walter LaFeber, "Johnson, Vietnam, and Tocqueville," in Warren I. Cohen and Nancy Bernkopf Tucker, eds, *Lyndon Johnson Confronts the World* (New York: Cambridge University Press, 1994), p. 49.

216. Quoted in Kevin Boyle, "The Price of Peace," *Diplomatic History*, XXVII (January 2003), 61.

217. Zhai, *China and the Vietnam Wars*, p. 218.

218. Quoted in James G. Hershberg and Chen Jian, "Informing the Enemy," in Priscilla Roberts, ed, *Behind the Bamboo Curtain* (Stanford: Stanford University Press, 2006), p. 215.

219. Quoted in William J. Duiker, "Victory by Other Means," in Gilbert, ed., *Why the North Won the Vietnam*, p. 68.

220. Quoted in Ivan V. Gaiduk, *The Soviet Union and the Vietnam War* (Chicago: Ivan R. Dee, 1996), p. 150.

221. Quoted in Robert Brigham, "Vietnam at the Center," in Lloyd C. Gardner and Ted Gittinger, eds, *International Perspectives on Vietnam* (College Station: Texas A & M Press, 2000), p. 98.

222. Quoted in Herring, *LBJ and Vietnam*, p. 37.

223. Quoted in Evan Thomas, *Robert Kennedy* (New York: Simon & Schuster, 2000), p. 350.

224. Quoted in James G. Hershberg, "Who Murdered 'Marigold,'" Working Paper no. 27, *Cold War International History Project* (April 2000), p. 74.

225. David Kaiser, "Discussion, Not Negotiations," in Gardner and Gittinger, *Search for Peace in Vietnam*, p. 118.

226. Boyle, "Price of Peace," p. 47.

227. Quoted in Beschloss, *Reaching*, p. 181.

228. Quoted in Robert K. Brigham, *Guerrilla Diplomacy* (Ithaca: Cornell University Press, 1998), p. 48.

229. Polish diplomat Jerzy Michalowski quoting Giap in Hershberg, "Who Murdered 'Marigold,'" p. 11.

230. Assistant Secretary of Defense John McNaughton quoted in Donald F. Lach and Edmund S. Wehrle, *International Politics in East Asia* (New York: Praeger, 1975), p. 338.

CHAPTER 10

Détente and Disequilibrium, 1969–1981

Richard M. Nixon (1913–1994) and Mao Zedong (1893–1976), 1972. *During his historic trip to China in February 1972, President Nixon shares a handshake with Chairman Mao Zedong. Both the Chinese and Americans wanted to erase the image of John Foster Dulles's famous snub of Zhou Enlai in 1954. "I like to deal with rightists," Mao later explained. They say what they really think—not like the leftists, who say one thing and mean another." (Nixon Presidential Materials Project/National Archives)*

DIPLOMATIC CROSSROAD

❖ *Richard M. Nixon's Trip to China, 1972*

"THERE IS NO Crowd," the advance man radioed from the Beijing airport. "Did you say, 'No crowd'?" the president's chief security office aboard the incoming plane replied.[1] Indeed, when President Richard M. Nixon's jet, the *Spirit of 76,* touched down that wintry morning of February 21, 1972, the reception was decidedly restrained. Apparently the Chinese wanted to suggest that Nixon desired this dramatic meeting more eagerly than did the People's Republic of China (PRC). Instead of cheering throngs, only "a vast silence" welcomed Nixon.[2] Greeting the president was trim seventy-three-year-old Premier Zhou Enlai, who had served Chairman Mao Zedong as a key administrator since 1949. The television cameras whirred, sending back home picture postcards of the historic encounter. The president's political team managed the event for maximum political effect. "The China trip was [White House Chief of Staff] Bob Haldeman's masterpiece, his Sistine chapel," bragged one White House staff member.[3] The presidential assistant for national security affairs, Henry Kissinger, feared that Nixon might overreach with his public-relations ambitions, warning Zhou "that China had survived barbarian invasions but had never encountered advance men."[4]

Nixon's "journey for peace" contrasted sharply with the previous quarter-century of icy relations between the two countries.[5] They had harangued each other as warmongers and had fought one another in Korea. Washington maintained close ties with the PRC's archenemy Jiang Jieshi in Taiwan, while China aided America's foe in Vietnam. Despite this history of hostility, Nixon and Mao now determined that cooperation best served their respective countries' interests.

In 1969, newly inaugurated President Nixon had asked Kissinger to review relations with China. When border fighting between the Soviet Union and China broke out that year, Nixon told his cabinet: "The worst thing ... would be for the Soviet Union to gobble up Red China."[6] He soon sent positive signals to Beijing by scaling back U.S. Seventh Fleet operations in the Taiwan Strait and relaxing trade restrictions with China. Early in 1970, PRC diplomats resumed talks with U.S. officials in Warsaw, which they had suspended two years earlier to protest U.S. intervention in Vietnam. Kissinger dismissed Nixon's hopes for an opening to Beijing as a "flight of fancy," but the president remained undeterred.[7] Later that year both countries used the press to signal openness to higher level talks. Nixon told *Time* magazine that the one thing "I want to do before I die ... [is] to go to China."[8] Mao then mentioned to American journalist Edgar Snow that he would welcome Nixon to China, "either as a tourist or as President."[9] In April 1971, a U.S. table tennis team accepted an invitation to visit China. Quips about "Ping-Pong diplomacy" did not detract from the event's symbolic significance. After the team's trip, Nixon became "excited to the point of euphoria" and wanted to skip straight to a presidential visit to Beijing with no preparatory discussions.[10] But he eventually relented and allowed Kissinger to go to China by himself. In Islamabad, Pakistan, in early July, the presidential aide secretly boarded a plane for Beijing. In his meetings with Zhou, Kissinger assured the Chinese premier that other than the issue of Taiwan, which they could resolve in the "relatively near future," Washington and Beijing had "no conflicting interests at all."[11] On July 15, President Nixon made the startling announcement that he would go to China to "seek the normalization of relations."[12]

Renewed relations seemed to promise many advantages. Because the Soviets had become China's "most dangerous and most important enemy," U.S. ties with Beijing might keep Moscow off balance.[13] "We're using the Chinese thaw to get the Russians shook," Nixon told an aide.[14] With the U.S. economy sagging, moreover, the legendary China market once again loomed large in American imaginations. U.S. recognition of China might also convince Beijing to press North Vietnam to accept a political settlement of the Vietnam War.

The China trip further promised Nixon political profits at home. With antiwar Democrats lambasting his continued intervention in Vietnam, Nixon could seize the peace issue prior to the first presidential primaries in March. Even though "the libs [liberals] will try to piss on it as an election year gimmick," Kissinger frankly remarked that Nixon's "political ass was on the line."[15] Having urged relations with China for years, liberal-left Americans soon applauded the China trip. At the same time, the right wing of the Republican party could hardly charge that Nixon, a proven anticommunist, had turned soft on communism.

Finally, the China journey was central to the general Nixon-Kissinger policy of "détente"—the relaxation of nternational tensions with communist nations to protect U.S. interests. The Chinese, still reeling from their destructive internal Cultural Revolution (1966–1969) and eager to avert an exhausting international conflict, now perceived the Americans as evolving from a "monkey" to a "human being."[16] Military skirmishes in 1969 along the shared 4,150-mile border with the USSR frightened many Chinese, who recalled the Soviet invasion of Czechoslovakia in 1968. As the Soviets constructed an air base in Mongolia, the Chinese dug bomb shelters and tunnel networks. Renewed ties, then, might deter the "polar bear" to the north.[17] "We can work together to commonly deal with a bastard," Mao told Kissinger.[18] A Sino-American rapprochement might also assure Beijing that Washington did not seek to rearm "Japanese militarists" by allowing Tokyo's economic expansion to fuel a more robust military.[19] China also wanted trade and a reduced U.S. commitment to Taiwan.

On the flight to China, Nixon studied notebooks about Chinese politics, culture, and diplomacy. Included were CIA analyses of Mao and Zhou and "talking points" that Nixon committed to memory. A press corps of eighty-seven, heavy with television news personalities, accompanied the presidential party of thirty-seven. Zhou sensed Nixon's eagerness for success, comparing him to a loose woman "tarting herself up and offering herself at the door."[20]

Nixon soon met Chairman Mao. Seated in overstuffed chairs, Nixon, Kissinger, Mao, and Zhou talked warmly for about an hour. Seventy-eight-year-old Mao, although suffering from congestive heart disease, remained an imposing figure, esteemed by the Chinese as the father of the People's Republic. "Your book, *Six Crises,* is not a bad book," Mao bantered. Responding to that lukewarm review of his prepresidential memoirs, Nixon looked at Zhou and joked: "He reads too much."[21]

Born into a well-to-do mandarin family, Zhou spoke English, Russian, French, and Japanese as well as his native Chinese. U.S. diplomats contrasted Zhou's quiet, patient style with the blunt, haggling manner of Soviet officials. Mao, for his part, came away impressed with Nixon as someone "who knows what he stands for, as well as what he wants," but dismissed Kissinger as "a funny little man" who shuddered "all over with nerves every time he comes to see me."[22]

That evening, in the Great Hall of the People, Zhou hosted a banquet for 800 guests. Sipping glasses of *mao tai,* a 150-proof rice liquor, Americans and their hosts toasted each other in the traditional "*gan bei*" ("dry glass") fashion.[23] The Chinese military band played "America the Beautiful"—as "a toast to your next Inaugural," Zhou whispered to Nixon.[24] The president called for a "long march together," even quoting Mao himself: "Seize the day, seize the hour. This is the hour."[25] While Nixon privately assured Zhou on February 22 that "I am removing this irritant [Vietnam] as fast as anyone in my position could," journalists filed reports on the Chinese lifestyle—clean streets, gauze masks to prevent infectious diseases, acupuncture techniques, anti-imperialist banners, expertise in table tennis, regimented schools, puritanical social habits, bicycles, the monotony of blue dress.[26] After years of thinking the Chinese a bestial enemy, Americans now found them living and suffering like the rest of humanity. Whereas in the 1960s, Americans used words such as "ignorant, warlike, treacherous, and sly" to describe the "Red Chinese," after the 1972 trip they described them as "hard-working, intelligent, progressive, artistic, and practical."[27]

After late-night social events, an exhausted Kissinger helped fashion language for a joint communiqué that followed Zhou's formula of "seeking common ground while reserving differences."[28] Affirming existing ties with South Korea and Japan, Nixon assured his hosts that a continued U.S. military presence in Asia was "China's [best] hope for Jap restraint."[29] The Americans then stated their opposition to "outside pressure or intervention" in Asia—meaning Vietnam. The Chinese declared that they would continue to support "the struggles of all oppressed people" against large nations that attempt to "bully" the small.[30] All foreign troops should withdraw from Asia, especially from Vietnam. As for Taiwan, which the United States still recognized as the official government of China, the Chinese part of the communiqué urged the withdrawal of all U.S. military forces from the island. There was only one China. Privately the president assured his hosts that he accepted their contention that "Taiwan is part of China," and he promised not to "support any Taiwan independence movement."[31] Kissinger also pledged that Washington would "oppose any Japanese military presence on Taiwan."[32] Zhou predicted that Taiwan would return to Beijing's control after Nixon's reelection. The president asked only that Beijing reject a military solution. Publicly, the Americans sugar-coated their position by endorsing a "peaceful settlement of the Taiwan question by the Chinese themselves."[33] Both parties agreed, however, that "neither should seek hegemony in the Asia-Pacific region" and both opposed "efforts by any other country" to establish "such hegemony"—a slap at the Soviet Union.[34]

As part of the show for the U.S. public, the president and his wife also played tourist, especially by visiting the Great Wall. On one occasion, Zhou pointed to the picture of pandas on his cigarette package, telling Patricia Nixon, "We will give you two."[35] She bubbled with joy. Diplomacy done, the president proclaimed that "this was the week that changed the world."[36] Kissinger privately boasted that Washington and China had become "in plain words ... tacit allies."[37] One negative headline proclaimed: "They Got Taiwan, We Got Eggroll."[38]

Nixon, Kissinger, and Their Critics

Nixon and Kissinger orchestrated this surprising turnabout in Sino-American relations. Richard Milhous Nixon, the grocer's son from Whittier, California, relished the big play in politics. His long political career as congressman, senator, and vice president had yielded many changes in his political persona, leading one historian to liken the search for the real Nixon to "a shell game without a pea."[39] A secretive, suspicious man once described as a "walking box of short circuits," Nixon raged at his many domestic "enemies." "One day we will get them," he told an aide, "get them on the floor and step on them, crush them, show no mercy ... stick our heels in ... and twist."[40] Nixon also wanted the Soviets and North Vietnamese to think him irrational and unpredictable. This "madman theory" would supposedly deter adversaries or cause them to settle on American terms.[41]

His administration guarded itself against its critics through secrecy, executive crimes, and corrupt political practices later known collectively as Watergate. Because he wanted documentation for his memoirs, Nixon secretly recorded conversations in the White House. When made public by court order, the tapes inspired an impeachment process that Nixon himself, caught in lies, terminated by resigning from the presidency on August 8, 1974, thereby elevating Vice President Gerald Ford to the White House. Exposure of criminality weakened the executive branch in its ongoing struggle with Congress over foreign policy. Watergate also caused bewilderment abroad, with Mao dismissing the affair as a "fart in the wind."[42]

After Nixon's ignoble departure, Henry A. Kissinger stayed on. Presidential assistant for national security affairs (1969–1976) and secretary of state (1973–1977), Kissinger thought Nixon an "egomaniac" who feared not receiving

Pinocchio and Jiminy Cricket. "A two-fisted, barefaced liar"—so Republican Senator Barry Goldwater described Nixon before the Watergate crisis forced the president from office. Using characters from the popular story of Pinocchio, the cartoonist Robert Grossman depicts Nixon as the untruthful youngster and Henry A. Kissinger as his faithful adviser. Nixon's biographer Richard Reeves writes: "So many layers of lies were needed to protect the layers of secrecy that no one, including the President himself, knew what the truth was anymore. ... It was hard to keep track of the deceptions, even for the deceivers." (© Robert Grossman)

"adequate credit" for foreign-policy triumphs such as the change in China policy.[43] One observer remarked that "Nixon and Kissinger were like two scorpions in the same bottle, sometimes friendly, often antagonistic, but almost inseparable."[44] This tense relationship led to a series of fierce disagreements about the proper path to take in negotiations.

Having escaped from Nazism in 1938, the German-born Kissinger became one of the most traveled diplomats in history. He reveled in personal diplomacy, in the give-and-take, the manipulation of power and people. His "devilish nimbleness" and evident rapport with people of different cultures brought him negotiating successes.[45] Kissinger managed an impressive number of roles: theorist, policymaker, negotiator, presidential adviser, bureaucratic infighter, and public spokesperson. He and Nixon agreed early that they would make policy in the White House, often sidestepping the foreign-affairs bureaucracy. William P. Rogers served as a loyal secretary of state until 1973, but Nixon granted him little authority. Resenting its exclusion from policymaking, Congress reasserted its prerogatives by passing the War Powers Resolution (1973): The president could commit U.S. troops abroad for no more than sixty days, after which he had to obtain congressional approval. Congress also vexed Kissinger by cutting foreign aid to Turkey, Cambodia, South Vietnam, and Angola. Without Watergate and without congressional meddling, Kissinger lamented, he could have accomplished so much more. He nonetheless shared with North Vietnamese negotiator Le Duc Tho the Nobel Peace Prize in 1973.

Kissinger still remained a popular figure. He charmed journalists and leaked secret information to generate favorable newspaper stories. A self-proclaimed "swinger" prior to his 1974 marriage, Kissinger once accused Anne Armstrong, the first U.S. female ambassador to Britain, of crying when he excluded her from negotiations. "I might have bitten him," recalled Armstrong, "but I wasn't going to cry."[46] State Department officials joked that working for Kissinger as secretary of state was like being a mushroom: "Because you're kept in the dark all the time, because you get a lot of shit dumped on you, and, in the end, you get canned."[47] Critics argued that Kissinger followed the ruthless maxim that the ends justify the means: He wiretapped aides and journalists; he defended the president in the lowest days of Watergate; he relied recklessly on huge arms sales; he sponsored CIA plots abroad that held America up to ridicule for advocating democracy but undermining it; and he approved the deadly bombings of Southeast Asia. "One must not confuse the intelligence business with missionary work" Kissinger explained.[48] He similarly

Makers of American Foreign Relations, 1969–1981

Presidents	Secretaries of State
Richard M. Nixon, 1969–1974	William P. Rogers, 1969–1973
Gerald Ford, 1974–1977	Henry A. Kissinger, 1973–1977
Jimmy Carter, 1977–1981	Cyrus R. Vance, 1977–1980
	Edmund Muskie, 1980–1981

urged the military leaders of Argentina to get the "terrorist problem under control as quickly as possible:" his main concern was not human rights but that they "get it over quickly."[49]

Kissinger and Nixon considered themselves pragmatists, not ideologues. The term that most generally described the thrust of their diplomacy was "détente": limited cooperation with the Soviet Union and the People's Republic of China within a general environment of rivalry. Détente became a means, a process, a climate in which to reduce international tensions and sustain U.S. leadership in world politics. Détente was supposed to produce a geopolitical "equilibrium," by expanding U.S. leverage to contain the Soviet Union and China and curb radical revolution worldwide.[50] To Nixon, the world divided into roughly five power centers (including Japan and Western Europe) with each keeping order among smaller states and clients in its region and each respecting one another's sphere. Nixon and Kissinger saw Soviet–American competition as the primary dynamic in world affairs. They understood that by 1970 the Soviet Union had achieved nuclear parity or equality with the United States, that the Soviets suffered severe internal economic problems and needed outside help, that the Sino-Soviet split had widened, and that world power (capital and weaponry) had become diffused as nations had recovered from World War II and colonies had broken away from empires. Recognizing that Washington could not "conceive *all* the plans, design *all* the programs, execute *all* the decisions," the duo sought to move the United States from containment through confrontation to containment through negotiation.[51]

Détente, SALT, and the Nuclear Arms Race

The Nixon administration emphasized the triangular relationship formed by the Soviet Union, China, and the United States and attempted to play the two communist states off each other. For the Soviets there would be both incentives (capital and trade) to encourage restraint, and penalties (large arms sales to Soviet adversaries and closer ties to China) to punish unacceptable behavior. Détente made sense to European allies who abhorred the U.S. "obsession with Southeast Asia."[52] Moscow and Beijing might help the United States extricate itself from war in Vietnam. Détente supposedly offered a cheaper way of pursuing containment by reducing the necessity for interventions, spiraling military expenditures, and new nuclear weapons systems. The Nixon administration cut the armed forces from 3.5 million in 1968 to 2.3 million in 1973, ended the draft, and in 1972 negotiated a strategic arms limitation treaty. Détente also conjured up images of expanded markets. Massive grain shipments flowed to the Soviet Union—in 1972, 25 percent of the American wheat crop. Corporations such as Pepsi-Cola and Chase Manhattan Bank started operations in the USSR. Exports to the Soviet Union reached $2.3 billion in 1976. "They want credits, they want trade, and we'll give it all to 'em," said Nixon. "But for a price."[53]

The Nixon–Kissinger grand strategy rested on some questionable assumptions. It overestimated the usefulness of China as a check on Moscow. It assumed wrongly that the Soviets could manage their "friends" in North Vietnam or the Middle East and that great-power cooperation could calm Third World problems. Still viewing small states as proxies of the great powers, Nixon paid too little attention to the local sources of disputes. Kissinger spent much of his time trying to keep détente glued together in the face of regional conflicts in Asia, Africa, and the Middle East and economic challenges from the Organization of Petroleum Exporting Countries (OPEC). Even America's friends caused difficulty: Iran insisted on huge arms shipments but raised oil prices, threatening the U.S. economy; Saudi Arabia demanded sophisticated weaponry but refused to help resolve the Arab-Israeli conflict.

Détente also ran afoul of domestic dissenters. In 1974 congressional conservatives and liberals cooperated to deny most-favored-nation trade status to the Soviet Union until it permitted Jewish emigration. Americans of Eastern European descent berated détente as an abandonment of their homelands to Soviet domination. Liberals criticized Kissinger's tolerance of authoritarian regimes that trampled on human rights. The Nixon and Ford administrations contradicted themselves by appealing for arms control while they broke records for arms sales abroad ($10 billion in 1976 alone). Hard-line anticommunists labeled Kissinger an appeaser who squandered U.S. supremacy in the international system.

The Nixon administration nonetheless claimed diplomatic triumphs. The opening to China ranked highest. The turnaround helped thwart reconciliation between the two communist giants. Moscow deployed more divisions in Asia—away from NATO. China received top-grade intelligence on the Soviets. "You don't need a master spy. We give you everything," said Kissinger.[54] New ties between China and Japan contributed to Asian stability. Sino-American trade flourished, reaching $700 million in 1973. Also, cultural exchanges and travel between the once-distant nations reduced mutual ignorance. In 1973 Washington and Beijing exchanged "Liaison Offices" or mini-embassies. Formal diplomatic relations had to wait until 1979, after Watergate, Nixon's resignation, the 1976 presidential election, the deaths of Mao and Zhou, and new political alignments within China.

The Sino-American rapprochement did have some tragic side effects. In 1971 the Bengalis of East Pakistan rebelled against the military dictatorship of (West) Pakistan and declared the independent nation of Bangladesh. The Pakistani government attempted to crush the revolution through what U.S. officials at the scene called "selective genocide."[55] India, which had just signed a treaty of friendship with the Soviet Union, intervened on behalf of the rebels. The White House thereupon ordered a "tilt" in favor of Pakistan.[56] As an ally, Pakistan had granted bases for U-2 flights over the Soviet Union and intelligence-gathering posts to monitor Soviet nuclear testing. Kissinger bluntly told Nixon: "We can't allow a friend of ours and China's to get screwed in a conflict with a friend of Russia's."[57] American weapons soon rushed to Pakistan, foreign aid to India stopped, and a naval task force steamed into the Bay of Bengal. The White House took a global rather than a regional view of the crisis and saw India acting as Moscow's pawn trying to "goat" Pakistan into full-scale war.[58] But India never attacked West Pakistan, and the Soviet Union never encouraged it to attack. Pakistan, India, China, and the Soviet Union all had indicated support for an agreement that matched the outcome: an end to hostilities, and independence for Bangladesh.

Despite sharp exchanges over the hotline during the Indo-Pakistani conflict, détente remained U.S. policy. At a summit meeting in Moscow in May 1972, Nixon

Anatoly Dobrynin (b. 1919) and Henry Kissinger (b. 1923). Dobrynin, the Soviet ambassador to the United States, served during six presidencies from John F. Kennedy to Ronald Reagan. His most important contributions came during the Cuban missile crisis and later during détente when he served as a "back channel" for secret negotiations between the White House and Kremlin that bypassed the State Department. Kissinger and Dobrynin developed a rapport through their extensive contacts. When Dobrynin congratulated him for sharing the Nobel Peace Prize with Le Duc Tho in 1973, Kissinger replied, "I figure it like Groucho Marx said, 'Any club that took him in, he does not want to join.' I would say anything that Le Duc Tho is eligible for, there must be something wrong with it." (Nixon Presidential Materials Project, National Archives and Record Administration)

told Soviet Chairman Leonid Brezhnev that capitalism and communism could "live together and work together."[59] They struck agreements on cooperation in space exploration (culminating in a joint space venture in 1975) and trade (large grain sales soon followed). On Vietnam, they concluded that small nations should not disrupt détente. Only a few weeks earlier, when Nixon had escalated the bombing of North Vietnam, he feared that an angry Moscow might cancel the summit. The Soviets did not; détente came first.

The Strategic Arms Limitation Talks (SALT) agreements dominated the summit. When the Nixon administration entered office, it inherited a legacy of doctrines and missiles that defined U.S. nuclear strategy. (See Glossary, p. 377.) In the 1960s, the doctrine of "massive retaliation" evolved into the concept of "mutual assured destruction," or MAD. MAD's viability depended on each side's "second-strike capability": the ability to absorb a first strike and still destroy the attacker with a retaliatory or second strike. By 1969 American strategists sought superiority through the triad: land-based intercontinental ballistic missiles (ICBMs), long-range B-52 bombers, and submarine-launched ballistic missiles (SLBMs), all armed with nuclear weapons. To help guarantee superiority, the United States had also begun to flight-test the "multiple independently targetable reentry vehicle" (MIRV). Finally, Nixon inherited plans for an "anti-ballistic missile" (ABM) system to defend cities and ICBMs vulnerable to Soviet attack. Because ABMs theoretically protected offensive weapons from attack, critics feared that they would stimulate the Soviets to build more missiles to overwhelm the ABM protection, further accelerating the nuclear arms race.

By 1968 Washington had deployed 1,054 ICBMs to the Soviets' 858; the United States also led in SLBMs 656 to 121, and in long-range bombers 545 to 155. The United States ranked first in total nuclear warheads, about 4,200 to 1,100, and in the accuracy of its weapons systems. Yet U.S. officials knew that the Soviets were constructing new missiles, submarines, and bombers at a pace that would soon give the Soviets nuclear parity with the United States. President Nixon soon abandoned the untenable doctrine of superiority and accepted parity of forces with the Soviet Union. Still, he decided to phase in the ABM system and ordered the installation of MIRVs. Thus the United States could enter the SALT talks, he said, from a position of strength.

The SALT-I talks began in Helsinki in November 1969 and culminated at the Moscow summit in May 1972 with two agreements. The first, a treaty, limited the deployment of ABMs for each nation to two sites. In essence the accord sustained the MAD doctrine by leaving urban centers in both countries vulnerable. The other accord, an interim agreement, froze the existing number of ICBMs already deployed or in construction. At the time, the Soviet Union led 1,607 to 1,054. The interim agreements also froze SLBMs at 740 for the USSR and 656 for the United States.

SALT-I did not limit the hydra-headed MIRVs, thus leaving the United States superior in deliverable warheads, 5,700 to 2,500. Nixon and Kissinger underestimated the speed with which the Soviets would deploy their own MIRVs on heavier missiles, and by not seeking a ban on MIRVs, they rendered American ICBMs theoretically vulnerable to a first strike. Nor did the agreement restrict long-range bombers, in which the United States held a 450 to 200 advantage. Finally, SALT-I did not prohibit the development of new weapons. The United States, for example, moved ahead on the Trident submarine (to replace the Polaris-Poseidon fleet), the B-1 bomber (to replace the B-52), and the cruise missile.

Still, SALT-I did begin frank talks to place limits on nuclear weapons. In August 1972, the Senate passed the ABM treaty by an 88 to 2 vote; a joint congressional resolution later endorsed the interim agreement. Détente's reputation soared. Conservative critics charged, however, that the United States lagged behind the Soviet Union in delivery vehicles (ICBMs, SLBMs, and strategic bombers). "What in the name of God is strategic superiority?" Kissinger challenged his detractors. "What do you do with it?"[60]

The Nuclear Arms Race: A Glossary

Anti-ballistic missile (ABM): A defensive missile designed to destroy an incoming enemy ballistic missile before its warhead reaches its target.

Ballistic missile: A rocket-propelled missile that leaves the atmosphere and returns to earth in a free fall.

Cruise missile: A guided missile that flies to its target within the earth's atmosphere, close to the surface. The cruise missile can carry a nuclear warhead and can be launched from the air, land, or sea.

Delivery vehicle: A missile or strategic bomber that delivers a warhead to its target.

Deployment: Installing weapons, making them ready for action.

First strike: An initial nuclear attack by one country intended to destroy an adversary's strategic nuclear forces.

Intercontinental ballistic missile (ICBM): A land-based missile capable of traveling more than 3,000 nautical miles to deliver one or more warheads.

Intermediate-range nuclear forces (INF): Sometimes called theater nuclear forces, these weapons have a range of about 3,000 miles.

Missile experimental (MX): An American ICBM capable of carrying as many as ten MIRVs.

Multiple independently targetable reentry vehicle (MIRV): A vehicle loaded with a warhead and mounted, along with similar vehicles, on one ballistic missile. Once separated from the missile, each MIRV can be directed against a different target.

Mutual assured destruction (MAD): The ability of both the United States and the Soviet Union to inflict damage so severe that neither is willing to initiate a nuclear attack.

Neutron bomb: An "enhanced radiation weapon," this nuclear bomb is designed primarily to kill people and to inflict less damage on buildings than other bombs.

Nonproliferation: The process of inhibiting the rapid spread of nuclear weapons to other powers. The Nuclear Nonproliferation Treaty of 1968 recognized five nuclear powers—the United States, USSR, Great Britain, France, and the People's Republic of China. All other states were treaty-bound to refrain from creating and deploying nuclear weapons.

Nuclear freeze: The immediate halt to the development, production, transfer, and deployment of nuclear weapons.

Second strike: A retaliatory nuclear attack launched after being hit by an opponent's first strike.

Strategic Defense Initiative (SDI): Popularly known as "Star Wars," SDI was President Ronald Reagan's 1983 proposal to build a space-based, defensive system that could establish a protective shield over the United States and its allies with the capability to shoot down incoming ballistic missiles.

Strategic weapons or arms: Long-range weapons capable of hitting an adversary's territory. ICBMs, SLBMs, and strategic bombers are so classified.

Submarine-launched ballistic missile (SLBM): A ballistic missile carried in and launched from a submarine.

Surface-to-air missile (SAM): A missile launched from the earth's surface for the purpose of knocking down an adversary's airplanes.

Tactical nuclear weapons: Low-yield nuclear weapons for battlefield use.

Triad: The three-part structure of American strategic forces (ICBMs, SLBMs, and strategic bombers).

Warhead: The part of a missile that contains the nuclear explosive intended to inflict damage.

Subsequent negotiations on SALT-II moved slowly. At Vladivostok, in November 1974, President Ford and Chairman Brezhnev agreed on two principles to guide the talks—a ceiling of 2,400 on the total number of delivery vehicles permitted each side and no more than 1,320 missiles equipped with MIRVs. Thereafter the SALT-II talks bogged down over which types of weapons should count in the 2,400 ceiling, with Washington insisting that the new Soviet Backfire bomber be included, and the Soviets demanding inclusion of the U.S. cruise missile.

By 1977 the United States wielded 8,500 warheads, compared with 5,700 in 1972; comparable Soviet figures equaled 4,000 and 2,500. Total strategic delivery vehicles by 1978 numbered 2,059 for the United States and 2,440 for the Soviet Union. Détente had not stopped the nuclear arms race.

In Europe, however, détente worked to ease tensions. Willy Brandt, the West German chancellor, pursued a policy of *Ostpolitik* to remove the two Germanies from great-power competition. A West German–Soviet treaty of August 1970 identified détente as the goal of both countries and recognized the existence of two Germanies. A few months later Brandt signed an agreement with Poland that confirmed the latter's postwar absorption of German territory. Then, in June 1972, the four powers occupying Berlin signed an agreement wherein the Soviet Union guaranteed Western access to the city. Finally, in December 1972, the two Germanies themselves initialed a treaty that provided for the exchange of diplomatic representatives and membership in the United Nations for both (effected in 1973). European East-West trade boomed, with the West German economy the chief beneficiary. Some scholars have argued that U.S.-Soviet détente emerged in part "to preclude a West German-led détente" that could exclude the United States and split the Western alliance.[61]

At the Conference on Security and Cooperation in Helsinki, Finland, in summer 1975, delegates from thirty-five nations accepted the permanence of existing European boundaries, including adjustments made in Germany and Eastern Europe three decades earlier. The conferees pledged themselves to détente and endorsed human rights for all Europeans. Kissinger blasted right-wing critics for their "bitching about the borders we had done nothing to change when we had a nuclear monopoly."[62] So-called Helsinki groups meanwhile pressed communist governments to honor their pledge about human rights. Such groups included Charter 77, headed by Václav Havel in Czechoslovakia, and Solidarity, led by Lech Walesa in Poland. Instead of the "consolidation of the postwar order that Moscow had so long desired," a Kissinger aide later noted, "the political status quo in Eastern Europe began to unravel."[63] In the short run, as "masters of our own house," the Kremlin arrested Soviet intellectuals who demanded freedom of speech.[64]

Regional Tails Wagging the Superpower Dogs: The Middle East

The Nixon Doctrine, announced in July 1969, declared that henceforth the United States would supply military and economic assistance but not soldiers to help nations defend themselves. To prevent new Vietnams, Washington sought to build up regional surrogate powers, such as Iran and Israel. Third World countries still mattered because of their apparent vulnerability to destabilizing radicalism and hence to pernicious Soviet influence. Moscow's endorsement of national liberation movements, according to Kissinger, connected the internal politics of developing nations with the "international struggle."[65] When troubles arose in the Third World, Nixon, Ford, and Kissinger reflexively interpreted them as moves in the game of great-power politics.

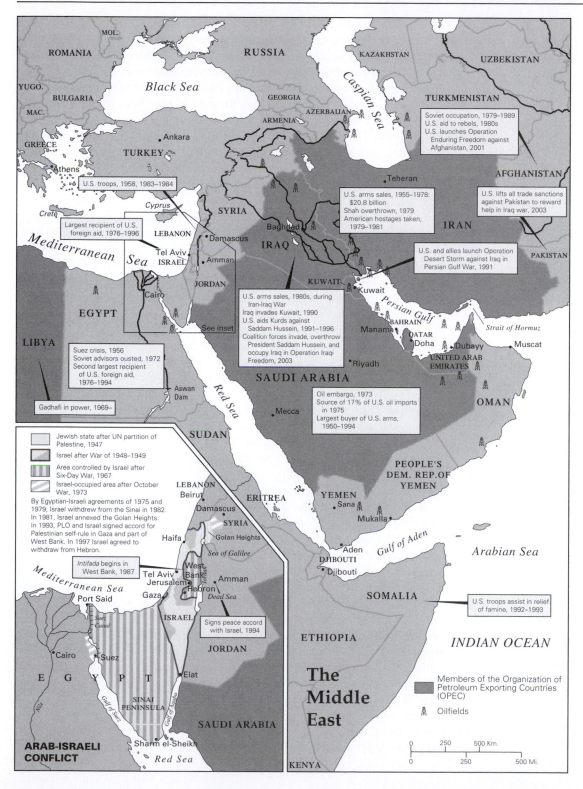

The Middle East

Map labels and annotations:

MOL.

ROMANIA

YUGO.

BULGARIA

MAC.

Black Sea

RUSSIA

KAZAKHSTAN

UZBEKISTAN

GREECE

•Ankara

TURKEY

GEORGIA

ARMENIA

AZERBAIJAN

Caspian Sea

TURKMENISTAN

Soviet occupation, 1979–1989
U.S. aid to rebels, 1980s
U.S. launches Operation
Enduring Freedom against
Afghanistan, 2001

•Teheran

AFGHANISTAN

Athens•

U.S. troops, 1958, 1983–1984

Crete

Cyprus

SYRIA

•Damascus

Baghdad•

IRAQ

U.S. arms sales, 1955–1978:
$20.8 billion
Shah overthrown, 1979
American hostages taken,
1979–1981

IRAN

U.S. lifts all trade sanctions
against Pakistan to reward
help in Iraq war, 2003

PAKISTAN

Largest recipient of U.S.
foreign aid, 1976–1996

LEBANON

Tel Aviv•

ISRAEL

•Amman

JORDAN

Mediterranean Sea

U.S. and allies launch Operation
Desert Storm against Iraq in
Persian Gulf War, 1991

KUWAIT

•Kuwait

Persian Gulf

Cairo•

EGYPT

See inset

U.S. arms sales, 1980s, during
Iran-Iraq War
Iraq invades Kuwait, 1990
U.S. aids Kurds against
Saddam Hussein, 1991–1996
Coalition forces invade, overthrow
President Saddam Hussein, and
occupy Iraq in Operation Iraqi
Freedom, 2003

BAHRAIN

•Manama

QATAR

•Doha

•Dubayy

UNITED ARAB
EMIRATES

Strait of Hormuz

•Muscat

LIBYA

Suez crisis, 1956
Soviet advisors ousted, 1972
Second largest recipient
of U.S. foreign aid,
1976–1994

Aswan
Dam

•Riyadh

Red Sea

SAUDI ARABIA

OMAN

Gadhafi in power, 1969–

Oil embargo, 1973
Source of 17% of U.S. oil imports
in 1975
Largest buyer of U.S. arms,
1950–1994

•Mecca

SUDAN

PEOPLE'S
DEM. REP. OF
YEMEN

YEMEN

•Sana

•Mukalla

ERITREA

•Aden

Gulf of Aden

Arabian Sea

DJIBOUTI

•Djibouti

SOMALIA

U.S. troops assist in relief
of famine, 1992–1993

ETHIOPIA

INDIAN OCEAN

**The
Middle
East**

KENYA

Members of the Organization of
Petroleum Exporting Countries
(OPEC)

Oilfields

0   250   500 Km.

0   250   500 Mi.

Inset — ARAB-ISRAELI CONFLICT:

Jewish state after UN partition of
Palestine, 1947

Israel after War of 1948–1949

Area controlled by Israel after
Six-Day War, 1967

Israel-occupied area after October
War, 1973

By Egyptian-Israeli agreements of 1975 and
1979, Israel withdrew from the Sinai in 1982.
In 1981, Israel annexed the Golan Heights.
In 1993, PLO and Israel signed accord for
Palestinian self-rule in Gaza and part of
West Bank. In 1997 Israel agreed to
withdraw from Hebron.

Intifada begins in
West Bank, 1987

LEBANON

Beirut•

•Damascus

SYRIA

Haifa•

Golan Heights

Sea of Galilee

Mediterranean Sea

Tel Aviv•

West
Bank

Jerusalem•

•Amman

Gaza•

•Hebron

Dead Sea

Port Said•

ISRAEL

Suez Canal

•Cairo

E G Y P T

•Suez

JORDAN

Signs peace accord
with Israel, 1994

SINAI
PENINSULA

Gulf of Suez

Gulf of Aqaba

•Elat

SAUDI ARABIA

Nile

Sharm el-Sheikh•

Red Sea

Problems in the Middle East sorely tested détente. Basic U.S. goals since World War II had been consistent for the region: ensure oil supplies; contain the Soviet Union; protect Israel; challenge neutralism; and blunt the appeal of Arab nationalism. After the 1956 Suez crisis, the Soviet Union and the United States armed Egypt and Israel respectively. In June 1967, after years of threats and counterthreats, Israel attacked Egypt and Syria. In the Six-Day War, the Israelis, using American-supplied weapons, captured the West Bank (including Jerusalem) from Jordan, the Golan Heights from Syria, and the entire Sinai Peninsula, including the eastern bank of the Suez Canal, from Egypt. Half of the Arab states broke diplomatic relations with Washington. Soviet vessels obtained access to Arab ports. Washington, in turn, sold fifty F-4 Phantom jets to Israel in December 1968 and winked at Israel's development of nuclear weapons.

Nixon's administration worried that the persistent Arab-Israeli "powder keg" would open a Soviet avenue into the Middle East.[66] As the Israelis deployed U.S. Phantom jets on bombing raids deep into Egypt in January 1970, the Soviets shipped surface-to-air missiles (SAMs) to Egypt to defend against the Phantoms. Thousands of Soviet troops, advisers, and pilots answered Egypt's call for assistance. Washington gave Israel more planes and more arms with military credits amounting to $1.2 billion from 1971 to 1973.

Meanwhile, Palestinian Arabs, many of them refugees ousted from their homes in 1948 by Israeli forces, grew more frustrated. The Palestine Liberation Organization (PLO), formed in 1964, came under the aggressive leadership of Yasir Arafat. Many Arab leaders backed the organization's demands for destruction of the Jewish state and for creation of a Palestinian homeland. In 1970 a radical wing of the PLO hijacked airliners and seized hostages. Palestinian terrorists murdered Israeli athletes at the 1972 Olympic Games in Munich. The Israelis retaliated, targeting PLO figures abroad.

From 1970 to 1973, the Nixon administration's "standstill diplomacy" seemed to work.[67] Israel possessed military superiority, Moscow displayed restraint, and a new, seemingly more moderate Egyptian government under the leadership of Anwar el-Sadat came to power after Gamal Nasser's death in September 1970. Fearful that détente would condemn Egypt to a "no war, no peace" paralysis, Sadat plotted a new strike against Israel.[68] After thwarting a Soviet-supported coup, he abruptly expelled several thousand Soviet technicians and military advisers in summer 1972. The United States continued to arm Israel; in early 1973 Washington promised more planes. Then on October 6, 1973 (Yom Kippur, the holiest day on the Jewish calendar), Egyptian forces struck across the canal into Sinai while Syrian troops attacked Israel's northern border. Taken by surprise, the Israelis suffered heavy losses, and the Arabs regained land lost in 1967. Although Nixon promised Tel Aviv more Phantoms, Kissinger speculated that the best result "would be if Israel came out a little ahead but got bloodied in the process, and if the U.S. stayed clean."[69] But when the Soviets rushed arms to Syria, Kissinger wondered if "those sons of bitches in Moscow are schnookering us."[70]

In a massive airlift of supplies, Nixon ordered "everything that will fly" to Israel on October 14.[71] As Israel counterattacked, Soviet premier Aleksei Kosygin went to Cairo to persuade Sadat to accept a cease-fire. Kissinger flew to Moscow

Golda Meir (1898–1978), Nixon, and Kissinger.
In early 1973, the prime minister of Israel met with the president, who promised more U.S. airplanes. On the Nixon-Meir relationship, White House counsel Leonard Garment later wrote: "How could Nixon resist this mother of all mothers, ... smart, spiky, and resolute in her simple schoolteacher frock?" (Department of State *Newsletter*)

on October 20, learning en route that the Saudis had embargoed oil to the United States. Other Arab states soon joined the embargo. With Nixon increasingly distracted by the Watergate crisis, Kissinger and the Soviets finally arranged a cease-fire on October 22. But the Israelis ignored the truce and surrounded the Egyptian Third Army. When Moscow pressed for Soviet and U.S. troops to enforce the truce jointly, Washington overreacted. An inebriated Nixon blurted: "Words won't do the job. We've got to act."[72] Kissinger thereupon ordered all U.S. forces on nuclear alert, a calculated ploy to shock Soviet decision makers. Angry Kremlin leaders chose not to intervene unilaterally. Kissinger pressed the Israelis to honor the truce. A new cease-fire held.

The Arab-Israeli contest had far-reaching economic repercussions. Arab states such as Saudi Arabia, which for years had supplied Western nations with inexpensive petroleum, now used their black riches as a weapon. They embargoed petroleum shipments to the United States and quadrupled the price of crude oil for Western Europe and Japan. The United States, importing between 10 and 15 percent of its oil from the Middle East, suffered an energy crisis. Gasoline prices spun upward as anxious drivers lined up, sometimes for hours, to fuel their automobiles. The embargo ended in March 1974, but prices remained high and U.S. vulnerability had been exposed.

Kissinger launched "shuttle diplomacy" to prevent another Mideast blowup. With impressive stamina, he bargained in Cairo and Tel Aviv and other capitals intermittently for two years. Finally, on September 1, 1975, Egypt and Israel initialed a historic agreement that provided for an eventual Israeli pullback from part of the Sinai, created a United Nations–patrolled buffer zone, and placed U.S. technicians in "early warning" stations to detect military activities. Washington also promised substantial aid to both Egypt and Israel.

Thorny problems remained. The Palestinian Arabs still demanded a homeland, while Israelis entrenched themselves in occupied territories, building farms and houses. Jordan still demanded return of the West Bank, and Syrian hostility persisted with the Golan Heights in Israel's hands. A bloody civil war broke out in Lebanon, which prompted Syria to send in troops in 1976. Washington continued to ship weapons to both Arabs and Israelis after the October war. In 1976, Sadat, who wanted U.S. technology and mediation, denounced Moscow, saying that "99 percent of the cards in the game are in America's hands whether the Soviet Union likes it or not."[73] Once Cairo turned emphatically toward Washington, U.S. Mideast policy looked more like old-fashioned containment than détente. Excluding the Soviets and Palestinians from Mideast diplomacy prevented a full Arab-Israeli settlement. The spectacular rescue by Israeli commandos of 259 hostages held captive by Palestinian terrorists in Entebbe, Uganda, on July 4, 1976, also galvanized U.S. public support for Israel. After Entebbe, it became axiomatic that "the United States should not only act *with* Israel on foreign policy but *like* Israel in matters of unconventional warfare."[74] Moscow, in turn, gave more support to Libya's President Moammar Gadhafi, a radical Pan Arabist who came to power in 1969 and denounced all Mideast peace efforts.

As a counterweight to the Soviets and radical Arabs, Washington fashioned a closer alliance with the Shah of Iran. After 1972, the Shah's military gorged itself on modern American arms, paid for by galloping oil revenues ("petro-dollars"). In 1977 his nation ranked as the largest foreign buyer of American-made arms, spending $5.7 billion that year alone. But doubters thought such excessive military spending foolhardy when the Iranian per capita income stood at only $350. Ruthlessly suppressing all dissent, the Shah hired a New York advertising agency to enhance his image as America's "unconditional ally" in the turbulent Middle East.[75] Washington did not see that "Iran was the regional tail wagging the superpower dog."[76]

Thinking Globally: Relations with Latin America and Africa

Latin America remained of intense interest to the United States. Latin American military officers still trained at the Inter-American Defense College in Washington, D.C., where they learned urban counterinsurgency and jungle warfare techniques. In the early 1970s, one-third of Latin American exports went to the United States, and two-fifths of the region's imports came from the United States. In 1976 Latin American countries supplied 34 percent of U.S. petroleum imports, 68 percent of its coffee, 57 percent of its sugar, 47 percent of its copper, and 98 percent of its bauxite. In that year U.S. direct investments in its southern neighbors totaled $17 billion. Latin American governments nonetheless increasingly challenged Washington. Soon after taking office, Nixon sent Governor Nelson Rockefeller on a fact-finding mission to Latin America that sparked protests. The governor reported in August 1969 that Latin Americans resented Washington's "paternalistic" efforts to "direct the internal affairs of other nations to an unseemly degree."[77] Mexico refused to honor the economic blockade of Cuba, boldly proclaimed the economic independence of small states and their right to expropriate foreign enterprises, and urged that developed nations share their wealth with poorer countries. In 1974 the United Nations approved these views by a 120 to 6 vote, with

Washington voting no. After 1968, a new, radical (noncommunist) military government in Peru nationalized an Exxon oil subsidiary and defiantly purchased Soviet MiGs. Venezuela, a founding member of the Organization of Petroleum Exporting Countries (OPEC) in 1960, joined the Arabs in drastically raising petroleum prices in the 1970s. In 1976 Caracas too nationalized American-owned oil companies.

Chile attracted Washington's rapt attention in September 1970. That month Chileans elected as their president Salvador Allende, a physician by profession and a founder of Chile's Socialist party. The CIA had sent hundreds of thousands of dollars in bribes and propaganda money to back a right-wing candidate. Nixon feared that socialist regimes in Cuba and Chile would make Latin America a "red sandwich," ignoring that "[f]our thousand miles of heterogeneous societies and regimes would lie between those two slabs of Marxist pumpernickel."[78] Nixon personally gave CIA official Richard Helms full authority to "make the [Chilean] economy scream."[79] With one corporate lawyer lamenting that "We used to be the fucker. ... Now we're the fuckee," the CIA worked with Kennecott and Anaconda, companies which feared nationalization of their assets.[80] Washington also cut off economic aid and denied Export-Import Bank loans to Chile. Military assistance continued as the CIA conspired with Chilean army officers and spent $6 million to subsidize newspapers and political parties opposed to Allende. In 1973 a military junta overthrew and murdered Allende. Declassified documents indicate that "sectors of the U.S. government" were directly involved in operations designed to create a "coup climate."[81] Vivid images of Allende's ouster recurred in the 1982 film *Missing,* a taut thriller in which Chilean authorities, with the complicity of U.S. embassy officials, kill an American journalist for exposing U.S. machinations. The new junta returned nationalized companies to private hands, suspended freedom of speech and press, and tortured and killed political opponents. When Congress threatened to cut off arms sales in 1976, Kissinger assured Chilean dictator Augusto Pinochet that "your greatest sin was to overthrow a government that was going Communist."[82]

The Nixon and Ford administrations also sought to keep Cuba isolated. Seeing Castro as a Soviet puppet, Nixon concluded in 1970 from sketchy U-2 evidence that the Soviets were building a nuclear submarine base at Cienfuegos, Cuba, in violation of their pledge after the 1962 missile crisis not to place offensive weapons on the island. Still Nixon wanted "to play it down" to keep "some 'clown senator' [from] asking for a Cuban blockade in the middle of an election."[83] When Moscow denied building a submarine facility, Nixon claimed a victory that "reaffirmed," "clarified," and "amplified" the 1962 understanding by prohibiting Soviet nuclear submarine facilities in Cuba.[84] Still seeking some accommodation with North America in the early 1970s, Castro deemphasized the export of revolution, and in 1973 he signed an antihijacking treaty with Washington to discourage terrorism in the airways. Two years later the Organization of American States lifted its economic blockade of Cuba. Following secret talks to explore possibilities for détente, Kissinger rejected baseball commissioner Bowie Kuhn's efforts in 1975 to arrange games between the United States and Cuba. When Cuban troops in Africa helped Angolan radicals seize control of that country, Kissinger concluded that Castro "was probably the most genuine revolutionary leader then in power," and hopes for Cuban-American normalization faded.[85]

Frank Church (1924–1984). Democratic senator from Idaho (1957–1981), Church became a major figure on the Foreign Relations Committee, serving as its chair (1979–1981). A critic of the Vietnam War and an effective orator, Church chaired Senate investigations that revealed U.S. complicity in the overthrow of Chile's Salvador Allende and exposed CIA abuses such as assassination attempts on foreign leaders. (Frank Church Collection, Boise State University Library)

Until the mid-1970s, Africa stood low on the Nixon-Ford-Kissinger list of diplomatic priorities. When he first entered office, Nixon told Kissinger, "Henry, let's leave the niggers to Bill [Secretary of State William Rogers] and we'll take care of the rest of the world."[86] Kissinger thought "the African liberation movements were communist 'stooges' because of their reliance on weapons from China, Cuba, and the Soviet Union," and he urged support for white minority regimes in Portuguese Angola, Rhodesia, and South Africa.[87] The National Security Council explained in a memorandum (NSSM 39) that the entrenched whites would approve only moderate change, and that the black majorities, fearing white military superiority, would refrain from major violent confrontation. Washington thus relaxed the arms embargo to white South Africa; Congress in 1971 passed the Byrd Amendment permitting the United States to buy chromium from Rhodesia despite UN sanctions against Ian Smith's white minority government. The Black Congressional Caucus blasted the "stifling hypocrisy" of Nixon's policies toward Africa.[88] In contrast to segregationist caricatures of African leaders as "boys in funny hats and monkey-skin coats" from "left-leaning hog-wallow and mangrove-swamp nations" only "slightly removed from cannibalism," dollar-conscious observers cited the more than $2 billion invested in black Africa and U.S. purchases of cobalt, oil, manganese, and platinum.[89]

Events in Angola eventually shattered American complacency. Since the early 1960s, black rebel groups had battled the Portuguese in Angola. Playing a double game, the CIA channeled funds to a faction of independence fighters while Washington officially backed Portugal and sold it military equipment to quell the nationalist rebellion. The Soviets began to support another guerrilla group, the Popular Movement for the Liberation of Angola (MPLA). When the CIA spent $32 million in 1975 on covert operations to defeat the MPLA, the State Department official in charge of African affairs, Nathaniel Davis, argued that such actions could not control the revolution but would stimulate increased Soviet activity. Davis urged a diplomatic solution. For "a test of strength with the Soviets," he advised Kissinger, "we should find a more advantageous place."[90] "You may be right in African terms, but I'm thinking globally," Kissinger retorted. He believed that "a great country that cannot give military aid in these revolutionary solutions is going to become irrelevant."[91] Davis resigned.

Gerald R. Ford (1913–2006). In October 1973 Vice President Spiro Agnew pleaded no contest to charges of income-tax evasion and acceptance of bribes and resigned. Ford then assumed the office of vice president. A long-time conservative member of Congress from Michigan, Ford aroused controversy when, as president, he pardoned Richard M. Nixon. Ford tried to maintain a U.S. presence in Vietnam and Angola, but Congress rejected funding. (The White House)

In November 1975, Portugal granted independence to Angola. The insurgent factions then fought one another in a civil war, with the U.S. clients performing poorly. South Africa and Zaire also dispatched troops, as did Cuba. Moscow hesitated (lest it scuttle détente) but also sent arms and advisers when South African forces intervened. Davis's resignation and leaks about the secret intervention stirred Congress. Another Vietnam? President Ford asked for $25 million for arms, but Congress "pulled the plug," by voting in January 1976 to stop military expenditures for Angola.[92]

Kissinger raged at "the probable loss to communism of a key developing country at a time of great uncertainty over our will and determination."[93] Yet critics thought it misleading to view an African civil war through a Cold War prism. The MPLA, after all, did not molest American oil companies and never became a Soviet puppet. Washington hurt itself by choosing the losing side. Discussions with the

MPLA—preventive diplomacy—might have reduced the violence. Cuba's conspicuous intervention actually goaded Moscow—heretofore very cautious about backing revolutionary movements "outside its neighboring countries"—to defend "global anti-imperialism" in far-off Angola. This success fueled further "limited interventions" in Africa and Asia, ultimately leading to the Soviets' disastrous incursion into Afghanistan during the 1980s.[94]

Ford's ban on using the word *détente* after Angola pointedly exposed the differing Soviet and American interpretations of that concept. What Nixon-Kissinger-Ford had intended as codes of conduct that would restrain Soviet expansion, Moscow saw as "the natural result of the correlation of forces in the world arena," nothing that would "change the laws of the class struggle."[95] Thus, as Washington sustained its regional clients in the Mideast peace process, for example, the Brezhnev regime sought "to perform our international duty" by assisting national liberation movements.[96]

In addition to Angola, the outbreak of racial violence in South Africa prompted a reappraisal of U.S. policy toward Africa. The United States, reasoned Kissinger, "must grab the initiative" or "we will be faced with the Soviets, and Cuban troops," even race wars.[97] Arms shipments went to Kenya and Zaire. Economic ties were strengthened through investments by companies such as Bethlehem Steel and Kaiser Aluminum, in pursuit of titanium and bauxite, respectively. Kissinger began to disengage from white minority regimes in Rhodesia and South Africa, urging the latter to abandon its segregationist policy of apartheid lest popular uprisings conducive to Marxist influence proliferate. Such changes underscored the fact that Africa had become a Cold War arena.

Number One Challenged: Economic Competition, Environmental Distress, and the North-South Debate

"It's terribly important we be number one economically," said Nixon, "because otherwise we can't be number one diplomatically or militarily."[98] In the 1970s, the international economic order created after World War II foundered. The Bretton Woods monetary mechanism (see page 204) faltered; the dollar skidded; famines starved millions; dwindling natural resources spawned political tensions; and the former colonies of the Third World challenged the industrial nations to share power. The global recession of the early 1970s became the worst since the 1930s. Inflation raised the cost of industrial goods for developing countries. Protectionist barriers rose. Dramatically climbing oil prices hit poor and rich nations alike, while the price of other commodities, such as copper, slumped, causing economic downturns in nations dependent on the export of one product. Economists coined the term "Fourth World"—poor, less developed countries (LDCs) that lacked profit making raw materials and built up large foreign debts. The Soviet Union and the People's Republic of China engaged in world trade as never before, in quest of agricultural products and high technology. Enlarged East-West trade became a headline issue.

In this chaotic economy, the United States produced about one-third of all the world's goods and services and remained the world's largest trading nation. In 1970

U.S. exports stood at $27.5 billion; by 1977 they had climbed to $121.2 billion. Coca-Cola, Gillette, and IBM earned more than half of their profits abroad. Many American jobs depended on healthy foreign trade. In 1976, for example, one out of every nine manufacturing workers produced goods for export. Exports accounted for one out of every four dollars of agricultural sales in 1977.

American industry also relied on imports of raw materials: 75 percent of the tin, 91 percent of the chrome, 99 percent of the manganese, and 64 percent of the zinc consumed by Americans in 1975 came from foreign sources. In 1977 the nation imported more than 40 percent of its petroleum. These import needs had become conspicuous in 1971 when, for the first time since the 1930s, the United States suffered a trade deficit, importing more than it exported. Six years later, the trade imbalance reached $26.5 billion, due mainly to oil imports. U.S. direct investments abroad—about half of the world's total foreign direct investments—equaled $75.5 billion in 1970 and $149.8 billion in 1977. The greatest part of these investments remained in developed countries (73 percent in 1975). Some investments faced political unrest, terrorist acts, and nationalization.

Despite its commanding status, the United States seemed to be losing its competitive edge. In the 1970s, ninety-eight nations had higher rates of economic growth. Japan and West Germany, strategic allies but commercial rivals, challenged America in the international marketplace. In fact, Japanese automobiles, televisions, and electronic equipment seized a large share of the U.S. markets. Once dominant, American producers of computers, high technology, and aerospace machinery now struggled to retain high rank. With millions of U.S. and European petro dollars flowing into their coffers, would wealthy Arabs buy up American banks, companies, and real estate?

The descent of the once mighty dollar further suggested decline. A "dollar glut" developed abroad, induced by U.S. foreign-aid programs, military expenditures ($90 billion in 1970 alone), private investments, inflation, and purchases of higher-priced oil. Foreigners held $78 billion in 1969; by 1977 the figure had jumped to $373 billion. Foreign holders of dollars exchanged them for gold, thus putting pressure on America's diminishing gold stock. The dollar declined in value against currencies such as the German mark and Swiss franc. Washington faced a serious balance-of-payments crisis.

The Nixon administration responded with unilateral economic measures. In August 1971, after the dollar had fallen to its lowest point since World War II, Nixon devalued the dollar (by increasing the dollar price of an ounce of gold) and suspended its convertibility into gold. He also cut foreign aid by 10 percent and imposed a 10 percent surtax on all imports, seeking thereby to reduce the influx of Japanese and European goods and to put diplomatic pressure on other nations to revalue their currencies to make them less competitive with the dollar. "We'll fix those bastards," vowed Nixon.[99]

In December representatives of ten leading trading nations gathered in Washington to try to stabilize the international monetary system. After stormy sessions in which Secretary of the Treasury George Schulz told the delegates that "Santa Claus is dead," America's economic competitors agreed to revalue their currencies to bring them more into line with the dollar.[100] The United States then lifted its import surcharge and once more made the dollar exchangeable for gold. But this agreement did not work for long; in early 1973 the United States again devalued the dollar, this time letting it "float," its value determined by supply and demand in the monetary marketplace. Efforts by the International Monetary Fund to restore an orderly system fell short.

International money problems intersected with foreign trade problems. Higher priced American goods could not easily compete with Japanese or European products, and the European Common Market engaged in preferential trade arrangements and export subsidies that hurt U.S. sales abroad. Japan too was highly protectionist at home yet aggressively penetrating global markets. In 1971 Tokyo averted a trade war by voluntarily limiting textile exports to America. Multilateral trade negotiations, under the auspices of the long-working General Agreement on Tariffs and Trade (1947), began in Tokyo in 1974. Five years later the "Tokyo Round" of negotiations finally produced accords that shrank tariffs about 30 percent. The signatories, including the United States, also wrote codes to regulate subsidies and dumping, but without liberalizing trade in agriculture.

In 1972 the developing world had 74 percent of the world's population, but accounted for only 17 percent of the world's combined gross national product (GNP). From the perspective of developing nations (the "South"), it seemed imperative that wealthier industrial nations (the "North") charge less for manufactured goods and technology, offer foreign assistance and loans at low rates, reduce tariffs, pay more for raw materials through commodity price agreements, and allow Third World nations to restrict foreign-owned corporations. Developing countries also insisted on a greater voice in international institutions such as the World Bank. "The object is to complete the liberation of the Third World countries from external domination," explained Tanzania's Julius K. Nyerere.[101] Kissinger, however, viewed the movement with total contempt, contending that the "axis of history starts in Moscow, goes to Bonn, crosses over to Washington, and then goes to Tokyo. What happens in the South is of no importance."[102]

The Group of 77 disagreed. This coalition of developing nations, organized in 1964, grew to more than one hundred countries in the 1970s. The consortium came to dominate the UN General Assembly, which in 1974 endorsed a New International Economic Order. The United States, Japan, and Western European nations struck some compromises. But charges of American greed rang hollow when many Third World leaders indulged in financial corruption and wasted resources on weaponry. India, for example, allotted billions to produce a nuclear bomb in 1974 instead of devoting those funds to alleviate severe food shortages.

Famine intensified. Insufficient fertilizer, inadequate farm acreage, pollution, droughts, and shrinking fish supplies condemned one-quarter of humankind to hunger. The drought that swept Africa in the early 1970s caused at least 10,000 deaths a day. A high birth rate and falling death rate put severe pressure on available food supplies. In 1975 the world's population passed 4 billion. Nutritionists estimated that nearly a quarter of the world's people ate less than the calories required to sustain ordinary physical activity.

At the 1974 World Food Conference in Rome, the United States voted to help finance an International Fund for Agricultural Development to expand food

Famine in Chad, Africa.   Chad, an impoverished former French colony, gained independence in 1960. Since 1965, civil wars, fueled by ethnic strife and opposition to dictatorial leaders, have wracked this landlocked country. Oil deposits attracted the interest of outside powers in recent years, but during the drought-plagued 1970s, Chad was only one of many poor nations that suffered food shortages and famine. Millions died in this world hunger crisis. (CARE, New York)

production in developing countries. But Americans continued to market surplus food for profit, most notably in large grain sales to the dollar-paying Soviet Union. And food aid, always political, became more so; in 1973–1974 most U.S. food assistance went to clients South Vietnam, Cambodia, and South Korea. At the same time, because of rising oil costs, the United States reduced its exports of petroleum-derived fertilizers, thus contributing to a worldwide decline in grain production in 1974. U.S. foreign-aid strategy in the early 1970s aimed to assist especially the most impoverished people through projects to improve nutrition, family planning, health, education, and food production. Although total foreign aid (economic and military) had increased from $6.6 billion in 1970 to $7.8 billion in 1977, the proportion of GNP devoted to development assistance actually decreased. In 1977 Americans spent about four times as much on tobacco products as their government expended on development aid. Kissinger attempted to meet some of the developing nations' demands; he nonetheless voiced a growing American impatience with their "confrontational" manner.[103]

North-South relations also became contentious over environmental issues. In the United States, books such as Rachel Carson's *Silent Spring* (1962), Paul Erlich's *The Population Bomb* (1968), and Barry Commoner's *The Closing Circle* (1971) raised public consciousness about environmental degradation and the growing imbalance between food supplies and burgeoning populations. In 1969 Greenpeace organized to protest nuclear-weapons tests, and the following year Americans celebrated the first Earth Day. Nixon bowed to congressional pressure to create the Environmental Protection Agency (EPA). Oil spills from oceangoing tankers, unsafe disposal of hazardous wastes, and the contamination of water sources underscored these borderless, transnational issues requiring international attention. Environmental groups around the world pressed for action.

The United Nations sponsored the Conference on the Human Environment in Stockholm in 1972. More than 100 nations, nineteen intergovernmental organizations (IGOs), and 400 nongovernmental organizations (NGOs) attended. Third World nations feared that measures to protect the environment would slow their economic development. The South demanded compensation for stricter environmental controls as well as more Northern aid earmarked for environmental projects. Developed nations in turn worried that Third World industrialization would overwhelm the biosphere. "People don't give a shit about the environment," said Nixon privately as he pledged U.S. monies to the new environmental fund and backed a moratorium on commercial whaling.[104] But he balked at more financial assistance to Third World countries and bristled at complaints that Washington had degraded the natural environment in Indochina. Still, the global conference spurred national environmental reforms, set up Earthwatch to monitor environmental conditions, and spotlighted transboundary pollution.

In the 1960s a new question became urgent: Who owned the rights to the gas, petroleum, and minerals such as manganese and nickel that rested in the deep seabed? Offshore oil drilling was well advanced, but the exploitation of the ocean's mineral riches was just beginning. American companies invested large sums in new technology for the ocean floor. Washington endorsed the principle that seabed resources were "a common heritage of mankind" in 1970, but at the UN-sponsored Law of the Sea Conference, which opened in 1973, U.S. officials rejected the South's call for a powerful international seabed agency with exclusive rights over the mining of ocean resources.[105] Because the new authority would operate on a one-nation, one-vote basis, industrial nations would lose their competitive advantage. In 1976–1977 Washington proposed a dual system: private development and an international authority, the latter to be assigned exclusive exploitation of certain mining sites. Until such an agreement, Kissinger insisted, the United States would explore and mine on its own.

The South and North also debated multinational corporations, the South seeking tighter controls and a larger proportion of profits earned from operations in developing nations. Ten of the top twelve multinationals in the mid-1970s were U.S.-based, including General Motors, Exxon, and Ford Motor. Lockheed Aircraft and Exxon, among others, spent millions to bribe overseas politicians—a practice Congress tried to halt through the 1977 Foreign Corrupt Practices Act. The multinationals' economic decisions—where to locate a plant, for example—held real importance for developing nations that welcomed multinational investments but resented outside control. The South also protested that the multinationals employed too few "locals" in high positions and exploited natural resources without adequate compensation. Defenders replied that multinational enterprises brought benefits to developing nations in higher wages, tax revenues, and technology transfers. Benign or not, multinational corporations by the early 1970s had become major actors in the international system.

No Mere Footnote: Vietnamization, Cambodia, and a Wider War

"What we are doing now with China is so great, so historic, the word 'Vietnam' will be only a footnote when it is written in history," Kissinger boasted in 1971.[106] Yet America's longest war claimed rapt attention until 1975. Nixon constantly worried that the persistent war could undermine support at home and spoil détente. "I'm not going to end up like LBJ," he assured his advisers. "I'm going to stop that war. Fast."[107] But under what terms would the United States withdraw?

At the outset, Nixon weighed his options. He could simply pull out of Vietnam, "lock, stock and barrel."[108] But Nixon would not sacrifice an ally, and he vowed "to avoid [the] defeat of America."[109] He hoped to capitalize on détente, persuading China and the Soviet Union to force Hanoi to compromise. Through military escalation, he signaled Ho Chi Minh that he intended to punish the enemy harshly where Johnson had not. Nixon's "madman" strategy sought concessions from Hanoi through hints of atomic blackmail. The president also proclaimed a policy of Vietnamization. He would strengthen South Vietnam through huge infusions of foreign aid and the training of a larger South Vietnamese army (ARVN), while he gradually withdrew U.S. troops from Vietnam. To counteract growing public disapproval of the war, Nixon gave flag-waving speeches and promised to end the draft.

The multifaceted scheme did not work. Hanoi's leaders did not bow to foreign wishes, whether from Washington, Moscow, or Beijing. Having outlasted the French, Ho's legions had no intention of surrendering to the Americans. As for dissent at home, every new escalation swelled the ranks of the critics, finally prompting Congress to limit the president's ability to enlarge the war. Although U.S. ships, planes, helicopters, rifles, and millions of dollars poured in, South Vietnam became dependent on U.S. aid to keep its army in the field, undermining the ultimate objective of standing on its own feet. Aid sustained the corrupt regime of General Nguyen Van Thieu, a government of self-serving officials, unpopular and ultimately incapable of conducting a winning effort. As the ranks of ARVN swelled to more than 1 million soldiers, some Vietnamese groups complained that "Vietnamization is only the change in the color of the dead."[110] The heavy draft calls in South Vietnam failed to improve ARVN's military fortunes and only served to alienate the peasantry, who lost their sons to the army. Finally, Vietnamization diminished *American* military effectiveness. "We're no longer here to win," said one U.S. military officer. "We're merely 'campaigning' to keep the [American] casualties down."[111]

Peace talks had started in summer 1968, but bogged down in frustrating arguments about seating arrangements. In early 1969, the negotiations remained stalled over Nixon's demand for North Vietnam to pull its forces out of the South and his refusal to abandon the Thieu government. With northern infiltration continuing, Nixon decided to bomb communist sanctuaries in Cambodia—but secretly, so that neither Congress nor the American people knew about it. The bombing of Cambodia began in March 1969 with punishing B-52 sorties. But leaks soon brought the story out. Nixon ordered the FBI to wiretap several journalists and government officials in a futile attempt to catch the leakers.

Kissinger, in August 1969, began a series of secret meetings with North Vietnamese representatives that lasted into 1973. Both sides publicly accused the other of negotiating in bad faith. Meanwhile, U.S. soldiers were coming home, so that by the end of 1971 the troop level had dropped to 139,000 from its peak of 543,400 in 1969. Protest against the war continued nonetheless. On October 15, 1969, a quarter-million people peacefully marched in Washington, calling for a moratorium on the war. The president asked the "great silent majority of my fellow Americans" to back him, and he urged Vice President Spiro Agnew to attack the news media.[112]

Events in Cambodia actually prompted Nixon to expand the war. In March 1970, a pro-American general, Lon Nol, prodded by U.S. operatives, overthrew the neutralist government. Nixon saw new opportunities: Aid Lon Nol against the Khmer Rouge (Cambodian communists) and the North Vietnamese, who used Cambodian territory to attack South Vietnam; step up the attack on the North Vietnamese in Cambodia, already targets of American bombing raids; send unmistakable signals to Hanoi that it had better relent; and show his critics "who's tough."[113] He ordered U.S. troops to invade Cambodia in late April.

A cascade of protest rolled across America. Antiwar demonstrations rocked college campuses. Inexperienced national guard troops killed four students at Kent State University in Ohio. Two students at all-black Jackson State College in Mississippi died when state police fired on a women's dormitory. Within the administration, three Kissinger aides resigned in protest against the Cambodian invasion. After the Senate terminated the Tonkin Gulf Resolution of 1964 (page 352) and Congress nearly cut off funds for military operations in Cambodia, Nixon chose Barry Goldwater and Bob Dole to defend him in the Senate, praising them as "gut fighters" who would willingly "use the stab in the back line."[114]

Nixon declared the Cambodian operation a success in terms of arms captured and enemy troops killed. Although the invasion probably bought time for Vietnamization, the venture also widened the war, caused the sanctuaries to spread out, and further ravaged Cambodia. Hanoi substantially increased its aid to the Khmer Rouge insurgents, who gained new recruits radicalized by the U.S. invasion. Lon Nol became another besieged Asian leader dependent on U.S. assistance. Both negotiations and the war dragged on. Nixon ordered "protective reaction strikes" against North Vietnam after U.S. reconnaissance planes were shot down. In early 1971, he approved a South Vietnamese invasion of Laos, where in six weeks of heavy fighting ARVN forces "got their tail beat off," thus turning Vietnamization's "first test" into its "biggest failure."[115]

At home the wider war wrought more turmoil. After a court-martial in March 1971 found First Lieutenant William Calley guilty of murdering unresisting children, women, and old men at My Lai in 1968 (see page 356), Nixon ordered him released from jail while he appealed his sentence. (A military court sentenced Calley to ten years house arrest, but he won release in 1974 after challenging his sentence in the federal courts.) Army officials dismissed murder and cover-up charges against all other personnel connected with the massacre. In June 1971, the *New York Times* printed the *Pentagon Papers,* a long, secret Defense Department history of U.S. intervention in Vietnam. Leaked by a former Pentagon official, Daniel Ellsberg, the papers fortified critics in their argument that U.S. presidents consistently had tried to win a military victory and frequently had withheld facts from the American public. After the Supreme Court refused to halt publication of the *Pentagon Papers,* Nixon, egged on by Kissinger who told him if he failed to act "it shows you're a weakling," set up a "plumbers" group to stop leaks and to find ways to discredit Ellsberg.[116] Watergate soon followed.

The year 1972 saw the presidential trip to China and SALT-I—and even greater escalation in Vietnam. In Paris, Kissinger continued to meet with the North Vietnamese, always rejecting the communist demand that the United States abandon Thieu. Hanoi launched a full-scale offensive in March that threw the Saigon government into disarray. Nixon ordered American B-52 bombers to pummel fuel depots around Hanoi and Haiphong, where four Soviet merchant ships were sunk. In May the president announced the mining of Haiphong harbor and more massive bombing raids code-named LINEBACKER-I. "We've got to use the maximum power of this country against a shit-asshole country [North Vietnam] to win the war," he growled.[117] North Vietnamese aid to the South slowed but did not stop.

The Peace Agreement, Withdrawal, and Defeat

In early October 1972, Kissinger and the North Vietnamese negotiator Le Duc Tho finally reached an agreement that provided for U.S. withdrawal sixty days after a cease-fire, the return of U.S. prisoners of war, and a political arrangement in the South that ultimately included elections. North Vietnam had given up its demand that Thieu resign, and Washington dropped its insistence that North Vietnamese troops pull out of the South. When Kissinger traveled to Saigon, however, Thieu balked. Resentful at not having been consulted, the South Vietnamese president said "if we accept the document as it stands, we will be committing suicide."[118] Hanoi, suspecting trickery, published the agreement that it had crafted with Kissinger. Still, on October 31, Kissinger told the press "peace is at hand."[119] Not quite.

Back in Paris, on November 20, Kissinger and Le Duc Tho resumed their meetings. In early December they reached terms very much like those Thieu and Nixon had torpedoed in October. But a final agreement faltered over the status of the Demilitarized Zone (DMZ). Washington broke off the talks. The carrot for Saigon (more arms), the stick for Hanoi. From December 18 to 28, LINEBACKER-II planes pounded North Vietnam hour upon hour in what Nixon told the Joint Chiefs it was "your last chance to use military power to win this war."[120] Everything from factories to water supplies took hits in the "Christmas bombing." Fifty-foot bomb craters gaped in Hanoi and Haiphong. At least 2,000 civilians perished. The bombings "made the world recoil in revulsion."[121] On December 22, Washington offered to stop the assaults if Hanoi agreed to reopen negotiations. Le Duc Tho resumed talks with Kissinger, and on January 27, 1973, the two men signed a peace accord, with Kissinger joking that "my successor … will have to meet with [Tho] and try to understand what we agree to here. … I pity my successor."[122] The United States promised to withdraw its remaining troops within sixty days; both sides would exchange prisoners; an international commission would oversee the cease-fire;

VICTORY'S JUST around THE corner.

Vietnam Refrain. Presidents Eisenhower through Ford kept predicting victory in Vietnam but kept losing the war. As the historian T. Christopher Jespersen has argued, even Gerald Ford "refused to acknowledge" the rapid disintegration of South Vietnam in April 1975 and "attempted to saddle Congress with the ultimate burden of having lost Southeast Asia." (MIKE PETERS EDTCTN (NEW) © King Features Syndicate)

and a coalition would conduct elections in the South. New language settled the DMZ issue. When Thieu again demurred, Nixon gave his secret promise that "we will respond with full force" if Hanoi violated the agreement.[123] He also made a secret threat that if Saigon rejected the accords, "it will be the end of everything—in other words the abandonment of South Vietnam."[124] In the four years of the Nixon-Kissinger war, 20,553 Americans and half a million Vietnamese had died when "we could have gotten essentially the same deal anytime after the 1968 bombing halt," as one diplomat judged.[125] Indeed, a Kissinger aide concluded: "We bombed the North Vietnamese into accepting our concessions."[126]

The cease-fire broke down quickly as each side moved to strengthen itself militarily. The United States maintained military and CIA "advisers" in Vietnam and transferred equipment and bases to the Saigon regime. One peace provision called for U.S. funded reconstruction in North Vietnam. But that promise died when the cease-fire collapsed. Warships still cruised off the coast, and the bombing of Cambodia continued. Congress acted again, this time against a president weakened by Watergate, voting in June 1973 to require the president to cease military actions in all parts of Indochina. Nixon vetoed the measure but accepted a compromise deadline of August 15. In November came the War Powers Resolution. In 1974 Congress rejected $1.5 billion in military aid for Thieu's collapsing government, voting $700 million instead.

Pressed by North Vietnamese advances, Thieu and his coterie seemed paralyzed by early 1975. Then the communists launched an offensive whose swift success even surprised them. Many ARVN troops deserted, were captured, or were killed. Refugees clogged highways; the turmoil in the countryside and cities left some civilians near starvation.

On April 30, 1975, the victorious North Vietnamese streamed into Saigon. For days, frantic Vietnamese had surged toward the Tan Son Nhut air base near Saigon, where U.S. planes loaded evacuees. Thousands of scrambling, crying Vietnamese engulfed the U.S. Embassy, whose roof served as a landing pad for helicopters from offshore ships. Thieu, the generals, and other high-ranking officials had managed to escape earlier, but many Vietnamese compromised by their years of cooperation with the United States were later sent to communist "reeducation camps." Approximately 1 million Vietnamese escaped as "boat people" and sailed away in unseaworthy craft with inadequate water and food. Human tragedy also struck Cambodia and Laos, where, in 1975, the communist insurgents also triumphed. In Cambodia the Khmer Rouge imposed a genocidal regime that killed millions.

The Americans exited from their longest war without victory. Some 58,219 Americans died in battle. At least 3 million Vietnamese died. Hundreds of thousands of people were maimed, and millions became refugees. Civilian deaths in Cambodia and Laos also numbered in the millions. The United States spent at least $170 billion in Southeast Asia and left environmental and biological devastation in its wake. Hanoi has claimed that 3 million Vietnamese became contaminated by the chemical Agent Orange, including 50,000 deformed children. Three hundred thousand American soldiers have sought testing for possible exposure and an estimated 2,000 of their children suffer from Spina Bifada. A 1984 class action suit in conjunction with the Agent Orange Act (1991), the Veterans' Benefits Improvement Act (1994), and the Agent Orange Benefits Act (1996) have provided compensation to the American victims, but Washington has not aided any afflicted Vietnamese.

The prolonged Vietnam War also alienated U.S. allies, undercut détente, and spoiled relations with the Third World. At home, the war fueled inflation and political instability. Nixon's Watergate abuses stemmed in large part from the strains the war placed on the White House and from frustrations over leaks. Believing that their highest officials had too often lied, Americans' trust in their government plummeted. Blaming others rather than their own flawed policies for the failure in Vietnam, Nixon and Kissinger added to the bitterness that infused debates over American foreign policy in the years ahead.

The Many Lessons and Questions of Vietnam

Americans only reluctantly searched for lessons after the Vietnam debacle, apparently more relieved that the war had ended than inquisitive about consequences. Hawkish leaders feared that defeat had weakened U.S. credibility, lamenting a "Vietnam syndrome" that allegedly prevented America from sustaining its role as world leader. "Do we get to win this time?" asked the fictional John Rambo as he returned to Vietnam in the popular film *Rambo: First Blood II* (1985).[127] Hawks claimed that they could have gained victory if only the American people had not suffered a failure of will during the Tet offensive: Just let the military do its job next time, unencumbered by fickle public opinion, inquisitive journalists, and congressional watchdogs. "We didn't know our ally [South Vietnam]," General Maxwell Taylor later admitted, but "we knew even less about the enemy. And, the last, most inexcusable of our mistakes, was not knowing our own people."[128]

Some political scientists, such as Graham Allison in *Essence of Decision* (1971), emphasized a bureaucratic politics model to interpret events. They suggested that it is difficult to hold individuals accountable for decisions and "outcomes," because of the way the impersonal, oversized bureaucracy resists change, follows standard operating procedures, and becomes rutted in traditional channels.[129] This bureaucracy had to be reformed to encourage more intragovernment debate, eschew fixed doctrines and knee-jerk anticommunism, and give more attention to the historical record to avoid making the same mistakes again and again. Critics of this analysis, however, blamed Vietnam on strong presidents such as Johnson, who actually controlled the bureaucracy through appointments, an overpowering personality, and a pervasive ideology. This viewpoint implied that a future change in presidents would bring about diplomatic reformation. A more assertive Congress, some argued, could rein in the "imperial presidency."[130]

Was Vietnam, as some suggested, a prime example of American global expansionism and arrogance that continually required intervention abroad? Two post-Vietnam incidents in 1975 seemed to suggest as much. With polls in Europe indicating major declines in U.S. standing after the fall of Saigon, Cambodian patrol boats seized the U.S. merchant ship *Mayaguez* in May. "Let's look ferocious," snarled Kissinger, intending to refute charges that Washington had become a helpless giant after Vietnam.[131] U.S. marines assaulted Koh Tang Island off the Cambodian coast, and U.S. warships and planes attacked Cambodian targets, nearly killing the *Mayaguez* crew (the lives of the sailors being "a secondary consideration," in Kissinger's view).[132] Cambodians released the *Mayaguez* and its crew of thirty-nine, but forty-one Americans died and fifty were wounded. Similarly, when the inhabitants of Portuguese East Timor tried to assert their independence in December 1975, Ford and Kissinger flashed a green light for the Indonesian military regime to annex the island, saying that "it is important that whatever you do succeeds quickly."[133] A bloody invasion and civil war followed, leaving some 200,000 Timorese dead.

The Vietnam War, said other critics, revealed the shortcomings of the containment doctrine, which had failed to make distinctions between peripheral and vital areas and which applied military force to political problems. Ronald Steel, an eloquent critic of *Pax Americana,* concluded: "Never confuse knights and bishops with pawns."[134] The historian Henry Steele Commager concluded that "some wars are so deeply immoral … that those who resist it are the truest patriots."[135] To some, then, defeat became a victory for humane values. In contrast to those who blamed the antiwar activists for encouraging the enemy and weakening congressional resolve, historians of the peace movement have offered a more modest judgment. Antiwar opponents "produced an awareness of an alternative America that stripped away through dissent and resistance the rational, moral, and political legitimacy of Washington's war in Indochina."[136] Thus: "The dissidents did not stop the war. But they made it stoppable."[137]

By the late 1970s, public discussion of the Vietnam experience and its consequences increased. Films such as *Coming Home* (1978), *The Deer Hunter* (1978), and *Apocalypse Now* (1979) heightened public attention. Depicting the soldiers' Vietnam were memoirs such as C. D. B. Bryan's *Friendly Fire* (1976), Ron Kovic's *Born on the Fourth of July* (1976), Philip Caputo's *A Rumor of War* (1977), and Michael Herr's

Dispatches (1977); oral histories such as Al Santoli's *Everything We Had* (1981) and Mark Baker's *Nam* (1981); and novels such as James Webb's *Fields of Fire* (1978).

The dedication of the Vietnam Veterans Memorial in Washington in November 1982 gave the 2.8 million survivors of service in the war "a wailing wall."[138] Yet some critics felt the dark, recessed design evoked shame for U.S. intervention in Vietnam and better served as a "tribute to [antiwar actress] Jane Fonda."[139] Early stereotypes of Vietnam veterans as emotional cripples unable to adjust to civilian life were soon replaced by gritty, can-do, take-charge supermen, as portrayed by Sylvester Stallone and Chuck Norris in the "back-to-Vietnam" films of the Reagan era. Recent studies disagree about the pervasiveness of post-traumatic stress disorder among Vietnam veterans, with some studies concluding that 2 percent of those who served contracted the condition; others place the figure at 19 percent.[140]

Most historical accounts of the war have emphasized the *American* experience in Vietnam, even as millions of Vietnamese, Cambodians, and Laotians suffered and died in the fighting, and hundreds of thousands more came to the United States and gained citizenship over the next two decades. Instead of a real country on the far side of the Pacific with its own history and culture, Vietnam had become, as one writer put it, "another word for mistakes or dishonesty or whatever."[141] The only "Vietnamese words we learned were the cusswords," recalled one veteran.[142]

This historical amnesia pushed many uncomfortable aspects of U.S. behavior into the shadows. After the United States found itself confronted with evidence of military abuses in the Iraq War (see page 496), Vietnam veterans came forward with evidence of such practices in Vietnam. A formerly classified Pentagon archive revealed seven massacres of at least 137 civilians from 1967 to 1971, 78 other attacks in which 57 noncombatants were killed, 56 wounded, and 15 sexually assaulted, and 141 instances in which U.S. soldiers tortured civilian detainees and prisoners of war with fists, sticks, bats, water, or electric shock. Of the 203 soldiers accused of harming Vietnamese civilians, only 22 suffered convictions at their court-martial hearings.

Debate on the war came to center on whether the United States could have won. Many conservatives articulated a "stab-in-the-back" theory, namely, that the United States could have won had protestors not sapped America's will to fight and had civilian officials not restrained the military.[143] President Ronald Reagan declared that American troops "were denied permission to win," and one historian charged that the United States had "forsaken" its victory in Vietnam.[144] Doubters have raised questions about such thinking. Because the bombing of North Vietnam did not significantly impede the flow of matériel and soldiers to the South, perhaps only a U.S. invasion of the North would have sufficed to defeat the enemy. This strategy would have entailed heavy American casualties and a long occupation of a hostile population that had fought against foreign domination for decades. Would Americans volunteer for a cause with such an uncertain end? Would they tolerate huge draft calls? An invasion of the North, moreover, would have risked war with both the Soviet Union and China. In fact, China sent substantial forces to North Vietnam between 1965 and 1969, credibly threatening intervention if the United States moved north with "dire consequences for the world."[145] To say that Washington lacked the "will" to win misses the real limits on U.S. power. "What

Vietnam Memorials. These statues, part of the memorial site in Washington, D.C., honor the men and women who served in the Vietnam War. On the left is the Three Soldiers Statue by Frederick Hart, and on the right is the Vietnam Women's Memorial by Glenna Goodacre. Both stand near the long black granite Memorial Wall designed by Maya Ying Lin, on which the names of Americans who died in Vietnam are etched. (National Park Service)

distinguishes me from [Lyndon] Johnson," Nixon once said, "is that I have the *will* in spades."[146] Yet Nixon wisely rejected tactical nuclear weapons or an invasion of the North because he recoiled from the domestic and international consequences.

To have won, suggested some, the United States would also have had to destroy what it was trying to save. What would remain after "victory"? Perhaps at best an internally divided, economically feeble nation needing huge infusions of U.S. aid but still vulnerable to collapse. Even with the military unleashed, it would still have faced intractable problems: an inhospitable terrain and climate; an elusive adversary deeply committed to its cause, battle-tested and able to live off the land (*its* land); and a South Vietnamese people who often sheltered communist soldiers. As for allies sharing the burden, most European partners urged Washington to stop wasting its resources on a fruitless venture. Of America's forty allies by treaty, only four— Australia, New Zealand, South Korea, and Thailand—sent combat troops.

The United States could not have won, others have argued, because of conditions in South Vietnam. As the South Vietnamese populace and government grew more war weary, Washington continually encouraged coups to ensure that Saigon would cooperate with its plans. The South Vietnamese desertion rate ran high.

Cyrus R. Vance (1917–2002).
"Cy" Vance brought extensive diplomatic experience to his post as secretary of state. Vance won plaudits for negotiating the Panama Canal treaties and SALT-II. His resignation in 1980 was the first such act made in protest by a secretary of state since that of William Jennings Bryan in 1915. (National Archives)

ARVN forces suffered the same problems that afflicted their government: poor morale, corruption, and nepotism. The "war of attrition" alienated many South Vietnamese, as did the unsettling strategic hamlet program, disruptive "search and destroy" missions, leveling of villages, bombings of innocents, and spraying of Agent Orange. Cultural differences also separated Americans from Vietnamese. Bars and prostitution flourished in a rural Buddhist society made rapidly urban by fleeing refugees. High-tech computers hummed and giant war machines rumbled in a land of water buffalo, rice paddies, and traditional peasant folk.

Problems in the U.S. military itself reduced the chances for victory. To reassure superiors that they were turning back the enemy, some officers submitted false reports on the numbers killed. "If he's dead and Vietnamese, he's VC [Vietcong]" became the prevailing assumption in the field.[147] The military also suffered from corruption and mismanagement—even a black market for equipment developed. By early 1971, some 40,000 GIs had become heroin addicts. "Fragging"—the murder of officers by enlisted soldiers by means of a hand grenade or other weapon—further reduced combat effectiveness. Educational deferments under the draft system meant that high school dropouts outnumbered college graduates in combat. The rotation system for officers—one year in Vietnam to "punch your ticket"—undermined military cohesion and the benefits of experience. Disgusted with the "groupthink pressure" and "pretense," General Colin Powell later wrote that many of "my generation ... vowed that when our turn came to call the shots, we would not quietly acquiesce in half-hearted warfare for half-baked reasons that the American people could not understand or support."[148]

The United States also faced tenacious adversaries who suffered staggering losses but kept coming. Defending their nation against outsiders, the Vietnamese enemy seemed indomitable. "Everything we knew commanded us to fight," a Vietcong veteran remembered. "Our ancestors called us to war. Our myths and legends called us to war."[149] Whatever the answer to the Vietnam tragedy, succeeding administrations would have to operate in a domestic political setting of uncertainty about the direction of American foreign relations. Conservative defenders of the war stood ready to criticize any policy that smacked of retrenchment or "another Munich." Liberals and radicals stood alert to dispute any policy that seemed to offer "another Vietnam." The 1976 presidential campaign passed with barely a word uttered about Vietnam. But its winner, Jimmy Carter, faced the challenge of reconstructing U.S. foreign policy in the wake of a lost war.

Mixed Signals: Carter's Contradictory Course

For the new president, the Nixon-Kissinger approach to international affairs contained too much bluster, too much military posturing, and too much insensitivity toward Third World peoples. Carter promised to reduce military budgets, bring some of America's overseas forces home, trim arms sales abroad, and slow nuclear proliferation. He berated the Republicans for supporting dictatorial regimes. Yet at times Carter sounded like an inveterate Cold Warrior, remarking that "when violence occurred in almost any place on earth, the Soviets or their proxies were most likely at the center of it."[150] After the downbeat years of Watergate, Vietnam, CIA abuses, and soaring oil prices, the election of the wealthy, Baptist peanut farmer with a toothy smile inspired hope. After graduating from the Naval Academy and serving on a nuclear submarine, Carter entered Georgia politics and became governor in 1970. Following a four-year term, this obscure Democrat set out to win the presidency. Carter cherished hard work, family responsibility, and religion. Energetic and self-confident, he seemed to some people sanctimonious and arrogant. A quick learner, he paid meticulous attention to details. Unwilling to prioritize, he tried to be "desk officer for everything."[151] Carter had little experience in foreign affairs beyond membership in the Trilateral Commission, which brought together business, political, and academic notables for discussions of global problems bedeviling industrial nations. Carter had followed the fractious debate over Vietnam and knew that a new national foreign-policy consensus had not yet taken form.

Carter selected Cyrus Vance as his secretary of state. A wealthy, West Virginia–born, Yale-educated lawyer, Vance held top posts in the Department of Defense in the 1960s, learning from Vietnam that Washington could not "prop up a series of regimes that lacked popular support."[152] He favored quiet diplomacy to improve Soviet-American relations. When Vance resigned in April 1980, he did so not only to protest a misguided hostage rescue mission in Iran but also to reprove Carter for embracing the "visceral anti-Sovietism" of Zbigniew Brzezinski, the national security affairs adviser.[153]

Jimmy Carter (b. 1924) and Zbigniew Brzezinski (b. 1928). A Warsaw-born son of a Polish diplomat, Brzezinski emigrated to the United States in 1953. A long-time professor of political science at Columbia University, he gained renown for his Cold War views before serving as Carter's adviser. Asked in 1998 if he regretted that U.S. aid to anti-Soviet Muslims in Afghanistan during the 1980s had helped install a hostile Taliban regime that sponsored terrorism against the West, Brzezinski replied: "What is more important in world history? The Taliban or the collapse of the Soviet empire? Some agitated [Muslims] or the liberation of Central Europe and the end of the Cold War?" (Courtesy Jimmy Carter Presidential Library)

Andrew Young (b. 1932).
A graduate of Howard University and the Hartford Theological Seminary, the Reverend Young had been Dr. Martin Luther King's right-hand man in the civil rights movement of the 1950s–1960s and a member of Congress from Georgia before Carter named him ambassador to the United Nations. Young was forced to resign in 1979 when he admitted meeting with representatives of the Palestine Liberation Organization, whose participation in negotiations he deemed essential to Middle East peace. (United Nations. Photograph by Y. Nagata)

Arrogant and aggressive, Brzezinski blamed most of the world's troubles on the Soviets. He sought military superiority and worked to play China off against the Soviet Union. To counter Vance's argument that a military coup in Iran would produce bloodshed, Brzezinski coldly pronounced that "world politics was not a kindergarten."[154] State Department officers often bristled over Brzezinski's strong-arm bureaucratic methods and his back-channel contacts with foreign leaders. "While Mr. Vance played by the Marquis of Queensberry rules," remarked one official, "Mr. Brzezinski was more of a street fighter." The president believed that Vance and Brzezinski would balance one another: "Zbig would be the thinker, Cy would be the doer, and Jimmy Carter would be the decider."[155] But acrimonious infighting rendered the administration's foreign policy inconsistent, marked by zigs and zags.

At the start Carter officials rejected the extreme options of Fortress America (isolationism) and Atlas America (global policeman) in favor of Participant America. That meant emphasizing preventive diplomacy: advancing the peace process in the Middle East; reducing nuclear arms; normalizing relations with China: stimulating improvements in human rights; and creating economic stability through talks on the law of the sea, energy, and clean air and water. The president wanted to avoid a reactive foreign policy enmeshed in day-to-day crises. Carter especially sought to restore U.S. influence in the Third World. He preferred to emphasize North-South rather than East-West issues and to make concessions to nationalists. Third World crises, he argued, sprang from deep-seated, indigenous economic, social, racial, and political problems. The appointment of Andrew Young as ambassador to the United Nations symbolized Carter's sympathetic approach. An African American veteran of the civil rights movement, Young gradually improved the U.S. dialogue with suspicious Third World diplomats. But in 1979, Carter had to fire him after Young made unauthorized contact with representatives of the Palestine Liberation Organization, a group that the United States refused to recognize.

The soul of American foreign policy, Carter insisted, should be the defense and expansion of human rights for foreign peoples. As one scholar noted, "Virtually all of the essential human rights legislation was already in place when he took office," but neither Nixon nor Ford had made much use of it.[156] Drawing on his own religious commitment, Carter vowed to win for all peoples the freedom to work, vote, worship, travel, speak, assemble, and receive a fair trial. Slavery, genocide, torture, forced labor, arbitrary arrest, rigged elections, and suspensions of civil liberties all became anathema. Dictators must respect human rights or face cutbacks in American foreign aid.

While telling Americans to put their "inordinate fear of communism" behind them, he actually reinvigorated the containment doctrine by initiating new weapons systems, by encouraging anti-Soviet nationalism in Eastern Europe, and by cultivating the friendship of Third World governments.[157] Carter believed improved Sino-American ties, continued strategic arms limitations talks, and public denunciations of Soviet violations of human rights also might check Moscow. By 1979 Carter, having moved closer to Brzezinski's views, sounded the familiar Cold War calls for "a more muscular foreign policy."[158] The following year he proclaimed the Carter

Doctrine, or containment in the Persian Gulf. Confrontation more than cooperation came to characterize Soviet-American relations under Carter.

Engaging the Third World: Latin America and Africa

Carter launched an active diplomacy toward Latin America and Africa. In Latin America, Carter championed human rights and worked to accommodate nationalism. Latin American governments petitioned Washington for lower tariffs, higher commodity prices, and less interference in disputes between their governments and American corporations. The Carter administration saw high stakes: $59 billion in trade (1979); investments of $24.4 billion (1979); vital imports of petroleum, copper, and tin; and Latin America's thirty votes in the United Nations. Foreign aid ($726 million in 1977–1978) continued as one means of exerting influence.

Panama became the first testing ground. Panamanians had long resented the 1903 treaty granting the United States the Canal Zone, a ten-mile-wide, 500-square-mile slice of territory that cut their nation in half— "a foreign flag piercing its own heart."[159] After bloody anti-American riots in 1964, President Lyndon B. Johnson had started talks, but they barely crawled forward. Carter brought the negotiations to fruition. Two treaties were signed in 1977 and ratified the following year. One treaty, abrogating the 1903 document, provided for the integration of the Canal Zone into Panama and increased Panama's percentage of the canal's revenues. The other treaty granted the United States the right to defend the "neutrality" of the canal forever. In a national vote, Panamanians approved the treaties by a 2 to 1 margin, but nationalistic sentiment against a continued U.S. role in Panamanian affairs ran high.

Conservative critics in the United States soon denounced the treaties as diabolical appeasement. Many Americans thought that the United States owned the canal. Former California Governor Ronald Reagan mangled the historical record: "We bought it, we paid for it, it's ours, and we're going to keep it."[160] Giving up a key waterway would supposedly weaken U.S. defense and leave Panama vulnerable to Soviet or Cuban subversion. Treaty advocates stressed the goodwill that Washington would gain. Nonratification could "poison" trade with Latin America and invite terrorist attacks on the canal.[161] The canal's value had diminished because modern aircraft carriers and supertankers could not squeeze through its locks. Moreover, less than 10 percent of U.S. foreign trade went through it.

As the debate peaked in early 1978, the administration used arguments that alarmed Panamanians. A "memorandum of understanding," signed by Panamanian General Omar Torrijos and Carter provided for U.S. intervention after the year 2000 to thwart "any aggression or threat directed against the Canal or against the peaceful transit of vessels through the Canal."[162] When asked what the United States would do if the Panamanians closed the canal for repairs, Brzezinski retorted: "Close down the Panamanian government for repairs."[163] On March 16, 1978, the Senate approved the neutrality treaty 68 to 32; the other treaty passed on April 18 by a similar count—in both cases with only one vote more than the

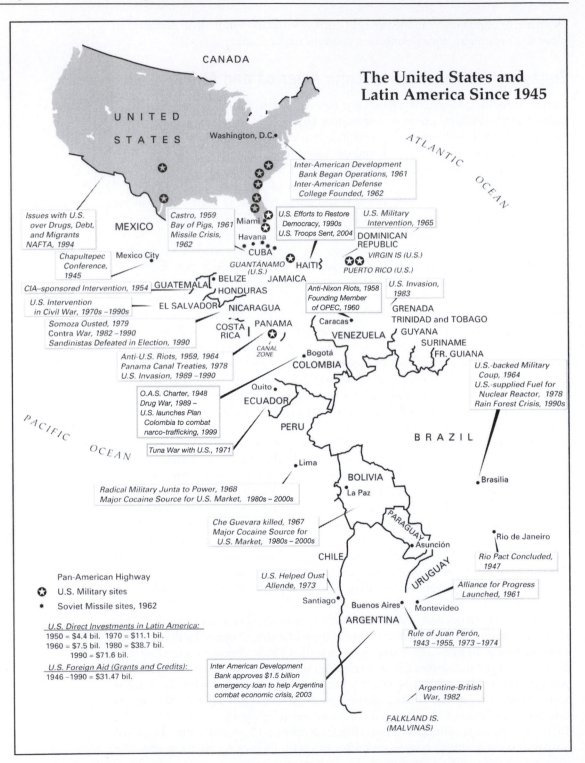

The United States and Latin America Since 1945

CANADA

UNITED STATES

Washington, D.C.

Inter-American Development Bank Began Operations, 1961 Inter-American Defense College Founded, 1962

Issues with U.S. over Drugs, Debt, and Migrants NAFTA, 1994

MEXICO

Castro, 1959 Bay of Pigs, 1961 Missile Crisis, 1962

Miami

Havana

U.S. Efforts to Restore Democracy, 1990s U.S. Troops Sent, 2004

U.S. Military Intervention, 1965

DOMINICAN REPUBLIC

VIRGIN IS (U.S.)

PUERTO RICO (U.S.)

Chapultepec Conference, 1945

Mexico City

CUBA

GUANTÁNAMO (U.S.)

HAITI

CIA–sponsored Intervention, 1954

GUATEMALA

BELIZE

HONDURAS

JAMAICA

U.S. Intervention in Civil War, 1970s –1990s

EL SALVADOR

NICARAGUA

Anti-Nixon Riots, 1958 Founding Member of OPEC, 1960

U.S. Invasion, 1983

GRENADA

Somoza Ousted, 1979 Contra War, 1982 –1990 Sandinistas Defeated in Election, 1990

COSTA RICA

PANAMA

Caracas

VENEZUELA

TRINIDAD and TOBAGO

GUYANA

SURINAME

FR. GUIANA

CANAL ZONE

Bogotá

COLOMBIA

U.S.-backed Military Coup, 1964 U.S.-supplied Fuel for Nuclear Reactor, 1978 Rain Forest Crisis, 1990s

Anti-U.S. Riots, 1959, 1964 Panama Canal Treaties, 1978 U.S. Invasion, 1989 –1990

O.A.S. Charter, 1948 Drug War, 1989 – U.S. launches Plan Colombia to combat narco-trafficking, 1999

Quito

ECUADOR

PERU

BRAZIL

Tuna War with U.S., 1971

Lima

Radical Military Junta to Power, 1968 Major Cocaine Source for U.S. Market, 1980s – 2000s

BOLIVIA

La Paz

Brasilia

Che Guevara killed, 1967 Major Cocaine Source for U.S. Market, 1980s – 2000s

PARAGUAY

Rio de Janeiro

Asunción

Rio Pact Concluded, 1947

CHILE

URUGUAY

U.S. Helped Oust Allende, 1973

Alliance for Progress Launched, 1961

Santiago

Buenos Aires

Montevideo

ARGENTINA

Rule of Juan Perón, 1943 –1955, 1973 –1974

PACIFIC OCEAN

ATLANTIC OCEAN

Pan-American Highway

⭐ U.S. Military sites

• Soviet Missile sites, 1962

U.S. Direct Investments in Latin America:
1950 = $4.4 bil. 1970 = $11.1 bil.
1960 = $7.5 bil. 1980 = $38.7 bil.
          1990 = $71.6 bil.

U.S. Foreign Aid (Grants and Credits):
1946 –1990 = $31.47 bil.

Inter American Development Bank approves $1.5 billion emergency loan to help Argentina combat economic crisis, 2003

Argentine-British War, 1982

FALKLAND IS. (MALVINAS)

two-thirds tally needed. Carter later acknowledged that "some fine members of Congress had to pay with their political careers for their votes."[164]

The Carter administration also contended with nationalist stirrings in Nicaragua. Since 1936 the Somoza family had ruled that Central American state (see page 164). Dictatorial and corrupt, the Somoza dynasty nevertheless had gained grudging U.S. support as a reliable anticommunist ally and had received military aid, which it often used to suppress critics. Nicaragua had served as a staging area for CIA operations against Guatemala (1954) and Cuba (1961). All the while, Nicaraguans suffered high rates of poverty, malnutrition, and illiteracy, and the Somozas amassed great wealth. A long-smoldering popular rebellion exploded in 1978, led by the leftist Sandinista National Liberation Front (FSLN). Business executives, Catholic clergy, and intellectuals joined the crusade to unseat the Somozas and reduce U.S. influence. General Anastasio Somoza Debayle, a graduate of West Point, answered with torture, executions, and bombings of civilians.

Carter tried to ease Somoza's departure and restrict the Sandinistas. Somoza balked and the effort failed. After the FSLN opened its final offensive in mid-1979, Washington encouraged the national guard—Somoza's hated personal army—to preserve order. When this tactic also misfired, Somoza fled the battle-scarred country in July 1979; he was later assassinated in Paraguay.

The new Nicaraguan government promised a mixed economy and pluralistic politics. But only after Mexico, Venezuela, and others offered loans did Carter ask Congress to appropriate $75 million in economic assistance. Not until July 1980 did Congress allocate funds, with conservatives calling the Sandinistas "communists" because they welcomed Cuban advisers. Tension soon ran high, especially when Carter suspended economic aid in early 1981 after the Sandinistas aided rebels who were challenging the U.S.-backed government of El Salvador.

Cuba continued to claim close U.S. scrutiny. Carter initially sought to reduce tensions with Fidel Castro. In March 1977, U.S. and Cuban negotiators began to discuss normalization of relations. In September, Cuba and the United States established "interests sections" in each other's country (essentially embassies without full diplomatic recognition). Carter also lifted the ban on travel to Cuba. Castro in 1978 made gestures toward improved relations by releasing 3,600 political prisoners. Several irritants diminished these positive steps. The Soviet Union was pouring about $3 million a day into Cuba to sustain the island's fragile economy, weakened by the longstanding U.S. trade embargo and Castro's mismanagement. Washington still viewed Cuba as a Soviet puppet and charged that Cuban troops in Angola and Ethiopia acted as Soviet surrogates. Secret, high-level U.S.-Cuba talks in 1978–1980 failed to normalize relations or relax the trade embargo. In spring 1980, Castro suddenly announced that Cubans wishing to leave the country could use Peruvian visas if they could get them. Thousands jammed into the Peruvian Embassy grounds in Havana. Carter thereupon announced that Cubans who wanted to join their families already in the United States would be welcome. Castro soon declared that Cubans who wanted to emigrate could do so by boat from the port of Mariel. A "freedom flotilla" began to shuttle between Cuba and Florida as 100,000 Cubans entered U.S. processing centers. Castro emptied his jails of "undesirables" and cynically put them on boats to the United States. "Fidel has flushed his toilet on us," the mayor of Miami bitterly charged.[165]

Elsewhere in Latin America, right-wing governments resisted Carter's efforts to improve human rights, although Haiti, Argentina, and the Dominican Republic did release hundreds of political prisoners. In 1977 Carter suspended military aid to Guatemala when its regime sanctioned the murder and torture of political opponents; two years later he froze U.S. aid to Bolivia after that nation's military seized power. Military assistance to Latin America dropped from $210 million in 1977 to only $54 million in 1979, as Carter kept dictators at arm's length. Jacobo Timerman, an Argentine journalist and political prisoner, remarked: "What a human rights policy does is save lives. And Jimmy Carter's policy did. … But the policy is even more important to you than to us. It builds up a democratic consciousness in the United States."[166]

Although sub-Saharan African issues lacked the urgency of Latin American problems, the Carter administration strove to identify the United States with black African nationalism and to end the "last vestiges of colonialism" in Zimbabwe/Rhodesia and Namibia.[167] UN Ambassador Andrew Young became the president's chief adviser, with "African solutions for African problems" as his motto. He believed that support for a strong and stable black Africa, through aid and trade, would reduce Soviet influence on the continent. African nationalism, not U.S. intervention, would contain the USSR and protect U.S. interests.

Much seemed at stake in Africa. The continent had political clout—a third of the membership in the United Nations. Africa possessed a bulging storehouse of raw materials. For example, Zaire ranked as the United States's largest supplier of cobalt; Nigeria became the second largest source of imported oil; Gabon supplied manganese; Namibia had the world's largest uranium mine; and South Africa shipped manganese, platinum, chromium, and antimony. By 1979 Americans had invested some $4 billion in black Africa and about $2 billion in South Africa. Total annual trade with Africa passed the $30 billion figure. Africa's ports and airfields also lay along strategic sea lanes. The region's political instability invited great-power competition.

The Carter administration worked especially hard to cultivate Nigerian friendship. Africa's most populous nation, Nigeria ranked seventh in world oil production and carried weight in African politics. Nigeria became independent in 1960 and in 1967 suffered a civil war in which victory over Biafran separatists cost half a million lives. World opinion, including that of the United States, grew hostile toward the military regime that had perpetrated this tragedy. But in the 1970s, when America suffered its energy crisis and Nigeria expanded its oil production, relations improved.

South Africa's riches, traditional ties to the United States, and white minority government ensured its continuing prominence on the U.S. diplomatic agenda. Carter chided white South African rulers for apartheid—an official system of segregating nonwhites and whites that included removals of blacks to designated homelands, discriminatory wages based on race, and denial of voting rights and civil liberties for blacks. Visiting South Africa, Vice President Walter Mondale

Cengage Learning CPM

U.S. Dependence on Imports of Raw Materials, 1980

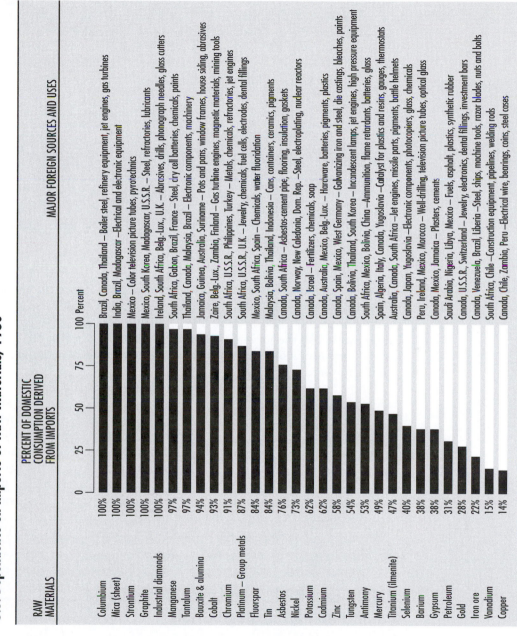

PERCENT OF DOMESTIC CONSUMPTION DERIVED FROM IMPORTS

RAW MATERIALS	Percent	MAJOR FOREIGN SOURCES AND USES
Columbium	100%	Brazil, Canada, Thailand — Boiler steel, refinery equipment, jet engines, gas turbines
Mica (sheet)	100%	India, Brazil, Madagascar — Electrical and electronic equipment
Strontium	100%	Mexico — Color television picture tubes, pyrotechnics
Graphite	100%	Mexico, South Korea, Madagascar, U.S.S.R. — Steel, refractories, lubricants
Industrial diamonds	100%	Ireland, South Africa, Belg.-Lux., U.K. — Abrasives, drills, phonograph needles, glass cutters
Manganese	97%	South Africa, Gabon, Brazil, France — Steel, dry cell batteries, chemicals, paints
Tantalum	97%	Thailand, Canada, Malaysia, Brazil — Electronic components, machinery
Bauxite & alumina	94%	Jamaica, Guinea, Australia, Suriname — Pots and pans, window frames, house siding, abrasives
Cobalt	93%	Zaire, Belg.-Lux., Zambia, Finland — Gas turbine engines, magnetic materials, mining tools
Chromium	91%	South Africa, U.S.S.R., Philippines, Turkey — Metals, chemicals, refractories, jet engines
Platinum — Group metals	87%	South Africa, U.S.S.R., U.K. — Jewelry, chemicals, fuel cells, electrodes, dental fillings
Fluorspar	84%	Mexico, South Africa, Spain — Chemicals, water fluoridation
Tin	84%	Malaysia, Bolivia, Thailand, Indonesia — Cans, containers, ceramics, pigments
Asbestos	76%	Canada, South Africa — Asbestos-cement pipe, flooring, insulation, gaskets
Nickel	73%	Canada, Norway, New Caledonia, Dom. Rep. — Steel, electroplating, nuclear reactors
Potassium	62%	Canada, Israel — Fertilizers, chemicals, soap
Cadmium	62%	Canada, Australia, Mexico, Belg.-Lux. — Hardware, batteries, pigments, plastics
Zinc	58%	Canada, Spain, Mexico, West Germany — Galvanizing iron and steel, die castings, bleaches, paints
Tungsten	54%	Canada, Bolivia, Thailand, South Korea — Incandescent lamps, jet engines, high pressure equipment
Antimony	53%	South Africa, Mexico, Bolivia, China — Ammunition, flame retardants, batteries, glass
Mercury	49%	Spain, Algeria, Italy, Canada, Yugoslavia — Catalyst for plastics and resins, gauges, thermostats
Titanium (Ilmenite)	47%	Australia, Canada, South Africa — Jet engines, missile parts, pigments, battle helmets
Selenium	40%	Canada, Japan, Yugoslavia — Electronic components, photocopiers, glass, chemicals
Barium	38%	Peru, Ireland, Mexico, Morocco — Well-drilling, television picture tubes, optical glass
Gypsum	38%	Canada, Mexico, Jamaica — Plasters, cements
Petroleum	31%	Saudi Arabia, Nigeria, Libya, Mexico — Fuels, asphalt, plastics, synthetic rubber
Gold	28%	Canada, U.S.S.R., Switzerland — Jewelry, electronics, dental fillings, investment bars
Iron ore	22%	Canada, Venezuela, Brazil, Liberia — Steel, ships, machine tools, razor blades, nuts and bolts
Vanadium	15%	South Africa, Chile — Construction equipment, pipelines, welding rods
Copper	14%	Canada, Chile, Zambia, Peru — Electrical wire, bearings, coins, steel cases

angered whites by calling for a one-person, one-vote policy because "perpetuating an unjust system is the surest incentive to increase Soviet influence and even racial war."[168] Critics chanted: "Carter, Carter cut the jive, cut the ties to apartheid," to protest the president's refusal to support economic sanctions.[169] U.S. trade stood at $4 billion in 1979 and America's top corporations operated there, including General Motors, Exxon, Ford, General Electric, and Firestone. Although critics argued for disinvestment, the meager concessions to their prodding came via a voluntary pledge from only 116 of the 300 Americans firms operating in South Africa to follow nondiscriminatory employment practices. Many black African leaders protested the sale of American aircraft to the regime and criticized Carter's approval of Export-Import Bank loans (subsequently stopped by Congress). Citing the flow of strategic minerals from South Africa, and claiming that disinvestment would hurt native blacks by causing unemployment, Carter officials argued that steady pressure, short of economic sanctions, would move South Africa to reform. The white regime's changes, however, amounted to little more than the "desegregation of the deck chairs on the *Titanic*."[170]

In Zimbabwe/Rhodesia, the civil war between whites and insurgent blacks finally ended. Ian Smith's white government, formed in 1965, had made token gestures to black majority rule, but Carter insisted on real change. The president persuaded Congress in 1977 to repeal the Byrd Amendment (1971), which had permitted U.S. trade with Zimbabwe/Rhodesia in chromium, despite the UN-declared economic boycott of Smith's regime. Carter in 1979 refused to endorse white-manipulated elections. Finally, British-led negotiations culminated in an all-race, nationwide election held in April 1980, which produced a new government for Zimbabwe led by the former black rebel Robert Mugabe. By the early twenty-first century, Mugabe's rule, which had begun with such optimism, had lapsed into dictatorship.

By the end of Carter's term, U.S. influence in Africa stood higher than ever, and trade was improving. Still Carter and Brzezinski worried about expanding Soviet and Cuban influence in sub-Saharan Africa. Moscow tried to balance relationships between rival regimes in Somalia and Ethiopia. One State Department official compared the Soviets to "the fellow who is pinned to two girls on the same campus. Let's see if they can pull it off."[171] When war erupted between the two countries in the Ogaden desert region, Moscow abandoned Somalia and backed the Marxist regime in Ethiopia. The Somali leader Siad Barre then expelled the Soviets in 1977 and the United States adopted him as a military client. As Ethiopia repelled the Somali attack, Brzezinski remarked that détente "lies buried beneath the sands of the Ogaden."[172]

Middle East Highs and Lows: Camp David and the Iranian Hostage Crisis

The Iranian revolution and hostage crisis, civil war in Lebanon, Arab-Israeli conflict, Iran-Iraq War, Soviet thrust into Afghanistan (see page 412), and Western reliance on Persian Gulf oil put the Middle East in the headlines. Saudi Arabia served as America's largest supplier of imported oil. In 1980 Israel and Egypt together received about one-third of all U.S. foreign aid. During the period 1971–1981, the United States sold $47.7 billion worth of arms to Mideast countries. U.S. weapons became the instruments of war in the region: Israel used U.S. warplanes to attack Palestinian communities in Lebanon and Iran used American arms to battle Iraq. Syrians and Iraqis brandished Soviet armaments.

Building on Kissinger's efforts, Carter concentrated on bringing Egypt and Israel to the peace table. President Anwar el-Sadat of Egypt, in November 1977, astonished the world by journeying to Jerusalem to offer peace and security in exchange for an Israeli withdrawal from lands occupied since 1967. When the Sadat initiative faltered, Carter interceded, inviting Sadat and Israeli prime minister Menachem Begin to Camp David. From September 5 to 17, 1978, the three leaders and their aides engaged in often heated discussion. Carter pressed Begin to withdraw to Israel's 1967 border so that the restored territories might provide a homeland for Palestinians. Israel could not have both peace and captured territories, Carter reasoned. He favored an agreement based on the 1967 United Nations Resolution 242, by which Arabs would recognize Israel's right to live in peace and security in exchange for Israeli withdrawal from seized territories. Playing "the role of draftsman, strategist, therapist, friend, adversary, and mediator," Carter wooed and cajoled.[173] He promised both sides huge amounts of aid if they would settle their differences.

Egypt and Israel signed two Camp David Accords. The first stated goals: negotiations leading to self-government for the West Bank and Gaza and subsequent participation of Jordanians and Palestinians in the peace process. The second, a "framework" for peace, provided for Israeli withdrawal from the Sinai in exchange for Egyptian diplomatic recognition. Following further protracted negotiations (in which Carter flew to the Middle East to meet separately with Begin and Sadat), the Egyptian-Israeli Peace Treaty was signed on March 26, 1979. It provided for the phased withdrawal of Israel from the Sinai, to be completed in 1982; the stationing of UN forces along the Egyptian-Israeli boundary; full economic and diplomatic relations between Cairo and Tel Aviv; and the opening of negotiations on Palestinian rights in the occupied West Bank and Gaza (see map, page 379). After thirty years of war, peace formally came to part of the Middle East. Other Arabs, especially the PLO, denounced the treaty as a "dead horse" for not recognizing the right of Palestinians to a homeland.[174] By the end of Carter's administration, Israeli and PLO forces, the latter with Syrian help, were shooting at one another in Lebanon (see page 438).

Elsewhere in the Middle East, Iran confronted Carter with the greatest setback of his presidency. On November 4, 1979, hundreds of Iranian students stormed the U.S. embassy in Tehran. "We're paying you back for Vietnam," snarled one attacker.[175] Sixty-six Americans were captured. According to the jubilant students, American hostages would go free only after Shah Mohammad Reza Pahlavi returned to Iran for trial. The admission of the Shah to a New York hospital two weeks earlier had provided the immediate catalyst for seizing the embassy. But Iranian hostility had been smoldering since the 1950s. When Prime Minister Mohammad Mossadegh nationalized the Anglo-Iranian Oil Company, the CIA plotted successfully with

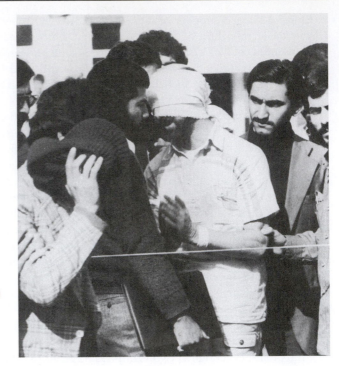

American Hostage in Iran. On November 8, 1979, this blindfolded, hand-tied American captive was paraded on the grounds of the U.S. Embassy in Teheran. A jeering crowd taunted the frightened American early in the Iranian hostage crisis. (AP Images)

royalist Iranians and British officials to oust him. The Shah, newly installed on his throne, soon became a staunch anticommunist U.S. ally.

In the 1970s popular discontent with the Shah swelled just as the Nixon administration elevated his status in the Middle East in the wake of the OPEC oil boycott. Muslim clerics, merchants, young workers, and feudal landholders felt aggrieved by the Shah's modernization of the economy, which brought Western cultural influences, inflation, unemployment, inadequate housing, and preferential jobs for skilled foreigners. SAVAK, the secret police organized with CIA help in 1957, committed untold brutalities that helped to unite disparate groups against the monarch and his sponsor, the United States. Massive purchases of American arms also fueled unrest. In the period 1973–1978, the Shah spent $19 billion of the nation's oil wealth to buy helicopters, fighter aircraft, destroyers, and missiles. Despite the mightiest military in the Middle East, many Iranians thought that the Shah squandered the nation's resources as a stooge of the United States. The Shah lapsed into fatalism and lethargy as doctors informed him that he had inoperable cancer.

President Carter, visiting Teheran in late 1977, "dumbfounded" observers and enraged Iranian dissidents when he praised the Shah for making Iran "an island of stability in one of the more troubled areas of the world."[176] In 1978 demonstrations, riots, and strikes shook Iran. "Hang firm and … count on our backing," Carter told the Shah after the latter had declared martial law.[177] U.S. officials ignored advice to open direct communication with the Islamic Ayatollah Ruhollah Khomeini, the evident leader of the revolution, then in exile in Paris. Not until senior "Wise Man" George Ball visited Iran in November did Washington fully understand "that the Shah was on the way to a great fall" and "like Humpty Dumpty, his regime could not be put together again."[178]

The Shah appointed a puppet government and flew to Egypt on January 16, 1979. Making it clear that Islamic clerics intended to govern Iran, the Ayatollah rejected the new regime and soon installed his own. He fueled rampant anti-Americanism in angry speeches. After leaving Teheran, the Shah discovered that few nations wanted to give sanctuary to a repudiated despot. In October Carter confronted pressure to allow the Shah to visit cancer experts in New York. After asking his aides, "What are you going to advise me to do if they overrun our embassy and take our people hostage," the president relented.[179] The Shah arrived in New York on October 22; on November 4 militant students seized the embassy.

As stunned Americans watched "America Held Hostage" each night on television, it became clear that the hostage-takers wanted more than the Shah.[180] First, the hostage-grabbing was Iran's way of preventing the Shah from launching a counter-revolution from the United States in a replay of 1953. Second, it helped Iran break diplomatic relations with the United States, which Khomeini called a "global Shah" never to be trusted.[181] Finally, the hostage drama permitted the eighty-one-year-old Khomeini to use anti-Americanism to overwhelm civilian moderates who competed for control of the revolution.

As the diplomats struggled to communicate with a dysfunctional Iranian government, the hostages suffered through an ordeal lasting 444 days. At first blindfolded with their hands and feet tied, they thought that they would be either released quickly or killed. For a long time they could not speak or read newspapers. The hostages lost weight and became sick. They constantly fought boredom, melancholy, and fear. The worst terror they endured was a mock execution, preceded by abusive interrogation. None were killed.

On April 7, 1980, after a series of failed secret overtures, the United States broke relations with Iran. Khomeini publicly taunted the White House, sneering, "Why should we be afraid? ... Carter does not have the guts to engage in military action."[182] The president kept his anger in check in public, but raged in private that he wanted "to punish them. ... They must know that they can't fool around with us."[183] Instead of air strikes, Carter ordered the Joint Chiefs of Staff to launch a secret rescue mission. "Stunned" that such a momentous decision had been "made in my absence," Vance blasted the plans as unnecessary since the hostages faced no immediate physical danger.[184]

On April 24, eight helicopters lifted off the supercarrier *Nimitz* in the Arabian Sea. Six C-130 Hercules transports took to the skies from Egypt. All headed for a rendezvous in the Iranian desert; from there rescue teams of Green Berets and Rangers planned to infiltrate Teheran and assault the U.S. Embassy to free the hostages. But the helicopters ran into dust storms; two malfunctioned before reaching Iran, and another lost a hydraulic line at the rendezvous point. The president accepted the commander's recommendation to abort the mission. In the hasty exit, a helicopter and a C-130 collided, killing eight crew members. The saddened president told the nation the news. Vance quietly resigned.

What if ...   *the Iranian Hostage Rescue Mission Had Succeeded?*

The Iranian hostage crisis and the failed rescue mission have come to symbolize the weaknesses of the Carter presidency—indecision, lack of toughness, and faulty planning. But what if the highly risky mission, which even its commander Colonel Charles Beckwith gave only a fifty percent chance of working, had succeeded? First, one has to define success. Even had the U.S. commandos reached the embassy, they likely would have had to force themselves in and out. As one member of the team noted: "The only difference between this and the Alamo is that Davy Crockett didn't have to fight his way in." Once the rescuers reached the embassy, the risk to the hostages' lives would have greatly increased. Some hostages could have been killed in the crossfire between U.S. troops and the Iranians, or the latter might have deliberately killed hostages to prevent their rescue. "Thank God for the sandstorm," remarked one hostage, who worried that her life would have been at risk if Delta force had reached Tehran.

Critics argue that even had the mission only produced minimal loss of American lives, the outcome might not have been wholly positive. As Vance pointed out in opposing the mission, nothing prevented the Iranians from seizing U.S. journalists and businesspeople who still remained in the country after the severing of diplomatic relations. Carter would then have faced another hostage crisis with little chance of mounting a successful rescue mission or negotiating a face-saving diplomatic resolution. The very fact that the United States used military means to free the hostages could have inflamed the Middle East and alienated even those Islamic countries enjoying good relations with the United States, such as Saudi Arabia and Egypt. Islamic radicals and Arab nationalists would have been better able to recruit new adherents to their cause.

Others argue that a successful mission, even if it resulted in the loss of U.S. life and angered many Middle Eastern nations, would still have had a positive effect over the long term. Much like in the *Mayaguez* incident in 1975, the fate of the hostages and rescuers would have been less important than demonstrating U.S. power and toughness. A successful mission might have made Islamic radicals think twice before taking more U.S. hostages, such as the twenty-five Americans kidnapped in Lebanon by Iranian-backed radical groups from 1982 to 1992. A consistent U.S. policy of zero-tolerance for terrorism might have also deterred other types of terrorism, such as hijackings and suicide bombings.

Carter's aides had urged him to act to ensure his reelection in 1980. The failure to free the hostages clearly hurt him in that year's presidential race whereas a successful mission would have excited public approval. But Carter's political problems went beyond Iran. Spiraling inflation, high gas prices, unemployment, criticism of the Panama Canal treaties, the failure of détente, and criticism of Carter's pessimism about the United States all hurt his chances to defeat Republican Ronald Reagan. A successful mission might have made Reagan's victory narrower, but Carter's troubles were so numerous as to make his reelection unlikely.

With hindsight, the odds of a successful hostage rescue mission validate Cyrus Vance's dissent. The risky mission, even if successful, promised few concrete positive effects. Measured against the much more probable negative outcomes, Carter's decision to mount the operation seems to have been motivated by personal frustration and political desperation.

Four events finally facilitated a resolution. First, the Shah died in Egypt in July 1980. Second, Khomeini's Islamic clerics won control of the parliament and thus no longer needed the hostages for their political purposes. Third, in September, Iraq and Iran went to war, and Iran found that it had few friends or funds. And fourth, Ronald Reagan, who promised a tougher posture, was elected president. On the day before Reagan took office, an agreement was secretly struck with the help of Algerian mediators: release of the hostages in exchange for unfreezing Iranian assets in the United States. On January 20, 1981—shortly after Reagan's inauguration—the hostages gained their freedom. They returned home to a relieved nation that celebrated briefly and then tried to forget.

Détente's Downfall: Soviet-American Rivalry, Afghanistan, and the Carter Record

Tension over Afghanistan and arms control along with conflicting interpretations of Soviet behavior led to détente's collapse. Some Carter officials believed that global problems did not always stem from Soviet intrigue and that Moscow suffered domestic troubles, an unimaginative and aged leadership, and nationalist stirrings in Eastern Europe. But Brzezinski and his NSC staff countered that Soviet expansionism in the Middle East and Africa had to be faced down, not negotiated away. The president eventually leaned toward the hard-line Brzezinski.

When Carter ostentatiously urged respect for human rights, the Kremlin responded by harassing Jews who applied to emigrate from the Soviet Union to Israel and dissident intellectuals who criticized the communist regime. From the American perspective, too, the Soviets seemed bent on a military buildup: Cuban troops and Soviet advisers stayed in Angola; the Soviet navy and Warsaw Pact forces modernized; and greater numbers of missiles pointed at NATO countries. "We were enthusiastically arming ourselves, like binging drunks, without any apparent political need," a Soviet official later admitted.[185] In this environment laced with suspicion and hostility, Secretary Vance journeyed to Moscow in March 1977 to reenergize SALT with a sudden, publicized proposal for deep cuts in ICBMs—precisely the category in which the Soviets were strongest. The Soviets thought Carter was saying: "Either you accept our position or we start an arms race and the Cold War again."[186] Vance went home empty-handed.

As Soviet-American trade increased, Moscow understandably expressed puzzlement over "constant zigzags" in U.S. behavior.[187] In the SALT-II talks of 1977–1979, the Soviets tried but failed to block American development of the new MX (missile experimental), an improved ICBM designed to carry ten MIRVs; the Trident-II submarine-launched ballistic missile, capable of carrying fourteen warheads; and the cruise missile (see Glossary, page 377). The Americans

Jimmy Carter's World.
The Iranian crisis joined domestic economic turmoil to trouble President Carter. A White House aide remembered that "before conferring with a foreign leader, Carter would often sit by his globe ... trying to imagine the political, economic, and military pressures experienced by the leader." (AUTH © 1978 The Philadelphia Inquirer. Reprinted with permission of UNIVERSAL PRESS SYNDICATE. All rights reserved)

failed to restrict the new Soviet supersonic "Backfire" bomber. Its range of 5,500 miles threatened Western Europe and China. Prolonged negotiations nonetheless culminated in the SALT-II treaty, signed at the Vienna summit in June 1979. The agreement for the first time established numerical equality in total strategic nuclear delivery vehicles, each limited to 2,250 by 1982. The treaty capped MIRVed launchers at 1,200 and limited the number of warheads per delivery vehicle. Whereas the treaty required the Soviets to dismantle more than 250 existing delivery vehicles, the Americans could expand from their current 2,060 to the ceiling of 2,250. Each nation could conduct technical verification of the other's compliance without interference.

But SALT-II soon fell victim to the deteriorating Soviet-American relationship. In the Senate, opponents argued that progress on nuclear-arms control should be linked to Soviet behavior on other issues, such as human rights and Africa. Democratic senator Henry Jackson of Washington and other hawks also claimed that the Soviets, by the mid-1980s, could exploit a "window of vulnerability" and destroy America's land-based missiles in a first strike.[188] Dovish critics, however, found SALT-II limitations too meager, permitting continued nuclear-weapons growth.

The Carter administration concentrated on rebutting conservative critics. Without SALT-II, the Soviets would enlarge their nuclear forces at a brisker pace. Compelled to keep up, the United States would fuel an expensive arms race. As for the alleged vulnerability of American ICBMs, Carter officials explained that the Soviets would have to deposit two warheads squarely on every ICBM silo to ensure destruction—an unlikely scenario: The timing would have to be near-perfect so that one incoming warhead would not explode and destroy other warheads before they reached their targets ("fratricide"). The president would not stand by and let American ICBMs be destroyed in their silos. Even if a Soviet first strike somehow destroyed the land-based ICBMs (only 30 percent of U.S. nuclear forces), SLBMs and strategic bombers would remain to annihilate tens of millions of Soviet people. "They [Soviets] are not supermen; they are not fools either," remarked one official.[189] Carter tried to win votes from hawks by announcing an expensive five-year military expansion program and a plan to deploy 572 Pershing-II ballistic missiles and ground-launched cruise missiles in Western Europe to counter the Soviet medium-range SS-20 missiles aimed at America's allies.

The Soviet invasion of Afghanistan in late December 1979 killed the SALT-II treaty and elevated to orthodoxy Brzezinski's hard-line views about a malevolent Soviet Union. Some 50,000 Red Army troops marched into neighboring Afghanistan to sustain a Soviet client challenged by Islamic rebels. The Soviets also intervened because they wanted to maintain Afghanistan as a "buffer" against the spread of Islamic fundamentalism in central Asia.[190] Covert CIA assistance to the insurgents since July also raised fears in Moscow that the Afghans might "do a Sadat on us" by aligning with the United States.[191] Brzezinski had backed the secret aid to the Afghani Islamic right, hoping to provoke a Soviet invasion. He told the president: "Now we can give the USSR its Vietnam war."[192] After inciting Moscow to invade, Carter publicly acted as if Afghanistan marked the first step in a Soviet master plan to take over the oil-rich Persian Gulf region, proclaiming their actions to be "the greatest threat to peace since the Second World War."[193] "Putting 'a Red thread' through the complexities of the Gulf area seemed to us to be a desirable and justified simplification" to arouse the American people, Brzezinski later admitted.[194] In retaliation, Carter withdrew the SALT-II treaty from the Senate, stopped high-technology sales and grain shipments to the USSR, and pulled the United States out of the Summer Olympic Games scheduled for Moscow. Carter also outlined military measures: arms assistance for Pakistan; creation of U.S. naval facilities in Oman, Kenya, Somalia, and Egypt; formation of a rapid deployment force for use in the Middle East; positioning of two aircraft carrier groups in the region; and a much increased defense budget. And last, CIA assistance increased and sustained Afghan resistance.

On January 24, 1980, the president proclaimed the Carter Doctrine: "An attempt by any outside force to gain control of the Persian Gulf region will be regarded as an assault on the vital interests of the United States of America" and "will be repelled by use of any means necessary, including military force."[195] As a statement of containment, it sounded familiar themes. But serious problems impeded implementation. When Washington offered $400 million to Pakistan, its prime minister scoffed "Peanuts!" and demanded more.[196] The Saudis refused to let the U.S. military use their facilities. Most nations rejected Carter's call for an Olympics boycott.

As Soviet-American relations deteriorated, Sino-American ties improved. Both Beijing and Washington sought to use each other to contain the Soviet Union. Following U.S. diplomatic recognition in early 1979, China embarked on a three-week incursion against Vietnam to show it "had no fear of the Soviet Union."[197] A U.S.-China trade agreement in 1980 enabled the Export-Import Bank to extend credits to the People's Republic. U.S. companies signed contracts to tap China's oil. In 1977–1980 China ranked fourth in the world as a buyer of U.S. agricultural exports, taking about half of the nation's cotton exports in 1979 alone. Mineral-short America eyed China's large deposits of tin, chrome, and tungsten. In 1980 American exports to China totaled $4 billion, up from $807 million in 1974. China replaced the Soviet Union as Washington's largest communist trading partner; in 1980 U.S. exports to the Soviet Union stood at a comparatively low $1.5 billion.

Taiwan's status, however, remained contentious. Washington severed formal diplomatic relations with the Republic of China on Taiwan, unilaterally terminated the 1954 mutual defense treaty, and withdrew all U.S. forces and military installations from the island. But private Americans maintained strong economic links, and low-level official ties continued through an "Institute." Washington also kept up the flow of military aid. The People's Republic still insisted on ultimately repossessing Taiwan. U.S. cultural interactions with Taiwan remained strong, especially so when Taiwanese teams won Little League baseball championships during the 1970s.

During the Carter presidency, many Americans sensed that the nation's role as the world's sheriff, banker, business manager, and teacher had eroded. High OPEC prices, huge deficits in the balance of payments, haunting memories of Vietnam, revolution in Nicaragua, return of the Canal Zone to Panama, Castro's defiance, Soviet nuclear equivalence and the jilted SALT-II, the Iranian hostage crisis, and Afghanistan—all seemed to project an image of American weakness. Carter could not persuade Americans that a decline in U.S. power was inevitable in an interdependent, multipolar world of some 150 nations. When he urged energy conservation as "the moral equivalent of war," wags spelled out the acronym MEOW.[198]

Carter left a mixed record. Too often, administration policy appeared erratic because of the constant feuding between the State Department and Brzezinski's National Security Council. One scholar quipped that Carter appeared "allergic to all efforts at eloquence," at times seeming to "lack the skill, energy or even the interest" to persuade the U.S. public to support his policies.[199] Carter also violated some of his stated goals. He promised to withdraw U.S. forces from South Korea but then reversed himself. Strongly advocating nuclear nonproliferation, he nonetheless agreed in 1980 to ship 38 metric tons of enriched uranium fuel to India, even though New Delhi had snubbed the nonproliferation treaty. He promised to reduce defense spending but actually increased the Pentagon's budget by 14.5 percent in his last year. Despite his pledge to reduce arms sales abroad, they climbed from $12.8 billion in 1977 to $17.1 billion in 1980.

Carter's human-rights policy also seemed selective. When Vietnamese armies overthrew the genocidal Pol Pot regime in Cambodia in late 1978, U.S. aid went to Khmer Rouge guerrillas to contain the perceived expansion of Soviet influence via Hanoi, even though Carter had called the Khmer Rouge "the worst violators of human rights in the world today."[200] Amnesty International, founded in 1961 to monitor the worldwide status of human rights, cited the governments of Argentina, Brazil, Guatemala, Indonesia, Iran, Morocco, the Philippines, South Korea, Taiwan, and Thailand for condoning or practicing torture, political terrorism, or arbitrary arrest. In 1976–1980 Washington delivered $2.3 billion in military aid to those ten nations and sold them weapons worth $13.7 billion. Carter's human-rights efforts led to the freeing of hundreds of political prisoners abroad, but the president's detractors faulted his effort as either too little or too meddlesome.

Carter officials believed that the administration pursued noble goals, achieved diplomatic successes, and infused morality into American foreign policy to prove that U.S. power lay not simply in military capabilities but also in the nation's values. The administration candidly explained the limits of U.S. influence in a world of diffused power and stressed the need to deal with long-range issues, not just immediate crises. Pointing to the Egyptian-Israeli peace, Panama Canal treaties, normalization of relations with China, North-South dialogue, end to civil war in Zimbabwe, and an improved American status in Africa, Professor Brzezinski proudly filled out the administration's report card: A–/B+. But in the 1980 presidential election Carter received only 41 percent of the popular vote. One longtime aide observed that "Carter is a complex man" and in 1980 "much to our dismay" even "after all the millions of words that had been written, and all the thousands of hours on television" the public "still did not have a clear picture of who he was."[201] Carter's standing domestically and internationally has improved since his electoral loss in 1980, but he remains controversial in the early twenty-first century because of his acts of private diplomacy and outspoken intervention in international affairs, including in Haiti, North Korea, and the Middle East. The criticism only mounted after his winning the Nobel Peace Prize in 2002. Heavily polarized opinions leave Carter's presidential legacy unsettled. Still, one commentator concluded that in the modern age when a "president leaves office with the Constitution more or less intact, and without a lot of dead American boys scattered around the planet, we ought to give him a medal."[202]

FURTHER READING FOR THE PERIOD 1969–1981

See works on the Cold War, the Third World, and other topics cited in earlier chapters.

For foreign relations during the Nixon and Ford presidencies, and for Richard M. Nixon the person, see Stephen E. Ambrose, *Nixon* (1989, 1991); Douglas Brinkley, *Gerald R. Ford* (2007); James Cannon, *Time and Chance* (1994) (Ford); Robert Dallek, *Nixon and Kissinger* (2007); Mark Feeney, *Nixon at the Movies* (2004); John R. Greene, *The Presidency of Gerald R. Ford* (1994); Joan Hoff, *Nixon Reconsidered* (1998); Fredrik Logevall and Andrew Preston, eds., *Nixon in the World* (2008); Roger Morris, *Richard Milhous Nixon* (1989); Richard Reeves, *President Nixon* (2001); Asaf Siniver, *Nixon, Kissinger, and U.S. Foreign Policy Making* (2008); and Melvin Small, *The Presidency of Richard Nixon* (1999).

For Henry A. Kissinger, see Jussi Hahnimäki, *Flawed Architect* (2004); Christopher Hitchens, *The Trial of Henry Kissinger* (2001); Walter Isaacson, *Kissinger* (1992); Roger Morris, *Uncertain Greatness* (1977); Robert D. Schulzinger, *Henry Kissinger* (1989); and Jeremi Suri, *Henry Kissinger and the American Century* (2007).

For Jimmy Carter and his foreign relations, see Brian J. Auten, *Carter's Conversion* (2008); Douglas Brinkley, *The Unfinished Presidency* (1998); Andrew DeRoche, *Andrew Young* (2003); John Drumbell, *The Carter Presidency* (1993); Gary M. Fink and Hugh Davis Graham, eds., *The Carter Presidency* (1998); Frye Gaillard, *Prophet from Plains* (2007); Burton I. Kaufman, *The Presidency of James Earl Carter, Jr.* (1993); Kenneth E. Morris, *Jimmy Carter, American Moralist* (1996); Herbert O. Rosenbaum and Alexej Ugrinsky, eds., *Jimmy Carter* (1993); David Skidmore, *Reversing Course* (1996); and Robert A. Strong, *Working in the World* (2000).

For Congress, see Loch K. Johnson, *Bombs, Bugs, Drugs, and Thugs* (2000); Robert G. Kaufman, *Henry M. Jackson* (2000); Kathryn S. Olmsted, *Challenging the Secret Government* (1997); and Keith W. Olson, *Watergate* (2003).

For Soviet-American relations, détente, and SALT, see Ann H. Cahn, *Killing Détente* (1998); Dan Caldwell, *The Dynamics of Domestic Politics and Arms Control* (1991) (SALT-II); Michael B. Froman, *The Development of the Idea of Détente* (1992); Raymond L. Garthoff, *Détente and Confrontation* (1995); Jonathan Haslam, *The Soviet Union and the Politics of Nuclear Weapons in Europe* (1990); Melvyn Leffler, *For the Soul of Mankind* (2007); Wilfred Loth, *Overcoming the Cold War* (2002); Keith L. Nelson, *The Making of Détente* (1995); Matthew J. Ouimet, *The Rise and Fall of the Brezhnev Doctrine in Soviet Foreign Policy* (2002); M. E. Sarotte, *Dealing with the Devil* (2001) (Ostpolitik); Jeremi Suri, *Power and Protest* (2003); Terry Terriff, *The Nixon Administration and the Making of U.S. Nuclear Strategy* (1995), and Vladislav Zubok, *A Failed Empire* (2007).

For China and Japan, see Rosemary Foot, *The Practice of Power* (1995); Arnold Xiangze Jiang, *The United States and China* (1988); Ronald C. Keith, *The Diplomacy of Zhou Enlai* (1989); William C. Kirby, et al., *The Normalization of U.S.-China Relations* (2005); Walter LaFeber, *The Clash* (1997) (Japan); James Lilly, *China Hands* (2004), Margaret MacMillan, *Nixon and Mao* (2007); James Mann, *About Face* (1999) (China); Robert S. Ross, *Negotiating Cooperation* (1995); Robert S. Ross and Jiang Changbin, eds., *Re-Examining the Cold War* (2001); Michael Schaller, *Altered States* (1997) (Japan); Ross Terrill, *Mao* (1993); Nancy B. Tucker, *Taiwan, Hong Kong, and the United States* (1994) and *China Confidential* (2001); Patrick Tyler, *A Great Wall* (2000); and Yafeng Xia, *Negotiating with the Enemy* (2006).

The end and lessons of the Vietnam War are explored in Dale Andrade, *America's Last Vietnam Battle* (2001); Pierre Asselin, *A Bitter Peace* (2002); Michael R. Belknap, *The Vietnam War on Trial* (2003); Larry Berman, *No Peace, No Honor* (2001); Kenton J. Clymer, *The United States and Cambodia, 1969–2000* (2004); Eric Dean, Jr., *Shook Over Hell* (1997); Susan Jeffords, *The Remasculinization of America* (1989); Rhodri Jeffreys-Jones, *Peace Now!* (1999); Ben Kiernan, *The Pol Pot Regime* (2002); Jeffrey Kimball, *Nixon's Vietnam War* (1998) and *Vietnam War Files* (2004); Michael Lind, *Vietnam: The Necessary War* (1999); Travor B. McCrisken, *American Exceptionalism and the Legacy of Vietnam* (2003); Deborah Nelson, *War Behind Me* (2008) (war crimes); John Prados and Margaret Pratt Porter, eds., *Inside the Pentagon Papers* (2004); Stephen P. Randolph, *Powerful and Brutal Weapons* (2007); Robert Schulzinger, *Time for Peace* (2004); William Shawcross, *Sideshow* (1979) (Cambodia); Wayne Thompson, *To Hanoi and Back* (2000); James Willbanks, *Abandoning Vietnam* (2004); and Randall B. Woods, ed., *Vietnam and the American Political Tradition* (2003). See also works listed in Chapter 9.

International economic questions, including the North-South debate, are covered in David P. Calleo, *The Imperious Economy* (1982); Albert L. Danielson, *The Evolution of OPEC* (1982); Francis J. Gavin, *Gold, Dollars, and Power* (2004); Jeffrey A. Hart, *The New International Economic Order* (1983); Diane B. Kunz, *Butter and Guns* (1997); Allen J. Matusow, *Nixon's Economy* (1998); and Robert K. Olson, *U.S. Foreign Policy and the New International Economic Order* (1981).

Environmental issues, population, food, and their intersection with the international economy and world politics are examined in Scott Barrett, *Environment and Statecraft* (2003); Lynton K. Caldwell, *International Environmental Policy* (1984); John McCormick, *Reclaiming Paradise* (1989); and Ross B. Talbott, *The Four World Food Agencies in Rome* (1990).

For Africa and some Third World issues, see Andrew DeRoche, *Black, White, and Chrome* (2001) (Zimbabwe); Piero Gleijeses, *Conflicting Missions* (2001); Fernando A. Guimarães, *The Origins of the Angolan Civil War* (1998); Gerald Horne, *From the Barrel of a Gun* (2001) (Zimbabwe); Donna R. Jackson, *Jimmy Carter and the Horn of Africa* (2007); Robert J. McMahon, *The Limits of Empire* (1999); and P. David Searles, *The Peace Corps Experience* (1997).

For the Middle East, oil, and the Arab-Israeli conflict, see Warren Bass, *Support Any Friend* (2003); George W. Breslauer, *Soviet Strategy in the Middle East* (1990); Rachel Bronson, *Thicker Than Oil* (2006); David Carlton, *The West's Road to 9/11* (2005); Avner Cohen, *Israel and the Bomb* (1998); Robert Dreyfuss, *Devil's Game* (2005); James F. Goode, *The United States and Iran* (1997); Douglas Little, *American Orientalism* (2002); Melani McAlister, *Epic Encounters* (2001); Yezid Sayigh, *Armed Struggle and the Search for State* (1998) (Palestinians); David Schoenbaum, *The United States and the State of Israel* (1993); Kenneth W. Stein, *Heroic Diplomacy* (1999); and Daniel Yergin, *The Prize* (1991) (oil).

For U.S.-Iranian relations and the hostage crisis, see Gholam Reza Afkhami, *The Life and Times of the Shah* (2009); Mark Bowden, *Guests of the Ayatollah* (2006); Charles-Phillippe David et al., *Foreign Policy in the White House* (1993); David Farber, *Taken Hostage* (2004); James E. Goode, *The United States and Iran* (1997); David Harris, *The Crisis* (2005); Daniel Patrick Houghton, *U.S. Foreign Policy and the Iran Hostage Crisis* (2001); Russell L. Moses, *Freeing the Hostages* (1996); Ofira Seliktat, *Failing the Crystal Ball Test* (2000) (Carter and Iran); William Shawcross, *The Shah's Last Ride* (1988); Gary Sick, *October Surprise* (1991) (hostages and Reagan election); and Marvin Zonis, *Majestic Failure* (1991).

Latin America–U.S. relations, including Chile and the Panama Canal Treaties, are treated in Adam Clymer, *Drawing the Line at the Big Ditch* (2008) (Panama Canal Treaties); David W. Engstrom, *Presidential Decision Making Adrift* (1997) (Mariel boatlift); Peter Kornbluh, *The Pinochet File* (2003); Walter LaFeber, *The Panama Canal* (1989); John Major, *Prize Possession* (2002) (Panama); Morris H. Morley, *Washington, Somoza, and the Sandinistas* (1994); Louis A. Pérez, Jr., *Cuba and the United States* (2003); Lubna Z. Qureshi, *Nixon, Kissinger, and Allende* (2009); Stephen G. Rabe, *The Road to OPEC* (1982) (Venezuela); Lars Schoultz, *National Security and United States Policy Toward Latin America* (1987), and *Beneath the United States* (1998); Paul E. Sigmund, *The United States and Democracy in Chile* (1993); Kathryn Sikkink, *Mixed Signals* (2007)(human rights); and Peter H. Smith, *Talons of the Eagle* (1996)

See also the General Bibliography; Robert L. Beisner, ed., *Guide to American Foreign Relations Since 1600* (2003); and the following notes.

NOTES TO CHAPTER 10

1. Quoted in Bernard Kalb and Marvin Kalb, *Kissinger* (Boston: Little, Brown, 1974), p. 266.
2. Hugh Sidey in *Life, LXXII* (March 3, 1972), 12.
3. Quoted in Margaret MacMillan, *Nixon and Mao* (New York: Random House, 2007), p. 273.
4. Quoted in Robert Dallek, *Nixon and Kissinger* (New York: HarperCollins, 2007), p. 330.
5. *Department of State Bulletin, LXVI* (March 6, 1972), 290.
6. Quoted in John Lewis Gaddis, *Strategies of Containment* (New York: Oxford University Press, 2005, 2nd ed.), p. 294
7. Quoted in Jussi Hanhimäki, *Flawed Architect* (New York: Oxford University Press, 2004), p. 32.
8. Yafeng Xia, "China's Elite Politics and Sino-American Rapprochement, January 1969–January 1972," *Journal of Cold War Studies, VIII* (Fall 2006), 14.
9. Quoted in John Maxwell Hamilton, *Edgar Snow* (Bloomington: Indiana University Press, 1988), p. 269.

10. Kissinger quoted in Jung Chang and Jon Halliday, *Mao* (New York: Knopf, 2005), p. 581.

11. Quoted in Evelyn Goh, *Contructing the U.S. Rapprochement with China, 1961–1974* (New York: Cambridge University Press, 2005), p. 167.

12. *Public Papers, Nixon, 1971* (Washington, D.C.: Government Printing Office, 1972), p. 819.

13. Mao quoted in Joseph Y. S. Cheng, "Mao Zedong's Perception of the World in 1968–1972," *Journal of American-East Asian Relations, VII* (Fall–Winter 1998), 254.

14. Entry of April 20, 1971 in H. R. Haldeman, *The Haldeman Diaries* (New York: Putnam, 1994), p. 275.

15. Quoted in Joan Hoff, "A Revisionist View of Nixon's Foreign Policy," *Presidential Studies Quarterly, XXVI* (Winter 1996), 117.

16. Mao quoted in Chen Jian, *Mao's China & the Cold War* (Chapel Hill: University of North Carolina Press, 2001), p. 267.

17. Mao quoted in the Li Zhisui, *The Private Life of Chairman Mao* (New York: Random House, 1994), p. 565.

18. Quoted in Rosemary Foot, *The Practice of Power* (New York: Oxford University Press, 1995), p. 137.

19. Zhou quoted in Goh, *Constructing,* p. 176.

20. Chang and Halliday, *Mao,* p. 588.

21. Quoted in Richard Nixon, *RN* (New York: Grosset & Dunlap, 1978), p. 564.

22. Quoted in MacMillan, *Nixon and Mao,* p. 74.

23. John H. Holdridge, *Crossing the Divide* (Lanham, Md. Rowman & Littlefield, 1997), p. 87.

24. Entry of February 22, 1972, *Haldeman Diaries,* p. 416.

25. Kissinger memorandum of conversation, February 21, 1972 in William Burr, ed., *The Kissinger Transcripts* (New York: New Press, 1998), p. 64.

26. Quoted in Jussi Hanhimäki, "Kissinger, Triangular Diplomacy, and the End of the Vietnam War, 1971–73," *Diplomacy and Statecraft, XIV* (March 2003), 170.

27. George Gallup in *Hartford Courant*, March 12, 1972.

28. Quoted in Ronald C. Keith, *The Diplomacy of Zhou Enlai* (New York: St. Martin's, 1989), p. 199.

29. Quoted in Michael A. Schaller, *Altered States* (New York: Oxford University Press, 1997), p. 227.

30. *Department of State Bulletin, LXVI* (March 20, 1972), 435–438.

31. Nixon quoted in Jaw-Ling Joanne Chang, "Taiwan's Policy Toward the United States," in William C. Kirby, Robert S. Ross, and Gong Li, eds., *Normalization of U.S.-China Relations* (Cambridge: Harvard University Press, 2005), p. 233.

32. Quoted in Nancy Bernkopf Tucker, "Taiwan Expendable?," *Journal of American History, XCII* (June 2005), 123.

33. Quoted in Nancy Bernkopf Tucker, *Taiwan, Hong Kong, and the United States* (New York: Twayne, 1994), p. 104.

34. *Department of State Bulletin, LXVI* (March 20, 1972), 435–438.

35. MacMillan, *Nixon and Mao,* p. 148.

36. Nixon, *RN,* p. 580.

37. Quoted in Michael Schaller, "Détente and the Strategic Triangle," in Robert S. Ross and Jiang Changbin, eds., *Re-examining the Cold War* (Cambridge: Harvard University Press, 2001), p. 358.

38. *Philadelphia Inquirer* quoted in Melvin Small, *The Presidency of Richard Nixon* (Lawrence: University Press of Kansas, 1999), p. 124.

39. William Appleman Williams quoted in Lance Morrow, *The Best Year of Their Lives* (New York: Basic Books, 2005), 159.

40. *Newsweek* reporter quoted in Dallek, *Nixon and Kissinger,* p. 546; Nixon quoted in Lewis Lapham, *The Theater of War* (New York: New Press, 2002), p. 18.

41. H. R. Haldeman, *The Ends of Power* (New York: Times Books, 1978), p. 98.

42. Quoted in Hanhimäki, *Flawed Architect,* p. 338.

43. Quoted in Richard Valeriani, *Travels with Henry* (New York: Berkeley, 1980), p. 123; Henry Kissinger, *White House Years* (Boston: Little, Brown, 1979), p. 1094.

44. Conrad Black, *Richard Nixon* (New York: PublicAffairs, 2007), p. 576.

45. Stanley Hoffmann, *Primacy or World Order* (New York: McGraw-Hill, 1978), p. 33.

46. Quoted in Ann Miller Morin, *Her Excellency* (New York: Twayne, 1994), p. 110.

47. Quoted in MacMillan, *Nixon and Mao,* p. 55.

48. Quoted in Thomas G. Paterson, "Oversight or Afterview?" in Michael Barnhart, ed., *Congress and United States Foreign Policy* (Albany: State University of New York Press, 1987), p. 155.

49. Quoted in Carlos Osorio, ed., "Argentine Military Believed U.S. Gave Go-Ahead for Dirty War," *National Security Archive Briefing Book No. 73* (August 21, 2002).

50. Kissinger, *White House Years,* p. 55.

51. Kissinger quoted in Robert J. McMahon, *The Limits of Empire* (New York: Columbia University Press, 1999), p. 157.

52. Memorandum of White House Meeting, December 7, 1970, Box 68, Dean Acheson Papers, Yale University, New Haven, Conn.

53. Quoted in Jeffrey Kimball, *The Vietnam War Files* (Lawrence: University Press of Kansas, 2003), p. 15.

54. Quoted in David M. Lampton, *Same Bed, Different Dreams* (Berkeley: University of California Press, 2001), p. 223.

55. Archer Blood quoted in Sajit Gandhi, ed., "The Tilt: The U.S. and the South Asian Crisis of 1971," *National Security Archive Electronic Briefing Book No. 79* (December 16, 2002).

56. Quoted in Robert J. McMahon, *The Cold War on the Periphery* (New York: Columbia University Press, 1994), p. 346.

57. Quoted in Evelyn Goh, "Nixon, Kissinger, and the 'Soviet Card' in the U.S. Opening to China, 1971–1974," in *Diplomatic History, XXIX* (June 2005), 481.

58. President's Briefing, November 16 and 17, 1971 in Gandhi, "The Tilt."

59. Nixon, *RN,* p. 527.

60. Quoted in Donald R. Baucom, *The Origins of SDI* (Lawrence: University Press of Kansas, 1992), p. 75.

61. Hope M. Harrison, "The Berlin Wall, Ostpolitik, and Détente," in David C. Geyer and Bernd Schaefer, eds., *American Détente and German Ostpolitik, 1969–1972* (Washington, D.C. German Historical Institute, 2004), p. 9.

62. Kissinger quoted in Piero Gleijeses, *Conflicting Missions* (Chapel Hill: University of North Carolina Press, 2002), p. 388.

63. William Hyland quoted in Walter Isaacson, *Kissinger* (New York: Simon & Schuster, 1992), p. 402.

64. Andrei Gromyko quoted in Matthew J. Ouimet, *The Rise and Fall of the Brezhnev Doctrine in Soviet Foreign Policy* (Chapel Hill: University of North Carolina Press, 2003), p. 87.

65. Kissinger, *White House Years,* p. 117.

66. Quoted in David Schoenbaum, *The United States and the State of Israel* (New York: Oxford University Press, 1993), p. 171.

67. William B. Quandt, *Decade of Decisions* (Berkeley: University of California Press, 1977), p. 127.

68. Sadat quoted in Yazid Sayigh, *Armed Struggle and the Search for State* (New York: Oxford University Press, 1997), p. 152.

69. Quoted in Rachel Bronson, *Thicker than Oil* (New York: Oxford University Press, 2006), p. 118.

70. Quoted in Henry Kissinger, *Crisis* (New York: Simon and Schuster, 2003), p. 96.

71. Quoted in Douglas Little, *American Orientalism* (Chapel Hill: University of North Carolina Press, 2002), p. 106.

72. Alexander Haig quoting Nixon in Raymond G. Garthoff, *Détente and Confrontation* (Washington D.C.: Brookings Institution, 1995; rev. ed.), p. 426.

73. Quoted in *New York Times*, March 15, 1976.

74. Melani McAlister, "A Cultural History of the War without End," *Journal of American History, LXXXIX* (September 2002), 445.

75. Kissinger quoted in James A. Bill, *The Eagle and the Lion* (New Haven: Yale University Press, 1988), p. 203.

76. Gary Sick quoted in Little, *American Orientalism*, p. 148.

77. Quoted in Samuel Baily, *The United States and the Development of South America* (New York: New Viewpoints, 1976), p. 118.

78. Quoted in Dallek, *Nixon and Kissinger*, p. 233.

79. Quoted in Christopher Andrew and Vasili Mitrokhin, *The World Was Going Our Way* (New York: Basic Books, 2005), p. 73.

80. Quoted in Stephen Kinzer, *Overthrow* (New York: Times Books, 2006), p. 187.

81. Peter Kornbluth, *The Pinochet File* (New York: New Press, 2003), p. 114.

82. Quoted in Christopher Hitchens, *The Trial of Henry Kissinger* (New York: Verso, 2001), p. 70.

83. Quoted in Dallek, *Nixon and Kissinger*, p. 229.

84. Quoted in Garthoff, *Détente and Confrontation*, p. 92.

85. Quoted in Piero Gleijeses, "Moscow's Proxy," *Journal of Cold War Studies, VIII* (Fall 2006), 103.

86. Quoted in David F. Schmitz, *The United States and Right-Wing Dictatorships, 1965–1989* (New York: Cambridge University Press, 2006), p. 82.

87. Francis Njubi Nesbitt, *Race for Sanctions* (Bloomington: Indiana University Press, 2004), p. 73.

88. Quoted in Steven Mertz, "Congress, the Anti-Apartheid Movement, and Nixon," *Diplomatic History, XII* (Spring 1988), 177.

89. Quoted in Thomas A. Noer, "Segregationists and the World," in Brenda Gayle Plummer, ed., *Window on Freedom* (Chapel Hill: University of North Carolina Press, 2003), pp. 143, 148.

90. Quoted in Gleijeses, *Conflicting Missions*, p. 291.

91. Quoted in Thomas W. McCormick, *America's Half Century* (Baltimore: Johns Hopkins University Press, 1996; rev. ed.), p. 189; quoted in Jeremi Suri, *Henry Kissinger and the American Century* (Cambridge: Harvard University Press, 2007), p. 238.

92. Gerald R. Ford, *A Time to Heal* (New York: Harper and Row, 1979), p. 345.

93. Quoted in John Prados, *Lost Crusader* (New York: Oxford University Press, 2003), p. 317.

94. Soviet Foreign Office quoted in Odd Arne Westad, "Moscow and the Angolan Crisis," *Cold War International History Project Bulletin*, no. 8–9 (Winter 1996/1997), pp. 27, 29.

95. Leonid Brezhnev quoted in Wilfred Loth, *Overcoming the Cold War* (New York: Palgrave, 2002), p. 133.

96. Anatoly Dobrynin, *In Confidence* (New York: Random House, 1995), p. 472.

97. Quoted in Gleijeses, *Conflicting*, p. 390.

98. Quoted in Richard Reeves, *President Nixon* (New York: Simon and Schuster, 2001), p. 343.

99. Quoted *ibid.*, p. 341.

100. Quoted in Francis J. Gavin, *Gold, Dollars, and Power* (Chapel Hill: University of North Carolina Press, 2004), p. 196.

101. Quoted in Thomas G. Paterson, *On Every Front* (New York: Norton, 1992; 2nd ed.), p. 217.

102. Quoted in Alan McPherson, *Intimate Ties, Bitter Struggles* (Washington, D.C. Potomac Books, 2006), p. 74.

103. Quoted in Elaine P. Adam and Richard P. Stebbins, eds., *American Foreign Relations, 1976* (New York: New York University Press, 1978), p. 478.

104. Quoted in Small, *Presidency*, p. 163.

105. United Nations, General Assembly, *Official Records*, 22nd Session, August 18, 1967, Document A/6695, p. 1.

106. Quoted in Michael Roskin, "An American Metternich," in Frank J. Merli and Theodore A. Wilson, eds., *Makers of American Diplomacy* (New York: Charles Scribner's Sons, 1974), p. 698.

107. Quoted in McMahon, *Limits*, p. 255.

108. Mike Mansfield quoted in Stanley Millet, ed., *South Vietnam* (New York: Facts on File, 1973–1974; 7 vols.), *IV*, 64.

109. H. R. Haldeman notes quoted in Michael A. Genovese, *The Nixon Presidency* (Westport, Conn.: Greenwood, 1990), p. 134.

110. Vietnamese Confederation of Labor quoted in Edmund F. Wehrle, *Between a River and a Mountain* (Ann Arbor: University of Michigan Press, 2005), p. 182.

111. Bernard Trainor quoted in Kenneth J. Hagen and Ian J. Bickerton, *Unintended Consequences* (London: Reaktion Books, 2007), p. 157.

112. *Public Papers, Nixon, 1969*, p. 909.

113. Quoted in Roger Morris, *Uncertain Greatness* (New York: Harper & Row, 1977), p. 175.

114. Quoted in Robert David Johnson, *Congress and the Cold War* (New York: Cambridge University Press, 2006), p. 165.

115. Ambassador William Sullivan and Foreign Minister Nguyen Co Thach quoted in McMahon, *Limits of Empire*, p. 264.

116. Quoted in Melvin Small, *At the Water's Edge* (Chicago: Ivan R. Dee, 2005), p. 176.

117. Quoted in Kimball, *Vietnam War Files*, p. 221.

118. Quoted in Hanhimäki, "Kissinger," p. 180.

119. Kissinger, *White House Years*, p. 1399.

120. Quoted in Dale Andrade, *America's Last Vietnam Battle* (Lawrence: University Press of Kansas, 2001), p. 480.

121. *The London Daily Mirror* quoted in George C. Herring, "Fighting without Allies," in Marc Jason Gilbert, ed., *Why the North Won the Vietnam War* (New York: Palgrave, 2002), p. 92.

122. Quoted in Pierre Asselin, *Bitter Peace* (Chapel Hill: University of North Carolina Press, 2002), p. 184.

123. Quoted in William Bundy, *A Tangled Web* (New York: Hill & Wang, 1998), p. 362.

124. Alexander Haig quoted in James H. Willbanks, *Abandoning Vietnam* (Lawrence: University Press of Kansas, 2004), p. 184.

125. Richard Holbrooke quoted in Isaacson, *Kissinger*, p. 483.

126. John Negroponte quoted in Marilyn Young, *The Vietnam Wars* (New York: HarperCollins, 1991), p. 279.

127. Quoted in George C. Herring, "Vietnam: The War That Never Seems to Go Away," *New England Journal of History, LIV* (Spring 1998), 8.

128. Quoted in Thomas G. Paterson, "Historical Memory and Illusive Victories," *Diplomatic History, XII* (Winter 1988), 14.

129. Quoted in J. Garry Clifford, "Bureaucratic Politics," in Michael J. Hogan and Thomas G. Paterson, eds., *Explaining the History of American Foreign Relations* (New York: Cambridge University Press, 2004; 2nd ed.), p. 91.

130. Arthur Schlesinger, Jr., *The Imperial Presidency* (Boston: Houghton Mifflin, 1973).

131. Quoted in John R. Greene, *The Presidency of Gerald R. Ford* (Lawrence: University Press of Kansas, 1994), p. 150.

132. Quoted in Cécile Mentétrey-Monchau, "The *Mayaguez* Incident as an Epilogue to the Vietnam War and its Reflection of the Post-Vietnam Political Equilibrium in Souteast Asia," in *Cold War History, V* (August 2005), 343.

133. Kissinger quoted in William Burr and Michael L. Evans, eds., "Ford, Kissinger, and the Indonesian Invasion, 1975–76," *National Security Archive Electronic Briefing Book No. 62* (December 6, 2001).

134. Ronald Steel, in "America Now: A Failure of Nerve?" *Commentary, LX* (July 1975), 83.

135. Henry Steele Commager, "The Defeat of America," *New York Review of Books,* October 5, 1972, p. 13.

136. Charles DeBenedetti, *The Peace Reform in American History* (Bloomington: Indiana University Press, 1980), p. 174.

137. Charles DeBenedetti, "On the Significance of Peace Activism," *Peace and Change, IX* (Summer 1983), 14.

138. Bruce Weigl quoted in Young, *Vietnam,* p. 328.

139. Phyllis Schlafly quoted in Robert D. Schulzinger, *A Time for Peace* (New York: Oxford University Press, 2006), p. 99.

140. Quoted in *ibid.,* pp. 83–84.

141. Kevin Farrell quoted in Arnold R. Isaacs, *Vietnam Shadows* (Baltimore: Johns Hopkins University Press, 1997), p. 147.

142. C. W. Bowman quoted in Eric Bergerud, *Red Thunder, Tropic Lightning* (New York: Penguin, 1994), p. 224.

143. Jeffrey P. Kimball, "The Stab-in-the-Back Legend and the Vietnam War," *Armed Forces and Society, XIV* (Spring 1988), 433; Mark Moyar, *Triumph Forsaken* (Cambridge University Press, 2006).

144. Quoted in George C. Herring, "The 'Vietnam Syndrome,'" *Virginia Quarterly Review, LVII* (Fall 1981), 595.

145. Qiang Zhai, "Reassessing China's Role in the Vietnam War," in Xiaobing Li and Hongshan Li, eds., *China and the United States* (Lanham, Md.: University Press of America, 1998), p. 111.

146. Quoted in Andrade, *America's Last,* p. 475.

147. Quoted in Philip Caputo, *A Rumor of War* (New York: Ballantine, 1977), p. 69.

148. Colin L. Powell, *My American Journey* (New York: Random House, 1995), p. 149.

149. Le Ly Hayslip, *When Heaven and Earth Changed Places* (Garden City, N.Y.: Doubleday, 1989), p. xiv.

150. Quoted in John A. Soares, "Strategy, Ideology, and Human Rights," *Journal of Cold War Studies, VIII* (Fall 2006), 67.

151. William Quandt in discussion of "Negotiations at Home and Abroad" in Herbert B. Rosenbaum and Alexej Urginsky, eds., *Jimmy Carter* (Westport, Conn.: Greenwood, 1994), p. 62.

152. Quoted in *Washington Post,* January 12, 1977; *New York Times,* May 2, 1979.

153. Cyrus Vance, *Hard Choices* (New York: Simon and Schuster, 1983), p. 394.

154. Zbigniew Brzezinski, *Power and Principle* (New York: Farrar, Straus & Giroux, 1985, rev. ed.), p. 380.

155. Hamilton Jordan, *Crisis* (New York: G. P. Putnam's Sons, 1982), p. 47.

156. Kathryn Sikkink quoted in Julie A. Mertus, *Bait and Switch* (New York: Routledge, 2004), p. 29.

157. Quoted in John Lewis Gaddis, *Strategies of Containment* (New York: Oxford University Press, 1982), p. 345.

158. Gaddis Smith, *Morality, Reason, & Power* (New York: Hill & Wang, 1986), p. 9.

159. Omar Torrijos quoted in Richard Hudson, "Storm Over the Canal," *New York Times Magazine,* May 16, 1976, p. 24.

160. Quoted in Lou Cannon, *President Reagan* (New York: Simon & Schuster, 1991), p. 342.

161. George Moffett Exit Interview, December 5, 1980, Jimmy Carter Presidential Library, Atlanta, Ga.

162. *Department of State Bulletin, LXXVIII* (May 1978), 52.

163. Brzezinski, *Power,* p. 136.

164. Quoted in Charles O. Jones, *The Trusteeship Presidency* (Baton Rouge: Louisiana State University Press, 1988), p. 160.

165. Quoted in Saul Landau, "The Bay of Pigs," *Los Angeles Times,* April 19, 1981.

166. Quoted in Kathryn Sikkink, *Mixed Signals* (Ithaca: Cornell University Press, 2004), p. xx.

167. Quoted in Elaine P. Adam and Richard P. Stebbins, eds., *American Foreign Relations, 1977* (New York: New York University Press, 1979), p. 301.

168. *Ibid.,* p. 309.

169. Quoted in Nesbitt, *Race,* p. 108.

170. Clyde Ferguson and William R. Cotter, "South Africa," *Foreign Affairs, LVI* (January 1978), 262.

171. Quoted in Donna R. Jackson, *Jimmy Carter and the Horn of Africa* (Jefferson, N.C.: McFarland, 2007), p. 50.

172. Quoted in Alex de Waal, "The Wrong Lessons," *Boston Review* (December 2003/January 2004).

173. William B. Quandt, *Camp David* (Washington, D.C.: Brookings, 1986), p. 258.

174. Quoted in *Hartford Courant,* December 22, 1980.

175. Quoted in Doyle McManus, *Free at Last!* (New York: New American, 1981), p. 16.

176. Pierre Salinger, *America Held Hostage* (Garden City, N.Y.: Doubleday, 1981), p. 5; quoted in Ussama Mukdisi, "'Anti-Americanism' in the Arab World," *Journal of American History, LXXXIX* (September 2002), 548.

177. Jimmy Carter, *Keeping Faith* (New York: Bantam, 1982), p. 439.

178. Ball quoted in Little, *American Orientalism,* p. 225.

179. Quoted in Mark Bowden, *Guests of the Ayatollah* (New York: Atlantic Monthly Press, 2006), p. 19.

180. Quoted in Daniel Yergin, *The Prize* (New York: Simon & Schuster, 1991), p. 701.

181. Quoted in Harold H. Saunders, "Diplomacy and Pressure," in Warren Christopher et al., *American Hostages in Iran* (New Haven: Yale University Press, 1982), p. 102.

182. Quoted in David Carlton, *The West's Road to 9/11* (New York: Palgrave Macmillan, 2005), p. 112.

183. Quoted in Bowden, *Guests,* p. 217.

184. Vance, *Hard Choices,* p. 409; Warren Christopher, *Chance of a Lifetime* (New York: Scribner's, 2001), p. 100.

185. Georgi Arbatov quoted in Thomas M. Nichols, "Carter and the Soviets," *Diplomacy & Statecraft, XIII* (June 2002), 28.

186. Georgy Kornienko quoted in Vladislav Zubok, "An Offered Hand Rejected?" in Rosenbaum and Ugrinsky, *Carter,* p. 365.

187. Quoted in George McGovern, "How to Avert a New 'Cold War'," *Atlantic Monthly, CCXLV* (June 1980), 52.

188. Quoted in Frances FitzGerald, *Way Out There in the Blue* (New York: Simon & Schuster, 2000), p. 87.

189. Leslie H. Gelb, "The Facts of SALT II," April 1979, Department of State Current Policy No. 65.

190. Garthoff, *Détente,* p. 928.

191. Leonid Shebarshim quoted in Odd Arne Westad, "New Russian Evidence on the Soviet Intervention in Afghanistan," *Cold War International History Project,* nos. 8–9 (Winter 1996/1997), p. 130.

192. Quoted in Robert Dreyfuss, *Devil's Game* (New York: Metropolitan Books, 2005), p. 265.

193. Quoted in Melvyn P. Leffler, *For the Soul of Mankind* (New York: Hill & Wang, 2007), p. 335.

194. George Urban, "A Long Conversation with Dr. Zbigniew Brzezinski," *Encounter, LVI* (May 1981), 18.

195. *Department of State Bulletin, LXXX* (February 1980), Special B.

196. Quoted in Smith, *Morality,* p. 232.

197. Deng Xiaoping quoted in Allen S. Whiting, "China's Use of Force," *International Security, XXVI* (Fall 2001), 120.

198. Quoted in Michael S. Sherry, *In the Shadow of War* (New Haven: Yale University Press, 1995), p. 350.

199. Quoted in James T. Patterson, *Restless Giant* (New York: Oxford University Press, 2005), p. 105; James Fallows quoted in Frye Gaillard, *Prophet from Plains* (Athens: University of Georgia Press, 2007), p. 42.

200. Quoted in Kenton Clymer, "Jimmy Carter, Human Rights, and Cambodia," *Diplomatic History, XXVII* (April 2003), 246.

201. Hamilton Jordan quoted in Gaillard, *Prophet,* p. 13.

202. James David Barber quoted *ibid.*, p. 55.

CHAPTER 11

A New World Order?
Reagan, Bush, and
Clinton, 1981–2001

The Berlin Wall Comes Down, 1989. *Berliners celebrate atop the partially dismantled Berlin Wall on November 12, 1989. East Germans (back to camera) crowd through the opening into West Berlin at Potsdamer Platz. The opening of the Wall three days earlier led to the reunification of East and West Germany. Watching the scene on television, Secretary of State James Baker found it "hard to hold back tears of joy as the trickle of people seeking freedom in the West turned into a torrent." (AP Images)*

DIPLOMATIC CROSSROAD

◆   *The Berlin Wall Comes Down, 1989*

THE PARTYING BEGAN at midnight. Earlier on that afternoon of November 9, 1989, the East Berlin Communist party boss had announced that starting at 12:00 A.M. on November 10, citizens of the German Democratic Republic (GDR) could leave the country at any spot, including the crossing points along the infamous 28-mile-long Berlin Wall. The news spread throughout the divided city, to the 1.3 million inhabitants of East Berlin and the 2 million in the West. At Checkpoint Charlie in the American sector of West Berlin, a raucous crowd gathered, carrying bottles of beer and sparkling wine to celebrate.

At midnight, thousands of East Berliners filed through. West Berlin exploded with trumpet blasts, fireworks, and dancing. Strangers embraced amidst honking horns. Atop the ten-foot wall in front of the Brandenburg Gate, Berliners linked arms and sang the popular folk song, "Such a Beautiful Day Should Last Forever."[1] New signs soon covered graffiti: "Stalin is Dead, Europe Lives" and "Only Today is the War Really Over."[2] During the ensuing three-day weekend, more than 2 million Easterners crossed into West Berlin to walk along the Kurfürstendamm boulevard, an upscale shopping district where migrants eagerly spent the hundred marks ($60) given them by West German authorities as welcome money. Everywhere people grasped at freedom. Thousands of East Germans in their two-cylinder Trabant cars wheezed onto the autobahns to visit loved ones inside West Germany.

The British scholar Timothy Garton Ash participated in "the greatest street party in the history of the world." As he strolled through the Potsdamer Platz on Sunday morning, November 12, he could see workers dismantling the famous platform where distinguished visitors, including John F. Kennedy and Ronald Reagan, had hurled defiant speeches across the Berlin Wall. Soon the platform disappeared "like an unneeded stage prop." To Garton Ash, the weekend had a "magic, Pentecostal quality … when you feel that somewhere an angel has opened his wings."[3] The German wife of a U.S. diplomat kept saying: "I don't believe it. I just don't believe it."[4] West German Chancellor Helmut Kohl told President George H. W. Bush by phone: "Without the United States this day would not have been possible."[5]

The foundations of the Wall had begun to crumble the previous May, when Hungary opened its border with Austria. In August tens of thousands of East Germans went on holiday to Hungary, then traveled across the Austro-Hungarian border and eventually to West Germany where they could obtain automatic rights of citizenship. East Germany banned travel to Hungary, but this restriction only temporarily stemmed the flood, as more East Germans voted with their feet, some escaping through Czechoslovakia. By late October, the number of refugees from the GDR had swelled to 200,000.

The day after the Wall came down, a bloodless coup in Sofia, Bulgaria, ousted Todor Zhivkov, the hard-line Communist party boss of the past thirty-five years. By the end of November, mass demonstrations were peacefully terminating communist

Exodus of East Germans.
On October 4, 1989, some 10,000 refugees from East Germany milled outside the West German Embassy in Prague, Czechoslovakia, waiting for special buses to take them to West Germany where they could obtain automatic citizenship. Five weeks later, the Berlin Wall opened.
(AP Images)

rule in Czechoslovakia, and during Christmas week a bloody popular uprising toppled the tyrannical regime of Nicolae Ceaușescu in Romania. It was "one of those rare times," according to *Time* magazine, "when the tectonic plates of history shift beneath men's feet, and nothing after is quite the same."[6]

Gorbachev and the Earthquakes of 1989–1991

The seismic events of the *annus mirabilis* (year of miracles) would not have occurred without major impetus from Soviet President Mikhail S. Gorbachev. Since ascending to leadership in the Kremlin in March 1985, Gorbachev's bold effort at reforming the Soviet Union had acquired a momentum of its own. To revive the sick Soviet economy, plagued by declining productivity and a demoralized work force, the Soviet leader warned that "everyone must change, from the worker to the minister to the secretary of the central committee."[7] What started out as a fairly limited foreign-policy agenda—ending a Soviet war in Afghanistan, improving relations with China, and negotiating arms-control agreements with the United States—quickly escalated.

Gorbachev identified the huge drain on Soviet resources caused by the superpower competition as one area of potential savings. He decided on military cuts *despite* a continued U.S. arms buildup—"wasteful expenditures that we were not going to match," he later insisted—and in December 1988, astonished the world by announcing that over the next two years his country would unilaterally cut its military forces by 500,000 men and 10,000 tanks.[8] Quietly he passed the word: Soviet troops would not intervene to put down any uprisings in Eastern Europe. The veteran communist oligarchs of Eastern Europe heard the message and lost their

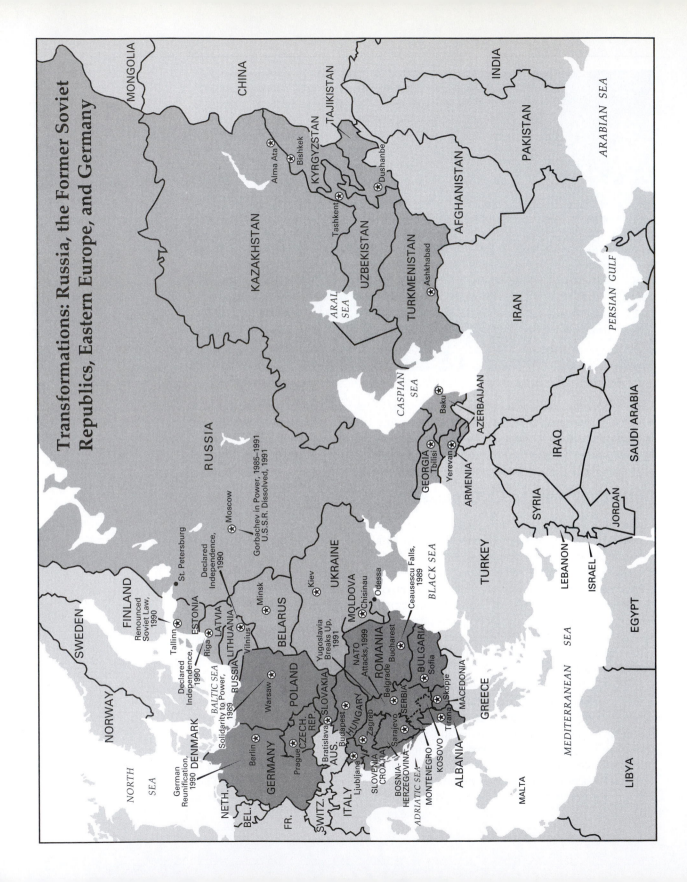

Transformations: Russia, the Former Soviet Republics, Eastern Europe, and Germany

MONGOLIA

CHINA

INDIA

RUSSIA

KAZAKHSTAN

TAJIKISTAN

KYRGYZSTAN

⊕ Alma Ata

⊕ Bishkek

⊕ Dushanbe

PAKISTAN

ARABIAN SEA

⊕ Tashkent

UZBEKISTAN

TURKMENISTAN

AFGHANISTAN

ARAL SEA

⊕ Ashkhabad

IRAN

PERSIAN GULF

CASPIAN SEA

⊕ Baku

AZERBAIJAN

Gorbachev in Power, 1985–1991
U.S.S.R. Dissolved, 1991

⊕ Moscow

GEORGIA ⊕ Tbilisi

ARMENIA

⊕ Yerevan

IRAQ

SAUDI ARABIA

SYRIA

JORDAN

LEBANON

ISRAEL

TURKEY

EGYPT

SWEDEN

FINLAND
Renounced
Soviet Law,
1990

● St. Petersburg

Declared
Independence,
1990

⊕ Kiev

UKRAINE

⊕ Minsk

BELARUS

MOLDOVA

⊕ Chisinau

● Odessa

Ceausescu Falls,
1989

BLACK SEA

NORWAY

NORTH SEA

DENMARK

German
Reunification,
1990

NETH.

BEL.

FR.

Declared
Independence,
1990

⊕ Tallinn

ESTONIA

⊕ Riga

LATVIA

Vilnius

LITHUANIA

BALTIC SEA

RUSSIA

Solidarity to Power,
1989

⊕ Warsaw

POLAND

CZECH. REP.

Prague

Berlin

GERMANY

SWITZ.

ITALY

Bratislava

SLOVAKIA

AUS.

Budapest

HUNGARY

Ljubljana

SLOVENIA

Zagreb

CROATIA

Yugoslavia
Breaks Up,
1991

NATO
Attacks, 1999

Belgrade

SERBIA

Sarajevo

BOSNIA-
HERZEGOVINA

MONTENEGRO

KOSOVO

ROMANIA

⊕ Bucharest

BULGARIA

⊕ Sofia

Skopje

MACEDONIA

Tirana

ALBANIA

GREECE

ADRIATIC SEA

MALTA

MEDITERRANEAN SEA

LIBYA

nerve. In December 1989, a large sign in Prague tallied the results: "Poland—10 Years / Hungary—10 Months / East Germany—10 Weeks / Czechoslovakia—10 Days / Romania—10 Hours."[9] Not expecting Eastern Europe to self-destruct "like a beheaded Hydra," Gorbachev had encouraged the process, advising East Germans to open the Wall and "avoid an explosion."[10]

The toppling of communist regimes in Eastern Europe reverberated inside the Soviet Union. During late August 1989, a million citizens of Estonia, Latvia, and Lithuania linked arms to form a human chain 400 miles long to protest the fiftieth anniversary of Stalin's annexation of the Baltic states. In March 1990, the Lithuanian Parliament declared formal independence from the Soviet Union, and Estonia's governing body renounced Soviet law. In May Latvia declared independence, and Ukraine proclaimed itself sovereign in July.

Gorbachev quickly went from confident master to bewildered victim of forces that he himself had unleashed. He won the Nobel Peace Prize (1990) but lost his country. By the end of 1991, the Soviet Union had disintegrated into fifteen competing nations. The Communist party disbanded, and the weakened central government recognized the independence of the three Baltic states. Russia declared its own independence and with many of the republics formed the Commonwealth of Independent States in December. Boris Yeltsin's Russian government took over the Kremlin, the KGB, and the Soviet Foreign Ministry. Gorbachev stepped down. On Christmas day 1991, at 7:32 P.M. (Moscow time), the red hammer-and-sickle flag atop the Kremlin fluttered downward for the last time, soon to be replaced by the red, white, and blue flag of the new Commonwealth.

The collapse of the Soviet Union ushered in the end of the Cold War, the multivalent U.S.-Soviet rivalry that had spanned the globe politically, economically, militarily, and culturally for nearly half a century. Optimistic observers predicted an age of transnational peace as communism ebbed and liberal democracy reached every shore. Gorbachev's American counterpart, President Ronald Reagan, participated in the historic transformations that brought the Cold War to a close. Yet his successors in the White House, George H. W. Bush (1989–1993) and William J. Clinton (1993–2001), faced supranational dilemmas that proved even more intractable than did the seemingly nation-based problems of old. What finally resounded in the United States during the 1990s was less a triumphant affirmation of the "end of history" than a discomfiting feeling of being caught, in the poet Matthew Arnold's words, "between two worlds, one dead, / the other powerless to be born."[11] The 1980s brought the Cold War towards its decisive finish. But the 1990s offered little in its place, as U.S. leaders vainly sought a political compass to help them navigate the bewildering post–Cold War world.

Ronald Reagan's Mission to Revive American Hegemony

President Ronald Reagan served eight years in office, and some have credited him with the momentous feat of ending the Cold War. Yet this Hollywood actor-turned-president had no foreign affairs experience before taking office in

Ronald Reagan (1911–2004).
Born in Illinois, a graduate of
Eureka College, a long-time
professional actor, and governor
of California (1967–1975),
Reagan displayed a sunny
disposition that helped return
optimism, even chauvinism, to the
national mood. As the vaunted
"Great Communicator," Reagan
proved adept at "using every
communcations medium save
Morse Code and smoke signals,"
according to one journalist.
Although opponents called him
"an amiable dunce" and "George
Wallace sprinkled with eau de
cologne," his wife Nancy remarked:
"He is more complex than
people think." (Ronald Reagan
Presidential Library)

1981. He preferred movies and television to reading books, riding horses to round-table discussions, and he often revealed ignorance of fundamental information, as when he marveled following his first South American trip: "They're all individual countries."[12] Reagan was prone to exaggeration, factual inaccuracy, and right-wing sloganeering. He acted more on instinct than on patient reasoning. His staff, fearing ill-thought utterances, managed his public performances. Surrounded by specialists who tapped his natural talent, Reagan proved an effective communicator. "Being a good actor pays off," he once told students at China's Fudan University.[13]

Reagan became a very popular president, winning a landslide reelection in 1984 against former Vice President Walter Mondale. Even when Reagan suffered setbacks, Americans applauded his speak-from-the-heart manner, his self-deprecating humor (especially about his age), and his dogged ideological consistency. Reagan made decisions like "a Turkish pasha," an aide recalled, "passively letting his subjects serve him, selecting only those morsels of public policy that were especially tasty."[14] "He treats us all the same," said Reagan's chief of staff James A. Baker III—"as hired help."[15]

Several beliefs guided the Reagan administration. First, the devil theory: A malevolent Soviet Union ignited civil wars, promoted terrorism, built an "evil empire," and sponsored "all the unrest that is going on in the world."[16] Such rhetoric overlooked the many successful Soviet-American agreements of the recent past. It also exposed the United States to accusations of a double standard, given Washington's own sponsorship of propaganda and covert skullduggery. Reagan officials thought in terms of bipolarity, global containment, and confrontation. "My idea of American policy toward the Soviet Union is simple," Reagan said. "We win and they lose. What do you think of that?"[17] There was one exception. The United States lifted the grain embargo so that U.S. farmers could sell billions of dollars of wheat and corn to the Soviet Union.

A second guiding principle was defense preparedness. Believing the Soviets had achieved "a definite margin" of military superiority, Reagan vowed to surpass them by advancing "peace through strength," a "forward strategy of freedom."[18] "Defense is not a budget item," he told the Pentagon. "Spend what you need."[19] They did— and more. Running up huge federal deficits, Reagan launched the largest peacetime arms buildup in American history, spending $2 trillion. "The objective," as one official put it, "was to find weak points in the Soviet structure, to aggregate the weaknesses, and to undermine the system."[20] Reagan pushed the B-1 bomber, ordered stockpiling of the neutron bomb, resumed production of poison gas for chemical warfare, expanded the navy, beefed up counterinsurgency units, and advanced the Trident-II submarine, MX, cruise missile, Stealth bomber, and mobile Midgetman missile programs. Military appropriations increased by 50 percent, growing from $143.9 billion in 1980 to $294.7 billion in 1985. That year the Pentagon spent $28 million an hour, twenty-four hours a day, seven days a week.

A belief in capitalist supremacy impelled decision making. Reagan and his advisers believed that nations must embrace capitalism and privatize managed economies. American leaders frequently lectured Third World nations on the "magic of the marketplace."[21] The United States accordingly cast the only "no" vote against a UN resolution to restrict baby formula sales in developing nations, where companies had marketed the product so aggressively that mothers were foregoing healthy breast-feeding in favor of the artificial liquid, which they mixed with polluted water.

A missionary impulse reinforced military and economic convictions. Reagan envisioned the United States as a "shining city on a hill," a model for other nations to emulate.[22] He quoted Tom Paine and Thomas Jefferson: "We have it in our power to begin the world over again" and "to spread the sacred fire of liberty" everywhere.[23] This reformist zeal found expression through such institutions as the National Endowment for Democracy (founded in 1983), which used federal and private funds to promote free enterprise and democratic politics abroad. The endowment gave millions of dollars to overseas political parties, labor unions, and publishers, many with an anti-leftist bias.

Political expediency lay behind lofty democratic idealism. Citing the failure of the Carter administration to support friendly dictators in Iran and Nicaragua, Reaganites accepted Ambassador to the United Nations Jeane Kirkpatrick's distinction between "authoritarian" and "totalitarian" regimes.[24] Authoritarian governments in countries such as the Philippines, Chile, South Korea, and South Africa, though antidemocratic, sustained capitalist economies and would eventually implement U.S. suggestions for reform. Communist totalitarian regimes imposed managed economies and presumably resisted change. Given such thinking, Reagan officials downgraded human-rights tests for friendly authoritarian governments.

Emotional patriotism enabled U.S. initiatives. Reagan believed it essential to gain public support for a more militarized, interventionist foreign policy. He implored the American people to abandon their post-Vietnam "self-doubt" in favor of a "national reawakening."[25] Whipping up latent triumphalism, Reagan reassured Americans that "we've closed the door on a long, dark period of failure."[26]

These six premises together formed the basis for the Reagan Doctrine. The president in 1985 pledged support for anticommunist "freedom fighters" who battled the Soviets or Soviet-backed governments.[27] The CIA, with congressional approval, funneled aid to insurgents in Afghanistan, Nicaragua, Angola, Cambodia, and Ethiopia. An heir to "rollback" arguments of the 1950s, the Reagan doctrine made overt what had been covert: the attempted overthrow of governments deemed threatening to U.S. interests. The policy emphasized "low-intensity" military action through allies, proxies, and paramilitary assets so that fewer American soldiers would fight and die in foreign lands as elite forces organized others to do the dirty work of shadow wars.

In pursuit of a U.S.- and capitalist-friendly international order, Reagan named the volatile General Alexander M. Haig, Jr., secretary of state, followed in June 1982 by George P. Shultz. An economist and business executive, Shultz often clashed with Secretary of Defense Caspar W. ("Cap") Weinberger, especially after Weinberger announced in 1984 that the United States should only use military force with long-term public support, for "clearly defined political and military objectives," and with "the clear intention of winning."[28] Though Weinberger hung a sign in his office quoting Churchill—"Never give in, never give in, never, never, never, never"—Shultz chastised Weinberger as a big spender who refused to put newly augmented U.S. forces in the field.[29] Shultz also battled hawkish CIA director William J. Casey, who once barked: "The business of Congress is to stay out of my business."[30]

Makers of American Foreign Relations, 1981–2001

Presidents	Secretaries of State
Ronald Reagan, 1981–1989	Alexander M. Haig, Jr., 1981–1982
	George P. Shultz, 1982–1989
George H. W. Bush, 1989–1993	James A. Baker III, 1989–1992
	Lawrence Eagleburger, 1992–1993
William J. Clinton, 1993–2001	Warren M. Christopher, 1993–1997
	Madeleine K. Albright, 1997–2001

Richard V. Allen, a business consultant, served as Reagan's assistant for national security affairs through 1982, when he departed under a cloud of scandal. The office of National Security Adviser remained unstable. Under William Clark, Reagan's political crony from California, NSC staffwork became so cumbersome that Shultz thought it "worse than a university."[31] Then came Robert C. McFarlane, a former marine who never argued against misguided policies because "if I'd done that, Bill Casey, Jeane Kirkpatrick, and Cap Weinberger would have said I was some kind of commie."[32] John M. Poindexter, an active-duty admiral with a Ph.D. in nuclear physics, succeeded McFarlane, but resigned in late 1986 amidst the Iran-Contra affair.

That debacle erupted because, despite strong opposition from Weinberger and Shultz, and despite explicit congressional legislation banning military trade with Iran and prohibiting U.S. aid to the Nicaraguan *contras*, national security operatives in 1985–1986 secretly traded weapons to Iran in order to press the release of U.S. hostages held in Lebanon, then used arms sale proceeds to fund the Nicaraguan rebels. To ensure secrecy, McFarlane, Poindexter, and Marine Lieutenant Colonel Oliver North ran both schemes almost completely outside the purview of the Defense and State Departments. Poindexter claimed not to have told Reagan about the arms sale diversions because he wanted the president "to have some deniability so that he would be protected."[33] "We did not—repeat did not—trade weapons or anything else for hostages, nor will we," Reagan announced on television soon after the scandal broke in November 1986.[34] But "Reagan's know-nothing case was a tough sell," a biographer writes.[35] The record shows that at top-level meetings on Iran-Contra, President Reagan made the basic decisions, without monitoring every operational detail. In March 1987, Reagan acknowledged publicly that he mistakenly "told the American people I did not trade arms for hostages. My heart and my best intentions still tell me that's true, but the facts and the evidence tell me it's not."[36]

Reagan's appointment of Frank C. Carlucci, a seasoned diplomat, and then General Colin Powell as his next NSC advisers did not quiet the crisis that besmirched the presidency. In 1989 North was found guilty of three felonies, and in early 1990 Poindexter was convicted of five felony charges, including lying to Congress. A federal appeals court overturned both convictions because Congress had granted

" WHAT DO I KNOW...AND WHEN WILL I KNOW IT?"

Reagan in Doubt. When the crisis over the arms sale to Iran and aid to the *contras* erupted in 1986–1987, Reagan could not remember the details of his decisions. Diagnosis of Alzheimer's disease in 1994 raised the question of whether Reagan had suffered any mental impairment during his presidency. Because doctors had apparently not tested him for Alzheimer's disease while president, it seemed impossible to judge whether Reagan's mental lapses were the result of dementia or simply the normal failings of an elderly president who remembered only the details that interested him. (Bill Schoor © 1987 United Featires Sundicate, Inc.)

immunity to the two men for testimony given to congressional committees. All told, some 190 Reagan officials were indicted or convicted of illegal activities, though only Thomas Cline, a former CIA officer found guilty of tax fraud, served jail time due to the Iran-Contra scandal. Reagan's successor, President George Herbert Walker Bush, pardoned the highest ranking figures complicit in the affair, including Weinberger, former National Security Advisor Robert McFarlane (who botched a suicide attempt during the investigation), State Department official Elliott Abrams, and three CIA officers complicit in the cover-up. The "common denominator of their motivation—whether their actions were right or wrong—was patriotism," Bush rationalized.[37] Bush's son, President George W. Bush (2001–2009), awarded administrative positions to Poindexter and to such implicated individuals as Abrams, Otto Reich, John Negroponte, and Richard Armitage, many of whom helped plan an invasion and occupation of Iraq "on the basis of arguments it knew to be false." Just as the philosopher George Santayana predicted, a critic wrote, "by ignoring history, Americans had condemned themselves to repeat it."[38]

Soviet-American Crises and the Antinuclear Movement

Though frequently and vigorously professing aversion to nuclear war, Reagan assumed that the Soviet Union outdistanced the United States in atomic weapons. The United States had to close the "window of vulnerability"—the theoretical

George Shultz (b. 1920).
A graduate of Princeton University and the Massachusetts Institute of Technology (Ph.D., 1949), Shultz served as secretary of labor, director of the Office of Management and Budget, and secretary of the treasury in the Nixon administration. In 1982 he joined the Reagan cabinet as secretary of state. One pundit said Shultz had "the charisma of a drowsy clam." (Department of State)

susceptibility of American land-based ICBMs to a Soviet first strike—by enlarging the American nuclear arsenal.[39] While the Soviets outranked the United States in ICBMs and SLBMs, they lagged in strategic bombers and nuclear warheads. At least two-thirds of Soviet nuclear arms consisted of easy targets: ICBMs in fixed silos. And Reagan failed to count on the American side the defense spending of NATO allies. In 1983 the president's own Commission on Strategic Forces reported that no window existed—that America's triad of air-, sea-, and land-based nuclear weapons provided sufficient deterrence.

Statements by Reagan officials about winning a nuclear war spurred transatlantic debate. The evangelist Billy Graham, the World Council of Churches, and the Union of Concerned Scientists urged restraint in the nuclear arms race. The American Medical Association declared that "there is no adequate medical response to a nuclear holocaust."[40] "Cease this madness," urged the veteran Kremlinologist George F. Kennan, who recommended an immediate 50 percent cut in nuclear arsenals on both sides, the denuclearization of much of Europe, and a complete ban on nuclear weapons testing and development.[41] The House of Representatives in 1983 passed a freeze resolution. Proponents argued that America's infrared satellites could verify a halt on the testing and deployment of ballistic missiles, rendering further arms proliferation unnecessary. "I would agree to a freeze if only we could freeze the Soviets' global desires," the president retorted.[42]

Still, calls for a halt to the nuclear arms race kept coming. Jonathan Schell's best-selling *Fate of the Earth* (1982) graphically depicted a hydrogen bomb attack on New York City. Celebrities Bruce Springsteen, Jackson Browne, Meryl Streep, Martin Sheen, and others lent their voices to the freeze movement, and in fall 1982, some 750,000 protesters crowded into Central Park, the largest antinuclear demonstration in U.S. history. In May 1983, the Roman Catholic Bishops of the United States issued a pastoral letter that called "the arms race one of the greatest curses on the human race."[43] Feminists ridiculed the sexual nature of the discourse on nuclear strategy wherein "white men in ties" talked about "missile size,… vertical erector launchers, thrust-to-weight ratios, soft lay downs, [and] deep penetrations."[44] And in November 1983, ABC television dramatized *The Day After*, a world where bewildered survivors of a nuclear war wandered amidst debris, dust, and smoke from mass fires that blocked the sun's rays and killed plant and animal life. "The d—n media has propagandized our people against our defense plans more than the Russians have," the president complained, though the film itself "left me greatly depressed."[45]

Antinuclear opposition also surfaced in Europe. Soon after taking office, Reagan mentioned the possibility of a limited nuclear war in Europe that spared the two great powers. He stated incorrectly that cruise missiles were defensive weapons—in fact, they were designed to strike deep inside the USSR—and that SLBMs could be recalled after firing. In 1981 huge crowds in Bonn, London, Rome, and Amsterdam called for a ban on the installation of Pershing and cruise missiles. Reflecting heightened emotions, West German novelist Günter Grass compared the Pershings' deployment with Nazi plans for the Final Solution. Activists demanded that both Washington and Moscow sit down to talk.

To satisfy Western European leaders who welcomed U.S. missiles but wanted less domestic protest, and to quiet the transnational antinuclear movement, Reagan reluctantly agreed to discussions in Geneva on intermediate-range nuclear forces (INF) in Europe. For these negotiations, which opened in November 1981, Washington proposed to stop planned deployment of the new Pershing and cruise missiles in NATO nations if Moscow would dismantle its SS-20, SS-4, and SS-5 missiles pointed at Western Europe. The Soviets initially rejected this "zero option," because it excluded British and French nuclear forces and U.S. weapons on submarines and aircraft. Moscow deployed more triple-warhead SS-20s, whereupon in 1983 Pershing-IIs were deployed first to Great Britain and then to West Germany. In November 1983, to express their displeasure over these new missiles, the Soviets suspended the INF talks. Meetings did not resume until early 1985, only to falter again. Negotiations on strategic nuclear weapons did not fare much better. Reagan replaced SALT with START—Strategic Arms Reduction Talks. Discussions began in Geneva in 1982, but because the American plan sought drastic reductions in those very weapons that constituted the bulk of Soviet deterrent power, negotiations stalled.

Then came President Reagan's announcement in March 1983 of the Strategic Defense Initiative (SDI). Soon dubbed "Star Wars," SDI envisioned an antiballistic missile defense system above the atmosphere—a laser or particle beam shield that could intercept Soviet ballistic missiles and destroy them in space. Even if such a device could incapacitate most incoming weapons, skeptical scientists noted, "the remaining 5 or 10 percent would be enough to totally destroy civilization."[46] Others

"Star Wars" in 1984. President Reagan made a passionate case for the Strategic Defense Initiative to prevent a "madman" with missiles from blackmailing "all of us." Some scientists assured him that they could create his "dream"—an effective ballistic missile defense system. In this artist's sketch, a space-based electromagnetic ray gun destroys a nuclear-armed reentry vehicle presumably launched from the Soviet Union. SDI development still limped along in the new century, with successful tests of weapons interception technology remaining elusive as of 2009. (U.S. Army/Department of Defense, Still Media Records Center)

argued that if SDI ever did work, it would undermine deterrence itself by eliminating the danger of Soviet attack, thus freeing the United States to use nuclear weapons without fear of retaliation. Schultz privately called the Strategic Defense Initiative "lunacy."[47] The president, however, optimistically viewed it as the perfect defense, similar to the fictional "Inertia Projector" of the 1940 film *Murder in the Air*, which had starred Ronald Reagan as the buccaneering secret service agent Brass Bancroft. As SDI research advanced, with some test results actually faked to keep congressional funds flowing, START sputtered.

Further tensions spoiled the negotiating environment. After months of strikes and protests by Poland's Solidarity labor movement, the Polish military cracked down in December 1981, imposing martial law and arresting Solidarity leaders. Washington quickly suspended U.S.-Polish economic agreements, cut back Soviet-American trade, and banned Soviet airline flights to the United States. NATO countries reacted cautiously, seeking to protect their lucrative trade with the Soviet Union and Soviet clients.

On September 1, 1983, Korean Air Lines Flight 007, en route from Anchorage, Alaska, to Seoul, South Korea, strayed some 300 miles off course and crossed Soviet airspace near a strategic nuclear base. Soviet planes scrambled. When the Korean pilot did not acknowledge warning shots, a Soviet jet blasted the Boeing 747 with one missile, killing all 269 passengers aboard. Reagan deplored this "barbarous act," urging UN member states to condemn the Soviet Union and to suspend airport services to Soviet planes.[48] Soviet officials claimed that KAL 007 was on a spy mission for the United States. Moscow later revealed that the shootdown had occurred in international airspace and that Soviet authorities had crudely covered up their error. Yet Reagan's heated response so alarmed Soviet officials that NATO military exercises in November caused the Kremlin to prepare for a nuclear first strike. Informed about this nuclear "near-miss," Reagan recited to aides the biblical story of Armageddon and made his first public plea to banish nuclear weapons "from the face of the earth."[49] Ambassador Anatoly Dobrynin thought that until tempers cooled, we "can't cook porridge together."[50]

Another obstacle to an arms-control agreement was the infirmity of Soviet leadership (Reagan quipped how could he meet with Kremlin leaders when "they keep dying on me") until the arrival of Mikhail S. Gorbachev in 1985.[51] Leonid Brezhnev died in 1982; his aging successors Yuri Andropov and Konstantin Chernenko died within three years. Gorbachev became the new general secretary of the Communist party, at age fifty-four one of the Soviet Union's youngest leaders, with a personality quite "different from the wooden ventriloquism of the average Soviet apparatchik."[52] Determined to reform the sluggish Soviet economy through restructuring (*perestroika*) and to open the suffocating authoritarian political system through liberalization (*glasnost*), Gorbachev initiated stunning changes in his own nation and across the globe.

"Deeply affected" by the disastrous accident at the Chernobyl nuclear power station in 1986, the new secretary general altered the Soviet position on nuclear weapons.[53] He unilaterally stopped further deployment of intermediate-range missiles, and he halted nuclear-weapons tests. In November 1985, Gorbachev and Reagan met in Geneva. Although they could not agree on SDI or an extension of

Mikhail Gorbachev (b. 1932) and Reagan. In May 1988, at the Moscow summit meeting. Although Gorbachev occasionally bristled at Reagan's sanctimonious manner, the two leaders enjoyed a warm personal relationship. Gorbachev reportedly laughed at Reagan's oft-quoted joke about a Russian lady who got into the Kremlin and told Gorbachev: "In America, I could go into the White House and say to Reagan, 'I don't like the way you're running the country.'" In the joke, Gorbachev replied: "Why, my dear, you can do the same thing in the Soviet Union. You can come up to my office *anytime* and say, 'I don't like the way Reagan's running his country.'" (Photo by Bill Fitzpatrick, The White House, Courtesy Ronald Reagan Library)

SALT-II, they established friendly personal relations. "I bet the hardliners in both our countries are bleeding," Reagan whispered as he shook Gorbachev's hand."[54] "We have no secret plans for world domination," Gorbachev assured the president.[55] Then in early 1986, Gorbachev called for an end to all nuclear weapons by the year 2000. At another summit meeting in Reykjavík, Iceland, in October 1986, the conferees made tremendous progress by agreeing to reduce warheads, missiles, and bombers and to remove all American and Soviet intermediate missiles from Europe. When Gorbachev said that "this all depends, of course, on your giving up SDI," Reagan quickly ended the meeting.[56] "I was mad," he wrote in his diary on October 12. "He tried to act jovial but I acted mad and it showed."[57] Still, Reagan found the results "breathtaking," and the atmosphere had clearly changed for the better.[58]

The Washington summit meeting in December 1987 finally saw the signing of the Intermediate-Range Nuclear Forces (INF) Treaty, which provided for the elimination of all U.S. and Soviet INF missiles everywhere and verification of their destruction through on-site inspections. What had changed? "Gorby—(I should say Mikhail)," the president wrote, had accepted the "zero option" and given Washington "120 percent of what it wanted" in negotiations.[59] "We will leave Afghanistan," promised Foreign Minister Eduard Sheverdnadze, a welcome change from the dour Andrei Gromyko.[60] The antinuclear movement had produced strong antinuclear public opinion in Europe and America. Most obvious, the two superpowers saw the treaty as beneficial to their quite different national interests. Both faced economic troubles spawned by the long Cold War. "Our economy," one Soviet official admitted, "has been literally eviscerated by military spending."[61] The Senate approved the

INF Treaty by a 95 to 5 vote in May 1988, and the dismantling of missiles began that summer.

Gorbachev boldly advanced other initiatives. In April 1988, he signed a UN-mediated accord providing for the withdrawal of all Soviet forces from Afghanistan. They departed early the next year, acknowledging a conspicuous defeat for the Soviet military, caused in part by the Stinger antiaircraft weapons that the United States had shipped to the Afghan *mujahedeen* (literally, "stragglers"). In December 1988, the Soviet leader announced a unilateral Soviet cut of 500,000 ground troops. Moscow reduced its support for the Sandinistas in Nicaragua and negotiated for the removal of Cuban troops from Angola. The Soviets also stopped jamming Voice of America broadcasts.

Civil Wars and Interventionism: Central America and the Caribbean

Central America figured prominently in Reagan's counterrevolutionary crusade. Long in the U.S. sphere but gripped by destabilizing economic and political divisions, Central America during the 1980s experienced intensifying civil strife and anti-Yankee nationalism that threatened U.S. hegemony in the region. Reagan likened the Caribbean to a "Communist lake" wherein the United States "resembles a giant, afraid to move."[62]

The State Department claimed that Moscow used Cuba to train insurgents and promote "Cuba-model states" that posed a direct military threat to the United States.[63] Reagan declared that the Caribbean provided "our lifeline to the outside world," and that "Soviet military theorists ... want to tie down our attention and forces on our own southern border and so limit our capacity to act in more distant places such as Europe, the Persian Gulf, the Indian Ocean, the Sea of Japan."[64] U.S. officials determined to defeat leftist insurgents in El Salvador, topple the Sandinista government in Nicaragua, and draw Guatemala and Honduras into a tighter U.S. military network. Through billions of dollars in aid, CIA operations, weapons and advisers, splashy military maneuvers, and support for the anti-Sandinista *contras,* Washington plunged more deeply into Central America.

Critics charged that Reagan exaggerated the Soviet-Cuban threat, underplayed the local causes of disorder, bypassed opportunities for negotiations, and nurtured the political right and the military. In veiled reference to the United States, Colombian President Belisario Betancur warned Reagan in 1982 that "in certain parts of Central America bonfires are lit by social injustice or provoked by foreign hands that do not belong to the area."[65] Such unwelcome interventionism possibly invited what Washington wanted most to prevent: countervailing Soviet influence in the area. Senator Christopher Dodd (Democrat of Connecticut) agreed that "if Central America were not racked with poverty, there would be no revolution."[66]

In El Salvador, the Reagan administration nonetheless found an apparent textbook "case of armed aggression against a small country by Communist powers acting through Cuba."[67] This impoverished nation suffered high infant mortality, illiteracy, and endemic violence. The army and the landed class had long ruled the nation. Two percent of the people owned half the land. In October 1979, however, reform-minded colonels seized power and organized a new government under José Napoleón Duarte, a Christian Democratic party leader. El Salvador's displaced political elite responded by organizing death squads to assassinate moderates and radicals alike. Leftists countered by forming the *Farabundo Martí Front for National Liberation* (FMLN). In 1980 Salvadoran national guard troops raped and killed four American nuns, but the Salvadoran government, cowed by right-wing violence, refused to prosecute the officers who ordered the murders. First Carter, then Reagan, extended economic and military aid to the Duarte government. Ambassador Jeane Kirkpatrick excused the slayings: "The nuns were not just nuns," she claimed, but "political activists for the FMLN."[68]

Reagan dramatically increased economic and military aid to El Salvador. Congress complied while demanding that the administration certify human-rights progress in the country. Every six months officials dutifully issued optimistic but disingenuous statements. "Everybody *knew*, Congress *knew*, what they [Salvadoran military forces] were doing," a U.S. embassy official recalled. "What's improvement, any

"Communism." Critics of Reagan's interventionism in Central America believed that the president misread the sources of instability in the region. (Dennis Renault, *Sacramento Bee*)

way? You kill eight hundred and it goes down to two hundred, that's improvement."[69] The UN Truth Commission reported in 1993 that 85 percent of the 75,000 people killed in the Salvadoran civil war died at the hands of government forces and gun-for-hire death squads. With U.S. military advisers training some of the units responsible for murdering civilians, American diplomats did not exert high-level pressure for change on Salvadoran military leaders. "El Salvador is Spanish for Vietnam," a popular bumper sticker read. Despite spending $4.5 billion in El Salvador during the 1980s, victory in the bloody civil war still eluded Reagan when he left office. Only after four more years of killing on both sides did the combatants finally negotiate a United Nations–sponsored peace in January 1992.

The Reagan administration blamed much of the Salvadoran trouble on Cuba and Nicaragua, which sent small supplies of arms to the insurgents. The Sandinistas invited thousands of Cuban medical specialists and teachers into their poor country, used Cuban advisers and Soviet weapons to build a strong military, and limited free speech as they moved to a one-party government. As the United States had long treated Cuba, so it treated Nicaragua during the 1980s: putting pressure on the nationalistic government of a small country to the point where it faced a choice between capitulation or seeking outside help for defense. Reagan first cut off all foreign aid. In November 1981, he ordered the CIA to train and arm the anti-Sandinista *contras*. "Let's make the bastards sweat," CIA director William Casey told his covert operatives.[70] A mercenary army of 15,000, including former supporters of Somoza, the *contras* were "a mixed bag," admitted General Colin Powell. "We worked with what we had."[71] Reagan hailed them as the "moral equivalent of the Founding Fathers."[72] From bases in Honduras and Costa Rica the *contras* raided Nicaragua, sabotaging bridges, oil facilities, and crops, and using CIA "coercive techniques" (including "direct physical brutality") against civilians.[73]

Although in 1982, Congress had prohibited the use of funds to overthrow the Nicaraguan government, Reagan officials winked at the restriction. In early 1984, Congress discovered that the CIA had worked with *contra* commandos to mine three Nicaraguan ports. "This is no way to run a railroad," Senator Barry Goldwater ranted in a note to Casey. "I am pissed."[74] When Nicaragua went to the World Court to charge a breach of international law, Washington refused to recognize the court's jurisdiction. (In June 1986, the court decided that the United States had violated international law by funding the *contras* and ordered Washington to pay an indemnity to Nicaragua; Reagan ignored the ruling.) In mid-1984, Congress banned aid to the *contras*.

The congressional prohibition did not stop aid to the *contras*. Following Reagan's explicit instructions "to do whatever you have to do to help these people keep body and soul together," CIA, Pentagon, and NSC officials rerouted money from defense appropriations and solicited funds from foreign countries and private donors to supply the rebels.[75] In 1985–1986 Colonel North of Reagan's NSC shifted to the *contras* profits from secret arms sales to Iran by using Israeli intermediaries and a Swiss bank account. North also coordinated a network of planes and ships and funded the building of a large airstrip in Costa Rica—all without informing Congress. "I don't think it was wrong," North later said. "I think it was a neat idea."[76] An independent federal prosecutor concluded that President Reagan "created the conditions which made possible the crimes committed by others" and "knowingly participated" in the illegal aid effort.[77] Defeating "Communism in Central America" took precedence over "obeying the law," so Reagan officials "lied about what they were doing—publicly, privately, repeatedly, egregiously."[78] "Here we are again," rued Republican Mark O. Hatfield of Oregon, "old men creating a monster for young men to destroy."[79]

In early 1985, Reagan admitted publicly what he had long denied: Washington sought to topple the Sandinista government. In May he imposed an economic embargo and blocked loans to Nicaragua from the World Bank and the Inter-American Development Bank. Congress appropriated $27 million for "humanitarian" aid to the *contras*. Still, the war did not go well. The insurgents feuded among themselves, generated little popular support, and could not seize and hold towns. But they forced the Sandinistas to shift funds from social programs to defense and to restrict civil liberties, slowing the revolution and rousing internal dissent.

Meanwhile, Nicaraguan-American talks in Mexico produced no agreement. Reagan officials treated negotiations as "nothing more than a necessary smoke-screen to quiet opposition to the paramilitary program."[80] Washington snubbed the Contadora group (Mexico, Venezuela, Panama, and Colombia), which in 1983 had persuaded the five Central American states to limit foreign advisers, reduce arms, and promote democracy. Reagan officials also stiff-armed the 1987 peace plan by Costa Rican president Oscar Arias Sánchez but had to negotiate when the *contras* agreed to a cease-fire in March 1988. Now hobbled by the public scandal, Reagan resisted appeals for more aid to the *contras*. When Reagan left office, the Sandinistas still governed. Under arrangements brokered by the Central American presidents, the Washington-backed candidate Violetta Barrios de Chamorro soundly defeated Sandinista President Daniel Ortega Saavedra in elections finally held in 1990. (Ortega later staged a comeback, winning the presidency in 2006.) After nearly a decade of civil war, 30,000 Nicaraguans had died and the ravaged economy had sunk to the second poorest in the hemisphere.

Secretary of State Haig blamed Cuba for "exporting revolution and bloodshed" to El Salvador and Nicaragua.[81] "I'll make that island a fucking parking lot," he thundered.[82] Reagan banned tourist and business visits to Cuba, denied Cuban officials visas for travel in the United States, and restricted importation of Cuban newspapers and magazines. Cuba actually endorsed the Contadora process and urged negotiations in order to forestall U.S. intervention. In December 1984, Washington did agree to return to Cuba about 2,700 criminals who had come by boat in the 1980 Mariel exodus, and Castro promised to let Cubans reunite with families in the United States. But when the United States, in mid-1985, started up Radio Martí to act as "an electronic Bay of Pigs" beaming propaganda into Cuba, Castro angrily abrogated the accord.[83]

On October 25, 1983, U.S. troops invaded the tiny Caribbean island of Grenada, with its population of 85,000 and GDP of less than $100 million, hoping to send "shivers up Castro's spine about whether or not they [the Cubans] might be next."[84] The administration justified the invasion as the rescue of 1,000 Americans, many of them medical students. Some 6,000 Americans went ashore to oust a Marxist regime that Reagan termed "a Soviet-Cuban colony."[85] More than 100 people died, including about 25 Cubans helping to build an airstrip that Reagan claimed would serve the Cuban and Soviet militaries but that British engineers said merely boosted Grenada's tourist trade. "We're mopping up," Reagan wrote in his diary. "Success seems to shine on us & I thank the Lord for it."[86] By mid-December, having deported surviving Cubans from the island and closed the Soviet Embassy, U.S. forces evacuated Grenada. The mission had cost $75.5 million. World opinion disapproved—even Reagan's staunchest Cold War ally, British Prime Minister Margaret Thatcher, thought the American response "exaggerated"—but North Americans celebrated victory only days after a bomb killed 241 U.S. soldiers in Lebanon.[87] The operation, one scholar writes, "signaled a new era" in post-Vietnam U.S. foreign policy, "one where the use of overwhelming force was back on the table."[88]

Hornets' Nests in the Middle East, Africa, and Asia

The Reagan administration failed to sustain Carter's momentum towards peace in the Middle East. Reagan did seek to gain some sort of homeland for the Palestinians and to guarantee Israel's security through a new Arab-Israeli accord. But Lebanon descended into brutal civil war and suffered a punishing Israeli invasion and Syrian occupation. The Iran-Iraq War disrupted oil shipments, Libya and the United States skirmished, Israel and the United States bickered, and terrorists victimized the innocent, including many Americans. Saudi Arabia and Jordan refused to relax tensions with Israel yet kept placing large orders for U.S. arms. In 1981 Reagan approved the sale to Saudi Arabia of high-tech military equipment valued at $8.5 billion. Reaganites assumed that the Soviet Union coveted the region. "If Israel was not there, the United States would have to be there," Reagan stated in the run-up to the 1980 election.[89] But Israel considered the PLO and Arab nationalism the greater threats, and Arab leaders designated Israel, not Moscow, as enemy number one.

In late 1981, in open defiance of the U.S. position, Israel suddenly announced its annexation of the Golan Heights, a disputed territory previously under Syrian control that bordered Israel, Lebanon, and Jordan. After Reagan suspended an Israeli-American military agreement and Americans protested Israeli bombing raids of PLO camps in Lebanon, Israeli Prime Minister Menachem Begin barked: "You don't have a right, from a moral perspective, to preach to us."[90] Then came Egyptian President Anwar Sadat's assassination in October 1981 at the hands of extremists opposed to the Camp David Accords, followed by Israel's invasion of Lebanon the following year.

Lebanon had long been caught in the middle of Israeli-Palestinian tensions. For decades, displaced Palestinians had moved into the country, and in 1970–1971 PLO fighters driven from Jordan had joined them. When civil war erupted in the mid-1970s, Lebanon invited Syria, which also backed the PLO, to restore order. Syrian troops arrived and stayed. From bases in Lebanon the PLO harassed and murdered Israelis. Israel invaded Lebanon in June 1982 and captured Beirut, helping to destroy much of the capital city. Reagan telephoned Begin: "Menachem, this is a holocaust." "Mr. President," Begin countered, "I think I know what a holocaust is."[91] The bombing nonetheless stopped. U.S. officials arranged the withdrawal of both PLO and Israeli forces from Beirut and created a peacekeeping force that included U.S. marines. Israel's foes soon targeted Americans. In April 1983, bombs hit the U.S. Embassy in Beirut, killing 63 people. Then, in October, a terrorist drove a truck loaded with explosives into a building full of sleeping American troops, killing 241. Although the conflict was rooted in post–World War II tensions arising from Israel's creation, Weinberger's aide, General Colin Powell, thought the United States had "stuck its hand into a thousand-year-old hornet's nest."[92] In February 1984, with public criticism rising, Reagan withdrew the marines.

After 533 days and scores of deaths, U.S. troops could not quell Lebanon's multifaceted war. Critics chastised the administration for acquiescing in Israel's use of U.S. weapons in violation of contractual restrictions. When the veteran diplomat George Ball claimed that Israel's "rampaging Army" had "devastated" Lebanon, Cold War hawks accused him of anti-Semitism.[93] In 1985 Israel received the largest U.S. foreign-aid package of any nation—$3 billion.

Israeli-American relations soured again after the Palestinian uprising (in Arabic, the *intifada*) began in December 1987 in the West Bank and Gaza, which respectively bordered on the Dead and Mediterranean Seas. The Israelis had been ruling the 1.5 million inhabitants of these regions since 1967, when it seized the territories from Jordan and Egypt. Like other Palestinians in the Middle East (some 5 million), the PLO-backed participants in the *intifada* wanted a homeland.

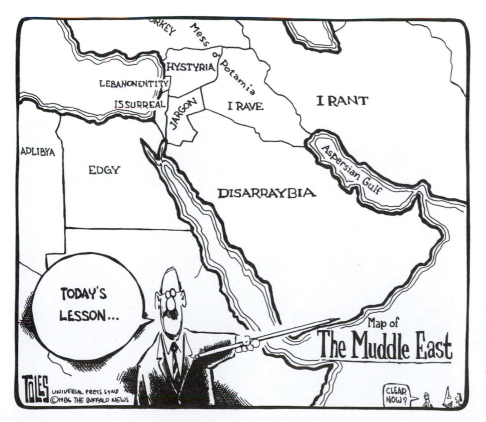

The Middle East. To many Americans, including the cartoonist Toles, the turbulent Middle East seemed a strange, even irrational region. (TOLES © 1986 The Washington Post. Reprinted with permission of UNIVERSAL PRESS SYNDICATE. All rights reserved.)

As youthful demonstrators were shot down by Israeli troops, Shultz urged an international conference to work out a "land for peace" solution. Both Israel and the PLO adamantly rejected the idea. Jordan instead relinquished the West Bank to the PLO, which declared an independent Palestinian state and endorsed UN Resolution 242. When PLO leader Yasir Arafat asked to speak before the General Assembly, Shultz denied him a visa. UN members thereupon voted to hear Arafat in Geneva, Switzerland, where the PLO leader recognized Israel's right "to exist in peace and security" and renounced "all forms of terrorism."[94] Accepting Arafat's pledge, U.S. diplomats in December 1988 opened talks in Tunisia with the PLO for the first time. Israel denounced the negotiations.

Reagan had declared in his first inaugural that "terrorism" would replace Carter's focus on "human rights" as the principal concern of foreign policy.[95] In 1985 alone, more than 800 terrorist incidents in the world claimed some 900 lives, 23 of them Americans. Mideast terrorists drew the greatest attention. Passengers on American commercial jets became hijack and murder victims, and U.S. citizens were taken hostage. In one case in 1985, U.S. warplanes forced to the ground an Egyptian airliner known to be carrying four Palestinians who had earlier seized the Italian cruise ship *Achille Lauro* and murdered a wheelchair-bound American. "You can run but you can't hide," warned Reagan.[96]

The Reagan administration blamed the Libyan ruler Moammar Gadhafi for much of the terrorism because Gadhafi strongly supported the PLO and backed liberation movements worldwide that used terrorist tactics. The United States severed relations with Libya in early 1981. The following year Washington imposed an embargo on Libyan oil imports, and in early 1986 Reagan banned trade altogether. After a series of terrorist attacks at busy European airports, the United States sent warships into the Gulf of Sidra. When a makeshift bomb killed a GI in a West

Shaking Hands with Saddam Hussein. Iraqi President Saddam Hussein (1937–2006) greets Donald Rumsfeld (b. 1932), then special envoy of President Ronald Reagan, in Baghdad on December 20, 1983. The Reagan administration extended aid to Iraq in its war with Iran, even though Saddam Hussein was a known dictator who abused human rights. As secretary of defense twenty years later, Rumsfeld directed more bellicose policies toward Saddam Hussein and Iraq. (CNN TV photo from National Security Archive, © Getty Images)

Berlin disco in April, U.S. intelligence established a Libyan connection. Hoping, in Casey's words, to "get lucky" and kill him, American fighter-bombers demolished Gadhafi's Soviet-built air force and bombed his official residence, killing dozens, including Gadhafi's adopted baby daughter.[97] That same year audiences cheered Hollywood heartthrob Tom Cruise as he went from "hot dog" to *Top Gun* (1986) in celluloid dogfights against Libyan MiGs.[98]

Reagan also tilted toward Iraq in the Iran-Iraq War, a bloody eight-year cross-border conflict. Iraq had begun the war in 1980 to seize Iranian oil lands and topple the Khomeini regime, which had incited Shiite Muslims in Iraq to rebel. Washington quietly supplied Iraq with military intelligence, a half-billion dollars in credits, and dual-use technology, even though "we knew" that Saddam Hussein "was an S.O.B."[99] In May 1987, two sea-skimming missiles fired by an Iraqi aircraft hit the U.S. frigate *Stark,* killing 37 crewmen. Iraq apologized. Reagan beefed up the U.S. naval presence in the Persian Gulf and reflagged Kuwaiti oil tankers as American vessels. The next year, in July, the crew of the U.S.S. *Vincennes,* thinking itself under attack, shot down a civilian Iranian airliner, killing all 290 aboard. Washington admitted error while covering up the fact that the *Vincennes* was inside Iranian territorial waters at the time of the shootdown. Simultaneous with these pro-Iraq endeavors, the United States secretly sold the Iranian government weapons to secure its cooperation in gaining the release of American hostages in Lebanon (see pp. 428–429). "Among other things," a scholar writes, "the Reagan administration found itself exposed as having worked with the country with which it was at war. Convoluted, indeed."[100] Not until August 1988 did Iran and Iraq agree to end a conflict that had killed hundreds of thousands.

In Africa, too, Reagan confronted knotty, protracted problems: death-dealing famine in Ethiopia and Sudan; civil wars in Ethiopia and Angola, where Soviet and Cuban troops assisted ruling regimes and covert CIA aid helped insurgents; the unresolved status of South Africa–dominated Namibia; and the dehumanizing policy of apartheid in South Africa. Toward white-ruled South Africa Reagan at first launched "constructive engagement"—official disapproval of apartheid without economic sanctions.[101] The policy amounted to a "kid-glove" approach, said critics.[102] Nonetheless, when Pretoria rejected serious reform, black South Africans marched, protested, and died, demanding that people around the world take sides. As violence spread across South Africa, Reagan worried that Moscow might exploit the turmoil. Protest in the United States, led by the Free South Africa Movement, a broad-based coalition, forced the issue onto the American political agenda. Claiming that "sanctions may hurt, but apartheid kills," members of Congress joined with church, labor, and intellectual leaders to picket the South African embassy in Washington, D.C.[103] The Nobel Prize–winning South African bishop Desmond M. Tutu toured the United States, condemning constructive engagement as "immoral" and calling the United States "an accessory before and after the fact of apartheid."[104] Cities and states passed divestiture laws requiring the sale of stock they owned in U.S. companies operating in South Africa. Such black entertainers as Ray Charles, the O'Jays, the Temptations, Roberta Flack, and Stephanie Mills also pressed U.S. corporations to divest from South Africa. Some companies pulled out; by 1986, U.S. investments had dropped to $1.3 billion from $2 billion in 1981. To head off congressional action,

Reagan, in September 1985, added new sanctions on nuclear and computer sales to the earlier (1962) embargo on arms transactions with South Africa. But in October 1986, with an unusual bipartisan consensus and over Reagan's veto, Congress passed even stiffer sanctions, including a ban on new American investments in and oil exports to South Africa and on imports of certain South African products.

Good news did come from Namibia. South Africa had governed this former German colony since World War I, defying the United Nations when it revoked Pretoria's mandate in 1966 and demanded independence. Since the early 1970s, the radical South West African People's Organization (SWAPO), with Cuban and Soviet support, had battled South African armies from bases in Angola and Zambia. After twelve years of sporadic negotiations, Angola, Cuba, and South Africa in December 1988 signed a U.S.-mediated agreement for a Cuban troop withdrawal from Angola and black majority rule in Namibia. Formal independence came in March 1990.

Trouble persisted in Asia, however, where Ferdinand Marcos's Philippines became a nettlesome ally. Elected president in 1965, Marcos had created a dictatorship marked by corruption, martial law, and personal enrichment. By the early 1980s, his country groaned under a foreign debt of more than $20 billion, high unemployment, and economic stagnation. He jailed, tortured, and murdered critics. Business, Roman Catholic, civil libertarian, and professional leaders demanded reform. The accelerating discontent with Marcos came to a head in August 1983, after assassins gunned down the anti-Marcos leader Benigno S. Aquino. The evidence pointed to a successful military conspiracy.

American investments of $2 billion, trade sales of similar value, and outstanding debts owed to American banks seemed in jeopardy. So, too, did two major U.S. bases: Subic Bay Naval Station and Clark Air Base. The Reagan administration distanced itself from Marcos and pressed for reforms. When Marcos stole an election from Benigno Aquino's widow, Corazon Aquino, turmoil tore across the Philippines. Besieged by his own people and abandoned by Washington, which decided the "time has come" to "divorce" its erstwhile ally, Marcos on February 25, 1986, went into exile in Hawai'i.[105] U.S. aid soon flowed to the Aquino government.

An altogether different kind of issue agitated Japanese-American relations: a huge trade deficit as Tokyo emerged as a major economic competitor. "We send Japan low-value soybeans, wheat, coal and cotton," one business leader complained. "They send us high-value autos, motorcycles, TV sets, and oil-well casings. It's 1776 and we're a colony again."[106] In 1985 the total U.S. trade deficit (more imports than exports) mounted to an all-time high of $148.5 billion—$50 billion of it with Japan. The overall deficit derived in large part from the strong dollar abroad (making American goods expensive in other countries) and the indebtedness of Third World nations, which forced them to buy fewer U.S. products. Japan's tariff barriers, cartels, and government subsidies also made it difficult for American goods to penetrate Japanese markets. Protectionists demanded retaliatory tariffs on Japanese goods so that ailing American industry could better meet import competition and American workers could hold their jobs. In 1985 Japan voluntarily set quotas on automobile and carbon-steel shipments to the United States and promised trade liberalization at home, but Washington wanted more. The 1988 Omnibus Trade and Competitiveness Act implicitly targeted Japan in authorizing U.S. retaliation against nations that refused to negotiate reductions in trade barriers. As the Reagan era came to a close, Japan's foreign minister characterized the Japanese-American trade relationship as "at its worst since the war."[107]

Indispensable Nation: Bush, Clinton, and the Post–Cold War World

Reagan claimed foreign-policy successes, especially in the twilight of his presidency: Namibia, the INF Treaty, the departure of dictators in Haiti (Jean-Claude Duvalier) and the Philippines (Ferdinand Marcos), termination of the Iran-Iraq War, talks with the PLO, and Cuban withdrawal from Angola. At the end, Reagan seemed less ideological, more adaptable, while improved relations with the Soviet Union suggested that the Cold War was winding down. But Reagan also bequeathed to his successors, Republican President George H. W. Bush (1989–1993) and Democratic President William Jefferson Clinton (1993–2001), several unresolved international issues, including major environmental problems neglected throughout Reagan's presidency. Soil erosion, reduced food production, population growth, toxic waste, acid rain, clean water shortages, forest depletion, and environmental warming due to the "greenhouse effect" of carbon dioxide and other gases building up in the atmosphere—all augured competition for scarce resources that spawned political unrest. So, too, the Iran-Contra scandal, the fiasco in Lebanon, enduring Israeli-Palestinian strife, continued civil war in Latin America, and yawning trade and budget deficits belied Reagan's promise to purify an imperfect world. In his upbeat farewell address, Ronald Reagan declared that "America is respected again in the world, and looked to for leadership."[108] Less sanguine observers wondered whether he "may have left time bombs ticking away for the future."[109]

One such time bomb went off in 1989 when, to the surprise of most analysts in the U.S. political and intelligence establishments, communism collapsed in Eastern Europe. Studied nonchalance was the official American response. By the time the Berlin Wall came down, the Bush administration—initially divided between hardline "squeezers" and "dealers" over the correct response to Gorbachev—had made up its mind that the Russian leader was "for real" and that Washington would cooperate with Moscow in smoothing the transition to a post–Cold War world.[110] American "strategic silence" signaled that the United States would not exploit the upheaval in Eastern Europe.[111] "Our marching orders," noted the U.S. ambassador to Moscow: "Don't do something, *stand there!*"[112]

Prudence became Bush's watchword—a president's "first duty," he said.[113] Bush and his foreign-policy team were cautious about almost everything. Resembling "an English Conservative politician of the old school," Bush was born in Massachusetts in 1924 to a wealthy, old Yankee family.[114] He became a decorated navy pilot in World War II, attended Yale (B.A., 1948), and then moved to Texas, where he amassed greater wealth in the booming oil industry of the 1950s. After serving in Congress (1967–1971) and as ambassador to the United Nations (1971–1973), U.S. representative to China (1974–1975), and CIA director (1976–1977), he unsuccessfully challenged Ronald Reagan for the Republican presidential nomination in 1980 and then accepted second spot on the ticket. Always a Republican loyalist, Bush supported Reagan's policies, not always to his own benefit. Reflecting an Eisenhoweresque capacity for linguistic slipups (Texas Governor Ann Richards remarked that Bush had been born with a "silver foot in his mouth"), Bush in 1989 summarized his enduring relationship with Reagan: "For seven and a half years I've worked alongside him, and I'm proud to be his partner. We've had triumphs, we've made mistakes, we've had sex." He quickly corrected himself: "Setbacks. We've had setbacks."[115] Still, the president remained saddled throughout his single term with the task of "Fighting the Wimp Factor," as *Newsweek* put it—reversing an appearance of patrician unmanliness by constructing a public image of decisiveness and

George H. W. Bush (b. 1924).
Bush once said that "in foreign affairs ... it's sometimes easier to get things done than with problems at home, because you don't have to go up against a hostile Congress for everything you want." (National Archives)

strength—hence Bush's professed masculine passion for fried pork rinds and his exclamation following U.S. victory in Persian Gulf War: "By God, we've kicked the Vietnam Syndrome once and for all."[116]

Bush selected a compatible secretary of state in James A. Baker III, a close friend from Texas who had skillfully managed his political campaigns. Like Bush, born to the elite (1930), Baker had become a Texas corporate lawyer following graduation from Princeton University. "A man I can accomplish things with," Soviet foreign minister Eduard Shevardnadze pronounced after their first meeting.[117] National Security Adviser Brent Scowcroft worked easily with Baker and with Baker's successor, Lawrence Eagleburger, without the feuding of previous administrations. A former army general "with few edges and fewer enemies," Scowcroft acted as facilitator, broker, and coordinator, not as architect of policy.[118] "Between Scowcroft, Baker, [Defense Secretary Richard] Cheney, and [Joint Chiefs of Staff Chair General Colin] Powell, this was not a group of shrinking violets," the president's daughter observed.[119] Bush himself favored face-to-face relationships with leaders—"Rolodex diplomacy," in the words of two scholars—to cultivate international alliances and stability.[120]

The election as president of five-term Arkansas governor William J. Clinton in 1992 seemed to bring a different generational perspective to the White House. Graduate of Georgetown University and Yale Law School, Rhodes scholar, Vietnam War protester and draft avoider, and at age forty-six the second youngest elected president, this first post–Cold War commander in chief became known for his "uncanny ability to charm people"—some called it "Clinton charisma"—while exciting antipathy from opponents who viewed him as hypocritical and inept.[121] Clinton confronted a new era in U.S. foreign relations, one marked by unprecedented American global dominance but racked by sectarian and religious strife. A pragmatist in foreign as in domestic politics, Clinton pledged to maintain America's global leadership by advancing multilateral solutions to worldwide problems of human rights, trade, weapons proliferation, terrorism, and war. Declaring that "I refuse to be part of a generation that celebrates the death of communism abroad with the loss of the American dream at home," he prioritized bread-and-butter issues of taxes, deficits, economic growth, health care, and welfare reform.[122] His campaign slogan "It's the economy, stupid" might also have applied to Russian relations, for Clinton later regretted that "we should have done more—*much* more" to underwrite Russia's transition to a market economy.[123] Notwithstanding Clinton's election to a second term in 1996, Republican congressional majorities after 1994 cut foreign aid, delayed ambassadorial appointments, and rejected the Comprehensive Nuclear Test Ban Treaty (1999). Also plaguing the president in 1998–1999 were impeachment proceedings started by Congress after Clinton's apparent perjury over a sex scandal.

Clinton favored a loosely structured foreign policy bureaucracy that one presidential scholar likened to "a little boys' soccer team with no assigned positions and each player chasing the ball"—"ad-hocracy in action," said another analyst.[124] The first president since World War II who had not served in the military and who in his youth had penned a letter to a draft coordinator stating that he "loathed the military," Clinton roused the armed forces' disdain in turn.[125] One two-star general at an Air Force banquet characterized Clinton as a "gay-loving," "pot-smoking," "draft-dodging," "womanizing" commander in chief, the first charge referring to Clinton's controversial and failed effort to allow homosexuals to serve openly in the military.[126] "He was so inexperienced he would have us grab a rattlesnake by the tail because that was where the noise was coming from," a contemptuous colonel claimed.[127]

Sixty-seven-year-old Warren M. Christopher became Clinton's first secretary of state. This alumnus of the University of Southern California and Stanford Law School had served as deputy secretary of state during the Carter years and had negotiated the release of American hostages from Iran in 1980–1981. Disciplined, dignified, and dour, Christopher proved an indefatigable negotiator. Replacing Christopher for the second term was UN ambassador Madeleine Albright, a former Georgetown University professor who resurrected Cold War certitudes. The blunt-speaking Albright quickly earned a hawkish reputation. "If we have to use force," she declared, "it is because we are America. We are the indispensable nation."[128]

Christopher maintained collegial relations with Clinton's national security affairs adviser, Anthony Lake. This Harvard and Princeton graduate exhibited little of the egotism often found in White House advisers. Asked to define a new grand strategy for the post–Cold War era, Lake in 1993 proposed the expansion of free markets and democracies as a substitute for containment. Lake's successor Samuel R. "Sandy" Berger outlined more concrete goals for Clinton's second term: integrating

Madeleine Korbel Albright (b. 1937).   Born in Prague, the daughter of a Czech diplomat who defected to the United States in 1948, Albright was raised as a Roman Catholic and apparently did not learn until she became secretary that her parents had been born Jewish and three of her grandparents had died in the Holocaust. After attending Wellesley College (B.A. 1959) and earning a Ph.D. at Columbia University (1976), Albright served on the National Security Council staff during the Carter administration and later taught political science at Georgetown University. As Clinton's ambassador to the United Nations (1993–1996), she at first supported the UN's expanded role in international peacekeeping. In her memoir *Madame Secretary* (2003), she summed up Clinton's foreign policy as "determined to do the right thing but in a tough-minded way." (Bureau of Public Affairs, U.S. Department of State)

Eastern and Western Europe without provoking Russia; liberal trade expansion; cooperation against such supranational threats as terrorism and drugs; and working toward a "strong, stable Asia Pacific Community."[129]

As the U.S. economy improved in the 1990s, Clinton adopted the view of his foreign policy advisers that the "new virility symbols are exports and productivity and growth rates" rather than nuclear missiles.[130] He skillfully lobbied through Congress the North American Free Trade Agreement (NAFTA). In 1994 Washington signed the "Uruguay Round" of GATT accords liberalizing world trade. The agreement also created the World Trade Organization, which Clinton hailed as promoting "economic renewal" for the United States and the world.[131] In pushing as well for U.S. participation in both a future Free Trade Area of the Americas and the Asia Pacific Economic Cooperation forum, the president preached the "gospel of geoeconomics."[132] Worrisome, however, was the 1998 U.S. trade deficit of $233.4 billion—a record.

Nowhere was the primacy of geoeconomics more evident than in American initiatives, in conjunction with the International Monetary Fund (IMF), to act as the engine of the international political economy. When the Mexican peso collapsed in 1994, Washington fashioned an international financial bailout that included a $50 billion credit, with the United States ($20 billion) and the IMF ($18 billion) the chief backers. The announcement of a $10.2 billion credit line to Russia during Boris Yeltsin's reelection campaign in 1996 clearly reflected Washington's policy preferences. The United States contributed $5 billion to an overall $41.5 billion loan to Brazil in fall 1998, provided that Brazil implement IMF-approved measures to balance its huge budget deficit.

During the Asian financial crisis of 1997–1998, U.S. Treasury officials, working through the IMF, orchestrated a financial package of $115 billion, in return for which Asian countries promised banking and budget reforms. With financial markets gyrating wildly in January 1998, Deputy Treasury Secretary Lawrence Summers jetted to China, Hong Kong, Thailand, Malaysia, Singapore, and South Korea to quarantine the "Asian economic flu."[133] Despite leftist complaints that IMF requirements undercut social welfare reforms and increased unemployment, Summers contrasted Clinton's successful rescue with the Coolidge-Hoover failure to assist the war-stricken European economies in the 1920s and 1930s.

Russian Disintegration, German Reunification, NATO Expansion, Balkan Hell

The turning point in Soviet–American relations seems to have come in early May 1989 during Secretary Baker's visit to Moscow, when Gorbachev offered specific reductions for the Conventional Forces in Europe negotiations (CFE) that came close to NATO's proposals. Bush spoke hopefully of moving "beyond containment" and of integrating the Soviet Union "into the community of nations."[134] A cordial meeting in September between Baker and Foreign Minister Shevardnadze in Jackson Hole, Wyoming, broke the impasse over Strategic Arms Reduction Talks (START) when the Soviets dropped their demand that the United States abandon its SDI research. Gorbachev prompted jubilation at the Malta summit in December by renouncing Soviet "bridgeheads in Cuba and Central America" and recognizing America's permanent role in Europe.[135] At the Washington summit of June 1990, Bush and Gorbachev signed agreements to improve trade, reduce chemical weapons, expand university undergraduate exchanges, and negotiate deeper cuts in strategic arms. During Germany's reunification Bush helped ensure Soviet acquiescence by emphasizing that only membership in NATO could keep the new Germany from moving aggressively eastward. When Iraq invaded Kuwait in early August 1990, Washington and Moscow jointly called for an "international cutoff of all arms supplies" to Iraq, and Bush kept in touch with Gorbachev throughout the crisis. The START-I accord signed in Moscow in July 1991 limited each nuclear superpower to 1,600 delivery vehicles and 6,000 strategic nuclear devices. Only 4,900 such devices could be carried by intercontinental ballistic missiles (ICBMs) or sea-launched missiles (SLBMs). The remaining 1,100 devices permitted under the treaty included warheads and bombs carried by cruise missiles and strategic bombers.

Then came the abortive coup against Gorbachev of August 18–21. With Gorbachev under house arrest in his Crimean vacation home, the president of the Russian Soviet Republic, Boris Yeltsin, holed up with top aides in the Russian parliament building to deflect an attempted takeover by disaffected Communist hardliners. Bush ordered the National Security Agency to help Yeltsin make "secure calls" to Soviet military commanders in order to defuse the crisis.[136] When the revolt fizzled, legitimate authority shifted from the Kremlin to Yeltsin and the Russian Republic, paving the way for the Soviet Union's collapse in December 1991. Even though Bush saw a strong central government as essential for keeping control over the Soviet nuclear arsenal, he quickly adapted to a Yeltsin-led Russia, as evidenced by a $24-billion Western aid package to that state. Just before Bush left office in January 1993, he and Yeltsin signed a START-II agreement in Moscow that provided for the cutting of nuclear warheads and bombs to 3,500 (U.S.) and 2,997 (Russia) and for eliminating all multiple warhead (MIRV) intercontinental missiles by the year 2003.

Clinton, too, pursued a "Russia first" policy, calling Russia's transition to democracy "the greatest strategic challenge of our time."[137] His chief expert on Russian affairs, Strobe Talbott, urged "shock therapy" and tightfisted monetarism to create "the kind of Russia we want," despite attendant high unemployment and the removal of social safety nets for the Russian people.[138] Noting that Yeltsin was "up to his ears in alligators" in the sharply divided Russian Duma (parliament), Clinton gave the Russian leader unconditional support when he dissolved that lawmaking body in October 1993 and then turned army guns on recalcitrant legislators.[139]

Critics claimed that by sticking by Yeltsin, Clinton repeated Bush's mistake with Gorbachev. Such criticism seemed valid, as Russia's gross national product fell by 20 percent during the first four years of reforms, inflation ate up personal savings, thousands of Russian troops failed to suppress a revolt in the breakaway republic of Chechnya in 1994–1996, and a Russian Mafia exploited a growing black market in Russia's cities. Notwithstanding several U.S.-Soviet summit meetings, Yeltsin's failing health and inability to cope with Russia's economic crisis made him an unreliable partner. Nor could more than $60 billion in Western loans prevent the

Russian economy from collapsing. Yeltsin's successor after 1999, former KGB officer Vladimir Putin, brought a modicum of stability to the Kremlin, but his authoritarian style exposed the limits of political liberalization in the new Russia.

Germany also faced post–Cold War questions of identity and leadership. Chancellor Kohl put forward a plan for confederation between East and West, making reunification "a matter for Germans to decide."[140] East Germany's citizens migrated westward at an alarming rate. Local government, public services, the economy, and civic morale in the GDR steadily eroded. In early 1990, West German politicians and parties built alliances in the East for an anticipated post-election unification. The Kohl-supported center-conservative coalition won a landslide victory in the March GDR elections. Kohl initiated currency union and economic merger in July 1990. Then, in September, the four powers agreed to end their postwar occupation. In October East and West Germany formally reunited.

Bush's advisers believed that "an unattached Germany on the loose in Central Europe" looked more threatening to Moscow "than one embedded in NATO."[141] Gorbachev dropped objections to a reunited Germany in NATO in exchange for a promise of Western economic aid and a smaller German army. Kohl, too, moved quickly to dispel fears of "hob–nailed boots and spike helmets" by limiting future troop strength and pledging never to build nuclear, chemical, or biological weapons.[142] Germany became the dominant voice in the European Community (EC), pressed for aid to Eastern Europe and the former Soviet republics, and pledged billions of dollars (but not troops) to the Gulf War. Steadfast in their commitment to European integration and NATO, Germans later contributed to peacekeeping missions in the Persian Gulf, Somalia, Yugoslavia, and Afghanistan. Kohl's successor, Gerhard Schroeder, continued to cooperate by deploying troops and warplanes in the Kosovo conflict in 1999, though differences over Iraq in 2002–2003 temporarily poisoned relations (see p. 509).

The conversion of the Economic Community into the European Union (EU) through ratification of the Maastricht Treaty in fall 1993 advanced economic integration in the West. The EU Council decided in 1995 to establish a European Central Bank, issue a common currency (the "Euro"), and complete European Monetary Union by July 2002. But political disunity persisted. Most West European states proved reluctant to intervene in Bosnia and Herzegovina, where, on the ashes of the old Yugsolavia, a bloody war raged that featured genocidal killing. Of the former Soviet bloc nations, Poland, Hungary, and Czechoslovakia (divided into Czech and Slovak republics in 1993) progressed most quickly in organizing market economies and democratic governments. The other ex-Soviet republics and clients faced smoldering ethnic and national rivalries long frozen by the Cold War.

Touting the slogan "enlargement and engagement," President Clinton announced in 1994 that the question of NATO expansion eastward was no longer "whether" but "when and how."[143] He publicly designated Poland, Hungary, and the Czech Republic as the first beneficiaries of NATO membership. European leaders proceeded to rubber-stamp Clinton's proposals, notwithstanding George F. Kennan's prediction that this "most fateful error" would "impel Russian foreign policy in directions decidedly not to our liking."[144] The three new members officially joined NATO in March 1999.

President William Jefferson Clinton (b. 1946) and Richard C. Holbrooke (b. 1941). Photographed in 1997, President Clinton (right) was using crutches because of a knee injury. Clinton's presidency subsequently suffered a serious blow when a sex scandal caused him to become only the second president to be impeached. A former aide to Henry Kissinger, Holbrooke served in Jimmy Carter's State Department and later as ambassador to Germany, assistant secretary of state for Europe, and chief diplomatic troubleshooter in the Balkans for the Clinton administration. President Barack Obama named him a special envoy to Afghanistan and Pakistan in 2009. After successfully negotiating the 1995 Dayton agreement, which ended the war in Bosnia, Holbrooke in 1998 helped to broker a temporary cease-fire in the southern Yugoslavian province of Kosovo, where Muslim ethnic Albanians battled their Serbian overlords. (White House Photo)

NATO had already displayed ineffectiveness in dealing with the Balkan crisis. Despite CIA predictions of bloody ethnic violence in Yugoslavia, the Bush administration deferred to European allies when they recognized an independent Croatia and Slovenia in summer 1991. "We've got no dog in this fight," Secretary of State Baker said.[145] Serbia proclaimed a new Federal Republic of Yugoslavia (including Montenegro) and incited Serbs living in the other republics—especially in Bosnia—to take up arms. Croats and Muslims living in Bosnia declared an independent state. After Bosnia–Herzegovina became independent in April 1992, Serbs began to shell Sarajevo, the city where in 1914 an assassination had triggered World War I. Bosnian Serbs grabbed territory and displaced Bosnian Muslims through the horrors of "ethnic cleansing," which included the mass rape of Muslim women by Serbian soldiers.[146] Serbian militia seized approximately 70 percent of the Bosnian hinterland. France and Britain dispatched "Blue Helmets" (UN troops) to safeguard relief supplies but eschewed military intervention. By 1993 as many as 150,000 people had perished.

Clinton inherited this "problem from hell."[147] Ambassador Madeleine Albright asked: "What's the point of having this superb military … if we can't use it?"[148] But the Pentagon noted the rugged terrain and told Clinton: "We do deserts, we don't do mountains."[149] The president issued warnings to the Serbs and proclaimed America's humane concern, but he lacked both foreign and domestic support for intervention in a region where ethnic rivalries seemed impervious to outside influence and where U.S. interests appeared uncertain. When Clinton proposed lifting the arms embargo against Bosnia and launching air strikes against the Bosnian Serbs, NATO balked because of its own peacekeeping forces on the ground. Starting in February 1994, NATO did carry out air strikes against Serbian planes in "no-fly" zones and against Serb artillery shelling Sarajevo. Bosnian Serbs nonetheless succeeded in displacing Muslims from much of Bosnia. After Bosnian Serbs in July 1995 seized the safe havens of Srebenica and Zepa and massacred over 8,000 Muslims within sight of UN peacekeepers, Clinton adopted an "endgame strategy" of more forceful diplomatic and military action.[150] While the Croatian army, with covert American support, overran Serb-held territory in northwest Bosnia, a U.S. negotiated agreement to end UN vetoes of NATO military action led to intensified air attacks. Yugoslav president Slobodan Milosevic imposed his authority over the Bosnian Serbs and agreed to a cease-fire that October. A peace conference convened at Wright-Patterson Air Force Base in Ohio. The Dayton Accords of December 14, 1995 retained a Croat-Muslim Federation and a Serb Republic within a single Bosnian state, with Sarajevo to remain as a multiethnic capital. The United States agreed to contribute 20,000 personnel as part of a 60,000-member NATO implementation force that would separate the parties and assist in reconstruction.

In 1999, another Balkan crisis drew international attention. In the largely ethnic Albanian, Muslim province of Kosovo (Yugoslavia), President Milosevic ordered further ethnic cleansing. When Milosovic rejected NATO's demands to halt the persecution and preserve Kosovo's autonomy, Clinton ruled out U.S. ground forces and chose air power. The NATO bombing campaign unleashed even more cruelties in Kosovo, as the Serbs systematically burned, looted, raped, and forced 800,000 Muslim refugees to flee to neighboring Albania and Macedonia. Pounded by air attacks, encircled by hostile nations, and suffering a NATO-imposed oil embargo, Milosevic relented in early June under an agreement to withdraw his forces from Kosovo, permit the return of refugees, accept a NATO security presence, and grant greater autonomy to Kosovo. The International War Crimes Tribunal at The Hague indicted and later tried Milosevic and his top aides for war crimes against the peoples of Kosovo and Bosnia.

Hope and Tragedy in Africa

While communism collapsed in Eastern Europe, apartheid began its descent in South Africa. As in Europe, the main impetus for reversing decades of social, political, and economic discrimination came from within—in this case, from within a nation of 35 million blacks, people of mixed race, and Asians ruled by 6.7 million whites. Washington played a modest role in nurturing the process.

The Namibia-Angola agreement in 1988 prepared the way by withdrawing Cuban and South African troops from Angola. With South Africa no longer at war, and with the Cold War itself coming to an end, antiapartheid organizations found it increasingly difficult to obtain outside assistance and weapons to mount guerrilla campaigns inside South Africa. Harsh measures by Pretoria's security police also neutralized most armed black nationalist activity. When South Africa's white leaders P. W. Botha and his successor F. W. de Klerk recommended negotiating an end to apartheid, beleaguered black activists thus responded positively.

Nelson Mandela (b. 1918).
A founder of the African National Congress (ANC), this attorney and member of the Xhosa tribe was a young man when the white South African government jailed him in November 1962. Often compared to Mahatma Gandhi in his commitment to human rights, democracy, and peace, he served nearly three decades in prison to protest the injustices and cruelty of racial apartheid in South Africa. (© Reuters/Corbis)

White leaders' own openness to change came as a result of a decades-long struggle by South African activists determined to bring an end to segregation, combined with more recent economic sanctions by antiapartheid allies in the international community. The United States under President Bush applied such economic pressures. From 1986 to 1989, sanctions cost South Africa $32 billion to $40 billion. When de Klerk became president in September 1989, he lifted prohibitions against dissent, stopped executions, freed selected political prisoners, legalized banned organizations such as the African National Congress (ANC), and desegregated beaches and some housing areas. Of greatest symbolic importance, de Klerk released the political prisoner and ANC leader Nelson Mandela in February 1990.

Twenty-six parties entered serious talks for a democratic South Africa in early 1993. Four straight years of zero economic growth helped spur compromises. Agreement finally came in September 1993, and South Africa's first all-race elections were held in April 1994. The ANC handily won, and the septuagenarian Mandela became South Africa's first black president. After the parliament drew up a constitution, the U.S. Congress repealed sanctions. Mandela and de Klerk shared the Nobel Peace Prize in 1993. Mandela's regime welcomed U.S. aid and investment. Firms that had previously disinvested, such as Ford, Honeywell, General Electric, Sara Lee, and Citibank, quickly returned. By 1996 more than 500 U.S. companies were operating in South Africa, with a total asset value of $3.5 billion. A Truth and Reconciliation Commission attempted to heal the past by gathering testimony that bore witness to the atrocities of the apartheid regime.

Overshadowing much of sub-Saharan Africa was a growing HIV/AIDS pandemic, which, alongside chronic starvation and dislocation, was linked with ongoing neocolonial exploitation and political strife. Ghastly television pictures of emaciated African children had helped spur U.S. intervention a decade earlier. In December 1992, George Bush ordered 28,150 U.S. troops to the Horn of Africa on a humanitarian mission to feed the starving population of civil-war-torn Somalia. "We can get in," Scowcroft said. "But how do we get out?"[151] Bush hoped that U.S. forces could restore order, move relief supplies to desperate Somalis, and then turn peace-keeping duties over to the United Nations. Operation Restore Hope succeeded at first. U.S. officials initiated cooperative relations with the most powerful Somali warlord, General Mohamed Farah Aidid, who controlled Mogadishu. Relief operations fed the hungry, and mediation efforts progressed with clan leaders agreeing to negotiate national reconciliation. The United Nations then tried to restore political stability. President Clinton left 8,000 U.S. logistical troops in Somalia, along with a 1,000-person quick-reaction force. Such attempts at nation-building, even under UN auspices, aroused nationalist resentment. In mid-1993 Aidid's forces attacked Pakistani peacekeeping troops, killing twenty-four. U.S. forces under UN command tried unsuccessfully to kill Aidid in a "decapitation mission."[152]

In early October, nineteen U.S. Army Rangers died in a bloody firefight. A shocked Clinton watched television pictures of dead U.S. soldiers being dragged through the streets of Mogadishu by jubilant Somalis. Though as many as 1,000 Somalis died versus 18 American soldiers, Clinton was convinced that public opinion opposed the sacrifice of even one American life. He withdrew all U.S. forces by April 1994, leaving the mission to the UN. Critics identified a new syndrome—"Vietmalia, combining *Vietnam* and *Somalia*."[153] That African nation remained tumultuous.

Just a month after U.S. personnel departed Somalia, mass killing erupted in the central African republic of Rwanda. A suspicious April 1994 plane crash that killed the presidents of Rwanda and Burundi, both members of the dominant Hutu majority, touched off massacres of the Tutsi minority that left more than 800,000 dead in eighty-nine days. The Clinton administration resisted proposals for vigorous intervention, concentrated on evacuating U.S. citizens, and even instructed officials to avoid the term *genocide*, a label that invoked purposeful mass killing and possibly carried both a moral and a legal obligation to intervene.[154] Not until the massacres had ended did Clinton order U.S. troops in July to secure the airport in Kigala so that relief supplies could flow directly to Rwanda and stem the flood of refugees into neighboring Burundi, Tanzania, and Zaire.

The Rwanda massacres embarrassed Washington by exposing the moral relativism that underlay much U.S. foreign policy. On visiting Africa in 1998, President Clinton apologized for not "calling these crimes by their rightful name: genocide."[155] Washington helped create the African Crisis Response Initiative, designed to assist African countries to organize joint forces for rapid intervention in the future. Despite such plans, fighting flared between Hutus and Tutsis in Burundi in 1996, and the next year a revolt, backed by Rwanda, Uganda, and Eritrea, toppled long-time U.S. client Mobutu Sese Seko in Zaire (renamed the Democratic Republic of Congo). The new government of Laurent Kabila promptly slaughtered thousands of Hutu *genocidaires* exiled in the eastern provinces. Over the next five years the Democratic Republic of the Congo suffered some 3.3 million "excess deaths" from combat, disease, and malnutrition.[156]

U.S. relations also fared badly with Sudan. The Islamic government of that nation temporarily sheltered Osama bin Laden, the wealthy Saudi financier whose radical anti-Western organization al Qaeda perpetrated numerous terrorist acts against the United States during the 1990s. In August 1998, Washington fired cruise missiles at a Sudanese pharmaceutical plant in retaliation for al Qaeda attacks on U.S. embassies in Kenya and Tanzania that killed 224 people, including 12 Americans. U.S. missiles also struck targets in Afghanistan, apparently just missing bin Laden. Skeptics suggested that the president, facing impeachment, followed a "*Wag the Dog*" strategy—so named for a contemporary movie in which a president foments a phony war to deflect attention from a sex scandal.[157]

Elsewhere in Africa the U.S. record was mixed. Washington maintained close ties with General Sani Abachi's repressive military regime in Nigeria, which exported $6.3 billion in oil, gas, and other commodities to the United States in 1997, making it the fifth largest supplier of foreign oil. Abachi's death in 1998 began a turbulent transition to civilian rule. Although civil wars destabilized former Cold War clients such as Liberia, Sudan, Somalia, and Zaire (Congo), recent targets of U.S. assistance (South Africa, Ghana, Ethiopia, Mozambique, Uganda, and Mali) made significant political and economic progress in the 1990s. In 1996 American trade with the eleven countries of southern Africa totaled $9 billion, the equivalent of U.S. trade with Russia and former Soviet republics. During a six-nation visit in March 1998, President Clinton hailed an "African Renaissance," but Congress killed his proposed Africa Trade and Investment Act.[158]

What if ... the United States had killed Osama bin Laden in August 1998?

Once the CIA established that Saudi millionaire Osama bin Laden had funded and directed the terrorist bombings of the U.S. embassies in Tanzania and Kenya in August 1998, President Bill Clinton authorized missile strikes on bin Laden training camps in Afghanistan and on a pharmaceutical plant in Khartoum that presumably manufactured nerve gas agents for al Qaeda. The Afghan attacks missed bin Laden by several hours, and the U.S. government failed to prove that the demolished Sudanese plant had ever made chemical weapons components. Clinton, just three days from grand jury testimony concerning his affair with White House intern Monica Lewinsky, was accused by critics of attempting a public diversion by exaggerating al Qaeda's threat to the United States. Only after September 11, 2001, when pilots trained in terrorist tactics at bin Laden camps used airplanes to incinerate thousands of people in New York City and Washington, D.C. (see p. 481), did the scope of Clinton's possible missed opportunity of August 1998 become apparent. Could anything, with hindsight, have turned out differently?

The August 1998 raids came amidst a series of failed efforts by the Clinton administration to "get" bin Laden. Since mid-1996, when al Qaeda's bombing of U.S. military barracks in Dhahran, Saudi Arabia, killed 19 Americans, the CIA, FBI, and other agencies hatched schemes to contain bin Laden's power. U.S. officials contemplated freezing bin Laden's assets, capturing and prosecuting him in the United States, and having him assassinated. The United States also pressured the Taliban (a faction in Afghanistan's civil war) to stop sheltering bin Laden. Time and again, plans were stymied—by flawed intelligence, bureaucratic rivalries, political constraints, and other contingencies. In spring 1998, for instance, the CIA trained Afghan Pashtun agents to capture bin Laden at his Tarnak Farms compound in rural Afghanistan, but the principals canceled the raid, fearing that failure could jeopardize lives and trigger a coup in neighboring Pakistan. A missile strike on another bin Laden camp in Afghanistan scheduled for February 1999 was scuttled to protect visiting Emirati dignitaries, while a near shootout between Taliban MiGs and American Predator surveillance craft in fall 2000 thwarted plans for a missile attack on Tarnak Farms. In the case of the 1998 strikes, bin Laden may have slipped away because Washington officials notified Pakistan that it was lobbing missiles over its territory lest Islamabad misinterpret the assault as coming from India and launch a retaliatory—even nuclear—counterattack. Pakistani informers might have leaked to bin Laden that a raid was coming, hence his escape.

Suppose bin Laden had been killed? The most optimistic possibility is that 9/11 might not have happened and that the ensuing U.S.-led wars in Afghanistan and Iraq might also have been avoided. Bin Laden reportedly told Khalid Sheikh Mohammed, architect of the planes operation, to proceed with planning in late 1998. Bin Laden's death that August would likely have complicated training for 9/11. But Mohammed or bin Laden's deputy Ayman al-Zawahiri might still have guided the scheme to fruition. Bin Laden's money itself may not have been critical; the operation cost no more than $500,000, from start to finish. Killing bin Laden in 1998 might not have prevented a 9/11-style attack, though it might have obviated a U.S. invasion of Afghanistan. Because neoconservative designs for regime change in Iraq predated 9/11, another pretext for invading that country might eventually have been found.

Clinton, in any case, never took the ultimate step of deploying Special Forces to capture bin Laden in Afghanistan. For American officials to have judged that the gain in doing so outweighed the risk, they would have had to fathom fully the danger that bin Laden posed. Even after the embassy attacks, bin Laden had been responsible for fewer than 50 American deaths, most of them overseas. U.S. leaders perceived bin Laden as capable of causing hundreds of casualties, not thousands. Moreover, the potential costs of assassination were considerable. Killing bin Laden—whom few Westerners had ever heard of but who had built a substantial following in anti-Western Muslim circles during the 1980s and 1990s—would likely have yielded little political capital to Clinton, while martyring bin Laden and inviting additional anti-American attacks worldwide. A U.S.-sponsored assassination could have intensified political unrest in Afghanistan (valued for its future Eurasian oil pipeline) and Pakistan (newly armed with nuclear weapons) and inflamed Pakstani-Indian tensions. International condemnation of U.S. action might also have complicated American efforts to end war in the Balkans, force Iraqi concessions on its own nuclear program, and secure Israeli-Palestinian peace.

The costs associated with bin Laden's killing were high, even if the stakes, in retrospect, were higher. Yet if Clinton deserves blame for bin Laden's escape, so, too must Republican President George W. Bush, who assumed office in January 2001. Clinton recalled telling Bush: "Your biggest threat is bin Ladin and the al Qaeda" and "One of the great regrets of my presidency is that I didn't get him for you, because I tried to." But Bush's government held no high-level meetings on bin Laden, nor did it execute any cohesive plan to find bin Laden or weaken al Qaeda in the eight months prior to September 11, 2001. Bin Laden remained at large throughout Bush's two terms as president; he remained at large still when President Barack Obama took office in January 2009.

Invasions and Implosions in Latin America

The Bush administration slowly reversed past policies toward Latin America. Narcotics continued to flow into the profitable U.S. marketplace despite expensive antidrug operations; debt, rampant inflation, and sluggish growth rates imperiled economies; a graying Fidel Castro still vexed Washington; and an escalating crisis with Panama threatened further instability in the Caribbean. But the Western Hemisphere seemed to be advancing from military regimes to popularly elected governments, as in Argentina, Chile, and Brazil. After the Sandinistas lost elections in 1990 to U.S.-backed Violeta Barrios de Chamorro and her National Opposition Union, the civil war in Nicaragua finally ended. The civil war in El Salvador terminated under a UN-brokered agreement in 1992. Both wars left Central America with staggering costs of reconstruction and reconciliation and tens of thousands dead. Latin America's economic linkage with the United States nonetheless remained strong: in 1990, 40 percent of the region's exports flowed to the United States.

Bush's and Clinton's sponsorship of NAFTA, as well as the agreement to implement a Free Trade Area of the Americas (FTAA) by 2005, held the promise of a more prosperous Latin America. "A rising tide lifts all boats," Clinton declared at the Summit of the Americas in 1994, prompting the prime minister of Barbados to reply that "a rising tide can … overturn small boats."[159] Disagreements over farm subsidies, as well as financial crises in Brazil and Argentina, slowed integration so that only a U.S.-Chile free-trade agreement was achieved by late 2003. Debts also thwarted progress. In 1990 Latin American countries owed more than $400 billion. Brazil, Mexico, and Argentina owed the most, and much of it to U.S. banks. The debt crisis hurt the United States. As debtors struggled to meet debt-service payments, they trimmed their imports. U.S. exports then slumped by billions of dollars, and North American jobs were lost. Latin migrants trying to escape grinding poverty pressed against U.S. immigration gates. The narcotics trade expanded as poor farmers turned to lucrative drug crops for income. Because health services and educational outlays had to be reduced and economic-development projects scuttled throughout Latin America, political unrest spread.

Treasury Secretary Nicholas F. Brady instituted a program in 1989 that provided for some debt relief and lower interest rates. Several agreements between commercial banks and Latin American governments, backed by the IMF, cut debt burdens by about one-third. In return, Latin American debtors accepted market-opening requirements—controlling inflation, attracting foreign investment, and reducing trade restrictions. Brady's initiatives seemed to work. Spurred by NAFTA and planning for the Free Trade Area of the Americas, Latin American exports grew from an average 4.5 percent during the 1980s to 9.9 percent in the 1990s, while foreign investments leaped from $6.7 billion in 1990 to $22.4 billion in 1996. Political corruption and a growing fiscal crisis, however, triggered an implosion in Argentina in December 2001 when that country defaulted on its $140 billion foreign debt (see p. 511). The financial meltdown threatened to infect Uruguay, Paraguay, and even Brazil. Not until the summer of 2003—after the war against Iraq that several Latin American countries opposed—did the administration of George W. Bush encourage the IMF to restructure Argentina's debt repayments.

When President Carlos Salinas of Mexico proposed a free trade agreement with Washington in 1990, he reversed more than a century of "building walls to keep out U.S. goods, investment, and influence."[160] Embraced by the Bush administration, signed by Canada, Mexico, and the United States in 1992, and approved by Congress in 1993, the resulting North American Free Trade Agreement created the world's largest free trade bloc, comprising 370 million people with a combined gross domestic product of $6.5 trillion. President Clinton subsequently negotiated side agreements with Mexico to protect workers' rights and environmental standards, and he mobilized an effective lobbying effort that included former presidents and secretaries of state. Bilateral trade rose by $17 billion annually between 1993 and 1996, with a $7 billion net surplus for U.S. exports. Statistics revealed 100,000 U.S. jobs lost due to NAFTA by 1997, but unemployment rates reached historic lows as the revived U.S. economy created 2.5 million new jobs per year in the mid-1990s. Despite continuing bilateral problems with drugs and illegal immigration, NAFTA promised to expand an already burgeoning "Mexamerica," the 2,000-mile border society where two cultures blended "like reluctant lovers in the night, embracing for fear that letting go could only be worse."[161]

Many Americans believed that the flourishing drug trade endangered international stability and U.S. security. Between 1985 and 1995 the world production of opium and coca leaves roughly tripled, as drug prices dropped and U.S. prisons filled to capacity with people convicted of drug-related crimes. With 489 million people, 128 million passenger cars, 11.5 million trucks, and 2.2 million railroad cars passing through U.S. border inspections per year, actually finding drugs was "like trying to catch minnows at the base of Niagara Falls."[162]

The United States spent upwards of $3 billion a year in a supply-side war against foreign sources and middlemen. Under Bush and Clinton, U.S. counternarcotics aid went to the Andean nations of Peru, Bolivia, and Colombia, but Washington also increasingly stressed stanching demand inside the United States itself. This apparent change stemmed in part from pressure from Latin Americans who contended that North Americans unfairly blamed them for the drug problem. "No one is forcing the gringos to snort coke, so let Washington deal with it," they seemed to say.[163] An estimated 72 million Americans (34 percent of the population) had used illegal drugs, while only 3.9 percent of Mexico's population had done the same.

Mexico had become a major source of marijuana and heroin and a major highway for South American cocaine shipments. From Bolivia, Peru, and Colombia came coca, which was processed into cocaine and crack. (Tons of opium/heroin also entered the United States from the "Golden Triangle" of Burma, Thailand, and Laos and the "Golden Crescent" of Iran, Afghanistan, and Pakistan.) Any nation that came into contact with the drug trade became exposed to corruption, drug addiction, violence, and death. Illegal drug money bribed politicians in some Latin American states. In Colombia the sharpshooters of the militarized drug cartels assassinated judges, journalists, police officers, and public officials. Leftist guerrillas called the *Sendero Luminoso* (Shining Path) used the drug trade to help finance their rebellion in Peru. Drug profits, not reinvested in long-term development, distorted regional economies, while the laundering of "narcodollars" befouled banking systems. Colombia took courageous steps to defeat the drug lords of the Medellín and Cali cartels, only to produce the "hydra effect" of more dispersed operations and new drug fiefdoms in Mexico, Venezuela, and Brazil.[164] By 1998, 75 percent of U.S.-imported cocaine arrived through Mexico. Authorities confiscated an estimated 15 percent of the five to seven tons of illegal drugs crossing the southwest border every day.

The drug issue became central to Panamanian–United States relations after General Manuel Antonio Noriega took power in 1983. As the intelligence chief of the Panama Defense Forces, he had come to know Panama's thriving world of drug trafficking. Panamanian banks laundered drug money, and Noriega became a millionaire by cutting deals with Colombia's cocaine barons. By the late 1980s, his autocratic rule and drug-running had stirred anger in North Americans eager to blame the swaggering dictator for U.S. drug problems.

The American Addiction.
This political cartoon from a Honduran newspaper reflected the Latin American perspective that the drug crisis in the United States stemmed not from the production of cocaine in Latin America but from the consumption of dangerous drugs in North America. Could the cartoonist also be suggesting that the drug trade was destroying Latin America? (McDonald/Diario El Heraldo, San Pedro Sula, Honduras)

Official Washington and Noriega had long been covert allies. As a young officer in the 1960s, Noriega received regular payments from the CIA; during the 1980s he helped train the *contras*. Thus Washington turned a blind eye to his drug trafficking until 1988, when two Florida grand juries indicted the dictator for shipping Colombian drugs to the United States. Washington froze Panamanian assets in the United States and offered Noriega a safe haven in Spain. The defiant Panamanian strongman stirred anti-*yanqui* rallies in the fall of 1989, and the shooting death of a U.S. marine in December by Panamanian Defense Force guards roused a heretofore cautious General Powell to line up with Cheney, Baker, and Scowcroft in urging a massive military response. "Okay, let's do it," the president declared. "The Hell with it."[165]

In the early hours of December 20, 1989, President Bush launched Operation Just Cause. The invasion of Panama by 22,500 troops achieved its intended goal of removing Noriega from power. A billion dollars' worth of property in Panama City was damaged and 516 Panamanians died. The resistance proved greater than anticipated. When U.S. troops finally located Noriega in the Vatican Embassy in Panama City, the psychological operations team employed rock-and-roll to induce surrender. As part of the acoustic assault, operatives blasted "Born to Run," "Crying in the Chapel," "I Fought the Law and the Law Won," and "We Gotta Get Outta This Place."[166] Foiled in his efforts to reveal CIA secrets and embarrass President Bush, Noriega in April 1992 was convicted of cocaine smuggling, money laundering, and racketeering and sentenced to 30 years in U.S. federal prison.

Bush's popularity soared after the military invasion of Panama. Democrats and Republicans alike cheered even though Bush had not consulted Congress. Critics, however, reproached the administration for violating the UN Charter and the Organization of American States Charter, which contain nonintervention provisions. The OAS censured the United States, and only a U.S. veto prevented passage of a UN Security Council resolution condemning the invasion.

The U.S. military also intervened in poverty-stricken Haiti to restore a deposed president. Elected in 1990, the Reverend Jean-Bertrand Aristide fled nine months later when Haitian military leaders resisted his plans for demilitarization and social reform. A junta headed by General Raul Cedras terrorized and tortured political opponents, as refugees scrambled to escape on makeshift boats. Clinton, fearing an immigration crisis, denounced the junta but ordered the U.S. Coast Guard to turn back refugees seeking asylum. "A total fuck-up," admitted Anthony Lake, as "shell-shocked" Pentagon planners hesitated to use force so soon after the Somalia debacle.[167] Not until late summer 1994 did Clinton act decisively. With a 20,000-strong invasion force set to land within thirty-six hours, a negotiating team headed by Jimmy Carter and Colin Powell persuaded the junta to step down to avert bloodshed. Operation Uphold Democracy disarmed the Haitian military, returned Aristide to power, then left on schedule in April 1995. Haiti's living standards remained the poorest in the hemisphere. Another coup in early 2004 deposed Aristide a second time, whereupon U.S. forces once again intervened to restore order.

As for Cuba, the end of the Cold War caused Castro's Cuba to retrench but not repent. Castro announced in 1992 that Cuba would no longer give military support to revolutionary movements, that Cuba was "desovietized forever."[168]

The end of Soviet subsidies produced tremendous economic hardship and increased the number of Cubans fleeing in makeshift rafts across the Florida Straits. After thirty-seven refugees drowned when Cuban authorities sank their hijacked boat in August 1994, rioting in Havana prompted Castro to denounce Washington for encouraging hijackers. Henceforth Cuban police would not stop people from leaving so long as they did not hijack boats or planes. More than 35,000 departed in the next month. Clinton tried to "demagnetize" the United States by barring entry to the *balseros* (rafters).[169] He then reached an agreement with Havana that increased to 20,000 the legal immigrants permitted into the United States annually, required Cuba to halt illegal immigration, and placed refugees under detention. To discourage a new exodus, Washington promised to return all future boat people to Cuba.

Bilateral efforts to resolve the refugee problem ended abruptly. Three civilian aircraft piloted by a Cuban-American group called Brothers to the Rescue flew toward Cuba in February 1996 in search of boat people. Because the Brothers organization had been warned about previous violations of Cuban air space, Cuban MiGs gave chase and shot down two of the planes, killing four crew members. "This is not *cojones* [testicles]," Madeleine Albright lectured Havana, "this is cowardice."[170]

Congress passed the Helms–Burton bill in March 1996 by large majorities. The legislation not only allowed U.S. citizens (including naturalized Cuban-Americans) to sue foreign companies that did business using properties confiscated by the Castro regime; it also barred any relaxation of sanctions until a democratic government ruled in Cuba. When the EU claimed that Helms-Burton violated the rules of the new World Trade Organization, Clinton temporarily suspended suits against foreign firms while maintaining the punishing embargo. Castro meanwhile railed about North America's "canned culture" invasion that "transmits poisonous messages … to all families, to all homes, to all children."[171] Clinton instituted a modest thaw in early 1999 by authorizing U.S. citizens to send at least $1,200 a year to Cuban families and increasing passenger flights to and from Cuba. But additional Clinton reforms ran afoul of the legal-political controversies surrounding six-year-old refugee Elián González, rescued off the Florida coast and eventually returned to his Cuban father in spring 2000 against the angry protests of Cuban Americans.

Mideast Imbroglios

The invasion of Kuwait by Iraq on August 2, 1990, led to a significant exercise of U.S. power in the Persian Gulf. Saddam Hussein cited old territorial claims to occupy Kuwait in the name of all "zealous Arabs who believe in one Arab nation."[172] Washington feared that Hussein might next invade Saudi Arabia—a major strategic and petroleum-producing ally—and control 40 percent of the world's oil. Bush pledged: "This will not stand."[173] He organized an international coalition of thirty countries to liberate Kuwait from Iraqi occupation. By November the UN had imposed economic sanctions and demanded Iraqi withdrawal. Bush initially sent some 200,000 American troops as part of a multinational peacekeeping force to defend Saudi Arabia (Operation Desert Shield). In early November he increased the expeditionary force (including allied contingents) to 700,000. The

Security Council commanded Iraq to evacuate Kuwait by January 15, 1991, or else face military attack. UN sanctions cut off 90 percent of Iraq's imports and 97 percent of its exports. Iraq replied that it would consider withdrawal from Kuwait only if Israel relinquished its occupied territories. When Bush asked for authorization to send U.S. troops into combat under a UN resolution, Congress debated for four days. Senator George Mitchell of Maine cited the risks: "an unknown number of casualties and deaths, billions of dollars spent, a greatly disrupted oil supply and oil price increases, the possible long-term American occupation of Iraq, long-lasting Arab enmity against the United States, a possible return to isolationism at home."[174] Senator Robert Dole of Kansas rebutted that "Saddam … may think he's going to be rescued, maybe by Congress."[175] Despite mass protests chanting "hell no, we won't go—we won't fight for Texaco," a majority in both houses narrowly approved Bush's request to use force.[176]

Described by one critic as a "Pentagon trade show with live ammunition," Operation Desert Storm commenced with an aerial bombardment of Iraq and Kuwait on January 16.[177] For five weeks satellite television coverage via Cable News Network (CNN) enabled Americans to watch Tomahawk cruise missiles driving towards Iraqi targets and U.S. Patriot missiles intercepting Iraqi Scuds. Bush and Baker masterfully managed the coalition, persuading Israel not to retaliate after Iraqi Scud attacks, keeping Gorbachev "on the right track" as allied bombs devastated Russia's longtime client, and conducting a rhetorical campaign of "national unity" that portrayed Hussein as an "anti-agent," opposed to civilized norms, laws, and moral codes.[178] Finally, on February 23, hundreds of thousands of allied ground forces invaded Kuwait and eastern Iraq. Iraqi troops scrambled to leave Kuwait, blowing up 800 oil wells as they retreated. Allied aircraft flew hundreds of sorties along the "Highway of Death" from Kuwait City to Basra. After only 100 hours

World Orders, Old and New. In 1991, as the United States fought the Persian Gulf War, the cartoonist Jim Borgman linked past (Theodore Roosevelt) and present (George H. W. Bush) to suggest that the United States still saw itself as—and acted like—an international policeman. (JIM BORGMAN © 1991 Cincinnati Enquirer. Reprinted with permission of UNIVERSAL PRESS SYNDICATE. All rights reserved.)

of fighting on the ground, Iraq accepted a UN-imposed cease-fire. Iraq's casualties numbered at least 25,000 military dead. Survivors battled cholera and typhoid fever. U.S. forces suffered only 148 deaths and 458 wounded, but 140,000 service personnel were exposed to low levels of the nerve agent sarin; by 2002 more than half of Gulf War veterans had sought medical care or filed disability claims.

The Gulf war was "like teenage sex," a senator quipped. "We got in too soon and out too soon."[179] Though urged by Cheney to "think big," Bush did not order troops to Baghdad to capture Saddam Hussein because he wanted to maintain Iraq as buffer to still-hostile Iran.[180] He hoped that the Iraqi military or disgruntled associates in the Ba'ath party would oust Hussein in a coup. Yet when Kurds in northern Iraq and Shi'ites in the south rebelled, Bush did little to help. Hussein crushed both rebellions. Public pressure persuaded Bush to send thousands of U.S. troops to northern Iraq, where the United Nations designated a "no-fly" zone prohibiting Iraqi aircraft from attacking Kurds. Hussein's survival dissatisfied Americans who associated "regime change" with victory.

Under Security Council Resolution 687, Iraq had to accept the inviolability of the boundary with Kuwait; tolerate the presence of UN peacekeepers on its borders; and fully disclose all chemical, biological, and nuclear weapons, including missiles, and cooperate in their destruction. What allied bombs had missed, UN inspectors tried to locate. Hussein's scientists and engineers had built nuclear facilities that were within months of producing nuclear weapons when the Gulf War began. Inspectors found and destroyed more than 100 Scud missiles, 70 tons of nerve gas, and 400 tons of mustard gas.

Saddam Hussein nonetheless continued "making trouble" for Washington.[181] In retaliation for an apparent Iraqi assassination plot against former president Bush, Clinton ordered missile attacks on Baghdad in 1993. He sent 36,000 troops to Kuwait the following year to deter Iraqi military movements southward, then bombed Iraq again in 1996 when Hussein crushed a Kurdish revolt in northern Iraq. UN sanctions to force removal of all weapons of mass destruction reportedly contributed to the deaths of many Iraqi civilians, including half a million children. Asked about the human costs, Secretary Albright avowed that "the price is worth it."[182] Baghdad played a six-year shell game by interfering with UN inspectors as they searched for chemical weapons and biological stores of anthrax, botulinum, and aflatoxin. The Iraqi government protested the UN inspection teams' sharing of intelligence data with U.S. officials—information later used to target sites for U.S. air strikes. In February and November 1998, the United States rushed forces to the Persian Gulf, each time deferring attack when Iraq promised complete access for inspectors.

When Saddam Hussein again stiff-armed UN inspectors on the eve of Clinton's impeachment in December 1998, the president launched a joint Anglo-American bombing campaign aimed at reducing Iraq's military capabilities. Several hundred Tomahawk missiles (more than in the Gulf War) fired over a period of four days targeted suspected weapons sites but also provoked criticism from China, Russia, and France. Clinton weighed options for a government overthrow in Iraq, but the war in Kosovo and renewed violence between Israelis and Palestinians in autumn 2000 diverted his attention while Saddam Hussein continued defying the new UN Monitoring and Verification Commission (UNMOVIC).[183]

Not surprisingly, war against Iraq impacted the Arab-Israeli peace process. When Bush took office in 1989, Secretary Baker pressed both sides but especially implored Israel: "Forswear annexation. Stop settlement activity."[184] The end of the Cold War actually improved the diplomatic climate. No longer subsidized by the Soviet Union, Yasir Arafat also alienated oil-rich Saudi Arabia and the Gulf emirates by his ill-fated backing of Iraq during the 1991 war. When Israel showed restraint in the face of Iraqi missile attacks and Washington promised an expanded peace process after the war, Arafat reluctantly cooperated.

A breakthrough followed secret meetings between Israeli and PLO representatives in Oslo, Norway. In September 1993, Israeli Prime Minister Yitzhak Rabin and Arafat exchanged a "kissless handshake" on the South Lawn of the White House after signing a historic declaration of principles for eventual Palestinian self-rule in the Gaza Strip and part of the West Bank.[185] Israel and Jordan signed a peace accord in July 1994 after the United States agreed to forgive Jordan's foreign debt, but Syria refused to make peace despite a visit by Clinton to Damascus.

Rabin's assassination in November 1995, Palestinian terrorist bombings, and the election of hard-line prime minister Benjamin Netanyahu in 1996 stalled the peace process. At a nine-day summit in Maryland in October 1998, Arafat and Netanyahu did agree to some Israeli pullbacks in return for changes in the PLO Charter calling for Israel's destruction. Secret Israeli-PLO negotiations in Stockholm set the stage for what was supposed to be a final peace agreement at Camp David in July 2000. Despite Israel's apparent willingness to cede much of the West Bank, the Camp David summit foundered over principles, process, and particulars. The Likud leader Ariel Sharon's visit in September to Jerusalem's Temple Mount, a disputed area,

PLO-Israeli Agreement.
On September 13, 1993, President Clinton acted as stage manager on the South Lawn of the White House when Israeli prime minister Yitzhak Rabin (left), and Palestine Liberation Organization chair Yasir Arafat (right), signed a historic accord for Palestinian self-rule in the Gaza Strip and Jericho—first steps, perhaps, toward a Palestinian homeland. After Rabin and Arafat affixed their signatures, Clinton shook hands with both men and then stepped back and gestured with his arms. Arafat reached his hand out, and after several long seconds, Rabin responded. (The White House)

ignited Palestinian clashes that quickly escalated into a second *intifada* that persisted through the administration of George W. Bush and further impeded the peace process (see p. 504).

Feuding and Trading with China, Vietnam, and Japan

Human rights and trade issues continued to dominate U.S. relations with Asia under Bush and Clinton. During the night of June 3–4, 1989, Chinese soldiers and tanks stormed into Beijing's Tiananmen Square. Hundreds—perhaps thousands—of demonstrators lay dead. For weeks unarmed students had been holding peaceful prodemocracy rallies and appealing for talks with government leaders. China's octogenarian rulers saw the students' call for political liberalization to match economic reforms as an attempt "to create chaos."[186] Deng Xiaoping crushed the prodemocracy movement and ordered the arrest and execution of protesters. World opinion seethed.

Bush signaled China that he wanted to keep relations intact. He suspended weapons sales and deferred new World Bank loans to China but continued Beijing's most-favored-nation trade status. Convinced that global security required stable and friendly Sino-American ties, Bush sent Brent Scowcroft secretly to Beijing on June 30 with the message that "we can do a lot more for them when they aren't killing their own people."[187] Critics charged that the United States was shortsightedly siding with China's elderly clique while alienating the nation's younger, progressive, future leaders. Bush encouraged such leaders in Prague but snubbed them in Beijing.

Despite China's negative record on human rights, its economy boomed during the 1990s. U.S. trade with China reached $33.1 billion in 1992, with an $18.3 billion surplus in China's favor; by 1997 the figures climbed to $63 billion and $39.5 billion. Candidate Clinton in 1992 faulted Bush for siding "with the status quo against democratic change ... with the old geography of repression rather than a new map of freedom."[188] He vowed to link PRC human rights improvements with free trade privileges. But the Clinton administration renewed China's most-favored-nation trading privileges in June 1993 after the Beijing government released several prominent dissidents and established diplomatic ties with South Korea (1992), despite continued human rights abuses. Beijing's growing trade with Seoul and its pressure on North Korea to permit international nuclear inspection also pleased Washington. When Clinton again granted China most-favored-nation status in 1994, he frankly declared that human rights and trade issues were henceforth decoupled. A *San Francisco Chronicle* editorial, "America: The Pushover Country," accused Clinton of "out-Bushing Bush" in coddling China.[189]

Tensions nonetheless increased after a visit in May 1995 by Taiwan's president to his Cornell University alma mater. Accusing Washington of a plot to "divide, weaken, and contain China," Beijing precipitated a crisis in March 1996 by firing three ballistic missiles close to Taiwan and conducting military exercises in the Taiwan Strait.[190] Secretary of Defense William Perry warned of "grave consequences," as two U.S. carrier task forces steamed ostentatiously toward the region.[191] Both sides

Prodemocracy Courage, Tiananmen Square, Beijing, China.   In early 1989 university students and sympathizers camped in Beijing's great square. They made hopeful speeches about democracy and even built a towering replica of the Statue of Liberty. Drawing inspiration from Poland's Solidarity movement, the young prodemocracy activists pleaded with their nation's aged leaders to liberalize China's politics. In June the military swept into the square. After the massacre, one person—probably a student— braved tanks in a sobering example of the classic contest between the courageous individual and the powerful state. (AP Images/Jeff Widener)

soon backed off, as the United States reaffirmed its support of "one China," and the Chinese agreed not to sell nuclear technology to states that supported terrorism.[192] A week-long state visit to the United States by Chinese president Jiang Zemin in October 1997 promised a "constructive strategic partnership."[193]

U.S. relations with Vietnam also improved. In the fall of 1992, President Bush announced the "last chapter of the Vietnam War" after a full accounting of the 2,265 U.S. military personnel still listed as missing in action (MIAs).[194] The Clinton administration lifted the nineteen-year-old trade embargo in February 1994. Within hours PepsiCo erected a giant, inflated can of soda in the middle of Ho Chi Minh City and gave away 40,000 cans of the international soft drink. General Electric set up offices two blocks from the infamous "Hanoi Hilton" prison where American POWs, including 2008 Republican presidential candidate John McCain, had been detained and tortured. Despite a devastating war and two decades of isolation, many of the 71 million Vietnamese apparently retained a certain attraction to things American. Hanoi undoubtedly saw a strong U.S. economic presence as a possible counter to its giant neighbor China.

President Clinton established full diplomatic relations in July 1995, and his appointment as ambassador of Pete Peterson, a former prisoner of war in North Vietnam for seven years, defused much of the resentment against normalization. Ironically, the economic growth fueled by foreign investment ($8.6 billion in 1996) most benefited the south where Nike and other companies utilized infrastructure left by the Americans. Just as joint historical symposia on the Vietnam War helped to reconcile the past, so did Colin Powell's visit to Hanoi in 2001 wherein the former U.S. soldier wowed his hosts by singing the country classic "El Paso" during an off-the-record talent show.[195]

Trade issues dominated the Japanese-American relationship as well. Anti-Americanism in Japan and "Japan bashing" (*Nihon tataki*) in the United States afflicted the world's two major economies. In 1990 the world's ten largest banks had headquarters in Japan. Japan's biggest company, NTT, was more than twice the size of America's leading corporation, IBM. By 1990 the dollar-rich Japanese controlled 25 percent of California's banking assets and owned almost half of downtown Los Angeles. Japanese firms acquired the MCA and Columbia movie studios as well. Michael Crichton's bestselling novel *Rising Sun* (1992) reflected American anxieties in ominously depicting a Japanese takeover of the American high-tech sector.

Predictions of Japan's global economic hegemony soon faded. The Japanese variant of capitalism, with close ties among corporate "families" of manufacturers, suppliers, exporters, and banks, proved insufficiently flexible in the face of fast-moving globalization. Japan's highly structured society encouraged high production and savings from its citizens but discouraged bold Japanese entrepreneurs equivalent to America's Ted Turner or Bill Gates. As the New York stock exchange soared in the mid-1990s, Tokyo's Nikkei average slumped to half the levels of the late 1980s. U.S. exports to Japan jumped from $27 billion in 1986 to $47.8 billion in 1992 to $66 billion in 1997, even though the trade deficit (in Japan's favor) still hovered around $50 billion in the mid-1990s. McDonald's ranked as Japan's largest restaurant chain by 1995 and Apple Computer became the second largest vendor of personal computers. After Japanese banking losses during the Asian financial crisis of 1997–1998, the $8 trillion U.S. economy stood roughly twice as large as Japan's. Nonetheless, Tokyo still maintained large trade surpluses, with every dollar earned adding to Japan's huge foreign investments.

Washington valued Japan's close military alliance with the United States and its shouldering of more of the mutual defense costs. American officials praised Tokyo for providing economic assistance to developing nations such as the Philippines. North Korea's nuclear ambitions and China's potential menace to Taiwan reinforced Tokyo's desire for continuing military ties even in the absence of a Soviet enemy. Relations were temporarily strained by the rape of a twelve-year-old girl on Okinawa by three U.S. servicemen in 1995. Apologies helped to maintain the U.S.-Japan security alliance, including Tokyo's $40 billion per year self-defense forces (plus paying 70 percent of burden sharing for U.S. troops in Japan). As the new millennium began, many Americans still held ambivalent attitudes about their erstwhile enemy and long-time ally—as "miracle and menace, docile and aggressive, fragile blossom and Tokyo Rose."[196]

Between Two Worlds: Reagan, Bush, Clinton, and the Legacies of the Cold War

"Gosh, I miss the Cold War," President Clinton half-joked after American soldiers were killed in Somalia.[197] Indeed, the post–Cold War era seemed less wieldy than the bipolar system it replaced—so full of violence, so rife with religious and ethnic tensions, so overarmed, so wracked by economic catastrophe, so plagued by illicit drugs, crime, and AIDS, so threatened by the proliferation of nuclear weapons and the deterioration of the natural environment, so burdened by overpopulation and famine.

Reflecting widespread nostalgia for the seeming simplicity of the U.S.-Soviet conflict, and evincing the triumphalist mood that attended the Cold War's end, admiring biographers quickly began mythologizing Reagan's presidency. Because Reagan "lured the Russians into the serious negotiations that really ended the Cold War," while "massive military spending forced the economically crippled Soviets to make concessions," Reagan allegedly ranked with Abraham Lincoln and Franklin D. Roosevelt as "one of the three great liberators in American history."[198] And unlike those predecessors, Reagan achieved victory "through conversation and dialogue" rather than through "total war."[199] Critics told another story, deploring the wasted money (especially on SDI) and noting that the remarkable changes initiated by Gorbachev sprang less from U.S. pressure than from a new generation of Soviet leaders and from courageous Eastern European dissidents. The large U.S. defense buildup may actually have delayed the end of the Cold War by undermining Soviet moderates in their struggle against Kremlin hawks. Reagan possibly undercut America's own power and prestige by running up a tremendous debt and neglecting to repair the American economy or to improve American education for the competitive international marketplace. The president's militaristic foreign policy stimulated warrior fantasies at home, shown in a slew of war-themed films of the 1980s (*Rambo* and *Missing in Action*, for instance) that sanctioned violent solutions to complex social and national problems. Even more sobering was that the celebrated collapse of communism in Eastern Europe and the Soviet Union came to obscure decades of disastrous Third World interventions. For peoples of Asia, Latin America, and Africa caught in the crossfire of decolonization and Cold War strife, resultant human suffering was enormous—as, for instance, in Vietnam, where enough landmines and other weapons remain in place "to destroy lives well into a generation yet to be born."[200]

The Bush and Clinton administrations that followed were tasked not only with "cleaning up" in the aftermath the Reagan Doctrine, but also with managing the complex legacies of a half-century of U.S. overextension and war.[201] Caught between the Cold War and an embryonic "new world order," Bush and Clinton confronted a dizzying array of challenges.[202] Weapons of mass destruction posed one dilemma. Arms sales accelerated across the post–Cold War world. Showing up in the world arms market were U.S. Stinger missiles that the Reagan administration had given in the 1980s to radical Islamic rebels in Afghanistan. After the Soviet withdrawal, Reagan's Afghan "freedom fighters" used the weapons against rivals, became traffickers in heroin, trained *jihad* terrorists and assassins, and suppressed indigenous Afghan women's rights. The United States continued exporting $15 billion in weapons each year as Third World governments lined up to buy Patriot missiles with money better spent on health and education.

Other weapons posed deadly threats. The release of sarin gas into the Tokyo subway by a Japanese religious cult in 1995 raised the chilling specter of biological and chemical terrorism. With biological weapons banned since 1972, the 1993 Chemical Convention (ratified by Washington in 1997) required signatories to destroy all chemical weapons by the year 2005 and to submit to rigorous inspection. More than 100 nations in 1997 signed a treaty banning antipersonnel land mines, but President Clinton refused to sign it because U.S. troops in Korea relied on mines to protect against a North Korean attack.

Nuclear proliferation remained a grave peril to all nations. Even though South Africa dismantled its nuclear weapons after 1993, Israel, Pakistan, and India had all

World Arms Exports, 1992–1994

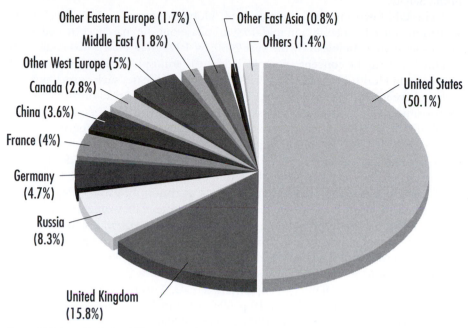

Other Eastern Europe (1.7%)
Middle East (1.8%)
Other West Europe (5%)
Canada (2.8%)
China (3.6%)
France (4%)
Germany (4.7%)
Russia (8.3%)
United Kingdom (15.8%)
Other East Asia (0.8%)
Others (1.4%)
United States (50.1%)

Source: U.S. Arms Control and Disarmament Agency

joined the nuclear club, and others such as Iran, Iraq, and North Korea aspired to do so. Congress provided nearly $1.5 billion to help Russia, Belarus, Ukraine, and Kazakhstan dismantle much of the former Soviet nuclear arsenal and safeguard the remaining nuclear materials inside Russia. In a "Megatons to Megawatts" arrangement, President Clinton promised to buy from Russia 500 metric tons of highly enriched uranium over a 20-year period for $12 billion.[203] Calling nonproliferation "one of our nation's highest priorities," Clinton did what he could to prevent "nuclear yardsales" and to maintain nuclear security inside Russia.[204]

Environmental hazards also presented borderless dilemmas. Population pressures taxed scarce resources, bringing more pollution, more disease, and more famines such as those that wracked Africa in the 1980s and 1990s. Overgrazing and tree-cutting in countries such as Bangladesh produced quick runoffs of rainfalls and flooding, washing away precious topsoil and killing many. Ecological problems in turn generated economic turmoil, political instability, and social disintegration. Yet the Bush administration vetoed monies for the UN Population Fund in 1989 because the agency supported birth-control programs that allowed abortions. Because Washington did not want the 1982 Convention on the Law of the Sea to restrict private American business, not until fall 1997 did President Clinton transmit the treaty to the Senate, where it remains pending. At the 1992 Earth Summit in Rio de Janeiro, attended by 178 nations, Bush opposed strong environmental protection rules, charging that they would cost jobs. He refused to sign the Biodiversity Treaty designed to slow the loss of endangered species. Clinton signed the treaty in 1993; it, too, languishes in the Senate.

The UN Environmental Program kept "global commons" issues alive. Eighty-six nations agreed at Helsinki in mid-1989 to phase out the manufacture and use of ozone-destroying chemicals by the year 2000; by 1994 their efforts had reduced by half the *increase* in the concentration of CFCs in the atmosphere. Through the efforts of the World Health Organization (WHO), infectious diseases such as smallpox and malaria have nearly been eliminated. Combating the global spread of AIDS became the organization's next daunting task. Genetic-engineering programs funded by the World Bank labored to improve farm productivity. At a conference in Kyoto in 1997 attended by 166 countries, the United States agreed to a Global Warming Convention under which developed nations must reduce carbon dioxide, methane, and other greenhouse gas emissions by 6 to 8 percent below their 1990 levels.

Sexual violence and inequality also gained attention. In early 1994, the State Department focused for the first time on the treatment of women in its annual human-rights report. Its grim findings included forced sterilizations and abortions in China; coerced prostitution in Thailand and Burma; husbands killing their wives because of insufficient dowries in India; laws making adultery illegal for women but not for men in Morocco. The United Nations reported in 2000 that two-thirds of the world's 876 million illiterate people were female. Worldwide, women held only 14 percent of top managerial jobs, 10 percent of seats in national legislatures, and 6 percent of cabinet-level posts. In 1996 the United States joined Canada in making genital mutilation (an estimated 2 million victims per year) and other gender-based abuses grounds for asylum. With UN conventions on the rights of women still unratified by the United States, the State Department in November 2001 indicted Afghanistan's Taliban regime for "egregious acts of violence against women, including rape, abduction, and forced marriage."[205]

Because "information, ideas, and money now pulse across the planet at light speed," international communications issues assumed new importance.[206] Since the 1970s, developing nations had been calling for a "New Information Order" in which the powerful Northern and Western nations would have to report news accurately and fairly. Third World critics charged that the control of information by developed states—especially the United States—created dependency and retarded economic growth. Because of its remote-sensing satellites, the United States allegedly could marshal greater information than weaker states in negotiations on tariffs and other issues. Through the International Telecommunications Satellite Consortium (INTELSAT), founded in 1964 to coordinate the use of satellites, the United States has also preserved control of the majority of the electromagnetic spectrum for itself and its allies. By 1999 Time Warner, the world's largest TV producer, was selling thousands of hours of programs to 175 countries. Such dominance helped, for example, to increase sales of sneakers to China through video images of Michael Jordan slam-dunking a basketball. An international agreement in 1997 opened the $600 billion global telephone market to greater competition, with U.S. companies poised to increase their one-third share. Although 90 percent of the 610 billion e-mail messages on the World Wide Web were in English by 2000, experts predicted that Internet traffic in other languages will soon predominate. Electronic commerce (or "e-business") totaled $145 billion in 1999 and was expected to reach $7.29 trillion worldwide by 2004.

Powerful governments were vulnerable to opponents with easy access to the new technology. In 1989 protesting Chinese students used fax machines to communicate with the outside world. International revulsion against the Chinese crackdown was so extensive largely because the ghastly events appeared on worldwide television. Nor could Islamic censorship in Iran stem the "tide of godlessness" represented by bootleg videocassettes of *Baywatch* and *Titanic*.[207] In 2000 a young hacker from the Philippines launched a virus that cost some $15 billion in damages in the United States alone. Computers seized after 9/11 would reveal al Qaeda plans to destroy U.S. power grids by attacking the computer systems that controlled them—a form of "e-jihad," or holy war on-line.[208]

Globalization (roughly defined as the process of integrating peoples politically, culturally, and economically into a larger community) made foreign relations less foreign. The impact of NAFTA on both St. Joseph, Missouri, and Racine, Wisconsin, for example, was the loss of manufacturing jobs when textiles and refrigeration plants relocated to Mexico, and the addition of employees by high-tech firms eager to take advantage of the booming export market. Even college sports became globalized, as nearly 300 student athletes from 59 countries had accepted basketball scholarships at American universities by 1998. Street protests against the effects of globalization began with the "Battle in Seattle" in 1999 and were repeated at subsequent economic summits. Many critics saw globalization as "neoimperialism wearing Bill Gates's face and Mickey Mouse's ears," exploiting "women, minorities, the poor, and developing regions. It fouls ecosystems, displaces local cultures … and deepens the divide (digital and otherwise) between the global haves and have-nots."[209] A French sheep farmer became a national hero in 1999 by destroying a McDonald's restaurant to "protect culinary sovereignty."[210] Yet the widespread popularity of the Japanese game Pokemon suggested "true cultural globalization, not just Americanization."[211] For good or ill, contemporary globalization grew "farther, faster, cheaper and deeper."[212]

What the veteran analyst George F. Kennan called the global "bewilderments" of the new millennium were accompanied by pressing domestic problems.[213] Americans ballyhooed victory in the Cold War, but "why doesn't it feel better?" asked one journalist.[214] The United States in 1998 trailed twenty-two other leading industrialized nations in high school graduation rates. Even with a revived economy and balanced budget by 2000, America suffered an increasing division between rich and poor; millions unable to afford medical insurance and adequate health care; workers losing jobs as corporations "outsourced" abroad. Clinton warned that the "currency of national strength in this new era will be denominated not only in ships and tanks and planes, but in diplomas and patents and paychecks."[215]

By the year 2000, however, America's military might and global reach had grown even more predominant. Despite talks of a post–Cold War "peace dividend" during the Clinton years, the defense budget remained on "Cold War autopilot" ($270 billion in 1999) and the Pentagon developed new weapons systems and strategies for use against "rogue" states and terrorists.[216] The Air Force emphasized "stealth" aircraft that could deliver "smart" bombs and missiles without alerting enemy radar. The Navy reluctantly planned new generations of cruise missileships to replace its aging supercarriers. The Army stressed hand-to-hand combat by small units of "Rangers" at some cost to historically preferred large-scale battles of maneuver by division and corps, and the Marine Corps rose to a new level of parity with the other services as the arm that could most readily attack from the sea. Dubbed "Tomahawk Diplomacy" after the American cruise missile of choice, the new strategy smacked of nineteenth-century gunboat diplomacy—the arbitrary application of military and naval force to teach less "civilized" peoples proper behavior. The military increasingly took on the roles of peacekeepers and nation builders in faraway places, with mixed results.

In the end, neither Clinton nor Bush seemed able to translate the promises of a new world order into a cohesive program for international progress and renewal. More managers than architects of change, Bush and Clinton helped transition Eastern Europe and the Soviet Union from communism towards capitalism and South Africa from apartheid towards democracy. Both guided the United States toward normalized relations with Vietnam; both rejected Reagan's largely pro-Iraq foreign policy. But Bush and Clinton perpetuated many policies of their Cold War predecessors—in Cuba, where they continued isolating Castro's regime; in the Middle East, where they tenuously balanced pro-Israel concerns with strategic Arab alliances; and in Latin America, where U.S. economic and political interventionism continued apace. Both invoked bold and visionary language. Bush hailed the end of a "world divided—a world of barbed wire and concrete block, conflict and cold war," proposing in its place "a world in which freedom and respect for human rights find a home among all the nations."[217] Clinton described the end of the Cold War as "a moment of miracles. The United States must and will serve as a fulcrum for change and a pivot point for peace. I know that together we can extend this moment of miracles into an age of great work and new wonders."[218] Yet neither president captured the popular imagination the way that Reagan did with his Cold War certitudes—even as Reagan's own antipodal language accompanied a risky brinkmanship and masked a leader who did not control crucial details of his foreign policy.

Perhaps the post–Cold War decade offered the wrong historical moment for grand visionaries to occupy the White House. As ideological and political bipolarity receded, the nation apparently needed problem-solvers, not prophets—practical leaders who could put aside inflamed rhetoric and concentrate on governing America in an ever-more complex world, one in which enemies no longer seemed to emanate from a single, adversarial state. But just as the Cold War had provided an "alibi" to "neglect complex global issues," it also had provided a convenient pretext for a globalist foreign policy.[219] Without a foreign menace to justify dictatorial double-dealing (as in China) or intervention in Third World trouble spots (such as Somalia and Haiti), the contradictions of U.S. foreign policy were laid bare, and Americans showed little willingness to sacrifice money and lives for faraway others. Only when victory could be assured rapidly with little or no loss of American life (as in Panama and the Persian Gulf) did citizens rally around the flag, calling forth sepia-colored memories of Cold War unity, only to retreat once more to private lives of insularity and abundance. In a decade liberated from dichotomy and marked by the intensified blurring of boundaries—political, economic, environmental, and personal—some welcomed liberation from dictates of the past and embraced the chance, in Thomas Paine's words, to "begin the world over again." Others experienced vertigo, seeking certainty that the enemy did not, after all, lie within, and that the mantle of greatness that the nation had folded around itself throughout its history remained whole. That mantle had always shone most brightly when the country was or imagined itself under attack. As Americans stood, Janus-faced, before the new millennium, those who craved a new external force against which the nation could define itself did not have long to wait.

FURTHER READING FOR THE PERIOD 1981–2001

For overviews and topical surveys on the period, see Dean Baker, *The United States since 1980* (2007); William C. Berman, *America's Right Turn* (1994); Meena Bose and Rosanna Perotti, eds., *From Cold War to World Order* (2002); Zbigniew Brzezinski, *Second Chance* (2007); Andrew Busch, *Reagan's Victory* (2005) (conservative ascendency); Robert M. Collins, *Transforming America* (2007); Fraser Cameron, *US Foreign Policy After the Cold War* (2002); Derek Chollet and James Goldgeier, *America Between the Wars* (2008); James E. Cronin, *The World the Cold War Made* (1996); Ivo H. Daalder and James M. Lindsay, *American Unbound* (2003); Stephen Ducat, *The Wimp Factor* (2004); John Ehrman, *The Rise of Neoconservatism* (1995) and *The Eighties* (2005); H. Bruce Franklin, *War Stars* (2008); Raymond Garthoff, *The Great Transition* (1994); Fred Greenstein, ed., *The George W. Bush Presidency* (2003); William Greider, *Fortress America* (1998); P. Edward Haley, *Strategies of Dominance* (2006); George Herring, *From Colony to Superpower* (2008); Mark Hertsgaard, *The Eagle's Shadow* (2002); Michael Hirsh, *At War with Ourselves* (2003); Stanley Hoffmann, *World Disorders* (1999); Chalmers Johnson, *The Sorrows of Empire* (2004); Paul Krugman, *The Great Unraveling* (2003); Charles Kupchan, *The End of the American Era* (2002); Lewis Lapham, *Theater of War* (2002); Robert J. Lieber, ed., *Eagle Adrift* (1997); Robert S. Litwak, *Rogue States and U.S. Foreign Policy* (2000); Wilfred Loth, *Overcoming the Cold War* (2002); Michael Mandelbaum, *The Dawn of Peace in Europe* (1997); Joseph S. Nye, *The Paradox of American Power* (2002); Don Oberdorfer, *From the Cold War to a New Era* (1998); James T. Patterson, *Restless Giant* (2005); David Reynold, *Summits* (2007); Michael Schaller, *Right Turn* (2007); James M. Scott, *After the End* (1999); Ronald Steel, *Temptations of a Superpower* (1995); Jessica Stern, *The Ultimate Terrorists* (1999); Emmanuel Todd, *After the Empire* (2004); Robert W. Tucker and David C. Henrickson, *The Imperial Temptation* (1992); Jules Tygiel, *Ronald Reagan and the Triumph of American Conservatism* (2006); Odd Arne Westad, ed., *The Fall of Détente* (1995); Sean Wilentz, *The Age of Reagan* (2008); and William C. Wohlforth, *Cold War Endgame* (2003).

Ronald Reagan and his policies are studied in John Arquilla, *The Reagan Imprint* (2006); Michael K. Bohn, *The Achille Lauro Hijacking* (2004); Lou Cannon, *President Reagan* (1991); Richard S. Conley, *Reassessing the Reagan Presidency* (2003); Robert Dallek, *Ronald Reagan* (1984); John P. Diggins, *Ronald Reagan* (2007); Theodore Draper, *A Very Thin Line* (1991) (Iran-Contra); Beth A. Fischer, *The Reagan Reversal* (1997); Frances FitzGerald, *Way Out There in the Blue* (2000); Allan Gerson, *The Kirkpatrick Mission* (1991) (UN); Nigel Hey, *The Star Wars Enigma* (2006); Richard J. Jensen, *Reagan at Bergen-Belsen and Bitburg* (2007); Haynes Johnson, *Sleepwalking Through History* (1991); Paul Kengor, *The Crusader* (2006), *God and Ronald Reagan* (2004), and *The Reagan Presidency* (2005); Peter Kornbluh and Malcolm Byrne, eds., *The Iran-Contra Scandal* (1993); Mark P. Lagon, *The Reagan Doctrine* (1994); Edmund Morris, *Dutch* (1999); William E. Pemberton, *Exit with Honor* (1997); Richard Reeves, *President Reagan* (2005); Michael Schaller, *Reckoning with Reagan* (1992); Peter Schweitzer, *Reagan's War* (2002); James M. Scott, *Deciding to Intervene* (1996) (Reagan Doctrine); Gil Troy, *Morning in America* (2005); Nicholas Wapshott, *Ronald Reagan and Margaret Thatcher* (2007); and David C. Wills, *The First War on Terrorism* (2004).

On George H. W. Bush, consult Ryan J. Barilleaux and Mark J. Rozell, *Power and Prudence* (2004); Colin Campbell and Bert A. Rockman, *The Bush Presidency* (1991); Anthony J. Eksterowicz and Glenn P. Hastedt, *The Presidencies of George Herbert Walker Bush and George Walker Bush* (2008); John Robert Greene,

The Presidency of George Bush (2000) and *The George H. W. Bush Years* (2006); Christopher Maynard, *Out of the Shadow* (2008); Martin J. Medhurst, *The Rhetorical Presidency of George H. W. Bush* (2006); Timothy J. Naftali, *George H. W. Bush* (2007); Herbert S. Parmet, *George Bush* (1998); Tom Wicker, *George Herbert Walker Bush* (2004); Kenneth W. Thompson, ed., *The Bush Presidency* (1998); Craig Unger, *House of Bush, House of Saud* (2004); and Steve A. Yetiv, *Explaining Foreign Policy* (2004) (First Gulf War).

For William J. Clinton's presidency, see William C. Berman, *From the Center to the Edge* (2001); Sidney Blumenthal, *The Clinton Wars* (2004); Terry L. Deibel, *Clinton and Congress* (2000); Michael Dobbs, *Madeleine Albright* (1999); John Dumbrell, *Clinton's Foreign Policy* (2008); Jason A. Edwards, *Navigating the Post-Cold War World* (2008); Nigel Hamilton, *Bill Clinton* (2007); John F. Harris, *The Survivor* (2005); William G. Hyland, *Clinton's World* (1999); Haynes Johnson, *The Best of Times* (2001); Joe Klein, *The Natural* (2002); Donald T. Phillips, *The Clinton Charisma* (2007); Flavio Romano, *Clinton and Blair* (2006); Todd G. Shields and Jeannie M. Whayne, *The Clinton Riddle* (2004); Shirley Anne Warshaw, *The Clinton Years* (2004).

For the Cold War's end and its impact on the former Soviet Union, in Eastern Europe, and U.S. foreign relations, see Dana H. Allin, *Cold War Illusions* (1995); Timothy Garton Ash, *The Uses of Adversity* (1989) and *The Magic Lantern* (1990); Ronald D. Asmus, *Opening NATO's Door* (2002); Michael Beschloss and Strobe Talbott, *At the Highest Levels* (1993); Archie Brown, *The Gorbachev Factor* (1996); Stephen F. Cohen, *Failed Crusade* (2000) and *Soviet Fates and Lost Alternatives* (2009); Timothy Colton, *Yeltsin* (2008); Matthew Evangelista, *Unarmed Forces* (1999); Andrew Felkey, *Yeltsin's Russia and the West* (2002); David S. Foglesong, *The American Mission and the "Evil Empire"* (2007); John Lewis Gaddis, *The United States and the End of the Cold War* (1992); A.S. Grachev, *Gorbachev's Gamble* (2008); Norman A. Graebner et al., *Reagan, Bush, Gorbachev* (2008); Richard K. Hermann, *Ending the Cold War* (2004); Michael Hogan, ed., *The End of the Cold War* (1992); Jerry F. Hough, *Democratization and Revolution in the U.S.S.R., 1985–1991* (1997); Robert G. Kaiser, *Why Gorbachev Happened* (1991); Charles W. Kegley, Jr., ed., *The Long Postwar Peace* (1991); Richard Lebow and Janice Gross Stein, *We All Lost the Cold War* (1993); Melvyn P. Leffler, *For the Soul of Mankind* (2007); Allen George A. MacLean, *Clinton's Foreign Policy in Russia* (2006); Michael Mandelbaum, ed., *Central Asia and the World* (1994) (former Soviet republics); Jack Matlock, *Reagan and Gorbachev* (2004); Michael MccGwire, *Perestroika and Soviet National Security* (1991); Olva Njølstad, *The Last Decade of the Cold War* (2004); Matthew Ouimet, *The Rise and Fall of the Brezhnev Doctrine in Soviet Foreign Policy* (2003); Thomas G. Paterson, *On Every Front* (1992); David Remnick, *Lenin's Tomb* (1993); Robert Service, *Russia* (2003); Leon V. Sigal, *Hang Separately* (2000); Kiron K. Skinner, ed., *Turning Points in Ending the Cold War* (2008); Helene Sjursen, *The United States, Western Europe and the Polish Crisis* (2003); Odd Arne Westad, *The Global Cold War* (2005); William C. Wohlforth, *Cold War Endgame* (2003); Christopher I. Xenakis, *What Happened to the Soviet Union* (2002); and Ivan Zasoursky, *Media and Power in Post-Soviet Russia* (2002) and Vladislav Zubok, *A Failed Empire* (2007).

For the wars in the former Yugoslavia and the international response, see Norman Cigar and Paul Williams, *Indictment at the Hague* (2002); Donald C. F. Daniel et al., *Coercive Inducement and the Containment of International Crises* (1999); James Gow, *The Triumph of the Lack of Will* (1997); John Hagan, *Justice in the Balkans* (2003); David Halberstam, *War in a Time of Peace* (2001); Dag Henriksen, *NATO's Gamble* (2007) (Kosovo); Tim Judah, *Kosovo* (2008); Matthew McAllester, *Beyond the Mountains of the Damned* (2002) (Kosovo); Elizabeth Pond, *Endgame in the Balkans* (2006); Sabrina P. Ramet, *The Three Yugoslavias* (2006); Miron Rezan, *Europe's Nightmare* (2001) (Kosovo); Cees Wiebes, *Intelligence and War in Bosnia, 1992–1995* (2003); and Susan L. Woodward, *Balkan Tragedy* (1995).

On Asia, see Zachary Abuza, *Militant Islam in Southeast Asia* (2003); Raymond Bonner, *Waltzing with a Dictator* (1987) (Marcos); H. W. Brands, *Bound to Empire* (1992) (Philippines); Roger Buckley, *U.S.-Japan Alliance Diplomacy* (1992); Chae-ho Chong, *Between Ally and Partner* (2007) (China, South Korea); Stephen D. Cohen, *Cowboys and Samurai* (1991); Warren I. Cohen, ed., *Pacific Passage* (1996); Bruce Cumings, *Divided Korea* (1995); Jean A. Garrison, *Making China Policy* (2005); William H. Gleysteen, Jr., *Massive Entanglement, Marginal Influence* (1999) (South Korea); Richard J. Kessler, *Rebellion and Repression in the Philippines* (1989); Walter LaFeber, *The Clash* (1997) (Japan); David M. Lampton, *Same Bed, Different Dreams* (2000) (U.S.-China); Robert S. McMahon, *The Limits of Empire* (1999) (Southeast Asia); Andrew Nathan and Perry Link, eds., *The Tiananmen Papers* (2001); Michael Schaller, *Altered States* (1997) (Japan); Patrick Smith, *Japan*

(1997); and Robert L. Suettinger, *Beyond Tiananmen* (2004); Robert G. Sutter, *The United States in Asia* (2009); Edith Terry, *How Asia Got Rich* (2002); and Nancy B. Tucker, *Strait Talk* (2009).

For South America and the Caribbean, see Richard Crandall, *Driven by Drugs* (2002) (Colombia); David W. Engstrom, *Presidential Decision Making Adrift* (1997) (Mariel boatlift); H. Michael Erisman, *Cuba's Foreign Relations in a Post–Soviet World* (2002); Philippe R. Girard, *Clinton in Haiti* (2004); Eldon Kenworthy, *America/Américas* (1995); Walter LaFeber, *Inevitable Revolutions* (1993); William M. LeoGrande, *Our Own Backyard* (1998); Juan J. Lopez, *Democracy Delayed* (2002) (Cuba); Abraham F. Lowenthal, ed., *Exporting Democracy* (1991); Morris Morley and Christopher McGillion, *Unfinished Business* (2002) (Cuba); Leigh A. Payne, *Uncivil Movements* (2000); Louis A. Pérez, Jr., *Cuba and the United States* (1997); Ralph Pezzullo, *Plunging into Haiti* (2006); Brenda Gayle Plummer, *Haiti and the United States* (1992); Joaquin Roy, *Cuba, the United States, and the Helms-Burton Doctrine* (2000); Bert Ruiz, *The Colombian Civil War* (2002); Lars Schoultz, *Beneath the United States* (1998) and *That Infernal Little Cuban Republic* (2009); Peter H. Smith, *Talons of the Eagle* (2007); and Gary Williams, *U.S.-Grenada Relations* (2007).

On Central America see Sergio Aguayo, *Myths and (Mis)Perceptions* (1998) (Mexico); Peter Andreas, *Border Games* (2000) (Mexico); Ariel C. Armony, *Argentina, the United States, and the Anti-Communist Crusade in Central America* (1997); Kevin Buckley, *Panama* (1991); Kenneth M. Coleman and George C. Herring, eds., *Understanding the Central American Crisis* (1991); Russell Crandall, *Driven by Drugs* (2008) (Colombia); Timothy J. Dunn, *The Militarization of the U.S.-Mexico Border* (1996); Lesley Gill, *The School of the Americas* (2004); Michael Grow, *U.S. Presidents and Latin American Interventions* (2008); Martha Honey, *Hostile Acts* (1994) (Costa Rica); Susanne Jonas, *The Battle for Guatemala* (1991); Stephen Kinzer, *Blood of Brothers* (1991) (Nicaragua); Peter Kornbluh, *Nicaragua* (1988); John Lindsey-Poland, *Emperors in the Jungle* (2003); Jacqueline Mazza, *Don't Disturb the Neighbors* (2001) (Mexico); Abraham F. Lowenthal and Katrina Burgess, eds., *The California-Mexico Connection* (1993); Morris H. Morley, *Washington, Somoza, and the Sandinistas* (1994); Robert A. Pastor, *Whirlpool* (1992), *Integration with Mexico* (1993), and *Exiting the Whirlpool* (2001); W. Dirk Raat, *Mexico and the United States* (1996); Fred Rosen, *Empire and Dissent* (2008); Margaret E. Scranton, *The Noriega Years* (1991); Christian Smith, *Resisting Reagan* (1996); Peter H. Smith, *Talons of the Eagle* (2008); and Gaddis Smith, *The Last Years of the Monroe Doctrine, 1945–1993* (1994).

Middle East topics are examined in Rachel Bronson, *Thicker Than Oil* (2006) (Saudi Arabia); Richard J. Chasdi, *Tapestry of Terror* (2002); Lawrence A. Freedman, *A Choice of Enemies* (2008); Burton I. Kaufman, *The Arab Middle East and the United States* (1996); Nicholas Laham, *Selling AWACS to Saudi Arabia* (2002), *Crossing the Rubicon* (2004), and *The American Bombing of Libya* (2008); David Lesch, *The Arab-Israeli Conflict* (2007); Aaron David Miller, *The Much Too Promised Land* (2008); Debra A. Miller, *Iraq* (2004); Tim Niblock, *"Pariah States" and Sanctions in the Middle East* (2002); Michael B. Oren, *Power, Faith, and Fantasy* (2007); William B. Quandt, *The Peace Process* (1993); Yezid Sayad, *Armed Struggle and the Search for State* (1997); David Schoenbaum, *The United States and the State of Israel* (1993); Shimon Shamir and Bruce Maddy-Weitzman, *The Camp David Summit—What Went Wrong?* (2005); Joseph T. Stanik, *El Dorado Canyon* (2002); Michael Tracy Tomas, *American Policy Toward Israel* (2007); Patrick Tyler, *A World of Trouble* (2009); Bernard Wasserman, *Israelis and Palestinians* (2003); Steven M. Wright, *The United States and Persian Gulf Security* (2007); Daniel Yergin, *The Prize* (1991) (oil); Steve A. Yetiv, *The Absence of Grand Strategy* (2008) and *Crude Awakenings* (2004) (Persian Gulf); and Eyal Zisser, *Assad's Legacy* (2002).

Iraqi-U.S. relations and the Persian Gulf War are treated in Stephen R. Graubard, *Mr. Bush's War* (1992); Khihir Hamza, *Saddam's Bombmaker* (2000); Avigdor Haselkorn, *The Continuing Storm* (1999); Jean E. Krasno and James D. Sutterlin, *The United Nations and Iraq* (2002); John R. MacArthur, *Second Front* (1992) (censorship); Debra A. Miller, *Iraq* (2004); Morris M. Mottale, *The Origins of the Gulf Wars* (2001); John Mueller, *Policy and Opinion in the Gulf War* (1994); Geoff Simons, *Targeting Iraq* (2002); Jean Edward Smith, *George Bush's War* (1992); Philip M. Taylor, *War and the Media* (1992); and Kenneth R. Timmerman, *The Death Lobby* (1991).

African issues are studied in Michael Barnett, *Eyewitness to a Genocide* (2003) (Rwanda); Christina Fisanick, *The Rwanda Genocide* (2004); John L. Hirsch and Robert B. Oakley, *Somalia and Operation Restore Hope* (1995); Richard W. Hull, *American Enterprise in South Africa* (1990); Jeffrey A. Lefebvre, *Arms for the Horn* (1991) (Ethiopia and Somalia); Fatima Meer, *Higher Than Hope* (1990) (Mandela); Robert K. Massie, *Loosing the Bonds* (1997) (South Africa); Larry Minear and Thomas G. Weiss, *Humanitarian Politics* (1995); Samantha Power, *"A Problem from Hell"* (2002) (Genocide); Peter J. Schraeder, *United States Foreign Policy Toward Africa* (1994); and Jonathan Stevenson, *Losing Mogadishu* (1995).

For the nuclear arms race, arms control, and the antinuclear movement, see Donald C. Baucom, *The Origins of SDI* (1992); Ronald J. Bee, *Nuclear Proliferation* (1995); William E. Burrows and Robert Windrem, *Critical Mass* (1994); Dan Caldwell, *The Dynamics of Domestic Politics and Arms Control* (1991) (SALT-II); James E. Goodby, *At the Borderline of Armageddon* (2006); Paul Lettow, *Ronald Reagan and the Quest to Abolish Nuclear Weapons* (2005); David S. Meyer, *A Winter of Discontent* (1990) (freeze); Ronald E. Powaski, *Return to Armageddon* (2000); Stephen I. Schwartz, ed., *Atomic Audit* (1998); Raju Thomas, *The Nuclear Nonproliferation Regime* (1997); and Daniel Wirls, *Buildup* (1992).

Economic issues and globalization are discussed in Royce J. Ammon, *Global Television and the Shaping of World Politics* (1999); C. Fred Bergsten, *Dilemmas of the Dollar* (1996); Maxwell A. Cameron and Brian W. Tomlin, *The Making of NAFTA* (2001); Alfred E. Eckes, Jr. and Thomas W. Zeiler, *Globalization and the American Century* (2003); Thomas L. Friedman, *The Lexus and the Olive Tree* (1999); Kent Jones, *Who's Afraid of The WTO* (2003); Mary Cusimano Love, ed., *Beyond Sovereignty* (2003); John R. MacArthur, *The Selling of Free Trade* (2002); William A. Orme, Jr., *Understanding NAFTA* (1996); Louis W. Pauly, *Who Elected the Bankers?* (1997); Maryse Robert, *Negotiating NAFTA* (2002); Peter Singer, *One World* (2002); Robert Solomon, *Money on the Move* (1999); and Joseph E. Stiglitz, *Globalization and Its Discontents* (2002) and *The Roaring Nineties* (2003).

On environmental issues, consult Richard E. Benedick, *Ozone Diplomacy* (1998); Lee-Anne Broadhead, *International Environmental Politics* (2002); Laurie Garrett, *Microbes Versus Mankind* (1997); Edward Goldsmith and Nicolas Hildyard, eds., *The Earth Report* (1988); Thomas F. Homer-Dixon, *Environmental Scarcity and Global Security* (1993); Jeremy Leggett, *Carbon War* (2001) (global warming); Ralph B. Levering and Miriam L. Levering, *Citizen Action for Global Change* (1999); George D. Moffett, *Global Population Growth* (1994); Joachim Radkau, *Nature and Power* (2008); Spencer Weart, *The Discovery of Global Warming* (2004); and Donald Worster, ed., *The Ends of the Earth* (1989).

For population and immigration issues, see Frank B. Bean et al., *At the Crossroads* (1998) (Mexico); Matthew Connelly, *Fatal Misconception* (2008) (population); John F. Hutchinson, *Champions of Charity* (1996) (Red Cross); Christopher Mitchell, ed., *Western Hemisphere Immigration and United States Foreign Policy* (1992); Michael S. Teitelbaum and Myron Weiner, eds., *Threatened Peoples, Threatened Borders* (1995); and Reed Ueda, *Postwar Immigrant America* (1994).

See also the General Bibliography, Robert L. Beisner, ed., *Guide to American Foreign Relations Since 1600* (2003), and the following notes:

NOTES TO CHAPTER 11

1. *Newsweek, CXIV* (November 20, 1989), 28.
2. Timothy Garton Ash, "The German Revolution," *New York Review of Books*, December 21, 1989, p. 14.
3. *Ibid.*
4. Gaby Greenwald quoted in G. Jonathan Greenwald, *Berlin Witness* (University Park: Penn State University Press, 1993), p. 264.
5. Quoted in George Bush and Brent Scowcroft, *A World Transformed* (New York: Knopf, 1998), p. 151.
6. Quoted in *Time, CXXXIV* (November 20, 1989), 29.
7. Quoted in *Washington Post National Weekly Edition*, January 1–7, 1990.
8. Quoted in Richard Ned Lebow and Janice Gross Stein, "Reagan and the Russians," *The Atlantic Monthly, CCLXXIII* (February 1994), 36.
9. Quoted in *Time, CXXXV* (January 1, 1990), 53.

10. Vladislav M. Zubok, "New Evidence on the End of the Cold War," *Cold War International History Project*, nos. 12–13 (Fall/Winter 2001), p. 11; quoted in Michael Beschloss and Strobe Talbott, *At the Highest Levels* (Boston: Little, Brown, 1993), p. 134.
11. Francis Fukuyama, *The End of History and the Last Man* (New York: Penguin, 1992), p. 5; Matthew Arnold, "Stanzas from the Grande Chartreuse," 1855.
12. Quoted in Robert G. Kaiser, "Your Host of Hosts," *New York Review of Books*, June 28, 1984, p. 38.
13. Quoted *ibid.*, p. 39.
14. Martin Anderson, *Revolution* (Stanford: Stanford University Press, 1990), p. 290.
15. Quoted in Richard Reeves, *President Reagan* (New York: Simon & Schuster, 2005), p. xv.

16. Reagan quoted in Strobe Talbott, *The Russians and Reagan* (New York: Vintage, 1984), p. 32, and in Michael Schaller, *Right Turn* (New York: Oxford University Press, 2007), p. 78.

17. Quoted in Sean Wilentz, *The Age of Reagan* (New York: Harper Collins, 2008), p. 151.

18. Reagan quoted in David Wirls, *Buildup* (Ithaca: Cornell University Press, 1992), pp. 32–33 and Elizabeth Edwards Spalding, "The Origins and Meaning of Reagan's Cold War," in Paul Kengor and Peter Schweizer, eds., *The Reagan Presidency* (New York: Rowman & Littlefield, 2005), pp. 53–54.

19. Quoted in Michael Schaller, *Reckoning with Reagan* (New York: Oxford University Press, 1992), p. 4.

20. Richard V. Allen quoted in Robert M. Collins, *Transforming America* (New York: Columbia University Press, 2007), p. 197.

21. *Department of State Bulletin, LXXXIV* (May 1984), 4.

22. Quoted in Gary Scott Smith, *Faith and the Presidency* (New York: Oxford University Press, 2007), p. 325.

23. *Department of State Bulletin, XXII* (November 1984), 7; quoted in Michael J. Mazarr, "George W. Bush, Idealist," *International Affairs, LXXIX* (June 2003), 515.

24. Quoted in Walter LaFeber, *Inevitable Revolutions* (New York: Norton, 1993; 2nd ed.), p. 276.

25. *Public Papers, Reagan, 1981*, p. 464; *ibid., 1983* (Washington, D.C.: Government Printing Office, 1984–1985, 2 vols.), I, 265.

26. *Public Papers, Reagan, 1983, II*, 1189.

27. Quoted in David F. Schmitz, *The United States and Right-Wing Dictatorships, 1965–1989* (New York: Cambridge University Press, 2006), p. 195.

28. Quoted in Michael McClintock, *Instruments of Statecraft* (New York: Pantheon, 1992), p. 378.

29. Quoted in Collins, *Transforming*, p. 197.

30. Quoted in Robert David Johnson, "Congress and the Cold War," *Journal of Cold War Studies, III* (Spring 2001), 96.

31. George P. Schultz, *Turmoil and Triumph* (New York: Charles Scribner's Sons, 1992), p. 275.

32. Quoted in Robert A. Pastor, "The Centrality of Central America," in Larry Berman, ed., *Looking Back on the Reagan Presidency* (Baltimore: Johns Hopkins University Press, 1990), p. 40.

33. Quoted in Theodore S. Draper, *A Very Thin Line* (New York: Simon & Schuster, 1991), p. 560.

34. Quoted in Jules Tygiel, *Ronald Reagan* (New York: Pearson Longman, 2005), p. 174.

35. Reeves, *President Reagan*, p. 379.

36. Quoted in Troy Gil, *Morning in America* (Princeton: Princeton University Press, 2005), p. 235.

37. Quoted in Timothy Naftali, *George H. W. Bush* (New York: Times Books, 2007), p. 154.

38. Eric Alterman, *When Presidents Lie* (New York: Viking, 2004), p. 293.

39. Quoted in Robert E. Osgood, "The Revitalization of Containment," *Foreign Affairs: America and the World, 1981, LX* (1982), 475.

40. Quoted in *New York Times*, December 10, 1981.

41. George F. Kennan, "Cease This Madness," *Atlantic Monthly, CCXLVII* (January 1981), 25–28.

42. Quoted in Spalding, "Origins," p. 56.

43. Quoted in Allen M. Winkler, *Life Under a Cloud* (New York: Oxford University Press, 1993), p. 200.

44. General William Odum quoted in Carol Cohn, "Sex and Death in the Rational World of Defense Intellectuals," *Signs, XII* (Autumn 1987), 692–693.

45. Ronald Reagan Diary, March 7, 1983 and October 10, 1983, in Douglas Brinkley, ed., *The Reagan Diaries* (New York: HarperCollins, 2007), pp. 135, 186.

46. Gregory Fossedal of the Heritage Foundation quoted in Wirls, *Buildup*, p. 149.

47. Quoted in James T. Patterson, *Restless Giant* (New York: Oxford University Press, 2005), p. 194.

48. Quoted in John Patrick Diggins, *Ronald Reagan* (New York: Norton, 2007), p. 351.

49. Reagan quoted in Beth A. Fischer, *The Reagan Reversal* (Columbia: University of Missouri Press, 1997), p. 135.

50. Anatoly Dobrynin, *In Confidence* (New York: Random House, 1995), p. 538.

51. Quoted in Schaller, *Right Turn*, p. 79.

52. Margaret Thatcher, *The Downing Street Years* (New York: HarperCollins, 1993), p. 461.

53. George Schultz quoted in Archie Brown, *The Gorbachev Factor* (New York: Oxford University Press, 1996), p. 231.

54. Quoted in Robert G. Kaiser, *How Gorbachev Happened* (New York: Simon & Schuster, 1991), p. 119.

55. Quoted in Reeves, *President Reagan*, p. 286.

56. Quoted in Jack F. Matlock, *Autopsy on an Empire* (New York: Random House, 1995), p. 97.

57. Reagan Diary, October 12, 1986, in Brinkley, ed., *Reagan Diaries*, p. 444.

58. Ronald Reagan, *An American Life* (New York: Simon & Schuster, 1990), p. 675.

59. Reagan Diary, December 9, 1987, in Brinkley, ed., *Reagan Diaries*, p. 555; Ambassador Jack Matlock quoted in Carolyn M. Ekedal and Melvin A. Goodman, *The Wars of Eduard Shevardnadze* (University Park: Penn State University Press, 1997), p. xix.

60. Quoted in Leon V. Sigal, *Hang Separately* (New York: Century Foundation Press, 2000), p. 91.

61. Georgi Arbatov, *The System* (New York: Times Books, 1992), p. 350.

62. Quoted in Michael J. Sullivan III, *American Adventures Abroad* (Malden, Mass.: Blackwell, 2008), p. 180.

63. Quoted in Harold Molineu, *U.S. Policy toward Latin America* (Boulder, Colo.: Westview Press, 1986), p. 176.

64. *Public Papers, Reagan, 1983, I*, 373, 601.

65. Quoted in Jim Kuhn, *Ronald Reagan in Private* (New York: Sentinel, 2004), p. 104.

66. Quoted in *New York Times*, April 28, 1983.

67. White Paper quoted in Doug Stokes, "Countering the Soviet Threat?" *Cold War History, III* (April 2003), 82.

68. Quoted in LaFeber, *Inevitable Revolutions*, p. 277.

69. Howard Lane quoted in Mark Danner, "The Truth of El Mozote," *The New Yorker, LXIX* (December 6, 1993), 118.

70. Quoted in Bob Woodward, *Veil* (New York: Simon & Schuster, 1987), p. 281.

71. Colin L. Powell, *My American Journey* (New York: Random House, 1995), p. 339.

72. Quoted in Patterson, *Restless Giant*, p. 209.

73. CIA manual quoted in *New York Times*, January 29, 1997.

74. Quoted in Patterson, *Restless Giant*, p. 208.

75. Quoted in William E. Pemberton, *Exit with Honor* (Armonk, N.Y.: Sharpe, 1998), p. 173.

76. Quoted in Alan McPherson, *Intimate Ties, Bitter Struggles* (Washington, D.C.: Potomac Books, 2006), p. 103.

77. Lawrence Walsh quoted in Theodore Draper, "Walsh's Last Stand," *New York Review of Books*, March 3, 1994, p. 27.

78. William M. LeoGrande, *Our Own Backyard* (Chapel Hill: University of North Carolina Press, 1998), p. 587.

79. Quoted *New York Times*, February 23, 1985.

80. Robert M. Gates, *From the Shadows* (New York: Simon & Schuster, 1996), p. 273.

81. Quoted in Peter Kornbluh, "The Haig-Rodríguez Secret Talks," *Cold War International History Project Bulletin*, nos. 8–9 (Winter 1996/1997), p. 219.

82. Michael Deaver quoting Haig in Schaller, *Reckoning*, p. 123.

83. Laurien Alexandre, *The Voice of America* (Norwood, N.J.: Ablex, 1988), p. 139.

84. Robert McFarlane quoted in Deborah H. Strober and Gerald S. Strober, eds., *Reagan* (Boston: Houghton Mifflin, 1998), p. 290.

85. Quoted in Lars Schoultz, *Beneath the United States* (Cambridge: Harvard University Press, 1998), p. 365.

86. Reagan Diary, October 27, 1985, in Brinkley, ed., *Reagan Diaries*, p. 191.

87. Quoted in *Ronald Reagan and Margaret Thatcher* (New York: Penguin, 2007), p. 201.

88. Russell Crandall, *Gunboat Democracy* (New York: Rowman & Littlefield, 2006), p. 162.

89. Quoted in Michael Thomas, *American Policy Toward Israel* (New York: Routledge, 2007), p. 61.

90. Quoted in *New York Times*, December 21, 1981.

91. Quoted in David Schoenbaum, *The United States and the State of Israel* (New York: Oxford University Press, 1993), p. 273.

92. Powell, *My American Journey*, p. 281.

93. Quoted in James A. Bill, *George Ball* (New Haven: Yale University Press, 1997), pp. 194–195.

94. Quoted in Yezid Sayid, *Armed Struggle and the Search for State* (New York: Oxford University Press, 1997), p. 624.

95. Quoted in Melani McAlister, "A Cultural History of the War Without End," *Journal of American History*, LXXXIX (September 2002), 448.

96. Quoted in *New York Times*, October 15, 1985.

97. Quoted in Nicholas Laham, *The American Bombing of Libya* (Jefferson, N.C.: McFarland, 2008), p. 115.

98. Tom Engelhardt, *The End of Victory Culture* (New York: BasicBooks, 1995), p. 201

99. Geoffrey Kemp quoted in Douglas Little, *American Orientalism* (Chapel Hill: University of North Carolina Press, 2002), p. 227.

100. Bruce W. Jentleson, *With Friends Like These* (New York: Norton, 1994), p. 59.

101. Chester A. Crocker, "South Africa: Strategy for Change," *Foreign Affairs*, LIX (Winter 1980/1981), 346.

102. Donald Rothchild and John Ravenhill, "From Carter to Reagan," in Kenneth Oye et al., eds., *Eagle Defiant* (Boston: Little, Brown, 1983), p. 349.

103. Democratic Representative from Pennsylvania William H. Gray quoted in Stephen R. Weissman, *A Culture of Deference* (New York: BasicBooks, 1995), p. 171.

104. Quoted in Francis Njubi Nesbitt, *Race for Sanctions* (Bloomington: Indiana University Press, 2004), p. 127.

105. Republican Senator from Nevada Paul Layatt quoted in William E. Kline and James Worthen, "The Philippines," in Ernest R. May and Philip D. Zelikow, eds., *Dealing with Dictators* (Cambridge: MIT Press, 2006), p. 137; Kline and Worther, *ibid.*, p. 165.

106. Lee Iacocca quoted in Donald W. White, *The American Century* (New Haven: Yale University Press, 1996), p. 395.

107. Abe Shintaro quoted in Walter LaFeber, *The Clash* (New York: Norton, 1997), p. 380.

108. Quoted in Foreign Policy Association, *Great Decisions 1990* (New York: Foreign Policy Association, 1990), p. 16.

109. Terry Deibel, "Reagan's Mixed Legacy," *Foreign Policy*, no. 75 (Summer 1989), 49.

110. Arnold L. Horelick, "U.S. Soviet Relations," *Foreign Affairs, LXIX* (America and the World,1989/90; quoted in Elizabeth Drew, "Letter from Washington," *The New Yorker, LXV* (November 22, 1989), 122.

111. William Forrest Harlow, "And the Wall Came Tumbling Down," in Martin J. Medhurst, ed., *The Rhetorical Presidency of George H. W. Bush* (College Station: Texas A&M Press, 2006), p. 39.

112. Jack Matlock quoted in John Robert Greene, *The Presidency of George Bush* (Lawrence: University Press of Kansas, 2000), p. 90.

113. Quoted in Mary E. Stuckey, *Defining Americans* (Lawrence: University Press of Kansas, 2004), p. 293.

114. Erwin C. Hargrove, *The Effective Presidency* (Boulder: Paradigm, 2008), p. 173.

115. Richards quoted in Tom Wicker, *George Herbert Walker Bush* (New York: Penguin, 2004), p. 5; Bush quoted in Stephen J. Ducat, *The Wimp Factor* (Boston: Beacon Press, 2004), p. 85.

116. Quoted in Ducat, *ibid.*, pp. 85, 102.

117. Quoted in Beschloss and Talbott, *Highest*, p. 205.

118. David Halberstam, *War in a Time of Peace* (New York: Scribners, 2001), p. 65.

119. Doro Bush Koch, *My Father, My President* (New York: Warner Books, 2006), p. 277.

120. Ryan J. Barilleaux and Mark J. Rozell, *Power and Prudence* (College Station: Texas A&M University Press, 2006), pp. 121–122.

121. Donald T. Phillips, *The Clinton Charisma* (New York: Palgrave, 2007), p. 4.

122. Quoted in William A. De Gregorio, *The Complete Book of U.S. Presidents*, 6th ed. (Fort Lee, NJ: Barricade Books, 2005), p. 751.

123. Quoted in Strobe Talbott, *The Russian Hand* (New York: Random House, 2002), p. 407.

124. Fred I. Greenstein and John Burke quoted in Dale R. Herspring, *The Pentagon and the Presidency* (Lawrence: University Press of Kansas, 2004), p. 332.

125. Quoted *ibid.*, p. 335.

126. *Ibid.*, p. 336.

127. Col. David Hackworth quoted *ibid.*, p. 331.

128. Quoted in Jussi M. Hanhimäki, "Global Visions and Parochial Politics," *Diplomatic History, XXVII* (September 2003), 440.

129. Quoted in *Washington Post National Weekly Edition*, July 4, 1997.

130. Martin Walker, "The Clinton Doctrine," *The New Yorker, LXXII* (October 7, 1996), 7.

131. Quoted in *Hartford Courant*, December 16, 1993.

132. Douglas Brinkley, "Democratic Enlargement: The Clinton Doctrine," *Foreign Policy*, no. 106 (Spring 1997), 125.

133. Richard Brookhiser, "The Mind of George W. Bush," *Atlantic Monthly, CCLXXXIX* (April 2003), 59.

134. Quoted in Barilleaux and Rozell *Power and Prudence*, p. 123.

135. Quoted in Zubok, "New Evidence," p. 14.

136. John B. Dunlap, "The August 1991 Coup and Its Impact on Soviet Politics," *Journal of Cold War Studies, V* (Winter 2003), 112.

137. Quoted in Paul D. Wolfowitz, "Clinton's First Year," *Foreign Affairs, LXXIII* (January/February 1994), 41; Robert Legvold, "Clinton Foreign Policy and the Revolution in the East," in Todd G. Shields et al., eds., *The Clinton Riddle* (Fayetteville: University of Arkansas Press, 2004), p. 182.

138. Talbott quoted in Stephen F. Cohen, *Failed Crusade* (New York: Norton, 2000), pp. 7, 250.

139. Quoted in Hargrove, *Effective Presidency,* p. 216.

140. Jim Hoagland, "Europe's Destiny," *America and the World, 1989*.

141. Brent Scowcroft quoted in James Chace, "New World Disorder," *New York Review of Books*, December 17, 1998, p. 60.

142. John S. Duffield, *World Power Forsaken* (Stanford: Stanford University Press, 1998), p. viii.

143. Quoted in Hargrove, *Effective Presidency*, p. 216; quoted in James Goldgeier, "NATO Expansion: Anatomy of a Decision," *The Washington Quarterly, XXI* (Winter 1998), 94.

144. William Perry quoted in Victor Israelyan, "Don't Tease a Wounded Bear," *The Washington Quarterly, XXI* (Winter 1998), 53; Kennan quoted in *New York Times*, February 5, 1997.

145. Quoted in Elizabeth Pond, *Endgame in the Balkans* (Washington, D.C.: Brookings Institution Press, 2006), p. 30.

146. Andrew Bell Fialkoff, "A Brief History of Ethnic Cleansing," *Foreign Affairs, LXXII* (Summer 1993), 120.

147. Warren Christopher quoted in Samantha Power, *"A Problem from Hell"* (New York: BasicBooks, 2002), p. xii.

148. Quoted in Colin L. Powell, *My American Journey* (New York: Random House, 1995), pp. 576–577.

149. Quoted in John Newhouse, "No Exit, No Entrance," *The New Yorker, LXIX* (June 28, 1993), 46.

150. Anthony Lake quoted in John F. Harris, *The Survivor* (New York: Random House, 2005), p. 199.

151. Quoted in Herspring, *Pentagon and the Presidency*, p. 343.

152. Quoted in *Washington Post National Weekly Edition*, October 18–24, 1993.

153. Quoted in Halberstam, *War in a Time of Peace*, p. 265.

154. Quoted in David F. Gordon and Howard Wolpe, "The Other Africa," *World Policy Journal, XV* (Spring 1998), 52.

155. Quoted in *Hartford Courant*, March 26, 1998.

156. International Rescue Committee quoted in "Primary Sources," *The Atlantic Monthly* (July/August 2003), 38.

157. David Benjamin and Stephen Simon quoted in *Washington Post National Weekly Edition*, January 7–13, 2002.

158. Quoted in *Washington Post National Weekly Edition*, December 21–28, 1998.

159. Quoted in *New York Times*, December 12, 1994.

160. Robert A. Pastor, "The Clinton Administration and the Americas," in Robert Lieber, ed., *Eagle Adrift* (New York: HarperCollins, 1996), p. 101.

161. Tom Miller, *On the Border* (1981), quoted in W. Dirk Raat, *Mexico and the United States* (Athens: University of Georgia Press, 1992), p. 173.

162. Stephen Flynn, "America the Vulnerable," *Foreign Affairs, LXXXI* (January/February 2002), 75.

163. Patrick Lloyd Hatcher, "The Unwinnable War on the Drug Trade," *Orbis, XLI* (Fall 1997), 659.

164. Eva Bertram and Kenneth Sharpe, "The Unwinnable Drug War," *World Policy Journal, XIII* (Winter 1996/1997), 45.

165. Quoted in Herspring, *Pentagon and the Presidency*, p. 308.

166. Public Affairs Action Report, December 20, 1989–January 31, 1990, National Security Archive, Washington, D.C.

167. Quoted in Joe Klein, *The Natural* (New York: Doubleday, 2002), p. 73; Richard Feinberg (NSC) quoted in Philippe R. Girard, *Clinton in Haiti* (New York: Palgrave, 2004), p. 44.

168. Jorge Domínguez, "U.S.-Cuban Relations: From the Cold War to the Colder War," *Journal of Interamerican Studies and World Affairs, XXXIX* (Fall 1997), 54.

169. Quoted in William M. LeoGrande, "From Havana to Miami," *ibid., XL* (Spring 1998), 77.

170. Quoted in Ann Blackman, *Seasons of Her Life* (New York: Charles Scribner's Sons, 1998), p. 246.

171. Quoted in *Washington Post National Weekly Edition*, November 30, 1998.

172. Quoted in Deborah Amos, *Lines in the Sand* (New York: Simon & Schuster, 1992), p. 82.

173. Quoted in Michael Howard, "The Prudence Thing," *Foreign Affairs, LXXVII* (November/December 1998), 131.

174. Quoted in Lawrence Freedman and Efraim Karsh, *The Gulf Conflict* (Princeton: Princeton University Press, 1993), p. 293.

175. Quoted in John T. Rourke, *Presidential Wars and American Democracy* (Washington, D.C.: Paragon, 1993), p. 59.

176. Quoted in Greene, *Presidency of George Bush*, p. 123.

177. Lewis Lapham, *Theater of War* (New York: New Press, 2002), p. 132.

178. Rachel Martin Harlow, "Agency and Agent in George Bush's Gulf War Rhetoric," in Medhurst, ed., *Rhetorical Presidency*, pp. 63, 65.

179. Thomas Harkin quoted in *Hartford Courant*, March 20, 2003.

180. Quoted in Herspring, *Pentagon and the Presidency*, p. 314.

181. Bill Clinton, *My Life* (New York: Knopf, 2004), p. 728.

182. Quoted in Ussama Makdisi, "'Anti-Americanism' in the Arab World," *Journal of American History, LXXXXIX* (September 2002), 556.

183. Quoted in Kenneth M. Pollock, *The Threatening Storm* (New York: Random House, 2002), p. 94.

184. James Baker, "Principles and Pragmatism," May 22, 1989, Department of State Current Policy no. 1176.

185. Clinton, *My Life*, p. 544.

186. Quoted in Roderick MacFarqhuar, "The End of the Chinese Revolution," *New York Review of Books*, July 20, 1989, p. 8.

187. Lawrence Eagleburger quoted in James A. Baker III, *The Politics of Diplomacy* (New York: G. P. Putnam's Sons, 1995), p. 110.

188. Quoted in June Teufel Dreyer, "Clinton's China Policy," in Shields et al., eds., *The Clinton Riddle*, p. 154.

189. Quoted in Dreyer, "Clinton's China Policy," p. 168.

190. Quoted in Jonathan D. Pollock, "The United States and Asia in 1996," *Asian Survey, XXXVII* (January 1997), 97.

191. William Perry quoted *ibid*.

192. Quoted in Lucien W. Pye, "The United States and Asia in 1997," *Asian Survey, XXXVII* (January 1998), 99.

193. Quoted in Yoichi Funabashi, "Tokyo's Depression Diplomacy," *Foreign Affairs, LXXVII* (November/December 1998), 32.

194. Quoted in Robert B. Oxnam, "Asia & Pacific Challenges," *Foreign Affairs: America and the World 1992–1993, LXXII* (January 1993), 72.

195. John T. Rourke, *International Politics on the World Stage*, 9th ed. (New York: McGraw Hill, 2003), p. 288.

196. Bruce Cumings quoted in Benjamin Schwartz, "Why America Thinks It Has to Run the World," *The Atlantic Monthly, CCLXXVII* (June 1996), 94.

197. Quoted in *Washington Post National Weekly Edition*, October 25, 31, 1993.

198. John Arquilla, *The Reagan Imprint* (Chicago: Ivan R. Dee, 2006), p. 55; Diggins, *Ronald Reagan*, p. xx.

199. Diggins, *ibid*.

200. Odd Arne Westad, *The Global Cold War* (New York: Cambridge University Press, 2007), p. 404.

201. Naftali, *George H. W. Bush*, p. 65.

202. Bush quoted in Medhurst, *Rhetorical Presidency*, p. 81.

203. Quoted in Arjun Makhijani et al., "Dismantling the Bomb," in Stephen I. Schwartz, ed., *Atomic Audit* (Washington, D.C.: Brookings, 1998), p. 346.

204. Quoted in Josiah M. Marshall, "The Power Rangers," *The New Yorker, LXXIX* (February 2, 2004), 88.

205. Quoted in Emily S. Rosenberg, "Rescuing Women and Children," *Journal of American History, LXXXIX* (September 2002), 456.

206. Anthony Lake quoted in Brinkley, "Democratic Enlargement," p. 117.

207. Quoted in *Washington Post National Weekly Edition*, December 14, 1998.

208. Richard A. Love, "The Cyberthreat Continuum," in Maryann Cusimano Love, ed., *Beyond Sovereignty* (Belmont, Calif.: Thompson-Wadsworth, 2003), p. 196.

209. Maryann Cusimano Love, "Global Problems, Global Solutions," in *ibid*, p. 5.

210. Rob Kroes, "American Empire and Cultural Imperialism," in Thomas Bender, ed., *Rethinking American History in a Global Age* (Berkeley: University of California Press, 2002), pp. 303–304; *New York Times*, August 29, 1999.

211. Thomas Zeiler, "Globalization," in Alexander DeConde et al., *Encyclopedia of American Foreign Policy,* 3 vols. (New York: Scribner's, 2002), *II*, 146.

212. Thomas Friedman, *The Lexus and the Olive Tree* (New York: Farrar, Straus, and Giroux, 1999), pp. 7–8.

213. George F. Kennan, "Correspondence," *World Policy Journal, XV* (Spring 1998), 107.

214. Maureen Dowd in *New York Times*, March 4, 1990.

215. Quoted in Jonathan Clarke, "The Conceptual Poverty of U.S. Foreign Policy," *Atlantic Monthly, CCLXXII* (September 1993), 62.

216. George Andrew MacLean, *Clinton's Foreign Policy in Russia* (Burlington, Vt.: Ashgate, 2006), p. 17; Charles Krauthammer quoted in Nye, *Paradox*, p. 2; quoted in Robert Worth, "Clinton's Warriors," *World Policy Journal, XV* (Spring 1998), 47.

217. Quoted in Medhurst, *Rhetorical Presidency*, p. 81.

218. Quoted in Phillips, *Clinton Charisma*, p. 120.

219. Strobe Talbott in *Time, CXXXV* (January 1, 1990), 72.

CHAPTER 12

Millennial America: Foreign Relations Since 2001

September 11, 2001. *Billowing smoke over the Manhattan skyline marked the first hostile attacks on the American mainland since British forces burned Washington in 1814. One scholar has argued: "September 11 was an apolitical act. What was the terrorists' next step, what was their strategy, how would the chief terrorists know when they had achieved their goals?" The seeming lack of rational military purpose marked the attacks as "acts of catastrophic nihilism." (© Reuters/Corbis)*

DIPLOMATIC CROSSROAD

❖ *9/11 and After*

A PRESIDENTIAL SPEECHWRITER called it "the worst crime ever recorded on videotape."[1] Early in the morning of September 11, 2001, fifteen Saudi Arabians and four Egyptians, secretly armed with box-cutters, boarded four commercial airliners. Two planes took off from Boston, the other two from Newark, New Jersey, and Washington, D.C. At 8:46 A.M. and 9:03 A.M., respectively, the two hijacked Boston aircraft exploded into the north and south towers of the World Trade Center in New York City. "Another plane hit! Another plane hit the building!" shouted an emergency dispatcher at the nearby Port Authority building.[2] At 9:39 A.M., the Washington jetliner struck and destroyed a portion of the Pentagon. At 10:10 A.M., the Newark aircraft, possibly intended for the White House or Capitol, plunged to a fiery demise in a field in western Pennsylvania as passengers tried to overpower the plane's hijackers. By midday both World Trade Center towers had collapsed and the death toll (including airline passengers) numbered 2,823 in New York City, 45 in Pennsylvania, and 189 in Washington, D.C. The victims came from more than eighty countries around the world.

Stunned Americans gaped in disbelief as television networks played and replayed the horrific montage. The novelist John Updike watched from a tenth-floor apartment in Brooklyn Heights as the south tower "fell straight down like an elevator, with a tinkling shiver and a groan of concussion distinct across the mile of air."[3] New York Mayor Rudy Giuliani, rushing to the World Trade Center, "looked up and saw a man jump out—above the fire, must have been at least hundred stories—and my eye followed him, almost transfixed, all the way down."[4] An anguished police officer reported "body parts ... five blocks away."[5] For those conditioned by films such as *Black Sunday* (1977) or *Air Force One* (1997), the images seemed "right out of a big-budget Hollywood production," making reality "almost impossible to believe."[6] In Florida at the time of the attacks, President George W. Bush viewed replays of the second New York explosion and commented tersely: "We're at war."[7] With the president away from Washington, Vice President Dick Cheney became "the dominant figure on September 11."[8] He took command of the Presidential Emergency Operations Center in the basement of the White House, ordering the president and his party to an air force base in Nebraska. Chief congressional leaders moved to an underground installation in the Blue Ridge Mountains. Cheney also grounded all nongovernment aircraft and instructed military pilots to shoot down any planes that did not comply. That evening the president returned to Washington and, over national television, announced: "We will make no distinction between the terrorists who committed these acts and those who harbor them."[9] Before going to bed he noted in his diary: "The Pearl Harbor of the twenty-first century took place today."[10]

In the nation's capital, the intelligence community belatedly "connected the dots."[11] Only minutes before the attacks, CIA Director George L. Tenet told a member of Congress that the Saudi exile Osama bin Laden and his terrorist network al Qaeda (Arabic for "the Base") were "going to do something big."[12] Tenet proved prophetic. The passenger manifests of the plane that plowed into the Pentagon listed three known al Qaeda operatives. Federal investigators pieced together evidence that the nineteen hijackers—trained at al Qaeda bases in Afghanistan, organized and financed in Germany, England, and Spain with money sent from around the world—had entered the United States on tourist or student visas. They adopted American lifestyles (including the consumption of alcohol, forbidden in the Muslim religion) to avoid suspicion, in some cases living in quiet, middle-class communities for several years prior to the attacks. Some took rudimentary flight training in California and Florida, which enabled them to operate the jetliners after they had killed or intimidated pilots and crews. The hijack leaders believed that they were participating in a "martyrdom operation."[13] Communicating primarily through the Internet, the terrorists epitomized the "declining importance of states"—"transnational, united not by their national citizenships or even the desire to form a state, but by religious and ideological beliefs."[14] Osama bin Laden, wearing a military fatigue jacket, soon appeared on videotape to praise the hijackers: "Here is America struck by God Almighty in one of its vital organs. ... God has blessed a group of vanguard Muslims, the forefront of Islam, to destroy America!"[15]

As al Qaeda's responsibility for the attacks became clear, many Americans wondered what had prompted such horrible deeds. George W. Bush quickly answered: "Why do they hate us? They hate our freedoms."[16] But others disputed this formula as simplistic. One journalist who knew bin Laden scoffed: "Bin Laden is not some 'AY-rab' who woke up one morning in a bad mood, his turban all in a twist, only to decide America was the enemy." Despite contrary claims from pundits, he "does not rail against the pernicious effects of Hollywood movies, or against Madonna's midriff," but condemns "the continued [U.S.] presence in Arabia, U.S. support for Israel, its continued campaign against Iraq, and its support for regimes such as Egypt and Saudi Arabia that bin Laden regards as apostates from Islam."[17] Neither Bush nor the American public seemed ready for such self-reflection. Anti-bin Laden songs flooded the Internet, including one modeled after Paul Simon's "Fifty Ways to Leave Your Lover" that offered the same number of methods to kill the Saudi terrorist ("You know, it's really not my habit to be rude, but a battery acid enema would surely kill this dude").[18] Bush, overcome with "testosterone and anger," shared the sentiment, proclaiming: "I don't care what the international lawyers say, we are going to kick some ass."[19] Cofer Black, the CIA counterterrorism chief, told his agents to get "[bin Laden's] head in a box" so he could "take it down and show the President."[20] Bush placed the country on a war footing, as Cheney predicted that defeating terrorism might require military action against "forty or fifty countries" and last more than fifty years.[21]

After 9/11, most of the world expressed deep sympathy and offered America assistance. German Chancellor Gerhard Schroeder called the attacks "a declaration of war against the whole civilized world," and the French newspaper *Le Monde* editorialized, "We are all Americans now."[22] NATO allies quickly invoked Article V for collective defense and promised Washington aid after Bush declared a global war "to rid the world of evil."[23] As Washington demanded that the Islamic fundamentalist

**WANTED DEAD OR ALIVE.
Osama bin Laden (b. 1957).**
The mastermind behind 9/11 and al Qaeda's earlier attacks on the U.S. embassies in Kenya and Tanzania (1998) and the U.S. navy destroyer *Cole* (2000), bin Laden had declared a *jihad* (literally "struggle," often translated "holy war") against Americans. Distributed by the Rewards for Justice Program through the State Department, matchbook covers bearing the al Qaeda leader's likeness offered payments of up to $5 million for information leading to his capture. (Robert E. Goodrich/State Department)

George W. Bush (b. 1946). Looking pensive, the president viewed the damaged Pentagon from a helicopter on September 14, 2001. Characterizing himself as a person who did not "sit around trying to analyze myself a lot," Bush reportedly did not ask hard questions of his advisers. Asked if he consulted his father, the ex-president, Bush replied: "There is a higher father I appeal to." Treasury Secretary Paul O'Neill described the president in NSC meetings as "a blind man in a roomful of deaf people." (AP Images/ The White House, Eric Draper)

Taliban government of Afghanistan hand over bin Laden and his followers, the Bush administration warily accepted minimal aid against that country because it did not want other nations dictating terms or conditions. "At some point," Bush told aides, "we may be the only ones left. That's okay with me. We are America."[24]

After a period of anger and grief, Americans asked whether the attacks could have been prevented. Congressional investigations and press reports revealed an administration that ignored warnings and discounted threats from bin Laden and al Qaeda. Bush had dismissed Bill Clinton's antiterrorist efforts as "swatting at flies" while the presidential assistant for national security affairs, Condoleezza Rice, initially disdained al Qaeda and bin Laden as "chump change."[25] Richard Clarke, the counterterrorism coordinator for the National Security Council, recounted Rice's incredulity when she learned that rather than just "a guy with a few camp followers," bin Laden actually led an organization with "tens of thousands of followers and millions of dollars in scores of countries."[26] Pentagon officials also had felt no need to worry about a "little terrorist in Afghanistan."[27]

This dismissive attitude was already apparent in July 2001, when Tenet and an undercover CIA official told Rice they had overwhelming evidence that al Qaeda during the coming weeks or months planned a "spectacular" attack with mass casualties. Rice tepidly responded that nothing "pointed to an attack on the homeland."[28] The National Security Agency picked up chatter about "another Hiroshima," and Jordanian intelligence overheard the name of the operation: "The Big Wedding. In the culture of suicide bombers, the day of a martyr's death is his wedding day, when he greets the maidens of Paradise."[29] On August 6, when a CIA agent verbally briefed Bush on a report titled "Bin Laden Determined to Strike in the US," the president looked him in the eye and said: "All right, you've covered your ass, now."[30]

Rice later claimed that the CIA briefing had been "historical" based on old reporting—"an explosive title on a nonexplosive piece."[31] Although critics wonder what might have happened if the Bush administration had reacted more alertly to these warnings, preventing the attacks would have been difficult, if not impossible. Intelligence suggested a spectacular attack, but none of the pieces coalesced clearly to anticipate suicidal assaults on the Twin Towers and the Pentagon. For critics, however, the pattern of administrative behavior loomed more important than its failure to stop the attacks. In its first year, the Bush team displayed the same "absence of self-doubt" that later prompted it to plunge ahead with risky overseas ventures despite warnings from people with years of experience and knowledge.[32]

Rise of the Vulcans: Bush and His War Cabinet

Fifty-four-year-old George W. Bush, eldest son of the ex-president, entered the White House in 2001. The second Bush graduated from Yale University and Harvard Business School, drilled for oil in Texas, served as an Oval Office factotum to his father, and briefly owned the Texas Rangers baseball team. An excessive drinker in his youth, Bush embraced religion at age forty and modeled himself on Sam Houston, another famous Texan, whose victory over alcohol had been "transformative."[33] His lack of experience in foreign affairs embarrassed him during the 2000 campaign. Once a local television reporter quizzed him on the leaders of Chechnya, Taiwan, Pakistan, and India, and he flunked—badly. When a magazine reporter later asked his view of the Taliban, he stared blankly until she prompted him with hints about "repression of women in Afghanistan." He replied, "Oh, I thought you said some band."[34] But Bush tried to disarm his critics by suggesting that he would not pursue an activist international agenda. During one presidential debate, he contended: "If we're an arrogant nation, they'll view us that way, but if we're a humble nation, they'll respect us."[35] Bush also argued that no candidate could master everything about the world so what mattered was the national security team he could assemble.

That team, recruited with some help from his father, followed him to Washington in 2001. They dubbed themselves "the Vulcans" after the Roman god of fire, whose statue stood prominently in Condoleezza Rice's hometown of Birmingham, Alabama. Rice had served on George H. W. Bush's national security staff. Trained as an expert on the Soviet Union and Eastern Europe, she had played a key role in U.S. deliberations regarding the unification of Germany. During the Clinton years, she served as provost of Stanford University and sat on corporate boards, including the

Makers of American Foreign Relations Since 2001

President	Secretaries of State
George W. Bush, 2001–2009	Colin L. Powell, 2001–2005
	Condoleezza Rice, 2005–2009
Barack Obama, 2009-	Hillary R. Clinton, 2009-

oil company Chevron which named a tanker after her. The elder Bush invited her to meet with his son at his summer home in Kennebunkport, Maine. They quickly "bonded" over their mutual affection for sports, with a friend remarking that one thing Rice "found most endearing about George W. is that he used sports metaphors and Condi does too."[36] Bush appointed her foreign policy coordinator for his campaign, then national security adviser, and later secretary of state. For Bush, who valued loyalty above all qualities, Rice seemed "like my sister" and she grew closer to him personally than any one else in his administration.[37]

Prominent veterans from the Ford, Reagan, and elder Bush administrations enhanced Bush's credibility in foreign affairs. Dick Cheney chaired Bush's vice presidential selection committee and promptly picked himself for the job. His résumé included stints as chief of staff to President Gerald Ford, member of Congress from Wyoming, defense secretary under the elder Bush, and chief executive officer of the multinational firm Halliburton. His seemingly unflappable demeanor had earned him an undeserved reputation as a moderate, despite a congressional voting record that placed him among the most conservative members of the Republican party. "A self-described and proud-of-it hawk," Cheney bragged that he had "never met a weapons system he didn't vote for."[38] He quickly emerged as the most powerful vice president in U.S. history with a major role in shaping foreign policy. The vice president rarely shared his views in large meetings, with one senator describing him sitting mute and motionless "like a big bullfrog on a log," only breaking his silence to croak: "No, Mr. President, that's not right."[39]

Cheney also staffed the national security bureaucracy with like-minded colleagues including his own mentor, Donald Rumsfeld. A rising star in the Republican party in the early 1970s, Rumsfeld had served first as Gerald Ford's chief of staff and then as secretary of defense. He had hired a young Cheney as his deputy and persuaded Ford to promote him after Rumsfeld moved to the Pentagon. Even though George H. W. Bush considered Rumsfeld "arrogant, self-important, too sure of himself and Machiavellian," the younger Bush seemed eager to prove his father wrong by naming Rumsfeld to head the Defense Department.[40]

For his first term, Bush chose Colin Powell as secretary of state. The "most politically adroit general since … Eisenhower," Powell had served as national security adviser under Reagan and as chair of the Joint Chiefs of Staff under the elder Bush and Clinton.[41] The Vietnam War veteran accepted Bush's appointment despite having castigated "the sons of the powerful" who had avoided service in Vietnam by wangling "slots in Reserves and National Guard units," as Bush had done.[42]

A reluctant warrior, Powell often clashed with the hawkish Rumsfeld, who once said that Powell's job "is to talk them to death, and mine is to hit them over the head."[43] Despite "all the Texas, Alamo macho that made Powell uncomfortable," his soldierly code of obedience kept him in his "own lane," as he put it.[44] Once, however, when told that his boss slept early and soundly, Powell retorted: "I sleep like a baby, too—every two hours I wake up screaming."[45] Powell and Bush never developed close personal ties. Some insiders thought Powell's "stratospheric poll ratings" and status among the most admired men in the country threatened the president.[46] The White House quickly dubbed Powell the "black sheep" of the administration, and it became Rice's job to chastise and bring him back to the fold.[47] Just a week before 9/11, *Time* ran an article asserting that Powell "was isolated and out of step" with many in the administration. A friend said of the article: "It sucks" but "if it had shown you were in charge," then "you would have been totally fucked."[48] Powell burst out in laughter.

The frosty relationship between the secretary of state and president undercut Bush's boast that he had the "finest foreign policy team ever assembled."[49] Cheney's claim to be the "real national security adviser" created immediate tensions with Rice, who allegedly "threw a fit" when the vice president sought to chair National Security Council meetings in the president's absence.[50] Rice won that battle, but she failed to prevent Cheney and Rumsfeld from dominating the policy process. Neither Cheney nor Rumsfeld respected Rice, the latter viewing her as "a glorified Russian studies graduate student … not up to the job." Even Bush's gentlemanly chief of staff Andrew Card admitted that Rumsfeld behaved "a little bit sexist" in his treatment of the national security adviser.[51] Yet, other participants also labeled Rice the "weakest" and "the worst" national security adviser in the history of the office.[52] Even Rice's aides testified to her difficulties in "following up problems," while Powell blasted Rice for thinking that she "has two cabinet secretaries to fuck with."[53] Some concluded, however, that Rice had not failed. Instead she was fulfilling the president's wishes "in a particularly agile way" by allowing an alternative NSC process to emerge that enabled her to manipulate "the secretary of defense and secretary of state to further what were in fact the vice president's and the president's goals."[54] Powell and Rumsfeld eventually resigned, but Rice grew more powerful and influential over time. She proved more effective than Powell as secretary of state, in part because "foreign diplomats" assumed "her words reflect[ed] the view of her very close friend, the president of the United States."[55]

Beyond personal and bureaucratic rivalries, the administration split over the proper approach to national security itself. Powell and Rice had reputations as realists who believed in power politics and dismissed attempts to demand internal changes in regimes before negotiating with them. But Cheney, Rumsfeld, and such key aides as Deputy Secretary of Defense Paul Wolfowitz wanted to change fundamentally Washington's attitudes and policies toward the rest of the world. When Cheney and Wolfowitz had served in the first Bush Pentagon, they had drafted a Defense Planning Guidance document calling for continued U.S. military preeminence and the prevention of new rivals, with Germany and Japan cast as potential threats. The authors brushed aside permanent international organizations, such as NATO and the UN, as antiquated and instead praised "ad hoc assemblies" that would dissolve once a crisis had passed.[56] The first Bush ordered the document rewritten after it was leaked to the press. But the ideas reemerged in 2002 in George W. Bush's National Security Strategy paper. This new philosophy of unapologetic U.S. hegemony combined with a messianic desire to transform regimes defined what came to be known as the neoconservative approach to international relations. Advocates rejected "the utopian multilateralism of Woodrow Wilson and Bill Clinton" and lavished praise on the "muscular patriotism of Teddy Roosevelt and Ronald Reagan."[57] As one critic translated it, "every ten years or so, the United States needs to pick up some crappy little country and throw it against the wall, just to show the world we mean business."[58] Still, no one should fear Washington becoming a malevolent hegemon because "the exercise of American power is inherently virtuous because of the self-evident legitimacy of American political values."[59]

Such imperial views contradicted Bush's humbler comments as a presidential candidate. How to explain the disjunction? Some observers argued that 9/11 served as a conversion experience for a president who had not yet embraced neoconservatism. Others pointed to a clear pattern of behavior that predated 9/11 of claiming "limited sovereignty for the rest of the world and absolute sovereignty for the United States."[60] Bush had rejected numerous multilateral efforts soon after entering office, including the Kyoto Protocol on global warming, the International Criminal Court, the ABM treaty, the Comprehensive Test Ban Treaty, nonproliferation of small arms and light weapons, and protocols to verify the banning of biological and chemical weapons. If these decisions did not spring from doctrinaire neoconservatism, they certainly suggested a unilateralism that would only intensify after 9/11. In any case, as the war on terror began in late 2001, Bush had clearly exchanged his professedly reserved approach to the rest of the world for one based on much more forceful engagement.

Donald Rumsfeld (b. 1932) and Dick Cheney (b. 1941). As secretary of defense and vice president, these men became the most powerful advocates of the neoconservative position in the Bush administration. They embraced what one analyst called the Cheney doctrine: If there's just a 1 percent chance of the unimaginable happening, act as if it is a certainty. Cheney defended this position because "it's not about our analysis or finding preponderance of evidence. It's about our response." (U.S. Army photo by Staff Sgt. Gary Hillard, Defense Visual Information Center)

Present at a New Creation: The War on Terror, Afghanistan, and the Bush Doctrine

For Bush and his national security team, 9/11 had changed the world. The Vulcans saw themselves at a key juncture in history, much like America's generation of leaders after 1945. The historical moment demanded a new strategy and approach to the world. They immediately reversed the traditional practice of treating terrorists as criminals—guilty of individual acts—claiming that terrorist groups were incapable of mounting sophisticated operations on their own. Hostile or "rogue" states hid behind terrorist groups, using them for their own nefarious purposes. Wolfowitz hence called "for a strategy of ending states that sponsor terrorism."[61] Bush accordingly issued an ultimatum to Afghanistan's Taliban regime to turn over bin Laden and other al Qaeda operatives to the United States or else share their fate. He whisked aside Taliban requests for evidence of guilt, and combat operations began on October 7, 2001.

A rousing military campaign against the Taliban obscured some troubling questions about prior U.S. policy toward Afghanistan and neighboring Islamic states. The Taliban had taken control with material support from Saudi Arabia and Pakistan after the Soviet withdrawal in 1989. Many in Taliban ranks had attended all male, Islamic fundamentalist schools funded with Saudi money and based across the border in Pakistan. The CIA and the Pakistan intelligence agencies had trained tens of thousands of transnational jihadi fighters (Algerians, Egyptians, Indonesians, Filipinos, and British Muslims) to harass the Soviet occupiers beginning in 1979. When that war ended, bin Laden and others in the jihadi vanguard scattered across the globe to continue their battle against infidel forces. The United States now had to slay a monster partially of its own making.

Saudi Arabia broke off relations with the Taliban soon after the president's ultimatum, but Pakistan's military regime maintained its Taliban ties and cooperated only reluctantly with Washington. The United States and Britain then mounted massive air attacks on mountainous Afghanistan while the anti-Taliban Northern Alliance provided ground forces. At first the war progressed slowly, but in early November Taliban authority began to collapse. By early December, bin Laden and the remnants of al Qaeda in Afghanistan had taken refuge in caves near Tora Bora. Northern Alliance forces attacked by ground while U.S. planes pounded the area from the air, and al Qaeda abandoned the site on December 16. Bin Laden and key supporters, however, escaped into the remote tribal regions of northwest Pakistan. The escape may have been more than bad luck. Without Pashto speakers, U.S. intelligence had to rely heavily on Pakistani intelligence officers to interrogate Taliban defectors, problematic given that the CIA suspected that Pakistani intelligence had helped bin Laden to avoid capture. The airlifting of Pakistani operatives out of Afghanistan prior to the final assault on Tora Bora may well have provided cover for bin Laden's escape.

Hailed as a great success in 2001, the Afghan campaign actually sowed the seeds of failure. Rumsfeld pointed to Afghanistan as validation for his "revolution in military affairs," proving that small numbers of ground troops, coupled with air power, could win decisive battles.[62] At war's end, however, with "more cops in

New York City than soldiers on the ground in Afghanistan," the meager United Statesand NATO forces accorded warlords control over much of the country and made the president of Afghanistan the functional equivalent of the "mayor of Kabul," the Afghan capital.[63] Bush had so little regard for nation building in Afghanistan that he requested no reconstruction funds in his budget of January 2003. Congress eventually appropriated $295 million, but experts estimated the need for at least $14 billion. Without U.S. aid, Afghan peasants resumed planting poppies (opium) as their cash crop. By 2005 Afghanistan had again become the world's number one opium supplier, producing 90 percent of the global total. The flood of heroin produced from Afghan opium raised serious questions about whether the Bush administration had sent the message "help fight the Taliban and no one will interfere with your [drug] trafficking."[64] The drug money also enriched al Qaeda and Taliban insurgents, who intensified their efforts against the U.S. and NATO forces. Eight years after ousting the Taliban, the fighting persisted (with 651 U.S. fatalities and almost 2,700 wounded along with over 10,000 Afghani civilian deaths), drug trafficking expanded, and political stability remained elusive. The UN Security Council warned that Afghanistan might become a failed state if these conditions endured.

Captured al Qaeda and Taliban prisoners also posed new dilemmas. Because President Bush had never asked for a declaration of war, he claimed that personnel captured in Afghanistan belonged to no official armed force so as to classify them as "enemy combatants" outside the control of international law, rather than as prisoners of war. He thereupon created a prison camp at Guantánamo Bay, Cuba, in January 2002. According to Justice Department memoranda, neither U.S. nor international law, including the Geneva Convention, applied to the detainees. More disturbing, the memoranda defined torture as "only extreme acts" that produced pain equivalent "to death or organ failure" or lasting psychological harm "like post-traumatic stress disorder." Interrogation techniques that might be considered "cruel, inhuman, or degrading" would not be banned as torture.[65]

Such brutal treatment often began immediately after capture. The American interrogators of John Walker Lindh, a twenty-year-old American who had joined the Taliban, "stripped him, gagged him, strapped him to a board, and exhibited him to the press and to any soldier who wished to see him."[66] U.S. authorities brought 775 detainees to Guantánamo; over the subsequent six years, 420 were later released without charge. But the camp aroused limited public attention until the news media uncovered similar information about prisoner abuse in Iraq (see page 498).

The campaign in Afghanistan, however, proved to be "phase one" in "a larger war."[67] The new global war on terror led Washington to forge military ties and base agreements with former Soviet clients from Eastern Europe to Central Asia. All told, some half million uniformed and civilian personnel served in 725 military installations abroad under Bush. In 2003 U.S. Army Special Operations Command deployed in sixty-five countries—from training Nepalese troops to fight Maoist rebels to pursuing Abu Sayaf guerrillas in the Philippines to helping Colombian soldiers in their war against narco-traffickers. One American solider, whose unit saw deployments in Liberia, Afghanistan, and Bosnia, bragged: "We're like tourists with guns."[68]

"Homeland security" (including a new Cabinet-level department) became part of national security, as Congress passed the Patriot Act in autumn 2001 that expanded the federal government's power to conduct electronic surveillance, hold military trials for suspected terrorists, and carry out other activities that arguably infringed on basic civil rights. The Bush administration also implemented new financial regulations and monitoring systems to curb terrorist activities. But these proved largely ineffective because the U.S. Treasury Department lacked sufficient personnel to follow up reports from banks and other financial institutions. Underground financial networks continued to flourish in the Islamic world and acts of terror were cheap to carry out. The October 2002 bombings at an Indonesian resort, for example, cost $50,000, while a series of bombings in Spain in 2004, carried out with dynamite and cell phones, expended less than $10,000. Rumsfeld admitted the financial disadvantage: "Our cost is billions against the terrorist cost of millions."[69] Although counterterrorist activities provided important, if not always effective, means to prevent future attacks, they did not rally public support in the manner of the Afghan war. Rumsfeld urged that the larger war on terror be managed "like a political campaign with daily talking points."[70]

Bush ushered in "phase two" in his State of the Union address in January 2002. Modeled after FDR's "day of infamy" speech, Bush's rhetoric singled out Iraq, Iran, and North Korea "and their terrorist allies" as "an axis of evil, arming to threaten the peace of the world [with] weapons of mass destruction." Iraq especially posed a "grave and growing danger." Bush vowed: "I will not stand by as peril grows closer and closer."[71] The speech took many U.S. allies by surprise, especially those in Europe, which had existing relationships with Iran, and Japan and South Korea, where they hoped to pursue productive negotiations with North Korea. When asked if allies had been consulted about the speech beforehand, Wolfowitz snapped: "They could read it."[72] Bush was treating his European partners "as if they were part of some Warsaw Pact," groused Zbigniew Brzezinski.[73]

The president followed his "axis of evil" pronouncements with a new strategic vision for the United States built around the doctrine of preemptive self-defense, including the possible first use of nuclear weapons. This Bush Doctrine also endorsed ad hoc alliances and selective multilateralism. Bush had abandoned the main linchpins of American Cold War policy: containment, deterrence, and permanent regional alliances, replacing them with "Wilsonianism in boots."[74] By spring 2002, leading neoconservatives wrote obituaries for NATO, claiming "the proximal cause of NATO's death was victory in Afghanistan … [which] made clear America's military dominance and Europe's consequent military irrelevance."[75]

This "go it alone" posture proved prophetic. International opinion, which had rallied heavily in Bush's favor immediately after 9/11, became increasingly negative. In France, a book alleged that the U.S. government had fabricated the attack on the Pentagon and planted explosives at the base of the World Trade Center towers; it quickly became a best seller, and by 2003, some 20 percent of Germans subscribed to the same false theory. "With poll after poll" showing the United States "as the chief threat to world peace," one observer noted, "within months of September 11, the indispensable nation was becoming the indefensible nation."[76]

Bush paired his expansive vision of American power with an equally broad definition of executive authority. His Justice Department argued that no limits existed on the president's power to wage the war on terror. Bush could "deploy force preemptively" against a terrorist group or state regardless of their links to 9/11 or to any other terrorist incidents, and his actions would be "unreviewable" by any other body.[77] Bush carried these imperial notions with him as he steered the nation toward war with Iraq.

"Slam Dunk": Justifying the Iraq War

Bush had made it clear in his State of the Union address that he intended to overthrow Saddam Hussein. Cheney, Powell, and Wolfowitz had all publicly supported the elder Bush's decision not to capture Baghdad in 1991, with Wolfowitz later explaining that Saddam's ouster would have required "more or less permanent occupation of a country that could not govern itself, but where the rule of a foreign occupier would increasingly be resented."[78] During the 1990s, Wolfowitz and other neoconservatives gradually persuaded themselves that Washington could avoid occupation by quickly turning the country over to a government led by Iraqi exiles. In 1998, Wolfowitz, Rumsfeld, and allies at the neocon Project for a New American Century successfully lobbied Congress to pass the Iraqi Liberation Act, making regime change an official goal of U.S. policy. Until 9/11, however, Bush followed Powell's moderate strategy of pressuring Saddam Hussein economically through "smart sanctions."[79] With Pentagon debris still burning, Wolfowitz and Rumsfeld instantly suspected Iraqi complicity in the attacks, with Rumsfeld telling aides, "judge whether good enough [to] hit S[addam] H[ussein] at same time. ... Go massive. Sweep it all up. Things related and not."[80] Bush also "believe[d] Iraq was involved."[81]

Linkages between Saddam Hussein's regime and 9/11 proved elusive, despite claims by Bush officials that they had "bulletproof" evidence of Hussein's ties to al Qaeda.[82] When pressed for proof, one CIA Middle East expert bluntly told a senior NSC official: "If you want to go after that son of bitch to settle old scores, be my guest. But don't tell us he is connected to 9/11 or to terrorism because there is no evidence to support that."[83] Richard Clarke likened a diversionary war against Iraq to "invading Mexico" after Pearl Harbor.[84]

Administration hawks apparently saw an opportunity to build a new pillar of U.S. power in the Middle East, replacing Saudi Arabia with a democratic Iraq that was friendly to Israel, harbored no terrorists, and could pump oil for the world economy "at the right price."[85] Rumsfeld, Wolfowitz, and Cheney switched their emphasis from links to al Qaeda to weapons of mass destruction (WMD). They warned that the Iraqi dictator threatened "America and the world with horrible poisons and diseases and gases and atomic weapons." "Imagine a September eleventh with weapons of mass destruction," cautioned Rumsfeld. "It's not three thousand— it's tens of thousands of innocent men, women, and children." It was "a slam dunk" that Iraq had the weapons, Tenet assured Bush, and Condoleezza Rice warned that "we don't want the smoking gun to be a mushroom cloud."[86]

Critics from many quarters challenged these claims. The liberal historian Arthur Schlesinger, Jr., recalled that the Cold War advocates of preventive war "were regarded as loonies."[87] Dick Armey, a conservative Republican from Texas, thought an invasion would produce "a quagmire" and later admitted: "If I'd gotten the same briefing from President Clinton … I probably would have said, 'Ah, bullshit.'"[88] Jack Straw, the British foreign minister, privately contended that Iran, Korea, and Libya posed greater threats than Iraq, which might have a small offensive WMD capability but no "nukes."[89] According to Arab League Secretary General Amr Moussa an invasion would "open the gates of hell," and Egypt's leader Hosni Mubarak predicted that war would spawn "a hundred bin Ladens."[90] Some of the harshest criticism came from Germany where Chancellor Gerhard Schroeder maligned Washington's unilateral "adventure" and his justice minister compared President Bush to the "Nazi Adolf."[91] The most startling rebuke came from former National Security Adviser Brent Scowcroft, Rice's mentor and one of the elder Bush's closest friends. In what many interpreted as guidance from a worried father to a rebellious son, Scowcroft publicly warned that an Iraq invasion would destabilize the Middle East. "Scowcroft has become a pain in the ass in his old age," the president reportedly scoffed.[92]

Bush nonetheless roused support at home and abroad. British Prime Minister Tony Blair provided early and full backing for Saddam Hussein's ouster. In the U.S. Senate, John McCain (Republican of Arizona) repeated administration claims that Iraq had "developed stocks of germs and toxins in sufficient quantities to kill the entire population of Earth multiple times," and Hillary Clinton (Democrat of New York) accused the Iraqi dictator of giving aid and comfort to terrorists, "including al Qaeda members."[93] The historian John Lewis Gaddis rejoiced that "a conservative Republican administration" had embraced "a liberal Democratic ideal—making the world safe for democracy," which he predicted should "provide the basis for a renewed grand strategic bipartisanship."[94]

Bush had already decided to invade. As early as March 2002, he had told several senators that he intended to "take [Saddam] out," and, in July, Rice confided to a State Department official that "the decisions were made" and Iraq could stave off war only if it completely capitulated to Washington's demands.[95] The president waved aside critics at home and abroad, and on the first anniversary of 9/11 he admonished the United Nations: "If [other governments] do not act, America will."[96] With Congress passing a joint resolution authorizing military force against Iraq on October 11, Bush challenged the UN Security Council to enforce Iraqi disarmament. The Security Council passed a new resolution in November and sent inspection teams into Iraq. Then Bush grew impatient with Baghdad's apparent stalling and pressured the UN to act. In mid-December 2002, when Powell counseled patience until the inspections ended, Bush barked: "War is inevitable."[97]

The president once again pounded the bully pulpit. In January 2003, he used his State of the Union Address to hype more evidence for war, and, in the process, uttered seventeen words that turned out to be utterly false: "The British government has learned that Saddam Hussein has recently sought significant quantities of uranium from Africa."[98] Forged documents and faulty intelligence underlay that claim. Continued questions and press scrutiny annoyed Bush. "Did you tell her

Colin Powell (b. 1937) Presenting U.S. Evidence at the UN, 2003. Holding up a model vial of anthrax, on February 5, 2003, Powell made a powerful presentation that Iraq possessed dangerous stockpiles of biological and chemical weapons. His claims deviated from his earlier testimony to the U.S. Senate in May 2002 that although Saddam Hussein sought weapons of mass destruction, "the best intelligence estimates suggest that [he has] not been terribly successful." Bowing to pressure from the president and Pentagon neocons ("fucking crazies," he called them), Powell agreed to make the administration's case for war before an international television audience. After leaving office, he understood that he would be remembered mainly for promoting the false case at the United Nations, lamenting: "I'm the one who made the television moment." (AP Images)

[a reporter] I don't like motherfuckers who gas their own people? … Did you tell her I don't like assholes who lie to the world?" he erupted to his press secretary.[99]

"Maybe they'll believe you," said Bush as he enlisted Powell to speak to the UN about Iraq's WMDs.[100] The soldier-turned-diplomat worked hard to ensure that he did not repeat the president's earlier misstatements. His friend Joe Biden, Democratic senator of Delaware, told Powell "just stick to what you know" with "none of that crazy shit about buying uranium from Africa." The secretary replied wearily: "Joe, someday when you're retired and I'm retired, I'll tell you about all the pressures I've been put under over here."[101] As the secretary's televised lecture began, the CIA's chief weapons expert told a friend that the evidence for Iraqi WMDs had been oversold, insisting: "We just don't have it."[102] Powell's presentation, which stressed chemical and biological weapons allegedly possessed by Saddam Hussein, produced impressive results at home, with public opinion shifting overnight in favor of an invasion.

Overseas opinion still remained skeptical. And many Americans proved unconvinced that war was necessary. Bush and his allies spurned the opposition. When 10 million people in 600 cities around the world marched on February 15 against the impending invasion of Iraq, probably the largest one-day peace protest in history, the president claimed never to listen to "focus groups."[103] While the UN Security Council debated a resolution for war against Iraq later that month, U.S. diplomats told allies that the decision "is ours, and we have made it. The only question now is whether the Council will go along with it or not."[104] Calling Bush a "reckless," "naïve," "simplistic," and "unilateralist … cowboy," France, Germany, Russia, and China mustered a majority to defeat a UN resolution backing war.[105] Bush went ahead and attacked Iraq anyway.

Mission Accomplished? The Invasion and Occupation of Iraq

Operation Iraqi Freedom began on March 20, 2003, with forty cruise missiles and several satellite-guided bombs striking a compound near Baghdad where Saddam Hussein and his sons were reportedly meeting. Even though this "decapitation" attempt failed to kill the Iraqi dictator, the ensuing twenty-six day "shock and awe" campaign quickly overthrew Hussein's regime. At a cost of only 161 dead, the U.S.- and British-led coalition, numbering some 250,000 troops, conquered Iraq in "almost half the time, with one-third the casualties, and at one-fourth the cost" of the first Gulf War of 1991 (see p. 461).[106] Despite initial delays because of sand storms and gloomy prognostications that Baghdad would become another Stalingrad, superior weapons and tactics turned the war into a rout. Iraqi civilian deaths were reportedly near 3,000. The toppling of Saddam Hussein's statue in the heart of Baghdad on April 9 signaled the end of his brutal regime. Coalition forces occupied the rest of battered Iraq within a week. On May 1, greeted by a huge banner spelling MISSION ACCOMPLISHED, Bush made a flashy tail-hook landing in a navy jet aboard the returning aircraft carrier *Abraham Lincoln* off the California coast and pronounced the official end of major combat operations.

Military triumph brought gloating and grand expectations. "Not since Rome has one nation loomed so large over the others," wrote a scholar who called "American empire" the "dominant narrative of the twenty-first century."[107] One neoconservative exulted: "America and the world owe George W. Bush a debt of thanks.

U.S. Marines Topple Saddam Hussein's Statute, Baghdad, 2003. On April 9, 2003, U.S. Marines captured Baghdad, and U.S. television screens soon displayed the dramatic razing of Saddam Hussein's statute in Firdus Square. Many Americans immediately recalled similar images from 1989 when Eastern European regimes fell along with statues of Lenin. But journalists soon revealed how the media and government had collaborated to manipulate television viewers. Tom Shales of the *Washington Post* noted that of all the Saddam Hussein statues scattered throughout the city the Iraqi crowds had conveniently chosen the one located across from the hotel where most of the international media resided. Wide angle shots clearly showed that the Square never attracted more than a few hundred people, many of them reporters. Early shots also demonstrate that U.S. marines actually toppled the statute, initially wrapping Saddam's "head" in a U.S. flag before replacing it with an Iraqi flag and using a tank to pull it down. For most of April 9, CNN and Fox News favored tight shots suggesting an Iraqi crowd spontaneously celebrating its freedom—and replaying similar versions of the event every five minutes from 11:00 A.M. to 8:00 P.M. (AP Images) (Wathiq Khuzaie/Getty Images)

Nothing so avenged the victims of September 11 or so shielded Americans from the recurrence of similar disaster" as did the conquest of Iraq.[108] Victory proved that virile Americans were "from Mars" and hesitant Europeans ("old Europe," in Rumsfeld's dismissive words) were "from Venus."[109] Bush officials likened the coming democratization of Iraq to that of Germany or Japan after World War II, a "demonstration effect" for the Arab world so that "it will no longer produce ideologies of hatred that lead men to fly airplanes into buildings in New York and Washington."[110] Bush did not "expect Thomas Jefferson to come out of this, but I believe people will be free."[111]

Yet problems quickly emerged. Massive looting began within hours of U.S. forces reaching Baghdad. One mob stripped the Ministry of Industry of computers, telephones, furniture, and file cabinets. Similar scenes occurred across Baghdad, including the National Museum of Antiquities where artifacts dating to ancient Mesopotamia were stolen, while U.S. troops stood by without orders or enough numbers to intervene. Having dismissed the Army's claim that several hundred thousand troops would be needed to secure Iraq, Rumsfeld and Wolfowitz rationalized that "freedom's untidy" and "stuff happens."[112] The looting and chaos helped squander any chance that Americans would be "greeted as liberators."[113] Some Iraqis "saw no reason to thank the United States for removing" a leader that Washington had propped up in the past.[114]

Displaying "spectacular incompetence in planning for the aftermath," the Pentagon and State Department struggled to devise a scheme to transfer sovereignty to a provisional government, to train a professional army and police forces, and to plan economic reconstruction in a country where the unemployment rate reached as high as 60 percent.[115] Jay Garner, a retired general, led the initial reconstruction efforts. He followed the Pentagon's plan of a brief U.S. occupation and a quick handover of authority to a provisional government of former Iraqi exiles. But escalating crime and disorder, along with State Department and CIA fears that an exile-led government would be seen as illegitimate, drove Bush to replace him in May 2003. On his return to Washington, Bush asked if "you want to do Iran?" Garner replied: "We want to hold out for Cuba."[116]

Both neoconservatives and their allies in the Iraqi exile community expressed dismay when Bush sought to restore stability by creating an American-led occupation government, the Coalition Provisional Authority (CPA). Some Iraqi leaders thought that "the United States had been duplicitous" from the beginning and sought to make the CPA head L. Paul Bremer a "'pro-consul figure."[117] Bremer's first two decisions—de-Baathification (the removal of all members of Saddam's party from government) and dissolving the Iraqi army—spawned turmoil and fueled a growing insurgency. The occupation authority squandered years of administrative experience when they de-Baathified Iraq's ministries, generating confusion and inefficiency. Eliminating the Iraqi army decreased the number of soldiers available to maintain the peace, removed the last symbol of Iraqi sovereignty, and sent tens of thousands disgruntled men with combat training into the streets. Bush reportedly had no advance knowledge of Bremer's actions, which contradicted the recommendations of the National Security Council but complied with Rumsfeld's wishes.

Evidence of the CPA's incompetence proliferated. Malnutrition among children doubled, and homes endured sporadic electricity and little potable water, with garbage and sewage filling the streets. Both literacy and household income declined during the CPA's reign. In 2008, after five years of U.S. occupation, Iraq still ranked fifth on the Fund for Peace's index of failed states (Afghanistan ranked seventh). A country swimming in oil suffered gasoline shortages because its refineries stood unrepaired. At the CPA headquarters in Baghdad's fortified Green Zone, "the less one knew about Iraq, the more influence one had."[118] Ideological conformity proved more important than expertise in the Middle East. Bremer embraced "free-market nation building" to make Iraq's economy "the most open to trade and capital flows in the world, and put it among the lowest taxed in the world, rich or poor."[119]

From the moment they invaded Iraq, American forces faced an escalating "guerrilla-type campaign"—a "long, hard slog," in Rumsfeld's phrase.[120] During the push from Kuwait to Baghdad, hit-and-run attacks fouled supply lines, and some Iraqi civilians who welcomed U.S. forces fell victim to murder and abuse. Suicide bombing and improvised explosive devices (IEDs) soon followed. Such threats should not have come as a surprise. The CIA had issued numerous prewar warnings that the invasion might breed an insurgency. Indeed, Saddam Hussein had instructed his top ministers to hold out for days and then allow the insurgency to take over. He and his top generals reportedly had studied Vietnamese manuals on guerrilla tactics in preparation. IEDs (low-tech, roadside bombs) became the signature weapon of the insurgency and the "single greatest threat" to occupation forces, accounting for one-third of all U.S. troops killed in the first year of the insurgency.[121] A defiant Bush boasted: "Bring 'em on."[122]

A terrorist "network of networks" soon augmented die-hard Saddam loyalists.[123] Foreign Islamicists, including members of al Qaeda who "weren't there before," took advantage of Iraq's porous border to join in the violence.[124] Terrorism experts dubbed Iraq "the Super Bowl for jihadists" and warned that "we have provided war games … against the best-trained military on earth."[125] The belated capture of Saddam Hussein ("We got him!") in December 2003 did nothing to ease the increasingly dangerous tasks of military occupation.[126] By late 2007, the violence had transformed approximately 20 percent of Iraq's prewar population into refugees. Three million had left the country and another 2 million had been displaced within Iraq.

Deteriorating conditions accelerated the U.S. public's disillusionment with the war. After months of futile searching, even after interviewing captured Iraqi scientists, David Kay, the chief inspector of the 1,400-strong U.S. Iraq Survey Group, admitted in January 2004 that "we were all wrong" about the WMD that had supposedly posed such an imminent threat.[127] Kay resigned in disgust, calling for an investigation into the intelligence used to justify the war and claiming that the public had a right to feel "abused."[128] The White House initially blamed the CIA and the intelligence community for providing flawed data. Extensive congressional and press investigations concluded, however, that the administration should have known that Iraqi WMD program "were nascent, moribund, or non-existent."[129] Bush's inner circle had rejected the intelligence community consensus and pressured analysts to change their opinions or cherry-picked questionable evidence to "justify a decision

U.S. Prisoner Abuse at Abu Ghraib Prison, Baghdad. In April 2004, in images so shocking some were deemed unsuitable for newspapers and television, pictures of hooded prisoners with dangling electric wires or attacking dogs shocked the world. As one scholar contended, Abu Ghraib revealed more than "simple sadism or a breakdown of military discipline" but instead exposed "standard interrogation practice[s] inside … secret CIA prisons that have operated on executive authority since the start of the war on terror." (AP Images)

already made."[130] Wolfowitz, in a moment of candor, confessed: "For bureaucratic reasons, we settled on one issue, weapons of mass destruction, because it was the one reason everyone could agree on."[131] In fact, Saddam Hussein had deliberately spread disinformation about WMDs in order to deter an invasion from Iran and to help maintain his own political authority. "The much maligned, relatively low-cost policy of containment had worked, and the high-cost policy of counter-proliferation had not been needed," noted one UN official.[132]

No sooner had Iraqi WMDs been exposed as a mirage than shocking images of prisoner maltreatment splashed across U.S. television screens. In April 2004, several news organizations reproduced gruesome photographs of U.S. military police abusing Iraqi prisoners at Abu Ghraib prison in Baghdad. The previous January a soldier had leaked a compact disc full of horrific images to the Army's Criminal Investigation Division, and these images became public three months later. Major General Antonio Taguba's final report enumerated instances of "sadistic, blatant, and wanton criminal abuse," including "breaking chemical lights and pouring the phosphoric liquid on detainees; pouring cold water on naked detainees; beating detainees with a broom handle and a chair, threatening male detainees with rape; … sodomizing a detainee with … a broom stick, and using military dogs to frighten and intimidate detainees."[133] Rumsfeld blamed the abuse on a handful of "bad apples."[134] Fewer than twenty-five officers and soldiers were subsequently punished or discharged. Photographs and documents exposing abuse of women and children remain classified, according to congressional aides who had viewed all the evidence, to maintain the fiction of "the prisoners as al Qaeda."[135] Multiple sources including a former officer at Abu Ghraib have contended that "between 70 percent and 90 percent" of Iraqi detainees were arrested by mistake.[136] Official investigations balked at pinning responsibility for the abuse on the higher echelons. Nonetheless, one former intelligence official contended that the reserve military police were incapable of devising sophisticated psychocultural techniques; instead he attributed them to top-secret counterterrorism operatives inside that cell block.

Abu Ghraib prompted further questions about other military and CIA prisons. Congressional investigators discovered that detainee abuse began after officers decided to "Gitmoize" the detention system in Iraq, a reference to prisons at Guantánamo Bay, Cuba.[137] As one FBI agent put it: "For a lack of a camera, you could have seen in Guantánamo what was seen at Abu Ghraib."[138] Some interrogators at the prison actually studied Chinese techniques used to extract false confessions from U.S. POWs during the Korean War. After a CIA analyst "found people lying in their own feces," including elderly captives clearly suffering from dementia, he feared the United States was committing war crimes.[139] The administration first denied UN officials' request to visit Guantánamo. Bush officials also dismissed criticism from the International Red Cross and Amnesty International regarding the indefinite detention and harsh treatment of prisoners at Guantánamo. A series of federal court cases challenged Bush's contention that his powers as commander in chief permitted him to hold detainees without the protections of the Constitution or international law, including the Geneva Convention. On June 12, 2008, the U.S. Supreme Court ultimately ruled that all constitutional protections, including habeas corpus and the right to trial, extended to the Guantánamo detainees.

The scandal continued in 2005 when newspapers and human rights organizations further reported on secret CIA prisons and "enhanced interrogation techniques." After 9/11 Bush granted the CIA "operational flexibility" to carry out "extraordinary renditions"—the shipping of prisoners to countries with "questionable or blatantly horrible" human rights records, where they were often tortured.[140] Given this evidence, the president could not deflect responsibility for this "torture by proxy" by blaming the "unauthorized actions by ill-trained personnel."[141] Key administration figures closely monitored and approved the renditions and the tortuous treatment of "high-value detainees" in CIA prisons. Cheney, Rumsfeld, Powell, Rice, CIA Director George Tenet, and Attorney General John Ashcroft personally approved the most severe interrogation tactics, including simulated drowning through "water boarding"—with instructions so detailed that some interrogation "sessions were almost choreographed."[142] Congress in October 2005 passed the Detainee Treatment Act requiring the Defense Department to adhere to the Geneva Convention, but Cheney worked successfully to exempt CIA personnel from the law's restrictions.

Guerrilla war, pictures of prisoner abuse, and worldwide protests against the United States recalled images from the 1960s. Certainly the vocabulary of Vietnam seemed to have returned: "credibility gap; seek (rather than search) and destroy; the difficulty of telling friend from foe; military resentment at civilian interference; … winning and losing hearts and minds."[143] Yet Bush and his defenders adamantly rejected comparisons between Vietnam and Iraq. Senator John McCain railed against "a totally false comparison," citing such differences as jungle versus desert fighting or an all-volunteer force versus a force of draftees.[144] But these denials ignored important similarities, including the inability of overwhelming military firepower to produce political stability, the growing antipathy of the indigenous society to U.S. occupation, and declining public support at home. The rejection of any parallels between Iraq and Vietnam also hampered prosecution of the war. Rumsfeld punished those who publicly acknowledged that an insurgency or guerrilla war existed in Iraq, thus losing a chance to adapt U.S. strategy to a different war than the one he anticipated. When a military counterinsurgency expert suggested some programs that had worked in Vietnam, Paul Bremer exploded: "I don't want to talk about Vietnam. This is not Vietnam. This is Iraq!"[145] Both Rumsfeld and Bremer tried to exorcise the specters of Vietnam, but in refuting history they failed to learn any lessons from it. Soldiers on the ground sounded eerily like their predecessors from the 1960s. One combatant confessed to "no dilemma when it came to shooting people who were not in uniform, I just pulled the trigger. ... If they were there, they were the enemy."[146] Counterinsurgency expert John Nagl acknowledged Iraqi anger towards Americans: "We're into the behavior-modification phase. I want their minds right now. Maybe we'll get their hearts later."[147] In 2007 Bush claimed that the principal historical lesson of Vietnam should stress the lives of "millions of innocent citizens" who paid the price of America's hasty withdrawal and terms "like 'boat people,' 'reeducation camps,' and 'killing fields.'"[148] His conflation of the Khmer Rouge in Cambodia with Vietnam and his suggestion that the United States abandoned a war that it was winning "is not revisionist history," one scholar claimed, "it is fantasy history."[149] The military historian Andrew Bacevich suggested that "the news is actually much worse. Iraq may be shaping up to be America's Algeria."[150] In that conflict, the French believed that the traditional laws of war conceded victory to the Algerian nationalists and in frustration employed "systematic torture, extrajudicial killings, and their own brand of terrorism."[151]

Following Abu Ghraib and the undeniable failures of the CPA, the Bush administration abruptly changed course and turned authority over to an Iraqi interim government in June 2004. The insurgency continued unabated as Iraq prepared for January 2005 elections. The neocons had high expectations for these elections despite ongoing sectarian strife. The minority Sunni Muslims threatened to boycott the elections because they feared majority Shiite domination of the new government. Optimistic neocons dismissed such fears because they believed that Iraqi Shiites, unlike their counterparts in Iran, were proto-democrats who would maintain a "thick wall" between mosque and state.[152] In the January elections, however, the Shi'a did not vote for secular, liberal, or pro-western parties. One scholar summed up the election results: "This is a government that will have very good relations with Iran," which "is not the outcome that the United States was hoping for."[153] "Throughout Iraq," a senior Iranian intelligence officer crowed, "the people we supported are in power."[154] Sunnis immediately regretted their boycott. Kurds and Shi'a dominated the transitional government, and Sunnis scrambled to gain positions in the new government slated to assume power in 2006. Ethnic and sectarian violence escalated to civil war levels and left some wondering if Iraq should be allowed to break up into separate enclaves—Kurdistan in the North, Sunni in the center, and the Shi'a in the south.

Bush himself remained upbeat. Presidential aides openly mocked critics, claiming "We're an empire now, and when we act, we create our own reality."[155] After his reelection, Bush remained even more convinced that "one of the great gifts of the Almighty is the desire in everybody's soul ... to be free."[156] A promise to "support the growth of democracy" across the globe became the centerpiece of his second inaugural address.[157] Skeptics pointed out that "you've got to be a coherent society before you can be a democracy."[158] But "the President believes so firmly that he is President for just this mission—and there's something religious about it," his aides stressed.[159] The following year, he hailed Afghanistan and Iraq as examples of the advance of freedom, noting that the number of democracies had increased from two dozen in 1945 to one hundred and twenty two in 2006. He failed to mention that neither Iraq nor Afghanistan had qualified as a democracy in the survey he cited.

By 2006, aides and allies appreciated the dire conditions in Iraq even if the president did not. Rice acknowledged "tactical errors—thousands of them," while Britain's Tony Blair admitted the war had been "pretty much a disaster."[160] After Democratic gains in the 2006 elections, Bush accepted Rumsfeld's resignation, and he appointed Robert Gates, a close associate of his father during the first Gulf War, as the new Secretary of Defense. An original member of the bipartisan Iraq Study Group created by Congress in March 2006 to assess the Iraq War, Gates was expected to follow that panel's recommendations to engage Syria and Iran in a regional security dialogue and to begin a gradual troop withdrawal. Pentagon strategists soon offered the president three options: Go Big (a sharp increase in troops), Go Long (reduce the U.S. combat role and concentrate on the military training and advisory missions), and Go Home (swift withdrawal of U.S. troops).

Bush chose a hybrid plan—a "surge" of 30,000 additional troops with continued training and advisory missions so Iraqis could become more responsible for their own security. Impatient congressional leaders demanded that General David Petraeus, the new military commander in Iraq, give them periodic updates on Iraqi military conditions. The surge did appear to reduce violence by spring 2008, and Petraeus claimed the Iraqi government had met some of its legislative and economic benchmarks. A Government Accountability Office Study and the State Department's annual report on terrorism, however, indicated that daily attacks against civilians remained unchanged from 2006 to 2007 and that most benchmarks had not been met. Other observers noted three separate wars in Iraq: one against al Qaeda, which was going well in 2007–2008; a second against a domestic Sunni insurgency in the center, which became dormant after the United States began paying Sunni militias to put down their arms; and a third against Shiite extremist militias in the south that could turn ugly rapidly. Although militia violence had dropped, discontent among Sunni politicians grew, leading to a mass resignation from the government—a sign that any alleged progress might be fleeting. Even U.S. success in training Iraqi security forces could backfire if it turned out that U.S. advisers "are basically arming potential factions in the civil wars" that might eventually break out.[161]

As Bush continued to urge victory, the Iraqi government became restive. In May 2007, a majority of the Iraqi parliament called for a timetable for troop

Bush Dodges Reporter's Shoe, December 2008. During his so-called "legacy" tour, President Bush held a Baghdad press conference hailing U.S. success in Iraq and soon found himself dodging insults and shoes. Iraqi journalist Muntadhar al-Zeidi became a folk hero in Iraq for his act of defiance. In Islamic culture, the throwing of shoes ranks as a supreme insult. In 2003, images of Iraqis throwing shoes at statues and posters of Saddam Hussein had been used to justify the U.S. invasion. After the incident, Iraqi guards beat and arrested al-Zeidi. A Saudi businessman offered to buy the shoes for $10 million, but U.S and Iraqi security forces destroyed them during a search for explosives. On January 29, 2009, officials in the Iraqi city of Tikrit unveiled an enormous, foliage-filled bronze shoe in the city square as tribute to al-Zeidi's act. Iraqi security forces dismantled the monument the following day. (AP Images)

withdrawal and a freeze on the size of foreign forces. Despite Bush's claim that U.S. troops remained in Iraq at the invitation of its government, he repeatedly ignored Iraqi calls for troop withdrawals and pressed Baghdad to sign a status of forces agreement that would authorize indefinite U.S. military occupation, more than fifty permanent American bases, U.S. *carte blanche* to conduct military operations and to arrest Iraqis, legal immunity for American forces and private contractors, control of Iraq's airspace below 29,000 feet, and unlimited freedom to pursue the "war on terror" through operations in Iraq.

The Iraqi parliament refused to approve the agreement without substantial U.S. concessions, including the elimination of permanent bases and a firm deadline for U.S. withdrawal. Meanwhile, opinion polls indicated that 70 percent of Iraqis believed the surge had failed and nearly 50 percent wanted the United States to leave immediately. The Iraqi government balked at any agreement until after the U.S. presidential election in November 2008. Democrat Barack Obama's victory provided Baghdad with the leverage to win major concessions. The final status of forces pact required U.S. forces to withdraw from Iraqi cities by June 2009 and all U.S. troops to leave the country by December 31, 2011. The agreement also made U.S. military contractors and off-duty military personnel subject to Iraqi criminal law. Despite Washington's concessions, the pact remained deeply unpopular in Iraq. When Bush traveled to Baghdad on December 14, 2008, Iraqi journalist Muntadhar al-Zeidi threw both of his shoes at Bush, shouting, "This is a farewell kiss from the Iraqi people, you dog."[162] Bush managed to dodge both projectiles, but al Zeidi's act elicited cheers throughout Iraq and much of the Middle East.

The costs of the Iraq War continued to accumulate for both Americans and Iraqis. The number of U.S. combatants killed during the occupation soon surpassed the death toll (138) during the combat war, exceeding 4,200 by early 2009, with

"So?" Cartoonist Ben Sargent captures public disgust with the Iraq War and the Bush administration's apparent indifference to its toll. When a reporter confronted Vice President Cheney with surveys indicating that almost two-thirds of Americans did not believe the Iraq War worth the costs, he replied "So? You can't be blown off course by polls." (SARGENT© 2008 Austin American-Statesman. Reprinted with permission of UNIVERSAL PRESS SYNDICATE. All rights reserved.)

more than 30,000 wounded. Even personnel who returned home struggled. The suicide rate among soldiers hit a record high in 2007, with 115 deaths and another 166 attempted suicides among troops deployed in Iraq and Afghanistan. Cases of posttraumatic stress disorder also swelled, with 40,000 troops diagnosed with the condition since 2003. Iraqi civilian deaths reached an estimated 90,000 to 99,000 by early 2009. Financial costs also mounted, with monthly expenditures climbing to $12.5 billion in 2008. Together the wars in Iraq and Afghanistan had cost taxpayers $645 billion, with economists estimating that the total budgetary figures would eventually reach $2.655 trillion. If one adds macroeconomic costs, such as the impact on oil prices, and social costs, such as the wars' disruption of families, the total may increase to $4.4995 trillion. Analysts noted additional negative consequences: setting a precedent for other states to wage preemptive war, undermining rules of international behavior, and actually aiding al Qaeda in destroying a secular Iraqi regime. A military analyst offered his blunt opinion: "I voted for these guys. But I think they are incompetent. ... Certainly in the long run we have harmed ourselves. We are playing to the enemy's political advantage."[163] The government's own statistics indicated that five years in Iraq and seven years in Afghanistan produced little positive impact on terrorism. Worldwide terrorist attacks increased from slightly more than 11,000 in 2005 to nearly 14,500 in 2007. Terror attacks in Iraq nearly doubled from almost 3,500 in 2005 to 6,212 in 2007. The report told the same story for Afghanistan, where 491 terrorist attacks in 2005 jumped to more than 1,100 in 2007.

Containing Evil and Spreading Freedom: The Bush Policy Toward the Middle East and Asia

While Bush focused on Iraq, his neocon advisers pushed for "regime change" in Sudan, North Korea, Iran, China, and even Saudi Arabia. They believed that "Saddam's Iraq was the most challenging" rogue regime and victory there had "increase[d] the range of options" in confronting Syria and Iran.[164] Tehran's inclusion in Bush's "axis of evil" actually startled Iranians. After 9/11, Iran's leaders had immediately criticized the "terrorist Taliban" and permitted public demonstrations of sympathy for America.[165] The Iranian government also announced its willingness to normalize diplomatic relations. Cooperation continued during the Afghan invasion with Tehran offering help for stranded pilots, opening up its ports to humanitarian aid, and encouraging its ally, the Northern Alliance, to work with U.S. forces. After the Taliban fell, Iran helped broker a deal by which the U.S. favorite, Hamid Karzai, became the new president of Afghanistan. Improved relations seemed likely. Then Bush ostentatiously inducted Iran into the "axis of evil."

The moderate Iranian President Mohammad Khatami nonetheless persisted in reaching out to the United States. In March 2003, he offered to meet "one-on-one" regarding Iranian nuclear research, support for militant groups, such as Hezbollah in Lebanon, and recognition of Israel's right to exist. But the Bush administration rejected bilateral talks, contending that Khatami had little power and insisting that any contacts include European representatives. Later in 2003, a furor erupted when International Atomic Energy Agency (IAEA) inspectors found remnants of weapons-grade uranium on some Iranian equipment, which the IAEA subsequently concluded had predated Iranian acquisition of that apparatus. With Bush on the sidelines, Britain, France, and Germany negotiated an agreement whereby Iran would accept more rigorous IAEA inspections, suspend its uranium enrichment program, gain the European Union's recognition of Iran's right to develop peaceful nuclear energy, and begin a dialogue on regional security and stability. Hard-liners in Washington and Tehran helped scuttle the agreement. Bush officials disputed the IAEA's conclusion about the weapons-grade uranium's origins, while conservative Iranian clerics rigged parliamentary elections in 2005 to reduce Khatami's authority. Having stiff-armed Khatami's diplomatic entreaties, the neoconservatives earned a new president, Mahmoud Ahmadinejad, "who shared their belief in the Clash of Civilizations."[166] Ahmadinejad halted IAEA inspections, staged theatrical propaganda events implying that he coveted nuclear weapons, and inflamed international opinion with outrageous statements about the Holocaust and the destruction of Israel. Despite UN Security Council sanctions levied in December 2006, Ahmadinejad refused to curtail his nuclear program. A split emerged between Rice, who wanted to engage Iran and reach out to moderates, and Cheney, who insisted on a policy of isolation and military threats. Reports circulated about a possible military strike against Iran to warn against exploiting the chaos in Iraq. Yet Washington itself had created a regional power vacuum that allowed Iran's influence to grow. "The only army capable of containing Iran"—the Iraqi Army—"has been destroyed by the United States," experts pointed out.[167]

In December 2007, a National Intelligence Estimate concluded that Iran actually had halted its nuclear weapons program in 2003, revelations that Cheney had worked to suppress for more than a year. The Bush administration spoke with one voice in doubting the estimate's conclusions, unashamedly pointing to earlier intelligence mistakes regarding Iraq's WMD programs. Washington insisted that Iran must halt its uranium enrichment program, while the Pentagon and CIA escalated covert activities inside Iran both to acquire information about its nuclear program and to

SPREADING DEMOCRACY IN THE MIDDLE EAST

Spreading Democracy in the Middle East. Secretary of State Condoleezza Rice argued that Washington needed to be "committed to values," using both the sword and the olive branch. But cartoonist Ann Telnaes suggests that Rice's diplomatic efforts in the Middle East relied more on U.S. firepower than on its democratic values. (© Ann Telnaes. Used with the permission of AnnTelnaes and the Cartoonist Group. All rights reserved.)

destabilize the Ahmadinejad regime. In 2008, as Cheney reportedly quizzed his aides on "how to create a casus belli between Tehran and Washington," Gates warned congressional leaders that a preemptive strike "would create generations of jihadists, and our grandchildren will be battling our enemies here in America."[168] Yet both officials agreed that the alleged Iranian threat had to be neutralized before conditions in Iraq could improve. Iranian nuclear development, real or imagined, also threatened to unleash a regional nuclear arms race. Hedging against a nuclear Iran, Turkey, Syria, Saudi Arabia, Kuwait, Egypt, Libya, and Morocco all have expressed interest in obtaining nuclear reactors, ostensibly for domestic power production.

While Bush rattled sabers at Iran, he preached democracy to U.S. allies in the region. After his reelection in 2004, the president and Rice, now secretary of state, struck an "evangelical tone," contending that "liberty" was "not America's gift to the world, it is God's gift to humanity."[169] This ambitious freedom agenda appeared to reap results: Iraq held elections; a popular uprising in Lebanon ousted a pro-Syrian government and forced Syrian troops to withdraw from that country; and U.S. protests prompted Egypt to free opposition leader Ayman Nour—all within the first months of 2005. But "the hopeful narrative of Arab countries holding free elections" had its denouement.[170] When Egypt held its first multicandidate presidential election in September 2005, the incumbent Hosni Mubarak manipulated the process (winning nearly 89 percent of the vote) and quickly jailed his leading opponent, Nour, on trumped-up charges. When Rice visited Cairo in February 2006, she declined even to mention Nour's name. Egypt remained the second

President Bush and Saudi Crown Prince Abdullah (b. 1924), 2005. After the 9/11 attacks, U.S.-Saudi relations hit a low point. Prince Abdullah's visit to Bush's Texas ranch in 2005 sought to rebuild strong ties, but Bush's missionary agenda continued to nettle conservative Arabs. Abdullah became king in August 2005 after the death of his half-brother, Fahd. When Rice proposed criticizing the oil-rich kingdom for jailing dissidents, one of her aides interjected: "Do you want eleven-dollar-a-gallon gasoline?" (AP Images)

leading recipient of U.S. foreign aid, and when Lebanon elected a democratic government, Washington offered no investments to shore up the fledgling regime. Other observers argued that Bush and Rice underestimated resistance from such allies as Saudi Arabia, and overestimated the positive effect of Iraq's January 2005 elections. With more than 80 percent of the Arab public registering an unfavorable attitude toward the United States, dissident movements in the Middle East espoused openly anti-U.S. agendas. Democracy, realist critics noted, might actually hurt U.S. interests in the region.

Arab anger toward the United States stemmed both from the Iraq War and from Washington's response to the Arab-Israeli conflict. When Bush entered office in 2001, a violent Palestinian uprising caused Israel's governing coalition to unravel. If Washington did not intervene, "the consequences could be dire, especially for the Palestinians," warned Powell. But the president countered: "Sometimes a show of strength by one side can really clarify things."[171] After 9/11, with the war on terror taking on contours of the Cold War, Israel became its Berlin with Prime Minister Ariel Sharon hailed as an indispensable ally. In 2002, Bush urged the Palestinians to reject leaders "compromised by terror," but he did not personally intercede until June 2003, when he arranged a summit between Sharon and the new Palestinian Prime Minister Mahmoud Abbas.[172] No sooner had Bush promised to "ride herd" on the resulting recommendations (or "road map") than escalating violence on both sides derailed the process.[173] In 2004 Palestinian suicide bombings against Israelis, Israeli assassinations of Palestinian leaders, and Sharon's insistence on retaining Jewish settlements in occupied territory kept the levels of death and destruction high. Yasir Arafat's death and Abbas's election as Palestinian president in early 2005 led to a cease-fire and raised hopes for progress. But Sharon angered members of his own party when he proposed abandoning Jewish settlements in Gaza. Then in January 2006 Sharon suffered an incapacitating stroke, and Hamas, an avowed enemy of Israel long designated a terrorist organization by Washington, won a majority in the Palestinian parliament. Chastened by Hamas's victory, both Bush and Rice muted their millennial rhetoric about democratizing the Middle East and returned to bolstering friendly, albeit authoritarian, regimes in the region.

The Bush administration faced a new test when fighting broke out in July 2006 between Israel and the Iranian-backed terrorist organization, Hezbollah. It began when Hezbollah fired rockets into Israel from its bases in southern Lebanon and crossed the border to attack Israeli units. Hezbollah captured two Israeli soliders. Israel retaliated by sending troops across the Lebanese border to take out rocket launching sites. The Bush administration initially did little except ask each side to show restraint. Cheney backed an aggressive Israeli response, which might facilitate a preemptive strike against Iran by removing Hezbollah's ability to retaliate against Israel. Despite massive bombing raids that killed numerous Lebanese civilians, Hezbollah continued to fire rockets on northern Israel. Rice successfully worked with the United Nations to broker a cease-fire in August. But every step forward in the region seemed to result in a step backward. Washington pressured Abbas to dissolve the Palestinian government and expel Hamas. Learning of U.S. covert aid to rival Palestinian militias and fearing a coup, Hamas struck first in mid-2007, setting off a brief but bloody civil war in Gaza. Abbas declared a state of emergency and dismissed all Hamas members from the government, but the latter group still controlled Gaza.

With the Palestinian territories split between two competing factions and with corruption allegations dogging Israeli Prime Minister Ehud Olmert, the prospects for peace already seemed dim before Israel began a massive assault on Gaza in late December 2008, ostensibly provoked by Hamas rocket attacks on southern Israel and coinciding with the transition from the Bush to Obama presidencies. When the U.N. Security Council endorsed a cease-fire on January 9, 2009, Washington point-edly abstained while publicly stating that it supported the resolution. Israeli leaders wanted to avoid a repeat of their failed attacks on Hezbollah in 2006 and vowed to continue the military operation until it eliminated Hamas's military threat. Israel declared a unilateral cease-fire on January 17 and pulled its troops out of Gaza on January 21. International reaction proved mixed, with some defending Israel's right to defend itself from Hamas's terror attacks and others decrying a disproportionate response that killed 1,200 Palestinians in retaliation for 14 Israeli deaths.

Bush bequeathed other regional tensions to his successor. In September 2007, Israel launched a preemptive strike against an alleged Syrian nuclear reactor and hinted at a possible similar attack against Iranian facilities. International Atomic Energy Agency (IAEA) inspectors later tentatively concluded that the Syrian site had housed a reactor.

Nuclear proliferation also fomented instability elsewhere in Asia. The discovery that North Korea had accumulated enough plutonium from its Yongbyon reactor to make several atomic bombs had triggered a short-lived crisis in the early 1990s. Pyongyang refused to cooperate with the IAEA and threatened to withdraw from the Nuclear Non-Proliferation Treaty (NPT), which North Korea had signed in 1985. As the Pentagon readied plans for a preemptive "surgical strike" in 1994 and a second Korean war "whose costs would far exceed" the first, a "private" visit by for-mer president Jimmy Carter to North Korea that October brokered an agreement whereby North Korea agreed to halt its nuclear weapons program and submit to international inspection; in return the United States promised $4 billion in energy aid.[174] The accord collapsed when North Korea in a missile test of September 1998 lobbed a three-stage rocket over Japan's main island. Refusing to swallow the bait, the Clinton administration continued humanitarian aid to starving North Koreans. IAEA inspectors reported no new evidence of nuclear weapons development. An accord to halt North Korea's nuclear and missile programs seemed within reach.

The Bush team, however, condemned Clinton's "appeasement" of North Ko-rea and chose to isolate Pyongyang.[175] The new president vetoed bilateral talks and expressed contempt for the North Korean leader, Kim Jong Il, calling him a "pygmy" who "acts like a spoiled child" while "starving his own people" in a "gulag the size of Houston."[176] North Korea's inclusion among the "axis of evil" followed. Bush bowed to pressure from his Asian allies, and six-party talks among the United States, China, Japan, Russia, South Korea, and North Korea continued but made little progress. North Korea remained adamant that only bilateral talks paired with a noninvasion pledge would produce compromise. The confrontation escalated in October 2006 when Kim finally made good on his threat to test a nuclear weapon. "Thank God for Kim Jong Il," one hard-line official reportedly exclaimed, hoping that the test would provoke U.S. military action.[177] The test shocked U.S. allies and prompted both UN sanctions and more productive six-party talks. By February 2007, North Korea agreed to terminate its nuclear program, and by July 2008 it had turned over important files on its nuclear efforts and began disabling the Yongbon reactor. Despite this seeming success, conservatives lambasted Bush for kowtowing to nuclear blackmail, and liberals charged that he had squandered earlier opportunities to reach a similar agreement. As Bush left office, Pyongyang renounced its pledge to abandon its nuclear ambitions, bragged that it had 5 nuclear weapons, and issued threats against South Korea in January 2009 and then declared itself opened to new nuclear talks the next month.

Pakistan evoked nuclear fears as well. Washington needed Islamabad's cooperation in Afghanistan, during the invasion and after. But the connections between Pakistani intelligence, the Taliban, and al Qaeda ran deep. Soon ominous warnings circulated that Islamic fundamentalists in Pakistan's nuclear establishment might funnel nuclear weapons to terrorists. In 2004 Pakistan admitted that its principal nuclear scientist, A. Q. Khan, had given illegal nuclear assistance to Iran, Libya, and North Korea. In fact, Islamabad had known of Khan's crimes for more than three years, and after four years of claiming he acted alone, Khan changed his story and implicated President Pervez Musharraf in his activities. Islamabad had placed Khan under unofficial house arrest in 2004, but Pakistani courts ordered him freed in early 2009. Khan left his home smiling, but refused to answer questions, claiming "we don't want to talk about the past."[178] The Khan scandal also exposed the United States as having befriended Pakistan, a country that had never signed the NPT and had proffered nuclear aid to two members of the "axis of evil." Worries about Pakistan mounted as political instability and violence erupted in 2007, including the assassination of the pro-American former prime minister Benazir Bhutto as she campaigned for a return to office. A new democratically elected government assumed power in 2008, but tensions with Islamabad continued over Afghanistan and al Qaeda's presence in the remote northwestern regions of Pakistan.

Bush pursued a different course with India, the other nuclear power on the subcontinent. He reached out to New Delhi, promising not to be a "nagging nanny" on nuclear matters.[179] The 9/11 attacks cemented the budding entente as both powers perceived Islamic extremists as a growing threat. Once Rice became secretary of state, she vowed to usher India "out of the nuclear netherworld."[180] India's refusal to sign the NPT, she argued, should not outweigh the enormous benefits of close bonds with the most populous democracy in the world. When Bush encountered Indian Prime Minister Manmohan Singh during a ceremony in Moscow in 2005, he casually mentioned that "you and I need to talk civilian nukes."[181] So eagerly did Washington seek an agreement that India essentially gained all it wanted—U.S. nuclear fuel and technology and official status as nuclear state without signing the NPT. India actually faced a uranium shortage that Rice could have used as leverage. Afterward Russia sold India all the uranium it needed. The pact did bring Indian civilian nuclear reactors under international inspection for the first time, but it also freed domestic nuclear resources for Indian's weapons program. Congressional amendments and other complications delayed implementation until late 2008.

Rice and Bush offered further proof of their commitment to New Delhi when they immediately expressed sympathy and support in November 2008 as India reacted to terrorist attacks in Mumbai (formerly Bombay). A Pakistani-based terrorist organization used automatic weapons and grenades to kill at least 173 people while injuring almost twice that number. Islamabad denied any links to the attack, but under U.S. pressure eventually admitted that the attackers were Pakistani nationals. Bush sent a team of FBI investigators to help India hunt down those responsible. During his last days in office, the departing president touted India as "a major world power in the 21st century," in part to check the growth of Chinese global influence.[182]

Indeed, Bush had labeled China a "strategic competitor" as early as the 2000 campaign.[183] Many neoconservatives believed that only Beijing posed a serious challenge to U.S. military and economic hegemony. But no one in the Bush administration wanted to push China too hard and jeopardize a thriving trade relationship. A mini-crisis ignited in early 2001 when a U.S. surveillance aircraft collided with a Chinese jet and crash-landed on Hainan Island. No sooner did Bush apologize than he announced arms sales and "whatever it takes to help Taiwan defend itself."[184] Again 9/11 altered the landscape, as Bush made two fruitful trips to China and President Jiang Zemin visited Bush's Texas ranch in October 2002. With China becoming a full member of the World Trade Organization, Secretary Powell promised the "three Cs"—a "candid, constructive, and cooperative relationship."[185] Beijing played a key role in persuading North Korea to restrain its nuclear program, and Chinese products flooded the U.S. market, resulting in $202 billion trade deficit in 2005. But the two global giants also clashed over the U.S. invasion of Iraq, as well as UN sanctions aimed at controlling Iran's nuclear ambitions, Chinese aid to Sudan in its genocidal war in Darfur (see page 513), and Beijing's violent suppression of protestors in Tibet. Notwithstanding China's dismal human rights record, Bush waved aside public calls to boycott the opening ceremonies of the Beijing Summer Olympic Games in 2008. As Beijing prepared for the Olympics, Americans and the world looked on in horror as China's Sichuan province suffered a massive earthquake in May 2008 that killed more than 69,000 people and left 4.8 million people homeless. In the weeks that followed, the United States, South Korea, Japan, Singapore, Russia, and Taiwan all sent aid or joined in the effort to rescue survivors pinned under rubble.

The Chinese quake marked only the latest in a series of massive natural disasters in Asia and the Indian Ocean region. An earthquake near Sumatra in December 2004 triggered tidal waves (or tsunamis) that killed some 230,000 people around the Indian Ocean littoral and elicited an outpouring of aid from across the globe. The massive damage inspired calls for a global tsunami early warning system. Bush weathered criticism when his initial offer of $350 million in monetary aid lagged behind other less wealthy nations. He eventually increased U.S. aid to $950 million and asked two former presidents, his father and Bill Clinton, to help raise money for private relief efforts. Just days prior the Chinese earthquake in 2008, the second deadliest cyclone in recorded history hit Burma (also known as Myanmar). The country's military rulers resisted international aid and balked at giving an accurate accounting of the more than 100,000 dead. Aid workers along with their supplies waited for days in Thailand as the Burmese junta refused them entry visas. India, one of the few countries that maintained close relations with Burma, urged its leaders to open its borders. The United States, Malaysia, Thailand, and Britain joined New Delhi in directly aiding the cyclone's victims.

This train of natural disasters, however, did not dissuade many experts from predicting Asian global dominance by the end of the twenty-first century. China and India both posted impressive economic growth rates and demonstrated mounting military strength during the first decade of the new century. As multinational firms sought cheap labor, China became the manufacturing hub of the world. But the economic plaudits heaped on Beijing and New Delhi tended to obscure Japan's superior rank as the world's second wealthiest state. Japanese Prime Minister Junchiro Koizumi and his successors, Shinzo Abe, Yasuo Fukuda, and Taro Aso, made a strong alliance with the United States their first priority. All four leaders supported the U.S. war on terror, with Koizumi sending 600 Japanese troops to Iraq, where they focused on humanitarian and reconstruction efforts until their withdrawal in 2006. Koizumi left a lasting impression with Americans when he visited Elvis Presley's Graceland mansion in 2006, where he donned oversized golden sunglasses and regaled Bush and gawking reporters with an Elvis impersonation that featured hand movements, leg shakes, and snippets from his favorite songs. Given the close ties between Tokyo and Washington, some analysts predicted that Japan would use its considerable resources to blunt either Chinese or Indian hegemony and preserve U.S. influence in the region.

Getting a Sense of Their Souls: Europe, Latin America, and Africa in the Twenty-First Century

To some observers, the Japanese-American relationship in Asia mirrored the U.S.-British relationship in Europe. British Prime Minister Tony Blair had maintained close bonds with Bill Clinton and quickly developed similar ties with Bush. London emerged as Washington's most trusted ally in Afghanistan and Iraq. While other European allies criticized Bush's unilateralism, Blair insisted that Britain "must steer close to America" or risk losing "our influence to shape what they do."[186] But Blair met heavy opposition in Parliament (where some called him "Bush's poodle") and from the British public, which opposed the war by a large margin and took to the streets to protest.[187] Britain sent 45,000 troops to Iraq, making it the second largest force in the coalition. Blair's steadfast commitment increased in July 2005 after two rounds of terrorist bombings targeted the London public transit system, killing fifty-six people. He publicly vowed to "pull [out] this evil ideology by its roots."[188] After Blair resigned in 2007, his successor Gordon Brown admitted mistakes in Iraq, but he pledged to continue the close relationship with Washington.

Britain joined sixteen other NATO nations in the multinational coalition occupying Iraq. But no other power sent more than 3,200 troops and twelve sent less than 1,000. All but eight NATO nations (including Britain) withdrew their troops by 2008. The most steadfast allies turned out to be former members of the Warsaw Pact: Poland, Romania, Bulgaria, the Czech Republic, Estonia, Latvia,

Slovakia, Lithuania, and Hungary. Key U.S. partners during the Cold War—France and Germany—distanced themselves from Washington's increasingly imperial presence.

Germany and France first dissented from Bush's "axis of evil" speech, labeling it "simplistic," whereupon neocons dubbed them "an axis of petulance."[189] When France's veto threat scuttled a UN resolution authorizing the Iraq War, Cheney bluntly asked the French ambassador if his country was "an ally or a foe."[190] Resentful superpatriots retaliated by relabeling French fries as "freedom fries," shunning champagne, and calling the French "cheese-eating surrender monkeys."[191] French and German leaders nonetheless reflected the sentiments of their publics, of which 86 percent opposed the U.S. invasion of Iraq. In no European country did public support for the Iraq war exceed 40 percent. In Turkey, a NATO member that bordered Iraq, 4 million people paid to see a sensational movie *The Valley of the Wolves—Iraq* (2006), in which U.S. soldiers were depicted killing Iraqis to supply an illegal trade in human organs. German Chancellor Schroeder lamented Europe's missed opportunity to help "the United States avoid making a mistake with heavy consequences."[192]

As the Iraq War began, Condoleezza Rice reportedly threatened to "ignore Germany and punish France."[193] The Atlantic alliance tottered but did not fall apart. Over time, Europeans showed more animosity toward President Bush and the specific policy of invading Iraq than they did the United States in general. Both France and Germany sent troops to Afghanistan, and French intelligence developed "one of the best" relationships in the world with the CIA counterterrorism division.[194] Economic ties also remained strong and vital. Americans invested five times as much money in Germany as they did in China in 2006 and four times as much in Belgium as they did in India. Europeans likewise provided three-quarters of all foreign investment in the United States. In Germany and France, the avowedly pro-American Angela Merkel became German chancellor in 2005, and Nicolas Sarkozy, who earned the nickname "*Sarko l'americain,*" ascended to the French presidency in 2007.

Although Western Europe remained central to the world economy, the addition of East European nations into NATO and the European Union (EU) reshaped the identity of the continent and its relationship to the world. In 2002 the EU invited Estonia, Latvia, Lithuania, Cyprus, the Czech Republic, Hungary, Malta, Poland, Slovenia, and Slovakia to join, with full integration achieved in May 2004. That same year seven more countries joined NATO: Estonia, Latvia, Lithuania, Slovenia, Slovakia, Romania, and Bulgaria. Russia accepted partnership status. Eastern European economies slowly recovered after the wrenching transition from communism to capitalism, with Russia's economic transformation benefitting from its massive oil and natural gas reserves and a rapid rise in global energy prices.

President Bush especially sought a productive relationship with Russia. After meeting President Vladimir Putin in 2001, Bush told reporters he had looked him in the eye and "was able to get a sense of his soul."[195] Putin gave strong support to U.S. efforts in Afghanistan, telling a group of Americans—in English—that when the Taliban asked for Russian assistance, "We gave them only one answer," gesturing with the Russian version of "the finger."[196] Nonetheless, Putin joined his French and German counterparts in vigorously opposing the Iraq War.

Condoleezza Rice (b. 1954), and Robert Gates (b. 1943), 2008.   When Donald Rumsfeld resigned as secretary of defense in November 2006, Cheney stood as the last bastion of neoconservative orthodoxy in the administration. Bush immediately appointed former CIA director Robert Gates to manage the Pentagon. Some observers believed that the elder Bush and his close friend Brent Scowcroft had engineered the selection to provide "adult supervision" and to "isolate Cheney and give their girl Condoleezza Rice a chance to perform." Beginning in 2007, Rice's influence did seem to increase, and the administration's approach to both North Korea and Iran became less bellicose. When Barack Obama assumed the presidency in 2009, he retained Gates at the Pentagon. (© Matthew Cavanaugh/epa/Corbis)

Nuclear weapons caused the greatest strain on U.S.-Russian relations. Bush advocated shrinking the U.S. nuclear arsenal, but he saw no need for a treaty with Russia and jettisoned the Strategic Arms Reduction Talks that his father had initiated. The president also dismissed the Anti-Ballistic Missile Treaty (ABM) treaty as a "relic" of the Cold War because it blocked deployment of national missile defense.[197] Putin responded with a pledge to counter any U.S. missile defense with more advanced offensive weapons. Despite Secretary Powell's admonition that effective missile defense lay years if not decades in the future, Bush unilaterally withdrew from the ABM treaty in December 2001. Under pressure from Congress and with Putin still seeking arms reduction, Bush eventually reversed his opposition to a formal agreement. The so-called Moscow Treaty, signed in 2002, could more accurately be labeled a gentlemen's agreement. The two-and-half-page document promised that by 2012 both powers would cut their arsenals to 1,700–2,200 deployed nuclear warheads, but it contained no formal schedule for reductions and no verification measures. Nuclear warheads and missiles were to be placed in storage intact and thus could easily be redeployed in a crisis.

The Moscow Treaty proved the highpoint of U.S.-Russian relations under Bush. Moscow's complaints about encirclement greeted NATO invitations to former Soviet republics Ukraine and Georgia along with plans for missile defense bases in Poland and the Czech Republic. Putin first tried compromise on national missile defense by offering to share a Soviet-era radar system in Azerbaijan as a substitute for NATO bases in Eastern Europe. But when Bush stiff-armed his offer, Russia withdrew from the Conventional Forces in Europe treaty (negotiated by the elder Bush and Mikhail Gorbachev). In February 2007, Putin blasted Washington's "uncontained hyper use of force" in international relations.[198] Critics tagged Russia as "a semiauthoritarian regime in democratic clothing," especially after Putin avoided the constitutional bar against a third term by becoming prime minister when his protégé Dmitry Medvedev won election to the presidency in 2008.[199] Russia's suspected complicity in the dioxin poisoning of Ukrainian president Viktor Yushchenko in 2004 and the apparent assassination of a former Russian intelligence officer in Britain two years later conjured up fears of a new Cold War where the battle lines would not be in Berlin, Africa, or Asia but on Russia's own borders. Tensions escalated in August 2008 when the former Soviet republic of Georgia attacked the breakaway provinces of South Ossetia and Abkhazia, thereby prompting Moscow to send troops to protect rebel leaders in both areas. President Bush immediately decried Russia's "bullying and intimidation."[200] After a week of fighting, French President Sarkozy brokered a cease-fire that left Russian troops in South Ossetia and Abkhazia. The Bush administration continued to portray Georgia as a victim of Russian aggression and supported its claim to both provinces. Secretary of Defense Gates remarked that for the first time, both the defense secretary (himself) and secretary of state (Rice) had "doctorates in Russian studies. A fat lot of good that's done us."[201]

Elsewhere, the Cuban-American relationship remained frozen in Cold War rigidity. Bush continued a hard-line policy toward Fidel Castro even when the latter offered to cooperate in the housing of Taliban and al Qaeda prisoners at Guantánamo Bay. "A façade [and] all cosmetics," sniffed Washington.[202] In fall 2003, with a political eye toward the Cuban-American vote in the next presidential election, Bush tightened sanctions against Castro, prompting a Cuban diplomat to scold the Texan for "acting like a cowboy."[203] The administration later listed Cuba among the states accused of sponsoring terrorism and admonished Havana for befriending the "axis of evil." In 2008, when an increasingly ill Castro stepped down as Cuban president and his younger brother Raúl succeeded him, Bush ritualistically rejected any changes so long as either Castro brother remained in power. Nonetheless, the U.S. Chamber of Commerce and key corporations continued to press Washington to end the embargo.

Even as Castro faded from the scene, a new generation of leftist leaders gained power in numerous Latin American countries. During the 1990s, most Latin American governments embraced liberal capitalist economic policies touted in Washington. But beginning in December 2001, a major fiscal crisis in Argentina threatened the economies of Uruguay, Paraguay, and even Brazil. Latin America in 2002 then suffered its worst economic performance in two decades, with a negative growth rate of 1.1 percent. In its aftermath, Latin American social democrats won elections in Brazil (2002), Argentina (2003), Uruguay (2004), Bolivia (2005), Chile (2006), Nicaragua (2006), and Ecuador (2007). The governments varied widely in their approaches and in their attitudes toward the United States. Brazilian President Luiz Inácio Lula de Silva (commonly referred to as Lula) and Chilean President Michelle Bachelet pursued amicable relations with Washington, while Bolivian President Evo Morales joined the Venezuelan president Hugo Chávez in denouncing Bush and praising Castro's resistance to U.S. hegemony. Despite differences on regional issues, this new group of leftist leaders joined in opposing U.S. efforts to create a Free Trade Area of the Americas (FTAA). The FTAA collapsed in 2005, and Washington concluded a bilateral free-trade agreement with Chile (2003), and pursued others with Panama and Colombia.

These new left-wing governments opposed the United States on multiple fronts. In 2005, they rejected the former Mexican foreign minister Luis Ernesto Derbez, Washington's candidate for general secretary of the Organization of American States, and instead selected José Miguel Insulza, a Chilean socialist. Morales nationalized Bolivia's natural gas reserves in 2006, scuttling agreements with U.S. and Chilean companies, and Ecuador's president Rafael Correa pledged to terminate the U.S. lease at Eloy Alfaro Air Base. Chávez, Bush's most nettlesome critic, proposed a Bolivarian Alternative for the Americas, a plan for regional economic integration that emphasized social welfare and mutual economic aid rather than simple trade liberalization. Cuba, Nicaragua, Bolivia, Antigua and Barbuda, Dominica, and St. Vincent and the Grenadines signed onto the project, with Rafael Correa announcing his intention to join. The Bush administration charged that the democratically elected Chávez endangered democracy in his country and the hemisphere. In return, Chávez accused the United States of masterminding a coup that briefly removed him from power in 2002. Despite political wrangling, economic relations, especially Venezuelan oil exports to the United States, remained vibrant.

Mexico best symbolized Bush's rocky relationship with the rest of the Americas. Having sampled U.S.-Mexican relations as governor of Texas, the new president entered office pledged to cooperate with Mexico City on trade, drugs, and immigration. But relations soured quickly. In 2002, Mexico withdrew from the Rio Pact on hemispheric defense shortly after Washington invoked it in response to 9/11. The next year, Mexico cast its UN Security Council vote against the U.S invasion of Iraq. Bush's diplomatic efforts with Mexican President Vincente Fox to reach an agreement on illegal immigration, including a guest worker program, met strong opposition from his own Republican party, which insisted on increased funding for border control and construction of a 700-mile fence between the two countries—"like East Germany with its wall," scoffed one Texan.[204] With 664,000 people and 12,338 trucks crossing the border daily, some business leaders worried that curtailing illegal immigration would end up impeding commerce. The border patrol stopped 1.3 million people from entering the United States illegally in 2004, but an estimated 485,000 eluded them. Interdiction efforts did nothing to reduce the economic incentives. Many Mexican families relied on the $20 billion their migrant relatives sent home every year.

Drug policy stressed interdiction with equally dismal results. The Mexican border accounted for 90 percent of the cocaine smuggling into the United States. The arrest in 2002 of the principal Mexican drug lord Benjamin Arellano Felix did little to stem the traffic. "It would stop being a business if the United States didn't want drugs," said Arellano.[205] Nor did Washington's direct participation in Plan Colombia reap much benefit. Despite $700 million per year in U.S. military aid after 1998, the Colombian government's war against narco-trafficking guerrillas had the reverse effect of increasing the production of coca and poppies (heroin). As the pressure increased, smugglers abandoned routes in Colombia for new ones in Venezuela. Farther south, the triborder region of Paraguay, Argentina, and Brazil had become by 2003 "the world's new Libya," where drug lords and terrorists with "widely disparate ideologies" met to "swap tradecraft."[206] Narcotics had become "a shared tragedy for both halves of the hemisphere."[207] Cash proved more effective than coercion in inducing drug cartels to reduce cocaine shipments to the United States. As the value of the dollar plummeted against the euro, the common European currency, Colombian drug traffickers began targeting wealthier European consumers, using small, impoverished African nations such as Guinea-Bissau as smuggling hubs. Issues other than drugs drew increasing U.S. attention to Africa. With a large Muslim population and with eleven central governments ranked among the twenty most likely to collapse, Africa became a key front in the Bush war on terror. In 2005 the Pentagon announced a $500 million plan to train soldiers in Morocco, Algeria, Tunisia, Mauritania, Mali, Senegal, Niger, Nigeria, and Chad to confront five regional terrorist networks with links to al Qaeda. The growing strength of Islamic radicals in Somalia helped spark a civil war in 2006. The Islamist Court Union, allegedly linked to al Qaeda and Hezbollah, took control of southern Somalia and vowed to rule according to Islamic religious codes. U.S.-backed warlords battled back, and eventually Ethiopia invaded in December. By 2008 Somalia remained divided among four competing factions, including a separatist group in the Northwest, an Ethiopian-backed transitional government holding the capital of Mogadishu and sections of the north, warlord-led clans, and the Islamic resistance. Most of the South remained in hostile hands. The renewed violence in Somalia, a brief U.S. intervention in Liberia's civil war in 2003, the growing terrorist presence, and corporate interest in African oil reserves helped produce in September 2008 a new U.S. military command solely dedicated to African threats.

Sudan's twenty-year civil war finally elicited vigorous political attention from the Bush administration. Some of the southern rebels battling the central government, the National Islamic Front (NIF), professed to be Christians. In the United States, conservative evangelicals "saw the conflict in caricaturist terms"—as an Islamic government persecuting good Christians.[208] With an important segment of his political base pressing for action, Bush made brokering peace in Sudan one of his first foreign policy initiatives. Fearing an aggressive response because of its previous relationship with bin Laden (see page 453), Sudan turned over its vast intelligence files on al Qaeda to win U.S. goodwill. The NIF also cooperated with U.S. efforts to end the civil war, signing a comprehensive peace agreement in January 2005.

With Washington concentrating on the NIF's war in the South, the Khartoum government felt emboldened to engage in "ethnic cleansing" in Darfur, a region the size of France in its western territories. Rooted in conflict over land and water, herders who considered themselves Arab took up arms against farmers who considered themselves African. Both groups practiced Islam and, to the outsider, seem physically indistinguishable. But in 2003, when insurgents formed the Sudanese People's Liberation Army to fight for the right of African farmers, the NIF responded by arming Arab militias. Government forces bombed farming villages from the air while Janjaweed militias on horseback or camel comprised the ground forces. The militias torched homes, raped women and girls, killed livestock, and threw children into burning houses. They polluted wells with dead bodies and branded raped women "to make permanently visible their humiliation."[209] Many Sudanese fled to refugee camps in Sudan and neighboring Chad. From 2003 to 2008, an estimated 350,000 to 400,000 people died in the violence. In 2004 Colin Powell publicly labeled the killings in Darfur as genocide. A UN commission rejected claims of genocide, but ordered prosecutors at the International Criminal Court (ICC) to investigate massive human rights violations. As the rest of the world contented itself with "walking loudly and carrying a toothpick," the NIF inhibited humanitarian efforts by confiscating food meant for refugees, feeding it to animals, and impounding it as genetically modified.[210] Bush's personal envoy to Sudan brokered a tentative peace agreement in 2006, but it quickly collapsed. China, which coveted Sudanese oil, supported Khartoum, as did the Arab League, which claimed that Sudan must fend off potential colonial occupiers. The NIF in 2007 reluctantly accepted a joint UN/African Union peacekeeping force. With the "developed world gladly wash[ing] its hands of Darfur," agitation from nongovernmental organizations, interested legislators, and concerned individuals was insufficient to stop the killing.[211] In July 2008, the ICC investigators indicted Sudanese president Omar Hassan al-Bashir, contending: "His alibi was 'counterinsurgency.' His intent was genocide."[212] The indictment, however, remained largely symbolic unless the UN Security Council decided to enforce it.

Western interest in undeveloped African oil deposits may have trumped concern for human rights abuses in Sudan, Equatorial Guinea, and Nigeria. Yet the same noninterventionist pattern persisted in petroleum-poor Zimbabwe where Robert Mugabe, Zimbabwe's president since it overturned white minority rule in 1980, engaged in systematic human rights abuses for most of his rule. In 1982, he used massive force against a Matabele tribal uprising killing at least 10,000 people, and in 1987 his brutal tactics suppressed a rival political party. He nonetheless received praise as a freedom fighter until 1998 when criticism mounted over his confiscation of land from white farmers, discrimination against homosexuals, and violent liquidation of political opponents. In 2008, after Mugabe's main political rival Morgan Tsvangirai and his Movement for Democratic Change won both the first round of the presidential election and a majority in parliament, Mugabe initiated waves of violence, murder, and torture. Tsvangirai took refuge in the Dutch embassy and withdrew from the second round of balloting, calling any vote a sham and leaving Mugabe unopposed. "I will not surrender power until death do part us," vowed Mugabe.[213] Despite the terror campaign, South African president Thabo Mbeki and other African leaders hesitated to condemn Mugabe, and Russia and China vetoed Bush's efforts to pass UN Security Council sanctions.

However ineffectual in healing African political conflicts, the Bush administration recognized the AIDs crisis as a leading security threat. Sub-Saharan Africa contained two-thirds of all HIV infected people worldwide and 20 million people had died from AIDS since 1983. In the Republic of South Africa alone, 5.5 million lived with HIV among a population of 48 million, making it the country with the world's deadliest AIDS epidemic. At first the Bush administration moved slowly. The head of USAID doubted the effectiveness of AIDS treatment, inaccurately claiming that "African villagers couldn't tell time" and could not "be expected to take drugs according to the prescribed schedule."[214] But Rice and Powell persuaded Bush to support a five-year, $15 billion program to fight AIDS in Africa and other impoverished countries. The president announced his pledge during a visit to South Africa and Botswana in July 2003. Four years later, he claimed the program had paid to treat 1.1 million people in fifteen nations, out of the nearly 40 million people worldwide whom the UN reported lived with HIV. Worried about the impact on African militaries, the Pentagon also joined the battle against AIDS, aiding Uganda and other nations to fund HIV education and prevention programs. With the armies of Uganda, South Africa, and Malawi all reporting high infection rates, those countries risked losing their ability to maintain domestic security. The African AIDS epidemic could create failed states vulnerable to terrorism and civil conflicts. Because AIDS killed mainly adults between twenty and forty-five years old, "we're creating a generation of orphans," warned Mark R. Dybul, the U.S. global AIDS coordinator.[215] Despite combined economic growth rates of 6 percent since 2004 (higher than the world average) and notwithstanding plans for continentwide cooperation through the new African Union, Africa's future depended on solving the AIDS crisis and ending civil wars.

Transnational Challenges and Opportunities

The global AIDS pandemic reflected the growing importance of transnational issues—problems that elided national boundaries. A disease that spread only through intimate human contact had rapidly traversed the globe. In 2007 about 36 million people were living with HIV/AIDS; 2.4 million died of AIDS in 2007. Forty-five million may become infected by 2010. Confronting the deadly epidemic required world leaders to think in global terms, for solutions confined to single states proved woefully inadequate.

Nobel Peace Prize Winners, 2001–2008

2001	The United Nations and Secretary General Kofi Annan for efforts at securing a more peaceful world.
2002	Jimmy Carter for efforts to find peaceful solutions to international conflicts.
2003	Shirin Ebadi, Iranian human rights activist and judge who worked to improve the rights of women and children.
2004	Wangari Maathai, Kenyan environmental and political activist for her contribution to sustainable development and peace.
2005	International Atomic Energy Agency and Director General Mohammed ElBaradei for their efforts to prevent nuclear proliferation and ensure the safe use of peaceful nuclear energy.
2006	The Grameen Bank and its founder, Bangladeshi economist Muhammed Yunis, for advancing economic and social opportunities for the poor, especially women, through their pioneering microcredit work.
2007	The Intergovernmental Panel on Climate Change and former U.S. vice president Al Gore for their efforts to increase knowledge about man-made climate change and advance measures to counteract such change.
2008	Martti Ahtisaari, former President of Finland and UN diplomat for his works to resolve conflicts in Namibia, Indonesia, Kosovo, and Iraq.

Global warming emerged as another key transnational problem in the new millennium. Scientists predicted that emissions from power plants and the effects of economic enterprises would rapidly increase planetary temperatures with potentially devastating effects on the climate. The Kyoto Pact, negotiated in 1997 and approved by the Clinton administration, pledged developed nations to cutting carbon dioxide, methane, and other greenhouse gases that trapped solar heat. But Congress had not ratified the accord when Bush took office. Despite his campaign promises to cut power plant emissions and to regulate carbon dioxide as a pollutant, the new president formally withdrew from the Kyoto pact in 2001, saying that "we will not do anything that harms our economy, because first things first are the people who live in America."[216] The move angered European allies and provided no effective replacement for Kyoto. With the United States consuming 22 percent of the world's energy, serious attempts to control climate change required Washington's participation. In May 2007, Bush reversed himself and called for multilateral efforts to reduce greenhouse gases. But by that point, 182 countries were seeking to fulfill the Kyoto standards, and the news on climate change had become even more ominous.

The turnaround in U.S. policy came in reaction to a UN Intergovernmental Panel on Climate Change report released in early 2007. The Bush administration had disputed earlier scientific data, claiming "we don't have enough information to quantify the level of risk."[217] But the UN panel, which collected assessments from more than 2,500 scientists, had a reputation for being conservative and even out-of-date. Its previous reports had hedged on responsibility for climate change, but its new findings stressed with more than 90 percent probability that human activity had caused global warming. The report concluded that even with immediate changes in human behavior, the existing level of greenhouse gases in the atmosphere would increase planetary temperatures, causing glaciers and polar ice caps to melt and sea levels to rise. The cycle would continue for more than a millennium "due to the timescales associated with climate processes."[218] Without effective curtailment of greenhouse gases, average global temperatures were expected to increase between 2 and 11.5 degrees Fahrenheit by the end of the twenty-first century, with sea levels

Whitechuck Glacier, 1973 and 2006. These two photographs of the Whitechuck Glacier in North Cascades National Park (in Washington State) illustrate how one branch of the ice mass retreated 1.2 miles from 1973 to 2006. Global warming could produce widespread and rapid glacial retreat, causing sharp decreases in fresh water for irrigation and domestic use as well as for animals and plants that depend on seasonal glacier melt. (Courtesy Marui Pelto, Nichols College, North Cascade Glacier Climate Project)

rising from 7 to 23 inches. These changes will also produce more frequent heat waves, heavy rainfall, droughts, tropical cyclones, and extreme high tides.

With 2005 the warmest year on record, some observers thought it was already too late to stave off the worst consequences of climate change. Elevated sea temperatures could destroy coral reefs that shelter many fish vital to the world food supply; melting glaciers and prolonged droughts could affect world water supplies creating shortages and devastating agriculture. As regional climates altered, the global distribution of money and power might also shift. Experts speculated that "rising world temperatures might throw Indonesia, Mexico, Nigeria, and other low latitude nations into generations of misery, while causing Canada, Greenland, and Scandinavia to experience a rip-roarin' economic boom."[219] Drought and violent storms could create numerous refugees from affected regions, while melting ice caps might expose new land masses and natural resources setting off aggressive land grabs in the Arctic and Antarctica. Rising sea levels could flood significant portions of Bangladesh, the Netherlands, and completely submerge some small Pacific islands. Coastal cities, including economic hubs such as Shanghai and Hong Kong, could also be swamped. In 2007, the security implications of climate change prompted the *Bulletin of the Atomic Scientists,* which had monitored the danger of nuclear annihilation since 1946, to add global warming as another menace ticking away on its Doomsday Clock.

The UN panel warned that Africa could suffer the most extreme effects with a quarter of a billion people losing their water supply and food production falling by 50 percent in many countries. The Darfur conflict and a global food crisis in 2007–2008 offered a preview of things to come. In fact, drought in the 1980s had bred tensions in Sudan between herders and farmers that only later mutated into racial conflict. World food prices spiked in 2007–2008 with costs for rice increasing by 217 percent, wheat by 136 percent, maize (corn) by 125 percent, and soybeans by 107 percent. Experts pointed to a perfect storm of poor harvests caused by unseasonable droughts, rising oil prices, growing consumer demand in Asia, and increasing

Bono (b. 1960) and Al Gore (b. 1948) Share a Laugh, 2008.   Pictured here at the World Economic Forum in Davos, Switzerland, the lead singer for U2, an Irish rock band, and the former U.S. vice president both sought to raise public awareness of global issues. Bono (born Paul David Hewson) parlayed his celebrity and wealth into his philanthropic causes, befriending political figures as diverse as conservative Republican Senator Jesse Helms of North Carolina and Lula, the democratic socialist president of Brazil, in order to win support for his campaign to aid Africa. Gore also won worldwide acclaim, including the 2007 Nobel Peace Prize, for his environmental activism. After losing the 2000 presidential election, he "fell out of love" with politics and focused on "the moral issue" of global climate change. (Courtesy Robert Scoble)

use of food grains to create alternative fuels. Food riots broke out in fifteen countries, including Egypt, Mexico, Bolivia, Bangladesh, Pakistan, and South Africa. The director general of the World Bank cautioned that growing global poverty and hunger acted like "a time bomb lodged against the heart of liberty."[220]

Climate change also increased the threat of disease. By the early twenty-first century, 8 million people died of AIDS, tuberculosis, and malaria annually, predominantly in poor countries—"approximately one Holocaust each year."[221] Global warming potentially could increase that number by creating more habitats for disease-bearing insects. Private philanthropy augmented governmental efforts to meet these dangers. From 2000 to 2005, software multi-billionaire Bill Gates spent $6 billion to address health issues in the developing world. Former president Bill Clinton created a foundation to help people confront the challenges of global interdependence, especially the AIDS pandemic and global warming. Embracing market-based solutions, the foundation organized a purchasing consortium to reduce prices for AIDS drugs and pooled resources in large cities so they could more quickly apply new technologies to reduce carbon emissions. Entertainers also sponsored benefit concerts such as Live 8 in 2005 dedicated to eliminating global poverty and Live Earth in 2007 to raise awareness about global climate change.

What if ...   *Al Gore had become president in 2001?*

The 2000 presidential election stands as one of the most controversial in U.S. history. Vice President Al Gore narrowly won the popular vote, receiving some 500,000 more votes than George W. Bush. Florida, where the official results showed the two candidates separated by less than 450 votes, seemed to give Bush victory in the Electoral College. But his victory margin proved so small it prompted automatic recounts. Bush challenged the recount procedures and before all the contested ballots could be examined, the U.S. Supreme Court ruled in a 5 to 4 decision that Florida's procedures violated the Constitution's equal protection clause, effectively making Bush president. What if Al Gore had won instead? How might events have turned out differently?

The 9/11 attacks undoubtedly still would have occurred. The failures to prevent the attacks rested on the inability of the FBI, CIA, and other intelligence agencies to share and interpret information more than it did presidential decision making. Richard Clarke did present Condoleezza Rice with a strategy paper for confronting al Qaeda, but his proposals would not have prevented 9/11 because operational preparations had advanced too far by that point. Confronted with the aerial attacks on the World Trade towers and the Pentagon, Gore likely would have issued a similar ultimatum to the Taliban and attacked Afghanistan from the air. He might have welcomed European offers of assistance. Nonetheless, European complaints about U.S. unilateralism and "hyper power" pretentions began in the 1990s after Clinton's refusal to join the International Criminal Court and Congress's rejection of the Comprehensive Nuclear Test Ban Treaty. Strains in the Atlantic alliance likely would have surfaced. After defeating the Taliban, Gore likely would have focused more on nation-building in Afghanistan than did Bush.

Even though the Clinton administration had listed Iran, Iraq, and North Korea as "rogue states," Gore would likely have hesitated to identify an "axis of evil." Instead Gore could have continued Clinton's diplomatic efforts with North Korea, evidenced in Secretary Madeleine Albright's historic meeting with Kim Jong Il in October 2000. A follow-up visit to Pyongyang by Clinton, cancelled because of the controversy surrounding the 2000 election, might have been undertaken later by Gore. The former vice president might also have accepted Iran's proposal for direct talks in 2002 and 2003.

The two issues where a Gore presidency would have produced the most marked change were Iraq and global warming. In contrast to hawks in the Clinton administration who pushed for regime change in Iraq, Gore preferred to work through the UN to return inspectors and modify sanctions so they targeted Saddam Hussein and the ruling elite rather than ordinary Iraqi people. His prior legislative and vice-presidential record in favor of multilateralism, moreover, make it less likely that had Gore become president, a doctrine of preemptive war would have been articulated or implemented along the lines of the Bush doctrine in Afghanistan and Iraq. As a U.S. senator, Gore had written *Earth in the Balance* (1992), which warned of the world's ecological challenges and proposed a Global Marshall Plan to address them. A President Gore most certainly would not have denied climate change and global warming for more than six years. With the Senate narrowly split between Democrats and Republicans from 2001 through 2008, he still might not have mustered the two-thirds vote needed to ratify the Kyoto Pact. As president, however, he could have used his executive authority to implement other measures to control U.S. carbon emissions. Yet Gore may well have exerted greater influence on these issues as a private citizen, having dedicated his public career after 2000 to raising awareness about the threat of global warming. Whereas a politician must temporize or revise positions to build public support and legislative coalitions, as a private citizen he had the freedom to voice his uncompromising assessment of global warming. Gore's film, *An Inconvenient Truth* (2006), which depicted his public presentations on environmental dangers, won the Academy Award for Best Documentary, and, in 2007, he shared the Nobel Peace Prize with the Intergovernmental Panel on Climate Change.

Philanthropy and the global reach of popular entertainers exemplified what some scholars call soft power. The United States still led the world in traditional measures of power, with its annual defense outlay amounting to 40 percent of global expenditures and its control of over 29 percent of global wealth. For some, however, American domination of film and television exports, its status as the largest publisher of books, its huge profits from music sales, its leadership in scientific research, and the 1.6 million international students enrolled in U.S. colleges and universities symbolized a milder form of hegemony that helped build a global empire of consumption. U.S. culture even proved alluring to its enemies. Just before the 2003 invasion, a foreign visitor in Baghdad riding in a taxi heard a disc jockey denounce President Bush just before making a "zippy intro for a song by Madonna."[222] Kim Jong Il made no secret of his adoration of basketball superstar Michael Jordan, and in 2001 his son Kim Jong Nam was detained when he tried to enter Japan under a fake passport, explaining that he merely wanted to visit Tokyo Disneyland.

With the U.S. economy serving as the engine of globalization, with American products from Velcro to Viagra popular everywhere, America's soft power complemented and extended its hard power. Despite U.S. advantages, cultural exchange flowed in all directions, with the world's second largest economy, Japan, sending the United States such cultural phenomena as karaoke, Pokémon cartoons and cards, 1,400 different manga titles (Japanese comic books), animé, including the 2002 Academy Award winner for best animated film, *Spirited Away,* and baseball stars, including Daisuke Matsuzaka, Hideki Matsui, Ichiro Suzuki, and Kosuke Fukudome. China contributed basketball star Yao Ming, who became a fixture at the NBA All-Star game.

Some scholars suggested that global interconnections would help prevent wars. The journalist Thomas Friedman posited the Golden Arches Theory of Conflict Prevention, arguing that "people in McDonald's countries don't like to fight wars any more, they prefer to wait in line for burgers."[223] Skeptics pointed out that although none of the axis of evil had a McDonald's, a Golden Arches restaurant stood conspicuously in the center of Belgrade when NATO bombed it in 2000, and both Israelis and Lebanese had hamburgers readily available when they squared off in 2006. The United States, the biggest "Big Mac" consumer of all, invaded both Afghanistan and Iraq after Friedman proffered his flawed theory.

While not denying the reach of soft power, some commentators argued that its effects were not always positive. Beginning in the 1990s, MTV, a U.S.-based network built around music and youth programming, launched channels in India, China, Italy, Spain, France, the Netherlands, Russia, Brazil, Japan, Korea, Poland, Latin America, Central Europe, and channels in Mandarin and Arabic. These stations did feature some local programming, but they relied heavily on U.S. music videos that often included racist, sexist, and violent imagery. A poll of young people in twelve countries indicated that they developed a negative impression of the United States after encountering these images. Others lamented U.S. fast food chains crowding out local cuisine in China, where 41 percent reported eating at the restaurants at least once a week. As U.S. tobacco companies lost customers at home because of public health concerns, they ramped up their cigarette exports from 50 billion cigarettes in 1975 to 220 billion in 1994. World health officials hence predicted that tobacco-related deaths in the developing world would rise from 2 million in 2000 to 7 million in 2030.

The World Wide Web and the expansion of global broadcasting also offered benefits and challenges. Although the Internet developed via global collaboration, the United States quickly became the dominant player in cyberspace, with 56 percent of all Web content in English. The Web's proponents have celebrated its democratic nature, where blogs allow anyone to offer their opinions. Sites such as You Tube have bypassed government censorship and exposed government violence in

Barack Obama (b. 1961) and Nobel Laureate Wangari Maathai (b. 1960), 2006. Then Senator Barack Obama, later elected president in November 2008, visited with Kenyan Nobel Laureate Professor Wangari Maathai during an African tour in 2006. Maathai earned an international reputation for her environmental and political activism. She founded the Green Belt Movement in 1977, which subsequently planted over 40 million trees across Kenya to prevent soil erosion. She also worked to bring multiparty democracy to her country. The son of a Kenyan economist and an American anthropologist from Kansas, Obama made history as the first African American president. In July 2008, Obama spoke to a crowd of 200,000 in Berlin near where the infamous wall once split the city, issuing a challenge to the world: "The walls between old allies on either side of the Atlantic cannot stand. The walls between the countries with the most and those with the least cannot stand. The walls between races and tribes; natives and immigrants; Christian and Muslim and Jew cannot stand. These now are the walls we must tear down." (Fredrick Omondi Onyango)

Zimbabwe; soldiers in Iraq posted footage that contradicted the rosy pictures provided in Washington; and critics of the war debated supporters. Yet, the Web's democratic and anarchic character also allowed terrorist networks to plan attacks and extol their exploits via on-line videos. The website Ana al-Muslim called on members of the global jihad to wage "a media war that is parallel to the military war."[224] Al Jazeera, a television network based in Qatar, broadcasting in Arabic and English, ranked as the third largest international news channel in the world after BBC World and CNN International. The network came under fire from the Bush administration for airing statements from Osama bin Laden and for what Washington contended was biased coverage of the Afghan and Iraqi invasions. Many conservatives considered Al Jazeera enemy media and have urged the Pentagon to take action to end its broadcasts. After U.S. missiles struck the Al Jazeera offices in Kabul and Baghdad, a British tabloid claimed that in 2004 Bush had discussed bombing Al Jazeera headquarters with Tony Blair. True or not, former House Speaker New Gingrich lamented the Bush team's insufficient appreciation of soft power. "The real key is not how many enemies I kill," said Gringrich, "The real key is how many allies do I grow. And that is a very important metric that they just don't get."[225]

At times, Washington's push to spread products and expertise around the globe melded together its soft and hard power. U.S. arms exports reached $7.4 billion in 2007 and totaled almost $53 billion since 2000. This quest for profits sometimes

"... And Then We Just Kept on Fencing ...". Cartoonist Tom Toles links calls for a border fence to cut off illegal immigration with other issues that Americans refused to confront, including global warming, Darfur, European allies, and free trade. (TOLES © 2006 Washington Post. Reprinted with permission of UNIVERSAL PRESS SYNDICATE. All rights reserved.)

undercut U.S. national security policy, with surplus parts from U.S. fighter jets making their way to Iran. In the late twentieth century, private military contractors joined more traditional defense industries in earning profits from war. These companies, such as Kellogg, Brown & Root, can "deploy troops, build and run military bases, train guerrilla forces, conduct air surveillance, mount coups, stave off coups, and put back together the countries wars have destroyed (or at least try to)."[226] Erik Prince, the founder of Blackwater Security, boasted: "Our corporate goal is to do for the national security apparatus what FedEx did to the postal service."[227] With "the active Army ... about broken" in its inability to confront the multiple threats from terrorists, private military companies have taken on tasks that soldiers had performed in earlier conflicts and supplemented the 1.389 million military personnel deployed worldwide.[228] In Iraq, Blackwater received contracts to protect the CPA and then the U.S. embassy staff, earning almost $2 billion in fees. But the company also provoked controversy. In March 2004, insurgents in Fallujah attacked four Blackwater employees and hanged their dead bodies from a bridge over the Euphrates River. Fallujah immediately became a flashpoint where battles raged for months. Three years later, Blackwater snipers killed seventeen people in Baghdad. The FBI investigation concluded that at least fourteen of the shootings had no justification. Excessive reliance on private contractors "motivated by bottom line profits" might result in foreign policy by default.[229]

Other critics worried about American foreign policy's "excessively military cast. Delighted to own the biggest hammer on the planet, policymakers tend to treat every problem as if it were a nail."[230] U.S. military power overshadowed all potential rivals for the near term, perhaps prolonging what political scientists call a "unipolar moment" through "command of the commons" (seas, space, and air).[231] A British journalist noted the "paradox" of American power—"too great to be challenged by any other state, yet not great enough to solve problems such as global terrorism and nuclear proliferation."[232] As diplomacy receded as a method to resolve differences, even Secretary of Defense Robert Gates lamented in 2007 that the total budget for the State Department was $36 billion—"less than what the Pentagon spends on healthcare" while the "6,600 professional Foreign Service officers" numbered fewer than the personnel required "for one aircraft carrier strike group."[233] While domestic programs starved, military spending ballooned under Bush—$304.8 billion in 2001 to $696.3 billion in 2008, while no other country's defense budget exceeded $60 billion. This growth, combined with a massive tax cut since 2001, boosted the national debt to $9 trillion. With 44 percent of the publicly held debt owed to foreign creditors, especially in Japan, China, and OPEC nations, warnings of American decline that had been mocked in the 1990s became fashionable again. Americans also wondered what they had gained from massive defense spending. One attempt to measure quality of life ranked the United States ninety-seventh out of 141 nations, citing as negatives the wars in Afghanistan and Iraq along with a high violent crime rate and one of the world's largest prison populations.

As the U.S. economy plunged into recession in 2008 and the global economy reeled from a massive credit crunch, stock markets crashed around the globe and businesses shed jobs at rates not experienced in decades. Analysts feared a global depression that might rival the Great Depression of the 1930s. The economic crisis helped contribute to Bush's historically low job approval ratings. As his presidency concluded, scholars debated Bush's legacy, with a majority ranking him among the very worst presidents in history—Richard Nixon, Herbert Hoover, James Buchanan, and Warren G. Harding. Bush's defenders argued that he would be vindicated, much like Harry Truman who weathered bouts of heavy public disapproval but rose in public estimations decades later. The president ignored his critics, perceiving "himself as doing the Lord's work."[234] Any appraisal of the Bush presidency must grapple with the Iraq War and its stormy aftermath, the precipitous decline in U.S. standing in world opinion, the expansion of presidential authority to conduct the war on terror without congressional authorization, and the dangerous precedent of waging preventive war under false premises. One analyst contended that "history judges good presidents by what they do, bad ones by how long they take to undo."[235]

Bush has bequeathed to his successor Barack Obama an uncertain future in Iraq and Afghanistan. Obama's presidential candidacy had benefited from his early opposition to the Iraq War. But he declared he did not oppose all wars, just "dumb wars."[236] Indeed, he pledged to withdraw U.S. troops from Iraq within sixteen months while expanding the U.S. military commitment in Afghanistan. He also promised to strengthen the U.S. commitment to nuclear nonproliferation and arms control, take a more active approach to ending violence in Darfur, pursue peace between Israelis and Palestinians, raise the profile of U.S.-African relations, and end wasteful spending on ineffective missile defense systems. Overall, he expressed a willingness to replace confrontation with conversation, asserting in his Inaugural Address: "To those who cling to power through corruption in deceit and the silencing of dissent, know that you are on the wrong side of history; but that we will extend a hand if you are willing to unclench your fist."[237] Obama announced during his first week in

Hillary Rodham Clinton (b. 1947), 2009. Barack Obama selected Clinton, a former First Lady, Democratic senator from New York, and his leading rival for the 2008 Democratic nomination, as his secretary of state. Pictured here testifying during her confirmation hearings, Clinton pledged a renewed emphasis on diplomatic over military solutions to security problems. She also voiced a deep commitment to human rights, especially to alleviating "the plight of women and girls, who comprise the majority of the world's unhealthy, unschooled, unfed, and unpaid." (© Kevin LaMarque/Reuters/Corbis)

office that he would close the Guantánamo Bay prison camp within twelve months and end interrogation practices that many had condemned as torture. One of the greatest obstacles facing Obama was high expectations amidst a tangle of domestic and international problems. He would have to prioritize some problems over others, and partisans on all sides would inevitably be disappointed. Whatever course the new president selects, the United States will remain at the center of world politics. And Americans will vigorously debate their choices, as they have throughout their history.

FURTHER READING FOR THE PERIOD SINCE 2001

Some works listed in Chapter 11 also cover topics in this period.

For studies of 9/11 and after, see Abdel Bari Atwan, *The Secret History of Al Qaeda* (2008); Anny Bakalian and Mehdi Bozorgmehr, *Backlash 9/11* (2009); Stephen Brill, *After* (2003); Steve Coll, *Ghost Wars* (2004); Robert D. Crews and Armin Tarzi, eds., *The Taliban and the Crisis in Afghanistan* (2007); Richard Crockatt, *America Embattled* (2003); Mary L. Dudziak, ed., *September 11 in History* (2003); Jim Dwyer and Kevin Flynn, *102 Minutes* (2005); Anthony Feinstein, *Journalists Under Fire* (2007); Norman Friedman, *Terrorism, Afghanistan, and America's New Way of War* (2003); Rohan Gunaratna, *Inside Al Qaeda* (2002); Dilip Hiro, *War Without End* (2002); Gilles Kepel, *Jihad* (2002); Gilles Kepel and Jean-Pierre Milelli, eds., *Al Qaeda in Its Own Words* (2007); Bruce Lincoln, *Holy Terrors* (2003); David S. New, *Holy War* (2002); Omar Nasiri, *Inside the Jihad* (2008); Jonathan Randall, *Osama* (2004); Ahmed Rashid, *Jihad* (2002) and *Taliban* (2001); Bob Woodward, *Bush at War* (2002); and Lawrence Wright, *The Looming Tower* (2006).

For George W. Bush, his administration, and his foreign policy, see Hal Brands, *From Berlin to Baghdad* (2008); Elisabeth Bumiller, *Condoleezza Rice* (2007); Laurent Cohen-Tanugi, *An Alliance at Risk* (2003) (NATO); Ivo H. Daalder and James M. Lindsay, *America Unbound* (2003); Karen DeYoung, *Soldier* (2006) (Colin Powell); Robert Draper, *Dead Certain* (2007) (George W. Bush); Elizabeth Drew, *Fear and Loathing in George W. Bush's Washington* (2004); Craig R. Eisendrath and Melvin A. Goodman, *Bush League Diplomacy* (2004); John C. Fortier and Norman J. Ornstein, eds., *Second-Term Blues* (2007); Barton Gellman, *Angler* (2008) (Cheney); Fred Greenstein, ed., *The George W. Bush Presidency* (2003); Stefan Halper and Jonathan Clarke, *America Alone* (2004); George C. Herring, *From Colony to Superpower* (2008); Dale R. Herspring, *Rumsfeld's Wars* (2008); Mark Hertsgaard, *The Eagle's Shadow* (2002); Michael Hirsh, *At War with Ourselves* (2003); Chalmers Johnson, *The Sorrows of Empire* (2004); John B. Judis, *The Folly of Empire* (2004); Lawrence Kaplan, *NATO United, NATO Divided* (2004); Peter J. Katzenstein and Robert O. Keohane, eds., *Anti-Americanisms in World Politics* (2007); Glenn Kessler, *The Confidante* (2007) (Condoleezza Rice); James Kitfield, *War and Destiny* (2005); Paul Krugman, *The Great Unraveling* (2003); Charles Kupchan, *The End of the American Era* (2002); Lewis Lapham, *Theater of War* (2002); Marcus Mabry, *Twice as Good* (2007) (Condoleezza Rice); James Mann, *The Rise of the Vulcans* (2004); Alexander Markovitz, *Uncouth Nation* (2006); Peter Merkl, *The Rift Between America and Old Europe* (2005); Julie A. Mertus, *Bait and Switch* (2004); John Nichols, *Dick* (2004) (Cheney); Joseph S. Nye, *The Paradox of American Power* (2002); Christopher D. O'Sullivan, *Colin Powell* (2009); Elizabeth Pond, *Friendly Fire* (2004); Andrew Ross and Kristin Ross, eds. *Anti-Americanism* (2004); Stephen Schier, ed., *High Risk and Big Ambition* (2004); Peter Singer, *The President of Good & Evil* (2004); Ron Suskind, *The One Percent Doctrine* (2006), *The Price of Loyalty* (2004), and *The Way of the World* (2008); Emmanuel Todd, *After the Empire* (2004), and Jacob Weisberg, *The Bush Tragedy* (2008).

For the War on Terror and the Bush Doctrine, see John Agnew, *Hegemony* (2005); Andrew Bacevich, *American Empire* (2002); Walter Brasch, *America's Unpatriotic Acts* (2004); Matthew Brzezinski, *Fortress America* (2004); Roger Burbach and Jim Tarbell, *Imperial Overstretch* (2004); Stephen Burman, *The Shape of the American Empire* (2007); Clark Butler, ed., *Guantánamo Bay and the Judicial-Moral Treatment of the Other* (2007); Angelo M. Codevilla, *No Victory, No Peace* (2005); Anthony H. Cordesman, *Terrorism, Asymmetric Warfare, and Weapons of Mass Destruction* (2001); Bruce Cumings, Ervand Abrahamian, and Moshe Ma'Oz, *Inventing the Axis of Evil*

(2004); David Farber, ed., *What They Think of Us* (2007); Karen J. Greenberg and Joshua L. Dratel, eds., *The Torture Papers* (2005); Derek Gregory, *The Colonial Present* (2004); Robert Jervis, *American Foreign Policy in a New Era* (2005); Robert D. Kaplan, *Imperial Grunts* (2005); Robert Kaufman, *In Defense of the Bush Doctrine* (2007); Gilles Kepel, *The War for Muslim Minds* (2004); Jon Kraus et al., eds., *Transformed by Crisis* (2004); Melvyn P. Leffler, and Jeffrey W. Legro, eds., *To Lead the World* (2008); Charles Maier, *Among Empires* (2007); Mahmood Mamdani, *Good Muslim, Bad Muslim* (2004); Alfred W. McCoy, *A Question of Torture* (2006); Walter Russell Mead, *Power, Terror, Peace, and War* (2004); Cullen Murphy, *Are We Rome* (2007); Paul Murphy, *The Wolves of Islam* (2004); Timothy Naftali, *Blind Spot* (2005); Donald Nuechterlein, *Defiant Superpower* (2005); John Newhouse, *Imperial America* (2004); Anne Norton, *Leo Strauss and the Politics of American Empire* (2004); Bernard Porter, *Empire and Superempire* (2006); Stanley Renshon and Peter Suedfeld, eds., *Understanding the Bush Doctrine* (2007); Paul Rutherford, *Weapons of Mass Persuasion* (2004); and Patwant Singh, *The World According to Washington* (2005).

For Iraq and the Iraq War, see Nadje Al-Ali and Nicola Pratt, *What Kind of Liberation?* (2009); Tariq Ali, *Bush in Babylon* (2003); Jon Lee Anderson, *The Fall of Baghdad* (2004); Anonymous, *Imperial Hubris* (2005); Andrew Arato, *Constitution Making Under Occupation* (2008); James Bamford, *A Pretext for War* (2004); Sara Beck and Malcolm Downing, eds., *The Battle for Iraq* (2003); James DeFronzo, *The Iraq War* (2009); Charles Duelfer, *Hide and Seek* (2009); Wayne H. Bowen, *Undoing Saddam* (2007); Robert K. Brigham, *Iraq, Vietnam, and the Limits of American Power* (2008); Joseph Cirincione et al., *WMD in Iraq* (2004); John K. Cooley, *An Alliance Against Babylon* (2005); Mark Danner, *Torture and Truth* (2005); Mark R. DePue, *Patrolling Baghdad* (2007); James Fallows, *Blind into Baghdad* (2006); Charles. H. Ferguson, *No End in Sight* (2008); Lloyd Gardner and Marilyn B. Young, eds., *Iraq and the Lessons of Vietnam* (2008); Michael R. Gordon and Bernard E. Trainor, *Cobra II* (2006); Ahmed S. Hashim, *Insurgency and Counter-Insurgency in Iraq* (2006); Eric Herring and Glen Rangwala, *Iraq in Fragments* (2006); Seymour M. Hersh, *Chain of Command* (2004); Michael Isikoff and David Corn, *Hubris* (2006); Sandra Mackey, *The Reckoning* (2002); Peter Mansour, *Baghdad at Sunrise* (2008); Tara McKelvey, *Monstering* (2007); Thomas Mowle, ed., *Hope is not a Plan* (2007); Williamson Murray and Robert H. Scoles, Jr., *The Iraq War* (2003); George Packer, *The Assassins' Gate* (2006); Stephen Pelletière, *America's Oil Wars* (2004); Kenneth M. Pollack, *The Threatening Storm* (2002); John Prados, *Hoodwinked* (2004); Jeffrey Record, *Dark Victory* (2004); Thomas Ricks, *Fiasco* (2006); James Risen, *State of War* (2006); Gary Rose, ed., *The Right War?* (2005); Aram Roston, *The Man Who Pushed America to War* (Ahmad Chalabi) (2008); Jeremy Schahill, *Blackwater* (2007); Simon Serfaty, *Architects of Delusion* (2008); Joseph E. Stiglitz and Linda J. Bilmes, *The Three Trillion Dollar War* (2008); and Bob Woodward, *Plan of Attack* (2004) and *State of Denial* (2006).

International economic issues are discussed in Alfred E. Eckes, Jr., and Thomas W. Zeiler, *Globalization and the American Century* (2003); David Harvey, *The New Imperialism* (2003); Kent Jones, *Who's Afraid of The WTO* (2003); Mary Cusimano Love, ed., *Beyond Sovereignty* (2003); John R. MacArthur, *The Selling of Free Trade* (2002); Peter Singer, *One World* (2002); Benn Steil and Robert E. Litan, *Financial Statecraft* (2006); and Joseph E. Stiglitz, *Globalization and Its Discontents* (2002).

For North Korea, Japan, China, and Asia, see Zachary Abuza, *Militant Islam in Southeast Asia* (2003); Jasper Becker, *Rogue Regime* (2005) (North Korea); Ted Galen Carpenter, *America's Coming War with China* (2005); Victor Cha and David Kang, *Nuclear North Korea* (2004); Bruce Gilley, *China's Democratic Future* (2004); Peter Hays Gries, *China's New Nationalism* (2004); Selig Harrison, *Korean Endgame* (2003); Chae-Jin Lee, *A Troubled Peace* (2006) (Korea); Michael O'Hanlon and Mike Mochizuki, *Crisis on the Korean Peninsula* (2003); Charles Perry and Toshi Yoshihara, *US-Japan Alliance* (2003); Charles L. Pritchard, *Failed Diplomacy* (2007) (North Korea); and Robert L. Suettinger, *Beyond Tiananmen* (2004).

The Palestinian question, Israel, Iran, and the Middle East are discussed in Irvine Anderson, *Biblical Interpretation of Middle East Policy* (2005); Ali M. Ansari, *Confronting Iran* (2006); Fakhreddin Azimi, *The Quest for Democracy in Iran* (2007); Rachel Bronson, *Thicker than Oil* (2006); Richard J. Chasdi, *Tapestry of Terror* (2002); Andrew Hammond, *What the Arabs Think of America* (2007); Tim Niblock, *"Pariah States" and Sanctions in the Middle East* (2002); Anne Marie Oliver and Paul Steinberg, *The Road to Martyrs' Square* (2005); Marc J. O'Reilly, *Unexceptional* (2008) (Persian Gulf); Kenneth Pollack, *The Persian Puzzle* (2004); Barry Rubin, *The*

Tragedy of the Middle East (2004); William A. Rugh, *American Encounters with Arabs* (2006); Bernard Wasserman, *Israelis and Palestinians* (2003); and Eyal Zisser, *Assad's Legacy* (2002).

For U.S. relations with Latin America, see Richard Crandall, *Driven by Drugs* (2002) (Colombia); Patrick J. Haney and Walt Vanderbush, *The Cuban Embargo* (2005); Alfredo Molano, *Loyal Soldiers in the Cocaine Kingdom* (2004); Morris Morley and Christopher McGillion, *Unfinished Business* (2002) (Cuba); Robert Pastor, *Cuba, the United States, and the Post-Cold War World* (2005); and Bert Ruiz, *The Colombian Civil War* (2002).

For Africa, including Darfur, see M. W. Daley, *Darfur's Sorrow* (2007); Julie Flint and Alex deWaal, *Darfur* (2008); Douglas Johnson, *The Root Causes of Sudan's Civil Wars* (2004); Adam LeBor, *Complicity with Evil* (2007); Tom Lodge, *Politics in South Africa* (2004); Susan Collin Marks, *Watching the Wind* (2000) (South Africa); Francis Njubi Nesbitt, *Race for Sanctions* (2004); Andrew Norman, *Robert Mugabe and the Betrayal of Zimbabwe* (2004); Sherene Razack, *Dark Threats and White Knights* (2004) (Somalia); and James Traub, *The Best Intentions* (2007).

For transnational issues, including global warming, see Allan M. Brandt, *The Cigarette Century* (2007); Kurt M. Campbell, ed., *Climatic Cataclysm* (2008); Jared Diamond, *Collapse* (2005); Tim Flannery, *The Weather Makers* (2006); Matthew Fraser, *Weapons of Mass Distraction* (2005); Elizabeth Hanson, *The Information Revolution and World Politics* (2008); Niklas Höhne, *What's Next After the Kyoto Protocol* (2006); Elizabeth Kolbert, *Field Notes from a Catastrophe* (2006); Eugene Linden, *Winds of Change,* (2006); Joseph S. Nye, Jr., *Soft Power* (2004); Spencer Weart, *The Discovery of Global Warming* (2004); and Ernesto Zedillo, *Global Warming* (2008).

See also the General Bibliography, Robert L. Beisner, ed., *Guide to American Foreign Relations Since 1600* (2003), and the following notes.

NOTES TO CHAPTER 12

1. David Frum, *The Right Man* (New York: Random House, 2003), p. 114.
2. Quoted in *Hartford Courant,* August 30, 2003.
3. John Updike, "Comment," *The New Yorker, LXXVII* (September 24, 2001), 28.
4. Quoted in "Mayor of the World," *Time, CLVIII* (December 31, 2001/January 7, 2002), 44.
5. Port Authority transcripts quoted in *Hartford Courant,* August 29, 2003.
6. David Von Drabble in *Washington Post National Weekly Edition,* September 17–23, 2001.
7. Quoted in Nicholas Lemann, "The Options," *The New Yorker, LXXVII* (October 1, 2001), 72.
8. James Mann, *Rise of the Vulcans* (New York: Penguin, 2004), p. 296.
9. Quoted in Walter LaFeber, "The Bush Doctrine," *Diplomatic History, XXVI* (Fall 2002), 143.
10. Quoted in Bob Woodward, *Bush at War* (New York: Simon & Schuster, 2002), p. 7.
11. CIA official quoted in *Washington Post National Weekly Edition,* May 27–June 2, 2002.
12. Quoted in Woodward, *Bush at War,* p. 3.
13. Osama bin Laden quoted in Kathleen Hall Jamieson and Paul Waldman, *The Press Effect* (New York: Oxford University Press, 2003), p. xi.
14. Robert Jervis, *American Foreign Policy in a New Era* (New York: Routledge, 2005), p. 41.
15. Quoted in Woodward, *Bush at War,* p. 211.
16. Presidential Address to a Joint Session of Congress and the American People, September 20, 2001 (www.whitehouse.gov).
17. Peter Bergen quoted in David Corn, *Lies of George W. Bush* (New York: Three Rivers Press, 2004), p. 136.
18. Quoted in Paul Lewis, *Cracking Up* (Chicago: University of Chicago Press, 2006), p. 181.
19. Quoted in Greg Grandin, *Empire's Workshop* (New York: Metropolitan, 2006), p. 197; quoted in Alfred W. McCoy, *A Question of Torture* (New York: Metropolitan Books, 2006), p. 113.
20. Quoted in Stephen Kinzer, *Overthrow* (New York: Times Books, 2006), p. 277.
21. Cheney quoted in William K. Tabb, "Two Wings of the Eagle," *Monthly Review, LV* (Summer 2003), 80.
22. Schröder and *Le Monde* quoted in Peter Merkl, *The Rift Between American and Old Europe* (New York: Routledge, 2005), p. 1.
23. Quoted in Elizabeth Drew, "Hung Up in Washington," *New York Review of Books,* February 12, 2004, p. 18.
24. Quoted in Woodward, *Bush at War,* p. 81.
25. Bush quoted in Timothy Naftali, *Blind Spot* (New York: Basic Books, 2005), p. 289; former official quoted in Seymour M. Hersh, "The Iraq Hawks," *The New Yorker, LXXVII* (December 24 & 31, 2001), 59.
26. Quoted in Elisabeth Bumiller, *Condoleezza Rice* (New York: Random House, 2007), p. 143.
27. Quoted in Richard H. Immerman, "Intelligence and Strategy," *Diplomatic History, XXXII* (January 2008), p. 18.
28. CIA agent and Rice quoted in Bumiller, *Rice,* pp. 156–157.
29. Lawrence Wright, *The Looming Tower* (New York: Knopf, 2006), p. 337–338.
30. Quoted in Ron Suskind, *The One Percent Doctrine* (New York: Simon & Schuster, 2006), p. 2.
31. Quoted in Bumiller, *Rice,* p. 161.
32. Marcus Mabry, *Twice as Good* (New York: Modern Times, 2007), p. 209.
33. Richard Brookhiser, "The Mind of George W. Bush," *The Atlantic Monthly, CCLXXXIX* (April 2003), 59.

34. Quoted in Kinzer, *Overthrow*, p. 276.
35. Quoted in Julie A. Mertus, *Bait and Switch* (New York: Routledge, 2004), p. 53.
36. Quoted in Mann, *Rise*, 250.
37. Bush quoted in Glenn Kessler, *The Confidante* (New York: St. Martin's Press, 2007), p. 5.
38. Quoted in Mann, *Rise*, p. 201.
39. Senator Joseph Biden quoted in George Packer, *The Assassins' Gate* (New York: Farrar, Straus and Giroux, 2006), p. 44.
40. Bob Woodward, *State of Denial* (New York: Simon & Schuster, 2006), pp. xii–xiii.
41. Eliot Cohen quoted in *Washington Post National Weekly Edition*, December 25, 2000/January 1, 2001.
42. Quoted in Michael Hirsh, *At War with Ourselves* (New York: Oxford University Press, 2003), p. 52.
43. Quoted *ibid.*, p. 54
44. Woodward, *Bush at War*, p. 322; Powell quoted in *Washington Post National Weekly Edition*, April 7–13, 2003.
45. Quoted in Hendrik Hertzberg, "Blixxkrieg," *The New Yorker*, LXXIX (February 10, 2003), 33.
46. Bob Woodward, *Plan of Attack* (New York: Simon & Schuster, 2004), p. 79.
47. Mabry, *Twice as Good*, p. 172.
48. Quoted in Woodward, *Plan of Attack*, p. 79.
49. Bush quoted in Mann, *Rise of the Vulcans*, p. ix.
50. CIA official quoted in James Risen, *State of War* (New York: Free Press, 2006), p. 64; former administration official quoted in Bumiller, *Rice*, p. 137.
51. Rumsfeld and Card quoted in Bumiller, *Rice*, p. 178.
52. Kessler, *Confidante*, p. 3; *Washington Post National Weekly Edition*, November 12–18, 2007.
53. Kessler, *Confidante*, p. 7; Powell quoted in John Bolton, *Surrender is not an Option* (New York: Threshold Editions, 2007), p. 76.
54. Packer, *Assassins' Gate*, p. 113.
55. Kessler, *Confidante*, p. 2
56. Packer, *Assassins' Gate*, pp. 13–14.
57. William Kristol quoted in John Judis, *The Folly of Empire* (New York: Scribner, 2004), p. 169.
58. Michael Ledeen quoted in Ervand Abrahamian, "Empire Strikes Back," in Bruce Cumings, Ervand Abrahamian, and Moshe Ma'oz, *Inventing the Axis of Evil* (New York: New Press, 2004), p. 93.
59. Jeffrey Record, *Dark Victory* (Annapolis: Naval Institute Press, 2004), p. 69.
60. Marilyn B. Young, "Ground Zero," in Mary L. Dudziak, ed., *September 11 in History* (Durham: Duke University Press, 2003), p. 21.
61. Quoted in Mann, *Rise*, p. 300.
62. Quoted in *Washington Post National Weekly Edition*, April 26–May 4, 2003.
63. Richard Clarke quoted in Seymour Hersh, *Chain of Command* (New York: HarperCollins, 2004), p. 146–147.
64. Risen, *State of War*, p. 157.
65. Quoted in Karen J. Greenberg and Joshua L. Datel, eds., *The Torture Papers* (New York: Cambridge University Press, 2005), pp. 213–214.
66. Hersh, *Chain of Command*, p. 4.
67. Colin Powell quoted in Mann, *Rise*, p. 309.
68. Quoted in Robert D. Kaplan, *Imperial Grunts* (New York: Random House, 2005), p. 205.
69. Quoted in Benn Steil and Robert E. Litan, *Financial Statecraft* (New Haven: Yale University Press, 2007), p. 41.
70. Quoted in Jon Western, *Intervention and War* (Baltimore: Johns Hopkins University Press, 2005), p. 194.
71. Quoted in Frum, *Right Man*, p. 239.
72. Quoted in Mann, *Rise*, p. 320.
73. Quoted in Mary Nolan, "Anti-Americanization in Germany," in Andrew Ross and Kristin Ross, eds., *Anti-Americanism* (New York: New York University Press, 2004), p. 130.
74. Stanley Hoffman quoted in George C. Herring, *From Colony to Superpower* (New York: Oxford University Press, 2008), p. 944.
75. Charles Krauthammer quoted in Elizabeth Pond, *Friendly Fire* (Washington, DC: Brookings Institution Press, 2004), p. 38.
76. Walter Russell Mead, *Power, Terror, Peace, and War* (New York: Knopf, 2004), p. 5.
77. Justice Department memo quoted in Michael Isikoff and David Corn, *Hubris* (New York: Crown Publishers, 2006), p. 22.
78. Quoted in Mann, *Rise*, p. 190.
79. Quoted in Kenneth M. Pollack, *The Threatening Storm* (New York: Random House, 2002), p. 106.
80. Rumsfeld notes quoted in Packer, *Assassins' Gate*, p. 40.
81. Quoted *ibid.*, p. 41.
82. Rumsfeld quoted in Spencer Ackerman and John B. Judis, "The First Casualty," *New Republic*, CCXXVII (June 30, 2003), 14.
83. Quoted in George Tenet, *At the Center of the Storm* (New York: HarperCollins, 2007), p. 307.
84. Quoted in Carolyn Eisenberg, "The New Cold War," *Diplomatic History*, XXIX (June 2005), 424.
85. Michael Ignatieff, "Why Are We in Iraq? (And Liberia? And Afghanistan?)," *New York Times Magazine* (September 7, 2003), p. 71.
86. Bush, Rumsfeld, and Rice quoted in Ackerman and Judis, "First Casualty," pp. 14, 17; Tenet quoted in Bob Woodward, *Plan of Attack* (New York: Simon & Schuster, 2004), p. 249.
87. Quoted in Abrahamian, "Empire Strikes Back," p. 97.
88. Quoted in Isikoff and Corn, *Hubris*, pp. 24, 125.
89. Quoted in Alastair Campbell, *The Blair Years* (New York: Knopf, 2007), p. 630.
90. Quoted in Andrew Hammond, *What the Arabs Think of America* (Westport, Conn: Greenwood, 2007), pp. 87–88.
91. Gerhard Schröder and Herta Daubler-Gmein quoted in Martin Walker, "The Winter of Germany's Discontent," *World Policy Journal*, XIX (Winter 2002/03), 2–3.
92. Quoted in Jacob Weisberg, *The Bush Tragedy* (New York: Random House, 2008), p. 69.
93. Quoted in Isikoff and Corn, *Hubris*, p. 150.
94. Quoted in Lloyd E. Ambrosius, "Woodrow Wilson and George W. Bush," *Diplomatic History*, XXX (June 2006), 522.
95. Bush quoted in Record, *Dark Victory*, p. 29; Rice quoted in Tenet, *At the Center of the Storm*, p. 309.
96. Quoted in Michael Dunne, "The United States, the United Nations, and Iraq," *International Affairs*, LXXIX (March 2003), 271.
97. Quoted in Douglas J. Feith, *War and Decisions* (New York: Harper, 2008), p. 342.
98. Quoted in Woodward, *Plan of Attack*, p. 294.
99. Quoted in Isikoff and Corn, *Hubris*, p. 3.
100. Quoted in *Washington Post National Weekly Edition*, October 16–22, 2006.
101. Quoted in Robert Draper, *Dead Certain* (New York: Free Press, 2007), p. 186.
102. Quoted in Risen, *State of War*, p. 110.
103. Quoted in William Finnegan, "Marches and Parades," *The New Yorker*, LXXIX (May 19, 2003), 33.

104. Quoted in Dana H. Allin, Philip H. Gordon, and Michael O'Hanlon, "The Democratic Party and Foreign Policy," *World Policy Journal,* *XIX* (Spring 2003), 12.

105. Quoted in Samuel F. Wells, "The Transatlantic Illness," *Wilson Quarterly, XXVII* (Winter 2003), 42.

106. Max Boot, "The New American Way of War," *Foreign Affairs, LXXXII* (July/August 2003), 44.

107. Joseph S. Nye, Jr. "U.S. Power and Strategy After Iraq," *Foreign Affairs, LXXXII* (July/August 2003), 60.

108. Angelo M. Codevilla, *No Victory, No Peace* (Lanham, Md.: Rowman & Littlefield, 2005), p. 111.

109. Michael Cox, "Martians and Venutians in the New World Order," *International Affairs, LXXIX* (Spring 2003), 523–532.

110. Condoleezza Rice and Paul Wolfowitz quoted in Mark Danner, "Iraq: The New War," *New York Review of Books,* September 25, 2003, pp. 90–91; Bush quoted in Ron Suskind, *The Price of Loyalty* (New York: Simon & Schuster, 2004), p. 187.

111. Quote in Michael H. Hunt, *The American Ascendancy* (Chapel Hill: University of North Carolina Press, 2007), p. 279.

112. Rumsfeld quoted in Peter J. Boyer, "Downfall," *The New Yorker, LXXXII* (November 20, 2006), 62.

113. Cheney quoted in Packer, *Assassins' Gate,* p. 97.

114. Ibrahim Al-Marashi and Abdul Hadi al-Khalili, "Iraqis' Bleak Views of the United States," in David Farber, ed. *What They Think of Us* (Princeton: Princeton University Press, 2007), p. 12.

115. Arthur M. Schlesinger, Jr., "Eyeless in Iraq," *New York Review of Books,* October 23, 2003, p. 26.

116. Quoted in Woodward, *State of Denial,* p. 224.

117. Ali A. Allawi, *The Occupation of Iraq* (New Haven: Yale University Press, 2007), p. 107.

118. Anonymous Iraqi quoted in Packer, *Assassins' Gate,* p. 198.

119. *Wall Street Journal* quoted in Grandin, *Empire's Workshop,* p. 160.

120. General John Abizaid quoted in Danner, "Iraq," p. 88; *New York Times,* October 22, 2003.

121. Thomas E. Ricks, *Fiasco* (New York: Penguin Press, 2006), p. 217.

122. CNN.com, July 3, 2003.

123. *The Iraq Study Group Report* (Filiquarian Publishing, 2006), p. 17.

124. Nicholas Lemann, "Comment: Real Reasons," *The New Yorker, LXXIX* (September 22, 2003), 82.

125. CIA official quoted in Risen, *State of War,* p. 147; Jessica Stern quoted in Charles H. Ferguson, *No End in Sight* (New York: PublicAffairs, 2008), p. 435.

126. Paul Bremer quoted in *New York Times,* December 15, 2003.

127. David Kay quoted in *New York Times,* February 1, 2004.

128. Quoted in Suskind, *One Percent Doctrine,* p. 299.

129. John Prados, *Hoodwinked* (New York: New Press, 2004), p. xi.

130. Immerman, "Intelligence and Strategy," 22.

131. Quoted in *USA Today,* May 30, 2003.

132. Hans Blix, *Disarming Iraq* (New York: Pantheon Books, 2004), p. 269.

133. Quoted in Hersh, *Chain of Command,* p. 22.

134. Quoted in McCoy, *Question of Torture,* p. 142.

135. Steven Miles quoted in Tara McKelvey, *Monstering* (New York: Carroll & Graf, 2007), p. 197.

136. Quoted in McCoy, *Question of Torture,* p. 142.

137. Quoted in Hersh, *Chain of Command,* p. 31.

138. Quoted in Seymour Hersh, "The General's Report," *The New Yorker, LXXXIII* (June 25, 2007), 66.

139. Quoted in Hersh, *Chain of Command,* p. 2.

140. Jeremy Scahill, *Blackwater* (New York: Nation Books, 2007), p. 271.

141. Quoted in McCoy, *Question of Torture,* p. 175; Jane Mayer, "The Black Sites," *The New Yorker, LXXXIII* (August 13, 2007), 49.

142. ABCNews.go.com, April 9, 2008.

143. Marilyn B. Young, "Two, Three, Many Vietnams," *Cold War History, VI* (November 2006), 416.

144. Quoted in Robert K. Brigham, *Is Iraq Another Vietnam?* (New York: PublicAffairs, 2006), p. 35.

145. Quoted in *Washington Post National Weekly Edition,* July 31–August 6, 2006.

146. Specialist Corporal Michael Richardson quoted in Roger Burbach and Jim Tarbell, *Imperial Overstretch* (New York: Zed Books, 2004), p. 2.

147. Quoted in Young, "Two, Three, Many Vietnams," 417.

148. Quoted in *Boston Globe,* August 23, 2007.

149. Quoted *ibid.*

150. Quoted in Robert D. Shulzinger, *Time for Peace* (New York: Oxford University Press, 2006), p. 200.

151. *Ibid.*

152. Ahmed S. Hashim, *Insurgency and Counter-Insurgency in Iraq* (Ithaca: Cornell University Press, 2006), p. 283.

153. Juan Cole quoted in Allawi, *Occupation of Iraq,* p. 393.

154. Quoted in Kinzer, *Overthrow,* p. 313.

155. Quoted in Frank Rich, *The Greatest Story Ever Sold* (New York: Penguin Press, 2006), pp. 3–4.

156. Quoted in George Packer, "Not Wise," *The New Yorker, LXXXII* (May 8, 2006), 24.

157. Quoted in Jeffrey Goldberg, "Breaking Ranks," *The New Yorker, LXXXI* (October 31, 2005), 60.

158. Quoted in Jeffrey Goldberg, "The Lorax," *The New Yorker, LXXXII* (February 12, 2007), 36.

159. Quoted in George Packer, "Betrayed," *New Yorker, LXXXIII* (March 26, 2007), 72.

160. Rice quoted in Bumiller, *Rice,* p. 284; Blair quoted in Simon Serfaty, *Architects of Delusion* (Philadelphia: University of Pennsylvania Press, 2008), p. 114.

161. Joost Hilterman quoted in Ferguson, *No End in Sight,* p. 476.

162. BBC News, December 14, 2008.

163. Quoted in James Fallows, *Blind into Baghdad* (New York: Vintage Books, 2006), p. 115.

164. Victor Davis Hanson, "Has Iraq Weakened Us?" in Gary Rosen, ed., *The Right War?* (New York: Cambridge University Press, 2005), p. 220.

165. Quoted in Abrahamian, "Empire Strikes Back," p. 96.

166. Quoted in Ali M. Ansari, *Confronting Iran* (New York: Basic Books, 2006), p. 230.

167. Vali Nasr quoted in Seymour M. Hersh "The Redirection," *The New Yorker, LXXXIII* (March 5, 2007), 58.

168. Quoted in Seymour M. Hersh, "Preparing the Battlefield," *The New Yorker, LXXXIV* (July 7, 2008) <www.newyorker.com>.

169. Brent Scowcroft quoted in *Washington Post National Weekly Edition,* September 10–16, 2007; Bush quoted in Mertus, *Bait and Switch,* p. 58.

170. David Samuels, "Grand Illusions," *Atlantic Monthly, CCICIX* (June 2007), 52.

171. Powell and Bush quoted in Suskind, *Price of Loyalty,* p. 71–72.

172. Quoted in Donald E. Nuechterlein, *Defiant Superpower* (Washington, D.C. Potomac Books, 2005), p. 34.

173. Quoted in *New York Times,* June 15, 2003.

174. Carter Diary quoted in Douglas Brinkley, *The Unfinished Presidency* (New York: Viking, 1998), p. 399.

175. Bolton, *Surrender,* p. 101.

176. Quoted in Jasper Becker, *Rogue Regime* (New York: Oxford University Press, 2005), p. 254.

177. Quoted in Kessler, *Confidante,* p. 87.

178. Quoted in *Boston Globe,* February 7, 2009.

179. Quoted in *New York Times,* September 7, 2001.

180. Kessler, *Confidante,* p. 50.

181. Quoted *ibid.,* p. 58.

182. Quoted in *Washington Post National Weekly Edition,* April 10–16, 2006.

183. Quoted in Mann, *Rise,* p. 281.

184. Quoted in Elizabeth Economy, "Changing Course on China," *Current History, CII* (September 2003), 246.

185. Quoted in Oleksandr Gladky, "American Foreign Policy and U.S. Relations with Russia and China," *World Affairs, CLXVI* (Summer 2003), 7.

186. Quoted in Serfaty, *Architects of Delusion,* p. 59.

187. Charles Kennedy quoted in *BBC News World Edition,* February 3, 2003.

188. Quoted in *Manchester Guardian,* July 14, 2005.

189. French Foreign Minister Hubert Védrine and Charles Krauthammer quoted in Mann, *Rise,* p. 321.

190. Quoted *ibid.,* p. 355.

191. Quoted in Merkl, *The Rift Between America and Old Europe,* p. 2.

192. Quoted in Serfaty, *Architects of Delusion,* p. 121.

193. Quoted in Time.com, May 4, 2003.

194. CIA official quoted in *Washington Post National Weekly Edition,* July 11–17, 2005.

195. Quoted in Mann, *Rise,* p. 288.

196. Quoted in Bolton, *Surrender,* p. 71.

197. Quoted in *New York Times,* June 13, 2001.

198. Speech and the Following Discussion at the Munich Conference on Security Policy, February 10, 2007, <president.kremlin.ru>.

199. Ivan Krastev, "What Russia Wants," *Foreign Policy,* no. 166 (May/June 2008), 49.

200. Quoted in *Los Angeles Times,* August 8, 2008.

201. Quoted in *New York Times,* September 20, 2008.

202. Vicki Huddleston quoted in Morris Morley and Chris McGillion, *Unfinished Business* (New York: Cambridge University Press, 2002), p. 199.

203. Dagoberto Rodriguez quoted in *Miami Herald,* October 10, 2003.

204. Quoted in *Washington Post National Weekly Edition,* May 29–June 4, 2006.

205. Quoted in *Washington Post National Weekly Edition,* November 11–17, 2002.

206. Jessica Stern, "The Protean Enemy," *Foreign Affairs, LXXXII* (July/August 2003), 32.

207. Sol M. Linowitz, "Latin America," *Foreign Affairs, LXVII* (Winter 1988/1989), 56

208. United Nations Africa expert quoted in Adam LeBor, *"Complicity with Evil"* (New Haven: Yale University Press, 2006), p. 195.

209. Quoted in M.W. Daly, *Darfur's Sorrow* (New York: Cambridge Univeristy Press, 2007), p. 284.

210. John Prendergast quoted in *Washington Post National Weekly Edition,* November 27–December 3, 2006.

211. Daly, *Darfur's Sorrow,* pp. 292–293.

212. ICC Prosecutor Luis Moreno-Ocampo quoted in *New York Times,* July 14, 2008.

213. Quoted in *African Press International,* April 4, 2008.

214. James Traub, *The Best Intentions* (New York: Farrar, Straus, and Giroux, 2006), p. 155.

215. Quoted in Stephan Faris, "Containment Strategy," *Atlantic Monthly, CCICVIII* (December 2006), 34.

216. Quoted in Charles A. Kupchan, "The Rise of Europe," *Political Science Quarterly, CXVIII* (Summer 2003), 223.

217. Presidential Science Advisor John H. Marburger III quoted in *Washington Post National Weekly Edition,* February 6–12, 2006.

218. Intergovernmental Panel on Climate Change, "Summary for Policymakers," in *Climate Change 2007* <ippc-wg1.ucar.edu>.

219. Greg Easterbrook, "Global Warming: Who Loses—and Who Wins?" *Atlantic Monthly, CCICIX* (April 2007), 56.

220. Mike Moore quoted in Bruce R. Kuniholm, "9/11, the Great Game, and the Vision Thing," *Journal of American History, LXXXIX* (September 2002), 437.

221. Maryann Cusimano Love, "Mind the Gap," in Mary Cusimano Love, ed., *Beyond Sovereignty* (Belmont, Calif: Thomson-Wadsworth, 2003), p. 323.

222. Matthew Fraser, *Weapons of Mass Distraction* (New York: St. Martin's, 2005), pp. 212–213.

223. Quoted *ibid.,* p. 256.

224. Quoted in Elizabeth Hanson, *The Information Revolution and World Politics* (Lanham, Md.: Rowman & Littlefield, 2008), p. 1.

225. Quoted in Joseph S. Nye, Jr., *Soft Power* (New York: PublicAffairs, 2004), p. ix.

226. Cullen Murphy, *Are We Rome?* (Boston: Houghton Mifflin, 2007), p. 87.

227. Quoted in Jeremy Scahill, *Blackwater* (New York: Nation Books, 2007), p. xix.

228. Colin Powell quoted *ibid.,* p. xxii.

229. Quoted in Mertus, *Bait and Switch,* p. 105.

230. Andrew J. Bacevich in *Washington Post National Weekly Edition,* April 28–May 4, 2003.

231. Barry R. Posen, "Command of the Commons," *International Security, XXVIII* (Summer 2003), 7.

232. Sebastian Mallaby quoted in Joseph S. Nye, Jr. *The Paradox of American Power* (New York: Oxford University Press, 2002), p. 40.

233. Remarks Delivered by Secretary of Defense Robert M. Gates, Manhattan, Kansas, November 26, 2007 <www.defenselink.mil>.

234. Michael Novak quoted in *Washington Post National Weekly Edition,* July 9–15, 2007.

235. Jonathan Rauch, "Unwinding Bush," *Atlantic Monthly, CCICVIII* (October 2006), 27.

236. Quoted in *Boston Sunday Globe,* February 8, 2009.

237. Quoted in *Boston Globe,* January 21, 2009.

Makers of American Foreign Relations

Presidents	Secretaries of State	Chairs of the Senate Foreign Relations Committee
George Washington (1789–1797)	Thomas Jefferson (1790–1793) Edmund Randolph (1794–1795) Timothy Pickering (1795–1797)	
John Adams (1797–1801)	Timothy Pickering (1797–1800) John Marshall (1800–1801)	
Thomas Jefferson (1801–1809)	James Madison (1801–1809)	
James Madison (1809–1817)	Robert Smith (1809–1811) James Monroe (1811–1817)	James Barbour (1816–1817)
James Monroe (1817–1825)	John Quincy Adams (1817–1825)	James Barbour (1817–1818) Nathaniel Macon (1818–1819) James Brown (1819–1820) James Barbour (1820–1821) Rufus King (1821–1822) James Barbour (1822–1825)
John Quincy Adams (1825–1829)	Henry Clay (1825–1829)	Nathaniel Macon (1825–1826) Nathan Sanford (1826–1827) Nathaniel Macon (1827–1828) Littleton W. Tazewell (1828–1829)
Andrew Jackson (1829–1837)	Martin Van Buren (1829–1831) Edward Livingston (1831–1833) Louis McLane (1833–1834) John Forsyth (1834–1837)	Littleton W. Tazewell (1829–1832) John Forsyth (1832–1833) William Wilkins (1833–1834) Henry Clay (1834–1836) James Buchanan (1836–1837)
Martin Van Buren (1837–1841)	John Forsyth (1837–1841)	James Buchanan (1837–1841)
William H. Harrison (1841)	Daniel Webster (1841)	William C. Rives (1841)

Makers of American Foreign Relations *(continued)*

Presidents	Secretaries of State	Chairs of the Senate Foreign Relations Committee
John Tyler (1841–1845)	Daniel Webster (1841–1843) Abel P. Upshur (1843–1844) John C. Calhoun (1844–1845)	William C. Rives (1841–1842) William S. Archer (1842–1845)
James K. Polk (1845–1849)	James Buchanan (1845–1849)	William Allen (1845–1846) Ambrose H. Sevier (1846–1848) Edward A. Hannegan (1848–1849) Thomas H. Benton (1849)
Zachary Taylor (1849–1850)	John M. Clayton (1849–1850)	William R. King (1849–1850)
Millard Fillmore (1850–1853)	Daniel Webster (1850–1852) Edward Everett (1852–1853)	Henry S. Foote (1850–1851) James M. Mason (1851–1853)
Franklin Pierce (1853–1857)	William L. Marcy (1853–1857)	James M. Mason (1853–1857)
James Buchanan (1857–1861)	Lewis Cass (1857–1860) Jeremiah S. Black (1860–1861)	James M. Mason (1857–1861)
Abraham Lincoln (1861–1865)	William H. Seward (1861–1865)	Charles Sumner (1861–1865)
Andrew Johnson (1865–1869)	William H. Seward (1865–1869)	Charles Sumner (1865–1869)
Ulysses S. Grant (1869–1877)	Elihu B. Washburne (1869) Hamilton Fish (1869–1877)	Charles Sumner (1869–1871) Simon Cameron (1871–1877)
Rutherford B. Hayes (1877–1881)	William M. Evarts (1877–1881)	Hannibal Hamlin (1877–1879) William W. Eaton (1879–1881)
James A. Garfield (1881)	James G. Blaine (1881)	Ambrose E. Burnside (1881) George F. Edmunds (1881)
Chester A. Arthur (1881–1885)	Frederick T. Frelinghuysen (1881–1885)	William Windon (1881–1883) John F. Miller (1883–1885)
Grover Cleveland (1885–1889)	Thomas F. Bayard (1885–1889)	John F. Miller (1885–1887) John Sherman (1887–1889)
Benjamin Harrison (1889–1893)	James G. Blaine (1889–1892) John W. Foster (1892–1893)	John Sherman (1889–1893)
Grover Cleveland (1893–1897)	Walter Q. Gresham (1893–1895) Richard Olney (1895–1897)	John T. Morgan (1893–1895) John Sherman (1895–1897)
William McKinley (1897–1901)	John Sherman (1897–1898) William R. Day (1898) John Hay (1898–1901)	William P. Frye (1897) Cushman K. Davis (1897–1901)
Theodore Roosevelt (1901–1909)	John Hay (1901–1905) Elihu Root (1905–1909) Robert Bacon (1909)	William P. Frye (1901) Shelby M. Cullom (1901–1909)

Makers of American Foreign Relations *(continued)*

Presidents	Secretaries of State	Chairs of the Senate Foreign Relations Committee
William Howard Taft (1909–1913)	Philander C. Knox (1909–1913)	Shelby M. Cullom (1909–1913)
Woodrow Wilson (1913–1921)	William Jennings Bryan (1913–1915) Robert Lansing (1915–1920) Bainbridge Colby (1920–1921)	Augustus O. Bacon (1913–1915) William J. Stone (1915–1919) Henry Cabot Lodge (1919–1921)
Warren G. Harding (1921–1923)	Charles E. Hughes (1921–1923)	Henry Cabot Lodge (1921–1923)
Calvin Coolidge (1923–1929)	Charles E. Hughes (1923–1925) Frank B. Kellogg (1925–1929)	Henry Cabot Lodge (1923–1924) William E. Borah (1925–1929)
Herbert C. Hoover (1929–1933)	Henry L. Stimson (1929–1933)	William E. Borah (1929–1933)
Franklin D. Roosevelt (1933–1945)	Cordell Hull (1933–1944) Edward R. Stettinius, Jr. (1944–1945)	Key Pittman (1933–1940) Walter F. George (1940–1941) Tom Connally (1941–1945)

Presidents	Secretaries of State	Chairs of the Senate Foreign Relations Committee	Secretaries of Defense	Assistants to the President for National Security Affairs
Harry S. Truman (1945–1953)	Edward R. Stettinius, Jr. (1945) James F. Byrnes (1945–1947) George C. Marshall (1947–1949) Dean G. Acheson (1949–1953)	Tom Connally (1945–1947) Arthur H. Vandenberg (1947–1949) Tom Connally (1949–1953)	James V. Forrestal (1947–1949) Louis A. Johnson (1949–1950) George C. Marshall (1950–1951) Robert A. Lovett (1951–1953)	
Dwight D. Eisenhower (1953–1961)	John F. Dulles (1953–1959) Christian A. Herter (1959–1961)	Alexander Wiley (1953–1955) Walter F. George (1955–1957) Theodore F. Green (1957–1959) J. William Fulbright (1959–1961)	Charles E. Wilson (1953–1957) Neil H. McElroy (1957–1959) Thomas S. Gates, Jr. (1959–1961)	Robert Cutler (1953–1955 & 1957–1958) Dillon Anderson (1955–1956) William H. Jackson (1956) Gordon Gray (1958–1961)
John F. Kennedy (1961–1963)	Dean Rusk (1961–1963)	J. William Fulbright (1961–1963)	Robert S. McNamara (1961–1963)	McGeorge Bundy (1961–1963)
Lyndon B. Johnson (1963–1969)	Dean Rusk (1963–1969)	J. William Fulbright (1963–1969)	Robert S. McNamara (1963–1968) Clark M. Clifford (1968–1969)	McGeorge Bundy (1963–1966) Walt W. Rostow (1966–1969)

Makers of American Foreign Relations *(continued)*

Presidents	Secretaries of State	Chairs of the Senate Foreign Relations Committee	Secretaries of Defense	Assistants to the President for National Security Affairs
Richard M. Nixon (1969–1974)	William P. Rogers (1969–1973) Henry A. Kissinger (1973–1974)	J. William Fulbright (1969–1974)	Melvin R. Laird (1969–1973) Elliot L. Richardson (1973) James R. Schlesinger (1973–1974)	Henry A. Kissinger (1969–1974)
Gerald R. Ford (1974–1977)	Henry A. Kissinger (1974–1977)	J. William Fulbright (1974–1975) John Sparkman (1975–1977)	James R. Schlesinger (1974–1976) Donald Rumsfeld (1976–1977)	Henry A. Kissinger (1974–1975) Brent Scowcroft (1975–1977)
James E. Carter (1977–1981)	Cyrus R. Vance (1977–1980) Edmund Muskie (1980–1981)	John Sparkman (1977–1979) Frank Church (1979–1981)	Harold Brown (1977–1981)	Zbigniew Brzezinski (1977–1981)
Ronald W. Reagan (1981–1989)	Alexander M. Haig, Jr. (1981–1982) George P. Shultz (1982–1989)	Charles Percy (1981–1985) Richard G. Lugar (1985–1987) Claiborne Pell (1987–1989)	Caspar Weinberger (1981–1987) Frank C. Carlucci (1987–1989)	Richard Alien (1981) William P. Clark, Jr. (1981–1983) Robert C. McFarlane (1983–1985) John M. Poindexter (1985–1986) Frank C. Carlucci (1986–1987) Colin L. Powell (1987–1989)
George H. W. Bush (1989–1993)	James A. Baker III (1989–1992) Lawrence Eagleburger (1992–1993)	Claiborne Pell (1989–1993)	Richard B. Cheney (1989–1993)	Brent Scowcroft (1989–1993)
William J. Clinton (1993–2001)	Warren M. Christopher (1993–1997) Madeleine K. Albright (1997–2001)	Claiborne Pell (1993–1995) Jesse Helms (1995–2001)	Les Aspin (1993–1994) William J. Perry (1994–1997) William S. Cohen (1997–2001)	Anthony Lake (1993–1996) Samuel R. Berger (1996–2001)
George W. Bush (2001–2009)	Colin L. Powell (2001–2005) Condoleezza Rice (2005–2009)	Joseph R. Biden, Jr. (2001–2003) Richard G. Lugar (2003–2007) Joseph R. Biden, Jr. (2007–2009)	Donald Rumsfeld (2001–2006) Robert Gates (2006–2009)	Condoleezza Rice (2001–2005) Stephen Hadley (2005–2009)
Barack H. Obama (2009–)	Hillary R. Clinton (2009–)	John F. Kerry (2009–)	Robert Gates (2009–)	James L. Jones, Jr. (2009–)

General Bibliography

General Reference Works

See also "Overviews of Relations with Countries, Regions, and Other Places of the World" and "Overviews of Subjects," both below, and your library's computer-based sources. Comprehensive bibliographies also appear in Robert L. Beisner, ed., *Guide to American Foreign Relations Since 1600* (2003) and Bruce W. Jentleson and Thomas G. Paterson, eds., *Encyclopedia of U.S. Foreign Relations* (1997).

Annual Surveys: *Environmental Resource Handbook* (2001–); *Facts on File* (1941–); *Human Development Report* (1990–); *Keesing's Record of World Events* (also titled *Keesing's Contemporary Archives*) (1931–); London Institute of World Affairs, *The Yearbook of World Affairs* (1947–); Alan F. Pater and Jason R. Pater, eds., *What They Said In ...: The Yearbook of World Opinion* (1971–); *Political Handbook of the World* (1928–); *The Statesmen's Year-Book World Gazetteer* (1864–); United Nations, *Demographic Yearbook* (1948–); *The World Bank Atlas* (1967–); *World Development Report* (1978–). See also "Statistics."

Atlases and Gazetteers: Ewan W. Anderson and Don Shewan, *An Atlas of World Political Flashpoints* (1993); Andrew Boyd, *An Atlas of World Affairs* (1998); Saul B. Cohen, *Columbia Gazetteer of the World* (1998); Rodger Doyle, *Atlas of Contemporary America* (1994); Robert Ferrell and Richard Natkiel, *Atlas of American History* (1987); *Hammond Atlas of the World* (1992); Derek Hayes, *The Historical Atlas of the United States* (2007); Eric Homberger, *The Penguin Historical Atlas of North America* (1995); Michael Kidron and Ronald Segal, *The State of the World Atlas* (1995); Catherine Mattson and Mark T. Mattson, *Contemporary Atlas of the United States* (1998); David Munro, ed., *Chambers World Gazetteer* (1988); *National Geographic Atlas of the World* (1992); Stuart Murray, *Atlas of American Military History* (2005); Richard Natkiel et al., eds., *Atlas of the Twentieth Century* (1982); *The New York Times Atlas of the World* (1992); *Oxford Atlas of the World* (2000); Rand McNally, *Today's World* (1996); Dan Smith, *The State of War and Peace Atlas* (1997); Dean Smith and Michael Kidron, *The State of the World Atlas* (1999); U.S. Military Academy, *West Point Atlas of American Wars* (1997).

Bibliographies: Samuel Flagg Bemis and Grace Gardner Griffin, *Guide to the Diplomatic History of the United States, 1775–1921* (1935); Richard Dean Burns, ed., *A Guide to American Foreign Relations Since 1700* (1982); Congressional Information Service, *American Foreign Policy Index* (1994–); Council on Foreign Relations, *Foreign Affairs Bibliography* (1933–1972); Byron Dexter, ed., *The Foreign Affairs 50-Year Bibliography* (1972); Frank Freidel, ed., *Harvard Guide to American History* (1974); Mary Beth Norton, ed., *Guide to Historical Literature* (1995); Francis P. Prucha, *Handbook for Research in American History* (1987). The journal *Diplomatic History* regularly publishes articles that review the historiography of major topics and periods and provide extensive bibliographical guidance. The *Journal of American History* regularly lists recent publications. Journals such as *Foreign Affairs* and *Political Science Quarterly* regularly publish reviews of recent books.

Biographical Aids: John S. Bowman, *The Cambridge Dictionary of American Biography* (1995); Asa Briggs, *A Dictionary of Twentieth Century World Biography* (1990); Mari Jo Buhle et al., eds., *The American Radical* (1994); David Crystal, ed., *The Cambridge Biographical Encyclopedia* (1994); *Current Biography* (1940–); *Dictionary of American Biography* (1928–); *Encyclopedia of World Biography* (1998); John A. Garraty and Mark C. Carnes, eds., *American National Biography* (1999); John Garraty and Jerome L. Sternstein, eds., *The Encyclopedia of American Biography* (1996); *International Who's Who* (1935–); Bernard K. Johnpoll and Harvey Klehr, eds., *Biographical Dictionary of the American Left* (1986); Warren F. Kuehl, ed., *Biographical Dictionary of Internationalists* (1983); *National Cyclopedia of American Biography* (1898–); Alan Palmer, *Who's Who in Modern History* (1980); Philip Rees, *Biographical Dictionary of the Extreme Right Since 1890* (1991); Frank W. Thackery and John E. Findling, eds., *Statesmen Who Changed the World* (1993); U.S. Department of State, *Biographic Register* (1860–1974) and *Foreign Service List* (1929–); *Who Was Who in America* (1963–); *Who's Who in America* (1899–); *Who's Who in the World* (1971–).

Chronologies: Lester H. Brune, *Chronological History of U.S. Foreign Relations* (2002); Gorton Carruth, *The Encyclopedia of American Facts and Dates* (1993) and *The Encyclopedia of World Facts and Dates* (1993); Council on Foreign Relations, *Foreign Affairs Chronology, 1978–1989* (1990) and *The United States in World Affairs* (1932–1972);

Robert H. Ferrell and John S. Bowman, eds., *The Twentieth Century* (1984); Bernard Grun, *The Timetables of History* (1991); John E. Jessup, *A Chronology of Conflict and Resolution, 1945–1985* (1989); Royal Institute of International Affairs, *Survey of International Affairs, 1920–1963* (1972–1977); Laurence Urdang, ed., *The Timetables of American History* (1996). See also "Annual Surveys."

Documentary Collections and Series: Martin P. Claussen, ed., *The National State Papers of the United States: Texts of Documents (1789–1817)* (1980–); Council on Foreign Relations, *Documents on American Foreign Relations, 1938/1939–1970* (1939–1973); Jussi M. Hanhimäki and Odd Arne Westad, eds., *The Cold War* (2004); Royal Institute of International Affairs, *Documents on International Affairs, 1928–1963* (1929–1973); Arthur M. Schlesinger, Jr., ed., *The Dynamics of World Power: A Documentary History of U.S. Foreign Policy, 1945–1973* (1973); U.S. Congress, *American State Papers* (1852–1859); U.S. Department of State, *A Decade of American Foreign Policy: Basic Documents, 1941–1949* (1985), *American Foreign Policy: Basic Documents, 1950–1955* (1957), *American Foreign Policy: Basic Documents, 1977–1980* (1983–1986), *American Foreign Policy: Current Documents, 1956–1967* (1956–1967), *American Foreign Policy: Current Documents, 1981–* (1984–), *Bulletin* (1938–), *Dispatch* (1990–), *Foreign Relations of United States 1861–* (1862–), and *Press Conferences of the Secretaries of State, 1922–1974* (n.d.); *Vital Speeches of the Day* (1934–).

Encyclopedias and Dictionaries: John Whiteclay Chambers, ed., *Oxford Companion to American Military History* (1999); Alexander DeConde et al., eds., *Encyclopedia of American Foreign Policy* (2002); *Encyclopedia of the World's Nations* (2002); John Drexel, ed., *The Facts on File Encyclopedia of the 20th Century* (1991); Graham Evans and Jeffrey Newnham, *The Penguin Dictionary of International Relations* (1999); John M. Farragher, ed., *The American Heritage Encyclopedia of American History* (1998); John E. Findling, *Dictionary of American Diplomatic History* (1989); Paul Finkelman and Joseph C. Miller, eds., *MacMillan Encyclopedia of World Slavery* (1998); Charles W. Freeman, Jr., *The Diplomat's Dictionary* (1997); Kenneth L. Hill, *Encyclopedia of Conflicts Since World War II* (1998); Bruce W. Jentleson and Thomas G. Paterson, eds., *Encyclopedia of U.S. Foreign Relations* (1997); Stanley I. Kutler, ed., *Encyclopedia of the United States in the Twentieth Century* (1995); Jeffrey A. Larson and James M. Smith, eds., *Historical Dictionary of Arms Control and Disarmament* (2005); Leonard Levy and Louis Fisher, eds., *Encyclopedia of American Presidents* (1994); Robert A. Meyers, ed., *The Encyclopedia of Environmental Analysis and Remediation* (1998); Richard B. Morris et al., *Encyclopedia of American History* (1996); Immanuel Ness, *The Encyclopedia of Global Population and Demographics* (1999); Cathal J. Nolan, *The Greenwood Encyclopedia of International Relations* (2002); Bruce Norton, *Encyclopedia of American War Heroes* (2002); James H. Olson, *Historical Dictionary of the Great Depression* (2001); Norman Polmar and

Thomas B. Allen, *Spybook: The Encyclopedia of Espionage* (2004); David Robertson, *A Dictionary on Human Rights* (2004); Jerry K. Sweeney et al., *America and the World, 1776–1998* (2000); Ruud van Dijk et al, eds., *Encyclopedia of the Cold War* (2008); Thomas G. Weiss and Sam Davis, eds., *The Oxford Handbook on the United Nations* (2007).

Statistics: Erik W. Austin and Jerome C. Clubb, *Political Facts of the United States Since 1789* (1986); International Monetary Fund, *International Financial Statistics* (1948–); George T. Kurian, ed., *The Illustrated Book of World Rankings* (1996); Robert D. Schulzinger, ed., *A Companion to American Foreign Relations* (2003); Victor Showers, *World Facts and Figures* (1989); Ruth L. Sivard, *World Military and Social Expenditures* (1974–); Charles L. Taylor and David A. Jodice, *World Handbook of Political and Social Indicators* (1983); United Nations, *Demographic Yearbook* (1948–), *Report on the World Social Situation* (1952–), and *Statistical Yearbook* (1948–); U.S. Agency for International Development, *United States Overseas Loans and Grants and Assistance from International Organizations, July 1, 1945–Sept. 30, 1980* (1981); U.S. Bureau of the Census, *Historical Statistics of the United States* (1975) and *Statistical Abstract of the United States* (1878–); U.S. Central Intelligence Agency, *Handbook of International Economic Statistics* (1971–) and *The World Factbook* (1981–); World Bank, *World Tables* (1974–); World Resources Institute, *World Resources* (1990–). See also "Annual Surveys."

Overviews of Relations with Countries, Regions, and Other Places of the World, Including Atlases and Gazetteers (A), Annual Surveys and Chronologies (AS), Bibliographies (B), Biographical Aids (BA), Chronologies (C), Encyclopedias and Dictionaries (E), and Statistics (S)

Afghanistan: Larry Goodson, *Afghanistan's Endless War* (2001); M. Hassar Kakar, *Afghanistan: The Soviet Invasion and the Afghan Response* (1995); William Maley, ed., *Fundamentalism Reborn* (2002); Nancy P. Newell and Richard S. Newell, *The Struggle for Afghanistan* (1981); Leon B. Poullada, *The Kingdom of Afghanistan and the United States, 1828–1973* (1995); Ahmed Rashid, *Taliban* (2001) and *Descent into Chaos* (2008); Jeffrey J. Roberts, *The Origins of the Conflict in Afghanistan* (2002); Barnet Rubin, *The Fragmentation of Afghanistan* (2002).

Africa: Thomas Borstelmann, *Cold War and the Color Line* (2001); Chris Cook and David Killinway, *African Political Facts Since 1945* (1991) (E); Howard F. French, *Continent for the Taking* (2004); Peter Duignan and Lewis H. Gann, *The United States and Africa* (1987); David F. Gordon et al., *The United States and Africa* (1998); Piero Gleijeses, *Conflicting Missions* (2001); Dennis Hickey and Kenneth White, *An*

Enchanting Darkness (1993); Lawrence C. Howard, *American Involvement in Africa South of the Sahara, 1800–1860* (1988); Henry F. Jackson, *From the Congo to Soweto* (1982); Zaki Laidi, *The Superpowers and Africa* (1990); Colin Legum, ed., *Africa Contemporary Record* (1968–) (AS); Michael McCarthy, *Dark Continent* (1983); Lysle E. Meyer, *The Farther Frontier* (1992); Thomas Noer, *Cold War and Black Liberation* (1985); Anthony G. Pazzanita and Tony Hodges, *Historical Dictionary of Western Sahara* (1994) (E); Peter J. Schraeder, *United States Foreign Policy Toward Africa* (1994); Elliot P. Skinner, *African-Americans and U.S. Policy Toward Africa, 1850–1924* (1992); George White, *Holding the Line* (2005); U.S. Library of Congress, *The United States and Sub-Saharan Africa* (1984) (B); Robert Anthony Waters, Jr., *Historical Dictionary of United State-Africa Relations* (2009) (E). See also countries.

Alaska: Paul S. Holbo, *Tarnished Expansion* (1983); Ronald J. Jensen, *The Alaska Purchase* (1975); Walter A. McDougall, *Let the Sea Make a Noise* (1993). See also Kushner and Saul in "Russia and the Soviet Union."

Albania: William B. Bland, *Albania* (1988) (B); Nicholas J. Costa, *Shattered Illusions* (1998).

Algeria: Charles-Robert Ageron, *Modern Algeria* (1992); Matthew Connelly, *A Diplomatic Revolution* (2002); R. Cameron Hume, *Mission to Algiers* (2007); Martin Stone, *The Agony of Algeria* (1997); Irwin W. Wall, *France, the United States, and the Algerian War* (2001). See also "North Africa."

Angola: Richard Black, *Angola* (1992) (B); Susan H. Broadhead, *Historical Dictionary of Angola* (1992) (E); Chester A. Crocker, *U.S. and Angola* (1986); Thomas Collelo, ed., *Angola* (1990); Fernando A. Guimãres, *The Origins of the Angolan Civil War* (1998); Lawrence W. Henderson, *Angola* (1979); John A. Marcum, *The Angolan Revolution* (1969, 1978); Kenneth Mokoena and Nicole Gaymon, eds., *The Angola Crises* (1991); Inge Tvedten, *Angola* (1997); George Wright, *Destruction of a Nation* (1997). See also "Africa."

Antarctica: Peter J. Beck, *The International Politics of Antarctica* (1986); Robert Headland, *Chronological List of Antarctic Expeditions* (1989) (E and C); Christopher C. Joyner and Ethel R. Theis, *Eagle over the Ice* (1997); Frank G. Klotz, *America on the Ice* (1990); Jeffrey D. Myhre, *The Antarctic Treaty System* (1986); John Stewart, *Antarctica* (1990) (E); Gilligan D. Triggs, ed., *The Antarctic Treaty Regime* (1987).

Arab World: See "Israel, Palestine, and Arab-Israeli Conflict" and "Middle East."

Arctic: Elizabeth B. Elliot-Meisel, *Arctic Diplomacy: Canada and the United States in the Northwest Passage* (1998); Clive Holland, *Arctic Exploration and Development* (1993) (E). See also "Canada."

Argentina: Alan Biggs, *Argentina* (1991) (B); Glen Dorn, *Peronistas and New Dealers* (2005); Deborah Norden and Robert Guillermo Russell, *Argentina and the United States* (2002); Harold F. Peterson, *Argentina and the United States* (1964); David Rock, *Argentina* (1985); David Sheinin, *Searching for Authority* (1998) and *United States and Argentina* (2006); Joseph Tulchin, *Argentina and the United States* (1990); Arthur P. Whitaker, *The United States and the Southern Cone* (1976). See also "Latin America."

Armenia: James B. Gidney, *A Mandate for Armenia* (1967); Vrej Nerses Neressian, *Armenia* (1993) (B).

Asia and Pacific Islands: Alexander Besher, *The Pacific Rim Almanac* (1991) (E); Jessica S. Brown et al., eds., *The United States in East Asia* (1985) (B); Frederica M. Bunge and Melinda W. Cooke, eds., *Oceania* (1985); I. C. Campbell, *A History of the Pacific Islands* (1989); Warren I. Cohen, *The Asian American Century* (2002); Donald Denoon and Stewart Firth, eds., *The Cambridge History of the Pacific Islanders* (1997); John C. Dorance, *The United States and the Pacific Islands* (1992); Norman Douglas and Ngaire Douglas, eds., *Pacific Islands Yearbook* (1932–) (AS); Arthur P. Dudden, *The American Pacific* (1992); Ainslie T. Embree, *Encyclopedia of Asian History* (1988) (E); John R. Eperjesi, *Imperialist Imaginary* (2005); Gerald Fry, *Pacific Basin and Oceania* (1987) (B); Roger W. Gale, *The Americanization of Micronesia* (1979); Marc Gallichio, *The Scramble for Asia* (2008); Arrell M. Gibson, *Yankees in Paradise* (1993); David Hanlon, *Remaking Micronesia* (1998); Donald D. Johnson, *The United States in the Pacific* (1995); Christina Klein, *Cold War Orientalism* (2003); James I. Matray, *Encyclopedia of U.S.–East Asian Relations* (2002) (E); John C. Perry, *Facing West* (1994); Priscilla Roberts, *Behind the Bamboo Curtain* (2006); Deryck Scarr, *The History of the Pacific Islands* (1990); Gerald Segal, *Rethinking the Pacific* (1990); David Shavit, *The United States in Asia* (1990) (E); Roger C. Thompson, *The Pacific Rim Since 1945* (1994); Howard Willens and Deanne C. Seimar, *National Security and Self-determination* (2000) (Micronesia). See also countries and "Vietnam and Southeast Asia."

Australia: Glen St. John Barclay, *Friends in High Places* (1985); Philip Bell, *Implicated* (1993); Norman Harper, *A Great and Powerful Friend* (1987); E. C. Paul, *Little America* (2006); Joseph Siracusa and Yeong-Han Cheong, *America's Australia, Australia's America* (1997).

Austria: Günter Bischof and Anton Pelinka, *The Americanization/Westernization of Austria* (2003); James Jay Carafano, *Waltzing into the Cold War* (2002); Audrey K. Cronin, *Great Power Politics and the Struggle over Austria, 1945–1955* (1986); Barbara Jelavich, *Modern Austria* (1988); Mellany A. Sully, *A Contemporary History of Austria* (1990); Reinhold Wagnleitner, *Coca-Colonization and the Cold War* (1994). See also "Europe."

Azerbaijan: Ian Bremmer and Ray Taras, eds., *Nations and Politics in the Soviet Successor States* (1993) Edmund Herzog, *The New Caucasus* (1999). See also "Russia and the Soviet Union."

Baltic States: Walter C. Clemens, Jr., *Baltic Independence and Russian Empire* (1991); David Flint, *The Baltic States* (1992); Kristian Gerner, *The Baltic States and the End of the Soviet Empire* (1993); Walter R. Iwaskiw, ed., *Estonia, Latvia, and Lithuania* (1996); Anatol Lieven, *The Baltic Revolution* (1993); Inese A. Smith and Marita V. Grunts, *The Baltic States* (1993).

Belarus: Helen Fedor, *Belarus and Moldova* (1995).

Belgium: Jonathan E. Helmreich, *United States Relations with Belgium and the Congo* (1998); Frank E. Hugget, *Modern Belgium* (1969). See also "Europe."

Bolivia: Rex A. Hudson and Dennis M. Haggerty, eds., *Bolivia* (1991); Kenneth D. Lehman, *Bolivia and the United States* (1999); Waltraud Q. Morales, *Bolivia* (1992).

Bosnia–Herzegovina: Ivo Daalder, *Getting to Dayton* (2000); Noel Malcolm, *Bosnia* (1994).

Brazil: Jan Black, *United States Penetration of Brazil* (1977); Elizabeth A. Cobbs, *The Rich Neighbor Policy* (1992); John Dickenson, ed., *Brazil* (1997) (B); Gerald K. Haines, *The Americanization of Brazil* (1989); Stanley Hilton, *Brazil and the Great Powers* (1975); Rex A. Hudson, ed., *Brazil* (1998); Frank McCann, *The Brazilian-American Alliance, 1937–1945* (1973); Micol Siegel, *Uneven Encounters* (2009); Joseph Smith, *Unequal Giants* (1991); Steven C. Topik, *Trade and Gunboats* (1996); W. Michael Weis, *Cold Warriors and Coups d'État* (1993).

Bulgaria: Glenn A. Curtis, ed., *Bulgaria* (1993).

Cambodia: MacAlister Brown and Joseph J. Zasloff, *Cambodia Confronts the Peacemakers, 1979–1998* (1998); David P. Chandler, *The Tragedy of Cambodian History* (1991); Kenton J. Clymer, *Troubled Relations* (2007); Michael Haas, *Cambodia, Pol Pot, and the United States* (1991); Henry Kamm, *Cambodia* (1998); Ben Kiernan, *How Pol Pot Came to Power* (1985) and *The Pol Pot Regime* (1996); Russell R. Ross, ed., *Cambodia* (1990); William Shawcross, *The Quality of Mercy* (1984) and *Sideshow* (1979).

Cameroon: Julius A. Amin, *The Peace Corps in Cameroon* (1992); Mark DeLancey, *Cameroon* (1986) (B); Mark DeLancey and H. Mbella Mokeba, *Historical Dictionary of Cameroon* (1990) (E). See also "Africa."

Canada: David J. Bercuson and J. L. Granatstein, *The Collins Dictionary of Canadian History* (1988) (E); Robert Bothwell, *Canada and the United States* (1992); Stephen Clarkson, *Uncle Sam and Us* (2003); Charles Doran, *Forgotten Partnership* (1984); John Findlay and Ken S. Coates, eds., *Parallel Destinies* (2002); J. L. Granatstein and Robert Bothwell, *Pirouette* (1990); J. L. Granatstein and Norman Hillmer, *For Better or For Worse* (1992); Lansing Lamont and Duncan Edmonds, eds., *Friends So Different* (1989); Seymour Martin Lipset, *Continental Divide* (1990); Lawrence Martin, *The Presidents and the Prime Ministers* (1982); Graeme S. Mount, *Invisible and Inaudible in Washington* (1999); Denis Smith, *Diplomacy of Fear* (1988); Reginald C. Stuart, *United States Expansionism and British North America 1775–1871* (1988); John H. Thompson and Stephen J. Randall, *Canada and the United States* (1998). See also "Great Britain."

Caribbean: Charles D. Ameringer, *The Caribbean Legion* (1974); David Healy, *Drive to Hegemony* (1988); Roger Hughes, *The Caribbean* (1987) (B); Lester D. Langley, *The United States and the Caribbean, 1900–1970* (1980) and *The United States and the Caribbean in the Twentieth Century* (1989); Sandra W. Meditz and Dennis M. Hanratty, eds., *Islands of the Commonwealth Caribbean* (1989); Harvey Neptune, *Caliban and the Yankees* (2008) (Trinidad); Robert F. Smith, *The Caribbean World and the United States* (1994).

Central African Republic: Pierre Kalck, *Historical Dictionary of the Central African Republic* (1992) (E).

Central America: Tom Barry, *Central America Inside Out* (1991) (C and E); Leslie Bethel, ed., *Central America Since Independence* (1991); Morris J. Blachman et al., eds., *Confronting Revolution* (1986); John Booth and Thomas Walker, *Understanding Central America* (1993); John Coatsworth, *Central America and the United States* (1994); Kenneth M. Coleman and George C. Herring, eds., *Understanding the Central American Crisis* (1991); John E. Findling, *Close Neighbors, Distant Friends* (1987); Kenneth J. Grieb, *Central America in the Nineteenth and Twentieth Centuries* (1988) (B); Walter LaFeber, *Inevitable Revolutions* (1993); Thomas M. Leonard, *Central America and the United States* (1991) and *Central America and U.S. Policies, 1820s–1980s* (1985) (B); Mark B. Rosenberg and Luis G. Solis, *United States and Central America* (2007); Thomas D. Schoonover, *The United States in Central America, 1860–1911* (1991); Ralph L. Woodward, *Central America* (1985).

Chad: Mario J. Azevedo, *Roots of Violence* (1998); Thomas Collelo, ed., *Chad* (1990); Samuel Decalo, *Historical Dictionary of Chad* (1987) (E).

Chile: Lubna Z. Qureshi, *Nixon, Kissinger, and Allende* (2009); Michael Francis, *The Limits of Hegemony* (1977); David Mares and

Francisco Rosas Arevena, *United States and Chile* (2001); Michael Monteon, *Chile in the Nitrate Era* (1982); Heraldo Munoz and Carlos Portales, *Elusive Friendship* (1991); William F. Sater, *Chile and the United States* (1990); Paul E. Sigmund, *The United States and Democracy in Chile* (1993).

China (and Taiwan): Gordon Chang, *Friends and Enemies* (1990); Warren I. Cohen, *America's Response to China* (2000); Jacques Downs, *The Golden Ghetto* (1997); Jonathan Fenby, *Modern China* (2008); Rosemary Foot, *The Practice of Power* (1995); Jonathan Goldstein et al., eds., *America Views China* (1991); Harry Harding, *A Fragile Relationship* (1992); Michael H. Hunt, *The Making of a Special Relationship* (1983); Chen Jian, *Mao's China and the Cold War* (2001); Arnold Xiangze Jiang, *The United States and China* (1988); Noam Kochavi, *A Conflict Perpetuated* (2002); David M. Lampton, *Same Bed Different Dreams* (2000); Wei-chin Lee, *Taiwan* (1990) (B); Ernest R. May and John K. Fairbank, eds., *America's China Trade in Historical Perspective* (1986); Thomas D. Lutze, *China's Inevitable Revolution* (2007); James Peck, *Washington's China* (2006); Simei Qing, *From Allies to Enemies* (2007); Robert S. Ross, *Negotiating Cooperation* (1995); Michael Schaller, *The United States and China* (2002); Robert Suettinger, *Beyond Tiananmen* (2003); David Shambaugh, *Beautiful Imperialist* (1991); Nancy B. Tucker, *Taiwan, Hong Kong, and the United States* (1994) and *Dangerous Strait* (2005); Qiang Zhai, *China and the Vietnam Wars* (2000); Shu Guang Zhang, *Deterrence and Strategic Culture* (1992).

Colombia: Marcelo Bucheli, *Bananas and Business* (2005); David Bushnell, *The Making of Modern Colombia* (1993); Bradley Lynn Coleman, *Colombia and the United States* (2008); Robert H. Davis, *Colombia* (1990) (B); Dennis M. Hanratty and Sandra W. Meditz, eds., *Colombia* (1990); Richard L. Lael, *Arrogant Diplomacy* (1987); Stephen J. Randall, *Colombia and the United States* (1992) and *The Diplomacy of Modernization* (1977); Bert Ruiz, *Colombia's Civil War* (2002).

Congo (Kinshasa): David N. Gibbs, *The Political Economy of Third World Intervention* (1991); Madeline G. Kalb, *The Congo Cables* (1982); Sean Kelly, *America's Tyrant: The CIA and Mobutu of Zaire* (1993); Sandra W. Meditz and Tim Merrill, eds., *Zaire* (1994); Michael G. Schatzberg, *Mobutu or Chaos* (1991); Crawford Young and Thomas Turner, *The Rise and Decline of the Zairian State* (1985).

Costa Rica: Theodore S. Creedman, *Historical Dictionary of Costa Rica* (1991) (E); Martha Honey, *Hostile Acts* (1994); Kyle Longley, *The Sparrow and Hawk* (1997); Charles L. Stansifer, *Costa Rica* (1991) (B).

Cuba: James G. Blight and Philip Brenner, *Sad and Luminous Days* (2002); James G. Blight et al., *Cuba on the Brink* (2002); Ronald H. Chilcote and Sheryl Lutjens, eds., *Cuba, 1953–1978* (1986) (B); Juan del Aguilar, *Cuba* (1988); Esteban Morales Dominguez and Gary Prevost, *United States-Cuban Relations* (2008); Jorge Domínguez, *To Make the World Safe for Revolution* (1989); Jesse J. Dossick, ed., *Cuba, Cubans, and Cuban-Americans, 1902–1991* (1992) (B); José M. Hernández, *Cuba and the United States* (1993); Howard Jones, *Bay of Pigs* (2008); Morris H. Morley, *Imperial State and Revolution* (1987); Morris Morley and Christopher McGillon, *Unfinished Business* (2002) and *Cuba, the United States, and the Post-Cold War World* (2005); Thomas G. Paterson, *Contesting Castro* (1994); Louis A. Pérez, Jr., *Cuba* (1995), *Cuba* (1988) (B), *Cuba and the United States* (2003), and *Cuba in the American Imagination* (2008); Lars Schoultz, *That Infernal Little Cuban Republic* (2008); Sheldon M. Stern, *Averting the "Final Failure"* (2003); Jaime Suchlicki, *Historical Dictionary of Cuba* (1988) (E); Victor Anders Triay, *Fleeing Castro* (1998).

Cyprus: Tozun Bahcheli, *Greek-Turkish Relations Since 1955* (1990); Henry A. Richter, *Greece and Cyprus Since 1920* (1991) (B); Eric Solsten, ed., *Cyprus* (1991).

Czech Republic (and Czechoslovakia): David Short, *Czechoslovakia* (1986) (B); Gordon Skilling, *Czechoslovakia* (1991); Walter Ullmann, *The United States in Prague, 1945–1948* (1978); Betty Miller Unterberger, *The United States, Revolutionary Russia, and the Rise of Czechoslovakia* (1989).

Dominican Republic: G. Pope Atkins and Larman C. Wilson, *The Dominican Republic and the United States* (1998) and *The United States and the Trujillo Regime* (1972); Ian Bell, *The Dominican Republic* (1981); Bruce J. Calder, *The Impact of Intervention* (1984); Lauren Derby, *The Dictator's Seduction* (2009); Eric Thomas Chester, *Rag-Tags, Scum, Riff-Raff, and Commies* (2001); Piero Gleijeses, *The Dominican Crisis* (1978); Richard A. Haggerty, ed., *Dominican Republic and Haiti* (1991); Eric P. Roorda, *The Dictator Next Door* (1998); Kai Schoenhals, *Dominican Republic* (1990) (B); Howard J. Wiarda, *The Dominican Republic* (1992).

Eastern Europe: Robert F. Byrnes, *U.S. Policy Toward Eastern Europe and the Soviet Union* (1989); Stephen A. Garrett, *From Potsdam to Poland* (1986); Bennett Kovrig, *Of Walls and Bridges* (1991); Geoffrey Swain and Nigel Swain, *Eastern Europe Since 1945* (1993).

Ecuador: David Corkill, *Ecuador* (1989) (B); Dennis M. Hanratty, ed., *Ecuador* (1991); Ronn Pineo, *Ecuador and the United States* (2007); David W. Schodt, *Ecuador* (1987).

Egypt: Gregory L. Aftandilian, *Egypt's Bid for Arab Leadership* (1993); Geoffrey Aronson, *From Sideshow to Center Stage* (1986); William J. Burns, *Economic Aid and American Policy Toward Egypt, 1955–1981*

(1985); Peter L. Hahn, *The United States, Great Britain, and Egypt, 1945–1956* (1991); Matthew F. Holland, *America and Egypt* (1996); Ragai N. Makar, *Egypt* (1988) (B); Helen C. Metz, ed., *Egypt* (1991); Gail E. Meyer, *Egypt and the United States* (1980); William B. Quandt, *The United States and Egypt* (1990).

El Salvador: America's Watch, *El Salvador's Decade of Terror* (1991); Cynthia Arnson, *El Salvador* (1982); Enrique A. Baloyra, *El Salvador in Transition* (1982); Martin Diskin and Kenneth Sharpe, *The Impact of U.S. Policy in El Salvador, 1979–1986* (1986); Richard A. Haggerty, ed., *El Salvador* (1990); T. S. Montgomery, *Revolution in El Salvador* (1982); Ralph Lee Woodward, *El Salvador* (1988) (B).

Estonia: Toivo U. Raun, *Estonia and the Estonians* (1991).

Ethiopia: David A. Korn, *Ethiopia, the United States, and the Soviet Union* (1986); Jeffrey S. Lefebvre, *Arms for the Horn* (1991); Harold G. Marcus, *Ethiopia, Great Britain, and the United States, 1941–1974* (1983); Thomas P. Ofcansky, ed., *Ethiopia* (1993); Chris Prouty and Eugene Rosenfeld, *Historical Dictionary of Ethiopia* (1994) (E).

Europe: Peter Coffey, *The EC and the United States* (1993); Carol Fink and Frank Hadler, *1956* (2006); Victoria de Grazia, *Irresistible Empire* (2005); Jeffrey Glen Giauque, *Grand Designs and Visions of Unity* (2002); John L. Harper, *American Visions of Europe* (1994); William I. Hitchcock, *The Struggle for Europe* (2003); Robert Kagan, *Of Paradise and Power* (2003); Ethan B. Kapstein, *The Insecure Alliance* (1990); John Killick, *The United States and European Integration, 1945–1960* (1998); Deborah Kisatsky, *The United States and the European Right, 1945–1955* (2005); Geir Lundestad, *"Empire" by Integration* (1998) and *United States and Western Europe Since 1945* (2003); Elizabeth Pond, *Friendly Fire* (2004); Kevin Ruane, *The Rise and Fall of the European Defense Community* (2000); Thomas A. Schwartz, *Lyndon Johnson and Europe* (2003); William Shawcross, *Allies* (2004); Marc Trachtenberg, ed., *Between Empire and Alliance* (2003) and *A Constructed Peace* (1999); Pascaline Winand, *Eisenhower, Kennedy, and the United States of Europe* (1993).

Finland: Jussi M. Hanhimäki, *Containing Coexistence* (1997); Robert Rinehart, ed., *Finland and the United States* (1993); Eric Solsten and Sandra W. Meditz, *Finland* (1990).

France: Henry Blumenthal, *A Reappraisal of Franco-American Relations, 1830–1871* (1959), *France and the United States* (1970), and *Illusion and Reality in Franco-American Diplomacy, 1914–1945* (1986); Charles Cogan, *Oldest Allies, Guarded Friends* (1994); Frank Costigliola, *The Cold Alliance* (1992); Michael Creswell, *Question of Balance* (2006); William Hitchcock, *France Restored* (2001); Brian McKenzie,

Remaking France (2005); Robert O. Paxton and Nicholas Wahl, eds., *De Gaulle and the United States, 1930–1970* (1994); Jacques Portes, *Fascination and Misgiving* (2000); Irwin M. Wall, *The United States and the Making of Postwar France* (1991); Marvin Zahniser, *Uncertain Friendship* (1975) and *Then Came Disaster* (2002).

Gabon: David E. Gardinier, *Historical Dictionary of Gabon* (1994) (E).

Germany and Berlin: David E. Barclay and Elisabeth Glaser-Schmidt, eds., *Transatlantic Image and Perceptions* (1997); Steven Casey, *Cautious Crusade* (2001); Hans W. Gatzke, *Germany and the United States* (1980); Petra Goedde, *GIs and Germans* (2003); William Glenn Gray, *Germany's Cold War* (2003); Wolfram F. Hanrieder, *Germany, America, Europe* (1989); Maria Hohn, *GIs and Fräuleins* (2002); Patrick Thaddeus Jackson, *Civilizing the Enemy* (2006); Manfred Jonas, *The United States and Germany* (1984); Margrit Krewson, *German-American Relations* (1995) (B); James McAlister, *No Exit* (2002); Frank Ninkovich, *Germany and the United States* (1995); M. E. Sarotte, *Dealing with the Devil* (2001); Timothy Schroer, *Recasting Race after World War II* (2007); Hans-Jürgen Schröder, ed., *Confrontation and Cooperation* (1993); Thomas A. Schwartz, *America's Germany* (1991); Eric Solsten, ed., *Germany* (1996); W. R. Smyser, *Kennedy and the Berlin Wall* (2009); Stephen F. Szabo, *Parting Ways* (2004); Ian Wallace, *Berlin* (1993) (B); Peter Wyden, *Wall* (1989).

Ghana: LaVerde Berry, ed., *Ghana* (1995); Kevin Kelly Gaines, *American Africans in Ghana* (2006); Daniel McFarland, *Historical Dictionary of Ghana* (1985).

Great Britain: C. J. Bartlett, *"The Special Relationship"* (1992); David Dimbleby and David Reynolds, *An Ocean Apart* (1989); Alan P. Dobson, *Anglo-American Relations in the Twentieth Century* (1995); John Dumbrell, *Special Relationship* (2006); Sylvia Ellis, *Historical Dictionary of Anglo-American Relations* (2009) (E); Robert M. Hathaway, *Great Britain and the United States* (1990); David A. Lincove and Gary R. Treadway, eds., *The Anglo-American Relationship* (1988) (B); William Roger Louis and Hedley Bull, eds., *The Special Relationship* (1986); Jonathan Hollowell, ed., *Twentieth Century Anglo-American Relations* (2001); B. J. C. McKercher, *Transition of Power* (1999); John Moser, *Twisting the Lion's Tail* (1999); Anne Orde, *The Eclipse of Great Britain* (1996); Richie Ovendale *Anglo-American Relations in the Twentieth Century* (1998); David Reynolds, *Britannia Overruled* (2000); Andrew Roberts, *A History of the English-Speaking Peoples Since 1900* (2008); Mark Stoler, *Allies at War* (2005).

Greece: Louis Cassimatis, *American Influence in Greece, 1917–1929* (1988); Theodore A. Couloumbis, *The United States, Greece, and Turkey* (1983); Theodore A. Couloumbis and John O. Iatrides, eds.,

Greek-American Relations (1980); Glenn E. Curtis, ed., *Greece* (1995); John O. Iatrides, ed., *Ambassador MacVeagh Reports* (1980); Jon V. Kofas, *Intervention and Underdevelopment* (1989); Monteagle Stearns, *Entangled Allies* (1991); Lawrence S. Wittner, *American Intervention in Greece, 1943–1949* (1982).

Grenada: Peter M. Dunn and Bruce W. Watson, eds., *American Intervention in Grenada* (1985); Gordon K. Lewis, *Grenada* (1987); Kai P. Schoenhals and Richard A. Melanson, eds., *Revolution and Intervention in Grenada* (1985); Gary Williams, *U.S.-Grenada Relations* (2007).

Guam: Timothy P. Maga, *Defending Paradise* (1988); Earl S. Pomeroy, *Pacific Outpost* (1951); Robert F. Rogers, *Destiny's Landfall* (1995).

Guatemala: Nick Cullather, *Secret History* (1999); Paul J. Dosal, *Doing Business with the Dictators* (1993); Piero Gleijeses, *Shattered Hope* (1991); Jim Handy, *Gift of the Devil* (1985); Richard Immerman, *The CIA in Guatemala* (1982); Stephen M. Streeter, *Managing the Counterrevolution* (2001).

Guyana: Tim Merrill, ed., *Guyana and Belize* (1993); Stephen G. Rabe, *U.S. Intervention in British Guiana* (2005).

Haiti: Gordon S. Brown, *Toussaint's Clause* (2005); Frances Chambers, *Haiti* (1983) (B); Tim Matthewson, *Proslavery Foreign Policy* (2003); David Nicholls, *From Dessalines to Duvalier* (1979); Brenda Gayle Plummer, *Haiti and the United States* (1992); Ralph Pezzullo, *Plunging into Haiti* (2006); Mary Renda, *Taking Haiti* (2001); Robert I. Rotberg, *Haiti* (1971).

Hawai'i: Helena G. Allen, *The Betrayal of Queen Lilioukalani* (1982); Stephen Kinzer, *Overthrow* (2006); Ralph S. Kuykendall, *The Hawaiian Kingdom* (1938–1967); Nancy Morris and Love Dean, *Hawai'i* (1992) (B); Gary Okihiro, *Island World* (2008); Noenoe K. Silva, *Aloha Betrayed* (2004).

Honduras: Alison Acker, *Honduras* (1988); Pamela F. Howard-Reguindin, *Honduras* (1992) (B); Harvey Meyer and Jessie Meyer, *Historical Dictionary of Honduras* (1994) (E).

Hungary: László Borhi, *Hungary in the Cold War, 1945–1956* (2004); Stephan R. Burant, ed., *Hungary* (1990); Charles Gati, *Failed Illusions* (2006); Johanna C. Granville, *The First Domino* (2004).

India: William J. Barnds, *India, Pakistan, and the Great Powers* (1972); H. W. Brands, *India and the United States* (1990); W. Norman Brown, *The United States and India, Pakistan, and Bangladesh* (1972); Srinivas M. Chary, *The Eagle and the Peacock* (1994); Kenton J. Clymer, *Quest for Freedom* (1995); James Heitzman and Robert L. Worden, eds., *India* (1996); Dennis Kux, *India and the United States* (1992); Robert J. McMahon, *The Cold War on the Periphery* (1994); Dennis Merrill, *Bread and the Ballot* (1990); Norman D. Palmer, *The United States and India* (1984); Andrew Rotter, *Comrades at Odds* (2000); Santosh C. Saha, *Indo-U.S. Relations, 1947–1988* (1990) (B); Strobe Talbott, *Engaging India* (2004).

Indian Ocean: Helen C. Metz, ed., *Indian Ocean: Five Island Countries* (1995).

Indonesia: Theodore Friend, *Indonesian Destinies* (2003); Paul F. Gardner, *Shared Hopes, Separate Fears* (1997); Frances Gouda, *American Visions of the Netherlands East Indies/Indonesia* (2002); Michael Leifer, *Indonesia's Foreign Policy* (1983); Robert J. McMahon, *Colonialism and Cold War* (1981); Andrew Roadnight, *United States Policy Toward Indonesia in the Truman and Eisenhower Years* (2002); Robert L. Worden, ed., *Indonesia* (1993).

Iran: Gholam Reza Afkhami, *The Life and Times of the Shah* (2008); Ali M. Ansari, *Confronting Iran* (2006); James A. Bill, *The Eagle and the Lion* (1988); Richard W. Cottam, *Iran and the United States* (1988); Mark J. Gasiorowski, *U.S. Foreign Policy and the Shah* (1991); Sīrūs Ghanī, *Iran and the West* (1987) (B); James F. Goode, *The United States and Iran, 1946–51* (1989); Nikki R. Keddie and Mark J. Gasiorowski, eds., *Neither East nor West* (1990); Mark H. Lytle, *The Origins of the Iranian-American Alliance, 1941–1953* (1987); Rouhollah K. Ramazani, *The United States and Iran* (1982); Barry Rubin, *Paved with Good Intentions* (1980); Kuross A. Samii, *Involvement by Invitation* (1987); Abraham Yeselson, *United States–Persian Diplomatic Relations, 1883–1921* (1956).

Iraq: Rick Atkinson, *Crusade* (1993); Robert Brigham, *Is Iraq Vietnam?* (2006); Lawrence Freedman and Efraim Karsh, *The Gulf Conflict, 1990–1991* (1993); Kenneth J. Campbell, *A Tale of Two Quagmires* (2007); Bruce Jentleson, *With Friends like These* (1994); Barry Lando, *Web of Deceit* (2007); Sandra Mackey, *The Reckoning* (2002); Helen C. Metz, ed., *Iraq* (1990); Morris M. Mottale, *The Origins of the Gulf Wars* (2001); Geoff Simons, *Targeting Iraq* (2002); William Stivers, *Supremacy and Oil* (1982).

Ireland: Thomas N. Brown, *Irish-American Nationalism, 1870–1890* (1966); Francis M. Carroll, *American Opinion and the Irish Question, 1910–1923* (1978) and *The American Presence in Ulster: A Diplomatic History, 1796–1996* (2005); Sean Cronin, *Washington's Irish Policy, 1916–1986* (1987); Troy D. Davis, *Dublin's American Policy* (1998).

Israel, Palestine, and Arab-Israeli Conflict: George W. Ball and Douglas B. Ball, *The Passionate Attachment* (1992); Abraham Ben-Zvi,

The United States and Israel (1994); Ian J. Bickerton and Carla L. Klausner, *A Concise History of the Arab-Israeli Conflict* (1998); Herbert Druks, *The Uncertain Friendship* (2001); William Roger Louis and Robert W. Stookey, eds., *The End of the Palestine Mandate* (1986); Michael I. Karpin, *The Bomb in the Basement* (2006); Camille Mansour, *Beyond Alliance* (1994); Michelle Mart, *Eye on Israel* (2006); John J. Mearsheimer and Stephen M. Walt, *Israel Lobby and U.S. Foreign Policy* (2007); Donald Neff, *Fallen Pillars: U.S. Policy Towards Palestine and Israel Since 1945* (1995); Ilan Pappe, *The Israel/Palestine Question* (1999); William B. Quandt, *Peace Process* (1993); John Quigley, *Palestine and Israel* (1990); Bernard Reich, ed., *An Encyclopedia of the Arab-Israeli Conflict* (1996) (E) and *The United States and Israel* (1984); Cheryl Rubenberg, *Israel and the American National Interest* (1986); David Schoenbaum, *The United States and the State of Israel* (1993); Charles D. Smith, *Palestine and the Arab-Israeli Conflict* (1992); Steven Spiegel, *The Other Arab-Israeli Conflict* (1985); Michael W. Suleiman, ed., *U.S. Policy on Palestine* (1995); Mark Tessler, *A History of the Israeli-Palestinian Conflict* (1994); Edward Tivnan, *The Lobby* (1987).

Italy: Alessandro Brogi, *A Question of Self-esteem* (2002); Alexander DeConde, *Half-Bitter, Half-Sweet* (1971); H. Stuart Hughes, *The United States and Italy* (1979); James E. Miller, *The United States and Italy, 1940–1950* (1986); David F. Schmitz, *The United States and Fascist Italy, 1922–1940* (1988); Leo J. Wollemborg, *Stars, Stripes, and Italian Tricolor* (1990).

Japan: Sadao Asada, *Japan and the World* (1989) (B); Michael A. Barnhart, *Japan and the World Since 1868* (1995); John H. Boyle, *Modern Japan* (1993); Roger Buckley, *US-Japan Alliance Diplomacy, 1945–1990* (1992); Donald E. Dolan and Robert L. Worden, eds., *Japan* (1992); Tsuyoshi Hasegawa, *Racing the Enemy* (2005); Akira Iriye and Robert A. Wampler, eds., *Partnership* (2001); Walter LaFeber, *The Clash* (1997); Takeshi Matsuda, *Soft Power and Its Perils* (2007); Gavan McCormack, *Client State* (2007); Rita E. Neri, *U.S. and Japan Foreign Trade* (1988) (B); Charles E. Neu, *The Troubled Encounter* (1975); Ian Nish, *Japanese Foreign Policy in the Interwar Period* (2002); Michael Schaller, *Altered States* (1997) and *The American Occupation of Japan* (1985); Sayuri Shimizu, *Creating People of Plenty* (2001); Naoko Shibusawa, *America's Geisha Ally* (2006); John Swenson-Wright, *Unequal Allies?* (2005); and John Van Sant et al., *Historical Dictionary of United States-Japan Relations* (2007) (E).

Jordan: Madiha Rashid al-Madfai, *Jordan, the United States, and the Middle East Peace Process* (1993); Miriam Joyce, *Anglo-American Support for Jordan* (2008); Helen C. Metz, ed., *Jordan* (1991).

Kazakhstan: Glenn E. Curtis, *Kazakhstan, Kyrgyzstan, Tajikistan, Turkmenistan, and Uzbekistan* (1997); Michael Mandelbaum, ed., *Central Asia and the World* (1994).

Korea and Korean War: Greg Brazinsky, *Nation Building in South Korea* (2007); Jongsuk Chay, *Diplomacy of Asymmetry* (1990); Bruce Cumings, *Korea's Place in the Sun* (1997) and *The Origins of the Korean War* (1981, 1990); Paul M. Edwards, *The Korean War* (1998) (B); David Halberstam, *Coldest Winter* (2007); Burton I. Kaufman, *The Korean War* (1997); Chae-Jin Lee, *Troubled Peace* (2006); Yun-Bok Lee and Wayne Patterson, eds., *Korean-American Relations, 1866–1997* (1998); Mitchell B. Lerner, *The "Pueblo" Incident* (2002); Peter Lowe, *The Korean War* (2000); Donald S. Macdonald, *U.S.-Korean Relations* (1992); James I. Matray, ed., *Historical Dictionary of the Korean War* (1991) (E); Keith McFarland, *The Korean War* (1986) (B); Katherine H. S. Moon, *Sex Among Allies* (1997); Andrew C. Nahm, *Historical Dictionary of the Republic of Korea* (1993) (E); Stanley Sandler, *The Korean War* (1995) (E); Andrea M. Savada, ed., *North Korea* (1994) and *South Korea* (1992); Andre Schmid, *Korea Between Empires* (2002); Leon V. Sigal, *Disarming Strangers* (1998); William Stueck, *The Korean War* (1995), *Rethinking the Korean War* (2002), and *The Korean War in World History* (2004); Harry G. Summers, Jr., *Korean War Almanac* (1990) (C and E); Spencer Tucker, *Encyclopedia of the Korean War* (E) (2000).

Kuwait: Abdul-Reda Assiri, *Kuwaiti Foreign Policy* (1990); Jill Crystal, *Kuwait* (1992) and *Oil and Politics in the Gulf* (1995).

Laos: Timothy N. Castle, *At War in the Shadow of Vietnam* (1993); Helen Cordell, *Laos* (1993) (B); Arthur J. Dommen, *Laos* (1985); Jane Hamilton-Merritt, *Tragic Mountains* (1993); Andrea M. Savada, ed., *Laos* (1995); Charles A. Stevenson, *The End of Nowhere* (1972).

Latin America: G. Pope Atkins, *Encyclopedia of the Inter-American System* (1997) (E) and *Latin America in the International System* (1995); John A. Britton, *The United States and Latin America* (1997) (B); Peter Calvert, *The International Politics of Latin America* (1994); David W. Dent, *U.S.–Latin American Policymaking* (1995) (B); Mark T. Gilderhus, *The Second Century* (2000); Greg Grandin, *The Last Colonial Massacre* (2004); Jack W. Hopkins, ed., *Latin America and Caribbean Contemporary Record* (1983–) (AS); John J. Johnson, *A Hemisphere Apart* (1990); Gilbert Joseph and Daniela Spenser, *In From the Cold* (2007); Lester D. Langley, *America and the Americas* (1989); William M. LeoGrande, *Our Own Backyard* (1998); Thomas M. Leonard, ed., *United States–Latin American Relations, 1850–1903* (1999); Kyle Longley, *In the Eagle's Shadow* (2002); Abraham F. Lowenthal, ed., *Exporting Democracy* (1991); Alan McPherson, *Yankee No!* (2003) and *Intimate Ties, Bitter Struggles* (2006); Nancy Mitchell, *The Danger of Dreams* (1999); Fredrick B. Pike, *The United States and Latin America* (1992); David M. Pletcher, *The Diplomacy of Trade and Investment* (1998); Henry Raymont, *Troubled Neighbors* (2005); Fred Rosen, *Empire and Dissent* (2008); Lars Schoultz, *Beneath the United States* (1998); David Shavit, *The United States in Latin America* (1992) (E); David Sheinin, ed., *Beyond the Ideal*

(2000); Joseph Smith, *United States and Latin America* (2005); Peter H. Smith, *Talons of the Eagle* (1996).

Lebanon: C. H. Bleaney, *Lebanon* (1991) (B); Thomas L. Friedman, *From Beirut to Jerusalem* (1989); Irene Gendzier, *Notes from the Minefield* (1997); Dilip Hiro, *Lebanon* (1993); Itamar Rabinovich, *The War for Lebanon, 1970–1985* (1986).

Liberia: D. Elwood Dunn, *The Foreign Policy of Liberia During the Tubman Era, 1944–1971* (1979); Katherine Harris, *The United States and Liberia* (1985); Richard Moose, *U.S. Policy Toward Liberia* (1980); Hassan B. Sisay, *Big Powers and Small Nations* (1985); Charles M. Wilson, *Liberia* (1985).

Libya: Scott L. Bills, *The Libyan Arena* (1995); Mahmoud G. El Warfally, *Imagery and Ideology in U.S. Policy Toward Libya, 1969–1982* (1988); P. Edward Haley, *Qaddafi and the United States Since 1969* (1984); Ronald Bruce St. John, *Two Centuries of Strife* (2002); Dirk Wandewalle, ed., *Qadhafi's Libya* (1995).

Lithuania: Saulius Sužiedelis, *Historical Dictionary of Lithuania* (1997) (E); Robert A. Vitas, *United States and Lithuania* (1990).

Mauritania: Robert E. Handloff, ed., *Mauritania* (1990).

Mauritius: Larry Bowman, *Mauritius* (1991).

Mexico: Peter Andreas, *Border Games* (2000); Leslie Bethel, ed., *Mexico Since Independence* (1991); Jorge Domínguez and Rafael Fernandez de Castro, *United States and Mexico* (2001); John D. Dwyer, *The Agrarian Dispute* (2008); Donald S. Frazier, ed., *The United States and Mexico at War* (1998) (E); John M. Hart, *Empire and Revolution* (2002); Lester D. Langley, *Mexico and the United States* (1991); Krystina M. Libura et al, *Echoes of the Mexican American War* (2004); David E. Lorey, ed., *United States–Mexico Border Statistics Since 1900* (1990) (S) and *The U.S.–Mexican Border in the Twentieth Century* (2000); Jacqueline Mazza, *Don't Disturb the Neighbors* (2001); Robert A. Pastor and Jorge G. Castañeda, *Limits to Friendship* (1988); George D. C. Philip, *Mexico* (1993) (B); W. Dirk Raat, *Mexico and the United States* (1997); Clint E. Smith, *Inevitable Partnership* (2000); Daniela Spenser, *The Impossible Triangle* (1999).

Middle East: Robert J. Allison, *The Crescent Observed* (1995); Warren Bass, *Support Any Friend* (2003); Martin Gilbert, *Atlas of the Arab-Israeli Conflict* (1993) (A); Peter Hahn, *Caught in the Middle East* (2006) and *Historical Dictionary of United States-Middle East Relations* (2007) (E); Gregory Harms, *The Palestine Israel Conflict* (2008); Burton I. Kaufman, *The Arab Middle East and the United States* (1996); Colin Legum et al., eds.,

Middle East Contemporary Survey (1978–) (AS); George Lenczowski, *American Presidents and the Middle East* (1989); David Lesch, *The Arab-Israeli Conflict* (2008); Douglas Little, *American Orientalism* (2008); Melani McAllister, *Epic Encounters* (2001); Marc J. O'Reilly, *Unexceptional* (2008); Michael B. Oren, *Power, Faith, and Fantasy: America in the Middle East* (2007); Reeva S. Simon et al., eds., *The Encyclopedia of the Modern Middle East* (1996) (E); Kenneth Stein, *Heroic Diplomacy* (1999); Alan R. Taylor, *The Superpowers and the Middle East* (1991).

Mongolia: Robert C. Worden and Andrea M. Savada, eds., *Mongolia* (1991).

Morocco: Leon B. Blair, *Western Window in the Arab World* (1970); Luella J. Hall, *The United States and Morocco, 1776–1956* (1961).

Mozambique: Mario Azevedo, *Historical Dictionary of Mozambique* (1991) (E); Chester A. Crocker, *U.S. Policy Toward Mozambique* (1987); Margaret Hall and Tom Young, *Confronting Leviathan* (1997); Malyn Newitt, *A History of Mozambique* (1995).

Myanmar: John F. Cady, *The United States and Burma* (1976); Patricia M. Herbert, *Burma* (1991) (B).

Namibia: John J. Grotpeter, *Historical Dictionary of Namibia* (1994) (E).

Nepal: Andrea M. Savada, ed., *Nepal and Bhutan* (1993).

Netherlands: Doeko Bosscher et al., eds., *American Culture in the Netherlands* (1996); Hans Loeber, ed., *Dutch-American Relations, 1945–1969* (1992); J. W. Schulte Nordholt and Robert P. Swierenga, eds., *A Bilateral Centennial: A History of Dutch-American Relations, 1783–1982* (1982); Gertrude Reichenbach-Consten and Abraham Noordergraaf, eds., *Two Hundred Years of Netherlands-American Interaction* (1985); Cornelius van Minnen, *American Diplomats in the Netherlands, 1815–50* (1993).

Nicaragua: Karl Berman, *Under the Big Stick* (1986); E. Bradford Burns, *Patriarch and Folk* (1991); Paul C. Clark, Jr., *The United States and Somoza* (1992); Michael D. Gambone, *Eisenhower, Somoza, and the Cold War in Nicaragua* (1997); Michel Gobat, *Confronting the American Dream* (2005); Peter Kornbluh, *Nicaragua* (1987); Tim L. Merrill, ed., *Nicaragua* (1994); Morris H. Morley, *Washington, Somoza, and the Sandinistas* (1994); Neil Narr, *Sandinista Nicaragua* (1990) (B); Robert Pastor, *Condemned to Repetition* (1987); Mauricio Salaún, *U.S. Intervention and Regime Change in Nicaragua* (2005); Thomas W. Walker, *Nicaragua* (1991), ed., *Reagan Versus the Sandinistas* (1987), and ed., *Revolution and Counterrevolution in Nicaragua* (1991); Knut Walter, *The Regime of Anastasio Somoza* (1993); Ralph Lee Woodward, *Nicaragua* (1994) (B).

Nigeria: Bassey E. Ate, *Decolonization and Dependence* (1987); Helen C. Metz, ed., *Nigeria* (1992); Robert B. Shepard, *Nigeria, Africa, and the United States* (1991); Joseph E. Thompson, *American Policy and African Famine* (1990).

North Africa: Charles F. Gallagher, *The United States and North Africa* (1963); Richard S. Parker, *North Africa* (1984).

Norway: Mats Berdal, *The United States, Norway, and the Cold War* (1997); Wayne S. Cole, *Norway and the United States* (1989); Ronald C. Popperwell, *Norway* (1972); Sigmund Skard, *The United States in Norwegian History* (1976); Rolf Tamnes, *The United States and the Cold War in the High North* (1991).

Oman: Joseph A. Kechichian, *Oman and the World* (1995).

Pakistan: David Armstrong and Joseph Trento, *America and the Islamic Bomb* (2007); Peter R. Blood, ed., *Pakistan* (1995); Dennis Kux, *The United States and Pakistan, 1947–2000* (2001); Adrian Levy, *Deception* (2007); Iftikhar Malik, *U.S.–South Asian Relations, 1940–1947* (1991); Shirin Tahir-kheli, *The United States and Pakistan* (1982); David D. Taylor, *Pakistan* (1990) (B); M. S. Venkataramani, *The American Role in Pakistan, 1947–1958* (1982).

Panama (and Panama Canal): Michael L. Conniff, *Panama and the United States* (1992); David N. Farnsworth and James W. McKenney, *U.S.-Panama Relations, 1903–1978* (1983); Walter LaFeber, *The Panama Canal* (1990); Thomas M. Leonard, *Panama, the Canal, and the United States* (1993) (B); John Lindsay-Poland, *Emperors in the Jungle* (2003); John Major, *Prize Possession* (1993); David McCullough, *The Path Between the Seas* (1977); Aims McGuiness, *Path of Empire* (2007); Matthew Parker, *Panama Fever* (2008).

Paraguay: Anibal Miranda, *United States–Paraguay Relations* (1990); Frank O. Mora and Jerry W. Cooney, *Paraguay and the United States* (2007); Riordan Roett and Richard S. Sacks, *Paraguay* (1991).

Persian Gulf: Bruce R. Kuniholm, *The Persian Gulf and United States Policy* (1984) (B); Charles A. Kupchan, *The Persian Gulf and the West* (1987); Helen C. Metz, ed., *Persian Gulf States* (1993); Marc O'Reilly, *Unexceptional* (2008); Michael A. Palmer, *Guardians of the Gulf* (1992).

Peru: Lawrence A. Clayton, *Peru and the United States* (1999); Rex A. Hudson, ed., *Peru* (1993); Cynthia McClintock and Fabian Vallas, *The United States and Peru* (2003); Fredrick B. Pike, *The United States and the Andean Republics* (1977); Ronald B. St. John, *The Foreign Policy of Peru* (1992).

Philippines: David H. Bain, *Sitting in Darkness* (1984); H. W. Brands, *Bound to Empire* (1992); Nick Cullather, *Illusions of Influence* (1994); Ronald E. Dolan, ed., *Philippines* (1993); Julian Go and Anne L. Foster, eds., *The American Colonial State in the Philippines* (2003); Stanley Karnow, *In Our Image* (1989); Paul A. Kramer, *Blood of Government* (2006); Brian M. Linn, *The Philippine War* (2000); Glenn A. May, *Battle for Batangas* (1991); Jim Richardson, *Philippines* (1989) (B).

Poland: Debra J. Allen, *The Oder-Neisse Line* (2003); Glenn E. Curtis, ed., *Poland* (1994); Richard Lukacs, *Bitter Legacy* (1982); Helene Sjursen, *The United States, Western Europe, and the Polish Crisis* (2003); Anthony Kemp-Welch, *Poland Under Communism* (2008).

Portugal: Scott B. MacDonald, *European Destiny, Atlantic Transformations* (1993); Kenneth Maxwell and Michael H. Haltzel, eds., *Portugal* (1990); Eric Solsten, ed., *Portugal* (1994).

Puerto Rico: Rafael Bernabe, *Puerto Rico in the American Century* (2007); Laura Briggs, *Reproducing Empire* (2002); Raymond Carr, *Puerto Rico* (1984); Arturo Morales Carríon, *Puerto Rico* (1984); Elena E. Cevallos, *Puerto Rico* (1985) (B); Truman B. Clark, *Puerto Rico and the United States, 1917–1933* (1975); Ronald Fernandez, *The Disenchanted Island* (1996); A. W. Maldonado, *Teodora Moscoso and Puerto Rico's Operation Bootstrap* (1997); José Trías Monge, *Puerto Rico* (1997).

Romania: Ronald D. Bachman, ed., *Romania* (1990); Joseph F. Harrington and Bruce J. Courtney, *Tweaking the Nose of the Russians* (1991); Elizabeth W. Hazard, *Cold War Crucible* (1996).

Russia and the Soviet Union: N. N. Bolkhovitinov and J. Dane Hartgrove, *Russia and the United States* (1987) (B); Peter G. Boyle, *American-Soviet Relations* (1993); Archie Brown et al., eds., *The Cambridge Encyclopedia of Russia and the Soviet Union* (1994) (E); Donald Davis and Eugene P. Trani, *The First Cold War* (2000); Philip J. Funigiello, *American-Soviet Trade in the Cold War* (1988); A.A. Fursenko and Timothy J. Naftali, *Khrushchev's Cold War* (2006); John Lewis Gaddis, *Russia, the Soviet Union, and the United States* (1990); Raymond L. Garthoff, *Détente and Confrontation* (1985) and *The Great Transition* (1994); Yoram Gorlizki and O.V. Khlevniuk, *Cold Peace* (2004); Hope M. Harrison, *Driving the Soviets up the Wall* (2003); Walter LaFeber, *America, Russia, and the Cold War* (2002); James K. Libbey, *American-Russian Economic Relations* (1989) (B); J. D. Parks, *Culture, Conflict, and Coexistence* (1983); Norman E. Saul, *Concord and Conflict* (1996), *The United States and Russia, 1763–1867* (1991), *War and Revolution* (2002), and *Historical Dictionary of United States-Russian/Soviet Relations* (2009) (E); David Shavit, *United States Relations with Russia and the Soviet Union* (1993) (E); V. M. Zubok, *A Failed Empire* (2007).

Rwanda: Jared Cohen, *One Hundred Days of Silence* (2007); Learthen Dorsey, *Historical Dictionary of Rwanda* (1994) (E).

Samoa (American): J. A. C. Gray, *Amerika Samoa* (1960); Paul Kennedy, *The Samoan Tangle* (1974); George H. Ryden, *The Foreign Policy of the United States in Relation to Samoa* (1933).

Saudi Arabia: Irvine H. Anderson, *Aramco, the United States, and Saudi Arabia* (1981); Rachel Bronson, *Thicker Than Oil* (2006); Nathan J. Citino, *From Arab Nationalism to OPEC* (2002); Parker T. Hart, *Saudi Arabia and the United States* (1999); Helen C. Metz, ed., *Saudia Arabia* (1993); Aaron D. Miller, *Search for Security* (1980); Nadav Safran, *Saudi Arabia* (1986); Craig Unger, *House of Bush, House of Saud* (2004); Robert Vitalis, *America's Kingdom* (2007).

Scandinavia: Jussi M. Hanhimäki, *Scandinavia and the United States* (1997); Geir Lundestad, *America, Scandinavia, and the Cold War* (1980); Franklin D. Scott, *Scandinavia* (1975) and *The United States and Scandinavia* (1950).

Senegal: R. M. Dilley and J. S. Eades, *Senegal* (1994) (B).

Somalia: John L. Hirsch and Whert B. Oakley, *Somalia and Operation Restore Hope* (1995); Helen C. Metz, ed., *Somalia* (1993).

South Africa: James Barber and John Barratt, *South Africa's Foreign Policy* (1990); Thomas Borstelmann, *Apartheid's Reluctant Uncle* (1993); Rita M. Byrnes, ed., *South Africa* (1997); Christopher Coker, *The United States and South Africa, 1968–1985* (1986); Jeffrey V. Davis, *South Africa* (1994) (B); Terrell D. Hale, *United States Sanctions and South Africa* (1993) (B); Richard W. Hull, *American Enterprise in South Africa* (1990); C. T. Keto, *American–South African Relations, 1784–1980* (1985) (B); Y. G. M. Lulat, *U.S. Relations with South Africa* (1991) (B); Princeton N. Lyman, *Partner to History* (2002); Robert K. Massie, *Loosing the Bonds* (1997); William Minter, *King Soloman's Mines Revisited* (1986); Francis N. Nesbitt, *Race for Sanctions* (2004); Thomas J. Noer, *Briton, Boer, and Yankee* (1978) and *Cold War and Black Liberation* (1985).

Spain: Michael Alpert, *A New International History of the Spanish Civil War* (1998); Rodrigo Botero, *Ambivalent Embrace* (2001); Thomas Chavez, *Spain and the Independence of the United States* (2002); James W. Cortada, *Two Nations over Time* (1978) and ed., *Spain in the Twentieth-Century World* (1980); Robert W. Kern, *Historical Dictionary of Modern Spain* (1990) (E); Boris N. Liedtke, *Embracing a Dictatorship* (1998).

Sudan: Carolyn Fkuehr-Lobban et al., *Historical Dictionary of Sudan* (1992) (E); Julie Flint and Alex deWaal, *Darfur* (2008); Helen C. Metz, ed., *Sudan* (1992); Peter Woodward, *Sudan* (1989).

Sweden: Sture Kindmark and Tore Tallroth, eds., *Swedes Looking West* (1983).

Switzerland: Heinze K. Meier, *Friendship Under Stress* (1970) and *The United States and Switzerland in the Nineteenth Century* (1963).

Syria: David W. Lesch, *Syria and the United States* (1992); Moshe Ma'oz, *Syria and Israel* (1995); Andrew Rathwell, *Secret War in the Middle East* (1995); Bonnie Saunders, *The United States and Arab Nationalism* (1996); Eyal Zisser, *Assad's Legacy* (2002).

Thailand: Richard Aldrich, *The Key to the South* (1993); Daniel Fineman, *Special Relationship* (1997); Barbara L. LePoer, ed., *Thailand* (1989); Robert J. Muscat, *Thailand and the United States* (1990).

Trieste: Bogdan C. Novak, *Trieste, 1941–1954* (1970); Roberto Rabel, *Between East and West* (1988).

Turkey: David J. Alvarez, *Bureaucracy and Cold War Ideology* (1980); William Hale, *Turkey, the U.S., and Iraq* (2007); George S. Harris, *Troubled Alliance* (1972); Harry H. Howard, *Turkey, the Straits, and U.S. Policy* (1974); Helen C. Metz, ed., *Turkey* (1996); Nasa Uslu, *Turkish-American Relationship between 1947 and 2003* (2003).

Uganda: Rita M. Byrnes, ed., *Uganda* (1992).

Ukraine: Lubomyr A. Hajda, ed., *Ukraine in the World* (1998); Steven Woehrel, *Ukraine* (1994).

Uruguay: Kitty L. Drummond, *Relations Between Uruguay and the United States* (1936); Rex A. Hudson and Sandra W. Meditz, eds., *Uruguay* (1992); Martin Weinstein, *Uruguay* (1987).

Venezuela: Judith Ewell, *Venezuela and the United States* (1996); Eva Golinger, *Bush Versus Chávez* (2008); Janet Kelley and Carlos A. Romero, *United States and Venezuela* (2001); Sheldon B. Liss, *Diplomacy and Independence* (1978); Stephen G. Rabe, *The Road to OPEC* (1982); Darlene Rivas, *Missionary Capitalist* (2002); Miguel Tinker Salas, *The Enduring Legacy* (2009).

Vietnam and Southeast Asia: David L. Anderson, ed., *Shadow on the White House* (1993); David Anderson, *The Columbia Guide to the Vietnam War* (2002) (E); Pierre Asselin, *A Bitter Peace* (2002); Larry Berman, *No Peace, No Honor* (2001); James G. Blight, janet M. Lang, and David A. Welch, *Vietnam If Kennedy Had Lived* (2009); John S. Bowman, ed., *The Vietnam War* (1986) (C); Mark Philip Bradley, *Making Sense of the Vietnam Wars* (2008); Robert Brigham, *Guerrilla Diplomacy* (1998); Lester H. Brune and Richard Dean Burns, eds., *America and* the Indochina Wars, 1945–1990 (1991) (B); Peter Busch, *All the Way with JFK* (2003); Robert Buzzanco and Marilyn Young, eds., *A Companion to the Vietnam War* (2002) (E); Philip E. Catton, *Diem's Final Failure* (2002); William J. Duiker, *Historical Dictionary of Vietnam* (1989) (E); H. Bruce Franklin, *Vietnam and Other American Fantasies* (2002); Joseph A. Fry, *Debating Vietnam* (2008); Lloyd C. Gardner, *Approaching Vietnam* (1988); George C. Herring, *America's Longest War* (2000); Gary R. Hess, *Vietnam and the United States* (1998) and *Vietnam* (2009); George McT. Kahin, *Intervention* (1986); David Kaiser, *American Tragedy* (2000); Gabriel Kolko, *Anatomy of a War* (1985); Stanley I. Kutler, ed., *Encyclopedia of the Vietnam War* (1995) (E); Frederik Logevall, *Choosing War* (1999); Robert J. McMahon, *The Limits of Empire* (1999); Edwin F. Moise, *Historical Dictionary of the Vietnam War* (2001) (E); Mark Moyar, *Triumph Forsaken* (2006); Charles E. Neu, *After Vietnam* (2000); James S. Olson, *Dictionary of the Vietnam War* (1988) (E) and *The Vietnam War* (1993) (B); Andrew J. Rotter, *The Path to Vietnam* (1987); Robert D. Schulzinger, *A Time for War* (1997); Harry G. Summers, Jr., *Vietnam War Almanac* (1985) (C); Spencer C. Tucker, ed., *Encyclopedia of the Vietnam War* (1998) (E); Donald E. Weatherbee, *Historical Dictionary of United States-Southeast Asia Relations* (2008) (E); Randall B. Woods, ed., *Vietnam and the American Political Tradition* (2003); Marilyn Young, *The Vietnam Wars* (1991).

Virgin Islands and West Indies: William W. Boyer, *America's Virgin Islands* (1983); Cary Fraser, *Ambivalent Anti-Colonialism* (1994); Verna P. Moll, *Virgin Islands* (1991) (B); Andrew Jackson O'Shaughnessy, *An Empire Divided* (2000); Stephen J. Randall and Graeme Malent, *The Caribbean Basin* (1998); Charlie Witham, *Bitter Rehearsal* (2002).

Yemen: Ahmed Nomen Al-Madhaqi, *Yemen and the USA* (1994); Fred Halliday, *Revolution and Foreign Policy* (1989).

Yugoslavia: Leonard Cohen, *Broken Bonds* (1993); Misha Glenny, *The Balkans* (2000); Lorraine M. Lees, *Keeping Tito Afloat* (1997); Miron Rezan, *Europe's Nightmare* (2001); Ivo Tasovic, *American Policy and Yugoslavia, 1939–1941* (1999); Susan Woodward, *Balkan Tragedy* (1995).

Zimbabwe: Andrew DeRoche, *Black, White, and Chrome* (2001); Gerald Horne, *From the Barrel of a Gun* (2001); R. Kent Rasmussen, *Historical Dictionary of Zimbabwe* (1990) (E).

Overviews of Subjects, Including Atlases (A), Annual Surveys (AS), Bibliographies (B), Biographical Aids (BA), Chronologies (C), Encyclopedias (E), and Statistics (S)

African Americans: Carol Anderson, *Eyes Off the Prize* (2003); Thomas Borstelmann, *The Cold War and the Color Line* (2001); Chris

Dixon, *African America and Haiti* (2000); Mary Dudziak, *Cold War Civil Rights* (2000); Robert Gallicho, *The African American Encounter with Japan and China* (2001); Gerald Horne, *Black and Red* (1986); Michael L. Krenn, *Black Diplomacy* (1998); Azza Salema Layton, *International Relations and Civil Rights* (2000); James H. Meriwether, *Proudly We Can Be Africans* (2002); Kenneth O'Reilly, *Nixon's Piano* (1995); Brenda Gayle Plummer, *Rising Wind* (1996); "Symposium: African Americans and U.S. Foreign Relations," *Diplomatic History, XX* (Fall 1996); Jonathan Rosenberg, *How Far the Promised Land?* (2006); Lamin Sanneh, *Abolitionists Abroad* (2000); Timothy Schroer, *Recasting Race after World War II* (2007) (Germany); Penny Von Eschen, *Race Against Empire* (1997).

AIDS Pandemic: Jonathan Engel, *Epidemic: A Global History of AIDS* (2006); J. Mann, Daniel Tarantola, and T. Netter, eds., *AIDS in the World* (1992, 1996); Matthew Smallman-Raynor et al., *Atlas of AIDS* (1992) (A).

Air Force and Air Power: Charles D. Bright, ed., *Historical Dictionary of the U.S. Air Force* (1992) (E); Alan P. Dobson, *Peaceful Air Warfare* (1991); Richard P. Hallion, *The Literature of Aeronautics, Astronautics, and Air Power* (1984) (B); John B. Rae, *Climb to Greatness* (1968); Michael S. Sherry, *The Rise of American Air Power* (1987); Jeffrey S. Underwood, *The Wings of Democracy* (1991); Bruce W. Watson and Susan W. Watson, *The United States Air Force* (1992) (E).

Alliance for Progress: Jerome Levinson and Juan de Onís, *The Alliance That Lost Its Way* (1970); L. Ronald Scheman, ed., *The Alliance for Progress* (1988); Jeffrey F. Taffet, *Foreign Aid as Foreign Policy* (2007).

American Revolution: Richard Blanco, ed., *The American Revolution* (1993) (E); Mark M. Boatner III, *Encyclopedia of the American Revolution* (1974) (E); Lester J. Cappon, ed., *Atlas of Early American History: The Revolutionary Era, 1760–1790* (1976) (A); John M. Faragher, ed., *The Encyclopedia of Colonial and Revolutionary America* (1990) (E); Jack P. Greene and J. R. Pole, eds., *The Blackwell Encyclopedia of the American Revolution* (1991) (E); John W. Raimo, ed., *Biographical Directory of American Colonial and Revolutionary Governors, 1607–1789* (1980) (BA).

Anti-Americanism: Seth D. Armas, *French Anti-Americanism (1930–1948)* (2007); Dan Diner, *German Anti-Americanism* (1995); Peter J. Katzenstein and Robert O. Keohane, *Anti-Americanisms in World Politics* (2007); Rob Kroes and Maarten van Rossem, eds., *Anti-Americanism in Europe* (1986); Denis Lacorne et al., eds., *The Rise and Fall of Anti-Americanism* (1990); Andrei Markovits, *Uncouth Nation* (2007); Richard Pells, *Not Like Us* (1997); Philip Roger, *The American Enemy* (2005); Alvin Z. Rubenstein and Donald E. Smith, eds., *Anti-Americanism in the Third World* (1985); Andrew Ross and Kristin

Ross, *Anti-Americanism* (2004); Barry Rubin and Judith Colp Rubin, *Hating America* (2006).

Anticommunism and McCarthyism: Jeff Broadwater, *Eisenhower and the Anti-Communist Crusades* (1992); Peter H. Buckingham, *America Sees Red* (1987) (B); Thomas P. Doherty, *Cold War, Cool Medium* (2003); Richard M. Fried, *Nightmare in Red* (1990); Robert Griffith, *The Politics of Fear* (1987); Joel Kovel, *Red Hunting in the Promised Land* (1994); Stanley I. Kutler, *The American Inquisition* (1982); David K. Johnson, *The Lavender Scare* (2003); Ted Morgan, *Reds* (2003); Richard G. Powers, *Not Without Honor* (1995); Athan Theoharis, *Chasing Spies* (2002); Stephen J. Whitfield, *The Culture of the Cold War* (1996); Michael J. Ybarra, *Washington Gone Crazy* (2004).

Arms Sales and Trade: Michael Broszka and Thomas Ohlson, *Arms Transfers to the Third World* (1987); Michael T. Klare, *American Arms Supermarket* (1984); Edward J. Laurence, *The International Arms Trade* (1992); Andrew J. Pierre, *The Global Politics of Arms Sales* (1982).

Biological and Chemical Warfare: G. M. Burck and Charles C. Flowerree, *International Handbook on Chemical Weapons Proliferation* (1991) (E); Anthony H. Cordesman, *Weapons of Mass Destruction in the Middle East* (1991); Arthur J. Dommen et al., *The United States and Biological Warfare* (1999); Stephen Endicott and Edward Hagerman, *The United States and Biological Warfare* (1999); Sheldon H. Harris, *Factories of Death* (1994); John Norris and Will Fowler, *NBC: Nuclear, Biological, and Chemical Warfare on the Modern Battlefield* (1998) (E); Amy E. Simpson, ed., *The Chemical Weapons Convention Handbook* (1993).

Civil Defense: Laura McEnany, *Civil Defense Begins at Home* (2000); Kenneth D. Rose, *One Nation Underground* (2001).

Civil War (American): Mark M. Boatner III, *The Civil War Dictionary* (1988) (E); D. P. Crook, *The North, the South, and the Powers* (1974); Richard N. Current, ed., *Encyclopedia of the Confederacy* (1993) (E); David S. Heidler et al., *Encyclopedia of the American Civil War* (2000) (E); John T. Hubbell and James W. Geary, eds., *Biographical Dictionary of the Union* (1995) (BA); David C. Roller and Robert W. Twyman, eds., *The Encyclopedia of Southern History* (1979) (E); Jon L. Wakelyn, ed., *Biographical Dictionary of the Confederacy* (1977) (BA); Steven E. Woodworth, ed., *The American Civil War* (1996) (B).

Coast Guard, U.S.: Irving H. King, *The Coast Guard Expands* (1996), *The Coast Guard Under Sail* (1989), and *George Washington's Coast Guard* (1978); Robert E. Johnson, *Blood Stained Sea* (2004) and *Guardians of the Sea* (1987).

Cold War: Thomas S. Arms, *Encyclopedia of the Cold War* (1994) (E); H. W. Brands, *The Devil We Knew* (1993); John Lewis Gaddis, *We Now Know* (1997) and *The Cold War* (2005); Michael H. Hunt, *The World Transformed* (2004); Michael Kort, *The Columbia Guide to the Cold War* (2001) (E); Walter LaFeber, *America, Russia, and the Cold War* (2001); Tom Lansfors, *Historical Dictionary of the Cold War* (2007) (E); Melvyn P. Leffler, *For the Soul of Mankind* (2007); Ralph B. Levering, *The Cold War* (2005); Ralph B. Levering et al., *Debating the Origins of the Cold War* (2002); Wilford Loth, *Overcoming the Cold War* (2002); Thomas J. McCormick, *America's Half-Century* (1995); Robert J. McMahon, *The Cold War* (2003); Wilson D. Miscamble, *From Roosevelt to Truman* (2007); Richard Schwartz, *Cold War Culture* (E) (1998); Joseph Smith and Simon Davis, *Historical Dictionary of the Cold War* (E) (2000); Thomas G. Paterson, *Meeting the Communist Threat* (1988) and *On Every Front* (1992); Odd Arne Westad, *The Global Cold War* (2008); Vladislav M. Zubok, *A Failed Empire* (2007). See also "Disarmament and Arms Control," "Nuclear Arms," "Russia and the Soviet Union," and "Threat Perception and Calculation."

Communications: James L. Baughman, *The Republic of Mass Culture* (1992); Menahem Blondheim, *New Over the Wires* (1994); David H. Culbert, *News for Everyman* (1976) (radio); Wilson Dizard, Jr., *Digital Diplomacy* (2001); Paul R. Edwards, *The Closed World* (1996) (computers); Howard H. Frederick, *Global Communications and International Relations* (1992); Bradley S. Greenberg, ed., *Communication and Terrorism* (2001); Julian Hale, *Radio Power* (1975); Elizabeth C. Hanson, *The Information Revolution and World Politics* (2008); Daniel R. Headrick, *The Invisible Weapon* (1991); David Paull Nickles, *Under the Wire* (2003); James G. Savage, *The Politics of International Telecommunications Regulation* (1989); James Schwoch, *The American Radio Industry and Its Latin American Activities* (1990); Philip M. Taylor, *Global Communications* (1997).

Congress (House and Senate): Betty Austin, *J. William Fulbright* (1995) (B); David M. Barrett, *The CIA and Congress* (2005); Stephen G. Christianson, *Facts About the Congress* (1996); Congressional Quarterly, *Biographical Directory of the American Congress* (1997) (BA) and *Congress and the Nation, 1945–1984* (1965–1985) (E); Robert U. Goehlert and John R. Sayre, *The United States Congress* (1981) (B); Lewis L. Gould, *The Most Exclusive Club* (2005) (Senate); Ronald L. Hatzenbeuhler and Robert L. Ivie, *Congress Declares War* (1983); Barbara Hinckley, *Less Than Meets the Eye* (1994); Robert David Johnson, *Congress and the Cold War* (2006); James M. Lindsey, *Congress and the Politics of U.S. Foreign Policy* (1994); Goran Rystad, ed., *Congress and American Foreign Policy* (1982); U.S. Congress, *Biographical Directory of the United States Congress, 1774–1989* (1989) (BA); Gerald F. Warburg, *Conflict and Consensus* (1989); Stephen R. Weissman, *A Culture of Deference* (1995).

Constitution and Constitutional Interpretation: David G. Adler and Larry N. George, eds., *The Constitution and American Foreign Policy*

(1996); Henry B. Cox, *War, Foreign Affairs, and Constitutional Power, 1829–1901* (1984); Louis Fischer, *Constitutional Conflicts Between the President and Congress* (1985); Thomas M. Franck and Michael J. Glennon, *Foreign Relations and National Security Law* (1993); Louis Henkin, *Constitutionalism, Democracy, and Foreign Affairs* (1990) and *Foreign Affairs and the United States Constitution* (1996); Harold Honggju Koh, *The National Security Constitution* (1990); Leonard W. Levy et al., eds., *Encyclopedia of the American Constitution* (1986) (E); Gordon Silberstein, *Imbalance of Powers* (1997); Joan E. Smith, *The Constitution and American Foreign Policy* (1989); Abraham Sofaer, *War, Foreign Affairs, and Constitutional Power* (1976).

Containment: Terry L. Deibel and John Lewis Gaddis, eds., *Containment* (1986); John Lewis Gaddis, *Strategies of Containment* (2005); Charles Gati, ed., *Caging the Bear* (1974); Deborah Larson, *Origins of Containment* (1985).

Counterinsurgency: Benjamin R. Beede, *Intervention and Counterinsurgency* (1984) (B); Douglas S. Blaufarb, *The Counterinsurgency Era* (1977); Larry E. Cable, *Conflict of Myths* (1986); Anthony James Joes, *America and Guerrilla Warfare* (2000); Gil Merom, *How Democracies Lose Small Wars* (2003); Michael T. Klare and Peter Kornbluh, eds., *Low-Intensity Warfare* (1988); Michael McClintock, *Instruments of Statecraft* (1992); D. Michael Shafer, *Deadly Paradigms* (1988).

Credibility: Robert J. McMahon, "Credibility and World Power," *Diplomatic History, XV* (Fall 1991), 455–471; Jonathan Mercer, *Reputation and International Politics* (1996).

Cultural Relations: Christian G. Appy, ed., *Cold War Constructions* (2000); Jongsuk Chay, ed., *Culture and International Relations* (1990); Heidi Fehrenbach and Uta G. Poiger, eds., *Transactions, Transgressions, and Transformations* (2000); Jessica C. E. Gienow-Hecht, *Transmission Impossible* (1999); Petra Goedde, *GIs and Germans* (2003); Gilbert G. Gonzales, *Culture of Empire* (2004); Akira Iriye, *Cultural Internationalism and World Order* (1997); Robert D. Johnson, ed., *On Cultural Ground* (1994); Gilbert M. Joseph et al., eds., *Close Encounters of Empire* (1998); Amy Kaplan and Donald E. Pease, eds., *Cultures of United States Imperialism* (1993); Michael Krenn, *Fall-out Shelters for the Human Spirit* (2005); Rob Kroes, *If You've Seen One You've Seen the Mall* (1996); Peter J. Kuznick and James Gilbert, eds., *Rethinking Cold War Culture* (2001); Naima Prevots, *Dance for Export* (1998); Uta G. Poiger, *Jazz, Rock, and Rebels* (2000); Yale Richmond, *Cultural Exchange and the Cold War* (2003); Emily Rosenberg, *Spreading the American Dream* (1982); Frances Sauders, *The Cultural Cold War* (1999); Leonard Sussman, *The Culture of Freedom* (1992); Penny Von Eschen, *Satchmo Blows Up the World* (2004); Reinhold Wagnleitner and Elaine T. May, eds., *"Here, There, and Everywhere": The Foreign Politics of American Popular Culture* (2000).

Decolonization: Franz Ansprenger, *The Dissolution of Colonial Empires* (1989); Prosser Gifford and William Roger Louis, eds., *Decolonization and African Independence* (1988); D. A. Low, *Eclipse of Empire* (1991); David P. Newsom, *Imperial Mantle* (2001); David Ryan and Victor Pugong, eds., *The United States and Decolonization* (2000); Hendrik Spruyt, *Ending Empire* (2005); Brian Urquhart, *Decolonization and World Peace* (1989).

Department of State, Foreign Service, and Diplomatic Practice: Robert Dean, *Imperial Brotherhood* (2001); Robert U. Goehlert and Elizabeth Hoffmeister, *The Department of State and American Diplomacy* (1986) (B); Charles S. Kennedy, *The American Consul* (1990); Henry E. Mattox, *The Twilight of Amateur Diplomacy* (1989); Edward S. Mihalkanin, *American Statesmen* (2004); Robert H. Miller et al., *Inside an Embassy* (1992); Cathal Nolan, ed., *Notable U.S. Ambassadors Since 1775* (1998); Elmer Plischke, *United States Diplomats and Their Mission* (1979) and *U.S. Department of State* (1999); Martin Weil, *A Pretty Good Club* (1978); Richard H. Werking, *The Master Architects* (1977).

Dependency: Fernando Henrique Cardoso and Enzo Faletto, *Dependency and Development in Latin America* (1979); Andre Gunder Frank, *Capitalism and Underdevelopment in Latin America* (1967); Vincent A. Mahler, Dependency Approaches to International Political Economy (1980); Robert A. Packenham, *The Dependency Movement* (1992); Richard Peet, *Theories of Development* (1999).

Deterrence: Alexander L. George and Richard Smoke, *Deterrence in American Foreign Policy* (1974); Ted Hopf, *Peripheral Visions* (1994); Robert Jervis et al., *Psychology and Deterrence* (1985); Derek Smith, *Deterring America* (2006).

Dictatorships: H. E. Chehabi and Juan J. Linz, *Sultanistic Regimes* (1998); Ernest R. May, et al., *Dealing With Dictators* (2006); David F. Schmitz, *Thank God They're on Our Side* (1999) and *The United States and Right-Wing Dictatorships, 1965–1989* (2006).

Diplomatic Immunity: Linda S. Frey and Marsha L. Frey, *The History of Diplomatic Immunity* (1999); Grant V. McClanahan, *Diplomatic Immunity* (1989).

Disarmament and Arms Control: Sheikh Rustum Aki, *The Peace and Nuclear War Dictionary* (1989) (E); Stephen E. Atkins, *Arms Control and Disarmament* (1989) (B); Richard Dean Burns, ed., *Encyclopedia of Arms Control and Disarmament* (1993) (E); Jeffrey M. Elliot and Robert Reginald, *The Arms Control, Disarmament, and Military Security Dictionary* (1989) (E); Milton S. Katz, *Ban the Bomb* (1986); Jeffrey A. Larson and James M. Smith, eds., *Historical Dictionary of Arms Control and Disarmament* (2005) (D); Kendrick Oliver, *Kennedy, MacMillan, and the*

Nuclear Test Ban Treaty, 1961–63 (1998); Henry D. Sokoloski, *Best of Intentions* (2001); Stockholm International Peace Research Institute, *SIPRI Yearbook: International Armaments and Disarmament* (1969–) (AS and S); David Tal, *The American Nuclear Disarmament Dilemma, 1945–1963* (2008) United Nations, *Disarmament Yearbook* (1976–) (AS); Lawrence S. Wittner, *The Struggle Against the Bomb* (1993–2003).

Dollar Diplomacy: Emily S. Rosenberg, *Missionaries to the World* (1999); Cyrus Veeser, *A World Safe for Capitalism* (2002).

Drug Trafficking: Bruce M. Bagley, ed., *Drug Trafficking Research in the Americas* (1997) (B); Ted Galen Carpenter, *Bad Neighbor Policy* (2003); Richard Crandall, *Driven by Drugs* (2002); Jurg Gerber and Eric L. Benson, *Drug War, American Style* (2001); Donald J. Mabry, ed., *The Latin American Narcotics Trade and U.S. National Security* (1989); Scott B. MacDonald and Bruce Zagaris, eds., *International Handbook on Drug Control* (1992) (E); Alfred W. McCoy, *The Politics of Heroin* (2003) and *War on Drugs* (1992); Katherine Meyer and Terry Parssinen, *Webs of Smoke* (2002); Peter Dale Scott, *Drugs, Oil, and War* (2002); Arnold H. Taylor, *American Diplomacy and the Narcotics Traffic, 1900–1931* (1969); William O. Walker III, *Drug Control in the Americas* (1981), ed., *Drugs in the Western Hemisphere* (1996), and *Opium and Foreign Policy* (1991).

Economic Relations and Business: William H. Becker and Samuel F. Wells, eds., *Economics and World Power* (1984); Alfred E. Eckes, Jr., *Opening America's Market* (1995); Niall Ferguson, *The Ascent of Money* (2008); Dana Frank, *Buy American* (1999); Michael J. Freeman, *Atlas of the World Economy* (1991) (A); Francis J. Gavin, *Gold, Dollars, and Power* (2003); Carolyn Gibson, *The McGraw-Hill Dictionary of International Trade* (1994) (E); Robert Gilpin, *Global Political Economy* (2002); Judith Goldstein, *Ideas, Interests, and American Trade Policy* (1993); Bernard Hoekman and Michel Kostecki, *The Political Economy of the World Trading System* (1996); John N. Ingham, *Biographical Dictionary of American Business Leaders* (1983) (BA); John N. Ingham and Lyness B. Feldman, *Contemporary American Business Leaders* (1990) (BA); Edward S. Kaplan and Thomas W. Ryley, *Prelude to Trade Wars* (1994); Diane Kunz, *Butter and Guns* (1997); Thelma Liesner, *One Hundred Years of Economic Statistics* (1989) (S); Charles R. Morris, *The Trillion Dollar Meltdown* (2008); Wahib Nasrallah, *United States Corporation Histories* (1991) (B); Timothy O'Donnell et al., eds., *World Economic Data* (1991) (S); James S. Olsen, *Dictionary of American Economic History* (1992) (E); Robert Soloman, *Money on the Move* (1999); Joan E. Spero and Jeffrey A. Hart, *The Politics of International Economic Relations* (1997); Amy Staples, *The Birth of Development* (2007); United Nations, *International Trade Statistics Yearbook* (1985– (AS and S), *World Economic Survey* (1955–) (AS and S), and *Yearbook of International Trade Statistics* (1950–1982) (AS and S); Malcolm Warner, ed., *International Encyclopedia of Business and Management* (1996) (E); Mira Wilkins, *The Emergence of Multinational Enterprise* (1970) and *The Maturing of Multinational Enterprise* (1975); Thomas W. Zeiler, *Free Trade, Free World* (1999).

Economic Sanctions and Export Controls: Alan P. Dobson, *U.S. Economic Statecraft for Survival, 1933-1999* (2002); Gary C. Hufbauer and Jeffrey J. Schott, *Economic Sanctions Reconsidered* (1990); William J. Long, *U.S. Export Control Policy* (1989); Donald Losman, *International Economic Sanctions* (1979); Homer E. Moyer, Jr., and Linda L. Mabry, *Export Controls as Instruments of Foreign Policy* (1988); R. T. Naylor, *Economic Warfare* (2001); Meghan O'Sullivan, *Shrewd Sanctions* (2003); Thomas G. Weiss, *Political Gain and Civilian Pain* (1998); Ka Zeng, *Trade Threats, Trade Wars* (2004).

Environment: Scott Barrett, *Environment and Statecraft* (2003); Lee-Anne Broadhead, *International Environmental Politics* (2002); Robert Broadman, *International Organization and the Conservation of Nature* (1981); Lester R. Brown et al., *State of the World* (1984–) (AS); Lynton K. Caldwell, *International Environmental Policy* (1990); André R. Cooper, Sr., ed., *Cooper's Comprehensive Environmental Desk Reference* (1996) (E); Kurkpatrick Dorsey, *The Dawn of Conservation Diplomacy* (1999); Thomas Friedman, *Hot, Flat, and Crowded* (2008); Michael T. Klare, *Rising Powers, Shrinking Planet* (2008); Fridtjof Nansen Institute (Norway), *Green Globe Yearbook* (1992–) (AS); John McCormick, *The Global Environment* (1995) and *Reclaiming Paradise: The Global Environmental Movement* (1989); Organisation for Economic Co-operation and Development, *The State of the Environment* (1991) (E and S); Robert Paehlke, ed., *Conservation and Environmentalism* (1995) (E); Kirkpatrick Sale, *The Green Revolution* (1993); Philip Shabecoff, *Earth Rising* (2000); Richard P. Tucker, *Insatiable Appetite* (2007); World Resources Institute, *Environmental Almanac* (1992) (E); World Resources Institute (or International Institute for Environment and Development), *World Resources* (1976–); Ernest Zedillo, ed., *Global Warming* (2008).

Ethics: Gerald Elfstrom, *Ethics for a Shrinking World* (1990); J. E. Hare and Carey B. Joynt, *Ethics and International Affairs* (1982); Dorothy V. Jones, *Code of Peace* (1991); Kenneth W. Thompson, ed., *Ethics and International Relations* (1985) and *Moral Dimensions of American Foreign Policy* (1984).

Ethnic Conflict: David Callahan, *Unwinnable Wars* (1997); Human Rights Watch, *Slaughter Among Neighbors* (1995); David A. Lake and Donald Rothchild, eds., *The International Spread of Ethnic Conflict* (1998); Robin M. Williams, Jr., *Wars Within* (2003); Stefan Wolff, *Ethnic Conflict* (2006).

Ethnic Groups and Immigration: Gerald Chaliand and Jean-Pierre Rageau, *The Penguin Atlas of Diasporas* (1995) (A); Francesco Cordasco, ed., *Dictionary of American Immigration History* (1990) (E);

Alexander DeConde, *Ethnicity, Race, and American Foreign Policy* (1992); Izumi Hirobe, *Japanese Pride, American Prejudice* (2001); R. Kent Rasmussen, ed., *Immigration in U.S. History* (2006); David M. Reimers, *Still the Golden Door* (1992); Abdul Aziz Said, ed., *Ethnicity and U.S. Foreign Policy* (1977); Tony Smith, *Foreign Attachments* (2000); Stephen Thernstrom, ed., *Harvard Encyclopedia of American Ethnic Groups* (1980) (E); Robert W. Tucker et al., eds., *Immigration and U.S. Foreign Policy* (1990).

Expansion: See "Imperialism," "Manifest Destiny and Imperialism," and "West (U.S) and Frontier."

Export-Import Bank: Frederick C. Adams, *Economic Diplomacy* (1976); William H. Becker, *The Market, the State, and the Export-Import Bank of the United States, 1934–2000* (2003); Richard E. Feinberg, *Subsidizing Success* (1982); Rita M. Rodriquez, ed., *The Export-Import Bank at Fifty* (1987).

Extraterritoriality: Wesley R. Fishel, *The End of Extraterritoriality* (1952); Dietr Lange and Gary Born, eds., *The Extraterritorial Application of National Laws* (1987); Elaine Scully, *Bargaining with the State from Afar* (2001).

Films, Television, and Cultural Expansion: Royce J. Ammon, *Global Television and the Shaping of World Politics* (1999); Robert Burgoyne, *Film Nation* (1997); David A. Cook, *Lost Illusions* (2000); Thomas Doherty, *Cold War, Cool Medium* (2003) and *Projections of War* (1999); Susan Jeffords, *Hard Bodies* (1993); James F. Larson, *Global Television and Foreign Policy* (1988); Thomas J. Saunders, *Hollywood in Berlin* (1994); Robert Brent Toplin, *Reel History* (2002).

Food Diplomacy and Relief: Kristin L. Ahlberg, *Transplanting the Great Society* (2008); Nicole Ball, ed., *World Hunger* (1981) (B); Raymond F. Hopkins and Donald J. Puchala, *Global Food Interdependence* (1980); Don Paarlberg, *Toward a Well-Fed World* (1988); Vernon W. Ruttan, ed., *Why Food Aid?* (1993); Hans W. Sinder et al., *Food Aid* (1987); Claire Stanford, ed., *World Hunger* (2007); Ross B. Talbott, *The Four World Food Agencies in Rome* (1990).

Foreign Aid: David H. Lumsdaine, *Moral Vision in International Politics* (1993); Robert A. Packenham, *Liberal America and the Third World* (1973); Roger Riddell, *Foreign Aid Reconsidered* (1987); Vernon W. Ruttan, *United States Development Assistance Policy* (1995).

Foreign Investment in the United States: Mira Wilkins, *The History of Foreign Investment in the United States to 1914* (1989).

French and Indian War: Fred Anderson, *Crucible of War* (2001); Frank W. Brecher, *Losing a Continent* (1998); Ronald J. Dale, *The Fall of New France* (2004); Jonathan Dull, *The French Navy and the Seven Years' War* (2005); Frank McLynn, *1759* (2004); Matt Schumann and Karl W. Schweizer, *The Seven Years' War* (2008); Seymour I. Schwartz, *The French and Indian War, 1754–1763* (1995) (E); Franz A.J. Szabo, *The Seven Years' War in Europe, 1756–1763* (2008).

Genocide: Patrick Brantlinger, *Dark Vanishings* (2003); Israel Charney, ed., *Genocide* (1988) (B) and *Encyclopedia of Genocide* (1999) (E); Ben Kiernan, *Blood and Soil* (2007); Leo Kuper, *Genocide* (1981); Lawrence J. LeBlanc, *The United States and the Genocide Convention* (1991); Samantha Power, *The Problem from Hell* (2002); Charles B. Stroozier and Michael Flynn, eds., *Genocide, War, and Human Survival* (1996); Benjamin A. Valentino, *Final Solutions* (2004). See also "Holocaust," "Humanitarian Relief and Intervention," and "War Crimes and Trials."

Good Neighbor Policy: Irwin Gellman, *Good Neighbor Diplomacy* (1979); David Green, *The Containment of Latin America* (1971); Fredrick B. Pike, *FDR's Good Neighbor Policy* (1995); Bryce Wood, *The Dismantling of the Good Neighbor Policy* (1985).

Health and Medical History of Leaders: Kenneth R. Crispell and Carlos F. Gomez, *Hidden Illness in the White House* (1988); Robert H. Ferrell, *Ill-Advised* (1992); Robert E. Gilbert, *The Mortal Presidency* (1992); Bert E. Park, *Ailing, Aged, Addicted* (1993) and *The Impact of Illness on World Leaders* (1986).

Health Organizations: Kelly Lee, *Historical Dictionary of the World Health Organization* (1998) (E); Javid Siddiqi, *World Health and World Politics* (1994); Paul Weindling, ed., *International Health Organizations and Movements* (1995).

Holocaust: Yehudi Bauer, *Rethinking the Holocaust* (2001); Richard Breitman, *Official Secrets* (1998); Richard Breitman and Alan M. Kraut, *American Refugee Policy and European Jewry* (1987); Henry L. Feingold, *Bearing Witness* (1995); Saul Friedlander, *The Years of Extermination* (2007); Martin Gilbert, *Auschwitz and the Allies* (1981); Israel Gutman, ed., *Encyclopedia of the Holocaust* (1990) (E); Deborah E. Lipstadt, *Beyond Belief* (1993); Michael R. Marrus, *The Holocaust in History* (1987); David Wyman, *The Abandonment of the Jews* (1984) and *Paper Walls* (1968).

Hostage-Taking: Russell D. Buhite, *Lives at Risk* (1995); David R. Farber, *Taken Hostage* (2005); David P. Houghton, *U.S. Foreign Policy and the Iran Hostage Crisis* (2001); Russell Lee Moses, *Freeing the Hostages* (1996).

Humanitarian Relief and Intervention: Gary J. Best, *Freedom's Battle* (2008); Robert C. DiPrizo, *Armed Humanitarians* (2002); David

Kennedy, *The Dark Side of Virtue* (2004); Larry Minear and Thomas G. Weiss, *Humanitarian Politics* (1995); David Rieff, *Bed for the Night* (2002); Robert I. Rotberg and Thomas G. Weiss, eds., *From Massacres to Genocide* (1996).

Human Rights: Amnesty International, *The Amnesty International Report* (1977–) (AS); Elizabeth Borgwardt, *A New Deal for the World* (2007); Peter R. Baehr, *The Role of Human Rights in Foreign Policy* (1994); Jack Donnelly and Rhoda E. Howard, eds., *International Handbook of Human Rights* (1987) (E); Carole Fink, *Defending the Rights of Others* (2007); Charles Humana, *World Human Rights Guide* (1992); Human Rights Watch, *World Report* (1983–) (AS); Michael Ignatieff, *American Exceptionalism and Human Rights* (2005); Natalie Kaufman, *Human Rights Treaties and the Senate* (1990); William Korey, *The Promises We Keep* (1993); Edward Lawson, *Encyclopedia of Human Rights* (1991) (E); A. Glenn Mower, *Human Rights and American Foreign Policy* (1987) and *The United States, the United Nations, and Human Rights* (1979); A. H. Robertson and J. G. Merrills, *Human Rights in the World* (1997) (B); Roger Normand and Sarah Zaidi, *Human Rights at the UN* (2008); David Robertson, *A Dictionary on Human Rights* (2004) (E); Lars Schoultz, *Human Rights and United States Policy Toward Latin America* (1981); Kathryn Sikkink, *Mixed Signals* (2004).

Ideology: Richard J. Barnet, *Roots of War* (1972); David C. Engerman, *Staging Growth* (2003); John Fousek, *To Lead the Free World* (2002); Joan Hoff, *A Faustian Foreign Policy* (2008); Richard T. Hughes, *Myths America Lives By* (2003); Michael H. Hunt, *Ideology and U.S. Foreign Policy* (1987); Jacob Heilbrun, *They Knew They Were Right* (2008) (neo-conservatives); Christina Klein, *Cold War Orientalism* (2003); Michael E. Latham, *Modernization as Ideology* (2000); Ron Robin, *The Making of the Cold War Enemy* (2001); William A. Williams, *The Tragedy of American Diplomacy* (1962); Nicholas Xenos, *Cloaked in Virtue* (2008).

Imperialism: Michael B. Brown, *The Economics of Imperialism* (1974); Philip Darby, *Three Faces of Imperialism* (1987); Michael Doyle, *Empires* (1986); Niall Ferguson, *Empire* (2003) and *Colossus* (2006); Peter L. Hahn and Mary Ann Heiss, eds., *Empire and Revolution* (2001); Eric Hinderaker, *Elusive Empires* (1997); Amy Kaplan, *The Anarchy of Empire in the Making of U.S. Culture* (2002); Gabriel Kolko, *The Roots of American Foreign Policy* (1969); Frank Ninkovich, *The United States and Imperialism* (2001); Marc J. O'Reilly, *Unexceptional* (2008); Tony Smith, *The Pattern of Imperialism* (1981).

Indians (Native Americans): Brian W. Dippie, *The Vanishing American* (1982); Michael Green, *The Politics of Indian Removal* (1982); Barry Klein, ed., *Reference Encyclopedia of the American Indian* (1993) (E); Calvin Martin, ed., *The American Indian and the Problem of History* (1986); Jane T. Merritt, *At the Crossroads* (2003);

Francis Paul Prucha, *Atlas of American Indian Affairs* (1990) (A) and *The Indian in American Society* (1985); Jayme Sokolow, *The Great Encounter* (2002); Paul Stuart, *Nation Within a Nation* (1987) (S); Carl Waldman, *Atlas of the North American Indian* (1985) (A); Anthony F. C. Wallace, *Jefferson and the Indians* (2001); Philip Weeks, *"They Made Us Many Promises"* (2002).

Intelligence, CIA, and Covert Action: David Alvarez, *Secret Messages* (2000); Christopher Andrew, *For the President's Eyes Only* (1995); Christopher Andrew and Vasili Mitrokhin, *The World Was Going Our Way* (2005); T. H. Bagley, *Spy Wars* (2007); James Bamford, *Body of Secrets* (2001) and *The Shadow Factory* (2008); Richard Breitman, *U.S. Intelligence and the Nazis* (2005); Marjorie W. Cline et al., *Scholar's Guide to Intelligence Literature* (1983) (B); Steve Coll, *Ghost Wars* (2004); George C. Constantinides, *Intelligence & Espionage* (1983) (B); Arthur B. Darling, *The Central Intelligence Agency* (1990); John Diamond, *The CIA and the Culture of Failure* (2008); William J. Daugherty, *Executive Secrets* (2004); Melvin A. Goodman, *The Failure of Intelligence* (2008); Kristian Gustafson, *Hostile Intent* (2007); John Earl Haynes, *Early Cold War Spies* (2006); Rhodri Jeffreys-Jones, *The CIA and American Democracy* (2003) and *Cloak and Dollar* (2002); Rhodri Jeffreys-Jones and Andrew Lownie, eds., *North American Spies* (1991); Loch K. Johnson, *Secret Agencies* (1996) and *Bombs, Bugs, Drugs, and Thugs* (2000); Loch Johnson and James Wirtz, eds., *Intelligence and National Security* (2007); Stephen Kinzer, *Overthrow* (2006); Stephen F. Knott, *Secret and Sanctioned* (1996); Mark Lowenthal, *U.S. Intelligence* (1992); Thomas Mahnken, *Uncovering the Ways of War* (2002); Ernest R. May, ed., *Knowing One's Enemies* (1985); Ernest R. May et al., *Dealing with Dictators* (2006); Alfred W. McCoy, *A Question of Torture* (2006); Elizabeth McIntosh, *Sisterhood of Spies* (2009); Gregory Mitrovich, *Undermining the Kremlin* (2000); John Jacob Nutter, *CIA's Black Ops* (2008); Norman Polmar and Thomas B. Allen, *Spy Book* (2004); Neal H. Petersen, *American Intelligence, 1775–1990* (1992) (B); Walter Pforzheimer, *Bibliography of Intelligence Literature* (1985) (B); Thomas Powers, *Intelligence Wars* (2003); John Prados, *The Presidents' Secret Wars* (1986) and *Safe for Democracy* (2006); John Ranelagh, *The Agency* (1986); James Risen, *State of War* (2006); Jeffrey T. Richelson, *A Century of Spies* (1995), *Spying on the Bomb* (2006), and *The U.S. Intelligence Community* (1995); Frank J. Smist, Jr., *Congress Oversees the United States Intelligence Community* (1994); Bradley F. Smith, *The Shadow Warriors* (1983); Michael J. Sullivan, *American Adventurism Abroad* (2008); William Taubman, *Secret Empire* (2003); Athan Theoharis, *The Quest for Absolute Security* (2007); Evan Thomas, *The Very Best Men* (1995); Gregory F. Treverton, *Covert Action* (1987); David Tucker and Christopher Lamb, *United States Special Operations* (2008); Nigel West, *Historical Dictionary of Cold War Counterintelligence* (2007) (E); Hugh Wilford, *The Mighty Wurlitzer* (2007); Robin W. Winks, *Clock & Gown* (1987).

International Law and Hague Conferences: Robert L. Bledsoe and Boleslaw A. Boczek, *The International Law Dictionary* (1987) (E); Calvin D. Davis, *The United States and the First Hague Conference* (1962) and *The United States and the Second Hague Conference* (1976); Ingrid Delupis, ed., *Bibliography of International Law* (1975) (B); Richard Falk et al., eds., *International Law* (1985); James Fox, *Dictionary of International and Comparative Law* (1991) (E); Daniel P. Moynihan, *The Law of Nations* (1990).

International Monetary Fund and System: Michael N. Barnett, *Rules for the World* (2004); Barry Eichengreen, *Globalizing Capital* (1996); Harold James, *International Monetary Cooperation Since Bretton Woods* (1996); Mary E. Johnson, *The International Monetary Fund* (1993) (B); Robert Soloman, *Money on the Move* (1999); Jean Tirole, *Financial Crises, Liquidity, and the International Monetary Fund System* (2002); Ngaire Woods, *The Globalizers* (2006).

International Organizations: Sheikh Ali, *The International Organization and World Order Dictionary* (1992) (E); John Boli and George M. Thomas, eds., *Constructing World Culture* (1999); George W. Baer, ed., *International Organizations, 1918–1945* (1981) (B); Akira Iriye, *Global Community* (2002); Edward C. Luck, *Mixed Messages* (1999); Edward J. Osmanczyk, *The Encyclopedia of the United States and International Organizations* (1990) (E); Hans-Albrecht Schraepler, *Directory of International Organizations* (1996); Union of International Associations, *Yearbook of International Organizations* (1948–) (AS).

Isolationism: Wayne S. Cole, *Roosevelt and the Isolationists* (1983); Justus D. Doenecke, *Anti-Intervention* (1987) (B), *The Battle Against Intervention, 1939–1941* (1997), and *Storm on the Horizon* (2001); Thomas N. Guinsburg, *The Pursuit of Isolationism in the United States Senate* (1982); Manfred Jonas, *Isolationism in America, 1935–1941* (1966).

Journalism and Media: James L. Baughman, *Henry R. Luce and the Rise of the American News Media* (1988); Robert Herzstein, *Henry R. Luce* (1994) and *Henry R. Luce, Time, and the American Crusade in Asia* (2005); Gerd Horten, *Radio Goes to War* (2002); Joseph P. McKerns, ed., *Biographical Dictionary of American Journalism* (1989) (BA); Brigitte Lebens Nacos, *The Press, Presidents, and Crises* (1990); Johanna Neuman, *Lights, Camera, War* (1995); David D. Permutter, *Photojournalism and Foreign Policy* (1998); Arch Puddington, *Broadcasting Freedom* (2000); Michael Schudson, *The Power of News* (1995); Simon Serfaty, *The Media and Foreign Policy* (1990); Michael S. Sweeney, *Secrets of Victory* (2000); William H. Taft, ed., *Encyclopedia of Twentieth-Century Journalists* (1986) (BA); John Tebbel and Sarah Miles Watts, *The Press and the Presidency* (1985).

Labor: Robert W. Cherny and William Issel, *American Labor and the Cold War* (2004); Philip S. Foner, *U.S. Labor Movement and Latin America* (1988); Ronald Radosh, *American Labor and United States Foreign Policy* (1969); Federico Romero, *The United States and the European Trade Union Movement, 1944–1951* (1992); Shelton Stromquist, ed., *Labor's Cold War* (2008); Edmund F. Wehrle, *Between a River and a Mountain* (2005).

Law of the Sea: Jack N. Barkenbus, *Deep Seabed Resources* (1979); Ann L. Hollick, *U.S. Foreign Policy and the Law of the Sea* (1981); Ralph B. Levering and Miriam L. Levering, *Citizen Action for Global Change* (2002); D. P. O'Connell, *The International Law of the Sea* (1982); Clyde Sanger, *Ordering the Oceans* (1987); United Nations, *The Law of the Sea* (1991) (B); Harry N. Scheiber, ed., *The Law of the Sea* (2000).

League of Nations: John Milton Cooper, *Breaking the Heart of the World* (2001); Warren F. Kuehl, *Seeking World Order* (1969); F. S. Northedge, *The League of Nations* (1986).

Manifest Destiny and Expansion: Laura E. Gomez, *Manifest Destinies* (2007); Amy S. Greenberg, *Manifest Manhood and the Antebellum American Empire* (2005); Thomas R. Hietala, *Manifest Design* (2003); Reginald Horsman, *Race and Manifest Destiny* (1981); Linda S. Hudson, *Mistress of Manifest Destiny* (2001); Robert W. Johannsen, ed., *Manifest Destiny* (1998); Robert E. May, *Manifest Destiny's Underworld* (2002); Christopher Morris and Sam W. Haynes, eds., *Manifest Destiny and Empire* (1998); Ivan Musicant, *Empire by Default* (1998); Frank Ninkovich, *The United States and Imperialism* (2001); Walter Nugent, *Habits of Empire* (2008); Anders Stephanson, *Manifest Destiny* (1995); Albert K. Weinberg, *Manifest Destiny* (1935).

Marshall Plan: John Bledsoe Bonds, *Bipartisan Strategy* (2002); Michael J. Hogan, *The Marshall Plan* (1987); Brian McKenzie, *Remaking France* (2005); Alan S. Milward, *The Reconstruction of Western Europe, 1945–51* (1984); Martin A. Schain, ed., *The Marshall Plan* (2001); Imanuel Wexler, *The Marshall Plan Revisited* (1983).

Marine Corps, U.S.: Joseph H. Alexander et al., *A Fellowship of Valor* (1997); Allan R. Millett, *Semper Fidelis* (1980).

Merchant Marine: John A. Butler, *Sailing on Friday* (1997); Rene De La Pedraja, *A Historical Dictionary of the U.S. Merchant Marine and Shipping Industry* (1994) (E).

Military, U.S. Army, and Wars: William M. Arkin et al., *Encyclopedia of the U.S. Military* (1990) (E); Andrew Bacevich, *The Limits of Power* (2008); Benjamin R. Beede, *Military and Strategic Policy* (1990) (B); Susan Brewer, *Why America Fights* (2009); John W. Chambers, *To Raise an Army* (1987) and *Oxford Companion to American Military History* (1999) (E); Edward M. Coffman, *The Regulars* (2005);

E. Ernest Dupuy and Trevor N. Dupuy, *The Harper Encyclopedia of Military History* (1993) (E); John C. Fredriksen, *Shield of the Republic/Sword of Empire* (1990) (B); Kenneth J. Hagan and William R. Roberts, eds., *Against All Enemies* (1986); Christopher Layne, *The Peace of Illusions* (2006); Robin Higham and Donald J. Mrozek, eds., *A Guide to the Sources of United States Military History* (1975–) (B); International Institute for Strategic Studies, *Strategic Survey* (1966–) (AS) and *The Military Balance* (1959/1960–) (AS); *International Military and Defense Encyclopedia* (1993) (E); John E. Jessup and Louise B. Ketz, eds., *Encyclopedia of the American Military* (1994) (E); Michael Lind, *The American Way of Strategy* (2008); Brian M. Linn, *The Echo of Battle* (2008); Allan R. Millett and Peter Maslowski, *For the Common Defense* (1994); Jay M. Shafritz et al., eds., *Dictionary of Military Science* (1989); Roger J. Spiller and Joseph G. Dawson III, eds., *Dictionary of American Military Biography* (1984) (BA); Jerry K. Sweeney, ed., *A Handbook of American Military History* (1996) (E); Herbert K. Tillema, *International Armed Conflict Since 1945* (1991) (B); Peter G. Tsouras et al., *The United States Army* (1991) (E); Cynthia Watson, *U.S. National Security Policy Groups* (1990) (E); Russell F. Weigley, *History of the United States Army* (1984).

Minerals: Alfred E. Eckes, *The United States and the Global Struggle for Minerals* (1979); Jordan E. Helmreich, *Gathering Rare Ores* (1986); David Hollett, *More Precious Than Gold* (2008); Mark Kurlansky, *Salt: A World History* (2002); Ronnie Lipschutz, *When Nations Clash* (1989).

Missionaries: Henry Bowden, *Dictionary of American Religious Biography* (1993) (BA); John K. Fairbank, ed., *The Missionary Enterprise in China and America* (1974); Gael Graham, *Gender, Culture, and Christianity* (1995); Patricia Hill, *The World Their Household* (1985); Jane Hunter, *The Gospel of Gentility* (1984); William R. Hutchison, *Errand to the World* (1987); Paul A. Varg, *Missionaries, Chinese, and Diplomats* (1958).

Monroe Doctrine: James E. Lewis, Jr., *The American Union and the Problem of Neighborhood* (1998); Ernest R. May, *The Making of the Monroe Doctrine* (1975); Gretchen Murphy, *Hemispheric Imaginings* (2004); Gaddis Smith, *The Last Years of the Monroe Doctrine* (1994).

Nation-Building: James Dobbins et al., *America's Role in Nation-Building* (2003); Cynthia Watson, *Nation-building* (2004).

National Security Council: Gerry Andrianopoulos, *Kissinger and Brzezinski* (1991); John Prados, *Keepers of the Keys* (1991); David Rothkopf, *Running the World* (2005); Andrew Preston, *War Council* (2006); Douglas Stuart, *Creating the National Security State* (2008); Bromley K. Smith, *Organizational History of the National Security Council During the Kennedy and Johnson Administrations* (1988).

Navy, U.S., and Sea Power: George W. Baer, *One Hundred Years of Sea Power* (1994); James C. Bradford, *Admirals of the New Steel Navy* (1990), *Captains of the Old Steam Navy* (1986), and *Command Under Sail* (1985); William B. Cogan, *Dictionary of Admirals of the United States Navy* (1989) (BA); Paolo E. Coletta, *A Selected and Annotated Bibliography of American Naval History* (1988) (B); Paolo E. Coletta et al., eds., *American Secretaries of the Navy* (1980) (BA); Michael J. Crawford and Christine F. Hughes, *The Reestablishment of the Navy, 1787–1801* (1995) (B); Kenneth J. Hagan, ed., *In Peace and War* (2008) and *This People's Navy* (1991); John B. Hattendorf and Lynn C. Hattendorf, *A Bibliography of the Works of Alfred Thayer Mahan* (1986) (B); David F. Long, *Gold Braid and Foreign Relations* (1988); Barbara A. Lynch and John E. Vajda, *United States Naval History* (1993) (B); Franklin D. Margiotta, ed., *Brassey's Encyclopedia of Naval Forces and Warfare* (1996) (E); Nathaniel Philbrick, *Sea of Glory* (2003); Jack Sweetman, ed., *American Naval History* (1984) (C); Bruce W. Watson and Susan M. Watson, *The United States Navy* (1991) (E).

Neutralism and Nonalignment: H. W. Brands, *The Specter of Neutralism* (1989); K. C. Chaudhary, *Non-aligned Summitry* (1988); Steven R. David, *Choosing Sides* (1991); Richard L. Jackson, *The Non-aligned, the UN, and the Superpowers* (1983); Lawrence W. Martin, ed., *Neutralism and Nonalignment* (1962).

Nobel Peace Prize: Irwin Abrams, *The Nobel Peace Prize and the Laureates* (1988); Oaula McGuire, ed., *Nobel Prize Winners Supplement* (1992); Judith Stiehm, *Champions for Peace* (2006); Tyler Wasson, ed., *Nobel Prize Winners* (1987).

North American Free Trade Agreement (NAFTA): Maxwell A. Cameron and Brian W. Tomlin, *The Making of NAFTA* (2001); Allan Metz, *A NAFTA Bibliography* (1996) (B); John R. Macarthur, *The Selling of "Free Trade"* (2002); John S. Odell, ed., *Negotiating Trade* (2006); William A. Orme, Jr., *Understanding NAFTA* (1996); Maryse Robert, *Negotiating NAFTA* (2002); Jerry M. Rosenberg, *Encyclopedia of the North American Free Trade Agreement* (1984) (E).

North Atlantic Treaty Organization (NATO): Ronald A. Asmus, *Opening NATO's Door* (2002); Timothy Ireland, *Creating the Entangling Alliance* (1981); Robert S. Jordan, Jr., ed., *Generals in International Politics* (1987); Lawrence S. Kaplan, *NATO 1948* (2007), *NATO United, NATO Divided* (2004), and *The Long Entanglement* (1999); Augustus R. Norton et al., *NATO* (1985) (B); S. V. Papacosma et al., *NATO After Fifty Years* (2001); S. V. Papacosma and Mary Ann Heiss, *NATO and the Warsaw Pact* (2008); Joseph Smith, ed., *The Origins of NATO* (1990).

Nuclear Arms: Timothy Botti, *Ace in the Hole* (1996); Paul Boyer, *By the Bomb's Early Light* (1985); McGeorge Bundy, *Danger and*

Survival (1990); Joseph Cirincione, *Bomb Scare* (2008); Campbell Craig, *Destroying the Village* (1998); Gerard J. De Groot, *The Bomb: A Life* (2005); Robert A. Divine, *The Sputnik Challenge* (1993); Lawrence Freedman, *The Evolution of Nuclear Strategy* (1989); Gregg Herken, *Counsels of War* (1985); David Holloway, *The Soviet Union and the Arms Race* (1984); Robert S. Morris, *Racing for the Bomb* (2002); John Newhouse, *War and Peace in the Nuclear Age* (1989); Septimus Paul, *Nuclear Rivals* (2000); William G. M. Pearson, *The Nuclear Arms Race* (1989) (E); Ronald E. Powaski, *March to Armageddon* (1987) and *Return to Armageddon* (2000); Richard Rhodes, *Arsenals of Folly* (2007); Scott D. Sagan, *The Limits of Safety* (1993); Stephen I. Schwartz, ed., *Atomic Audit* (1998); S. S. Schweber, *In the Shadow of the Bomb* (2000); Richard Smoke, *National Security and the Nuclear Dilemma* (1987); Spencer R. Weart, *Nuclear Fear* (1988); Allan M. Winkler, *Life Under a Cloud* (1993).

Oil: M. A. Adelman, *The Genie out of the Bottle* (1995); Jeremy Leggett, *Carbon War* (2002); Michael T. Klare, *Blood and Oil* (2005); David S. Painter, *Oil and the American Century* (1986); Stephen J. Randall, *United States Foreign Oil Policy, 1919–1984* (1985); Anthony Sampson, *The Seven Sisters* (1991); Fiona Venn, *Oil Diplomacy in the Twentieth Century* (1986); Daniel Yergin, *The Prize* (1991).

Olympics: Allen Guttmann, *The Games Must Go On* (1984) and *The Olympics* (1992); Christopher R. Hill, *Olympic Politics* (1996); Kristine Toohey, *Olympic Games* (2000); David Wallechinsky, *The Complete Book of the Summer Olympics* (1996) (E) and *The Complete Book of the Winter Olympics* (1993) (E).

Organization of American States (OAS): David Sheinin, *The Organization of American States* (1996) (B).

Organization of Petroleum Exporting Countries (OPEC): M. E. Ahrari, *OPEC* (1986); Albert L. Danielson, *The Evolution of OPEC* (1982); Ian Skeet, *OPEC* (1988).

Peace Corps: Fritz Fischer, *Making Them Like Us* (1998); Elizabeth Cobbs Hoffman, *All You Need Is Love* (1998); T. Zane Reeves, *The Politics of the Peace Corps & Vista* (1988); Gerald T. Rice, *Bold Experiment* (1985); Robert Ridinger, *The Peace Corps* (1989) (B): D. David Searles, *The Peace Corps Experience* (1997).

Peacekeeping: Jane Boulden, *Peace Enforcement* (2002); Paul F. Diehl, *International Peacekeeping* (1993); William J. Durch, ed., *The Evolution of UN Peacekeeping* (1993); Frederick H. Fleitz, Jr., *Peacekeeping Fiascoes of the 1990s* (2002); Rachel Gisselquist, *To Rid the Scourge of War* (2003); Alan James, *Peacekeeping in International Politics* (1990); Zisk Martin, *Enforcing the Peace* (2003). William G. O'Neill, *New Challenge for Peacekeepers* (2004).

Peace Movements: Harriet Hyman Alonso, *Peace as a Women's Issue* (1993); Scott H. Bennett, *Radical Pacifism* (2003); Peter Brock, *Pacifism in the United States from the Colonial Era to the First World War* (1968); Peter Brock and Nigel Young, *Pacifism in the Twentieth Century* (1999); Charles Chatfield, *The American Peace Movement* (1992); Charles DeBenedetti, ed., *Peace Heroes in Twentieth Century America* (1986) and *The Peace Reform in American History* (1980); Matthew Evangelista, *Unarmed Forces* (1999); Michael S. Foley, *Confronting the War Machine* (2003); Catherine Foster, *Women for All Seasons* (1989); Charles F. Howlett, *The American Peace Movement* (1990) (B); Rhodri Jeffreys-Jones, *Peace Now!* (1999); Harold Josephson et al., eds., *Biographical Dictionary of Modern Peace Leaders* (1985) (BA); Robert Kleidman, *Organizing for Peace: Neutrality, the Test Ban, and the Freeze* (1993); Elvin Laszlo and Jong Youl Yoo, eds., *World Encyclopedia of Peace* (1986) (E); Robert S. Meyer, *Peace Organizations Past and Present* (1988) (E); David S. Patterson, *Toward a Warless World* (1976); Nancy L. Roberts, *American Peace Writers, Editors, and Periodicals* (1991) (BA); Lawrence S. Wittner, *Rebels Against War* (1984) and *The Struggle Against the Bomb* (1993–2003); Valarie H. Ziegler, *The Advocates of Peace in Antebellum America* (1992).

Pearl Harbor, 1941: Stanley L. Falk, "Pearl Harbor," *Naval History* (1988) (B); Richard F. Hill, *Hitler Attacks Pearl Harbor* (2002); Robert W. Love, Jr., ed., *Pearl Harbor Reexamined* (1990); Martin V. Melosi, *The Shadow of Pearl Harbor* (1977); Frank P. Mintz, *Revisionism and the Origins of Pearl Harbor* (1985); James W. Morley, ed., *The First Confrontation* (1995); Gordon W. Prange, *Pearl Harbor* (1986); Emily Rosenberg, *A Date Which Will Live* (2003); Myron J. Smith, Jr., *Pearl Harbor* (1991) (B).

Philanthropy and Foundations: Robert Arnove, *Philanthropy and Cultural Imperialism* (1980); Edward H. Berman, *The Influence of the Carnegie, Ford, and Rockefeller Foundations on American Foreign Policy* (1983); Marcos Cueto, ed., *Missionaries of Science: The Rockefeller Foundation and Latin America* (1994); Robert L. Daniel, *American Philanthropy in the Near East, 1820–1960* (1970); Raymond Fosdick, *The Story of the Rockefeller Foundation* (1989); Helen Laville, *Cold War Women* (2002).

Population: *The Encyclopedia of Global Population and Demographics* (1998) (E); Matthew Connelly, *Fatal Misconception* (2008); William Peterson and Renee Peterson, *Dictionary of Demography* (1986) (E).

President (General): Eric Alterman, *When Presidents Lie* (2004); James Barber, *The Presidential Character* (1992); Michael R. Beschloss, *Presidential Courage* (2007); Meena Bose, *Shaping and Signaling Presidential Policy* (1998); J. Garry Clifford and Theodore A. Wilson, eds., *Presidents, Diplomats, and Other Mortals* (2007); Alexander DeConde,

Presidential Machismo (2000); Robert U. Goehlert and Fenton S. Martin, *The Presidency* (1985) (B); Louis Gould, *The Modern American Presidency* (2003); Stephen Graubard, *Command of Office* (2004); Mark Grossman, *Encyclopedia of the United States Cabinet* (E) (2000); Dale R. Herspring, *The Pentagon and the Presidency* (2005); Gary Hess, *Presidential Decisions for War* (2001); George T. Kurian, *A Historical Guide to the U.S. Government* (1997) (E); Leonard W. Levy and Louis Fisher, eds., *Encyclopedia of the American Presidency* (1993) (E); Theodore Lowi, *The Personal President* (1985); John E. Mueller, *War, Presidents, and Public Opinion* (1973); Anna K. Nelson, ed., *The Policy Makers* (2009); Richard E. Neustadt, *Presidential Power and the Modern Presidents* (1990); Richard M. Pious, *Why Presidents Fail* (2008); Arthur M. Schlesinger, Jr., *The Imperial Presidency* (1973) and *War and the American Presidency* (2004); Robert Sobel, ed., *Biographical Directory of the United States Executive Branch, 1774–1977* (1977) (BA).

Privateering: Donald B. Chidsey, *The American Privateers* (1962); Reuben E. Stivers, *Privateers and Volunteers* (1975); Carl E. Swanson, *Predators and Prizes* (1991).

Propaganda and Public Diplomacy: Laura A. Belmonte, *Selling the American Way* (2008); Lori Lyn Bogle, *The Pentagon's Battle for the American Mind* (2004); Nicholas Cull, *Selling War* (1995); Robert Cole, *The Encyclopedia of Propaganda* (1997) (E); Andrew Defty, *Britain, America, and Anti-Communist Propaganda, 1945–1953* (2004); Walter Hixson, *Parting the Curtain* (1997); David F. Krugler, *The Voice of America and the Domestic Propaganda Battles, 1945–1953* (2000); Alexandre Lauien, *The Voice of America* (1988); Clayton D. Laurie, *The Propaganda Warriors* (1996); Gifford Malone, *Political Advocacy and Cultural Communication* (1988); Jarol B. Manheim, *Strategic Public Diplomacy and American Foreign Policy* (1994); Sig Mickelson, *America's Other Voice* (1983); Michael Nelson, *War of the Black Heavens* (1997); Caroline Page, *Propaganda and Foreign Policy in the 20th Century* (2007); Shawn J. Parry-Giles, *The Rhetorical Presidency, Propaganda, and the Cold War, 1945–1955* (2002); Holly C. Shulman, *The Voice of America* (1990); Chris Tudda, *The Truth is Our Weapon* (2006); Allen M. Winkler, *The Politics of Propaganda* (1978).

Public Opinion: Eric Alterman, *Who Speaks for America* (1998); Richard J. Barnet, *The Rockets' Red Glare* (1990); H. Schuyler Foster, *Activism Replaces Isolationism: U.S. Public Attitudes, 1940–1975* (1983); George Gallup, *The Gallup Poll: Public Opinion* (1972–) (AS and S); Ole R. Holsti, *Public Opinion and American Foreign Policy* (1996); David D. Newsom, *The Public Dimension of Foreign Policy* (1996); Melvin Small, *Democracy and Diplomacy* (1996). Robert Sobel, *The Impact of Public Opinion on U.S Foreign Policy Since Vietnam* (2001).

Race and Racism: Kate A. Baldwin, *Beyond the Color Line and Iron Curtain* (2002); Gerald Horne, *Race War* (2004); Michael L. Krenn,

ed., *Race and U.S. Foreign Policy* (1998); Yukiko Koshiro, *Transpacific Racisms* (1999); Paul Gordon Lauren, *Power and Prejudice* (1988); Eric L. Love, *Race over Empire* (2004); Hazel M. McFerson, *The Racial Dimension of American Overseas Colonial Policy* (1997); Jason C. Parker, *Brother's Keeper* (2008); Brenda Gayle Plummer, ed., *Window on Freedom* (2003); Cheryl Russell, ed., *Racial and Ethnic Diversity* (2002); George E. Shepherd, ed., *Racial Influence on American Foreign Policy* (1971); Jay A. Sigler, ed., *International Handbook on Race and Race Relations* (1987) (E); Megan Weinberg, *World Racism and Related Inhumanities* (1992); George White, *Holding the Line* (2005).

Red Cross: Nicholas O. Berry, *War and the Red Cross* (1997); Pierre Bossier, *From Solferino to Tsushima* (1985); John F. Hutchinson, *Champions of Charity* (1996).

Refugees: Anna Bramwell, ed., *Refugees in the Age of Total War* (1988); Gil Loescher, *Beyond Charity* (1993); Gil Loescher and John A. Scalan, *Calculated Kindness* (1986); J. Bruce Nichols, *The Uneasy Alliance: Religion, Refugee Work, and U.S. Foreign Policy* (1988); Michael S. Teitelbaum and Myron Weiner, eds., *Threatened Peoples, Threatened Borders* (1995); U.S. Committee on Refugees, *World Refugee Survey* (1980–) (AS).

Scientists and Science: Michael Adas, *Dominance by Design* (2006); Greta Jones, *Science, Politics and the Cold War* (1988); Clarence Lasby, *Operation Paperclip* (1971); Joseph Rotblat, ed., *Scientists, the Arms Race, and Disarmament* (1982).

Slave Trade and Slavery: David Brion Davis, *Inhuman Bondage* (2006); William Dusinberre, *Slavemaster President* (2003); Don E. Fehrenbacher, *The Slaveholding Republic* (2001); Randall Miller and John Smith, eds., *Dictionary of Afro-American Slavery* (1988) (E); Junius P. Rodriguez, ed., *The Historical Encyclopedia of World Slavery* (1997) (E).

The South (U.S.): Joseph A. Fry, *Dixie Looks Abroad* (2002); Alfred Hero, *The Southerner and World Affairs* (1965); Charles O. Lerche, *The Uncertain South* (1964); Tim Mathewson, *A Proslavery Foreign Policy* (2003); Tennant S. McWilliams, *The New South Faces the World* (1988); Peter Trubowitz, *Defining the National Interest* (1998).

Space and Satellites: William E. Burrows, *Deep Black* (1986); Walter A. McDougall, *The Heavens and the Earth* (1985); Jeffrey T. Richelson, *America's Secret Eyes in Space* (1990); Paul B. Stares, *The Militarization of Space* (1985).

Spanish-American-Cuban-Filipino War: Benjamin R. Beede, ed., *The War of 1898 and U.S. Interventions, 1899–1934* (1994) (B); James C. Bradford, ed., *Crucible of Empire* (1993); Kristin Hoganson,

Fighting for American Manhood (1998); Jerry Keenan, ed., *Encyclopedia of the Spanish-American and Philippine-American War* (E) (2001); Louis A. Peréz, Jr., *The War of 1898* (1998); Anne C. Venzon, *The Spanish-American War* (1990) (B).

Sports: David Goldblatt, *The Ball Is Round* (2008) (soccer); Allen Guttmann, *Games and Empires* (1994); Barbara Keys, *Globalizing Sports* (2006); Walter LaFeber, *Michael Jordan and the New Global Capitalism* (2002); Thomas W. Zeiler, *Ambassadors in Pinstripes* (2006).

Summit Conferences: Elmer Plischke, *Diplomat in Chief* (1986) and *Summit Diplomacy* (1958); Robert D. Putnam and Nicholas Bayne, *Hanging Together: The Seven-Power Summits* (1984); Gordon R. Weihmiller and Dusko Doder, *U.S.-Soviet Summits* (1986).

Tariffs and Protectionism: David A. Lake, *Power, Protection, and Free Trade* (1988); James M. Lutz, *Protectionism* (1988) (B); Paul Wolman, *Most Favored Nation* (1992); Thomas Zeiler, *American Trade and Power in the 1960s* (1992).

Terrorism: Susan K. Anderson et al., *Historical Dictionary of Terrorism* (2002) (E); Stephen Brill, *After* (2003); Richard J. Chasdi, *Tapestry of Terror* (2002); Anthony H. Cordesman, *Terrorism, Asymmetric Light Warfare, and Weapons of Mass Destruction* (2001); Martha Crenshaw and John Pimlott, eds., *Encyclopedia of World Terrorism* (1996) (E); Richard Crockett, *American Embattled* (2003); Christopher Dobson and Ronald Payne, *The Never Ending War* (1987); Norman Friedman, *Terrorism, Afghanistan, and America's New Way of War* (2003); Rohan Gunaratna, *Inside Al Qaeda* (2002); Dilip Hiro, *War Without End* (2002); Giles Kepel, *Jihad* (2002); Robert Kumamoto, *International Terrorism and American Foreign Relations, 1945–1976* (1999); Walter Laqueur, *The Age of Terrorism* (1987); Cecilia Menjívar and Néstor Rodriguez, *When States Kill* (2005); Edward F. Mickolus et al., *International Terrorism in the 1980s* (1989) (C), *Terrorism, 1988–1991* (1993) (C), and *Transnational Terrorism, 1968–1979* (1980) (C); Suzanne R. Ontiveros, *Global Terrorism* (1986) (B); Ahmed Rashid, *Jihad* (2002; Barry Rubin, ed., *The Politics of Terrorism* (1990); Mark Selden and Alvin Y. So, *War and State Terrorism* (2004); Jeffrey D. Simon, *The Terrorist Trap* (1994); Jessica Stern, *The Ultimate Terrorists* (1999); John R. Thackrah, *Encyclopedia of Terrorism and Political Violence* (1987) (E); Lawrence Wright, *The Looming Tower* (2006).

Threat Perception and Calculation: Noel E. Firth and James H. Noren, *Soviet Defense Spending: A History of CIA Estimates, 1950–1990* (1998); Robert H. Johnson, *Improbable Dangers* (1994).

Think Tanks: Donald E. Abelson, *American Think-Tanks and Their Role in US Foreign Policy, 1976–88* (1996); Peter Grose, *Continuing the Inquiry* (1996); David M. Ricci, *The Transformation of American Politics* (1993); Robert D. Schulzinger, *The Wise Men of Foreign Affairs* (1984); Christopher Simpson, ed., *Universities and Empire* (1999); Bruce L. R. Smith, *The Rand Corporation* (1966); James A. Smith, *The Idea Brokers* (1991); Michael Wala, *The Council on Foreign Relations and American Foreign Policy in the Early Cold War* (1994).

Tourism and Travel: James Clifford, *Routes* (1997); Christopher Endy, *Cold War Holidays* (2004) (France); Cynthia Enloe, *Bananas, Beaches, and Bases* (1990); Maxine Fieffer, *Tourism in History* (1985); Marie-Franáoise Lanfant et al., *International Tourism* (1995); Sara Mills, *Discourses of Difference* (1991); Margaritte S. Shaffer, *See America First* (2001); David Spurr, *The Rhetoric of Empire* (1993); John Urry, *The Tourist Gaze* (1990).

United Nations: Carol Anderson, *Eyes Off the Prize* (2003); Joseph P. Baratta, *Strengthening the United Nations* (1987) (B); Seymour M. Finger, *American Ambassadors at the United Nations* (1987); Thomas M. Frank, *Nation Against Nation* (1985); Robert F. Gorman, *Great Debates at the United Nations* (2001); Max Harrelson, *Fires All Around the Horizon* (1989); Robert C. Hilderbrand, *Dumbarton Oaks* (1990); Evan Luard and Derek Herter, *The United Nations* (1993); Kumiko Matsuura et al., *Chronology and Fact Book of the United Nations, 1941–1991* (1992) (C); Edmund Jan Osmanczyk, *The Encyclopedia of the United Nations and International Relations* (1990) (E); Gary B. Ostrower, *The United States and the United Nations* (1998); William Preston, Jr., et al., *Hope and Folly* (1989) (UNESCO); Caroline Pruden, *Conditional Partners* (1998); Stephen Schlesinger, *Act of Creation* (2003).

War Crimes and Trials: Omar Bartov et al., eds., *Crimes of War* (2002); Gary Jonathan Bass, *Stay the Hand of Vengeance* (2002); Norman Cigar and Paul Williams, *Indictment at the Hague* (2002); Richard L. Lael, *The Yamashita Precedent* (1982); John R. Lewis, *Uncertain Judgment* (1979) (B); Timothy Maga, *Judgment at Tokyo* (2002); Philip R. Piccigallo, *The Japanese on Trial* (1979); Telford Taylor, *Nuremberg and Vietnam* (1970); Norman E. Tutorow, ed., *War Crimes, War Criminals, and War Crimes Trials* (1986) (B).

War of 1812: John C. Fredriksen, *Free Trade and Sailors' Rights* (1985) (B); John Latimer, *1812* (2007); Dwight L. Smith, *The War of 1812* (1985) (B).

War Powers: Louis Fischer, *Presidential War Power* (1995); Christopher N. May, *In the Name of War* (1989); Gary M. Stein and Morton H. Halperin, eds., *The U.S. Constitution and the Power to Go to War* (1994); John H. Sullivan, *The War Powers Resolution* (1982); Francis D. Wormuth and Edwin B. Firmage, *To Chain the Dog of War* (1989).

West (U.S.) and Frontier: William A. Beck and Ynez D. Haase, *Historical Atlas of the American West* (1989) (A); William Goetzmann and Glyndwr Williams, *The Atlas of North American Exploration* (1992) (A); J. Norman Heard, *Handbook of the American Frontier* (1987) (E); Adrian Johnson, *America Explored* (1974) (E); Howard R. Lamar, ed., *The New Encyclopedia of the American West* (1998) (E); Patricia Nelson Limerick et al., eds., *Trials* (1991); Clyde A. Milner III et al., eds., *The Oxford History of the American West* (1994) (E); Charles Phillips and Alan Axelrod, eds., *Encyclopedia of the American West* (1996) (E); Dan L. Thrapp, *The Encyclopedia of Frontier Biography* (1988–) (BA).

Women and Gender Issues: Homer L. Calkin, *Women in the Department of State* (1978); Kyle A. Courdileone, *Manhood and American Political Culture in the Cold War* (2005); Edward P. Crapol, ed., *Women and American Foreign Policy* (1992); Rebecca Grant and Kathleen Newland, eds., *Gender and International Relations* (1991); Human Rights Watch, *Global Report on Women's Human Rights* (1995); Susan Jeffords, *The Remasculinization of America* (1989); Rhodri Jeffreys-Jones, *Changing Differences* (1995); Nancy W. McGlen and Meredith Reid Sarkes, *Women in Foreign Policy* (1993); Linda Schott, *Reconstructing Women's Thoughts* (1997); Mari Yoshihara, *Embracing the East: White Women and American Orientalism* (2003).

World Court: Michael Dunne, *The United States and the World Court, 1920–1935* (1988); D. F. Fleming, *The United States and the World Court* (1945); Shabtai Rosenne, *The World Court* (1989) (E).

World's Fairs: John E. Findling, ed., *Historical Dictionary of World's Fairs and Expositions* (1990); Robert H. Haddow, *Pavilions of Plenty* (1997); Robert W. Rydell, *All the World's a Fair* (1987) and *World of Fairs* (1993); Robert W. Rydell and Nancy Gwinn, eds., *Fair Representations* (1994).

World-System Analysis: Thomas J. McCormick, *America's Half-Century* (1995); Immanuel Wallerstein, *Geopolitics and Geoculture* (1991), *The Modern World-System* (1974), *Politics of the World-Economy* (1984), and *World Inequality* (1975).

World War I: Arthur Banks, *A Military History Atlas of the First World War* (1975) (A); Martin Gilbert, *Atlas of World War I* (1994) (A); Holger H. Herwig and Neil M. Heyman, *Biographical Dictionary of World War I* (1982) (BA); George T. Kurian, *Encyclopedia of the First World War* (1990) (E); Stephen Pope and Elizabeth-Anne Wheal, *The Dictionary of the First World War* (1995) (E); Anne C. Venzon, ed., *The United States and the First World War* (1995) (B).

World War II: Marcel Baudot et al., eds., *The Historical Encyclopedia of World War II* (1980) (E); I. C. B. Dear and M. R. D. Foot, eds., *The Oxford Companion to World War II* (1995) (E); John Keegan, ed., *The Times Atlas of the Second World War* (1989) (A) and *World War II* (2000) (E); Williamson Murray and Allen Millet, *A War to Be Won* (2000); Norman Polmar and Thomas B. Allen, *World War II* (1991) (E); John J. Sbrega, *The War Against Japan* (1989) (B); U.S. Military Academy, *Campaign Atlas to the Second World War* (1980) (A); Peter Young, ed., *Atlas of the Second World War* (1973) (A); Gerhard Weinberg, *A World at Arms* (1995); David T. Zabecki, *World War II in Europe* (1997) (E).

Index

Italic page numbers indicate maps, photos, illustrations, or captions.

Abachi, Sani, 453
Abbas, Mahmoud, 504
ABC powers, 51. *See also* Argentina;
    Brazil; and Chile
ABC television, 430
Abdullah, Saudi crown prince, *504*
Abdullah, Fahd, *504*
Abe, Shinzo, 508
Abkhazia, 511
Abraham Lincoln (aircraft carrier), 493
Abraham Lincoln brigade, 132
Abu Ghraib (Baghdad), 496–497, *496*
Acheson, Dean, 217, 233, *250,* 254,
    278, 287; on China, 256; Cuban
    missile crisis and, 340, 342; as
    Johnson's advisor, *323,* 323, 349;
    Korean War and, 268, 272, 275
Achille Lauro (cruise ship), 440
Addams, Jane, 20, 85
Ad Hoc Task Force on Vietnam, 323
Afghanistan, 300, 454–455, 457;
    Al-Qaeda in, 481; arms sales to,
    466; bombing of, 453; Central
    Intelligence Agency in, 412, 427;
    future of, 523; loans to, 249;
    Soviets in, 384–385, 406,
    411–414, 423, 433, 434, 466;
    Taliban regime in, 468, 487; U.S.
    invasion of, 487–490
Africa, *333;* AIDS in, 452, 514–515;
    Cold War in, 385; drug trade and,
    513; famine in, 387, *388,* 441, 467;
    human rights and, 514; Italian
    colonies in, 131; Kennedy and,
    329; nationalism in, 404, 406; in
    1945, map, *296;* oil, 513, 514;
    post-Cold War, 508–515; Soviets
    in, 406; trade with, 384–385, 404,
    406; in 2000, map, *297. See also
    specific countries and regions*

African Americans, 336, *356;* in
    government, 384, 400; invasion
    of Ethiopia and, 137; in military,
    17, 87–88, 255; racism against,
    87–88, 255, 258, 298–299;
    school segregation and, 298–299
African Crisis Response Initiative, 453
African National Congress (ANC),
    452, 452
Africa Trade and Investment Act, 453
Agent Orange, 354, 398
Agnew, Spiro, *384,* 391
Aguinaldo, Emilio, 16, 18, 19, *21,* 21–22
Ahmadinejad, Mahmoud, 502–503
Aidid, Mohamed Farah, 452
AIDS. *See* HIV/AIDS
Aircraft, 165, 283; A-20 ("Boston")
    bomber, *111,* 112–113, 138; B-1
    bomber, 376; B-29 bomber, 226,
    227, 241; B-52 bomber, 275,
    321, 322, 341, 376, 390, 392;
    Berlin airlift and, 241, *242;*
    C-130 Hercules transport, 409;
    Cuban MiGs, 459; F-4 Phantom
    jets, 380; Japanese, 189, *228;*
    Korean Air Lines 007, 432; long-
    range bombers, 376; MiG-15
    fighter jets, 342, 383; sales of, to
    World War II belligerents,
    112–115, 138–139; Soviet, 338,
    342, 343, 378, 383, 412; stealth
    bombers, 426, 469–470; strategic
    bombers, 412, 430; in 9/11
    (2001) terrorist attacks, 480;
    terrorists and, 440; U-2 spy
    planes, 283, 287, 290–291, *291,*
    328, 331, 374, 383
Aircraft carriers, 351
Air force, 112, 114, 138, 172;
    Chinese, 153, 198; German, 113;

stealth aircraft and, 469–470;
    Strategic Air Command,
    275, 287
Air Force One (film), 480
Alaska boundary dispute, 57
Albania, 451
Al-Bashir, Omar Hassan, 514
Albiza Campos, Pedro, 168
Albright, Madeleine K., *446,* 446,
    459, 461, 519; Balkan crisis
    and, 450
Alcohol, U.S. soldiers and, 87
Algeria, 287
Al Jazeera, 521
Allen, George, 305
Allen, Richard V., 428
Allende, Salvador, *383,* 383
Alliance for Progress, 329, 334, 350
Allies, World War I, 77, 78–79, 81,
    89–90; Atlantic Charter and,
    179; debts of, 105, 122, 124;
    peace and, 91, 93
Allies, World War II, 126, 181–182,
    186; at Atlantic Charter
    Conference, 178–181; Japanese
    containment and, map, *212;* at
    Potsdam Conference, 214–217;
    strategy of, 190–192, 193–196;
    at Yalta Conference, 207–210.
    See also France; Great Britain;
    Soviet Union
Allison, Graham, 395
al Qaeda, 454–455, 469, *481,* 481,
    482, 487, 495, 499, 501, 513,
    518; aid/funding for, 488, 491;
    Hussein and, 490; Pakistan and,
    506; prisoners, 488, 496–497,
    496, 511; weapons of mass
    destruction and, 490
Alsace-Lorraine, 82

Al-Zeidei, Muntadhar, *500*

American Asiatic Association, 24, 25

American Century (magazine), 191

American Committee for the
    Outlawry of War, 125

American Federation of Labor, 201

America First Committee, 182, 185

Americanization, 121, 148, 251,
    307–310

American Medical Association, 430

American Peace Commission, 91

American Relief Administration, 128

American Tragedy, An (Dreiser), 128

American Union Against
    Militarism, 85

AM/LASH (CIA program), 343

Amnesty International, 414, 497

Ana al-Muslim website, 521

Anaconda Copper, 121, 383

Andropov, Yuri, 432

Anglo-Iranian Oil Company, 407

Anglo-Japanese alliance (1902), 53, 57

Anglophobia, 77. *See also* Great
    Britain

Angola, 384, 442; Central
    Intelligence Agency in, 384, 427,
    441; Cuban/Soviet influence in,
    384, 411, 434, 441, 451; Portugal
    and, 384

Anthrax, *492*

Anti-Americanism, 105, 121, 145,
    151, 167–168, 249, 284, 300–302,
    307–308, 406–409, 511–512

Anti-ballistic missile (ABM) system,
    376–378

Anti-ballistic missile (ABM) treaty,
    448, 486, 510

Anti-Comintern Pact, 131

Anticommunism. *See* McCarthyism;
    Red Scare

Anti-imperialism, 4, 5, 8–10, 19–20,
    19, 21, 151; women's
    organizations and, 40

Anti-Imperialist League, 19, *20*

Anti-Semitism, 200, 244, 439. *See also*
    Jews

Antiwar movement: Gulf War and, 460;
    during interwar years, 125–127,
    134; invasion of Iraq and, 492;
    Vietnam War and, 356–358, *356*.
    See also Pacifist organizations

ANZUS Pact, 275

Apartheid, 257, 384, 385, 441,
    451–453; end of, 451–452

Apocalypse Now (film), 395

Appeasement policy, 113,
    130–133, 135

Apple Computer, 465

Aquino, Benigno S., 442

Aquino, Corazon, 442

Arabian-American Oil Company
    (Aramco), 213

*Arabic (*ship), 80

Arab League, 491, 514

Arabs: conflicts with Israel, 301, 374,
    379, 380–382, 406–407, 504;
    founding of Israel and, 244–246;
    Nasserite, 303; nationalism and,
    300, 380, 438; peace talks with
    Israel, 462; purchase of U.S.
    properties by, 386; stereotypes
    of, 299. *See also* Middle East;
    specific countries

Arafat, Yasir, 380, 440, 462, 504;
    PLO-Israeli agreement and,
    462, 462

Arbenz Guzmán, Jacobo, 304–306

Argentina, 50, 158, 213; debt of, 45;
    democracy in, 511; drug trade,
    512–513; financial crisis in, 456,
    511; Germany and, 172; human
    rights in, 414; military aid to,
    257; Pan Americanism and,
    171–172; terrorism in, 373;
    United Nations' membership of,
    205; U.S. hegemony and, 172

Arias Sánchez, Oscar, 437

Aristide, Jean-Bertrand, 458

Aristocracy, 40

Armey, Dick, 491

Armour company, 105

Arms embargoes, 51, 138–139, 181; of
    Bosnia, 451; of Iraq, 448; of
    Italy, 130; of South Africa, 384;
    of Spain, 137; of World War II
    belligerents, 115, 135, 138–139

Arms limitation: Eisenhower and,
    278; Geneva Summit (1955),
    283–284; interwar conferences
    for, 125–127; Rapacki plan for,
    288, 309; Washington Naval
    Conference, 127, 146, 148,

149–152. *See also* Strategic Arms
    Limitation Talks

Arms manufacturers, 134. *See also*
    Military–industrial complex

Arms race, 278, 309. *See also* Cold
    War; Military buildup; Missiles;
    Nuclear weapons

Arms sales, 466–467, *467*; to
    belligerents, World War II,
    112–115, 138–139, 181; Carter
    era, 407, 408, 411, 413, 414; to
    East Africa, 385; to Egypt, 380;
    to Iran, 374, 382, 407, 408, 411,
    436; to Israel, 303, 380, 382; to
    Latin America, 213; to Pakistan,
    374, 413; to Saudi Arabia, 374,
    438; to South Africa, 441; Soviet
    deals, 154, 380, 407; to Taiwan,
    463; to Third World, 466–467,
    467. *See also* Military aid

Armstrong, Anne, 372

Army, 139; African Americans in, 17,
    87–88; Chinese, 270–272;
    Criminal Investigation Division,
    496; Cuba and, 44; doughboys,
    World War I, 87–90; in
    Formosa, 254; Green Berets,
    331, 334, 409; intervention in
    Russia, 101–103; Iraqi, 502; in
    Korea, 270–275; Mexican
    revolution and, 51; North
    Korean, 274; Rangers, 409, 452,
    470; Rough Riders, 16, 17;
    women in, 87; before World
    War I, 85; World War I
    expansion of, 85–86. *See also*
    Red (Soviet) Army

Army Appropriation
    Bill (1901), 44

Army of the Republic of Vietnam
    (ARVN), 351, *353,* 390–391,
    393, 398

Arnold, Henry, 112, 113, 115

Ash, Timothy Garton, 422

Asia: Co-Prosperity Sphere in, 153,
    187; financial crisis in, 447, 465;
    great powers in, map, *27;*
    Japanese power in, 150;
    nationalism in, 172, 216; natural
    disasters in, 507–508; U.S.
    interests in, 53–55, 122, 252;

U.S. military in, 370; after World War II, 213, map, *253;* World War II deaths in, 215. *See also* Indochina; Southeast Asia; *specific countries*

Asia Pacific Economic Cooperation Forum, 447

Aso, Taro, 508

Assassinations: of Benigno Aquino, 442; Central Intelligence Agency and, 338; of Kennedy, 347; of Lumumba, 306; of Rabin, 462; of Sadat, 438

Associated Press, 121

Aswan Dam (Egypt), 300, 301

Atlantic Charter Conference, *177,* 178–181, 191, 203

Atomic bomb, 231; development of, 217, 240–241, 309; diplomacy and, 230; in Hiroshima and Nagasaki, 215, *225,* 226–231, *227, 230,* 398; in Korean War, 272; Manhattan Project and, 226, *228,* 228, 231; Soviet development of, 250, 258–259; testing, 214, 229, 230, 251, 257, 294. *See also* Nuclear weapons

"Atoms for Peace" speech, 278

Attlee, Clement, 270

Auchincloss, Louis, *92*

"Aunties" (anti-imperialists), 18–21

Auschwitz extermination camp, 203

Australia, 213, 397; in ANZUS pact, 275; in Southeast Asia Treaty Organization, 292, 326

Austria, *93, 132, 200, 201, 238;* aid to, 204; Cold War neutrality of, 283; German annexation of, 132

Austro-Hungarian Empire, 76–77, 90, 93 104; collapse of, 93, *95*

Authoritarian regimes, 427

Aviation industry, 112–113. *See also* Aircraft

Axis, World War II, 179–180, 186, 187; demilitarization of, 205; Latin America and, 172, 213; Rome-Berlin, 131. *See also* Germany; Italy; Japan

"Axis of evil," 489, 502, 505, 506, 509, 511

Azerbaijan, 510

Ba'ath party (Iraq), 461, 494

Bacevich, Andrew, 498

Bachelet, Michelle, 511

Baez, Joan, 356

Baghdad Pact, 283, 299, 309

Baker, James A., III, *421,* 426, 445, 447, 458; Arab-Israeli conflict and, 460, 462; Balkan crisis and, 450; Gulf War and, 460

Baker, Josephine, *298*

Baker, Mark, 396

Baker, Newton, 88–89

Baker, Ray Stannard, 100

Balance of power, 26, 28, 29, 39, 60, 232–233, 373

Balkans, 185, 211, 450. *See also specific countries*

Ball, George W., 340, 353, 439; Iran and, 409

Baltic states,194, 425. *See also specific state or country*

Bandung Conference (1955), 293, 300

Bangladesh, 374, 467; food riots in, 518

Banking, 164, 166, 373, 406, 449, 452; in China, 55–56; development and, 276, 305, 437; in Haiti, 47; World War I loans and, 105. *See also* Export-Import Bank; Inter-American Bank; World Bank

Bao Dai, emperor of Vietnam, 325–327

Baruch, Bernard, 240

Baruch Plan, 240–242

Baseball, 153, 156, 383, 418

Basketball, 520

Batista, Fulgencio, *167,* 167–168, 304; overthrow of, 305, 336–337

Battle Cry of Peace (film), 85

Bay of Pigs invasion (1961), 337–338, *339,* 339, 344

BBC World, 521

Beckwith, Charlie, 410

Begin, Menachem, 407, 438

Beirut (Lebanon) bombing of, 439

Beisner, Robert L., 248

Belarus, 467

Belgium, 131, 149, 208; Congo and, 335–336; Ruhr Valley seizure by, 125; in World War I, 76–77, 82

Bell, J. Franklin, 23

Bemis, Samuel Flagg, 81

Benelux nations, 249. *See also* Belgium; Luxembourg; Netherlands

Beneš, Eduard, 236

Ben-Gurion, David, *245*

Berger, Samuel R., 446–447

Berlin, 331–333 378; airlift to, 241, *242;* crisis in, 289–290; East, 281, 289; West, 288–289, 331–333

Berlin Wall, *332,* dismantling of, *421,* 422–423

Bernstorff, Johann von, 74, 80

Bethlehem Steel (company), 385

Bethmann-Hollweg, Theobold von, 73, 77

Beveridge, Albert, 4, 20, 28

Bevin, Ernest, 247

Bhutto, Benazir, 506

Bidault, Georges, 247

Bikini atomic test, 251, 294

Bin Laden, Osama, 454–455, 481–483, *481,* 487, 513, 521; in Sudan, 453

Biological weapons, 461, 466, 486, *492*

Bipartisanship, 257

Black, Cofer, 481

Black Africans, apartheid and, 257, 384, 385, 441, 451–453

Black Chamber code-breakers, 149

Black Hand, 76–77

Black Power, *356*

Black Sunday (film), 480

Black Tom munitions factories, 83

Blackwater Security, 522

Blair, Tony, 491, 499, 508, 521

Blight, David W., *17,* 17

Boaz, Franz, 165

Boer War (1899–1902), 28

Bok, Edward, 125

Bolivia, 105, 211; aid to, 404; democracy in, 511; drug trade in, 457; food riots in, 518

Bolshevism, 93, 100–103, 105, 124, 127, 128; Asia and, 150, 151; Coolidge and, 116, 163. *See also* Soviet Union (USSR)

Bolton, Herbert E., 169

Bombers. *See* Aircraft

Bombing: of Afghanistan, 453; of Beirut, 439; of Cambodia, 390–391; of China, by Nationalists, 292; of Dresden, 216, 228; of France, *216;* of Guatemala City, 305; of Hiroshima and Nagasaki, 215, 226–231, *230;* of Indonesia, 489; of Iraq, 461; of Lebanon, by Israel, 438–439; of Libya, 440–441; of London subway, 508; of North Vietnam, 392–393, 396; Palestinian terrorists, 462; of Serbia, by NATO, 451; of Shanghai, 153, *154;* of Southeast Asia, 373, 398; of Spain, 489; of Sudan, 453; suicide, 495, 504; of Tokyo, 216, 228; of Vietnam, 321–324, 353, 354, 376

Bono (rock star), *517*

"Boondocks," 24

Borah, William E., 118, 126, *144,* 158; anti-war sentiment of, 96, 126, *357;* Latin America and, 158; Manchurian Crisis and, 147

Border control, 512

Borgman, Jim, *460*

Borno, Louis, 166

Born on the Fourth of July (Kovic), 395

Borodin, Michael, 151

Borstelmann, Thomas, 336

Bosch, Juan, 350

Bosnia, 61, 76–77, 449

Bosnia-Herzegovina, 449–451

Botha, P. W., 451

Boxer Rebellion (China), 26, 53, 56, 269

Boy Scouts of America, 63

Bradley, Omar, 272

Brady, Nicholas F., 456

Brandegee, Frank, 94

Brandt, Willy, *332,* 378

Brazil, 51, 161, 211, 466; debt of, 456; democracy in, 511; drug trade in, 457, 512–513; financial crisis in, 456, 511; Germany and, 172; human rights in, 414; loans to, 447; military coup in, 350; political upheaval in, 172

Bremer, L. Paul, 494, 498

Brest-Litovsk, Treaty of (1918), 89, 100

Bretton Woods Agreement Act (1945), 204, 385

Brezhnev, Leonid, 375, 377, 385; death of, 432; Strategic Arms Limitation Talks and, 375

Briand, Aristide, 126

Bricker, John, 309

Bricker Amerndment, 309

Bridges, Styles, 254, 280

Brinkley, David, 240, 275, 322

Brinkmanship, 280, 293

Britain. *See* Great Britain

British Aggressions in Venezuela, or the Monroe Doctrine on Trial (pamphlet), 5

British Guiana, 5

Brothers to the Rescue, 459

Brown, Gordon, 508

Brussels Treaty (1948), 249

Brussels World's Fair (1958), 299

Bryan, C. D. B., 395

Bryan, William Jennings, 42, *50,* 60, 85; as anti-imperialist, 19, 21; China and, 56; Dominican Republic and, 46; *Lusitania* and, 73, 75, *80,* 81; Nicaragua and, 49, 50; as presidential candidate, 12

Bryan-Chamorro Treaty (1916), 49

Brzezinski, Zbigniew, *399,* 399, 400, 401, 414; on Bush, 489; Iran and, 411–414; Middle East peace and, 411; Panama Canal and, 401; Trilateral Commission and, 399

Bucareli Agreements (1923), 169

Buchenwald concentration camp, 200, *202*

Buchwald, Art, 307–308.

Buck, Pearl, 150

Buddhists, Vietnam War and, *346,* 346–347, 398

Buenos Aires Conference (1936), 171

Bulgaria, 90, *95,* 235; fall of communism in, 422; after World War II, 211

Bulletin of the Atomic Scientists, 259, 517

Bullitt, William C., 103, 119, 129–130

Bunau-Varilla, Philippe, 34, 35, 36, 38

Bundy, McGeorge, 330, 342, 347, 349

Bunker, Ellsworth, 320

Burdick, Eugene, 299

Burma, 196, 216, 232, 300, 457, 468; cyclone disaster, 507–508

Burundi, 453

Bush, George H. W., 422, 443–447, *444,* 466, *500;* cabinet of, 445; China and, 463; on environmental issues, 443; Gorbachev and, 443; Gulf War and, 459–461, *460;* Iran-Contra affair and, 429; Latin America and, 455; New World Order of, *460;* North American Free Trade Agreement and, 456–457; Panama invasion and, 458; personal style of, 443–445; Somalian civil war and, 452–453; Vietnam and, 464

Bush, George W., *482;* AIDS in Africa and, 452; appraisal of, 523; cabinet of, 483–486, *486;* global warming and, 468, 516; Iraq invasion and occupation, 459–461; media censorship and, 521; Mexico and, 512; Middle East and, 470; military buildup under, 522–523; North Korea and, 467, 505–506; preemptive war doctrine, 489, 490, 501, 503, 504, 505; Putin and, 449, 509; Russia and, 509–511; 9/11 terrorist attacks and, 480–483, *482;* war on terrorism of, 447, 455, 486, 487–490, *496, 500,* 504, 508, 513, 523

Bush Doctrine, 487–490

Business: corporatism, 116, 159–160; e-business, 468–469; expansion of, 134; Japanese purchase of, 465; multinational corporations, 386, 389; Nazi collaboration with, 134; Sino-Soviet détente and, 373; in South Africa, 406, 452; in Vietnam, 464; World War I and, 134

Butler, Smedley D., 166

Byrd Amendment (1971), 384, 406

Byrnes, James F., 238–239

Byroade, Henry, 301

C. Turner Joy (destroyer), 351
Cable, John, 112
Cable News Network (CNN), 460, *493*, 521
Cairo Conference (1943), *197,* 197–198
Calder, Bruce, 47
California, racism in, 54–55
Calley, William, 354, 391
Cambodia, 326, 395; Central Intelligence Agency in, 427; food aid for, 388; French and, 324; genocide in, 394; Khmer Rouge in, 391, 394, 414; *Mayaguez* incident and, 395; U.S. thrust into, 391, 384, 414
Cambridge American Cemetery and Memorial, *104*
Camp David, 290–291, 406–411, 438, 462
Canada, 41, 249; Alaska boundary and, 57; environmental concerns in, 443; free trade agreements and, 456
Canal Zone. *See* Panama Canal
Can Lao (Vietnam), 327
Cannon, Joe, 2
Caperton, William B., 47, 165
Caputo, Philip, 356, 395
Cárdenas, Lázaro, *170,* 170
Caribbean region, 434; Good Neighbor Policy in, 163; U.S. interests in, 9; U.S. interventions in, *48,* 157–158, *160,* 257; U.S. power in, 9, 59, 60, 77, 148, 157–158, *339, 341. See also* Latin America; Central America; *specific countries*
Carlucci, Frank C., 428
Carnegie, Andrew, 19, 20, 23, 28
Carnegie Endowment for International Peace, 125
Carranza, Venustiano, 49, 50–53
Carson, Rachel, 388
Cartagena (ship), 34
Carter, Jimmy, 435; Africa and, 404–406; cabinet of, *398, 399,* 399–400; China and, 400; Cuba and, 401–404; Haiti and, 458; human rights and, 400, 401, 411, 412, 414; Iranian hostage crisis

and, 406–411, *408;* Latin America and, 401–406; Middle East and, 406–411; North Korea and, 505; Panama and, 401; political style of, 399–400; Soviet Union and, 399, 400, 404–406, 410–414
Carter Doctrine, 413
Casablanca Conference (1943), 192, 194
Casey, William J., 427, 428, 436, 441
Castillo Armas, Carlos, 304, 305
Castro, Cipriano, 45
Castro, Fidel, 15, 383, 403–404, 437, 455, 511; Bay of Pigs invasion and, 337–338, *339;* Carter and, 403–404; Central Intelligence Agency plots against, 278, 336, 337–338, 343; Cuban revolution and, 305, 336–338; Mariel exodus (1980) and, 403, 437, 459; missile crisis (1962) and, 338–343. *See also* Cuba
Castro, Raúl, 338, 511
Ceauşescu, Nicolae, 423
Cédras, Raul, 458
Censorship, 520–521
Central America, 148, 158; civil wars in, 455–456; communism in, *435,* 437; German investment in, 39, 113; Reagan and, 434–438, 443; underdevelopment in, 434–435; United Fruit Company and, 42, 160; U.S. intervention in, 45–49. *See also* Caribbean, Latin America; *specific countries*
Central Intelligence Agency (CIA), 217, 369; in Afghanistan, 412, 427; in Angola, 384, 427, 441; assassination plots of, 277–278, 338, 343; and Balkan crisis, 450; in Cambodia, 427; in Central America, 304–305, 434; in Chile, 383, 427; in Congo, 336; counterterrorism efforts, 481, 483, 509; creation of, 217, 249; Cuba and, 278, 336, 337–338, 343, 383; in Ethiopia, 427, 441; expansion of, 310; Free Europe Committee and, *285;* in Guatemala, 277, 306, 309; in

Indonesia, 277; interventions by, 412; in Iran, 277, 306, 309; Iran-Contra affair and, 428–429; Iranian hostage crisis and, 407–408, 412; Iraq invasion and, 483, 490, 494, 495, 502; Kissinger and, 372; in Laos, 344; in Nicaragua, 403, 427, 436–437; Noriega and, 458; Pakistan and, 487; in Philippines, 277; prisons, 497, 497; Radio Free Europe and, 286; under Reagan, 427; Syria and, 303; U-2 spy plane mission, 290–291; Vietnam and, 309, 320, 327, 352, 354, 393
Central Powers, World War I. *See* Austro-Hungary; Germany; Turkey
Ceylon (Sri Lanka), 216
Chad: famine in, *388;* Sudanese refugees in, 513
Chamberlain, Neville, 132, 135; appeasement and, 113, 132, 135, 137, 210
Chamorro, Violeta Barrios de, 437, 455
Chaplin, Charlie, *131*
Chapultepec, Act of (1945), 206, 213
Charles, Ray, 441
Charter 77, 378
Chase Manhattan Bank, 373
Château-Thierry, battle of, 89
Chávez, Hugo, 511, 512
Chechnya, war in, 448
Checkpoint Charlie, 332
Chemical Convention (1993), 466
Chemical weapons, 426, 461, 466, 486, *492;* in Vietnam, 354, 398; World War I, 87, *89*
Cheney, Richard, 480, 481, *486,* 509, 510; antiwar sentiments and, *501;* Bush and, 484–486, *486;* 490, 497, 502; Middle East goals and, 503, *503,* 504
Chennault, Claire Lee, 153, 198
Chernenko, Konstantin, 432
Chernobyl nuclear disaster, 243, 432
Chiang Kai-shek. *See* Jiang Jieshi
Chile, 51, 105, 172, 213, 306, 383; authoritarianism in, 427; Central Intelligence Agency in, 383, 427;

copper in, 121, 159, 162, 383;
democracy in, 511; economy of,
383; Peru and, 159; political
upheaval in, 172; U.S. trade
agreement with, 456, 511
China, 24–26, 196–200; aid to,
155–156, 186, 188, 204, *253;*
cigarette sales in, *25;* civil war
in, 251–254; communists in,
151, 154; immigration from,
198; Iraq War and, 492; Japan
and, 25, 129, 137, 153–156, 186;
Liaodong Province, 25, 53; loans
to, 155–156, 413; Manchuria
and, 53–54, 145–147, 158;
nationalism in, 105, 145, 151;
Open Door for, 9, 26, 53, 55, 56,
57, 149, 150, 156, 196;
Philippines and, 150; revolution
in, 56; Russia and, 53; Shandong
province, 25, 56, 92, 149, 150;
trade with, 151; United Nations
and, 204, 205, 210; U.S. interests
in, 213; war with Japan, 129,
137, 208; World War I peace
and, 92; World War II deaths in,
215. *See also* Nationalist China;
People's Republic of China
(PRC)
China Incident, 153
China Lobby, 254
China White Paper, 254
Chlorofluorocarbons (CFCs), 468
Chomsky, Noam, 356
Christian-Muslim rivalry, in
Lebanon, 303
Christopher, Warren M., 446
Church, Frank, *357, 383*
Churchill, Randolph, 63
Churchill, Winston S., 63, *114,* 183,
207, 239, 249, 283; Atlantic
Charter and, *171,* 178–181, *180,*
185; atomic bomb and, 230–231;
British empire and, 211, 325; at
Cairo Conference, *197,* 197–198;
China and, 196–197, *197;* "Iron
curtain" speech of, 239; Lend-
Lease and, 178, 184; Middle East
and, 213–214; Pearl Harbor
attack and, *189,* 189; percentage
agreement with Stalin, 211; at

Potsdam Conference, 214–217;
on Soviet threat to Greece, 244;
United Nations and, 205; World
War II strategy and, 191–192,
194, 196; at Yalta Conference,
207–210, *207*
Citibank, 452
City of Memphis (ship), 83
Civil Service Loyalty Review
Board, 281
Civil wars: in Africa, 384, 406, 453,
513–514; in Angola, 441; in
China, 150, 151, 154, 154, 197,
251, 252, 274; in Congo,
335–336, 453; in Darfur,
513–514; in East Timor, 395; in
Ethiopia, 441; in Greece,
243–244; in Laos, 343–344; in
Lebanon, 303, 382, 438; in
Liberia, 513; in Nicaragua, 453;
in Nigeria, 404; in El Salvador,
453, 455–456; in Somalia,
452–453, 513; in Spain, 132,
135, 137; in Sudan, 513; in
Zimbabwe/Rhodesia, 406. *See
also* Korean War; Vietnam War
Clark, William, 428
Clarke, Richard, 482, 518
Clay, Lucius, *238,* 241, 332
Clayton-Bulwer Treaty (1850), 36
Clemenceau, Georges, 88, 91, 93, *96*
Cleveland, Grover, 8–10, *10,* 29;
Cuba and, 10–15; Venezuelan
crisis and, 5–8, *6, 7*
Clifford, Clark, 245, 322, 323
Climate change, 516–517
Clinton, Hillary, 491, *523*
Clinton, William J., 445, *450,*
454–455, *462,* 468, 518–519;
Africa and, 453; and arms
proliferation, 467; and bin Laden,
454–455; Balkan crisis and, 450;
cabinet of, 446–447; China and,
463; counterterrorism efforts of,
482; Cuba and, 459; on domestic
troubles, 469; global warming
and, 468, 516; Haiti and, 458;
Kosovo and, 451; NATO
expansion and, 449; North Korea
and, 466, 505; personal style of,
445–446; philanthropy of, 518;

Russia and, 445, 448, 467;
Rwanda genocide and, 453;
Somalia and, 453, 465; trade
agreements and, 447, 456–457;
united Germany and, 449;
Vietnam and, 464
Closing Circle, The (Commoner), 388
CNN (Cable News Network), 460,
493, 521
Coca-Cola Company, *295,* 386
Cocaine trade, *457,* 457, 458,
512–513
Cock-eyed World (film), 164
Cody, Buffalo Bill, 26, 57, 62
Cold War, 235, 325, 443, 489, 491,
510, 511; Africa and, 385;
Americanization, 307–310;
Berlin crisis and, 241, *242;*
brinkmanship, 280, 293; China
and, 251–254; Cuban missile
crisis and, 338–343; and détente,
290, 373; Dulles and, 275,
279–281; Eastern Europe and,
235–238; economic troubles
and, 433; Eisenhower and,
309–310, 331; emerging culture
of, 256–259; end of, 449, 458,
465, 466; in Europe, 246–250;
Germany in, 241; globalization
of; Gorbachev and, *433;* Iranian
crisis and, 240; Japan and,
251–252; Kennedy and, 347;
Khrushchev and, 282–286,
290–291, 300; Korean War and,
267, 268–275; nonalignment in,
295–300, 344; race and,
298–299; Truman Doctrine and,
243–246, 254; U-2 crisis and,
290–291; Vietnam and, 328,
350. *See also* Arms race;
Communism; Containment;
Military buildup; Soviet Union
Colleges. *See* Universities and colleges
Colombia, 159, 437; drug trade in,
457, 512–513; isthmian canal
and, 16, 34–39, 59, 60
Colonialism, 191, 196, 300, 308; in
Africa, 404; Coca-colonization,
295; corporate, 160–161; French,
in Indochina, 324, 325. *See also*
Imperialism

Columbia Pictures, 465
Coming Home (film), 395
Commager, Henry Steele, 395
Commerce. *See* Trade
Commerce Department, 122
Commission on Strategic Forces, 430
Committee to Defend America by
    Aiding the Allies, 182
Commoner, Barry, 388
Commonwealth of Independent
    States, 425. *See also* Russia; *and
    specific former Soviet Republics*
Communications, international, 121,
    468–469, 520–521. *See also*
    Propaganda
Communism, 346; in Central
    America, *435,* 437; in Cuba, 337;
    Dulles and, 103, 278, 279, 301,
    310; in Eastern Europe,
    235–238; Eisenhower and, 278,
    279–281, 303; end of, in Eastern
    Europe, 422–423; end of, in
    Russia, 425; in Greece,
    243–244; Korean War and, 271,
    272; in Laos, 344; in Latin
    America, 163–164, 304–305; in
    Middle East, 303; NSC-68 and,
    250; in Philippines, 442; in
    Poland, 211; Reagan and, *435;*
    Red Fascism and, *235,* 235;
    Third World and, 295–300, 328;
    in Vietnam, 324, 325, 326, 327,
    350, 394. *See also* Cold War;
    Containment policy; Mao
    Zedong; People's Republic of
    China; Soviet Union; Stalin,
    Joseph
Comprehensive Nuclear Test Ban
    Treaty (1999), 44, 486, 518.
Computer viruses, 469
Concentration camps, 200, *202*
Conference on Security and
    Cooperation (1975), 378
Conference on the Human
    Environment (1972), 389
Congo (Zaire), 82, 278, 384, 385,
    404, 453; civil war in, 335–336,
    453; Democratic Republic
    of, 453
Congress: 18, 137; bipartisanship in,
    257; Black Caucus, 384; Byrd

Amendment, 384, 406; China
    Lobby in, 254, 310; Cold War
    and, 309–310; Cuba and, 4, 7, 9,
    10, 12; Formosa Resolution,
    292, 293; Gulf War and, 460;
    immigration reform by,
    403–404; Iran-Contra scandal
    and, 428–429; Jewish refugees
    and, 201; League of Nations and,
    94, 97, 103–104; Lend-Lease
    and, 184; Marshall Plan and,
    247; Neutrality Acts and,
    134–135, 185–186; Nicaraguan
    contras and, 437; Panama Canal
    and, 36, 38, 40, 59; Puerto Rico
    and, 61; Republican control of,
    445; on Salvadoran death squads,
    436; South Korea and, 274; tariff
    reduction by, 124; Venezuelan
    crisis and, 7, 9, 10; Vietnam War
    and, 326, 351, 352, 357, 358,
    393; War Debt Commission,
    124; war powers of, 372; World
    War I and, *83,* 83–84; World
    War II and, 190. *See also* Senate
Congress for Cultural Freedom, 249
Connally, Tom, 269
Conrad, Paul, *321*
Conservatives, 403, 412
Constitutionalists (Mexico), 49, 51, 52
Consumerism, 307
Contadora group, 437
Containment policy, 252, 257, 328,
    373; under Carter, 400–401,
    413; under Eisenhower-Dulles,
    275, 279–281, 288, 303, 308; in
    Middle East, 382, 413; post-
    World War II, 246, *248,* 250;
    Third World and, 296–297;
    Vietnam War and, 357, 395. *See
    also* Cold War
Contras (Nicaragua), 428–429, *429,*
    434, 436–437, 443, 458
Conventional Forces in Europe (CFE)
    negotiations, 447
Coolidge, Calvin, 116, 163–164,
    170, 171
Copper, Chilean, 121, 159, 162, 383
Corporatism, 116, 160–161
Corporations, multinational, 386,
    389. *See also* specific corporations

Correa, Rafael, 512
Costa Rica, 436, 437
Costigliola, Frank, 239
Cotton trade, 128, 301, 413
Coughlin, Charles E., 201
Crichton, Michael, 465
Croatia, 450–451
Cromwell, William Nelson, 36, 37
Cronkite, Walter, 322
Cruise, Tom, 441
Cruise missiles, 377, 412, 426, 431,
    453; Tomahawk, 460, 461, 470
Cuba: Angola and, 384, 403, 411,
    434; Bay of Pigs invasion and,
    337–338; Brothers to the Rescue
    and, 459; Carter and, 403, 411;
    Central Intelligence Agency and,
    278, 306, 336, 337–338, 343,
    384; embargo of, 337, 338, 384,
    459, 511; immigration from, 403,
    459; independence of, 4, 10–15;
    Josephine Baker in, *298;*
    Machado regime in, 167, 171;
    Mexico and, 403; missile crisis
    and, 243, 338–343, *340,*
    Namibia and, 441, 442;
    nationalism in, 167–168, 305,
    309; under Platt Amendment,
    43–45, 61, 167; political
    upheaval in, 172, 309; post-Cold
    War, 511; Reagan and, 436–438;
    revolution in, 336–338; Soviet
    aid to, 337, 403, 459; Spanish-
    American-Cuban-Filipino War
    and, 2, 15–16; sugar and, 10, 11,
    12, 42, 44, 45, 159, 162, 167,
    336, 337, *339;* U.S. interests in,
    2–5, 336. *See also* Castro, Fidel
Cubela Secades, Rolando, 343
Cultural exchanges: economic
    expansion and, 120–125;
    Fulbright Program, 249; jazz
    tours of Soviet bloc, 276; with
    Mexico, 169
Cultural relations: Africa and, 276;
    Asia and, 276; Britain and,
    57–63, 178; China and, 26, 151,
    369–370, 414; Cuba and, 43–45,
    167–168, 383, 459; Europe and,
    121, 134, 430–431; with France,
    509; Latin America and, 159–160,

165; Japan and, 251–252, 295, 463, 508; Mexico and, 51, 169; Philippines and, 23–24, *25;* soft power and, 519–520; Soviet Union and, 102–103, 190, 284, 307–309. See also *Culture*
Cultural stereotypes, 169, 298–299
Culture: American invasion and, 178; Americanization and, 121, 128, 133, 148, 251, 307–310, 469; globalization of, 469, 519–521; Western Europe, 307. *See also* Films
Cunard Line, 71
Curtin, John, 213
Czech legion, 102
Czechoslovakia, 93, *95,* 200, 238, 247, 378; arms deal with Egypt, 301; division of, 449; East German refugees in, 422, *423;* fall of communism in, 422; German annexation of, 112–113, 132–133, 137; Guatemala and, 305; Soviet Union and, 208, 236, 350. *See also* Slovak Republic
Czech Republic, 449

Dachau concentration camp, 200
Daniels, Josephus, *170,* 170
Darfur, 507, 513–514
Darlan, Jean-François, 194
Dartiguenave, Philippe Sudre, 166
Darwinism, 40, 57
Davies, John Paton, 281
Davies, Joseph E., 130, *163*
Davis, Nathaniel, 384
Dawes, Charles G., 125
Dawes Plan (1924), 99, 125
Day After, The (film), 430
Dayton Accords, 451
Death squads, 436
Debs, Eugene, 103
Debt: Argentine, 45; Haitian, 166; information dependency, 468; Jordanian, 462; Latin American, 456; modern economy and, 523; Philippine, 442, 466; post–World War I, 105, 122, 124–125; Third World, 385, 442. *See also* Loans

Declaration of Panama (1939), 172, 211
Declaration of the United Nations (1942), 179
Deer Hunter, The (film), 395
Defense Department, 249, 278, 287; Korean War and, 275; *Pentagon Papers* and, 391–392
Deforestation, 467
De Gaulle, Charles, 309, 324, 344, 346, 347, *348,* 349
De Grazia, Victoria, 248
De Klerk, F. W., 451, 452
De Lesseps, Ferdinand, 36
Delivery vehicles, for nuclear weapons, 377, 412, 448
De Lôme, Enrique Dupuy, 15
Democracy, 251, 404; prosperity and, 233
Democratic Party, 42, 91, 119, 139; Cold War and, 310; Geneva summit and, 283–284; League of Nations and, 97; prosperity and, 116; Venezuela crisis and, 5
Democratic People's Republic of Korea. *See* North Korea
Democratic Republic of Congo, 453
Democratic Republic of Vietnam (DRV), 325, 326. *See also* North Vietnam
Deng Xiaoping, 463
Denmark, 61
Deployment of weapons, 377
Depression, 6, 9, 523. *See also* Great Depression
Detainee Treatment Act, 497
Détente: Carter and, 400; with China, 369, 373, 390; Cold War and, 290; Cuba and, 383; Ford and, 385; Kissinger and, 373–378; McCarthyism and, 309; Middle East and, 382; SALT-I and, 373–377; with Soviet Union, 283, 290, 373–388, 390; Vietnam War and, 390, 394
Detzer, Dorothy, 126, 134
Developing nations. *See* Third World; *specific countries and regions*
Dewey, George, *14,* 16–18, 21 45
Dewey, John, 84
Dewey, Thomas E., 205

Díaz, Adolfo, 48
Díaz, Porfirio, 49
Diem, Ngo Dinh, 326–328, *327,* 344–348, *345*
Dienbienphu, battle at, 326
Dieppe, Allied raid on, 193
Diplomacy, 4, 9, 12; atomic, 236; cultural, *308;* decline of, 523; dollar, 42, 45, 46, 53–57, 59, *249;* preventive, 385, 400; Tomahawk, 470
Disarmament conferences, in interwar years, 125–127. *See also* Arms limitation; Washington Naval Conference
Disease: climate change and, 518; flu epidemic, 87; HIV/AIDS, 452, 468, 514–515, 518; malaria, 518; tuberculosis, 518; venereal, 88–89; World Health Organization and, 249, 468; yellow fever, 16, 121
Dispatches (Herr), 396
Displaced persons. *See* Refugees
Dobrynin, Anatoly, *375,* 432
Dodd, Christopher, 434
Dole, Robert, 460
Dollar devaluation, 386–387
Dollar diplomacy, 42, 45, 46, 53–57, 59, *249*
Dominican Republic; human rights in, 404; political upheaval in, 172; U.S. interests in, 45–47, 159, 211, 213; U.S. troops in, 162–167, 350
Domino theory, 308, 326; Third World and, 280
Doughboys, in Europe, 87–90. *See also* World War I
Douglas, William O., 327
Douglas Company, 112, 113
Dow Chemical, 356
Dower, John W., 251
Draft, 86–87, 182
Drago, Luis M., 45
Dresden, bombing of, 216, 228
Drought, 517
Drug trade, Latin American, 456, *457,* 457, 512–513
Duarte, José Napoleón, 435–436
Du Bois, W. E. B., 47

Dubrow, Elbridge, 327
Dudziak, Mary, *298*
Duiker, William, *325*
Duke, James B., *25*
Dulles, Allen W., 103, 277, 337
Dulles, John Foster, *278*, 280, *282*, *327;* anticommunist stance of, 103, 279, 280, 299, 310; brinkmanship and, 280, China and, 292, 293, 308, 368; Cold War and, 275, 279–281, 282; on Japan, 294–295; Korean War and, 268; Latin American nationalism and, 304, 308; Middle East and, 302, 303; on racial strife, 299; on Sino-Soviet split, 292; on Vietnam, 326
Dumbarton Oaks Conference (1944), 204–205
Du Pont, 128, 134
Dutch East Indies, 105, 186
Duvalier, "Baby Doc," 167, 443
Duvalier, François "Papa Doc," 167
Dybul, Mark R., 515

Eagleburger, Lawrence, 445
Earth Day, 388
Earth in the Balance (Gore), 519
Earth Summit (Rio, 1992), 467
Earthwatch, 389
East Berlin, 281, 289
Eastern Europe, 214; aid to, 204, 449; anti-Soviet propaganda for, *285;* boundaries of, 191; communism in, 235–238, 275; détente and, 373; dissidents in, 443; economic recovery, 509; European Union and, 449, 509; fall of communism in, 422–243, 423–425; human rights in, 378; Marshall Plan and, 247; nationalism in, 285–286, 400; Rapacki Plan for, 288; revolution in, 423–425; self-determination in, 301; Soviet troops in, 232, 281, 423; Soviet Union and, 196, 204, 211, 230, 257, 443; trade with, 236, 276;Warsaw Pact of, 250, 285; after World War II, 249. *See also specific countries*

East Germany, 241, 331–332; Berlin crisis and, 289, 331–332; German reunification and, 449; opening of Berlin Wall and, *421*, 422–423; refugees from, 331, *423*, 423
East Timor, 395
Economic aid. *See* Foreign aid
Economic Conference (London), 124
Economic cooperation, 117, 181–182
Economic Cooperation Act (1948), 247
Economic depression, 6, 9. *See also* Great Depression
Economic nationalism, 123, 125, 167, 304
Economic sanctions: against Cuba, 383, 383, 403, 437, 511; against Iraq, 459; against Italy, 131; against Japan, 147, 153, 154, 156, 187–188; against Nicaragua, 437; against Rhodesia, 384, 406; against Serbia-Montenegro, 450–451; against South Africa, 384, 404, 406, 442, 452. *See also* Trade embargoes
Economists, 159
Economy: Arab oil embargo and, 381; Asian financial crisis (1997–1998), 447; Chilean, 383; China trade and, 369; Chinese trade and, 463; cultural expansion and, 120–125; environmental issues and, 517–518; European recovery, 214, 307, 509; German, 241; globalization and, 470; global recession (1970s) 385–386; global recession (2008), 523; globalization and, 521–522; Japanese, 295, 307, 386, 464–465; Latin American, 159, 336, 456; Mexican, 456–457; Russian collapse, 448; South African, 452; Soviet, 127–130, *129*, 423, 433; Third World and, 385–389, 426–427; U.S. loss of competitive edge in, 386; U.S. military spending and, 443; U.S. share of World (1925–1929), *122;* Vietnamese, 464; Vietnam War and, 323;

after World War I, 105; after World War II, 216–217, 233, 247
Ecuador, 511
Eden, Anthony, *137, 181
Edge Act (1919), 105, 122
Edison, Thomas A., 16
Egypt, 303, 380, 381, 413; Anglo-French invasion of, 60, 301–302; Czech arms deal with, 301; food riots in, 518; Israel and, 301, 302, 380–381, 407; Soviet Union and, 300, 380–381; in United Arab Republic, 303
Egyptian-Israeli Peace Treaty (1979), 407
Eisenhower, Dwight D., 103, 193, *202, 279–280, 294, *299, 306;* Americanization and, 307; Berlin crisis and, 290–291; Castro and, 337, *339,* Central Intelligence Agency and, 277–278; Cold War and, 309–310, 331; Eastern Europe and, 286, 287; Korean War and, 275–276; Laos and, 344; Latin American nationalism and, 305; military buildup under, 278, 280, *289;* personal style of, 275–276; racism and, 299; Suez crisis and, 301–302; Taiwan Strait crisis and, 292, 293; U-2 crisis and, 290–291; Vietnam and, 326–328, *393;* World War II and, 191, *202,* 216, 276; Eisenhower Doctrine, 280, 303, 308
Eisenstein, Sergei, 128
Electronic business, 468–469
Eliot, Charles W., 19
Ellsberg, Daniel, 391
El Salvador, 171, 403, 434; civil war in, 435–436, 455–456
Embargoes. *See* Arms embargoes; Economic sanctions; Naval blockades; Trade embargoes
Emigration, Jewish, from Soviet Union, 374, 411. *See also* Immigration; Refugees
Energy conservation, 413
Englebrecht, Helmuth, 134
English language, 468, 520

Enola Gay (bomber), 226, *227*

Entebbe, Uganda, 382

Environmental issues, 59; books about, 388; global concern with, 388–389, 443, 467–468, 516–518

Environmental Protection Agency (EPA), 389

Eritrea, 131, 453

Erlich, Paul, 388

Espionage and Sedition Acts, 103

Essen, Germany, *248*

Essence of Decision (Allison), 395

Estonia, 93, *95*, 425,

Estrada Palma, Tomás, 44

Ethiopia, 406, 453; Central Intelligence Agency in, 427, 441; Italian invasion of, *137*, 131, 135, 137; Soviet/Cuban influence in, 403, 406, 441

"Ethnic cleansing," 450–451, 513. *See also* Genocide

Ethnic conflicts: in Balkans, 450; Hutu-Tutsi in Africa, 453

Europe: Americanization of, 121; antinuclear protests in, 430–431; Cold War in, 246–250, 308; détente in, 378; line of defense in, 113–114; post-Cold War, 508–515; Soviet Union and, 127; terrorism in, 380; trade with, 233; U.S. tariffs and, 122; World War I, map, *78*; World War I debt of, 124; before World War II, map, *95*; after World War II, map, *238. See also* Eastern Europe; North Atlantic Treaty Organization (NATO); Western Europe; *specific countries*

European Advisory Commission, 194

European Central Bank, 449

European Common Market, 387

European Community (EC), 449

European Defense Community (EDC), 283

European Monetary Union, 449

European Recovery Program (ERP). *See* Marshall Plan

European Union (EU), 449, 459; expansion of, 509

Evans, Robley D., 62

Everything We Had (Santolini), 396

Exodus (ship), 244

Expansion,18–21; U.S. in Asia, 252; Cold War and, 257; U.S. economic, 233; of European Union (EU), 509; U.S. during interwar years, 134; Japanese, during interwar years, 151, *155;* Soviet, 411–414; Vietnam War and, 394. *See also* Colonialism; Imperialism

Explorer I (satellite), 287

Export-Import Bank, 124, 276

Export-Import Bank loans: to Afghanistan, 249; to Chile, 383; to China, 413; to Cuba, 167–168; to Czechoslovakia, 238; to Greece, 243–244; to Haiti, 166; to Latin America, 159, 162, 211; to Mexico, 171; to South Africa, 406; to Soviet Union, 129

Extraterritoriality, 151, 197

Exxon, 383, 389, 406

Falaba (ship), 80, 81

Fairs. *See* World's fairs

Fallujah, 522

Famine: in Africa, 387, *388,* 441, 517; climate change and, 517–518

Farabundo Martí Front for National Liberation (FMLN), 434

I.G. Farben Company, 134

Farouk, king of Egypt, 300

Fascism, 134, *235*, 235. *See also* Nazi Germany; Italy

FBI (Federal Bureau of Investigation), 390, 522

Federal Republic of Germany (FRG). *See* West Germany

Federal Republic of Yugoslavia. *See* Yugoslavia

Felix, Benjamin Arellano, 512

Fellowship of Reconciliation, 125

Ferebee, Thomas, 226

Ferrell, Robert H., *207*

Fields of Fire (Webb), 396

Films, 16, 85, 133, 172, 203, 441, 453, 465, 509; Americanization and, 121, 520; about Cuba, 168; Cold War and, 257, 258, 307; about Haiti, 165; in Japan, 251, 294; Japanese investment in, 465; Mexican stereotypes in, 169; about Nicaragua, 164; Soviet-American relations and, 128, 307; terrorist actions in, 480; about Vietnam War, 394, 395–396; about World War II, 190

Finland, *95,* 125, 182, 257; Soviet Union and, 93, 100, 235–236

Firestone corporation, 406

First strike, nuclear weapons, 377, 430, 432

First Yank in Tokyo (film), 157

Fischer, Fritz, *335*

Fisher, John, 59

Fisheries disputes, 59

Five Power Treaty (1922), 149

Flack, Roberta, 441

Flagg, James Montgomery, *160, 191*

Fletcher, Henry P., 62

Flight (film), 164

Flooding, climate change and, 517

Flu epidemic (1918), 87

Flying Tigers (China), 153, 198

Food: famine in Africa, 387, *388,* 441, 467, 517; climate change and, 517–518; Food for Peace Program, 276, 344; Indian self-sufficiency in, 443; population growth and, 467; riots, 518; World Food Conference (1974), 388–389

Foraker Act (1900), 62

Forbes, W. Cameron, 166

Ford, Gerald R., 371, 383, *384*, 384, 385, *393*, 395, 400; Africa and, 385; Cuba and, 384*;* Strategic Arms Limitation Talks and, 374, 377, 378

Ford, Henry, 85, 121, 128, 133, 161

"Fordlandia," 161

Ford Motor Company, 389, 406, 452

Fordney-McCumber Act (1922), 122

Foreign Affairs (journal), 163, 246

Foreign aid, 233, 387–388; to Angola, 372; to Bolivia, 404; to Cambodia, 372, 388; Cold War rivalry in, 309; to Eastern Europe, 204, 449; to Egypt, 301,

407, 503–504; to El Salvador,
435–436; to Haiti, 458; increase
in, 276, 386; to India, 333–334;
to Israel, 301, 407, 439; Japanese,
442; to Latin America, 304, 305,
400; linked to human rights,
400; to Nicaragua, 403, 436; to
Philippines, 442; to Poland, 204,
284–285; to Russia, 448; to
South Korea, 274, 388; to South
Vietnam, 328, 372, 388, 390;
Soviet, to Egypt, 303; Soviet, to
India, 300; Soviet, to Indonesia,
300; to Taiwan, 292; to Third
World, 300; to Turkey, 372. *See
also* Export-Import Bank; Lend-
Lease aid; Loans; Military aid
Foreign Corrupt Practices Act (1977),
389
Foreign investment, 386; in Africa,
384–385, 406; in Cuba, 459; in
Germany, 509; in interwar years,
121–123, 152–153; in India, 509;
Japanese, 145, 465; in Latin
America, 159, 160–162, 304,
382–385, 400–401, 456; in
Mexico, 51, 456–457; in
Nicaragua, 164; in Philippines,
148, 442; in South Africa, 441;
in Vietnam, 464
Foreign policy public, 10
Forests, 467
Formosa. *See* Taiwan
Forrestal, James V., 236, 244
Fortuny, José Manuel, 304
Four Policemen, 196, 198
Four Power Treaty (1922), 149
Fourteen Points, 90–93, 94
Fourth World, 385
Fousek, John, *189*
Fox, Vincente, 512
Fox News, *493*
France, 116, 146, 283, 309; aircraft
sales to, 112–115, 138; Algeria
and, 287; alliance with, 292;
appeasement policy of, 113–114,
131–132; arms sales to, 181;
Balkan crisis and, 450; Brussels
Treaty and, 249; colonies of,187;
disarmament and, 149; Geneva
summit and, 283–284; Germany

and, 241; Great Britain and, 57;
Haiti and, 47; Indochina and, 25,
92, 105, 179, 191, 232; Iraq War
and, 492, 509; Kellogg-Briand
Pact and, 126; mandate system
and, 92; Marshall Plan and, 247;
Morocco and, 60; nuclear forces
of, 431; nuclear weapons of, *348*,
350; Ruhr valley seizure by, 125;
Southeast Asia Treaty
Organization and, 326; Soviet
Union and, 127; Spanish civil
war and, 132; United Nations
and, 205, 210; Vietnam and, 216,
257, 278, 324, 326–328; World
War I and, 76, 77, 78, 81, 82, 83,
104; World War I peace and,
91–93; after World War II, 210;
World War II and, 182, 191,
192, 203
France, Anatole, 83
Francis, David, 100
Franco, Francisco, 132, 137
Frankfurter, Felix, 201, 202
Franz Ferdinand, archduke of
Austria-Hungary, 77
Free elections, 236, 289; in Egypt,
503–504
Free Europe Committee, *285*
Free South Africa Movement, 441
Free Trade Area of the Americas, 447,
456, 511
Friedman, Thomas, 520
Friendly Fire (Bryan), 395
Fukuda, Yasuo, 508
Fulbright, J. William, 249, 330, 337;
Vietnam and, *357,* 357
Fulbright Program, 249
Fund for Peace, 495

Gabon, 404
Gaddis, John Lewis, 491
Gadhafi, Moammar, 382, 440–441
Gaither Report, 287
Galbraith, John Kenneth, 342
Garbo, Greta, 130
Garment, Leonard, *381*
Garner, Jay, 494
Gas warfare, 87, *89,* 426, 461. *See also*
Chemical weapons

Gates, Bill, 469, 518
Gates, Robert, 499, *510;*511, 523
Gaza. *See* West Bank and Gaza
Gbedemah, K. A., 298
Gender, 4, 20, 28–29, 55, 63–64, *83,*
87, *88, 238,* 252, *281, 299,* 382,
400, 430, 444–445; 468; cultural
bias and, 298–299. *See also*
Masculine ethos
Gender stereotypes: cultural bias and,
299; masculinity, 159–160,
245, 299
General Agreement on Tariffs and
Trade (GATT), 387, 447
General Electric, 121, 128, 406,
452, 464
General Motors, 121, 389, 406
Genet, Charles Clinton, 88
Geneva Conference on Indochina
(1954), 292, 326, 327, 344, 359
Geneva Convention, 488, 497
Geneva Disarmament Conference, 127
Geneva summit meeting (1955),
283–284
Genocide: Balkan ethnic cleansing,
450–451; Cambodian, 394, 414;
Darfur, 507, 513–514; Nazi
Holocaust, 200–203; in
Rwanda, 453
George V, King of England, *72*
George Washington (ship), 91, 100
Georgia, 510, 511
Gerard, James W., 82
German Democratic Republic
(GDR). *See* East Germany
Germany, 25, 26, 28, 60, 130–133;
air force of, 113; alliance with
Italy, 132; al Qaeda in, 481;
appeasement policy toward, 113,
130–133; atomic bomb and, 228;
Bolsheviks and, 100; bombing of
Dresden, 216; China and, 25;
foreign investment in, 509;
France and, 241; Great Britain
and, 241; Haiti and, 47;
Holocaust and, 200–203;
invasion of Czechoslovakia by,
132–133, 137; Latin America
and, 45, 113, 172, 211, 213;
Lusitania and, 52, 71–75, 80;
Mexico and, 50, 51, 53, 83, 84;

Morocco and, 60; pact with Japan, 131, 157, 187; Poland and, 115, 133, 139, 181, 211; rearmament of, 127, 130; rehabilitation of, 116, 241; reunification of, 283, *421*, 422–423, 448, 449; Rhineland, 116, 131; Russia and, 100; Soviet Union and, 127, *132*, 133, 232; Spanish civil war and, 132; submarine warfare of, 71–75, 79–80, 81–84, 179, 185; threat from, 39, 113, 124–125, 187; trade with Soviet bloc by, 413; transformations, map, *424;* U.S. businesses and, 121; U.S. invasion of Iraq and, 481, 491, 492, 502, 509; World War I and, 76–79, 89–90; World War I peace and, 90, 92–93, *95;* World War I reparations and, 124;World War II and, 182, map, *183,* 187; World War II deaths in, 215–216; World War II peace and, 206–207, 209, 210–214, *238. See also* Berlin; East Germany; Nazis; West Germany

Ghana, *329,* 336, 453

Giap, Vo Nguyen, 321, 322, 359

Gillespie, Dizzy, 276

Gillette corporation, 386

Gilpatrick, Roswell, 331

Gingrich, Newt, 521

Glasgow, Ellen, 104

Glasnost (Soviet policy), 432

Globalization, 465, 469; of Cold War, 307–310; communications and, 121, 468–469; as neoimperialism, 469; U.S. economy as engine of, 470, 519–521

Global challenges, 515–524

Global warming, 443, 468, 486, 516–517

Godzilla (film), 294

Goedde, Petra, *242*

Gold crisis, 323, 386

Golden Arches Theory of Conflict Prevention, 520

Goldman, Emma, 86

Goldwater, Barry, 333, 351, *371,* 391, 436

Gómez, Máximo, 11

Gompers, Samuel, 18

Gomulka, Wladyslaw, 284

Goncharov, German, 243

Gonzalez, Elian, 459

Goodacre, Glenna, *397*

Good Earth, The (Buck), 150; (film) 157.

Good Neighbor Policy, 159, 172, 304; in Cuba, 167; in Dominican Republic, 164; in Mexico, 169; in Nicaragua, 164; Pan Americanism and, 171–172

Goodwin, Richard, 340

Goodyear corporation, 105

Gorbachev, Mikhail S., 443, 423–425, 460; coup against, 448; Reagan and, 432–434, *433;* 1989 revolutions and, 423, 425; Soviet arms reductions and, 423, 447

Gore, Al, *517;* 518–519

Gore, Thomas P., 82

Government Accountability Office, 499

Graham, Billy, 430

Graham, Martha, *308*

Grayson, Cary, 97–99

Great Britain, 60, *74,* 137, 187, 200; alliance with, 292; al Qaeda in, 481;American cultural invasion of, 178; appeasement policy of, 113, 130–133, 135; arms sales to, 113, 181–182; atomic bomb of, 309; Baghdad Pact and, 300; Balkan crisis and, 450; Boer War and, 28; Brussels Treaty and, 249; Canadian border disputes and, 57; China and, 25, 56; Cuba and, 438; disarmament and, 126–127, 149; empire of, 63, 216, 232, 326; France and, 60; Geneva summit and, 283–284; German partition and, 241; Greece and, 211, 215; India and, 105, 135; Indochina and, 325; invasion of Iraq by, 508; Iranian oil crisis and, 240; Israel and, 244–246; Japan and, 57; Jewish refugees and, 202; Korean War and, 270; Latin America and, 5,

36; Lend-Lease to, 178, 184; loan to, 240; mandate system and, 92; Mexico and, 50; Middle East and, 213–214, 287; naval blockade, World War I, 79–81; nuclear forces of, 431; Panama Canal and, 36; rapprochement with, 40, 57–63; Spanish civil war and, 132; Suez crisis and, 301–302; trade of, 120, 179; U.S. neutrality and, 77–79;Venezuela crisis and, 5, 46; World War I and, 75, 76, 77–79, 80–81, 91;World War I deaths, 104, 215;World War I debts of, 124; World War II aftermath, 204, 210, 216;World War II strategies and, 191–192; Zimbabwe/Rhodesia and, 406

Great Depression, 116, 117, 128, 145, 162, 523; global effects of, 123–124, *123,* 160, 172

Greater East Asia Co-Prosperity Sphere, 153, 187

Great Society, 349

Greece, 204, 281; civil war in, 243–244; Great Britain and, 211, 215; Turkey and, 243–244

Green Berets, 331, 409

Greenhouse gas emissions, 443, 468, 516

Greenpeace, 388

Greer (destroyer), 179, 185

Grenada, U.S. invasion of, 437–438

Gresham, Walter Q., 10

Grew, Joseph C., 62, 153, 186, 187, 190

Grey, Sir Edward, 59, 81

Gromyko, Andrei, 293, 433

Grossman, Robert, *371*

Group of 77, 387

Groves, Leslie, 226, *228*

Gruening, Ernest, 352

Guam, 19, 62, 149

Guangzhou Bay (China), 25

Guantánamo Bay naval base, 15, 44, 341, 488, 511, 524

Guatemala, 304–306; Central Intelligence Agency in, 277, 309; human rights in, 404, 414; U.S. interests in, 159, 211, 434

Guerin, Fritz W., *17*

Guevara, Che, 338
Guiliani, Rudolph, 480
Guinea-Bissau, 513
Gulflight (ship), 81
Gulf War (1991), 449, 459–461
Gusterson, Hugh, *229*
Guomindang (China), 150, 151, 153, 154, 255; supply routes to, 186; U.S. China policy and, 197, 198

Hague, The. *See* World Court
Haig, Alexander M., Jr., 427, 437
Haiti, 45, 46, 443; human rights in, 404; U.S. interests in, 159; U.S. occupation of, 162–163, 164–165, *166*, 458, 470
Haitian National Bank, 47
Halberstam, David, *325*
Halifax, Lord, 202
Hamas, 504–505
Hamm, Clifford, *165*
Hanighen, Frank, 134
Harding, Warren G., 98, *117*, 117, 149, 162
Harriman, E. H., 55
Harriman, W. Averell, 128, *240*, 344, 354; on Soviet Union, 211, 234; Truman and, 234
Hart, Frederick, *397*
Harvard University, 61
Hatfield, Mark O., 437
Havana Conference (1928), 171
Havel, Václav, 378
Hawai'i, 55; annexation of, 5, 6, 10, 13, 18, 19–20, 28
Hay, John M., 26, 41, 60; Open Door notes and, *26*, 26, 53, 56; Panama Canal and, 34–38
Hay-Bunau-Varilla Treaty (1903), 38
Hay-Herrán Treaty (1903), 36
Hay-Pauncefote Treaty (1900), 36
Hearst, William Randolph, 4, 15, 118
Helms, Jesse, 459
Helms, Richard, 383
Helms-Burton Act, 459
Helsinki conferences (1975), 376–378
Hemingway, Ernest, *104*
Henry, prince of Prussia, 62
Heroin trade, 457, 466, 488, 512–513
Herr, Michael, 395

Herrán, Thomás, 36
Hezbollah, 504–505
Hindenburg, Paul von, 90
Hippisley, Alfred, 26
Hirohito, emperor of Japan, *231, 251*, 251
Hiroshima, bombing of, 215, 226–231, *230*
Hiss, Alger, 208, 268
Hitler, Adolf, 130–133, *131, 132, 133,* 137, 185, 186, 189, 190, 192–193; Allied unity and, 179–180, 185, 194; appeasement policy toward, 113, 130–133; *blitzkrieg* of, 139, 182; German rearmament under, 127; Jews and, 179, 200–203; Latin America and, 171–172; Soviet invasion and, 130; Stalin compared to, 235; view of America by, 133. *See also* Nazis
HIV/AIDS, 468; in Africa, 452, 514–515
Hmong clans (Laos), 344
Hoar, George F., 4, 19
Hobart, Garrett, 3
Ho Chi Minh, *325,* 326, 347, 351, 359, 390; French and, 92, 105, 324–328; Nixon and, 390–392; Tet offensive and, *321, 322*
Ho Chi Minh Trail, *355, 359*
Hoffman, Paul, 247
Hogan, Michael J., 247
Hoganson, Kristin, *13*
Holbrooke, Richard, *450*
Hollywood movies. *See* Films
Holocaust, 200–203
Honduras, 159, 434, 436
Honeywell corporation, 452
Hong Kong, 25
Hoover, Herbert, 78, 117–118, *118, 164;* economic nationalism and, 124; Haiti and, *166;* Manchurian crisis and, 145, 147, 148; oil reserves and, 162; postwar Germany and, 241; on Soviet Union, 127
Hoover, J. Edgar, *170,* 170–171
Hopkins, Harry, 180–181, 191, 210, *214,* 214
Hornbeck, Stanley K., 188

House, Edward M., *72,* 73, 77, 80–81, *81;* World War I peace and, 91, 102, 105
House-Grey Memorandum (1916), 81
Hubbard, John, 34
Huerta, Victoriano, 49–51, 59
Hughes, Charles Evans, *117,* 118, 127, 163, 171; at Washington Conference, 149
Hughes, Langston, 137
Huguang Railroad, 56
Hull, Cordell, 119, *120,* 137, *138,* 185, 187, 188; Atlantic Charter and, 179, 181; embargo of Japan and, 154, 156; on Haiti, 165; on Jewish refugees, 201, 203; Latin America and, 162, 171, 172; Soviet Union and, 137; tariff reduction and, 124; World War II peace and, 194, 205, 206
Human rights, 80, 384; Africa and, 514; authoritarianism and, 427; Bricker Amendment on, 309; Carter and, 400, 401, 411, 412, 414; in China, 463, 507; in El Salvador, 436; European conference on, 378; prisoners/detainees, 341, 488, 496–497, *496,* 511; U.N. Declaration on, 258; women's rights and, 468
Humphrey, Hubert, *319, 358,* 359
Hungary, 422, 449; revolution in, 102, 285–286; Soviet Union and, 208, 211, 235, *286,* 302; war refugees in, 200–203; after World War I, 93, *95*
Hurley, Patrick J., 198–199, *199,* 200, 252
Hu Shi, 151
Hussein, king of Jordan, 276, 303
Hussein, Saddam, *440;* al Qaeda ties, 490; capture of, 495; invasion of Kuwait by, 459–461; economic sanctions against, 490; Iraq invasion and, 493, 495, 519; statue of, *493,* 493; weapons of mass destruction and, 491, *492,* 492, 496
Hutu-Tutsi rivalry (Rwanda), 453
Hydrogen bomb, 250, 259, 294. *See also* Atomic bomb

IBM (International Business Machines), 386, 465

Ice caps, 516–517

Iceland, 185, 433

IEDs (improvised explosive devices), 495

Igarashi, Yoshikuni, *251*

Illinois (ship), 83

Immigration: Chinese, 198; Cuban, 437, 459; Haitian, 458; illegal, from Mexico, 403, 512; Japanese, 55, 153; Jewish, 200–203, 244–245, 374, 411; quota system, 119, 200. *See also* Refugees

Immigration Act (1924), 153

Imperialism, 135, 151, 302; reaction to, 4, 8–10, 12, 19–21, 28–29. *See also* Colonialism; Expansion

Improvised explosive devices (IEDs), 495

Inconvenient Truth, An (film), 519

Independent internationalism, 115–120, 148

India, 213, 299; aid to, 333–334; British in, 105, 135, 216, 232; food self-sufficiency in, 443; foreign investment in, 509; independence of, 59; nuclear arms of, 347, 387, 414, 466–467, 506–507; Pakistan and, 334, 466–467; Soviet Union and, 374; women's rights in, 468

Indochina, 292; environmental damage in, 389; French in, 25, 92, 105, 179, 191, 232, 278, 325; Japanese in, 179; military aid to, 269, 393; Vietnam War and, 395; after World War II, 251. *See also* Southeast Asia; *specific countries*

Indonesia, 215, 251, 277; bombing of, 489; Dutch and, 216, 232; East Timor and, 395; human rights in, 414; Soviet aid to, 300

Industry, environment and, 388–389. *See also* Business; Military-industrial complex; Trade; *specific industries*

Information, global revolution in, 468–469

Inland Fisheries Treaty (1908), 59

Insular Cases (1901–1904), 62

Insulza, José Miguel, 512

Intelligence, *188*, 188. *See also* Central Intelligence Agency; U-2 spy planes

Inter-American Defense College, 382

Inter-American Development Bank, 276, 305, 437

Intercontinental ballistic missiles (ICBMs), 287, *288, 289,* 331; defined, 377; limitations on, 376–378, 411–412, 448; vulnerability of, 430

Intergovernmental Committee on Refugees, 201

Intergovernmental organizations (IGOs), 389

Intergovernmental Panel on Climate Change, 516

Intermediate-range ballistic missiles (IRBMs), 287

Intermediate-range nuclear forces (INFs), 377, 431–434

Intermediate-Range Nuclear Forces (INF) Treaty (1987), 433–434, 443

International Atomic Energy Agency, 502, 505

International Bank for Reconstruction and Development. *See* World Bank

International Business Machines (IBM), 386, 465

International communications issues, 468–469

International competition, 20

International Criminal Court, 486, 514, 518

International Fund for Agricultural Development, 387–388

International Harvester, 128

International Red Cross, 497

Internationalists, 96, 98, 115–120, 148

International Ladies Garment Workers Union, 127

International Monetary Fund (IMF), 204, 217, 246, 447; Latin America and, 456; regulation by, 387

International Non-Intervention Committee, 132

International Telecommunications Satellite Consortium (INTELSAT), 468

International Telephone and Telegraph (ITT), 121, 161

Internet, 481, 520–521

Interwar years (1920–1939), 111–139; appeasement policy in, 113, 130–133; arms sales to belligerents in, 112–115, 138–139; China in, 119, 129, 137, 150–152; economic and cultural expansion in, 120–125; Germany in, 113, 115, 124, 130–133, 137–139; independent internationalism in, 115–120; isolationism and neutrality in, 115, 133–135; Japan in, 113, 127, 129, 137, 152–156; Latin America in, 157–162; Mexico in, 169–171; Pan Americanism in, 171–172, 181; peace initiatives in, 125–127; U.S.-Soviet relations in, 120, 127–130

Intifada (Palestinian uprising), 439, 463

Investment. *See* Foreign investment

Iran, 214, 303, 306, 378, 457; alliance with, 382; arms sales to, 374, 382, 407, 408, 411, 437; Azerbaijan and, 240; Baghdad Pact and, 300; censorship in, 469; Central Intelligence Agency in, 277, 309; hostage crisis in, 406–411, *408;* human rights in, 400, 414; Iran-Contra affair and, 428–429, *429;* nuclear arms and, 466–467; oil in, 240, 406–407, 408, 412; Soviet Union and, 240; war with Iraq, 406, 409–410, 441

Iran-Contra affair, 428–429, *429,* 443

Iraq, 214, 303; army of, 502; Baghdad Pact and, 300; Coalition Provisional Authority in, 494–495, 498, 522; economic sanctions against, 459; freedom and democracy movement in, 503–504; future of, 523; George W. Bush and, 489–490, 492; Gulf War and, 449, 459–461,

493; invasion of Kuwait by, 448, 459–461; Kurds in, 461; nuclear arms and, 466–467; oil in, 213–214; U.S. invasion and occupation of, 490–402, 493–500, 501; war with Iran, 406, 409–410, 441; weapons of mass destruction in, 461, *492*, 502

Iraq Study Group, 499

Ireland, 200

Irish Americans, 77

Irish Easter Rebellion (1916), 82

Iron and steel production, 9

"Iron curtain" speech (Churchill), 239

Ishii, Kikujiro, 57

Islamic fundamentalism, 412, 469, 481–482, 487, 506

Islamist Court Union, 513

Isolationism, 115, 133–135, 154, 186, 190, 248. *See also* Neutrality

Isolationists, *144*, 154, 181, 182

Israel, 203, 378, 438–440; aid to, 301, 407, 439; Arab conflicts with, 301, 462, 504; creation of, 244–246, *245*; Egypt and, 301, 302, 380–381, 40; nuclear weapons of, 466–467; stereotypes of, 299; weapons sales to, 301–302, 380, 382. *See also* Middle East

Italy, 149; alliance with Germany, 132; invasion of Ethiopia by, 100, 131, 136–137; Latin America and, 171; menace from, 113, 124; post–World War II, 211, 213; rearmament of, 127; refugees in, 200, 203, 204; Spanish civil war and, 132; World War I and, 77, 90–91; World War II and, 187, 191, 192

ITT (International Telephone and Telegraph), 121, 161

Iwo Jima, 251

Jackson, Henry M., 412

Jagan, Cheddi, *336*

Jamaica, 59

James, Jack, 268

James, William, 23

Japan, 60, 309; alliance with, 275, 293–295, 465; Allies' containment of, map, *212*; anti-Americanism in, 464; Asian expansion of, 52, 152–156, map, *155*; bombing of, *225*, 226–231, *230*; China and, 25, 129, 137, 152–156, 186, 197, 199, 508; economic sanctions of, 147, 153, 154, 156, 186, 187–188; economy of, 295, 307, 386; foreign investments of, 464–465; German pact with, 131, 167; Great Britain and, 57; India and, 508; Indochina and, 179; interwar years (1920–1939), 152–156; Iraq, troops in, 508; Korea and, 25, 53, 54, 55, 251, 442; Latin America and, 171; Manchuria and, 126, 145–147, *146*, 158, 172; menace from, 113, 124; oil needs of, 147, 152, 18–187, 381; Pacific war and, 208–210; People's Republic of China and, *367*, 369, 374; Soviet Union and, 196; trade with, 153, 386, 387, 442–443; Tripartite Pact and, 187; U.S. occupation of, 251–252, 294; Washington Conference and, 148, 149; World War I and, 77; World War II and, 186–190, 191, 210, *212*, 231; after World War II, 215

Jefferson, Thomas, 20, 427, 494

Jenner, William E., 269

Jerome, Jenny, 63

Jespersen, T. Christopher, *393*

Jewish Welfare Board, 87

Jews: anti-Semitism and, 200, 244, 439; creation of Israel and, 244–246, *245*; Holocaust and, 200–203; masculinity and, *245*, 299; Nazis and, 130, 132, 138, 179; settlements of, Palestine, 504; Soviet emigrants, 374, 411. *See also* Israel

Jiang, Madame (Meiling Soong), 151, *152*, 157, *197*

Jiang Jieshi (Chiang Kai-shek), 156–157, 187, 189, 197, 210, 252–254, 281; communists and, 151, 154; Japan and, 145; Korean War and, 272, 273, 274; Stilwell and, 197–198; Taiwan Strait crisis and, 292–293; "two Chinas" policy and, 310; U.S. support for, *197*, 198–199, 252–254, 292, 309, 368

Jiang Zemin, 464

Jiaozhou (Kiaochow), 25, 56

Jihad (Muslim holy war or "struggle"), 466, 469

Jihadi fighters, *481*, 495, 503, 521

Jim Crow, 298–299. *See also* Racism

Jingoism, 3, 7, 9, 77

Jinmen (Quemoy), 292–293

Johnson, Hiram, 97, 101, *134*, 184

Johnson, James Weldon, 165

Johnson, Lyndon, *319*, 324, 334, 343, 344, 401; Dominican Republic and, 350; on Peace Corps, 334; personal style of, *347*, 349–350; Tet offensive and, 320–324, *321*, *323*; Vietnam War and, *323*, 324, 344, 347, 348–350, *358*, *393*, 395

Joint Chiefs of Staff, 293; Cuba and, 337, 338, 340; directive 1067, 206–207, 214; Iran hostage crisis and, 409; Korean War and, 270, 272; Laos and, 344; Vietnam and, 353

Jones Act of 1916, 24

Jones Act of 1917, 168

Jordan, 303, 382, 438; Israel peace accord and, 462

Jordan, David Starr, 20

Jordan, Michael, 468

Judd, Walter, 254

Judt, Tony, 231

Jusserand, Jules, *41*

Kabila, Laurent, 453

Kaiser Aluminum, 385

Kamikaze air attacks, 229

Karski, Jan, 202

Karzai, Hamid, 502

Katsura, Taro, 54

Katyn (Poland) massacre, 193

Kazakhstan, 467
Kearny (destroyer), 185
Kelley, Jay W., *279*
Kellogg, Frank B., 97, 117–118, 126, 159
Kellogg, Brown & Root, 522
Kellogg-Briand Pact (1928), 126, 127, 146, 147, 153
Kemmerer, Edward, 159
Kennan, George F., 239, 250, 358, 449; anti-nuclear movement and, 430; containment policy and, *246,* 246, 287–288; on new millennium, 469; Potsdam accord and, 215; on Soviet threat, 120, 130, 232
Kennedy, John F., 310, *328,* 359; Africa and, *329;* Alliance for Progress and, 329, 334; Berlin crisis and, 331–332; Cuba and, 336–343; Laos and, 343–345; military buildup under, 331–332; policy style of, 328–330; Third World and, 328, 333–336; Vietnam and, 327, *328,* 328, 330, 343–349, *348, 393*
Kennedy, Joseph P., 329
Kennedy, Robert F., 322, 330, *347,* 358; Cuban missile crisis and, 340, 342
Kenya, 385, 413; U.S. embassy in, *481*
Kerensky, Alexander, 100
Khan, A. Q., 506
Khanh, Nguyen, 351
Khartoum, 513–514
Khatami, Mohammad, 502
Khe Sanh, battle for, 321–322
Khmer Rouge, 391, 394, 414
Khomeini, Ruhollah, 408, 409, 411, 441
Khrushchev, Nikita S., 103, 281, *283,* 293; Cold War diplomacy of, 281, 284, *289,* 290–291, 300; Cuba and, 337, 338, *339,* 339, 341–343; debate with Nixon, *284,* 284, 307, *328;* deStalinization and, 284; Kennedy and, 331–332, 334; U-2 crisis and, 290–291, *291*
Kim Il Sung, 273, 274

Kim Jong Il, 505–506, 519–520
Kim Jong Nam, 520
King, Ernest, 191
King, Martin Luther, Jr., 356
Kirkpatrick, Jeane, 427, 428, 435
Kissinger, Henry A., 368–370, *371, 375,* 380–381, *381,* 407; Africa and, 384–385; Cuba and, 383; détente and, 373–376; on foreign aid, 387–388; Iran and, 380–381; *Mayaguez* incident and, 395; Middle East and, 380–381; Nixon's visit to China and, 368–371, *371;* on ocean mining, 389; personal style of, 371–373; Pinochet and, 383; shuttle diplomacy of, 381; Vietnam War and, 391–392, 394, 395, 398
Kitchen debate, *284,* 284, 307, 328
Kitchin, Claude, 85
Knapp, Harry, 162
Knowland, William E., 293
Knox, Frank, 136, 182
Knox, Philander C., 42, 46, 48, 56
Kohl, Helmut, 422, 449
Koizumi, Junchiro, 508
Kolchak, A. V., 102
Konoe, Fumimaro, 187
Korea, Japan and, 25, 53, 54, 55, 251, 442. *See also* North Korea; South Korea
Korean Air Lines (KAL) Flight 007, 432
Korean War, *267,* 268–275, map, *271;* casualties in, 272–273; China and, *267,* 270–275, 292; Japan and, 295; MacArthur and, 268, 269, 270–272; peace talks for, 272, 292; Soviet Union and, 269, 270–271, 273–275, 281; U.S. entry in, 270–272; Vietnam and, 326
Kosovo conflict, 449, *450*
Kosygin, Alexei, 350, 380
Kovic, Ron, 395
Kristallnacht, 200
Kuhn, Bowie, 383
Kun, Bela, 102
Kung, H. H., 151
Kurds, in Iraq, 461, 498–499
Kuwait; Iraqi invasion of, 448, 459–461

Kyoto Global Warming Convention (1997), 468
Kyoto Protocol, 486, 516

LaFollette, Robert M., 39, 83, 85, *86, 97*
LaFollette, Robert M., Jr., 136
Lake, Anthony, 446, 458
Lambert, Jack, *234*
Land mines treaty, 466
Langley (aircraft carrier), *213*
Lansdale, Edward, 327, 338
Lansing, Robert, 42, 75, 79, 81; Asia and, 57; World War I peace and, 91, 102
Laos, 326, 343–344, 391, 394, 457; Central Intelligence Agency in, 344; French and, 324
Latin America, 119, 121, 202, 309; Alliance for Progress and, 329, 334, 350; alliances with, 205; anti-American sentiment in, 511–512; anticommunism in, 257, 300; Britain and, 5, 36; Carter administration and, 401–406; communists in, 163–164, 304–305; debt of, 456; democracy in, 511–512; drug trade in, 456, *457,* 457; economic expansion and, 39, 122, 511; foreign investment in, 159, 160–162, 303–304, 382–385, 401, 456; Germany and, 45, 113, 171–172; Good Neighbor Policy, 159–160, 172; Great Britain and, 5, 36; leftist leaders, 511–512; nationalism in, 303–305; Pan Americanism and, 171–172, 181; post-Cold War, 508–515; racism in, 57; trade with, 160–162, 401, 456, 511; U.S. interests in, 39, 59, 105, 116, 152, 382–385; U.S. intervention in, 135, map, *402,* 457; U.S. power in, 148, 350. *See also* Caribbean; Central America; *specific countries*
Latvia, 93, *95,* 425
Law of the Sea Conference (1970), 389
Law of the Sea Treaty (1982), 467
Lea, Tom, *209*

League of Nations, 94−98, 118, 194; appeasement policy and, 130; Congress and, 94, 96, 103−104; Italy and, 131; Manchurian crisis and, 146, 147; pacifism and, 125, 127; Soviet Union in, 127; Wilson and, 91−93, 96−97, 118

Lebanon, 303, 443; civil war in, 382, 406, 438−439; hostages in, 428; Palestine Liberation Organization in, 438−439; Syria and, 438−439, 503

Le Duc Tho, 372, *375,* 392

Lee, Fitzhugh, 2, 12

LeMay, Curtis, *343,* 354

Lend-Lease aid, 190; to Britain, 178, 184; to China, 198, 253−254; to Soviet Union, *184,* 185, 194, 196, 214, 240

Lend-Lease Bill, 184

Lenin, Vladimir Ilyich, 100, *101,*

Less developed countries (LDCs), 385. *See also* Third World

Levinson, Salmon, 126

Lewis, Ross, *288*

Lewinsky, Monica, 454

Liaodong Province (China), 25, 53

Liberia, 58, 60, 453, 513

Libya, 440−441; nuclear weapons of, 506

Life magazine, 190

Lima Conference (1938), 172, 211

Limited Test Ban Treaty (1963), 343, 349

Lin Bao, 357

Lind, John, 50

Lindbergh, Charles, *158,* 170

Lindh, John Walker, 488

LINEBACKER (bombing raids), 392−393

Lippmann, Walter, 250, 288; on Soviet containment, 246

Lithuania, 82, 93, *95,* 425, 479

"Little Boy" (atomic bomb), 226, *227*

Litvinov, Maxim, *129*

Liu Shaoqi, *267*

Live Earth concert, 518

Live 8 concert, 518

Lloyd George, David, 75, *91, 103*

Loans: to belligerents, World War II, 105−106, 135; to Brazil, 447; to

China, 197, 463; defaulted, 125; to Great Britain, 240; to Mexico, 171, 447, 456; to Russia, 447, 448. *See also* Debt; Export-Import Bank; Foreign aid; World Bank

Lockhart, Bruce, 103

Lockheed Aircraft, 389

Lodge, Henry Cabot, 4, 18, 20, 21, 23, 57; League of Nations and, 94, 96−97, *97,* 99

Lodge, Henry Cabot, Jr., 347

London Conference of Foreign Ministers, 238−239

London Economic Conference (1933), 119

Long, Breckinridge, 201−202

Long, John D., 2

Long March (China), 154

"Long peace," 243

Lon Nol, 391

Loo, Richard, 157

Loomis, Francis B., 34

Louis, Joe, 137

Lovett, Robert, 340

Low, David, *138*

Lowenthal, Max, 245

Luce, Henry R., 157, 191

Lucky Dragon (fishing boat), 294

Ludlow, Louis, 134

Lula de Silva, Luiz Inácio, 511

Lumumba, Patrice, 278, 306, 335−336

Lusitania (ship), 52, 56, *70,* 71−75, *72, 73, 74, 80,* 80, 81

Lytton Commission, 146, 147

Maastricht Treaty (1993), 449

MacArthur, Douglas, 192, 209; Korean War and, 268, 269, 270−272, *272;* occupation of Japan and, 251

Mbeki, Thabo, 514

McCain, John, 491, 498

McCarthy, Eugene, 322−323, 358

McCarthy, Joseph, 252, 258, 268, 279−281, *280,* 310; State Department and, 252, 275, 279, *280*

McCarthyism, 258, 269, 275, 281, 287, 309

McCormack, John W., 184

McCoy, Frank R., 62, 164

McCrea, John, *104*

MacDonald, James G., *245*

McDonald's restaurants, 465, 468, 520

McFarlane, Robert C., 428, 429

Machado, Gerardo, 167, 171

McKinley, William, 2−5, *3,* 8−10, *13,* 18−21, 29; Asia and, 21−27; China and, 24−26; Cuba and, 10−15, 42; Philippines and, 20, 21, 26; Spanish-American-Cuban-Filipino War and, 15−18

McKinley Tariff (1890), 13

McLaglen, Victor, 164

McLemore, Jeff, 82

MacMillan, Harold, 303

McNamara, Robert Strange, *330,* 331, 349; Cuban missile crisis and, 338, 340, 341, 342, 343, 350; Vietnam War and, 322, 351, 354, 358

Madame Secretary (Albright), *446*

Maddox (destroyer), 351

Madero, Francisco I., 49

Madman strategy, 371, 390

Maginot Line, 131

Magoon, Charles E., 44

Mahan, Alfred Thayer, 40

Maine (battleship), *1,* 2−5, 15

Malaria, 518

Malawi, 515

Malta, 448

Manchuria, 154, 252, 255, 256; crisis in, 100, 126, 145−147; Japan and, 53, 145−147, 152, 172; Russia and, 53−54; Soviet Army in, 209, 230, 253

Mandate system, 92, 93

Mandela, Nelson, *452,* 452

Manela, Erez, 105

Manhattan Project, 226, *228,* 228, 231

Mann, Thomas, 305, 350

Mansfield, Mike, 327, *357*

Mao Zedong, *199,* 199, 255−256, *293,* 358, 374; Chinese civil war and, 154, 197, 253−254, 255,

274; Korean War and, *267,* 270, 274; Nixon and, *367,*368, 369; Republic of China and, 293; Stalin and, 210, 250, 252–254. *See also* People's Republic of China (PRC)

Marco Polo Bridge incident, 153

Marcos, Ferdinand, 442

Mariel boatlift (1980), 403, 437, 459

MARIGOLD (peace initiative), 359

Marines, *160,* 470; in Cuba, 44; in Dominican Republic, 46, 47, 162–163; in Haiti, 47, 48–49, 164–165, *166;* in Lebanon, 438; in Mexico, 51; in Nicaragua, 164, *165;* in Somalia, 452–453

Marshall, George C., 151, 179, *232,* 245; China and, 252–254; European recovery plan of, 247–248; Korean War and, 270; World War II and, 182, 190, 192

Marshall, Thomas, 99

Marshall Islands, 251

Marshall Plan, 247–248

Mart, Michelle, *245*

Martí, José, 11, 45

Masaryk, Jan, 236

Masaryk, Thomas, 102, 105

Masculine ethos, 63–64, 159–160, 444–445; Jews and, *245, 299*

Matsuoka, Yosuke, 187

Mayaguez (ship), 395, 410

May Fourth Movement (China), 92

Mayo, Henry T., 51

May 30th Movement (China), 151

Mazu (Matsu), 292–293

MCA (corporation), 465

Mead, Lucia True Ames, 20

Medvedev, Dmitry, 511

Mehta, G. L., 298

Meir, Golda, *381*

Merchant Marine Act (1920), 122

Merchants of Death (Englebrecht & Hanighen), 134

Merkel, Angela, 509

Meuse-Argonne offensive, 89

Mexico, 163, 172, 437; Bush and, 512; Cuba and, 383; drug trade in, 457; financial bailout of, 447; food riots in, 518; Germany and, 49, 50, 51, 83, 84; Good

Neighbor Policy in, 169; immigrants from, 403, 512; loans to, 171, 447, 456; nationalism and, 61, 171; Nicaragua and, 403; North American Free Trade Agreement and, 456–457, 469; oil production in, 49, 50, 169, 170, 403; revolution in, 49–53, 169; Spanish civil war and, 132; trade with, 456–457; U.S. influence in, 60, 158

Mexico City, 50, 169

Micronesia, 251

Middle East, 308, 378–382, *439;* arms sales to, 407; Bush plan for, 470; Carter Doctrine and, 413; Eisenhower Doctrine and, 303; Great Britain and, 213–214, 287; mandate system and, 92; map, *379, 439;* nationalism in, 300–302; oil in, 240; peace process in, 385, 443; Soviets in, 411; U.S. interests in, 122, 240, 300; U.S. intervention in, 280. *See also* Arabs; Muslims; *specific countries*

Midway Island, 153

Migratory Bird Treaty (1916), 58

Mikolajczyk, Stanislas, 208

Miles, Nelson A., 18

Military: American, in Britain, 178; draft, 86, 182–183; Japanese, 294; nation building by, 470; Nixon's reduction of, 373; privatization of, 522; problems in, 398; rearmament, for World War II, 113, 179; Rhineland occupation and, 116; Tomahawk diplomacy of, 470; World War I preparedness, 84–87. *See also* Air force; Arms limitation; Arms race; Army; Defense Department; Joint Chiefs of Staff; Marines; Navy

Military aid, 276; to Angola, 384–385; to Argentina, 257; Axis powers to Spain, 132; to Chile, 383; to China, 253–254; Chinese, to North Vietnam, 327, 358; to *contras,* 428–429, *429,* 434, 436–437; to El Salvador,

435–436; to Europe, 250; to Greece, 244; human rights violations and, 414; to Indochina, 269, 394; to Latin America, 305, 401; to Nationalist China (Taiwan), 292; to Nicaragua, 403, 436–437; to North Atlantic Treaty Organization, 258; to Philippines, 269; to South Korea, 274; to South Vietnam, 325–326, 327, 344–345; Soviet, to Cuba, 338–343; Soviet, to North Vietnam, 327; to Taiwan, 413. *See also* Arms sales

Military bases, 182, 331; in Central America, 211; in Cuba, 44, 338; in Czech Republic, 5610; in Egypt, 413; in former Soviet bloc, 470; in Haiti, 166–167, *166;* in Japan, 251, 294, 442; in Kenya, 413; in Morocco, 275; in Oman, 413; at Pearl Harbor, 149, 153; in Philippines, 442; in Poland, 510; in Saudi Arabia, 275; in Somalia, 413; in Spain, 275; on Taiwan, 413; in Vietnam, 320, 394

Military buildup: under Bush, 522–523; under Carter, 414; under Eisenhower, 278, 280; under Johnson, 323; under Kennedy, 331–332; in Korean War, 275; in Nazi Germany, 130; under Reagan, 426, 442, 443; Soviet, 431. *See also* Arms race

Military-industrial complex, 103, 217, 278

Military preemption, doctrine of, 489, 490, 501, 503, 504, 505

Mills, Stephanie, 441

Milosevic, Slobodan, 451

Missiles: arms race and, 287, *289,* 331–332; Chinese, 463; in Cuba, 338–343; glossary of, 377; in Gulf War, 460, 461; intermediate range nuclear forces, 287, 377, 433–434; Iraqi, 441; Iraqi Scud missiles, 461, 462; Jupiter, *341,* 342; Midgetman program, 426; Minuteman, *279;* Missile experimental (MX), 377, 411; Multiple independently targetable reentry vehicles (MIRVs), 376–378, 411–412, 448; Patriot missiles, 460, 466; Pershing missiles, 412, 430, 431; Soviet, 287, *341,* 340–343, 411, 431; Strategic Arms Limitation Talks and, 411–414; Stinger missiles, 466; submarine launched ballistic (SLBMs), 376–378, 448; surface-to-air (SAMs), 338, 377, 380; Titan II missile, *279;* world market for, 465. *See also* Cruise missiles; Intercontinental Ballistic Missiles; Intermediate Range Ballistic Missiles

Missing (film), 383

Missionaries, 4; in China, 22, 25, 26, *50,* 151

Mission to Moscow (film), 190

Mitchell, George, 460

MKULTRA (CIA program), 278

Mobil corporation, 406

Mobutu Sese Seko, 453

Molotov, V. M., 191, 199, 208, *234,* 234, *247,* 247; at London conference, 238–239; Marshall Plan and, 247; meeting with Truman, 215, 234; Yalta and, 236

Mondale, Walter, 404, 406, 426

Monetary system, 386–387. *See also* Bretton Woods

Mongolia, 154, 256, 369

Monnet, Jean, 113

Monroe, James, 46

Monroe, Marilyn, 307, 329

Monroe Doctrine, 11, 12, 94, *339;* Roosevelt Corollary to, 28, 45–47, 158, *460;* Venezuela crisis and, 5, 7, 9

Montevideo Conference (1933), 171

Moral Equivalent of War (MEOW), 413

Morales, Evo, 511

Morgan, J. P., 56

J. P. Morgan Company, 125

Morgenthau, Henry, Jr., 119, 206, 356; on arms sales to

belligerents, 112, 113; on Jewish refugees, 201, 203

Morgenthau Plan, 206–207, 214, 241

Morocco, 60, 203, 275; human rights in, 414, 468

Moros (Philippines), 23

Morrow, Dwight W., *158,* 170

Morse, Wayne, *281,* 352, *357*

Moscow: Conference (1945), 194, *195,* 238; exhibition (1959), *284,* 284, 307; Treaty (2002), 510; Youth Festival (1957), 284

Mossadegh, Mohammed, 301, 306, 407

Most-favored-nation status, 151, 463

Motion pictures. *See* Films (Hollywood movies)

Motorola corporation, 295

Moussa, Amr, 491

Movement for Democratic Change, 514

MTV, 520

Mubarak, Hosni, 491, 503

Muccio, John J., 268

Mugabe, Robert, 406, 514

Mukden incident, 145–146

Multinational corporations, 386, 389

Multiple independently targetable reentry vehicle (MIRV), 376–378, 411–412, 448

Munich Conference (1938), 112, 132, 136–137, 328

Muños Marín, Luis, 169

Musharraf, Pervez, 506

Musashi (warship), 153

Muslims, 408, 498–499; in former Yugoslavia, 450–451; and *jihad,* 466, 469; in Iran, 408; Islamic fundamentalism, 412, 469; Lebanon civil war and, 303; Moros, in Philippines, 23; Shi'ite, 441, 461. *See also* Arabs; Sunni Muslims; and Shi'ite Muslims

Mussolini, Benito, 131, *137,* 138

Mutual Defense Assistance Bill, 250

Mutually assured destruction (MAD), 376–378

Mutual Security Administration, 248, 276

Mutual Security Treaty, 294

My Lai massacre, 355–356, 391

Nagasaki, atomic bombing of, 215, *225,* 226–231, *230*

Nagl, John, 498

Nagy, Ferenc, 235, 236

Nahl, Perham, *33*

Naimark, Norman, *238*

Nam (Baker), 396

Namibia, 441, 442; South Africa and, 404, 441, 451

Nanjing, 153

Nashville (ship), 34, 38

Nasser, Gamal Abdel, 300, 301, *301,* 302–303

National Aeronautics and Space Administration (NASA), 287

National Association of Manufacturers, 6

National Basketball Association, 520

National City Bank, 163, 166

National Council for the Prevention of War, 126

National Defense Act (1916), 86

National Defense Education Act (1958), 287

National Endowment for Democracy, 427

National Intelligence Estimate, 502

National Islamic Front, 513–514

Nationalism, 4, 234, 309; African, 404, 406; Arab, 300–301, 380, 438; Asian, 172; communism and, 251, 275; Cuban, 167–168; Eastern European, 286, 400; economic, 123, 125, 167, 304; Greek, 243–244; Laotian, 344; Latin American, 159, 172, 303–305, 336, 344, 401–406; Mexican, 49, 171; in Middle East, 300–302; Nicaraguan, 403; Panamanian, 401; Puerto Rican, 168–169; Russian, 232; in Somalia, 452; in Spain, 132; Third World, 296, 300, 303–305, 357, 400; U.S. insensitivity to, 61; Vietnamese, 324, 325, 327, 346; after World War I, 92–93, 105

Nationalist China, 151, 198–199, 252–254, 274, 310; Taiwan Strait crisis and, 292–293. *See also* Taiwan

National Liberation Front (NLF) (North Vietnam), 321, 327, 344–345, 346, 347, 350–354, *352, 353*; Tet offensive and, 320–324, *352*

National Museum of Antiquities, 494

National Origins Act (1924), 200

National security, 258

National Security Agency, 482,

National Security Council (NSC), 333, 414; creation of, 249; Cuba and, 340–342; Iran hostage crisis and, 411; Paper 68 (NSC-68), 250, 272; under Reagan, 428; Southern Africa and, 384

National Student Association, 278

Nation building, *333,* 333–336, 470; in Africa, *333,* 334, 336, 452; in Vietnam, 345

Nation (magazine), 166

Natural disasters, 507–508; climate change and, 517

Naval blockades, World War I, 79–81

Naval War College, 39, 153

Navy, 9, 18, 28, 185; aircraft carriers, 351; Anglo-American cooperation, 182–183; arms race and, *58,* 149; British, 71, 130; Chinese guerrillas and, 197; in Dominican Republic, 47; German, 130, 185; Great White Fleet, 59; Guantánamo Bay base, 44, 341; Haiti and, 47; Japanese, 149, 153; in Mediterranean, 243–244, 303; Pacific expansion of, 55, 149, 187, *213;* Panama Canal and, 39; Pearl Harbor and, 189–190, *189;* Seventh Fleet, 269, 270, 273, 292, 368; Six Fleet, 303; Washington conference and, 149–150; World War I expansion, 85. *See also* Marines; Submarines; *and specific ships*

Navy Act of 1896, 9

Nazis, 133, 179–180, 185, *235;* business collaboration with, 134. *See also* Germany, World War II and; Hitler, Adolf

Nazi-Soviet Pact (1939), 130, 187

NBA (National Basketball Association), 520

NBC news program, 322

Nehru, Jawaharlal, *299,* 300

Netanyahu, Benjamin, 462

Netherlands (Dutch), 149; empire of, 105, 187; Indonesia and, 216, 232

Neutrality and Neutralism, 134–135; Austria, in Cold War, 283; Cold War nonalignment, 295–300, 344; Latin American, 171; nonentanglement and, 134; in World War I, 75, 75–79, 171

Neutrality Acts (1935, 1936, 1937), 116, 134–136, 139, 186; revision of, 181–182, 188–186

Neutron bomb, 377, 426

New Deal, 124, 134, 153, 168–169

Newfoundland fisheries, 59

New Information Order, 468–469

New International Economic Order, 387

New Mexico, 214, 229, 230

New Panama Canal Company, 36

New People's Army (Philippines), 442

Newspapers, yellow press, 4, 10

New York, 9/11 terrorist attacks in, *479,* 480–483

New York Journal, 4, 15, 17

New York (ship), 71

New York Times, 391

New York World, 4, 8, 11, 37

New Zealand, 213, 275, 397; in Southeast Asia Treaty Organization, 292, 326

Nguyen Ngoc Loan, 322

Nhu, Madame, 345

Nhu, Ngo Dinh, 327, 346–348

Nicaragua, 47–49, 162, 436–437; Central Intelligence Agency in, 403, 427, 436; civil war in, 453; democracy in, 511; Panama Canal and, 36; Sandinistas in, 403, 455, 434, 436–437; U.S. aid to *contras* in, 428–429, *429,* 434, 436–437; U.S. military intervention in, 152, 163–164, 171, 403, 413

Nicholas II, tsar of Russia, 100

Nigeria, 404, 453; oil production in, 404, 404, 453

Nike (shoe manufacturer), 465

Nikkei, 465

Nimitz, Chester, 209

Nimitz (supercarrier), 409

9/11, terrorist attack (2001), *479,* 480–483. *See also* World Trade Center attack (2001)

Nine Power Treaty (1922), 148, 149

Ninotchka (film), 130

Nitze, Paul, 250, 340

Nixon, Richard M., 275, *276,* 296, 359, 376; Cuba and, 383; debate with Khrushchev, *284,* 307, 328; dollar devaluation and, 386–387; environment and, 389; Kissinger and, 371–373, *371;* Middle East and, 380–382, *381;* personal style of, 371–373; tour of Latin America by, 305, 307; trip to China, *367,* 368–371, 392; Vietnam and, 370, 371, 373, 374, 390–398, 400

Nixon Doctrine, 378

Nkrumah, Kwame, *329*

Nobel Peace Prize, 414, 425, 452, 452, 519; list of winners, 515

Nomura, Kichisaburo, 187

Nonalignment, 295–300

Nonentanglement, 59, 134. *See also* Isolationism; Neutrality

Nongovernmental organizations (NGOs), 389

Nonintervention pledge, 171–172

Noriega, Manuel Antonio, 457–458

Norris, Chuck, 396

Norris, George, 83, 97, 136, 158

North, Oliver, 428, 436

North Africa, 191, 192. *See also specific countries*

North American Free Trade Agreement (NAFTA), 447, 456–457, 469

North Atlantic Treaty Organization (NATO), 411, 447; U.S. joining of, 249–250; Balkan crisis and, 447–451; defense spending of, 287, 430; expansion of, 447–451; Iraq invasion and, 508–509; nuclear weapons and, 331, 431–434; Soviet Union and, 249–250; united Germany in, 448, 449; West Germany in, 250, 283

North Cascades National Park, *516*

North Korea, *267,* 466–467, 519; China and, 270–272, 273–274; invasion of South Korea by, 268–270; Korean War and, 268–275; nuclear weapons of, 463, 466–467, 505–506; *Pueblo* affair and, 322. *See also* Korean War

North Pacific Fur Seal Convention (1911), 59

North Vietnam, 327–328, 351–352, 390; bombing of, 392–393, 396; Cambodia and, 390–392; Chinese aid to, 327, 354; Laos and, 344; peace talks with, *358,* 358, 369; Tonkin Gulf and, 351–352. *See also* Ho Chi Minh; Vietnam War

Nour, Ayman, 503

Novgorod automobile factory, 128

Novikov, Nikolai, 241

NTT (Japanese firm), 464

Nuclear arms race, 231, *288;* glossary for, *377. See also* Arms race

Nuclear nonproliferation, 240–241, 287, 309, 350, 461, 466–467, 523. *See also* Nuclear Nonproliferation Treaty; nuclear weapons

Nuclear Nonproliferation Treaty (1968), 350, 505

Nuclear weapons, 230–231, 241–242, 466–467; brinkmanship, 280, 293; Chinese development of, 292, 293; Cuban missile crisis and, 338–343; delivery vehicles for, 377, 411–412; in Europe, 287; first strike of, 377, 430, 432; former Soviet Union, 467; freeze on, 377, 430; Indian development of, 350, 387, 506–507; Iran's development of, 502–503; in Iraq, 461; Korean War and, 272; limitations on, 278, 343, 448; Middle Eastern nations, development of, 503; nonproliferation of, 350, 414, 467; proliferation of, 258–259, 283, 310, 331, 466–467, 505–506; protests against, 294, 389, 430–431; Reagan and,

430–434, *431;* in Russia, 510–511; Strategic Arms Limitation Talks (SALT), 373–378, 411–414; Taiwan Strait crisis and, 293; testing of, 291, 343, 430, *431,* 432; Vietnam and, 354, 397, 397. *See also* Atomic bomb; Missiles

Nuremberg Laws, 200

Nye, Gerald P., 112, 114, 134, 136

Nyerere, Julius, 387

Obama, Barack, *450, 523,* 523–524

Obregón, Alváro, 169

Ocean resources, 389. *See also* Fisheries disputes

Office of Strategic Services (OSS), *199,* 217, 324

Oil industry and trade: African, 513, 514; Chinese, 413; embargo (1973), 381; environment and, 388–389; Iranian, 240, 406–407, 408, 412; Italy and, 137; Japanese imports, 147, 152, 187–188; Mexican, 49, 50, 169, 170, 171, 403; Middle Eastern, 213–214, 240, 302, 382; nationalization of, 383; Nigerian, 404, 453; Organization of Petroleum Exporting Countries and, 374, *379,* 383, 408, 413; Peruvian, 383; Saudi, 381, 406–407, 462; U.S. import of, 386, 406–407; Venezuelan, 159, 160, 169, 211. *See also* Standard Oil Company

O'Jays, the, 441

Okinawa, 251, 465; battle for, 228

Olmert, Ehud, 505

Olney, Richard, 6, 6, 11, 12, 13

Olympia (warship), *14,* 17

Olympic Games, 63, 131, 380, 413

Oman, 413

Omnibus Trade and Competitiveness Act (1988), 442–443

O'Neill, Paul, *482*

Open Door notes, *26,* 26, 53, 55

Open Door policy, 122, 156, 215; in China, 9, 26, 53, 55, 56, 57, 149, 150, 156, 196; during Cold War, 236, 257; Manchurian crisis and,

146, 146, 147, 148; Roosevelt and, 42, 60–61; Wilson and, 76, 84

Operation Castration, 337

Operation Desert Shield, 459

Operation Desert Storm, 460

Operation Iraqi Freedom, 493–501

Operation Just Cause, 458

Operation MAGIC, *188,* 188, 190

Operation Mongoose, 338

Operation Northwoods, 338

Operation OVERLORD, 191, 194, 196

Operation Restore Hope, 452–453

Operation Rolling Thunder, 353

Operation TORCH, 191

Operation Uphold Democracy, 458

Operation Vittles, *242*

Opium trade, 457, 488

OPLAN 34-A (covert operation), 351

ORANGE (war plan), 172

Oregon (warship), 40

Organization of American States (OAS), 304, 383, 458

Organization of Petroleum Exporting Countries (OPEC), 374, *379,* 383, 408, 413

Orinoco River, 5, 8

Orlando, Vittorio, 91

Orozco, José Clemente, 169

Ortega Saavedra, Daniel, 437

Oscar II (ship), 85

Ostpolitik, 332, 378

Ouimet, Francis, 61

Owens, Jesse, 131

Pacific Ocean: line of defense in, 113, 157–158, 186; World War II in, 189–190, 208–210, *212;* post-World War II, 251, map, *253.* See also *specific islands*

Pacifist organizations, 190; during interwar years, 125–127, 134; women in, *83, 85,* 125, 134; World War I and, 85, 90. *See also* Antiwar movement; Nuclear weapons, protests against

Page, Walter Hines, 77, 83

Paine, Tom, 427

Pakistan, 275, 368, 413, 454–455, 457; arms sales to, 374, 413; Baghdad Pact and, 299, 300; Bangladesh and, 374; food riot in, 518; India and, 334, 466–467; Iraq invasion and, 487, 506–507; nuclear arms of, 466–467; in Southeast Asia Treaty Organization, 292, 326

Palestine, 504–505; Jewish state in, 202, 203, 244–246. *See also* Israel

Palestine Liberation Organization (PLO), 380, 407; Arab-Israeli peace and, *462,* 462; bases in Lebanon, 438–439; Iranian hostages and, 411

Palestinians, *intifada* (uprising) by, 439, 463; in Lebanon, 439; as refugees, 301, 380; in West Bank and Gaza, 407, 439

Palmer, A. Mitchell, *102*

Panama, 34–39, 61, 257, 437; canal zone and, 350, 401; crisis in, 455; Declaration of (1939), 172, 211; nationalism in, 305; U.S. invasion of, 458

Panama Canal, *33,* 57, 59, 60–61, 305, 350; Carter and, 401; map, *37;* neutrality of, 401; site selection for, 34–39, *38*

Panama-Pacific Exhibition, *33*

Pan American Conferences (1923–1938), 171–172

Pan American Conference (1939), 181

Panay (gunboat), 154

Panther (warship), 47

Paraguay, 403, 456, 511; drug trade, 512–513

Paramount Pictures, 128

Paris, peace negotiations (1969–1973), 392–394

Paris, Treaty of (1899), 21

Paris, Treaty of (1919), 94, 102

Paris summit meeting (1960), 290–291

Pathet Lao, 344

Patriot Act (2001), 489

Paul, Alice, 103

Pauncefote, Julian, 36

Peace Corps, *329,* 334

Pearl Harbor, 149, 153, 189–190, *189, 213, 229,* 480

Pentagon, 352, 356; Africa and, 513, 515; Balkan crisis and, 450; new weapons systems of, 469–470; occupation of Iraq and, 482, 485, 489, *492,* 494, 499, 502, 505, 510; under Reagan, 426; 9/11 (2001) terrorist attack on, 480. *See also* Defense Department; Joint Chiefs of Staff

Pentagon Papers, 391–392

People's Republic of China (PRC), aid to North Vietnam by, 327, 357–358; Carter and, 400; Congo and, 336; détente with, 368, 373, 390; hard-line toward, 310; Johnson and, 350; Korean War and, *267,* 269–275; Nixon's trip to, *367,* 368–371; nonrecognition of, 254–256, 308; nuclear weapons of, 309; Soviet Union and, 254–256, 292–295, 368, 373–374; Taiwan Strait crisis and, 292–293; threat to Taiwan by, 463, 465; Tiananmen Square massacre, 463, *464;* trade with, 309, 385, 413, 463–464, 469; U.S. interests in, 413; U.S. invasion of Iraq and, 492, 505; Vietnam and, 324, 326, 350, 351, 396. *See also* Mao Zedong

PepsiCo, 373, 464

Percentages agreement, 211

Perestroika (Soviet policy), 432

Pérez, Louis A., Jr., 3, 18

Pérez Jiménez, Marcos, 305

Perkins, Dexter, *10*

Permanent Court of International Justice. *See* World Court

Perón regime, 257

Perry, William, 463

Pershing, John J., 23, 53, 87, 88

Peru, 172, 383; Chile and, 159; narcoterrorism in, 457

Peterson, Pete, 464

Petraeus, David, 499

Petroleum. *See* Oil industry and trade

Peurifoy, John, 304

Philanthropy, 518, 519–520

Philippine Islands, 26, 54, 55, 61, 172, 292, 469; authoritarian regimes in, 427, 442; Central Intelligence Agency, 277; economic expansion and, 122; human rights in, 414; military aid to, 269; Moros in, 23–24; Southeast Asia Treaty Organization and, 326; Spanish-American-Cuban-Filipino War and, 16–18; U.S. control of, 20; U.S. investment in, 148, 442; U.S. protection of, 149, 150; World War II deaths in, 215; World War II in, 188

Phillips, Cabell, *280*

Phillips, William, 62

Phoenix program, 354

Pike, Fredrick, 160

Ping-Pong diplomacy, 368

Pinochet, Augusto, 383

Pittman, Key, 138

Plan Colombia, 512

Plan of San Diego, 51

Platt Amendment (1934), 15, 41, 43–45, 49, 61, 63, 167

Poindexter, John M., 428, 429

Point Four Program, 249, 257

Pokemon (computer game), 469

Poland, 82, 93, *95,* 205, 449; aid to, 204, 284–285; boundary with Germany, 215, 378; German invasion of, 115, 133, 139, 181; Holocaust in, 200, 202–203; nationalism in, 284–285; Solidarity in, 378, 432; Soviet Union and, 133, 193–194, 208, 211, 235; World War II and, 196, 215; Yalta agreement on, 207–210, 214, 234

Pollution. *See* Environmental issues

Ponce (Puerto Rico) Massacre, *168*

Popular Movement for the Liberation of Angola (MPLA), 384

Population Bomb (Erlich), 388

Population growth, 387, 443, 467

Portsmouth Conference (1905), 40

Portugal, 149, 298; Angola and, 384

Potsdam Conference (1945), 214–217, 231

Potter, David, 295

Poverty, 467. *See also* Third World

Powell, Colin, 398, 464, 504, 507, 510; Africa and, 514; Bush and, 445, 484–485; Darfur and, 513; Haiti and, 458; Iraq invasion and, 490–492, *492*; Panama invasion and, 458*;* Reagan administration and, 428, 436, 439

Power, balance of, 26, 28, 29, 39, 60, 232–233, 373

Powers, Francis Gary, 290, *291*

Preemption, doctrine of, 489, 490, 501, 503, 504, 505

President's Committee on Civil Rights, 258

Prevots, Naima, *308*

Prince, Elk, 522

Prince of Wales (ship), *177, 178*

Prisoners of War (POWs), 272

Proctor, Redfield, 2

Profiles in Courage (Kennedy), *328*

Progressive era, 40, 76

Project for a New American Century, 490

Project Paperclip, 241

Propaganda, 179; anti-American, 249, 284, 305; anti-Soviet, 100, *267, 284, 285,* 304; CIA and, 327, 384; communist, 128, 257; free enterprise, 427; pro-Western, 300, 437; USIA and, 276; wartime, 134, 196, 213. *See also* Voice of America

Prosperity and democracy, 233

Prostitution, U.S. soldiers and, 88

Public health, 121. *See also* Disease Public opinion, 9, 10, 19 *Pueblo* (spy ship), 322 Puerto Rico, 19, 47, 61, *168,* 168–169 Pulitzer, Joseph, 4

PURPLE (code machine), *188*

Purple Heart (film), 157 Putin, Vladimir, 449, 509–511

Pyle, Ernie, *209*

Quezon, Manuel, 24

Qualia, Tom, *335*

"Quarantine speech" (Roosevelt), 137, 154

Quebec Conference (1944), 206

Quemoy (Jinmen), 292–293

Rabin, Yitzhak, *462,* 462

Race riots (1919), 103

Racism and race, 28; African apartheid, 257, 385, 404, 406; against black Americans, 87–88, 255, 258, 276, *356;* against Filipinos, 22, 23; against Africans, 336; against Haitians, 165, 458; against Japanese, 54–55, 229–230; against Jews, 130; Cold War and, 276, 298–299; pseudoscientific thinking about, 40, 57. *See also* Anti–Semitism *and* Cultural stereotypes

Radford, Arthur, 326

Radio Corporation of America (RCA), 121

Radio Free Europe, 276, 286

Radio Liberty, 276

Radio Martí, 437

Railroads, 102; in China, 53–54, 145

RAINBOW (war plan), 172

Rambo (film), 394

Ramsay, Harold V., 89

Rangers, 409, 452, 470

Rankin, Jeannette, *83*

Rapacki, Adam, 287–288

Rapacki Plan, 288, 309

Raw materials, 324; U.S. import of, 233, 257, 386, 404, 405

Ray, Ted, 63

Rea, Charles, *228*

Reagan, Ronald, 396, 410, *426, 429*; Afghanistan and, 466; Africa and, 441–442; beliefs of, 425–427; Bush and, 425; cabinet of, 427–429; Central America and, 434–438, *435;* Cuba and, 436–438*;* El Salvador and, 434–436; Gorbachev and, *433;* Iran-Contra affair and, 428–429, *429;* Iran-Iraq war and, 441; Japan and, 442; legacy of, 443–444; Libyan terrorism and, 440–441; Middle East and, 438–441; military buildup under, 426, 443; Nicaragua and, 436–437; on Panama Canal, 401;

personal style of, 425–427; Philippines and, 442; Soviet Union and, 426; Third World and, 434–438

Reagan Doctrine, 427, 466

Reciprocal Trade Agreements Act (1934), 124, 162

Reciprocity Treaty (1902), 44

Reconstruction Finance Corporation, 128

Red Fascism, *235,* 235. *See also* Communism

Red Scare, 100–103. *See also* Bolshevism; communism; McCarthyism

Red (Soviet) Army, 193–194, 208, 211; in Afghanistan, 412; cutbacks in, 423; in Eastern Europe, 232, 281–283, 423; in Hungary, 285–286, *285;* in Manchuria, 209, 230, 253; in Romania, 235

RED SOX/RED CAP (CIA program), 286

Reed, James, 96

Reeves, Richard, *371*

Refugees: Cuban, 459; East German, 331, 422; ethnic Albanian, 451; Haitian, 458; Hungarian, 286; Palestinian, 301, 380, 382; Rwandan, 453; Sudanese, 513; Vietnamese, 394, 398; World War II, 200–203

Regime change, 501–508

Reid, Whitelaw, 60

Rekjavík summit (1986), 433

Renda, Mary, *166*

Report to the Secretary on the Acquiescence of This Government in the Murder of the Jews, 203

Republican Party, 91, 116, 275; control of Congress by, 445; imperialism and, 21

Republic of the Congo, 453. *See also* Zaire (Congo)

Republic of Vietnam, 327. *See also* South Vietnam

Reuben James (destroyer), 185

Revolutions: anticolonial, 295; Cuban, 336–338; Eastern European, 422–423, 425;

Hungarian, 102, 285–286;
Mexican, 48–51, 169; Russian,
84, 100
Reza Shah Pahlavi, Mohammad, 306,
382, 407
Rhee, Syngman, 274
Rhineland, 93, 116, 131
Rhodesia. *See* Zimbabwe/Rhodesia
Ribbentrop, Joachim von, *132*
Ricarte, Artemio, 23
Rice, Condoleezza, *503, 510*, 518;
Africa and, 514; Bush and,
483–485; Cheney and, 502;
Egypt and, 503; India and,
506–507; Iraq invasion and, 490,
491, 497, 499, 504
Ridgeway, Matthew, 326
Rio de Janeiro Conference
(1942), 213
Rio Earth Summit (1992), 467
Rio Pact (1947), 304
Ripka, Hubert, 238
Rising Sun (film), 465
Robb, Chuck, *319*
Roberts, Grace, *54*
Robin, Ron, *267*
Robins, Raymond, 100
Rockefeller, Nelson A., 160–161, *161,*
172, 382
Rockefeller Foundation, 121, 151
Rockhill, William H., 26
Rogers, Will, 170
Rogers, William P., 372, 384
Rogers Act (1924), 119
Roman Catholic bishops, 430
Romania, 93, *95,* 200; fall of
communist regime in, 423;
Soviet dominance in, 208, 209,
211, 235
Rome-Berlin Axis, 131. *See
also* Axis
Rommel, Erwin, 193
Roosevelt, Eleanor, *152,* 258
Roosevelt, Franklin D., *50,* 116, 127,
163; on arms sales to belligerents,
111, 112–115, *114,* 115; at
Atlantic Charter conference,
*177, 178–181, 203; atomic bomb
and, 230–231; at Cairo
Conference, *197;* China and, 51,
186, 196–200; entry into World

War II and, 114–115, 189–190;
foreign policy style of, *111,*
118–119; Good Neighbor Policy
and, 159–160, 167; Haiti and,
166; Indochina and, 325; Japan
and, 154–155, 187, 189–190;
Jewish refugees and, 200–203;
Lend-Lease and, 178, 184–185,
194; Mexico and, 171; Middle
East and, 213–214; at Moscow
Conference, 194; naval buildup
under, 156, 185; neutrality and,
134–136; New Deal of, 124, 134,
153, 168–169; Nicaragua and,
164; "quarantine" speech of, 137,
154; repudiation of isolationism
by, 181, 182, 186; Soviet Union
and, *129,* 129, 153; United
Nations and, 204–205; at Yalta
Conference, 199, 207–210, *207*
Roosevelt, Theodore, 40, 55, 59, 60,
63–64, *460;* Anglo-American
entente and, 57–63; "big stick"
policy of, 40, 118; Cuba and, 2,
3, 16, 17, 44–45; as imperialist,
3, 4, 7, 9, 16, 17, 20, 21, 28;
Japan and, 53–57; *Lusitania* and,
73; Monroe Doctrine and, 16,
28, 44–45; Panama Canal and,
35, 35–38; personal style of,
39–41; Philippines and, 23;
World War I and, 85, 86
Roosevelt, Theodore, Jr., 168
Roosevelt Corollary, 158, *460. See
also* Monroe Doctrine
Root, Elihu, *35,* 41, 46, 47, 55, *56,*
57, 60, 62, 118; Cuba and, 41,
42, 44
Root-Takahira declaration (1908), 55
Rosskam, Edwin, *168*
Rostow, Walter, 323, 343, 345, 349,
351, 359
Rotary International, 160
Rotter, Andrew, *299*
Rough Riders, 16, 17, *43,* 62
Ruhr Valley, 125, 206
Rumor of War, A (Caputo),
356, 395
Rumsfeld, Donald, *440, 486*; George
W. Bush and, 484–486; on
occupation of Iraq, 489, 490,

494, 495, 496, 497, 498, 499;
resignation of, *510*
Rusk, Dean, 256, 322, *323,* 349;
Cuban missile crisis and, 337,
339, 342; on Kennedy, 329;
Vietnam War and, 322, 330, 345,
350, 357
Russia, 28; Bush and, 509–511;
China and, 26, 53; economic
collapse in, 448; Japan and, 53;
loans to, 447, 448; nationalism
in, 232; nuclear weapons in, 467,
510–511; revolution in, 84, 100;
transformations in, map, *424;*
U.S. invasion of Iraq and, 487,
488; World War I and, 77, 89,
91, 93, *95, 104. See also*
Bolshevism; Soviet Union
(USSR)
Russo-Japanese War, 145
Ruth, George Herman ("Babe"),
153, 156
Rwanda, genocide in, 453

Sadat, Anwar el-, 380, 382, 407, 438
St. Louis (ship), 201
St. Louis World's Fair, 24
Sakhalin Island, 149, 210
Salinas, Carlos, 456
Salisbury, Lord, *7, 7,* 8
Sam, Guillaume, 47
Sandinista National Liberation Front
(FSLN), 403
Sandino, César Augusto, 164, *164*
Sands of Iwo Jima (film), 257
San Francisco Conference (1945), 205
San Francisco Examiner, 54
San Francisco School Board, 55
San Juan Hill, battle for, 17
San Martín, Ramón Grau, 167
Santoli, Al, 396
Santos Zelaya, José, 47–48
Sarajevo, Bosnia, 63, 76–77
Sara Lee corporation, 452
Sarin gas, 466
Sarkozy, Nicolas, 509, 511
Satellites: communications, 468–469;
launches of, 287, *288*
Saudi Arabia, 213–214, 301, 303,
406–407, 481; arms sales to, 374,

438; Gulf War and, 459; oil in, 381, 406–407, 462; Taliban and, 487; U.S. Iraq invasion and, 480, 481, 487, 490, 501, 503, 504; U.S. military base in, 275, 413; women's rights in, 468

SAVAK (Iranian secret police), 408

Scali, John, 342

Schindler's List (film), 203

Schlesinger, Arthur M., Jr., 329, 337, 356, 491

Schmeling, Max, 137

School segregation, 298–299

Schrecker, Ellen, *280*

Schroeder, Gerhard, 449, 481, 509

Schuler, Friedrich E., *170*

Schurz, Carl, *20*

Schwartz, Thomas A., *248*

Schweiger, Walter, 71, *73,* 80

Scowcroft, Brent, 445, 452, 458, 463

Scruggs, William L., 5, 8

Sea levels, climate change and, 517

Second strike, 376, 377

Security Council, United Nations, 204–205, 210, 482, 485, 488, 491, 492, 494, 512; Gulf War and, 460; Israeli-Palestine conflict, 505; Korean War and, 273–274

Seeger, Pete, 356

Selassie, Haile, 131

Selective Service Act (1917), 86–87

Selective Service Act (1940), 182

Senate: ABM treaty and, 376; Foreign Relations Committee, 138; Military Affairs Committee, 112, 113; treaty-making power of, 310, 401–402; Vietnam War and, 391. *See also* Congress

Sendero Luminoso (Shining Path), 457

September 11 (9/11) terrorist attacks, *479,* 480–483

Serbia-Montenegro, 450–451

Service, John S., 198

Shah of Iran. *See* Reza Shah Pahlavi, Mohammad

Shales, Tom, *493*

Shandong province (China), 25, 56, 92, 149, 150

Shanghai, bombing of, 153, *154*

Sharon, Ariel, 462, 504

Sherry, Michael, *126*

Shevardnadze, Eduard, 445, 447

Shi'ite Muslims, 441, 461, 498–499

Shining Path (Peru), 457

Shotwell, James T., 126

Shriver, Sargent, *335*

Shultz, George P., 427, 428, 432

Siberia, 102, 149

Sicily, 191

Silent Spring (Carson), 388

Simon Bolivar (film), 172

Singer Sewing Company, 42

Singh, Manmohan, 506

Sino-Japanese War, 10, 25

Six Crises (Nixon), 369

Six-Day War (1967), 380

Slovakia, 449

Slovenia, 450

Smith College Junior Year in France, 125

Smith, Ian, 384, 406

Smith, Jacob, 22

Smith, Margaret Chase, *281*

Smoot-Hawley Tariff (1930), 123, 167

Snow, Edgar, 368

Soft power, 519–521

Solidarity (Poland), 378, 432

Somalia, 131, 413, 452–453; civil war in, 513; Soviets and, 406, 413; U.S. intervention in, 452–453, 465, 470, 513

Somoza Debayle, Anastasio, 403

Somoza family, 403

Somoza García, Anastasio, *161, 164*

Soong, Meiling (Madame Jiang), 151, *197*

Soong, T.V., 151

South Africa, 384–385; apartheid in, 257, 384, 385, 404, 406, 441, 451–453; authoritarianism in, 427; Boer War in, 28; food riots in, 518; HIV/AIDS in, 514–515; majority rule in, 451–452; Namibia and, 404, 441; nuclear weapons of, 466; trade and investment in, 404–406, 452; white minority rule in, 385, 404, 406

South America, 105, 161; German investment in, 39, 114. *See also* Latin America

Southeast Asia: bombing of, 375; Japan and, 152, 179, 186, 190; military aid to, 394; U.S. interests in, 325; Vietnam War and, map, *355. See also* Indochina; *specific countries*

Southeast Asia Treaty Organization (SEATO), 283, 292, 299, 326

South Korea: aid to, 274, 388; authoritarianism in, 427; China and, 463; human rights in, 414, 427; North Korean invasion of, 268–275; Soviet Union and, 432; U.S. ties to, 370, 388, 397, 414. *See also* Korean War

South Manchuria Railway, 145

South Ossetia, 511

South Vietnam, 306, 309, 344–345, *345,* 346, 347, 351, 352, 354; aid to, 372, 388, 390; Vietcong in, 344, 354. *See also* Vietnam

South Vietnamese Army (ARVN), 320–324

South West African People's Organization (SWAPO), 442

Souvanna Phouma, 344

Soviet Union (USSR), 120, 146, 190; Afghanistan and, 385, 406, 411–414, 433, 434, 466; aircraft/bombers of, 338, 342, 343, 378, 383, 411–412; in Angola and Ethiopia, 403, 406; anti-Bolshevism and, 100–103; armament spending in, 283; Atlantic Charter and, 179, 181; atomic bomb and, 230–231, 240–241, 250; Austria and, 283; Berlin and, 288–289, 378; Carter administration and, 399, 400, 404–406, 411–414; Central America and, 434, 437–438; China and, 199, 254–256, 292–295, 368–371; Cold War rivalry with U.S., 232, 235, 309; Congo and, 336; containment of (*See* Containment policy); Cuba and, 337, 403, 459; Czechoslovakia and, 102, 208, 236, 350; détente and, 283, 290, 373–378, 390; disintegration of,

422–423; Eastern Europe and, 196, 204, 211, 235, 236, 301–302; economy of, 433; Egypt and, 380; Eisenhower and, 216, 279–281; expansion of, 411; Finland and, 182; Ford plant in, 121; Geneva summit and, 283–284; Germany and, 127, 130, 133; under Gorbachev, 423–425, 432–434; grain sales to, 373, 375, 388, 413; Greece and, 243–244; human rights in, 400; Hungary and, 208, 211, 235, *286*; India and, 374; during interwar years, 116, 127–130; Iran and, 240; isolation of, 150; Japan and, 150, 151, 153, 154, 251, 252; Jewish emigration from, 374, 411; Johnson and, 350; Korea Air Lines 007 and, 432; Korean War and, 269, 270, 272–275, 281; Latin America and, 304; Lend-Lease aid to, *184*, 185, 194, 214, 240; Marshall Plan and, 240, 247–248; Middle East and, 245–246, 381–382; missiles of, 287, 331, 411; Namibia and, 441, 442; national liberation and, 378, 385; Nazi pact with, 130, 187; North Atlantic Treaty Organization and, 249–250; Poland and, 133, 193–194, 207, 211, 235; Potsdam accords and, 214–217; Reagan and, 426, 430–434, *433*, 443; 1989 revolutions and, 423–425, 469; Spanish civil war and, 132; Strategic Arms Limitation Talks and, 373–378, 411–414; Syria and, 382, 407; Taiwan Strait crisis and, 293; Third World and, 300; trade with, 385, 413, 432; transformations, map, *424;* Turkey and, 243–244; U-2 crisis and, 290–291, *291;* United Nations and, 205; U.S. propaganda and, 284, *285;* Vietnam War and, 326, 396; Warsaw Pact and, 250; Watergate scandal and, 371; West Germany and, 283, 288–289, 378; World

War II and, 203, 216; Yalta Conference and, 207–210, 235. *See also* Cold War; Red (Soviet) Army; Russia; Stalin, Joseph
Smithsonian Institution, 276
Space exploration, 375
Spain, 275, 481; bombing of, 489; civil war in, 132, 135, 137; Cuba and, 2–5, 8, 9, 10, 11, 12, 13
Spanish-American-Cuban-Filipino War, 10, 16–18, 28, 39; events leading to, 11–15
Special Forces, 331, 334, 343, 344, 488. *See also* Green Berets; Rangers
Speck von Sternburg, Hermann, 45
Spellman, Francis Cardinal, 327
Spielberg, Steven, 203
Spirited Away (film), 520
Spock, Benjamin, 356
Sputnik (satellite), 287
Stalin, Joseph, 130, 190, 193, 232, 240, 256; Atlantic Charter and, 181; Berlin blockade and, 241; China and, 154, 252–253, 254, 280; Cold War and, 232, 251; compared to Hitler, 235; death of, 272, 281; denouncement of, 286; Eastern Europe and, 235, 236, 238, 247; on German containment, 194–195; Greek communists and, 243–244; Korean War and, *267,* 270, 272–275; Lend-Lease and, 196, 214; as obstructionist, 255–256; pact with Hitler, 130, *132;* percentage agreement and, 211; at Potsdam Conference, 214–217, 235; purges of, 130; at Teheran Conference, 196; on Truman, *234;* Warsaw uprising and, 211; at Yalta Conference, 199, 207–210, 244
Stalingrad, siege of, 192–193
Stallone, Sylvester, 396
Standard Oil Company, 42, 49, 134, 154, 160, 170
Stark, Harold R., 182
Stark (frigate), 441
"Star Wars" (SDI), 377, 431–434, *431*
State, U.S. Department of, 103, 204, 214; Africa and, 384; Brzezinski

and, 400, 406; budget of, 2007, 523; China and, 197; on Cuban/ Soviet threat, 434; defense establishment and, 217; Dominican Republic and, 163; Egypt and, 301; elite inner circle of, 62; Guatemala and, 304; Haiti and, 47; Iranian crisis and, 240; Israel and, 246; Jewish refugees and, 201, 203; Korean War and, 268; Latin America and, 334; *Lusitania* disaster and, 71; McCarthyism and, 252, 281, *282;* Nicaragua and, 47, 48–49; nuclear arms race and, 414; occupation of Iraq and, *481,* 491, 494, 499, 523; Panama Canal and, 36; race and, 299; Roosevelt and, 118, 138; Soviet affairs and, 119–120, 129; U-2 spy plane and, *291;* women's rights, 468; World War I reparations and, 125
Steel, Ronald, 395
Steffens, Lincoln, 103
Steiner, Zara, 125
Stereotypes, and cultural bias, 169, 229–230, 298–299
Stettinius, Edward R., Jr., 205
Stevenson, Adlai E., 275, 280, *341,* 341
Stilwell, Joseph W., 196–200, *197*
Stimson, Henry L., 62, *118,* 118, 126, 136, 206, *232,* 330; atomic diplomacy and, 236; Japan and, 182; Manchurian crisis and, *144,* 145–147, 148, 158; Nicaragua and, 164; post-World War II Europe and, 236; as Secretary of War, 182; Soviet Union and, 127, 153
Stimson Doctrine, 147
Stinger missiles, 466
Stockdale, James B., 351
Straight, Willard, 55, 62
Strategic Air Command, 275, *279,* 287
Strategic Arms Limitation Talks (SALT), 242, 431; under Carter, 411–414; under Ford, 377–378; under Nixon, 373–377

Strategic Arms Reduction Talks (START), 431, 432, 447, 448

Strategic Defense Initiative (SDI-Star Wars), 377, 431–434, *431*

Strategic weapons, 377

Straw, Jack, 491

Stuart, J. Leighton, 255

Submarine-launched ballistic missiles (SLBMs), 376–378, 430; limitations on, 412, 448

Submarines, 51; *Lusitania* disaster and, 71–75, 81; Soviet, 342; Trident series, 376, 411, 426; World War I, 79–84; World War II, 179, 185

Sudan, 441; bombing of, 453; civil war in, 513–514

Suez crisis, 301–302

Sugar trade: Cuban, 110, 11, 12, 42, 44, 45, 159, 162, 167, 336, 337, *339;* Haitian, 165; Puerto Rican, 167

Suicide bombings, 495, 504

Summers, Lawrence, 447

Summit of the Americas (1994), 456

Sunday, Billy, 84

SUNFLOWER (peace initiative), 359

Sun Zhongshan (Sun Yat-Sen), 105, 150, 151

Sunni Muslims, 498–499

Supreme Court, 62, 298, 392

Surface-to-air missiles (SAMs), 338, 377, 380

Sussex (ship), 82

Sweden, 203

Swift company, 105

Switzerland, 203

Syria, 301, 303, 380, 382, 407, 502; Arab-Israeli conflict and, 462; Lebanon and, 438–439, 503; nuclear weapons of, 505

Tactical nuclear weapons, 377

Taft, Robert, 249–250, 269

Taft, William Howard, 40, 42, 44, 45, 46, 48, 49, 54, 59, 60, 62; China trade and, 55, 56, 57; Philippines and, *22, 23*

Taft-Katsura memorandum, 54

Taguba, Antonio, 496

Taiwan (Formosa), 24, 198, 254, 292, 309; arms sales to, 463; Army Advisory Group on, 254; Chinese threat to, 463, 465; human rights in, 414; Korean War and, 270, 273; People's Republic of China and, 292–293, 414, 507; Taiwan Strait crisis and, 292–293; U.S. commitment to, 369, 370, 413. *See also* Jiang Jieshi; Nationalist China

Taiwan Strait crisis, 292–293

Takahira, Kogoro, 53, 55

Taking Haiti (Renda), *166*

Talbott, Strobe, 448

Taliban, 468, 482, 487–488, 502; Bush on, 483; prisoners, 488, 496–497, *496,* 511

Tanzania, 387, 453; U.S. embassy in, *481*

Tariffs, 13, 190; Chinese, 150, 151; General Agreement on Trade and, 387, 447; interwar years' policy, 122–123; Japanese, 442; reduction in, 276, *328,* 387, 401

Taxation, 122, 169

Taylor, Maxwell, 345, 394

Technology transfer, 389

Teheran, hostage crisis in (1979–1981), 406–411, *408*

Teheran Conference (1943), 196

Teller Amendment, 3–4

Telnaes, Ann, *503*

Temptations, the, 441

Tenet, George L., 480–481, 482, 490, 497

Terrorism, 466; in Argentina, 373; CIA and, 481, 483; in Europe, 380; hijackings, 440, 480–483; increase in, 501; in India, 507; Internet and, 521; Iran hostage crisis, 406–411, *408;* Libyan-sponsored, 440; Palestinian, 462; September 11 (2001), *479,* 480–483; in Uganda, 382; war on, 447, 486, 487–490, *496,* 500, 504, 508, 513, 523; world trade and, 447

Tet offensive, 320–324, *352,* 359, 394

Texaco (Texas Oil Company), 49

Texas, 51

Thailand, 292, 326, 344, 397, 457, 468; human rights in, 414, 468

Thant, U, 341

Thatcher, Margaret, 438

Thieu, Nguyen Van, *358,* 390, 392–394

Third World, 256, 295–300; aid to, 387–388; arms sales to, 466–467; Cold War and, 434; communism and, 295–300, 328; Cuban support for revolution in, 403–404; cultural bias and, 298–299; debt of, 385, 442; decolonization in, 232, 295–296, 300; domino theory and, *277,* 280; economic relations with, 385–389, 436–427, 466; environment and, 388–389, 467–468; global communications and, 468–469; Kennedy and, 328, 331, 333; multinational corporations and, 389; nationalism in, 295, 300, 303–305, 357; nonalignment and, 295–300; Peace Corps and, 334; power-sharing with, 385, 387; as proxies of great powers, 374; racism and, 298–299; raw materials from, 256–257; Soviet influence in, 378; trade with, 385–386, 387;Vietnam War and, 394

Thorpe, Jim, 63

Tiananmen Square massacre, 463, *464*

Tibbets, Paul, 226, *227*

Ticonderoga (aircraft carrier), *213,* 351

Tillman, John, 59

Time magazine, 163, 423

Times of India, 300

Time Warner, 468

Tipitapa, Peace of (1927), 164

Tito, Josip Broz, 211, 236, 244, 257, 285

Tobacco, 43, 520

Tobey, Charles, 181

Togo, Nakagori, 53

Tojo, Hideki, 187

Tokyo: bombing of, 216, 228; sarin gas release, 466

Toles, Tom, *439, 522*

Tomahawk cruise missiles, 460, 461, 470

Tonkin Gulf Resolution, 352, 357, 391

Top Gun (film), 441

Torrijos, Omar, 401

Torture, 488, 496–497, *496*, 511

Trade, 9; with Africa, 384–385, 404–406; British, 123, 179; with Canada, 456; with Chile, 456; with China, 24–25, 55, 368, 369, 413, 463, 507; with Cuba, 12; dollar diplomacy and, 42; with Eastern Europe, 236, 276, 378; East-West, 422; expansion and, 256–257; global, 204, 385–389; Great Depression and, 116; with Japan, 153, 187–188, 386, 387, 442–443; with Latin America, 160–162, 382, 401, 403, 456; Marshall Plan and, 246–248; most-favored-nation status, 151, 463; multinational corporations and, 386; neutrality and, 76; with Nicaragua, 164; with Philippines, 442; post-World War I expansion, 120; in raw materials, 233, 256–257, 323, 386, 404, 405; Soviet, with Cuba, 337; with Soviet Union, 127–128, 373, 406, 413, 432; with Third World, 385–386; with Venezuela, 5–6; in World War I, 79. *See also* Business; Open Door policy; Tariffs; *specific commodities*

Trade agreements, 447, 456–457. *See also specific agreements*

Trade embargoes, 153; against China, 292; against Cuba, 337, 338, 403, 459; oil embargo (1973), 381; against Vietnam, 464. *See also* Economic Sanctions

Trade Expansion Act (1962), *328*

Trading Corporation, 128

Transcontinental Peace Caravan, 126

Transnational challenges and opportunities, 515–524

Trans-Siberian Railroad, 102

Trask, David, *345*

Triad, 377

Trilateral Commission, 399

Tripartite Pact, 187, 188

Triple Alliance (Central Powers), 77

Triple Entente, 77

Trotsky, Leon, 128

Trujillo, Rafael Leonidas, 163–164, *163*, 211, 213

Truman, Harry S., 104, 207, *232*, *234*, *239*, 240, *249*; atomic bomb and, 227–231, *249*; Berlin airlift and, 241, *242*; bipartisanship and, 258; China and, 254, 255–256; communism and, 275; European military aid and, 250; Israel and, 244–246; Korean War and, 268–270, 273–274; Morgenthau Plan and, 241; personal style of, 233–234; Point Four Program of, 249; at Potsdam Conference, 214–217, 231; Soviet Union and, 214, 239, 240, 244; Vietnam and, 325

Truman Doctrine, 243–246, 254, 308, 328

Truth and Reconciliation Commission (South Africa), 452

Tshombe, Moise, 335, 336

Tsvangirai, Morgan, 514

Tuberculosis, 518

Tugwell, Rexford, 169

Turkey, 90; Baghdad Pact and, 300; Soviet Union and, 243–244, 281; U.S. missiles in, 339, *341*, 341, 342; World War I and, 77

Turner, William T., 71–72, *73*

Tutsi-Hutu rivalry (Rwanda), 453

Tutu, Desmond M., 441

Twain, Mark, 19, 20

Twelve O'Clock High (film), 257

Twenty-One Demands (1915), 56

U-boats. *See* Submarines

Uganda, 453, 515

Ugarte, Manuel, 159

Ugly American, The (Lederer & Burdick), 299

Ukraine, 100, 425, 467, 510

Ulbricht, Walter, 332

Unilateralism, 124, 486, 491, 492, 508

Union Carbide, 134

Union of Concerned Scientists, 430

Union of Socialist Soviet Republics. *See* Russia; Soviet Union (USSR)

United Arab Republic, 303

United Fruit Company (UFCO), 42, 161, 304, 305

United Nations (UN), *204,* 204–205, *206,* 210, 217, 382–383; African membership in, 404; arms negotiations and, 283; baby formula resolutions, 426–427; Balkan crisis and, 450; on colonialism, 300; Conference on the Human Environment, 389; Declaration on Human Rights, 258; economic sanctions on Iraq, 459; Egypt-Israeli peace and, 381–382, 407; El Salvador civil war and, 436; Environmental Program, 468; German membership in, 378; Group of 77 and, 387; human rights and, 258, 309; invasion of Iraq and, 461, 509; Iran crisis and, 240; Israel and, 244–246, 407, 440; Khrushchev speech at, 290; Korean War and, *267,* 268, 269, 270–275; Latin American votes in, 205, 401; launching of, 204–205; Monitoring and Verification Commission, 461; North Korea and, 506; peacekeeping by, 302, 335–336, 458, 461, 514; Population Fund, 467; Relief and Rehabilitation Administration (UNRRA), 204, 217, 246; Resolution 242, 407, 440; Resolution 687, 461; Security Council, 204–205, 210, 273, 460, 461; Somalia and, 453–453; Soviet Union and, 204–205; U.S. invasion of Grenada and, 437–438; U.S. invasion of Panama and, 458; weapons inspection by, 461, 466; women's rights and, 468; World Health Organization, 249, 468

United Press (UP), 121, 268

U.S. News & World Report, 307

U.S. Rubber, 121

United States Embassies: in Beirut, 439; in Kenya, *481*; in Saigon, 394; in Tanzania, *481*

United States Information Agency (USIA), 276, 307

Universities and colleges, 62, 134; anti-American sentiment in, 305; Central Intelligence Agency and, 278; in China, 42, 151; globalization of sports and, 469; high-tech research by, 287; military contracts and, 217; Naval, 39, 153; in Puerto Rico, 169; Vietnam War protests at, 356, 391

Updike, John, 480

Uruguay, 305, 456, 511; democracy in, 511; Pan Americanism and, 171–172

U-20 submarines. *See* Submarines

U-2 spy planes, 328, 331, 374; Cold War crisis, 290–291, *291*; Cuba and, 331, *340*, 340, 342, 383

Valley of the Wolves—Iraq (film), 509

Vance, Cyrus, *396*, 399, 409; Iran and, 400, 409–410

Vandenburg, Arthur H., 134, 190, 205, 249

Vanderlip, Frank, 24

Van Kirk, Theodore, 226

Vardon, Harry, 63

Venereal disease, soldiers and, 88–89

Venezuela, 45, 162, 305, 383, 403, 437, 511; boundary dispute in, 5–8, 9, 10, 12, 28; drug trade in, 457, 512–513; oil industry in, 159, 160, 169, 211

Versailles, Treaty of (1919), 94, 98, 103, 116, 130

Veterans of Future Wars, 134

Vienna summit meetings: (1961), 331–332; (1979), 377–378, 412

Vietcong (VC), 320, 321, 322, *345*, 344, *345*, 354, 356, 357, 398

Vietminh, 324–328

Vietnam, 215, 368, 369; Cambodia and, 414; China and, 413; France and, 216, 257, 274, 278; MIAs in, 464

Vietnam syndrome, 445

Vietnam Veterans Memorial, 396

Vietnam War: antiwar protest, *346*, 356–359, *356*, 391, 396, *398;* background of, 324–328; Cambodia and, 390–392; casualties in, 321, 322, 356, 394; China and, 368; films and books about, 395–396; Iraq War parallels, 497–498; Johnson and, 349–356; Kennedy and, 327, *328*, 328, 330, 343–348; legacy of, 394–398; map, *355;* MIAs in, 464; military problems in, 398; Nixon and, 370, 371, 373, 374, 390–398, 400; peace efforts, 369, 391, 392–394; post-traumatic stress disorder and, 396; Rusk and, 322, 330, 345, 350, 357; strategic hamlet program in, *345*, 345, 351, 398; Tet offensive, 320–324, *352*, 359, 394; Vietnamization of, 390–392

Vietnam Women's Veterans Memorial, *397*

Vigilancia (ship), 83

Villa, Francisco (Pancho), 51–53, *52*

Villard, Oswald Garrison, 85

Vincennes (ship), 441

Vincent, John Carter, 281

Virgin Islands, 61

Voice of America, 179, 276, 286, 434

Von Eschen, Penny, 276

Wagner, Robert, 201

Wag the Dog (film), 453

Wald, Lillian, 85

Walesa, Lech, 378

Walker Isthmian Canal Commission, 36

Wallace, Henry A., 236, 241; as Cold War dissenter, 241, 258

War Debt Commission, 124

Warheads, 377. *See also* Missiles

War Powers Resolution (1973), 372, 393

War Refugee Board, 203

War Resisters League, 125

Warsaw: talks with China, 368; in World War II, 202, 211

Warsaw Pact, 250, 285, 350, 411

Washington Naval Conference (1922), 127, 146, 148, 149–152

Watergate scandal, *371*, 371, 372, 374, 381, 393, 394

Weapons of mass destruction (WMD), 461, 489, 490, *492*, 496; al Qaeda and, 490; Hussein and, 491, *492*, 492, 496; in Iraq, *492*, 495–496, 502. *See also specific weapons*

Webb, James, 396

Webb-Pomerene Act (1918), 105, 122

Wedemeyer, Albert C., 254

Weinberger, Caspar W., 427, 428, 429, 439

Weizman, Chaim, *245*, 245

Welles, Sumner, 119, *120*, 137, 139, 162, 179; Cuba and, 167

West Bank and Gaza, 301, 407, 439, 462, 504–505

West Berlin, 288–289, 331–332

Western Europe: anti-nuclear protests in, 430–431; defense of, 287; economic recovery in, 214, 307; Marshall Plan for, 246–248; nuclear weapons in, 412; oil crisis and, 381; Third World and, 387; U.S. culture and, 247. *See also* North Atlantic Treaty Organization; *specific countries*

West Germany, 241; Berlin crisis and, 241; German reunification and, 449; Marshall Plan and, 247, 250; missiles in, 431; North Atlantic Treaty Organization and, 250, 283; opening of Berlin Wall and, *421*, 422–423 rearmament of, 275, 289; Soviet Union and, 283, *285*, 378; U.S. military pact with, 289; as U.S. trade rival, 386. *See also* Berlin; East Berlin; Germany

Westmoreland, William C., 354; Tet offensive and, 320, 321, 322, 354, 394

Weyler, Valeriano y Nicolau, 11, 14

What Me Befell (Jusserand), 41

Wheeler, Burton K., 163, 184

Wheeler, Earl, *321*

Wherry, Kenneth, 280

White, Henry, 91
White, Mark, *341*
White, Theodore H., 217, 281, 330
White, William Allen, 134, 181, 182
Whitechuck Glacier, *516*
Why England Slept (Kennedy), 328
Wilbur, Curtis D., 164
Wilhelm II, kaiser of Germany, 39, 60, 75, 77, *86*
Wilkins, Mira, 120
Williams, G. Mennen "Soapy", 287, *333*
Willkie, Wendell L., 182
Wilson, Henry Lane, 49
Wilson, Hugh, 138, 147–148
Wilson, Woodrow, 29, 39, 40, 59, 64, 324; Asia and, 53–57; Bolshevism and, 101–103; business and World War I, 134; cabinet of, 40–42, 118–119; Cuba and, 45; Dominican Republic and, 47; Haiti and, 164; health of, 97–98, *98,* League of Nations and, 91–93, *92, 94,* 96–97, 99–100, 118; *Lusitania* and, 73–75; Mexican revolution and, 51–53; missionary diplomacy of, *50;* neutrality and, 75, 79; Nicaragua and; Soviet Union and, 127; World War I and, 80–81, *81,* 81–84, 85–86, 116; World War I peace and, 90–93, 105
Wilson (film), 100, 203
Wilsonianism, 75, 119, 190
Wolfowitz, Paul, 485, 487, 489, 490, 494, 496
Wolff, H. Drummond, 12
Women: anti-imperialist, 20; feminists, 430; German, *238;* global rights of, 468; in government, *281;* Hitler's view of, 134; as missionaries, *54;* organizations of, 40, 85, 125, 134, 184; as pacifists, *83, 85,* 125, 134; in warfare, 87, *88, 397. See also* Gender
Women's International League for Peace and Freedom (WILPF), 125, 134

Women's Peace Union, 125
Wood, Leonard, *43,* 43, 44,63, 85
Woodford, Stewart L., 2, 14
Woodling, Sam, 128
Woodring, Harry, 112, 113
Woolley, Mary, 126
Woolworth, F.W., 121
Worcester, Dean, *24*
World Bank, 217, 437, 463, 468; Aswan Dam funding and, 301; creation of, 204; loans to China, 463; post–World War II loans from, 246; poverty and hunger and, 518; Third World and, 387
World Council of Churches, 430
World Court (the Hague), 125, 436; Milosevic trial at, 451; U.S. membership in, 127
World Economic Conference, 119
World Economic Forum, *517*
World Food Conference (1974), 387–388
World Health Organization (WHO), 249, 468
World's fairs, 24, 299
World Trade Center attack (2001), *479,* 480–483. *See also* 9/11
World Trade Organization, 447, 459
World War I, 119, 126; big business and, 134; casualties in, 76, 103, 104; economic ties in, 75–76, 105–106; Europe after, map, *95;* legacies of, 103–106; outbreak of, map, *78;* peace conference after, 90–94; preparedness for, 84–87; reparations following, 93, 124–125; submarine warfare in, 79–84; U.S. entry into, 81–84; U.S. neutrality and, 75–79; women in, 87, *88*
World War II, 190–210; arms sales to belligerents in, 112–115; Asia after, map, *253;* battles in Pacific, *212;* casualties of, 194, *209,* 215–216; conferences during, 194, *195,* 199, 206–210; D-Day invasion, 203; Europe after, map, *238;* Germany in, 182–183, *183;* Haiti in, 166–167; Holocaust in,

200–203; legacy of, 126, 214–217; peace, 203–207; strategies in, 190–196. *See also* Allies, World War II; *and specific belligerent*
World Wide Web, 468–469, 520–521
Wright, Wilbur, 62

Yale University-in-China, 42
Yalta Conference (1945), 199, 205, 207–210, *207,* 214, 234, 235
Yamato (warship), 153
Yellow fever, 16, 121
"Yellow press," 4, 10
Yeltsin, Boris, 425, 447–448
Yemen, 301
Yihequan (Boxers), 26, 53, 56
Yohn, Jeff, *339*
Yom Kippur War (1973), 380
You Tube, 520
Young, Andrew, *400, 400,* 404
Young Men's Christian Association (YMCA), 41, 87
Young Plan, 125
Yugoslavia, 93, *95,* 215, 281; ethnic violence in, 450–451; Tito regime in, 211, 236, 244
Yushchenko, Viktor, 511

Zaire (Congo), 82, 278, 384, 385, 404, 453; civil war in, 335–336, 453
Zambia, 405, 442
Zeiger, Susan, *88*
Zemin, Jiang, 507
Zhivkov, Todor, 422
Zhang, Hong, *255*
Zhou Enlai, 198, 199, 254, 292; Korean War and, *267,* 270; Nixon and, *367,* 368, 369–370; Vietnam and, 326
Zimbabwe/Rhodesia, 384, 404, 514; white minority rule in, 385, 404, 406
Zimmermann telegram, 53, 83
Zionists, 245. *See also* Israel